DSM-5 Diagnoses

Neurodevelopmental Disorders

Intellectual Disability

Intellectual Disability (Intellectual Development Disorder)

Communication Disorders

Language Disorder / Social (Pragmatic) Communication Disorder / Speech Sound Disorder / Childhood Onset Fluency Disorder (Stuttering)

Autism Spectrum Disorder

Autism Spectrum Disorder

Attention-Deficit / Hyperactivity Disorder

Attention-Deficit / Hyperactivity Disorder

Specific Learning Disorder

Motor Disorders

Developmental Coordination Disorder / Stereotypic Movement Disorder / Tourette's Disorder / Persistent (Chronic) Motor or Vocal Tic Disorder / Provisional Tic Disorder

Schizophrenia Spectrum Disorders

Schizophrenia / Schizotypal (Personality) Disorder / Schizophreniform Disorder / Brief Psychotic Disorder / Delusional Disorder / Schizoaffective Disorder

Bipolar and Related Disorders

Bipolar I Disorder / Bipolar II Disorder / Cyclothymic Disorder

Depressive Disorders

Disruptive Mood Dysregulation Disorder / Major Depressive Disorder / Persistent Depressive Disorder (Dysthymia) / Premenstrual Dysphoric Disorder

Anxiety Disorders

Panic Disorder / Agoraphobia / Specific Phobia / Social Anxiety Disorder (Social Phobia) / Generalized Anxiety Disorder / Separation Anxiety Disorder / Selective Mutism

Obsessive-Compulsive and Related Disorders

Obsessive-Compulsive Disorder / Body Dysmorphic Disorder / Hoarding Disorder / Trichotillomania (Hair-Pulling Disorder) / Excoriation (Skin-Picking Disorder)

Trauma- and Stressor-Related Disorders

Reactive Attachment Disorder / Disinhibited Social Engagement Disorder / Acute Stress Disorder / Posttraumatic Stress Disorder / Adjustment Disorders

Dissociative Disorders

Depersonalization-Derealization Disorder / Dissociative Amnesia / Dissociative Identity Disorder

Somatic Symptom and Related Disorders

Somatic Symptom Disorder / Illness Anxiety Disorder / Conversion Disorder / Psychological Factors Affecting Other Medical Conditions / Factitious Disorder

Feeding and Eating Disorders

Pica / Rumination Disorder / Avoidant/Restrictive Food Intake Disorder / Anorexia Nervosa / Bulimia Nervosa / Binge Eating Disorder

Elimination Disorders

Enuresis / Encopresis

Sleep-Wake Disorders

Insomnia Disorder / Hypersomnolence Disorder / Narcolepsy / Obstructive Sleep Apnea Hypopnea / Central Sleep Apnea / Sleep-related Hypoventilation / Circadian Rhythm Sleep-Wake Disorders / Nightmare Disorder / Rapid Eye Movement Sleep Behavior Disorder / Restless Legs Syndrome / Non-Rapid Eye Movement Sleep Arousal Disorders

Sexual Dysfunctions

Erectile Disorder / Female Orgasmic Disorder / Delayed Ejaculation / Early Ejaculation / Female Sexual Interest/Arousal Disorder / Male Hypoactive Sexual Desire Disorder / Genito-Pelvic Pain / Penetration Disorder

Gender Dysphoria

Gender Dysphoria in Children, in Adolescents, or Adults

Disruptive, Impulse-Control, and Conduct Disorders

Oppositional Defiant Disorder / Intermittent Explosive Disorder / Conduct Disorder

Substance Use and Addictive Disorders

Alcohol Use Disorder / Amphetamine Use Disorder / Cannabis Use Disorder / Stimulant Use Disorder / Other Hallucinogen Use Disorder / Inhalant Use Disorder / Nicotine Use Disorder / Opioid Use Disorder / Phencyclidine Use Disorder / Sedative, Hypnotic, or Anxiolytic Use Disorders / Tobacco Use Disorder / Gambling Disorder

Neurocognitive Disorders

Delirium / Mild Neurocognitive Disorder / Major Neurocognitive Disorder

Personality Disorders

Antisocial Personality Disorder / Avoidant Personality Disorder / Borderline Personality Disorder / Narcissistic Personality Disorder / Obsessive-Compulsive Personality Disorder / Schizotypal Personality Disorder / Dependent Personality Disorder / Schizoid Personality Disorder / Paranoid Personality Disorder / Histrionic Personality Disorder

Paraphilic Disorders

Exhibitionistic Disorder / Fetishistic Disorder / Frotteuristic Disorder / Pedophilic Disorder / Sexual Masochism Disorder / Sexual Sadism Disorder / Transvestic Disorder / Voyeuristic Disorder

Conditions for Further Study

Attenuated Psychosis Syndrome / Depressive Episodes with Short-Duration Hypomania / Persistent Complex Bereavement Disorder / Caffeine Use Disorder / Internet Gaming Disorder / Neurobehavioral Disorder Associated with Prenatal Alcohol Exposure / Suicidal Behavior Disorder / Non-Suicidal Self Injury

DSM-5 Classification System

Neurodevelopmental Disorders
Schizophrenia Spectrum and Other Psychotic Disorders
Bipolar and Related Disorders
Depressive Disorders
Anxiety Disorders
Obsessive-Compulsive and Related Disorders
Trauma- and Stressor-Related Disorders
Dissociative Disorders
Somatic Symptom and Related Disorders
Feeding and Eating Disorders
Elimination Disorders
Sleep-Wake Disorders
Sexual Dysfunctions
Gender Dysphoria
Disruptive, Impulse-Control, and Conduct Disorders
Substance-Related and Addictive Disorders
Neurocognitive Disorders
Personality Disorders
Paraphilic Disorders
Other Mental Disorders
Medication-Induced Movement Disorders and Other Adverse Effects of Medication
Other Conditions That May Be a Focus of Clinical Attention

WileyPLUS Learning Space

An easy way to help your students **learn, collaborate,** and **grow.**

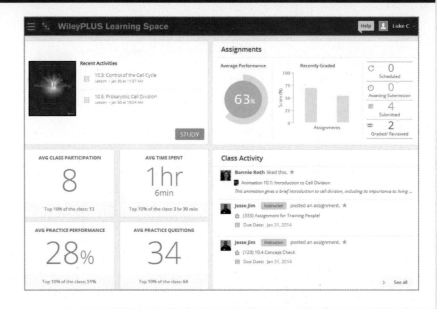

Personalized Experience

Students create their own study guide while they interact with course content and work on learning activities.

Flexible Course Design

Educators can quickly organize learning activities, manage student collaboration, and customize their course—giving them full control over content as well as the amount of interactivity among students.

Clear Path to Action

With visual reports, it's easy for both students and educators to gauge problem areas and act on what's most important.

Instructor Benefits

- Assign activities and add your own materials
- Guide students through what's important in the interactive e-textbook by easily assigning specific content
- Set up and monitor collaborative learning groups
- Assess learner engagement
- Gain immediate insights to help inform teaching

Student Benefits

- Instantly know what you need to work on
- Create a personal study plan
- Assess progress along the way
- Participate in class discussions
- Remember what you have learned because you have made deeper connections to the content

We are dedicated to supporting you from idea to outcome.

WILEY

Abnormal Psychology

The Science and Treatment of Psychological Disorders

Thirteenth Edition

Abnormal Psychology

The Science and Treatment of Psychological Disorders

Thirteenth Edition

Ann M. Kring
University of California, Berkeley

Sheri L. Johnson
University of California, Berkeley

With former contributions from

Gerald C. Davison
University of Southern California

John M. Neale
State University of New York at Stony Brook

WILEY

Vice President & Executive Publisher	George Huffman
Executive Editor	Christopher T. Johnson
Senior Marketing Manager	Margaret Barrett
Product Designer	Beth Tripmacher
Associate Editor	Kyla Buckingham
Editorial Assistant	Kristen Mucci
Senior Content Manager	Dorothy Sinclair
Senior Production Editor	Sandra Rigby
Design Director	Harry Nolan
Senior Designer	Thomas Nery
Senior Photo Editor	Billy Ray

Cover Photo: Image provided by the USGS EROS Data Center Satellite Systems Branch/Visible Earth/NASA/htrtp://visibleearth.nasa.gov/view_rec.php?id=2939

This book was set in 10/12 Berkeley Book by codeMantra and was printed and bound by Quad/Versailles.
This book is printed on acid free paper.

Founded in 1807, John Wiley & Sons, Inc. has been a valued source of knowledge and understanding for more than 200 years, helping people around the world meet their needs and fulfill their aspirations. Our company is built on a foundation of principles that include responsibility to the communities we serve and where we live and work. In 2008, we launched a Corporate Citizenship Initiative, a global effort to address the environmental, social, economic, and ethical challenges we face in our business. Among the issues we are addressing are carbon impact, paper specifications and procurement, ethical conduct within our business and among our vendors, and community and charitable support. For more information, please visit our website: www.wiley.com/go/citizenship.

ISBN - 9781118-85909-4
BRV ISBN - 978-1118-95398-3

Printed in the United States of America

10 9 8 7 6 5 4 3 2 1

To
_____

Angela Hawk

Daniel Rose

About the Authors

ANN M. KRING is Professor of Psychology at the University of California at Berkeley, where she will assume the role of Department Chair in July 2015. She received her B.S. from Ball State University and her M.A. and Ph.D. from the State University of New York at Stony Brook. Her internship in clinical psychology was completed at Bellevue Hospital and Kirby Forensic Psychiatric Center, in New York. From 1991 to 1998, she taught at Vanderbilt University. She joined the faculty at UC Berkeley in 1999 and has served two terms as Director of the Clinical Science Program and Psychology Clinic. She received a Distinguished Teaching Award from UC Berkeley in 2008. She is on the editorial board of *Schizophrenia Bulletin, Journal of Abnormal Psychology,* and *Psychological Science in the Public Interest*, and is a former Associate Editor for *Journal of Abnormal Psychology, Cognition and Emotion,* and *Applied and Preventive Psychology.* She was elected President of the Society for Research in Psychopathology, and she is a member of the Executive Board of the Society for Affective Science.

She has won several awards, including a Young Investigator Award from the National Alliance for Research on Schizophrenia and Depression in 1997 and the Joseph Zubin Memorial Fund Award in recognition of her research in schizophrenia in 2006. In 2005, she was named a fellow of the Association for Psychological Science. Her research has been supported by grants from the Scottish Rite Schizophrenia Research program, the National Alliance for Research on Schizophrenia and Depression, and the National Institute of Mental Health. She is a co-editor (with Denise Sloan) of the book *Emotion Regulation and Psychopathology* (Guilford Press) and co-author (with Janelle Caponigro, Erica Lee, and Sheri Johnson) of the book *Bipolar Disorder for the Newly Diagnosed* (New Harbinger Press). She is also the author of more than 100 articles and chapters. Her current research focus is on emotion and psychopathology, with a specific interest in the emotional features of schizophrenia, assessing negative symptoms in schizophrenia, and the linkage between cognition and emotion in schizophrenia.

SHERI L. JOHNSON is Professor of Psychology at the University of California at Berkeley, where she directs the Cal Mania (Calm) program, and she is a visiting professor at the University of Lancaster, England. She received her B.A. from Salem College and her Ph.D. from the University of Pittsburgh. She completed an internship and postdoctoral fellowship at Brown University, and she was a clinical assistant professor at Brown from 1993 to 1995. From 1995 to 2008, she taught in the Department of Psychology at the University of Miami, where she was recognized three times with the Excellence in Graduate Teaching Award. In 1993, she received the Young Investigator Award from the National Alliance for Research in Schizophrenia and Depression. She is a consulting editor for *Clinical Psychological Science* and *Journal of Abnormal Psychology,* she was an associate editor for *Applied and Preventive Psychology* and *Cognition and Emotion,* and she has served on editorial boards for six journals, including *Psychological Bulletin.* She is has served as the secretary for the Society for Research in Psychopathology and is a Fellow of the Academy of Behavioral Medicine Research and the Association for Psychological Science.

For the past 25 years, her work has focused on understanding the factors that predict the course of mania and depression. She uses social, psychological, and neurobiological paradigms to understand these processes. Her work has been funded by the National Alliance for Research on Schizophrenia and Depression, the National Cancer Institute, the National Science Foundation, and by the National Institute of Mental Health. She has published over 175 articles and chapters, and her findings have been published in leading journals such as the *Journal of Abnormal Psychology, Psychological Bulletin,* and the *American Journal of Psychiatry.* She is co-editor of several books, including *Psychological Treatment of Bipolar Disorder* (Guilford Press), *Bipolar Disorder for the Newly Diagnosed* (New Harbinger Press), and *Emotion and Psychopathology* (American Psychological Association).

A bit of authorship history…

For the past 10 years, Ann Kring and Sheri Johnson have been the sole authors of the book. However, the book's history dates back 40 years. Back then, Gerald Davison and John Neale sat down to share their experiences teaching the undergraduate abnormal psychology course at the State University of New York at Stony Brook. Arising from that conversation was the outline of a textbook on which they decided to collaborate, one that was different from the texts available at the time. The first edition of this book, co-authored by Davison and Neale, was published in 1974. Ann Kring joined the team in 2001, and she invited Sheri Johnson to join in 2004, when Kring and Johnson took over full authorship responsibilities. The legacy of Davison and Neale remains in this and every edition, and we are forever indebted to these two pioneering authors who developed and wrote many editions of this textbook. Near the end of our work on the twelfth edition, we learned that John Neale had passed away after a long illness. He is greatly missed by many.

Photo by Christine McDowell

GERALD C. DAVISON is Professor of Psychology at the University of Southern California. Previously he was Professor and Chair of the Department of Psychology at USC and served also as Director of Clinical Training. He recently served as Dean of the USC Davis School of Gerontology. He earned his B.A. in social relations from Harvard and his Ph.D. in psychology from Stanford. He is a Fellow of the American Psychological Association, a Charter Fellow of the Association for Psychological Science, and a Distinguished Founding Fellow of the Academy of Cognitive Therapy. Among his other honors are the USC Associates Award for Excellence in Teaching, and the Outstanding Educator Award and the Lifetime Achievement Award of the Association for Behavioral and Cognitive Therapies. Among his more than 150 publications is his book *Clinical Behavior Therapy*, co-authored in 1976 with Marvin Goldfried and reissued in expanded form in 1994. It is one of two publications that have been recognized as Citation Classics by the Social Sciences Citation Index. He is also on the editorial board of several professional journals. His research has emphasized experimental and philosophical analyses of psychopathology, assessment, therapeutic change, and the relationships between cognition and a variety of behavioral and emotional problems via his articulated thoughts in simulated situations paradigm.

Photo by John M. Neale

JOHN M. NEALE was Professor of Psychology at the State University of New York at Stony Brook, retiring in 2000. He received his B.A. from the University of Toronto and his M.A. and Ph.D. from Vanderbilt University. He won numerous awards, including the American Psychological Association's Early Career Award (1974), the Distinguished Scientist Award from the American Psychological Association's Society for a Science of Clinical Psychology (1991), and the Sustained Mentorship Award from the Society for Research in Psychopathology (2011). Besides his numerous articles in professional journals, he published books on the effects of televised violence on children, research methodology, schizophrenia, case studies in abnormal psychology, and psychological influences on health. Schizophrenia was a major focus of his research, and he also conducted research on the influence of stress on health.

Preface

It has been nearly 40 years since the first edition of this book was published. From the beginning, the focus of the book has always been on the balance and blending of research and clinical application; on the use of paradigms as an organizing principle; and on the effort to involve the reader in the problem solving engaged in by clinicians and scientists. These qualities have continued to be the cornerstones of subsequent editions, and we have been both surprised and delighted at the favorable reception the book has received and, perhaps more importantly, the impact it has had on the lives of so many students of psychopathology throughout the years.

With the thirteenth edition, we continue to emphasize the recent and comprehensive research coverage that has been the hallmark of the book as well as to expand the pedagogical features. We have added more questions to the Check Your Knowledge boxes, additional clinical cases, figures, tables, and clear writing to make this material accessible to a broad audience. Now more than ever, we emphasize an integrated approach, showing how psychopathology is best understood by considering multiple perspectives and how these varying perspectives can provide us with the clearest accounting of the causes of these disorders as well as the best possible treatments.

The cover image is a kaleidoscope of lights chosen to represent the myriad factors that contribute to psychological disorders. This image illustrates a number of key principles about our book. Just as a kaleidoscope offers an extensive and diverse array of colorful patterns, many people are differently impacted by psychological disorders. People are shaped by the interaction of their neurobiology and environment, which is what the study of psychological disorders is all about: different paradigms (genetic, neuroscience, cognitive behavioral) coming together to shape the development and course of different psychological disorders. This is also how science works. New discoveries help to reshape the domains of scientific inquiry, shifting the perspective of our current understanding of psychological disorders in the same way as moving the lights in a kaleidoscope changes the way we see the colors. Our book is first and foremost grounded in the latest science of psychological disorders. As new discoveries and new treatments are developed, our understanding moves toward a better conceptualization of psychological disorders.

Goals of the Book

With each new edition, we update, make changes, and streamline features to enhance both the scholarly and pedagogical characteristics of the book. We also devote considerable effort to couching complex concepts in prose that is sharp, clear, and vivid. The domains of psychopathology and intervention continue to become increasingly multifaceted and technical. Therefore, a good textbook covering psy-chological disorders must engage the careful and focused attention of students so that they can acquire a deep and critical understanding of the issues and the material. Some of the most exciting breakthroughs in psychopathology research and treatment that we present in the book have come in areas that are complex, such as molecular genetics, neuroscience, and cognitive science. Rather than oversimplify these complex issues, we have instead added a number of pedagogical features to enhance understanding of this vital material.

We endeavor to present up-to-date theories and research in psychopathology and intervention as well as to convey some of the intellectual excitement that is associated with the search for answers to some of the most puzzling questions facing us today. We try to encourage students to participate with us in a process of discovery as we sift through the evidence on the origins of psychopathology and the effectiveness of specific interventions.

In this edition, we continue to emphasize ways in which we can do away with the stigma that is unfortunately still associated with psychological disorders. Despite the ubiquity of psychopathology, the stigma associated with it can keep some individuals from seeking treatment, keep our legislatures from providing adequate funding for treatment and research, and keep some terms as accepted popular vernacular (e.g., *crazy, nuts*). Thus, another of our goals for the book is to combat this stigma and present a positive and hopeful view on the causes and treatments of mental illness.

Another change to this edition is the broadening of our title. Older terms such as abnormal psychology reflect vestiges of the past in many ways, even though many courses that cover the causes and treatment of psychological disorders retain this title. It is our hope that the term *abnormal psychology* will soon be replaced, as it can unwittingly perpetuate the stigma that people with psychological disorders are "abnormal" in many ways. Our contention is that people with psychological disorders are first and foremost people and that the term *abnormal* can be overly broad and misconstrued to the detriment of people impacted by psychological disorders.

Organization of the Thirteenth Edition

In Chapters 1 through 4, we place the field in historical context, present the concept of paradigms in science, describe the major paradigms in psychopathology, describe the fifth edition of the *Diagnostic and Statistical Manual of Mental Disorders* (DSM-5), crit-ically discuss its validity and reliability, provide an overview of major approaches and techniques in clinical assessment, and then describe the major research methods of the field. These chapters are the foundation on which the later chapters can be interpreted and understood. As in the twelfth edition, specific psychological disorders and their treatment are discussed in Chapters 5 through 15.

A recurrent theme in the book is the importance of perspectives, or, to use Kuhn's (1962/1970) phrase, paradigms. Throughout the book we discuss three major paradigms: genetic, neuroscience, and cognitive behavioral. We also emphasize the importance of factors that are important to all paradigms, including emotion, gender, culture, ethnicity, and socioeconomic status. A related issue is the use of more than one paradigm in studying psychological disorders. Rather than force an entire field into, for example, a cognitive behavioral paradigm, we argue from the available information that different problems in psychopathology are amenable to analyses within different frameworks. For instance, genetic factors are important in bipolar disorder and attention-deficit/hyperactivity disorder, but genes do their work via the environment. In disorders such as depression, cognitive behavioral factors are essential, but neurotransmitters also exert an influence. For still other disorders—for example, dissociative disorders—cognitive factors involving consciousness are important to consider. Furthermore, the importance of a diathesis–stress approach remains a cornerstone to the field. Emerging data indicate that nearly all psychological disorders arise from subtle interactions between genetic or psychological predispositions and stressful life events.

We continue to emphasize that psychopathology is best understood by considering how genes do their work via psychological processes and the environment. Thus, rather than asking whether genes or the environment is more important in a particular disorder, we emphasize that both of these factors are important. Exciting new discoveries have made it clear that nature and nurture work together, not in opposition to each another. Without the genes, a behavior might not be possible. But without the environment, genes could not express themselves and thus contribute to the behavior. Genes are remarkably flexible at responding to different types of environments. In turn, human beings are quite flexible at adapting to different environments. In this edition, we have added several examples to highlight how genetic, social, and cognitive risk factors operate in tandem.

We continue to include considerable material on culture and ethnicity in the study of causes and treatment of psychological disorders. In Chapter 2, we present a separate section that emphasizes the importance of culture and ethnicity in all paradigms. We point to the important role of culture and ethnicity in the other chapters as well. For example, in the Diagnosis and Assessment chapter (3), we discuss cultural bias in assessment and ways to guard against this selectivity in perception. We have updated coverage of culture and ethnicity in substance use disorders (Chapter 10).

New to This Edition

The thirteenth edition has many new and exciting additions and changes. We have added significant new material about the impact of DSM-5 in every chapter, and we continue to organize the chapters to reflect the organization of the DSM-5. Now that DSM-5 is in use, material on DSM-IV-TR has been largely removed. In addition, we continue to update and innovate. We no longer apologetically

cover theories that don't work or don't have empirical support. As the research on each disorder has burgeoned, we've moved to just highlighting the most exciting and accepted theories, research, and treatments. This edition, as always, contains hundreds of updated references. Throughout the book, we have further streamlined the writing to increase the clarity of presentation and to highlight the key issues in the field. We have included new figures to carefully illustrate the genetics and brain networks involved in different disorders. Finally, we have added new photos to illustrate current events and news regarding mental health.

We have continued to add additional pedagogy based on feedback from students and professors. In addition to multiple new Clinical Case boxes, we have also included a number of new Focus on Discovery boxes in order to illustrate what the different disorders look like in the context of real people's lives as well as to showcase cutting-edge research on particular topics. In addition, we have modified and added new Check Your Knowledge questions in nearly all chapters so that students can do a quick check to see if they are learning and integrating the material. Drawing on evidence for the importance of generative thinking for learning, many of the new questions are open-ended. There are many new photos to provide students with additional real-world examples and applications of psychopathology, including examples of some of the highly successful and well-known people who have come forward in the past several years to discuss their own psychological disorders. The end-of-chapter summaries continue to be consistent across the chapters, using a bulleted format and summarizing the descriptions, causes, and treatments of the disorders covered.

New and Expanded Coverage

We are really excited about the new features of this edition. Some of the major new material in this edition includes:

Chapter 1: Introduction and Historical Overview

New material on stigma, including updates to current legislation and support/advocacy groups and stigma reduction efforts
Some of the history sections are streamlined
New section on what we can learn from history
New material on the mental health professions

Chapter 2: Current Paradigms in Psychopathology

New material on cultural factors that cut across paradigms
New material on cutting-edge molecular genetics, including single nucleotide polymorphisms (SNPs), copy number variations (CNVs), and genome-wide association studies
Updated coverage of the latest neuroscience findings
Updated coverage on cognitive science contributions to the cognitive behavioral paradigm
Updated material in the Focus on Discovery boxes on gender and health and socioeconomics and health

Chapter 3: Diagnosis and Assessment

New information on DSM-5, including reliability from the field trials, additional material on cultural assessment, and cross-cutting symptom assessment materials

New information on the Research Domain Criteria (RDoC)

Clinical cases presented with DSM-5 diagnoses

Older diagnostic information moved to the Focus on Discovery box covering the history of diagnosis

Updated data on cultural bias in assessment

Updated information on assessment measures

Updated information on underreporting of stigmatized behaviors

Chapter 4: Research Methods

New material on genome-wide association studies (GWAS)

New content on the efficacy of culturally competent psychotherapies

Chapter 5: Mood Disorders

Added a dual-factor model of seasonal affective disorder

Described the high prevalence of depression in the offspring of mothers with depression

Added a population-based study that supports the link of creativity with bipolar disorder

Added a richer clinical description of mania

Updated findings on the mechanisms through which the serotonin transporter polymorphism may interact with environmental risk factors to influence neurobiological and cognitive risk factors for depression

New discussion of the importance of childhood adversity in depression

New material on the role of interpersonal stress in depression, and the debate about whether bereavement-related depressive symptoms should be distinguished from other forms of depression

New studies on the prospective evidence for cognitive models of depression

New theory and data regarding the mechanisms driving rumination in depression

New Focus on Discovery Box on how research on cytokines serves as a link between biological and social risk factors for depression

Updates on the number of people who have tried antidepressants

New data on mindfulness treatment for depression

New findings on deep brain stimulation

New data on transcranial magnetic stimulation, now licensed by the FDA for treatment-resistant depression

New material on public health approaches to suicide prevention

Chapter 6: Anxiety Disorders

New data on the prevalence and functional outcomes of anxiety disorders

Enhanced clinical description of generalized anxiety disorder

New evidence regarding a specific genetic polymorphism relevant across the anxiety disorders (PPARGC1A gene) and one that is relevant to panic disorder (neuropeptide S NPSR gene)

Better discussion of the nature of attentional impairment in anxiety disorder

New evidence that attentional training can reduce cortisol response to daily stress

Summary of findings on mindfulness and acceptance-based treatments

Chapter 7: Obsessive-Compulsive-Related and Trauma-Related Disorders

More detail and a new clinical case to enrich understanding of the clinical picture of obsessions and compulsions

New data on the high rate of absenteeism associated with body dysmorphic disorder

New section more concisely reviewing the epidemiology of obsessive-compulsive disorder (OCD) and related disorders as a whole, given the substantial parallels across the three disorders

New data on the heritability of the obsessive-compulsive and related disorders

New studies showing that hoarding disorder is related to neural activation in regions that are similar to those implicated in OCD and body dysmorphic disorder

New behavioral model for OCD, emphasizing difficulties stopping engagement in a behavior that effectively warded off threat in the past

Greater detail on the process of conducting exposure and ritual prevention for a person with OCD, with less emphasis on the historical development of this approach

New section on deep brain stimulation for OCD

New information on the definition of complex posttraumatic stress disorder (PTSD) and on the reasons this was not included as a subtype in the DSM-5

New clinical case for PTSD focused on a college student who was raped

Refined discussion of the hippocampus as helping organize memories but also placing them in context, and how this might lead to PTSD

Coverage of the PTSD specifier for depersonalization or derealization

Chapter 8: Dissociative Disorders and Somatic Symptom-Related Disorders

More description of the different forms of dissociation

More detail on the difficulties in estimating the prevalence of dissociative disorders

Reorganized to cover controversies about memory as part of the discussion of dissociative amnesia

New case study for dissociative amnesia, fugue subtype

Updates on the high prevalence of depersonalization and derealization symptoms among college students, and the most typical dissociative experiences

New criticisms regarding the case of Sybil

New evidence on the medical costs of treating somatic symptom disorders

More detail on how somatic symptom disorders relate to disorders with contentious etiology

Updated theory on whether conversion disorder has truly changed in prevalence over time

Neurofeedback for pain control discussed

New example of mass hysteria, illustrating an important social facet of conversion disorder

Enhanced description of cognitive techniques for somatic symptom disorders

New treatment outcome data for somatic symptom disorders

Chapter 9: Schizophrenia

New research on genetics

New material on schizophrenia and the brain

New section on brain connectivity

New material on culture and expressed emotion

New findings on clinical high risk for schizophrenia

New material on cannabis use as a risk factor for schizophrenia

Updated material on first and second-generation antipsychotic medications

Updated material on psychosocial treatments for schizophrenia

New Focus on Discovery Box on misdiagnosis of schizophrenia

Chapter 10: Substance Use Disorders

New material on DSM-5 indicators of severity of alcohol and drug use disorders

New statistics on use of all drugs

New material on e-cigarettes

New material on marijuana

New material on the neuroscience of addiction

New material on tobacco and stimulants, including cocaine

New treatment studies for smoking, alcohol, and cocaine

New section on delayed versus immediate rewards in the neurobiology of addiction

Chapter 11: Eating Disorders

Expanded section on binge eating disorder, consistent with its inclusion in DSM-5, including physical consequences and prognosis

Updated and expanded material on obesity

New information on cognitive behavior therapy for anorexia

New information on DSM-5 severity ratings for all eating disorders

New material on prevention of eating disorders

Chapter 12: Sexual Disorders

Description of a more accurate penile plethysmograph

New case studies of orgasmic disorder and voyeuristic disorder

New data on the prevalent use of testosterone off-label, and the sexual side effects of such usage

Now noted that more than 20 trials have tested cognitive behavioral therapy (CBT) for sexual dysfunction disorders

Updated statistics on success rates with directed masturbation treatment for orgasmic disorders

Additional detail regarding cognitive interventions for sexual dysfunction

New data on the percentage of people who have engaged in sado-masochistic sexual practices

More detail on the DSM-5 diagnostic criteria for pedophilia

New data on lower IQ and neurocognitive problems among men diagnosed with pedophilia

Updated material on the etiology of pedophilia and sexual coercion, with attention to the idea that there may be multiple pathways to both problems

Research evidence for the role of impulsivity in paraphilias added

Satiation treatment described for paraphilias

New information about civil liberties and diagnoses of paraphilias

Chapter 13: Disorders of Childhood

Updated material on attention-deficit/hyperactivity disorder (ADHD)

New material on prevalence rates, risk factors, and treatment in childhood ADHD and expanded information on ADHD in adulthood

New information on genetics and conduct disorder

New information on preventing conduct disorder

New material on intermittent explosive disorder

New material on disruptive mood dysregulation disorder

New information on genetics, neuroscience, and prevention of conduct disorder

New information on treatment of anxiety in childhood

New information on etiology of depression in childhood

Updated material on dyslexia

New clinical case box on dyslexia

New material on stimulant medications in children

Updated prevalence data for all disorders

Updated material on genetics in autism spectrum disorder

Updated material in the Focus on Discovery box covering controversies in the field

New information on autism spectrum disorder

Chapter 14 Late Life and Neurocognitive Disorders

New section on the negative consequences of internalizing negative stereotypes about aging

New data regarding specific genes and immune function in Alzheimer's disease

New information about the prevalence of frontotemporal dementia (FTD)

Updated information about prevention trials

New information about training programs for memory in dementia

Chapter 15 Personality Disorders

Emphasis on the pervasive influence of personality on a broad range of outcomes

Added data on unstructured clinical interviews, noting poor inter-rater reliability in the DSM-5 field trials and poor validity compared to structured interviews

Discussion of findings from several studies showing that personality disorders are more common during adolescence and that the prevalence decreases over the life course, and that many people recover from personality disorders

Richer clinical descriptions throughout the chapter and new case vignettes to illustrate paranoid personality disorder, antisocial personality disorder, and obsessive-compulsive personality disorder

Reorganized to discuss evidence that heritability, parenting styles, and child abuse are important as common risk factors across the personality disorders. The etiology of more specific personality disorders is then focused strictly on those disorders with more available research.

New Focus on Discovery box on media images of psychopathy

New Focus on Discovery box on whether narcissism is increasing over time among college students

New data from discordant twin studies regarding the relative weight of family risk and abuse in risk for borderline personality disorder

Data on parenting styles related to narcissism and dependent personality disorder

More discussion of the implications of dependent personality disorder for outcomes

Streamlined discussion of the risk factors for antisocial personality disorder and borderline personality disorder, and of psychotherapy for borderline personality disorder

Chapter 16: Legal and Ethical Issues

Reorganized for better readability

New material on intellectual disability and capital punishment

New Clinical Case box

New information on specific states and the insanity defense

Special Features for the Student Reader

Several features of this book are designed to make it easier for students to master and enjoy the material.

Clinical Case Boxes We have updated for DSM-5 and added a number of new Clinical Cases throughout the book to provide a clinical context for the theories and research that occupy most of our attention in the chapters and to help make vivid the real-life implications of the empirical work of psychopathologists and clinicians.

Focus on Discovery Boxes There are many in-depth discussions of selected topics throughout the book. This feature allows us to involve readers in specialized topics in a way that does not detract from the flow of the regular text. Sometimes a Focus on Discovery box expands on a point in the text; sometimes it deals with an entirely separate but relevant issue, often a controversial one. We have added a number of new boxes in this edition, replacing a number of the older ones. Additional boxes feature real-life examples of individuals living with different disorders.

Quick Summaries We include short summaries throughout the chapters to allow students to pause and assimilate the material. These should help students keep track of the multifaceted and complex issues that surround the study of psychopathology.

End-of-Chapter Summaries Summaries at the end of each chapter are in bulleted form. In Chapters 5–15, we organize these by clinical descriptions, etiology, and treatment—the major sections of every chapter covering the disorders. We believe this format will make it easier for readers to review and remember the material. In fact, we even suggest that students read the summary before beginning the chapter itself in order to get a good sense of what lies ahead. Then rereading it after completing the chapter itself will enhance students' understanding and provide an immediate sense of what has been learned in just one reading of the chapter.

Check Your Knowledge Questions Throughout each chapter, we provide between three and six boxes that ask questions about the material covered in the chapter. These questions are intended to help students assess their understanding and retention of the material as well as provide them with samples of the types of questions that often are found in course exams. The answers to the questions in these boxes are at the end of each chapter, just before the list of key terms. We believe that these will be useful aids for students as they make their way through the chapters.

Glossary When an important term is introduced, it is boldfaced and defined or discussed immediately. Most such terms appear again later in the book, in which case they will not be highlighted in this way. All these terms are listed again at the end of each chapter, and definitions appear at the end of the book in a glossary.

DSM-5 Table The endpapers of the book contain a summary of the psychiatric nomenclature for the fifth edition of the *Diagnostic and Statistical Manual of Mental Disorders*, known as DSM-5. This provides a handy guide to where particular disorders appear in the "official" taxonomy or classification. We make considerable use of DSM-5, though in a selective and sometimes critical vein. Sometimes we find it more effective to discuss theory and research on a particular problem in a way that is different from DSM's conceptualization.

Teaching and Learning Environment

WileyPlus Learning Space

What is *WileyPLUS Learning Space*? It's a place where students can learn, collaborate, and grow. Through a personalized experience, students create their own study guide while they interact with course content and work on learning activities.

WileyPLUS Learning Space combines adaptive learning functionality with a dynamic new e-textbook for your course—giving you tools to quickly organize learning activities, manage student collaboration, and customize your course so that you have full control over content as well as the amount of interactivity between students.

Instructors can:

- Assign activities and add their own materials
- Guide students through what's important in the e-textbook by easily assigning specific content
- Set up and monitor collaborative learning groups
- Assess student engagement
- Benefit from a sophisticated set of reporting and diagnostic tools that give greater insight into class activity

Learn more at www.wileypluslearningspace.com. If you have questions, please contact your Wiley representative.

What do students receive with *WileyPLUS Learning Space*?

- A **digital version** of the complete textbook with integrated media and quizzes.

- The **ORION** adaptive learning module that maximizes study time.

- **Case Study Videos** present an encompassing view of 16 psychological disorders, updated for DSM-5. Produced by documentary filmmaker Nathan Friedkin in collaboration with Ann Kring and Sheri Johnson, each case study video is about 7 to 10 minutes long and features people with psychological disorders and their families, in the context of their lives, describing symptoms from their own perspectives. In addition each video also provides concise information about the available treatment options and commentary from a mental health professional.

- **Wiley Psychology Videos** present a collection of over 50 brief clips applying the concepts of clinical psychology to current events.

- **Practice Exams.** These learning features give students a way to test themselves on course material before exams. Each practice exam contains fill-in-the-blank, application, and multiple-choice questions that provide immediate feedback. Each question is also linked to a learning objective within the book to aid students in concept mastery.

- **Flashcards.** This interactive module gives students the opportunity to easily test their knowledge of vocabulary terms.

- **Web Resources.** Annotated web links put useful electronic resources for psychology into the context of your Developmental Psychology course.

What do instructors receive with *WileyPLUS Learning Space*?

Pre-created teaching materials and assessments help instructors optimize their time:

- A wealth of brief **video segments** perfect for classroom use.

- The **Instructor's Manual,** prepared by Robert Egbert of Walla Walla University, is designed to help instructors maximize student learning. It presents teaching suggestions for each chapter of the text, including lecture starters, lecture extensions, classroom discussions and activities, out of the classroom assignments, Internet and print resources, and more!

- Every chapter contains a **Lecture PowerPoint presentation,** prepared by Stephanie Sitnick of the University of Pittsburgh, with a combination of key concepts, figures and tables, and examples from the textbook.

- **Media Enriched PowerPoint presentations,** available in *WileyPLUS,* contain embedded links to multimedia sources and can be easily modified according to your needs.

- The **Test Bank,** prepared by Rebecca Howell of Forsyth Technical Community College, is available in a Word document format or through Respondus or Diploma. The questions are available to instructors to create and print multiple versions of the same test by scrambling the order of all questions found in the Word version of the test bank. This allows users to customize exams by altering or adding new problems. The test bank has over 100 multiple-choice, true-false, text entry, and essay questions per chapter. Each question has been linked to a specific student learning outcome, and the correct answers are provided with section references to its source in the text.

- **Gradebook:** *WileyPLUS* provides instant access to reports on trends in class performance, student use of course materials, and progress toward learning objectives, helping info

To Learn More

To review samples of the **Abnormal Psychology: The Science and Treatment of Psychological Disorders** rich program of teaching and learning material, please visit www.wiley.com/college/sc/kring or contact your local Wiley representative to arrange a live demonstration of WileyPLUS.

Acknowledgments

We are grateful for the contributions of our colleagues and staff, for it was with their assistance that this edition was able to become the book that it is. In particular, we are extremely appreciative of the work done by Jordan Tharp, who did a huge amount of work to create, manage, and edit our ever-expanding reference section. Sheri is deeply thankful for the peaceful retreat provided by the Center for Advanced Study in the Behavioral Sciences at Stanford University, and to Tricia Soto and Amanda Thomas for their tireless help with literature searches. Sheri is also thankful to Paul Blanc for his innumerable suggestions for how to bring the material to life, to Kate Harkness for her thoughts about exciting new findings, and to Andrew Peckham for his impeccable solutions for simplifying complex material. We have also benefited from the skills and dedication of the folks at Wiley. For this edition, we have many people to thank. Specifically, we thank Executive Editor, Chris Johnson; Senior Marketing Manager, Margaret Barrett; Senior Production Editor, Sandra Rigby; and Senior Photo Editor, Billy Ray. We also are extremely grateful for the generous help and timely support from Kristen Mucci, Editorial Assistant.

From time to time, students and faculty colleagues have written us their comments on the book; these communications are always welcome. Readers can e-mail us at akring@berkeley.edu, sljohnson@berkeley.edu.

Finally and most importantly, our heartfelt thanks go to the most important people in our lives for their continued support and encouragement along the way. A great big thanks to Angela Hawk (AMK) and Daniel Rose (SLJ), to whom this book is dedicated with love and gratitude.

SEPTEMBER 2014
Ann M. Kring, *Berkeley, CA*
Sheri L. Johnson, *Berkeley, CA*

Brief Contents

Contents

7

Obsessive-Compulsive-Related and Trauma-Related Disorders 200

8

Dissociative Disorders and Somatic Symptom-Related Disorders 224

9

Schizophrenia 250

10

Substance Use Disorders 286

Introduction and Historical Overview

1. Be able to explain the meaning of stigma as it applies to people with psychological disorders.
2. Be able to describe and compare different definitions of psychological disorder.
3. Be able to explain how the causes and treatments of psychological disorders have changed over the course of history.
4. Be able to describe the historical forces that have helped to shape our current view of psychological disorders, including biological, psychoanalytic, behavioral, and cognitive views.
5. Be able to describe the different mental health professions, including the training involved and the expertise developed.

Clinical Case: Jack

Jack dreaded family gatherings. His parents' house would be filled with his brothers and their families, and all the little kids would run around making a lot of noise. His parents would urge him to "be social" and spend time with the family, even though Jack preferred to be alone. He knew that the kids called him "crazy Uncle Jack." In fact, he had even heard his younger brother Kevin call him "crazy Jack" when he'd stopped by to see their mother the other day. Jack's mother admonished Kevin, reminding him that Jack had been doing very well on his new medication. "Schizophrenia is an illness," his mother had said.

Jack had not been hospitalized with an acute episode of schizophrenia for over 2 years. Even though Jack still heard voices, he learned not to talk about them in front of his mother because she would then start hassling him about taking his medication or ask him all sorts of questions about whether he needed to go back to the hospital. He hoped he would soon be able to move out of his parents' house and into his own apartment. The landlord at the last apartment he had tried to rent rejected his application once he learned that Jack had schizophrenia. His mother and father needed to cosign the lease, and they had inadvertently said that Jack was doing very well with his illness. The landlord asked about the illness, and once his parents mentioned schizophrenia, the landlord became visibly uncomfortable. The landlord called later that night and said the apartment had already been rented. When Jack's father pressed him, the landlord admitted he "didn't want any trouble" and that he was worried that people like Jack were violent.

Clinical Case: Felicia

Felicia didn't like to think back to her early school years. Elementary school was not a very fun time. She couldn't sit still or follow directions very well. She often blurted out answers when it wasn't her turn to talk, and she never seemed to be able to finish her class papers without many mistakes. As if that wasn't bad enough, the other girls often laughed at her and called her names. She still remembers the time she tried to join in with a group of girls during recess. They kept running away, whispering to each other, and giggling. When Felicia asked what was so funny, one of the girls laughed and said, "You are hyper, girl! You fidget so much in class, you must have ants in your pants!"

When Felicia started fourth grade, her parents took her to a psychologist. She took a number of tests and answered all sorts of questions. At the end of these testing sessions, the psychologist diagnosed Felicia with attention-deficit/hyperactivity disorder (ADHD). Felicia began seeing a different psychologist, and her pediatrician prescribed the medication Ritalin. She enjoyed seeing the psychologist because she helped her learn how to deal with the other kids' teasing and how to do a better job of paying attention. The medication helped, too—she was able to concentrate better and didn't seem to blurt out things as much anymore.

Now in high school, Felicia is much happier. She has a good group of close friends, and her grades are better than they have ever been. Though it is still hard to focus sometimes, she has learned a number of ways to deal with her distractibility. She is looking forward to college, hoping she can get into the top state school. Her guidance counselor has encouraged her, thinking her grades and extracurricular activities will make for a strong application.

WE ALL TRY TO understand other people. Determining why another person does or feels something is not easy to do. In fact, we do not always understand our own feelings and behavior. Figuring out why people behave in normal, expected ways is difficult enough; understanding seemingly abnormal behavior, such as the behavior of Jack and Felicia, can be even more difficult.

In this book, we will consider the description, causes, and treatments of a number of different **psychological disorders**. We will also demonstrate the numerous challenges professionals in this field face. As you approach the study of **psychopathology**, the field concerned with the nature, development, and treatment of psychological disorders, keep in mind that the field is continually developing and adding new findings. As we proceed, you will see that the field's interest and importance are ever growing.

One challenge we face is to remain objective. Our subject matter, human behavior, is personal and powerfully affecting, making objectivity difficult. The pervasiveness and potentially disturbing effects of psychopathology intrude on our own lives. Who has not experienced irrational thoughts, or feelings? Most of us have known someone, a friend or a relative, whose behavior was upsetting or difficult to understand, and we realize how frustrating and frightening it can be to try to understand and help a person suffering psychological difficulties. You can see that this personal impact of our subject matter requires us to make a conscious, determined effort to remain objective.

The other side of this coin is that our closeness to the subject matter adds to its intrinsic fascination; undergraduate courses in clinical or abnormal psychology are among the most popular in the entire college curriculum, not just in psychology departments. Our feeling of familiarity with the subject matter draws us to the study of psychopathology, but it also has a distinct disadvantage: we bring to the study our preconceived notions of what the subject matter is. Each of us has developed certain ways of thinking and talking about psychological disorders, certain words and concepts that somehow seem to fit. As you read this book and try to understand the psychological disorders it discusses, we may be asking you to adopt different ways of thinking and talking from those to which you are accustomed.

Perhaps most challenging of all, we must not only recognize our own preconceived notions of psychological disorders, but we must also confront and work to change the **stigma** we often associate with these conditions. Stigma refers to the destructive beliefs and attitudes held by a society that are ascribed to groups considered different in some manner, such as people with psychological disorders. More specifically, stigma has four characteristics (see Figure 1.1):

1. A label is applied to a group of people that distinguishes them from others (e.g., "crazy").

2. The label is linked to deviant or undesirable attributes by society (e.g., crazy people are dangerous).

3. People with the label are seen as essentially different from those without the label, contributing to an "us" versus "them" mentality (e.g., we are not like those crazy people).

4. People with the label are discriminated against unfairly (e.g., a clinic for crazy people can't be built in our neighborhood).

The case of Jack illustrates how stigma can lead to discrimination. Jack was denied an apartment because of his schizophrenia. The landlord believed Jack's schizophrenia meant he would be violent. This belief is based more in fiction than reality, however. A person with a psychological disorder is not necessarily any more likely to be violent than a person without such a disorder (Steadman, Mulvey, Monahan, et al., 1998; Swanson, Holzer, Ganju, & Jono, 1990), even though people with psychological disorders can be violent if they do not receive treatment (Torrey, 2014).

As we will see, the treatment of people with psychological disorders throughout recorded history has not generally been good, and this has contributed to their stigmatization, to the extent that they have often been brutalized and shunned by society. In the past, torturous treatments were held up to the public as miracle cures, and even today, terms such as *crazy, insane, retard,* and *schizo* are tossed about without thought of the people who actually suffer from psychological disorders and for whom these insults and the intensely distressing feelings and behaviors they refer to are a reality of daily life. The cases of Jack and Felicia illustrate how hurtful using such careless and mean-spirited names can be.

Psychological disorders remain the most stigmatized of conditions in the twenty-first century, despite advances in the public's knowledge about the origins of psychological disorders (Hinshaw, 2007). In 1999, then Surgeon General of the United States David Satcher, in his groundbreaking report on mental illness, wrote that stigma is the "most formidable obstacle to future progress in the arena of mental illness and mental health" (U.S. Department of Health and Human Services, 1999). Sadly, this remains true more than 15 years later.

Throughout this book, we hope to fight this stigma by showing you the latest evidence about the nature and causes of these disorders, together with treatments, dispelling myths and other misconceptions as we proceed. As part of this effort, we will try to put a human face on psychological disorders by including descriptions of actual people with these disorders Additional ways to fight stigma are presented in Focus on Discovery 1.1.

But you will have to help in this fight, for the mere acquisition of knowledge does not ensure the end of stigma (Penn, Chamberlin, & Mueser, 2003). As we will see in Chapter 2, in the last 20 years we have learned a great deal about neurobiological contributors to psychological disorders, such as neurotransmitters and genetics. Many mental health practitioners and advocates hoped that the more people learned about the neurobiological causes of psychological disorders, the less stigmatized these disorders would be. However, results from an important study show that this may not be true (Pescosolido, Martin, Long, et al., 2010). People's knowledge has increased, but unfortunately stigma has not decreased. In the study, researchers surveyed people's attitudes and knowledge about psychological disorders at two points in time: 1996 and 2006. Compared to 1996, people in 2006 were more likely to believe that psychological disorders such as schizophrenia, depression, and alcohol addiction had a neurobiological cause, but stigma toward these disorders did not decrease. In fact, in some cases it increased. For example, people in 2006 were less likely to want to have a person with schizophrenia as their neighbor compared to people in 1996. Clearly, there is work to be done to reduce stigma.

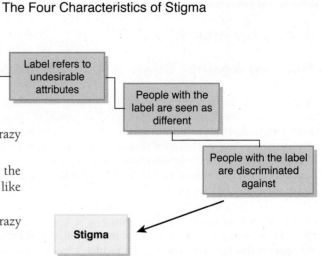

The Four Characteristics of Stigma

Figure 1.1 The four characteristics of stigma.

FOCUS ON DISCOVERY 1.1

Fighting Against Stigma: A Strategic Approach

In 2007, psychologist Stephen Hinshaw published a book entitled *The Mark of Shame: The Stigma of Mental Illness and an Agenda for Change*. In this important book, Hinshaw outlines several steps that can be taken to end stigma surrounding psychological disorders. Here we briefly discuss some of the key suggestions for fighting stigma across many arenas, including law and policy, community, mental health professions, and individual/family behaviors and attitudes.

Policy and Legislative Strategies

Parity in Insurance Coverage In 1996, the Federal Mental Health Parity Act required that insurance coverage for mental illness be at the same level as for other illnesses, which was an important first step. However, the law had a number of problems (e.g., addiction was not included; companies could set limits on coverage). In 2008, an even broader parity bill, the Mental Health Parity and Addiction Equity Act (MHPAE), came closer to offering true parity. With this law, insurance companies cannot charge higher co-payments or deductibles for mental illness than they do for other types of illnesses. Rules regarding the implementation of the law were put into place in 2010. The Affordable Care Act, the large expansion of all types of health care in the United States, continues to honor the provisions set forth by the MHPAE with a set of regulations signed by President Barack Obama in 2013. These regulations specify that insurers cannot approve fewer doctor visits or less time in a hospital for people with psychological disorders than for people with other disorders and illnesses. Unfortunately, however, these regulations do not yet apply to the broad health care programs in the United States for the elderly (Medicare) and the poor (Medicaid). One recent study found that the number of **psychiatrists** who accepted new people under Medicare or Medicaid declined by nearly 20 percent between 2005 and 2010 (Bishop, Press, Keyhani, & Pincus, 2014).

Discriminatory Laws Some states have rules banning people with a psychological disorder from voting, marrying, serving on juries, or holding public office. In an analysis of bills submitted for consideration in state legislatures in 2002, there were about as many bills to take away liberties as there were to grant liberties to people with psychological disorders. Similarly, there were roughly equal numbers of new bills that would effectively increase discrimination against people with psychological disorders as there were bills that would diminish discrimination (Corrigan, Watson, Heyrman, et al., 2005). Speaking to state legislators about the importance of nondiscriminatory laws is something we can all do to help fight stigma in this arena.

Employment Unemployment rates among people with psychological disorders are extremely high, despite provisions of the Americans with Disabilities Act (ADA) that make it illegal to keep someone with a psychological disorder from obtaining or keeping a job. The cruel irony here is that only a small number of ADA claims deal with job discrimination for people with a psychological disorder (likely because people with psychological disorders are afraid to come forward due to the stigma surrounding their illness). Yet these claims are among the easiest, at least in terms of cost, to fix (e.g., contrast the cost of allowing time off for therapy to the cost of redesigning and building a wheelchair-accessible area). Further training in job-relevant skills, such as provision of extra educational benefits to those whose education might have been curtailed

by a psychological disorder, would help with employment opportunities. Similarly, training in social skills relevant to the workplace and other structured programs to enhance workplace success is an important goal.

Decriminalization People with psychological disorders, particularly substance use disorders, often end up in jail rather than a hospital. Large urban jails, such as the Los Angeles County jail, Riker's Island in New York, and Cook County jail in Chicago, now house more people with psychological disorders than any hospital, public or private, in the United States. Many substance use problems are first detected within the criminal justice system, and people may need more intensive treatment to address these issues. Minimal or no treatment is provided in jail, and so this is not an optimal place for people with psychological disorders. Many states have adopted assisted outpatient treatment (AOT) laws that provide court-mandated outpatient treatment rather than jail time for people with psychological disorders.

Community Strategies

Housing Options Rates of homelessness in people with psychological disorders are too high, and more programs to provide community residences and group homes are needed. However, many neighborhoods are reluctant to embrace the idea of people with a psychological disorder living too close by. Lobbying legislatures and community leaders about the importance of adequate housing is a critically important step toward providing housing for people with psychological disorders and reducing stigma.

Personal Contact Providing greater housing opportunities for people with psychological disorders will likely mean that people with these disorders will shop and eat in local establishments alongside people without these disorders. Research suggests that this type of contact—where status is relatively equal—can reduce stigma. Informal settings, such as local parks and churches, can also help bridge the personal contact gap between people with and without psychological disorders.

Education Educating people about psychological disorders (one of the goals of this book!) is an important step toward reducing stigma. Education alone won't completely eradicate stigma, however. By learning about psychological disorders, though, people may be less hesitant to interact with people who have different disorders. Many of you already know someone with a psychological disorder. Sadly, though, stigma often prevents people from disclosing their history with a psychological disorder. Education may help lessen people's hesitancy to talk about their illnesses.

Mental Health and Health Profession Strategies

Mental Health Evaluations Many children see their pediatricians for well-baby or well-child exams. The goal of these visits is to prevent illness before it occurs. Hinshaw (2007) makes a strong case for including similar preventive efforts for psychological disorders among children and adolescents by, for example, including rating scale assessments from parents and teachers in order to help identify problems before they become more serious.

Education and Training Mental health professionals should receive training in stigma issues. This type of training would undoubtedly help professionals recognize the pernicious signs of stigma, even within the very profession that is charged with helping people with psychological disorders. In addition, mental health professionals need to keep current on the descriptions, causes, and empirically supported treatments for psychological disorders. This would certainly lead to better interactions with people and might also help educate the public about the important work being done by mental health professionals.

Individual and Family Strategies

Education for Individuals and Families It can be frightening and disorienting for families to learn that a loved one has been diagnosed with an illness, and this may be particularly true for psychological disorders. Receiving current information about the causes and treatments of psychological disorders is crucial because it helps to alleviate blame and stereotypes families might hold about psychological disorders. Educating people with a psychological disorder is also extremely important. Sometimes termed *psychoeducation*, this type of information is built into many types of treatments, whether pharmacological or psychosocial. In

order for people to understand why they should adhere to certain treatment regimens, it is important for them to know the nature of their illness and the treatment alternatives available.

Support and Advocacy Groups Participating in support or advocacy groups can be a helpful adjunct to treatment for people with psychological disorders and their families. Websites such as Mind Freedom International (http://www.mindfreedom.org) and the Icarus Project (http://www.theicarusproject.net) are designed to provide a forum for people with psychological disorders to find support. Some such groups also encourage people not to hide their disorders, but rather to consider it a point of pride—"Mad Pride" events are scheduled all over the world (Quart, 2013). These sites, developed and run by people with psychological disorders, contain useful links, blogs, and other helpful resources. In-person support groups are also helpful, and many communities have groups supported by the National Alliance on Mental Illness (http://www.nami.org). Finding peers in the context of support groups can be beneficial, especially for emotional support and empowerment.

Recent efforts to reduce stigma have been quite creative in their use of social media and other means to get the message out that psychological disorders are common and affect us all in one way or another. Indeed, one of the largest and most recent epidemiological studies (see Chapter 4 for more on epidemiology) reported that the lifetime prevalence of any psychological disorder in the United States was 46.4 percent (Kessler, Berglund, Demler, et al., 2005), suggesting that nearly half of the U.S. population may experience some type of psychological disorder in their lifetimes. Many people with blogs have talked poignantly about their lives with different psychological disorders, and these accounts help to demystify and therefore destigmatize it. For example, Allie Brosh writes a blog called Hyperbole and a Half and discusses her experiences with depression on her blog (http://hyperboleandahalf.blogspot.com) and in a book (Brosh, 2013). The site Patients Like Me (http://www.patientslikeme.com) is a social networking site for people with all sorts of different illnesses. Other creative efforts include the design of T-shirts by a graphic designer named Dani Balenson (http://danibalenson.com). In her work, she seeks to use color and graphics to depict the symptoms, behaviors, and struggles that characterize psychological disorders such as ADHD, obsessive-compulsive disorder, depression, and bipolar disorder (http://www.livingwith.co).

In this chapter, we first discuss what we mean by the term *psychological disorder*. Then we look briefly at how our views of psychological disorders have evolved through history to the more scientific perspectives of today. We conclude with a discussion of the current mental health professions.

Defining Psychological Disorder

A difficult but fundamental task facing those in the field of psychopathology is to define psychological disorder. The best current definition of psychological disorder is one that contains several characteristics. The definition of *mental disorder* presented in the fifth edition of the American diagnostic manual, the *Diagnostic and Statistical Manual of Mental Disorders* (DSM-5), which was released in May 2013, includes a number of characteristics essential to the concept of psychological disorder (Stein, Phillips, Bolton, et al., 2010), including the following:

- The disorder occurs within the individual.
- It involves clinically significant difficulties in thinking, feeling, or behaving.
- It usually involves personal distress of some sort, such as in social relationships or occupational functioning.
- It involves dysfunction in psychological, developmental, and/or neurobiological processes that support mental functioning.
- It is not a culturally specific reaction to an event (e.g., death of a loved one).
- It is not primarily a result of social deviance or conflict with society.

In the following sections, we consider four key characteristics that should be part of any comprehensive psychological disorder definition: personal distress, disability, violation of social norms, and dysfunction (see Figure 1.2). We will see that no single characteristic can fully define the concept, although each has merit and each captures some part of what might be a full definition. Consequently, psychological disorder is usually determined based on the presence of several characteristics at one time.

Defining Psychological Disorder

Figure 1.2 Four characteristics of a comprehensive definition of psychological disorder.

Personal Distress

One characteristic used to define psychological disorder is personal distress—that is, a person's behavior may be classified as disordered if it causes him or her great distress. Felicia felt distress about her difficulty in paying attention and the social consequences of this difficulty—that is, being called names by other schoolgirls. Personal distress also characterizes many of the forms of psychological disorder considered in this book—people experiencing anxiety disorders and depression suffer greatly. But not all psychological disorders cause distress. For example, an individual with the antisocial type of personality disorder may treat others coldheartedly and violate the law without experiencing any guilt, remorse, anxiety, or other type of distress. And not all behavior that causes distress is disordered—for example, the distress of hunger due to religious fasting or the pain of childbirth.

Clinical Case: José

José didn't know what to think about his nightmares. Ever since he returned from the war, he couldn't get the bloody images out of his head. He woke up nearly every night with nightmares about the carnage he witnessed as a soldier stationed in Fallujah. Even during the day, he would have flashbacks to the moment his Humvee was nearly sliced in half by a rocket-propelled grenade. Watching his friend die sitting next to him was the worst part; even the occasional pain from shrapnel still embedded in his shoulder was not as bad as the recurring dreams and flashbacks. He seemed to be sweating all the time now, and whenever he heard a loud noise, he jumped out of his chair. Just the other day, his grandmother stepped on a balloon left over from his

"welcome home" party. To José, it sounded like a gunshot, and he immediately dropped to the ground.

His grandmother was worried about him. She thought he must have *ataque de nervios*, just like her father had back home in Puerto Rico. She said her father had been afraid all the time and felt like he was going crazy. She kept going to Mass and praying for José, which he appreciated. The army doctor said he had posttraumatic stress disorder (PTSD). José was supposed to go to the Veterans Administration (VA) hospital for an evaluation, but he didn't really think there was anything wrong with him. Yet his buddy Jorge had been to a group session at the VA, and he said it made him feel better. Maybe he would check it out. He wanted these images to get out of his head.

Disability

Disability—that is, impairment in some important area of life (e.g., work or personal relationships)—can also characterize psychological disorder. For example, substance use disorders are defined in part by the social or occupational disability (e.g., serious arguments with one's spouse or poor work performance) created by substance abuse. Being rejected by peers, as Felicia was, is also an example of this characteristic. Phobias can produce both distress and disability—for example, if a severe fear of flying prevents someone living in California from taking a job in New York. Like distress, however, disability alone cannot be used to define psychological disorder because some, but not all, disorders involve disability. For example, the disorder bulimia nervosa involves binge eating and compensatory purging (e.g., vomiting) in an attempt to control weight gain, but it does not necessarily involve disability. Many people with bulimia lead lives without impairment, while bingeing and purging in private. Other characteristics that might, in some circumstances, be considered disabilities—such as being blind and wanting to become a professional race car driver—do not fall within the domain of psychopathology. We do not have a rule that tells us which disabilities belong in our domain of study and which do not.

Personal distress can be part of the definition of psychological disorder.

© michele piacquadio/iStockphoto

Violation of Social Norms

In the realm of behavior, social norms are widely held standards (beliefs and attitudes) that people use consciously or intuitively to make judgments about where behaviors are situated on such scales as good–bad, right–wrong, justified–unjustified, and acceptable–unacceptable. Behavior that violates social norms might be classified as disordered. For example, the repetitive rituals performed by people with obsessive-compulsive disorder (see Chapter 7) and the conversations with imaginary voices that some people with schizophrenia engage in (see Chapter 9) are behaviors that violate social norms. José's dropping to the floor at the sound of a popping balloon does not fit within most social norms. Yet this way of defining psychological disorder is both too broad and too narrow. For example, it is too broad in that criminals violate social norms but are not usually studied within the domain of psychopathology; it is too narrow in that highly anxious people typically do not violate social norms.

Also, of course, social norms vary a great deal across cultures and ethnic groups, so behavior that clearly violates a social norm in one group may not do so at all in another. For example, in some cultures but not in others, it violates a social norm to directly disagree with someone. In Puerto Rico, José's behavior would not likely have been interpreted in the same way as it would be in the United States. Throughout this book, we will address this important issue of cultural and ethnic diversity as it applies to the descriptions, causes, and treatments of psychological disorders.

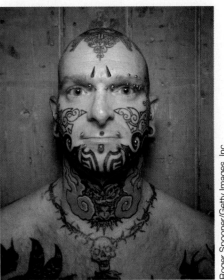

Roger Spooner/Getty Images, Inc.

To some people, extreme tattoos are a violation of the social norm. However, social norm violations are not necessarily signs of a psychological disorder.

Dysfunction

In an influential and widely discussed paper, Wakefield (1992) proposed that psychological disorders could be defined as **harmful dysfunction**. This definition has two parts: a value judgment ("harmful") and an objective, scientific component—the "dysfunction." A judgment that a behavior is harmful requires some standard, and this standard is likely to depend on social norms and values, the characteristic just described. Dysfunctions are said to occur when an internal mechanism is unable to perform its natural function—that is, the function that it evolved to perform. By grounding this part of the definition of psychological disorder in evolutionary theory, Wakefield hoped to give the definition scientific objectivity.

Numerous critics have argued that the dysfunction component of Wakefield's definition is not so easily and objectively identifiable in relation to psychological disorders (e.g., Houts, 2001; Lilienfeld & Marino, 1999). One difficulty is that many internal mechanisms involved in psychological disorders are unknown; thus, we cannot say exactly what may not be functioning properly.

Wakefield (1999) has tried to meet this objection by, in part, referring to plausible dysfunctions rather than proven ones. In the case of Jack, for example, hallucinations (hearing voices) could be construed as a failure of the mind to "turn off" unwanted sounds. Nevertheless, we have a situation in which we judge a behavior or set of behaviors to be harmful and then decide that the behavior represents a psychological disorder because we believe it is caused by a dysfunction of some unknown internal mechanism. Clearly, like the other definitions of psychological disorder, Wakefield's concept of harmful dysfunction has its limitations.

The DSM definition provides a broader concept of dysfunction, which is supported by our current body of evidence. Specifically, the DSM definition of dysfunction refers to the fact that developmental, psychological, and biological dysfunctions are all interrelated. That is, the brain impacts behavior, and behavior impacts the brain; thus dysfunction in these areas is interrelated. This broadening does not entirely avoid the problems associated with Wakefield's definition, but it is an attempt to formally recognize the limits of our current understanding.

Indeed, it is crucial to keep in mind that this book presents human problems that are currently considered psychological disorders. Over time, because the field is continually evolving, the disorders discussed in books like this will undoubtedly change, and so will the definition of psychological disorder. It is also quite possible that we will never be able to arrive at a definition that captures psychological disorder in its entirety and for all time. Nevertheless, at the current time, the characteristics included in the definition constitute a useful partial definition, but keep in mind that they do not equally or invariably apply to every diagnosis.

Quick Summary

This book focuses on the description, causes, and treatments of a number of different psychological disorders. It is important to note at the outset that the personal impact of our subject matter requires us to make a conscious, determined effort to remain objective. Stigma remains a central problem in the field of psychopathology. Stigma has four components that involve the labels for psychological disorders and their uses. Even the use of everyday terms such as *crazy* or *schizo* can contribute to the stigmatization of people with psychological disorders.

Defining psychological disorder remains difficult. A number of different definitions have been offered, but none can entirely account for the full range of disorders. Whether or not a behavior causes personal distress can be a characteristic of psychological disorder.

But not all behaviors that we consider to be part of psychological disorders cause distress. Behaviors that cause a disability or are unexpected can be considered part of a psychological disorder. But again, some behaviors do not cause disability, nor are they unexpected. Behavior that violates social norms can also be considered part of a psychological disorder. However, not all such behavior is considered part of a psychological disorder, and some behaviors that are characteristic of psychological disorders do not necessarily violate social norms. Harmful dysfunction involves both a value and a scientific component. Like the other definitions, however, it cannot fully account for what we study in psychopathology. Taken together, each definition of psychological disorder has something helpful to offer in the study of psychopathology.

Check Your Knowledge 1.1 (Answers are at the end of the chapter.)

1. Characteristics of stigma include all of the following *except*:
   a. a label reflecting desirable characteristics
   b. discrimination against those with the label
   c. focus on differences between those with and without the label
   d. labeling a group of people who are different
2. Which of the following definitions of psychological disorder is currently thought best?
   a. personal distress
   b. harmful dysfunction
   c. norm violation
   d. none of the above

3. Why is the DSM definition of psychological disorder perhaps the best current definition?
   a. It includes information about both violation of social norms and dysfunction.
   b. It includes many components, none of which alone can account for psychological disorder.
   c. It is part of the current diagnostic system.
   d. It recognizes the limits of our current understanding.

History of Psychopathology

Many textbooks begin with a chapter on the history of the field. Why? It is important to consider how concepts and approaches have changed (or not) over time, because we can learn from mistakes made in the past and because we can see that our current concepts and approaches are likely to change in the future. As we consider the history of psychopathology, we will see that many new approaches to the treatment of psychological disorders throughout time appear to go well at first and are heralded with much excitement and fanfare. But these treatments eventually fall into disrepute. These are lessons that should not be forgotten as we consider more contemporary approaches to treatment and their attendant excitement and fanfare.

The search for the causes of psychological disorders has gone on for a considerable period of time. At different periods in history, explanations for psychological disorders have been supernatural, biological, and psychological. As we quickly travel through these different periods, ask yourself what level of explanation was operating at different times.

Early Demonology

Before the age of scientific inquiry, all good and bad manifestations of power beyond human control—eclipses, earthquakes, storms, fire, diseases, the changing seasons—were regarded as supernatural. Behavior seemingly outside individual control was also ascribed to supernatural causes. Many early philosophers, theologians, and physicians who studied the troubled mind believed that disturbed behavior reflected the displeasure of the gods or possession by demons.

The doctrine that an evil being or spirit can dwell within a person and control his or her mind and body is called **demonology**. Examples of demonological thinking are found in the records of the early Chinese, Egyptians, Babylonians, and Greeks. Among the Hebrews, odd behavior was attributed to possession of the person by bad spirits, after God in his wrath had withdrawn protection. The New Testament includes the story of Christ curing a man with an unclean spirit by casting out the devils from within him and hurling them onto a herd of swine (Mark 5:8–13).

The belief that odd behavior was caused by possession led to treating it by **exorcism**, the ritualistic casting out of evil spirits. Exorcism typically took the form of elaborate rites of prayer, noisemaking, forcing the afflicted to drink terrible-tasting brews, and on occasion more extreme measures, such as flogging and starvation, to render the body uninhabitable to devils.

Early Biological Explanations

In the fifth century B.C., Hippocrates (460?–377? B.C.), often called the father of modern medicine, separated medicine from religion, magic, and superstition. He rejected the prevailing Greek belief that the gods sent mental disturbances as punishment and insisted instead that such illnesses had natural causes and hence should be treated like other, more common maladies, such as colds and constipation. Hippocrates regarded the brain as the organ of consciousness, intellectual life, and emotion; thus, he thought that disordered thinking and behavior were indications of some kind of brain pathology. Hippocrates is often considered one of the earliest proponents of the notion that something wrong with the brain disturbs thought and action.

Hippocrates classified psychological disorders into three categories: mania, melancholia, and phrenitis, or brain fever. Further, Hippocrates believed that normal brain functioning, and therefore mental health, depended on a delicate balance among four humors, or fluids of the body, namely, blood, black bile, yellow bile, and phlegm. An imbalance of these humors produced disorders. If a person was sluggish and dull, for example, the body supposedly contained a preponderance of phlegm. A preponderance of black bile was the explanation for melancholia; too much yellow bile explained irritability and anxiousness; and too much blood, changeable temperament.

The Greek physician Hippocrates held a biological view of psychological disorders, considering psychological disorders to be diseases of the brain.

Through Hippocrates' teachings, the phenomena associated with psychological disorders became more clearly the province of physicians rather than priests. The treatments he suggested were quite different from exorcism. For melancholia, for example, he prescribed tranquility, sobriety, care in choosing food and drink, and abstinence from sexual activity. Because Hippocrates believed in natural rather than supernatural causes, he depended on his own keen observations and made valuable contributions as a clinician. He also left behind remarkably detailed records clearly describing many of the symptoms now recognized in seizure disorders, alcohol dependence, stroke, and paranoia.

Hippocrates' ideas, of course, did not withstand later scientific scrutiny. However, his basic premise—that human behavior is markedly affected by bodily structures or substances and that odd behavior is produced by some kind of physical imbalance or even damage—did foreshadow aspects of contemporary thought. In the next seven centuries, Hippocrates' naturalistic approach to disease and disorder was generally accepted by other Greeks as well as by the Romans, who adopted the medicine of the Greeks after the Roman Empire became the major power in the ancient European world.

The Dark Ages and Demonology

Historians have often pointed to the death of Galen (A.D. 130–200), the second-century Greek who is regarded as the last great physician of the classical era, as the beginning of the so-called Dark Ages in western European medicine and in the treatment and investigation of psychological disorders. Over several centuries of decay, Greek and Roman civilization ceased to be. The Church now gained in influence, and the papacy was declared independent of the state. Christian monasteries, through their missionary and educational work, replaced physicians as healers and as authorities on psychological disorder.[1]

The monks in the monasteries cared for and nursed the sick, and a few of the monasteries were repositories for the classic Greek medical manuscripts, even though the monks may not have made use of the knowledge in these works. Monks cared for people with psychological disorders by praying over them and touching them with relics; they also concocted fantastic potions for them to drink in the waning phase of the moon. Many people with psychological disorders roamed the countryside, destitute and progressively becoming worse. During this period, there was a return to a belief in supernatural causes of psychological disorders.

Galen was a Greek physician who followed Hippocrates' ideas and is regarded as the last great physician of the classical era.

The Persecution of Witches Beginning in the thirteenth century, in response to widespread social unrest and recurrent famines and plagues, people in Europe turned to demonological explanations to account for these disasters. Witchcraft, now viewed as instigated by Satan, was seen as a heresy and a denial of God. Then, as today, when faced with inexplicable and frightening occurrences, people tended to seize on whatever explanation seemed most plausible. The times conspired to heap enormous blame on those regarded as witches, who were persecuted with great zeal.

In 1484, Pope Innocent VIII exhorted the clergy of Europe to leave no stone unturned in the search for witches. He sent two Dominican monks to northern Germany as inquisitors. Two years later they issued a comprehensive and explicit manual, *Malleus Maleficarum* ("the witches' hammer"), to guide the witch hunts. This legal and theological document came to be regarded by Catholics and Protestants alike as a textbook on witchcraft. Those accused of witchcraft should be tortured if they did not confess; those convicted and penitent were to be imprisoned for life; and those convicted and unrepentant were to be handed over to the law for execution. The manual specified that a person's sudden loss of reason was a symptom of demonic possession and that burning was the usual method of driving out the supposed demon. Records of the period are not considered reliable, but it is thought that over the next several centuries hundreds of thousands of people, particularly women and children, were accused, tortured, and put to death.

---

[1]The teachings of Galen continued to be influential in the Islamic world. For example, the Persian physician al-Razi (865–925) established a facility for the treatment of people with psychological disorders in Baghdad and was an early practitioner of psychotherapy.

Contemporary investigators initially believed that many of the people accused of being witches during this period were mentally ill (Zilboorg & Henry, 1941). The basis for this belief was the confessions of the accused that investigators interpreted as delusional beliefs or hallucinations.

More detailed research into this historical period, however, indicates that many of the accused were not mentally ill. Careful analyses of the witch hunts reveal that more healthy than ill people were tried. Confessions were typically obtained during brutal torture, having been suggested to the accused witches both by their accusers and by the prevailing beliefs of the times. Indeed, in England, where torture was not allowed, the confessions did not usually contain descriptions resembling delusions or hallucinations (Schoeneman, 1977).

Lunacy Trials Evaluations of other sources of information also indicate that a psychological disorder was not primarily ascribed to witchcraft. From the thirteenth century on, as the cities of Europe grew larger, hospitals began to come under secular jurisdiction. Municipal authorities, gaining in power, tended to supplement or take over some of the activities of the Church, one of these being the care of people who were mentally ill. The foundation deed for the Holy Trinity Hospital in Salisbury, England, dating from the mid-fourteenth century, specified the purposes of the hospital, one of which was that the "mad are kept safe until they are restored of reason." English laws during this period allowed people with psychological disorders to be hospitalized. Notably, the people who were hospitalized were not described as being possessed (Allderidge, 1979).

In the dunking test, if the woman did not drown, she was considered to be in league with the devil (and punished accordingly); this is the ultimate no-win situation.

Beginning in the thirteenth century, lunacy trials to determine a person's mental health were held in England. As explained by Neugebauer (1979), the trials were conducted under the Crown's right to protect the people with psychological disorders, and a judgment of insanity allowed the Crown to become guardian of the lunatic's estate. The defendant's orientation, memory, intellect, daily life, and habits were at issue in the trial. Usually, strange behavior was attributed to physical illness or injury or to some emotional shock. In all the cases that Neugebauer examined, only one referred to demonic possession. Interestingly, the term *lunacy* comes from a theory espoused by the Swiss physician Paracelsus (1493–1541), who attributed odd behavior to a misalignment of the moon and stars (the Latin word for "moon" is *luna*). This lunar explanation, even if unsubstantiated, was a welcome alternative to explanations involving demons or witches. Even today, many people believe that a full moon is linked to odd behavior; however, there is no scientific evidence to support this belief.

Development of Asylums

Until the fifteenth century, there were very few hospitals for people with psychological disorders in Europe. However, there were many hospitals for people with leprosy. As leprosy gradually disappeared from Europe (probably because with the end of wars came a break with the sources of the infection), these buildings were now underused. Attention seems to have turned to people with psychological disorders, and the old leprosy hospitals were converted to **asylums**, refuges for the housing and care of people with psychological disorders.

Bethlehem and Other Early Asylums The Priory of St. Mary of Bethlehem was founded in 1243. Records indicate that in 1403 it housed six men with psychological disorders. In 1547, Henry VIII handed it over to the city of London, thereafter to be a hospital devoted solely to the confinement of people with psychological disorders. The conditions in Bethlehem were deplorable. Over the years the word *bedlam*, the popular name for this hospital, came to mean a place or scene of wild uproar and confusion. Bethlehem eventually became one of London's great tourist attractions, by the eighteenth century rivaling both Westminster Abbey and the Tower of London. Even as late as the nineteenth century, viewing the people housed

Corbis-Bettmann

In this eighteenth-century painting by Hogarth, two upper-class women find amusement in touring St. Mary's of Bethlehem (Bedlam).

in Bethlehem was considered entertainment, and people bought tickets to see them. Similarly, in the Lunatics Tower, which was constructed in Vienna in 1784, people were confined in the spaces between inner square rooms and the outer walls, where they could be viewed by passersby.

Obviously, confining people with psychological disorders in hospitals and placing their care in the domain of medicine did not necessarily lead to more humane and effective treatment. Medical treatments were often crude and painful. Benjamin Rush (1745–1813), for example, began practicing medicine in Philadelphia in 1769 and is considered the father of American psychiatry. Yet he believed that psychological disorder was caused by an excess of blood in the brain, for which his favored treatment was to draw great quantities of blood from disordered individuals (Farina, 1976). Rush also believed that many people with psychological disorders could be cured by being frightened. Thus, one of his recommended procedures was for the physician to convince the patient that death was near!

Pinel's Reforms Philippe Pinel (1745–1826) has often been considered a primary figure in the movement for more humane treatment of people with psychological disorders in asylums. In 1793, while the French Revolution raged, he was put in charge of a large asylum in Paris known as La Bicêtre. A historian described the conditions at this particular hospital:

> [The patients were] shackled to the walls of their cells, by iron collars which held them flat against the wall and permitted little movement. They could not lie down at night, as a rule. Oftentimes there was a hoop of iron around the waist of the patient and in addition chains on both the hands and the feet. These chains [were] sufficiently long so that the patient could feed himself out of a bowl, the food usually being a mushy gruel—bread soaked in a weak soup. Since little was known about dietetics, [no attention] was paid to the type of diet given the patients. They were presumed to be animals and not to care whether the food was good or bad. (Selling, 1940, p. 54)

Many texts assert that Pinel removed the chains of the people imprisoned in La Bicêtre. Historical research, however, indicates that it was not Pinel who released the people from their chains. Rather, it was a former patient, Jean-Baptiste Pussin, who had become an orderly at the hospital. In fact, Pinel was not even present when the people were released (Weiner, 1994). Several years later, though, Pinel praised Pussin's efforts and began to follow the same practices.

Pinel came to believe that people in his care were first and foremost human beings, and thus these people should be approached with compassion and understanding and treated with dignity. He surmised that if their reason had left them because of severe personal and social problems, it might be restored to them through comforting counsel and purposeful activity. Thus, light and airy rooms replaced dungeons. People formerly considered dangerous now strolled through the hospital and grounds without creating disturbances or harming anyone. Some people who had been incarcerated for years were apparently restored to health and eventually discharged from the hospital.

Although Pinel did much good for people with psychological disorders, he was no paragon of enlightenment and egalitarianism. He reserved the more humanitarian treatment for the upper classes; people of the lower classes were still subjected to terror and coercion as a means of control, with straitjackets replacing chains.

Corbis Images

In the nineteenth century, Dorothea Dix played a major role in establishing more mental hospitals in the United States.

Moral Treatment For a time, mental hospitals established in Europe and the United States were relatively small, privately supported, and operated along the lines of the humanitarian changes at La Bicêtre. In the United States, the Friends' Asylum, founded in 1817 in Pennsylvania, and the Hartford Retreat, established in 1824 in Connecticut, were

FOCUS ON DISCOVERY 1.2

The Mental Hospital Today

More people with psychological disorders are found in jails and prisons than in mental hospitals in the United States—a national disgrace.

In the late 1960s and early 1970s, concerns about the restrictive nature of confinement in a mental hospital along with unrealistic enthusiasm about community-based treatments (Torrey, 2014) led to the so-called deinstitutionalization (i.e., release from the hospital) of a large number of people with psychological disorders. Budget cuts beginning in 1980 and continuing today have caused this trend to continue. But sometimes people with a psychological disorder do need treatment in a hospital setting, and unfortunately, we still do not do a good job of this, even in the twenty-first century (as we will discuss in more detail in Chapter 16). Treatment in public mental hospitals today is often "just enough" to provide some protection, food, shelter, and in most cases medication. Indeed, people with psychological disorders in a public hospital may receive little treatment beyond medication; their existence is monotonous and sedentary for the most part.

Public mental hospitals in the United States are funded either by the federal government or more likely by the state in which they are located. Many Veterans Administration hospitals and general medical hospitals also contain units for people with psychological disorders. Since the mid-1950s, the number of public mental hospitals has decreased substantially. In 1955 there were 340 beds in public hospitals for people with psychological disorders for every 100,000 people; by 2010 there were just 14 beds for every 100,000 people (Torrey, 2014).

With the decreasing numbers of state and county hospitals, you might guess that more private mental hospitals were built to provide services once available through public hospitals. This was indeed the case beginning in the 1970s. In 1969, there were 150 private hospitals, but in 1998, there were 348 (Geller, 2006). This trend toward increasing private hospitals, however, peaked in 1992. Since then, private hospitals have also declined in number. The physical facilities and professional care in private hospitals tend to be superior to those of public hospitals for one reason: the private hospitals have more money. And prior to the Patient Protection and Affordable Care Act (2010), or the ACA, only those who have health insurance or their own money could afford to stay there. Time will tell if the "insurance for all" promise of the ACA will translate into stays in private psychiatric hospitals for all.

A somewhat specialized mental hospital, sometimes called a forensic hospital, is reserved for people who have been arrested and judged unable to stand trial and for those who have been acquitted of a crime by reason of insanity (see Chapter 16). Although these people have not been sent to prison, security staff and other tight security measures regiment their lives even as they receive treatment during their stay. There is some evidence to suggest that people who receive treatment at forensic hospitals are less likely to reoffend than people who are sent to regular prisons and do not receive treatment (Harris, 2000).

One of the many unfortunate consequences of fewer public and private mental hospitals today is overcrowding in existing hospitals. One longitudinal study of 13 public mental hospitals in Finland showed that nearly half the hospitals were overcrowded (defined as having 10 percent more occupancy than the hospital was designed for). The researchers also found that overcrowding was associated with an increased risk of violence against hospital staff by patients (Virtanen, Vahtera, Batty, et al., 2011). Although we have developed more effective treatments for many psychological disorders, as we will see throughout this book, the mental hospital of today is still in need of improvement.

Another very unfortunate consequence of fewer mental hospitals is the fact that jails have become the *de facto* mental hospitals in many cities in the United States (Baillargeon, Binswanger, Penn, et al., 2009; Torrey, 2014). Sadly, jails in Los Angeles County and Cook County (in Chicago) are now the largest "mental hospitals" in the United States in that they house more people with psychological disorders than any actual mental hospital. Moreover, a report from the Treatment Advocacy Center and the National Sheriffs Association that drew from 2004–2005 data in the United States indicated that there are more people with psychological disorders in jails or prisons than in mental hospitals (Torrey, Kennard, Eslinger, et al., 2010). Furthermore, of the people currently in prison or jail, over half have a psychological disorder (James & Glaze, 2006).

© Amanda Brown/Star Ledger/© Corbis

Most rooms at state mental hospitals are bleak and unstimulating.

established to provide humane treatment. In accordance with this approach, which became known as **moral treatment**, people had close contact with attendants, who talked and read to them and encouraged them to engage in purposeful activity; residents led lives as close to normal as possible and in general took responsibility for themselves within the constraints of their disorders. Further, there were to be no more than 250 people in a given hospital (Whitaker, 2002).

Moral treatment was largely abandoned in the latter part of the nineteenth century. Ironically, the efforts of Dorothea Dix (1802–1887), a crusader for improved conditions for people with psychological disorders who fought to have hospitals created for their care, helped effect this change. Dix, a Boston schoolteacher, taught a Sunday school class at the local prison and was shocked at the deplorable conditions in which the inmates lived. Her interest spread to the conditions at mental hospitals and to people with psychological disorders who had nowhere to go for treatment. She campaigned vigorously to improve the lives of people with psychological disorders and personally helped see that 32 state hospitals were built. These large public hospitals took in many of the people whom the private hospitals could not accommodate. Unfortunately, the small staffs of these new hospitals were unable to provide the individual attention that was a hallmark of moral treatment (Bockhoven, 1963). Moreover, the hospitals came to be administered by physicians, most of whom were interested in the biological aspects of illness and in the physical, rather than the psychological, well-being of people with psychological disorders. The money that had once paid the salaries of personal attendants now paid for equipment and laboratories. (See Focus on Discovery 1.2 for an examination of whether the conditions in today's mental hospitals have improved.)

Quick Summary

Early concepts of psychological disorders included not only demonology (possession by demons) but also biological approaches, as evidenced by the ideas of Hippocrates. During the Dark Ages, some people with psychological disorders were cared for in monasteries, but many simply roamed the countryside. Some were persecuted as witches, but this was relatively rare (later analyses indicated that many of the people accused of being witches were not mentally ill). Treatments for people with psychological disorders have changed over time, though not always for the better. Exorcisms did not help. Treatments in asylums could also be cruel and unhelpful, but pioneering work by Dix and others made asylums more humane places for treatment. Unfortunately, their good ideas did not last, as the mental hospitals became overcrowded and understaffed.

Check Your Knowledge 1.2

True or false?
1. Benjamin Rush is credited with beginning moral treatment in the United States.
2. The most recent historical research has found that nearly all of the people persecuted as witches were mentally ill.
3. Hippocrates was one of the first to propose that psychological disorders had a biological cause.
4. The term *lunatic* is derived from the ideas of Paracelsus.

The Evolution of Contemporary Thought

As horrific as the conditions in Bethlehem Hospital were (and in many ways continue to be; see Focus on Discovery 1.2), the physicians at the time were nonetheless interested in what caused the maladies of their patients. Table 1.1 lists the hypothesized causes of the illnesses exhibited by people in 1810 that were recorded by William Black, a physician working at Bethlehem at the time (Appignannesi, 2008). It is interesting to observe that about half of the presumed causes were biological (e.g., fever, hereditary, venereal) and half were psychological (e.g., grief, love, jealousy). Only around 10 percent of the causes were spiritual.

Contemporary developments in biological and psychological approaches to the causes and treatments of psychological disorders were heavily influenced by theorists and scientists working in the late nineteenth and early twentieth centuries. We will discuss, compare, and evaluate these approaches more fully in Chapter 2. In this section, we review the historical antecedents of these more contemporary approaches.

Recall that in the West, the death of Galen and the decline of Greco-Roman civilization temporarily ended inquiries into the nature of both physical and mental illness. Not until much later did any new facts begin to come to light, thanks to an emerging empirical approach to medical science, which emphasized gathering knowledge by direct observation.

Biological Approaches

Discovering Biological Origins in General Paresis and Syphilis
The anatomy and workings of the nervous system were partially understood by the mid-1800s, but not enough was known to let investigators conclude whether or not the structural brain abnormalities presumed to cause various psychological disorders were present. Perhaps the most striking medical success was the elucidation of the nature and origin of syphilis, a venereal disease that had been recognized for several centuries.

The story of this discovery regarding syphilis provides a good illustration of how an empirical approach, the basis for contemporary science, works. Since the late 1700s, it had been known that a number of people with psychological disorders manifested a syndrome

Table 1.1 Causes of Maladies Observed among People in Bethlehem in 1810

Cause	Number of People
Childbed*	79
Contusions/fractures of skull	12
Drink/intoxication	58
Family/hereditary	115
Fevers	110
Fright	31
Grief	206
Jealousy	9
Love	90
Obstruction	10
Pride	8
Religion/Methodism	90
Smallpox	7
Study	15
Venereal	14
Ulcers/scabs dried up	5

Source: Adapted from Appignanesi (2008), Hunter & Macalpine (1963).
*Childbed refers to childbirth—perhaps akin to what we now call postpartum depression.

characterized by a steady deterioration of both mental and physical abilities, and progressive paralysis; the presumed disease associated with this syndrome was given the name general paresis. By the mid-1800s, it had been established that some people with general paresis also had syphilis, but a connection between the two conditions had not yet been made.

In the 1860s and 1870s, Louis Pasteur established the germ theory of disease, which posited that disease is caused by infection of the body by minute organisms. This theory laid the groundwork for demonstrating the relation between syphilis and general paresis. Finally, in 1905, the specific microorganism that causes syphilis was discovered. For the first time, a causal link had been established between infection, damage to certain areas of the brain, and a form of psychopathology (general paresis). If one type of psychopathology had a biological cause, so could others. Biological approaches gained credibility, and searches for more biological causes were off and running.

Genetics Francis Galton (1822–1911), often considered the originator of genetic research with twins as a result of his study of twins in the late 1800s in England, attributed many behavioral characteristics to heredity. He is credited with coining the terms *nature* and *nurture* to talk about differences in genetics (nature) and environment (nurture). In the early twentieth century, investigators became intrigued by the idea that psychological disorders may run in families, and beginning at that time, a number of studies documented the heritability of psychological disorders such as schizophrenia, bipolar disorder, and depression. These studies would set the stage for later theories about the causes of psychological disorders.

Unfortunately, Galton is also credited with creating the eugenics movement in 1883 (Brooks, 2004). Advocates of this movement sought to eliminate undesirable characteristics from the population by restricting the ability of certain people to have children (e.g., by enforced sterilization). Many of the early efforts in the United States to determine whether psychological disorders could be inherited were associated with the eugenics movement, and this stalled research progress. Indeed, in a sad page from U.S. history, state laws in the late 1800s and early 1900s prohibited people with psychological disorders from marrying and forced them to be sterilized in order to prevent them from "passing on" their illness. Such laws were upheld by the U.S. Supreme Court in 1927 (Chase, 1980), and it wasn't until the middle of the twentieth century that these abhorrent practices were halted. Nevertheless, much damage had been done: by 1945, more than 45,000 people with psychological disorders in the United States had been forcibly sterilized (Whitaker, 2002).

Biological Treatments The general warehousing of people in mental hospitals earlier in the twentieth century, coupled with the shortage of professional staff, created a climate that allowed, perhaps even subtly encouraged, experimentation with radical interventions. In the early 1930s, the practice of inducing a coma with large dosages of insulin was introduced by Sakel (1938), who claimed that up to three-quarters of the people with schizophrenia whom he treated showed significant improvement. Later findings by other researchers were less encouraging, and insulin-coma therapy—which presented serious risks to health, including irreversible coma and death—was gradually abandoned.

In the early twentieth century, **electroconvulsive therapy (ECT)** was originated by two Italian physicians, Ugo Cerletti and Lucino Bini. Cerletti was interested in epilepsy and was seeking a way to induce seizures experimentally. Shortly thereafter he found that by applying electric shocks to the sides of the human head, he could produce full epileptic seizures. Then, in Rome in 1938, he used the technique on a person with schizophrenia.

In the decades that followed, ECT was administered to people with schizophrenia and severe depression, usually in hospital settings. As we will discuss in Chapter 5, it is still used today for people with severe depression. Fortunately, important refinements in the ECT procedures have made it less problematic, and it can be an effective treatment.

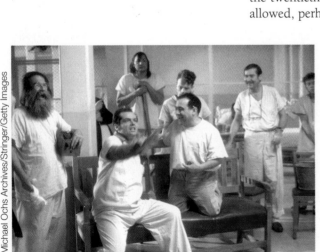

Francis Galton is considered the originator of genetics research.

© Bettmann/Corbis

Michael Ochs Archives/Stringer/Getty Images

Scene from *One Flew over the Cuckoo's Nest.* The character portrayed by Jack Nicholson was lobotomized in the film.

In 1935, Egas Moniz, a Portuguese psychiatrist, introduced the *prefrontal lobotomy*, a surgical procedure that destroys the tracts connecting the frontal lobes to other areas of the brain. His initial reports claimed high rates of success (Moniz, 1936), and for 20 years thereafter thousands of people with psychological disorders underwent variations of this psychosurgery. The procedure was used especially for those whose behavior was violent. Many people did indeed quiet down and could even be discharged from hospitals, but largely because their brains were damaged. During the 1950s, this intervention fell into disrepute for several reasons. After surgery, many people became dull and listless and suffered serious losses in their cognitive capacities—for example, becoming unable to carry on a coherent conversation with another person—which is not surprising given the destruction of parts of their brains that support thought and language.

Psychological Approaches

The search for biological causes dominated the field of psychopathology until well into the twentieth century, no doubt partly because of the discoveries made about the brain and genetics. But beginning in the late eighteenth century, various psychological points of view emerged that attributed psychological disorders to psychological malfunctions. These theories were fashionable first in France and Austria, and later in the United States, leading to the development of psychotherapeutic interventions based on the tenets of the individual theories.

Mesmer and Charcot During the eighteenth century in western Europe, many people were observed to be subject to *hysteria*, which referred to physical incapacities, such as blindness or paralysis, for which no physical cause could be found. Franz Anton Mesmer (1734–1815), an Austrian physician practicing in Vienna and Paris in the late eighteenth century, believed that hysteria was caused by a particular distribution of a universal magnetic fluid in the body. Moreover, he felt that one person could influence the fluid of another to bring about a change in the other's behavior.

Mesmer conducted meetings cloaked in mystery and mysticism, at which afflicted people sat around a covered wooden tub, with iron rods protruding through the cover from bottles underneath that contained various chemicals. Mesmer would enter the room, take various rods from the tub, and touch afflicted parts of a person's body. The rods were believed to transmit animal magnetism and to adjust the distribution of the universal magnetic fluid, thereby removing the hysterical disorder. Later, Mesmer perfected his routines by simply looking at people rather than using rods. Whatever we may think of this questionable explanation and strange procedure, Mesmer apparently helped many people overcome their hysterical problems.

Although Mesmer regarded hysteria as having strictly biological causes, we discuss his work here because he is generally considered one of the earlier practitioners of modern-day hypnosis. (The word *mesmerism* is a synonym for *hypnotism*; the phenomenon itself was known to the ancients of many cultures, where it was part of the sorcery and magic of conjurers and faith healers.)

Mesmer came to be regarded as a quack by his contemporaries, which is ironic, since he had earlier helped discredit an exorcist, Father Johann Gassner, who was performing similar rituals (Harrington, 2008). Nevertheless, hypnosis gradually became respectable. The great Parisian neurologist Jean Martin Charcot (1825–1893) also studied hysterical states. Although Charcot believed that hysteria was a problem with the nervous system and had a biological cause, he was also persuaded by psychological explanations. One day, some of his enterprising students hypnotized a healthy woman and, by suggestion, induced her to display certain hysterical symptoms. Charcot was deceived into believing that she was an actual patient with hysteria. When the students showed him how readily they could remove the symptoms by waking the woman, Charcot became interested in psychological interpretations of these very puzzling phenomena. Given Charcot's prominence in Parisian society, his support of hypnosis as a worthy treatment for hysteria helped to legitimize this form of treatment among medical professionals of the time (Harrington, 2008; Hustvedt, 2011).

Mesmer's procedure for manipulating magnetism was generally considered a form of hypnosis.

Corbis-Bettmann

Josef Breuer, an Austrian physician and physiologist, collaborated with Freud in the early development of psychoanalysis.

Breuer and the Cathartic Method In the nineteenth century, a Viennese physician, Josef Breuer (1842–1925), treated a young woman, whose identity was disguised under the pseudonym Anna O., with a number of hysterical symptoms, including partial paralysis, impairment of sight and hearing, and, often, difficulty speaking. She also sometimes went into a dreamlike state, or "absence," during which she mumbled to herself, seemingly preoccupied with troubling thoughts. Breuer hypnotized her, and while hypnotized, she began talking more freely and, ultimately, with considerable emotion about upsetting events from her past. Frequently, on awakening from a hypnotic session she felt much better. Breuer found that the relief of a particular symptom seemed to last longer if, under hypnosis, she was able to recall the event associated with the first appearance of that symptom and if she was able to express the emotion she had felt at the time. Reliving an earlier emotional trauma and releasing emotional tension by expressing previously forgotten thoughts about the event was called catharsis, and Breuer's method became known as the **cathartic method**. In 1895, Breuer and a younger colleague, Sigmund Freud (1856–1939), jointly published *Studies in Hysteria*, partly based on the case of Anna O.

The case of Anna O. became one of the best-known clinical cases in the psychoanalytic literature. Ironically, later investigation revealed that Breuer and Freud reported the case incorrectly. Historical study by Ellenberger (1972) indicates that Breuer's talking cure helped the young woman only temporarily. This claim is supported by Carl Jung, a renowned colleague of Freud's, who is quoted as saying that during a conference in 1925, Freud told him that Anna O. had never been cured. Hospital records discovered by Ellenberger confirmed that Anna O. continued to rely on morphine to ease the "hysterical" problems that Breuer is reputed to have cured by catharsis.

Freud and Psychoanalysis The apparently powerful role played by factors of which people seemed unaware led Freud to postulate that much of human behavior is determined by forces that are inaccessible to awareness. The central assumption of Freud's theorizing, often referred to as **psychoanalytic theory**, is that psychopathology results from **unconscious** conflicts in the individual. In the next sections, we take a look at Freud's theory. See Focus on Discovery 1.3 for a discussion of Freud's theory of personality development and Focus on Discovery 1.4 for Freud's ideas about depression.

Structure of the Mind Freud divided the mind, or the **psyche**, into three principal parts: **id**, **ego**, and **superego**. According to Freud, the id is present at birth and is the repository of all of the energy needed to run the psyche, including the basic urges for food, water, elimination, warmth, affection, and sex. Trained as a neurologist, Freud saw the source of the id's energy as biological, and he called this energy **libido**. The individual cannot consciously perceive this energy—it is unconscious, below the level of awareness.

Corbis Images

Sigmund Freud developed psychoanalytic theory, a theory of the structure and functions of the mind (including explanations of the causes of psychological disorders), and psychoanalysis, a method of therapy based on it.

The id seeks immediate gratification of its urges, operating on what Freud called the **pleasure principle**. When the id is not satisfied, tension is produced, and the id impels a person to eliminate this tension as quickly as possible. For example, a baby feels hunger and is impelled to move about, sucking, in an attempt to reduce the tension arising from the unsatisfied drive. A person may also attempt to obtain gratification by generating images—in essence, fantasies—of what is desired. For instance, the hungry baby imagines sucking at the mother's breast and thereby obtains some substitute, short-term satisfaction. Of course, fantasizing cannot really satisfy such urges. This is where the ego comes in.

According to Freud, the ego begins to develop from the id during the second 6 months of life. Unlike the contents of the id, those of the ego are primarily conscious. The id may resort to fantasy when seeking satisfaction, but the task of the ego is to deal with reality. The ego thus operates on what Freud termed the **reality principle** as it mediates between the demands of reality and the id's demands for immediate gratification.

The superego—the third part of the psyche in Freud's theory—can be roughly conceived of as a person's conscience. Freud believed that the superego develops throughout childhood,

Table 1.2 Selected Defense Mechanisms

Defense Mechanism	Definition	Example
Repression	Keeping unacceptable impulses or wishes from conscious awareness	A professor starting a lecture she dreaded giving says, "In conclusion."
Denial	Not accepting a painful reality into conscious awareness	A victim of childhood abuse does not acknowledge it as an adult.
Projection	Attributing to someone else one's own unacceptable thoughts or feelings	A man who hates members of a racial group believes that it is they who dislike him.
Displacement	Redirecting emotional responses from their real target to someone else	A child gets mad at her brother but instead acts angrily toward her friend.
Reaction formation	Converting an unacceptable feeling into its opposite	A person with sexual feelings toward children leads a campaign against child sexual abuse.
Regression	Retreating to the behavioral patterns of an earlier stage of development	An adolescent dealing with unacceptable feelings of social inadequacy attempts to mask those feelings by seeking oral gratification.
Rationalization	Offering acceptable reasons for an unacceptable action or attitude	A parent berates a child out of impatience, then indicates that she did so to "build character."
Sublimation	Converting unacceptable aggressive or sexual impulses into socially valued behaviors	Someone who has aggressive feelings toward his father becomes a surgeon.

arising from the ego much as the ego arises from the id. As children discover that many of their impulses—for example, biting and bed-wetting—are not acceptable to their parents, they begin to incorporate parental values as their own in order to receive the pleasure of parental approval and avoid the pain of disapproval.

Defense Mechanisms According to Freud, and as elaborated by his daughter Anna (A. A. Freud, 1946/1966), herself an influential psychoanalyst, discomforts experienced by the ego as it attempts to resolve conflicts and satisfy the demands of the id and superego can be reduced in several ways. A **defense mechanism** is a strategy used by the ego to protect itself from anxiety. Examples of defense mechanisms are presented in Table 1.2.

Psychoanalytic Therapy **Psychotherapy** based on Freud's theory is called **psychoanalysis** or psychoanalytic therapy. It is still practiced today, although not as commonly as it once was. In psychoanalytic and newer psychodynamic treatments, the goal of the therapist is to understand the person's early-childhood experiences, the nature of key relationships, and the patterns in current relationships. The therapist is listening for core emotional and relationship themes that surface again and again (see Table 1.3 for a summary of psychoanalysis techniques).

Freud developed a number of techniques in his efforts to help people resolve repressed conflicts. With *free association*, a person reclines on a couch, facing away from the analyst, and

Table 1.3 Major Techniques of Psychoanalysis

Technique	Description
Free association	A person tries to say whatever comes to mind without censoring anything.
Interpretation	The analyst points out the meaning of certain of a person's behaviors.
Analysis of transference	The person responds to the analyst in ways that the person has previously responded to other important figures in his or her life, and the analyst helps the person understand and interpret these responses.

FOCUS ON DISCOVERY 1.3

Stages of Psychosexual Development

Freud conceived of the personality as developing through a series of four distinct psychosexual stages. He used the term *psychosexual* because, at each stage, a different part of the body is the most sensitive to sexual excitation and, therefore, the most capable of satisfying the id.

During the **oral stage**, which lasts from birth to about 18 months, the demands of an infant's id are satisfied primarily by feeding and the sucking and biting associated with it. The body parts through which the infant receives gratification at this stage are the lips, mouth, gums, and tongue. During the **anal stage**, from about 18 months to 3 years of age, a child receives pleasure mainly via the anus, by passing and retaining feces. The **phallic stage** extends from age 3 to age 5 or 6; during this stage, maximum gratification of the id is obtained through genital stimulation. Between the ages of 6 and 12, the child is in a **latency period**; during these years the id impulses do not play a major role in motivating behavior. The final and adult stage is the **genital stage**, during which heterosexual interests predominate.

During each stage, the developing person must resolve the conflicts between what the id wants and what the environment will provide. How this is accomplished is believed, in Freud's view, to determine basic personality traits that last throughout the person's life. A person who experiences either excessive or deficient amounts of gratification at a particular stage develops a **fixation** and is likely to regress to that stage when stressed.

Jennie Woodcock; Reflections Photolibrary/ Corbis Images

According to Freud, too much or too little gratification during one of the psychosexual stages may lead to regression to this stage during stress.

Banana Stock/SuperStock, Inc.

In Freud's theory, the first stage of psychosexual development is the oral stage, during which pleasure is obtained from feeding.

is encouraged to give free rein to his or her thoughts, verbalizing whatever comes to mind, without censoring anything.

Another key component of psychoanalytic therapy is the analysis of **transference**. Transference refers to the person's responses to his or her analyst that seem to reflect attitudes and ways of behaving toward important people in the person's past. For example, a person might feel that the analyst is generally bored by what he or she is saying and as a result might struggle to be entertaining; this pattern of response might reflect the person's childhood relationship with a parent rather than what's actually going on between the person and the analyst. Through careful observation and analysis of these transferred attitudes, Freud believed the analyst could gain insight into the childhood origins of a person's repressed conflicts. In the example above, the analyst might suggest that the person was made to feel boring and unimportant as a child and could only gain parental attention through humor.

In the technique of *interpretation*, the analyst points out to the patient the meanings of certain of a person's behaviors. Defense mechanisms are a principal focus of interpretation. For instance, a man who appears to have trouble with intimacy may look out the window and change the subject whenever anything touches on closeness during the course of a session.

The analyst will attempt at some point to interpret the patient's behavior, pointing out its defensive nature in the hope of helping the patient acknowledge that he is in fact avoiding the topic.

Neo-Freudian Psychodynamic Perspectives Several of Freud's contemporaries met with him periodically to discuss psychoanalytic theory and therapy. As often happens when a brilliant leader attracts brilliant followers and colleagues, disagreements arose about many general issues, such as the relative importance of id versus ego, of biological versus socio-cultural forces on psychological development, of unconscious versus conscious processes, and of childhood versus adult experiences; whether sexual urges drive behaviors that are not obviously sexual; and the role of reflex-like id impulses versus that of purposive behavior governed primarily by conscious ego deliberations. We discuss two influential historical figures here: Carl Jung and Alfred Adler.

Jung and Analytical Psychology Carl Gustav Jung (1875–1961), a Swiss psychiatrist originally considered Freud's heir apparent, broke with Freud in 1914 on many issues. After a 7-year period of intense correspondence about their disagreements, Jung proposed ideas radically different from Freud's, ultimately establishing *analytical psychology*.

Jung hypothesized that in addition to the personal unconscious postulated by Freud, there is a **collective unconscious**, the part of the unconscious that is common to all human beings and that consists primarily of what Jung called *archetypes*, or basic categories that all human beings use in conceptualizing about the world. In addition, Jung asserted that each of us has masculine and feminine traits that are blended and that people's spiritual and religious urges are as basic as their id urges. Jung also catalogued various personality characteristics; perhaps most important among them are extraversion (an orientation toward the external world) versus introversion (an orientation toward the inner, subjective world). This personality dimension continues to be regarded as very important, and we will encounter it again in our discussion of personality disorders in Chapter 15.

Carl Jung was the founder of analytical psychology.

Adler and Individual Psychology Alfred Adler (1870–1937), also an early adherent of Freud's theories, came to be even less dependent on Freud's views than was Jung, and Freud remained quite bitter toward Adler after their relationship ended. Adler's theory, which came to be known as *individual psychology*, regarded people as inextricably tied to their society because he believed that fulfillment was found in doing things for the social good. Like Jung, he stressed the importance of working toward goals (Adler, 1930).

A central element in Adler's work was his focus on helping people change their illogical and mistaken ideas and expectations. He believed that feeling and behaving better depend on thinking more rationally, an approach that anticipated contemporary developments in cognitive **behavior therapy** (discussed in Chapter 2).

Continuing Influences of Freud and His Followers Freud's original ideas and methods have been heavily criticized over the years. For example, Freud conducted no formal research on the causes and treatments of psychological disorders. This remains one of the main criticisms today: because they are based on anecdotal evidence gathered during therapy sessions, some psychodynamic theories are not grounded in objectivity and therefore are not scientific. However, other contemporary psychodynamic theories, such

Alfred Adler was the founder of individual psychology.

FOCUS ON DISCOVERY 1.4

Freud's Ideas on Depression

In his celebrated paper "Mourning and Melancholia," Freud (1917/1950) drew from clinical observations to develop a model of depression. He theorized that the potential for depression is created early in childhood, during the oral period. If the child's needs are insufficiently or excessively gratified, the person becomes fixated in the oral stage. This arrest in development may cause the person to become excessively dependent on other people for the maintenance of self-esteem.

Why do people with this childhood history come to suffer from depression? Freud hypothesized that after the loss of a loved one—whether by death, separation, or withdrawal of affection—the mourner identifies with the lost one, perhaps in a fruitless attempt to undo the loss. Freud asserted that the mourner unconsciously resents being deserted and feels anger toward the loved one for the loss. In addition, the mourner feels guilt for real or imagined sins against the lost person. According to the theory, the mourner's anger toward the lost one becomes directed inward, developing into ongoing self-blame and depression. In this view, depression can be described as anger turned against oneself. Overly dependent persons are believed to be particularly susceptible to this process, and, as noted above, people fixated in the oral stage are overly dependent on others.

Although this theory was interesting at the time, not much research has been carried out to test it, and the little information available does not strongly support it. Contrary to the idea that depression is a result of anger turned inward, people with depression express much more anger than do people without depression (Biglan, Hops, & Sherman, 1988). Despite this, some of Freud's ideas continue to influence more recent models of depression, as we discuss in Chapter 5. For example, Freud maintained that depression could be triggered by the loss of a loved one. A large body of evidence indicates that episodes of major depressive disorder are precipitated by stressful life events, which often involve losses. Researchers have consistently shown that people who are high in dependency are prone to depressive symptoms after a rejection (Nietzel & Harris, 1990), a finding that is also congruent with Freud's theory. Although some of Freud's ideas still influence theories of depression, researchers have gone far beyond the clinical observations that were the foundation of his ideas.

as object relations theory (discussed in Chapter 2), have built a limited base of supportive research. Offshoots of object relations theory, such as attachment theory and the idea of the relational self (discussed in Chapter 2), have accumulated a good bit of research support, both in children and adults.

Though perhaps not as influential as it once was, the work of Freud and his followers continues to have an impact on the field of psychopathology (Westen, 1998). This influence is most evident in the following three commonly held assumptions:

1. *Childhood experiences help shape adult personality.* Contemporary clinicians and researchers still view childhood experiences and other environmental events as crucial. They seldom focus on the psychosexual stages about which Freud wrote, but some emphasize problematic parent–child relationships in general and how they can influence later adult relationships in negative ways.

2. *There are unconscious influences on behavior.* As we will discuss in Chapter 2, the unconscious is a focus of contemporary research in cognitive neuroscience and psychopathology. This research shows that people can be unaware of the causes of their behavior. However, most current researchers and clinicians do not think of the unconscious as a repository of id instincts.

3. *The causes and purposes of human behavior are not always obvious.* Freud and his followers sensitized generations of clinicians and researchers to the nonobviousness of the causes and purposes of human behavior. Contemporary psychodynamic theorists continue to caution us against taking everything at face value. A person expressing disdain for another, for example, may actually like the other person very much, yet be fearful of admitting positive feelings. This tendency to look under the surface, to find hidden meanings in behavior, is perhaps Freud's best-known legacy.

Quick Summary

The nineteenth and twentieth centuries saw a return to biological explanations for psychological disorders. Developments outside the field of psychopathology, such as the germ theory of disease and the discovery of the cause of syphilis, illustrated how the brain and behavior are linked. Early investigations into the genetics of psychological disorders led to a tragic emphasis on eugenics and the enforced sterilization of many thousands of people with psychological disorders. Such biological approaches to treatment as induced insulin coma and lobotomy eventually gave way to drug treatments. Psychological approaches to psychopathology began with Mesmer's manipulation of "magnetism" to treat hysteria (late eighteenth century), proceeded through Breuer's conceptualiza-

tion of the cathartic method in his treatment of Anna O. (late nineteenth century), and culminated in Freud's psychoanalytic theories and treatment techniques (early twentieth century). Jung and Adler took Freud's basic ideas in a variety of different directions. The theories of Freud and other psychodynamic theorists do not lend themselves to systematic study, which has limited their acceptance by some in the field. Although Freud's early work is often criticized, his theorizing has been influential in the study of psychopathology in that it has made clear the importance of early experiences, the notion that we can do things without conscious awareness, and the insight that the causes of behavior are not always obvious.

Check Your Knowledge 1.3

Fill in the blanks.

1. _____ was a French neurologist who was influenced by the work of _____.

2. _____ developed the cathartic method, which _____ later built on in the development of psychoanalysis.

3. The _____ is driven by the pleasure principle, but the _____ is driven by the reality principle.

4. In psychoanalysis, _____ refers to interpreting the relationship between therapist and client as indicative of the client's relationship to others.

5. _____ developed the concept of the collective unconscious; _____ developed the technique of free association; _____ is associated with individual psychology.

The Rise of Behaviorism After some years, many in the field began to lose faith in Freud's approach. This dissatisfaction was brought to a head by John B. Watson (1878–1958), who in 1913 revolutionized psychology with his views.

Watson looked to the experimental procedures of the psychologists who were investigating learning in animals, and because of his efforts, the dominant focus of psychology switched from thinking to learning. **Behaviorism** focuses on observable behavior rather than on consciousness or mental functioning. We will look at three types of learning that influenced the behaviorist approach in the early and middle parts of the twentieth century and that continue to be influential today: **classical conditioning**, **operant conditioning**, and **modeling**.

Classical Conditioning Around the turn of the twentieth century, the Russian physiologist and Nobel laureate Ivan Pavlov (1849–1936) discovered classical conditioning, quite by accident. As part of his study of the digestive system, Pavlov gave a dog meat powder to make it salivate. Before long, Pavlov's laboratory assistants became aware that the dog began salivating when it saw the person who fed it. As the experiment continued, the dog began to salivate even earlier, when it heard the footsteps of its feeder. Pavlov was intrigued by these findings and decided to study the dog's reactions systematically. In the first of many experiments, a bell was rung behind the dog and then the meat powder was placed in its mouth. After this procedure had been repeated a number of times, the dog began salivating as soon as it heard the bell and before it received the meat powder.

John B. Watson, an American psychologist, was the major figure in establishing behaviorism.

Corbis-Bettmann

Ivan Pavlov, a Russian physiologist and Nobel laureate, made important contributions to the research and theory of classical conditioning.

In this experiment, because the meat powder automatically elicits salivation with no prior learning, the powder is termed an **unconditioned stimulus (UCS)** and the response of salivation an **unconditioned response (UCR)**. When the offering of meat powder is preceded several times by a neutral stimulus, the ringing of a bell, the sound of the bell alone (the **conditioned stimulus**, or **CS**) is able to elicit the salivary response (the **conditioned response**, or **CR**) (see Figure 1.3). As the number of paired presentations of the bell and the meat powder increases, the number of salivations elicited by the bell alone increases. What happens to an established CR if the CS is no longer followed by the UCS—for example, if repeated soundings of the bell are not followed by meat powder? The answer is that fewer and fewer CRs (salivations) are elicited, and the CR gradually disappears. This is termed *extinction*.

Classical conditioning can even instill pathological fear. A famous but ethically questionable experiment conducted by John Watson and Rosalie Rayner (1920) involved introducing a white rat to an 11-month-old boy, Little Albert. The boy showed no fear of the animal and appeared to want to play with it. But whenever the boy reached for the rat, the experimenter made a loud noise (the UCS) by striking a steel bar behind Albert's head. This caused Little Albert great fright (the UCR). After five such experiences, Albert became very frightened (the CR) by the sight of the white rat, even when the steel bar was not struck. The fear initially associated with the loud noise had come to be elicited by the previously neutral stimulus, the white rat (now the CS). This study suggests a possible relationship between classical conditioning and the development of certain disorders, in this instance a phobia. It is important to note that this type of study could never be done today because it breaches ethical standards.

Operant Conditioning In the 1890s, Edward Thorndike (1874–1949) began work that led to the discovery of another type of learning. Rather than investigate the association between stimuli, as Pavlov did, Thorndike studied the effects of consequences on behavior. Thorndike formulated what was to become an extremely important principle, the **law of effect**: behavior that is followed by consequences satisfying to the organism will be repeated, and behavior that is followed by noxious or unpleasant consequences will be discouraged.

B. F. Skinner (1904–1990) introduced the concept of operant conditioning, so called because it applies to behavior that operates on the environment. Renaming Thorndike's "law of effect" the "principle of reinforcement," Skinner distinguished two types of reinforcement. **Positive reinforcement** refers to the strengthening of a tendency to respond by virtue of the presentation of a pleasant event, called a positive reinforcer. For example, a water-deprived pigeon will tend to repeat behaviors (operants) that are followed by the availability of water. **Negative reinforcement** also strengthens a response, but it does so via the removal of an aversive event, such as the cessation of electric shock.

Operant conditioning principles may contribute to the persistence of aggressive behavior, a key feature of conduct disorder (see Chapter 13). Aggression is often rewarded, as when one child hits another to secure the possession of a toy (getting the toy is the reinforcer). Parents may also unwittingly reinforce aggression by giving in when their child becomes angry or threatens violence to achieve some goal, such as staying up late to watch TV.

Modeling Learning often goes on even in the absence of reinforcers. We all learn by watching and imitating others, a process called modeling. In the 1960s, experimental work demonstrated that witnessing someone perform certain activities can increase or decrease diverse kinds of behavior, such as sharing, aggression, and fear. For example, Bandura and Menlove (1968) used a modeling treatment to reduce fear of dogs in children. After witnessing a

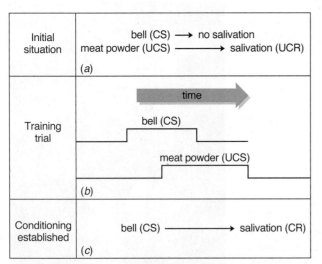

Figure 1.3 The process of classical conditioning. **(a)** Before learning, the meat powder (UCS) elicits salivation (UCR), but the bell (CS) does not. **(b)** A training or learning trial consists of presentations of the CS, followed closely by the UCS. **(c)** Classical conditioning has been accomplished when the previously neutral bell elicits salivation (CR).

fearless model engage in various activities with a dog, initially fearful children showed an increased willingness to approach and touch a dog. Children of parents with phobias or substance abuse problems may acquire similar behavior patterns, in part through observation.

Behavior Therapy Behavior therapy emerged in the 1950s. In its initial form, this therapy applied procedures based on classical and operant conditioning to alter clinical problems. Sometimes the term *behavior modification* is used as well, and therapists who use operant conditioning as a treatment often prefer that term. Behavior therapy was an attempt to change behavior, thoughts, and feelings by applying in a clinical context the methods used and the discoveries made by experimental psychologists.

One important behavior therapy technique that is still used to treat phobias and anxiety today is called **systematic desensitization**. Developed by Joseph Wolpe in 1958, it includes two components: (1) deep muscle relaxation and (2) gradual exposure to a list of feared situations, starting with those that arouse minimal anxiety and progressing to those that are the most frightening. Wolpe hypothesized that a state or response opposite to anxiety is substituted for anxiety as the person is exposed gradually to stronger and stronger doses of what he or she fears. We will cover this technique in more detail in Chapter 2, as it remains an important part of current forms of cognitive behavior therapy.

Modeling was also included in behavior therapy starting in the 1960s. For example, people reduced their fear of snakes by viewing both live and filmed encounters in which other people gradually approached and successfully handled snakes (Bandura, Blanchard, & Ritter, 1969). Fears of surgery and dental work have also been treated in a similar manner (Melamed & Siegel, 1975).

Operant techniques such as systematically rewarding desirable behavior and extinguishing undesirable behavior have been particularly successful in the treatment of many childhood problems (Kazdin & Weisz, 1998). Once contingencies shape a behavior, a key goal is to maintain the effects of treatment. If a therapist or a teacher has been providing reinforcement, one might not expect this person to keep providing reinforcement forever. This issue has been addressed in several ways. Because laboratory findings indicate that intermittent reinforcement—rewarding a response only a portion of the times it appears—makes new behavior more enduring, many operant programs move away from continuous schedules of reinforcement once desired behavior is occurring regularly. For example, if a teacher has succeeded in helping a disruptive child spend more time sitting by praising the child generously for each math problem finished while seated, the teacher will gradually reward the child for every other success, and ultimately only infrequently.

The Importance of Cognition Although behaviorism remains influential in many ways today, clinicians and researchers have recognized the limitations of focusing only on behavior. Human beings don't just behave; they think and feel, too! Early behavior theories did not leave much room for cognition and emotion. Beginning in the 1960s, the study of cognition began to become very prominent. Researchers and clinicians realized that the ways in which people think about, or *appraise,* situations can influence behavior in dramatic ways. For example, walking into a room of strangers can elicit thoughts such as "Great! I am so excited to meet all sorts of new and interesting people" or "I do not know any of these people and I am going to look and sound like a complete moron!" A person who has the first thought is likely to join a group of people enthusiastically and join in the conversation. The

B. F. Skinner originated the study of operant conditioning and the extension of this approach to education, psychotherapy, and society as a whole.

Kathy Bendo for John Wiley & Sons

Aggressive responses in children are often rewarded, which makes them more likely to occur in the future. In this photo, the more aggressive child gets to keep the toy.

Ken Cavanagh/Photo Researchers

Appraisals are an important part of cognitive therapy. As illustrated, appraisals can change the meaning of a situation.

person who has the second thought, however, is likely to turn right around and leave the room.

Cognitive Therapy Cognitive therapy, as mentioned earlier, is based on the idea that people not only behave, but also think and feel. All cognitive approaches have one thing in common. They emphasize that how people construe themselves and the world is a major determinant of psychological disorders. In cognitive therapy, the therapist typically begins by helping clients become more aware of their maladaptive thoughts. By changing cognition, therapists hope that people can change their feelings, behaviors, and symptoms.

The roots of cognitive therapy included Aaron Beck's cognitive therapy (discussed in Chapter 2) and Albert Ellis's *rational-emotive behavior therapy (REBT)*. Ellis's (1913–2007) principal thesis was that sustained emotional reactions are caused by internal sentences that people repeat to themselves; these self-statements reflect sometimes unspoken assumptions—irrational beliefs—about what is necessary to lead a meaningful life. In Ellis's REBT (Ellis, 1993, 1995), the aim is to eliminate self-defeating beliefs. A person with depression, for example, may say several times a day, "What a worthless jerk I am." Ellis proposed that people interpret what is happening around them, that sometimes these interpretations can cause emotional turmoil, and that a therapist's attention should be focused on these beliefs rather than on historical causes or, indeed, on overt behavior.

Ellis later (1991; Kendall, Haaga, Ellis, et al.,1995) shifted from a cataloguing of specific irrational beliefs to the more general concept of "demandingness," that is, the musts or shoulds that people impose on themselves and on others. Ellis hypothesized that it is this unrealistic, unproductive demand that creates the kind of emotional distress and behavioral dysfunction that bring people to therapists.

Quick Summary

Behaviorism began its ascendancy in the 1920s and continues to be an important part of various psychotherapies. John Watson built on the work of Ivan Pavlov in showing how some behaviors can be conditioned. B. F. Skinner, building on the work of Edward Thorndike, emphasized the contingencies associated with behavior, showing how positive and negative reinforcement could shape behavior. Research on modeling helped to explain how people can learn even when no obvious reinforcers are present. Early behavior therapy techniques that are still used today include systematic desensitization, intermittent reinforcement, and modeling. The study of cognition became popular beginning in the 1960s. Cognitive therapy was developed, and one of its pioneers, Albert Ellis, developed an influential treatment that is still used today. Rational-emotive behavior therapy emphasizes that the thoughts and "demands" that people impose on themselves (I should do this; I must do that) are counterproductive and lead to different types of emotional distress.

Check Your Knowledge 1.4

True or false?

1. Positive reinforcement refers to increasing a desired behavior, while negative reinforcement refers to eliminating an undesirable behavior.
2. Systematic desensitization involves meditation and relaxation.
3. A cat comes running at the sound of a treat jar rattling, and his human friend then gives him a treat. The conditioned stimulus in this example is the sound of the jar rattling.
4. REBT focuses on changing emotions first so that thoughts can then change.

Have We Learned from History?

Many students of psychopathology grumble about having to read about the history of our field; they are excited to get right into learning about the clinical descriptions, causes, and treatments for psychological disorders. After all, many students of psychopathology aspire to a career as a mental health professional, not a historian. As we began our tour of history, however, we noted that it was important for us to consider the history of our field so that we could see how things have and have not changed over time. Ideally, we will learn from our historical mistakes.

Certainly, we have made many advancements over the centuries. We've learned that more than half of people will experience a psychological disorder in their lifetime, and major models are available that integrate biology, psychology, and social influences for almost every psychopathology we will cover in this book. Many psychological treatments have been developed, and thousands of publications per year focus on the genetic and neurobiological roots of psychological disorders.

Despite these advances, we still have much to learn from history when it comes to reducing stigma and treating people with psychological disorders with respect, compassion, and dignity. Consider for example recent popular "reality" television shows of today such as *Hoarders, Beyond Scared Straight, Obsessed,* or *Intervention* that, respectively, showcase the lives of people with hoarding disorder (see Chapter 7), conduct disorder (see Chapter 13), obsessive compulsive disorder (see Chapter 7), or substance use disorder (see Chapter 10). Perhaps these shows help to educate people about psychological disorders, but perhaps also they perpetuate stigma by serving as the twenty-first-century version of viewing people in asylums for entertainment as was done in the eighteenth century. On the other hand, other television shows present realistic and compassionate portrayals of psychological disorders, such as *Homeland* (bipolar disorder; see Chapter 5) or *The United States of Tara* (dissociative identity disorder; see Chapter 8). Yet even these shows can simplify or magnify some of the rarer aspects of psychological disorders, perhaps to amplify their entertainment value.

Are contemporary television shows such as *Hoarders* a modern equivalent of aristocrats viewing people in St. Mary's of Bethlehem (aka Bedlam) for entertainment?

What about the living conditions for people with psychological disorders? People with serious disorders, such as schizophrenia, bipolar disorder, or severe depression, are often in need of short stays in hospitals. Unfortunately, many hospitals have closed since the 1950s, making it extremely difficult to be able to stay in a hospital when needed. As we will discuss in more detail in Chapter 16, many of the conditions inside the hospitals were deplorable. Yet, instead of improving these conditions, many hospitals simply closed, leaving a large gap in treatment services for people with particularly severe disorders. In 2014, the new "hospital" for psychological disorders is jail. That is, people with severe psychological disorders are more likely to be housed in jails than in a hospital (Torrey, 2014). Many people with psychological disorders are not able to work and thus have very little income. These economic realities increase the likelihood of living in low-income housing, such as a single-room occupancy hotel, or SRO, in order to avoid homelessness. A recent study of such living accommodations found that nearly 75 percent of the residents of an SRO in Vancouver, Canada, had some type of psychological disorder and that 95 percent of the residents had a substance use disorder (Vila-Rodriguez, Panenka, Lang, et al., 2013).

As we will see in the following chapters, we still have a ways to go when it comes to finding effective treatments with a tolerable set of side effects. For example, medications commonly used to treat schizophrenia have many unpleasant side effects, such as weight gain, dry mouth, blurred vision, and extreme fatigue. Imagine your life as a student if you had blurred vision nearly all of the time! Some of these side effects contribute to the development of other health problems (e.g., weight gain increases the risk of developing type 2 diabetes). It is perhaps not surprising then, that some people with schizophrenia opt not to take these medications to avoid the side effects. Of course, current medications may not be as horrid as treatments of old like bleeding or prefrontal lobotomy. In addition, there are effective psychotherapy treatments that do not involve medication at all for some psychological disorders. However, even though we will see in the coming chapters that cognitive behavior therapy is an effective treatment for several psychological disorders, it does not help all people.

Have we learned from history? It seems that the answer is both yes and no. These lessons of history are therefore important for those who are headed toward careers as clinical scientists and mental health professionals. And we hope that readers of this book, regardless of their current or future careers, will recognize that we can all do something to reduce stigma, first and foremost by understanding that our current approaches to psychological disorders can and must continue to improve.

The Mental Health Professions

© PhotoStock-Israel/Alamy

Clinical psychologists are trained to deliver psychotherapy.

As views of psychological disorders have evolved, so, too, have the professions associated with the field. Professionals authorized to provide psychological services include **clinical psychologists**, psychiatrists, **psychiatric nurses**, **counseling psychologists**, **social workers**, and **marriage and family therapists**. The need for such professions has never been greater. For example, the cost of psychological disorders in the United States is nearly $200 billion a year in lost earnings (Kessler, Heeringa, Lakoma et al., 2008). People with serious psychological disorders are often not able to work due to their illness, and as a result their yearly earnings are substantially less than those of people without psychological disorders (by as much as $16,000 a year!). In addition, people with psychological disorders used to be much more likely to be without health insurance than people without psychological disorders (Garfield, Zuvekas, Lave, & Donohue, 2011), a situation that will hopefully change in the United States with the new health care legislation (the ACA) passed in 2010. In this section, we discuss the different types of mental health professionals who treat people with psychological disorders, the different types of training they receive, and a few related issues.

Clinical psychologists (such as the authors of this textbook) must have a Ph.D. or Psy.D. degree, which entails 4 to 8 years of graduate study. Training for the Ph.D. in clinical psychology is similar to that in other psychological specialties, such as developmental or cognitive neuroscience. It requires a heavy emphasis on research, statistics, neuroscience, and the empirically based study of human behavior. As in other fields of psychology, the Ph.D. is basically a research degree, and candidates are required to write a dissertation on a specialized topic. But candidates in clinical psychology learn skills in two additional areas, which distinguish them from other Ph.D. candidates in psychology. First, they learn techniques of assessment and diagnosis of psychopathology; that is, they learn the skills necessary to determine whether a person's symptoms or problems indicate a particular disorder. Second, they learn how to practice psychotherapy, a primarily verbal means of helping people change their thoughts, feelings, and behavior to reduce distress and to achieve greater life satisfaction. Students take courses in which they master specific techniques and treat people under close professional supervision; then, during an intensive internship, they assume increasing responsibility for the care of people.

Another degree option for clinical psychologists is the Psy.D. (doctor of psychology), for which the curriculum is similar to that required of Ph.D. students, but with less emphasis on research and more on clinical training. The thinking behind this approach is that clinical psychology has advanced to a level of knowledge and certainty that justifies intensive training in specific techniques of assessment and therapeutic intervention rather than combining practice with research. On the other hand, conducting assessment or therapy without a sufficient research basis is professionally dubious. The American Psychological Association estimates that there are currently 93,000 practicing psychologists (www.apa.org), and in 2014, the Bureau of Labor Statistics estimated that the growth rate of jobs in clinical and counseling psychology will be 12 percent between 2012 and 2022, which is the average rate of job increase for most occupations (http://www.bls.gov/ooh/life-physical-and-social-science/psychologists.htm). However, as of 2003, estimates suggested that there were more clinical psychologists than needed to adequately deliver services and that this was negatively impacting clinical psychologists' salaries (Robiner, 2006). Nevertheless, psychologists are three times as likely to be providers of psychotherapy compared to social workers, according to a survey of nearly 2,000 people receiving mental health services (Olfson & Marcus, 2010).

Psychiatrists hold an M.D. degree and have had postgraduate training, called a residency, in which they have received supervision in the practice of diagnosis and pharmacotherapy (administering medications). By virtue of the medical degree, and in contrast to psychologists, psychiatrists can function as physicians—giving physical examinations, diagnosing medical problems, and the like. Most often, however, the only aspect of medical practice in which psychiatrists engage is prescribing **psychoactive medications**, chemical compounds that can influence how people feel and think. Psychiatrists may receive some training in psychotherapy as well, though this is not a strong focus of their training. In contrast to clinical psychologists, there is a shortage of psychiatrists, largely due to budget cuts in residency training programs. In 2013, the Bureau of Labor Statistics, using data from 2012 (http://www.bls.gov/oes/current/oes291066.htm#nat), estimated that there were under 25,000 psychiatrists in the United States.

Over the past 20 years, there has been a lively and sometimes acrimonious debate about whether to allow clinical psychologists with suitable training to prescribe psychoactive medications. Such a move is opposed not only by psychiatrists, whose turf would be invaded, but also by many psychologists, who view it as an ill-advised dilution of the basic behavioral science focus of psychology. Also at issue is the question of whether a non-M.D. can learn enough about neurobiology and neurochemistry to monitor the effects of drugs and protect people from adverse side effects and drug interactions. Currently, two states (New Mexico and Louisiana) allow psychologists to prescribe medication following the receipt of additional training; several other states are considering similar legislation.

A psychiatric nurse typically receives training at the bachelor's or master's level. Nurses can also receive more specialized training as nurse practitioner that will allow them to prescribe psychoactive medications. There are currently over 18,000 psychiatric nurses in the United States, but the trend appears to be more toward emphasizing training as a nurse practitioner in order to secure prescription privileges (Robiner, 2006).

Other graduate programs are more focused on clinical practice than are the traditional Ph.D. programs. One of these programs is counseling psychology. Counseling psychologists originally dealt mostly with vocational issues; their focus today may be quite similar to that in clinical psychology, though still with less of an emphasis on psychological disorders and more of an emphasis on prevention, education, and general life problems. Counseling psychologists work in a variety of settings, including schools, mental health agencies, industry, and community health centers. In 2012, the Bureau of Labor Statistics estimated that there were over 103,000 counseling and clinical psychologists in the United States (http://www.bls.gov/oes/current/oes193031.htm).

Social workers have an M.S.W. (master of social work) degree. Training programs are shorter than Ph.D. programs, typically requiring 2 years of graduate study. The focus of training is on psychotherapy. Those in social work graduate programs do not receive training in psychological assessment. In 2002, there were close to 100,000 social workers in the United States who provided direct mental health services and were also members of the National Association of Social Workers (Duffy, West, Wilk, et al., 2004).

Marriage and family therapists treat families or couples, focusing on the ways in which these relationships impact a variety of mental health issues. Specialized programs in marriage and family therapy can be at the master's or doctoral level. Some M.S.W. programs offer specialized training and certification in marriage and family therapy. According to the Bureau of Labor Statistics data from 2012, there were over 166,000 mental health counselors (which includes social workers) and marriage and family therapists working in the United States.

Summary

- The study of psychopathology is a search to explain why people behave, think, and feel in unexpected, sometimes odd, and possibly self-defeating ways. Unfortunately, people who have a psychological disorder are often stigmatized. Reducing the stigma associated with psychological disorders remains a great challenge for the field.

- In evaluating whether a behavior is part of a psychological disorder, psychologists consider several different characteristics, notably, personal distress, disability, violation of social norms, and dysfunction. Each characteristic tells us something about what can be considered psychological disorder, but no one by itself provides a fully satisfactory definition.

- Since the beginning of scientific inquiry into psychological disorders, supernatural, biological, and psychological points of view have vied for attention. More supernatural viewpoints included early demonology, which posited that people with psychological disorders are possessed by demons or evil spirits, leading to treatments such as exorcism. Early biological viewpoints originated in the writings of Hippocrates. After the fall of Greco-Roman civilization, the biological perspective became less prominent in western Europe, and demonological thinking gained ascendancy, as evidenced by the persecution of so-called witches. Beginning in the fifteenth century, people with psychological disorders were often confined in asylums, such as London's Bethlehem; treatment in asylums was generally poor or nonexistent until various humanitarian reforms were instituted in the eighteenth century. In the twentieth century, genetics and psychological disorders became an important area of inquiry, though the findings from genetic studies were used to the detriment of people with psychological disorders during the eugenics movement.

- Psychological viewpoints emerged in the nineteenth century from the work of Charcot and the writings of Breuer and Freud. Freud's theory emphasized stages of psychosexual development and the importance of unconscious processes, such as repression and defense mechanisms that are traceable to early-childhood conflicts. Therapeutic interventions based on psychoanalytic theory make use of techniques such as free association and the analysis of transference in attempting to overcome repression so that people can confront and understand their conflicts and find healthier ways of dealing with them. Later theorists such as Jung and Adler made various modifications to Freud's basic ideas and emphasized different factors in their perspectives on therapy.

- Behaviorism suggested that behavior develops through classical conditioning, operant conditioning, or modeling. B. F. Skinner introduced the ideas of positive and negative reinforcement and showed that operant conditioning can influence behavior. Behavior therapists try to apply these ideas to change undesired behavior, thoughts, and feelings.

- The study of cognition became widespread in the 1960s. Appraisals and thinking are part of cognitive therapy. Ellis was an influential theorist in cognitive therapy.

- There are a number of different mental health professions, including clinical psychologist, psychiatrist, counseling psychologist, psychiatric nurse, social worker, and marriage and family therapist. Each involves different training programs of different lengths and with different emphases on research, psychological assessment, psychotherapy, and psychopharmacology.

Answers to Check Your Knowledge Questions

1.1 1. a; 2. d; 3. b
1.2 1. F; 2. F; 3. T; 4. T

1.3 1. Charcot, Mesmer; 2. Breuer, Freud; 3. id, ego; 4. transference; 5. Jung, Freud, Adler
1.4 1. F; 2. F; 3. T; 4 F

Key Terms

anal stage
asylums
behavior therapy
behaviorism
cathartic method
classical conditioning
clinical psychologist
collective unconscious
conditioned response (CR)
conditioned stimulus (CS)
counseling psychologist
defense mechanism
demonology

ego
electroconvulsive therapy (ECT)
exorcism
extinction
fixation
genital stage
harmful dysfunction
id
latency period
law of effect
libido
marriage and family therapist

modeling
moral treatment
negative reinforcement
operant conditioning
oral stage
phallic stage
pleasure principle
positive reinforcement
psyche
psychiatric nurse
psychiatrist
psychoactive medications
psychoanalysis

psychoanalytic theory
psychological disorder
psychopathology
psychotherapy
reality principle
social worker
stigma
superego
systematic desensitization
transference
unconditioned response (UCR)
unconditioned stimulus (UCS)
unconscious

2 Current Paradigms in Psychopathology

AS WE NOTED IN Chapter 1, we face an enormous challenge to remain objective when we are trying to understand and study psychopathology scientifically. Science is a human enterprise that is bound by scientists' human limitations; it is also bound by the current state of scientific knowledge. We cannot ask questions or investigate phenomena that go beyond what human beings can understand, and it is very difficult even to go beyond what we currently understand. Our view is that every effort should be made to study psychopathology according to scientific principles. But science is not a completely objective and certain enterprise. Rather, as suggested by philosopher of science Thomas Kuhn (1970), subjective factors as well as our human limitations enter into the conduct of scientific inquiry.

Central to scientific activity, in Kuhn's view, is the notion of a **paradigm**, a conceptual framework or approach within which a scientist works—that is, a set of basic assumptions, a general perspective, that defines how to conceptualize and study a subject, how to gather and interpret relevant data, even how to think about a particular subject.[1] A paradigm has profound implications for how scientists operate at any given time. Paradigms specify what problems scientists will investigate and how they will go about the investigation.

In this chapter we consider current paradigms of psychopathology and treatment. We present three paradigms that guide the study and treatment of psychopathology: genetic, neuroscience, and cognitive behavioral. We also consider the important role of emotion and sociocultural factors in psychopathology. These factors cut across all the paradigms and are significant in terms of the description, causes, and treatments of all the disorders we will discuss in this book.

Current thinking about psychopathology is multifaceted. The work of clinicians and researchers is informed by an awareness of the strengths and limitations of all the paradigms. For this reason, current views of psychopathology and its treatment typically integrate several paradigms. At the end of this chapter we describe another paradigm—diathesis–stress—that provides the basis for an integrative approach.

---

[1] O'Donohue (1993) has criticized Kuhn's use of the concept of paradigm, noting that he was inconsistent in its definition. The complexities of this argument are beyond the scope of this book. Suffice to say that we find it useful to organize our thinking about psychological disorders around the paradigm concept. We use the term to refer to the general perspectives that constrain the way scientists collect and interpret information in their efforts to understand the world.

For researchers and clinicians, the choice of a paradigm has important consequences for the way in which they define, investigate, and treat psychopathology. Our discussion of paradigms will lay the groundwork for the topics covered in the rest of the book. We note at the outset that no one paradigm offers the "best" conceptualization of psychopathology. Rather, for most disorders, each paradigm offers some important information with respect to etiology and treatment, but only part of the picture.

The Genetic Paradigm

Genes do not, on their own, make us smart, dumb, sassy, polite, depressed, joyful, musical, tone-deaf, athletic, clumsy, literary or incurious. Those characteristics come from a complex interplay within a dynamic system. Every day in every way you are helping to shape which genes become active. Your life is interacting with your genes. (Shenk, 2010, p. 27)

It has been over 10 years since researchers decoded the human genome. That exciting milestone has been augmented with the virtual explosion of information regarding human genetics. The changes that have occurred in the **genetic paradigm** have transformed the way we think about genes and behavior. We no longer have to wonder, "Is nature or nurture responsible for human behavior?" We now know that (1) almost all behavior is heritable to some degree (i.e., it involves genes) and (2) despite this, genes do not operate in isolation from the environment. Instead, throughout the life span, the environment shapes how our genes are expressed, and our genes also shape our environments (Plomin, DeFries, Craig, & McGuffin, 2003; Rutter & Silberg, 2002; Turkheimer, 2000).

The current way to think about genes and the environment is cast as "nature via nurture" (Ridley, 2003). In other words, researchers are learning how environmental influences, such as stress, relationships, and culture (the nurture part), shape which of our genes are turned on or off and how our genes (the nature part) influence our bodies and brain. We know that without genes, a behavior might not be possible. But without the environment, genes could not express themselves and thus contribute to the behavior.

When the ovum, the female reproductive cell, is joined by the male's sperm, a zygote, or fertilized egg, is produced. It has 46 chromosomes, the number characteristic of a human being. Each chromosome is made up of many **genes**, the carriers of the genetic information (DNA) passed from parents to child.

People have between 20,000 and 25,000 genes; the absolute number is hard to fully estimate (Human Genome Project, 2008). At first, this news was surprising; since the mere fruit fly has around 14,000 genes, researchers had thought that surely human beings were several times more complex than that! As it turns out, however, one of the exciting things about this discovery was the revelation from dozens of other genetic labs that the number of genes was not all that important. Instead, it is the sequencing, or ordering, of these genes as well as what the genes actually *do* that make us unique. What genes do is make proteins that in turn make the body and brain work. Some of these proteins switch, or turn, on and off other genes, a process called **gene expression**. Learning about the flexibility of genes and how they switch on or off has closed the door on beliefs about the inevitability of the effects of genes, good or bad. And with respect to most psychological disorders, there is not one gene that contributes vulnerability. Instead, psychopathology is **polygenic**, meaning several genes, perhaps operating at different times during the course of development, turning themselves on and off as they interact with a person's environment, is the essence of genetic vulnerability.

We now know that we do not inherit psychological disorders from our genes alone; we develop them through the interaction of our genes with our environments (Shenk, 2010). This is a subtle but very important point. It is easy to fall into the trap of thinking a person inherits a disorder like schizophrenia from his or her genes. What genetics research today is telling us, however, is that a person *develops* schizophrenia from the interaction between genes and the environment [as well as the body (e.g. hormones), brain, and other genes].

An important term that will be used throughout the book is **heritability**. Unfortunately, it is a term that is easily misunderstood and often misused. Heritability refers to the extent to which variability in a particular behavior (or disorder) in a population can be accounted for by genetic factors. There are two important points about heritability to keep in mind.

1. Heritability estimates range from 0.0 to 1.0: the higher the number, the greater the heritability.
2. Heritability is relevant *only* for a large population of people, not a particular individual. Thus, it is incorrect to talk about any one person's heritability for a particular behavior or disorder. Knowing that the heritability of attention-deficit/hyperactivity disorder (ADHD) is around 0.70 does not mean that 70 percent of Jane's ADHD is the product of her genes and 30 percent, other factors. Rather, it means that in a population (e.g., a large sample in a study), the variation in ADHD is understood as being attributed to 70 percent genetic factors and 30 percent environmental factors. There is no heritability in ADHD (or any disorder) for a particular individual.

Shared environment refers to things families have in common, like marital quality.

Other factors that are just as important as genes in genetic research are environmental factors. **Shared environment** factors include those things that members of a family have in common, such as family income level, child-rearing practices, and parents' marital status and quality. **Nonshared environment** (sometimes referred to as *unique environment*) factors are those things believed to be distinct among members of a family, such as relationships with friends or specific events unique to a person (e.g., being in a car accident or on the swim team), and these are believed to be important in understanding why two siblings from the same family can be so different. Consider an example. Jason is a 34-year-old man who is dependent on alcohol and struggling to keep his job. His sister Joan is a 32-year-old executive in a computer company in San Jose and has no alcohol or drug problems. Jason did not have many friends as a child; Joan was one of the most popular girls in high school. Jason and Joan shared several influences, including their family atmosphere growing up. They also had unique, nonshared experiences, such as differences in peer relationships. Behavior genetics research suggests that the nonshared, or unique, environmental experiences have much more to do with the development of psychological disorders than the shared experiences.

We now turn to review two broad approaches in the genetic paradigm, including behavior genetics and molecular genetics. We then discuss the exciting evidence on the ways in which genes and environments interact. This sets the stage for our discussion of an integrative paradigm later in the chapter.

Behavior Genetics

Behavior genetics is the study of the degree to which genes and environmental factors influence behavior. To be clear, behavior genetics is not the study of *how* genes or the environment determine behavior. Many behavior genetics studies estimate the heritability of a psychological disorder without providing any information about how the genes might work. The total genetic makeup of an individual, consisting of inherited genes, is referred to as the **genotype** (physical sequence of DNA); the genotype cannot be observed outwardly. In contrast, the totality of observable behavioral characteristics, such as level of anxiety, is referred to as the **phenotype**.

Nonshared environment refers to factors that are distinct among family members, such as having different groups of friends.

Behavior genetics studies the degree to which characteristics, such as physical resemblance or psychopathology, are shared by family members with shared genes.

We defined gene expression earlier: the genotype should not be viewed as a static entity. Genes switch off and on at specific times, for example, to control various aspects of development. Indeed, genetic programs are quite flexible—they respond in remarkable ways to things that happen to us.

The phenotype changes over time and is the product of an interaction between the genotype and the environment. For example, a person may be born with the capacity for high intellectual achievement, but whether he or she develops this genetically given potential depends on environmental factors such as upbringing and education. Hence, intelligence is an index of the phenotype.

A study by Turkheimer and colleagues (2003) shows how genes and environment may interact to influence IQ. A number of studies have demonstrated high heritability for IQ (e.g., Plomin, 1999). What Turkheimer and colleagues found, though, was that heritability depends on environment. The study included 319 twin pairs of 7-year-olds (114 identical, 205 fraternal). Many of the children were living in families either below the poverty line or with a low family income. Among the families of lower socioeconomic status (SES), 60 percent of the variability in children's IQ was attributable to the environment. Among the higher SES families, the opposite was found. That is, variability in IQ was more attributable to genes than to environment. Thus, being in an impoverished environment may have deleterious effects on IQ, whereas being in a more affluent environment may not help out all that much. It is important to point out that these interesting findings deal with IQ scores, a measure of what psychologists consider to be intelligence, not achievement (we discuss this issue in more detail in Chapter 3). In Chapter 4, we will discuss the major research designs used in behavior genetics research—including family, twin, and adoption studies—to estimate the heritability of different disorders.

Molecular Genetics

Molecular genetics studies seek to identify particular genes and their functions. Recall that a human being has 46 chromosomes (23 chromosome pairs) and that each chromosome is made up of hundreds or thousands of genes that contain DNA (see Figure 2.1). Different

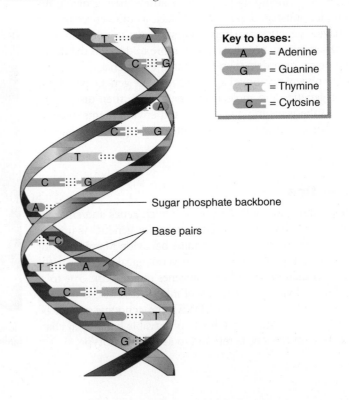

Key to bases:
A = Adenine
G = Guanine
T = Thymine
C = Cytosine

Sugar phosphate backbone

Base pairs

Figure 2.1 This figure shows a strand of DNA with four chemical bases: A (adenine), T (thymine), G (guanine), and C (cytosine).

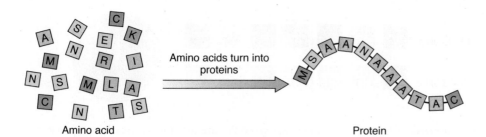

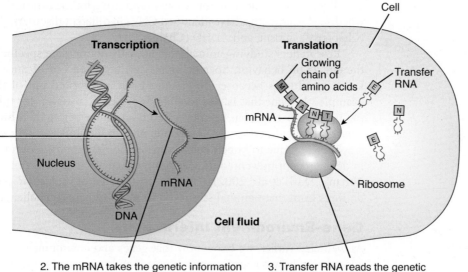

Figure 2.2 This figure shows gene **transcription**, the process by which DNA is transcribed to RNA. In some cases, the RNA is then translated into amino acids, which then form proteins, and proteins make cells.

Amino acids turn into proteins

Amino acid

Protein

Cell

Transcription

1. The first step in protein synthesis occurs inside the nucleus. It involves transferring, or transcribing, the blueprint or code for the protein from the DNA gene into a molecule of messenger RNA (mRNA). This process is called **transcription**.

Nucleus

mRNA

DNA

Cell fluid

Translation

Growing chain of amino acids

Transfer RNA

mRNA

Ribosome

2. The mRNA takes the genetic information from the nucleus of the cell to structures called ribosomes in the cell fluid, where proteins are made.

3. Transfer RNA reads the genetic code and delivers the needed amino acids to the ribosome to form a polypeptide chain. This process is called translation.

forms of the same gene are called **alleles**. The alleles of a gene are found at the same location, or locus, of a chromosome pair. A genetic **polymorphism** refers to a difference in DNA sequence on a gene that has occurred in a population.

The DNA in genes is transcribed to RNA. In some cases, the RNA is then translated into amino acids, which then form proteins, and proteins make cells (see Figure 2.2). Gene expression involves particular types of DNA called *promoters*. These promoters are recognized by particular proteins called *transcription factors*. Promoters and transcription factors are the focus of much research in molecular genetics and psychopathology. All of this is a remarkably complex system, and variations along the way, such as different combinations or sequences of events, lead to different outcomes.

In the past 10 years, molecular genetics research has focused on identifying differences between people in the *sequence* of their genes and in the *structure* of their genes. One area of interest in the study of gene sequence involves identifying what are called **single nucleotide polymorphisms** or **SNPs** (pronounced *snips*). A SNP refers to differences between people in a single nucleotide (A, T, G, or C; see Figure 2.3) in the DNA sequence of a particular gene. Figure 2.1 illustrates what a SNP looks like in a strand of DNA. The SNP is circled, pointing to the single nucleotide difference between the two strands. These are the most common types of polymorphisms in the human genome, with nearly 10 million different SNPs identified thus far. SNPs have been studied in schizophrenia, autism, and the mood disorders, to name but a few disorders.

Another area of interest is the study of differences between people in gene structure, including the identification of so-called **copy number variations (CNVs)**. A CNV can be present in a single gene or multiple genes. The name refers to an abnormal copy of one or more sections of DNA within the gene(s). These abnormal copies can be *additions*, where extra

Figure 2.3 Illustration of what a single nucleotide polymorphism, or SNP, looks like in a comparison of two people. The two strands are the same except for a single nucleotide. To the right, an illustration showing that the position of G in the sequence is far more common in a large population of people than the position of A in the sequence.

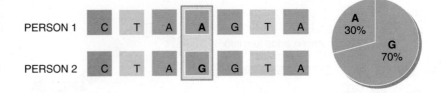

copies are abnormally present, or *deletions*, where copies are missing. As much as 5 percent of the human genome contains CNVs, which can be inherited from parents or can be what are called spontaneous (*de novo*) mutations—appearing for the first time in an individual. Later we will discuss studies that have identified CNVs in different disorders, particularly schizophrenia (Chapter 9), autism, and ADHD (Chapter 13).

Researchers studying animals can actually manipulate specific genes and then observe the effects on behavior. Specific genes can be taken out of mice DNA—these are called knockout studies because a particular gene is knocked out of the animal's system. For example, the gene that is responsible for a specific receptor for the neurotransmitter serotonin, called 5-HT$_{1A}$, has been knocked out in mice before their birth. As adults, they show what could be described as an anxious phenotype. Interestingly, one study that employed a novel technique to knock out this gene only temporarily found that its restoration early in development prevented the development of anxious behavior in the adult mice (Gross, Zhuang, Stark et al., 2002). This is a major area of molecular genetic work. Linking the findings from these animal studies to humans remains a challenge for the field, however.

Gene–Environment Interactions

As we noted earlier, we know now that genes and environments work together. Life experience shapes how our genes are expressed, and our genes guide us in behaviors that lead to the selection of different experiences. A **gene–environment interaction** means that a given person's sensitivity to an environmental event is influenced by genes.

Take a simple (and made-up) example. If a person has gene XYZ, he or she might respond to a snakebite by developing a fear of snakes. A person without the XYZ gene would not develop a fear of snakes after being bitten. This simple relationship involves both genes (the XYZ gene) and an environmental event (snakebite).

A different (and true) example of a gene–environment interaction involves depression. In one longitudinal study, a large sample of children in New Zealand was followed across time from the age of 5 until their mid-20s (Caspi, Sugden, Moffitt et al., 2003). Across this time, the researchers assessed a number of variables, including early childhood maltreatment (abuse) and depression as an adult. They also measured a particular gene called the **serotonin transporter gene** (5-HTT). This gene has a polymorphism such that some people have two short alleles (short–short), some have two long alleles (long–long), and some have one short and one long allele (short–long). Caspi and colleagues found that those individuals who had either the short–short allele or the short–long allele combinations of the 5-HTT gene *and* were maltreated as children were more likely to have major depressive disorder as adults than either those people who had the same gene combination but no childhood maltreatment or those people who were maltreated as children but had the long–long allele combination of the gene (see Figure 2.4). Thus, having the gene was not enough to predict an episode of depression, nor was the presence of childhood maltreatment. Rather, it was the specific combination of the gene configuration and environmental events that predicted depression. They found the same gene–environment interaction for having at least one short allele of the gene and reports of stressful life events. That is, those people who reported more severe stressful life events and had at least one

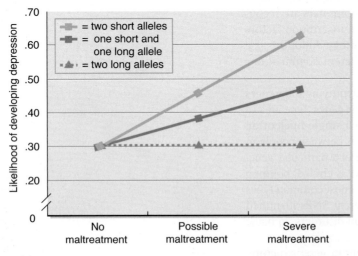

Figure 2.4 A gene–environment interaction is illustrated here. Having both the short allele of the 5-HTT gene and childhood maltreatment was associated with the greatest probability of developing depression as an adult. Adapted from Caspi et al. (2003).

short allele of the 5-HTT gene were at greater risk of developing depression.

Other exciting developments in this area have emerged in animal research. In these studies, different environments are manipulated, and then changes in behavior and gene expression are measured. The study of how the environment can alter gene expression or function is called **epigenetics**. The term *epigenetic* means "above or outside the gene" and refers to the chemical "marks" that are attached to and protect the DNA in each gene. These epigenetic marks are what control gene expression, and the environment can directly influence the work of these marks (Karg, Burmeister, Shedden, & Sen, 2011; Zhang & Meaney, 2010).

In a series of fascinating studies with rats, Darlene Francis has shown that parenting behaviors can be passed on to offspring in a nongenetic way. Good parenting among rats consists of a lot of licking and grooming (LG) and what is called arched-back nursing (ABN). Mothers differ in the extent to which they do these LG-ABN behaviors, but mothers who do it more tend to have pups that grow up to be less reactive to stress. Francis and colleagues (1999) found that pups born to mothers who were low in this LG-ABN behavior but raised by mothers high in LG-ABN (called a cross-fostering adoptee method; discussed in more detail in Chapter 4) grew up to be low in stress reactivity and as mothers themselves exhibited the high LG-ABN style.

Baby rats who are raised by a mother who does a lot of licking are more likely to do this when they grow up to be mothers, even if they were raised by an adoptive mother.

Courtesy of Darlene Francis

And when they had their own pups, these "grandpups" were also low in stress reactivity and became high LG-ABN mothers. Thus, this parenting style was transmitted across two generations after an adoption. Does this suggest that genes are not important? The adoptive parent's behavior was what was transmitted across generations, not the biological parent's behavior, which would suggest that this is an environmental effect.

However, a later study showed that this transmission of good mothering was due in part to the fact that it triggered an increase in the expression of a certain gene among the adopted offspring (Weaver, Cervoni, Champagne, D'Allesio et al., 2004). Using cross-fostering again, pups with a low LG-ABN biological mother who were raised by a high LG-ABN mother had increases in expression of a certain gene (glucocorticoid receptor) in the same way that pups with a biological high LG-ABN mother did (but pups with a biological low LG-ABN mother did not). The environment (mothering) was responsible for turning on (or turning up) the expression of a particular gene. Once it was on, the mothering style seemed to continue across generations.

We will continue to see these types of studies in animals and humans. Understanding how environments influence the expression of genes will be important for understanding the causes of psychopathology.

Evaluating the Genetic Paradigm

Our discussion of each paradigm will conclude with an evaluation section. Genetics is an important part of the study of psychopathology, and there are many ways in which genes might be involved in psychopathology. The models that will help us understand how genes are implicated in psychopathology are the ones that take the contemporary view that genes do their work through the environment. There are two huge challenges facing scientists working within the genetic paradigm. The first is to specify exactly how genes and environments reciprocally influence one another. Currently, this is more easily done in tightly controlled laboratory studies with animals. Making the leap to understanding how genes interact with complex human environments throughout the course of development is of course a greater challenge. The second is to recognize the complexity of the task, knowing that several genes (not just one) will contribute to a specific disorder and that currently there is a long pathway between the genes and the complex behaviors that make up psychological disorders, with several biological processes unfolding along the way. For example, the pathway between genes and eye color is short: genes give instructions for production of the chemicals that produce pigment. Indeed just one SNP accounts for blue eye color (Sturm, Duffy, Zhao et al., 2008). By contrast, the pathway between genes and the behavioral phenotypes of psychological disorders is a long and winding road, filled with many biological and psychosocial processes, each of which is influenced by multiple genes. Thus, each individual gene or genetic mutation may reveal a very small effect. Putting all the small genetic pieces together in order to tell the gene via environment story for psychological disorders remains a very big challenge (Chabris, Lee, Benjamin et al., 2013).

Although findings from the gene–environment interaction study of Caspi and colleagues described earlier have been replicated by several different groups of researchers, particularly when studies have incorporated careful interview measures of stress (Caspi, Hariri, Holmes, Uher, & Moffitt, 2010) as we discuss in Chapter 3, there have also been a number of failures to replicate these findings. This raises two more general and important issues in science: sample size and replication. Findings from any scientific study are more believable when they come from studies with larger samples of people who are representative of the general population (see Chapter 4 for more on these issues). In addition, findings are more believable when other researchers have independently replicated them. A study can be *directly* replicated by using the same measures and definitions of concepts, or it can be *indirectly* replicated by including broader measures of related constructs. For example, a direct replication of Caspi et al. (2003) would include the same genes and measures of stress; an indirect replication of Caspi et al. might include a different measure of stress, say poverty instead of childhood maltreatment. A related issue is that our field tends to prioritize the publication of new findings rather than replications, even if the new findings come from a study with a smaller sample size. By favoring the publication of only positive results, many studies that yield negative results do not get published, thus inflating the field's confidence in a set of findings. This tendency to publish only positive results is called publication bias, and as we will see in the remaining chapters, researchers are now figuring publication bias into their review of research findings. A current controversy in the field concerns how to consider these issues when interpreting the evidence for and against gene–environment interactions. Some researchers argue that direct replications of original studies with large sample sizes should be weighted more heavily when reviewing the evidence (Duncan & Keller, 2011), whereas others contend that including indirect replication studies is important for the broader generalizability of the findings (Caspi et al., 2010; Karg et al., 2011).

This is an exciting time for genetics research, and important discoveries about genes, environments, and psychopathology are being made at a rapid rate. In addition, some of the most exciting breakthroughs in genetics have involved a combination of methods from genetics and neuroscience. Although we present the genetic and neuroscience paradigms separately, they go hand in hand when it comes to understanding the possible causes of psychopathology.

Quick Summary

The genetic paradigm focuses on questions such as whether certain disorders are heritable and, if so, what is actually inherited. Heritability is a population statistic, not a metric of the likelihood a particular person will inherit a disorder. Environmental effects can be classified as shared and not shared (sometimes called unique). Molecular genetics studies seek to identify differences in the sequence and structure of genes as well as gene polymorphisms, such as SNPs, that may be involved in psychopathology.

Research has emphasized the importance of gene–environment interactions. In most cases genes do their work via the environment. Recent examples of genetic influence being manifested only under certain environmental conditions (e.g., poverty and IQ; early maltreatment, and depression) make clear that we must look not just for the genes associated with psychological disorders but also for the conditions under which these genes may be expressed.

Check Your Knowledge 2.1 (Answers are at the end of the chapter.)

1. The process by which genes are turned on or off is referred to as:
   a. heritability
   b. gene expression
   c. polygenic
   d. gene switching

2. Sam and Sally are twins raised by their biological parents. Sam excelled in music and was in the high school band; Sally was the star basketball player on the team. They both received top-notch grades, and they both had part-time jobs at the bagel store. An example of a shared environment variable would be _____; an example of a nonshared environment variable would be _____.
   a. school activities; their parents' relationship
   b. band for Sam; basketball for Sally
   c. their parents' relationship; work
   d. their parents' relationship; school activities

3. _____ refers to different forms of the same gene; _____ refers to different genes contributing to a disorder.
   a. Allele; polygenic
   b. Polygenic; allele
   c. Allele; polymorphism
   d. Polymorphism; allele

4. SNPs tell us about the _____ of genes, and CNVs tell us about the _____ of genes.
   a. DNA; RNA
   b. sequence; structure
   c. structure; sequence
   d. DNA; polymorphism

5. In the Caspi and colleagues (2003) gene–environment interaction study of depression, those who were at highest risk for developing depression were:
   a. those who were maltreated as children and had a biological parent with depression
   b. those who were maltreated as children and had at least one long allele of the 5-HTT gene
   c. those who were maltreated as children and had at least one short allele of the 5-HTT gene
   d. those who were not maltreated as children but had at least one short allele of the 5-HTT gene

The Neuroscience Paradigm

The **neuroscience paradigm** holds that psychological disorders are linked to aberrant processes in the brain. Considerable literature deals with the brain and psychopathology. For example, aspects of depression are associated with neurotransmitter problems; anxiety disorders may be related to a problem within the autonomic nervous system; dementia can be traced to impairments in structures of the brain. In this section, we look at three components of this paradigm in which the data are particularly interesting: neurons and neurotransmitters, brain structure and function, and the neuroendocrine system. We then consider some of the key treatments that follow from the paradigm.

Neurons and Neurotransmitters

The cells in the nervous system are called neurons, and the nervous system is comprised of billions of neurons. Although neurons differ in some respects, each **neuron** has four major parts: (1) the cell body; (2) several dendrites, the short and thick extensions; (3) one or more axons of varying lengths, but usually only one long and thin axon that extends a considerable distance from the cell body; and (4) terminal buttons on the many end branches of the axon (Figure 2.5). When a neuron is appropriately stimulated at its cell body or through its dendrites, a nerve impulse travels down the axon to the terminal endings. Between the terminal endings of the sending axon and the cell membrane of the receiving neuron there is a small gap, called the **synapse** (Figure 2.6).

For neurons to send a signal to the next neuron so that communication can occur, the nerve impulse must have a way of bridging the synaptic space. The terminal buttons of each axon contain synaptic vesicles, small structures that are filled with **neurotransmitters.** Neurotransmitters are chemicals that allow neurons to send a signal across the synapse to another neuron. As the neurotransmitter flows into the synapse, some of the molecules reach the receiving, or postsynaptic, neuron. The cell membrane of the postsynaptic neuron contains receptors. Receptors are configured so that only specific neurotransmitters can fit into them.

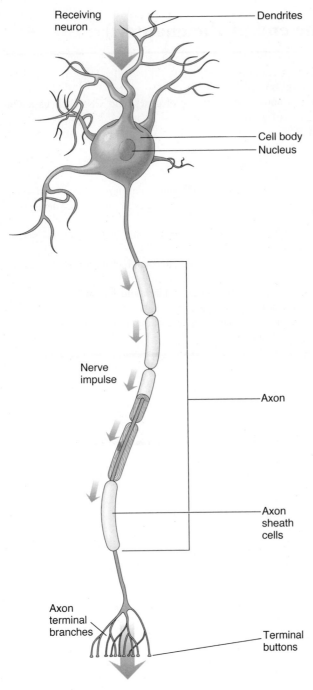

Figure 2.5 The neuron, the basic unit of the nervous system.

When a neurotransmitter fits into a receptor site, a message can be sent to the postsynaptic cell. What actually happens to the postsynaptic neuron depends on integrating thousands of similar messages. Sometimes these messages are excitatory, leading to the creation of a nerve impulse in the postsynaptic cell; at other times the messages are inhibitory, making the postsynaptic cell less likely to create a nerve impulse.

Once a presynaptic neuron (the sending neuron) has released its neurotransmitter, the last step is for the synapse to return to its normal state. Not all of the released neurotransmitter has found its way to postsynaptic receptors. Some of what remains in the synapse is broken down by enzymes, and some is taken back into the presynaptic cell through a process called **reuptake**.

Several key neurotransmitters have been implicated in psychopathology, including **dopamine**, **serotonin**, **norepinephrine**, and **gamma-aminobutyric acid (GABA)**. Serotonin and dopamine may be involved in depression, mania, and schizophrenia. Norepinephrine is a neurotransmitter that communicates with the sympathetic nervous system, where it is involved in producing states of high arousal and thus may be involved in the anxiety disorders and other stress-related conditions (see Focus on Discovery 2.1 for more on the sympathetic nervous system). GABA inhibits nerve impulses throughout most areas of the brain and may be involved in the anxiety disorders.

Early theories linking neurotransmitters to psychopathology sometimes proposed that a given disorder was caused by either too much or too little of a particular transmitter (e.g., mania is associated with too much norepinephrine, anxiety disorders with too little GABA). Later research has uncovered the details behind these overly simple ideas. Neurotransmitters are synthesized in the neuron through a series of metabolic steps, beginning with an amino acid. Each reaction along the way to producing an actual neurotransmitter is catalyzed by an enzyme. Too much or too little of a particular neurotransmitter could result from an error in these metabolic steps. Similar disturbances in the amounts of specific transmitters could result from alterations in the usual processes by which transmitters are deactivated after being released into the synapse. For example,

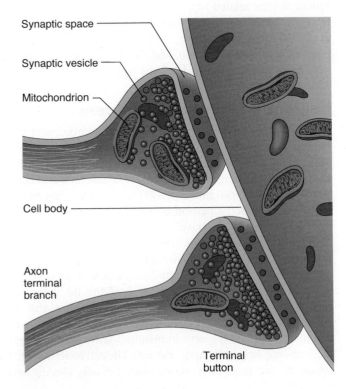

Figure 2.6 A synapse, showing the terminal buttons of two axon branches in close contact with a very small portion of the cell body of another neuron.

a failure to pump leftover neurotransmitter back into the presynaptic cell (reuptake) would leave excess neurotransmitter in the synapse. Then, if a new nerve impulse causes more neurotransmitter to be released into the synapse, the postsynaptic neuron would, in a sense, get a double dose of neurotransmitter, making it more likely for a new nerve impulse to be created.

Other research has focused on the possibility that the neurotransmitter receptors are at fault in some disorders. If the receptors on the postsynaptic neuron were too numerous or too easily excited, the result would be akin to having too much transmitter released. There would simply be more sites available with which the neurotransmitter could interact, increasing the chances that the postsynaptic neuron would be stimulated.

One method that investigators use to study how neurotransmitters are working in the brain is to have people take a drug that stimulates a particular neurotransmitter's receptors. This kind of drug is referred to as an **agonist**. A serotonin agonist, for example, is a drug that stimulates serotonin receptors to produce the same effects as serotonin does naturally. By contrast, an **antagonist** is a drug that works on a neurotransmitter's receptors to dampen the activity of that neurotransmitter. For example, many drugs used to treat schizophrenia are dopamine antagonists that work by blocking dopamine receptors (see Chapter 9).

Structure and Function of the Human Brain

The brain is located within the protective coating of the skull and is enveloped with three protective layers of membranes referred to as meninges. Viewed from the top, the brain is divided by a midline fissure into two mirror-image cerebral hemispheres; together they constitute most of the cerebrum. The major connection between the two hemispheres is a band of nerve fibers, called the **corpus callosum**, that allows the two hemispheres to communicate. Figure 2.7 shows the surface of one of the cerebral hemispheres. The cortex is comprised of the neurons that form the thin outer covering of the brain, the so-called **gray matter** of the brain. The cortex consists of six layers of tightly packed neurons, estimated to number close to 16 billion. The cortex is vastly convoluted; the ridges are called gyri, and the depressions between them sulci, or fissures. If unfolded, the cortex would be about the size of a formal dinner napkin. The sulci are used to define different regions of the brain, much like guide points on a map. Deep fissures divide the cerebral hemispheres into four distinct areas called lobes. The **frontal lobe** lies in front of the central sulcus; the **parietal lobe** is behind it and above the lateral sulcus; the **temporal lobe** is located below the lateral sulcus; and the **occipital lobe** lies behind the parietal and temporal lobes (see Figure 2.7). Different functions tend to be associated with particular brain areas: vision with the occipital lobe; discrimination of sounds with the temporal lobe; reasoning, problem solving, working memory, and emotion regulation with the frontal lobe. One important area of the cortex is called the **prefrontal cortex**. This region, in the very front of the cortex, helps to regulate the amygdala (discussed below) and is important in many different disorders.

If the brain is sliced in half, separating the two cerebral hemispheres, additional important structures can be seen. The gray matter of the cerebral cortex does not extend throughout the interior of the brain (see Figure 2.8). Much of the interior is **white matter**, made up of large tracts of myelinated (sheathed) fibers that connect cell bodies in the cortex with those in the spinal cord and in other centers lower in the brain. In certain areas, called *nuclei*, sets of nerves converge and messages are integrated from different centers.

One important set of areas, collectively referred to as the *basal ganglia*, is located deep within each hemisphere. The basal ganglia help regulate start-

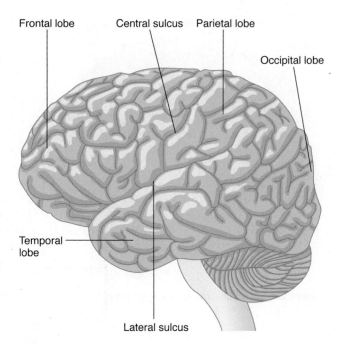

Figure 2.7 Surface of the left cerebral hemisphere, showing the four lobes and the central and lateral sulci.

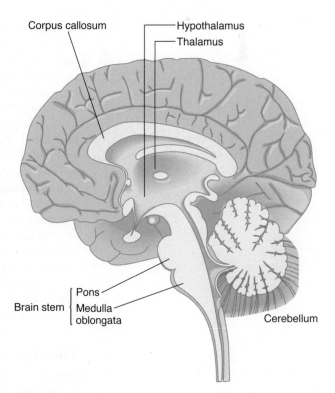

Figure 2.8 Slice of brain showing some of the internal structures.

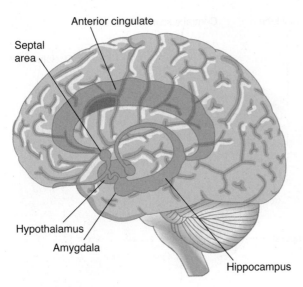

Figure 2.9 Subcortical structures of the brain.

ing and stopping both motor and cognitive activity. Also deep within the brain are cavities called **ventricles**. These ventricles are filled with cerebrospinal fluid. Cerebrospinal fluid circulates through the brain through these ventricles, which are connected with the spinal cord.

The **thalamus** is a relay station for all sensory pathways except the olfactory. The nuclei making up the thalamus receive nearly all impulses arriving from the different sensory areas of the body before passing them on to the cortex, where they are interpreted as conscious sensations. The **brain stem,** comprised of the *pons* and the *medulla oblongata,* functions primarily as a neural relay station. The pons contains tracts that connect the cerebellum with the spinal cord and with motor areas of the cerebrum. The medulla oblongata serves as the main line of traffic for tracts ascending from the spinal cord and descending from the higher centers of the brain. The **cerebellum** receives sensory nerves from the vestibular apparatus of the ear and from muscles, tendons, and joints. The information received and integrated relates to balance, posture, equilibrium, and the smooth coordination of the body when in motion.

A set of deeper, mostly subcortical, structures are often implicated in different forms of psychopathology. There is a long history of referring to different groupings of these structures as the *limbic system,* a term that most contemporary neuroscientists consider outdated. These structures, shown in Figure 2.9, support the visceral and physical expressions of emotion—quickened heartbeat and respiration, trembling, sweating, and alterations in facial expressions—and the expression of appetitive and other primary drives, namely, hunger, thirst, mating, defense, attack, and flight. Important structures are the **anterior cingulate**, the **septal area**, the **hippocampus**, which is associated with memory; the **hypothalamus**, which regulates metabolism, temperature, perspiration, blood pressure, sleeping, and appetite; and the **amygdala**, which is an important area for attention to emotionally salient stimuli. This is one of the key brain structures for psychopathology researchers, given the ubiquity of emotional problems in the psychological disorders. For example, people with depression show more activity in the amygdala when looking at pictures of emotional faces than do people without depression (Sheline, Barch, Donnelly et al., 2001).

The development of the human brain is a complex process that begins early in the first trimester of pregnancy and continues into early adulthood. It has been estimated that about a third of our genes are expressed in the brain, and many of these genes are responsible for laying out the structure of the brain. The development of the cells and the migration of these cells to the appropriate layers of cortex comprise an intricate dance. Unfortunately, missteps can happen, and current thinking about a number of disorders, such as schizophrenia, places the beginnings of the problem in these early developmental stages. Brain development continues throughout childhood, adolescence, and even into adulthood. What is happening during this time is cell development and a honing of the connections between cells and brain areas. The gray matter of the brain continues to develop, filling with cells, until early adolescence. Then, somewhat surprisingly, a number of synaptic connections begin to be eliminated—a process called **pruning**. Throughout early adulthood, the connections in the brain may become fewer, but they also become faster. The areas that develop the quickest are areas linked to sensory processes, like the cerebellum and occipital lobe. The area that develops last is the frontal lobe.

We will discuss a number of these brain areas throughout the book. For example, people with schizophrenia have been found to have enlarged ventricles of the brain (Chapter 9); the size of the hippocampus is reduced among some people with posttraumatic stress disorder, depression, and schizophrenia, perhaps due to overactivity of their stress response systems (Chapters 5, 7, and 9); brain size among some children with autism expands at a much greater rate than it should in typical development (Chapter 13).

The Neuroendocrine System

The neuroendocrine system has been implicated in psychopathology as well, and we will consider this evidence throughout this book. One of the systems we will return to again and again is the hypothalamic-pituitary-adrenal (HPA) axis (shown in Figure 2.10). The **HPA axis** is central to the body's response to stress, and stress figures prominently in many of the disorders we discuss in this book.

When people are faced with threat, the hypothalamus releases corticotropin-releasing factor (CRF), which then communicates with the *pituitary gland*. The pituitary then releases adrenocorticotropic hormone, which travels via the blood to the adrenal glands. The outer layers of the adrenal glands are referred to as the *adrenal cortex*; this area promotes the release of the hormone cortisol. **Cortisol** is often referred to as the stress hormone. This is not a fast-moving system, like the autonomic nervous system, to be reviewed shortly. Rather, it takes about 20 to 40 minutes for cortisol release to peak. After the stress or threat has remitted, it can take up to an hour for cortisol to return to baseline (i.e., before the stress) levels (Dickerson & Kemeny, 2004).

Studies of stress and the HPA axis are uniquely integrative. That is, they begin with a psychological concept (stress) and examine how stress is manifested in the body (the HPA axis). For example, in a series of animal studies, researchers have shown that rats and primates that are exposed to early trauma, such as being separated from their mothers, show elevated activity in the HPA axis when they are exposed to stressors later in life (Gutman & Nemeroff, 2003). As in our discussion of gene–environment interactions earlier, it is hard to consider biology and environment separately—biology may create increased reactivity to the environment, and early experiences may influence biology. As we will see, chronic stress and its effects on the HPA axis are linked to disorders as diverse as schizophrenia, depression, and posttraumatic stress disorder.

Another important system, the **autonomic nervous system (ANS)**, is discussed in Focus on Discovery 2.1. Much of our behavior is dependent on a nervous system that operates very quickly, generally without our awareness, and that has traditionally been viewed as beyond voluntary control; hence, the term *autonomic*.

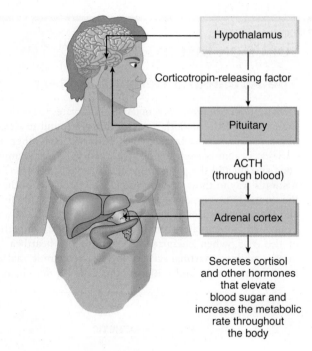

Figure 2.10 The HPA axis.

The Immune System

Stress also has effects on the immune system. The field that studies how psychological factors impact the immune system is called **psychoneuroimmunology.** Reviews of nearly 300 studies confirmed that a wide range of stressors produce problematic changes in the immune system, including medical school examinations, depression and bereavement, marital discord and divorce, job loss, caring for a relative with Alzheimer's disease, and the Three Mile Island nuclear disaster, among others (Kiecolt-Glaser & Glaser, 2002; Segerstrom & Miller, 2004). As we shall see throughout, changes in the immune system are also associated with different psychological disorders.

The immune system involves a broad array of cells and proteins that respond when the body is infected or invaded. A useful way of thinking about the immune system is to consider two broad types of immunity, natural and specific (Segerstrom & Miller, 2004).

Natural immunity is the body's first and quickest line of defense against infectious microorganisms or other invaders. A number of different cells, such as macrophages and natural killer cells, are unleashed on the invaders and begin to destroy them. Inflammation or swelling is a sign of these natural immunity cells at work. Activation of macrophages in turn stimulates the release of substances called **cytokines,** which help initiate such bodily responses to infection as fatigue, fever, and activation of the HPA axis. Although unpleasant, fever is actually a sign that the body is responding as it should to an infection.

Specific immunity involves cells that respond more slowly to infection, such as lymphocytes, which are involved in responding to specific pathogens or invading agents. Lymphocytes include T-helper cells and B cells. T-helper cells promote the release of cytokines; B cells release antibodies that deal with specific pathogens.

FOCUS ON DISCOVERY 2.1

The Autonomic Nervous System

The autonomic nervous system (ANS) innervates the endocrine glands, the heart, and the smooth muscles that are found in the walls of the blood vessels, stomach, intestines, kidneys, and other organs. This nervous system is itself divided into two parts, the **sympathetic nervous system** and the **parasympathetic nervous system** (Figure 2.11). A simple way to think about these two components of the ANS is that the sympathetic nervous system prepares the body for "fight or flight" and the parasympathetic nervous system helps "calm down" the body. Things are not actually that simple, though. The sympathetic portion of the ANS, when energized, accelerates the heartbeat, dilates the pupils, inhibits intestinal activity, increases electrodermal activity (i.e., sweat on the skin), and initiates other smooth muscle and glandular

responses that prepare the organism for sudden activity and stress. Division of activities is not quite so clear-cut, however, for it is the parasympathetic system that increases blood flow to the genitals during sexual excitement.

The autonomic nervous system figures prominently in many of the anxiety disorders, such as panic disorder and posttraumatic stress disorder. For example, people with panic disorder tend to misinterpret normal changes in their nervous system, such as shortness of breath after running up a flight of stairs. Instead of attributing this to being out of shape, people with panic disorder may think they are about to have another panic attack. In essence, they come to fear the sensations of their own autonomic nervous system.

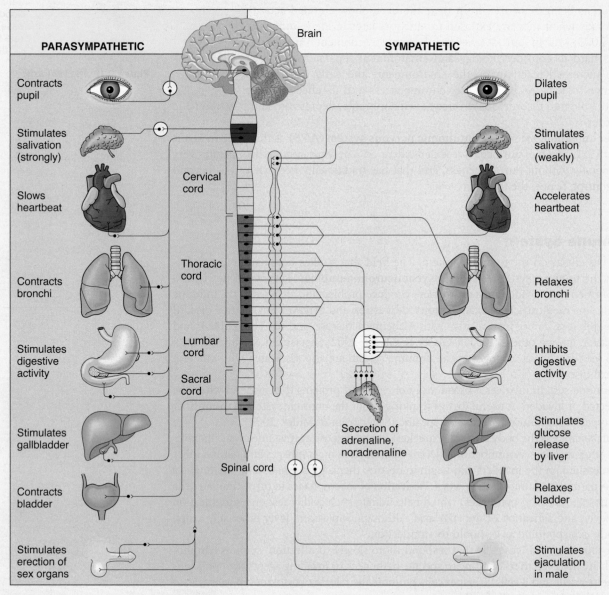

Figure 2.11 The autonomic nervous system.

Figure 2.12 shows the components of the immune system. The effects of stress on the immune system are direct, and they can happen very early in life. In fact, a series of studies with animals has convincingly demonstrated that prenatal stress experienced by a mother can produce long-lasting changes in behavior and the immune system in her offspring (Coe & Lubach, 2005).

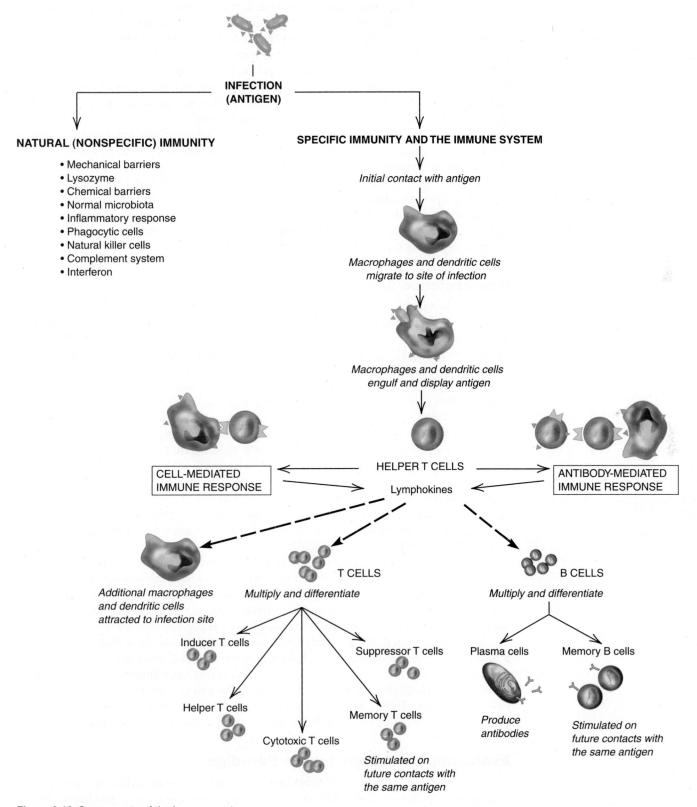

Figure 2.12 Components of the immune system.

For example, compared to infants of mothers who experienced no stress during pregnancy, the infants of rhesus monkey mothers who were exposed to chronic stress during pregnancy (exposure to loud and unpredictable noises 5 days a week for one-quarter of their pregnancy) were observed to have emotion regulation difficulties as babies and adolescents that negatively impacted their place in the social group (Coe, Lubach, & Schneider, 1999; Roughton, Schneider, Bromley, & Coe,1998). In addition, these babies exhibited immune system disturbances that continued into adolescence, including a deficiency of pro-inflammatory cytokines, such as **interleukin-6** (Coe, Kramer, Kirschbaum et al., 2002). Interleukin-6 (IL-6) promotes inflammation in response to infection and is importantly linked to human diseases as well as psychological disorders such as major depressive disorder. In addition, exposure to stress also slows the process of wound healing, which relies on the immune system (Kiecolt-Glaser, McGuire, Robles, & Glaser, 2002). Across a number of studies, age appears to be a factor—that is, older adults are more likely than younger adults to show a harmful immune response to stress.

Other evidence indicates that stress can trigger the release of cytokines such as interleukin-1 and interleukin-6, as if the body were fighting off an infection (Maier & Watkins, 1998). Why is this important? The link between stress and the immune system has several direct implications for overall health. Inflammation and higher levels of IL-6 have been linked to a number of diseases in older adults, such as coronary heart disease, arthritis, multiple myeloma, non-Hodgkin's lymphoma, osteoporosis, and type 2 diabetes. Thus, if stress increases the release of IL-6, the impact on health is likely to be negative. In short, the effects of stress on the immune system can be substantial.

Neuroscience Approaches to Treatment

The use of psychoactive drugs has been increasing dramatically. For example, between 2005 and 2010, just over 6 percent of adolescents in the United States ages 12–19 took some type of psychotropic medication (Jonas, Gu, & Albertorio-Diaz, 2013), and use of antidepressant medication among all ages increased 400 percent between 2005 and 2008 (Pratt, Brody, & Gu, 2011). Antidepressants were the third most commonly prescribed medication for any type of health issue in 2013, behind only blood pressure and cholesterol medications (IMS Health, 2014). Spending on antipsychotic drugs increased from $1.3 billion in 1997 to $5.6 billion in 2006 (Barber, 2008). Antidepressants, such as Prozac, increase neural transmission in neurons that use serotonin as a neurotransmitter by inhibiting the reuptake of serotonin. Benzodiazepines, such as Xanax, can be effective in reducing the tension associated with some anxiety disorders, perhaps by stimulating GABA neurons to inhibit other neural systems that create the physical symptoms of anxiety. Antipsychotic drugs, such as Olanzapine, used in the treatment of schizophrenia, reduce the activity of neurons that use dopamine as a neurotransmitter by blocking their receptors and also impact serotonin. Stimulants, such as Adderall, are often used to treat children with attention-deficit/hyperactivity disorder; they operate on several neurotransmitters that help children pay attention.

Although you might assume that we have learned which neurotransmitters are involved in a disorder and then used that to determine pharmacological treatments, this is often not the case. Rather, the reverse has often happened: a drug is found that influences symptoms, and then researchers are inspired to study the neurotransmitters influenced by that drug. But as we will see, the evidence linking neurotransmitters as causal factors in psychopathology is not very strong.

It should be noted that a person could hold a neuroscience view about the nature of a disorder and yet recommend psychological intervention. Contemporary scientists and clinicians also appreciate that nonbiological interventions can influence brain functioning. For example, psychotherapy that teaches a person how to stop performing compulsive rituals, which is an effective and widely used behavioral treatment for obsessive-compulsive disorder, has measurable effects on brain activity (Baxter,Ackerman, Swerdlow et al., 2000).

Evaluating the Neuroscience Paradigm

Over the past three decades, neuroscientists have made great progress in elucidating brain–behavior relationships. Neuroscience research on both the causes and treatment of psychopathology is proceeding at a rapid rate, as we will see when we discuss specific disorders in later chapters. Although we view these developments in a positive light, we also want to caution against reductionism.

Reductionism refers to the view that whatever is being studied can and should be reduced to its most basic elements or constituents. In the case of psychological disorders, reductionism happens when scientists try to reduce complex mental and emotional responses to biology. In its extreme form, reductionism asserts that psychology and psychopathology are ultimately nothing more than biology.

Basic elements, such as individual nerve cells, are organized into more complex structures or systems, such as neural networks or circuits. The properties of these neural circuits cannot be deduced from the properties of the individual nerve cells. The whole is greater than the sum of its parts. A good example is provided by computers. Students writing papers for their courses use word-processing programs like Google Docs. These software programs consist of many levels of code that communicate with the computer. The word-processing program necessarily involves low-level communication with the computer, involving a series of 0's and 1's and even electronics. Yet we don't conceptualize the program in terms of binary digits or electrical impulses. If the spell-checker stopped working, our first place to begin repairs would not be with the computer chips. Instead, we would want the programmer to fix the bug in the program. To be sure, the program could not run without the computer, but the program is more than just the impulses sent by the chips. In the same way, although a complex behavior like a hallucination necessarily involves the brain and nerve impulses, it is not likely that we can fully capture this by knowing about specific nerve impulses.

Certain phenomena emerge only at certain levels of analysis and will be missed by investigators who focus only on the molecular level. In the field of psychopathology, problems such as delusional beliefs, dysfunctional attitudes, and catastrophizing cognitions may well be impossible to explain neurobiologically, even with a detailed understanding of the behavior of individual neurons (Turkheimer, 1998).

Quick Summary

The neuroscience paradigm is concerned with the ways in which the brain contributes to psychopathology. Neurotransmitters such as serotonin, norepinephrine, dopamine, and GABA have been implicated in a number of disorders. A number of different brain areas are also a focus of research. The autonomic nervous system, which includes the sympathetic and parasympathetic nervous systems, is also implicated in the manifestations of some disorders. The HPA axis is responsible for the body's response to stress and thus is relevant for several stress-related disorders. Stress can also produce problematic changes in the immune system, and this can impact a number of psychological disorders, such as major depressive disorder. Cytokines help initiate such bodily responses to infection as fatigue, fever, and activation of the HPA axis. Inflammation and higher levels of the cytokine IL-6 have been linked to a number of diseases in older adults. Biological treatments, primarily medications, are effective for different disorders, but they are not necessarily treating the cause of the problems. Although the brain plays an important role in our understanding of the causes of psychopathology, we must be careful to avoid reductionism.

Check Your Knowledge 2.2

Fill in the blanks.
1. The so-called limbic system of the brain includes the following brain areas: _____, _____, _____, _____, and _____.
2. The _____ matter of the brain consists of the tracts of myelinated fibers that connect cells; the _____ matter of the brain refers to the brain's cells or neurons.
3. Neurotransmitters that are studied in psychopathology include _____, which can produce states of high arousal, and _____, which inhibits nerve impulses.
4. The HPA axis consists of the _____, _____, and _____.
5. _____ is the body's quick response immune system to stress; _____ is the slower response system.

The Cognitive Behavioral Paradigm

The **cognitive behavioral paradigm** traces its roots to learning principles and to cognitive science. As we will see, the basic principles from classical and operant conditioning (see Chapter 1) as well as cognitive science have shaped the development of many cognitive behavioral therapies.

Influences from Behavior Therapy

One of the key influences from behaviorism is the notion that problem behavior is likely to continue if it is reinforced. Generally, problem behavior is thought to be reinforced by four possible consequences: getting attention, escaping from tasks, generating sensory feedback (such as results from the hand flapping often seen in children with autism spectrum disorder), and gaining access to desirable things or situations (Carr, Levin, McConnachie et al., 1994). Once the source of reinforcement has been identified, treatment is then tailored to alter the consequences of the problem behavior. For example, if it was established that getting attention reinforced the problem behavior, the treatment might be to ignore the behavior. Alternatively, the problem behavior could be followed by **time-out**—the person is sent for a period of time to a location where positive reinforcers are not available. Today, time-out is a commonly used parenting technique for children who exhibit a problematic behavior of some sort.

Operant techniques such as systematically rewarding desirable behavior and extinguishing undesirable behavior have been particularly successful in the treatment of many childhood problems (Kazdin & Weisz, 1998). Once contingencies shape a behavior, a key goal is to maintain the effects of treatment. If a therapist or a teacher has been providing reinforcement, one might not expect this person to keep providing reinforcement forever. This issue has been addressed in several ways. Because laboratory findings indicate that intermittent reinforcement—rewarding a response only a portion of the times it appears—makes new behavior more enduring, many operant programs move away from continuous schedules of reinforcement once desired behavior is occurring regularly. For example, if a teacher has succeeded in helping a disruptive child spend more time sitting by praising the child generously for each math problem finished while seated, the teacher will gradually reward the child for every other success, and ultimately only infrequently.

Another successful example of operant conditioning is **behavioral activation (BA) therapy** of depression (Dimidjian, Barrera, Martell et al., 2011), which involves helping a person engage in tasks that provide an opportunity for positive reinforcement.

We introduced the technique called systematic desensitization in Chapter 1. Recall that this involves two components: (1) deep muscle relaxation and (2) gradual exposure to a list of feared situations, starting with those that arouse minimal anxiety and progressing to those that are the most frightening. The still-influential contribution from this behavioral approach is the **exposure** component of this treatment. The basic idea is that the anxiety will extinguish if the person can face the object or situation long enough with no actual harm occurring. Sometimes this exposure can be conducted **in vivo**—that is, in real-life situations. For example, if someone has a fear of flying, you might have him or her take an actual flight. At times, exposure cannot be conducted in real life, so *imaginal exposure* will be used to address fears, such as rape, trauma, or contamination. In other situations, both types of exposure are used.

Exposure continues to be a centrally important component of many forms of cognitive behavior therapy today, as we discuss in more detail in Chapters 6 and 7. In the years since exposure treatments were first developed, much has been learned about them.

Time-out is a behavioral therapy technique based on operant conditioning; the consequence for misbehavior is removal to an environment with no positive reinforcers.

Exposure treatment is one of the most well-supported approaches for anxiety disorders.

For instance, exposure to the real thing (in vivo exposure), when practical, is more effective than imagining situations. Also, even though relaxation training helps people experience less arousal when they first face the feared stimulus, there is no evidence that such training is required for good outcomes. As a result, it has been possible to develop briefer psychological treatments that do not include relaxation training.

As influential as these behavior therapy techniques were (and still are), behaviorism and behavior therapy were often criticized for minimizing the importance of two important factors: thinking and feeling. In other words, the way we think and feel about things undoubtedly influences our behavior. These limitations of behavioral points of view led some behavioral researchers and clinicians to include cognitive and emotion variables in their conceptualizations of psychopathology and therapy.

Cognitive Science

Cognition is a term that groups together the mental processes of perceiving, recognizing, conceiving, judging, and reasoning. Cognitive science focuses on how people (and animals) structure their experiences, how they make sense of them, and how they relate their current experiences to past ones that have been stored in memory.

At any given moment, we are bombarded by far more stimuli than we can possibly respond to. How do we filter this overwhelming input, put it into words or images, form hypotheses, and arrive at a perception of what is out there?

Cognitive scientists regard people as active interpreters of a situation, with people's past knowledge imposing a perceptual funnel on the experience. A person fits new information into an organized network of already accumulated knowledge, often referred to as a **schema**, or cognitive set (Neisser, 1976). New information may fit the schema; if not, the person reorganizes the schema to fit the information or construes the information in such a way as to fit the schema. The following situation illustrates how a schema may alter the way in which information is processed and remembered.

> *The man stood before the mirror and combed his hair. He checked his face carefully for any places he might have missed shaving and then put on the conservative tie he had decided to wear. At breakfast, he studied the newspaper carefully and, over coffee, discussed the possibility of buying a new washing machine with his wife. Then he made several phone calls. As he was leaving the house he thought about the fact that his children would probably want to go to that private camp again this summer. When the car didn't start, he got out, slammed the door and walked down to the bus stop in a very angry mood. Now he would be late. (Bransford & Johnson, 1973, p. 415)*

Now read the excerpt again, but add the word *unemployed* before the word *man*. Now read it a third time, substituting *investment banker* for *man*. Notice how differently you understand the passage. Ask yourself what parts of the newspaper these men read. If you were asked on a questionnaire to recall this information and you no longer had access to the excerpt, you might answer "the want ads" for the unemployed man and "the financial pages" for the investment banker. Since the passage does not specify which part of the paper was read, these answers are wrong, but in each instance the error would have been a meaningful, predictable one.

Other important contributions from cognitive science include the study of attention. As we will see, people with disorders as diverse as anxiety disorders, mood disorders, and schizophrenia have problems with attention. For example, individuals with anxiety disorders tend to focus their attention on threatening or anxiety-producing events or situations in the environment. People with schizophrenia have a hard time concentrating their attention for a period of time.

One of the ways in which researchers have studied attention is with the Stroop task. In this task, the participant sees a set of color names printed in inks of *different* colors and must name the ink color of each word as rapidly as possible (see Figure 2.13). To do this, participants have to resist the natural impulse to say the printed word. For example, a participant might see the word *blue* written in green ink. The participant is instructed to name the ink color (green) as fast as possible without making mistakes (saying the word *blue*). It is difficult to say *green*

Black	Pink
Red	White
Blue	Red
Green	**Black**
Yellow	Purple
Blue	Green
Red	Blue
White	Yellow

Figure 2.13 In the Stroop task, participants must name the color of the ink instead of reading the words.

and "inhibit" the more natural tendency to say *blue*. Interference, measured as a lengthening of response time, occurs because the words are more "attention grabbing" than the ink color.

The Stroop task has been modified to focus on emotion rather than colors. In this emotion Stroop task, participants are still instructed to name the color of the ink rather than saying the word. However, the list of words now contains emotion words instead of color words. So, for example, words such as *threat, danger, happy*, or *anxious* are written in different ink colors. In such an emotion Stroop task, individuals with anxiety disorders find that some of the emotion words are so attention grabbing that the impulse to say the word is especially strong. As in the original Stroop task, the more attention grabbing the word is, the more interference and the slower the response. Research has shown that people with anxiety disorders show more interference for threatening words (i.e., they say these words more slowly) than for nonthreatening words; this is used as evidence of an attention bias toward threatening information (see Chapter 6).

Of course, the concepts of schema and attention are related to each other. If a person has a particular set or schema about the world (e.g., the world is dangerous), that person may be more likely to pay attention to threatening or dangerous things in the environment. Furthermore, this person may be more likely to interpret ambiguous things in the environment as threatening. For example, seeing a stranger standing on a front porch may be interpreted as a sign of danger to someone with such a "danger" schema. For someone without such a schema, this person may be viewed simply as the person who lives in that house.

Cognitive explanations are central in the search for the causes of psychopathology and for new methods of intervention. Cognitive theorizing will be included in discussions of most of the disorders presented in subsequent chapters.

The Role of the Unconscious

As far back as Freud (see Chapter 1), much of human behavior was presumed to be unconscious, or outside the awareness of the individual. Later followers of Freud continued to emphasize the role of the unconscious in human behavior and psychopathology, but the way in which the unconscious has been discussed and even empirically studied has changed throughout the years.

The unconscious has been a hot topic of study among cognitive psychologists for over 30 years. For example, in one study, participants were presented with different shapes for 1 millisecond (one-thousandth of a second) (Kunst-Wilson & Zajonc, 1980). Later they showed virtually no ability to recognize the shapes they had seen, but when they rated how much they liked the shapes, they preferred the ones they had been shown to other ones. We know that familiarity affects judgments of stimuli; people tend to like familiar stimuli more than unfamiliar ones. This study indicates that some aspects of the stimuli must have been absorbed, even though participants said that they did not recognize the shapes.

Cognitive neuroscientists have more recently explored how the brain supports behavior that is outside conscious awareness. For example, the concept of *implicit memory* refers to the idea that a person can, without being aware of it, be influenced by prior learning. A person may be shown a list of words so quickly that he or she cannot identify the words. Later, the person will be able to recall those words even though the words were not consciously perceived during the rapid initial presentation. Thus, a memory is formed implicitly (i.e., without conscious awareness). Implicit memory paradigms have been adopted by psychopathology researchers, who have found, for example, that people with social anxiety and depression have trouble with these tasks (Amir, Foa, & Coles, 1998; Watkins, 2002).

Contemporary studies of the unconscious, such as studies of implicit memory, are a long way from Freud's original theorizing about the unconscious. For cognitive neuroscientists, the unconscious reflects the incredible efficiency and automaticity of the brain. That is, there are simply too many things going on around us all the time for us to be aware of everything.

Thus, our brains have developed the capacity to register information for later use even if we are not aware of it.

Cognitive Behavior Therapy

Cognitive behavior therapy (CBT) incorporates theory and research on cognitive processes. Cognitive behavior therapists pay attention to private events—thoughts, perceptions, judgments, self-statements, and even tacit (unconscious) assumptions—and have studied and manipulated these processes in their attempts to understand and modify overt and covert disturbed behavior. **Cognitive restructuring** is a general term for changing a pattern of thought. People with depression may not realize how often they think self-critically, and those with anxiety disorders may not realize that they tend to be overly sensitive to possible threats in the world. Therapists hope that people can change their feelings, behaviors, and symptoms by changing their cognition. The therapist begins by tracking the daily thoughts a person experiences but then moves to understanding more about core cognitive biases and schemata that might shape those daily negative thoughts.

Beck's Cognitive Therapy Psychiatrist Aaron Beck, one of the leading cognitive behavior therapists, developed a cognitive therapy for depression based on the idea that depressed mood is caused by distortions in the way people perceive life experiences (Beck, 1976; Salkovskis, 1996). For example, a person with depression may focus exclusively on negative happenings and ignore positive ones. Imagine that a woman's romantic partner both praises

Aaron Beck developed a cognitive theory of depression and a cognitive behavioral therapy for people with depression.

Dr. Aaron T. Beck, University Professor of Psychiatry, University of Pennsylvania.

Clinical Case: An Example of Beck's Cognitive Therapy

The following examples illustrate ways of beginning to help a person change negative cognitions.

Therapist: You said that you feel like a failure since Bill left you. How would you define "failure"?

Patient: Well, the marriage didn't work out.

Therapist: So, you believe that the marriage didn't work out because you, as a person, are a failure?

Patient: If I had been successful, then he would still be with me.

Therapist: So, would we conclude that we can say, "People whose marriages don't work out are failures"?

Patient: No, I guess I wouldn't go that far.

Therapist: Why not? Should we have one definition of failure for you and another for everyone else?

People who define *failure* as less than "extraordinarily successful" can see that their definitions are polarized in all-or-nothing terms—that is, "complete success" versus "complete failure." A variation on this technique is to ask the patient how others would define "success" or "failure."

Therapist: You can see that your definition of failure is quite different from the way other people might see it. Few people would say that a person who is divorced is a failure. Let's focus on the positive end

right now. How would most people define "success" in a person?

Patient: Well, they might say that someone has success when they accomplish some of their goals.

Therapist: OK. So, would we say that if someone accomplishes some goals they have success?

Patient: Right.

Therapist: Would we also say that people can have different degrees of success? Some people accomplish more goals than others?

Patient: That sounds right.

Therapist: So, if we applied this to you, would we say that you have accomplished some of your goals in life?

Patient: Yes, I did graduate from college and I have been working for the past six years. I've been busy raising Ted—he had some medical problems a couple of years ago, but I got the right doctors for him.

Therapist: So, would we call these some successful behaviors on your part?

Patient: Right, I've had some successes.

Therapist: Is there a contradiction, then, in your thinking—calling yourself a "failure" but saying that you have had several successes?

Patient: Yes, that doesn't make sense, does it? (quoted in Leahy, 2003, pp. 38–39).

and criticizes her. If the woman attends to the praise and remembers it the next day, she is likely to feel happy. But if she focuses on the criticism and continues to dwell on it the next day, she is likely to feel unhappy. Beck's therapy, which has now been adapted for many other disorders in addition to depression, is a collaborative treatment between therapist and the person seeking treatment. When a person with depression expresses feelings that nothing ever goes right, for example, the therapist offers counterexamples, pointing out how the person has overlooked favorable happenings. The general goal of Beck's therapy is to provide people with experiences, both inside and outside the therapy room, that will alter their negative schemas, enabling them to have hope rather than despair.

There have also been many recent innovations in CBT. These treatments include dialectical behavior therapy (see Chapter 15), mindfulness-based cognitive therapy (see Chapter 5), and acceptance and commitment therapy. The newer treatments differ from traditional CBT by incorporating a focus on spirituality, values, emotion, and acceptance. Another theme involves strategies to minimize emotional avoidance. For example, in acceptance and commitment therapy (Hayes, 2005), a person might be taught that much of the destructive power of emotions lies in the way we respond to them cognitively and behaviorally. An overarching goal of these therapies is to help a person learn to be more aware of emotions but to avoid immediate, impulsive reactions to that emotion. In the case of mindfulness-based cognitive therapy, this is facilitated through the use of meditation (Segal, Williams, & Teasdale, 2003). Overall, a rich array of cognitive behavioral approaches has been developed.

Evaluating the Cognitive Behavioral Paradigm

Cognitive behavioral explanations of psychopathology have generated a great deal of research over the past several decades. Yet, some cognitive explanations do not appear to explain much. That a person with depression has a negative schema tells us that the person thinks gloomy thoughts. But such a pattern of thinking is actually part of the diagnosis of depression. What is distinctive in the cognitive behavioral paradigm is that the thoughts are given causal status; that is, the thoughts are regarded as causing the other features of the disorder, such as sadness. Left unanswered is the question of where the negative schema came from in the first place. Much of the current research is focused on understanding what types of mechanisms sustain the biased thoughts shown in different psychopathologies.

Quick Summary

The cognitive behavioral paradigm reflects influences from behavior therapy and cognitive science. Treatment techniques designed to alter the consequences or reinforcers of a behavior, such as in time-out and exposure, are still used today. Cognitive science focuses on concepts such as schemas (a network of accumulated knowledge or set), attention, memory, and the unconscious, and these concepts are part of cognitive behavioral theories and treatments of psychopathology. For example, research on implicit memory promoted acceptance of the ideas of unconscious influences on behavior. Cognitive behavior therapy uses behavior therapy techniques and cognitive restructuring. Aaron Beck is an influential cognitive behavior therapist.

Check Your Knowledge 2.3

True or false?
1. In the Stroop task, interference is measured by how long it takes to name the color of the ink in a list of words.
2. Beck's theory suggests that people have distortions in the way they perceive life's experiences.
3. Current research on the unconscious is conducted in much the same way as it was when Freud talked about the unconscious.

Factors That Cut Across the Paradigms

Three important sets of factors that we will consider throughout this book are emotion, sociocultural, and interpersonal factors. Some type of disturbance in emotion can be found in nearly all psychological disorders. In addition, we will see that gender, culture, ethnicity, and social relationships bear importantly on the descriptions, causes, and treatments of the different disorders. In the next sections, we introduce these concepts and give some examples of why they are so important in psychopathology, regardless of what paradigm has been adopted.

Emotion and Psychopathology

Emotions influence how we respond to problems and challenges in our environment; they help us organize our thoughts and actions, both explicitly and implicitly, and they guide our behavior. Perhaps because our emotions exert such widespread influence, we spend a good deal of time trying to regulate how we feel and how we present our emotions to others. Given their centrality, it is not surprising that disturbances in emotion figure prominently in many different forms of psychopathology. By one analysis, as many as 85 percent of psychological disorders include disturbances in emotional processing of some kind (Thoits, 1985).

What is emotion? The answer to that question could fill an entire textbook on its own. Emotions are believed to be fairly short-lived states, lasting for a few seconds, minutes, or at most hours. Sometimes the word *affect* is used to describe short-lasting emotional feelings. Moods, on the other hand, are emotional experiences that endure for a longer period of time.

Most contemporary emotion theorists and researchers suggest that emotions have a number of components, including (but not limited to) expressive, experiential, and physiological components. The *expressive,* or *behavioral, component* of emotion typically refers to facial expressions of emotion. Many people with schizophrenia display very few facial expressions. The *experience,* or *subjective feeling, component* of emotion refers to how someone reports he or she feels at any given moment or in response to some event. For example, learning that you received an A on your midterm might elicit feelings of happiness, pride, and relief. Learning you received a C might elicit feelings of anger, anxiety, or embarrassment. The *physiological component* of emotion involves changes in the body, such as those due to the autonomic nervous system activity that accompanies emotion. For example, if a car almost runs you down as you are crossing the street, you may show a frightened look on your face, feel fear, and experience an increase in your heart rate and breathing rate.

When we consider emotional disturbances in psychological disorders, it is important to consider which of the emotion components are affected. In some disorders, all emotion components may be disrupted, whereas in others, just one might be problematic. For example, people with schizophrenia do not readily express their emotions outwardly, but they report feeling emotions very strongly. People with panic disorder experience excessive fear and anxiety when no actual danger is present. People with depression may experience prolonged sadness and other negative feelings. A person with antisocial personality disorder may not feel empathy. We will try to be clear in the book as to what component of emotion is being considered.

Another important consideration in the study of emotion and psychopathology is the concept of *ideal affect*, which simply refers to the kinds of emotional states that a person ideally wants to feel. At first glance, you might presume that happiness is the ideal affect for everyone. After all, who doesn't want to feel happy? However, research shows that ideal affects vary depending on cultural factors (Tsai, 2007). Thus, people from Western cultures, such as the United States, do indeed value happiness as their ideal state. However, people from East Asian cultures, like China, value less arousing positive emotions, such as calmness, more than happiness (Tsai, Knutson, & Fung, 2006). Tsai and colleagues have also shown a linkage between people's ideal affect and drug usage; if the ideal affect is a state of low arousal,

Emotion consists of many components, including expression (shown here), experience, and physiology.

© SensorSpot/iStockphoto

like calmness, a person is less likely, for example, to use cocaine (Tsai, Knutson, & Rothman, 2007). Cross-nationally, more people in the United States seek treatment for cocaine and amphetamines, drugs that are stimulating and associated with feelings of excitement and happiness; more people in China seek treatment for heroin, a drug that has calming effects (Tsai, 2007; for more on the effects of these drugs, see Chapter 10).

The study of emotion figures prominently in the work of neuroscientists who are examining the ways in which the brain contributes to the different emotion components. Geneticists have also begun to examine how tendencies to experience a lot of positive or negative emotion may run in families. Emotions such as anger figured prominently in Freud's views; more contemporary psychodynamic treatments also focus on changing emotion. Even cognitive behavioral therapies consider how emotion influences thinking and behavior. Emotion thus cuts across the paradigms and can be studied from multiple perspectives, depending on the paradigm that is adopted.

Sociocultural Factors and Psychopathology

A good deal of research has focused on the ways in which sociocultural factors, such as gender, race, culture, ethnicity, and socioeconomic status, can contribute to different psychological disorders. Researchers who study such sociocultural factors and psychopathology all share the premise that environmental factors can trigger, exacerbate, or maintain the symptoms that make up the different disorders. But the range of variables considered and the ways of studying those variables cover a lot of ground.

Several studies consider the role of gender in different disorders. These studies have shown that some disorders affect men and women differently. For example, depression is nearly twice as common among women as among men. On the other hand, antisocial personality disorder and alcohol use disorder are more common among men than women. Childhood disorders, such as attention-deficit/hyperactivity disorder, affect boys more than girls, but some researchers question whether this reflects a true difference between boys and girls or a bias in the diagnostic criteria. Current research is looking beyond whether men and women differ in the prevalence rates of certain disorders to asking questions about risk factors that may differently impact men and women in the development of certain disorders. For example, father-to-son genetic transmission appears to be an important risk factor in the development of alcohol use disorder for men, whereas sociocultural standards of thinness may be a risk factor in the development of eating disorders for women.

Other studies show that poverty is a major influence on psychological disorders. For example, poverty is related to antisocial personality disorder, anxiety disorders, and depression. We discuss the role of these factors in overall health in Focus on Discovery 2.2.

Cultural and ethnic factors in psychopathology have also been examined. Some questions, such as whether or not the disorders we diagnose and treat in the United States are observed in other parts of the world, have been fairly well studied. This research has demonstrated that a number of disorders are observed in diverse parts of the world. Indeed, no country or culture is without psychopathology of some sort. For example, Murphy (1976) examined whether schizophrenia symptoms could be observed in cultures as diverse as the Eskimo and Yoruba. She found that both cultures have a concept of being "crazy" that is quite similar to the Western definition of schizophrenia. The Eskimo's *nuthkavihak* includes talking to oneself, refusing to talk, delusional beliefs, and bizarre behavior. The Yoruba's *were* encompasses similar symptoms. Notably, both cultures also have shamans but draw a clear distinction between their behavior and that of mentally ill people. In Chapter 6, we discuss a number of anxiety conditions across the world that look very similar to the symptoms of panic disorder.

Although some disorders appear to occur in different cultures, other disorders are apparently specific to particular cultures. In Chapter 11, we consider the evidence that eating disorders are specific to Western culture. The Japanese term *hikikomori* refers to a condition in which a person completely withdraws from his social world (although women are affected, it is observed predominantly among men). People with hikikomori may completely shut themselves into their room or house—in some cases, for many years—refusing to interact with other people and leaving only occasionally to buy food. As we discuss in the next chapter, the current diagnostic system includes cultural factors in the discussion of every category of disorder, and this may be an important step toward increasing research in this area.

Even though there are some cross-cultural similarities in psychological disorders across cultures, there are also a number of profound cultural influences on the symptoms expressed in different disorders, the availability of treatment, and the willingness to seek treatment. We consider these issues throughout this book.

We must also consider the role of ethnicity in psychopathology. Some disorders, such as schizophrenia, are diagnosed more often among African Americans than Caucasians. Does this mean schizophrenia occurs more often in this group, or does it mean that some type of ethnic bias might be operating in diagnostic assessments? The use of drugs and their effects vary by ethnicity. Whites are more likely to use or abuse many drugs, such as nicotine, hallucinogens, methamphetamine, prescription painkillers, and, depending on the age group, alcohol. Yet African American smokers are more likely to die from lung cancer. Eating disturbances and body dissatisfaction are greater among white women than black women, particularly in college, but differences in actual eating disorders, particularly bulimia, do not appear to be as great. The reasons for these differences are not yet well understood and are the focus of current research. Table 2.1 shows data on ethnic and racial differences in the lifetime prevalence of different disorders.

Sociocultural factors have become more prominent in recent years in genetics and neuroscience. For example, *social neuroscience* seeks to understand what happens in the brain during complex social situations. Culture, too, has figured into neuroscience research (Kitayama & Uskul, 2011). Gene–environment interaction studies are uncovering the ways in which the social environment in combination with certain genes can increase the risk for disorders, as illustrated by the Caspi and colleagues (2003) study of childhood maltreatment, adult depression, and the 5-HTT gene discussed earlier. A multinational project called the 1000 Genomes Project (http://www.1000genomes.org) seeks to sequence the genomes of a representative sample of people around the world. In one study from this project, researchers found that people from each country had about the same number of rare variants in the genomes (Gravel, Henn, Gutenkunst et al., 2011). However, the rare variants were not the same in the different countries, suggesting that culture may also be influencing gene expression. For example, the short–short allele combinations of the 5-HTT gene studied by Caspi et al. (2003) varies across cultures (Chiao & Blizinsky, 2010, 2013). Cognitive behavioral traditions have tended to focus more on the individual rather than on how the individual interacts with the social world. However, this, too, is changing. Efforts are under way, for example, to develop cognitive behavior therapy for people from different cultures and ethnicities.

Culture and ethnicity play an important role in the descriptions, causes, and treatments of psychological disorders.

Betsie Van der Meer/Stone/Getty Images

Table 2.1 Lifetime Prevalence Rates of DSM-IV-TR Disorders Among Different Ethnic Groups

Disorder	White	Hispanic	Black
ADHD	4.6	4.6	3.4
Alcohol abuse or dependence	13.4	15.0*	9.5
Bipolar disorder	3.2	4.3	4.9*
Depression	17.9*	13.5	10.8
Drug abuse or dependence	7.9	9.1	6.3
Generalized anxiety disorder	8.6*	4.8	5.1
Panic disorder	4.9	5.4	3.1
PTSD	6.8	5.9	7.1

Table values are percentages. * indicates group with significantly highest prevalence rate.

Source: Adapted from Breslau, Lucia, & Alvarado (2006). Sample came from the National Comorbidity Survey-Replication study, which included a representative sample of people age 18 or older in the United States

FOCUS ON DISCOVERY 2.2

Sociocultural Factors and Health

Sociocultural factors such as gender, race, ethnicity, and socioeconomic status are important for understanding not only psychopathology, but also overall health. The many demonstrations of the pervasive role of these types of factors in health form the basis for the fields of **behavioral medicine** and **health psychology**. Here we consider how sociocultural factors have been studied in health psychology.

Gender and Health

At every age from birth to 85 and older, more men die than women. Men are more than twice as likely to die in automobile accidents and of homicide, cirrhosis, heart disease, lung cancer and other lung diseases, and suicide. Women, however, have higher rates of morbidity (i.e., poor health). That is, general poor health is more frequent among women, and women have a higher incidence of several specific diseases. For example, women have higher rates of diabetes, anemia, gastrointestinal problems, depression, and anxiety; and they report more visits to physicians, use more prescription drugs, and account for two-thirds of all surgical procedures performed in the United States. What are some of the possible reasons for the differences in mortality and morbidity rates in men and women?

Thomas Langreder/VISUM/The Image Works

Research shows that women live longer than men but women have more health problems than men.

It might be that women have some biological mechanism that protects them from certain life-threatening diseases. For example, epidemiological and observational studies suggested that estrogen might offer protection from **cardiovascular disease**. Based on this evidence, many women began hormone replacement therapy (HRT) following menopause (when estrogen naturally declines) in an attempt to reduce the risk of cardiovascular disease. However, randomized clinical trials of HRT for postmenopausal women (Hulley, Grady, Bush et al., 1998; Writing Group for the Women's Health Initiative Investigators, 2002) failed to find any such protective effects. In fact, the large prospective study called the Women's Health Initiative (WHI) had to end earlier than planned because women receiving estrogen plus progesterone therapy (so-called combined therapy) actually had an *increased* risk of breast cancer. Follow-up studies, which are still ongoing, reveal that the risk of HRT varies quite a bit depending on a number of factors, such as a woman's age and other health risk factors. For example, one follow-up study (Heiss, Wallace, Anderson et al., 2008) concluded that women taking HRT were not at greater risk for developing cardiovascular disease, but neither were they at decreased

risk for disease (Women's Health Initiative Screening Committee, 2004). The most recent follow-up study suggests that in general, neither estrogen alone nor the combined therapy is helpful in reducing disease risk, but that small subgroups of women may benefit from particular types and timings (e.g., for a few years postmenopause) of HRT (Manson, Chlebowski, Stefanick et al., 2013).

Other research has examined psychological risk factors for cardiovascular disease, such as anger and hostility. The evidence suggests that anger is not necessarily more commonly experienced and expressed by men, contrary to stereotypes about gender and emotion (Kring, 2000; Lavoie, Miller, Conway, & Fleet, 2001). However, increased hostility and both the suppression and expression of anger are associated with risk factors for cardiovascular disease among women (Matthews, Owens, Kuller et al., 1998; Rutledge, Reis, Olson et al., 2001). In addition, anxiety and depression are more common among women than men (see Chapters 5, 6, and 7) and are also linked to cardiovascular disease (e.g., Suls & Bunde, 2005).

Although the mortality rate is higher for men than women, the gender difference is shrinking. Why? In the early twentieth century, most deaths were due to infectious diseases, but now most deaths result from diseases that are affected by lifestyle. One possibility, then, is that lifestyle differences between men and women account for the sex difference in mortality and that these lifestyle differences are decreasing. Although men still smoke more than women and consume more alcohol, women are catching up in their use of alcohol and cigarettes. Not surprisingly, then, these behavior changes in women are paralleled by increases in lung cancer and by the failure of the mortality rate for cardiovascular disease to decrease among women (lung cancer has been the leading cause of cancer death among women in the United States since 1987; it will surpass breast cancer in the European Union in the next several years (Malvezzi, Bertuccio, Levi et al., 2014)).

Other explanations focus on the identification and treatment of disease in women. For example, even though cardiovascular disease is the number-one killer of women and more women than men have died from heart disease since 1984 (nearly one in four women who died in 2010 died of cardiovascular disease), there is still a widespread belief that men should be more concerned about heart disease than women. Furthermore, a common diagnostic procedure for heart disease risk, the so-called stress test, which involves measuring heart rate while on a treadmill, is not a good predictor of heart problems among women (Mora, Redberg, Cui et al., 2003), particularly women who do not have chest pains (Shaw, Bairy Merz, Pepine et al., 2006). In addition, a low dose of aspirin does not appear to prevent myocardial infarction in women as it does in men (though it does appear to prevent stroke in women, which is not true for men) (Ridker, Cook, Lee et al., 2005). Other research shows that women are less likely to be referred to a cardiovascular rehabilitation program following a heart attack, per-haps contributing to their persistent rates of mortality from cardiovascular disease (Abbey & Stewart, 2000).

Why do women have poorer health in general than men? There are sev-eral possible explanations. First, because women live longer than men, they may be more likely to experience certain dis-eases that are associated with aging, like Alzheimer's disease (see Chapter 14). Second, women may be more attentive to their health than are men and thus may be more likely to visit physicians and be diagnosed. Third, women are exposed to more stress than men, and they rate stress as having a greater impact on them, par-ticularly stress related to major life events (Davis, Matthews, & Twamley, 1999). Fourth, physicians tend to treat women's health concerns and complaints less seri-ously than men's concerns (Weisman & Teitelbaum, 1985). Finally, evidence indicates that women's morbidity dif-fers depending on socioeconomic and demographic variables, such as income, education, and ethnicity. For example, having more education and having a higher income are associated with fewer risk factors for cardiovascular disease, including obesity, smoking, hypertension, and reduced amounts of exercise. In the United States, women still have lower income than men (Goldin, 2014). Prior to the enactment of the Affordable Care Act in the United States, 16.5 million women did not have health insurance.

Jeff Greenberg/PhotoEdit

Poverty is stressful and is associated with poor health.

Socioeconomic Status, Ethnicity, and Health

Low socioeconomic status (SES) is associated with higher rates of health problems and mortality from all causes. One study attributed 133,000 deaths in the year 2000 to poverty (Galea, Tracy, Hoggatt et al., 2011). That may not seem like a large number, but in 2010 fewer people died from accidents (121,000) and only slightly more died from lung cancer (158,000). A number of explanations have been proposed for the correla-tion between SES and poor health and mortality, but many of these pro-posals are still in need of empirical support. Recent research attempts to trace the connections between health and SES, encompassing economic, societal, relationship, individual, and biological factors. For example,

one risk factor for poor health has to do with environmental factors that reinforce poor health behaviors. Poorer neighborhoods often have high numbers of liquor stores, grocery stores offering fewer healthy food choices, and fewer opportunities for exercise at health clubs or parks. Given these environmental constraints, it is perhaps not surprising to learn that lower-SES people are more likely than higher-SES people to engage in behaviors that increase the risk of disease, such as smoking, eating fewer fruits and vegetables, and drinking more alcohol (Lantz, House, Lepkowski et al., 1998).

Other risk factors include limited access to health services and greater expo-sure to stressors. Certainly, discrimination and prejudice are sources of chronic stress, and these abhorrent social condi-tions continue to affect people of color as well as people of lower SES and, in turn, impact health (Mayes, Cochran, & Barnes, 2007). Since people of color are found in high numbers among lower-SES groups, ethnicity has also been a feature of research into the relationship of SES to health. Consider, for example, that the mortality rate for African Americans is 1.2 times as high as it is for whites in the United States, according to the Centers for Disease Control (http://www.cdc.gov/nchs/deaths.htm). Why might this be? The reasons are complex and not com-pletely understood. Some research sug-gests that certain risk factors for disease are more common in people of color. For example, risk factors for cardiovascular disease (such as smoking, obesity, hyper-tension, and reduced exercise) are higher among women from ethnic minorities than among white women. This finding holds even when members of the two groups are comparable in SES (Winkleby, Kraemer, Ahn, & Varady, 1998). The increased prevalence of some of these risk factors shows up in studies of children as young as 6 to 9 years of age. For example, African American and Mexican American girls in this age range have higher body mass indices and higher fat intake than do non-Hispanic white girls (Winkleby, Cubbin, Ahn, & Kraemer, 1999). Other studies have found that increased stress associated with discrimination is linked to cardio-vascular reactivity among African American women (Guyll, Matthews, & Bromberger, 2001).

Consideration of SES at multiple levels, including the individual, family, and neighborhood, is also important (Mayes, Cochran, & Barnes, 2007). For example, lower family SES and neighborhood SES were found to be associated with greater cardiovascular reactivity for African American children and adolescents, but only lower family SES was asso-ciated with greater cardiovascular reactivity among white children and adolescents (Gump, Matthews, & Räikkönen, 1999). In sum, both SES and ethnicity are important factors in health.

Interpersonal Factors and Psychopathology

Beyond the role of culture, ethnicity, and poverty, thousands of articles have been published on how the quality of relationships influences different disorders. Family and marital relationships, social support, and even the amount of casual social contact all play a role in influencing the course of disorders. In Focus on Discovery 2.3, we discuss couples and family approaches to psychotherapy. Within relationships, researchers have looked for ways to measure not only the relative closeness and support offered but also the degree of hostility.

Other researchers are interested in understanding the role of trauma, serious life events, and stress in psychopathology. We will describe some of the ways people measure life events in the next chapter. But the influence of stress within the context of social relationships plays a role in just about all the disorders we will consider.

FOCUS ON DISCOVERY 2.3

Couples and Family Therapies

Given that interpersonal factors are important in nearly all disorders we discuss in this book, it is not surprising that therapies have been developed to focus on these relationships. In addition to interpersonal therapy, discussed in the text, we consider here two other types of therapies: couples therapy and family therapy.

Couples Therapy

Conflict is inevitable in any long-term partner relationship. About 50 percent of marriages in the United States end in divorce, and most of these divorces happen within the first seven years of marriage (Snyder, Castellani, & Whisman, 2006). People in a distressed marriage are two to three times as likely to experience a psychological disorder (Whisman & Uebelacker, 2006). In some couples, distress may be a consequence of the psychological disorder, but it is also clear that distress can contribute to psychological disorders. Couples therapy is often used in the treatment of psychological disorders, particularly when they occur in the context of major relationship distress.

Gary Conner/Alamy

When a problem involves a couple, treatment is most effective if the couple is seen together.

In couples therapy, the therapist works with both partners together to reduce relationship distress. Treatments for most couples focus on improving communication, problem solving, satisfaction, trust, and positive feelings.

Family Therapy

Family therapy is based on the idea that the problems of the family influence each member and that the problems of each member influ-

ence the family. As such, family therapy is used to address specific symptoms of a given family member, particularly for the treatment of childhood problems.

Some family therapists focus on roles within the family, asking questions about whether parents assume an appropriate level of responsibility. Sometimes family therapists attend to whether a given person in the family has been "scapegoated," or unfairly blamed for a broader issue in the family. Many family therapists teach strategies to help families communicate and problem-solve more effectively.

Family therapy is often tailored to the specific disorder. In family approaches for conduct disorder, the therapist may focus on improving parental monitoring and discipline. For adolescents with other externalizing problems, the goal of family therapy may be to improve communication, to change roles, or to address a range of family problems. With disorders like schizophrenia and bipolar disorder, family therapy often includes psychoeducation as a supplement for the medication treatment provided to the individual. Psychoeducation focuses on improving understanding of the disorder, reducing expressed family criticism and hostility, and helping families learn skills for managing symptoms, as in the clinical case of Clare (Miklowitz, George, Richards et al., 2003). In anorexia nervosa, family members are used strategically to help the adolescent gain weight. In sum, the goals and strategies of family therapy will be adjusted to meet the needs of different clients.

Clinical Case: Clare

Clare, a 17-year-old girl who lived with her parents and her 15-year-old brother, was referred for family-focused treatment (FFT) of bipolar disorder as an adjunct to medication treatment. She had received a diagnosis of bipolar I disorder in early adolescence and was treated with lithium carbonate and quetiapine but had never fully responded to medications.

During an individual assessment session, Clare explained that she thought about suicide almost daily and had made two prior attempts, both by overdosing on her parents' medications. Clare had kept both attempts secret from her parents. Ethically, clinicians need to take steps to keep a client safe, and in this case, one measure would be to let Clare's parents know about her suicidality. The clinician explained this to Clare.

The first goal in FFT is to provide psychoeducation about bipolar disorder. As the symptoms of bipolar disorder were being reviewed, the clinician asked Clare to discuss her suicide attempts with her parents. When Clare did so, her parents were surprised. Her father, who had experienced his own father's suicide, was particularly concerned.

After psychoeducation, a goal in FFT is to choose one problem for the family to address and to help them learn new problem-solving skills in the process. In this family, the focus of problem solving was how to keep Clare safe from her suicidal impulses. To begin problem solving, the therapist worked with the family to define the problem and its context. The therapist asked the family to discuss situations that seemed to place Clare at most risk for suicide. The family was able to pinpoint that both previous attempts had followed interpersonal losses.

The next phase of problem solving is to generate potential solutions. To help with this process, the clinician framed questions in the problem-solving process for the family, including whether Clare could share her suicidal thoughts with her parents, how to establish whether she was safe, what responses would be helpful from them, and what other protective actions should be taken. Using this structure, the family was able to agree on the plan that Clare would phone or page her parents when she was feeling self-destructive. Clare and her parents generated a plan in which her parents would help Clare engage in positive and calming activities until her suicidal thoughts were less intrusive. Clare and her parents reported feeling closer and more optimistic.

The therapist then began to conduct the next phase of therapy, which focused directly on symptom management. This phase consisted of training Clare to monitor her moods, to identify triggers for mood changes, and to help her cope with those triggers.

As is typical in FFT, the clinician introduced the communication enhancement module during session eight. A goal of this module is to role-play new communication skills. Family members practice skills such as "active listening" by paraphrasing and labeling the others' statements and by asking clarifying questions. At first, Clare and her brother protested against the role-play exercises.

Clare experienced another loss during this period when her one and only close long-term friend announced that she was going to be moving out of state. Clare took an overdose of Tylenol in a suicide attempt. Soon after overdosing, she became afraid, induced vomiting, and later told her parents about the attempt.

The next session focused on the suicide attempt. Her parents, particularly her father, were hurt and angry. Clare in turn reacted angrily and defensively. The therapist asked the family to practice active listening skills regarding Clare's suicidality. Clare explained that she had acted without even thinking about the family agreement because she had been so distressed about the idea of losing her friend. Clare's parents were able to validate her feelings using active listening skills. The therapist reminded the parents that suicidal actions are common in bipolar disorder and noted that Clare's ability to be honest about her suicide attempt was an indicator of better family connectedness. The therapist also recommended that Clare see her psychiatrist, who increased her dosage of lithium.

By the end of treatment after nine months, Clare had not made any more suicide attempts, had become more willing to take her medications, and felt closer to her parents. Like many people with bipolar disorder, though, she remained mildly depressed. Clare and her family continued to see the therapist once every three months for ongoing support. [Adapted from Miklowitz and Taylor (2005) with permission of the authors.]

Children who are securely attached to parents are more likely to be psychologically healthy adults.

Recall from Chapter 1 that one of the central features of psychoanalysis is transference, which refers to a person's responses to the analyst that seem to reflect attitudes and ways of behaving toward important people in the patient's past, rather than reflecting actual aspects of the relationship between the person and the analyst. Contemporary psychodynamic theorists have built on the concept of transference to emphasize the importance of a person's interpersonal relationships for psychological well-being. One example is **object relations theory,** which stresses the importance of long-standing patterns in close relationships, particularly within the family, that are shaped by the ways in which people think and feel. The "object" refers to another person in most versions of this theory. This theory goes beyond transference to emphasize the way in which a person comes to understand, whether consciously or not, how the self is situated in relation to other people. For example, a woman may come to understand herself as a worthless person based on her cold and critical relationship with her mother.

Another influential theory, **attachment theory,** grew out of object relations theory. John Bowlby (1907–1990) first proposed this theory in 1969, and Mary Ainsworth (1913–1999) and colleagues (1978) developed a method to measure attachment styles in infants. The essence of the theory is that the type or style of an infant's attachment to his or her caregivers can set the stage for psychological health or problems later in life. For example, infants who are securely attached to their caregivers are more likely to grow up to be psychologically healthy adults, whereas infants who are anxiously attached to their caregivers are more likely to experience psychological difficulties. Attachment theory has been extended to adults (Main, Kaplan, & Cassidy, 1985; Pietromonaco & Barrett, 1997), and couples (e.g., Fraley & Shaver, 2000); and therapies based on attachment theory have been developed for children and adults, though these treatments have not yet been empirically scrutinized.

Social psychologists have integrated both of these theories into the concept of the *relational self,* which refers to the self in relation to others (Chen, Boucher, Andersen, & Saribay, 2013; Chen, Boucher, & Parker Tapias, 2006). The concept of the relational self has garnered a tremendous amount of empirical support. For example, people will describe themselves differently depending on what other close relationships they have been asked to think about (Chen et al., 2006). Other studies show that describing a stranger in terms that are similar to a description of a close significant other will trigger positive feelings and facial expressions, presumably linked to the view of the self in relation to the close other person (Andersen, Reznik, & Manzella, 1996). Thus, if you are given a description of a stranger you must interact with that resembles a description of a close friend from high school, you will be more likely to smile, perhaps as a result of thinking about yourself and your interactions with your high school friend. The idea of the relational self has not yet been fully extended to the study of psychopathology, but given its theoretical basis and empirical support, it is ripe for translation to the study of interpersonal difficulties across many different psychological disorders.

Interpersonal Therapy Interpersonal therapy (IPT) emphasizes the importance of current relationships in a person's life and how problems in these relationships can contribute to psychological symptoms. The therapist first encourages the patient to identify feelings about his or her relationships and to express these feelings, and then helps the patient generate solutions to interpersonal problems. IPT has been shown to be an effective treatment for depression (a topic we turn to in more detail in Chapter 5). IPT has also been used to treat eating disorders, anxiety disorders, and personality disorders.

In IPT, four interpersonal issues are assessed to examine whether one or more of them might be impacting symptoms:

- *Unresolved grief*—for example, experiencing delayed or incomplete grieving following a loss
- *Role transitions*—for example, transitioning from child to parent or from worker to retired person
- *Role disputes*—for example, resolving different relationship expectations between romantic partners
- *Interpersonal or social deficits*—for example, not being able to begin a conversation with an unfamiliar person or finding it difficult to negotiate with a boss at work

In sum, the therapist helps the patient understand that psychopathology occurs in a social or relationship context and that getting a better handle on relationship patterns is necessary to reduce symptoms of psychopathology.

Unresolved grief is one of the issues discussed in interpersonal therapy.

Quick Summary

Disturbances in emotion figure prominently in psychopathology, but the ways in which emotions can be disrupted vary quite a bit. Emotions guide our behavior and help us to respond to problems or challenges in our environment. It is important to distinguish between components of emotion, including expression, experience, and physiology. In addition, mood can be distinguished from emotion. The concept of ideal affect points to important cultural differences in emotion that may be important in psychopathology. Psychological disorders have different types of emotion disturbances, and thus it is important to consider which of the emotion components are affected. In some disorders, all emotion components may be disrupted, whereas in others just one might be problematic. Emotion is an important focus in the paradigms.

Sociocultural factors, such as culture, ethnicity, gender, and socioeconomic status, are important factors in the study of psychopathology. Some disorders, like schizophrenia or anxiety, appear to be universal across cultures, yet their manifestations may differ somewhat and the ways in which society regards them may also differ. Other disorders, like eating disorders or hikikomori, may be specific to particular cultures. Some disorders are more frequently diagnosed in some ethnic groups than in others. It is not clear whether this reflects a true difference in the presence of disorder or perhaps a bias on the part of diagnosticians.

Current research is also examining whether risk factors associated with various disorders differ for men and women. Sociocultural factors have recently become the focus of people working in the other paradigms, and this trend will continue. Interpersonal relationships can be important buffers against stress and have benefits for physical and mental health. Object relations theory, which stresses the importance of relationships, and its offshoot, attachment theory, which emphasizes the role of attachment styles in infancy through adulthood, are also important in psychopathology research.

Check Your Knowledge 2.4

True or false?
1. Emotion consists of at least three components: expression, experience, and physiology.
2. Sociocultural factors such as gender, culture, ethnicity, and social relationships are less important to consider in the neuroscience paradigm.
3. Examining the problem-solving interactions of family members is useful for understanding key dimensions in relationships.
4. The relational self is a concept from social psychology that incorporates ideas from object relations and attachment theories.
5. Interpersonal therapy may focus on four types of interpersonal problems: unresolved grief, role transitions, role disputes, and social deficits.

Diathesis–Stress: An Integrative Paradigm

Psychopathology is much too diverse to be explained or treated adequately by any one of the current paradigms. Most of the disorders we will discuss in this book likely develop through an interaction of neurobiological and environmental factors, a view that we turn to next.

Stressors that may activate a diathesis range from minor, such as having car trouble, to major, such as the aftermath of a tornado.

The **diathesis–stress** paradigm is an integrative paradigm that links genetic, neurobiological, psychological, and environmental factors. It is not limited to one particular school of thought, such as cognitive behavioral, genetic, or neurobiological. The diathesis–stress concept was introduced in the 1970s as a way to account for the multiple causes of schizophrenia (Zubin & Spring, 1977). Its appeal continues today for many disorders, however, because, like the gene–environment interaction model reviewed above, it is a model that focuses on the interaction between a predisposition toward disease—the **diathesis**—and environmental, or life, disturbances—the stress. Diathesis refers most precisely to a constitutional predisposition toward illness, but the term may be extended to any characteristic or set of characteristics of a person that increases his or her chance of developing a disorder.

In the realm of neurobiology, for example, a number of disorders considered in later chapters appear to have a genetically transmitted diathesis. Other neurobiological diatheses include oxygen deprivation at birth, poor nutrition, and a maternal viral infection or smoking during pregnancy. Each of these conditions may lead to changes in the brain that predispose the individual toward psychopathology.

In the psychological realm, a diathesis for depression may be a particular cognitive schema or the chronic feeling of hopelessness sometimes found in people with depression. Other psychological diatheses include the ability to be easily hypnotized, which may be a diathesis for dissociative identity disorder (formerly called multiple personality disorder), and an intense fear of becoming fat, which is a vulnerability factor for some eating disorders.

Possessing the diathesis for a disorder increases a person's risk of developing it but does not by any means guarantee that a disorder will develop. The stress part of diathesis–stress is meant to account for how a diathesis may be translated into an actual disorder. In this context, stress generally refers to some noxious or unpleasant environmental stimulus that, in combination with the diathesis, triggers psychopathology. Psychological stressors include major traumatic events (e.g., becoming unemployed, divorce, death of a spouse, serving in combat) as well as more chronic stressors (e.g., living in poverty throughout childhood).

The key point of the diathesis–stress model is that both diathesis and stress are necessary in the development of disorders. Some people, for example, have inherited a predisposition that places them at high risk for mania (see Chapter 5): a certain amount of stress increases the possibility of developing mania. Other people, those at low genetic risk, are not likely to develop mania regardless of how difficult their lives are.

Another major feature of the diathesis–stress paradigm is that psychopathology is unlikely to result from the impact of any single factor. A genetically transmitted diathesis may be necessary for some disorders, but it is embedded in a network of other factors that also contribute to the disorder. These factors could include genetically transmitted diatheses for other personality characteristics; childhood experiences that shape personality; the development of behavioral competencies, and coping strategies; stressors encountered in adulthood; cultural influences; and numerous other factors.

Finally, we should note that within this framework, the data gathered by researchers holding different paradigms are not incompatible with one another. For example, stress may be needed to activate a predisposition toward a problem in neurotransmitter systems. Some of the differences between the paradigms also appear to be more semantic than substantive. A cognitive behavioral theorist may propose that maladaptive cognitions cause depression, whereas a neurobiological theorist may speak of the activity of a certain neural pathway. The two positions are not contradictory but merely reflect different levels of description, just as we could describe a table as pieces of wood in a particular configuration or as a collection of atoms.

In Focus on Discovery 2.4 we illustrate how adopting one paradigm to the exclusion of others can bias your view of the critical targets for treatment.

FOCUS ON DISCOVERY 2.4

Multiple Perspectives on a Clinical Problem

To provide a concrete example of how it is possible to conceptualize a clinical case using multiple paradigms, we present a case and discuss how the information provided is open to a number of interpretations, depending on the paradigm adopted.

Clinical Case: Arthur

Arthur's childhood had not been a particularly happy one. His mother died suddenly when he was only 6, and for the next 10 years he lived either with his father or with a maternal aunt. His father drank heavily, seldom managing to get through any day without some alcohol. His father's income was so irregular that he could seldom pay bills on time or afford to live in any but the most run-down neighborhoods. At times Arthur's father was totally incapable of caring for himself, let alone his son. Arthur would then spend weeks, sometimes months, with his aunt in a nearby suburb.

Despite these early life circumstances, Arthur completed high school and entered college. He qualified for student loans and other financial aid, but he also needed to wait tables and tend bar to make ends meet. During these college years, he felt an acute self-consciousness with people he felt had authority over him—his boss, his professors, and even some of his classmates, with whom he compared himself unfavorably.

Like many people in college, Arthur attended his fair share of parties. He pledged a fraternity at the end of his freshman year, and this was the source of most of his socializing. It was also the source of a lot of alcohol. He drank heavily at the weekend parties. By his senior year, however, he was drinking daily, often as a way to deal with the stress of being in school and working at the same time.

Two years after college, Arthur married his college girlfriend. He could never quite believe that his wife, as intelligent as she was beautiful, really cared for him. As the years wore on, his doubts about himself and about her feelings toward him would continue to grow. He felt she was far brighter than he, and he worried that she would make more money than he would.

After college, Arthur began a job at a publishing company, serving as an assistant editor. This job proved to be even more stressful than college. The deadlines and demands of the senior editors were difficult. He constantly questioned whether he had what it took to be an editor. Like his father, he often drank to deal with this stress.

Several years later, when it seemed that life should be getting easier, he found himself in even greater turmoil. Now 32 years old, with a fairly secure job that paid reasonably well, he was arguing more often with his wife. She continually complained about his drinking; he denied that there was a problem. After all, he was only drinking four beers a night. His wife wanted to start a family, but he was not sure if he wanted to have this additional stress in his life. His brooding over his marriage led him to drink even more heavily until finally, one day, he realized he was drinking too much and needed to seek help.

Depending on the paradigm you adopt, your conceptualization of this case may differ. If you hold a genetic point of view, you are attentive to the family history, noting that Arthur's father had similar difficulties with alcohol. You are probably aware of the research (to be reviewed in Chapter 10) that suggests a genetic contribution to alcohol use disorder. You do not discount environmental contributions to Arthur's problems, and you hypothesize about the ways in which genetic factors interact with different environmental factors (e.g., stress and work and in his relationships), which may in turn increase the likelihood that he will turn to alcohol to cope.

Now suppose that you are committed to a cognitive behavioral perspective, which encourages you to approach psychological disorders in terms of reinforcement patterns as well as cognitive variables. You may focus on Arthur's self-consciousness at college, which seems related to the fact that compared with his fellow students, he grew up with few advantages. Economic insecurity and hardship may have made him unduly sensitive to criticism and rejection. Alcohol has been his escape from such tensions. But heavy drinking, coupled with persistent doubt about his own worth as a human being, has worsened an already deteriorating marital relationship, further undermining his confidence. As a cognitive behavior therapist, you may decide on cognitive behavior therapy to convince Arthur that he need not obtain universal approval for every undertaking.

If you adopt an integrative perspective, you might follow more than one of these strategies. You would acknowledge the likely genetic contribution to Arthur's alcohol use disorder, but you would also identify key triggers (e.g., job stress) that might lead to greater bouts of drinking. You would likely employ many of the therapeutic techniques noted in this chapter.

Summary

- A paradigm is a conceptual framework or general perspective. Because the paradigm within which scientists and clinicians work helps to shape what they investigate and find, understanding paradigms helps us to appreciate subjective influences that may affect their work.
- The genetic paradigm holds that psychopathology is influenced by heritable factors. Recent genetic findings show how genes and the environment interact, and it is this type of interaction that will figure prominently in psychopathology. Molecular genetics research is identifying differences in gene sequence and structure that may be associated with vulnerability to psychopathology.
- The neuroscience paradigm emphasizes the role of the brain, neurotransmitters, and other systems, such as the HPA axis. Biological treatments, including medications, attempt to rectify the specific problems in the brain.
- The cognitive behavioral paradigm emphasizes schemas, attention, and cognitive distortions about life experiences and their influence on behavior as major factors in psychopathology. Cognitive neuroscience research follows from the early work of Freud, highlighting the importance of childhood experiences, the unconscious, and the fact that the causes of behavior are not always obvious. Cognitive behavior therapists focus on altering patients' negative schemas and thoughts about events in their lives.
- Emotion plays a prominent role in many disorders. It is important to distinguish among components of emotion that may be disrupted, including expression, experience, and physiology. Emotion disturbances are the focus of study across the paradigms.

- Sociocultural factors, including culture, ethnicity, gender, and poverty, are also important in conceptions of psychopathology. The prevalence and meaning of disorders may vary by culture and ethnicity, men and women may have different risk factors for different disorders, and social relationships can be an important buffer against stress.
- Interpersonal factors, including social support and relationships, are also factors that cut across paradigms. Social relationships can be an important buffer against stress, and relationships, including current conceptualizations of attachment and the relational self, are important. Sociocultural and interpersonal factors are included in the work of geneticists, neuroscientists, and cognitive behaviorists.
- Because each paradigm seems to have something to offer in enhancing our understanding of psychological disorders, an integrative paradigm is perhaps the most comprehensive. The diathesis–stress paradigm, which integrates several points of view, assumes that some people are predisposed to react adversely to environmental stressors. The diathesis may be genetic, neurobiological, or psychological and may be caused by early-childhood experiences, genetically influenced personality traits, or sociocultural influences, among other things.

Answers to Check Your Knowledge Questions

2.1 1. b; 2. d; 3. a; 4. b; 5.c

2.2 1. hypothalamus, anterior cingulate, septal area, hippocampus, amygdala; 2. white, gray; 3. norepinephrine, GABA; 4. hypothalamus, pituitary gland, adrenal cortex; 5. natural, specific

2.3 1. T; 2. T; 3. F

2.4 1. T; 2. F; 3. T; 4. T; 5. T

Key Terms

agonist	epigenetics	occipital lobe
allele	exposure	paradigm
amygdala	frontal lobe	parasympathetic nervous system
antagonist	gamma-aminobutyric acid (GABA)	parietal lobe
anterior cingulate	gene	phenotype
attachment theory	gene expression	polygenic
autonomic nervous system (ANS)	gene–environment interaction	polymorphism
behavior genetics	genetic paradigm	prefrontal cortex
behavior medicine	genotype	pruning
behavioral activation (BA) therapy	gray matter	reuptake
brain stem	health psychology	schema
cardiovascular disease	heritability	septal area
cerebellum	hippocampus	serotonin
cognition	HPA axis	serotonin transporter gene
cognitive behavior therapy (CBT)	hypothalamus	shared environment
cognitive behavioral paradigm	in vivo	single nucleotide polymorphism (SNP)
cognitive restructuring	interpersonal therapy (IPT)	sympathetic nervous system
copy number variation (CNV)	molecular genetics	synapse
corpus callosum	neuron	temporal lobe
cortisol	neuroscience paradigm	thalamus
diathesis	neurotransmitters	time-out
diathesis–stress	nonshared (unique) environment	transcription
dopamine	norepinephrine	ventricles
emotion	object relations theory	white matter

3 Diagnosis and Assessment

LEARNING GOALS

1. Be able to describe the purposes of diagnosis and assessment.
2. Be able to distinguish the different types of reliability and validity.
3. Be able to identify the basic features, historical changes, strengths, and weaknesses of the DSM.
4. Be able to describe the goals, strengths, and weaknesses of psychological and neurobiological approaches to assessment.
5. Be able to discuss the ways in which culture and ethnicity impact diagnosis and assessment.

Clinical Case: Aaron

Hearing the sirens in the distance, Aaron realized that someone must have called the police. He didn't mean to get upset with the people sitting next to him at the bar, but he just knew that they were talking about him and plotting to have his special status with the CIA revoked. He could not let this happen again. The last time people conspired against him, he wound up in the hospital. He did not want to go to the hospital again and endure all of the evaluations. Different doctors would ask him all sorts of questions about his work with the CIA, which he simply was not at liberty to discuss. They asked other odd questions, such as whether he heard voices or believed others were putting thoughts into his head. He was never sure how they knew that he had those experiences, but he suspected that there were electronic bugging devices in his room at his parents' house, perhaps in the electrical outlets.

Just yesterday, Aaron began to suspect that someone was watching and listening to him through the electrical outlets. He decided that the safest thing to do was to stop speaking to his parents. Besides, they were constantly hounding him to take his medication. But when he took this medication, his vision got blurry and he had trouble sitting still. He reasoned that his parents must somehow be part of the group of people trying to remove him from the CIA. If he took this medication, he would lose his special powers that allowed him to spot terrorists in any setting, and the CIA would stop leaving messages for him in phone booths or in the commercials on Channel 2. Just the other day, he found a tattered paperback book in a phone booth, which he interpreted to mean that a new assignment was imminent. The voices in his head were giving him new clues about terrorist activity. They were currently telling him that he should be wary of people wearing the color purple, as this was a sign of a terrorist. If his parents were trying to sabotage his career with the CIA, he needed to keep out of the house at all costs. That was what had led him to the bar in the first place. If only the people next to him hadn't have laughed and looked toward the door. He knew this meant that they were about to expose him as a CIA operative. If he hadn't yelled at them to stop, his cover would have been blown.

DIAGNOSIS AND ASSESSMENT are the critically important "first steps" in the study and treatment of psychopathology. In the case of Aaron, a clinician may begin treatment by determining whether he meets the diagnostic criteria for a mood disorder, schizophrenia, or perhaps a substance use disorder. Diagnosis can be the first major step in good clinical care. Having a correct **diagnosis** will allow the clinician to describe base rates, causes, and treatment for Aaron and his family, all of which are important aspects of good clinical care. More broadly, imagine that your doctor told you, "There is no diagnosis for what you have." Rather than this alarming scenario, hearing a diagnosis can provide relief in several different ways. Often, a diagnosis can help a person begin to understand why certain symptoms are occurring, which can be a huge relief. Many disorders, such as depression and anxiety, are extremely common; knowing that his or her diagnosis is common can also help a person feel less unusual.

Diagnosis enables clinicians and scientists to communicate accurately with one another about cases or research. Without agreed-on definitions and categories, our field would face a real dilemma because different scientists and clinicians would be unable to understand each other.

Diagnosis is important for research on causes and treatments. Sometimes researchers discover unique causes and treatments associated with a certain set of symptoms. For example, autism spectrum disorder (ASD) was only recognized in the *Diagnostic and Statistical Manual* in 1980. Since that time, research on the causes and treatments of ASD has grown exponentially.

To help make the correct diagnosis, clinicians and researchers use a variety of assessment procedures, beginning with a clinical interview. Broadly speaking, all clinical assessment procedures are more or less formal ways of finding out what is wrong with a person, what may have caused problems, and what can be done to improve the person's condition. Assessment procedures can help in making a diagnosis, and they can also provide information beyond a diagnosis. Indeed, a diagnosis is only a starting point. In the case of Aaron, for example, many other questions remain to be answered. Why does Aaron behave as he does? Why does he believe he is working for the CIA? What can be done to resolve his conflicts with his parents? Has he performed up to his intellectual potential in school and in his career? What obstacles might interfere with treatment? These are also the types of questions that mental health professionals address in their assessments.

In this chapter, we will describe the official diagnostic system used by many mental health professionals, as well as the strengths and weaknesses of this system. We will then turn to a discussion of the most widely used assessment techniques, including interviews, psychological assessment, and neurobiological assessment. We then conclude the chapter with an examination of a sometimes neglected aspect of assessment, the role of cultural bias. Before considering diagnosis and assessment in detail, however, we begin with a discussion of two concepts that play a key role in diagnosis and assessment: reliability and validity.

Cornerstones of Diagnosis and Assessment

The concepts of reliability and validity are the cornerstones of any diagnostic or assessment procedure. Without them, the usefulness of our methods is seriously limited. That said, these two concepts are quite complex. Here, we provide a general overview.

Reuters/NewMedia Inc./Corbis Images

Reliability is an essential property of all assessment procedures. One means of establishing reliability is to determine whether different judges agree, as happens when two umpires witness the same event in a baseball game.

Reliability

Reliability refers to consistency of measurement. An example of a reliable measure would be a wooden ruler, which produces the same value every time it is used to measure an object. In contrast, an unreliable measure would be a flexible, elastic-like ruler whose length changes every time it is used. Several types of reliability exist, and here we will discuss the types that are most central to assessment and diagnosis.

Interrater reliability refers to the degree to which two independent observers agree on what they have observed. To take an example from baseball, two umpires may or may not agree as to whether the ball is fair or foul.

Test–retest reliability measures the extent to which people being observed twice or taking the same test twice, perhaps several weeks or months apart, receive similar scores. This kind of reliability makes sense only when we can assume that the people will not change appreciably between test sessions on the underlying variable being measured; a prime example of a situation in which this type of reliability is typically high is in evaluating intelligence tests. On the other hand, we cannot expect people to be in the same mood at a baseline and a follow-up assessment 4 weeks later, and thus the test–retest reliability of a mood measure would likely be low.

Sometimes psychologists use two forms of a test rather than giving the same test twice, perhaps when there is concern that test takers will remember their answers from the first round of taking the test and aim merely to be consistent. This approach enables the tester to determine **alternate-form reliability**, the extent to which scores on the two forms of the test are consistent.

Finally, **internal consistency reliability** assesses whether the items on a test are related to one another. For example, one would expect the items on an anxiety questionnaire to be interrelated or to correlate with one another, if they truly tap anxiety. A person who reports a dry mouth in a threatening situation would be expected to report increases in muscle tension as well, since both are common characteristics of anxiety.

Reliability is typically measured on a scale from 0 to 1.0; the closer the number is to 1.0, the higher the reliability. For all types of reliability, the higher the number the better the reliability. For example, a test with an internal consistency reliability of .65 is only moderately reliable; a different test with an internal consistency reliability of .91 is very reliable.

Validity

Validity is a complex concept, generally related to whether a measure measures what it is supposed to measure. For example, if a questionnaire is supposed to measure a person's hostility, does it do so? Before we describe types of validity, it is important to note that validity is related to reliability—unreliable measures will not have good validity. Because an unreliable measure does not yield consistent results (recall our example of a ruler whose length is constantly changing), it will not relate very strongly to other measures. For example, an unreliable measure of coping is not likely to relate well to how a person adjusts to stressful life experiences. Reliability, however, does not guarantee validity. Height can be measured very reliably, but height would not be a valid measure of anxiety.

Content validity refers to whether a measure adequately samples the domain of interest. For example, a test to assess social anxiety ought to include items that cover feelings of anxiety in different social situations. It has excellent content validity because it contains questions about all the symptoms associated with social anxiety (see Chapter 6). For certain uses, though, the test might have poor content validity. The test doesn't cover questions about anxiety in nonsocial situations, and if one were trying to assess specific phobias about heights or snakes, this test would have poor content validity.

Criterion validity is evaluated by determining whether a measure is associated in an expected way with some other measure (the criterion). If both variables are measured at the same point in time, the resulting validity is referred to as **concurrent validity**. For example, later we will describe a measure of the overly negative thoughts that are believed to play an important role in depression. Criterion validity for this measure of negative thoughts could be established by showing that people with depression score higher on the test than do people without depression. In this example, the criterion is the diagnosis of depression. Another way to show concurrent validity is by showing that the measure of negative thoughts is correlated with a measure of depression symptoms.

Alternatively, criterion validity can be assessed by evaluating the ability of the measure to predict some other variable that is measured at some point in the future, often referred to as **predictive validity**. For example, IQ tests were originally developed to predict future school performance. Similarly, a measure of negative thoughts could be used to predict the development of depression in the future. In summary, concurrent and predictive validity are both types of criterion validity.

Construct validity is a more complex concept. It is relevant when we want to interpret a test as a measure of some characteristic or construct that is not observed simply or overtly (Cronbach & Meehl, 1955; Hyman, 2002). A construct is an inferred attribute, such as anxiousness or distorted cognition. Consider an anxiety-proneness questionnaire as an example. If the questionnaire has construct validity, people who obtain different scores on our test really will differ in anxiety proneness. Just because the items seem to be about the tendency to become anxious ("I find that I become anxious in many situations"), it is not certain that the test is a valid measure of the construct of anxiety proneness.

As shown in Figure 3.1, construct validity is evaluated by looking at a wide variety of data from multiple sources (compare this to criterion validity, where a test is typically evaluated against just one other piece of data). For example, people diagnosed as having an anxiety disorder and people without such a diagnosis could be compared on their scores on our self-report measure of anxiety proneness. The self-report measure would achieve some construct validity if the people with anxiety disorders scored higher than the people without anxiety disorders. Greater construct validity would be achieved by showing that the self-report measure was related to other measures thought to reflect anxiety, such as observations of fidgeting and trembling, and physiological indicators, such as increased heart rate and rapid breathing. When the self-report measure is associated with these multiple measures (diagnosis, observational indicators, physiological measures), its construct validity is increased.

More broadly, construct validity is related to theory. For example, we might hypothesize that being prone to anxiety is in part caused by a family history of anxiety. We could then obtain further evidence for the construct validity of our questionnaire by showing that it relates to a family history of anxiety. At the same time, we would also have gathered support for our theory of anxiety proneness. Thus, construct validation is an important part of the process of theory testing.

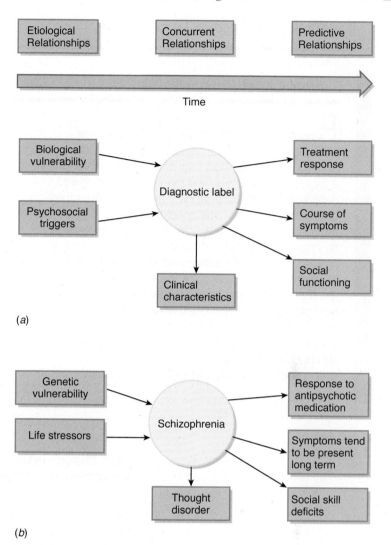

(a)

(b)

Figure 3.1 Construct validity. An example of the types of information a diagnosis might help predict.

Classification and Diagnosis

Clinical Case: Roxanne

Roxanne is a middle-aged woman who was brought to the local psychiatric emergency room by the police. They had found her running through a crowded street, laughing loudly and running into people. Her clothes were dirty and torn. When they questioned her, she was speaking rapidly, and her thoughts were hard to follow. At the ER, she wrestled free of the police and began running down the hallway. She knocked over two staff members during her flight, while bellowing at the top of her lungs, "I am the resurrection! Come follow me!" Police brought her back to the exam room, and the staff began to form hypotheses. Clearly, she was full of energy. Had she been through some trauma? She believed she had special religious powers—could this be a delusion? Unfortunately, the staff was unable to gain much information from an interview due to her rapid and incoherent speech. Roxanne sat restlessly, occasionally laughing and shouting; treatment could not proceed without understanding the reason for her unusual behavior. When efforts to calm Roxanne failed, police helped the staff to contact family members, who were relieved to hear that Roxanne was safe. She had disappeared from home the day before. Family members described a long history of bipolar disorder (formerly known as manic depression), and they reported having been concerned for the past couple weeks because Roxanne had stopped taking medications for both her bipolar disorder and her high blood pressure. Treatment was able to proceed based on the idea that Roxanne was experiencing a new manic episode of her long-standing bipolar disorder.

The Diagnostic System of the American Psychiatric Association: DSM-5

In this section, we focus on the diagnostic system used by many mental health professionals, the *Diagnostic and Statistical Manual of Mental Disorders* (**DSM**). In 1952, the American Psychiatric Association published its first *Diagnostic and Statistical Manual* (DSM). The publication of the DSM was informed by earlier systems of classification (see Focus on Discovery 3.1), and it has been revised five times since 1952. The fifth edition of the DSM, referred to as DSM-5, was released in 2013 (www.dsm5.org). In this chapter, we will review the major features of DSM-5, and then we will outline some strengths and criticisms of the DSM as well as of diagnosis in general. Because DSM-5 is new, we will note major differences between the DSM-IV-TR and the DSM-5 throughout the chapters of this book.

Each version of the DSM has included improvements. Beginning with the third edition of DSM and continuing today, an effort was made to create more reliable and valid diagnostic categories. Two major innovations were introduced in DSM-III that have been retained by each edition since.

1. Specific diagnostic criteria—the symptoms for a given diagnosis—are spelled out precisely, and clinical symptoms are defined in a glossary. Table 3.1 compares the descriptions of a manic episode given in DSM-II to those given in DSM-5. Notice how DSM-5 is much more detailed and concrete.

2. The characteristics of each diagnosis are described much more extensively in DSM-5 than they were in DSM-II. For each disorder there is a description of diagnostic features as well as associated features, such as laboratory findings (e.g., enlarged ventricles in schizophrenia) and results from physical exams (e.g., electrolyte imbalances in people who have eating disorders). Next, a summary of the research literature provides information about age of onset, course, prevalence, risk and prognosis factors, cultural and gender factors and differential diagnosis (i.e., how to distinguish similar diagnoses from each other).

FOCUS ON DISCOVERY 3.1

A History of Classification and Diagnosis

By the end of the nineteenth century, medical diagnostic procedures were improving as physicians began to understand the advantages of tailoring treatments to different illnesses. During the same period, other sciences, such as botany and chemistry, advanced after classification systems were developed. Impressed by these successes, investigators of psychological disorders also sought to develop classification schemes. Unfortunately, progress in classifying psychological disorders did not come easily.

Early Efforts at Classification of Psychological Disorders

Emil Kraepelin (1856–1926) authored an influential early classification system in his textbook of psychiatry first published in 1883. His classification system attempted to definitively establish the biological nature of psychological disorders. Kraepelin noted that certain symptoms clustered together as a *syndrome*. He labeled a set of syndromes and hypothesized that each had its own biological cause, course, and outcome. Even though effective treatments had not been identified, at least the course of the disease could be predicted.

Kraepelin proposed two major groups of severe psychological disorders: dementia praecox (an early term for schizophrenia) and manic-depressive psychosis (an early term for bipolar disorder). He postulated a chemical imbalance as the cause of dementia praecox and an irregularity in metabolism as the explanation of manic-depressive psychosis. Though his theories about causes were not quite correct, Kraepelin's classification scheme nonetheless influenced the current diagnostic categories.

Development of the WHO and DSM Systems

In 1939 the World Health Organization (WHO) added psychological disorders to the *International List of Causes of Death.* In 1948 the list was expanded to become *the International Statistical Classification of Diseases, Injuries, and Causes of Death,* a comprehensive listing of all diseases, including a classification of psychological disorders. Unfortunately, the psychological disorders section was not widely accepted. Even though American psychiatrists had played a prominent role in the WHO effort, the American Psychiatric Association published its own *Diagnostic and Statistical Manual* (DSM) in 1952.

In 1969 the WHO published a new version, now referred to as the *International Classification of Disease* (ICD), which was more widely accepted. In the United Kingdom, a glossary of definitions was produced to accompany the WHO system (General Register Office, 1968). A second version of the American Psychiatric Association's DSM, DSM-II (1968), was similar to the WHO system. But true consensus still eluded the field. Even though DSM-II and the British Glossary of Mental Disorders specified some symptoms of diagnoses, the two systems defined different symptoms for a given disorder! Thus diagnostic practices still varied widely. A new version of the ICD, the ninth, was released in 1975. The next editions of the DSM, continuing with the present edition, have tried to achieve greater consensus with the ICD, which is currently in its tenth edition (the eleventh edition is expected in 2017).

In 1980 the American Psychiatric Association published an extensively revised diagnostic manual, DSM-III, and a somewhat revised version, DSM-III-R, followed in 1987. One of the big changes in DSM-III that remained in place for 33 years was the introduction of the multiaxial system. Diagnoses were listed on separate dimensions, or axes. As shown in Figure 3.2, older versions of the DSM included five axes. This multiaxial classification system, by requiring judgments on each of the five axes, forced the diagnostician to consider a broad range of information. DSM-5 no longer uses these distinct axes.

In 1988 the American Psychiatric Association began work on DSM-IV, which was published in 1994. Thirteen working groups, which included many psychologists, were established to critique DSM-III-R, review literature, analyze previously collected data, and collect new data. Each work group tackled a different cluster of disorders. The committee adopted an important new approach—the reasons for changes in diagnoses would be explicitly stated and supported by data. In previous versions of the DSM, the reasons for diagnostic changes had not always been explicit. A revision to the supporting text of the DSM-IV, not the actual diagnostic criteria, was published in 2000 and named DSM-IV-TR, with the "TR" standing for text revision.

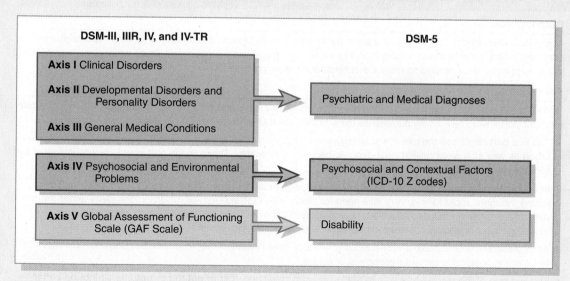

Figure 3.2 DSM-5 does not use the five axes of DSM-IV-TR.

As shown in Figure 3.3, the development of DSM-5 began in 1999. As with the process for DSM-IV, work groups reviewed each set of diagnoses. A series of study groups were also formed to consider issues that cut across diagnostic categories, such as life-span developmental approaches, gender and cross-cultural issues, general medical issues, impairment and disability, and diagnostic assessment instruments. These study groups conducted literature reviews and analyses and then provided feedback to the work groups regarding issues with specific diagnoses. As was done with DSM-IV, field trials were conducted on the new DSM-5 criteria in order to assess how they were performing in mental health settings. Additional revisions were made based on these data.

Although all changes were to be based on research data, the leaders emphasized that a high priority was to make the DSM-5 useful for clinicians. In the final stages of DSM-5 development, the leaders made changes that were not always consistent with the data and recommendations of the work groups (see Chapter 15 on Personality Disorders for a stark example of this problem). To protect the process from commercial interests, all work group members signed conflict-of-interest agreements, stating that they would limit their income to $10,000 or less per year from pharmaceutical and technology companies and similar industry groups. The crafters of the DSM-5 aimed to create a living document that will change as new research evidence emerges. New editions, then, are already on the horizon even as DSM-5 emerges, and the DSM-5 website (www.dsm5.org) continues to post such changes.

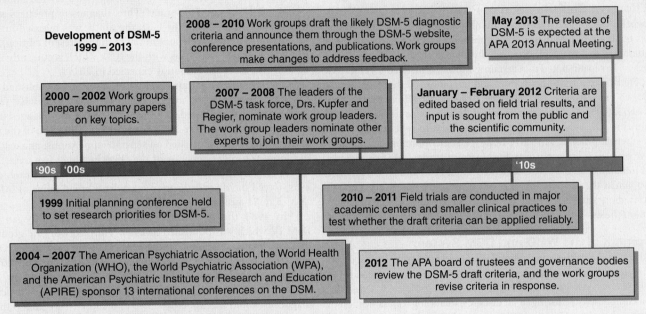

Development of DSM-5 1999 – 2013

2008 – 2010 Work groups draft the likely DSM-5 diagnostic criteria and announce them through the DSM-5 website, conference presentations, and publications. Work groups make changes to address feedback.

May 2013 The release of DSM-5 is expected at the APA 2013 Annual Meeting.

2000 – 2002 Work groups prepare summary papers on key topics.

2007 – 2008 The leaders of the DSM-5 task force, Drs. Kupfer and Regier, nominate work group leaders. The work group leaders nominate other experts to join their work groups.

January – February 2012 Criteria are edited based on field trial results, and input is sought from the public and the scientific community.

'90s '00s '10s

1999 Initial planning conference held to set research priorities for DSM-5.

2010 – 2011 Field trials are conducted in major academic centers and smaller clinical practices to test whether the draft criteria can be applied reliably.

2004 – 2007 The American Psychiatric Association, the World Health Organization (WHO), the World Psychiatric Association (WPA), and the American Psychiatric Institute for Research and Education (APIRE) sponsor 13 international conferences on the DSM.

2012 The APA board of trustees and governance bodies review the DSM-5 draft criteria, and the work groups revise criteria in response.

Figure 3.3 Timeline for the development of DSM-5.

Table 3.1 Mania in DSM-II Versus DSM-5

DSM-II (1968)

Mania was described in DSM-II in just a short paragraph. The paragraph described mania with five symptoms (elevated mood, irritable mood, racing thoughts, rapid talking and rapid movement). There was no mention of how many symptoms were needed to meet the criteria for a manic episode.

DSM-5 (2013)

DSM-5 provides a list of symptoms with descriptive detail for each symptom. The symptom description is divided into four parts, which we briefly summarize here. In the actual DSM-5, there is more detail for all four parts.

1. The first part describes the mood and energy symptoms for mania. A person must show an elevated or irritable mood as well as a great deal of goal-directed behavior and energy. These mood and energy symptoms must last for at least one week.

2. In addition to the mood and energy symptoms, a person must also have three or more symptoms, including racing thoughts, rapid talking, very little need for sleep, very high self-esteem or grandiose ideas about the self, difficulty maintaining focused attention, participating in behaviors that can get a person into trouble (e.g., excessive spending or sexual encounters), and excessive movements.

3. All of these symptoms make it very difficult to work or have healthy social relationships. Some people may need to be in the hospital to protect themselves or others.

4. The last part of the diagnosis is a "rule out" section to clarify whether or not the symptoms cannot be better accounted for by something else, such as another disorder or the effects of a drug (legal or not).

Changes in DSM-5

The DSM-5 includes many changes from the last edition, DSM-IV-TR. Indeed, even conventions for labeling the edition have shifted—the Roman numerals used to denote the edition (e.g., DSM-IV) are replaced with Arabic numbers (i.e., DSM-5) to facilitate electronic printing. We will cover many of the changes as we discuss specific disorders in the chapters throughout this book. Here, then, we cover some of the major debates and changes that have implications across diagnoses.

Removal of the Multiaxial System As shown in Figure 3.2, the multiaxial system first developed for DSM-III in 1980 was removed in DSM-5. In place of the first three axes, clinicians are simply to note psychiatric and medical diagnoses. The codes for the Psychosocial and Environmental Problems Axis were changed to be more similar to those used by the international community in the World Health Organization's (WHO) International Classification of Diseases (ICD). Axis V is removed in DSM-5; instead, the World Health Organization Disability Assessment Schedule (WHODAS) is included in the DSM-5 appendix of assessment measures in need of further study.

Organizing Diagnoses by Causes DSM-5 defines diagnoses on the basis of symptoms. Some have argued that advances in our understanding of etiology (causes) could help us rethink this approach. For example, schizophrenia and schizotypal personality disorder share a great deal of genetic overlap. Could these ties be reflected in the diagnostic system? Others have proposed organizing diagnoses based on parallels in neurotransmitter activity, temperament, emotion dysregulation, or social triggers. After considerable review during the development of DSM-5, it became clear that our knowledge base is not yet strong enough to organize diagnoses around etiology (Hyman, 2010). With the exception of IQ tests to help with the diagnosis of intellectual disability (formerly known as mental retardation) or polysomnography for sleep disorders, we have no laboratory tests, neurobiological markers, or genetic indicators to use in making diagnoses. The DSM-5 will continue to use symptoms as the basis for diagnosis.

On the other hand, changes were made to reflect growing knowledge of etiology. The DSM-IV-TR diagnoses were clustered into chapters based on similarity of symptoms, but in the DSM-5, the chapters were reorganized to reflect patterns of comorbidity and shared etiology (see Figure 3.4). For example, in DSM-IV-TR, obsessive-compulsive disorder was included in the chapter on anxiety disorders because it contained anxiety symptoms. The etiology of this disorder, though, seems to involve distinct genetic and neural influences compared to other anxiety disorders, as we discuss in Chapter 7. To reflect this, the DSM-5 included a new chapter for obsessive-compulsive and other related disorders. This new chapter includes disorders that often co-occur and share some risk factors, including obsessive-compulsive disorder, hoarding disorder, and body dysmorphic disorder.

Enhanced Sensitivity to the Developmental Nature of Psychopathology In DSM-IV-TR, childhood diagnoses were considered in a separate chapter. Most of those diagnoses have now been moved into other relevant chapters of DSM-5, to highlight the continuity between childhood and adulthood forms of disorder. For example, children who

Teri Stratford/Six-Cats Research Inc.

DSM-5 is the current diagnostic system of the American Psychiatric Association. It was released in 2013.

experience separation anxiety may be at greater risk for developing anxiety disorders as adults. In DSM-5, separation anxiety disorder was moved to the chapter on anxiety disorders. Across diagnoses, more detail is provided about the expression of symptoms in younger populations.

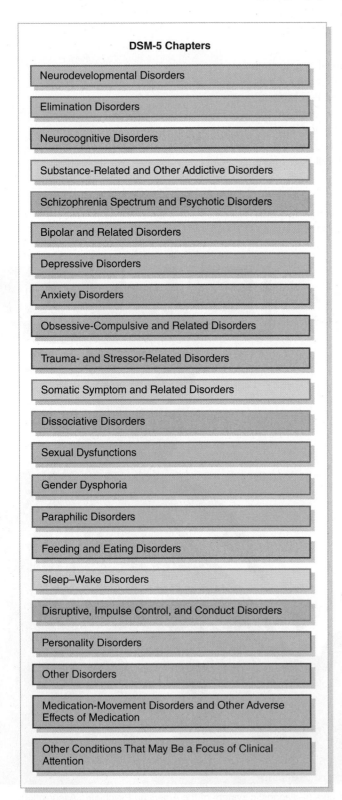

DSM-5 Chapters

Neurodevelopmental Disorders

Elimination Disorders

Neurocognitive Disorders

Substance-Related and Other Addictive Disorders

Schizophrenia Spectrum and Psychotic Disorders

Bipolar and Related Disorders

Depressive Disorders

Anxiety Disorders

Obsessive-Compulsive and Related Disorders

Trauma- and Stressor-Related Disorders

Somatic Symptom and Related Disorders

Dissociative Disorders

Sexual Dysfunctions

Gender Dysphoria

Paraphilic Disorders

Feeding and Eating Disorders

Sleep–Wake Disorders

Disruptive, Impulse Control, and Conduct Disorders

Personality Disorders

Other Disorders

Medication-Movement Disorders and Other Adverse Effects of Medication

Other Conditions That May Be a Focus of Clinical Attention

Figure 3.4 Chapters in DSM-5.

New Diagnoses Several new diagnoses were added to DSM-5. For example, disruptive mood dysregulation disorder was added to address the growing number of children and adolescents who are seen by clinicians due to severe mood changes and irritability as well as some of the symptoms of mania. Many of these youth do not meet the full criteria for mania (the defining feature of bipolar disorder) but were often incorrectly diagnosed with bipolar disorder because no other category seemed to fit their symptoms. It is hoped that by including this diagnosis, the overdiagnosis of bipolar disorder in children and adolescents will be lessened. Other new diagnoses include hoarding disorder, binge eating disorder, premenstrual dysphoric disorder, and gambling disorder.

Combining Diagnoses Some of the DSM-IV-TR diagnoses were combined because there was not enough evidence for differential etiology, course, or treatment response to justify separate diagnostic categories. For example, the DSM-IV-TR diagnoses of substance abuse and dependence were replaced with the DSM-5 diagnosis of substance use disorder. The DSM-IV-TR diagnoses of hypoactive sexual desire disorder and female sexual arousal disorder were replaced with the DSM-5 diagnosis of female sexual interest/arousal disorder. The DSM-IV-TR diagnoses of autism and Asperger's disorder were replaced with the DSM-5 diagnosis of autism spectrum disorder.

Ethnic and Cultural Considerations in Diagnosis Psychological disorders are universal. There is not a single culture in which people are free of psychological disorders. But there are many different cultural influences on the risk factors for psychological disorders (e.g., social cohesion, poverty, access to drugs of abuse, and stress), the types of symptoms experienced, the willingness to seek help, and the treatments available. Sometimes these differences across cultures are profound. For example, although mental health care is widely available in the United States, it is estimated that there is only one psychiatrist for every 2 million people living in sub-Saharan Africa (World Health Organization, 2001).

Cultural differences do not always play out in the way one might expect. For example, even with the access to medical care in the United States, a major study found that outcomes for schizophrenia were more favorable in Nigeria, India, and Colombia than in more industrialized countries, including the United States (Sartorius, 1986). People who immigrate from Mexico to the United States are initially about half as likely to meet the criteria for a psychological disorder as native-born citizens in the United States, but over time, they and their children begin to show an increase in certain disorders, such as substance abuse, such that their risk for disorder begins to approximate that of people born in the United States (Alegria, Canino, Shrout et al., 2008). As shown in Table 3.2, rates of psychological disorders tend to be higher in the United States than in many other countries. If we hope to understand how culture influences risk, symptom expression, and outcomes, we need a diagnostic system that can be applied reliably and validly in different countries and cultures. To facilitate international communication, the DSM-5 includes a list that cross-references the DSM diagnoses with the International Statistical Classification of Diseases and Related Health Problems (ICD) codes.

Table 3.2 Twelve-Month Prevalence Rates of the Most Common DSM-IV-TR Diagnoses by Country

Country	Anxiety Disorders	Mood Disorders	Substance Disorders	Any Psychological Disorder
Americas				
Colombia	10.0	6.8	2.8	17.8
Mexico	6.8	4.8	2.5	12.2
United States	18.2	9.6	3.8	26.4
Europe				
Belgium	6.9	6.2	1.2	12.0
France	12.0	8.5	0.7	18.4
Germany	6.2	3.6	1.1	9.1
Italy	5.8	3.8	0.1	8.2
Netherlands	8.8	6.9	3.0	14.9
Spain	5.9	4.9	0.3	9.2
Middle East and Africa				
Lebanon	11.2	6.6	1.3	16.9
Nigeria	3.3	0.8	0.8	4.7
Asia				
Japan	5.3	3.1	1.7	8.8
China	3.2	2.5	2.6	9.1

Source: The WHO World Mental Health Survey Consortium (2004).

Anxiety disorders include agoraphobia, generalized anxiety disorder, obsessive-compulsive disorder, panic disorder, posttraumatic stress disorder, social phobia, and specific phobia. Mood disorders include bipolar I and II disorders, dysthymia, and major depressive disorder. Substance disorders include alcohol or drug abuse or dependence. Diagnoses were assessed with the Composite International Diagnostic Interview. Values are percentages.

Note: In the European countries, bipolar disorders and non–alcohol-related substance use disorders were not assessed. Obsessive-compulsive disorder was not assessed in Asian countries.

Previous editions of the DSM were criticized for their lack of attention to cultural and ethnic variations in psychopathology. DSM-5 added features to enhance cultural sensitivity by including a section on culture-related diagnostic issues for nearly all disorders and an appendix devoted to developing a culturally informed case formulation. This appendix includes a cultural formulation interview consisting of 16 questions clinicians can use to help understand how culture may be shaping the clinical presentation. There is also a section on cultural concepts of distress that distinguishes syndromes that appear in particular cultures, culturally specific ways of expressing distress, and cultural explanations about the causes of symptoms, illness, and distress.

In the cultural formulation, clinicians are cautioned not to diagnose symptoms unless they are atypical and problematic within a person's culture. People vary in the degree to which they identify with their cultural or ethnic group. Some value assimilation into the majority culture, whereas others wish to maintain close ties to their cultural background. In general, clinicians are advised to be constantly mindful of how culture and ethnicity influence diagnosis and treatment.

Attention is paid to how culture can shape the symptoms and expression of a given disorder. For example, the symptoms of both schizophrenia (e.g., delusions and hallucinations) and depression (e.g., depressed mood and loss of interest or pleasure in activities) are similar cross-culturally (Draguns, 1989). But as we will discuss in Chapter 6, it is more likely in Japan than in the United States for anxiety to be focused around fears of offending others (Kirmayer, 2001). In evaluating symptoms, clinicians also need to be aware that cultures may shape the language used to describe distress. In many cultures, for example, it is common to describe grief or anxiety in physical terms—"I am sick in my heart" or "My heart is heavy"—rather than in psychological terms.

The core symptoms of depression appear to be similar cross-culturally.

The DSM-5 includes nine cultural concepts of distress in the Glossary of Cultural Concepts of Distress to describe syndromes that are likely to be seen within specific regions. The following are some examples of syndromes listed in the DSM-5 glossary.

- *Dhat Syndrome.* A term used in India to refer to severe anxiety about the discharge of semen.
- *Shenjing shuairuo* (neurasthenia). A common diagnosis in China, a syndrome characterized by fatigue, dizziness, headaches, pain, poor concentration, sleep problems, and memory loss.
- *Taijin kyofusho.* The fear that one could offend others through inappropriate eye contact, blushing, a perceived body deformation, or one's own foul body odor. This disorder is most common in Japan, but cases have been reported in the United States. Japanese cultural norms appear to prescribe more careful attention to social appropriateness and hierarchy, perhaps intensifying the risk of these symptoms (Fabrega, 2002).
- *Ataque de nervios.* Intense anxiety and fear of screaming and shouting uncontrollably found among people from Latino/Latina cultures (e.g., Lewis-Fernandez, Gorritz, Raggio et al., 2010).

Although not listed in the DSM-5 glossary, other culturally-relevant syndromes have been the focus of research. These include the following.

- *Amok.* A dissociative episode in which there is a period of brooding followed by a violent and sometimes homicidal outburst. The episode tends to be triggered by an insult and is found primarily among men. Persecutory delusions are often present as well. The term is Malaysian and is defined by the dictionary as a murderous frenzy. You may have heard the phrase "run amok."

Clinical Case: Lola: An Example of Diagnosis

Lola is a 17-year-old high school junior. She moved to the United States from Mexico with her parents and brother when she was 14 years old. A few months after they arrived, Lola's father returned to Mexico to attend the funeral of his brother. He was denied reentry to the United States due to a problem with his visa, and he has been unable to reunite with the family for nearly 3 years. Lola's mother found it difficult to make ends meet on her salary as a bookkeeper, and the family was forced to move to a rougher neighborhood a year ago. Lola's English was fairly good when she came to the United States, and she picked up many of the nuances of the language since arriving in the country. For the past 2 years, she has been dating a boy in her school. They have been fairly constant companions, and she describes him as the one person she would turn to if she was feeling upset. If her mother had any previous concern about Lola, it was that she seemed to rely on her boyfriend too much— she asked for his advice on both small and large decisions, and she seemed wary of social interactions when he wasn't present. Lola's mother stated, "It is as though she is afraid to think for herself." Lola's mother noted that she had always been a bit shy and had tended to count on her brother a lot for decisions and social support when she was younger.

With little warning, her boyfriend announced that he wanted to break up with her. Lola was extremely distressed by this change and reported that almost immediately she was unable to sleep or eat. She lost weight rapidly and found herself unable to concentrate on her schoolwork. Friends complained that she no longer wanted to talk during lunch or by phone. After 2 weeks of steadily feeling worse, Lola left a suicide note and disappeared. Police found her the next day in an abandoned home, holding a bottle of medicines. She reported that she had been sitting there all night, considering ending her life. Lola's mother reported that she had never seen her in so distressed a state but noted that a few other family members had struggled with periods of sadness. Still, these family members in Mexico had neither attempted suicide nor received any formal treatment. Instead, the family learned to give these family members support and time to heal on their own. After the police found Lola, she was hospitalized for intensive treatment.

DSM-5 Diagnosis
Diagnoses: Major depressive disorder, dependent personality disorder
Important Psychosocial/Contextual Factors:
Low income (ICD-10 Z59.6)

- *Ghost sickness.* An extreme preoccupation with death and those who have died, found among certain Native American tribes.
- *Hikikomori* (withdrawal). A syndrome observed in Japan, Taiwan, and South Korea in which an individual, most often an adolescent boy or young adult man, shuts himself into a room (e.g., bedroom) for a period of 6 months or more and does not socialize with anyone outside the room.

Some have argued that we should try to identify broad syndromes that can be identified across cultures and, in this light, have argued against differentiating cultural concepts of distress from other diagnostic syndromes (Lopez-Ibor, 2003). In support of this position, they point toward a number of cultural concepts of distress that are not so different from the main DSM diagnoses. For example, Kleinman (1986) interviewed 100 Chinese people who had been diagnosed with *shenjing shuairuo* and found that 87 percent of them met criteria for major depressive disorder. Many of these people responded to anti-depressant medications. Suzuki and colleagues (2003) pointed out that the symptoms of *taijin kyofusho* overlap with those of social anxiety disorder (excessive fear of social interaction and evaluation) and body dysmorphic disorder (the mistaken belief that one is deformed or ugly), which are more commonly diagnosed in the United States. Other syndromes may reflect the common concerns of anxiety and distress, with the content shaped by life circumstances and values (Lopez-Ibor, 2003). Hence, some researchers believe it is important to look for commonalities across cultures.

In contrast, others believe that culturally relevant concepts of distress are central, because local and personal meanings are a key issue in understanding psychological disorders (Gaw, 2001). Still others have argued that many of the diagnostic categories from the DSM systems have been "exported" across the world, often with little consideration of how culture impacts the symptom presentations, causes, and treatment decisions (Watters, 2010). Whether one advocates for a cross-cultural or culture-specific approach to diagnosis, all mental health professionals ought to, at the very least, be aware of the cultural influences that can and do influence diagnostic practices (Sue, Yan Cheng, Saad et al., 2012).

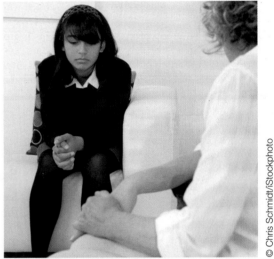

A therapist must be mindful of the role of cultural differences in the ways in which people describe their problems.

Returning to Clinical Case: Roxanne: A Second Example of a Diagnosis

Previously, we described the case of Roxanne, who was brought to the psychiatric emergency room by the police. The DSM-5 and DSM-IV-TR diagnosis for Roxanne might look as follows.

DSM-5 Diagnosis
Diagnoses: Bipolar I disorder, current or most recent episode manic; high blood pressure
Psychosocial/Contextual Factors: Problems with housing (homeless; ICD-10 Z 59.0)

Quick Summary

Because diagnosis can provide the first step in thinking about the causes of symptoms, it is often the first step in planning treatment. Because psychopathology is diagnosed on the basis of symptoms, clinical interviews are used to make diagnoses.

With all assessments, the reliability (the consistency of measurement) and validity (whether an assessment measures what it is designed to measure) should be evaluated. Reliability can be estimated by examining how well raters agree, how consistent test scores are over time, how alternate forms of a test compare, or how well items correlate with each other. There are many different forms of validity, including content, criterion, and construct validity.

Diagnostic systems for psychological disorders have changed a great deal in the past 100 years. Drawing on research evidence, the order of chapters in the DSM-5 is reorganized to reflect current knowledge of etiology. Some disorders are added, some are removed, and others are combined. DSM-5 continues to emphasize culturally sensitive case formulations.

Check Your Knowledge 3.1 (Answers are at the end of the chapter.)

Answer the questions.

1. Major changes in the DSM-5 include (circle all that apply):
   a. removal of the multiaxial system
   b. reorganization of the chapters
   c. many fewer diagnoses
   d. none of the above
2. Which type of reliability or validity is tested with the following procedures?
   _____ A group of high school students is given the same IQ test 2 years in a row.
   _____ A group of high school students is given an IQ test, and their scores are correlated with a different IQ test they took the year before.

_____ A measure of the tendency to blame oneself is developed, and researchers then test whether it predicts depression, whether it is related to childhood abuse, and whether it is related to less assertiveness in the workplace.

_____ People are interviewed by two different doctors. Researchers examine whether the doctors agree about the diagnosis.

a. interrater reliability
b. test–retest reliability
c. criterion validity
d. construct validity

Specific Criticisms of the DSM

Some specific questions and concerns have been raised about the DSM. We review some of these concerns in the following sections.

Too Many Diagnoses? DSM-5 contains more than 300 different diagnoses. Some have criticized the burgeoning number of diagnostic categories (see Table 3.3). As one example, the DSM-5 continues to include a category for acute stress disorder in order to capture symptoms in the first month after a severe trauma. Should these relatively common reactions to trauma be pathologized by diagnosing them as a psychological disorder (Harvey & Bryant, 2002)? Gambling disorder is added to DSM-5 under the chapter Substance-Related and Other Addictive Disorders. By expanding its coverage, the authors of the DSM seem to have made too many problems into psychological disorders without good justification for doing so.

Others argue that the system includes too many minute distinctions based on small differences in symptoms. One side effect of the huge number of diagnostic categories is a phenomenon called **comorbidity**, which refers to the presence of a second diagnosis. Comorbidity is the norm rather than the exception. Among people who met criteria for at least one DSM-IV-TR psychiatric diagnosis, 45 percent meet criteria for at least one more psychiatric diagnosis (Kessler, Berglund, Demler et al., 2005). Some argue that this overlap is a sign that we are dividing syndromes too finely (Hyman, 2010).

A more subtle issue about the large number of diagnoses is that many risk factors seem to trigger more than one disorder. For example, some genes are associated with an increase in the risk of externalizing disorders (see Chapter 13) as a whole (Kendler et al., 2003). Early trauma, dysregulation of stress hormones, tendencies to attend to and remember negative information about the self, and neuroticism all seem to increase risk for many anxiety disorders as well as mood disorders (Harvey, Watkins, Mansell et al., 2004). Anxiety and mood disorders also seem to share overlap in genetic risk (Kendler, Jacobson, Prescott et al., 2003), diminished function of a brain region called the prefrontal cortex (Hyman, 2010), and low serotonin function (Carver, Johnson, & Joormann, 2008). Similarly, selective serotonin reuptake inhibitors (SSRIs), such as Prozac, often seem to relieve symptoms of anxiety as well as depression (Van Ameringen, Lane, Walker et al., 2001). Different diagnoses do not seem to be distinct in their etiology or treatment.

Does this mean that we should lump some of the disorders into one category? Beliefs about lumping versus splitting differ. Some think we should keep the finer distinctions, whereas others believe we should lump (Caspi, Houts, Belsky et al., 2014; Watson, 2005).

Table 3.3 Number of Diagnostic Categories per Edition of DSM

Edition of DSM	Number of Categories
DSM I	106
DSM-II	182
DSM-III	265
DSM-III-R	292
DSM-IV-TR	297
DSM-5	347

Among people who think there are too many diagnostic categories, several researchers have considered ways to collapse disorders into broader categories. To begin, some disorders seem to co-occur more frequently than do others. For example, a person with antisocial personality disorder is highly likely to meet the diagnostic criteria for a substance use disorder. In the DSM, these are diagnosed as separate disorders. Some have argued that childhood conduct disorder, adult antisocial personality disorder, alcohol use disorder, and substance use disorder co-occur so often that they should be considered different manifestations of one underlying disease process or vulnerability (Krueger, Markon, Patrick et al., 2005). These different types of problems could be jointly considered "externalizing disorders."

The authors of DSM-5 took modest steps toward addressing these concerns. First, in a few cases, two disorders were combined into one disorder. For example, as noted previously, the DSM-IV-TR diagnoses of substance abuse and dependence are replaced with the DSM-5 diagnosis of substance use disorder. The changes in DSM-5 are small, though. Comorbidity will remain the norm. Second, the authors created a cross-cutting symptom assessment measure to allow clinicians to assess for those symptoms that cut across the DSM-5 diagnostic boundaries, such as depressed or anxious mood, sleep problems, and anger (Narrow, Clarke, Kuramoto et al., 2013).

The National Institute of Mental Health is tackling this problem by working on a new diagnostic system that seeks to create (many fewer) categories based on common causes. Termed the **Research Domain Criteria**, or RDoC, this system is currently conceived as a roadmap for research that will lead to the development of a new classification system that is based on neuroscience and genetic data rather than just clinical symptoms (Insel, 2014).

Categorical Classification Versus Dimensional Classification In the DSM-5, clinical diagnoses are based on **categorical classification**. Does the person have schizophrenia or not? Do the symptoms fit the category of mania or not? For example, in Table 3.1 we see that the diagnosis of mania requires the presence of three symptoms plus mania and excessive energy. But why require three symptoms rather than two or five? A categorical system forces clinicians to define one threshold as "diagnosable." There is often little research support for the threshold defined. Categorical diagnoses foster a false impression of categories with actual, hard boundaries. Indeed, up to half of the people seeking treatment have mild symptoms that fall just below the threshold for a diagnosis (Helmuth, 2003). Fortunately, many of these people with subthreshold symptoms of a diagnosis still receive extensive treatment (Johnson, Weissman, & Klerman, 1992).

It may be more helpful to know the severity of symptoms as well as whether they are present. In contrast to categorical classification, **dimensional** systems describe the *degree* of an entity that is present (e.g., a 1-to-10 scale of anxiety, where 1 represents minimal and 10, extreme). (See Figure 3.5 for an illustration of the difference between dimensional and categorical approaches.)

One reason categorical systems are popular is that they define a threshold for treatment. Consider high blood pressure (hypertension). Blood pressure measurements form a continuum, which clearly fits a dimensional approach; yet by defining a threshold for high blood pressure, doctors can feel more certain about when to offer treatment. Similarly, a threshold for clinical depression may help demarcate a point where treatment is recommended. Although the cutoffs are likely to be somewhat arbitrary, they can provide helpful guidance.

Despite some debate, particularly for personality disorders, DSM-5 preserved a categorical approach to diagnosis. A dimensional approach to personality disorders has been included in the appendix, but other diagnoses are based on categorical classification. DSM-5 did add severity ratings for nearly all disorders, however. Thus, DSM-5 is taking a first step toward including dimensions alongside the current categories.

The DSM-5 includes the category "unspecified," which is to be used when a person meets many but not all of the criteria for a diagnosis (this was called "not

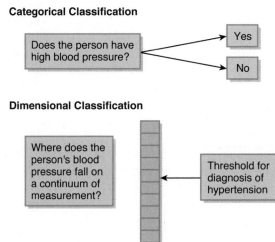

Figure 3.5 Categorical versus dimensional systems of diagnosis.

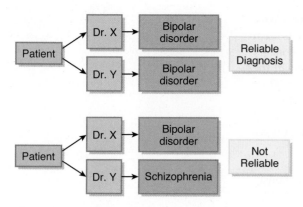

Figure 3.6 Interrater reliability. In this example, the diagnosis of the first person is reliable—both clinicians diagnose bipolar disorder—whereas the diagnosis of the second is not reliable.

Table 3.4 Reliability Data from the DSM-5 Field Trials	
Diagnosis	**Pooled Reliability Estimate**
Schizophrenia	.46
Bipolar I disorder	.56
Posttraumatic stress disorder	.67
Borderline personality disorder	.54
ADHD	.61
Autism spectrum Disorder	.69

Source: Adapted from Regier et al. (2013). Numbers are kappa statistics—the closer to 1.0, the better the reliability.

otherwise specified" in DSM-IV-TR). Unfortunately, far too many people will probably fit the "unspecified" category.

Reliability of the DSM in Everyday Practice   Suppose you were concerned about your mental health, and you went to see two psychologists. Consider the distress you would feel if the two psychologists disagreed—one told you that you had schizophrenia, and the other told you that you had bipolar disorder. Diagnostic systems must have high interrater reliability to be useful. Before DSM-III, reliability for DSM diagnoses was poor, mainly because the criteria for making a diagnosis were not clear (see Figure 3.6 for an illustration of interrater reliability).

The increased explicitness of the DSM criteria has improved reliability for many diagnoses (see Table 3.1). Nonetheless, because clinicians might not rely on the criteria precisely, the reliability of the DSM in everyday usage may be lower than that seen in research studies. Even when following criteria, there is some room for disagreement in DSM-5. For example, in the criteria for mania, mood is supposed to be "abnormally" elevated. What is abnormal? Such judgments set the stage for the insertion of cultural biases as well as the clinician's own personal ideas of what the average person should be doing. Because different clinicians may adopt different definitions for symptoms such as "abnormally elevated mood," achieving high reliability can be a challenge.

Evidence from the DSM-5 field trials where the diagnostic criteria were tested at several different mental health treatment facilities across the country suggests that the DSM still has work to do when it comes to reliability (see Table 3.4). Some have argued that expecting high reliability is unrealistic, particularly since the reliability of many medical diagnoses is not all that great either (Kraemer, Kupfer, Clarke et al., 2012). Although this may be true, it is disconcerting to think that mental health professionals may not agree on a particular person's diagnosis.

How Valid Are Diagnostic Categories?   The DSM diagnoses are based on a pattern of symptoms. A diagnosis of schizophrenia, then, does not have the same status as a diagnosis of, say, diabetes, for which we have laboratory tests.

One way of thinking about diagnosis is to ask whether the system helps organize different observations (see Figure 3.1). Diagnoses have construct validity if they help make accurate predictions. What types of predictions should a good diagnostic category facilitate? One would hope that a diagnosis would inform us about related clinical characteristics and about functional impairments. The DSM specifies that impairment or distress must be present to meet criteria for a diagnosis, so perhaps it is not surprising that diagnoses are related to functional impairments such as marital distress and missed days at work (see Table 3.5). Beyond capturing the most common difficulties for a person with a diagnosis, one would hope that a diagnosis would inform us about what to expect next—the likely course of the disorder and response to different treatments. Perhaps most importantly, one would hope that the diagnosis relates to possible causes of the disorder, for example, a genetic predisposition or a biochemical imbalance. A diagnosis with strong construct validity should help predict a broad range of characteristics.

We have organized this book around the major DSM diagnostic categories because we believe that they do indeed possess some construct validity. Certain categories have less validity than others, however, and we will discuss these gaps in the validity of specific diagnostic categories in later chapters.

General Criticisms of Diagnosing Psychological Disorders

Although we described some advantages of diagnosis in the beginning of this chapter, it is also clear that diagnoses can have negative effects. Consider how your life might be changed by receiving the diagnosis of schizophrenia. You might become worried that someone will recognize your disorder. Or you might fear the onset of another episode. You might worry about your ability to deal with new challenges. The fact that you have a diagnosis of a psychological

Table 3.5 Rates of Marital Distress and Missed Work Days Among People with Psychological Disorders in the Past Year

Disorder	Odds of Marital Distress for a Given Diagnosis Compared to No Psychological Disorder	Odds of Missed Work Days for a Given Diagnosis Compared to No Psychological Disorder
Panic disorder	1.28	3.32
Specific phobia	1.34	2.82
Social phobia	1.93	2.74
Generalized anxiety disorder	2.54	1.15
Posttraumatic stress disorder	2.30	2.05
Major depressive disorder	1.68	2.14
Bipolar I or II disorder	3.60	Not assessed
Alcohol use disorder	2.78	2.54

Note: Age, gender, education, and race/ethnicity are controlled for in marital distress analyses, and age and gender are controlled for in work-loss analyses. Diagnoses were based on the Composite International Diagnostic Interview. Marital distress was measured using a 14-item version of the Dyadic Adjustment Scale. Missed work days were measured during the month before the interview.

Source: Information on marital distress drawn from Whisman (2007). Information on work-loss days drawn from the ESEMeD/MHEDEA 2000 investigators (2004).

disorder could have a stigmatizing effect, as we discussed in Chapter 1. Friends and loved ones might treat you differently, and employment might be hard to find.

Without doubt, hearing a diagnosis can be difficult. Research shows that people with psychological disorders are widely viewed negatively, and they and their families often encounter stigma as a result (Wahl, 1999), which, as we discussed in Chapter 1, remains a huge problem. Many have raised concerns that a diagnosis might contribute to stigma. To study this problem, researchers have given people brief written descriptions of a person. Beyond including a bit of information about the person's life and personality, the descriptions include either a psychological disorder diagnosis (such as schizophrenia or bipolar disorder), a description of their symptoms (such as periods of high moods, decreased sleep, and restlessness), both (a diagnosis and symptoms), or neither. In this way, researchers can examine whether people tend to be more negative about diagnostic category labels or behavior. Research suggests that people tend to view the behaviors negatively more than the category labels. Sometimes labels may actually relieve stigma by providing an explanation for the symptomatic behavior (Lilienfeld, Lynn, Ruscio et al., 2010). Of course, making a diagnosis is still a serious process that warrants sensitivity and privacy. But it may not be fair to presume that diagnostic labels are the major source of stigma.

Another concern is that when a diagnostic category is applied, we may lose sight of the uniqueness of that person. Because of this concern, the American Psychological Association recommends that people avoid using words like *schizophrenic* or *depressive* to describe people. After all, we do not call people with medical illnesses by their disease (e.g., you aren't likely to hear someone with cancer described as the *canceric*). Rather, psychologists are encouraged to use phrases such as *a person with schizophrenia*.

Even with more careful language, some maintain that diagnosis leads us to focus on disorders and, in doing so, to ignore important differences among people. Unfortunately, this criticism ignores a fundamental truth: it is human nature to categorize whenever we think about anything. Some would argue, then, that if we use categories anyway, it is best to develop the categories systematically. If one accepts this perspective, then the question is how well the current system does in grouping disorders.

Quick Summary

Despite improvements in the DSM-5, a number of problems remain. Some argue that there are too many diagnoses. Others challenge the use of a categorical rather than a dimensional approach. Reliability is higher than it was in earlier editions of the DSM, but clinicians still disagree regarding some diagnoses, and the reliability achieved in practice may not be as high as the reliability achieved in research studies. Finally, the field as a whole faces a huge challenge; researchers are focused on validating this diagnostic system by trying to identify the causal patterns, symptom patterns, and treatment that can be predicted by a given diagnosis. In sum, although the DSM is continually improving, it is far from perfect. Regardless of which diagnostic system is used, there are certain problems inherent in diagnosing people with psychological disorders. It is important to be aware of the tendency to ignore a person's strengths when focusing on diagnoses. The American Psychological Association recommends using phrases such as *person with schizophrenia* rather than *schizophrenic* as one way to acknowledge that a person is much more than his or her diagnosis. Although many worry that applying labels may increase stigma, diagnoses can sometimes relieve stigma by providing a way of understanding symptoms.

Check Your Knowledge 3.2

Answer the questions.

1. List three reasons why some think DSM should lump diagnoses.

2. What are three broad types of characteristics that a valid diagnosis should help predict?

Psychological Assessment

Ryan McVay/Getty Images, Inc.

Although it is illegal to discriminate against those with psychological disorders, many employers do so. Stigma must be considered when giving a person a diagnosis of a psychological disorder.

To make a diagnosis, mental health professionals can use a variety of assessment measures and tools. Beyond helping to make a diagnosis, psychological assessment techniques are used in other important ways. For example, assessment methods are often used to identify appropriate therapeutic interventions. And repeated assessments are very useful in monitoring the effects of treatment over time. In addition, assessments are fundamental to conducting research on the causes of disorder.

We will see that beyond the basic interview, many of the assessment techniques stem from the paradigms presented in Chapter 2. Here we discuss clinical interviews; measures for assessing stress; personality tests, including objective and projective tests; intelligence tests; and behavioral and cognitive assessment techniques. Although we present these methods individually, a complete psychological assessment of a person will often entail combining several assessment techniques. The data from the various techniques complement each other and provide a more complete picture of the person. In short, there is no one best assessment measure. Rather, using multiple techniques and multiple sources of information will provide the best assessment.

Clinical Interviews

Most of us have probably been interviewed at one time or another, although the conversation may have been so informal that we did not regard it as an interview. Mental health professionals use both formal and structured as well as informal and less structured clinical interviews in psychopathological assessment.

Characteristics of Clinical Interviews One way in which a **clinical interview** is different from a casual conversation is the attention the interviewer pays to how the respondent answers questions—or does not answer them. For example, if a person is recounting marital conflicts, the clinician will generally be attentive to any emotion accompanying the comments. If the person does not seem upset about a difficult situation, the answers probably will be understood differently from how they would be interpreted if the person was crying or agitated while relating the story.

Carrying out good clinical interviews requires great skill. Clinicians, regardless of the paradigm adopted, recognize the importance of establishing rapport with a person who seeks their professional help. The interviewer must obtain the trust of the person; it is naive to assume that a person will easily reveal information to another, even to an authority figure with the title "Doctor." Even a person who sincerely, perhaps desperately, wants to recount intensely personal problems to a professional may not be able to do so without help.

Most clinicians empathize with their clients in an effort to draw them out and to encourage them to elaborate on their concerns. An accurate summary statement of what a person has been saying can help sustain the momentum of talk about painful and possibly embarrassing events and feelings, and an accepting attitude toward personal disclosures dispels the fear that revealing "secrets of the heart" (London, 1964) to another human being will have disastrous consequences.

Interviews vary in the degree to which they are structured. In practice, most clinicians probably operate from only the vaguest outlines. Exactly how information is collected is left largely up to the particular interviewer and depends, too, on the responsiveness and responses of the interviewee. Through years of training and clinical

Structured interviews are widely used to make reliable diagnoses.

experience, each clinician develops ways of asking questions that he or she is comfortable with and that seem to draw out the information that will be of maximum benefit to the person. Thus, to the extent that an interview is unstructured, the interviewer must rely on intuition and general experience. As a consequence, unstructured clinical interviews are less reliable than structured interviews; that is, two interviewers may reach different conclusions about the same person.

Structured Interviews At times, mental health professionals need to collect standardized information, particularly for making diagnostic judgments based on the DSM. To meet that need, investigators use a **structured interview,** in which the questions are set out in a prescribed fashion for the interviewer. One example of a commonly used structured interview is the Structured Clinical Interview (SCID) (Spitzer, Gibbon, & Williams, 1996). The SCID is currently being revised for DSM-5, but the general format of this interview for DSM-IV-TR is shown in Figure 3.7.

The SCID is a branching interview; that is, a person's response to one question determines the next question that is asked. It also contains detailed instructions to the interviewer concerning when and how to probe in detail and when to go on to questions about another diagnosis. Most symptoms are rated on a three-point scale of severity, with instructions in the interview schedule for directly translating the symptom ratings into diagnoses. The initial questions pertaining to obsessive-compulsive disorder (discussed in Chapter 7) are presented in Figure 3.7. The interviewer begins by asking about obsessions. If the responses elicit a rating of 1 (absent), the interviewer turns to questions about compulsions. If the person's responses again elicit a rating of 1, the interviewer is instructed to go to the questions for posttraumatic stress disorder. On the other hand, if positive responses (rating of 2 or 3) are elicited about obsessive-compulsive disorder, the interviewer continues with further questions about that problem.

In practice, most clinicians review the DSM symptoms in an informal manner without using a structured interview. Note, however, that clinicians using unstructured diagnostic interviews tend to miss comorbid diagnoses that often accompany a primary diagnosis (Zimmerman, 1999). When clinicians use an informal interview rather than a structured interview, the

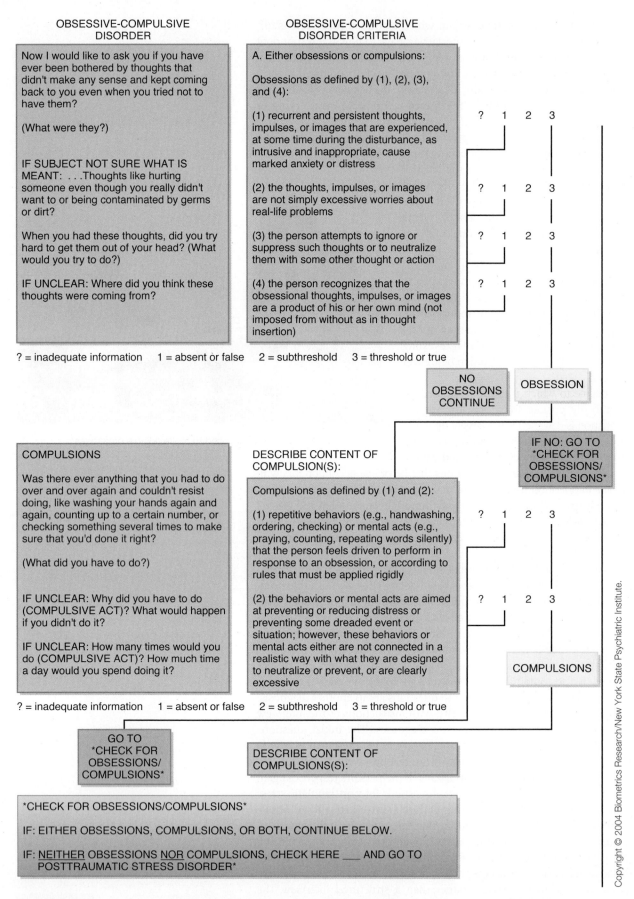

Figure 3.7 Sample item from the SCID. Reprinted by permission of New York State Psychiatric Institute Biometrics Research Division.

reliability of diagnoses also tends to be much lower (Garb, 2005). With adequate training, inter-rater reliability for structured interviews is generally quite good (Blanchard & Brown, 1998).

Assessment of Stress

Given its centrality to nearly all the disorders we consider in this book, measuring stress is clearly important in the total assessment picture. To understand the role of stress, we must first be able to define and measure it. Neither task is simple, as stress has been defined in many ways. See Focus on Discovery 3.2 for influential antecedents to our current conceptualizations of stress. Broadly, **stress** can be conceptualized as the subjective experience of distress in response to perceived environmental problems. Life stressors can be defined as the environmental problems that trigger the subjective sense of stress. Various scales and methods have been developed to measure life stress. Here we examine the most comprehensive measure of life stress: the Life Events and Difficulties Schedule (LEDS) as well as self-report checklist measures of stress.

The Bedford College Life Events and Difficulties Schedule This assessment is widely used to study life stressors (Brown & Harris, 1978). The LEDS includes an interview that covers over 200 different kinds of stressors. Because the interview is only semistructured, the interviewer can tailor questions to cover stressors that might only occur to a small number of people. The interviewer and the interviewee work collaboratively to produce a calendar of each of the major events within a given time period (see Figure 3.9 for an example). After the interview, raters evaluate the severity and several other dimensions of each stressor.

Stress can include major life events or daily hassles.

FOCUS ON DISCOVERY 3.2

A Brief History of Stress

The pioneering work by the physician Hans Selye set the stage for our current conceptualizations of stress. He introduced the term *general adaptation syndrome* (GAS) to describe the biological response to sustained and high levels of stress (see Figure 3.8). In Selye's model there are three phases of the response:

1. During the first phase, the alarm reaction, the autonomic nervous system is activated by the stress.
2. During the second phase, resistance, the organism tries to adapt to the stress through available coping mechanisms.
3. If the stressor persists or the organism is unable to adapt effectively, the third phase, exhaustion, follows, and the organism dies or suffers irreversible damage (Selye, 1950).

In Selye's syndrome, the emphasis was on the body's response, not the environmental events that trigger that response. Psychological researchers later broadened Selye's concept to account for the diverse stress responses that people exhibited, including emotional upset, deterioration of performance, or physiological changes such as increases in the levels of certain hormones. The problem with these response-focused definitions of stress is that the criteria are not clear-cut. Physiological changes in the body can occur in response to a number of things that we would not consider stressful (e.g., anticipating a pleasurable event).

Other researchers defined stress as a stimulus, often referred to as a stressor, rather than a response, and identified stress with a long list of environmental conditions, such as electric shock, boredom, catastrophic life events, daily hassles, and sleep deprivation. Stimuli that are considered stressors can be major (the death of a loved one), minor (daily hassles, such as being stuck in traffic), acute (failing an exam), or chronic (a persistently unpleasant work environment). For the most part, they are experiences that people regard as unpleasant, but they can also be pleasant events.

Like response-based definitions of stress, stimulus-based definitions present problems. It is important to acknowledge that people vary widely in how they respond to life's challenges. A given event does not elicit the same amount of stress in everyone. For example, a family that has lost its home in a flood but has money enough to rebuild and strong social support from a network of friends nearby will experience less stress from this event than will a family that has neither adequate money to rebuild nor a network of friends to provide social support.

Current conceptualizations of stress emphasize that how we perceive, or *appraise*, the environment determines whether a stressor is present. Stress is perhaps most completely conceptualized as the subjective experience of distress in response to perceived environmental problems. A final exam that is merely challenging to some students may be highly stressful to others who do not feel prepared to take it (whether or not their concerns are realistic).

Phase 1 The Alarm Reaction	Phase 2 Resistance	Phase 3 Exhaustion
ANS activated by stress	Damage occurs or organism adapts to stress	Organism dies or suffers irreversible damage

Figure 3.8 Selye's general adaptation syndrome.

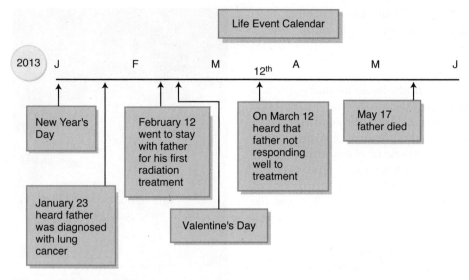

Life Event Calendar

2013 J   F   M   A   M   J
                            12th

New Year's Day

February 12 went to stay with father for his first radiation treatment

On March 12 heard that father not responding well to treatment

May 17 father died

January 23 heard father was diagnosed with lung cancer

Valentine's Day

Figure 3.9 Example of a life events timeline. The LEDS interview is designed to capture the major stressors a person has encountered in the past year.

The LEDS was designed to address a number of problems in life stress assessment, including the need to evaluate the importance of any given life event in the context of a person's life circumstances. For example, pregnancy might have quite a different meaning for an unmarried 14-year-old girl compared to a 38-year-old woman who has been trying to conceive for a long time. A second goal of the LEDS is to exclude life events that might just be consequences of symptoms. For example, if a person misses work because he or she is too depressed to get out of bed, any consequent job problems should really be seen as symptoms of the disorder rather than a triggering life event. Finally, the LEDS includes a set of strategies to carefully date when a life stressor occurred. Using this more careful assessment method, researchers have found that life stressors are robust predictors of episodes of anxiety, depression, schizophrenia, and even the common cold (Brown & Harris, 1989; Cohen, Frank, Doyle et al., 1998).

Self-Report Stress Checklists Because intensive interview measures like the LEDS are so comprehensive, they take a good deal of time to administer. Often clinicians and researchers want a quicker way to assess stress and thus may turn to self-report checklists, such as the List of Threatening Experiences (LTE; Brugha & Cragg, 1990) or the Psychiatric Epidemiological Research Interview Life Events Scale (PERL; Dohrenwend, Krasnoff, Askenasy et al., 1978). These checklists typically list different life events (e.g., death of a spouse, serious physical illness, major financial crisis), and participants are asked to indicate whether or not these events happened to them in a specified period of time. One difficulty associated with these types of measures is that there is a great deal of variability in how people view these events (Dohrenwend, 2006). For example, the death of a spouse could be the most horrible event ever for someone in a loving relationship. However, for someone in an abusive relationship, it might be the source of relief rather than stress. Other problems with such self-report checklists include difficulties with recall (Dohrenwend, 2006). For example, people may forget about some events. There is also evidence that people who are feeling depressed or anxious when they complete the measure may be biased in their responses. Perhaps because of these various issues influencing recall, test–retest reliability for life stress checklists can be low (McQuaid, Monroe, Roberts et al., 1992).

Personality Tests

Psychological tests further structure the process of assessment. The two most common types of psychological tests are personality tests and intelligence tests. Here we will examine the two types of personality tests: self-report personality inventories and projective personality tests.

Self-Report Personality Inventories In a **personality inventory**, the person is asked to complete a self-report questionnaire indicating whether statements assessing

The LEDS focuses on major stressors, such as deaths, job losses, and romantic breakups.

© Wavebreak Media LTD/Wavebreak Media Ltd./Corbis Images

habitual tendencies apply to him or her. When these tests are developed, they are typically administered to many people to analyze how certain kinds of people tend to respond. Statistical norms for the test can thereby be established. This process is called **standardization.** The responses of a particular person can then be compared with the statistical norms.

Perhaps the best known of these tests is the **Minnesota Multiphasic Personality Inventory (MMPI),** developed in the early 1940s by Hathaway and McKinley (1943) and revised in 1989 (Butcher, Dahlstrom, Graham et al., 1989). The MMPI is called multiphasic because it was designed to detect a number of psychological problems. Hundreds of items were tested in very large samples of people with and without a diagnosis. Sets of these items were established as scales. If a person answered many of the items in a scale in the same way as had people from a certain diagnostic group, his or her behavior was expected to resemble that of the particular diagnostic group. These 10 scales are described in Table 3.6.

The MMPI-2 (Butcher, Dahlstrom, Graham et al., 1989) was designed to improve validity and acceptability. The original sample from the MMPI was composed mainly of white people from Minnesota and lacked representation of ethnic minorities. The 1989 version

Table 3.6 Typical Clinical Interpretations of Items Similar to Those on the MMPI-2

Scale		Sample Item	Interpretation
	(Cannot say)	This is merely the number of items left unanswered or marked both true and false.	A high score indicates evasiveness, reading difficulties, or other problems that could invalidate results of the test. A very high score could also suggest severe depression or obsessional tendencies.
L	(Lie)	I approve of every person I meet. (True)	Person is trying to look good, to present self as someone with an ideal personality.
F	(Infrequency)	Everything tastes sweet. (True)	Person is trying to look abnormal, perhaps to ensure getting special attention from the clinician.
K	(Correction)	Things couldn't be going any better for me. (True)	Person is guarded, defensive in taking the test, wishes to avoid appearing incompetent or poorly adjusted.
1.	Hs (Hypochondriasis)	I am seldom aware of tingling feelings in my body. (False)	Person is overly sensitive to and concerned about bodily sensations as signs of possible physical illness.
2.	D (Depression)	Life usually feels worthwhile to me. (False)	Person is discouraged, pessimistic, sad, self-deprecating, feeling inadequate.
3.	Hy (Hysteria)	My muscles often twitch for no apparent reason. (True)	Person has somatic complaints unlikely to be due to physical problems; also tends to be demanding and histrionic.
4.	Pd (Psychopathy)	I don't care about what people think of me. (True)	Person expresses little concern for social mores, is irresponsible, has only superficial relationships.
5.	Mf (Masculinity–Femininity)	I like taking care of plants and flowers. (True, female)	Person shows nontraditional gender characteristics (e.g., men with high scores tend to be artistic and sensitive).
6.	Pa (Paranoia)	If they were not afraid of being caught, most people would lie and cheat. (True)	Person tends to misinterpret the motives of others, is suspicious and jealous, vengeful and brooding.
7.	Pt (Psychasthenia)	I am not as competent as most other people I know. (True)	Person is overanxious, full of self-doubts, moralistic, and generally obsessive-compulsive.
8.	Sc (Schizophrenia)	I sometimes smell things others don't sense. (True)	Person has bizarre sensory experiences and beliefs, is socially reclusive.
9.	Ma (Hypomania)	Sometimes I have a strong impulse to do something that others will find appalling. (True)	Person has overly ambitious aspirations and can be hyperactive, impatient, and irritable.
10.	Si (Social Introversion)	Rather than spend time alone, I prefer to be around other people. (False)	Person is very modest and shy, preferring solitary activities.

Note: The first four scales assess the validity of the test; there are seven other scales and methods for assessing validity not shown here. The numbered scales are the clinical or content scales. The Restructured Clinical (RC) Scales are not shown here.

Sources: Hathaway & McKinley (1943); revised by Butcher et al. (1989).

was standardized using a sample that was much larger and more representative of 1980 U.S. Census figures. Several items containing allusions to sexual adjustment, bowel and bladder functions, and excessive religiosity were removed because they were judged in some testing contexts to be needlessly intrusive and objectionable. Sexist wording was eliminated, along with outmoded idioms. New scales deal with substance abuse, emotions, and marital problems.

The MMPI-2 was subsequently revised and updated in 2001, 2003, and 2009. In these revisions, new profiles with revised clinical scales were added. An extensive research literature shows that the MMPI-2 is reliable and has adequate criterion validity when it is related to diagnoses made by clinicians and to ratings made by spouses (Graham, 2011).

Like many other personality inventories, the MMPI-2 is typically administered and scored by computer. Figure 3.10 shows a hypothetical profile. Such profiles can be used in conjunction with other assessment measures to help with diagnosis, assessment of personality functioning and coping style, and identification of potential obstacles to treatment.

You may wonder whether it would be easy to fake answers that suggest no psychopathology. For example, a superficial knowledge of contemporary psychopathology research could alert someone that to be regarded as psychologically healthy, he or she must not admit to worrying a great deal about receiving messages from television.

As shown in Table 3.6, the MMPI-2 includes several "validity scales" designed to detect deliberately faked responses. For example, an item on the lie scale might be, "I read the news-

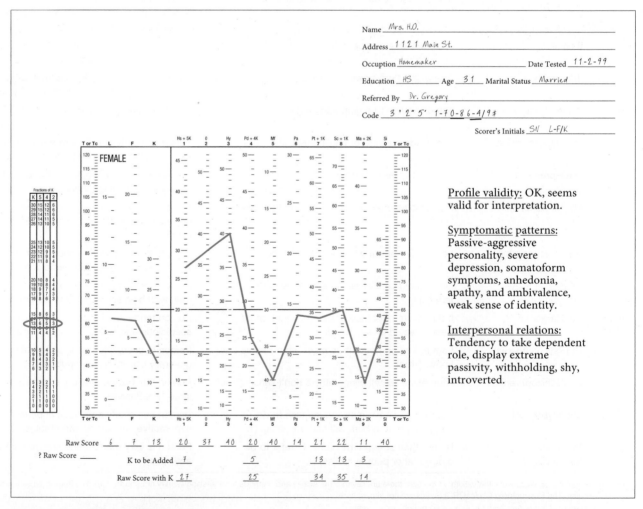

Profile validity: OK, seems valid for interpretation.

Symptomatic patterns: Passive-aggressive personality, severe depression, somatoform symptoms, anhedonia, apathy, and ambivalence, weak sense of identity.

Interpersonal relations: Tendency to take dependent role, display extreme passivity, withholding, shy, introverted.

Figure 3.10 Hypothetical MMPI-2 profile.

FOCUS ON DISCOVERY 3.3

Underreporting of Stigmatized Behaviors

Studies of self-reported drug use, sexual behavior, and violence on questionnaires or in face-to-face interviews highlight the importance of the setting in establishing the validity of what people will tell about their actions and attitudes (Ghanem, Hutton, Zenilman et al., 2005; Turner, Ku, Rogers et al., 1998).

In one study (Turner et al., 1998), findings from self-report questionnaires were compared with results from a novel self-report method—boys and young men (ages 15 to 19) listened by themselves through headphones to questions probing risky, often stigmatized behavioral practices and then indicated whether they had engaged in those behaviors by pressing keys on a computer keyboard labeled Yes and No. Compared to a matched control group who responded to the same items on a paper-and-pencil questionnaire, many more of the computer respondents admitted to having engaged in a range of high-risk behaviors. For example, they were almost 14 times more likely to report having had sex with an intravenous drug user (2.8 percent versus 0.2 percent), more than twice as likely to report having been paid for sex (3.8 percent versus 1.6 percent), and almost twice as likely to report having used cocaine (6.0 percent versus 3.3 percent). (One can safely assume that the differences would have been even greater if the boys had been interviewed by an adult researcher facing them across a table, another method that has been used to collect such survey data.) No significant differences showed up on questions directed at nonstigmatized or legal behaviors such as having had sex with a female in the preceding year (47.8 percent for computer users versus 49.6 percent for paper-and-pencil questionnaires) or having drunk alcohol in the past year (69.2 percent versus 65.9 percent).

In another study (Ghanem et al., 2005), men attending a clinic for sexually transmitted diseases treatment were randomly assigned to a face-to-face interview or an audio computer-assisted self interview (ACASI) when interviewed about high-risk sexual practices. Compared to the men who participated in the face-to-face interviews, those who participated in the ACASI were more likely to disclose sensitive information, such as same-sex sexual contact, number of sex partners in the past month, and receptive anal sexual contact. Interestingly, though, men in both conditions were equally likely to disclose illicit drug use behaviors.

If these findings show nothing else, they strongly suggest that the frequencies of sensitive behavior as determined by questionnaire or interview studies may be underestimates and that behaviors such as needle sharing and unsafe sex may be considerably more common than most people believe.

In an effort to obtain more accurate reports about stigmatized, sensitive, risky, or even illegal behaviors, investigators may apply for a Certificate of Confidentiality from the U.S. Department of Health and Human Services. These certificates provide additional protection for research participants by ensuring that sensitive information can be revealed during the research study without fear that the researchers will report their responses to legal or other authorities.

paper editorials every day." The assumption is that few people would be able to endorse such a statement honestly. Persons who endorse a large number of the statements in the lie scale might be attempting to present themselves in a good light. High scores on the infrequency (F) scale also discriminate between people trying to fake psychopathology and people who actually have a psychological disorder (Bagby, Nicholson, Bacchionchi et al., 2002). If a person obtains high scores on the lie or infrequency (F) scale, his or her profile might be viewed with skepticism. People who are aware of these validity scales, however, can still effectively fake their profile (Baer & Sekirnjak, 1997; Walters & Clopton, 2000). In most testing circumstances, however, people do not want to falsify their responses because they want to be helped. Focus on Discovery 3.3 discusses other issues surrounding the validity of self-report questionnaires.

Projective Personality Tests A **projective test** is a psychological assessment tool in which a set of standard stimuli—inkblots or drawings—ambiguous enough to allow variation in responses is presented to the person. The assumption is that because the stimulus materials are unstructured and ambiguous, the person's responses will be determined primarily by unconscious processes and will reveal his or her true attitudes, motivations, and modes of behavior. This notion is referred to as the **projective hypothesis.**

If a person reports seeing eyes in an ambiguous inkblot, for example, the projective hypothesis might be that the person tends toward paranoia. The use of projective tests assumes that the respondent would be either unable or unwilling to express his or her true feelings if asked directly. As you might have guessed, projective techniques are derived from the work of Freud and his followers (see Chapter 1).

The **Thematic Apperception Test (TAT)** is a projective test. In this test a person is shown a series of black-and-white pictures one-by-one and asked to tell a story related to each. For example, a person seeing a picture of a boy observing a youth baseball game from behind a fence may tell a story that contains angry references to the boy's parents. The clinician may, through the projective hypothesis, infer that the person harbors resentment toward his or her parents. There are few reliable scoring methods for this test, and the norms are based on a small and limited sample (i.e., few norms for people of different ethnic or cultural backgrounds). The construct validity of the TAT is also limited (Lilienfeld, Wood, & Garb, 2000). The **Rorschach Inkblot Test** is perhaps the best-known projective technique. In the Rorschach test, a person is shown 10 inkblots (for similar inkblots, see Figure 3.11), one at a time, and asked to tell what the blots look like. Half the inkblots are in black, white, and shades of gray; two also have red splotches; and three are in pastel colors.

Exner (1978) designed the most commonly used system for scoring the Rorschach test. The Exner scoring system concentrates on the perceptual and cognitive patterns in a person's responses. The person's responses are viewed as a sample of how he or she perceptually and cognitively organizes real-life situations (Exner, 1986). For example, Erdberg and Exner (1984) concluded from the research literature that respondents who express a great deal of human movement in their Rorschach responses (e.g., "The man is running to catch a plane") tend to use inner resources when coping with their needs, whereas those whose Rorschach responses involve color ("The red spot is a kidney") are more likely to seek interaction with the environment. (Rorschach suggested this approach to scoring in his original manual, *Psychodiagnostics: A Diagnostic Test Based on Perception* (1921), but he died only eight months after publishing his 10 inkblots, and his immediate followers devised other methods of interpreting the test.)

The Exner scoring system has norms, although the sample on which they are based was rather small and did not represent different ethnicities and cultures well. Regarding its reliability and validity, this work has enthusiastic supporters as well as equally harsh critics

Figure 3.11 In the Rorschach test, the person is shown a series of inkblots and is asked what the blots look like.

(Hunsley & Bailey, 1999; Lilienfeld Wood, & Garb, 2000; Meyer & Archer, 2001). Perhaps trying to make a blanket statement about the validity of the Rorschach (or the MMPI-2) is not the right approach. The test appears to have better validity in assessing some issues more than others. For example, limited evidence suggests that the Rorschach may have validity in identifying schizophrenia, borderline personality disorder, and dependent personality traits, but it remains unclear whether it does so better than other assessment techniques (Lilienfeld et al., 2000). In other words, it is unclear whether the Rorschach provides information that could not be obtained more simply—for example, through an interview.

Intelligence Tests

Alfred Binet, a French psychologist, originally constructed tests to help the Parisian school board predict which children were in need of special schooling. Intelligence testing has since developed into one of the largest psychological industries. An **intelligence test**, often referred to as an IQ test, is a way of assessing a person's current mental ability. IQ tests are based on the assumption that a detailed sample of a person's current intellectual functioning can predict how well he or she will perform in school, and most such tests are individually administered. The most commonly administered tests include the Wechsler Adult Intelligence Scale, 4th edition (WAIS-IV, 2008); the Wechsler Intelligence Scale for Children, 4th edition (WISC-IV, 2003); the Wechsler Preschool and Primary Scale of Intelligence, 4th edition (WPPSI-IV, 2012); and the Stanford–Binet, 5th edition (SB5, 2003); IQ tests are regularly updated, and, like personality inventories, they are standardized.

Beyond predicting school performance, intelligence tests are also used in other ways:

- In conjunction with achievement tests, to diagnose learning disorders and to identify areas of strengths and weaknesses for academic planning
- To help assess whether a person has intellectual disability (formerly known as mental retardation; see Chapter 13)
- To identify intellectually gifted children so that appropriate instruction can be provided them in school
- As part of neuropsychological evaluations; for example, periodically testing a person believed to be suffering from dementia so that deterioration of mental ability can be followed over time

IQ tests tap several functions believed to constitute intelligence, including language skills, abstract thinking, nonverbal reasoning, visual-spatial skills, attention and concentration, and speed of processing. Scores on most IQ tests are standardized so that 100 is the mean (i.e., the average score) and 15 or 16 is the standard deviation (a measure of how scores are dispersed above and below the average). Approximately 65 percent of the population receives scores between 85 and 115. Approximately 2.5 percent of the population falls below 70 or above 130 (i.e., 2 standard deviations below or above the mean score of 100).

IQ tests are highly reliable (Canivez & Watkins, 1998) and have good criterion validity. For example, they distinguish between people who are intellectually gifted and those with intellectual disability and between people with different occupations or educational attainment (Reynolds, Chastain, Kaufman et al., 1997). They also predict educational attainment and occupational success (Hanson, Hunsley, & Parker, 1988), at least among Caucasians (see below for a discussion of cultural bias in assessment). Although IQ and educational attainment are positively correlated (see Chapter 4 for a discussion of correlational methods), what remains less clear is whether more education causes an increase in IQ or whether IQ causes one to attain more education (Deary & Johnson, 2010). Furthermore, although correlations between IQ scores and school performance are statistically significant, IQ tests explain only a small part of school performance; much more is unexplained by IQ test scores than is explained.

Of interest to the subject matter of this book, IQ is also correlated with health. In one study of over one million Scandinavian men, lower IQ scores at age 20 were associated with a greater risk of hospitalization for schizophrenia, mood disorders, or substance dependence some 20 years

IQ tests have many subtests, including this test to assess spatial ability.

later, even after controlling for other possible contributing factors, such as the participants' families' socioeconomic status (Gale, Batty, Tynelius et al., 2010). A meta-analysis of 16 prospective, longitudinal studies (see Chapter 4 for a description of these methods) found that lower IQ scores in early adulthood were associated with greater mortality risk (i.e., death) later in life, even after controlling for other variables such as socioeconomic status and educational attainment (Calvin, Deary, Fenton et al., 2010).

Regarding construct validity, it is important to keep in mind that IQ tests measure only what psychologists consider intelligence. Factors other than what we think of as intelligence, however, also play an important role in how people will do in school, such as family and circumstances, motivation to do well, expectations, performance anxiety, and difficulty of the curriculum. Another factor relevant to IQ test performance is called stereotype threat. It suggests that the social stigma of poor intellectual performance borne by some groups (e.g., African Americans do poorly on IQ tests; women perform more poorly than men on mathematics tests) actually interferes with their performance on these tests. In one study demonstrating this phenomenon, groups of men and women were given a difficult mathematics test. In one condition, the participants were told that men scored higher than women on the test they were going to take (stereotype threat condition), while in the other condition they were told there were no gender differences in performance on the test. Only when the test was described as yielding gender differences did the women perform more poorly than the men (Spencer, Steele, & Quinn, 1999).

Unfortunately, awareness of these stereotypes develops early. For example, a study revealed that children develop awareness of stereotypes regarding ethnicity and ability between the ages of 6 and 10, with 93 percent of children being aware of such stereotypes by age 10 (McKown & Weinstein, 2003). This awareness seems to influence stereotype threat (and performance). In the McKown and Weinstein (2003) study, children were asked to complete a puzzle task. Half of the children received instructions that the task reflected their ability (stereotype threat condition), and half the children received instructions that the test did not reflect their ability. African American children who were aware of the stereotype about ethnicity and ability showed evidence of stereotype threat. Specifically, among African American children, those who received the ability instructions performed more poorly on the puzzle task than the children who did not, suggesting that the instructions activated the stereotype and thus influenced their performance.

Behavioral and Cognitive Assessment

Thus far, we have discussed assessment methods that measure personality traits and intellectual ability. Other types of assessment focus on behavioral and cognitive characteristics, including the following:

- Aspects of the environment that might contribute to symptoms (e.g., an office location next to a noisy hallway might contribute to concentration problems)

- Characteristics of the person (e.g., a person's fatigue may be caused in part by a cognitive tendency toward self-deprecation manifested in such statements as "I never do anything right, so what's the point in trying?")

- The frequency and form of problematic behaviors (e.g., procrastination taking the form of missing important deadlines)

- Consequences of problem behaviors (e.g., when a person avoids a feared situation, his or her partner offers sympathy and excuses, thereby unwittingly keeping the person from facing up to his or her fears)

The information necessary for a behavioral or cognitive assessment is gathered by several methods, including direct observation of behavior in real life as well as in laboratory or office settings, interviews and self-report measures, and various other methods of cognitive assessment (Bellack & Hersen, 1998). We turn to these now.

Direct Observation of Behavior In formal behavioral observation, the observer divides the sequence of behavior into various parts that make sense within a learning framework, including such things as the antecedents and consequences of particular behaviors. Behavioral observation is also often linked to intervention (O'Brien & Haynes, 1995).

It is difficult to observe most behavior as it actually takes place, and little control can be exercised over where and when it may occur. For this reason, many therapists contrive somewhat artificial situations in their consulting rooms or in a laboratory so that they can observe how a person or a family acts under certain conditions. For example, Barkley (1981) had a mother and her child spend time together in a laboratory living room, complete with sofas and a television. The mother was given a list of tasks for the child to complete, such as picking up toys or doing math problems. Observers behind a one-way mirror watched the proceedings and reliably coded the child's reactions to the mother's efforts to control as well as the mother's reactions to the child's compliant or noncompliant responses. These **behavioral assessment** procedures yielded data that could be used to measure the effects of treatment.

Behavioral assessment often involves direct observation of behavior, as in this case, where the observer is behind a one-way mirror.

Self-Observation Cognitive behavior therapists and researchers often ask people to observe and track their own behavior and responses, an approach called **self-monitoring**. Self-monitoring is used to collect a wide variety of data, including moods, stressful experiences, coping behaviors, and thoughts (Hurlburt, 1979; Stone, Schwartz, Neale et al., 1998)

Another method of self-observation is called **ecological momentary assessment,** or **EMA.** EMA involves the collection of data in real time as opposed to the more usual methods of having people reflect back over some time period and report on recently experienced thoughts, moods, or stressors. With EMA, a person is signaled (via text message or smartphone alert most typically) several times a day and asked to enter responses directly into the device (Stone & Shiffman, 1994).

EMA can be useful in clinical settings, revealing information that traditional assessment procedures might miss. For example, Hurlburt (1997) describes a case of a man with severe panic attacks. In clinical interviews, the man reported that his life was going very well, that he loved his wife and children, and that his work was both financially and personally rewarding. No cause of the panic attacks could be discerned. The man was asked to record his thoughts as he went about his daily routine. Surprisingly, about a third of his thoughts were concerned with annoyance with his children (e.g., "He left the fence gate open again and the dog got out").

> Once the high frequency of annoyance thoughts was pointed out to him, he . . . accepted that he was in fact often annoyed with his children. However, he believed that anger at his children was sinful and felt unfit as a father for having such thoughts and feelings. . . . [He] entered into brief therapy that focused on the normality of being annoyed by one's children and on the important distinction between being annoyed and acting out aggressively. Almost immediately, his anxiety attacks disappeared. (Hurlburt, 1997, p. 944)

Although some research indicates that self-monitoring or EMA can provide accurate measurement of such behavior, considerable research indicates that behavior may be altered by the very fact that it is being self-monitored—that is, the self-consciousness required for self-monitoring affects the behavior (Haynes & Horn, 1982). The phenomenon wherein behavior changes because it is being observed is called **reactivity.** In general, desirable behavior, such as engaging in social conversation, often increases in frequency when it is self-monitored (Nelson, Lipinski, & Black, 1976), whereas behavior a person wishes to reduce, such as cigarette smoking, diminishes (McFall & Hammen, 1971). Therapeutic interventions can take advantage of the reactivity that is a natural by-product of self-monitoring. Smoking, anxiety, depression, and health problems have all undergone beneficial changes in self-monitoring studies (Febbraro & Clum, 1998). Beyond reactivity, self-monitoring with portable electronic

Self-monitoring generally leads to increases in desirable behaviors and decreases in undesirable ones.

Table 3.7 Psychological Assessment Methods

Interviews	Clinical interviews	The clinician learns about the person's problems through conversation. The paradigm of the interviewer shapes the content of the interview.
	Structured interviews	Questions to be asked are spelled out in detail in a booklet. The Structured Clinical Interview for Axis I Disorders is a structured interview that is commonly used to make a diagnosis.
Stress measures		Self-report scales or interviews that assess stressful events and responses to these events.
Psychological tests	Personality tests	Self-report questionnaires, used to assess either a broad range of characteristics, as in the MMPI-2, or a single characteristic, such as dysfunctional attitudes.
	Projective tests	Ambiguous stimuli, such as inkblots (Rorschach test), are presented and responses are thought to be determined by unconscious processes.
	Intelligence tests	Assessments of current mental functioning. Used to predict school performance and identify cognitive strengths and weaknesses.
Direct observation		Used by clinicians to identify problem behaviors as well as antecedents and consequences.
Self-observation		People monitor and keep records of their own behavior, as in ecological momentary assessment.

Fuse/Getty Images, Inc.

Cognitive assessment focuses on the person's perception of a situation, realizing that the same event can be perceived differently. For example, moving could be regarded as a very negative event or a very positive one, resulting in very different levels of stress.

devices like smartphones has also been included effectively in cognitive behavior therapy for different anxiety disorders (Przeworski & Newman, 2006).

Cognitive-Style Questionnaires Cognitive questionnaires tend to be used to help plan targets for treatment as well as to determine whether clinical interventions are helping to change overly negative thought patterns as well as negative and positive emotions. In format, some of these questionnaires are similar to the personality tests we have already described.

One self-report questionnaire that was developed based on Beck's theory (see Chapters 2 and 5) is the Dysfunctional Attitude Scale (DAS). The DAS contains items such as "People will probably think less of me if I make a mistake" (Weissman & Beck, 1978). Supporting construct validity, researchers have shown that they can differentiate between people with and without depression on the basis of their scores on this scale and that scores decrease (i.e., improve) after interventions that relieve depression. Furthermore, the DAS relates to other aspects of cognition in ways consistent with Beck's theory (Glass & Arnkoff, 1997).

Quick Summary

The psychological assessments we have described are summarized in Table 3.7. A comprehensive psychological assessment draws on many different methods and tests. Interviews can be structured, with the questions predetermined and followed in a certain order, or unstructured, to follow more closely what the person tells the interviewer. Structured interviews are more reliable. Rapport is important to establish regardless of the type of interview.

Stress is best assessed via a semistructured interview that captures the importance of any given life event in the context of a person's life circumstances, as in the LEDS. Self-report checklists are also used to assess stress, but they have poorer reliability and validity than the LEDS.

The MMPI-2 is a standardized and objective personality inventory. The test has good reliability and validity and is widely used. Projective personality tests, like the Rorschach or TAT, are not as widely used today, likely due to their poor validity. Reliability can be achieved using scoring systems such as Exner's. Intelligence tests have been used for a number of years and are quite reliable. Like any test, there are limits to what an IQ test can tell a clinician or researcher.

Direct observation of behavior can be very useful in assessment, though it can take more time than a self-report inventory. Other behavioral and cognitive assessment methods include ecological momentary assessment (EMA) and questionnaires.

Check Your Knowledge 3.3

True or false?

1. If conducted properly, a psychological assessment typically includes just one measure most appropriate to the person.
2. Unstructured interviews may have poor reliability, but they can still be quite valuable in a psychological assessment.
3. The MMPI-2 contains scales to detect whether someone is faking answers.
4. The projective hypothesis is based on the idea that a person does not really know what is bothering him or her; thus, a subtler means of assessment is needed.
5. Intelligence tests are highly reliable.
6. EMA is a method to assess unwanted impulses.

Neurobiological Assessment

Recall from Chapters 1 and 2 that throughout history people interested in psychopathology have assumed, quite reasonably, that some symptoms are likely to be due to or at least reflected in malfunctions of the brain. We turn now to contemporary work in neurobiological assessment. We'll look at four areas in particular: brain imaging, neurotransmitter assessment, neuropsychological assessment, and psychophysiological assessment (see Table 3.8 for a summary of these methods).

Table 3.8 Neurobiological Assessment Methods	
Brain imaging	CT and MRI scans reveal the structure of the brain. PET reveals brain function and, to a lesser extent, brain structure. fMRI is used to assess both brain structure and brain function.
Neurotransmitter assessment	Includes postmortem analysis of neurotransmitters and receptors, assays of metabolites of neurotransmitters, and PET scans of neurotransmitter receptors.
Neuropsychological assessment	Behavioral tests such as the Halstead–Reitan and Luria–Nebraska assess abilities such as motor speed, memory, and spatial ability. Deficits on particular tests help point to an area of possible brain dysfunction.
Psychophysiological assessment	Includes measures of electrical activity in the autonomic nervous system, such as skin conductance, or in the central nervous system, such as EEG.

Brain Imaging: "Seeing" the Brain

Because many behavioral problems can be brought on by brain dysfunction, neurological tests—such as checking the reflexes, examining the retina for any indication of blood vessel damage, and evaluating motor coordination and perception—have been used for many years to identify brain dysfunction. Today, devices have become available that allow clinicians and researchers a much more direct look at both the structure and functioning of the brain.

Computerized axial tomography, the **CT** or **CAT scan**, helps to assess structural brain abnormalities (and is able to image other parts of the body for medical purposes). A moving beam of X-rays passes into a horizontal cross section of the person's brain, scanning it through 360 degrees; the moving X-ray detector on the other side measures the amount of radioactivity that penetrates, thus detecting subtle differences in tissue density. A computer uses the information to construct a two-dimensional, detailed image of the cross section, giving it optimal contrasts. Then the machine scans another cross section of the brain. The resulting images can show the enlargement of ventricles (which can be a sign of brain tissue degeneration) and the locations of tumors and blood clots.

Other devices for seeing the living brain include **magnetic resonance imaging**, also known as **MRI**, which is superior to the CT scan because it produces pictures of higher quality and does not rely on even the small amount of radiation required by a CT scan. In MRI the person

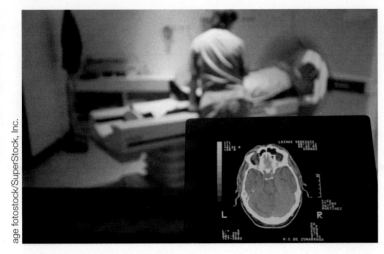

A person entering an fMRI scanner.

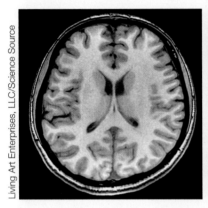

These two CT scans show a horizontal "slice" through the brain. The one on the left is normal; the one on the right has a tumor on the left side.

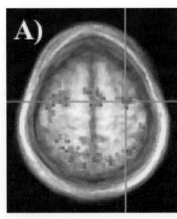
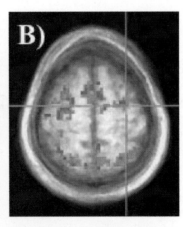

Functional magnetic resonance images (fMRI). With this method, researchers can measure how brain activity changes while a person is doing different tasks, such as viewing an emotional film, completing a memory test, looking at a visual puzzle, or hearing and learning a list of words.

is placed inside a large, circular magnet, which causes the hydrogen atoms in the body to move. When the magnetic force is turned off, the atoms return to their original positions and thereby produce an electromagnetic signal. These signals are then read by the computer andz translated into pictures of brain tissue. This technique provides an enormous advance. For example, it has allowed physicians to locate delicate brain tumors that would have been considered inoperable without such sophisticated methods of viewing brain structures.

An even greater advance has been a technique called **functional MRI (fMRI)**, which allows researchers to measure both brain structure and brain function. This technique takes MRI pictures so quickly that metabolic changes can be measured, providing a picture of the brain at work rather than of its structure alone. fMRI measures blood flow in the brain, and this is called the **BOLD** signal, which stands for blood oxygenation level dependent. As neurons fire, presumably blood flow increases to that area. Therefore, blood flow in a particular region of the brain is a reasonable proxy for neural activity in that brain region.

Positron emission tomography, the **PET scan**, a more expensive and invasive procedure, also allows measurement of both brain structure and brain function, although the measurement of brain structure is not as precise as with MRI or fMRI. A substance used by the brain is labeled with a short-lived radioactive isotope and injected into the bloodstream. The radioactive molecules of the substance emit a particle called a positron, which quickly collides with an electron. A pair of high-energy light particles shoot out from the skull in opposite directions and are detected by the scanner. The computer analyzes millions of such recordings and converts them into a picture of the functioning brain. The images are in color; fuzzy spots of lighter and warmer colors are areas in which metabolic rates for the substance are higher. Because this is more invasive than fMRI, it is now used less often as a measure of brain function.

Visual images of the working brain can indicate areas of degeneration, tumors, strokes, and trauma from head injuries, as well as disruptions in the neural connections between different brain regions, differences in volume (size) of various brain regions, and the distribution of psychoactive drugs in the brain. fMRI and to a lesser extent PET are being used to study neural deficits that are linked to various disorders, such as the failure of the prefrontal cortex of people with schizophrenia to become strongly activated while they attempt to perform a cognitive task. Current neuroimaging studies in psychopathology are attempting to identify not only areas of the brain that may be dysfunctional (e.g., the prefrontal cortex) but also deficits in the ways in which different areas of the brain communicate and connect with one another. This type of inquiry is often referred to as functional connectivity analysis since it aims to identify how different areas of the brain are connected with one another.

Neurotransmitter Assessment

It might seem that assessing the amount of a particular neurotransmitter or the quantity of its receptors in the brain would be straightforward. But as we began to discuss in Chapter 2, it is not. Most of the research on neurotransmitters and psychopathology has relied on indirect assessments.

In postmortem studies, the brains of deceased people are removed and the amount of specific neurotransmitters in particular brain areas can then be directly measured. Different brain areas can be infused with substances that bind to receptors, and the amount of binding can then be quantified; more binding indicates more receptors.

In studies of participants who are alive, one common method of neurotransmitter assessment involves analyzing the metabolites of neurotransmitters that have been broken down by enzymes. A **metabolite,** typically an acid, is produced when a neurotransmitter is deactivated. These by-products of the breakdown of neurotransmitters, such as norepinephrine, dopamine, and serotonin, are found in urine, blood serum, and cerebrospinal fluid (CSF; the fluid in the spinal column and in the brain's ventricles). For example, a major metabolite of dopamine is homovanillic acid (HVA); that of serotonin is 5-hydroxyindoleacetic acid (5-HIAA). A high level of a particular metabolite presumably indicates a high level of a neurotransmitter, and a low level indicates a low level of the neurotransmitter.

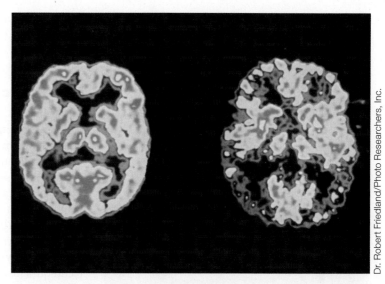

Dr. Robert Friedland/Photo Researchers, Inc.

The PET scan on the left shows a normal brain; the one on the right shows the brain of a person with Alzheimer's disease.

But there is a problem with measuring metabolites from blood or urine: such measures are not direct reflections of levels of neurotransmitters in the brain; metabolites measured in this way could reflect neurotransmitters anywhere in the body. A more specific measure can be taken of metabolites in the CSF fluid drawn from a person's spinal cord. Even with CSF fluid, however, metabolites reflect activity throughout the brain and spinal cord, rather than regions that are directly involved in psychopathology. We will see in Chapter 5 that studies of 5-HIAA, the main metabolite of serotonin, and depression have been inconsistent, perhaps owing to the fact that these metabolites are not directly reflecting serotonin levels of activity.

Another problem with metabolite studies is that they are correlational. In Chapter 4, we discuss the limits of correlational research, including the fact that causation cannot be determined from a correlational study. That is, when researchers find that neurotransmitter levels are low among people with a particular disorder, such as depression, this could be because neurotransmitter levels cause depression, because depression causes neurotransmitter changes, or because a third variable causes shifts in both neurotransmitters and depression. For example, dopamine, norepinephrine, and serotonin levels change in response to stress. To test whether neurotransmitter levels could cause symptoms, experimental evidence is needed.

To provide more experimental data on whether these neurotransmitter systems actually help cause psychopathology, one strategy is to administer drugs that increase or decrease levels of neurotransmitters. For example, a drug that raises the level of serotonin should alleviate depression; one reducing it should trigger depressive symptoms. This strategy also has its problems, though. One might wonder about whether it is ethical to conduct these studies if the goal of an experiment is to produce symptoms. Another issue is that drugs that change levels of one neurotransmitter often tend to influence other neurotransmitter systems. We will see examples of these types of studies throughout this book.

Clinicians and researchers in many disciplines are currently using brain-imaging and neurotransmitter assessment techniques both to discover previously undetectable brain problems and to conduct inquiries into the neurobiological contributions to thought, emotion, and behavior. It is a very lively and exciting area of research and application. Indeed, one might reasonably assume that researchers and clinicians, with the help of such procedures and technological devices as fMRI, could observe the brain and its functions more or less directly and thus assess all brain abnormalities. Results to date, however, are not strong enough for these methods to be used in diagnosing psychopathology. Moreover, many brain abnormalities involve alterations in structure so subtle or slight in extent that they have thus far eluded direct examination. Furthermore, the problems in some disorders are so widespread that finding the

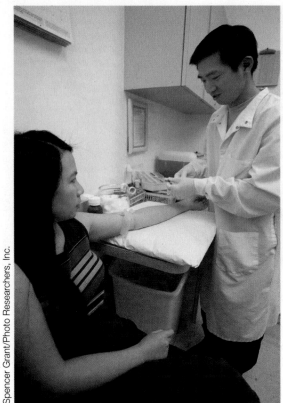

Measures of neurotransmitter metabolites in blood or urine levels do not provide a very accurate index of neurotransmitter levels in the brain.

Spencer Grant/Photo Researchers, Inc.

contributing brain dysfunction is a daunting task. Take, for example, schizophrenia, which affects thinking, feeling, and behavior. Where in the brain might there be dysfunction? Looking for areas that influence thinking, feeling, and behavior requires looking at just about the entire brain.

Neuropsychological Assessment

It is important at this point to note a distinction between neurologists and neuropsychologists, even though both specialists are concerned with the study of the central nervous system. A **neurologist** is a physician who specializes in diseases or problems that affect the nervous system, such as stroke, muscular dystrophy, cerebral palsy, or Alzheimer's disease. A **neuropsychologist** is a psychologist who studies how dysfunctions of the brain affect the way we think, feel, and behave. Both kinds of specialists contribute much to each other as they work in different ways, often collaboratively, to learn how the nervous system functions and how to ameliorate problems caused by disease or injury to the brain.

Neuropsychological tests are often used in conjunction with the brain-imaging techniques just described, both to detect brain dysfunction and to help pinpoint specific areas of behavior that are impacted by problems in the brain. Neuropsychological tests are based on the idea that different psychological functions (e.g., motor speed, memory, language) rely on different areas of the brain. Thus, for example, neuropsychological testing might help identify the extent of brain damage suffered during a stroke, and it can provide clues about where in the brain the damage may exist that can then be confirmed with more expensive brain-imaging techniques. There are numerous neuropsychological tests used in psychopathology assessment. Here, we highlight two widely used batteries of tests.

One neuropsychological test is Reitan's modification of a battery, or group, of tests previously developed by Halstead, called the Halstead–Reitan neuropsychological test battery. The following are three of the Halstead–Reitan tests.

1. **Tactile Performance Test—Time.** While blindfolded, the person tries to fit variously shaped blocks into spaces of a form board, first using the preferred hand, then the other, and finally both.

2. **Tactile Performance Test—Memory.** After completing the timed test, the person is asked to draw the form board from memory, showing the blocks in their proper location. Both this and the timed test are sensitive to damage in the right parietal lobe.

3. **Speech Sounds Perception Test.** Participants listen to a series of nonsense words, each comprising two consonants with a long-*e* sound in the middle. They then select the "word" they heard from a set of alternatives. This test measures left-hemisphere function, especially temporal and parietal areas.

Extensive research has demonstrated that the battery is valid for detecting behavior changes linked to brain dysfunction resulting from a variety of conditions, such as tumors, stroke, and head injury (Horton, 2008).

The Luria–Nebraska battery (Golden, Hammeke, & Purisch, 1978), based on the work of the Russian psychologist Aleksandr Luria (1902–1977), is also widely used (Moses & Purisch, 1997). The battery includes 269 items divided into 11 sections designed to determine basic and complex motor skills, rhythm and pitch abilities, tactile and kinesthetic skills, verbal and spatial skills, receptive speech ability, expressive speech ability, writing, reading, arithmetic skills, memory, and intellectual processes. The pattern of scores on these sections, as well as on the 32 items found to be the most discriminating and indicative of overall impairment, helps reveal potential damage to the frontal, temporal, sensorimotor, or parietal-occipital area of the right or left hemisphere.

The Luria–Nebraska battery can be administered in 2½ hours and can be scored in a highly reliable manner (e.g., Kashden & Franzen, 1996). Criterion validity has been established by findings that test scores can correctly distinguish 86 percent of people with and without neurological disease (Moses, Schefft, Wong et al., 1992). A particular advantage of the Luria–Nebraska tests is that one can control for educational level so that a less educated person will not receive a lower score solely because of limited educational experience (Brickman, McManus, Grapentine et al., 1984). Finally, a version for children ages 8 to 12 (Golden, 1981a, 1981b) has been found useful in helping to pinpoint brain damage and in evaluating the educational strengths and weaknesses of children (Sweet, Carr, Rossini et al., 1986).

Psychophysiological Assessment

The discipline of **psychophysiology** is concerned with the bodily changes that are associated with psychological events. Experimenters have used measures such as heart rate, tension in the muscles, blood flow in various parts of the body, and electrical activity in the brain (so-called brain waves) to study physiological changes when people are afraid, depressed, asleep, imagining, solving problems, and so on. Like the brain-imaging methods we have already discussed, the assessments we describe here are not sensitive enough to be used for diagnosis. They can, however, provide important information about a person's reactivity and can also be used to compare individuals. For example, in using exposure to treat a person with an anxiety disorder, it would be useful to know

Neuropsychological tests assess various performance deficits in the hope of detecting a specific area of brain malfunction. Shown here is the Tactile Performance Test.

the extent to which the person shows physiological reactivity when exposed to the stimuli that create anxiety. People who show more physiological reactivity may be experiencing more fear, which predicts more benefit from the therapy (Foa, Riggs, Marsie, et al., 1995).

The activities of the autonomic nervous system (also discussed in Chapter 2) are often assessed to understand aspects of emotion. One such measure is heart rate. Each heartbeat generates electrical changes, which can be recorded by electrodes placed on the chest that convey signals to an electrocardiograph or a polygraph. The signal is graphically depicted in an **electrocardiogram (EKG)**, which may be seen as waves on a computer screen.

A second measure of autonomic nervous system activity is **electrodermal responding,** or skin conductance. Anxiety, fear, anger, and other emotions increase activity in the sympathetic nervous system, which then boosts sweat-gland activity. Increased sweat-gland activity increases the electrical conductance of the skin. Conductance is typically measured by determining the current that flows through the skin as a small voltage is passed between two electrodes on the hand. When the sweat glands are activated, this current shows a pronounced increase. Since the sweat glands are activated by the sympathetic nervous system, increased sweat-gland activity indicates sympathetic autonomic excitation and is often taken as a measure of emotional arousal. These measures are widely used in research in psychopathology.

Brain activity can be measured by an **electroencephalogram (EEG).** Electrodes placed on the scalp record electrical activity in the underlying brain area. Abnormal patterns of electrical activity can indicate seizure activity in the brain or help in locating brain lesions or tumors. EEG indices are also used to measure attention and alertness.

As with the brain-imaging techniques reviewed earlier, a more complete picture of a human being is obtained when physiological functioning is assessed while the person is engaging in some form of behavior or cognitive activity. If researchers and clinicians are interested in psychophysiological responding in people with a specific phobia of spiders, for example, they would likely study the people while presenting stimuli, such as pictures of spiders or even actual spiders that would elicit the anxiety and fear responses.

A Cautionary Note About Neurobiological Assessment

A cautionary note regarding neurobiological assessment methods is in order here. Inasmuch as psychophysiology and brain imaging employ highly sophisticated electronic machinery, and many psychologists aspire to be as scientific as possible, researchers and clinicians sometimes

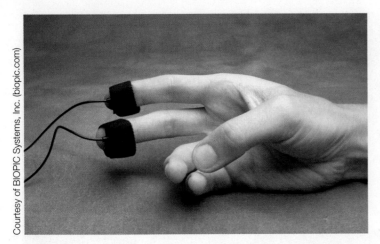

In psychophysiological assessment, physical changes in the body are measured. Skin conductance can be measured with sensors on two fingers.

believe uncritically in these apparently objective assessment devices without appreciating their real limitations and complications. Many of the measurements do not differentiate clearly among emotional states. Skin conductance, for example, increases not only with anxiety but also with other emotions—among them, happiness. In addition, being in a scanner is often a threatening experience. Thus, the investigator interested in measuring brain changes associated with emotion using fMRI must also take the scanning environment into account. It is also important to keep in mind that brain-imaging techniques do not allow us to manipulate brain activity and then measure a change in behavior (Feldman Barrett, 2003). In a typical study, we show people a list of emotionally evocative words and then measure blood flow in the brain. Does a person who fails to show the same level of activation in emotion regions during this task have a brain-based emotion deficit? Not necessarily. The person might not have paid attention, might not have understood the words, or might be focused on the loud clanging noises that the fMRI machine is making. It is important to be extremely careful in considering alternative explanations for the effects found in these studies.

Neither is there a one-to-one relationship between a score on a given neuropsychological test or a finding on an fMRI scan on the one hand and psychological dysfunction on the other. The reasons for these sometimes loose relationships have to do with such factors as how the person has, over time, developed different coping strategies. And the success of coping, in turn, has to do with the social environment in which the person has lived, for example, how understanding parents and friends have been or how well the school system has provided for the special educational needs of the person. Furthermore, the brain itself will change in response to these psychological and socioenvironmental factors over time. Therefore, in addition to the imperfect nature of the neurobiological assessment instruments themselves and our incomplete understanding of how the brain actually functions, clinicians and researchers must consider social and environmental factors that operate over time to contribute to the clinical picture. In other words, a complete assessment must include multiple methods (clinical interviews, psychological and neurobiological methods).

A final caution is reflected in the simple yet often unappreciated fact that in attempting to understand the consequences of any brain dysfunction, one must understand the preexisting abilities that the person had prior to diagnosis with a psychological disorder. This straightforward truth brings to mind the story of the man who, recovering from an accident that has broken all the fingers in both hands, earnestly asks the surgeon whether he will be able to play the piano when his wounds heal. "Yes, I'm sure you will," says the doctor reassuringly. "That's wonderful," exclaims the man, "I've always wanted to be able to play the piano."

Quick Summary

Advances in technology have allowed clinicians and researchers to "see" the living brain. Different imaging techniques, such as CT, MRI, and fMRI, have the potential to show areas of the brain that might not be working optimally. Direct assessment of neurotransmitters is not done often. Rather, examinations of the metabolites of neurotransmitters provide a rough way to estimate how neurotransmitters are functioning. Another approach is to administer drugs that increase or decrease the levels of a neurotransmitter. Postmortem exams also allow for measurements of neurotransmitters, particularly receptors.

Neuropsychological tests are tests that have been developed to show how changes in behavior may reflect damage or disturbance in particular areas of the brain. Psychophysiological assessment methods can show how behaviors and cognitions are linked to changes in nervous system activity, such as heart rate, skin conductance, or brain electrical activity. These methods have as many as or more limitations than other assessment measures, and the key concepts of reliability and validity are just as relevant with neurobiological assessment as with other forms of assessment.

Check Your Knowledge 3.4

True or false?
1. MRI is a technique that shows both the structure and function of the brain.
2. Neurotransmitter assessment is most often done using indirect methods.

3. A neuropsychologist is a psychologist who studies how dysfunctions of the brain affect the way we think, feel, and behave.
4. Brain activity can be measured with the psychophysiological method called EKG.

Cultural and Ethnic Diversity and Assessment

Studies of the influences of culture and ethnicity on psychopathology and its assessment have proliferated in recent years. As you read about some of this research, it is critical to keep in mind that there are typically more differences within cultural, ethnic, and racial groups than there are between them. Remembering this important point can help you avoid the dangers of stereotyping members of a culture or ethnic group.

We should also note that the reliability and validity of various forms of psychological assessment have been questioned on the grounds that their content and scoring procedures reflect the culture of white European Americans and so may not accurately assess people from other cultures. In this section we discuss problems of cultural bias and what can be done about them.

Cultural Bias in Assessment

The issue of cultural bias in assessment refers to the notion that a measure developed for one culture or ethnic group may not be equally reliable and valid with a different cultural or ethnic group. Some tests that were developed in the United States have been translated into different languages and used in different cultures successfully. For example, a Spanish-language version of the WAIS has been available for over 40 years (Wechsler, 1968) and can be useful in assessing the intellectual functioning of people from Hispanic or Latino cultures (Gomez, Piedmont, & Fleming, 1992). Additionally, the MMPI-2 has been translated into more than two dozen languages (Tsai, Butcher, Vitousek et al., 2001).

Simply translating words into a different language, however, does not ensure that the meaning of those words will be the same across different cultures. Several steps in the translation process, including working with multiple translators, back-translating, and testing with multiple native speakers, can help to ensure that the test is similar in different languages. This approach has been successful in achieving equivalence across different cultures and ethnic groups for some instruments, such as the MMPI-2 (Arbisi, Ben-Porath, & McNulty, 2002). Even with the MMPI-2, however, there are cultural differences that are not likely attributable to differences in psychopathology. For example, among Asian Americans who are not heavily assimilated into American culture, scores on most MMPI-2 scales are higher than those of Caucasians (Tsai & Pike, 2000). This is unlikely to reflect truly higher emotional disturbance among Asians. For children, the latest version of the WISC has been translated into Spanish (WISC-IV Spanish); in addition, it has a complete set of norms for Spanish-speaking children in the United States, and the items have been designed explicitly to minimize cultural bias.

Despite these efforts, the field has a way to go in reducing cultural and ethnic bias in clinical assessment. These cultural assumptions or biases may cause clinicians to over- or underestimate psychological problems in members of other cultures (Lopez, 1989, 1996). African American children are overrepresented in special education classes, which may be a result of subtle biases in the tests used to determine such placement (Artiles & Trent, 1994).

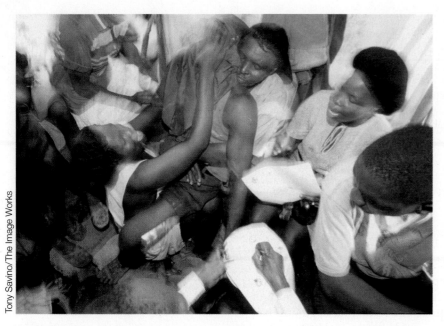

Tony Savino/The Image Works

Assessment must take the person's cultural background into account. Belief in spirit possession in some cultures should not always be taken to mean that the believer is psychotic.

At least since the 1970s, studies have found that African Americans are more likely to receive a diagnosis of schizophrenia than are Caucasian Americans; this does not likely reflect an actual difference but instead a form of ethnic bias on the part of clinicians (Arnold, Keck, Collins et al., 2004; Trierweiler, Neighbors, Munday et al., 2000). Yet take the example of an Asian American man who is very emotionally withdrawn. Should the clinician consider the notion that Asian cultures take a more positive view of lower emotional expressiveness in men than do European American cultures? A clinician who quickly attributes the behavior to a cultural difference may overlook an emotional problem that he or she would be likely to diagnose if the person were a white male. Indeed, recent evidence shows that clinicians confuse the absence of excitement in the facial expressions of Asian people as a sign of depression. Even though Asians are less likely to show such expressions than European Americans, this has nothing to do with whether or not they have depression (Tsai, 2014).

How do such biases come about? Cultural factors may affect assessment in various ways. Language differences, differing religious and spiritual beliefs, the alienation or presumed timidity of members of ethnic groups when being assessed by clinicians of the European American culture—all these factors can play a role. For example, clinicians who encounter people claiming to be surrounded by spirits might view this belief as a sign of schizophrenia. Yet in Puerto Rican cultures, such a belief is common; therefore, believing that one is surrounded by spirits should probably not be taken as a sign of schizophrenia in a Puerto Rican person (Rogler & Hollingshead, 1985).

Cultural and ethnic differences in psychopathology must be examined more closely. Unfortunately, the cultural and ethnic biases that can creep into clinical assessment do not necessarily yield efforts to compensate for them. There is no simple answer. The DSM-5's emphasis on cultural factors in the discussion of every category of disorder, along with its new cultural formulation interview, may well sensitize clinicians and researchers to the issue. When practitioners were surveyed, they overwhelmingly reported taking culture into account in their clinical work (Lopez, 1994), so it appears that the problem, if not the solution, is clearly in focus.

Strategies for Avoiding Cultural Bias in Assessment

Clinicians can—and do—use various methods to minimize the negative effects of cultural biases when conducting assessments. Perhaps the place to begin is with graduate training programs. Lopez (2002) has noted three important issues that should be taught to graduate students in clinical psychology programs. First, students must learn about basic issues in assessment, such as reliability and validity. Second, students must become informed about the specific ways in which culture or ethnicity may impact assessment rather than relying on more global stereotypes about a particular cultural or ethnic group. Third, students must consider that culture or ethnicity may not impact assessment in every individual case.

Assessment procedures can also be modified to ensure that the person truly understands the requirements of the task. For example, suppose that a Native American child performed poorly on a test measuring psychomotor speed. The examiner's hunch is that the child did not understand the importance of working quickly and was overly concerned with accuracy instead. The test could be administered again after a more thorough explanation of the importance of working quickly without worrying about mistakes. If the child's performance improves, the examiner has gained an important understanding of the child's test-taking strategy and avoids diagnosing psychomotor speed deficits.

Finally, when the examiner and client have different ethnic backgrounds, the examiner may need to make an extra effort to establish a rapport that will result in the person's best performance. For example, when testing a shy Hispanic preschooler, one of the authors was unable to obtain a verbal response to test questions. However, the boy was overheard talking in an animated and articulate manner to his mother in the waiting room, leading to a judgment that the test results did not represent a valid assessment of the child's language skills. When testing was repeated in the child's home with his mother present, advanced verbal abilities were observed.

As Lopez (1994) points out, however, "the distance between cultural responsiveness and cultural stereotyping can be short" (p. 123). To minimize such problems, clinicians are encouraged to be particularly tentative about drawing conclusions regarding people from different cultural and ethnic backgrounds. Rather, they are advised to make hypotheses about the influence of culture on a particular person, entertain alternative hypotheses, and then test those hypotheses.

Training in cultural awareness is truly important, as a clinician's biases can influence diagnosis. As an example, schizophrenia is often overdiagnosed among African Americans, leading to high dosages of antipsychotic medications and too many hospitalizations (Alarcon et al., 2009). One way to combat these biases is to use structured diagnostic interviews, like the SCID described above. When clinicians use structured interviews, they are less likely to overdiagnose people from different ethnic groups (Garb, 2005).

Cultural differences can lead to different results on an aptitude or IQ test. For example, Native American children may lack interest in the individualistic, competitive nature of IQ tests because of the cooperative, group-oriented values instilled by their culture.

© Marmaduke St. John/Alamy

Summary

- In gathering diagnosis and assessment information, clinicians and researchers must be concerned with both reliability and validity. Reliability refers to whether measurements are consistent and replicable, and validity refers to whether assessments are tapping into what they are meant to measure. Assessment procedures vary greatly in their reliability and validity. Certain diagnostic categories are more reliable than others.

Diagnosis

- Diagnosis is the process of assessing whether a person meets the criteria for a psychological disorder. Having an agreed-on diagnostic system allows clinicians to communicate effectively with each other and facilitates the search for causes and treatments. Clinically, diagnosis provides the foundation for treatment planning.
- *The Diagnostic and Statistical Manual of Mental Disorders* (DSM), published by the American Psychiatric Association, is an official diagnostic system widely used by mental health professionals. The latest edition of the manual, referred to as DSM-5, was published in 2013.
- Reliability of diagnosis has been improved dramatically by including specific criteria for each diagnosis. Criticisms of the DSM include the proliferation of diagnoses that are often related to the same risk factors and tend to co-occur; the absence of a dimensional approach to classification; the fact that reliability in practice may be lower than that achieved in research studies; and the ongoing need to validate diagnoses against etiology, course, and treatment. Most researchers and clinicians, though, recognize that the DSM is an enormous advance compared to previous systems.
- Some critics of the DSM argue against diagnosis in general. They point out that diagnostic classifications may ignore important information. Although many worry that diagnostic labels will increase stigma, there is some data that a diagnosis can reduce stigma by providing an explanation for worrisome behavior.

Assessment

- Clinicians rely on several modes of psychological and neurobiological assessment in trying to find out how best to describe an individual, search for the reasons the person is troubled, arrive at an accurate diagnosis, and design effective treatments. The best assessment involves multiple types of methods.
- Psychological assessments include clinical interviews, assessments of stress, psychological tests, and behavioral and cognitive assessments.
- Clinical interviews are structured or relatively unstructured conversations in which the clinician probes the person for information about his or her problems. Assessing stress is key to the field of psychopathology. A number of useful methods for assessing stress have been developed, including the LEDS.

- Psychological tests are standardized procedures designed to assess personality or measure performance. Personality assessments range from empirically derived self-report questionnaires, such as the Minnesota Multiphasic Personality Inventory, to projective tests in which the person interprets ambiguous stimuli, such as the Rorschach test. Intelligence tests, such as the Wechsler Adult Intelligence Scale, evaluate a person's intellectual ability and predict how well he or she will perform academically.

- Behavioral and cognitive assessment is concerned with how people act, feel, and think in particular situations. Approaches include direct observation of behavior, interviews, and self-report measures that are situational in their focus.

- Neurobiological assessments include brain-imaging techniques, such as fMRI, that enable clinicians and researchers to see various structures and access functions of the living brain; neurochemical assays that allow clinicians to make inferences about levels of neurotransmitters; neuropsychological tests, such as the Luria-Nebraska battery, that seek to identify brain defects based on variations in responses to psychological tests; and psychophysiological measurements, such as heart rate and electrodermal responding, that are associated with certain psychological events or characteristics.

- Cultural and ethnic factors play a role in clinical assessment. Assessment techniques developed on the basis of research with Caucasian populations may be inaccurate when used with people of differing ethnic or cultural backgrounds. Clinicians can have biases when evaluating people from different ethnic and cultural groups, which can lead to minimizing or exaggerating a person's psychopathology. Clinicians use various methods to guard against the negative effects of cultural biases in assessment.

Answers to Check Your Knowledge Questions

3.1 1. a, b; 2. b, c, d, a
3.2 1. high comorbidity, many different diagnoses are related to the same causes, symptoms of many different diagnoses respond to the same treatments; 2. any three of the following: etiology, course, social functioning, treatment

3.3 1. F; 2. T; 3. T; 4. T; 5. T; 6. F
3.4 1. F; 2. T; 3. T; 4. F

Key Terms

alternate-form reliability
behavioral assessment
BOLD
categorical classification
clinical interview
comorbidity
concurrent validity
construct validity
content validity
criterion validity
CT or CAT scan
diagnosis
Diagnostic and Statistical Manual of Mental Disorders (DSM)
dimensional diagnostic system
ecological momentary assessment (EMA)
electrocardiogram (EKG)

electrodermal responding
electroencephalogram (EEG)
functional magnetic resonance imaging (fMRI)
intelligence test
internal consistency reliability
interrater reliability
magnetic resonance imaging (MRI)
metabolite
Minnesota Multiphasic Personality Inventory (MMPI)
neurologist
neuropsychological tests
neuropsychologist
personality inventory
PET scan
predictive validity

projective hypothesis
projective test
psychological tests
psychophysiology
reactivity
reliability
Research Domain Criteria (RDoC)
Rorschach Inkblot Test
self-monitoring
standardization
stress
structured interview
test–retest reliability
Thematic Apperception Test (TAT)
validity

4 Research Methods in Psychopathology

LEARNING GOALS

1. Be able to define science and the scientific method.
2. Be able to describe the advantages and disadvantages of case studies, correlational designs, and experimental designs.
3. Be able to identify common types of correlational and experimental designs.
4. Be able to explain the standards and issues in conducting psychotherapy outcome research.
5. Be able to describe the basic steps in conducting a meta-analysis.

OUR ABILITY TO CONCEPTUALIZE and treat psychological disorders has improved vastly over the past 50 years. Nonetheless, important questions remain unanswered about the causes and treatments of psychological disorders. Therefore, it is important to pursue new discoveries using scientific research methods. This chapter discusses the methods used in psychopathology research.

Science and Scientific Methods

The term *science* comes from the Latin *scire*, meaning "to know." At its core, science is a way of knowing. More formally, it is the systematic pursuit of knowledge through observation. Science involves forming a theory and then systematically gathering data to test the theory.

A **theory** is a set of propositions meant to explain a class of observations. Usually, the goal of scientific theories is to understand cause–effect relationships. A theory permits the generation of more specific **hypotheses**—expectations about what should occur if a theory is true. For example, if the classical conditioning theory of phobias is valid, people with phobias should be more likely than those in the general population to have had traumatic experiences with the situations they fear, such as flying. By collecting such data, you could test this hypothesis.

People sometimes assume that a scientist formulates a theory by simply considering data that were previously collected and then deciding, in a rather straightforward fashion, that one way of thinking about the data is the most useful. Although some theory building follows this course, not all does. Theory building often involves creativity—a theory sometimes seems to leap into the scientist's head in a wonderful moment of insight. New ideas suddenly occur, and connections that were overlooked before are grasped. Formerly obscure observations might make a new kind of sense within the framework of the new theory.

What makes a good theory? A scientific approach requires that the theory and hypotheses be stated clearly and precisely. This is needed for scientific claims to be exposed to systematic tests that could negate the scientist's expectations. That is, regardless of how plausible a theory seems, it must be subject to disproof. Science proceeds by disproving theories, never by "proving theories." Consequently, it is not enough to assert that traumatic experiences during childhood cause psychological maladjustment in adulthood. This is no more than a possibility. According to a scientific point of view, a hypothesis must be amenable to systematic testing that could show it to be false. That is, the focus of testing is on disproving rather than proving a theory.

A set of principles must be considered in testing a theory. Each scientific observation must be replicable. Each facet of a study must be carefully defined so that findings can be replicated. Much of this depends on using assessments with strong reliability and validity, as discussed in Chapter 3. Beyond choosing measures carefully, though, researchers in psychopathology choose among different types of research designs. In this chapter, we discuss the pros and cons of some common types of research designs.

It is worth noting at the outset that many aspects of research involve ethical issues. For example, researchers must consider whether participants are fully informed, whether any coercion is involved in a study, and what the long-term implications of findings are. Ethical issues in the conduct of research are covered in Chapter 16.

As we review the theories and evidence about the causes of and treatments for psychological disorders, we will often encounter complexities and shortcomings in the research literature. Even if we knew all the variables controlling behavior—and no one would claim that we do—our ability to predict would be limited by many unexpected and uncontrollable factors that are likely to affect a person over a period of time. People do not behave in a social vacuum. Research participants and therapy clients live moment to moment in exquisitely complex interaction with others who themselves are affected on a moment-to-moment basis by hundreds of factors that are impossible to anticipate. We want to counsel humility, even awe, in an enterprise that tries to understand how things go awry with mental health.

Check Your Knowledge 4.1

True or false?
1. A good theory can be proven.
2. Researchers always build a theory by examining data, making rational assumptions, and then carefully testing the next small step—intuition is rarely involved.

3. Hypotheses are broader and more abstract than a theory is.

Approaches to Research on Psychopathology

In this section we describe the most common research methods in the study of psychopathology: the case study, correlational methods, and experimental methods. These methods will be seen in the studies described throughout this book, and we will describe some of the typical ways these different research methods are used in psychopathology research. Table 4.1 provides a summary of the strengths and weaknesses of each.

The Case Study

The **case study**, perhaps the most familiar method of observing human behavior, involves recording detailed information about one person at a time. The clinical cases described in the last chapter are examples of case studies. A comprehensive case study would cover developmental milestones, family history, medical history, educational background, employment history, marital history, social adjustment, personality, environment, and experiences in therapy across the life course.

Table 4.1 Research Methods in Psychopathology

Method	Description	Evaluation
Case study	Collection of detailed biographical information	Excellent source of hypotheses
		Can provide information about novel cases or procedures
		Can disconfirm a relationship that was believed to be universal
		Cannot provide causal evidence because alternative hypotheses cannot be eliminated
		May be biased by observer's theoretical viewpoint
Correlation	Study of the relationship between two or more variables, measured as they exist in nature	Widely used because we cannot manipulate many risk variables (such as personality, trauma, or genes) or diagnoses in psychopathology research with humans
		Often used by epidemiologists to study the incidence, prevalence, and risk factors of disorders in a representative sample
		Often used in behavioral genetics research to study the heritability of different disorders
		Cannot determine causality because of directionality and third-variable problems
Experiment	Includes a manipulated independent variable, a dependent variable, preferably at least one control group, and random assignment	Most powerful method for determining causal relationships
		Often used in studies of treatment
		Also used in analogue studies of the risk factors for psychological disorders
		Single-case experimental designs also common but can have limited external validity

Case studies lack the control and objectivity of other research methods. That is, the validity of the information gathered in a case study is sometimes questionable. The objectivity of case studies is limited because the clinician's paradigm will shape the kinds of information reported in a case study. To take one example, case studies by psychodynamic clinicians typically contain more information about the client's early childhood and parental conflicts than do reports by behavioral clinicians.

Despite their relative lack of control, case studies still play an important role in the study of psychological disorders. Specifically, the case study can be used:

1. To provide a rich description of a clinical phenomenon
2. To disprove an allegedly universal hypothesis
3. To generate hypotheses that can be tested through controlled research

We discuss each of these uses next.

The Case Study as a Rich Description Because it focuses on a single person, the case study can include much more detail than other research methods typically do. This is particularly helpful when a report covers a rare clinical phenomenon. Another typical use is to provide a detailed description of how a new intervention works. See Focus on Discovery 4.1 for an example of the level of detail that can be gathered with a case study.

The Case Study Can Disprove but Not Prove a Hypothesis Case histories can provide examples that contradict an assumed universal relationship. Consider, for example, the proposition that depressive episodes are always preceded by life stress. Finding even a single case of non–stress-related depression would negate the theory.

Even though case studies can disprove a hypothesis, they do not provide good evidence in support of a particular theory because they do not provide a way to rule out

FOCUS ON DISCOVERY 4.1

An Example of the Advantages and Disadvantages of Case Studies

Bipolar disorder, defined by episodes of mania, is one of the most severe of psychological illnesses. Manic episodes are defined by excessive goal-directed behavior accompanied by extreme happiness or anger, along with increased confidence, energy, talkativeness, and decreased need for sleep. Of particular concern, when people are manic they may not be aware of potential dangers, and so they are likely to engage in reckless behaviors, such as driving too fast, spending too much money, or being more sexual. Beyond the manic episodes, depressive episodes are also common for people with this disorder. The manic and the depressive symptoms both take a toll on jobs, relationships, and self-esteem.

Although bipolar disorder is believed to be inherited, sleep loss can trigger episodic symptoms of bipolar disorder (Colombo, Benedetti, Barbini et al., 1999). Wehr and his colleagues (1998) noted that electric lights might disrupt our natural sleep schedules and that this might be of particular concern for people with this disorder. Given this consideration, they theorized that a light–dark cycle that mirrored the natural rhythm of the sun might help protect sleep and thereby reduce symptoms of bipolar disorder. To test the influence of natural light–dark cycles on the course of bipolar disorder, Wehr's group tried a unique treatment idea: they asked a person with bipolar disorder to extend his hours of bedrest.

At the time the case study began, the patient was a 51-year-old married man who had worked as a chief engineer in a technology firm. He had always had a great deal of energy and drive. He reported that his mother had a history of depression. The patient developed depression in 1990 and was treated with two antidepressants. As is relatively common for people diagnosed with bipolar disorder (Ghaemi & Goodwin, 2003), the antidepressants triggered mild manic symptoms. In his case, though, the symptoms of depression and mania continued for more than 2 years, despite the addition of mood-stabilizing medications such as lithium and divalproex. Antidepressants were discontinued, but then he became depressed. When a new antidepressant was started, he developed manic symptoms again. Over a period of several years, he frequently shifted between depression and mania. During his manic periods, he was overly

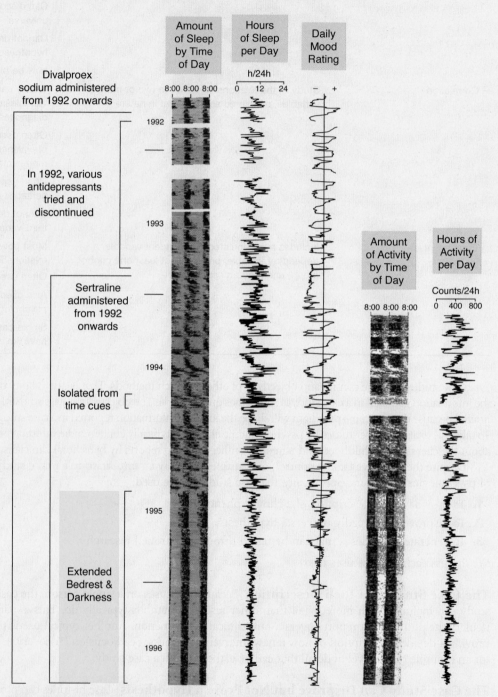

Figure 4.2 Sleep, mood, and activity patterns before and after a patient was treated with extended bedrest. Note that sleep, mood, and activity patterns improved once extended bedrest began in 1995. Adapted from Wehr (1998).

active, slept only 3–4 hours, and woke up before dawn. When he was depressed, he would spend long hours of the day inactive, then sleep for 10 or 12 hours, waking up late in the morning or even during the afternoon.

After several years of monitoring the client's symptoms and trying different medications, Wehr and his colleagues began the novel sleep/wake intervention in May 1995. For the first 3 months, the client slept in a bedroom on a research ward where lights could be carefully controlled. The room was sealed to protect against accidental light exposure. During the dark period, he was asked not to take part in any activities and even to avoid using the radio, TV, or telephone. During the first part of the intervention, he was asked to spend 14 hours resting in the dark each night. Over the next 18 months, the dark period was gradually reduced to 10 hours. Medications were kept stable throughout the sleep/wake intervention phase.

As shown in Figure 4.2, the number of hours per night that the client slept varied a good deal up until 1995, when the intervention began. At that point, the number of hours of sleep per night became much more routine. Also at that time, the amount of daily activity began to vary much less; the patient no longer displayed days of extreme inactivity or days of extreme hyperactivity. Most importantly, almost all of his mood ratings after the sleep/wake intervention began were in a neutral range, neither depressed nor manic. Hence the increased bedrest appeared to be an effective way to bolster the effects of medication.

Although the findings were encouraging, this case study leaves many questions unanswered. These include whether the critical ingredient in the intervention is time spent sleeping, time spent resting, or just a focus on calmer routines. It is also possible that something other than sleep/wake cycles changed for this patient during the period of the intervention, such that the symptom reductions were unrelated to sleep/wake. Perhaps most importantly, case studies can never reveal whether a treatment will work well for other patients.

Fortunately, several researchers have extended these findings. In other case studies (Wirz-Justice, Quinto, Cajochen et al., 1999) and uncontrolled studies (Barbini, Benedetti, Colombo et al., 2005), researchers have achieved good results with encouraging people with bipolar disorder to extend their time spent in bed. Other researchers have tried to help people with bipolar disorder to create more stable patterns of daily activities, along with improving sleep routines (Frank, Kupfer, Thase et al., 2005; Shen, Sylvia, Alloy et al., 2008; Totterdell & Kellett, 2008). Hence this early case report helped to generate interest in whether treatments focused on sleep could enhance the effects of medication in bipolar disorder. In short, case studies provide a way to illustrate new and interesting treatments. Case studies, though, cannot address whether treatment is the sole cause of the change, nor can they address whether findings can be applied to other people.

alternative hypotheses. To illustrate this problem, consider the sleep/wake intervention described in Focus on Discovery 4.1. Although it would be tempting to conclude that the therapy is effective, such a conclusion cannot be drawn legitimately because other factors could have produced the change. A stressful situation in the client's life may have resolved, or the client may have adopted better coping skills during the time period of the intervention. Thus, several plausible rival hypotheses could account for the clinical improvement. The data yielded by the case study do not allow us to determine the true cause of the change.

Using the Case Study to Generate Hypotheses Although the case study may not provide valid support for hypotheses, it does help generate hypotheses about causes and treatments for disorders. As they hear the life histories of many different clients, clinicians may notice patterns and then formulate important hypotheses that they could not have formed otherwise. For example, in his clinical work, Kanner (1943) noticed that some disturbed children showed a similar constellation of symptoms, including failure to develop language and extreme isolation from other people. He therefore proposed a new diagnosis—infantile autism—that was subsequently confirmed by larger-scale research and adopted into the DSM (see Chapter 13).

The Correlational Method

A great deal of psychopathology research relies on the **correlational method**. Correlational studies address questions of the form "Do variable X and variable Y vary together (co-relate)?" In correlational research, variables are measured as they exist in nature. This is distinct from experimental research (discussed later in this chapter), in which the researcher manipulates variables.

To illustrate the difference, consider that the role of stress in hypertension (high blood pressure) can be assessed with either a correlational or an experimental design. In a

Greg Smith/Cortis Images

Although the information yielded by a case study does not fare well as a source of evidence, it is an important source of hypotheses.

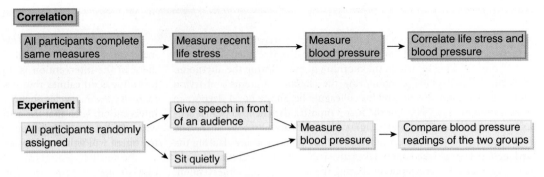

Figure 4.1 Correlational versus experimental studies.

correlational study, we might measure stress levels by interviewing people about their recent stressful experiences. Stress would then be correlated with blood pressure measurements collected from these same people. In an experimental study, in contrast, the experimenter might create stress in the laboratory; for example, some participants might be asked to give a speech to an audience about the aspect of their personal appearance that they find least appealing (see Figure 4.1). The key difference between these methods is whether or not a variable is manipulated. Psychopathologists will rely on correlational methods when there are ethical reasons not to manipulate a variable; for example, no researcher would try to manipulate genes, trauma, severe stressors, or neurobiological deficits in humans.

Numerous examples of **correlation** can be drawn from mental health research. For example, depression tends to correlate with anxiety; people who feel depressed tend to report feeling anxious. Comparisons of people with and without a diagnosis can be correlational as well. See Table 4.2 for a description of how such data might be coded. For example, two diagnostic groups may be compared to see how much stress was experienced before the onset of their disorders. In other words, questions are asked about relationships between a given diagnosis and some other variable; for example, "Is schizophrenia related to social class?" or "Are anxiety disorders related to neurotransmitter function?"

In the next sections, we discuss how to measure the relationship (correlation) between two variables, how to test whether the relationship is statistically and clinically significant, and some issues involved in determining whether variables are causally related. Then we discuss two specific types of research that tend to use correlational designs: epidemiology as well as behavior and molecular genetics.

Measuring Correlation The first step in determining a correlation is to obtain pairs of observations of the two variables in question. One example would be the height and weight of each participant. Another example would be the intelligence of mothers and daughters. Once such pairs of measurements are obtained, the strength of the relationship between the paired observations can be computed to determine the **correlation coefficient**, denoted by the symbol r. This statistic may take any value between -1.00 and $+1.00$, and it measures both the magnitude and the direction of a relationship. The higher the absolute value of r, the stronger the relationship between the two variables. That is, an r of either $+1.00$ or -1.00 indicates the strongest possible, or perfect, relationship, whereas an r of .00 indicates that the variables are unrelated. If the sign of r is positive, the two variables are said to be positively related; in other words, as the values for variable X increase, those for variable Y also tend to increase. Table 4.3 shows data for a correlation of $+.88$ between height and weight, indicating a very strong positive relationship; as height increases, so does weight. Conversely, when the sign of r is negative, variables are said to be negatively related; as scores on one variable increase, those for the other tend to decrease. For example, the number of hours spent watching television is negatively correlated with grade point average.

Table 4.2 Data for a Correlational Study with Diagnosis

Participant	Diagnosis	Stress Score
1	1	65
2	1	72
3	0	40
4	1	86
5	0	72
6	0	21
7	1	65
8	0	40
9	1	37
10	0	28

Note: Diagnosis of an anxiety disorder is coded as 1 if present and 0 if not present. Recent life stress is assessed on a 0–100 scale. Higher scores indicate greater recent stress. To make the point clearly, we present a smaller sample of cases than would be used in an actual research study. Notice that diagnosis is correlated with recent life stress. Patients with an anxiety disorder tend to have higher stress scores than people without an anxiety disorder. In this example, the correlation between stress and anxiety scores is +.60.

One way to think about the strength of a correlation is to plot the two variables. In Figure 4.3, each point represents the scores for a given person on variable *X* and variable *Y*. In a perfect correlation, all the points fall on a straight line; if we know the value of only one of the variables for a person, we can know the value of the other variable. Similarly, when the correlation is relatively large, there is only a small degree of scatter about the line of perfect correlation. The values tend to scatter increasingly far from the line as the correlations become lower. When the correlation reaches .00, knowledge of a person's score on one variable tells us nothing about his or her score on the other.

Statistical and Clinical Significance Thus far we have established that the magnitude of a correlation coefficient tells us the strength of a relationship between two variables. But scientists use **statistical significance** for a more rigorous test of the importance of a relationship. (Significance is considered with many different statistics. Here we focus on correlation coefficients, but significance is also relevant when we describe experiments below.) A statistically significant correlation is unlikely to have occurred by chance. A nonsignificant correlation may have occurred by chance, so it does not provide evidence for an important relationship. What do scientists mean by chance? Imagine that a researcher conducted the same study again and again. You would not expect to see exactly the same results every time. For example, there might be differences in who signed up for the study that would influence the pattern of findings. This random variation, or chance, must be considered in evaluating the findings of any study. When a correlation is not statistically significant, it is highly likely that no significant relationship will be observed if the study is repeated.

Table 4.3 Data for Determining a Correlation

	Height	Weight in Pounds
John	5'10"	170
Asher	5'10"	140
Eve	5'4"	112
Gail	5'3"	105
Jerry	5'10"	177
Gayla	5'2"	100
Steve	5'8"	145
Margy	5'5"	128
Gert	5'6"	143
Sean	5'10"	140
Kathleen	5'4"	116

Note: For this data set, the *r* of height and weight = +.88.

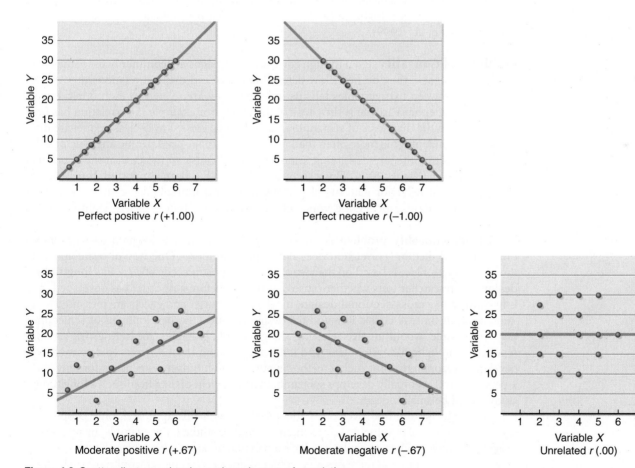

Figure 4.3 Scatter diagrams showing various degrees of correlation.

A statistical finding is usually considered significant if the probability that it is a chance finding is 5 or less in 100. This level of significance is called the alpha level, commonly written as $p < .05$ (the p stands for probability). In general, as the absolute size of the correlation coefficient increases, the result is more likely to be statistically significant. For example, a correlation of .80 (or –.80) is more likely to be significant than a correlation of .40.

Statistical significance is influenced not only by the size of the relationship between variables but also by the number of participants in a study. The fewer people studied, the larger the correlation needs to be to reach statistical significance. For example, a correlation of $r = .30$ is statistically significant when the number of observations is large—say, 300—but is not significant if only 20 observations were made. Thus, if the alcohol consumption of 30 men was studied and the correlation between depression and drinking was found to be .32, the correlation would not be statistically significant. The same correlation, however, would be significant if 300 men were studied.

Beyond statistical significance, it is important to consider **clinical significance.** Clinical significance is defined by whether a relationship between variables is large enough to matter. In a survey as large as the U.S. Census, almost every correlation you could conceive of would be statistically significant. Because of this issue, researchers also attend to whether a correlation is large enough to be of clinical significance. For example, one might want to see that a risk factor has a moderately strong relationship with the severity of symptoms. Clinical significance is also considered with statistics other than correlations. For a treatment effect to be considered clinically significant, a researcher might want to see that symptoms in the active treatment condition were decreased by 50 percent or that patients appeared comparable to those without disorder at the end of treatment. In other words, researchers should evaluate not only whether an effect is statistically significant but also whether the effect is large enough to be meaningful in predicting or treating a psychological disorder (Jacobson, Roberts, Berns et al., 1999).

Problems of Causality Even though correlational designs are commonly used, they have a critical drawback: they do not allow determination of cause–effect relationships. A large correlation between two variables tells us only that they are related to each other, but we do not know if either variable is the cause of the other. For example, a correlation has been found between the diagnosis of schizophrenia and social class; lower-class people are diagnosed with schizophrenia more often than middle- and upper-class people are. One possible explanation is that the stress of living in poverty could cause an increase in the prevalence of schizophrenia (Kwok, 2014). But a second hypothesis has been supported. It may be that the disorganized behavior patterns of persons with schizophrenia cause them to perform poorly in their occupational endeavors and thus to become impoverished (Dohrenwend & Dohrenwend, 1974).

The **directionality problem** is present in most correlational research designs—hence the often-cited dictum "correlation does not imply causation." One way of overcoming the directionality problem is based on the idea that causes must precede effects. In a **longitudinal design,** the researcher tests whether causes are present before a disorder has developed. This is in contrast to a **cross-sectional design,** in which the causes and effects are measured at the same point in time. A classic longitudinal design to study the development of schizophrenia, for example, would involve selecting a large sample of babies, measuring risk variables repeatedly throughout development, and following the sample for 45 years to determine who develops schizophrenia. But such a method would be prohibitively expensive, for only about 1 person in 100 eventually develops schizophrenia. The yield of data from such a longitudinal study would be small indeed.

The **high-risk method** overcomes this problem; with this approach, only people with above-average risk of developing schizophrenia would be studied. For example, many research programs involve studying people who have a parent diagnosed with schizophrenia (having a parent with schizophrenia increases a person's risk for developing schizophrenia). The high-risk method is also used to study several other disorders, and we will examine these findings in subsequent chapters.

Even if a high-risk study identifies a variable that precedes schizophrenia, a researcher still faces the **third-variable problem:** a third factor may have produced the correlation. Such factors are often labeled as *confounds*. Consider the following example, which points out an obvious third variable:

> One regularly finds a high positive correlation between the number of churches in a city and the number of crimes committed in that city. That is, the more churches a city has, the more crimes are committed in it. Does this mean that religion fosters crime, or does it mean that crime fosters religion? It means neither. The relationship is due to a particular third variable—population. The higher the population of a particular community, the greater . . . the number of churches and . . . the frequency of criminal activity. (Neale & Liebert, 1986, p. 109)

Psychopathology research offers numerous examples of third variables. Biochemical differences between people with and without schizophrenia are often reported. These differences could reflect the influence of medications used for schizophrenia or even dietary differences between groups; the differences might not reveal anything about the nature of schizophrenia. Are there ways to resolve the third-variable problem? Although some strategies can help reduce it, the solutions are only partially satisfactory. Take the example of diet as a potential confound in biochemical differences in schizophrenia. Researchers can try to control for diet in statistical analyses, but they may not measure the most important aspects of diet. It is not feasible to measure every possible confound. Because of the third-variable problem, causal claims cannot be made from correlational data.

In some epidemiological research, interviewers go door to door to conduct interviews.

© sturti/iStockphoto

One Example of Correlational Research: Epidemiological Research

Epidemiology is the study of the distribution of disorders in a population. That is, data are gathered about the rates of a disorder and its correlates in a large sample. Epidemiological research focuses on three features of a disorder:

1. **Prevalence.** The proportion of people with the disorder either currently or during their lifetime
2. **Incidence.** The proportion of people who develop *new* cases of the disorder in some period, usually a year
3. **Risk factors.** Variables that are related to the likelihood of developing the disorder

Epidemiological studies of risk factors are usually correlational studies because they examine how variables relate to each other without manipulating any of the variables.

Epidemiological studies are designed to be *representative* of the population being studied—researchers test a group of people who match the population on key characteristics, like gender, economic status, and ethnicity. Unfortunately, much of mental health research does not follow these principles but rather draws on samples that are not representative. For example, many studies use undergraduate samples. Undergraduates, though, are likely to be wealthier and more educated than the general population. If we only studied undergraduates with anxiety disorders, we could end up concluding that people with anxiety disorders are above average in intelligence. Other studies use samples drawn from treatment centers. But people who seek treatment may be those with the more severe forms of disorders. For example, estimates of suicide rates for a given disorder are much higher when measured in hospitalized samples as compared to rates in representative community samples. These types of bias can skew our perceptions of factors related to psychological disorders. Epidemiological studies, then, are needed to carefully identify risk variables and outcomes for disorders.

The National Comorbidity Survey–Replication is an example of one large-scale national survey that used structured interviews to collect information on the prevalence of several diagnoses (Kessler, Berglund, Demler et al., 2005). Parallel surveys in dozens of countries allow comparison of mental health prevalence and risk factors cross-nationally (Kessler, Angermeyer,

Epidemiological research has shown that mood disorders, anxiety disorders, and substance abuse are extremely common.

Table 4.4 Lifetime Prevalence Rates of Selected Diagnoses in the United States

Disorder	Male	Female	Total
Major depressive disorder	13.2	20.2	16.6
Bipolar I or II disorder	na	na	3.9
Dysthymia	1.8	3.1	2.5
Panic disorder	3.1	6.2	4.7
Specific phobia	11.1	13.0	12.1
Social phobia	8.9	15.8	12.5
Generalized anxiety disorder	na	na	5.7
Alcohol abuse	19.6	7.5	13.2
Drug abuse	11.6	4.8	7.9

Source: From data collected in the National Comorbidity Survey—Replication Study (Kessler et al., 2005).

Anthony et al., 2007). Table 4.4 shows some of the survey data that was gathered in the United States. The table presents lifetime prevalence rates—the proportion of people who experienced a disorder during their lifetime. From the table, we can see that major depression, alcoholism, and anxiety disorders are very common—so common, in fact, that as many as half (46.4 percent) of the people in the United States describe meeting criteria for a psychological disorder at some point during their lives. Knowing that psychological disorders will strike one out of every two people should help reduce stigma. People who experience the disorders may take comfort in knowing that so many other people struggle with similar issues.

Knowledge about risk factors may provide clues to the causes of disorders. For example, depression is about twice as common in women as in men. Thus, gender is a risk factor for depression. In Chapter 5, we will review theories about this gender difference. The results of epidemiological research may inform us about risk factors (like gender and social class) that can be more thoroughly investigated using other research methods.

Another Example of Correlational Research: Behavior and Molecular Genetics
Research on behavior genetics has relied on three basic methods to uncover whether a genetic predisposition for psychopathology is inherited—comparison of members of a family, comparison of pairs of twins, and investigation of adoptees. In each case, researchers are interested in whether relatives demonstrate similarity (correlations) in their patterns of disorder. Research on molecular genetics is designed to evaluate whether specific genes contribute to the presence of a disorder.

The **family method** can be used to study a genetic predisposition among members of a family because the average number of genes shared by two blood relatives is known. Children receive a random sample of half their genes from one parent and half from the other, so on average siblings as well as parents and their children share 50 percent of their genes. People who share 50 percent of their genes with a given person are called first-degree relatives of that person. Relatives who are not as closely related share fewer genes. For example, nephews and nieces share 25 percent of the genetic makeup of an uncle and are called second-degree relatives. If a predisposition for a psychological disorder can be inherited, a study of the family should reveal a relationship between the proportion of shared genes and the *concordance* of the disorder in relatives (that is, whether the relatives are matched on presence or absence of a disorder).

The starting point in such investigations is the collection of a sample of persons with the diagnosis in question. These people are referred to as **index cases** or **probands.** Then relatives are studied to determine the frequency with which the same diagnosis might be applied to them. If a genetic predisposition to the disorder being studied is present, first-degree relatives of the index cases should have the disorder at a rate higher than that found in the general population. This is the case with schizophrenia: about 10 percent of the first-degree relatives of index cases with schizophrenia can be diagnosed as having this disorder, compared with about 1 percent of the general population.

Although the methodology of family studies is clear, the data they yield are not always easy to interpret. For example, children of parents with agoraphobia—people suffering from a fear of being in places from which it would be hard to escape if they were to become highly anxious—are themselves more likely than average to have agoraphobia. Does this mean that a predisposition for this anxiety disorder is genetically transmitted? Not necessarily. The greater number of family members with agoraphobia could reflect the child-rearing practices and modeling of the phobic parents. In other words, family studies show that agoraphobia runs in families but not necessarily that a genetic predisposition is involved.

In the **twin method,** both **monozygotic (MZ) twins** and **dizygotic (DZ) twins** are compared. MZ, or identical, twins develop from a single fertilized egg and are genetically the same. DZ, or fraternal, pairs develop from separate eggs and are on average 50 percent alike genetically, no more alike than are any two siblings. MZ twins are always of the same sex, but DZ twins can be either the same sex or opposite in sex. Twin studies begin with diagnosed cases and then search for the presence of the disorder in the other twin. When the twins are alike diagnostically, they are said to be concordant. To the extent that a predisposition for a psychological disorder can be inherited, **concordance** for the disorder should be greater in genetically identical MZ pairs than in DZ pairs. When the MZ concordance rate is higher than the DZ rate, the characteristic being studied is said to be heritable. Heritability estimates range from 0 (no genetic contribution) to 1 (100% genetic contribution). We will see in later chapters that the concordance for many forms of psychopathology is higher in MZ twins than in DZ twins.

The **adoptees method** studies children who were adopted and reared completely apart from their biological parents. Though infrequent, findings from this method are more clear-cut because the child is not raised by the parent with a disorder. If a high frequency of agoraphobia was found in children reared apart from their parents who also had agoraphobia, we would have convincing support for the heritability of the disorder. In another adoptee method called **cross-fostering**, children are adopted and reared completely apart from their biological parents. In this case, however, the adoptive parent has a particular disorder, not the biological parent. The adoptee method is also used to examine gene–environment interactions. For example, one study found that adoptees who had a biological parent with antisocial personality disorder (APD) (Mudd, Cerone, Schiaffino et al., 2001) and were raised in an unhealthy adoptive family (e.g., parental conflict, abuse, alcohol/drugs in the adoptive family) were more likely to develop APD than two other groups of adoptees: (1) adoptees who had a biological parent with APD but were raised in a healthy family and (2) adoptees who had no biological parent with APD but were raised in an unhealthy adoptive family (Cadoret, Yates, Troughton et al., 1995). Thus, genes (APD in a biological parent) and environment (unhealthy adoptive family) worked together to increase the risk for developing antisocial personality disorder.

Molecular genetics methods are designed to identify specific genes or combinations of genes that may be associated with the presence of a particular disorder in a large population of people. One approach used in molecular genetics is called an **association study**. In these studies, researchers examine the relationship between a specific allele (i.e., different forms of the same gene; see Chapter 2) and a trait or behavior in the population. Because the researchers are measuring a specific allele rather than the general chromosome location, association studies can be precise. Association studies became common as technologies for measuring alleles became more affordable. In Chapter 14, we will describe a particular allele called APOE-4 that is related to late-onset Alzheimer's disease. Not all people with Alzheimer's have this allele, and not all people who have APOE-4 develop Alzheimer's. Still, there is an association between this allele and Alzheimer's disease (Williams, 2003).

Genome-wide association studies (**GWAS,** pronounced *gee-waas*) are a special type of association research. Using powerful computers, researchers look at all 20,000–25,000 genes to isolate differences in the sequence of genes between persons diagnosed with a disorder and a control group. Millions of sequences can be examined. The genome of individuals can be obtained from a simple swab on the inside of the cheek. The saliva is then analyzed to reveal millions of sequences across the thousands of genes for each person. GWAS studies require very large samples. GWAS studies with thousands of participants are available for schizophrenia, bipolar disorder, autism, depression, and Alzheimer's disease (Sullivan, Daly, & O'Donovan, 2012). GWAS researchers are most often looking for genetic variations called single nucleotide polymorphisms, or SNPs, but newer studies also focus on copy number variations (see Chapter 2). If certain SNPs are found more often in the group of people with certain diagnoses, such as schizophrenia, they are said to be associated with schizophrenia.

Quick Summary

Science is the systematic pursuit of knowledge through observation. The first step of science is to define a theory and related hypotheses. A good theory is precise and could be disproven.

The case study is an excellent way of examining the behavior of a single person in rich detail and of generating hypotheses that can be evaluated by controlled research. Sometimes the evidence disconfirms a theory; other times it illustrates a rare disorder or technique. But findings from a case study may or may not be valid—they may be biased by the observer's theories, and the patterns observed in one case may not apply to others. Furthermore, the case study cannot provide satisfactory evidence concerning cause–effect relationships because alternative hypotheses are not examined.

Correlational studies allow a researcher to gather data about variables and to see if these variables covary. No variables are manipulated; rather, the researcher assesses whether a naturally occurring relationship is large enough to appear statistically significant and clinically meaningful. Psychopathologists are forced to make heavy use of the correlational method because there are many key variables, including diagnosis, genes, trauma, and neurobiological deficits, that they do not have the freedom to manipulate in humans. But correlational findings are clouded by third-variable and directionality problems. High-risk designs, in which people with elevated risk of developing a psychological disorder are recruited and followed over time, overcome the directionality problem.

Studies of epidemiology and behavior genetics often use correlational designs. Researchers use epidemiological studies to assess how common disorders are (incidence and prevalence) and what risk factors are associated with them. Behavior genetics research uses the family method, to see how the presence of a disorder varies by the proportion of genes shared by family members; the twin method, to see whether monozygotic twins with more shared genes are at greater risk for developing a disorder than are dizygotic twins; and the adoptees method, to help separate genetic and environmental effects. Molecular genetics research includes genome-wide association studies to identify SNPs associated with a given disorder.

Check Your Knowledge 4.2

Answer the questions.
1. Which of the following are good uses of case studies (circle all that apply)?
   a. to illustrate a rare disorder or treatment
   b. to show that a theory does not fit for everyone
   c. to prove a model
   d. to show cause and effect
2. Correlational studies involve:
   a. manipulating the independent variable
   b. manipulating the dependent variable
   c. manipulating the independent and dependent variable
   d. none of the above
3. What is the most central problem that is unique to correlational studies, regardless of how carefully a researcher designs a study?
   a. Findings are qualitative rather than statistical.
   b. It is impossible to know which variable changes first.

c. Third variables may explain a relationship observed.
d. Findings may not generalize.
4. Incidence refers to:
   a. the number of people who will develop a disorder during their lifetime
   b. the number of people who report a disorder at the time of an interview
   c. the number of people who develop a disorder during a given time period
   d. none of the above
5. In behavior genetics studies, researchers can rule out the influence of parenting variables most carefully if they conduct studies using the:
   a. correlational method
   b. family method
   c. twin method
   d. adoptees method

The Experiment

The **experiment** is the most powerful tool for determining causal relationships. It involves the **random assignment** of participants to conditions, the manipulation of an **independent variable,** and the measurement of a **dependent variable.** We will begin with a brief overview of the basic features of an experiment. We will provide more detail on specific issues in designing experiments when we describe treatment outcome studies, the most common form of experiment in psychopathology research.

As an introduction to the basics of experimental research, consider a study of how emotional expression relates to health (Pennebaker, Kiecolt-Glaser, & Glaser, 1988). In this experiment, 50 undergraduates came to a laboratory for 4 consecutive days. On each of the 4 days, half the students wrote a short essay about a past traumatic event. They were instructed as follows:

> *During each of the four writing days. I want you to write about the most traumatic and upsetting experiences of your entire life. You can write on different topics each day or on the same topic for all four days. The important thing is that you write about your deepest thoughts and feelings. Ideally, whatever you write about should deal with an event or experience that you have not talked with others about in detail.*

The remaining students also came to the laboratory each day but wrote essays describing topics like their daily activities, a recent social event, the shoes they were wearing, and their plans for the rest of the day.

Information about how often the participants used the university health center was available for the 15-week period before the study began and for the 6 weeks after it had begun. Figure 4.4 shows these data. Members of the two groups had visited the health center about equally before the experiment. After writing the essays, however, the number of visits declined for students who wrote about their traumatic experiences and increased for the remaining students. (This increase may have been due to seasonal variation in rates of visits to the health center. The second measure of number of visits was taken in February, just before midterm exams.) From these data the investigators concluded that expressing emotions has a beneficial effect on health. The idea that daily writing (journaling) might help people cope with difficult experiences and emotions has become popular, and this article has been cited more than 1000 times.

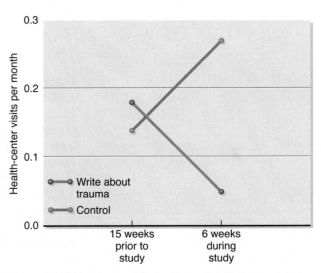

Figure 4.4 Health-center visits for the periods before and during the experiment. Visits for students who wrote about traumas decreased, while visits for those who wrote about mundane events actually rose. After Pennebaker (1988).

Basic Features of Experimental Design The emotional expression study just discussed illustrates many of the basic features of an experiment:

1. The investigator manipulates an independent variable. In this study, the independent variable was the writing topic.

2. Participants are assigned to the two conditions (traumatic experiences versus mundane happenings) by random assignment.

3. The researcher measures a dependent variable that is expected to vary with conditions of the independent variable. The dependent variable in this study was the number of visits to the health center.

4. Differences between conditions on the dependent variable are called the **experimental effect**. In this example, the experimental effect is the difference in the mean number of visits for those who wrote about traumatic experiences compared to those who wrote about mundane happenings.

Internal Validity **Internal validity** refers to the extent to which the experimental effect can be attributed to the independent variable. For a study to have internal validity, the researchers must include at least one **control group.** The control group does not receive the experimental treatment and is needed to claim that the effects of an experiment are due to the independent variable. In the Pennebaker study, the control group wrote about mundane happenings. The data from a control group provide a standard against which the effects of an independent variable can be assessed. We will describe control groups in more detail as we discuss treatment outcome studies.

The inclusion of a control group does not ensure internal validity, however. Random assignment is also important. To randomly assign participants in a two-group experiment, for example, the researchers could toss a coin for each participant. If the coin turned up heads, the participant would be assigned to one group; if tails, to the other group. Random assignment helps ensure that groups are similar on variables other than the independent variable.

Consider a treatment study in which participants can enroll in their choice of two experimental conditions—psychotherapy or medication. In this study, the researcher cannot claim that group differences are the result of treatment because a competing hypothesis cannot be disproven: patients in the two conditions might have differed in baseline characteristics such as their willingness to discuss difficult emotional issues or their beliefs about medications. This study design is poor because the researchers did not use random assignment. Without true random assignment, potential confounds make results hard to interpret, so that internal validity can be limited.

External Validity **External validity** is defined as the extent to which results can be generalized beyond the study. If investigators find that a particular treatment helps a particular group of patients, they will want to conclude that this treatment will be effective for other similar patients, at other times, and in other places. For example, Pennebaker and his colleagues would hope that their findings would generalize to other instances of emotional expression (e.g., confiding to a close friend), to other situations, and to people other than undergraduates.

Determining the external validity of the results of an experiment is extremely difficult. For example, participants in studies often behave in certain ways because they are being observed, and thus results that are produced in the laboratory may not automatically be produced in the natural environment. External validity may also be threatened by including only a select group of persons in a study, such as college students (Coyne, 1994) or Caucasian middle-class Americans (Hall, 2001). Indeed, in a review of articles published in six journals of the American Psychological Association between 2003 and 2007, 68 percent of participants in studies were from the United States and 96 percent were from Western industrialized countries (Arnett, 2008). Researchers must be alert to the extent to which they can claim findings are likely to generalize to people and settings other than those studied in the experiment. Often they must perform similar studies in new settings or with a different sample to test whether findings generalize.

Quick Summary

The experimental method entails manipulatimg an independent variable and measuring the effect on a dependent variable. Generally, participants are randomly assigned to one of at least two groups: an experimental group, which experiences the active condition of the independent variable, and a control group, which does not. The researcher tests to see if the independent variable had an effect (the experimental effect) by looking for differences between the experimental and control groups on the dependent variable.

Internal validity refers to whether an effect can be confidently attributed to the independent variable. External validity refers to whether experimental effects can be generalized to situations and people outside of this specific study. Experimental designs can provide internal validity, but external validity is sometimes of concern. Correlational studies can provide solid external validity but poorer internal validity.

One Example of Experimental Research: Treatment Outcome Research Treatment outcome research is designed to address a simple question: does treatment work? The clear answer is yes. Here we will focus on the issues in testing psychotherapy, but many of these same issues must be considered in evaluating medication treatments.

Hundreds of studies have examined whether people who receive psychotherapy fare better than those who do not. In meta-analyses of more than 300 studies, researchers have found that there is a moderately positive effect of treatment. About 75 percent of people who enter treatment achieve at least some improvement (Lambert & Ogles, 2004). As shown in Figure 4.5, these effects appear to be more powerful than the passage of time or support from friends and family. On the other hand, it is also clear from this figure that therapy does not always work. That is, about 25 percent of people do not improve in therapy.

What standards must treatment outcome research meet to be seen as valid? Several different working groups have come up with slightly different answers to this question. At a minimum, most researchers agree that a treatment study should include the following criteria:

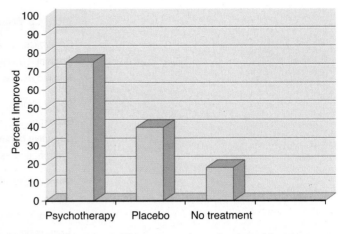

Figure 4.5 Summary of the percent of people who achieve improvement across outcome for psychotherapy, placebo, and no treatment across studies. Drawn from Lambert (2004). Psychotherapeutically speaking—updates from the Division of Psychotherapy (29). Downloaded from http://www.divisionofpsychotherapy.org/updates.php

- A clear definition of the sample being studied, such as a description of diagnoses
- A clear description of the treatment being offered, as in a treatment manual (described below)
- Inclusion of a control or comparison treatment condition
- Random assignment of clients to treatment or comparison conditions
- Reliable and valid outcome measures (see Chapter 3 for definitions of reliability and validity)
- A large enough sample for statistical tests

Studies in which clients are randomly assigned to receive active treatment or a comparison (either no treatment, a placebo, or another treatment) are called **randomized controlled trials (RCTs)**. In this type of experiment, the independent variable is the treatment and the dependent variable is the clients' outcome.

The American Psychological Association (APA) publishes a report on the therapies that have received empirical support using these standards (Task Force on Promotion and Dissemination of Psychological Procedures, 1995). The goal is to help clinicians, consumers, managed care agencies, and insurance companies draw more easily on this rapidly growing literature about **empirically supported treatments**. Some of the therapies the APA has found to have empirical support are shown in Table 4.5. We will describe empirically supported treatments throughout this book when we discuss specific psychological disorders.

Some aspects of the APA report on empirically supported treatments have been hotly debated. For example, a treatment's failure to appear on the APA list of empirically supported treatments (Table 4.5) could simply reflect a lack of careful studies. As you can see, most of the treatments listed are cognitive behavioral. Research on other treatments has not met the APA's strict research standards.

We now turn to some of the major decisions researchers face as they design treatment outcome studies. These issues include defining the treatment procedures, choosing the best possible control group, and recruiting an appropriate sample of patients. Once a treatment has been shown to work well in a tightly controlled treatment outcome study, effectiveness research is designed to test how well treatments fare in the real world. As evidence accrues that a treatment works, dissemination is needed to ensure that the treatment is adopted by therapists in the community. Throughout the process of testing a treatment, there is growing acknowledgment of the need to consider whether some treatments may be harmful (see Focus on Discovery 4.2).

Defining the Treatment Condition: The Use of Treatment Manuals Treatment manuals are detailed books on how to conduct a particular psychological treatment; they provide

Table 4.5 Examples of Empirically Supported Treatments for Adult Disorders

Generalized anxiety disorder	*Anorexia nervosa*
Cognitive therapy	Family-based treatment
Applied relaxation	
	Depression
Social phobia	Cognitive therapy
Exposure	Behavior therapy
Cognitive behavioral group therapy	Interpersonal psychotherapy
Systematic desensitization	Problem-solving therapy
	Self-management/self-control therapy
Simple phobia	
Exposure	*Schizophrenia*
Guided mastery	Family psychoeducation
Systematic desensitization	Cognitive behavior therapy
	Social learning/token economy programs
Obsessive-compulsive disorder	Cognitive remediation
Exposure and response prevention	Social skills training
Cognitive therapy	Behavioral family therapy
	Supported employment programs
Agoraphobia	Assertive community treatment
Exposure	
Cognitive behavior therapy	*Alcohol abuse and dependence*
	Community reinforcement approach
Panic	
Cognitive behavior therapy	*Relationship distress*
	Behavioral couples therapy
Posttraumatic stress disorder	Emotion-focused therapy
Prolonged exposure	Insight-oriented couples therapy
Cognitive processing therapy	
	Sexual dysfunctions
Bulimia	Partner-assisted sexual skills training
Cognitive behavior therapy	
Interpersonal psychotherapy	*Borderline personality disorder*
	Dialectical behavior therapy

Drawn from Task Force on Promotion and Dissemination of Psychological Procedures (1995).

Troubled people may talk about their problems with friends or seek professional therapy. Treatment is typically sought by those for whom the advice and support of family or friends have not provided relief.

specific procedures for the therapist to follow at each stage of treatment. With manuals, someone reading a psychotherapy study can have an idea of what happened in therapy sessions. The use of manuals is widely recommended for psychotherapy research (e.g. Nathan & Gorman, 2002) and for graduate training in clinical psychology (Crits-Christoph, 1995).

Treatment manuals are designed to help therapists achieve greater uniformity in how they conduct therapy. This leads to some debate. Some have expressed concern that manuals might constrain therapists to such an extent that they might not be sufficiently sensitive to a client's unique concerns (Haaga & Stiles, 2000). Evidence suggests that the manuals seem to be more helpful for novice therapists than for experienced therapists (Multon, Kivlighan, & Gold, 1996). The challenge, then, might be to provide manuals that give therapists both flexibility and a clear road map. One way to do so is to develop manuals that give therapists lots of freedom—for example, promoting the goal of exposure treatment for anxiety disorders but also giving a menu of options of how to conduct exposure (Kendall & Beidas, 2007).

FOCUS ON DISCOVERY 4.2

Can Therapy Be Harmful?

Despite the substantial evidence that therapies, on average, tend to be helpful, this does not mean that they help everyone. Indeed, a small number of people may be in worse shape after therapy. Estimating how often therapy is harmful is not easy. Up to 10 percent of people are more symptomatic after therapy than they were before therapy began (Lilienfeld, 2007). Does this mean that therapy harmed them? Maybe not. Without a control group, it is hard to know whether symptoms would have worsened even without therapy. Unfortunately, few researchers report the percentage of people who worsened in the different branches of treatment trials.

Nonetheless, it is important to be aware that several treatments have been found to be harmful to some people. Table 4.6 lists treatments identified as resulting in worsened outcomes in randomized controlled trials or in multiple case reports (Lilienfeld, 2007). We should note that harmful effects are not exclusive to therapy; the U.S. Food and Drug Administration has issued warnings that antidepressants and antiseizure medications can increase the risk of suicidality and that antipsychotic medications can increase the risk of death among the elderly.

Table 4.6 Examples of Treatments Found to Be Harmful in Multiple Studies or Case Reports

Treatment	Negative Effects
Critical incident stress debriefing	Heightened risk for posttraumatic symptoms
Scared Straight	Exacerbation of conduct problems
Facilitated communication	False accusations of child abuse against family members
Attachment therapies (e.g., rebirthing)	Death and serious injury to children
Recovered-memory techniques	Production of false memories of trauma
Dissociative identity disorder-oriented therapy	Induction of "alter" personalities
Grief counseling for people with normal bereavement reactions	Increases in depressive symptoms
Expressive-experiential therapies	Exacerbation of painful emotions
Drug Abuse Resistance Education (DARE) programs	Increased intake of alcohol and cigarettes

Drawn from Lilienfeld (2007).

Defining Control Groups To illustrate the importance of a control group, consider a study of a particular therapy for anxiety. Let us assume that persons with anxiety disorders receive therapy and that, from the start to the end of a 16-week program, their anxiety symptoms diminish. With no control group against which to compare the improvement, we cannot argue that changes are due to the treatment. The improvement in anxiety could have been due to factors other than the treatment, such as the passage of time or support from friends. Without a control group, any changes during treatment are difficult to interpret.

Many different types of control groups can be used in treatment outcome research. A no-treatment control group allows researchers to test whether the mere passage of time helps as much as treatment does. A stricter test compares the treatment group to a **placebo** control group. In psychotherapy research, the placebo might be a therapy that consists of support and encouragement (the "attention" component) but not the active ingredient of therapy under study (e.g., exposure to a feared stimulus in a behavioral treatment of a phobia). In medication studies, a placebo might be a sugar pill that is described to the patient as a proven treatment. A placebo condition allows researchers to control for expectations of symptom relief. The strictest type of design includes an active-treatment control group in which researchers compare the new treatment against a well-tested treatment. This type of design allows researchers to make comparative statements about two treatments.

Some have argued that placebos and no-treatment controls are unethical, in that active treatment is being withheld from patients who might suffer as a consequence (Wolitzky, 1995). An active-treatment control group may not raise ethical concerns, but it can be hard to show a difference between different types of active treatments. Choosing the best control group, then, is a difficult decision!

A treatment manual provides specific procedures for a therapist to use in working with a client. They are standard in treatment outcome studies.

Table 4.7 Percent of People Who Sought Treatment in the Past 12 Months for Emotions, Nerves, Mental Health, or Drug/Alcohol Concerns by Country (N = 84,850)

Country	Percent of People Seeking Treatment
Nigeria	1.6
China	3.4
Italy	4.3
Lebanon	4.4
Mexico	5.1
Colombia	5.5
Japan	5.6
Spain	6.8
Ukraine	7.2
Germany	8.1
Israel	8.8
Belgium	10.9
Netherlands	10.9
France	11.3
New Zealand	13.8
South Africa	15.4
United States	17.9

Drawn from a World Health Organization study reported by Wang, Aguilar-Gaxiola et al. (2007).

When including a placebo condition in a medication trial, researchers use a **double-blind procedure**. That is, the psychiatrist and the patient are not told whether the patient receives active medication or a placebo, so as to reduce bias in evaluating outcomes. A double-blind procedure can be hard to implement. Treatment providers and patients may guess who is getting the active treatment because medications are much more likely to produce side effects than are placebos (Salamone, 2000). Researchers often measure whether participants guessed that they were in the placebo condition, as well as how much they expected their treatment to help them.

The **placebo effect** refers to a physical or psychological improvement that is due to a patient's expectations of help rather than to any active ingredient in a treatment. The placebo effect is often significant and even long-lasting. For example, a meta-analysis of 75 research studies revealed that 29.7 percent of patients with depression improved after they received a placebo (Walsh, Seidman, Sysko et al., 2002). Among depressed patients who respond to antidepressant medication, many may actually be showing a placebo response (Kirsch, 2000). Because the placebo effect can be so powerful, many researchers continue to believe this is an important type of control condition to consider using.

Defining a Sample Randomized controlled trials (RCTs) typically focus on treating people who have a certain DSM diagnosis, such as major depressive disorder or panic disorder. Most studies, though, also exclude many potential participants, a process that can limit the external validity of findings. For example, researchers might exclude people who have more than one disorder or who are acutely suicidal (for ethical reasons). Some participants might be unwilling to enroll in a study in which they might be assigned to an ineffective treatment (the control condition). As it turns out, some studies exclude almost as many people as they enroll (Westen, Novotny, & Thompson-Brenner, 2004).

One of the major gaps in treatment outcome studies has been the failure to include people from diverse cultural and ethnic backgrounds. Most studies enroll predominantly white, non-Latino clients, so samples are often not diverse enough to examine how treatment effects vary for differing groups of people. This problem may reflect a more general tendency for members of minority groups and those from non-Western cultures to be less likely to seek treatment. For example, people from minority groups are about half as likely to receive mental health treatment as are white, non-Hispanic adults in the United States (U.S. Department of Health and Human Services, 2008). As shown in Table 4.7, there are also dramatic differences between countries in rates of treatment seeking among people with psychological disorders (Wang, Aguilar-Gaxiola, Alonso et al., 2007). Cultural and ethnic differences in willingness to seek treatment, particularly treatment in a research study, can limit the relevance of findings to minority populations.

Overall, far too few studies have been done on whether treatments are valid for any specific minority group (Chambless & Ollendick, 2001). Nonetheless, several studies have tested whether empirically supported treatments work well for culturally diverse populations. For example, a group version of interpersonal psychotherapy for depression was found to be efficacious for people living in Ugandan villages (Bolton, Bass, Neugebauer et al., 2003). Several studies support the efficacy of cognitive behavioral therapy (CBT) for anxiety disorders among African American clients (Miranda et al., 2006). Two studies have found comparable efficacy of CBT for childhood anxiety disorders across ethnicities, and findings of several studies indicate that the effects of treatments for childhood disruptive disorders, including CBT and family therapy, do not differ by ethnicity (Miranda, Bernal, Lau et al., 2005). In sum, at least some results from treatment outcome studies appear to generalize to minority populations. See Focus on Discovery 4.3 for other ways to consider culture and ethnicity in treatment.

Assessing How Well Treatments Work in the Real World RCTs, typically conducted in academic research settings, are designed to determine the **efficacy** of a treatment, that is, whether a treatment works under the purest of conditions. Because of the kinds of concerns just raised, some RCTs might not inform us about how these treatments work with broader samples in the hands of nonacademic therapists. That is, the external validity of controlled RCTs is sometimes criticized. We need to determine not just the efficacy of a treatment but

FOCUS ON DISCOVERY 4.3

The Importance of Culture and Ethnicity in Psychological Treatment

We have already mentioned that racial and ethnic minorities are less likely to seek mental health care (Wang et al., 2005). Even when they do seek care, they are more likely to stop treatment prematurely, and they are less likely to be provided state-of-the-art effective treatments (U.S. Department of Health and Human Services, 2001). A growing body of research is considering how to make treatments more applicable and effective for people from diverse backgrounds (Lopez, Barrio, Kopelowicz et al., 2012; Snowden, 2012). As we consider this area, we do want to raise one caveat about the risks of stereotyping. People from minority groups can differ as much from each other as their racial or ethnic group differs from another racial or ethnic group. It is important to consider the degree to which the person is *assimilated* into the majority culture and holds the same values as the majority culture (Sue & Sue, 2008).

Many minority clients report that they would prefer to see someone from a similar background (Lopez, Lopez, & Fong, 1991). Many clients believe that therapists of similar background, perhaps even of the same gender, will understand their life circumstances better and more quickly. Despite this assumption, it has *not* been demonstrated that better outcomes are achieved when client and therapist are similar in race or ethnicity (Griner & Smith, 2006) or that clients are more likely to continue treatment when there is such a match (Maramba & Nagayama-Hall, 2002). **Cultural competence** may matter more than ethnic matching. A therapist who is not a member of the same racial or ethnic group as the client might still understand the client and create a good therapeutic relationship if he or she is familiar with the client's culture (U.S. Department of Health and Human Services, 2002).

In developing cultural competence, therapists need to consider that many members of minority groups have encountered prejudice and racism, and many have been subjected to hate crimes (U.S. Department of Health and Human Services, 2002). Many families come to the United States from other countries to escape political turmoil and persecution, and these traumas may intensify the risks of posttraumatic stress disorder and emotional distress (Sue & Sue, 2008). Cultural background may shape values and beliefs about emotion (Boiger & Mesquita, 2012), as well as how to interact with authorities like treatment providers. These values and beliefs will influence the therapeutic interview. For example, Asian Americans may initially describe stress in physical terms, such as headaches and fatigue, even though they are aware of emotional symptoms and will endorse those when asked directly (Chang, Hahm, Lee et al., 2008). Latino cultural values may inhibit men from expressing weakness and fear (USDHHS, 2002). Native American children may avoid making eye contact with authorities as a way of expressing respect (Everett, Proctor, & Cartmell, 1989). Hence cultural background may shape not only experiences relevant to the development of symptoms but also how people will communicate in treatment.

Even though there is a small amount of evidence that established treatments are helpful for minority populations, many theorists argue

Although many minority clients report that they would like to see a minority therapist, cultural sensitivity appears to be more important to outcome than a match of ethnicity between client and therapist.

Lew Merrim/Photo Researchers, Inc.

that treatments should be adapted to be more culturally sensitive. In a meta-analysis, 76 studies comparing culturally competent psychotherapy to standard psychotherapy were identified (Griner & Smith, 2006). The culturally adapted interventions were consistently beneficial compared to the standard psychotherapies.

As an example of modifying the content of CBT for depression to be more specific to the concerns of African American women, one manual includes innovative suggestions, such as a focus on the social isolation, family concerns, and trauma that are common in this population, as well as strategies to challenge the myths of the superhuman African American woman. Among African American women, the tailored intervention was rated more positively and produced a larger reduction in depressive symptoms than a traditional CBT intervention (Kohn, Oden, Munoz et al., 2002).

Another approach to developing culturally sensitive interventions is to draw on the strengths of a given culture. For example, Latino culture emphasizes family values and spirituality. One team modified CBT for depression to incorporate more emphasis on family values. Puerto Rican adolescents who received culturally sensitive CBT demonstrated significantly more decrease in depressive symptoms than did those who received interpersonal psychotherapy or a control condition (Rossello, Bernal, & Rivera-Medina, 2008).

In sum, therapists can and should learn to work with people from many different backgrounds. This quest is helped by researchers who are adapting treatments for people from diverse backgrounds.

also its **effectiveness**—that is, how well the treatment works in the real world. Studies of effectiveness might include clients with a broader range of problems and provide less intensive supervision of therapists. Effectiveness studies often rely on briefer assessments as well. As you might expect, when clients have more serious diagnostic complications and providers have less support, psychotherapies and even medications tend to look less powerful than they do in careful efficacy studies (Rush, Trivedi, Wisniewski et al., 2006). Effectiveness studies do provide support for CBT in treating anxiety (Wade, Treat, & Stuart, 1998) and depression (Persons, Bostrom, & Bertagnolli, 1999), and for several psychotherapies as supplements to medication for bipolar disorder (Miklowitz, Otto, Frank et al., 2007).

The Need for Dissemination of Treatment Outcome Findings At this point, hundreds of studies have shown that certain psychological treatments work well. Many treatments have fared well not just in efficacy studies but in effectiveness studies as well. Even so, many therapists in the community report that they do not use empirically supported treatments. There is a large gap between science and practice in this field, and several approaches are being used to narrow this gap.

Dissemination is the process of facilitating adoption of efficacious treatments in the community, most typically by offering clinicians guidelines about the best available treatments along with training on how to conduct those treatments. Major policy efforts in England and in the U.S. Veterans Administration have focused on dissemination (McHugh & Barlow, 2010).

Even with better dissemination efforts, some clinicians find that the currently available empirically supported treatments are not applicable for some unique symptom presentations or for some clients from diverse backgrounds. What should a therapist do when a given client has a profile that does not fit with the available treatment studies? Evidence-based practice is a way of combining knowledge gained from treatment outcome research with clinical expertise, so that therapists can be sensitive to unique characteristics influencing the therapy process. In doing so, it is hoped that therapists consider the scientific evidence carefully, particularly knowing that inappropriate treatments could cause harm (Stuart & Llienfeld, 2007).

Check Your Knowledge 4.3

Circle all that apply for the following questions.
1. In an experimental design, the researcher manipulates:
   a. the independent variable
   b. the dependent variable
2. Dr. Jones is interested in whether a new treatment for autism will be helpful. She recruits 30 participants, and she randomly assigns 15 of them to receive drug X and 15 to receive a placebo. After 3 weeks of treatment, she measures social engagement. In this study, the independent variable is:
   a. medication condition
   b. drug X
   c. social engagement
   d. autism

3. The dependent variable in question 2 is:
   a. treatment
   b. drug X
   c. social engagement
   d. autism
4. Which of the following are the elements of an RCT by definition?
   a. randomization
   b. a comparison condition
   c. medications
   d. double-blind procedures
5. The goal of effectiveness studies is to determine whether a treatment works
   a. under the best possible conditions
   b. under real-world conditions

Analogue Experiments The experimental method is the clearest way to determine cause–effect relationships. Even though experiments are typically used to test treatments, there are many situations in which the experimental method cannot be used to understand the causes of psychological disorders. Why?

Suppose that a researcher has hypothesized that emotionally charged, overly dependent maternal relationships cause generalized anxiety disorder. An experimental test of this hypothesis would require randomly assigning infants to either of two groups of mothers. The mothers in one group would undergo an extensive training program to ensure that they would be able to create a highly emotional atmosphere and foster overdependence in children. The mothers in the second group would be trained not to create such a relationship with their children. The researcher would then wait until the participants in each group reached adulthood and determine how many of them had developed generalized anxiety disorder. Clearly, this is unethical.

In an effort to take advantage of the power of the experimental method, researchers sometimes use an **analogue experiment**. Investigators attempt to create or observe a related phenomenon—that is, an analogue—in the laboratory to allow more intensive study. Because a true experiment is conducted, results with good internal validity can be obtained. The problem of external validity arises, however, because the researchers are no longer studying the actual phenomenon of interest.

In one type of analogue study, temporary symptoms are produced through experimental manipulations. For example, lactate infusion can elicit a panic attack, hypnotic suggestion can produce brief symptoms of blindness similar to those seen in conversion disorder, and threats to self-esteem can produce anxiety or sadness. If mild symptoms can be experimentally induced by such manipulations, this may provide clues into the causes of more severe symptoms.

In another type of analogue study, participants are selected because they are considered similar to people with certain diagnoses. Thousands of studies, for example, have been conducted with college students who received high scores on questionnaire measures of anxiety or depression. (Not all of these studies are experimental; some use correlational designs.)

Studies of college students with mild symptoms may not provide a good analogue for major psychological disorders.

A third type of analogue study involves using animals as a way to understand human behavior. For example, researchers found that dogs that were exposed to electrical shocks the dogs could not control developed many of the symptoms of depression, including seeming despair, passivity, and decreased appetite (Seligman, Maier, & Geer, 1968). Similarly, researchers interested in studying anxiety disorders in humans sometimes study how animals become conditioned to fear previously unthreatening stimuli (Grillon, 2002). Such animal models have helped us understand more about the neurobiology of depression and anxiety disorders in humans.

The key to interpreting such studies lies in the validity of the analogue. Is a stressor encountered in the laboratory fundamentally similar to the death of a parent or other serious stressors? Are distressed college students similar to people with clinically diagnosable depression? Are lethargy and decreased eating in dogs akin to depressive symptoms in humans? Some would argue against such approaches overall, even when researchers are careful to discuss the limits of generalizability. For example, Coyne (1994) has argued that clinical depression is caused by different processes from those that cause common distress. He would argue that analogue studies with undergraduates have poor external validity.

We believe that analogue studies can be very helpful but that findings from these types of studies must be considered conjointly with studies that do not rely on analogues. Science often depends on comparing the results of experimental analogue studies to those of longitudinal correlational studies. For example, analogue studies have shown that people with depression respond more negatively to laboratory stressors (an analogue of life stress) than do those without depression, and correlational studies have shown that severe life events predict the onset of clinical depression. Because the findings from correlational and analogue studies complement each other, this provides strong support for life event models of depression. Analogue studies can provide the precision of an experiment (high internal validity), whereas correlational studies provide the ability to study very

Harlow's famous analogue research examined the effects of early separation from the mother on infant monkeys. Even a cloth surrogate mother is better than isolation for preventing subsequent emotional distress and depression.

important influences that cannot be manipulated, like the influence of death and trauma (high external validity).

Single-Case Experiments We have been discussing experimental research with groups of participants, but experiments do not always have to be conducted on groups. In **single-case experimental design**, the experimenter studies how one person responds to manipulations of the independent variable. Unlike the traditional case studies described above, single-case experimental designs can have high internal validity.

Chorpita, Vitali, and Barlow (1997) provide an example of how single-case studies can provide well-controlled data. They describe their treatment of a 13-year-old girl with a phobia (intense fear) of choking, such that she was no longer able to eat solid foods. At times, her fear was so intense that she would experience a fast heart rate, chest pain, dizziness, and other symptoms. She reported that the most frightening foods were hard foods, such as raw vegetables.

A behavioral treatment was designed based on exposure, a common strategy for treating anxiety. During the first 2 weeks, baseline assessments were taken of the amount of different foods eaten, along with her level of discomfort in eating those foods. Discomfort ratings were made on a subjective units of distress scale (SUDS) ranging from 0 to 9. Figure 4.6 shows her SUDS ratings and eating behavior over time for each food group. During the third week, she was asked to begin eating foods she described as mildly threatening—crackers and cookies—in three 4-minute blocks each day. The authors hoped that exposure to feared foods would reduce her anxiety. Despite this intervention, the patient's SUDS ratings and food consumption did not improve. When the therapist talked with the client and her parents, he discovered that the client was eating only the absolute minimum of foods, such that she was not getting enough exposure to the feared stimulus. To increase her exposure to foods, reinforcement was added to the program—her parents were instructed to give her ice cream at the end of any day in which the patient had consumed at least three servings of the target food. Within a week, she reported being able to consume crackers and cereals without distress. Gradually, she was asked to begin eating more frightening foods. One week she was asked to begin consuming soft vegetables, pasta, and cheese, followed the next week by meat, and the next week by raw vegetables, salad, and hard fruit. As shown by the graphs, as exposure to to each new food group was introduced, the client experienced a reduction in SUDS ratings within the next week; these effects do not appear to have been due simply to time or maturation, as anxiety was reduced only after the client was first exposed to the new food group. The repeated decrements in anxiety are hard to explain using any variable other than treatment. Gains were maintained through a 19-month follow-up.

In one form of single-case design, referred to as a **reversal design** or **ABAB design**, the participant's behavior must be carefully measured in a specific sequence:

1. An initial time period, the baseline (A)
2. A period when a treatment is introduced (B)
3. A reinstatement of the conditions of the baseline period (A)
4. A reintroduction of the treatment (B)

If behavior in the experimental period is different from that in the baseline period, reverses when the treatment is removed, and re-reverses when the treatment is again introduced, there is little doubt that the manipulation, rather than chance or uncontrolled factors, has produced the change. Hence, even though there is no control group, there are time periods that serve as control comparisons for the treatment (Hersen & Barlow, 1976).

The reversal technique cannot always be employed, however, because the initial state of a participant may not be recoverable. Remember that most treatments aim to produce enduring change, so just removing an intervention may not return a person to the pretreatment state. This reversal technique, then, is most applicable when researchers believe that the effects of their manipulation are temporary.

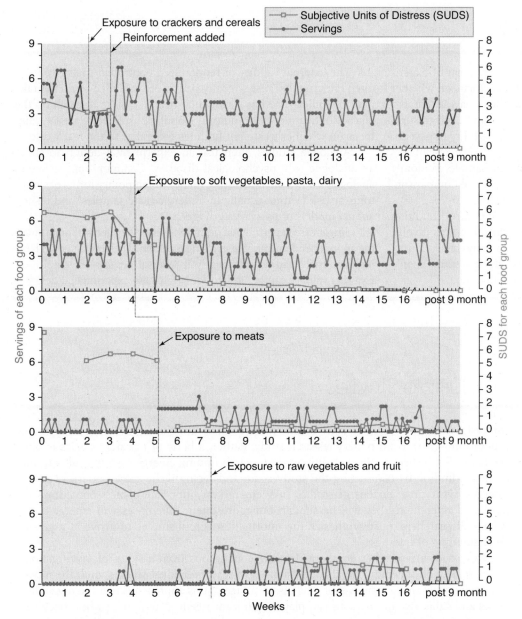

Figure 4.6 Effects of exposure treatment and reinforcement for food phobia in a single-case design. Note the rapid shifts in SUDS ratings as exposure for each new food group is introduced. From Chorpita et al., "Behavioral treatment of choking phobia in an adolescent: An experimental analysis," *Journal of Behavioral Therapy and Experimental Psychiatry, 38,* 307–315, copyright © 1997.

Perhaps the biggest drawback of single-case designs is the potential lack of external validity. The fact that a treatment works for a single person does not necessarily imply that it will be effective for others. Findings may relate to a unique aspect of that one person. Some researchers use single-case experimental research to decide whether research with larger groups is warranted. Other researchers conduct a series of single-case experiments to see if findings generalize. In doing so, it is important to include participants who differ. With replication across varied participants, single-case designs can provide a strong test of hypotheses. Indeed, single-case experimental research can be used as evidence that a treatment is efficacious. The APA task force (1995) considers a treatment to have gained empirical support if it has shown success compared to a well-designed control condition in at least nine single-case experiments.

Quick Summary

Treatment outcome studies are the most common form of experiment in the psychopathology field. These studies focus on whether a given treatment works well. A number of groups have attempted to provide clear standards for psychotherapy research and to summarize the current state of knowledge about the validity of psychotherapy. It is generally agreed that treatment outcome researchers should use treatment manuals, clearly define the sample, randomly assign participants to the active treatment or control comparison, and include reliable and valid measures of outcome.

There is some debate about the best type of control condition in that no-treatment and placebo-condition control groups involve withholding active treatments for those who may be suffering. Placebo conditions, however, are informative in that many people demonstrate symptom reduction after taking a placebo.

The external validity of randomized controlled trials (RCTs) is often criticized because so many people are excluded or do not take part in studies. There is a particular need for more research on the efficacy of treatments for minority populations. Effectiveness studies focus on whether treatment findings generalize to the real world.

Analogue studies often use an experimental design to study an analogue to a psychological disorder. Common approaches in analogue studies include testing milder or temporary forms of symptoms or risk factors (usually in undergraduate samples) and testing animal models of psychopathology.

Single-case experimental designs observe the effects of manipulating an independent variable in a single person. These designs can have high internal validity, particularly if reversal designs are employed. External validity can be limited for single-case experimental designs.

Integrating the Findings of Multiple Studies

Understanding the pros and cons of different research designs should suggest a natural conclusion—there is no perfect research study. Rather, a body of research studies is often needed to test a theory. When an important research finding emerges, a key goal is to replicate the finding by conducting the study again and seeing if the same pattern of results emerges. Over time, dozens of studies may emerge on important topics. Sometimes the results of different studies will be similar, but more often, differences will emerge across studies. Researchers must synthesize the information across studies to arrive at a general understanding of findings.

How does a researcher go about drawing conclusions from a series of investigations? A simple way of drawing general conclusions is to read individual studies, mull them over, and decide what they mean overall. The disadvantage of this approach is that the researcher's biases and subjective impressions can play a significant role in determining what conclusion is drawn. It is fairly common for two scientists to read the same set of studies and reach very different conclusions.

Meta-analysis was developed as a partial solution to this problem (Smith, Glass, & Miller, 1980). The first step in a meta-analysis is a thorough literature search, so that all relevant studies are identified. Because these studies have typically used different statistical tests, meta-analysis then puts all the results into a common scale, using a type of statistic called an *effect size*. For example, in treatment studies, the effect size offers a way of standardizing the differences in improvement between a therapy group and a control group so that the results of many different studies can be averaged. Figure 4.7 summarizes the steps in a meta-analysis.

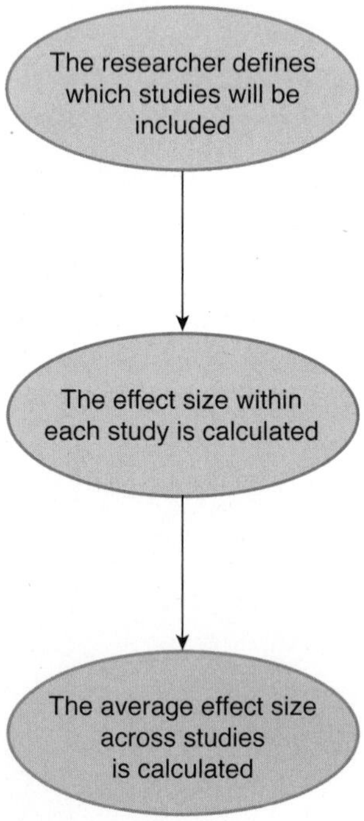

In their often-cited report, Smith and colleagues (1980) meta-analyzed 475 psychotherapy outcome studies involving more than 25,000 patients and 1,700 effect sizes; they came to conclusions that have attracted considerable attention and some controversy. Most importantly, they concluded that psychotherapies produce more improvement than does no treatment. Specifically, treated patients were found to be better off than almost 80 percent of untreated patients. Subsequent meta-analyses have confirmed that therapy appears to be effective (Lambert & Ogles, 2004).

The researcher defines which studies will be included

The effect size within each study is calculated

The average effect size across studies is calculated

Figure 4.7 Steps in conducting a meta-analysis.

Meta-analysis has been criticized primarily because researchers sometimes include studies that are of poor quality. For example, Smith and colleagues gave equal weight to all studies, so that a poorly controlled outcome study (such as one that did not evaluate what the therapists actually did in each session) received as much weight as a well-controlled one (such as a study in which therapists used a manual that specified what they did with each research participant). When Smith and colleagues attempted to address this problem by comparing the effect sizes of good versus poor studies and found no differences, they were further criticized for the criteria they employed in separating the good from the not so good (Rachman & Wilson, 1980). O'Leary and Wilson (1987) concluded that the ultimate problem is that someone has to make a judgment of good versus poor quality in research and that others can find fault with that judgment. A good meta-analysis, though, will be clear about the criteria for including or excluding studies.

Table 4.8 provides another example of a meta-analysis. In this meta-analysis, researchers integrated the findings of 27 epidemiological studies conducted in Europe on the 12-month prevalence of psychological disorders (Wittchen & Jacobi, 2005). Across these studies, more than 155,000 participants were interviewed. Prevalence estimates from the different studies were fairly varied. Tallying the findings across studies should give a stronger estimate of how common the disorders are.

Table 4.8 An Example of a Meta-Analysis: One-Year Prevalence Rates for Psychological Disorders across 27 European Studies

DSM-IV Diagnosis	Number of Studies	Combined N	12-Month Prevalence (%) Across the Combined Sample	Range of Prevalence Estimates Within Different Studies
Alcohol dependence	12	60,891	3.3	0.1–6.6
Illicit substance dependence	6	28,429	1.1	0.1–2.2
Psychotic disorders	6	27,291	0.9	0.2–2.6
Major depressive disorder	17	152,044	6.4	3.1–10.1
Bipolar I disorder	6	21,848	0.8	0.2–1.1
Anxiety disorders	12	53,597	1.6	0.7–3.1
Somatoform disorders	7	18,894	6.4	1.1–11
Eating disorders	5	19,761	4.8	0.2–0.7

Note: In this meta-analysis, researchers combined the findings of 27 major epidemiological studies on the 12-month prevalence of psychological disorders in European countries. Across these studies, more than 155,000 participants were interviewed. Researchers were able not only to determine the percentage of participants who met criteria for diagnoses but also to illustrate that there is a broad range of prevalence estimates across different studies.

Source: Adapted from Wittchen and Jacobi (2005).

Check Your Knowledge 4.4

Choose the best answer for each question.

1. Single-case experimental designs may lack:
   a. internal validity
   b. external validity
2. Correlational studies may lack:
   a. internal validity
   b. external validity

3. The step in meta-analysis that has received extensive criticism is:
   a. determining which studies should be included
   b. calculating the effect size of each study
   c. calculating the average effect size across studies
   d. none of the above

Summary

Science and Scientific Methods

- Science involves forming a theory and developing hypotheses based on that theory, and then systematically gathering data to test the hypotheses. It is important for researchers to replicate findings from a given study, which requires being precise about the methods used.

Approaches to Research on Psychopathology

- Common methods for studying psychopathology include case studies, correlational studies, and experimental studies. Each method has strengths and weaknesses.

Case Studies

- Case studies provide detailed descriptions of rare phenomena or novel procedures. Case studies also can disconfirm that a relationship is universal and can generate hypotheses that can be tested through controlled research. Case studies, however, may not always be valid, and they are of limited value in providing evidence to support a theory.

Correlational Research

- Correlational methods are the most common way to study the causes of psychological disorders, because we cannot manipulate most of the major risk factors in psychopathology, nor can we manipulate diagnosis.
- Conclusions drawn from cross-sectional correlational studies cannot be interpreted in cause–effect terms because of the directionality problem. Longitudinal studies help address which variable came first but can still suffer from the third-variable problem.
- One form of correlational study, epidemiological research, involves gathering information about the prevalence and incidence of disorders in populations and about risk factors that relate to higher probability of developing a disorder. Epidemiological studies avoid the sampling biases seen in studies of people drawn from undergraduate psychology classes or from treatment clinics.
- Studies of behavior genetics often rely on correlational techniques as well. The most common behavior genetics methods include the family method, the twin method, and the adoptees method. Molecular genetics research includes association studies and genome-wide association studies (GWAS) to identify specific genes that are related to a disorder.

Experimental Research

- In the experimental method, the researcher randomly assigns people to an experimental group or a control group. The effects of the independent variable on a dependent variable are then tested. Treatment outcome studies and analogue studies are common types of experimental research in psychopathology. Single-case experimental designs can provide well-controlled data.
- Generally, experimental methods help enhance internal validity, but correlational methods sometimes offer greater external validity.
- Research on the efficacy of various forms of psychological treatments has been conducted for many decades. Overall, this research suggests that about 80 percent of people gain some improvement from therapy. Therapy also seems to be more helpful than a placebo or the passage of time.
- Efforts have been made to define standards for research on psychotherapy trials and to summarize current knowledge on which psychological treatments work. These standards typically include the need to use a treatment manual, to randomly assign participants to treatment or a control condition, to define the sample carefully, and to use reliable and valid outcome measures. It is hoped that efforts to summarize these findings will help disseminate the best available therapeutic practices to clinicians, clients, and insurance companies.
- Researchers have also begun to identify treatments that may cause harm.
- Many people are excluded from or will not take part in clinical trials, and cultural diversity is lacking in most trials. A small number of studies demonstrate that established psychotherapies can be helpful with minority populations.
- A broader concern is that a gap exists between what happens in the research world and the real world. Efficacy research focuses on how well therapies work in carefully controlled experiments, whereas effectiveness research focuses on how well therapies work in the real world with a broader array of clients and therapists.

Integrating the Findings of Multiple Studies

- Meta-analysis is an important tool for reaching conclusions from a group of research studies. It entails putting the statistical comparisons from single studies into a common format—the effect size—so the results of many studies can be averaged.

Answers to Check Your Knowledge Questions

4.1 1. F; 2. F; 3. F
4.2 1. a and b; 2. d; 3. c; 4. c; 5. d

4.3 1. a; 2. a; 3.c; 4. a and b; 5. b
4.4 1. b; 2. a; 3. a

Key Terms

ABAB design
adoptees method
analogue experiment
association study
case study
clinical significance
concordance
control group
correlation
correlation coefficient
correlational method
cross-fostering
cross-sectional design
cultural competence

dependent variable
directionality problem
dissemination
dizygotic (DZ) twins
double-blind procedure
effectiveness
efficacy
empirically supported treatments
epidemiology
experiment
experimental effect
external validity
family method

genome-wide association studies (GWAS)
high-risk method
hypothesis
incidence
independent variable
index cases
internal validity
longitudinal design
meta-analysis
monozygotic (MZ) twins
placebo
placebo effect
prevalence

probands
random assignment
randomized controlled trials (RCTs)
reversal designs
risk factor
single-case experimental design
statistical significance
theory
third-variable problem
treatment outcome research
twin method

5 Mood Disorders

Clinical Case: Mary

Mary M., a 38-year-old mother of four children, had been deeply depressed for about 2 months when she first went to see a psychologist. Three years earlier, she had returned to work when health care bills made it hard for her family to get by on her husband's income as a high school teacher. About 7 months before her visit to the psychologist, she was laid off from her job as an administrative assistant, which was a serious blow to the family's finances. She felt guilty about the loss of her job and became preoccupied with signs of her overall incompetence. Each night, she struggled for more than an hour to fall asleep, only to wake up frequently throughout the night. She had little appetite and as a result had lost 10 pounds. She also had little energy for and no interest in activities that she had enjoyed in the past. Household chores became impossible for her to do, and her husband began to complain. Their marriage had already been strained for 2 years, and her negativity and lack of energy contributed to further arguments. Finally, realizing that Mary's symptoms were serious, Mr. M. cajoled her into making an appointment with a psychologist. (You will read about the outcome of Mary's treatment later in this chapter.)

MOOD DISORDERS INVOLVE DISABLING disturbances in emotion—from the extreme sadness and disengagement of depression to the extreme elation and irritability of mania. In this chapter, we begin by discussing the clinical description and the epidemiology of the different mood disorders. Next, we consider various perspectives on the etiology of these disorders, and then we consider approaches to treating them. We conclude with an examination of suicide, an action far too often associated with mood disorders.

Clinical Descriptions and Epidemiology of Mood Disorders

The DSM-5 recognizes two broad types of **mood disorders**: those that involve only depressive symptoms and those that involve manic symptoms (bipolar disorders). Table 5.1 presents a summary of the symptoms of each of these disorders. We will begin by discussing the depressive disorders, and then we will turn to the bipolar disorders. Within each, we will describe the core signs, the formal criteria for the specific disorders, and then the epidemiology and consequences of these disorders. After covering the clinical description and epidemiology of depressive and bipolar diagnoses, we describe the DSM-5 specifiers (subtypes) that are used to further define depressive disorders and bipolar disorders.

Depressive Disorders

The cardinal symptoms of depression include profound sadness and/or an inability to experience pleasure. Most of us experience sadness during our lives, and most of us say that we are "depressed" at one time or another. But most of these experiences do not have the intensity and duration to be diagnosable. The author William Styron (1992) wrote about his depression: "Like anyone else I have always had times when I felt deeply depressed, but this was something altogether new in my experience—a despairing, unchanging paralysis of the spirit beyond anything I had ever known or imagined could exist."

Ron Hoskins/Getty Images

In an interview with Oprah Winfrey, David Letterman talked about his personal battle with depression, saying "You get on an elevator and the bottom drops out, and you can't stand looking at the sun light, you can't wait to get back in bed at night. . . . It's a sink hole."

The symptoms of depression are varied. When people develop a depressive disorder, their heads may reverberate with self-recriminations. Like Mary, described in the Clinical Case, they may become focused on their flaws and deficits. Paying attention can be so exhausting that they have difficulty absorbing what they read and hear. They often view things in a very negative light, and they tend to lose hope. Initiative may disappear. Social withdrawal is common; many prefer to sit alone and be silent. Some people with depression neglect their appearance. When people become utterly dejected and hopeless, thoughts about suicide are common.

Physical symptoms of depression are also common, including fatigue and low energy as well as physical aches and pains. These symptoms can be profound enough to convince afflicted persons that they must be suffering from some serious medical condition, even though the symptoms have no apparent physical cause (Simon, Von Korff, Piccinelli et al., 1999).

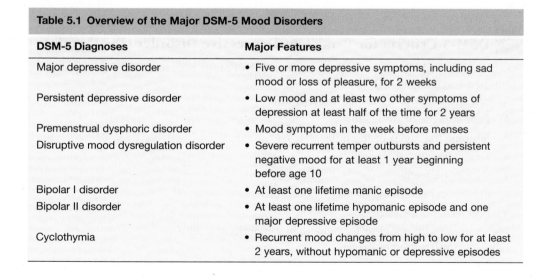

Table 5.1 Overview of the Major DSM-5 Mood Disorders

DSM-5 Diagnoses	Major Features
Major depressive disorder	• Five or more depressive symptoms, including sad mood or loss of pleasure, for 2 weeks
Persistent depressive disorder	• Low mood and at least two other symptoms of depression at least half of the time for 2 years
Premenstrual dysphoric disorder	• Mood symptoms in the week before menses
Disruptive mood dysregulation disorder	• Severe recurrent temper outbursts and persistent negative mood for at least 1 year beginning before age 10
Bipolar I disorder	• At least one lifetime manic episode
Bipolar II disorder	• At least one lifetime hypomanic episode and one major depressive episode
Cyclothymia	• Recurrent mood changes from high to low for at least 2 years, without hypomanic or depressive episodes

● DSM-5 Criteria for Major Depressive Disorder

Sad mood or loss of pleasure in usual activities.
At least five symptoms (counting sad mood and loss of pleasure):

- Sleeping too much or too little
- Psychomotor retardation or agitation
- Weight loss or change in appetite
- Loss of energy
- Feelings of worthlessness or excessive guilt
- Difficulty concentrating, thinking, or making decisions
- Recurrent thoughts of death or suicide

Symptoms are present nearly every day, most of the day, for at least 2 weeks. Symptoms are distinct and more severe than a normative response to significant loss.

Some people with depression have trouble falling asleep and staying asleep. Others find themselves sleeping for more than 10 hours but still feeling exhausted.

Although people with depression typically feel exhausted, they may find it hard to fall asleep and may wake up frequently. Other people sleep throughout the day. They may find that food tastes bland or that their appetite is gone, or they may experience an increase in appetite. Sexual interest disappears. Some may find their limbs feel heavy. Thoughts and movements may slow for some (**psychomotor retardation**), but others cannot sit still—they pace, fidget, and wring their hands (**psychomotor agitation**).

Major Depressive Disorder The DSM-5 diagnosis of **major depressive disorder (MDD)** requires five depressive symptoms to be present for at least 2 weeks. These symptoms must include either depressed mood or loss of interest and pleasure. As shown in the DSM-5 criteria, additional symptoms must be present, such as changes in sleep, appetite, concentration or decision making, feelings of worthlessness, suicidality, or psychomotor agitation or retardation.

MDD is an **episodic disorder**, because symptoms tend to be present for a period of time and then clear. Even though episodes tend to dissipate over time, an untreated episode may stretch on for 5 months or even longer. Some people improve enough that they no longer meet the criteria for diagnosis of MDD but continue to experience subclinical depression for years (Judd et al., 1998).

Major depressive episodes tend to recur—once a given episode clears, a person is likely to experience another episode. About two-thirds of people with an episode of major depression will experience at least one more episode during their lifetime (Solomon et al., 2000). The average number of episodes is about four (Judd, 1997). With every new episode that a person experiences, his or her risk for experiencing another episode goes up by 16 percent (Solomon et al., 2000).

Persistent Depressive Disorder People with **persistent depressive disorder** are chronically depressed—more than half of the time for at least 2 years, they feel blue or derive little pleasure from usual activities and pastimes. In addition, they have at least two of the other symptoms of depression. The central feature of this diagnosis is the chronicity of symptoms, which has been shown to be a stronger predictor of poor outcome than the number of symptoms. Among people who have experienced depressive symptoms for at least 2 years, those who do and do not have a history of major depressive disorder appear similar in their symptoms and treatment response (McCullough, Klein, Keller et al., 2000). Persistent depressive disorder is similar to a DSM-IV-TR diagnosis of dysthymia.

Kirsten Dunst's personal experience with major depressive disorder (MDD) provided her with insight for her role as an actress in the award-winning film Melancholia. One out of every five women will experience an episode of depression during her lifetime.

DSM-5 Criteria for Persistent Depressive Disorder (Dysthymia)

Depressed mood for most of the day more than half of the time for 2 years (or 1 year for children and adolescents).
At least two of the following during that time:
- Poor appetite or overeating
- Sleeping too much or too little
- Low energy
- Poor self-esteem
- Trouble concentrating or making decisions
- Feelings of hopelessness

The symptoms do not clear for more than 2 months at a time.
Bipolar disorders are not present.

FOCUS ON DISCOVERY 5.1

Gender Differences in Depression

Women are twice as likely as men are to experience major depression and persistent depressive disorder, and the gender ratio is particularly pronounced in countries and cultural groups with more traditional gender roles (Seedat et al., 2009). For example, this gender difference does not hold between Jewish adults, because depression is more common among Jewish men than among other men (Levav, Kohn, Golding et al., 1997). In ethnic and cultural groups where a gender difference is present, it typically begins to emerge during early adolescence and is consistently present by late adolescence. Some of you might wonder if these findings just reflect a tendency for men to be less likely to describe symptoms. So far, evidence does not support that idea (Kessler, 2003). Although a fair amount of research has focused on hormonal factors that could explain the vulnerability of women, findings have been mixed for this idea, too (Brems, 1995). Several social and psychological factors may help explain this gender difference (Nolen-Hoeksema, 2001):

- Twice as many girls as boys are exposed to childhood sexual abuse.
- During adulthood, women are more likely than men to be exposed to chronic stressors such as poverty and caretaker responsibilities.
- Acceptance of traditional social roles among girls may intensify self-critical attitudes about appearance. Adolescent girls worry more than adolescent boys about their body image, a factor that appears tied to depression (Hankin & Abramson, 2001).

The gender difference in depression does not emerge until adolescence. At that time, young women encounter many stressors and more pressure concerning social roles and body image, and they tend to ruminate about the resulting negative feelings.

- Traditional social roles may interfere with pursuit of some potentially rewarding activities that are not considered "feminine."
- Exposure to childhood and chronic stressors, as well as the effects of female hormones, could change the reactivity of the HPA axis, a biological system guiding reactions to stress.
- A focus on gaining approval and closeness within interpersonal relationships, which is more commonly endorsed by women, may intensify reactions to interpersonal stressors (Hankin, Mermelstein, & Roesch, 2007).
- Social roles promote emotion-focused coping among women, which may then extend the duration of sad moods after major stressors. More specifically, women tend to spend more time ruminating about sad moods or wondering about why unhappy events have occurred. Men tend to spend more time using distracting or action-focused coping, such as playing a sport or engaging in other activities that shake off the sad mood. As we discuss when we review cognitive factors in depression later in this chapter, a fair amount of research suggests that rumination will intensify and prolong sad moods.

In all likelihood, gender differences in depression are related to multiple factors. In considering these issues, bear in mind that men are more likely to demonstrate other types of disorders, such as alcohol and substance abuse as well as antisocial personality disorder (Seedat et al., 2009). Hence, understanding gender differences in psychopathology is likely to require attending to many different risk factors and syndromes.

Other DSM-5 Depressive Disorders The DSM-5 includes two depressive disorders that were not listed as mood disorders in the DSM-IV-TR. First, **disruptive mood dysregulation disorder** is a newly defined depressive disorder. Second, **premenstrual dysphoric disorder** has been moved from the DSM-IV appendix on conditions for further study to the main diagnostic section. We briefly discuss the rationale for disruptive mood dysregulation, a diagnosis specific to children and adolescents, in Focus on Discovery 13.4. Because so little is known, we do not discuss these two diagnoses further.

Epidemiology and Consequences of Depressive Disorders MDD is one of the most common psychological disorders. One large-scale epidemiological study estimated that 16.2 percent of people in the United States meet the criteria for diagnosis of MDD at some point in their lives. Although prevalence estimates are not yet available for the DSM-5 diagnosis of persistent depressive disorder, we do know that chronic forms of depression are rarer than MDD: about 2.5 percent of people meet the criteria for dysthymia as defined by DSM-IV-TR during their lives (Kessler, Berglund, Borges et al., 2005).

MDD and persistent depressive disorder are both twice as common among women as among men (Seedat et al., 2009; see Focus on Discovery 5.1 for a discussion of possible reasons for this gender difference). Socioeconomic status also matters—that is, MDD is three times as common among people who are impoverished compared to those who are not (Kessler, Berglund, Borges et al., 2005).

The prevalence of depression varies considerably across cultures. In a major cross-cultural study using the same diagnostic criteria and structured interview in each country, prevalence of MDD varied from a low of 6.5 percent in China to a high of 21 percent in France (Bromet, Andrade, Hwang et al., 2011). It is tempting to assume that differences in prevalence rates by country indicate a strong role for culture. It turns out that differences between countries in rates of depression may be fairly complex. As described in Focus on Discovery 5.2, one factor may be distance from the equator. Rates of winter depression, or seasonal affective disorder, are higher farther from the equator, where days are shorter. There is also a robust correlation of per-capita fish consumption with depression; countries with more fish consumption, such as Japan and Iceland, have much lower rates of MDD and bipolar disorder (Hibbeln, Nieminen, Blasbalg et al., 2006). Undoubtedly, cultural and economic factors, such as family cohesion and wealth disparity, play an important role in rates of depression as well.

The symptom profile of a depressive episode also varies across cultures, and one likely reason is the differences in cultural standards regarding acceptable expressions of emotional

FOCUS ON DISCOVERY 5.2

Seasonal Affective Disorder: The Winter Blues

Criteria for the seasonal specifier of MDD specify that a person experiences depression during two consecutive winters and that the symptoms clear during the summer. These winter depressions appear to be much more common in northern than in southern climates; while less than 2 percent of people living in sunny Florida report these patterns, about 10 percent of people living in New Hampshire report seasonal affective disorder (Rosen et al., 1990).

For mammals living in the wild, a slower metabolism in the winter could have been a lifesaver during periods of scarce food. For some unlucky humans, though, this same mechanism might contribute to **seasonal affective disorder**. It is believed that seasonal affective disorder is related to changes in the levels of melatonin in the brain. Melatonin is exquisitely sensitive to light and dark cycles and is only released during dark periods. People with seasonal affective disorder show greater changes in melatonin in the winter than do people without seasonal affective disorder (Wehr et al., 2001). Factors other than melatonin also are likely to contribute to seasonal mood shifts; for example, people with seasonal affective disorder show a change in their retinal sensitivity to light that appears to be genetically guided (Roecklein, Wong, Ernecoff et al., 2013).

Hibernation in animals typically involves sleeping long hours, along with lowered appetite

Media for Medical/UIG via Getty Images

This woman is having light therapy, which is an effective treatment for patients with seasonal depression.

Gilles Mingasson/Getty Images

Seasonal affective disorder is most common in regions far from the equator.

and energy. Indeed, the most common human response to seasonal shifts is sleep, appetite, and energy changes. Some people, though, seem to respond to those physical changes self-critically (Young, Watel, Lahmeyer et al., 1991). For example, faced with a lack of energy to tackle new projects, some people may feel guilty. People prone to self-criticism and other negative cognitions may be particularly likely to develop the full constellation of depressive symptoms in the face of the seasonal shifts in energy, sleep, and appetite.

Fortunately, several treatment options are available for seasonal affective disorder. Like other subtypes of depression, seasonal affective disorder responds to antidepressant medications and cognitive behavioral therapy (Rohan et al., 2007). Winter blues, though, are as likely to remit with 30 minutes of bright light each morning as with fluoxetine (Prozac) (Lam et al., 2006). At least eight high-quality studies have examined bright light as a treatment for seasonal affective disorder (Golden et al., 2005) and it is established as a first-line recommendation in the American Psychiatric Association treatment guidelines for depression. Intriguingly, light therapy has been shown to help relieve depression even among those without a seasonal pattern to their depressions (Lieverse et al., 2011).

distress. For example, people in South Korea are less likely to describe a sad mood or suicidal thoughts than are people in the United States (Chang et al., 2008). Complaints of nerves and headaches are common in Latino culture, and reports of weakness, fatigue, and poor concentration are common in some Asian cultures. On the other hand, these symptom differences do not appear to be major enough to explain the differing rates of depression across countries (Simon et al., 2002), particularly when careful studies are conducted.

In most countries, the prevalence of MDD increased steadily during the mid- to late twentieth century (Klerman, 1988); at the same time, the age of onset decreased (Kessler, Birnbaum et al., 2010). Figure 5.1 shows that the age of onset has become lower for each recent generation of people in the United States: among people in their 60s, less than 5 percent reported that they had experienced an episode of MDD by age 20, whereas among people ages 18–29, almost 10 percent reported that they had experienced an episode of MDD by age 20. The median age of onset is now the late teens to early 20s, and depression is now all too present on college campuses. One possible explanation for the increasing depression rates lies in the social changes that have occurred over the past 100 years. Support structures—such as tightly knit extended families and marital stability, which were more widespread in the past—are often absent for people today. Yet there are no clear data about why depression is striking earlier and earlier.

Both MDD and persistent depressive disorder are often associated, or comorbid, with other psychological disorders. About 60 percent of people who meet the criteria for diagnosis of MDD during their lifetime also will meet the criteria for diagnosis of an anxiety disorder at some point (Kessler et al., 2003). See Focus on Discovery 5.5 later in the chapter for more discussion of the overlap of anxiety disorders and depressive disorders. Other common comorbid conditions include substance-related disorders, sexual dysfunctions, and personality disorders.

Depression has many serious consequences. From the depths of a depression, getting to work may be far too effortful, parenting can feel like a burden, and suicide can seem like an option. As we will discuss later in this chapter, suicide is a real risk. MDD is also one of the world's leading causes of disability (Murray & Lopez, 1996); it is estimated that MDD is associated with $31 billion per year in lost productivity in the United States (Stewart, Ricci, Chee, Hahn, & Morganstein, 2003). MDD also has important effects for the next generation: offspring who are exposed to mother's MDD during early childhood are at high risk for developing depression (Hammen, Hazel, Brennan et al., 2012).

MDD is also related to a high risk of other health problems, including death from medical diseases (Mykletun et al., 2009). There is particularly strong evidence that depression is related to the onset and more severe course of cardiovascular disease. Across 22 prospective studies, depression has been found to predict a 60 percent increase in the severity of cardiovascular disease over time (Nicholson, Kuper, & Hemingway, 2006). Depression is also related to increased risk of death from cardiovascular disease, even after controlling for baseline cardiovascular health (Barth, Schumacher, & Herrmann-Lingen, 2004).

Although the diagnostic criteria for persistent depressive disorder require fewer symptoms than for MDD, do not make the mistake of thinking that persistent depressive disorder is a less severe disorder than MDD. One study found that these chronic depressive symptoms persisted on average for more than 5 years and that functioning declined as the symptoms persisted for more years (Klein, Shankman, & Rose, 2006). The chronicity of these symptoms takes a toll. Indeed, a study following patients for 5 years found that people with chronic depressive symptoms were more likely to require hospitalization, to attempt suicide, and to be impaired in their functioning than were people with MDD (Klein, Schwartz, Rose et al. 2000).

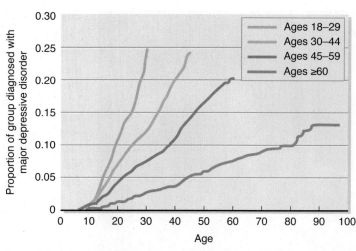

Source: Adapted from Kessler, Berglund, Demler et al., *JAMA*, 2003: 289, 3095–3105.

Figure 5.1 With each generation, the median age of onset for major depressive disorder gets younger.

Margaret Trudeau, the former first lady of Canada, has become an advocate for better mental health services since her own diagnosis with bipolar disorder.

Bipolar Disorders

The DSM-5 recognizes three forms of bipolar disorders: bipolar I disorder, bipolar II disorder, and cyclothymic disorder. Manic symptoms are the defining feature of each of these disorders. The bipolar disorders are differentiated by how severe and long-lasting the manic symptoms are.

These disorders are labeled "bipolar" because most people who experience mania will also experience depression during their lifetime (mania and depression are considered opposite poles). Contrary to what people may believe, an episode of depression is not required for a diagnosis of bipolar I (although two-thirds to three-fourths of people with an episode of mania will experience an episode of depression; see Cuellar, Johnson, & Winters, 2005). Depression is required for a diagnosis of bipolar II disorder.

Mania is a state of intense elation, irritability, or activation accompanied by other symptoms shown in the diagnostic criteria. During manic episodes, people will act and think in ways that are highly unusual compared to their typical selves. They may become louder and make an incessant stream of remarks, sometimes full of puns, jokes, rhymes, and interjections about nearby stimuli that have attracted their attention (like Wayne in the following Clinical Case). They may be difficult to interrupt and may shift rapidly from topic to topic, reflecting an underlying **flight of ideas**. During mania, people may become sociable to the point of intrusiveness. They can also become excessively self-confident. They may stop sleeping but remain incredibly energetic. Attempts by others to curb such excesses can quickly bring anger and even rage. Mania often comes on suddenly over a period of a day or two. For many, the boundless energy, bursts of joy, and incredible surge in goals can seem welcome, so that some fail to recognize the sudden changes as a sign of disorder. The following passage from Kay Redfield Jamison illustrates some of the rapid shifts that can occur.

> When you're high it's tremendous. The ideas and feelings are fast and frequent like shooting stars, and you follow them until you find better and brighter ones. Shyness goes, the right words and gestures are suddenly there, the power to captivate others a felt certainty. There are interests found in uninteresting people. Sensuality is pervasive and the desire to seduce and be seduced irresistible. Feelings of ease, intensity, power, well-being, financial omnipotence, and euphoria pervade one's marrow. But, somewhere, this changes. The fast ideas are far too fast, and there are far too many; overwhelming confusion replaces clarity. Memory goes. Humor and absorption on friends' faces are replaced by fear and concern. (Jamison, 1993, pp. 67–68)

Unfortunately, people can be oblivious to the potentially disastrous consequences of their manic behavior, which can include risky sexual activities, overspending, and reckless driving. The following quote, also from Kay Redfield Jamison, illustrates some of the impulsivity of this state.

> When I am high I couldn't worry about money if I tried. So I don't. The money will come from somewhere; I am entitled; God will provide. . . . So I bought twelve snakebite kits, with a sense of urgency and importance. I bought precious stones, elegant and unnecessary furniture, three watches within an hour of one another (in the Rolex rather than Timex class: champagne tastes bubble to the surface, are the surface, in mania), and totally inappropriate siren-like clothes. During one spree in London I spent several hundred pounds on books having titles or covers that somehow caught my fancy: books on the natural history of the mole, twenty sundry Penguin books because I thought it could be nice if the penguins could form a colony. Once I think I shoplifted a blouse because I could not wait a minute longer for the woman-with-molasses feet in front of me in line. Or maybe I just thought about shoplifting, I don't remember, I was totally confused. I imagine I must have spent far more than thirty thousand dollars during my two major manic episodes, and God only knows how much more during my frequent milder manias. But then back on lithium and rotating on the planet at the same pace as everyone else, you find your credit is decimated, your mortification complete. (Jamison, 1995, p. 75)

The DSM-5 also includes criteria for **hypomania** (see diagnostic criteria for manic and hypomanic episodes). *Hypo-* comes from the Greek for "under"; hypomania is "under"—less extreme than—mania. Although mania involves significant impairment, hypomania does not. Rather, hypomania involves a change in functioning that does not cause serious problems. The person with hypomania may feel more social, energized, productive, and sexually alluring.

Clinical Case: Wayne

Wayne, a 32-year-old insurance appraiser, had been married for 8 years. He lived happily with his wife and their two children in a middle-class neighborhood. He had not experienced any clear symptoms until one morning when he told his wife that he was bursting with energy and ideas, that his job was unfulfilling, and that he was just wasting his talent. That night he slept little, spending most of the time at his desk, writing furiously. The next morning he left for work at the usual time but returned home at 11:00 A.M., his car overflowing with aquariums and other equipment for tropical fish. He had quit his job, then withdrawn all the money from the family's savings account and spent it on tropical fish equipment. Wayne reported that the previous night he had worked out a way to modify existing equipment so that fish "won't die anymore. We'll be millionaires." After unloading the paraphernalia, Wayne set off to canvass the neighborhood for possible buyers, going door to door and talking to anyone who would listen.

Wayne reported that no one in his family had been treated for bipolar disorder, but his mother had gone through periods when she would stop sleeping and become extremely adventurous. For the most part, the family had regarded these episodes as unproblematic, with the exception of a period in which she had set off across the country without the children and had returned only after spending a major amount of money.

The following bit of conversation indicates Wayne's incorrigible optimism:

Therapist: *Well, you seem pretty happy today.*
Wayne: *Happy! Happy! You certainly are a master of understatement, you rogue! [Shouting, literally jumping out of his seat.] Why, I'm ecstatic! I'm leaving for the West Coast today, on my daughter's bicycle. Only 3100 miles. That's nothing, you know. I could probably walk, but I want to get there by next week. And along the way I plan to contact a lot of people about investing in my fish equipment. I'll get to know more people that way. . . . Oh, God, how good it feels.*

Bipolar I Disorder In the DSM-5, the criteria for diagnosis of **bipolar I disorder** (formerly known as manic-depressive disorder) include a single episode of mania during the course of a person's life. Note, then, that a person who is diagnosed with bipolar I disorder may or may not be experiencing current symptoms of mania. In fact, even someone who experienced only 1 week of manic symptoms years ago is still diagnosed with bipolar I disorder. Even more than episodes of MDD, bipolar episodes tend to recur. More than half of people with bipolar I disorder experience four or more episodes during their lifetimes (Goodwin & Jamison, 2007).

Bipolar II Disorder The DSM-5 also includes a milder form of bipolar disorder, called **bipolar II disorder**. To be diagnosed with bipolar II disorder, a person must have experienced at least one major depressive episode and at least one episode of hypomania (and no lifetime episode of mania).

Cyclothymic Disorder Also called *cyclothymia,* **cyclothymic disorder** is a second chronic mood disorder (the other is persistent depressive disorder). As with the diagnosis of persistent depressive disorder, the DSM-5 criteria require that symptoms be present for at least 2 years among adults. In cyclothymic disorder, the person has frequent but mild symptoms of depression, alternating with mild symptoms of mania. Although the symptoms do not reach the severity of full-blown hypomanic or depressive episodes, people with the disorder and those close to them typically notice the ups and downs.

Catherine Zeta-Jones has discussed her diagnosis of bipolar II disorder (*Telegraph*, April 30, 2013). As is common, her depression was recognized before the hypomanic episodes were.

DSM-5 Criteria for Cyclothymic Disorder

For at least 2 years (or 1 year in children or adolescents):

- Numerous periods with hypomanic symptoms that do not meet criteria for a hypomanic episode
- Numerous periods with depressive symptoms that do not meet criteria for a major depressive episode

The symptoms do not clear for more than 2 months at a time. Criteria for a major depressive, manic, or hypomanic episode have never been met. Symptoms cause significant distress or functional impairment.

DSM-5 Criteria for Manic and Hypomanic Episodes

Distinctly elevated or irritable mood.
Abnormally increased activity or energy.
At least three of the following are noticeably changed from baseline (four if mood is irritable):

- Increase in goal-directed activity or psychomotor agitation
- Unusual talkativeness; rapid speech
- Flight of ideas or subjective impression that thoughts are racing
- Decreased need for sleep
- Increased self-esteem; belief that one has special talents, powers, or abilities
- Distractibility; attention easily diverted
- Excessive involvement in activities that are likely to have painful consequences, such as reckless spending, sexual indiscretions, or unwise business investments
- Symptoms are present most of the day, nearly every day

For a manic episode:

- Symptoms last 1 week, require hospitalization, or include psychosis
- Symptoms cause significant distress or functional impairment

For a hypomanic episode:

- Symptoms last at least 4 days
- Clear changes in functioning are observable to others, but impairment is not marked
- No psychotic symptoms are present

Epidemiology and Consequences of Bipolar Disorders Bipolar I disorder is much rarer than MDD. In an epidemiological study that involved structured diagnostic interviews with a representative sample of 61,392 people across 11 countries, about 6 out of 1000 (0.6 percent) people met the criteria for bipolar I disorder (Merikangas et al., 2011). Rates of bipolar disorder appear to be higher in the United States than in other countries that have been studied. For example, in the United States, about 1 percent of people experience bipolar I disorder.

It is hard to estimate the prevalence of milder forms of bipolar disorder because some of the most commonly used diagnostic interviews are not reliable. When researchers conducted interrater reliability tests of bipolar II disorder using structured clinical interviews, the diagnosis was confirmed for less than half of the people tested (Kessler et al., 2006). (Many of those were diagnosed with other forms of bipolar disorder.) As you might expect given the low reliability, the prevalence estimates vary, with large-scale epidemiological studies suggesting that bipolar II disorder affects somewhere between 0.4 percent and 2 percent of people (Merikangas et al., 2007, 2011). It is estimated that about 4 percent of people experience cyclothymic disorder (Regeer et al., 2004).

More than half of those with bipolar spectrum disorders report onset before age 25 (Merikangas et al., 2011), but like depression, bipolar disorders are being seen with increasing frequency among children and adolescents (Kessler, Berglund, Demler et al., 2005). Although bipolar disorders occur equally often in men and women, women diagnosed with bipolar disorder experience more episodes of depression than do men with this diagnosis (Altshuler et al., 2010). About two-thirds of people diagnosed with bipolar disorder meet diagnostic criteria for a comorbid anxiety disorder, and many report a history of substance abuse.

Bipolar I disorder is among the most severe forms of psychological disorders. One-third of people remain unemployed a full year after hospitalization for mania (Harrow, Goldberg, Grossman et al., 1990). Suicide rates are high for both bipolar I and bipolar II disorders (Angst, Stassen, Clayton et al., 2002). People with these disorders are at high risk for a range of other medical conditions, including cardiovascular disease, diabetes, obesity, and thyroid disease

FOCUS ON DISCOVERY 5.3

Creativity and Mood Disorders

In her book *Touched with Fire: Manic-Depressive Illness and the Artistic Temperament* (1993), Kay Jamison, an expert on bipolar disorders and herself a longtime sufferer from bipolar I disorder, assembled evidence linking mood disorders, especially bipolar disorder, to artistic creativity. Of course, most people with mood disorders are not exceptionally creative, and most creative people do not have mood disorders—but the list of visual artists, composers, and writers who seem to have experienced mood disorders is impressive. The list includes Michelangelo, van Gogh, Tchaikovsky, Schumann, Gauguin, Tennyson, Shelley, Faulkner, Hemingway, F. Scott Fitzgerald, and Whitman. In recent years, many actors and actresses have also spoken out about their history of mania, including Stephen Fry, Carrie Fisher, and Linda Hamilton. The biographical findings dovetail with results from a population-based study of over 300,000 people in which those with bipolar disorder and their unaffected family members were overrepresented in creative occupations (Kyaga et al., 2011).

Many people assume that the manic state itself fosters creativity through elated mood, increased energy, rapid thoughts, and a heightened ability to make connections among seemingly unrelated events. Extreme mania, however, lowers creative output, and even if people produce more work during a manic period, the quality of that work might suffer, as seems to have been the case for the composer Robert Schumann (Weisberg, 1994). Moreover, studies have shown that people who have experienced episodes of mania tend to be less creative than those who have had the milder episodes of hypomania, and both groups tend to produce less creative output than do non-ill family members (Richards, Kinney, Lunde et al., 1988). Although many people with bipolar disorder worry that taking medications may limit their creativity, these findings suggest that reducing manic symptoms should help, rather than hurt, creativity.

Source: A. Summers & R. Swan, Sinatra: *The Life* (New York: Vintage Books, 2006), p. 218 (Getty Images, Inc.)

Photo Researchers

Frank Sinatra is quoted as having said this about himself: "Being an 18-karat manic depressive, and having lived a life of violent emotional contradictions, I have an over-acute capacity for sadness as well as elation."

Mood disorders are common among artists and writers. Tchaikovsky was affected.

(Kupfer, 2005), and these problems are often quite severe. People who have been hospitalized for bipolar I disorder are twice as likely to die from medical illnesses in a given year as are people without mood disorders (Osby, Brandt, Correia et al., 2001). These sad consequences of bipolar disorders are not offset by evidence that bipolar individuals and their family members possess heightened creativity or are high achievers (see Focus on Discovery 5.3).

People with cyclothymia are at elevated risk for developing episodes of mania and major depression. Even if full-blown manic episodes do not emerge, the chronicity of cyclothymic symptoms takes its toll.

Check Your Knowledge 5.1 (Answers are at the end of the chapter.)

Fill in the blanks.

1. Major depressive disorder is diagnosed based on at least _____ symptoms lasting at least _____ weeks.
2. Approximately _____ percent of people will experience major depressive disorder during their lifetime.
3. Worldwide, approximately _____ out of every 1000 people will experience a manic episode during their lifetime.

Answer the questions.

4. What is the key difference between the diagnostic criteria for major depressive disorder and persistent depressive disorder?
5. What is the key difference between the diagnostic criteria for bipolar I disorder and bipolar II disorder?

Table 5.2 Specifiers of Depressive Disorders and Bipolar Disorders

Subtype	Applicable to MDD?	Applicable to bipolar disorder?	Definition
Seasonal pattern	Yes	Yes	Episodes happen regularly at a particular time of the year
Rapid cycling	No	Yes	At least four episodes within the past year
Mood-congruent psychotic features	Yes	Yes	Delusions or hallucinations with themes that are consistent with the mood state (e.g., guilt, disease, or death themes accompanying depression)
Mood-incongruent psychotic features	Yes	Yes	Delusions or hallucinations with themes that do not match the valence of the depressive or manic episode
Mixed features	Yes	Yes	At least three manic symptoms are present during a depressive episode, or at least three depressive symptoms are present during a manic episode
Catatonia	Yes	Yes	Extreme physical immobility or excessive peculiar physical movement
Melancholic features	Yes	Yes (for depressive episodes)	Lack of pleasure in any activity, inability to gain relief from positive events, and at least three other symptoms of depression, such as a distinct quality of mood, depressive symptoms that are worse in the morning, waking at least 2 hours too early, loss of appetite/weight, psychomotor retardation or agitation, or guilt
Atypical features	Yes	Yes	Symptoms that are unusual for depressive or manic episodes are present
Peripartum onset	Yes	Yes	Onset during pregnancy or within 4 weeks postpartum
With anxious distress	Yes	Yes	At least two symptoms of anxiety are present
Suicide risk severity	Yes	Yes	Suicidal ideation, plans, or other risk indicators are present

Subtypes of Depressive Disorders and Bipolar Disorders

The mood disorders are highly heterogeneous—that is, people who have been diagnosed with the same disorder may show very different symptoms. The DSM-5 addresses this by providing criteria for dividing MDD and bipolar disorders into a number of specifiers (subtypes). See Table 5.2 for a list of specifiers and their definitions. Both the **rapid cycling** specifier (see Figure 5.2) and the seasonal specifier refer to the pattern of episodes over time, whereas other specifiers refer to the specific symptoms of the current episode. All of the specifiers can be applied to either MDD or bipolar disorders, with the exception of rapid cycling, which is diagnosed only for bipolar disorder. All of the episode specifiers can be applied to either depressed or manic episodes, with the exception of **melancholic**, which is only relevant for episodes of depression.

The seasonal specifier of MDD has achieved a fair amount of support (see Focus on Discovery 5.2 for discussion), but many of the other specifiers have not been well validated.

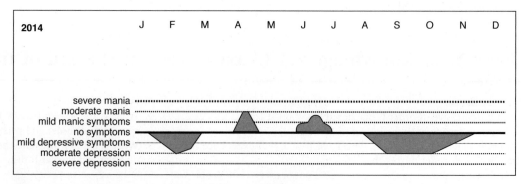

Figure 5.2 The rapid cycling specifier of bipolar disorder is defined by at least four mood episodes per year, as shown in this case.

For example, although about 14 percent of women meet criteria for the **peripartum specifier** of depression, depression is not much more common in the postpartum period compared to other periods in life, and about a half of depressive episodes that are present during pregnancy or after birth actually started before the pregnancy (Wisner et al., 2013). Similarly, problems exist with the rapid cycling specifier. In a longitudinal study, 95 percent of persons with rapid cycling bipolar disorder at baseline were no longer experiencing rapid cycling one year later (Schneck et al., 2008). As a third example of problems with specifiers, MDD with melancholic features may just be a more severe type of depression—that is, people with melancholic features have more comorbidity (e.g., with anxiety disorders), more frequent episodes of depression, and more impairment in everyday activities (Kendler, 1997).

Quick Summary

The DSM-5 contains two broad types of mood disorders: depressive disorders and bipolar disorders. Depressive disorders include major depressive disorder and persistent depressive disorder as well as two more recently recognized disorders: premenstrual dysphoric disorder and disruptive mood dysregulation disorder. Major depression is characterized by severe episodes lasting at least 2 weeks, whereas persistent depressive disorder is characterized by symptoms that last at least 2 years.

Bipolar disorders include bipolar I disorder, bipolar II disorder, and cyclothymic disorder. Bipolar I disorder is diagnosed on the basis of a single lifetime manic episode, and bipolar II disorder is diagnosed on the basis of hypomania and major depression. Cyclothymia is defined by frequent shifts between mild depressive and manic symptoms that last at least 2 years.

Specifiers of mood disorders are used to differentiate patterns of symptoms. Seasonal and rapid cycling specifiers are defined by the pattern of episodes over time; other specifiers are used to label the features of the current episode, including mood-congruent or mood-incongruent psychotic features, mixed features, catatonia, peripartum onset, with anxious distress, suicide risk severity, and, for depression, melancholia. The seasonal specifier has been well validated.

MDD is one of the most common psychological disorders, whereas bipolar I disorder affects 1 percent or less of the population. MDD and persistent depressive disorder affect twice as many women as men. Two-thirds of people with MDD will experience another episode. Bipolar disorder is even more recurrent than MDD—about 50 percent of people with bipolar I disorder experience four or more episodes.

Etiology of Mood Disorders

When we think of the profound extremes embodied in the mood disorders, it is natural to ask why these extremes happen. How can we explain Mary sinking into the depths of depression? What factors combined to drive Wayne into his frenzied state of unrealistic ambitions? Studies of etiology focus on why these disorders unfold. No single cause can explain mood disorders. A number of different factors combine to explain their onset.

While the DSM includes several different depressive disorders and bipolar disorders, the research on etiology and treatment has tended to focus on major depressive disorder and bipolar I disorder. For simplicity, we refer to these conditions as depression and bipolar disorder through the remainder of this chapter.

We begin by discussing biological factors involved in depression and bipolar disorder. As Table 5.3 shows, many different biological approaches have been applied to mood disorders, and we will describe genetic, neurotransmitter, brain-imaging, and neuroendocrine research. After describing these biological risk factors for depressive and bipolar disorders, we discuss psychosocial predictors of depression, and then turn to psychosocial models of bipolar disorder.

Genetic Factors

The more careful studies of MZ (identical) and DZ (fraternal) twins yield heritability estimates of 37 percent for MDD (Sullivan, Neale, & Kendler, 2000). As described in Chapter 2, heritability can be interpreted as the percent of the variance in depression that is explained

Table 5.3 Summary of Neurobiological Hypotheses About Major Depression and Bipolar Disorder

Neurobiological Hypothesis	Major Depression	Bipolar Disorder
Genetic contribution	Moderate	High
Serotonin and dopamine receptor dysfunction	Present	Present
Cortisol dysregulation	Present	Present
Changes in activation of emotion-relevant regions in the brain	Present	Present
Activation of the striatum in response to reward	Low	High

by genes. Heritability estimates are higher when researchers study more severe samples (e.g., when the people in the study are recruited in inpatient hospitals rather than outpatient clinics).

Bipolar disorder is among the most heritable of disorders. The most careful studies involve interviews with representative samples of twins selected from the community (rather than focusing only on people who seek treatment, who may have more severe cases of the disorder than those who are not treated). One community-based twin sample that used structured interviews to verify diagnoses obtained a heritability estimate of 93 percent (Kieseppa, Partonen, Haukka et al., 2004). Adoption studies also confirm the importance of heritability in bipolar disorder (Wender et al., 1986). Bipolar II disorder is also highly heritable (Edvardsen et al., 2008a).

Molecular genetics research (see Chapters 2 and 4) aims to identify the specific genes involved in mood disorders. To place molecular genetics research in context, it is worth pausing to consider the incredible range of depressive and bipolar symptoms that a person might experience. Because the mood disorders, and indeed most psychological disorders, are so complex and heterogeneous, it is highly unlikely that there is one single gene that explains these illnesses. Most researchers believe that these disorders will be related eventually to a set of genes, with each gene accounting for a minute proportion of risk.

Likely due to the very small effects of any one gene, genome-wide association studies (GWAS) involving more than 18,000 persons have failed to identify specific genes associated with MDD (Sullivan, Daly, & O'Donovan, 2012), and many of the specific genes identified in smaller studies have failed to replicate (Krishnan & Nestler, 2010). In studies involving thousands of people, several genetic polymorphisms related to bipolar disorder have been identified. These polymorphisms explain a very small proportion of the risk for bipolar disorder (Sullivan. et al., 2012), and some of the genetic polymorphisms identified appear to overlap with those involved in schizophrenia (CDGPGC, 2013).

A different approach is to consider whether a given gene might increase risk of depression in the presence of environmental risk factors. This approach shows that a polymorphism of the serotonin transporter gene does appear to be related to MDD. An initial study found that people with this polymorphism were at greater risk for depression after a stressful life event than those without the polymorphism (Caspi et al., 2003). That is, having at least one short allele was associated with elevated reactivity to stress (see Figure 5.3). In rhesus monkeys, the presence of at least one short allele in this gene is associated with poor serotonergic function. Thus, some people seem to inherit a propensity for a weaker serotonin system, which is then expressed as a greater likelihood to experience depression after childhood maltreatment or an adulthood severe stressor. This finding has been replicated in other large-scale studies, particularly when the studies involved careful measurement of maltreatment and life stressors (Karg, 2011; Uher & McGuffin, 2010). Intriguingly, this polymorphism in the serotonin transporter gene has also been related to risk factors for depression that we will be discussing later in this chapter, including activity in key brain regions (e.g., the amgydala, described below; Caspi, Hariri, Holmes et al., 2010) and negative cognitive tendencies (e.g., attention to negative information; Disner et al., 2013). This type of work, then, suggests that we should be considering genes for depression in concert with other risk factors.

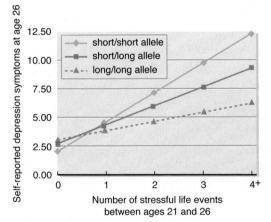

Source: Adapted from Caspi et al., *Science*, 2003: 301, 387.

Figure 5.3 Life events interact with the serotonin transporter gene to predict symptoms of depression.

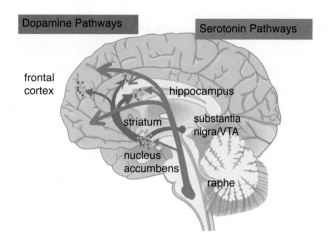

Dopamine Pathways

Serotonin Pathways

frontal
cortex

hippocampus

striatum

substantia
nigra/VTA

nucleus
accumbens

raphe

Figure 5.4 Serotonin and dopamine pathways are widespread in the brain.

Neurotransmitters   Three neurotransmitters have been studied the most in terms of their possible role in mood disorders: norepinephrine, dopamine, and serotonin. Each of these neurotransmitters is present in many different areas of the brain. Figure 5.4 illustrates how widespread serotonin and dopamine pathways are in the brain. For decades, researchers studied the idea that mood disorders would be related to having too much or too little of a neurotransmitter, with mixed results. More recent models have focused on the idea that mood disorders might involve changes in receptors that respond to the presence of neurotransmitters in the synaptic cleft (see Figure 5.5), with most of these newer studies focused on dopamine and serotonin.

How could one test the sensitivity of the postsynaptic receptors? If receptors are more or less sensitive, one might expect people to react differently to drugs that influence the level of a given neurotransmitter. For example, receptors that are overly sensitive may respond to even the smallest amount of a neurotransmitter in the synaptic cleft. If receptors are insensitive, a person may show a more pronounced response to a drop in neurotransmitter levels.

People with depression are less responsive than other people are to drugs that increase dopamine levels, and it is thought that the functioning of the dopamine might be lowered in depression (Naranjo, Tremblay, & Busto, 2001). Dopamine plays a major role in the sensitivity of the **reward system** in the brain, which is believed to guide pleasure, motivation, and energy in the context of opportunities to obtain rewards (Depue & Iacono, 1989). The diminished function of the dopamine system could help explain the deficits in pleasure, motivation, and energy in depression (Treadway & Zald, 2011).

Among people with bipolar disorder, several different drugs that increase dopamine levels have been found to trigger manic symptoms. One possibility is that dopamine receptors may be overly sensitive in bipolar disorder (Anand et al., 2000), which might help explain the excessive energy and enthusiasm seen during manic episodes.

In addition to dopamine, studies have also focused on the sensitivity of serotonin receptors. Researchers have conducted a set of studies that involve experimentally lowering serotonin levels. To lower serotonin levels, researchers deplete levels of **tryptophan**, the major precursor of serotonin. Tryptophan can be depleted with a drink that contains high levels of 15 amino acids but no tryptophan. Within hours, serotonin levels are lowered, an effect that lasts for several hours. Studies show that depleting tryptophan (and so lowering serotonin levels) causes temporary depressive symptoms among people with a history of depression or a family history of depression (Benkelfat, Ellenbogen, Dean et al., 1994; Neumeister et al., 2002). This effect is not observed among people with no personal or family history of depression. Current thinking is that people who are vulnerable to depression may have less sensitive serotonin receptors, causing them to respond more dramatically to lower levels of serotonin.

Like people diagnosed with MDD and their family members, relatives of those with bipolar disorder demonstrate stronger mood reactions to tryptophan depletion compared to matched controls (Sobczak, Honig, Nicolson et al., 2002). As with depression, it

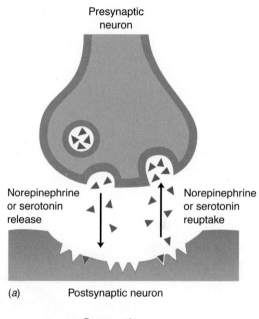

Presynaptic
neuron

Norepinephrine
or serotonin
release

Norepinephrine
or serotonin
reuptake

(a)   Postsynaptic neuron

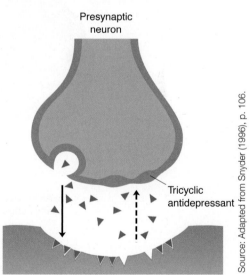

Presynaptic
neuron

Tricyclic
antidepressant

(b)   Postsynaptic neuron

Source: Adapted from Snyder (1996), p. 106.

Figure 5.5 (a) When neurotransmitters are released into a synapse, a pumplike reuptake mechanism begins to recapture some of the neurotransmitter before it reaches the postsynaptic neuron. (b) Tricyclic drugs block this reuptake process so that more neurotransmitter reaches the receptor. Selective serotonin reuptake inhibitors act more selectively on serotonin.

Table 5.4 Activity of Brain Structures Involved in Emotion Responses Among People with Mood Disorders

Brain Structure	Level in Depression	Level in Mania
Amygdala	Elevated	Elevated
Anterior cingulate	Elevated	Elevated
Dorsolateral prefrontal cortex	Diminished	Diminished
Hippocampus	Diminished	Diminished
Striatum	Diminished	Elevated

would appear that bipolar disorder may be related to diminished sensitivity of the serotonin receptors.

Brain Function: Regions Involved in Emotion

Functional brain-imaging studies suggest that episodes of MDD are associated with changes in many of the brain systems that are involved in experiencing and regulating emotion (Davidson, Pizzagalli, & Nitschke, 2002). Many of these studies examine brain responses to emotional stimuli, such as pictures of very positive or very negative scenes. Table 5.4 summarizes five primary brain structures that have been most studied in depression: the amygdala, the **anterior cingulate**, the **dorsolateral prefrontal cortex**, the hippocampus, and the **striatum** (see also Figure 5.6). We will discuss each of these regions, beginning with the amygdala.

Figure 5.6 Key brain regions involved in mood disorders.

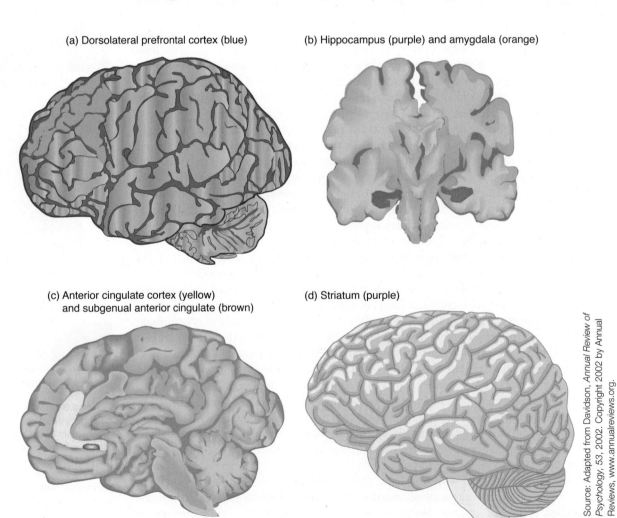

(a) Dorsolateral prefrontal cortex (blue)

(b) Hippocampus (purple) and amygdala (orange)

(c) Anterior cingulate cortex (yellow) and subgenual anterior cingulate (brown)

(d) Striatum (purple)

Source: Adapted from Davidson, *Annual Review of Psychology*, 53, 2002. Copyright 2002 by Annual Reviews, www.annualreviews.org.

The amygdala helps assess how salient and emotionally important a stimulus is. For example, animals with damage to the amygdala fail to react with fear to threatening stimuli and also fail to respond positively to food. In humans, the amygdala has been shown to respond when people are shown pictures of threatening stimuli. Functional brain activation studies show elevated activity of the amygdala among people with MDD. For example, when shown negative words or pictures of sad or angry faces, people with current MDD have a more intense and sustained reaction in the amygdala than do people with no MDD (Sheline et al., 2001). This pattern of amygdala overreactivity to emotional stimuli can be shown among relatives of people with depression who have no personal history of MDD, suggesting this might be part of the vulnerability to depression rather than just the aftermath of being depressed (Pilhatsch et al., 2014).

In addition to the amygdala, MDD is associated with greater activation of the anterior cingulate (Hamilton et al., 2012) and diminished activation of the hippocampus and dorsolateral prefrontal cortex when viewing negative stimuli (Hamilton et al., 2012; Schaefer, Putnam, Benca et al., 2006). Disturbances in these regions are believed to interfere with effective emotion regulation.

Finally, people with depression demonstrate diminished activation of the striatum during exposure to emotional stimuli (Hamilton et al., 2012), particularly when they are receiving positive feedback that they have earned a reward (Pizzagalli, Goetz, Ostacher et al., 2008). A specific region of the striatum (called the nucleus accumbens) is a central component of the reward system in the brain and plays a key role in motivation to pursue rewards (Salamone & Correa, 2012). The lack of activity of the striatum in response to positive feedback, then, may help explain why people with depression feel less motivated by and less engaged in the positive events in their life.

How might these findings fit together? One theory is that the overactivity in the amygdala during depression causes oversensitivity to emotionally relevant stimuli. At the same time, systems involved in regulating emotions are compromised (the anterior cingulate, the hippocampus, and the dorsolateral prefrontal cortex). Finally, neural regions involved in responding and mobilizing to rewards may also be underactive.

Many of the brain structures implicated in MDD also appear to be involved in bipolar disorder. Bipolar I disorder is associated with elevated responsiveness in the amygdala, increased activity of the anterior cingulate during emotion regulation tasks, and diminished activity of the hippocampus and dorsolateral prefrontal cortex (Houenou et al., 2011; Phillips et al., 2008). Although these patterns parallel those observed among people with MDD, one difference emerges. People with bipolar disorder tend to show high activation of the striatum (Chen, Suckling, Lennox et al., 2011), in contrast with the low activity observed for those with MDD.

The Neuroendocrine System: Cortisol Dysregulation

The HPA axis (hypothalamic–pituitary–adrenocortical axis; see Figure 2.12) may be overly active during episodes of MDD, which is consistent with the idea that stress reactivity is an important part of depression. As described above, there is evidence that the amygdala is overly reactive among people with MDD, and the amygdala sends signals that activate the HPA axis. The HPA axis triggers the release of cortisol, the main stress hormone. Cortisol is secreted at times of stress and increases the activity of the immune system to help the body prepare for threats.

Various findings link depression to high cortisol levels. For example, people with **Cushing's syndrome**, which causes oversecretion of cortisol, frequently experience depressive symptoms. A second line of research with animals has shown that when chemicals that trigger cortisol release are injected into the brain, many of the classic symptoms of depression are produced, including decreased interest in sex, decreased appetite, and sleep disturbance (Gutman & Nemeroff, 2003). In animals and humans, then, too much cortisol seems to produce depressive symptoms.

Even among people who are depressed but do not have Cushing's syndrome, cortisol levels are often poorly regulated—that is, the system does not seem to respond well to biological signals to decrease cortisol levels. To test this idea, researchers generally administer an agent such as dexamethasone, which suppresses cortisol secretion over the course of the night in healthy individuals. The dexamethasone suppression test (dex/CRH) is an even more sensitive test of the HPA system in which researchers administer both dexamethasone and corticotrophin-releasing hormone (which increases cortisol levels). About 80 percent of people hospitalized for depression show poor regulation of the HPA system on the dex/CRH test (Heuser, Yassouridis, & Holsboer, 1994). These abnormal responses to the dex/CRH test, though, normalize when the depressive episode ends for most people. People who continue to show elevated cortisol responses to the dex/CRH test after recovery from a depressive episode are more likely to relapse within the next year (e.g., Aubry et al., 2007).

Although cortisol helps mobilize beneficial short-term stress responses, prolonged high levels of cortisol can cause harm to body systems. For example, long-term excesses of cortisol have been linked to damage to the hippocampus—studies have found smaller-than-normal hippocampus volume among people who have experienced depression for years (Videbech & Ravnkilde, 2004).

Like people with MDD, people with bipolar disorder fail to demonstrate the typical suppression of cortisol after the dex/CRH test. This suggests that bipolar disorder is also characterized by a poorly regulated cortisol system (Watson, Thompson, Ritchie et al., 2006). Like those with MDD, people with bipolar disorder who continue to show abnormal responses to cortisol challenge tests after their episode clears are at high risk for more episodes in the future (Vieta et al., 1999).

In sum, both bipolar disorder and MDD are characterized by problems in the regulation of cortisol levels. Dysregulation in cortisol levels also predicts a more severe course of illness for bipolar disorder and MDD.

Quick Summary

Bipolar disorder is highly heritable. Major depression is modestly heritable. A polymorphism of the serotonin transporter gene may increase risk for depression, particularly in the context of environmental adversity.

Neurotransmitter models have traditionally focused on serotonin, dopamine, and norepinephrine. Current research focuses on receptor sensitivity of the serotonin and dopamine systems. Receptor sensitivity is often tested by manipulating the levels of neurotransmitters. Tryptophan depletion studies indicate that deficits in serotonin receptors are associated with depression and bipolar disorder. It also appears that depression may be related to diminished dopamine receptor sensitivity and that mania may be related to enhanced dopamine receptor sensitivity.

Neuroimaging studies suggest that depression and bipolar disorder are both associated with changes in regions of the brain that are involved in emotion. These changes seem consistent with a greater emotional reactivity (heightened activity of the amygdala) but less ability to regulate emotion (diminished activity of the dorsolateral prefrontal cortex and hippocampus, and greater activity of the anterior cingulate).

As noted, depression and bipolar disorder seem similar on many of these biological variables. One difference between the two conditions seems to be that depression appears to be related to lower activity of the striatum, whereas striatum activity appears to be high among those with bipolar disorder.

Depression and bipolar disorder are both related to poor regulation of cortisol when assessed using the dex/CRH test. Cortisol dysregulation also predicts a more severe course of mood symptoms over time.

Check Your Knowledge 5.2

Answer the questions.
1. Estimates of heritability are approximately _____ percent for MDD and _____ percent for bipolar I disorder.
   a. 60, 93
   b. 20, 100
   c. 37, 93
   d. 10, 59
2. Depression and mania both involve diminished receptor sensitivity of which of the following neurotransmitter systems?
   a. acetylcholine
   b. serotonin
   c. dopamine
   d. norepinephrine
3. In depression, dysregulation of the HPA axis is shown by:
   a. hypersensitivity of the pituitary gland
   b. failure to suppress cortisol by dexamethasone
   c. too little cortisol
   d. elevated parasympathetic nervous system activity
4. One brain region that appears to be overly active among people with mood disorders is the:
   a. hippocampus
   b. dorsolateral prefrontal cortex
   c. cerebellum
   d. amygdala
5. Serotonin levels can be diminished by depleting the amino acid, _____. [Fill in the blank]

Social Factors in Depression: Childhood Adversity, Life Events, and Interpersonal Difficulties

Interpersonal problems are very common for those with depression, but showing cause and effect takes much more than just documenting this correlation. The depressive symptoms could easily contribute to interpersonal difficulties, as the person withdraws, begins to feel irritable, and finds no joy when engaging with others. To show that interpersonal concerns are not just an effect of the depressive symptoms, longitudinal studies showing that an interpersonal factor is present before onset are extremely important. Fortunately, many large longitudinal studies are available, and we will focus on interpersonal variables that have been shown to precede and predict the onset of depressive episodes, including childhood adversity, negative life events, lack of social support, family criticism, and an excessive need for interpersonal reassurance.

Childhood adversity, such as early parental death, physical abuse, or sexual abuse, increases the risk that later, in their adolescence or adulthood, the person will develop depression (Daley, Hammen, & Rao, 2000) and that the depressive symptoms will be chronic (Klein et al., 2009). One aspect of childhood adversity, child abuse, can set the stage for many of the other risk factors in depression, including a negative cognitive style (Lumley & Harkness, 2007), poorer marital relationship quality (DiLillo, Giuffre, Tremblay et al., 2001), increased rates of life stress (Harkness, Bagby, & Kennedy, 2012), and altered activity in brain regions involved in depression (Hanson et al., 2013). Child abuse, though, appears even more strongly tied to anxiety disorders than to depression (Kessler, McLaughlin et al., 2010). This suggests that child abuse may increase the risk for different disorders, whereas other factors may shape whether depression occurs.

Beyond childhood adversity, the role of more recent stressful life events in triggering episodes of depression is well established. Prospective studies have shown that life events often precede a depressive episode. Even with a prospective study, though, it remains possible that some life events are caused by early symptoms of depression that have not yet developed into a full-blown disorder. Remember the case of Mary, who developed symptoms after she was laid off from her job. Maybe Mary lost her job because her trouble waking in the morning caused her to arrive at work late; disturbed sleep patterns can be an early sign of depression. Even when researchers exclude stressful life events that could have been caused by mild depressive symptoms, there is much evidence that stress can cause depression. In careful prospective studies, 42 to 67 percent of people report that they experienced a very serious life event that was not caused by symptoms in the year before their depression began. Common events include losing a job, a key friendship, or a romantic relationship (Brown & Harris, 1989).

Certain types of life events, such as those involving interpersonal loss and humiliation, appear particularly likely to trigger depressive episodes (Kendler, Hettema, Butera et al., 2003). As examples, the death of a close other or a breakup with one's partner both seem to triple the risk of a depressive episode within the next several months (Kendler et al., 2003). Animals also show depressive-type symptoms after loss.

If it is natural to become depressed after a loss, some have argued that we should not pathologize such a normative response by assigning a diagnostic label (Wakefield, 2011). Others argue that the depressions that do or do not unfold in response to interpersonal loss seem parallel in their symptoms, treatment response, and other core dimensions, such that we should consider interpersonal loss as just one of the many pathways into MDD (Kendler, Myers, & Zisook, 2008). The DSM-5 takes this latter approach, and so these episodes receive the same diagnostic label as those that do not follow an interpersonal life event. Regardless of the diagnostic guidelines, we would do well to remember that depressive symptoms may be a fairly common response to major losses. We discuss one model of the role of interpersonal loss and stress in provoking biological changes and depressive symptoms in Focus on Discovery Box 5.6.

Why do some people, but not others, become depressed after stressful life events? The obvious answer is that some people must be more vulnerable to stress than others.

Disturbances in many of the neurobiological systems we described above could increase reactivity to stress. Neurobiological factors, then, may be diatheses (preexisting vulnerabilities) that increase risk for mood disorders in the context of other triggers or stressors. Psychological and cognitive vulnerabilities also appear to be important. The most common models, then, consider both diatheses and stressors. Diatheses could be biological, social, or psychological.

One diathesis may be a lack of social support. People who are depressed tend to have sparse social networks and to regard those networks as providing little support (Keltner & Kring, 1998). Low social support may lessen a person's ability to handle stressful life events. One study showed that women experiencing a severely stressful life event without support from a confidant had a 40 percent risk of developing depression, whereas those with a confidant's support had only a 4 percent risk (Brown & Andrews, 1986). Social support, then, seems to buffer against the effects of severe stressors.

Family problems are another important interpersonal predictor of depression. A long line of research has focused on **expressed emotion (EE)**—defined as a family member's critical or hostile comments toward or emotional overinvolvement with the person with depression. High EE strongly predicts relapse in depression. Indeed, one review of six studies found that 69.5 percent of patients in families with high EE relapsed within 1 year, compared to 30.5 percent of patient in families with low EE (Butzlaff & Hooley, 1998). In a community study, marital discord also predicted the onset of depression (Whisman & Bruce, 1999).

The onset of depression can also be predicted by certain types of problems in a person's interpersonal style. In one line of longitudinal research, an excessive need for reassurance has been found to predict depression . Among a group of undergraduates who were not initially depressed, those who described themselves as needing unusually high amounts of reassurance were more likely to develop depressive symptoms over a 10-week period (Joiner & Metalsky, 2001). Among elementary school children, low social competence predicted the onset of depression (Cole, Martin, Powers et al., 1990); and among adolescents, poor interpersonal problem-solving skills predicted increases in depression (Davila, Hammen, Burge et al., 1995).

Clearly, interpersonal problems can trigger the onset of depressive symptoms, but it is also important to consider the flip side of the coin. Once depressive symptoms emerge, they can create interpersonal problems—that is, depressive symptoms seem to elicit negative reactions from others (Coyne, 1976). For example, roommates of college students with depression rated social contacts with them as less enjoyable, and they reported feeling hostility toward them (Joiner, Alfano, & Metalsky, 1992). Other research has shown that people respond poorly to constant reassurance seeking (Joiner, 1995). Taken together, it is clear that interpersonal loss, isolation, and relationship concerns can trigger depression, but it is good to be aware that the depression and the related vulnerability can also create challenges in interpersonal relationships.

Psychological Factors in Depression

Many different psychological factors may play a role in depressive disorders. In this section, we discuss personality and cognitive factors that operate as diatheses to increase the risk of depression in the context of stress. Here again, we will focus on some of the longitudinal findings documenting that personality and cognitive variables predict increases in depressive symptoms over time.

Neuroticism Several longitudinal studies suggest that **neuroticism**, a personality trait that involves the tendency to experience frequent and intense negative affect, predicts the onset of depression (Jorm et al., 2000). A large study of twins suggests that neuroticism explains at least part of the genetic vulnerability to depression (Fanous, Prescott, &

FOCUS ON DISCOVERY 5.4

Understanding the Overlap in Anxiety and Depression

One idea proposed for DSM-5 was to consider whether anxiety disorders and depressive disorders are distinct. There are several reasons to question whether anxiety disorders should be considered to be separable from depressive disorders. Chief among these reasons is the high rate of comorbidity. At least 60 percent of people with an anxiety disorder will experience major depressive disorder during their lifetime, and vice versa—about 60 percent of those with depression will experience an anxiety disorder (Kessler et al., 2003; Moffitt et al., 2007).

Certain anxiety disorders overlap with depressive disorders more than do others. Depression appears to be particularly likely to co-occur with generalized anxiety disorder (GAD; see Chapter 6) and posttraumatic stress disorder (PTSD; see Chapter 7) (Watson, 2009). Indeed, GAD is more correlated with depression than it is with other anxiety disorders (Watson, 2005). Beyond patterns of comorbidity, the etiology of GAD, PTSD, and depression overlaps. The genetic risk for GAD and depression overlaps substantially (Kendler et al., 2003). Major depression, persistent

depressive disorder, GAD, and PTSD each involve a propensity toward unhappiness and distress, whereas other anxiety disorders involve a propensity toward fear. Some risk factors seem tied to depression and to a range of anxiety disorders, such as neuroticism (Watson, 2005).

In response to this overlap, one group of researchers recommended that mood and anxiety disorders be subsumed into one larger chapter in the DSM-5 (Watson, O'Hara, & Stuart, 2008). Within that larger chapter, they recommended differentiating distress disorders: major depressive disorder, persistent depressive disorder, generalized anxiety disorder, and PTSD; fear disorders: panic, agoraphobia, social phobia, and specific phobia; and bipolar disorders (see Figure 5.7). Although this categorization was based on strong evidence from the epidemiological and genetic data, the crafters of DSM-5 decided not to make such a drastic change.

Rather, the DSM-5 includes the specifier "with anxious distress" to be used when depressive episodes are accompanied by at least two anxiety symptoms. Many patients will likely meet the criteria for this specifier.

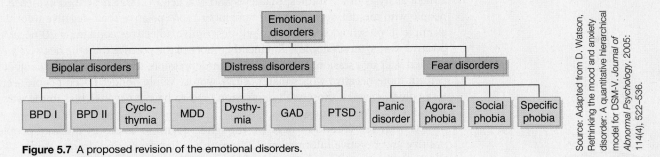

Figure 5.7 A proposed revision of the emotional disorders.

Source: Adapted from D. Watson, Rethinking the mood and anxiety disorder: A quantitative hierarchical model for DSM-V. *Journal of Abnormal Psychology*, 2005: 114(4), 522–536.

Kendler, 2004). As you would expect, neuroticism is also associated with anxiety (Kotov, Gamez, Schmidt, & Watson, 2010), an overlap we discuss in Focus on Discovery 5.4.

Cognitive Theories Pessimistic and self-critical thoughts can torture the person with depression. In cognitive theories, these negative thoughts and beliefs are seen as major causes of depression. We will describe three cognitive theories. Beck's theory and hopelessness theory both emphasize these types of negative thoughts, although the theories differ in some important ways. Rumination theory emphasizes the tendency to dwell on negative moods and thoughts. These models are not incompatible with the interpersonal and life stress research we discussed above; a person's negative thoughts may sometimes reflect genuinely stressful life circumstances. In cognitive models, though, the cognitions are seen as the most important force driving the depression.

Beck's Theory Aaron Beck (1967) argued that depression is associated with a **negative triad**: negative views of the self, their world, and the future (see Figure 5.8). According to this model, in childhood, people with depression acquired negative schemas through experiences such as loss of a parent, the social rejection of peers, or the depressive attitude of a parent. Schemas are different from conscious thoughts—they are an underlying set of beliefs that operate outside of a person's awareness to shape the way a person makes sense of his or her experiences. The negative schema is activated whenever the person encounters situations similar to those that originally caused the schema to form.

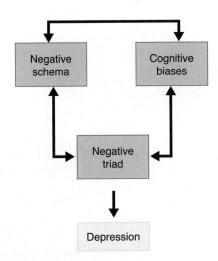

Figure 5.8 The interrelationships among different kinds of cognitions in Beck's theory of depression.

Once activated, negative schemas are believed to cause **cognitive biases**, or tendencies to process information in certain negative ways (Kendall & Ingram, 1989). That is, people with depression might attend to and remember even the smallest negative feedback about themselves, while at the same time failing to notice or remember positive feedback about themselves. People with a schema of ineptness might readily notice and remember signs that they are inept, while ignoring or forgetting signs that they are competent. Together, these cognitive errors lead them to make conclusions that are consistent with their underlying schema, which then maintains the schema (a vicious circle).

How has Beck's theory been tested? One widely used instrument in studies of Beck's theory is a self-report scale called the Dysfunctional Attitudes Scale (DAS), which includes items concerning whether people would consider themselves worthwhile or lovable. Hundreds of studies have shown that people demonstrate negative thinking on scales like the DAS during depression (Haaga, Dyck, & Ernst, 1991). Several major longitudinal studies suggest that people with negative cognitive styles are at elevated risk for developing depressive symptoms (Lewinsohn, Joiner, & Rohde, 2001), a first episode of MDD (Carter & Garber, 2011), and depressive relapse (Segal et al., 2006).

In studies of how people process information, depression is associated with a tendency to stay focused on negative information once it is initially noticed (Gotlib & Joormann, 2010) . For example, if shown pictures of negative and positive facial expressions, those with depression tend to look at the negative pictures longer than they look at the positive pictures. People with depression also tend to remember more negative than positive information. In a meta-analysis of 25 studies, Mathews and MacLeod (2002) described evidence that most people who are not depressed will remember more positive than negative information. For example, if presented with a list of self-descriptive adjectives containing 20 negative and 20 positive words, most people will remember more of the positive than the negative words when queried later in a session. People with major depression, though, tend to remember about 10 percent more negative words than positive words. While nondepressed people seem to wear rose-colored glasses, those with depression tend to have a negative bias in the way that they attend to and recall information.

As with self-reports of negative thoughts, cognitive biases in the way people process positive and negative information do seem to predict depression. In one study, 139 soldiers were tested before they went to the war in Iraq. Baseline tendencies to attend to sad faces were related to greater risk of developing depressive symptoms with exposure to the stresses of war (Beevers, Lee, Wells et al., 2011). Taken together, support has been obtained for Beck's model using a range of measures.

Hopelessness Theory According to **hopelessness theory** (see Figure 5.9; Abramson, Metalsky, & Alloy, 1989), the most important trigger of depression is hopelessness, which is defined by the belief that desirable outcomes will not occur and that there is nothing a person can do to change this. The model places emphasis on two key dimensions of **attributions**—the explanations a person forms about why a stressor has occurred (Weiner et al., 1971):

- Stable (permanent) versus unstable (temporary) causes
- Global (relevant to many life domains) versus specific (limited to one area) causes

Table 5.5 illustrates these dimensions by considering how different people might explain their low score on the Graduate Record Examination (GRE). People whose **attributional style** leads them to believe that negative life events are due to stable and global causes are likely to become hopeless, and this hopelessness will set the stage for depression.

Gerald Metalsky (1993) and colleagues conducted the first test of hopelessness theory. Early in the semester, college students

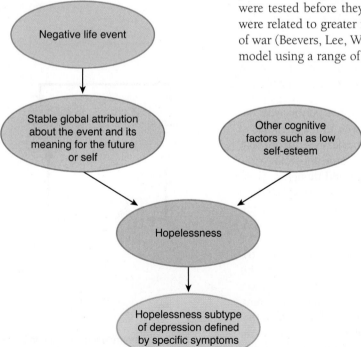

Figure 5.9 Major elements of the hopelessness theory of depression.

Table 5.5 An Example of Attributions: Why I Failed My GRE Math Exam

	Stable	Unstable
Global	I lack intelligence.	I am exhausted.
Specific	I lack mathematical ability.	I am fed up with math.

completed the Attributional Style Questionnaire (ASQ), as well as questionnaires to assess their grade aspirations, depressive symptoms, and hopelessness. These measures were used to predict depressive symptoms among students who received low grades on a test during the semester. Those who attributed poor grades to global and stable factors experienced more hopelessness, and in turn, hopelessness predicted depressive symptoms. Clearly, these results support the hopelessness theory. A similar study conducted with children in the sixth and seventh grades yielded almost identical results (Robinson, Garber, & Hillsman, 1995).

One large-scale study has assessed several different aspects of cognitive theories of depression. In the Temple–Wisconsin Cognitive Vulnerability to Depression study, the DAS, a measure used to test Beck's theory, and the ASQ, the measure used in tests of the hopelessness theory, were used to predict changes in depressive symptoms. Students with high scores on both the DAS and the ASQ were classified as high risk, whereas those with low scores on both measures were classified as low risk. Findings from this study provided support for cognitive theories: students in the high-risk group were more than six times as likely to develop first episodes of MDD in a two-year follow-up as were students in the low-risk group (Alloy, Abramson, Smith et al., 2006).

Rumination Theory While Beck's theory and the hopelessness model tend to focus on the nature of negative thoughts, Susan Nolen-Hoeksema (1991) suggested that a way of thinking called **rumination** may increase the risk of depression. Rumination is defined as a tendency to repetitively dwell on sad experiences and thoughts, or to chew on material again and again. The most detrimental form of rumination may be a tendency to brood regretfully about why a sad event happened (Treynor, Gonzalez, & Nolen-Hoeksema, 2003).

Tendencies to ruminate, as measured using self-report scales, have been found to predict the onset of major depressive episodes among initially nondepressed persons (Just & Alloy, 1997; Morrow & Nolen-Hoeksema, 1990; Nolen-Hoeksema, 2000). As described in Focus on Discovery 5.1, one interesting aspect of this theory is that women tend to ruminate more than men do, perhaps because of sociocultural norms about emotion and emotion expression. The tendency for women to ruminate more may help explain the higher rates of depression among women as compared to men (Nolen-Hoeksema, 2000).

Dozens of experimental studies have been conducted to see how inducing rumination affects moods. Typically, in the rumination–induction condition, participants are exposed to stress and then asked to dwell on their current feelings and on themselves (e.g., "Think about the way you feel inside"), whereas in a distraction (control) condition, participants are asked to think about topics unrelated to their self or feelings (e.g., "Think about a fire darting round a log in a fireplace"). The findings of dozens of such experimental studies indicate that rumination increases negative moods, particularly when people focus on negative aspects of their mood and their self (Watkins, 2008).

If rumination leads to sustained negative moods and even depression, why might people do it? According to one theory, it is evolutionarily adaptive to focus on negative events in order to solve problems (Andrews & Thomson, 2009). Although the findings of many experimental studies suggest that rumination can interfere with solving puzzles presented in the laboratory, no tests have examined whether rumination facilitates solving more major and complex life stressors. In contrast to the idea that rumination is evolutionarily adaptive, a different model suggests that getting stuck on negative thoughts results from a basic inability to control the focus of thoughts. Research shows that people with depression do have a hard time ignoring irrelevant information to complete a task, particularly when they are asked to ignore negative information (Gotlib & Joormann, 2010). Although there is still some debate about why people ruminate, it is clear that people who often ruminate are more likely to become depressed.

Check Your Knowledge 5.3

Answer the questions.

1. What types of recent life events are most likely to trigger major depressive episodes?

2. Name three interpersonal diatheses (during adulthood) that increase risk of depression.

3. Name three types of cognition related to risk for depression.

Social and Psychological Factors in Bipolar Disorder

Most people who experience a manic episode during their lifetime will also experience a major depressive episode, but not everyone will. For this reason, researchers often study the triggers of manic and depressive episodes separately within bipolar disorder.

Depression in Bipolar Disorder The triggers of depressive episodes in bipolar disorder appear to be similar to the triggers of major depressive episodes (Johnson, Cuellar, & Peckham, 2014). As in MDD, negative life events appear to be important in precipitating depressive episodes in bipolar disorder. Similarly, neuroticism, negative cognitive styles (Reilly-Harrington, Alloy, Fresco et al., 1999), expressed emotion (Miklowitz, Simoneau, Sachs-Ericsson et al., 1996), and lack of social support predict depressive symptoms in bipolar disorder.

Predictors of Mania Two factors have been found to predict increases in manic symptoms over time: reward sensitivity and sleep deprivation. Both of these models integrate psychological and biological facets of vulnerability to mania.

Reward Sensitivity The first model suggests that mania reflects a disturbance in the reward system of the brain (Depue, Collins, & Luciano, 1996). Researchers have demonstrated that people with bipolar disorder describe themselves as highly responsive to rewards on a self-report measure (Meyer, Johnson, & Winters, 2001). Being highly reward sensitive has also been shown to predict the onset of bipolar disorder (Alloy et al., 2008) and a more severe course of mania after onset (Meyer et al., 2001). In addition, a particular kind of life event predicts increases in manic symptoms among people with bipolar I disorder—specifically, life events that involve attaining goals, such as gaining acceptance to graduate school or getting married. How could successes like these promote increases in symptoms? Researchers have proposed that life events involving success may trigger cognitive changes in confidence, which then spiral into excessive goal pursuit (Johnson, Edge, Holmes et al., 2012). This excessive goal pursuit may help trigger manic symptoms among people who are biologically vulnerable to bipolar disorder.

Sleep Deprivation Researchers using a range of approaches have documented the intricate relationship of mania to disruptions in sleep and circadian (daily) rhythms (Murray & Harvey, 2010). Experimental studies indicate that sleep deprivation can precede the onset of manic episodes. In one study, participants who were experiencing bipolar depression were asked to stay at a sleep center, where they were kept awake all night. By the next morning, about 10 percent were experiencing at least mild symptoms of mania (Colombo, Benedetti, Barbini et al., 1999). In naturalistic studies, people often report that they had

FOCUS ON DISCOVERY 5.5

Integrating Biological and Social Risk Factors for Depression: Cytokines

Depression rates are very high among people with medical conditions such as obesity, cardiovascular disorder, cancer, diabetes, and Alzheimer's disease. For a long time, people thought that perhaps depression unfolded as a psychological response to the medical symptoms, but newer evidence suggests that this overlap in conditions may give us a clue about biological mechanisms in depression (Dantzer, O'Connor, Freund et al., 2008).

The key to this model is that medical conditions often trigger elevations in cytokines. As described in Chapter 2, cytokines are proteins that are released as part of an immune response. One set of these cytokines, pro-inflammatory cytokines, play a vital role in wound healing and fighting off infection by triggering inflammation. In the short term, this inflammation is adaptive. Problems arise, though, when the inflammation becomes prolonged. The current theory is that people may vary in how well and quickly they recover from the influence of pro-inflammatory cytokines and that this prolonged response might be tied to depression.

Two of these pro-inflammatory cytokines, IL-1Beta and TNF-alpha, have been shown to cause a syndrome called sickness behavior, which includes many of the symptoms that are seen in depression: decreased motor activity, reduced food consumption, social withdrawal, changes in sleep patterns, and reduced interest in rewards (like sugar, in the case of rats). A wide range of studies support the idea that pro-inflammatory cytokines can cause sickness behavior. For example, experimental administration of these two cytokines to animals triggers the symptoms of sickness behavior, which can be relieved by administering antidepressant medications. In humans, drugs such as interferon, which are used for severe medical conditions such as cancer, also increase levels of pro-inflammatory cytokines. Between a third and a half of patients treated with interferon develop the symptoms of major depressive disorder (Raison et al., 2006). In naturalistic studies without experimental manipulation, many people with major depressive disorder, and even those with no medical disorder, show elevated levels of cytokines (Raison, et al., 2006). High levels of pro-inflammatory cytokines can predict changes in depressive mood over time (van den Biggelaar et al., 2007).

Although researchers do not think that all depressions are related to cytokines, cytokines may be important for understanding some of the triggers of depression. One theory is that pro-inflammatory cytokines might be the culprit among people who develop a first episode of depression in the context of a major medical illness (Dantzer et al., 2008). Others have argued that inflammation may play a role in how life events trigger symptoms (Slavich & Irwin, 2014). Major life stresses, and particularly interpersonal life stressors, can provoke increases in pro-inflammatory cytokines. In experimental studies, harsh social feedback has been shown to produce temporary increases in pro-inflammatory cytokines (Dickerson, Gruenewald, & Kemeny, 2009). The social stressors that commonly trigger depression may operate in part through this inflammatory mechanism (Slavich & Irwin, 2014). A growing body of research is focused on developing treatments to reduce the activity of pro-inflammatory cytokines (Dantzer et al., 2008).

---

experienced a life event that disrupted their sleep just before the onset of manic episodes (Malkoff-Schwartz et al., 2000). Just as sleep deprivation can trigger manic symptoms, protecting sleep can help reduce symptoms of bipolar disorder (Frank, Swartz, & Kupfer, 2000). See Focus on Discovery 4.1 for a case study of an intervention that increased time spent in bed as a way of diminishing symptoms of bipolar disorder. Sleep and circadian rhythm disruption appear to be important aspects of mania risk.

Quick Summary

Research strongly suggests that childhood adversity and recent life events can increase the risk for MDD. Because many people do not become depressed after a life event, researchers have studied diatheses that could explain vulnerability to life events.

The interpersonal diatheses for depression include low social support, high expressed emotion, high need for reassurance, and poor social skills. Beyond social factors poor marital relationship quality,, psychological risk factors can help explain why some people become depressed. Evidence suggests that neuroticism, which involves frequent and intense negative affect, predicts the onset of depression. Cognitive factors include a negative schema; negative beliefs about the self, world, and future; biases to attend to and recall negative rather than positive information; stable and global attributions for stressors that lead to hopelessness; and tendencies to ruminate. Prospective evidence supports each of these cognitive models.

Many of the variables that predict MDD also appear to predict depressive symptoms within bipolar disorder. Mania appears to be predicted by sleep deprivation and by life events involving goal attainment.

Treatment of Mood Disorders

Most episodes of depression end after a few months, but the time may seem immeasurably longer to people with the disorder and to those close to them. With mania, even a few days of acute symptoms can create troubles for relationships and jobs. Moreover, suicide is a risk for people with mood disorders. Thus, it is important to treat mood disorders. Indeed, research suggests that it pays to treat depression. In one study, researchers ran a program at 16 large U.S. companies to identify depression, provide referrals for people with the condition, and even offer therapy by phone (Wang et al., 2007). Although the program cost several hundred dollars per worker, it saved about $1800 per employee in lost time at work, employee turnover, and other costs.

On one hand, more than 18.5 million prescriptions per year are filled for antidepressants in the United States (IMS Health, 2012), and about 25 percent of college students have tried antidepressant medication (Iarovici, 2014). On the other hand, community-based studies suggest that about half of people who meet diagnostic criteria for major depression do not receive care for their symptoms (Gonzalez et al., 2010).

Psychological Treatment of Depression

Several different forms of psychological treatment have been shown to help relieve depression. These treatments are similar in being relatively brief (3–4 months of weekly sessions) and focused on the here and now. As with studies of etiology, most of the research has focused on MDD. Available data, however, suggests that similar treatments can be helpful when depressive symptoms are more chronic.

Interpersonal Psychotherapy A treatment known as interpersonal psychotherapy (IPT) has fared well in clinical trials. As we described in Chapter 2, IPT builds on the idea that depression is closely tied to interpersonal problems (Klerman, Weissman, Rounsaville et al., 1984). The core of the therapy is to examine major interpersonal problems, such as role transitions, interpersonal conflicts, bereavement, and interpersonal isolation. Typically, the therapist and the patient focus on one or two such issues, with the goal of helping the person identify his or her feelings about these issues, make important decisions, and effect changes to resolve problems related to these issues. Like cognitive behavioral treatments, IPT is typically brief (e.g., 16 sessions). Techniques include discussing interpersonal problems, exploring negative feelings and encouraging their expression, improving both verbal and nonverbal communications, problem solving, and suggesting new and more satisfying modes of behavior. Several studies have found that IPT is effective in relieving MDD (Elkin et al., 1989) and that it prevents relapse when continued after recovery (Frank et al., 1990).

Cognitive Therapy In keeping with their theory that depression is caused by negative schema and cognitive biases, Beck and associates developed a cognitive therapy (CT) aimed at altering maladaptive thought patterns. To begin, the client is taught to understand how powerfully our thoughts can influence our moods and to see that the negative self-talk that they engage in day by day contributes to their low mood. To make this connection between thoughts and their mood, the client might be asked to complete daily monitoring homework that involves recording their negative thoughts throughout the week, so as to become more aware of how those thoughts are influencing their mood. The therapist then tries to help the person with depression to change his or her opinions about the self. When a person states that he or she is worthless because "nothing goes right, and everything I try to do ends in a disaster," the therapist helps the person look for evidence that contradicts this overgeneralization, such as abilities that the person is overlooking or discounting. The therapist then teaches the person to challenge negative beliefs and to learn strategies that promote making realistic and positive assumptions. Often, the client is asked to practice challenging overly negative thoughts in his or her day-to-day life, recording an initially negative thought and

Table 5.6 An Example of Daily Thought Monitoring, a Strategy Commonly Used in Cognitive Therapy

Date and Time	Situation *What was happening?*	Negative emotion *Note type of emotion (e.g., sad, nervous, angry) and the intensity of the emotion (0–100)*	Automatic negative thought	How much did you believe this initial thought (0–100)?	Alternative thought *Is there another view of the situation?*	Re-rate your belief in the initial thought	Outcome *Note type of emotion felt and emotion intensity (0–100) after considering the alternative*
Tuesday morning	I made a mistake on a report at work.	Sad–90 Embarrassed–80	I always mess things up. I'm never going to be good at anything.	90	My boss didn't give me enough time to prepare the report. I could have done a better job with more time.	50	Relief–30 Sad–30
Wednesday dinner	Eating dinner at a restaurant. An old friend from high school was at the next table and didn't recognize me.	Sad–95	I'm a nobody.	100	I've changed my hair drastically since then. Many people don't recognize me, but maybe she would have been happy to see me if I had reminded her of who I was.	25	Sad–25
Thursday breakfast	My husband left for work without saying goodbye to me.	Sad–90	Even the people I love don't seem to notice me.	100	I know that he had a huge presentation and he gets stressed.	20	Sad–20

then reconsidering whether this is the most accurate lens on the situation (see Table 5.6 for an example of a thought-monitoring homework assignment). Beck's emphasis is on cognitive restructuring (i.e., persuading the person to think less negatively).

Beck also includes a behavioral technique in his therapy called behavioral activation (BA) in which people are encouraged to engage in pleasant activities that might bolster positive thoughts about one's self and life. For example, the therapist encourages patients to schedule positive events such as going for a walk and talking with friends.

More than 75 randomized controlled trials have provided support for the efficacy of CT for depression (Gloaguen, Cottraux, Cucherat, & Blackburn, 1998). The strategies that clients learn in CT help diminish the risk of relapse even after therapy ends; this is an important issue given how common relapse is in MDD (Vittengl, Clark, Dunn, & Jarrett, 2007).

Computer-administered versions of CT have been developed. Typically, these interventions include at least brief contact with a therapist to guide the initial assessment, to answer questions, and to provide support and encouragement with the homework. Several randomized controlled trials provide evidence that computer-based CT is effective compared to treatment as usual in which patients were instructed to seek help from other sources, as they normally would (Andrews, Cuijpers, Craske et al., 2010). Because computer-based programs have varied in their effectiveness, it is important to ensure that consumers gain access to well-tested versions of computerized CT (Spek et al., 2007).

An adaptation of CT called **mindfulness-based cognitive therapy (MBCT)** focuses on preventing relapse after successful treatment for recurrent episodes of major depression (Segal, Williams, & Teasdale, 2001). MBCT is based on the assumption that a person becomes vulnerable to relapse because of repeated associations between sad mood and patterns of self-devaluing, hopeless thinking during major depressive episodes. As a result, when people who have recovered from depression become sad, they begin to think as negatively as they had when they were severely depressed. These reactivated patterns of thinking in turn intensify the sadness (Teasdale, 1988). Thus, in people with a history of major depression, sadness is more likely to escalate, which may contribute to the onset of new episodes of depression.

Clinical Case: An Example of Challenging a Negative Thought in Cognitive Therapy

The following dialogue is an example of one way that a therapist might begin to challenge a person's negative thoughts in CT, although it would take several sessions to help a client learn the cognitive model and to identify overly negative thoughts.

Therapist: *You said that you are a "loser" because you and Roger got divorced. Now we already defined what it is to be a loser—not to achieve anything.*

Patient: *Right. That sounds really extreme.*

Therapist: *OK. Let's look at the evidence for and against the thought that you have achieved something. Draw a line down the center of the page. On the top I'd like you to write, "I have achieved some things."*

Patient: *[draws line and writes statement]*

Therapist: *What is the evidence that you have achieved some things?*

Patient: *I graduated from college, I raised my son, I worked at the office, I have some friends, and I exercise. I am reliable. I care about my friends.*

Therapist: *OK. Let's write all of that down. Now in the right column let's write down evidence against the thought that you have achieved some things.*

Patient: *Well, maybe it's irrational, but I would have to write down that I got divorced.*

Therapist: *OK. Now in looking at the evidence for and against your thought that you have achieved some things, how do you weigh it out? 50–50? Differently than 50–50?*

Patient: *I'd have to say it's 95% in favor of the positive thought.*

Therapist: *So, how much do you believe now that you have achieved some things?*

Patient: *100%.*

Therapist: *And how much do you believe that you are a failure because you got divorced?*

Patient: *Maybe I'm not a failure, but the marriage failed. I'd give myself about 10%.*

(Quoted from R. Leahy, *Cognitive Therapy Techniques: A Practitioner's Guide* [New York: Guilford Press, 1991], Copyright Guilford Press. Reprinted with permission of the Guilford Press)

Note: As is typical, this dialogue challenges some, but not all, negative thoughts. Future sessions are likely to examine other negative thoughts.

The goal of MBCT is to teach people to recognize when they start to become depressed and to try adopting what can be called a "decentered" perspective—viewing their thoughts merely as "mental events" rather than as core aspects of the self or as accurate reflections of reality. For example, the person might say to himself or herself such things as "thoughts are not facts" and "I am not my thoughts" (Teasdale et al., 2000, p. 616). In other words, using a wide array of strategies, including meditation, the person is taught over time to develop a detached relationship to depression-related thoughts and feelings. This perspective, it is believed, can prevent the escalation of negative thinking patterns that may cause depression.

In one multisite study (Teasdale et al., 2000), people who formerly had depression were randomly assigned to MBCT or to "treatment as usual." The results of this study showed that MBCT was more effective than treatment as usual in reducing the risk of relapse among people with three or more previous major depressive episodes. MBCT does not, however, appear to protect against relapse among people with only one or two previous major depressive episodes (Ma & Teasdale, 2004). This may be one reason some of the randomized controlled trials have not supported the efficacy of mindfulness-based interventions (Hofmann, Sawyer, Witt et al., 2010). This treatment, then, seems most helpful when the MDD has been recurrent.

Behavioral Activation (BA) Therapy Earlier we mentioned that BA is one component of Beck's therapy. BA was originally developed as a standalone treatment, and it is based on the idea that many of the risk factors for depression interfere with receiving positive reinforcement (Lewinsohn, 1974). That is, life events, low social support, marital distress, poverty, and individual differences in social skills, personality, and coping may all lead to low levels of positive reinforcement. As depression begins to unfold, inactivity, withdrawal, and inertia are common symptoms, and these symptoms diminish the already low levels of positive reinforcement even further. Consequently, the goal of BA is to increase participation in positively reinforcing activities so as to disrupt the spiral of depression, withdrawal, and avoidance (Martell, Addis, & Jacobson, 2001).

BA has received a great deal of attention after positive findings in a study designed to identify the most effective ingredients in Beck's therapy (Jacobson & Gortner, 2000). The BA component of CT has been found to perform as well as the full package does in relieving MDD and preventing relapse over a 2-year follow-up period (Dobson et al., 2008). Group versions of behavioral therapy also appear to be effective (Oei & Dingle, 2008), and the treatment has now been successfully applied in many different settings for clients from a diverse range of backgrounds (Oei & Dingle, 2008). These findings challenge the notion that people must directly modify their negative thinking to alleviate depression and suggest instead that engaging in rewarding activities may be enough.

Behavioral Couples Therapy Because depression is often tied to relationship problems, including marital distress, researchers have studied **behavioral couples therapy** as a treatment for depression. In this approach, researchers work with both members of a couple to improve communication and relationship satisfaction. Findings indicate that when a person with depression is also experiencing marital distress, behavioral couples therapy is as effective in relieving depression as individual CT (Jacobson, Dobson, Fruzzetti et al., 1991) or antidepressant medication (Barbato & D'Avanzo, 2008). As you might expect, marital therapy has the advantage of relieving relationship distress more than does individual therapy.

Psychological Treatment of Bipolar Disorder

Medication is a necessary part of treatment for bipolar disorder, but psychological treatments can supplement medication to help address many of its associated social and psychological problems. These psychotherapies can also help reduce depressive symptoms in bipolar disorder.

Educating people about their illness is a common component of treating many disorders, including bipolar disorder and schizophrenia. **Psychoeducational approaches** typically help people learn about the symptoms of the disorder, the expected time course of symptoms, the biological and psychological triggers for symptoms, and treatment strategies. Studies confirm that education about bipolar disorder can help people adhere to treatment with medications such as lithium (Colom et al., 2003). This is an important goal because as many as half of people being treated for bipolar disorder do not take medication consistently (Regier, Narrow, Rae et al., 1993). Psychoeducation can help clients understand the rationale for taking these medications even after symptoms dissipate, can foster hope that the medications will help, and can target the internalized stigma that many clients experience when taking a medication such as lithium. Beyond helping people be more adherent with their medications, psychoeducational programs have been shown to help people avoid hospitalization (Morriss et al., 2007).

Several other types of therapy are designed to help build skills and reduce symptoms for those with bipolar disorder. Both CT and family-focused therapy (FFT) have received particularly strong support (Lam et al., 2000). CT draws on many of the types of techniques that are used in major depressive disorder, with some additional content designed to address the early signs of manic episodes. FFT aims to educate the family about the illness, enhance family communication, and develop problem-solving skills (Miklowitz & Goldstein, 1997).

In one large study, researchers recruited people who had bipolar disorder and who were depressed at treatment entry (Miklowitz et al., 2007). All of the patients in the trial received intensive medication treatment because researchers were interested in whether adding psychotherapy to medication treatment for bipolar disorder is helpful. Patients were randomly assigned to receive either psychotherapy or three sessions of a control treatment called collaborative care (psychoeducation about bipolar disorder). The 163 patients in the psychotherapy condition were further assigned to receive CT, FFT, or IPT. Each type of psychotherapy helped relieve depression more than the collaborative care condition did. There was no evidence that CT, FFT, or IPT differed in their effects on depression. These findings suggest that several types of psychotherapy are helpful for bipolar depression.

Biological Treatment of Mood Disorders

A variety of biological therapies are used to treat depression and mania. The two major biological treatments are electroconvulsive therapy and drugs. We will also briefly discuss transcranial magnetic stimulation, a technique that is FDA-approved for a small subset of people with MDD.

Electroconvulsive Therapy for Depression Perhaps the most controversial treatment for MDD is electroconvulsive therapy (ECT). For the most part now, ECT is only used to treat MDD that has not responded to medication. ECT entails deliberately inducing a momentary seizure by passing a 70- to 130-volt current through the patient's brain. Formerly, electrodes were placed on each side of the forehead, a method known as bilateral ECT. Today, *unilateral ECT*, in which the current passes only through the nondominant (typically the right) cerebral hemisphere, is often used because side effects are less pronounced than with bilateral ECT (McCall, Reboussin, Weiner, & Sackeim, 2000). In the past, the patient was usually awake until the current triggered the seizure, and the electric shock often created frightening contortions of the body, sometimes even causing bone fractures. Now the patient is given a muscle relaxant before the current is applied so that they sleep through the procedure and the convulsive spasms of muscles are barely perceptible. The patient awakens a few minutes later remembering nothing about the treatment. Typically, patients receive between 6 and 12 treatments, spaced several days apart.

Even with these improvements in procedures, inducing a seizure is drastic treatment. Why should anyone agree to undergo such radical therapy? The answer is simple. ECT is more powerful than antidepressant medications for the treatment of depression (UK ECT Review Group, 2003), particularly when psychotic features are present (Sackeim & Lisanby, 2001). Most professionals acknowledge that people undergoing ECT face some risks of short-term confusion and memory loss. It is fairly common for patients to have no memory of the period during which they received ECT and sometimes for the weeks surrounding the procedure. Unilateral ECT produces fewer cognitive side effects than bilateral ECT does. Nonetheless, even unilateral ECT is associated with deficits in cognitive functioning 6 months after treatment (Sackeim et al., 2007). In any case, clinicians typically resort to ECT only if less drastic treatments have failed. Given that suicide is a real possibility among people who are depressed, many experts regard the use of ECT after other treatments have failed as a responsible approach.

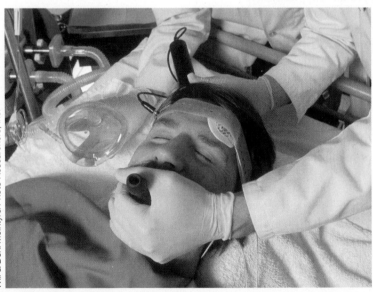

Electroconvulsive therapy is an effective treatment for depression that has not responded to medication. Using unilateral shock and muscle relaxants has reduced undesirable side effects.

Will & Deni McIntyre/Photo Researchers, Inc.

Medications for Depressive Disorders Drugs are the most commonly used and best-researched treatments—biological or otherwise—for depressive disorders (and, as we will see, for bipolar disorders as well). In the United States, about 75 percent of people receiving treatment for depression are prescribed antidepressant medications (Marcus & Olfson, 2010). As shown in Table 5.7, there are three major categories of **antidepressant** drugs:

Table 5.7 Medications for Treating Mood Disorders

Use	Category	Generic Name	Trade Name
Antidepressants	MAO inhibitors	tranylcypromine	Parnate
	Tricyclic antidepressants	imipramine, amitriptyline	Tofranil, Elavil
	Selective serotonin reuptake inhibitor (SSRI)	fluoxetine, sertraline	Prozac, Zoloft
Mood stablizers		lithium	Lithium
	Anticonvulsants	divalproex sodium	Depakote
	Antipsychotics	olanzapine	Zyprexa

monoamine oxidase inhibitors (MAOIs), **tricyclic antidepressants**, and **selective serotonin reuptake inhibitors (SSRIs)** (see Figure 5.5 for more detail on tricyclic antidepressants and SSRIs). The clinical effectiveness of all three classes of drugs is about the same (Depression Guidelines Panel, 1993). Dozens of double-blind studies have shown these medications to be effective in treating depressive disorders, with 50–70 percent of people who complete treatment showing major improvement (Nemeroff & Schatzberg, 1998).

Treatment guidelines recommend continuing antidepressant medications for at least 6 months after a depressive episode ends—and longer if a person has experienced several episodes. Continuing antidepressants after remission lowers the risk of recurrence from approximately 40 percent to about 20 percent (Geddes et al., 2003). To prevent recurrence, medication doses should be as high as those offered during acute treatment.

In the past several years, a number of controversies have developed regarding antidepressants. One major concern is that antidepressants do not appear to be more effective than are placebos for relieving mild or moderate symptoms of major depressive disorder. Antidepressants do offer a clear advantage compared to placebos in the treatment of severe major depressive disorder (Fournier et al., 2010) or persistent depressive disorder (Keller et al., 2000).

Beyond the evidence that these medications may not be helpful for those with mild levels of depression, published studies may overestimate how many people respond well to antidepressant medications. When pharmaceutical companies conduct studies to apply for either initial approval to market a medication or to support a change in the use of a medication in the United States, the data must be filed with the Food and Drug Administration (FDA). One research team examined what happened to the data from antidepressant studies conducted between 1987 and 2004 (Turner, Matthews, Linardatos et al., 2008). Of the 74 studies conducted, 51 percent were rated as having positive findings (i.e., supported the use of the antidepressant). All but one of the studies with positive findings were published. Of the studies with negative findings, less than half were published, and even in those reports, the published reports described the findings as positive even though the FDA had rated them as neutral or negative. Overall, then, the published findings were much more positive than the data in the FDA files.

In the face of these discouraging reports, one strategy is to conduct studies focused on what to do when a person does not gain relief from a first round of an antidepressant. In an attempt to answer this type of question, the STAR-D (Sequenced Treatment Alternatives to Relieve Depression) trial examined antidepressant response among 3671 patients across 41 sites, including 18 primary care facilities (Rush et al., 2006). In sharp contrast to the types of clean, non-comorbid depression histories reported in most medication trials, most of the patients enrolled in STAR-D suffered from chronic or recurrent depression, had comorbid psychiatric conditions, and had already received some (unsuccessful) treatment for the current episode. Rather than assessing whether antidepressant medication or psychotherapy was more helpful than a placebo treatment, the goal of the study was to consider the types of practical questions that physicians face in daily practice. Patients were all started on citalopram (Celexa), an SSRI. If they did not respond to citalopram, they were offered (1) a choice of a different medication to replace the citalopram, (2) a chance to add a second medication to the citalopram, or (3) CT if they were willing to pay part of the cost. The researchers provided patients who did not respond with a third type of antidepressant and if needed, even a fourth.

The findings were sobering. Only about one-third of patients achieved full symptom relief when treated with citalopram (Trivedi et al., 2006). Among those who did not respond to citalopram, very few wanted to pay for CT and only 30.6 percent who received a second medication (either alone or as a supplement to citalopram) achieved remission. Across the course of treatments, relapse rates were high, so that even with the complex array of treatments offered, only 43 percent of people achieved sustained recovery (Nelson, 2006). The findings from this study highlight the need to develop new treatments for those who do not respond well to currently available treatments.

Among patients who are prescribed an antidepressant, 40 percent stop taking the medication within the first month (Olfson, Blanco, Liu et al., 2006), most commonly because they have a hard time tolerating the side effects such as dizziness, headaches, erectile dysfunction, or gastrointestinal complaints (Thase & Rush, 1997). The MAOIs are the least used antidepressants because of their potentially life-threatening side effects if combined with certain foods or beverages. The SSRIs have become the most commonly prescribed antidepressants because they tend to produce fewer side effects than the other classes of antidepressants (Enserink, 1999). Nonetheless, the FDA required manufacturers to include packaging information warning people that SSRIs have been associated with case reports of suicidality, particularly during the early phases of treatment or after increases in dosage. There is specific concern about the potential for suicidality in children, adolescents, and young adults; researchers continue to look at this important issue, as findings have been controversial (see Chapter 13).

Transcranial Magnetic Stimulation for Depression In 2008, the FDA approved **transcranial magnetic stimulation** (rTMS) for a small subset of those with depression: patients who have failed to respond to a first antidepressant but have not yet tried a second antidepressant. In this approach, an electromagnetic coil is placed against the scalp, and intermittent pulses of magnetic energy are used to increase activity in the dorsolateral prefrontal cortex. Typical treatment lasts 30 minutes, with daily doses delivered for 5 to 10 days. In most randomized controlled trials, researchers have compared the treatment to a sham treatment in which the device is placed against the scalp at enough of an angle that the magnetic pulse will not increase brain activity. Multiple randomized controlled trials suggest that rTMS can help relieve treatment-resistant depression compared to the sham treatment (Slotema, Blom, Hoek et al., 2010).

Comparing Treatments for Major Depressive Disorder Combining psychotherapy and antidepressant medications bolsters the odds of recovery by more than 10–20 percent above either psychotherapy or medications alone for most people with depression (Hollon, Thase, & Markowitz, 2002). One study found that even offering CT by telephone for those beginning antidepressants could improve outcomes compared to medication alone (Simon, 2009). Each treatment offers unique advantages. Antidepressants work more quickly than psychotherapy, thus providing immediate relief. Psychotherapy may take longer but may help people learn skills that they can use after treatment is finished to protect against recurrent depressive episodes.

Many patients are interested in knowing whether medications or therapy will be more effective in relieving symptoms. In the most careful study to date comparing cognitive therapy to antidepressants, researchers focused on the treatment of severe depression. Two hundred and forty patients with severe depression were randomly assigned to receive antidepressant medication, CT, or a placebo for four months. Those who recovered were followed for another 12 months. CT was as effective as antidepressant medication for severe depression, and both treatments were more effective than placebo. CT had two advantages: it was less expensive than medication, and over the long term it helped protect against relapse once treatment was finished (Hollon et al., 2005).

Medications for Bipolar Disorder Medications that reduce manic symptoms are called *mood-stabilizing medications*. **Lithium**, a naturally occurring chemical element, was the first mood stabilizer identified. Up to 80 percent of people with bipolar I disorder experience at least mild benefit from taking this drug (Prien & Potter, 1993). Even though symptoms are usually decreased with medications, most patients continue to experience at least mild manic and depressive symptoms. Results of a major meta-analysis indicated that 40 percent of people relapsed while taking lithium as compared to 60 percent while taking a placebo (Geddes, Burgess, Hawton, Jamison, & Goodwin, 2004).

Because of possibly serious side effects, lithium has to be prescribed and used very carefully. Lithium levels that are too high can be toxic, so patients taking lithium must have regular blood tests. It is recommended that lithium be used continually for the person's entire life (Maj, Pirozzi, Magliano, & Bartoli, 1998).

Two classes of medications other than lithium have been approved by the FDA for the treatment of acute mania: anticonvulsant (antiseizure) medications such as divalproex sodium (Depakote) and antipsychotic medications such as olanzapine (Zyprexa). These other treatments are recommended for people who are unable to tolerate lithium's side effects. Like lithium, these medications help reduce mania and, to some extent, depression. Unfortunately, even these medications have serious side effects. As one example, anticonvulsants have been found to be related to a small increase in suicidal ideation compared to rates for placebo (Food and Drug Administration, January 31, 2008).

Typically, lithium is used in combination with other medications. Because lithium takes effect gradually, therapy for acute mania often begins with both lithium and an antipsychotic medication, such as olanzapine, which has an immediate calming effect (Scherk, Pajonk, & Leucht, 2007).

The mood-stabilizing medications used to treat mania also help relieve depression. Nonetheless, many people continue to experience depression even when taking a mood-stabilizing medication such as lithium. For these people, an antidepressant medication is often added to the regimen (Sachs & Thase, 2000), but two potential issues are associated with this practice. First, it is not clear whether antidepressants actually help reduce depression among persons who are already taking a mood stabilizer (the first type of treatment provided in bipolar disorder). Second, among people with bipolar disorder, antidepressants are related to a modest increase in the risk of a manic episode if taken without a mood stabilizer (Pacchiarotti et al., 2013).

Returning to Clinical Case: Treatment Decisions for Mary

Mary, the woman described at the beginning of this chapter, reported increasing problems because of her depression. Accordingly, her therapist referred her to a psychiatrist, who prescribed fluoxetine (Prozac). Both the psychologist and the psychiatrist agreed that medication might help by quickly relieving her symptoms. But after 2 weeks, Mary decided she did not want to continue taking Prozac because she found the side effects uncomfortable and did not like the idea of taking medication over the long term. She had not gotten much relief, maybe because her concerns about medication had led her to skip many doses.

With so many different types of treatment available, determining the best therapy for a given client can be a challenge. Mary had experienced a major life event and transition, suggesting that interpersonal psychotherapy might fit. But she was blaming herself for her job loss and other issues, suggesting that CT might help. Marital conflicts suggested behavioral

couples therapy could be appropriate. How does a therapist choose which approach to use? Sometimes this decision reflects the personal preferences and training of the therapist. Ideally, the approach incorporates the treatment preferences of the client as well. Her therapist began CT, in the belief that Mary's tendency to blame herself excessively when things went wrong was contributing to her depression. CT helped her learn to identify and challenge irrationally negative cognitions about herself. Therapy began by helping her identify times in her day-to-day life when her sad moods could be explained by overly negative conclusions about small events. For example, when her children would misbehave, Mary would quickly assume this was evidence that she was a bad mother. Over time, Mary began to examine and challenge long-held beliefs about her lack of competence. By the end of 16 weeks of treatment, she had obtained relief from her depression.

A Final Note on Treatment Many researchers are studying how treatments influence the psychological and biological mechanisms that seem to drive depression. For example, researchers have shown that antidepressants reduce negative thinking among persons with depression well before they influence mood state (Harmer, Goodwin, & Cowen, 2009). Researchers also have shown that successful treatments, whether with psychotherapy, medications, or ECT, change activity in the brain regions related to depression (Goldapple et al., 2004; Nobler et al., 2001).

In addition to considering the mechanisms through which treatments work, researchers have been developing new approaches to treatment. One newer approach is **deep brain stimulation**, a technique that involves implanting electrodes into the brain (Mayberg et al., 2005). By applying a small current to the electrodes, activity within that brain region can be manipulated. These studies are typically conducted only with small numbers of people who did not respond to other treatments for depression, and it is too early to consider deep brain stimulation as a standard treatment approach. Nonetheless, deep brain stimulation studies provide an important test of whether changing activity in a given region can help relieve depressive symptoms. Some researchers found that manipulating activity in the anterior cingulate and the nucleus accumbens using deep brain stimulation led to decreased depressive symptoms in about half of individuals who had failed to respond to previous depression treatments (Bewernick et al., 2010; Holtzheimer & Mayberg, 2011). The findings support the idea that the anterior cingulate and the nucleus accumbens play an important role in depression. Understanding more about how psychological and medication treatments change underlying neurobiological processes may help us refine treatments for the future.

Quick Summary

Many different treatments are available for depression. Cognitive therapy (CT), interpersonal psychotherapy (IPT), behavioral activation (BA) treatment, and behavioral couples therapy have all received support. ECT is effective, but there are concerns about cognitive side effects. The three forms of antidepressants have been found to be similarly effective; SSRIs have become more popular because they have fewer side effects than MAOIs and tricyclic antidepressants. CT appears to be as effective as antidepressant medication even in the treatment of severe MDD. IPT, though, does not appear to be as powerful as antidepressant medication for MDD.

Medication treatment is the first line of defense against bipolar disorder. The best-researched mood stabilizer is lithium, but anticonvulsants and antipsychotic medications are also effective mood stabilizers. Recent findings cast doubt on whether antidepressant medication is helpful in bipolar disorder. Some psychological treatments may help when offered as supplements to medications for the treatment of bipolar disorder. The best-validated approaches include psychoeducation, CT, and family therapy (FFT). IPT also fared well in the largest trial of psychological supplements to medications. These treatments appear particularly helpful in improving adherence to medication regimens and relieving depressive symptoms within bipolar disorder.

Check Your Knowledge 5.4

Circle all answers that apply.
1. Which of the following psychotherapies have obtained support in the treatment of MDD?
   a. interpersonal psychotherapy
   b. behavioral activation
   c. psychoanalytic therapy
   d. cognitive therapy
2. The most effective treatment for MDD with psychotic features is:
   a. Prozac
   b. any antidepressant medication
   c. ECT
   d. psychotherapy
3. Selective serotonin reuptake inhibitors (SSRIs) are more popular than other antidepressants because they:
   a. are more effective
   b. have fewer side effects
   c. are cheaper

Clinical Case: Steven

"Shannon Neal can instantly tell you the best night of her life: Tuesday, December 23, 2003, the Hinsdale Academy debutante ball. Her father, Steven Neal, a 54-year-old political columnist for The Chicago Sun-Times, was in his tux, white gloves, and tie. 'My dad 'walked me down and took a little bow,' she said, and then the two of them goofed it up on the dance floor as they laughed and laughed. A few weeks later, Mr. Neal parked his car in his garage, turned on the motor and waited until carbon monoxide filled the enclosed space and took his breath, and his life, away."

He had been under stress as he finished a book and had been hospitalized for heart problems. "Still, those who knew him were blindsided. 'If I had just 30 seconds with him now,' Ms. Neal said of her father, 'I would want all these answers.'"
(Cohen, 2008, p. 1)

Suicide

No other kind of death leaves friends and relatives with such long-lasting feelings of distress, shame, guilt, and puzzlement as does suicide (Gallo & Pfeffer, 2003). Survivors have an especially high mortality rate in the year after the suicide of a loved one.

We will focus on quantitative research on suicide, but those who study suicide learn from many different sources. Many philosophers have written searchingly on the topic, including Descartes, Voltaire, Kant, Heidegger, and Camus. In addition, novelists such as Herman Melville and Leo Tolstoy have provided insights on suicide, as have writers who have killed themselves, such as Virginia Woolf and Sylvia Plath. The study of suicide involves many different ethical questions and forces people to consider their own views on life and death.

We begin by defining terms (see Table 5.8). Suicidal ideation refers to thoughts of killing oneself and is much more common than attempted or completed suicide. Suicide attempts involve behaviors that are intended to cause death. Most suicide attempts do not result in death. **Suicide** involves behaviors that are intended to cause death and actually do so. **Nonsuicidal self-injury** involves behaviors that are meant to cause immediate bodily harm but are not intended to cause death (see Focus on Discovery 5.6).

Epidemiology of Suicide and Suicide Attempts

Suicide rates may be grossly underestimated because the circumstances of some deaths are ambiguous; for example, a seemingly accidental death may have involved suicidal intentions. Nonetheless, it has been estimated that, on average, every 20 minutes someone in the United States dies from suicide (Arias, Anderson, Kung et al., 2003).

Studies on the epidemiology of suicidality suggest the following:

- In the United States, the overall suicide rate is about 1 per 10,000 in a given year (Centers for Disease Control and Prevention, 2006).

Writers who killed themselves, such as Sylvia Plath, have provided insights into the causes of suicide. In perhaps an act that is at least partially related to the heritability of suicide, Sylvia Plath's son also killed himself.

Table 5.8 Key Terms in the Study of Suicidality

Suicidal ideation: thoughts of killing oneself
Suicide attempt: behavior intended to kill oneself
Suicide: death from deliberate self-injury
Nonsuicidal self-injury: behaviors intended to injure oneself without intent to kill oneself

FOCUS ON DISCOVERY 5.6

Nonsuicidal Self-Injury

Nonsuicidal self-injury (NSSI) is more common than previously thought (Nock, 2010), and contrary to previous thinking, it is practiced by many who do not have borderline personality disorder (Nock, Kazdin, Hiripi et al., 2006). Here we define this behavior and give some reasons it occurs.

There are two key issues to consider in defining NSSI. The first is that the person did not intend to cause death. The second is that the behavior is designed to immediately cause injury. Most commonly, people cut, hit, or burn their body (Franklin et al., 2010). When surveyed, anywhere from 13 to 45 percent of adolescents report having engaged in NSSI, but the higher estimates may be due to overly broad definitions. For example, some studies will include "scratching to the point of bleeding," without ruling out poison ivy or other reasons people might be scratching. Without a doubt, though, there is a group of people who engage in serious attempts to hurt themselves. The modal profile is of a person who tries NSSI infrequently (less than 10 times) during early adolescence and then stops (Nock, 2009). A subset of people seem to persist in self-injury, sometimes reporting more than 50 incidents of self-injury per year, and it is this profile of persistent NSSI that researchers are working to understand (Nock & Prinstein, 2004).

In a comprehensive review, Nock and colleagues (2010) argue that people will hurt

WireImage/Getty Images, Inc.

In an interview with the BBC, Princess Diana described reaching a point of such pain that she engaged in nonsuicidal self-injury.

themselves for many different reasons. For some, the injury seems to help quell negative emotions, such as anger. Some report feeling satisfied after self-injury because they have given themselves punishment that they believe they deserved. The behavior can also be reinforcing interpersonally—others may respond by increasing support or by reducing aggression. Several studies provide evidence that those who are prone to self-injury do seem to experience more intense emotions and provide more intense psychophysiological responses to stress than others do; believe that they deserve to be punished; and report difficulty managing relationships constructively (Nock & Mendes, 2008). In one study, people who engaged in NSSI were asked to record feelings, events, and NSSI incidents daily over time. Feelings of self-hatred and of being rejected were common just before incidents of self-injury took place (Nock, Prinstein, & Sterba, 2009). Taken together, NSSI may be reinforcing both psychologically (by relieving feelings of self-hatred and anger) and socially (by eliciting more supportive reactions from others). It is likely to require integrated social, emotional, and cognitive research to fully understand this complex behavioral pattern. To foster more attention to this issue, the DSM-5 includes a NSSI diagnosis in the appendix as a condition for further study.

- Worldwide, about 9 percent of people report suicidal ideation at least once in their lives, and 2.5 percent have made at least one suicide attempt. The rate of suicide attempts in the United States is about twice the rate in other countries (Nock & Mendes, 2008).

- Suicide rates are higher in regions where more people own guns. Guns are by far the most common means of suicide in the United States (Arias et al., 2003), accounting for about 60 percent of all suicides. States and countries where more people own guns tend to have higher suicide rates (Miller & Hemenway, 1999).

- Men are four times more likely than women to kill themselves (Arias et al., 2003).

- Women are more likely than men are to make suicide attempts that do not result in death (Nock & Mendes, 2008).

- Men usually choose to shoot or hang themselves; women are more likely to use pills, a less lethal method, which may account for their lower rate of completed suicide.

- The suicide rate increases in old age. The highest rates of suicide in the United States are for white males over age 50.

- The rates of suicide for adolescents and children in the United States are increasing dramatically but are still far below the rates of adults (see Figure 5.10). Some estimates suggest that at least 40 percent of children and adolescents experience suicidal ideation at least once. Because young people are less likely to die from other causes, suicide ranks as the third leading cause of death among those aged 10 to 24.

- Being divorced or widowed elevates suicide risk four- or fivefold.

Risk Factors for Suicide

Suicide is such a complex and multifaceted act that no single model can hope to explain it. Myths about suicide abound, highlighting the need for careful research (see Table 5.9). Increasingly, those who have survived suicide attempts have joined public advocacy and support movements to help inform this field, and their perspectives may enhance our ability to understand factors that lead up to suicide attempts (see livethroughthis.org).

Psychological Disorders Suicide is discussed in this chapter because many persons with mood disorders have suicidal thoughts and some engage in suicidal behaviors. More than half of those who try to kill themselves are depressed at the time of the act (Centers for Disease Control and Prevention, 2006), and as many as 15 percent of people who have been hospitalized with depression ultimately die from suicide (Angst et al., 2002). Other psychological disorders also are important in understanding suicide: as many as 90 percent of people who attempt suicide are suffering from a psychological disorder. About 5–7 percent of people diagnosed with bipolar disorder and 5 percent diagnosed with schizophrenia eventually die from suicide (Palmer, Pankratz, & Bostwick, 2005; Tondo, Isacsson, & Baldessarini, 2003). Impulse control disorders, substance use disorders, PTSD, and borderline personality disorder are also each related to a higher risk of suicidal actions (Linehan, 1997; Nock & Mendes, 2008; Nock et al., 2009). Even less severe psychological disorders, such as panic disorder and eating disorders, are associated with elevated risk of suicide (Linehan, 1997; Schmidt, Woolaway-Bickel, & Bates, 2000). With most of these disorders, though, suicides are most likely when a person is experiencing comorbid depression (Angst et al., 2002; Schmidt et al., 2000). Although understanding suicide within the context of psychological disorders is extremely important, most people with psychological disorders do not die from suicide.

Neurobiological Factors Twin studies suggest that heritability is about 48 percent for suicide attempts (Joiner, Brown, & Wingate, 2005). That is, genetic factors may explain about half of the variance in who will attempt suicide. Adoption studies also support the heritability of suicidality.

Source: Arias et al. (2003).

Figure 5.10 Annual deaths due to suicides per 100,000 people.

Lee Thompson Young, an actor well-known for his roles in the Famous Jett Jackson and Friday Night Lights, died from suicide in 2013. Researchers have shown that suicide rates increase in the month after a celebrity commits suicide. These findings provide evidence that the social environment is an influence on suicide.

Table 5.9 Myths About Suicide

Common Myth	Contrary Evidence
People who discuss suicide will not actually commit suicide.	Up to three-quarters of those who take their own lives communicate their intention beforehand.
Suicide is committed without warning.	People usually give many warnings, such as saying that the world would be better off without them or making unexpected and inexplicable gifts of highly valued possessions.
Suicidal people want to die.	Most people are thankful after suicide is prevented.
People who attempt suicide by low lethality means are not serious about killing themselves.	Many people are not well informed about pill dosages or human anatomy. Because of this misinformation, people who really want to die sometimes make nonlethal attempts.

Source: Fremouw, De Perzel, & Ellis (1990).

George C Beresford/Getty Images, Inc.

English novelist and critic Virginia Woolf (1882–1941).

On March 28, 1941, at the age of 59, Virginia Woolf drowned herself in the river near her Sussex home. Two suicide notes were found in the house, similar in content; one may have been written 10 days earlier, and it is possible that she may have made an unsuccessful attempt then, for she returned from a walk soaking wet, saying that she had fallen. The first was addressed to her sister Vanessa and the second to her husband, Leonard. To him, she wrote:

Dearest, I feel certain I am going mad again. I feel we can't go through another of those terrible times. And I shant recover this time. I begin to hear voices, and I can't concentrate. So I am doing what seems the best thing to do. You have given me the greatest possible happiness. You have been in every way all that anyone could be. I don't think two people could have been happier till this terrible disease came. I can't fight it any longer. I know that I am spoiling your life, that without me you could work. And you will I know. You see I can't even write this properly. I can't read. What I want to say is I owe all the happiness of my life to you. You have been entirely patient with me and incredibly good. I want to say that—everybody knows it. If anybody could have saved me it would have been you. Everything has gone from me but the certainty of your goodness. I can't go on spoiling your life any longer I don't think two people could have been happier than we have been. V.

Quoted from pp. 400–401, Briggs, J. (2005). Virginia Woolf: An Inner Life. Orlando, Fl: Harcourt, Inc.

Just as they are with depression, serotonin and cortisol are relevant to understanding suicidality. Researchers have found links between serotonin and suicide using an array of paradigms (Mann et al., 2000). Serotonin dysfunction appears to be particularly relevant for understanding violent suicide (Roy, 1994; Winchel, Stanley, & Stanley, 1990). Beyond the serotonin system, among patients with MDD, those who had an abnormal dexamethasone suppression test response had a 14-fold increase in the risk of suicide over the next 14 years (Coryell & Schlesser, 2001). Cortisol dysregulation and serotonin deficits, then, appear to be important predictors of suicidality.

Social Factors Economic and social events have been shown to influence suicide rates. As one example, across the past 100 years, suicide rates have been shown to increase modestly during economic recessions (Luo, Florence, Quispe-Agnoli, Ouyang, & Crosby, 2011). Some of the strongest evidence for the role of the social environment in suicide comes from the major effects of media reports of suicide. In one example of these effects, suicides rose 12 percent in the month after Marilyn Monroe's suicide (Phillips, 1985). A review of 293 studies found that media coverage of a celebrity suicide is much more likely to spark an increase in suicidality than coverage of a noncelebrity suicide (Stack, 2000). Media reports of natural deaths of famous people are not followed by increases in suicide, suggesting that it is not grief per se that is the influential factor (Phillips, 1974). These statistics suggest that sociocultural factors matter.

Social factors that are more directly relevant to the individual are also powerful predictors of suicidality. In a comprehensive review, Van Orden and colleagues (2010) argue that social isolation and a lack of social belonging are among the most powerful predictors of suicidal ideation and behavior. They maintain that the sensation of being alone, without others to turn to, is a major factor in the development of suicidality.

Psychological Factors Suicide may have many different meanings. It may be intended to induce guilt in others, to force love from others, to make amends for wrongs, to rid oneself of unacceptable feelings, to rejoin a deceased loved one, or to escape from emotional pain or an emotional vacuum. Undoubtedly, the psychological variables involved in suicide vary across people, but many researchers have attempted to identify risk factors that operate across them.

Several researchers relate suicide to poor problem-solving skills (Linehan & Shearin, 1988). Problem-solving deficits do predict suicide attempts prospectively (Dieserud, Roysamb, Braverman et al., 2003). Deficits also relate to the seriousness of previous suicide attempts, even after controlling for severity of depression, age, and intellectual functioning (Keilp et al., 2001).

A person who has trouble resolving problems can be expected to be more vulnerable to hopelessness. Hopelessness—the expectation that life will be no better in the future than it is in the present—is strongly tied to suicidality. High levels of hopelessness are associated with a fourfold elevation in the risk of suicide (Brown, Beck, Steer et al., 2000), and hopelessness is important even after controlling for depression levels (Beck, Kovacs, & Weissman, 1975).

Beyond these negative characteristics (e.g., poor problem solving, hopelessness), positive qualities may motivate a person to live and help a clinician to build a case for choosing life (Malone et al., 2000). One line of research builds on the Reasons for Living Inventory (Linehan, Goodstein, Nielsen et al., 1983). Items on this inventory tap into what is important to the person, such as responsibility to family and concerns about children. People with more reasons to live tend to be less suicidal than those with few reasons to live (Ivanoff, Jang, Smyth et al., 1994).

Although many people think about suicide, relatively few engage in suicidal actions. Additional variables predict the switch from thinking about suicide to acting on those thoughts (van Orden, Witte, Gordon, Bender, & Joiner, 2008). Among people who are experiencing suicidal thoughts, hundreds of studies demonstrate that people who are more impulsive are more likely to attempt suicide or to die from suicide (Brezo, Paris, & Turecki, 2006). Intense distress and hopelessness might set off thoughts about suicide, but suicidal actions might be driven by other factors, such as impulsivity.

Preventing Suicide

Many people worry that talking about suicide will make it more likely to happen. Rather, clinicians have learned that it is helpful to talk about suicide openly and matter-of-factly. Giving a person permission to talk about suicide may relieve a sense of isolation.

Because they are ambivalent about their suicidal intentions, most will communicate their intentions in some way. "The prototypical suicidal state is one in which a person cuts his or her throat, cries for help at the same time, and is genuine in both of these acts. . . . Individuals would be happy not to do it, if they didn't have to" (Shneidman, 1987, p. 170). Among those who attempt suicide but do not die, 80 percent report within the next two days that they are either glad to be alive or ambivalent about whether they want to die (Henriques, Wenzel, Brown et al., 2005). This ambivalence gives the clinician an important foothold.

Treating the Associated Psychological Disorder One approach to suicide prevention builds on our knowledge that most people who kill themselves are suffering from a psychological disorder. Thus when Beck's cognitive approach successfully lessens a patient's depression, that patient's suicidal risk is also reduced. Marsha Linehan's dialectical behavior therapy with borderline personality disorder patients provides another example of a treatment that is designed for a specific disorder but also provides protection from suicide (see Chapter 15).

Studies have found that medications for mood disorders reduce the risk of suicidality three- to fourfold (Angst et al., 2002). Specifically, lithium appears effective in suicide prevention for people with bipolar disorder (Cipriani, Pretty, Hawton et al., 2005). Among people who have been diagnosed with depressive disorders, ECT and antidepressants reduce suicidality (Bruce et al., 2004; Kellner et al., 2005). Risperidone, an antipsychotic medication, also appears to reduce the risk of suicide attempts among people with schizophrenia (Meltzer, 2003).

Treating Suicidality Directly Cognitive behavioral approaches appear to be the most promising therapies for reducing suicidality (van der Sande, Buskens, Allart, van der Graaf et al., 1997). These programs have been found to reduce the risk of a future attempt among those who have tried to kill themselves by 50 percent compared to treatment as usually offered in the community (Brown et al., 2005). They have also been found to reduce suicidal ideation (Joiner, Voelz, & Rudd, 2001). In a meta-analysis of 28 treatment trials, adults who received cognitive behavioral treatment reported less hopelessness, suicidal ideation, and suicidal behavior than those who received no treatment or other forms of treatment (Tarrier, Taylor, & Gooding, 2008).

Cognitive behavioral treatments include a set of strategies to prevent suicide (Brown, Henriques, Ratto et al., 2002). Therapists help clients understand the emotions and thoughts that trigger urges to commit suicide. Therapists work with clients to challenge their negative thoughts and to provide new ways to tolerate emotional distress. They also help clients solve problems they are facing. The goal is to improve problem solving and social support and thereby to reduce the feelings of hopelessness that often precede these episodes.

Professional organizations such as the American Psychiatric Association, the National Association of Social Workers, and the American Psychological Association charge their members with protecting people from suicide even if doing so requires breaking the confidentiality of the therapist–patient relationship. Therapists are expected to take reasonable precautions when they learn a patient is suicidal (Roy, 1995). One approach to keeping such patients alive is to hospitalize them as a short-term means of keeping them safe until they can begin to consider ways of improving their lives.

Granger Collection

After a broken engagement at age 31, Abraham Lincoln developed symptoms of depression that were so severe that his friends feared he would hurt himself, and they removed any sharp objects from his room. "I am now the most miserable man living," he confessed. "Whether I shall ever be better I cannot tell; I awfully forebode I shall not. To remain as I am is impossible; I must die or be better." (Cited in Goodwin, 2003.)

Golden Gate Bridge is one of the most popular locations for suicide in the world, with more than 1,600 people who have jumped to their death from its heights. In 2014, as evidence mounted that public health prevention programs can be highly effective, plans were made to construct a suicide barrier for the bridge.

Some have argued against involuntary hospitalizations and other efforts to keep people from killing themselves, seeing this as a violation of the right to liberty to make one's own choices, even if those end in death (Szasz, 1999). Most people who are prevented from killing themselves are grateful afterward for another chance at life. There are no easy answers here, but it is important to raise the questions.

Broader Approaches to Suicide Prevention It is exceedingly difficult to do controlled research on suicide prevention since the base rates are so low and the ability to track suicide in a large population is limited. One approach to this issue has been to study suicide prevention within the military, where rates of suicide are much higher than in the general population, programs can be offered to the entire community, and outcomes can be tracked carefully. In one study, researchers examined suicide rates in the Air Force before and after implementation of a comprehensive suicide prevention program. The program provided training for military leaders and for soldiers to encourage and destigmatize help seeking, to normalize the experience of distress, and to promote effective coping with distress. Implementation of the program led to a 25 percent drop in rates of completed suicide (Knox et al., 2010). It would appear that prevention efforts can reduce suicide rates.

Beyond prevention programs that target high-risk individuals, public health approaches to suicide prevention try to change how easily people can access the means they might use to commit suicide. For decades, the most common ovens in England relied on coal gas. Coal gas was cheap and widely available, but before it was burned, it released levels of carbon monoxide that were so high as to be deadly if one put one's head into a coal gas oven for even a couple of minutes. By the late 1950s, about 2500 suicides per year (almost half of the suicides in Britain) were committed in this manner. The British government phased out coal gas, and by the 1970s, almost no coal gas ovens remained. Over the course of those years, the British suicide rate dropped by a third and has remained at this lower rate.

Public health researchers often emphasize that most suicides tend to be impulsive—people often make a suicide attempt very quickly without much forethought. The more difficult it is to execute a suicidal action, the less likely it is to occur. For this reason, strategies such as erecting a barrier on a bridge, so that people cannot jump off the bridge on a moment's impulse, can be highly successful (Beautrais, Gibb, Fergusson et al., 2009).

Check Your Knowledge 5.5

True or false?
1. Men have higher rates of suicide than women.
2. Adolescents have higher rates of suicide than older adults do.
3. Most people with MDD will make a suicide attempt.

Answer the questions.
4. Which neurotransmitter is related to suicidality?
5. Which personality trait relates to suicidal action among those who are experiencing suicidal ideation?

Summary

Clinical Descriptions and Epidemiology

- There are two broad types of mood disorders: depressive disorders and bipolar disorders.
- Depressive disorders include major depression and persistent depressive disorder, along with the newer diagnoses of premenstrual dysphoric disorder and disruptive mood dysregulation disorder.
- Bipolar disorders include bipolar I disorder, bipolar II disorder, and cyclothymia. Bipolar I disorder is defined by mania. Bipolar II disorder is defined by hypomania and episodes of depression.
- Major depressive disorder, bipolar I disorder, and bipolar II disorder are episodic. Recurrence is very common in these disorders.
- Persistent depressive disorder and cyclothymia are characterized by low levels of symptoms that last at least 2 years.
- Major depression is one of the most common psychological disorders, affecting 16.2 percent of people during their lifetime. Rates of depression are twice as high in women as in men. Bipolar I disorder is much rarer, affecting 1 percent or less of the population.

Etiology

- Bipolar disorder is strongly heritable and depression is somewhat heritable. A polymorphism of the serotonin transporter gene is related to increased risk of depression when environmental adversity is also present.
- Neurobiological research has focused on the sensitivity of receptors rather than on the amount of various transmitters, with evidence for diminished sensitivity of the serotonin receptors in depression and mania. There is some evidence that mania is related to heightened sensitivity of the dopamine receptors and that depression is related to diminished sensitivity of dopamine receptors.
- Bipolar and unipolar disorders seem tied to elevated activity of the amygdala and the anterior cingulate and to diminished activity in the dorsolateral prefrontal cortex and hippocampus during tasks that involve emotion and emotion regulation. Bipolar disorder appears to be related to heightened activation of the striatum, but activity in this region appears to be low among those with depression.
- Overactivity of the hypothalamic–pituitary–adrenal axis (HPA), as indexed by poor suppression of cortisol by dexamethasone, is related to severe forms of depression and to bipolar disorder.
- Socioenvironmental models focus on the role of childhood adversity, negative life events, lack of social support, and family criticism as triggers for episodes but also consider ways in which a person with depression may elicit negative responses from others. People with less social skill and those who tend to seek excessive reassurance are at elevated risk for the development of depression.
- The personality trait that appears to be most closely related to depression is neuroticism. Neuroticism predicts the onset of depression.
- Influential cognitive theories include Beck's cognitive theory, hopelessness theory, and rumination theory. All argue that depression can be caused by cognitive factors, but the nature of the cognitive factors differs across theories. Beck's theory focuses on the cognitive triad, negative schemas, and cognitive biases. According to hopelessness theory, beliefs that a life event will have long-term meaningful consequences can instill a sense of hopelessness, which in turn results in depression. Rumination theory focuses on the negative effects of repetitively dwelling on the reasons for a sad mood. Prospective evidence is available for each model.
- Psychological theories of depression in bipolar disorder are similar to those proposed for unipolar depression. Some researchers have proposed that manic symptoms arise because of dysregulation in the reward system in the brain. Mania can be triggered by life events involving goal attainment. Mania also can be triggered by sleep deprivation.

Treatment

- Several psychological therapies are effective for depression, including interpersonal psychotherapy, cognitive therapy, behavioral activation therapy, and behavioral couples therapy.
- The major approaches that have been found to help as adjuncts to medication for bipolar disorder include psychoeducation, family therapy, and cognitive therapy, with some support for interpersonal psychotherapy as well.
- Electroconvulsive shock and several antidepressant drugs (tricyclics, selective serotonin reuptake inhibitors, and MAOIs) have proved their worth in lifting depression. Transcranial magnetic stimulation is FDA-approved for a small subset of people with depression. Lithium is the best-researched treatment for bipolar disorder, but antipsychotic and anticonvulsant medications also help decrease manic symptoms. Antidepressant medications have become controversial in the treatment of bipolar disorder.

Suicide

- Men, elderly people, and people who are divorced or widowed are at elevated risk for suicide. Most people who commit suicide meet diagnostic criteria for psychological disorders, with more than half experiencing depression. Suicide is at least partially heritable, and neurobiological models focus on serotonin and overactivity in the HPA. Environmental factors are also important: sociocultural events such as celebrity suicides and economic recessions can influence rates of suicide in the population, and social isolation is a robust predictor of suicide. Psychological vulnerability factors for suicidal ideation include poor problem solving, hopelessness, and lack of reasons to live; among those with suicidal ideation, suicidal action appears to be related to impulsivity.
- Several approaches have been taken to suicide prevention. For people with a psychological disorder, treatments targeting those symptoms help reduce suicidality. Many people, however, believe it is important to address suicidality more directly. CBT can help reduce suicidal ideation and behavior. Research suggests that suicide prevention can work. Public health interventions reduce the available means for committing suicide.

Answers to Check Your Knowledge Questions

5.1 five (including mood), two; 2. 16–17; 3. six; 4. MDD is diagnosed on the basis of five symptoms lasting at least 2 weeks; persistent depressive disorder requires only two symptoms, but they must be present for 2 years (or 1 year in children and adolescents). 5. Bipolar I disorder is diagnosed on the basis of manic episodes, which are more severe than the hypomanic episodes that are the core criterion for bipolar II disorder.

5.2 1. c; 2. b; 3. b; 4. d; 5. tryptophan

5.3 1. interpersonal life events; 2. social support, expressed emotion, reassurance seeking; 3. Beck's model of cognitive schemas guiding information processing errors in attention and memory that sustain the negative cognitive triad, Alloy's model of global and stable attributions guiding hopelessness, and rumination

5.4 1. a, b, d; 2. c; 3. b

5.5 1. T; 2. F; 3. F; 4. serotonin; 5. impulsivity

Key Terms

anterior cingulate
antidepressant
attribution
attributional style
behavioral couples therapy
bipolar I disorder
bipolar II disorder
cognitive biases
Cushing's syndrome
cyclothymic disorder
deep brain stimulation
disruptive mood dysregulation disorder
dorsolateral prefrontal cortex
episodic disorder
expressed emotion (EE)

flight of ideas
hopelessness theory
hypomania
lithium
major depressive disorder (MDD)
mania
melancholic
mindfulness-based cognitive therapy (MBCT)
monoamine oxidase inhibitors (MAOIs)
mood disorders
negative triad
neuroticism
nonsuicidal self-injury (NSSI)
persistent depressive disorder

peripartum onset
psychoeducational approaches
psychomotor agitation
psychomotor retardation
rapid cycling
reward system
rumination
seasonal affective disorder
selective serotonin reuptake inhibitors (SSRIs)
striatum
suicide
transcranial magnetic stimulation
tricyclic antidepressants
tryptophan

6 Anxiety Disorders

Clinical Case: Jenny

Jenny was a 23-year-old student completing her first year of medical school. The year had been a hard one, not only because of the long hours and academic challenges of medical school but also because her mother had developed cancer. One day, while attending rounds, Jenny found herself feeling lightheaded and dizzy. During rounds, the attending physician would ask students to diagnose and explain a given case, and on that day Jenny became extremely worried about whether she would be able to answer these questions when her turn came. As she thought about all this, her heart began to pound and her palms began to sweat. Overwhelmed by a deep sense of fear that something was horribly wrong, she abruptly fled the room without explaining her departure.

Later in the day, she wanted to explain leaving rounds but could not think of a good way to describe the situation to the attending physician. That night, she could not sleep, wondering what had happened and worrying about whether it would happen again. She worried about how this would affect her ability not only to take part in rounds but also to perform well in other roles, such as leading a small research group and meeting with other medical staff and clients. One week later, while driving to school, she experienced a sudden attack of similar symptoms, which forced her to pull off to the side of the road. She took the day off from school. Over the next several weeks, she began to avoid public situations as much as possible because she feared being humiliated by the return of these symptoms. She avoided study groups and going out with friends, and she turned down opportunities for training that involved public interviews of patients. She resigned from the choir that she had enjoyed being a part of for several years. Despite her withdrawal, she experienced three more attacks, each in unexpected situations. She began to think that maybe medical school was a poor choice for her because she had such deep fears about experiencing another attack during rounds. After she read about panic disorder in one of her textbooks, she decided to visit a psychologist. The psychologist confirmed that she was experiencing panic disorder, and they started cognitive behavioral treatment.

ERY FEW OF US go through even a week of our lives without experiencing anxiety or fear. In this chapter, we focus on a group of disorders called **anxiety disorders**. Both anxiety and fear play a significant role in these disorders, so it is important to understand some of the similarities and differences between these two emotions.

Anxiety is defined as apprehension over an anticipated problem. In contrast, **fear** is defined as a reaction to immediate danger. Psychologists focus on the "immediate" aspect of fear versus the "anticipated" aspect of anxiety—fear tends to be about a threat that is happening now, whereas anxiety tends to be about a future threat. Thus, a person facing a bear experiences fear, whereas a college student concerned about the possibility of unemployment after graduation experiences anxiety.

Both anxiety and fear can involve arousal, or sympathetic nervous system activity (see Focus on Discovery 2.1 for a brief overview of the sympathetic nervous system). Anxiety often involves moderate arousal, and fear involves higher arousal. At the low end, a person experiencing anxiety may feel no more than restless energy and physiological tension; at the high end, a person experiencing fear may sweat profusely, breathe rapidly, and feel an overpowering urge to run.

Anxiety and fear are not necessarily "bad"; in fact, both are adaptive. Fear is fundamental for "fight-or-flight" reactions—that is, fear triggers rapid changes in the sympathetic nervous system to prepare the body for escape or fighting. In the right circumstance, fear saves lives. (Imagine a person who faces a bear and doesn't marshal energy to run quickly!) In some anxiety disorders, though, the fear system seems to misfire—a person experiences fear at a time when there is no danger in the environment. This is most vividly seen in panic attacks, which we will discuss later in this chapter.

Anxiety is adaptive in helping us notice and plan for future threats—that is, to increase our preparedness, to help people avoid potentially dangerous situations, and to think through potential problems before they happen. In laboratory studies first conducted 100 years ago and since verified many times over, a small degree of anxiety has been found to improve performance on laboratory tasks (Yerkes & Dodson, 1908). Ask anyone with extreme test anxiety, though, and they will tell you that too much anxiety interferes with performance. Anxiety, then, provides a classic example of an inverse U-shaped curve with performance—an absence of anxiety is a problem, a little anxiety is adaptive, and a lot of anxiety is detrimental.

In this chapter, we examine the major anxiety disorders included in DSM-5: specific phobias, social anxiety disorder, panic disorder, agoraphobia, and generalized anxiety disorder. Obsessive-compulsive disorder and trauma-related disorders have a good deal in common with the anxiety disorders but are also distinct in some important ways. To recognize those distinctions, the DSM-5 places these conditions in chapters next to anxiety disorders. We will cover obsessive-compulsive and trauma-related disorders in Chapter 7. All of the anxiety disorders covered in this chapter involve excessive amounts of anxiety, and with the exception of generalized anxiety disorder, all involve tendencies to experience unusually intense fear (Cox, Clara, & Enns, 2002).

Anxiety disorders as a group are the most common type of psychological disorder. For example, in one study of over 8000 adults in the United States, approximately 28 percent of people endorsed having experienced symptoms at some point during their life that met criteria for diagnosis of an anxiety disorder (Kessler, Petukhova, Sampson et al., 2012). Phobias are particularly common. As a group, anxiety disorders are very costly to society and to people with the disorders. These disorders are associated with twice the average rate of medical costs (Simon, Ormel, VonKroff et al., 1995), higher risk of cardiovascular disease and other medical conditions (Roest, Martens, de Jonge et al., 2010; Stein, Aguilar-Gaxiola, Alonso et al., 2014), twice the risk of suicidal ideation and attempts (Sareen, Cox, Afifi et al., 2005), high rates of unemployment and days out of work (Alonso, Petukhova, Vilagut et al., 2011), and high rates of marital discord (Whisman & Bruce, 1999) compared to people without a psychological diagnosis. All of the anxiety disorders are associated with substantial decrements in the quality of life (Olatunji, Cisler, & Tolin, 2007). The following quote illustrates some of the ways that anxiety can influence daily life.

On ordinary days, doing ordinary things—reading a book, lying in bed, talking on the phone, sitting in a meeting, playing tennis—I have thousands of times been stricken by a pervasive sense of existential dread and been beset by nausea, vertigo, shaking, and a panoply of other physical symptoms. In these instances, I have sometimes been convinced that death, or something somehow worse, was imminent. (Stossel, 2014, p. 2)

We begin by defining the symptoms of the anxiety disorders before turning to the common themes in the etiology for the anxiety disorders as a group. We then describe specific etiological factors that shape whether a specific anxiety disorder develops. Like most disorders, many different paradigms have helped shed light on the anxiety disorders. Hence, throughout our discussions of etiology, we look at issues from various perspectives, with particular focus on genetic, neurobiological, personality, cognitive, and behavioral research. Finally, we consider the treatment of the anxiety disorders. We describe commonalities in the psychological treatment of the various anxiety disorders, and then we describe how these general treatment principles are modified to address specific anxiety disorders. Finally, we discuss biological treatments of the anxiety disorders.

Table 6.1 Overview of the Major DSM-5 Anxiety Disorders

Disorder	Description
Specific phobia	Fear of objects or situations that is out of proportion to any real danger
Social anxiety disorder	Fear of unfamiliar people or social scrutiny
Panic disorder	Anxiety about recurrent panic attacks
Agoraphobia	Anxiety about being in places where escaping or getting help would be difficult if anxiety symptoms occurred
Generalized anxiety disorder	Uncontrollable worry

Clinical Descriptions of the Anxiety Disorders

There is a lot of overlap in the way the various anxiety disorders are defined. For each disorder, several criteria must be met for a DSM-5 diagnosis to be made:

- Symptoms interfere with important areas of functioning or cause marked distress
- Symptoms are not caused by a drug or a medical condition
- Symptoms persist for at least 6 months or at least 1 month for panic disorder
- The fears and anxieties are distinct from the symptoms of another anxiety disorder.

Each disorder, though, is defined by a different set of symptoms related to anxiety or fear (see Table 6.1 for a brief summary).

Specific Phobias

A **specific phobia** is a disproportionate fear caused by a specific object or situation, such as fear of flying, fear of snakes, and fear of heights. The person recognizes that the fear is excessive but still goes to great lengths to avoid the feared object or situation. In addition to fear, the object of a phobia may elicit intense disgust (Olatunji, Etzel, Tomarken et al., 2011). The names for these fears consist of a Greek word for the feared object or situation followed by the suffix *-phobia* (derived from the name of the Greek god Phobos, who frightened his enemies). Two of the more common phobias are claustrophobia (fear of closed spaces) and acrophobia (fear of heights). Specific phobias tend to cluster around a small number of feared objects and situations (see Table 6.2). A person with a specific phobia for one type of object or situation is very likely to have a specific phobia for a second object or situation—that is, specific phobias are highly comorbid (Kendler, Myers, Prescott et al., 2001). The Clinical Case of Jan provides a glimpse of how specific phobias can interfere with important life goals.

DSM-5 Criteria for Specific Phobia

- Marked and disproportionate fear consistently triggered by specific objects or situations
- The object or situation is avoided or else endured with intense anxiety

Acrophobia, or phobia of heights, is common. People with this fear would find a glass elevator terrifying. Other specific phobias include fears of animals, injections, and enclosed spaces.

Table 6.2 Types of Specific Phobias

Type of Phobia	Examples of the Feared Object	Associated Characteristics
Animal	Snakes, insects	Generally begins during childhood
Natural environment	Storms, heights, water	Generally begins during childhood
Blood, injection, injury	Blood, injury, injections, or other invasive medical procedures	Clearly runs in families; profile of heart rate slowing and possible fainting when facing feared stimulus (LeBeau, Glenn, Liao et al., 2010)
Situational	Public transportation, tunnels, bridges, elevators, flying, driving, closed spaces	Tends to begin either in childhood or in mid-20s
Other	Choking, contracting an illness, etc.; children's fears of loud sounds, clowns, etc.	

Clinical Case: Jan

Jan, a 42-year-old woman, had been offered a high-paying job in Florida. She was considering declining the offer because it would force her to live in an area known for having snakes. Before making this decision, she decided to see a therapist. During her first meeting with the therapist, she described a litany of ways she had avoided any contact with anything remotely resembling a snake. She had steered clear of outdoor activities, TV programs on nature, and even her children's books on nature. Although she had been able to cope with her fears without too many negative consequences so far, the idea of living in an area with snakes had greatly increased her apprehension. Aside from her phobia, Jan reported that she had always been a bit of a nervous person, a trait she shared with her mother.

One form of specific phobia is an intense fear of blood, injection, or injuries.

Social Anxiety Disorder

The core feature of **social anxiety disorder** is a persistent, unrealistically intense fear of social situations that might involve being scrutinized by, or even just exposed to, unfamiliar people. Although this disorder is labeled social phobia in the DSM-IV-TR, the term *social anxiety disorder* is used in the DSM-5 because the problems caused by it tend to be much more pervasive and to interfere much more with normal activities than the problems caused by other phobias (Liebowitz, Heimberg, Fresco et al., 2000). In interpersonal interactions, people with social anxiety disorder feel as though "all eyes are watching them," with others waiting to evaluate them and record any embarrassing acts. Although this may sound like shyness, people with social anxiety disorder avoid more social situations, feel more social discomfort, and experience these symptoms for longer periods of their lifetime than do people who are shy (Turner, Beidel, & Townsley, 1990). Many fear that their anxiety will become apparent to others. The intense anxiety leads most such people to avoid social situations, as illustrated by Maureen in the next Clinical Case. The most common fears for those with social anxiety include public speaking, speaking up in meetings or classes, meeting new people, and talking to people in authority (Ruscio, Brown, Chiu et al., 2008). Forced to engage in one of these feared activities, the person may spend days in advance thinking about all the possible ways things could go wrong, and then spend days after the event reliving the small moments that did go badly with a sense of horror.

The manifestations and outcomes of social anxiety disorder vary greatly. Social anxiety disorder can range in severity from a few specific fears to a generalized host of fears. For example, some people might be anxious about speaking in public but not about other social situations. In contrast, others report fearing most social situations. Those with a broader array of fears are likely to experience more comorbid depression and alcohol abuse (Acarturk, de Graaf, van Straten et al., 2008). Although many who suffer with social anxiety are withdrawn and submissive, people vary in how they cope with the threat of social rejection, and a small proportion respond with overtly hostile and aggressive behavior (Kashdan & McKnight, 2010). People with social anxiety disorder often work in occupations far below their talents because of their extreme social fears. Many would rather work in an unrewarding job with limited social demand than deal with social situations every day.

Clinical Case: Maureen

Maureen, a 30-year-old accountant, sought psychotherapy after reading a newspaper notice advertising group therapy for people with difficulties in social situations. Maureen appeared nervous during the interview and described feeling intensely anxious in conversations with others. She described the problem as becoming worse over the years, to the point where she no longer interacted socially with anyone other than her husband. She would not even go to the supermarket for fear of having to interact with people. Maureen deeply feared being perceived as stupid. This fear made her so nervous that she would often stammer or forget what she was going to say while talking to others, thus adding to her apprehension that others would see her as stupid and creating a vicious circle of ever-increasing fear.

Among people with social anxiety disorder, at least a third also meet the criteria for a diagnosis of avoidant personality disorder (see Chapter 15; Chavira, Stein, & Malcarne, 2002). The symptoms of the two conditions overlap a great deal, as does the genetic vulnerability for the two conditions (Reichborn-Kjennerud, Czajkowski, Neale et al., 2007). Avoidant personality disorder, though, is a more severe disorder with an earlier onset and more pervasive symptoms.

Social anxiety disorder generally begins during adolescence, when peer relationships become particularly important. For some, however, the symptoms first emerge during childhood. Without treatment, social anxiety disorder tends to be chronic (Yonkers, Bruce, Dyck et al., 2003).

DSM-5 Criteria for Panic Disorder

- Recurrent unexpected panic attacks
- At least 1 month of concern or worry about the possibility of more attacks occurring or the consequences of an attack, or maladaptive behavioral changes because of the attacks

Spencer Grant/PhotoEdit

Social anxiety disorder typically begins in adolescence and interferes with developing friendships.

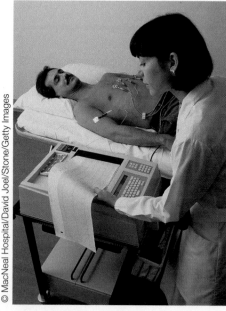

© MacNeal Hospital/David Joel/Stone/Getty Images

People with panic disorder often seek cardiac tests because they are frightened by changes in their heart rate.

Panic Disorder

Panic disorder is characterized by recurrent panic attacks that are unrelated to specific situations and by worry about having more panic attacks (see the Clinical Case of Jenny at the beginning of this chapter). A **panic attack** is a sudden attack of intense apprehension, terror, and feelings of impending doom, accompanied by at least four other symptoms. Physical symptoms can include shortness of breath, heart palpitations, nausea, upset stomach, chest pain, feelings of choking and smothering, dizziness, lightheadedness, faintness, sweating, chills, heat sensations, numbness or tingling sensations, and trembling. Other symptoms that may occur during a panic attack include **depersonalization** (a feeling of being outside one's body); **derealization** (a feeling of the world not being real); and fears of losing control, of going crazy, or even of dying. Not surprisingly, people often report that they have an intense urge to flee whatever situation they are in when a panic attack occurs. The symptoms tend to come on very rapidly and reach a peak of intensity within 10 minutes. Many people seek emergency medical care when they first experience a panic attack because they are terrified that they are having a heart attack.

As noted above, we can think about a panic attack as a misfire of the fear system: physiologically, the person experiences a level of sympathetic nervous system arousal matching what most people might experience when faced with an immediate threat to life. Because the symptoms are inexplicable, the person tries to make sense of the experience. A person who begins to think that he or she is dying, losing control, or going crazy is likely to feel even more fear. Among people with panic disorder, 90 percent report just these types of beliefs when panic attacks occur.

The diagnostic criteria for panic disorder require more than the presence of recurrent panic attacks. According to the DSM criteria for panic disorder, a person must experience recurrent panic attacks that are unexpected. Panic attacks that are triggered by specific situations, such as seeing a snake, are typically related to a phobia and should not be considered in diagnosing panic disorder. Beyond the occurrence of unexpected panic attacks, DSM criteria also specify that the person must worry about the attacks or change his or her behavior because of the attacks for at least 1 month. Hence, in making this diagnosis, the response to panic attacks is as important as the attacks themselves.

Remember that the criteria for panic disorder specify that panic attacks must be recurrent. It is fairly common for people to experience a single panic attack—more than a quarter of people in the United States report that they have experienced at least one panic attack during their lifetime (Kessler, Chiu, Jin et al., 2006). As Table 6.3 shows, though, many fewer people develop full-blown panic disorder. Among those who develop panic disorder, the onset is typically in adolescence. The symptoms of panic disorder tend to wax and wane over time (Nay, Brown, & Roberson-Nay, 2013). It can take a heavy toll; for example, as many as one-quarter of people with panic disorder report being unemployed for more than 5 years (Leon, Portera, & Weissman, 1995).

Table 6.3 Percent of Adults Ages 18–64 in the General Population Who Meet Diagnostic Criteria for Anxiety Disorders in the Past Year and in Their Lifetime

Anxiety Disorder	12-Month Prevalence Total	Lifetime Prevalence Total
Specific phobia	10.1	13.8
Social anxiety disorder	8.0	13
Panic disorder	3.1	5.2
Agoraphobia	1.7	2.6
Generalized anxiety disorder	2.9	6.2

Source: Kessler, Petukhova et al., 2012.

Agoraphobia

Agoraphobia (from the Greek *agora,* meaning "marketplace") is defined by anxiety about situations in which it would be embarrassing or difficult to escape if anxiety symptoms occurred. Commonly feared situations include crowds and crowded places such as grocery stores, malls, and churches. Sometimes the situations are those that are difficult to escape from, such as trains, bridges, or long road trips. As a consequence of their fear of these situations, many people with agoraphobia are virtually unable to leave their house, and even those who can leave do so only with great distress.

In the DSM-IV-TR, agoraphobia is coded as a subtype of panic disorder, but the DSM-5 includes agoraphobia as a separate diagnosis. This change brings the DSM in line with the International Classification of Diseases (ICD) diagnostic system, which has long recognized agoraphobia as a separate diagnosis. The new diagnosis also fits evidence from research studies. Indeed, five different large epidemiological studies suggest that at least half of people with agoraphobia symptoms do not experience panic attacks (Andrews, Charney, Sirovatka et al., 2009). Those who do not experience panic attacks are concerned about what will happen if other anxiety symptoms develop. The new diagnosis also fits with evidence that agoraphobia is related to significant impairment in daily functioning. The effects of agoraphobia on quality of life are as severe as those observed for the other anxiety disorders (Wittchen, Gloster, Beesdo-Baum et al., 2010).

Generalized Anxiety Disorder

The central feature of **generalized anxiety disorder** (GAD) is worry. Like Joe in the Clinical Case, people with GAD are persistently worried, often about minor things. The term *worry* refers to the cognitive tendency to chew on a problem and to be unable to let go of it (Mennin, Heimberg, & Turk, 2004). Often, worry continues because a person cannot settle on a solution to the problem. Most of us worry from time to time, but the worries of people with GAD are excessive, uncontrollable, and long-lasting. The worries of people with GAD center on the same types of threats that worry most of us: they worry about relationships, health, finances, and daily hassles (Roemer, Molina, & Borkovec, 1997)—but they worry more about these issues, as illustrated by the following passage.

> *I had graduated from college the year before, with honors. I had a prestigious job, loyal friends, a good apartment I shared with a bright and beautiful girlfriend, and as much money as I needed. Yet every day was torture. I slept fitfully, with recurring nightmares—tsunamis, feral animals, the violent deaths of loved ones. I had intestinal cramps and nausea and headaches. A sense of impending catastrophe colored every working moment. Worse, I had the distinct sense that catastrophe had already occurred. I had made the wrong decisions, gone down the wrong path, screwed up in a ruinous, irrevocable, epoch-making way. (Smith, 2012, pp. 3–4)*

DSM-5 Criteria for Generalized Anxiety Disorder

- Excessive anxiety and worry at least 50 percent of days about a number of events or activities (e.g., family, health, finances, work, and school)
- The person finds it hard to control the worry
- The anxiety and worry are associated with at least three (or one in children) of the following:
  - restlessness or feeling keyed up or on edge
  - easily fatigued
  - difficulty concentrating or mind going blank
  - irritability
  - muscle tension
  - sleep disturbance

DSM-5 Criteria for Agoraphobia

Disproportionate and marked fear or anxiety about at least two situations where it would be difficult to escape or receive help in the event of incapacitation, embarrassing symptoms, or panic-like symptoms, such as being outside of the home alone; traveling on public transportation; being in open spaces such as parking lots and marketplaces; being in enclosed spaces such as shops, theaters, or cinemas; or standing in line or being in a crowd

- These situations consistently provoke fear or anxiety
- These situations are avoided, require the presence of a companion, or are endured with intense fear or anxiety

People with agoraphobia often find crowds very distressing because escape would be difficult if anxiety symptoms occurred.

Beyond the uncontrollable worries, other symptoms of GAD include difficulty concentrating, tiring easily, restlessness, irritability, and muscle tension. GAD is not diagnosed if a person worries only about concerns driven by another psychological disorder; for example, a person with claustrophobia who only worries about being in closed spaces would not meet the criteria for GAD.

GAD typically begins in adolescence, though many people who have GAD report having had a tendency to worry all their lives (Barlow, Blanchard, Vermilyea et al., 1986). Once it develops, GAD is often chronic; in one study, about half of people with GAD reported ongoing symptoms eight years after an initial interview (Yonkers et al., 2003). Perhaps because of the chronicity, GAD is more strongly related to marital dissatisfaction than any other anxiety disorder (Whisman, Sheldon, & Goering, 2000), and people diagnosed with GAD report having few friendships compared to others (Whisman et al., 2000).

Clinical Case: Joe

Joe, a 24-year-old mechanic, was referred for psychotherapy by his physician, whom he had consulted because of difficulty falling asleep. He was visibly distressed during the entire initial interview, with a furrowed brow and continuous fidgeting. Although he first described worries about his health, a picture of pervasive anxiety soon emerged. He reported that he nearly always felt tense and he seemed to worry about everything. He was apprehensive of disasters that could befall him as he interacted with other people and worked, and he described worrying much of the time about his finances, his inability to establish a romantic relationship, and other issues. He reported a long history of difficulties relating to others, which had led to his being fired from several jobs. As he put it, "I really like people and try to get along with them, but I fly off the handle too easily. Little things upset me too much." Joe reported that he had always felt more nervous than other people but that his anxiety had become much worse after a romantic breakup 1 year ago.

Comorbidity in Anxiety Disorders

More than half of people with one anxiety disorder meet the criteria for another anxiety disorder during their life (Brown, Campbell, Lehman et al., 2001). Anxiety disorders are also highly comorbid with other disorders. Three-quarters of people with an anxiety disorder meet the diagnostic criteria for at least one other psychological disorder (Kessler, Crum, Warner et al., 1997). More specifically, about 60 percent of people in treatment for anxiety disorders meet the diagnostic criteria for major depression (Brown et al., 2001). We discuss this overlap in Focus on Discovery 5.5. Other conditions commonly comorbid with anxiety disorders include substance abuse (Jacobsen, Southwick, & Kosten, 2001) and personality disorders (Johnson, Weissman, & Klerman, 1992). As with many disorders, comorbidity is associated with greater severity and poorer outcomes of the anxiety disorders (Newman, Moffitt, Caspi et al., 1998; Newman, Schmitt, & Voss, 1997).

Gender and Cultural Factors in the Anxiety Disorders

It is well known that gender and culture are closely tied to the risk for anxiety disorders and to the specific types of symptoms that a person develops. As you will see, however, there are still some puzzles about why these patterns exist.

Gender

Women are more vulnerable to anxiety disorders than are men, with several studies documenting a 2 to 1 gender ratio (de Graaf, Bijl, Ravelli et al., 2002; Jacobi, 2004). Many different theories have been proposed to explain why women are more likely to develop anxiety disorders than men are. First, women may be more likely to report their symptoms. Social factors, such as gender roles, are also likely to play a role. For example, men may experience more social pressure than women to face fears—as you will see below, facing fears is the basis for one of the most effective treatments available. Women may also experience different life circumstances than do men. For example, women are much more likely than men to be sexually assaulted during childhood and adulthood (Tolin & Foa, 2006). These traumatic events may interfere with developing a sense of control over one's environment, and, as we will see below, having less control over one's environment may set the stage for anxiety disorders. Men may be raised to believe more in their personal control over situations as well. It also appears that women show more biological reactivity to stress than do men (Olff, Langeland, Draijer et al., 2007), perhaps as a result of these cultural and psychological influences. Although the gender gap is not fully understood, it is an important phenomenon.

Culture

People in every culture seem to experience problems with anxiety disorders, but culture and environment influence what people come to fear (Kirmayer, 2001). "If you live near a volcano you're going to fear lava. If you live in the rainforest you're going to fear malaria" (Smith, 2012, p. 72). *Kayak-angst*, a disorder that is similar to panic disorder, occurs among the Inuit people of western Greenland; seal hunters who are alone at sea may experience intense fear, disorientation, and concerns about drowning.

Several other culturally relevant syndromes provide examples of how culture and environment may shape the expression of an anxiety disorder. For example, in Japan a syndrome called *taijin kyofusho* involves fear of displeasing or embarrassing others; people with this syndrome typically fear such things as making direct eye contact, blushing, having body odor, or having a bodily deformity. The symptoms of this disorder overlap with those of social anxiety disorder, but the focus on others' feelings is distinct. Perhaps this focus is related to characteristics of traditional Japanese culture that encourage deep concern for the feelings of others (McNally, 1997). Other syndromes, such as *koro* (a sudden fear that one's genitals will recede into the body—reported in southern and eastern Asia), *shenkui* (intense anxiety and somatic symptoms attributed to the loss of semen, as through masturbation or excessive sexual activity—reported in China and similar to other syndromes reported in India and Sri Lanka), and *susto* (fright-illness, the belief that a severe fright has caused the soul to leave the body—reported in Latin America and among Latinos in the United States), also involve symptoms similar to those of the anxiety disorders defined in the DSM. As with the Japanese syndrome taijin kyofusho, the objects of anxiety and fear in these syndromes relate to environmental challenges as well as to attitudes that are prevalent in the cultures where the syndromes occur.

Beyond culturally relevant syndromes, the prevalence of anxiety disorders varies across cultures. This is not surprising given that cultures differ with regard to factors such as attitudes toward psychological disorders, stress levels, the nature of family relationships, and the prevalence of poverty—all of which are known to play a role in the occurrence or reporting of anxiety disorders. For example, in Taiwan and Japan, the prevalence of anxiety disorders seems to be quite low; however, this may reflect a strong stigma associated with having mental problems, which could lead to underreporting in those countries (Kawakami, Shimizu, Haratani et al., 2004). In Cambodia and among Cambodian refugees, very elevated rates of panic disorder (often diagnosed traditionally as *kyol goeu*, or "wind overload") have been reported, perhaps because of the extreme stress experienced by Cambodians over the past several decades (Hinton, Ba, Peou et al., 2000; Hinton, Um, & Ba, 2001).

For some time, researchers have thought that people from different cultures express symptoms of psychological distress and anxiety in different ways. For example, many thought that those from some cultures would express their emotional concerns through somatic

Disorders similar to panic attacks occur cross culturally. Among the Inuit, kayak-angst is defined by intense fear in lone hunters.

B & C Alexander/Photo Researchers

complaints, but it now seems that this conclusion might reflect sampling problems—that is, researchers often studied anxiety and depression in psychological clinics in the United States but in medical clinics in other cultures. One can imagine that a person seeing a medical doctor might be likely to emphasize somatic concerns! Indeed, many people, regardless of culture, tend to describe anxiety and depression initially in terms of bodily sensations when visiting a medical clinic. When researchers interview people in similar settings and ask specifically about psychological concerns, the ratio of somatic to psychological symptoms expressed appears to be much more similar across cultures (Kirmayer, 2001).

Quick Summary

As a group, anxiety disorders are the most common type of psychological disorder. Specific phobia is defined by an intense fear of an object or situation, social anxiety disorder by an intense fear of strangers or social scrutiny, panic disorder by anxiety about recurrent panic attacks, agoraphobia by a fear of places where escaping or getting help would be difficult if anxiety symptoms were to occur, and generalized anxiety disorder by worries lasting at least six months.

People with one anxiety disorder are very likely to experience a second anxiety disorder during their life. About 60 percent of people with anxiety disorders will experience major depression during their life. Women are much more likely than men to report an anxiety disorder. Culture influences the focus of fears, the ways that symptoms are expressed, and even the prevalence of different anxiety disorders.

Check Your Knowledge 6.1 (Answers are at the end of the chapter.)

For items 1–4, match the word to the definition.
1. fear
2. anxiety
3. worry
4. phobia
   a. an emotional response to immediate danger
   b. an excessive fear of a specific object or situation that causes distress or impairment

c. a state of apprehension often accompanied by mild autonomic arousal
d. thinking about potential problems, often without settling on a solution

Fill in the blank.
5. The percentage of people who will develop an anxiety disorder sometime during his or her lifetime is: _____
6. The key symptom of GAD is: _____

Common Risk Factors Across the Anxiety Disorders

As we consider risk factors associated with anxiety disorders, we begin by describing a set of factors that seem to increase risk for all of the anxiety disorders. The existence of such risk factors may help explain why people with one anxiety disorder are likely to develop a second one—that is, some risk factors increase the odds of having more than one anxiety disorder. For example, the factors that increase risk for social anxiety disorder may also increase risk for panic disorder.

Unlike the way we have organized most of the other chapters in this book, we have chosen to begin with the behavioral model. We do this because classical conditioning of a fear response is at the heart of many anxiety disorders. Many of the other risk factors, including genes, neurobiological correlates, personality traits, and cognition, influence how readily a person can be conditioned to develop a new fear response. Taken together, the risk factors combine to create an increased sensitivity to threat (Craske, Rauch, Ursano et al., 2009). Table 6.4 summarizes the general risk factors for anxiety disorders.

Table 6.4 Factors That Increase General Risk for Anxiety Disorders

Behavioral conditioning (classical and operant conditioning)

Genetic vulnerability

Disturbances in the activity in the fear circuit of the brain

Decreased functioning of gamma-aminobutyric acid (GABA) and serotonin; increased norepinephrine activity

Behavioral inhibition

Neuroticism

Cognitive factors, including sustained negative beliefs, perceived lack of control, and attention to cues of threat

Fear Conditioning

Earlier we mentioned that most anxiety disorders involve fears that are more frequent or intense than what most people experience. Where do these fears come from? The behavioral theory of anxiety disorders focuses on conditioning. **Mowrer's two-factor model** of anxiety disorders, published in 1947, continues to influence thinking in this area. Mowrer's model suggests two steps in the development of an anxiety disorder (Mowrer, 1947):

1. Through *classical conditioning*, a person learns to fear a neutral stimulus (the conditioned stimulus or CS) that is paired with an intrinsically aversive stimulus (the unconditioned stimulus or UCS).

2. A person gains relief by avoiding the CS. Through *operant conditioning*, this avoidant response is maintained because it is reinforcing (it reduces fear).

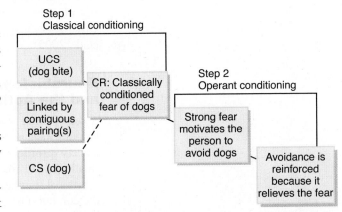

Figure 6.1 Two-factor model of conditioning as applied to dog phobia.

Consider the example shown in Figure 6.1. Imagine that a man is bitten by a dog and then develops a phobia of dogs. Through classical conditioning, he has learned to associate dogs (the CS) with painful bites (the UCS). This corresponds to step 1 above. In step 2, the man reduces his fear by avoiding dogs as much as possible; the avoidant behavior is reinforced by the reduction in fear. This second step explains why the phobia isn't extinguished. With repeated exposure to dogs that don't bite, the man would have lost his fear of dogs, but by avoiding dogs, the man gets little or no such exposure.

We should note that Mowrer's early version of the two-factor model does not actually fit the evidence very well; several extensions of this model, which we look at next, have been developed that fit the evidence better (Mineka & Zinbarg, 1998). One extension of the model considers different ways in which classical conditioning could occur (Rachman, 1977), including:

- Direct experience (like the dog bite in the example above)
- Modeling (e.g., seeing a dog bite a man or watching a video of a vicious dog attack)
- Verbal instruction (e.g., hearing a parent warn that dogs are dangerous).

Beyond considering these different sources of classical conditioning, researchers have shown that people with anxiety disorders seem to acquire fears more readily through classical conditioning and to show a slower extinction of fears once they are acquired (Craske et al., 2009). Most studies of this phenomenon use carefully controlled tests in a laboratory setting. For example, in one study, researchers conditioned people to fear a neutral picture of a Rorschach card (see Figure 3.11) by pairing the card with a shock six times (Michael, Blechert, Vriends et al., 2007). After receiving six shocks, most participants learned to fear the Rorschach card, as measured by using skin conductance responses to seeing the card—even those without an anxiety disorder developed this conditioned response. Those with and without an anxiety disorder (in this study, panic disorder) differed in the extinction phase

Courtesy Susan Mineka

Susan Mineka's research showed that when monkeys observe another monkey display fear of a snake, they also acquire the fear. This finding supports the idea that modeling plays a role in the etiology of phobias.

of the study, when the card was shown without any shock being provided. People who were not diagnosed with panic disorder showed a quick drop in their fear responses during the extinction phase, but people with panic disorder showed very little decrease in their fear response. Hence, people with panic disorder appear to sustain classically conditioned fears longer. Findings from a meta-analysis of 20 studies suggest that anxiety disorders are related to an elevated propensity to develop fears through classical conditioning and to a slow extinction of those fears once they are acquired (Lissek, Powers, McClure et al., 2005). Many of the risk factors we describe next could influence this sensitivity to fear conditioning.

Genetic Factors

Twin studies suggest a heritability of 20–40 percent for specific phobias, social anxiety disorder, and GAD, and about 50 percent for panic disorder (Hettema, Neale, & Kendler, 2001; True, Rice, Eisen et al., 1993). Some genes may elevate risk for several different types of anxiety disorder. For example, having a family member with a phobia is related to increased risk of developing not only a phobia but also other anxiety disorders (Kendler et al., 2001). Other genes may elevate risk for a specific type of anxiety disorder (Hettema, Prescott, Myers et al., 2005).

Neurobiological Factors: The Fear Circuit and the Activity of Neurotransmitters

A set of brain structures called the **fear circuit** is engaged when people feel anxious or fearful (Malizia, 2003). Key regions of the fear circuit, shown in Figure 6.2, are related to anxiety disorders. One important part of the fear circuit is the amygdala. The amygdala is a small, almond-shaped structure in the temporal lobe that appears to be involved in assigning emotional significance to stimuli. In animals, the amygdala has been shown to be critical for the conditioning of fear. The amygdala sends signals to a range of different brain structures involved in the fear circuit. Studies suggest that when shown pictures of angry faces (one signal of threat), people with several different anxiety disorders respond with greater activity in the amygdala than do people without anxiety disorders (Blair, Shaywitz, Smith et al., 2008; Monk, Nelson, McClure et al., 2006). Hence, elevated activity in the amygdala, a core part of the fear circuit, may help explain many different anxiety disorders.

The **medial prefrontal cortex** helps to regulate amygdala activity—it is involved in extinguishing fears and also appears to be engaged when people are regulating their emotions (Indovina, Robbins, Nunez-Elizalde et al., 2011; Kim, Loucks, Palmer et al., 2011). Researchers have found that adults who meet diagnostic criteria for anxiety disorders display less activity in the medial prefrontal cortex when viewing and appraising threatening stimuli (Britton, Grillon, Lissek et al., 2013) and when asked to regulate their emotional responses to threatening stimuli (Goldin, Manber-Ball, Werner et al., 2009). The pathway, or connectivity, linking the amygdala and the medial prefrontal cortex may be deficient among those with anxiety disorders (Kim et al., 2011). These deficits in connectivity between these two regions may interfere with the effective regulation and extinction of anxiety (Yehuda & LeDoux, 2007). We will discuss another part of the fear circuit, the locus coeruleus, when we discuss specific anxiety disorders.

Multiple neurotransmitters and neuropeptides are implicated in anxiety disorders, and many different techniques have been used to test their role. PET imaging provides a way to measure the receptor function of neurotransmitters, and findings of PET research link anxiety disorders to disruptions in serotonin and GABA receptors (Nikolaus, Antke, Beu et al., 2010). GABA is widely distributed throughout the brain and is believed to help inhibit anxiety (Sinha, Mohlman, & Gorman, 2004). Serotonin, which we discussed in Chapter 5 for its role in mood disorders, is believed to help

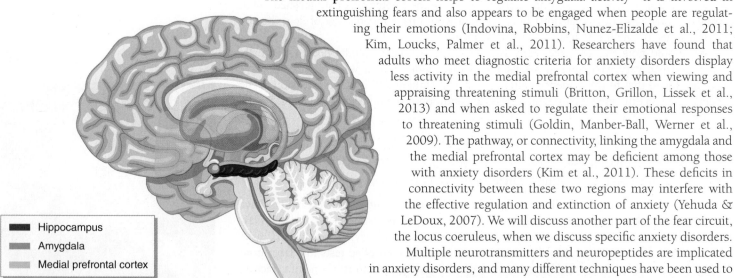

- ▬ Hippocampus
- ▬ Amygdala
- ▬ Medial prefrontal cortex

Figure 6.2 Fear and anxiety appear to be related to a set of structures in the brain called the fear circuit. The amygdala and medial prefrontal cortex are particularly involved in anxiety disorders.

modulate emotions (Carver, Johnson, & Joormann, 2008). Researchers have also used drug manipulation studies to show that anxiety disorders are related to increased levels of norepinephrine and changes in the sensitivity of norepinephrine receptors (Neumeister, Daher, & Charney, 2005). Norepinephrine is a key neurotransmitter in the activation of the sympathetic nervous system for "fight-or-flight" responses. In addition to human research, there is a huge body of animal research, using genetic paradigms and pharmacological manipulations, on the array of neurotransmitters and neuropeptides involved in the process of fear conditioning and extinction. Like the human research, this work supports the role of GABA, serotonin, and norepinephrine (Bukalo, Pinard, & Holmes, 2014).

Personality: Behavioral Inhibition and Neuroticism

Some infants show the trait of **behavioral inhibition**, a tendency to become agitated and cry when faced with novel toys, people, or other stimuli. This behavioral pattern, which has been described in infants as young as 4 months old, may be inherited and may set the stage for the later development of anxiety disorders. One study followed infants from 14 months through 7.5 years; 45 percent of those who showed elevated behavioral inhibition levels at 14 months showed symptoms of anxiety at age 7.5, compared to only 15 percent of those who had shown low behavioral inhibition levels (Kagan & Snidman, 1999). Behavioral inhibition appears to be a particularly strong predictor of social anxiety disorder: infants showing elevated behavioral inhibition were 3.79 times as likely as those with low behavioral inhibition to develop social anxiety disorder by adolescence (Chronis-Tuscano, Degnan, Pine et al., 2009).

Neuroticism is a personality trait defined by the tendency to experience frequent or intense negative affect. How does neuroticism relate to anxiety disorders? In a sample of 7076 adults, neuroticism predicted the onset of both anxiety disorders and depression (de Graaf et al., 2002). People with high levels of neuroticism were more than twice as likely to develop an anxiety disorder as those with low levels. In another study of 606 adults followed over 2 years, neuroticism was a major predictor of anxiety and depression (Brown, 2007).

Cognitive Factors

Researchers have focused on several separate cognitive aspects of anxiety disorders. Here, we concentrate on three: sustained negative beliefs about the future, a perceived lack of control, and attention to signs of threat.

Sustained Negative Beliefs About the Future People with anxiety disorders often report believing that bad things are likely to happen. For example, people with panic disorder might believe that they will die when their heart begins to pound, whereas people with social anxiety disorder might believe that they will suffer humiliating rejection if they blush. As pointed out by David Clark and colleagues (Clark, Salkovskis, Hackmann et al., 1999), the key issue is not why people think so negatively initially but, rather, how these beliefs are sustained. For example, by the time a person survives 100 panic attacks, you might expect the belief "this attack means I am about to die" would fade. One reason these beliefs might be sustained is that people think and act in ways that maintain these beliefs. That is, to protect against feared consequences, they engage in **safety behaviors**. For example, people who fear they will die from a fast heart rate stop all physical activity the minute they feel their heart race. They come to believe that only their safety behaviors have kept them alive. Hence, safety behaviors allow a person to maintain overly negative cognitions.

Perceived Lack of Control People who report experiencing little sense of control over their surroundings are at risk for a broad range of anxiety disorders (Mineka & Zinbarg, 1998). Childhood experiences, such as traumatic events (Green, McLaughlin, Berglund et al., 2010), punitive and restrictive parenting (Chorpita, Brown, & Barlow, 1998), or abuse (Chaffin, Silovsky, & Vaughn, 2005), may promote a view that life is not controllable.

Infants and toddlers showing behavioral inhibition—high anxiety about novel situations and people—are at greater risk of developing anxiety disorders during their lifetime.

Eric Audras/Onoky/Getty Images

Similarly, anxiety disorders often develop after serious life events that threaten the sense of control over one's life. Indeed, more than 70 percent of people report a severe life event before the onset of an anxiety disorder (Finlay-Jones, 1989). Other life experiences may shape the sense of control over the feared stimulus. For example, people who are used to dogs and feel comfortable about controlling dogs' behavior are much less likely to develop a phobia after a dog bite. On the whole, early and recent experiences of lack of control can influence whether a person develops an anxiety disorder (Mineka & Zinbarg, 2006).

Animal studies have illustrated that a lack of control over the environment can promote anxiety. For example, Insel and colleagues (1988) randomly assigned monkeys to one of two conditions. One group of monkeys grew up with the ability to choose whether and when they would receive treats. A second group of monkeys had no control over whether and when they received treats but received the same number of treats. In the third year of life, monkeys who had grown up without control behaved in ways that looked anxious when facing new situations and interacting with other monkeys; monkeys who had grown up with control showed less anxiety. In sum, animal and human studies both point toward the importance of perceived lack of control in the development of anxiety disorders.

Attention to Threat A large body of research indicates that people with anxiety disorders pay more attention to negative cues in their environment than do people without anxiety disorders (Williams, Watts, MacLeod et al., 1997). To test attention to threatening stimuli, researchers have used measures like the dot probe task (see Figure 6.3). In a meta-analysis of 172 studies, each of the specific anxiety disorders was associated with heightened attention to threatening stimuli on tasks such as the dot probe task (Bar-Haim, Lamy, Pergamin et al., 2007). For example, people with social anxiety disorder have been found to selectively attend to angry faces (Staugaard, 2010), whereas people with snake phobias selectively attend to cues related to snakes (McNally, Caspi, Riemann et al., 1990; Öhman, Flykt, & Esteves, 2001). Researchers have also shown that this heightened attention to threatening stimuli happens automatically and very quickly—before people are even consciously aware of the stimuli (Öhman & Soares, 1994; Staugaard, 2010). Once a threatening object captures their attention, anxious people have a difficult time pulling their attention away from that object; they tend to stay focused on a threatening object longer than others do (Cisler & Koster, 2010). In sum, anxiety disorders are associated with selective attention to signs of threat.

In one line of experimental research, investigators have examined whether attention to anxiety-related information can actually be created, and then whether this attention "bias" leads to more anxiety (MacLeod & Mathews, 2012). To train people to attend to threatening words, researchers used the dot probe task. To teach a negative bias, participants view hundreds of trials in which the dot is more likely to occur where the negative word was. For a control group, the dot is equally likely to appear where either the negative or neutral word was. People who were trained to attend to negative words reported a more anxious mood after training, especially when they were given a challenging task like an unsolvable puzzle to perform. The control group did not show an increase in anxious mood after training. The findings suggest that the way we focus our attention can foster an anxious mood.

Could these types of trained biases help us understand diagnosable levels of anxiety? Researchers have examined this question by training people diagnosed with generalized anxiety disorder to attend to positive information (Amir, Beard, Burns et al., 2009). To train a positive bias, the researchers used a version of the dot probe task in which dots appeared where the positive words had been. Participants in a control group completed an equivalent number of training sessions with a control version of the dot probe task. Participants completed 240 trials of training twice a week for four weeks. Anxiety levels did not change over the course of the study in the control group. Participants in the positive-bias training condition obtained lower anxiety scores on self-report and interview measures post-training: 50 percent of the people who received positive-bias training no longer met the diagnostic criteria for GAD. Parallel benefits of attention training have been shown among people with social anxiety (Schmidt, Richey, Buckner et al., 2009). This type of training also has been shown to help reduce cortisol responses when people encounter daily stressors (Dandeneau, Baldwin, Baccus et al., 2007).

First screen

Second screen

Figure 6.3 The computerized dot probe task is used to test biases in attention and, in some studies, to train attentional biases. On the first screen of each trial, participants see one neutral word and one negative word. On the second screen, a dot appears in the location where one of the two words was. The participant is asked to press a button as quickly as possible to indicate whether the dot appears on the left or right side of the screen. In the case shown here, a person who was looking at the word *death* will see the dot and respond more quickly than a person who was looking at the word *table*.

Etiology of Specific Anxiety Disorders

So far, we have discussed factors that might set the stage for development of anxiety disorders in general. Here, we turn to the question of how each of the specific anxiety disorders arises. That is, why does one person develop a specific phobia while another person develops generalized anxiety disorder? Keep in mind the common etiological factors already described and think about how these commonalities relate to and combine with the specifics described next.

Etiology of Specific Phobias

The dominant model of phobias is the two-factor model of behavioral conditioning, described earlier. Here we elaborate on how this model can be applied to understanding phobias. We'll describe some of the research evidence, as well as several refinements of the model.

In the behavioral model, specific phobias are seen as a conditioned response that develops after a threatening experience and is sustained by avoidant behavior. In one of the first illustrations of this model, John Watson and his graduate student Rosalie Rayner published a case report in 1920 in which they demonstrated creating an intense fear of a rat (a phobia) in an infant, Little Albert, using classical conditioning. Little Albert was initially unafraid of the rat, but after repeatedly seeing the rat while a very loud noise was made, he began to cry when he saw the rat.

Little Albert, shown here with Rayner and Watson, was classically conditioned to develop a fear of a white rat.

As already mentioned, behavioral theory suggests that phobias *could* be conditioned by direct trauma, modeling, or verbal instruction. But do most people with a phobia report one of these types of conditioning experiences? In one study, 1937 people were asked whether they had these types of conditioning experiences before the onset of their phobias (Kendler, Myers, & Prescott, 2002). Although conditioning experiences were common, about half of the people in the study could not remember any such experiences. Obviously, if many phobias start without a conditioning experience, this is a big problem for the behavioral model. But proponents of the behavioral model argue that people may forget conditioning experiences (Mineka & Öhman, 2002). Because of memory gaps, simple surveys of how many people remember a conditioning experience do not provide very accurate evidence about the behavioral model.

Even among those who have had a threatening experience, many do not develop a phobia. How might we understand this? To begin, the risk factors we have described, such as genetic vulnerability, neuroticism, negative cognition, and propensity toward fear conditioning, probably operate as diatheses—vulnerability factors that shape whether or not a phobia will develop in the context of a conditioning experience (Mineka & Sutton, 2006).

It also is believed that only certain kinds of stimuli and experiences will contribute to development of a phobia. Mowrer's original two-factor model suggests that people could be conditioned to be afraid of all types of stimuli. But people with phobias tend to fear certain types of stimuli. Typically, people do not develop phobias of flowers, lambs, or lamp shades! But phobias of insects or other animals, natural environments, and blood are common. As many as half of women report a fear of snakes; moreover, many different types of animals also fear snakes (Öhman & Mineka, 2003). Researchers have suggested that during the evolution of our species, people learned to react strongly to stimuli that could be life-threatening, such as heights, snakes, and angry humans (Seligman, 1971). That is, evolution may have "prepared" our fear circuit to learn fear of certain stimuli very quickly and automatically; hence, this type of learning is called **prepared learning**. In support of this idea of evolutionarily-adaptive fears, researchers have shown that monkeys can be conditioned to fear snakes and crocodiles but not flowers and rabbits (Cook & Mineka, 1989). As researchers have tested this model, some have discovered that people can be initially conditioned to fear many different types of stimuli (McNally, 1987). Fears of most types of stimuli fade quickly with ongoing exposure,

The prepared learning model suggests that we have evolved to pay special attention to signs of danger, including angry people, threatening animals, and dangerous natural environments.

though, whereas fears of naturally dangerous stimuli are sustained in most studies (Dawson, Schell, & Banis, 1986).

Etiology of Social Anxiety Disorder

In this section, we review behavioral and cognitive factors related to social anxiety disorder. The trait of behavioral inhibition may also be important in the development of social anxiety disorder.

Behavioral Factors: Conditioning of Social Anxiety Disorder Behavioral perspectives on the causes of social anxiety disorder are similar to those on specific phobias, insofar as they are based on a two-factor conditioning model. That is, a person could have a negative social experience (directly, through modeling, or through verbal instruction) and become classically conditioned to fear similar situations, which the person then avoids. The next step involves operant conditioning: avoidance behavior is reinforced because it reduces the fear the person experiences. There are few opportunities for the conditioned fear to be extinguished because the person tends to avoid social situations. Even when the person interacts with others, he or she may show avoidant behavior in smaller ways that have been labeled as safety behaviors. Examples of safety behaviors in social anxiety disorder include avoiding eye contact, disengaging from conversation, and standing apart from others. Although these behaviors are used to avoid negative feedback, they create other problems. Other people tend to disapprove of these types of avoidant behaviors, which then intensifies the problem (Wells, 1998). (Think about how you might respond if you were trying to talk to someone who looks at the floor, fails to answer your questions, and leaves the room in the middle of the conversation.)

Cognitive Factors: Too Much Focus on Negative Self-Evaluations Theory focuses on several different ways in which cognitive processes might intensify social anxiety (Clark & Wells, 1995). First, people with social anxiety disorders appear to have unrealistically negative beliefs about the consequences of their social behaviors—for example, they may believe that others will reject them if they blush or pause while speaking. Second, they attend more to how they are doing in social situations and their own internal sensations than other people do. Instead of attending to their conversation partner, they are often thinking about how others might perceive them (e.g., "He must think I'm an idiot"). In one study, researchers asked men to recount the thoughts that ran through their mind when they thought about introducing themselves to an attractive woman (Zanov & Davison, 2010). Men with social anxiety were much more likely to verbalize thoughts about their own performance than were those without social anxiety (Bates, Campbell, & Burgess, 1990; Zanov & Davison, 2009). As they focus on their performance, they often form powerfully negative visual images of how others will react to them (Hirsch & Clark, 2004). Of course, good conversation requires a focus on the other person, so too much thinking about inner feelings and evaluative cognitions can foster social awkwardness. The resultant anxiety interferes with their ability to perform well socially, creating a vicious circle. For example, the socially anxious person doesn't pay enough attention to others, who then perceive the person as not interested in them.

The evidence is clear that people with social anxiety disorder are overly negative in evaluating their social performance, even when they are not socially awkward (Stopa & Clark, 2000). For example, in one study, researchers assessed blushing in people with and without social anxiety disorder. Participants were asked to estimate how much they would blush during different tasks, such as singing a children's song. Then they were asked to engage in these different tasks. Participants with social anxiety disorder overestimated how much they would blush (Gerlach, Wilhelm, Gruber et al., 2001). Similarly, one research team asked people with social anxiety disorder to rate videos of their performance in giving a short speech. Socially anxious people rated their speeches more negatively than objective raters did, whereas people who were not socially anxious were not harsh in rating their own performance (Ashbaugh, Antony, McCabe et al., 2005). The evidence is clear that people with social anxiety disorder are unfairly harsh in their self-evaluations.

There is also evidence that people with social anxiety disorder attend more to internal cues than to external (social) cues. For example, people with social anxiety disorder appear to spend more time than other people do monitoring for signs of their own anxiety. In one study, researchers gave participants a chance to watch their own heart rate displayed on a computer screen or to view faces. Many of the faces were threatening. People diagnosed with social anxiety disorder attended more closely to their own heart rate than did the people who were not diagnosed with social anxiety disorder (Pineles & Mineka, 2005). Hence, rather than keeping their eye on potential external threats, people with this disorder tend to be busy monitoring their own anxiety levels.

How might all these risk variables fit together when we consider a person with social anxiety disorder, like Maureen? Maureen is likely to have inherited some tendency to be anxious when faced with new people. As she grew up, her anxiety may have interfered with her chances to acquire social skills and to gain self-confidence. Her fear of other people's opinions and her own negative thoughts about her social abilities created a vicious circle in which her intolerable anxiety led her to avoid social situations, and then the avoidance led to increased anxiety. Even when she is in social situations, her focus on her performance and anxiety levels may interfere with being fully engaged in the interaction.

Kim Basinger, the Oscar-winning actress, describes her experiences of anxiety in the video *Panic Attacks: A Film About Coping*. She is reported to have suffered from panic disorder and social anxiety disorder.

Etiology of Panic Disorder

In this section, we look at current thinking about the etiology of panic disorder from neurobiological, behavioral, and cognitive perspectives. As you will see, all of these perspectives focus on how people respond to somatic (bodily) changes like increased heart rate.

Neurobiological Factors We have seen that the fear circuit appears to play an important role in many of the anxiety disorders. Now we will see that a particular part of the fear circuit is especially important in panic disorder: the **locus coeruleus** (see Figure 6.4). The locus coeruleus is the major source of the neurotransmitter norepinephrine in the brain. Surges in norepinephrine are a natural response to stress, and when these surges occur, they are associated with increased activity of the sympathetic nervous system, reflected in a faster heart rate and other psychophysiological responses that support the fight-or-flight response. People with panic disorder show a more dramatic biological response to drugs that trigger releases of norepinephrine (Neumeister et al., 2005). Drugs that increase activity in the locus coeruleus can trigger panic attacks, and drugs that decrease activity in the locus coeruleus, including clonidine and some antidepressants, decrease the risk of panic attacks (Sullivan, Coplan, Kent et al., 1999).

Source: J. H. Martin, *Neuroanatomy Text and Atlas*, 4th ed. (1996), copyright McGraw Hill Education LLC with permission.

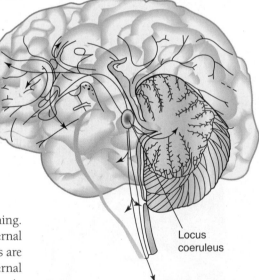

Behavioral Factors: Classical Conditioning

The behavioral perspective on the etiology of panic disorder focuses on classical conditioning. This model draws from an interesting pattern—panic attacks are often triggered by internal bodily sensations of arousal (Kenardy & Taylor, 1999). Theory suggests that panic attacks are classically conditioned responses to either the situations that trigger anxiety or the internal bodily sensations of arousal (Bouton, Mineka, & Barlow, 2001). Classical conditioning of panic attacks in response to bodily sensations has been called **interoceptive conditioning**: a person experiences somatic signs of anxiety, which are followed by the person's first panic attack; panic attacks then become a conditioned response to the somatic changes (see Figure 6.5).

Figure 6.4 The locus coeruleus is the major source of norepinephrine. Surges in norepinephrine lead to a number of physiological shifts, including faster heart rate.

Cognitive Factors in Panic Disorder Cognitive perspectives focus on catastrophic misinterpretations of somatic changes (Clark, 1996). According to this model, panic attacks develop when a person interprets bodily sensations as signs of impending doom (see Figure 6.6). For example, the person may interpret the sensation of an increase in heart rate as a sign of an impending heart attack. Obviously, such thoughts will increase the person's anxiety, which produces more physical sensations, creating a vicious circle.

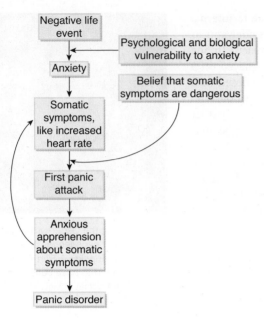

Figure 6.5 Interoceptive conditioning.

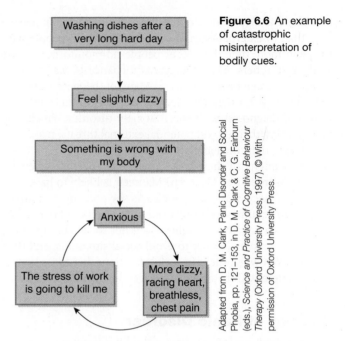

Figure 6.6 An example of catastrophic misinterpretation of bodily cues.

Adapted from D. M. Clark, Panic Disorder and Social Phobia, pp. 121–153, in D. M. Clark & C. G. Fairburn (eds.), *Science and Practice of Cognitive Behaviour Therapy* (Oxford University Press, 1997). © With permission of Oxford University Press.

Experiments demonstrate that panic attacks can be triggered by a variety of agents that change bodily sensations, including drugs and even exercise.

The evidence that these cognitive factors can contribute to panic attacks is quite strong. To understand the evidence, it is important to know that panic attacks can be experimentally induced in the laboratory. Research has focused on triggering panic attacks experimentally for more than 75 years. These studies suggest that an array of factors that create physiological sensations can trigger panic attacks among people with a history of panic attacks, including more than a dozen different medications (Swain, Koszycki, Shlik et al., 2003). Even drugs that have opposite physiological effects can set off panic attacks (Lindemann & Finesinger, 1938). Exercise alone, simple relaxation, or the physical sensations caused by an illness such as inner-ear disease also can induce panic attacks (Asmundson, Larsen, & Stein, 1998). Another commonly used procedure involves exposing people to air with high levels of carbon dioxide; in response to the diminished oxygen, breathing rate increases, and for some people this induces panic. In short, many different bodily sensations can trigger panic attacks (Barlow, 2004). Cognitive researchers have focused on how to differentiate the people who do and do not develop a panic attack in these experimental studies. People who develop panic attacks after being exposed to these agents seem to differ from those who do not develop panic attacks on only one characteristic—the extent to which they are frightened by the bodily changes (Margraf, Ehlers, & Roth, 1986).

To show the role of cognition as a predictor of panic attacks, researchers in one study used a paradigm described above, in which carbon dioxide levels are manipulated. Before breathing the carbon dioxide-manipulated air, some people were given a full explanation of the physical sensations they were likely to experience, and others were given no explanation. After breathing the air, those who had received a full explanation reported that they had fewer catastrophic interpretations of their bodily sensations, and they were much less likely to have a panic attack than those who did not receive an explanation (Rapee, Mattick, & Murrell, 1986). Catastrophic interpretations of bodily sensations, then, seem to be important in triggering panic attacks.

The propensity toward catastrophic interpretations can be detected before panic disorder develops. Many researchers have tested this idea using a scale called the **Anxiety Sensitivity Index**, which measures the extent to which people respond fearfully to their bodily sensations (Telch, Shermis, & Lucas, 1989). Sample items from this scale include "Unusual body sensations scare me" and "When I notice that my heart is beating rapidly, I worry that I might have a heart attack." In one study, college students with no history of panic attacks were divided into high and low scorers on the Anxiety Sensitivity Index (Telch & Harrington, 1992). Researchers then used the carbon dioxide manipulation described above to see who would develop panic attacks. As with the Rapee study just described, half of the participants were told that carbon dioxide would produce arousal symptoms, and half were not. When breathing carbon dioxide, panic attacks were most common among people who feared their bodily sensations, particularly if they were not warned about the physical effects of carbon dioxide on arousal. This result is exactly what the model predicts: unexplained physiological arousal in someone who is fearful of such sensations leads to panic attacks.

The Anxiety Sensitivity Index has also been shown to predict the onset of panic attacks in longer-term studies. In one study, researchers followed 1296 Air Force recruits as they went through the stressful experiences of basic training (Schmidt, Lerew, & Jackson, 1999). Consistent with the model, recruits with initially high scores on the Anxiety Sensitivity Index were more likely to develop panic attacks during basic training than were those with low scores.

Consistent with the idea that people with panic disorder are more attuned to small signs of body changes, several studies suggest that when heart rate is monitored using psycho-physiological equipment, people with panic disorder are more accurate than other people in knowing when an arrhythmia occurs and in detecting changes in their heart rate during periods of stress and arousal (Domschke, Stevens, Pfleiderer et al., 2010).

Putting It All Together: A Gene that Influences Neurobiological and Psychological Risk Factors for Panic Disorder The presence of a polymorphism in a gene guiding neuropeptide S function, the NPSR1 gene, has been tied to an increased risk of panic disorder (Donner, Haapakoski, Ezer et al., 2010). Considerable genetic and pharmacological research has shown that neuropeptide S is related to anxiety-like behaviors in mice (Donner et al., 2010). In humans, the NPSR1 gene has been related to increased amygdala response to threat stimuli (Kumsta, Chen, Pape et al., 2013), larger cortisol response to a laboratory stressor (Dannlowski, Kugel, Franke et al., 2011), and higher anxiety sensitivity scores (Domschke, Reif, Weber et al., 2011). Taken together, findings suggest that biological vulnerability may shape stress responses and hypersensitivity to somatic changes, and this may then increase the risk for panic disorder.

Etiology of Agoraphobia

Because agoraphobia was only recognized as a distinct disorder with the DSM-5, less is known about its etiology. As with other anxiety disorders, risk of agoraphobia appears to be related to genetic vulnerability and life events (Wittchen et al., 2010). One major model of how these symptoms evolves focuses on cognition.

The principal cognitive model for the etiology of agoraphobia is the **fear-of-fear hypothesis** (Goldstein & Chambless, 1978), which suggests that agoraphobia is driven by negative thoughts about the consequences of experiencing anxiety in public. There is evidence that people with agoraphobia think the consequences of public anxiety would be horrible (Clark, 1997). They seem to have catastrophic beliefs that their anxiety will lead to socially unacceptable consequences (e.g., "I am going to go crazy"; Chambless, Caputo, Bright et al., 1984).

Etiology of Generalized Anxiety Disorder

Generalized anxiety disorder (GAD) tends to co-occur with other anxiety disorders. Because the comorbidity is so high, researchers believe that many of the factors involved in predicting anxiety disorders in general are particularly important for understanding GAD. GAD, though, seems to differ from the other anxiety disorders in a few important ways. People who meet diagnostic criteria for GAD are much more likely to experience episodes of MDD than those with other anxiety disorders are. Moreover, GAD seems to involve a general tendency to experience general distress more than a specific pattern of intense fear. Indeed, whereas other anxiety disorders tend to be related to very intense psychophysiological responses to threatening stimuli, people diagnosed with GAD do not show this heightened psychophysiological response to threat (McTeague & Lang, 2012). Rather than fear, GAD is related to a more amorphous profile of general distress. Cognitive theory provides one way to make sense of the distress that is observed in GAD.

More specifically, cognitive factors may help explain why some people worry more than others. Worry is such an unpleasant emotion that one might ask why anyone would worry

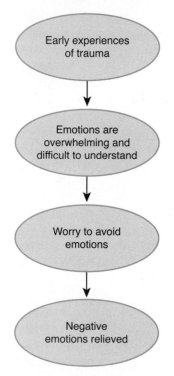

Figure 6.7 The excessive worry of GAD may be an attempt to avoid intense emotions.

a lot (Borkovec & Newman, 1998). Borkovec and colleagues have marshaled evidence that worry is actually reinforcing because it distracts people from more powerful negative emotions and images. The key to understanding this argument is to realize that worry does not involve powerful visual images and does not produce the physiological changes that usually accompany emotion. Rather, worry is more like a kind of repetitive self-talk about bad things that might happen but seems not to involve strong emotion. Indeed, worrying actually decreases psychophysiological signs of arousal (Freeston, Dugas, & Ladoceur, 1996). Thus, by worrying, people with GAD may be avoiding emotions that would be more unpleasant and more powerful than worry. But as a consequence of this avoidance, their underlying anxiety about these images does not extinguish.

What kinds of anxiety-evoking images might people with GAD be avoiding? A possible answer comes from studies showing that many people with GAD report a history of traumatic experiences (Borkovec & Newman, 1998). In one study in which more than 1000 participants were followed from age 3 to 32, researchers coded various forms of childhood maltreatment, including maternal rejection, harsh discipline, and childhood abuse. Maltreatment predicted a fourfold increase in the risk of developing GAD. It may be that worry distracts people with GAD from the distress of remembering these past traumas.

There is also support for the idea that people with GAD may be avoiding emotions. For example, people diagnosed with GAD report that they find it hard to understand and label their feelings (Mennin, Heimberg, Turk et al., 2002) and to regulate their negative emotions (Roemer, Lee, Salters-Pedneault et al., 2009), and they describe wanting to avoid intense emotion more than others do (Olatunji, Moretz, & Zlomke, 2010). See Figure 6.7 for an overview of how these processes might contribute to worry.

Some research suggests that people who have a hard time accepting ambiguity, that is, who find it intolerable to think that something bad *might* happen in the future, are more likely to worry and to develop GAD (Dugas, Marchand, & Ladouceur, 2005). This intolerance of uncertainty can predict increases in worry over time (Laugesen, Dugas, & Bukowski, 2003). Although intolerance of uncertainty is particularly strong for those with GAD, people with major depressive disorder and obsessive compulsive disorder also tend to struggle when the future is uncertain (Gentes & Ruscio, 2011).

Quick Summary

Many risk factors set the stage for anxiety disorders generally, rather than for a specific anxiety disorder. Behavioral models of anxiety disorders build from Mowrer's two-factor model (classical conditioning followed by operant conditioning). These models have been extended to consider that the classical conditioning may be driven by direct exposure to an event, observation of someone else experiencing an event (modeling), or verbal instruction. Other risk factors may increase the propensity toward fear conditioning. Genes increase risk for anxiety disorders. Neurobiological research on anxiety focuses on the brain's fear circuit. Anxiety disorders also appear to involve poor functioning of the GABA, norepinephrine, and serotonin systems. The personality traits of behavioral inhibition and neuroticism are both related to the development of anxiety disorders. From the cognitive perspective, anxiety disorders are associated with negative expectations about the future, beliefs that life is uncontrollable, and a bias to attend to negative information.

Specific phobias are believed to reflect conditioning in response to a traumatic event. Many people report that they experienced traumatic conditioning experiences before developing specific phobias,

but many people don't, perhaps because the conditioning experience has been forgotten. Prepared learning refers to the fact that people are likely to sustain conditioned responses to fear stimuli that have some evolutionary significance.

Social anxiety disorder appears to be related to conditioning and behavioral inhibition. Cognitive factors involved in social anxiety disorder include self-critical evaluations of social performance and tendencies to focus on internal thoughts and sensations.

Neurobiological research demonstrates that panic attacks are related to high activity in the locus coeruleus. Behavioral models emphasize the possibility that people could become classically conditioned to experience panic attacks in response to external situations or to internal somatic signs of arousal. Conditioning to somatic signs is called interoceptive conditioning. Cognitive perspectives focus on catastrophic misinterpretations of somatic symptoms.

A cognitive model of agoraphobia focuses on "fear of fear," or overly negative beliefs about what will happen if one experiences anxiety.

One cognitive model emphasizes that worry might actually protect people from intensely disturbing emotional images. People with GAD also appear to be intolerant of ambiguity.

Check Your Knowledge 6.2

Choose the best answer for each item.

1. Research suggests that genes can explain ——————— percent of the variance in anxiety disorders other than panic disorder.
   a. 0–20 percent
   b. 20–40 percent
   c. 40–60 percent
   d. 60–80 percent

2. ——————— is a personality trait characterized by a tendency to experience frequent and intense negative affect.
   a. Extraversion
   b. Neurosis
   c. Neuroticism
   d. Psychosis

Circle all that apply.

3. Cognitive factors found to correlate with anxiety disorders include:
   a. low self-esteem
   b. attention to signs of threat
   c. hopelessness
   d. lack of perceived control

4. A key structure in the fear circuit is the:
   a. cerebellum
   b. amygdala
   c. occipital cortex
   d. inferior colliculi

Match the theory to the model of etiology:

5. Panic disorder
6. GAD
7. Specific phobias
   a. anxiety sensitivity
   b. prepared learning
   c. avoidance of powerful negative emotions

Fill in the blanks.

8. The first step in Mowrer's two-factor model includes ——————— conditioning, and the second step involves ——————— conditioning.
   a. operant, operant
   b. classical, classical
   c. classical, operant
   d. operant, classical

Treatments of the Anxiety Disorders

Most people who seek treatment for anxiety disorders will only visit a family doctor. Most commonly, people will be offered a medication: in 2011, more than 80 million prescriptions were written for a class of anti-anxiety medications called benzodiazepines (IMS Health, 2012). As we shall see below, many other treatment options can be helpful for the anxiety disorders.

Commonalities Across Psychological Treatments

Effective psychological treatments for anxiety disorders share a common focus: exposure—that is, the person must face what he or she deems too terrifying to face. Therapists from varying perspectives all agree that we must face up to the source of our fear or, as an ancient Chinese proverb puts it, "Go straight to the heart of danger, for there you will find safety." Even psychoanalysts, who believe that the unconscious sources of anxiety are buried in the past, eventually encourage confronting the source of fears (Zane, 1984).

In a typical cognitive behavioral approach to exposure treatment, the therapist and the client make a list of triggers—situations and activities that might elicit anxiety or fear, and they create an "exposure hierarchy," a graded list of the difficulty of these triggers. Early sessions involve exposure to relatively less challenging triggers, and gradually, as the client learns that exposure will extinguish their anxiety, the more challenging triggers are faced. There have been more than 100 randomized controlled studies of CBT for anxiety disorders (Norton & Price, 2007), and dozens of these have compared CBT to a control treatment that involves some form of psychotherapy (Hofmann & Smits, 2008). Those studies suggest that CBT works well, even in comparison to other types of treatment. Exposure treatment is effective for 70–90 percent of clients.

The effects of CBT appear to endure when follow-up assessments are conducted six months after treatment (Hollon, Stewart, & Strunk, 2006) but in the years after treatment, many people experience some return of their anxiety symptoms (Lipsitz, Mannuzza, Klein et al., 1999).

A couple of key principles appear important in protecting against relapse (Craske & Mystkowski, 2006). First, exposure should include as many features of the feared object as possible. For example, exposure for a person with a spider phobia might include a focus on the hairy legs, the beady eyes, and other features of spiders. Second, exposure should be conducted in as many different contexts as possible (Bouton & Waddell, 2007). As an example, it might be important to expose a person to a spider in an office and also outside in nature.

The behavioral view of exposure is that it works by extinguishing the fear response. A good deal of work has focused on how extinction works at a neurobiological level and how this information might be used to refine exposure treatment (Craske, Kircanski, Zelikowsky et al., 2008). This work suggests that extinction does not work like an eraser. Let's take dog phobia as an example. Extinction will not erase the underlying fear of dogs altogether—the conditioned fear still resides deep inside the brain and it can resurface over time or in certain contexts. Rather, extinction involves learning new associations to stimuli related to dogs. These newly learned associations inhibit activation of the fear. Thus, extinction involves learning, not forgetting.

A cognitive view of exposure treatment has also been proposed. According to this view, exposure helps people correct their mistaken beliefs that they are unable to cope with the stimulus. In this view, exposure relieves symptoms by allowing people to realize that, contrary to their beliefs, they can tolerate aversive situations without loss of control (Foa & Meadows, 1997). Cognitive approaches to treatment of anxiety disorders typically focus on challenging (1) a person's beliefs about the likelihood of negative outcomes if he or she faces an anxiety-provoking object or situation, and (2) the expectation that he or she will be unable to cope. Thus cognitive treatments typically involve exposure in order to help people learn that they can cope with these situations. Because both behavioral and cognitive treatments involve exposure and learning to cope differently with fears, it is not surprising that most studies suggest that adding a cognitive therapy component to exposure therapy for anxiety disorders does not bolster results (Deacon & Abramowitz, 2004). Some very specific cognitive techniques, however, seem to help when added to exposure treatment; we will describe some of these below.

Virtual reality is sometimes used to simulate feared situations such as flying, heights, and even social interactions. Exposure treatment using virtual reality appears to provide substantial relief from anxiety disorders (Parsons & Rizzo, 2008). Findings of small randomized controlled trials indicate that exposure to these simulated situations appears to be as effective as **in vivo** (real-life) **exposure** (Klinger, Bouchard, Legeron et al., 2005; Rothbaum, Anderson, Zimand et al., 2006).

In addition to virtual reality programs, web-based programs have been developed to guide clients in CBT for the anxiety disorders. Computerized CBT programs for social anxiety disorder, panic disorder, and GAD achieve large effects compared to control conditions, and these effects appear to be sustained when clients are reassessed six months after they finish the program (Andrews, Cuijpers, Craske et al., 2010). These programs seem to work best when at least some human contact is provided (Marks & Cavanagh, 2009). For example, therapists might conduct the initial screening to ensure that a person is enrolled in the right type of program; they might help a person develop appropriate exposure hierarchy; or they might review homework assignments (Marks & Cavanagh, 2009). Even with this type of support, these programs substantially reduce the amount of professional contact time required to complete exposure treatment.

Although much of the work in this area is focused on exposure treatments, regardless of their format, several treatments have been developed more recently to help people take a more reflective, less reactive view of their intense anxiety and other emotions. These treatments include components such as mindfulness meditation and skills to promote acceptance of emotions, often in combination with some of the other CBT techniques. Although acceptance and mindfulness meditation treatments appear to be more powerful in reducing anxiety symptoms than are placebos, these treatments may not be as helpful as standard CBT approaches are (Vøllestad, Nielsen, & Nielsen, 2012). Findings regarding how these approaches compare to CBT have varied, and so more research is needed (Hofmann, Sawyer, Witt et al., 2010).

Psychological Treatments of Specific Anxiety Disorders

Next, we look at how psychotherapy can be tailored to the specific anxiety disorders. Even though exposure treatment is used with each anxiety disorder, how can it be tailored to specific anxiety disorders?

Psychological Treatment of Phobias Many different types of exposure treatments have been developed for phobias. Exposure treatments often include **in vivo** (real-life) **exposure** to feared objects. For phobias involving fear of animals, injections, or dental work, very brief treatments lasting only a couple of hours have been found to be highly effective—most people experience relief from phobic symptoms (Wolitzky-Taylor, Horowitz, Powers et al., 2008).

Psychological Treatment of Social Anxiety Disorder Exposure appears to be an effective treatment for social anxiety disorder. To provide a graded hierarchy of exposure, such treatments often begin with role playing or practicing with the therapist or in small therapy groups before undergoing exposure in more public social situations (Marks, 1995). With prolonged exposure, anxiety typically extinguishes (Hope, Heimberg, & Bruch, 1995). Social skills training, in which a therapist might provide extensive modeling of behavior, can help people with social anxiety disorder who may not know what to do or say in social situations. Remember that safety behaviors, like avoiding eye contact, are believed to interfere with the extinction of social anxiety (Clark & Wells, 1995). Consistent with this idea, the effects of exposure treatment seem to be enhanced when people with social anxiety disorder are taught to stop using safety behaviors (Kim, 2005). That is, not only are people asked to engage in social activities, but, while doing so, they are asked to make direct eye contact, to engage in conversation, and to be fully present. Doing so leads to immediate gains in how they are perceived by others, and it enhances the power of the exposure treatment (Taylor & Alden, 2011).

David Clark (1997) has developed a version of cognitive therapy for social anxiety disorder that expands on other treatments in a couple of ways. The therapist helps people learn not to focus their attention internally. The therapist also helps them combat their very negative images of how others will react to them. This cognitive therapy has been shown to be more effective than fluoxetine (Prozac) or than exposure treatment plus relaxation (Clark, Ehlers, McManus et al., 2003; Clark, Ehlers, Hackmann et al., 2006). In one study, people who had received cognitive therapy for social anxiety continued to show positive outcomes five years later (Mortberg, Clark, & Bejerot, 2011).

Psychological Treatment of Panic Disorder Like the behavioral treatments for phobias already discussed, cognitive behavioral treatments for panic disorder focus on exposure (White & Barlow, 2004). One well-validated cognitive behavioral treatment approach called **panic control therapy (PCT)** is based on the tendency of people with panic disorder to overreact to the bodily sensations (Craske & Barlow, 2001). In PCT, the therapist uses exposure techniques—that is, he or she persuades the client to deliberately elicit the bodily sensations associated with panic. For example, a person whose panic attacks begin with hyperventilation is asked to breathe rapidly for three minutes. Some examples of the techniques that can be used to provoke body sensations in this type of exposure therapy are shown in Table 6.5. When sensations such as dizziness, dry mouth, lightheadedness, increased heart rate, and other somatic signs of panic begin, the person experiences them under safe conditions; in addition, the person practices coping tactics for dealing with somatic symptoms (e.g., breathing from the diaphragm to reduce hyperventilation). With practice and encouragement from the therapist, the person learns to stop seeing physical sensations as signals of loss of control and to see them instead as intrinsically harmless sensations that can be controlled. The person's ability to create these physical sensations and then cope with them makes them seem more predictable and less frightening (Craske, Maidenberg, & Bystritsky, 1995).

Virtual reality technology is sometimes used to facilitate exposure to feared stimuli.

Social anxiety disorder is often treated in groups, which provide exposure to social threats and provide opportunities to practice new skills.

Table 6.5 Techniques for Provoking Somatic Symptoms During Exposure Treatment for Panic Disorder

Technique	Body Sensation
Rapid deep breathing for 90 seconds	Shortness of breath, sense of unreality
Attempt to swallow quickly 5 times in a row	Throat tightness, lump in throat
Run in place	Chest tightness, shortness of breath
Spin in chair	Dizziness

Source: Abramowitz & Braddock (2008).

In another version of cognitive treatment for panic disorder (Clark, 1996), the therapist helps the person identify and challenge the thoughts that make the physical sensations threatening (see Figure 6.6 for an example of one patient's thoughts). For example, if a person with panic disorder imagines that he or she will collapse, the therapist might help the person examine the evidence for this belief and develop a different image of the consequences of a panic attack. This treatment has been shown to work well in at least seven studies and appears to be a helpful supplement to exposure treatment (Clark et al., 1999).

A psychodynamic treatment for panic disorder also has been developed. The treatment involves 24 sessions focused on identifying the emotions and meanings surrounding panic attacks. Therapists help clients gain insight into areas believed to relate to the panic attacks, such as issues involving separation, anger, and autonomy. In one randomized controlled trial, patients who were assigned to receive psychodynamic treatment achieved more symptom relief than those who were assigned to a control condition of relaxation training (Milrod, Leon, Busch et al., 2007). In a separate trial, diminished rates of relapse were observed when psychodynamic therapy was added as a supplement to antidepressant treatment for panic disorder (Wiborg & Dahl, 1996). More research is needed, however, because both of these studies were small.

Psychological Treatment of Agoraphobia Cognitive behavioral treatments of agoraphobia also focus on exposure—specifically, on systematic exposure to feared situations. The person with agoraphobia may be coached to gradually tackle leaving home, then driving a couple of miles from home, then sitting in a movie theater for five minutes, and then staying for the full duration of a movie in a crowded theater. Exposure treatment of agoraphobia can be enhanced by involving the patient's partner (Cerny, Barlow, Craske et al., 1987). The partner without agoraphobia is taught that recovery rests upon exposure. Many will have sheltered the person from facing their fears, and through treatment, partners learn to foster exposure rather than avoidance.

Psychological Treatment of Generalized Anxiety Disorder Almost all tested treatments for GAD include several cognitive or behavioral components (Roemer, Orsillo, & Barlow, 2004). The most widely used behavioral technique involves relaxation training to promote calmness (DeRubeis & Crits-Christoph, 1998). Relaxation techniques can involve relaxing muscle groups one by one or generating calming mental images. With practice, clients typically learn to relax rapidly. Studies suggest that relaxation training is more effective than nondirective treatment or no treatment. One form of cognitive therapy includes strategies to help people tolerate uncertainty, as people with GAD seem to be more distressed by uncertainty than are those without GAD (Ladoceur, Dugas, Freeston et al., 2000). This treatment appears to be more helpful than relaxation therapy alone (Dugas, Brillon, Savard et al., 2010). Other cognitive behavioral strategies used to target worry include asking people to worry only during scheduled times, asking people to test whether worry "works" by keeping a diary of the outcomes of worrying, helping people focus their thoughts on the present moment instead of worrying, and helping people address core fears that they may be avoiding through worry (Borkovec, Alcaine, & Behar, 2004).

Quick Summary

Exposure treatment is the most validated psychological treatment for anxiety disorders. Cognitive treatments supplement exposure with interventions to challenge negative beliefs about what will happen when a person faces his or her fears.

For specific phobias, exposure treatments can work quite quickly. For social anxiety disorder, cognitive strategies, such as teaching a person to focus less on internal thoughts and sensations, are a helpful addition to exposure treatment. The most effective treatments for panic disorder include exposure to somatic sensations, along with cognitive techniques to challenge catastrophic misinterpretations of those symptoms. Exposure treatment for agoraphobia may be enhanced by including partners. Cognitive behavioral treatment of GAD can include relaxation training, strategies to help a person tolerate uncertainty and face core fears, and specific tools to combat tendencies to worry.

Medications That Reduce Anxiety

Drugs that reduce anxiety are referred to as **anxiolytics** (the suffix *-lytic* comes from a Greek word meaning "to loosen or dissolve"). Two types of medications are most commonly used for the treatment of anxiety disorders: **benzodiazepines** (e.g., Valium and Xanax) and antidepressants, including tricyclic antidepressants, selective serotonin reuptake inhibitors (SSRIs), and **serotonin–norepinephrine reuptake inhibitors (SNRIs)** (Hoffman & Mathew, 2008). Benzodiazepines are sometimes referred to as minor tranquilizers or sedatives. A large number of studies have now confirmed that benzodiazepines and antidepressants provide more benefit than do placebos for anxiety disorders (Kapczinski, Lima, Souza et al., 2002; Moylan, Staples, Ward et al., 2011; Stein, Ipser, & Balkom, 2004). Beyond these medications that seem to help the range of anxiety disorders, certain drugs seem to be effective for specific anxiety disorders. For example, buspirone (BuSpar) has received approval from the Food and Drug Administration for generalized anxiety disorder (Hoffman & Mathew, 2008).

Given the many effective treatments for anxiety, how does one decide which one to use? Generally, antidepressants are preferred over benzodiazepines. This is because people may experience severe withdrawal symptoms when they try to stop using benzodiazepines (Schweizer, Rickels, Case et al., 1990)—that is, they can be addictive. Benzodiazepines can have significant cognitive and motor side effects, such as memory lapses and drowsiness, and the side effects have been found to have real-world significance: benzodiazepines are related to an increased risk of car accidents (Rapoport, Lanctot, Streiner et al., 2009). Antidepressants tend to have fewer side effects than benzodiazepines. Nonetheless, as many as half of people discontinue tricyclic antidepressants because of side effects such as jitteriness, weight gain, elevated heart rate, and high blood pressure (cf. Taylor et al., 1990). Compared to tricyclic antidepressants, SSRIs and SNRIs tend to have fewer side effects. As a result, SSRIs and SNRIs are considered the first-choice medication treatments of most anxiety disorders. Some people, however, do experience side effects from SSRIs and SNRIs, including restlessness, insomnia, headache, and diminished sexual functioning (Bandelow, Zohar, Hollander et al., 2008). Many people stop taking anxiolytic medications because of the side effects.

This discussion leads us to the key problem: most people relapse once they stop taking medications. In other words, medications are only effective during the time when they are taken. Because of this fact, and because exposure treatments and medications provide comparable levels of relief from anxiety symptoms (Cuijpers, Sijbrandij, Koole et al., 2013), psychological treatments are considered the preferred treatment of most anxiety disorders, with the possible exception of GAD (Mitte, 2005).

Medication to Enhance Learning During Psychological Treatment

In contrast to anxiolytic medications, which dampen negative emotion, **D-cycloserine (DCS)** is a drug that enhances learning. Researchers have examined DCS as a way to bolster exposure

© Carlo Allegri/Getty Images

In an interview with Oprah Winfrey (September 24, 2009), Barbra Streisand described social anxiety so intense that she was unable to perform in public for 27 years.

Ricky Williams, the Heisman Trophy winner who became a star for his incredible skills as a running back, obtained relief of his social anxiety symptoms from antidepressant treatment.

treatment (Ressler, Rothbaum, Tannenbaum et al., 2004). In one study, 28 patients with acrophobia (fear of heights) were treated using two sessions of virtual reality exposure to heights. Half of the patients were randomly assigned to receive the medicine DCS while they completed the exposure sessions; the other half received a placebo. The patients who received DCS were less afraid of heights at the end of treatment and three months later than were the patients who did not receive DCS. Similarly, DCS has been found to enhance the effects of exposure treatment for social anxiety disorder and for panic disorder (Norberg, Krystal, & Tolin, 2008). Hence, this learning-enhancement medication appears to bolster the effects of a psychotherapy based on conditioning principles. Although this treatment is too new to be widely offered, the findings provide intriguing insight into how psychotherapy works.

Check Your Knowledge 6.3

Answer the questions.
1. What is the most common strategy used in CBT for anxiety disorders?
2. List two reasons psychological treatment is a better option than medication for anxiety disorders.

Circle all that apply.
3. Which of the following are valid treatment approaches to anxiety disorders?
   a. supportive listening
   b. benzodiazepines
   c. antidepressants
   d. exposure
4. D-cycloserine:
   a. cannot be used with exposure treatment
   b. has no effect on the outcome of exposure treatment
   c. bolsters the effects of exposure treatment

Summary

Clinical Descriptions of the Anxiety Disorders

- As a group, anxiety disorders are the most common type of psychological disorder.
- The five major DSM-5 anxiety disorders are specific phobia, social anxiety disorder, panic disorder, agoraphobia, and generalized anxiety disorder. Anxiety is common to all the anxiety disorders, and fear is common in anxiety disorders other than generalized anxiety disorder.
- Phobias are intense, unreasonable fears that interfere with functioning. Specific phobias commonly include fears of animals; natural environments such as heights; blood, injury, or injections; and situations such as bridges or flying.
- Social anxiety disorder is defined by intense fear of possible social scrutiny.
- Panic disorder is defined by recurrent attacks of intense fear that occur out of the blue. Panic attacks alone are not sufficient for the diagnosis; a person must be worried about the potential of having another attack.
- Agoraphobia is defined by fear and avoidance of being in situations where escaping or getting help would be difficult if anxiety symptoms were to occur.
- The key feature of generalized anxiety disorder is worry that lasts at least 6 months.

Gender and Sociocultural Factors in the Anxiety Disorders

- Anxiety disorders are much more common among women than men.
- The focus of anxiety, the prevalence of anxiety disorders, and the specific symptoms expressed may be shaped by culture.

Common Risk Factors across the Anxiety Disorders

- Mowrer's two-factor model suggests that anxiety disorders are related to two types of conditioning. The first stage involves classical conditioning, in which a formerly innocuous object is paired with a feared object. This can occur through direct exposure, modeling, or verbal instruction. The second stage involves operant conditioning, in which avoidance is reinforced because it reduces anxiety, and so the person does not gain the chance to have their fears extinguished. Many of the other risk factors may increase the propensity to develop and sustain these conditioned fears.
- Genes increase risk for a broad range of anxiety disorders. Beyond this general risk for anxiety disorders, there may be more specific heritability for certain anxiety disorders. In addition to genetic diatheses, other biological factors that are involved in a range of anxiety disorders

include disturbances in the activity in the fear circuit, poor functioning of the serotonin and GABA neurotransmitter systems, and increased norepinephrine activity.
- Cognitive factors include sustained negative beliefs about the future, lack of perceived control, and a heightened tendency to attend to signs of potential danger.
- Personality risk factors include behavioral inhibition and neuroticism.

Etiology of Specific Anxiety Disorders

- Behavioral models of specific phobias build on the two-factor model of conditioning. The learned preparedness model suggests that fears of objects with evolutionary significance may be more sustained after conditioning. Because not all people with negative experiences develop phobias, diatheses must be important.
- The behavioral model of social anxiety disorder expands the two-factor conditioning model to consider the role of safety behaviors. Other key risk factors include behavioral inhibition and cognitive variables such as excessively critical self-evaluations and a focus on internal sensations rather than social cues.
- Neurobiological models of panic disorder have focused on the locus coeruleus, the brain region responsible for norepinephrine release. Behavioral theories of panic attacks have posited that the attacks are classically conditioned to internal bodily sensations. Cognitive theories suggest that such sensations are more frightening due to catastrophic misinterpretation of somatic cues. A polymorphism of the NPSR1 gene also appears to increase risk of panic disorder.
- Cognitive models of agoraphobia focus on "fear of fear"—overly negative beliefs about the negative consequences of anxiety.

- One model of GAD suggests that worry actually helps people avoid more intense emotions. People with GAD also seem to have difficulty tolerating ambiguity.

Psychological Treatment for the Anxiety Disorders

- Behavior therapists focus on exposure to what is feared. For some anxiety disorders, cognitive components may also be helpful in therapy.
- Exposure treatment for specific phobias tends to work quickly and well.
- Adding cognitive components to exposure treatment may help for social anxiety disorder.
- Treatment for panic disorder often involves exposure to physiological changes.
- Treatment for agoraphobia may be enhanced by including partners in the treatment process.
- Relaxation and cognitive behavioral approaches are helpful for GAD.

Medications to Relieve Anxiety

- Antidepressants and benzodiazepines are the most commonly used medications for anxiety disorders. Benzodiazepines can be addictive.
- Discontinuing medications usually leads to relapse. For this reason, cognitive behavior therapy is considered a more helpful approach than medication treatment for most anxiety disorders.
- One new approach involves providing D-cycloserine during exposure treatment.

Answers to Check Your Knowledge Questions

6.1 1. a; 2. c; 3. d; 4. b; 5. 28 percent; 6. worry
6.2 1. b; 2. c; 3. b, d; 4. b; 5. a; 6. c; 7. b; 8. c
6.3 1. Exposure, sometimes supplemented with cognitive approaches; 2. Although efficacy of psychotherapy and medications is similar, medications have significant side effects, and relapse is common once medications are discontinued; 3. b, c, d; 4. c

Key Terms

agoraphobia
anxiety
anxiety disorders
Anxiety Sensitivity Index
anxiolytics
behavioral inhibition
benzodiazepines
D-cycloserine (DCS)
depersonalization
derealization

fear
fear circuit
fear-of-fear hypothesis
generalized anxiety disorder (GAD)
in vivo exposure
interoceptive conditioning
locus coeruleus
medial prefrontal cortex
Mowrer's two-factor model
panic attack

panic control therapy (PCT)
panic disorder
prepared learning
safety behaviors
serotonin–norepinephrine reuptake inhibitors (SNRIs)
social anxiety disorder
specific phobia

7 Obsessive-Compulsive-Related and Trauma-Related Disorders

LEARNING GOALS

1. Be able to define the symptoms and epidemiology of the obsessive-compulsive and related disorders and the trauma-related disorders.
2. Be able to describe the commonalities in the etiology of obsessive-compulsive and related disorders, as well as the factors that shape the expression of the specific disorders within this cluster.
3. Be able to summarize how the nature and severity of the trauma, as well as biological and psychological risk factors, contribute to whether trauma-related disorders develop.
4. Be able to describe the medication and psychological treatments for the obsessive-compulsive-related and trauma-related disorders.

Clinical Case: Jacob

Jacob was a 28-year-old graduate student when he sought treatment. Shortly after starting graduate school 2 years before, Jacob had begun to experience intrusive images of running over animals with his car. Although he knew that he had not done so, the images were so vivid that he could not get them out of his mind. Several times a week, he would be so disturbed by the idea that he could have hit animals that he would feel compelled to turn around and re-drive his route, looking for any signs of wounded or dead animals. If he spotted a wounded or dead animal, he would pull off the road and inspect his car for any signs that he might have been the person who hit the animal. Sometimes, when he finished his second trip, he would become concerned that he might have missed a wounded or dead animal, and he would feel the need to drive the route again. This often made him late for work or appointments, but if he didn't get the chance to look for wounded or dead animals, he would ruminate about the possibility of injured animals throughout the day. He had a number of other behaviors and thoughts he felt compelled to do, including elaborate bathing rituals, math problems that he solved again and again in his head, chewing his food a certain number of times, flipping his light switch on and off three times before he left his bedroom in the morning, and tapping his right elbow three times at the top of the hour. He knew these behaviors didn't make sense, but he still felt a terrible sense of anxiety if he didn't engage in them. The images occupied his mind and the behavioral rituals absorbed his time, such that his progress in graduate school had slowed to a crawl. Recently, his advisor had raised concerns that he was not making sufficient progress in his thesis research.

IN THIS CHAPTER, we examine obsessive-compulsive-related and trauma-related disorders. Obsessive-compulsive and related disorders are defined by repetitive thoughts and behaviors that are so extreme that they interfere with everyday life. The trauma-related disorders include posttraumatic stress disorder and acute stress disorder, two conditions that are triggered by exposure to severely traumatic events.

As you will see, people with these disorders report feeling anxious, and they often experience other anxiety disorders as well (Brakoulias, Starcevic, Sammut et al., 2011). Many of the risk factors for other anxiety disorders contribute to these disorders, and the treatment approaches overlap a good deal as well. Nonetheless, these disorders also have some distinct causes compared to other anxiety disorders. To highlight those differences, the authors of DSM-5 separated obsessive-compulsive and related disorders and trauma-related disorders from anxiety disorders. They placed their chapters covering obsessive-compulsive and trauma-related disorders next to their anxiety disorder chapter to highlight the overlap among all these disorders (Phillips, Stein, Rauch et al., 2010). As you read this chapter, it is important to consider parallels with the diagnoses described in our anxiety disorders chapter, Chapter 6.

Obsessive-Compulsive and Related Disorders

We will focus on three disorders in this section: obsessive-compulsive disorder (OCD), body dysmorphic disorder, and hoarding disorder (see Table 7.1). OCD, the prototypical disorder of this cluster, is defined by repetitive thoughts and urges (obsessions), as well as an irresistible need to engage in repetitive behaviors or mental acts (compulsions). Body dysmorphic disorder and hoarding disorder share symptoms of repetitive thoughts and behaviors. People with body dysmorphic disorder spend hours a day thinking about their appearance, and almost all engage in compulsive behaviors designed to address concerns about their appearance. People with hoarding disorder spend a good deal of their time repetitively thinking about their current and potential future possessions. They also engage in intensive efforts to acquire new objects, and these efforts can resemble the compulsions observed in OCD. For all three conditions, the repetitive thoughts and behaviors are distressing, feel uncontrollable, and require a considerable amount of time. For the person with these conditions, the thoughts and behaviors feel unstoppable.

Beyond similarities in the symptoms, these syndromes often co-occur. For example, about a third of people with body dysmorphic disorders meet diagnostic criteria for OCD during their lifetime. Similarly, up to a quarter of people with hoarding disorder will meet diagnostic criteria for OCD. About one-third of people with OCD experience at least some symptoms of hoarding (Steketee & Frost, 2003).

We will review the clinical features of these three disorders, and then we will describe research on their epidemiology and etiology. We end this section with a discussion of the biological and psychological treatment approaches to obsessive-compulsive and related disorders. As we will see, there are many parallels in the etiology and treatment of these three conditions (Phillips, Stein et al., 2010).

Table 7.1 Diagnoses of Obsessive-Compulsive and Related Disorders

DSM-5 Diagnoses	Key Features
Obsessive-compulsive disorder	• Repetitive, intrusive, uncontrollable thoughts or urges (obsessions) • Repetitive behaviors or mental acts that the person feels compelled to perform (compulsions)
Body dysmorphic disorder	• Preoccupation with imagined flaw in one's appearance • Excessive repetitive behaviors or acts regarding appearance (e.g., checking appearance, seeking reassurance)
Hoarding disorder	• Acquisition of an excessive number of objects • Inability to part with those objects

Clinical Descriptions of the Obsessive-Compulsive and Related Disorders

As mentioned, the obsessive-compulsive and related disorders all share a quality of repetitive thought as well as irresistible urges to engage repetitively in some behavior or mental act. As we will see next, though, the focus of thought and behavior takes a different form across the three conditions.

Obsessive-Compulsive Disorder The diagnosis of **obsessive-compulsive disorder (OCD)** is based on the presence of obsessions or compulsions. Most people with OCD experience both obsessions and compulsions. Although many think that the chief distinction here is of thoughts (obsessions) versus behaviors (compulsions), they are mistaken. Let's consider the technical definitions of obsessions and compulsions.

Obsessions are intrusive and recurring thoughts, images, or impulses that are persistent and uncontrollable (i.e., the person cannot stop the thoughts) and that often appear irrational to the person experiencing them. With a moment's reflection, most of you can likely think of a time when you had a repetitive thought. At least 80 percent of people experience brief intrusive thoughts from time to time—a terrible song or image gets stuck in your head (Rachman & DeSilva, 1978). And most of us also have urges now and then to behave in ways that would be embarrassing or dangerous. But few of us have thoughts or urges that are persistent and intrusive enough to qualify as obsessions. Like Jacob's images of animals (see the opening Clinical Case), the obsessions of most people with OCD have such force and frequency that they interfere with normal activities. Typically, the person spends hours out of the day immersed in these thoughts, images, or urges.

Obsessions often involve fear of contamination from germs or disease. Although most of us would like to avoid germs and disease, the fears of the person with OCD can be triggered by stimuli that are only remotely related to disease. One man with OCD was frightened by all cues that reminded him of cancer. He described seeing a bald cashier and thinking that the man's baldness might have been the result of chemotherapy. In response to these thoughts, he stopped shopping at the store lest he be exposed to whatever toxins could have contributed to the man's cancer (Woody & Teachman, 2000). Others with contamination fears describe the need to change clothes and shower after being in a room with someone who has coughed, and then to wash the clothes as well as any part of their home that the contaminated clothes might have touched.

To understand how contamination could spread so drastically from an initial threatening stimulus, researchers asked people with OCD to consider the building where the research was taking place and to identify the most contaminated object in the building. Most chose a trashcan or a toilet. In this regard, the people with OCD were similar to people with anxiety disorders and those with no disorder. With each participant, the researcher then removed a pencil from a new box of 12 pencils and rubbed the pencil against the contaminated object. The researcher then rubbed a second pencil against the first pencil, and then rubbed a third pencil against the second pencil, and so on through the 12 pencils. Participants were asked to rate the contamination level for each of the 12 pencils. Those without OCD generally rated the 6th pencil as free of contamination. Those with OCD rated even the 12th pencil as highly contaminated (Tolin, Worhunsky, & Maltby, 2004).

Other frequent foci for obsessions include sexual or aggressive impulses, body problems, religion, and symmetry or order (Bloch, Landeros-Weisenberger, Sen et al., 2008). Those with concerns about aggressive impulses might be haunted by disturbing images of hurting their loved ones, despite no anger or desire to do so. Terrified by a recurrent image of throwing her newborn baby down the stairs, one woman with OCD avoided standing on stairs for months (Belluck, 2014).

Compulsions are repetitive, clearly excessive behaviors or mental acts that the person feels driven to perform to reduce the anxiety caused by obsessive thoughts or to prevent some calamity from occurring. Jacob's need to revisit his route, described in the Clinical Case, fits this definition. Samuel Johnson, one of the most famous authors of the eighteenth century, has been described as suffering from multiple compulsions. For example,

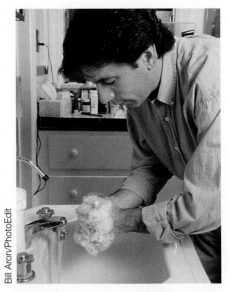

For people with obsessive-compulsive disorder, extreme fears of contamination can trigger abnormally frequent handwashing.

he felt compelled "to touch every post in a street or step exactly in the center of every paving stone. If he perceived one of these acts to be inaccurate, his friends were obliged to wait, dumbfounded, while he went back to fix it" (Stephen, 1900, cited in Szechtman & Woody, 2004). Like Samuel Johnson, many people with OCD feel compelled to repeat a ritual if they did not execute it with precision. The sheer frequency with which compulsions are repeated may be staggering. Commonly reported compulsions include the following:

- Pursuing cleanliness and orderliness, sometimes through elaborate rituals, such as showering for hours a day, wiping down all objects as they enter the house, or asking visitors to wash before they enter the house
- Performing repetitive, magically protective acts, such as counting, touching a body part, solving a math problem, or repeating a word again and again
- Repetitive checking, such as returning seven or eight times in a row to see that lights, stove burners, or faucets are turned off, windows fastened, and doors locked

We often hear people described as compulsive gamblers, compulsive eaters, and compulsive drinkers. Even though people may report irresistible urges to gamble, eat, and drink, clinicians do not regard these behaviors as compulsions because they are often experienced as pleasurable. In contrast, most people view their compulsive rituals as "rather silly or absurd," even though they are unable to stop performing them (Stern & Cobb, 1978). Although they may find their compulsions to be illogical, it is extremely difficult to stop—people with OCD feel as though something dire will happen if they do not perform the act.

OCD tends to begin either before age 10 or else in late adolescence/early adulthood (Conceicao do Rosario-Campos, Leckman, Mercadante et al., 2001). It has been described in children as young as age 2 (Rapoport, Swedo, & Leonard, 1992). Longitudinal research suggests that for most people, symptoms tend to be fairly chronic (Eisen, Sibrava, Boisseau et al., 2013). For those diagnosed with OCD, the pattern of symptoms appears to be similar across cultures (Seedat & Matsunaga, 2006). In addition to obsessions and compulsions, people with OCD are prone to extreme doubts, procrastination, and indecision.

Body Dysmorphic Disorder People with **body dysmorphic disorder** (BDD) are preoccupied with one or more imagined or exaggerated defects in their appearance. Although people with BDD may appear attractive to others, they perceive themselves as ugly or even "monstrous" in their appearance (Phillips, 2006). Women tend to focus on their skin, hair, facial features, hips, breasts, and legs, whereas men are more likely to focus on their height, penis size, or body hair (Perugi, Akiskal, Giannotti et al., 1997). Some men suffer from the preoccupation that their body is small or insufficiently muscular, even when others would not share this perception.

The concerns of people with BDD have an obsessional flavor in that they find it very hard to stop thinking about their concerns. As one woman wrote: "It's always in the back of my mind. I can't push it away. It's always there, taunting and haunting me" (Phillips, 2005, p. 69). On average, people with BDD think about their appearance for 3 to 8 hours per day (Phillips, Wilhelm, Koran et al., 2010). Also, like people with OCD, people with BDD find themselves compelled to engage in certain behaviors. The most common compulsive behaviors for those with BDD include checking their appearance in the mirror, comparing their appearance to that of other people, asking others for reassurance about their appearance, or using strategies to change their appearance or camouflage disliked body areas (grooming, tanning, exercising, changing clothes, and applying makeup) (Phillips, Wilhelm et al., 2010). While many spend hours a day checking their appearance, some try to avoid being reminded of their perceived flaws by avoiding mirrors, reflective surfaces, or bright lights (Phillips, 2005). Although most of us do things to feel better about our appearance, people with this disorder spend an inordinate amount of time and energy on these endeavors.

The symptoms are extremely distressing. About a third of patients with BDD have little insight into their overly harsh views, and so they are convinced that others will see

Howie Mandel describes his struggle with OCD in his book, *Here's the Deal: Don't Touch Me.* Deeply afraid of germs, he has been unable to shake hands with people, touch a glass, or use a handrail without feeling the intense urge to clean. At age 6, he had trouble learning to tie his shoes because he was afraid to touch his dirty shoe laces.

Criteria for Obsessive-Compulsive Disorder

- Obsessions and/or compulsions
- Obsessions are defined by
  - Recurrent, intrusive, persistent, unwanted thoughts, urges, or images
  - The person tries to ignore, suppress, or neutralize the thoughts, urges, or images
- Compulsions are defined by
  - Repetitive behaviors or thoughts that the person feels compelled to perform to prevent distress or a dreaded event
  - The person feels driven to perform the repetitive behaviors or thoughts in response to obsessions or according to rigid rules
  - The acts are excessive or unlikely to prevent the dreaded situation

The obsessions or compulsions are time consuming (e.g., at least 1 hour per day) or cause clinically significant distress or impairment

Clinical Case: Paul

After years of living with anxiety and shame over his appearance, Paul sought psychotherapy at age 33. He had first became "horrified" by his appearance during puberty when he noticed that he was not developing the square jaw lines that many of his male friends had begun to show. In the past several years, his shame was more focused on his nose, which he perceived as being too thin. He had sought surgery, but the surgeon refused to operate on his seemingly flawless nose. Over the past two decades, his preoccupation with his appearance had frequently interfered with socializing and altogether obstructed his ability to date. Even when he did venture out, he had to check his appearance repeatedly throughout the evening. Sometimes he was unable to go to work in his position as a physical therapist because he was overwhelmed by his anxiety. When he did go to work, he worried that his clients were too distracted by his physical flaws to attend to his instructions.
(Drawn with permission from Wilhelm, Buhlmann, Hayward et al., 2010.)

their flaws as grotesque (Phillips, Pinto, Hart et al., 2012). As many as a fifth endure plastic surgery, and many withstand multiple surgeries (Phillips, 2005). Unfortunately, plastic surgery does so little to allay their concerns that many report wanting to sue or hurt their physicians after the surgery (Veale, 2000). About a third of people with BDD endorse some history of suicidal ideation, and about 20% have attempted suicide (Buhlmann, Glaesmer, Mewes et al., 2010).

As is the case for Paul (see the Clinical Case), preoccupation with appearance can interfere with many aspects of occupational and social functioning. To cope with the intense shame they feel about their appearance, people with BDD may avoid contact with others. In one survey, about a third reported missing work or avoiding school in the past month due to concerns about their appearance (Phillips, 2005), and many take long breaks from work or interpersonal interactions to check their appearance or cope with the anxiety of being viewed by others. In another survey, about 40 percent of people with the disorder reported being unable to work (Didie, Menard, Stern et al. 2008), and some even become housebound.

BDD typically begins in adolescence. About 90 percent of persons diagnosed with the disorder still report symptoms 4 years after diagnosis (Phillips, Menard, Quinn et al., 2013). Many people never receive treatment, in part because mental health professionals often do not ask about these symptoms, and in part because those with the disorder often feel too ashamed to raise their concerns (Phillips, 2005).

Social and cultural factors surely play a role in how people decide whether they are attractive. Among college students, concerns about body appearance appear to be more common in America than in Europe—as many as 74 percent of American students report at least some concern about their body image, with women being more likely than men to report dissatisfaction (Bohne, Keuthen, Wilhelm et al., 2002). Most of these concerns, though, are not extreme enough to be characterized as psychological disorders. People with BDD experience agonizing distress over their perceived physical flaws.

Among those who develop BDD, case reports from around the world suggest that the symptoms and outcomes are similar across cultures (Phillips, 2005). The body part that becomes a focus of concern sometimes differs by culture, though. For example, eyelid concerns are more common in Japan than in Western countries. In addition, Japanese patients with BDD appear to be more concerned about offending others than are Western patients (Suzuki, Takei, Kawai et al., 2003).

Care should be taken to distinguish BDD from eating disorders. Most people with BDD are concerned about several different aspects of their appearance. When shape and weight concerns are the only foci, however, clinicians should consider whether the symptoms are better explained by an eating disorder.

DSM-5 Criteria for Body Dysmorphic Disorder

- Preoccupation with one or more perceived defects in appearance
- Others find the perceived defect(s) slight or unobservable
- The person has performed repetitive behaviors or mental acts (e.g., mirror checking, seeking reassurance, or excessive grooming) in response to the appearance concerns
- Preoccupation is not restricted to concerns about weight or body fat

Hoarding Disorder Collecting is a favorite hobby for many people, and almost all children go through a phase of collecting objects, but these hobbies are distinctly different from hoarding. What distinguishes the common fascination with collections from the clinical disorder of hoarding? Undoubtedly, the desire to acquire and save objects varies along a continuum (Timpano, Broman-Fulks, Glaesmer et al., 2013). For people with **hoarding disorder,** the need to acquire is clearly excessive, and it is only part of the problem. The bigger problem is that they abhor parting with their objects, even when others cannot see any potential value in them. Most typically, as illustrated in the Clinical Case of Dena, the person has acquired a huge range of different kinds of objects—collections of clothes, tools, or antiques may be gathered along with old containers and bottle caps. People with hoarding disorder are extremely attached to their possessions, and they are very resistant to efforts to get rid of them.

Many people who hoard are unaware of the severity of their behavior (Steketee & Frost, 2003), but to those surrounding them, the consequences of hoarding are clear and sometimes seem quite severe. The accrual of objects often overwhelms the person's home. In one study, case workers for elder services agencies were asked to describe their clients who suffered from hoarding disorder. Although the sampling strategy likely focused on particularly severe cases, the descriptions were notable. The case workers reported that the hoarding led to extremely filthy homes for about a third of their clients who had problems with hoarding, characterized by overpowering odors from rotten food or feces. More than 40 percent had accumulated so many items that they were no longer able to use their refrigerator, kitchen sink, or bathtub, and about 10 percent were unable to use their toilet (Kim, Steketee, & Frost, 2001). The poor hygiene, exposure to dirt, and difficulties with cooking can all contribute to poor physical health, such as respiratory problems. Many family members sever relationships, unable to understand the attachment to the objects. About three-quarters of people with hoarding disorder engage in excessive buying (Frost, Tolin, Steketee et al., 2009), and many are unable to work (Tolin, Frost, Steketee et al., 2008), making poverty all too common among people with this condition (Samuels, Bienvenu, Pinto et al., 2007). As the problem escalates, health officials often become involved in an effort to address safety and health concerns. About 10 percent of persons with hoarding disorder will be threatened with eviction at some point in their lives (Tolin et al., 2008). For some, the money spent on acquiring possessions leads to homelessness.

About one-third of people with hoarding disorder, much more often women than men, also engage in animal hoarding (Patronek & Nathanson, 2009). People who engage in animal hoarding sometimes view themselves as animal rescuers, but those who witness the problem see it differently—the accumulating number of animals often outstrips the person's ability to provide adequate care, shelter, and food. Animal hoarding is more likely to be associated with squalor than are other forms of hoarding. When animals are involved, animal protection agencies sometimes become involved.

Hoarding behavior usually begins in childhood or early adolescence (Grisham, Frost, Steketee et al., 2006). These early symptoms may be kept under control by parents and by limited income, so severe impairment from the hoarding often does not surface until later in life. Animal hoarding often does not emerge until middle age or older (Patronek & Nathanson, 2009).

Prevalence and Comorbidity of the Obsessive-Compulsive and Related Disorders

Although most of us have had a repetitive thought, have worried about our appearance, and have gone through a phase of collecting, these symptoms only lead to the genuine distress or impairment required for a diagnosis in a small proportion of people. Lifetime prevalence estimates are about 2 percent for OCD (Ruscio, Stein, Chiu et al., 2010) and for BDD (Buhlmann et al., 2010), and 1.5% for hoarding disorder (Nordsletten, Reichenberg, Hatch et al., 2013). OCD and BDD are both slightly more common among women than men (Nordsletten et al.,

DSM-5 Criteria for Hoarding Disorder

- Persistent difficulty discarding or parting with possessions, regardless of their actual value
- Perceived need to save items
- Distress associated with discarding
- The symptoms result in the accumulation of a large number of possessions that clutter active living spaces to the extent that their intended use is compromised unless others intervene.

© Bettmann/CORBIS

Hoarding captured the attention of the public in 1947, when the Collyer brothers were found dead, surrounded by 140 tons of objects, ranging from grand pianos to antique sculptures to a human skeleton, piled from floor to ceiling in their New York City brownstone.

Clinical Case: Dena

Dena was referred for treatment after animal care officials received reports from neighbors. A home inspection revealed over 100 animals living in her 3-acre yard and inside her house, many of them suffering from malnutrition, overcrowding, and disease. When interviewed, she reported that she was running a rescue mission for animals and that she was "just a little behind" because donations had diminished with the bad economy.

When the therapist visited her home, it became clear that her collections extended far beyond her animals. The rooms of her small home were so crowded that two of the doors to the outside could no longer be reached. Heaps of clothes and fabric mixed with miscellaneous furniture parts brimmed to the ceiling of her living room. In the kitchen, a collection of theater memorabilia crowded out access to the stove and refrigerator. The dining room was covered with assorted items—bags of trash, piles of bills, stacks of old newspapers, and several sets of china she had purchased "at a bargain" at yard sales.

When the therapist offered to help Dena organize and neaten her home, Dena became enraged. She said that she had only allowed the therapist to visit to help her broker an arrangement with the animal control authorities and that she did not want to hear any comments about her home. She described years of fighting with her family over her housekeeping, and she said she had done everything in her power to escape from their uptight rules and expectations. She denied needing the stove, stating that she wasn't about to start cooking hot meals as a single woman living alone. After the initial unsuccessful home visit, she refused any further contact with the therapist.

2013; Torres, Prince, Bebbington et al., 2006). Hoarding is equally common among men and women (Samuels et al., 2007), but very few men seek treatment (Steketee & Frost, 2003). In addition to the high rates of comorbidity within these three syndromes, all three of these syndromes tend to co-occur with depression and anxiety disorders. OCD and BDD also tend to co-occur with substance use disorders (Frost, Steketee, & Tolin, 2011; Gustad & Phillips, 2003; Ruscio et al., 2010).

Quick Summary

The major obsessive-compulsive and related disorders include obsessive-compulsive disorder (OCD), body dysmorphic disorder (BDD), and hoarding disorder. OCD is defined by obsessions and/or compulsions. BDD is defined by a preoccupation with an imagined defect in appearance and by intensive behavioral attempts to cope with the imagined defect. Hoarding disorder is defined by excessive acquisition of objects and severe difficulties in discarding objects, even when they are objectively without value.

People with BDD and hoarding disorder often have a history of OCD. Beyond this, the obsessive-compulsive and related disorders are commonly comorbid with anxiety disorders and major depressive disorder. OCD and BDD are often comorbid with substance abuse.

Check Your Knowledge 7.1 (Answers are at the end of the chapter.)

Answer the questions.

1. Describe the most typical course of the obsessive-compulsive and related disorders.

2. What is the chief difference between obsessions and compulsions?

Etiology of the Obsessive-Compulsive and Related Disorders

There is a moderate genetic contribution to OCD, hoarding, and body dysmorphic symptoms. Heritability is estimated to account for 40 to 50 percent of the variance in whether each of these conditions develops (Iervolino, Perroud, Fullana et al., 2009; Monzani, Rijsdijk, Iervolino et al., 2012; Taylor, Jang, & Asmundson, 2010).

Obsessive-compulsive disorder, body dysmorphic disorder, and hoarding disorder share some overlap in etiology that is particularly apparent for genetic and neurobiological risk factors. For example, people with BDD and hoarding disorder often have a family history of OCD (Gustad & Phillips, 2003; Taylor et al., 2010), which could be the result of a shared genetic vulnerability. In regard to neurobiological risk, OCD, BDD, and hoarding disorder seem to involve some of the same brain regions. Brain-imaging studies indicate that three closely related areas of the brain are unusually active in people with OCD (see Figure 7.1): the **orbitofrontal cortex** (an area of the medial prefrontal cortex located just above the eyes), the **caudate nucleus** (part of the basal ganglia), and the anterior cingulate (Menzies, Chamberlain, Laird et al., 2008; Rotge, Guehl, Dilharreguy et al., 2009). When people with OCD are shown objects that tend to provoke symptoms (such as a soiled glove for a person who fears contamination), activity in these three areas increases (McGuire, Bench, Frith et al., 1994). A similar pattern emerges when people with BDD view pictures of their own face. In those studies, BDD appears to be related to hyperactivity of the orbitofrontal cortex and the caudate nucleus (Feusner, Phillips, & Stein, 2010). When people with hoarding disorder are faced with decisions about whether to keep or discard possessions such as old mail, they show hyperactivity in the orbitofrontal cortex (Tolin, Kiehl, Worhunsky et al., 2009) and the anterior cingulate compared to a control group (Tolin, Stevens, Villavicencio et al., 2012).

While these genetic and neurobiological risk factors may set the stage for developing one of these disorders, why might one person develop OCD and another develop body dysmorphic disorder? Cognitive behavioral models focus on factors that might promote one disorder as compared to the other.

Etiology of Obsessive-Compulsive Disorder Cognitive behavioral models have been developed to explain how a person might get stuck repeating obsessions and compulsions again and again. A narrower cognitive model focuses on why obsessions might persist.

Cognitive Behavioral Models of Obsessions and Compulsions In moderation, many of the thoughts and behaviors that disrupt the days of those with OCD, such as checking, cleaning, or reconsidering a thought, have adaptive value. Cleaning, for example, can help reduce the risk of contamination and germs. The question, then, is why these thoughts and behaviors become so persistent, often in inappropriate contexts, so as to cause real distress or impairment. The central goal of cognitive behavioral theory is to understand why the person with OCD continues to show the behaviors or thoughts used to ward off an initial threat well after that threat is gone.

To gather data on how people with OCD respond once a threat is gone, researchers conducted a two-phase experiment. In the first phase, they created a threat by placing electrodes on participants' wrists and then teaching participants that they would receive a shock (an unconditioned stimulus) when a certain shape (the conditioned stimulus) appeared on the computer screen. To avoid the shock, participants had to press a foot pedal (the conditioned response). In this first phase, participants with and without OCD learned equally well to press the foot pedal to avoid shock. In the key second phase of the study, researchers unhooked the wrist electrodes so that

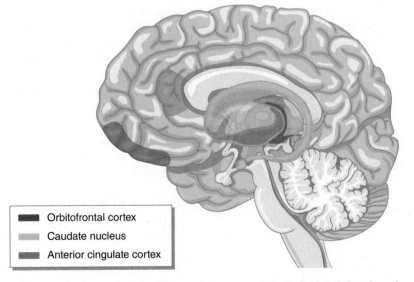

Orbitofrontal cortex
Caudate nucleus
Anterior cingulate cortex

Figure 7.1 Key brain regions in the obsessive-compulsive and related disorders: the orbitofrontal cortex, caudate nucleus, and anterior cingulate.

the participants could see that the threat of shock was gone. Even though they knew the threat was removed and even showed little psychophysiological response to the stimulus, many people with OCD either pressed the foot pedal or felt a strong urge to press the foot pedal when the conditioned stimulus (the shape) appeared on the screen. People without OCD quit pressing the foot pedal, and most didn't have an urge to press the foot pedal. The authors argue that for those with OCD, previously functional responses for reducing threat become habitual and hence difficult to override after the threat was gone (Gillan, Morein-Zamir, Urcelay et al., 2014). Consistent with this idea, other researchers have found that once someone with OCD develops a conditioned response to a stimulus, they are slower to change their response to that stimulus after it is no longer rewarded (Voon, Derbyshire, Ruck et al., 2014).

One cognitive model fits well with the idea that people with OCD continue to engage in behaviors to ward off threat, even after they can state that the threat is gone. According to this model, OCD is related to a deficit in the intuitive sense of feeling security and closure. Consider for a moment how we know to stop thinking about something or to quit studying for a test or organizing our desk. There is no absolute signal from the environment. Rather, most of us stop when we have the sense of "that is enough." **Yedasentience** is defined as this subjective feeling of knowing that you have thought enough, cleaned enough, or in other ways done what you should to prevent chaos and danger from low-level threats in the environment (Woody & Szechtman, 2011). It is theorized that people with OCD suffer from a biologically based deficit in yedasentience. Because they fail to gain the intuitive sense of completion and security, they have a hard time stopping their thoughts and behaviors. Objectively, they know that there is no need to check the stove or wash their hands again, but they suffer from an anxious internal sense that things are not complete. Compulsions are particularly reinforcing because they help relieve this sensation, and they do so even more effectively than self-statements do (Woody & Szechtman, 2011).

Thought Suppression: A Cognitive Model of Obsessions A different model focuses on obsessions. This model suggests that people with OCD may try harder to suppress their obsessions than other people and, in doing so, may actually make the situation worse. Several researchers have shown that people with OCD tend to believe that thinking about something can make it more likely to occur (Rachman, 1977). People with OCD are also likely to describe especially deep feelings of responsibility for what occurs (Ladoceur, Dugas, Freeston et al., 2000). As a consequence of these two factors, they are more likely to attempt **thought suppression** (Salkovskis, 1996). Consistent with theory, people with OCD report engaging in thought suppression more than others do (Amir, Cashman, & Foa, 1997).

Unfortunately, it is hard to suppress thoughts. Consider the findings of one study of what happens when people are asked to suppress a thought (Wegner, Schneider, Carter et al., 1987). Two groups of college students were asked either to think about a white bear or not to think about one; they were also told to ring a bell every time they thought about a white bear. The findings indicated that attempts to avoid thinking about the white bear did not work—students thought about the bear more than once a minute when trying not to do so. Beyond that, there was a rebound effect—after students tried to suppress thoughts about the bear for 5 minutes, they thought about the bear much more often during the next 5 minutes. Trying to suppress a thought may have the paradoxical effect of inducing preoccupation with it. Indeed, in one experimental study, suppressing thoughts even briefly led to more intrusions of that thought over the next four days (Trinder & Salkovaskis, 1994). Obviously, thought suppression is not a very good way to try to gain control over obsessions.

Etiology of Body Dysmorphic Disorder Why would Paul (see the Clinical Case) look in the mirror, see a nose that others see as perfectly reasonable, and respond with horror? Cognitive models of BDD focus on what happens when a person with this syndrome looks at his or her body. People with BDD can accurately see and process their physical features—the problem does not appear to be one of distortion of the physical features. Rather, people with BDD tend to be detail oriented, and this influences how they look at facial features (Feusner et al., 2010). Instead of considering the whole, they examine one feature at a time, which makes it more likely that they will become engrossed in considering a small flaw (Lambrou, Veale, & Wilson, 2011). They also consider attractiveness to be vastly more important than do control participants (Lambrou et al., 2011). Indeed, many people with BDD seem to believe that their self-worth is exclusively dependent on their appearance (Veale, 2004).

Etiology of Hoarding Disorder In considering hoarding, many take an evolutionary perspective (Zohar & Felz, 2001). Imagine you were a caveman with no access to grocery stores to replenish food reserves and no clothing stores to find warm clothes when the weather got cold. In those situations, it would be adaptive to store any resources you could find. The question, though, is how these basic instincts become so uncontrollable for some people. The cognitive behavioral model suggests a number of factors that might be involved. According to this model, hoarding is related to poor organizational abilities, unusual beliefs about possessions, and avoidance behaviors (Steketee & Frost, 2003). Let's review each of these factors, considering how they might lead to excessive acquisition as well as difficulties getting rid of objects.

People with hoarding disorder have several different types of problems with cognitive organizational abilities. Problems with attention interfere with staying focused on the task at hand (Tolin & Villavicencio, 2011), and even once they do focus on dealing with their possessions, they have difficulty categorizing objects and making decisions (Samuels, 2009). When asked to sort objects into categories in laboratory studies, people with hoarding disorder tend to be slow, to generate many more categories than others do, and to find the process highly anxiety-provoking (Wincze, Steketee, & Frost, 2007). These difficulties attending to the task at hand, organizing objects, and making decisions influence almost every aspect of acquiring objects, organizing the home, and removing excessive acquisitions. Faced with decisions about which object is the better one to acquire, many will go ahead and get two, three, or more of the same type of object. Many patients find it excruciatingly hard to sort through their objects and figure out what to discard, even with a supportive therapist present (Frost & Steketee, 2010).

Beyond these difficulties with organizational abilities, the cognitive model focuses on the unusual beliefs that people with hoarding disorder hold about their possessions. Almost by definition, people with hoarding disorder demonstrate an extreme emotional attachment to their possessions. They report feeling comforted by their objects, being frightened by the idea of losing an object, and seeing the objects as core to their sense of self and identity. They hold a deep sense of responsibility for taking care of those objects and are likely to resent it if others touch, borrow, or remove them (Steketee & Frost, 2003). Many feel a sense of grief when forced to part with an object (Frost, Steketee, & Tolin, 2012). These attachments may be even stronger when animals are involved. People who hoard animals often describe their animals as their closest confidants (Patronek & Nathanson, 2009). These beliefs about the importance of each and every object interfere with any attempt to tackle the clutter.

In the face of the anxiety of all these decisions, avoidance is common. Many people with this disorder find organizing their clutter so overwhelming that they delay tackling the chaos (Frost, Steketee, & Greene, 2003). Avoidance is considered one of the key factors that maintains the clutter.

Treatment of the Obsessive-Compulsive and Related Disorders

Treatments that work for obsessive-compulsive disorder, body dysmorphic disorder, and hoarding disorder are similar. Each of these disorders responds to antidepressant medications. The major psychological approach is exposure and response prevention, although this treatment is tailored for the specific conditions.

Medications Antidepressants are the most commonly used medications for the obsessive-compulsive and related disorders. Although they were initially developed to treat depression, randomized controlled trials support their effectiveness in the treatment of OCD (Steketee & Barlow, 2004) and BDD (Grant, Odlaug, & Schreiber, 2014).

In the treatment of OCD, clomipramine (Anafranil) is the most commonly used antidepressant (McDonough & Kennedy, 2002). In one study, it led to an approximately 50 percent reduction in OCD symptoms (Mundo, Maina, & Uslenghi, 2000), and it is helpful for youth as well as adults (Franklin & Foa, 2011). Most people, however, continue to experience at least mild symptoms of OCD even with antidepressant treatment (Grant et al., 2014).

Only two randomized controlled trials of medication treatment have been conducted for BDD. Both trials found that antidepressants were more helpful than placebo in reducing symptoms. These trials have provided support for both clomipramine and fluoxetine as treatments of BDD (Ipser, Sander, & Stein, 2009). As with OCD, many people continue to experience at least mild symptoms of BDD with antidepressant treatment.

No randomized controlled trials of medications are available for hoarding disorder. Much of our knowledge is based on studies of OCD patients who also have hoarding symptoms. Although most studies indicate that hoarding symptoms respond less to medication treatment than do other OCD symptoms (Steketee & Frost, 2003), findings of one study indicated that patients with hoarding disorder demonstrated as much of a response to an antidepressant as did those with OCD (Saxena, Brody, Maidment et al., 2007).

Psychological Treatment The most widely used psychological treatment for the obsessive-compulsive and related disorders is **exposure and response prevention (ERP)**. Victor Meyer (1966) developed this approach for OCD by tailoring the exposure treatment discussed in Chapter 6 to address the compulsive rituals that people with OCD use to ward off threats. We'll describe this cognitive behavioral treatment as it is applied to OCD, and then we will explain how it has been adapted for BDD and hoarding disorder.

Obsessive-Compulsive Disorder Many OCD sufferers hold an almost magical belief that their compulsive behavior will prevent awful things from happening. In the response prevention component of ERP, people expose themselves to situations that elicit the compulsive act and then refrain from performing the compulsive ritual—for instance, the person touches a dirty dish and then refrains from washing his or her hands. The reasoning behind this approach goes like this:

1. Not performing the ritual exposes the person to the full force of the anxiety provoked by the stimulus.
2. The exposure promotes the extinction of the conditioned response (the anxiety).

The exposure component of ERP uses the exposure hierarchy approach that we discussed in Chapter 6, in which a client begins with tackling less threatening stimuli and progresses to completing exposure sessions focused on more threatening stimuli. As an example, a client with a focus on contamination might start by being in a dirty room and progress to placing their hands on a sticky, grimy floor. Throughout the exposure sessions, the client is guided to avoid engaging in compulsions. Often, the therapist guides exposure to feared stimuli in the home, with help from family members (Foa & Franklin, 2001). Typically, ERP involves refraining from performing rituals during therapy sessions lasting up to 90 minutes as well as during home practice between sessions.

Refraining from performing a ritual is extremely unpleasant for people with OCD. (To get some idea of how unpleasant, try delaying for a minute or two before scratching an itch.) Given the intensity of treatment, it is not surprising that about 25 percent of clients refuse ERP treatment (Foa & Franklin, 2001).

A meta-analysis of 19 studies comparing ERP to control treatments suggested that ERP is highly effective in reducing obsessions and compulsions (Rosa-Alcazar, Sanchez-Meca, Gomez-Conesa et al., 2008). ERP is more effective than clomipramine for the treatment of OCD (Foa, Libowitz, Kozak et al., 2005), and it is effective for children and adolescents as well as adults (Franklin & Foa, 2011). Researchers have shown excellent outcomes for ERP offered by community therapists who do not specialize in OCD (Franklin & Foa, 2011). More than three quarters of people who receive this treatment show significant improvement (Mancebo, Eisen, Sibrava et al., 2011), although mild symptoms often persist.

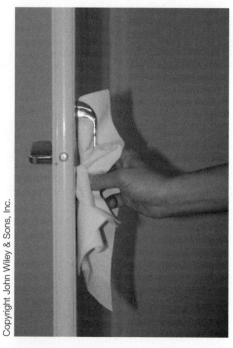

Exposure treatment for OCD involves confronting one's worst fears, such as contamination by dirty objects.

Cognitive approaches to OCD focus on challenging people's beliefs about what will happen if they do not engage in rituals (Van Oppen, de Haan, Van Balkom et al., 1995) or challenging their often inflated sense of responsibility (Clark, 2006). Eventually, to help test such beliefs, these approaches will use exposure. Several studies suggest that cognitive approaches perform as well as ERP (DeRubeis & Crits-Christoph, 1998).

Body Dysmorphic Disorder The basic principles of ERP are tailored in several ways to address the symptoms of BDD. For example, to provide exposure to the most feared activities, clients might be asked to interact with people who could be critical of their looks. For response prevention, clients are asked to avoid activities they engage in to reassure themselves about their appearance, such as looking in mirrors. As illustrated in the Clinical Case of Paul, these behavioral techniques are supplemented with strategies to address the cognitive features of the disorder, such as the excessively critical evaluations of physical features and the belief that self-worth depends on appearance.

Several trials have shown that ERP produces a major decrease in body dysmorphic symptoms compared to control conditions (cf. Wilhelm, Phillips, Didie et al., 2014). Treatments that include a cognitive component may be more powerful than those that address only behaviors (Williams, Hadjistavropoulos, & Sharpe, 2006), but both treatments produce lasting effects (Ipser et al., 2009).

Hoarding Disorder Treatment for hoarding is based on an adaptation of the ERP therapy that is employed with OCD (Steketee & Frost, 2003). The exposure element of treatment focuses on the most feared situation for people with hoarding disorder—getting rid of their objects. Response prevention centers on halting the rituals that they engage in to reduce their anxiety, such as counting or sorting their possessions. As with other exposure treatments, the client and the therapist work through a hierarchy, tackling increasingly difficult challenges as therapy progresses.

Despite the common elements, treatment is tailored in many ways for hoarding. As illustrated in the case of Dena, many people with hoarding disorder don't recognize the gravity of problems created by their symptoms. Therapy cannot begin to address the hoarding symptoms until the person develops insight. To facilitate insight, motivational strategies are used to help the person consider reasons to change. Once people decide to change, therapists help them make decisions about their objects and can provide tools and strategies to help them organize and remove their clutter. Therapists often supplement their office sessions with in-home visits, which can help them gain a better sense of the degree of hoarding but also allow for in vivo exercises on de-cluttering. In the first randomized controlled trial of this approach, patients who received CBT demonstrated significantly more improvement than did those assigned to a waiting list (Steketee, Frost, Tolin et al., 2010). With 26 weeks of treatment, about 70 percent of patients showed at least modest improvement in hoarding symptoms. Self-help groups, supplemented with structured readings, have been found to be a helpful approach that is less expensive than individual therapy (Muroff, Levis, & Bratiotis, 2014).

Early cognitive behavioral interventions focused on helping clients discard their objects as quickly as possible, hoping to avoid the quagmire of indecision and anxiety that might come from too much focus on evaluating possessions. Unfortunately, patients tended to drop out of treatment, and even those who did remain often showed little response (Abramowitz, Franklin, Schwartz et al., 2003; Mataix-Cols, Marks, Greist et al., 2002).

Despite the evidence that removing possessions too rapidly tends to fail, the TV show *Hoarders* featured many people who were faced with ridding themselves of objects under dire threat of eviction or other contingencies, and so were forced to discard their collections immediately.

Returning to Clinical Case: CBT Treatment for Paul

Paul and his therapist agreed to work together using CBT. To begin, they reviewed childhood and current influences on Paul's symptoms. Paul described his parents' extremely high standards for appearance, along with his father's obsessive and perfectionistic style. Throughout his life, Paul had felt that he could not live up to their standards.

He and the therapist then identified several cognitions (thoughts) that seemed to contribute to his anxiety, such as "Any flaw means I'm ugly" or "I know my client is thinking about how ugly my nose is." Paul was asked to record his most negative thoughts each day, and he was also taught ways to evaluate whether these thoughts might be overly harsh. He began to consider alternative ways of thinking.

As Paul developed more positive ways of thinking, the therapist began to target his avoidant and ritualistic behaviors. Paul tended to avoid social events, bright lights, and even eye contact with others, and he understood that these behaviors were interfering with his life. Treatment consisted of exposure, in which the therapist gradually coached Paul to make eye contact, to engage in social activities, and even to talk with others under bright light. Paul also had been conducting a series of rituals to try to reduce his anxiety, including engaging in facial exercises, studying others' noses, and surfing plastic surgery websites. The therapist helped him understand that the rituals did not actually relieve his anxiety. Rituals were tackled using response prevention: Paul was asked to stop conducting the rituals and to monitor his mood and anxiety as he did so.

After five sessions of treatment, Paul's therapist introduced perceptual retraining. When people with BDD look in the mirror, they focus on small details of their worst feature, and they are overly evaluative. As daily homework, Paul was asked to spend time looking in the mirror but focusing on the whole of his appearance. He was also asked to describe his nose using nonevaluative, objective language. The intense anxiety he initially experienced when completing this exercise diminished within a week. Soon, he was able to appreciate some of his features that he had previously ignored—for example, he noticed that he had nice eyes.

People with body dysmorphic disorder often focus excessive attention on their own appearance. Paul was trained to refocus his attention on people and events outside of himself. For example, when dining with a friend, he was coached to attend to the sound of his friend's voice, the flavor of the food, and the content of their conversation.

As Paul made gains, the therapist began to work on the more difficult and core aspects of cognitions—his deeply held beliefs about the meaning of his appearance. Paul described feeling that his physical flaws made him unlovable. The therapist helped him begin to consider his many positive qualities.

The tenth and final session consisted of reviewing the skills he had learned and discussing the strategies he would use if symptoms returned. Over the course of treatment, Paul's symptoms remitted so greatly that by the last session, he was no longer distressed about his nose.

(Drawn with permission from Wilhelm et al., 2010.)

The family relationships of those with hoarding disorder are often profoundly damaged. Relatives usually try various approaches to help clear the clutter, only to become more and more frustrated and angry as those attempts fail. Many resort to coercive strategies, including removing the hoarder's possessions while the person is away—strategies that typically create mistrust and animosity. Family approaches to hoarding begin by building rapport around these difficult issues (Tompkins & Hartl, 2009). Rather than aiming for a total absence of clutter, family members are urged to identify the aspects of hoarding and clutter that are most dangerous, for example, lack of access to an emergency exit. They can use their concern regarding these issues to begin dialogue and set priorities with the person with hoarding disorder. Support groups and online communities for family members of those with hoarding disorder (e.g., Children of Hoarders) have become increasingly common.

Deep Brain Stimulation: A Treatment in Development for OCD Researchers have tested deep brain stimulation, a treatment that involves implanting electrodes into the brain, for those with chronic OCD that fails to respond even after multiple pharmacological treatments. For the treatment of OCD, electrodes are typically implanted into either the nucleus accumbens or a region at the margin of the ventral striatum. Several small studies have found that about half of patients treated with deep brain stimulation attain significant relief with a couple months of treatment, and double-blind controlled studies support the efficacy of this treatment as well (Greenberg, Rauch, & Haber, 2010). The treatment remains experimental because complications can arise from implanting electrodes into the brain. Nonetheless, the gains from this approach provide support for neurobiological models of OCD.

Quick Summary

OCD, BDD, and hoarding disorder are moderately heritable. People with BDD and hoarding disorder often report a family history of OCD. OCD is characterized by high activity in the orbitofrontal cortex, the caudate nucleus, and the anterior cingulate. Body dysmorphic disorder involves heightened activity of the orbitofrontal cortex and the caudate nucleus. Hoarding disorder is related to heightened activity in the orbitofrontal cortex and the anterior cingulate.

Cognitive behavioral models help explain why one might develop a specific disorder in the cluster of obsessive-compulsive and related disorders. A behavioral model of OCD suggests that people sustain conditioned responses long after the contingencies that conditioned the initial behavior have shifted. Psychologically, OCD appears to be characterized by a deficit in yedasentience. Thought suppression may exacerbate tendencies toward obses-

sions. The cognitive model of BDD focuses on a detail-oriented analytic style, tendencies to overvalue the meaning of appearance for self-worth, and excessive attention to cues related to appearance. Cognitive behavioral models of hoarding disorder focus on poor organizational abilities (difficulties with attention, categorization, and decision making), unusual beliefs about possessions, and avoidance behaviors.

Antidepressants are the most supported medication treatment for the obsessive-compulsive and related disorders. The major psychological treatment approach for the obsessive-compulsive and related disorders is exposure and response prevention (ERP). ERP for hoarding disorder often involves motivational strategies to enhance insight and willingness to consider change. Deep brain stimulation is an experimental treatment for OCD.

Check Your Knowledge 7.2

Answer the questions.
1. List three reasons to consider OCD, BDD, and hoarding as related conditions.
2. What class of medication has been most carefully tested for the treatment of obsessive-compulsive and related disorders?

3. What is the most commonly used psychological treatment for obsessive-compulsive and related disorders?

Posttraumatic Stress Disorder and Acute Stress Disorder

Posttraumatic stress disorder and acute stress disorder are diagnosed only when a person develops symptoms after a traumatic event. These disorders, then, rest on the idea that horrific life experiences can trigger serious psychological symptoms. This diagnosis stands in contrast to all other major DSM diagnoses, which are defined entirely by symptom profiles. No other major DSM diagnosis places emphasis squarely on the cause.

Clinical Description and Epidemiology of Posttraumatic Stress Disorder and Acute Stress Disorder

Posttraumatic stress disorder (PTSD) entails an extreme response to a severe stressor, including recurrent memories of the trauma, avoidance of stimuli associated with the trauma, negative emotions and thoughts, and symptoms of increased arousal. Although people have known for many years that the stresses of combat can have powerful adverse effects on

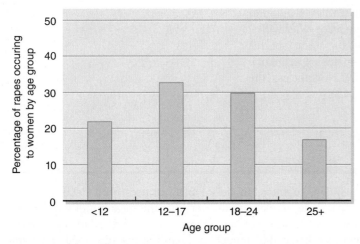

Figure 7.2 Annual rates of sexual assault victimization among women by age group. From Tjaden & Thoennes (2006).

Rescue workers, such as this firefighter who was at the World Trade Center in the aftermath of the 9/11 terrorist attack, could be vulnerable to PTSD.

soldiers, the aftermath of the Vietnam War spurred the development of this diagnosis.

The diagnostic criteria define serious trauma as an event that involved actual or threatened death, serious injury, or sexual violation. Far too many people have been exposed to these types of traumas. Since 2001, more than 2 million U.S. soldiers have served in Iraq and Afghanistan. Whereas military trauma is the most common type of trauma preceding PTSD for men, rape is the most common type of trauma preceding PTSD for women (Creamer, Burgess, & McFarlane, 2001), with at least one-third of women meeting the criteria for PTSD after a rape (Breslau, Chilcoat, Kessler et al., 1999). It has been estimated that one in every six American women will be raped during their lifetimes (Tjaden & Thoennes, 2006). As shown in Figure 7.2, these sexual assaults are disproportionately targeted at adolescent and young women. A discouraging 30 percent of female college students report that they have experienced the use of physical force, threats, or harm after they refused sexual contact with a person, with 8.7 percent reporting that they had experienced physical harm (Struckman-Johnson, 1988). About 70 percent of rapes are committed by someone known to the woman (National Center for Justice, 2003).

Exposure to trauma, however, is only the first part of considering this diagnosis. In addition to trauma, the diagnosis of PTSD requires that a set of symptoms be present. In the DSM-5, the symptoms for PTSD are grouped into four major categories:

- *Intrusively reexperiencing* the traumatic event. Like Ashley (see Clinical Case), many people with PTSD have dreams or nightmares about the trauma night after night. Others are haunted by painful and intrusive memories, often evoked by small sensory cues. Sensory reminders of the event can bring on a wave of psychophysiological arousal. For example, a veteran may tremble when he hears the sound of a helicopter that reminds him of the battlefield; for month after the event, a woman who was raped in a dark room may find her heart pounds when night falls.
- *Avoidance* of stimuli associated with the event. Most people with PTSD strive to avoid thinking about the event, and some try to avoid all reminders of the event. For example, a Turkish earthquake survivor stopped sleeping indoors after he was buried alive at night (McNally, 2003). Although most will say that they try to avoid remembering and reliving the event, avoidance usually fails: most people say that they do remember the event all too well and often (Rubin, Berntsen, & Bohni, 2008).
- Other signs of *negative mood and thought* that developed after the trauma. Many people with PTSD feel detached from friends and activities and find that nothing in life brings joy. As they wrestle with questions of blame about the event, many will come to believe that they are bad, and others will develop the belief that all people are untrustworthy.
- Symptoms of *increased arousal and reactivity.* The person with PTSD often feels continuously on guard, monitoring the environment for danger. Laboratory studies have confirmed that people with PTSD demonstrate heightened arousal, as measured by physiological responses to trauma-relevant images (Orr, Metzger, Lasko et al., 2003). This heightened arousal can be manifested in tendencies to be jumpy when startled, to have outbursts over small events, and to find it challenging to get to sleep or to sleep through the night.

The symptoms of PTSD may develop soon after the trauma but sometimes do not develop for years after the initial event. Once PTSD develops, symptoms are relatively chronic. In one study of people diagnosed with PTSD, about half continued to experience diagnosable symptoms when interviewed several years later (Perkonigg, Pfister, Stein et al., 2005). Suicidal thoughts are common among people with PTSD (Bernal, Haro, Bernert et al., 2007), as are incidents of nonsuicidal self-injury (Weierich & Nock, 2008). In a study of 15,288 army veterans followed for 30 years after their initial military service, PTSD predicted an elevated risk of early death from medical illness, accidents, and suicides (Boscarino, 2006).

● DSM-5 Criteria for Posttraumatic Stress Disorder

A. Exposure to actual or threatened death, serious injury, or sexual violence, in one or more of the following ways: experiencing the event personally, witnessing the event in person, learning that a violent or accidental death or threat of death occurred to a close other, or experiencing repeated or extreme exposure to aversive details of the event(s) other than through the media

B. At least 1 of the following **intrusion** symptoms:
   - Recurrent, involuntary, and intrusive distressing memories of the trauma(s), or in children, repetitive play regarding the trauma themes
   - Recurrent distressing dreams related to the event(s)
   - Dissociative reactions (e.g., flashbacks) in which the individual feels or acts as if the trauma(s) were recurring, or in children, reenactment of trauma during play
   - Intense or prolonged distress or physiological reactivity in response to reminders of the trauma(s)

C. At least 1 of the following **avoidance** symptoms:
   - Avoids internal reminders of the trauma(s)
   - Avoids external reminders of the trauma(s)

D. At least 2 of the following **negative alterations in cognitions and mood** began after the event:
   - Inability to remember an important aspect of the trauma(s)
   - Persistent and exaggerated negative beliefs or expectations about one's self, others, or the world
   - Persistently excessive blame of self or others about the trauma(s)
   - Persistently negative emotional state, or in children younger than 7, more frequent negative emotions
   - Markedly diminished interest or participation in significant activities
   - Feeling of detachment or estrangement from others, or in children younger than 7, social withdrawal
   - Persistent inability to experience positive emotions

E. At least 2 of the following changes in **arousal and reactivity:**
   - Irritable or aggressive behavior
   - Reckless or self-destructive behavior
   - Hypervigilance
   - Exaggerated startle response
   - Problems with concentration
   - Sleep disturbance

F. The symptoms began or worsened after the trauma(s) and continued for at least one month

G. Among children younger than 7, diagnosis requires criteria A, B, E, and F, but only 1 symptom from either category C or D

It has been argued that prolonged exposure to trauma, such as repeated childhood abuse, might lead to a broader range of symptoms than those covered by the DSM criteria for PTSD. This syndrome has been referred to as complex PTSD (Herman, 1992). Authors differ in the symptom profiles they link to prolonged trauma, but most write about negative emotions, relationship disturbances, and negative self-concept (Cloitre, Courtois, Charuvastra et al., 2011). What does the research suggest about the effects of prolonged trauma? Comprehensive review suggests that prolonged trauma may lead to more severe PTSD symptoms but does not seem to result in a distinct subtype with unique symptomatology (Resick, Bovin, Calloway et al., 2012). Given this, the DSM-5 does not include a diagnosis or a specifier for complex PTSD.

In addition to PTSD, the DSM includes a diagnosis for **acute stress disorder (ASD).** Like PTSD, ASD is diagnosed when symptoms occur after a trauma. The symptoms of ASD are fairly similar to those of PTSD, but the duration is shorter; this diagnosis is only applicable when the symptoms last for 3 days to one month.

The ASD diagnosis is not as well accepted as the PTSD diagnosis. There are two major concerns about the ASD diagnosis. First, the diagnosis could stigmatize short-term reactions to serious traumas, even though these are quite common (Harvey & Bryant, 2002). For example, after a rape, as many as 90 percent of women report at least some (subsyndromal) symptoms (Rothbaum, Foa, Murdock et al., 1992). Second, most people who go on to meet diagnostic criteria for PTSD do not experience DSM-IV-TR diagnoses of ASD in the first month after the trauma (Bryant, Creamer, O'Donnell et al., 2008). Nonetheless, those who do experience ASD are at elevated risk of developing PTSD within 2 years (Bryant, 2011). When we consider treatments, we will review evidence that treating ASD may help prevent the development of PTSD. Because less is known about ASD, we will focus on PTSD as we discuss epidemiology and etiology.

Clinical Case: Ashley

Ashley, a 20-year-old college student, sought help at the college counseling center. Three months before, she had been raped by a man whom she had met at a party earlier the same evening. She sought help when the ongoing terror and associated symptoms led her to fail her classes for the semester. Since the rape, she had felt as though she was on constant alert, scanning the environment for the man who had assaulted her. When she would see someone who looked even remotely like her attacker, her heart would pound, her knees would shake, and she would feel overwhelmed with terror. She had avoided social events because the thought of interacting with men frightened her. Most nights, she had tossed and turned for at least an hour before falling asleep, and then intense nightmares of the event would wake her. Her sleep loss often left her too exhausted to attend class, and even when she did attend class, she felt distracted and unable to concentrate. As she developed a newly cynical attitude toward people, she had withdrawn from most of her friends. She became unmotivated to be a part of campus life, and she stopped attending the club meetings that had been an important part of her social life before the trauma. Although she had tried hard to stop thinking about the event, she faced almost daily reminders, as sexual assaults were a constant issue in the school newspapers, activist rallies, and conversations in the cafeteria.

PTSD tends to be highly comorbid with other conditions. In one study of a representative community sample, researchers conducted diagnostic assessments repeatedly from ages 3 until age 26. Among people who had developed PTSD by age 26, almost all (93 percent) had been diagnosed with another psychological disorder before age 21. The most common comorbid disorders are other anxiety disorders, major depression, substance abuse, and conduct disorder (Koenen, Moffitt, Poulton et al., 2007). Two-thirds of those with PTSD at age 26 had experienced another anxiety disorder by age 21.

Among people exposed to a trauma, women are twice as likely to develop PTSD as are men (Breslau et al., 1999). This finding is consistent with the gender ratio observed for most anxiety disorders. Women may also face different life circumstances than do men. For example, women are much more likely than men to be sexually assaulted during childhood and adulthood (Tolin & Foa, 2006). In studies that control for a history of sexual abuse and assault, men and women have comparable rates of PTSD (Tolin & Foa, 2006).

Culture may shape the risk for PTSD in several ways. Some cultural groups may be exposed to higher rates of trauma and, as a consequence, manifest higher rates of PTSD. This seems to be the case for minority populations in the United States (Ritsher, Struening, Hellman et al., 2002). Culture also may shape the types of symptoms observed in PTSD. *Ataque de nervios,* originally identified in Puerto Rico, involves physical symptoms and fears of going crazy in the aftermath of severe stress and thus is similar to PTSD.

Etiology of Posttraumatic Stress Disorder

Would any of us break if exposed to severe enough life circumstances? Are some people so resilient that they could withstand whatever horrors life directs at them? Who is most likely to be haunted in the months and years after a terrible event? These are the questions we will consider as we review the etiology of PTSD.

Above, we mentioned that two-thirds of people who develop PTSD have a history of an anxiety disorder. Not surprisingly, then, many of the risk factors for PTSD overlap with the risk factors for anxiety disorders that we described in Chapter 6 (see Table 6.5). For example, PTSD appears to be related to genetic risk for anxiety disorders (Tambs, Czajkowsky, Roysamb et al., 2009), high levels of activity in areas of the fear circuit such as the amygdala (Rauch, Whalen, Shin et al., 2000), childhood exposure to trauma (Breslau, Davis, & Andreski, 1995), and tendencies to attend selectively to cues of threat (Bar-Haim, Lamy, Pergamin et al., 2007). Also parallel with anxiety disorders discussed in Chapter 6, neuroticism and negative affectivity predict the onset of PTSD (Pole, Neylan, Otte et al., 2009; Rademaker, van Zuiden, Vermetten et al., 2011).

Also parallel with anxiety disorders, PTSD has been related to Mowrer's two-factor model of conditioning (Keane, Zimering, & Caddell, 1985). In this model, the initial fear in PTSD is assumed to arise from classical conditioning. For example, a man may come to fear walking in the neighborhood (the conditioned stimulus) where he was assaulted (the unconditioned stimulus). This classically conditioned fear is so intense that the man avoids the neighborhood as much as possible. Operant conditioning contributes to the maintenance of this avoidance behavior; the avoidance is reinforced by the reduction of fear that comes from not being in the presence of the conditioned stimulus. This avoidant behavior interferes with chances for the fear to extinguish.

Keeping these parallels in mind, in this section we focus on factors that are uniquely associated with PTSD. We begin by describing evidence that certain kinds of traumas may be more likely to trigger PTSD than other types. Even among people who experience serious traumas, though, not everyone develops PTSD. Thus, a great deal of research has been conducted on neurobiological and coping variables that help predict the onset of PTSD.

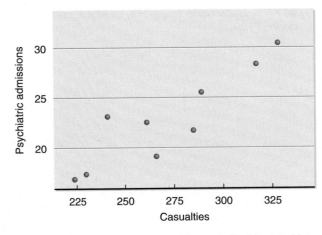

Figure 7.3 Percent of Canadian soldiers admitted for psychiatric care as a function of the number of casualties in their battalion during World War II. Drawn from Jones & Wessely (2001).

Nature of the Trauma: Severity and the Type of Trauma Matter The severity of the trauma influences whether or not a person will develop PTSD. Consider the case of people who are exposed to war. Among soldiers serving in Afghanistan or Iraq, the U.S. Veterans Administration estimates that rates of PTSD are doubled among those with a second tour of duty as compared to those with one tour of duty. About 20 percent of American fighters wounded in Vietnam developed PTSD, contrasted with 50 percent of those who were prisoners of war there (Engdahl, Dikel, Eberly et al., 1997). During Operation Desert Storm (in the 1990–1991 conflict following the Iraqi invasion of Kuwait), among those assigned to collect, tag, and bury scattered body parts of the dead, 65 percent developed PTSD (Sutker, Uddo, Brailey et al., 1994). As shown in Figure 7.3, the number of World War II soldiers admitted for psychiatric care was closely related to how many casualties occurred in their battalions (Jones & Wessely, 2001). During World War II, doctors estimated that 98 percent of men with 60 days of continuous combat would develop psychiatric problems (Grossman, 1995).

The occurrence of PTSD among residents of New York City after the terrorist attack on the World Trade Center on September 11, 2001, showed a similar correspondence with the severity of the trauma. Based on a telephone survey after the attack, researchers determined that 7 percent of the adults living within 8 miles of the World Trade Center in New York City reported symptoms that would have warranted a diagnosis of PTSD, but 20 percent of those living within a mile of the site reported such symptoms (Galea, Ahern, Resnick et al., 2002). In short, among people who have been exposed to traumas, those exposed to the most severe traumas are most likely to develop PTSD.

Beyond severity, the nature of the trauma matters. Traumas caused by humans are more likely to cause PTSD than are natural disasters (Charuvastra & Cloitre, 2008). For example, rapes, combat experience, abuse, and assault all are associated with higher risk than are natural disasters. Perhaps these events are seen as more distressing because they challenge ideas about humans as benevolent.

Neurobiology: The Hippocampus Above, we noted that PTSD appears to be related to dysregulation of the fear circuit, as with anxiety disorders discussed in Chapter 6. PTSD appears to be uniquely related to the function of the hippocampus (see Figure 7.4) (Shin & Liberzon, 2010). Brain-imaging studies show that the volume of the hippocampus is smaller among people with PTSD than among those who do not have the condition (Bremner, Vythilingam, Vermetten et al., 2003). A study of multiple pairs of identical twins, one of whom was a Vietnam veteran and the other not, is revealing of how hippocampal volume and PTSD are related (Gilbertson, Shenton, Ciszewski et al., 2002). As in previous studies of veterans, smaller hippocampal volume was associated with PTSD symptoms, but this study went on to find an additional important pattern. That is, smaller hippocampal volume in the nonveteran

Figure 7.4 A smaller hippocampus may be related to the risk of developing PTSD.

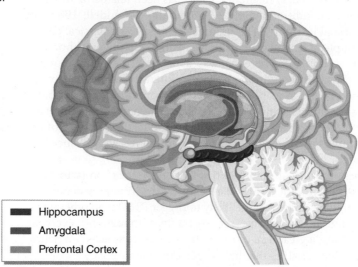

- Hippocampus
- Amygdala
- Prefrontal Cortex

twins was related to greater likelihood of PTSD in the veteran twins after military service. This suggests that smaller-than-average hippocampal volume probably precedes the onset of disorder.

The hippocampus plays a central role in our ability to locate autobiographical memories in space, time, and context, and in organizing our narratives of those memories. Difficulties in organizing memories and placing them in context could set the stage for PTSD.

Let's start with the idea of context. People with PTSD experience fear when they have any reminder of their trauma, even out of context. For example, the soldier who witnessed bombs dropping from a plane may remain frightened by all planes after he returns from the war. For those with PTSD, the cues that one is in a safe environment do not seem to work; the fear remains as intense as it did in the moment of the trauma. One argument is that hippocampal deficits could increase the risk that a person will experience this type of fear regardless of whether the context is safe or dangerous (Maren, Phan, & Liberzon, 2013).

Now consider the nature of memory in PTSD. Even though the person has intense memories cued by smells, sounds, and other sensory stimuli, he or she often has a hard time organizing these memories into well-organized narratives of the event. A meta-analysis of 27 studies found that people diagnosed with PTSD consistently demonstrate deficits on neuropsychological tests of verbal memory even while performing adequately on tests of visual memory (Brewin, Kleiner, Vasterling et al., 2007). Brewin (2014) theorizes that decreased hippocampal volume could help explain the deficits in verbal memory. Because other regions of the brain are involved in processing memories of physical sensations, the person with PTSD may sustain strong memories for sensory aspects of their trauma. This could help us understand how a person could simultaneously have a hard time describing the trauma and yet still be tortured by reminders of the trauma.

In sum, hippocampal deficits could contribute to psychological vulnerability to PTSD in two different ways. First, the hippocampal deficits could increase the risk that a person will respond to reminders of the trauma even when they occur in safe contexts. Second, the hippocampal deficits may interfere with organizing coherent narratives about the trauma.

Coping Several types of studies suggest that people who cope with a trauma by trying to avoid thinking about it are more likely than others to develop PTSD. Much of the work on avoidance coping focuses on symptoms of **dissociation** (such as feeling removed from one's body or emotions or being unable to remember the event). We discuss dissociation in more detail in Chapter 8. Dissociation may keep the person from confronting memories of the trauma. People who have

Survivors of natural disasters, such as the Japanese earthquake in 2011, are at risk for PTSD, but their risk may not be as high as those who experience traumas caused by humans, such as assaults.

symptoms of dissociation during and immediately after the trauma are more likely to develop PTSD, as are people who try to suppress memories of the trauma (Ehlers, Mayou, & Bryant, 1998). For example, in one study, researchers interviewed women within two weeks of a rape to ask questions about dissociation during the rape (e.g., "Did you feel numb?" and "Did you have moments of losing track of what was going on?"). Women with high levels of dissociation were much more likely to develop PTSD symptoms than were women with low levels of dissociation. The correlation between dissociation and PTSD has been confirmed in a meta-analysis of 16 studies involving 3534 participants (Ozer, Best, Lipsey et al., 2003). Many studies now show that symptoms of dissociation shortly after being raped predict the development of PTSD (Brewin & Holmes, 2003). Moreover, people who continue to use dissociation in the years after the trauma are at risk for ongoing PTSD symptoms (Briere, Scott, & Weathers, 2005).

To encourage clinicians to consider these coping patterns, the DSM-5 includes a dissociative symptom specifier in order to denote when PTSD is accompanied by persistent or recurrent symptoms of dissociation. About 10–15% of people meet the criteria for this specifier (Stein, Koenen, Friedman et al., 2013), and it is more common among people who have a history of childhood abuse (Wolf, Miller, Reardon et al., 2012).

Other protective factors may help a person cope with severe traumas more adaptively. Two factors that seem particularly important are high intelligence (Breslau, Lucia, & Alvarado, 2006; Kremen, Koenen, Boake et al., 2007) and strong social support (Brewin, Andrews, & Valentine, 2000). As an example, veterans returning from war who report a stronger sense of social support are less likely to develop PTSD (Vogt, Smith, Elwy et al., 2011). Having better intellectual ability to make sense of horrifying events, and more friends and family members to assist in that process, helps people avoid symptoms after traumatic events.

A surprisingly high proportion of people cope quite well with trauma. For some, trauma awakens an increased appreciation of life, renews a focus on life priorities, and provides an opportunity to understand one's strengths in overcoming adversity (Bonanno, 2004; Tedeschi, Park, & Calhoun, 1998).

Quick Summary

Posttraumatic stress disorder (PTSD) and acute stress disorder (ASD) are both severe reactions to trauma. The symptoms of PTSD and ASD are similar, but ASD can only be diagnosed if symptoms have lasted less than one month. Most people who develop PTSD have a history of other psychological disorders, and two-thirds have a history of anxiety disorders.

Some of the general risk factors for anxiety disorders appear to be involved in the development of PTSD. These general risk factors include genetic vulnerability, amygdala hyperactivity, neuroticism, childhood trauma exposure, and tendencies to attend to cues of threat in the environment. PTSD has also been related to Mowrer's two-factor model of conditioning.

More specific risk factors for PTSD have also been identified. The likelihood that a person will develop PTSD depends on the severity of the trauma. Neurobiological research has found that people with small hippocampal volume are more likely to develop PTSD. After exposure to trauma, people who rely on dissociative coping strategies (i.e., who avoid thinking about the trauma) are more likely to develop PTSD than people who rely on other strategies. Other resources that might promote adaptive coping, such as higher IQ and stronger social support, can protect against the development of PTSD.

Treatment of Posttraumatic Stress Disorder and Acute Stress Disorder

A good deal of work has focused on treatment of PTSD using medication and psychological treatments. Less research is available on ASD.

Medication Treatment of PTSD Dozens of randomized controlled trials have been conducted to examine medication treatments of PTSD (Stein, Ipser, & Seedat, 2000). One class

FOCUS ON DISCOVERY 7.1

Eye Movement Desensitization and Reprocessing

In 1989, Francine Shapiro began to promulgate an approach to trauma treatment called eye movement desensitization and reprocessing (EMDR). In this procedure, the client recalls a scene related to the trauma. Keeping the scene in mind, the client visually tracks the therapist's fingers as the therapist moves them back and forth about a foot in front of the person's eyes. This process continues for a minute or so, or until the client reports that the image is becoming less painful. At this point, the therapist tells the client to say whatever negative thoughts he or she is having, while continuing to track the therapist's fingers. Finally, the therapist tells the client to think a positive thought (e.g., "I can deal with this") and to hold this thought in mind, still tracking the therapist's fingers. This treatment, then, consists of classic imaginal exposure techniques, along with the extra technique of eye movement.

EMDR proponents argue that the eye movements promote rapid extinction of the conditioned fear and correction of mistaken beliefs about fear-provoking stimuli (Shapiro, 1999). The claims of dramatic efficacy have extended to disorders other than PTSD, including attention-deficit/hyperactivity disorder, dissociative disorders, panic disorder, public-speaking fears, test anxiety, and specific phobias (Lohr, Tolin, & Lilienfeld, 1998).

Despite the claims about this approach, several studies have indicated that the eye movement component of treatment is not necessary. Findings from a series of studies indicate that this therapy is no more effective than traditional exposure treatment of PTSD (Seidler & Wagner, 2006). The eye movement component is not supported by adequate theoretical explanations. Gerald Rosen made the following clever comparison. Imagine a practitioner begins to offer exposure treatment wearing a purple hat. We would hardly allow the "new" approach to merit labeling and marketing as "purple hat therapy" (Rosen & Davison, 2003). Given the lack of effective innovation in this approach, several researchers have argued that this approach should not be offered (Goldstein, de Beurs, Chambless et al., 2000).

of antidepressant, the selective serotonergic reuptake inhibitors (SSRIs), has received strong support as a treatment. Relapse is common if medications are discontinued.

Psychological Treatment of PTSD Parallel with the psychological treatment of anxiety disorders discussed in Chapter 6, exposure treatment is the primary psychological approach to treating PTSD. With the support of a therapist, the client is asked to face his or her worst fears, most typically by working up an exposure hierarchy from less intense fears to the most intense fears. One goal of treatment is to extinguish the fear response, particularly the over-generalized fear response; another goal is to help challenge the idea that the person could not cope with the anxiety and fear generated by those stimuli. As clients learn that they can deal with their anxiety, avoidance responses can be reduced.

In PTSD, the focus of exposure treatment is on memories and reminders of the original trauma, with the person being encouraged to confront the trauma to gain mastery and extinguish the anxiety. Where possible, the person is directly exposed to reminders of the trauma in vivo—for example, by returning to the scene of the event. In other cases, **imaginal exposure** is used—that is, the person deliberately remembers the event (Keane, Fairbank, Caddell et al., 1989). Therapists have also used virtual reality technology to treat PTSD; this technology can provide more vivid exposure than some clients may be able to generate in their imaginations (Rothbaum, Hodges, Alarcon et al., 1999).

Randomized controlled trials suggest that exposure treatment provides more relief from the symptoms of PTSD than supportive unstructured psychotherapy (Powers, Halpern, Ferenschak et al., 2010) or medication (Bradley, Greene, Russ et al., 2005). Despite the success of this approach, a great deal of controversy has arisen over another treatment of PTSD, and we discuss this controversy in Focus on Discovery 7.1.

Exposure therapy is hard for both the patient and the therapist because it requires such intense focus on traumatizing events. For example, women who have developed PTSD after rape might be asked to vividly recall the details of the worst moments of the attack. The patient's symptoms may even increase temporarily in the initial stages of therapy (Keane, Gerardi, Quinn et al., 1992).

Treatment is likely to be particularly hard and to require more time when the client has experienced recurrent traumas during childhood, as those experiences can interfere with learning to cope with emotions. In one randomized controlled trial, researchers examined whether teaching skills to regulate emotions would bolster the effects of exposure treatment for women who reported PTSD symptoms as a consequence of childhood abuse. The addition of emotion regulation skills led to several positive gains compared to standard exposure treatment, including diminished PTSD symptoms, improved emotion regulation, enhanced interpersonal functioning, and lower rates of post-treatment symptom relapse (Cloitre, Stovall-McClough, Nooner et al., 2010).

Several cognitive strategies have been used to supplement exposure treatment for PTSD. Interventions designed to bolster people's beliefs in their ability to cope with the initial trauma have been shown to fare well in a series of studies (Keane, Marshall, & Taft, 2006). Cognitive processing therapy is designed to help victims of rape and childhood sexual abuse dispute tendencies toward self-blame. This approach has also received empirical support (Chard, 2005; Resick, Nishith, Weaver et al., 2002) and appears to be particularly helpful in reducing guilt (Resick, Nishith, & Griffin, 2003) and dissociation (Resick, Suvak, Johnides et al., 2012).

A growing number of websites and support groups provide social support for those recovering from traumatic experiences. As one example, one website provides opportunities for veterans to discuss their experiences and learn basic information about the effects of military traumas (http://maketheconnection.net).

Psychological Treatment of Acute Stress Disorder   Is it possible to prevent the development of PTSD by offering treatment to people who have developed acute stress disorder (ASD)? Short-term (five- or six-session) cognitive behavioral approaches that include exposure appear to do so. For example, Richard Bryant and colleagues (1999) found that early intervention decreased the risk that ASD would develop into PTSD. The success of this approach has now been replicated. Across five studies, risk of PTSD among those who received exposure therapy was reduced to 32 percent, as compared to 58 percent for those who were assigned to a control condition (Kornør, Winje, Ekeberg et al., 2008).

The positive effects of early exposure treatment appear to last for years. Researchers examined the long-term effect of treatment on symptoms among adolescents who had survived a devastating earthquake. Even 5 years after the earthquake, adolescents who had received cognitive behavioral intervention reported less severe PTSD symptoms than did those who had not received treatment (Goenjian, Walling, Steinberg et al., 2005).

Exposure treatment appears to be more effective than cognitive restructuring in preventing the development of PTSD (Bryant, Mastrodomenico, Felmingham et al., 2008). Unfortunately, not all approaches to prevention work as well as exposure treatment (see Focus on Discovery 7.2).

FOCUS ON DISCOVERY 7.2

Critical Incident Stress Debriefing

Critical incident stress debriefing (CISD) involves immediate treatment of trauma victims within 72 hours of the traumatic event (Mitchell & Everly, 2000). Unlike cognitive behavioral treatment, CISD is usually limited to one long session and is given regardless of whether the person has developed symptoms. Therapists encourage people to remember the details of the trauma and to express their feelings as fully as they can. Therapists who practice this approach often visit disaster sites immediately after events, sometimes invited by local authorities (as in the aftermath of the World Trade Center attack) and sometimes not; they offer therapy both to victims and to their families.

Like EMDR, CISD is highly controversial. A review of six studies, all of which included randomly assigning clients to receive CISD or no treatment, found that those who received CISD tended to fare worse (Litz, Gray, Bryant et al., 2002). No one is certain why harmful effects occur, but remember that many people who experience a trauma do not develop PTSD. Many experts are dubious about the idea of providing therapy for people who have not developed a disorder. Some researchers raise the objection to CISD that a person's natural coping strategies may work better than those recommended by someone else (Bonanno, Wortman, Lehman et al., 2002).

Check Your Knowledge 7.3

Answer the questions.

1. List two major risk factors that contribute specifically to PTSD (as opposed to increasing general risk for anxiety disorders).
2. In conducting exposure treatment for PTSD, _____ exposure is sometimes used because _____ exposure cannot be conducted for experiences as horrific as war and rape.

3. Cognitive therapy when added to exposure for PTSD is particularly helpful in addressing (choose the answer that best fits):
   a. suicidal tendencies
   b. risk of relapse
   c. insomnia
   d. guilt

Summary

Obsessive-Compulsive and Related Disorders

- People with obsessive-compulsive disorder (OCD) have intrusive, unwanted thoughts and feel compelled to engage in rituals to avoid overwhelming anxiety. People with body dysmorphic disorder (BDD) experience persistent and severe thoughts that they have a flawed appearance, and they engage in intensive efforts to cope with their appearance. Hoarding disorder is characterized by tendencies to acquire an excessive number of objects and extreme difficulties in ridding oneself of those objects.

- OCD, BDD, and hoarding disorder are each moderately heritable. Family history studies suggest that there may be some shared genetic risk across these three disorders.

- OCD has been robustly linked to activity in the orbitofrontal cortex, the caudate nucleus, and the anterior cingulate. BDD also involves hyperactivity in regions of the orbitofrontal cortex and the caudate nucleus. Hoarding disorder involves hyperactivity in the orbitofrontal cortex and the anterior cingulate.

- Tendencies toward repetitive thought and behavior in OCD may be related to a tendency for conditioned responses to become habitual, such that they are sustained even after the threat is removed. OCD is also characterized by a lack of yedasentience. Obsessions may be intensified by attempts to suppress unwanted thoughts, in part because people with OCD tend to believe that thinking about something is as bad as doing it.

- The cognitive model relates BDD to a detail-oriented analytic style and an overvaluing of the importance of appearance to self-worth.

- Cognitive behavioral risk factors for hoarding include poor organizational abilities, unusual beliefs about the importance of possessions and responsibility for those possessions, and avoidance behaviors.

- ERP is a well-validated approach for the treatment of OCD that involves exposure, along with strategies to prevent engaging in compulsive behaviors. ERP has been adapted for the treatment of BDD and hoarding. For the treatment of BDD, ERP is supplemented with cognitive strategies to challenge people's overly negative views of their appearance, their excessive focus on their appearance, and their beliefs that self-worth depends on their appearance. For hoarding disorder, ERP is supplemented with strategies to increase insight and motivation.

- Antidepressants are the most commonly used medications for OCD, BDD, and hoarding disorder. Although these medications have received strong support for OCD and BDD, no randomized controlled trial has been conducted to examine medication treatment for hoarding disorder.

Trauma-Related Disorders

- Posttraumatic stress disorder (PTSD) is diagnosed only after a traumatic event. It is marked by symptoms of reexperiencing the trauma; avoidance of reminders of the trauma; negative alterations in cognitions and mood; and arousal. Acute stress disorder (ASD) is defined by similar symptoms with a duration of less than one month. PTSD is highly comorbid with other psychological disorders; about two-thirds of people who develop PTSD have a history of other anxiety disorders.

- Many of the risk factors involved in anxiety disorders are related to the development of PTSD, such as genetic vulnerability, hyperactivity of the amygdala, childhood trauma exposure, neuroticism, attention to negative cues in the environment, and behavioral conditioning. Research and theory on the causes that are specific to PTSD focus on the severity and nature of the traumatic event, and on risk factors such as small hippocampal volume, dissociation, and other factors that may enhance the ability to cope with stress, such as social support and intelligence.

- SSRIs are the most supported medication approach for PTSD.

- Psychological treatment of PTSD involves exposure, but often imaginal exposure is used. Psychological interventions for ASD can reduce the risk that PTSD will develop.

Answers to Check Your Knowledge Questions

7.1. 1. chronic; 2. Obsessions involve a repetitive and intrusive thought, urge, or image; compulsions involve either a thought or a behavior that the person feels the need to engage in to ward off threats.

7.2. 1. any three of these: (a) all share symptoms of uncontrollable repetitive thoughts and behavior; (b) the syndromes often co-occur; (c) people with BDD and hoarding disorder often have a family history of OCD; (d) similar brain regions are involved in all three syndromes; (e) all

three syndromes respond to antidepressants; (f) all three syndromes respond to exposure and response prevention; 2. antidepressants; 3. exposure and response prevention

7.3. 1. any two of the following: small volume of the hippocampus; avoidant coping strategies that prevent processing the trauma, such as dissociation; low IQ; poor social support; 2. imaginal, in vivo; 3. d

Key Terms

acute stress disorder (ASD)
body dysmorphic disorder
caudate nucleus
compulsion
dissociation

exposure and response prevention (ERP)
hoarding disorder
imaginal exposure
obsession
obsessive-compulsive disorder (OCD)

orbitofrontal cortex
posttraumatic stress disorder (PTSD)
thought suppression
yedasentience

8

Dissociative Disorders and Somatic Symptom-Related Disorders

Clinical Case: Gina

In December 1965, Dr. Robert Jeans was consulted by a woman named Gina Rinaldi, who had been referred to him by her friends. Gina, single and 31 years old, lived with another single woman and was working successfully as a writer at a large educational publishing firm. She was considered to be efficient, businesslike, and productive, but her friends had observed that she was becoming forgetful and sometimes acted out of character. Gina reported that she had been sleepwalking since her early teens; her present roommate had told her that she sometimes screamed in her sleep.

The youngest of nine siblings, Gina described her 74-year-old mother as the most domineering woman she had ever known. She reported that as a child she had been a fearful and obedient daughter. At age 28 she had an "affair," her first, with a former Jesuit priest, although it was apparently not physical in nature. Then she became involved with T.C., a married man who assured her he would get a divorce and marry her. She indicated that she had been faithful to him since the start of their relationship. T.C., however, fell out of her favor as he did not come through with his promised divorce and stopped seeing Gina regularly.

After several sessions with Gina, Dr. Jeans began to notice a second personality emerging. Mary Sunshine, as she came to be called by Gina and Dr. Jeans, was quite different from Gina. She seemed more childlike, more traditionally feminine, ebullient, and seductive. Gina felt that she walked like a coal miner, but Mary certainly did not. Some concrete incidents indicated Mary's existence. Sometimes while cleaning her home, Gina found cups that had had hot chocolate in them—neither Gina nor her roommate liked hot chocolate. There were large withdrawals from Gina's bank account that she could not remember making. She even discovered herself ordering a sewing machine on the telephone, although she disliked sewing; some weeks later, she arrived at her therapy session wearing a new dress that Mary had sewn. At work, Gina reported, people were finding her more pleasant, and her colleagues took to consulting her on how to encourage people to work better with one another. All these phenomena were entirely alien to Gina. Jeans and Gina came to realize that sometimes Gina was transformed into Mary.

More and more often, Jeans witnessed Gina turning into Mary in the consulting room. T.C. accompanied Gina to a session during which her posture and demeanor became more relaxed, her tone of voice warmer. Then Mary and Gina started having conversations with each other in front of Jeans.

A year after the start of therapy, an apparent synthesis of Gina and Mary began to emerge. At first it seemed that Gina had taken over entirely, but then Dr. Jeans noticed that Gina was not as serious as before, particularly about "getting the job done," that is, working extremely hard on the therapy. Dr. Jeans encouraged Gina to talk with Mary. The following is that conversation:

I was lying in bed trying to go to sleep. Someone started to cry about T.C. I was sure that it was Mary. I started to talk to her. The person told me that she didn't have a name. Later she said that Mary called her Evelyn. I was suspicious at first that it was Mary pretending to be Evelyn. I changed my mind, however, because the person I talked to had too much sense to be Mary. She said that she realized that T.C. was unreliable but she still loved him and was very lonely. She agreed that it would be best to find a reliable man. She told me that she comes out once a day for a very short time to get used to the world. She promised that she will come out to see you [Dr. Jeans] sometime when she is stronger. (Jeans, 1976, pp. 254–255)

Throughout January, Evelyn appeared more and more often, and Dr. Jeans felt that his patient was improving rapidly. Within a few months, she seemed to be Evelyn all the time; soon thereafter, this woman married a physician. Now, years later, she has had no recurrences of the other personalities.
(Drawn from Jeans, 1976)

IN THIS CHAPTER, WE discuss the dissociative disorders and the somatic symptom-related disorders. We cover these disorders together because both are hypothesized to be associated with stressful experiences, yet do not involve direct expressions of anxiety. In the dissociative disorders, the person experiences disruptions of consciousness—he or she loses track of self-awareness, memory, and identity. In the somatic symptom-related disorders, the person complains of bodily symptoms that suggest a physical defect or dysfunction, sometimes dramatic in nature. For some of the somatic symptom-related disorders, no physiological basis can be found, and for others, the psychological reaction to the symptoms appears excessive.

Beyond the idea that both types of disorders are related to stress, dissociative disorders and somatic symptom-related disorders tend to be comorbid. Patients with dissociative disorders often meet the criteria for somatic symptom-related disorders, and vice versa; those with somatic symptom-related disorders are more likely than those in the general population to meet the diagnostic criteria for dissociative disorders (Brown, Cardena, Nijenhuis et al., 2007; Dell, 2006).

Dissociative Disorders

The DSM-5 includes three major **dissociative disorders**: depersonalization/derealization disorder, dissociative amnesia, and dissociative identity disorder (formerly known as multiple personality disorder). Table 8.1 summarizes the key clinical features of the DSM-5 dissociative disorders. Dissociation, the core feature of each dissociative disorder, involves some aspect of emotion, memory, or experience being inaccessible consciously. Because dissociation is such a broad term (Allen, 2001), it is important to consider some of the different types of experience it encompasses.

Some types of dissociation are common. Many of you will have had experiences of studying so hard for a test that you lost track of time and might not even have noticed people coming and going from the room where you were studying. Some of you may have missed a turn on the road home when thinking about problems. These types of dissociative experiences are usually a harmless sign that one has been so focused on some aspect of experience that other aspects of experience are lost from awareness.

In contrast to common dissociative experiences like these, dissociative disorders are defined by more severe types of dissociation. Depersonalization/derealization involves a form of dissociation involving detachment, in which the person feels removed from the sense of self and surroundings. The person may feel "spaced out," numb, or as though in a dream (Holmes, Brown, Mansell et al., 2005). Dissociative amnesia and dissociative identity disorder involve a more dramatic form of dissociation, in which the person cannot access important aspects of memory. In dissociative identity disorder, the gaps in memory are so extensive that the person loses all sense of having a unified identity.

What causes dissociation to occur? At least mild levels of dissociation may be more likely when a person is sleep deprived (Giesbrecht, Smeets, Leppink et al., 2013). Both psychodynamic and behavioral theorists consider pathological dissociation to be an avoidance response that protects the person from consciously experiencing stressful events. Among people undergoing very intense stressors, such as advanced military survival training, many report brief moments of mild dissociation (Morgan, Hazlett, Wang et al., 2001).

It is very hard to estimate how common these disorders are. Only two studies assessed the lifetime prevalence of the dissociative disorders in community samples using face-to-face diagnostic interviews (Ross, 1991; Sar, Akyuz, & Dogan, 2007). Both of these studies relied on the Dissociative Disorders Interview Schedule (Ross, 1989), and the probes from this interview are so vague that the diagnostic rates might be overestimates. For example, the major probe to assess dissociative amnesia is, "Have you ever experienced sudden inability to recall important personal information or events that is too extensive to be explained by ordinary forgetfulness?" People vary in their definition of ordinary forgetfulness. Indeed, in one study, researchers found that twice as many cases were labeled as meeting dissociative amnesia with the Dissociative Disorders Interview Schedule as compared to a lengthier interview (Ross, Duffy, & Ellason, 2002). Bearing in mind that these are rough estimates, then, the two available community studies found that about 2.5 percent of people endorsed the lifetime diagnostic

Table 8.1 Diagnoses of Somatic Symptom and Related Disorders

DSM-5 Diagnosis	Description
Depersonalization/derealization disorder	• Alteration in the experience of the self and reality
Dissociative amnesia	• Lack of conscious access to memory, typically of a stressful experience. The fugue subtype involves traveling or wandering coupled with loss of memory for one's identity or past.
Dissociative identity disorder	• At least two distinct personalities that act independently of each other

criteria for depersonalization/derealization, about 7.5 percent for dissociative amnesia, and 1 to 3 percent for dissociative identity disorder (Ross, 1991; Sar et al., 2007). Other studies, however, have obtained much lower estimates of the prevalence of dissociative identity diagnoses in clinical practice. In a study involving unstructured diagnostic interviews of more than 11,000 psychiatric outpatients, about one in a thousand patients was diagnosed with a dissociative disorder (Mezzich, Fabrega, Coffman et al., 1989).

Researchers know less about dissociative disorders than about other disorders, and considerable controversy surrounds the risk factors for these disorders, as well as the best treatments. To some, this controversy may seem daunting. We believe, however, that issues like this present a fascinating focus, as researchers strive to untangle a complex puzzle. Because so little is known about dissociative disorders, though, we will focus on one of these disorders in more depth: dissociative identity disorder.

Depersonalization/Derealization Disorder

As described above, **depersonalization/derealization disorder** involves a disconcerting and disruptive sense of detachment from one's self or surroundings. Depersonalization is defined by a sense of being detached from one's self (e.g., being an observer outside of one's body). Derealization is defined by a sense of detachment from one's surroundings, such that the surroundings seem unreal (Heller, van Reekum, Schaefer et al., 2013). People with this disorder may have the impression that they are outside their bodies, viewing themselves from a distance or looking at the world through the fog. Sometimes they feel mechanical, as though they are robots. Although more than a third of college students report that they have experienced at least fleeting moments of depersonalization or derealization in the past year (Hunter, Sierra, & David, 2004), these mild and intermittent symptoms are rarely of concern. The DSM-5 criteria for depersonalization/derealization disorder specify that the symptoms must be persistent or recurrent. Unlike the other dissociative disorders, this disorder involves no disturbance of memory.

In *Spellbound*, Gregory Peck played a man with amnesia. Dissociative amnesia is typically triggered by a stressful event, as it was in the film.

The following quote, drawn from a 1953 medical textbook, captures some of the experience of this disorder:

> *The world appears strange, peculiar, foreign, dream-like. Objects appear at times strangely diminished in size, at times flat. Sounds appear to come from a distance. . . . The emotions likewise undergo marked alteration. Patients complain that they are capable of experiencing neither pain nor pleasure; love and hate have perished with them. They experience a fundamental change in their personality, and the climax is reached with their complaints that they have become strangers to themselves. It is as though they were dead, lifeless, mere automatons. (Schilder, 1953, pp. 304–305)*

The symptoms of depersonalization and derealization are usually triggered by stress. Depersonalization/derealization disorder usually begins in adolescence, and it can start either abruptly or more insidiously. Most people who experience depersonalization also experience derealization, and the course of symptoms is similar for both symptoms. Symptoms are often continuously present for years (Simeon, 2009). Comorbid personality disorders are frequent, and during their lifetime, about 90 percent of people with this disorder will experience anxiety disorders and depression (Simeon, Knutelska, Nelson et al., 2003). As in the case of Mrs. A., described below, childhood trauma is often reported (Simeon, Guralnik, Schmeidler et al., 2001).

The DSM-5 diagnostic criteria for depersonalization/derealization disorder specify that the symptoms can co-occur with other disorders but should not be entirely explained by those disorders. It is important to rule out disorders that commonly involve these symptoms, including schizophrenia, posttraumatic stress disorder, and borderline personality disorder (Maldonado, Butler, & Spiegel, 1998). Depersonalization is also relatively common during panic attacks (Marquez, Segui, Garcia et al., 2001) and during marijuana intoxication (Simeon et al., 2003).

DSM-5 Criteria for Depersonalization/Derealization Disorder

- **Depersonalization:** Experiences of detachment from one's mental processes or body, as though one is in a dream, or
- **Derealization:** Experiences of unreality of surroundings
- Symptoms are persistent or recurrent
- Reality testing remains intact
- Symptoms are not explained by substances, another dissociative disorder, another psychological disorder, or by a medical condition

Clinical Case: Mrs. A.

Mrs. A was a 43-year-old woman who lived with her mother and son and worked in a clerical job. She had experienced symptoms of depersonalization several times per year for as long as she could remember. "It's as if the real me is taken out and put on a shelf or stored somewhere inside of me. Whatever makes me *me* is not there. It is like an opaque curtain . . . like going through the motions and having to exert discipline to keep the unit together." She had found these symptoms to be extremely distressing. She had experienced panic attacks for one year when she was 35. She described a childhood trauma history that included nightly genital fondling and frequent enemas by her mother from her earliest memory to age 10. (Simeon, Gross, Guralnik et al., 1997, p. 1109)

● DSM-5 Criteria for Dissociative Amnesia

- Inability to remember important autobiographical information, usually of a traumatic or stressful nature, that is too extensive to be ordinary forgetfulness
- The amnesia is not explained by substances, or by other medical or psychological conditions
- Specify dissociative fugue subtype if the amnesia is associated with bewildered or apparently purposeful wandering

Dissociative Amnesia

The person with **dissociative amnesia** is unable to recall important personal information, usually information about some traumatic experience. The holes in memory are too extensive to be explained by ordinary forgetfulness. The information is not permanently lost, but it cannot be retrieved during the episode of amnesia, which may last as briefly as several hours or as long as several years. The amnesia usually disappears as suddenly as it began, with complete recovery and only a small chance of recurrence.

Most often the memory loss of amnesia involves information about some part of a traumatic experience, such as witnessing the sudden death of a loved one. More rarely the amnesia is for entire events during a circumscribed period of distress. During the period of amnesia the person's behavior is otherwise unremarkable, except that the memory loss may cause some disorientation. Procedural memory remains intact—the person remembers how to answer the phone, ride a bike, and execute other complex actions, even though he or she is unable to remember specific events.

In a more severe subtype of amnesia called **fugue** (from the Latin *fugere*, "to flee"), the memory loss is more extensive. The person typically disappears from home and work. Some may wander away from home in a bewildered manner. Others may take on a new name, a new home, a new job, and even a new set of personality characteristics. The person may even succeed in establishing a fairly complex social life. More often, however, the new life does not crystallize to this extent, and the fugue is more similar to the experience of Hannah Upp (see Clinical Case) in being of relatively brief duration, consisting of limited but apparently purposeful travel during which social contacts are minimal or absent. As in other forms of amnesia, recovery is usually complete, although it takes varying amounts of time; after recovery, people are fully able to remember the details of their life and experiences, except for those events that took place during the fugue. The first documented case of dissociative fugue appeared in the medical literature in 1887 in France of Albert Dadas, who traveled during his fugue states from France to Algeria, Moscow, and Constantinople (Hacking, 1998). The case received widespread attention at medical conferences, and a small epidemic of fugue cases were reported throughout Europe in the years that followed (Hacking, 1998).

In diagnosing dissociative amnesia, it is important to rule out other common causes of memory loss, such as dementia, substance abuse, and medication side effects. Heavy drinking can cause blackouts, and medications such as the benzodiazepines used in the treatment of anxiety (e.g., Valium) and the sedative-hypnotics used in the treatment of insomnia (e.g., Ambien) can cause amnesia, and so a key diagnostic consideration is whether any head injury, medication use, or substance use might have preceded the episode. Dementia can be fairly easily distinguished from dissociative amnesia. In dementia, memory fails slowly over time, is not linked to stress, and is accompanied by other cognitive deficits, such as an inability to learn new information.

Clinical Case: Hannah

In 2008, Hannah Upp's family and friends mounted an intensive search for her through media and Internet outlets after she had been missing for four days. As reported in the New York Times (Marx and Ddiziulis, February 27, 2009), Hannah, a 23-year-old Spanish teacher living in New York City, had gone out for a run on the last day before the new school year began leaving behind her ID and wallet. Almost 3 weeks later, she was rescued floating in the water about a mile southwest of Manhattan. She was suffering from dehydration and hypothermia, and she had large blisters on her heels. She had no memory of the events that occurred during those 3 weeks, and it is believed she suffered from an episode of dissociative amnesia, fugue subtype. When interviewed, Hannah could not identify any stressful trigger that would have provoked the episode—although her job was stressful, she loved teaching, and she was doing well in her pursuit of a master's degree. Some of the events from those three weeks could be retraced from public video footage and reports from people who had seen her wandering around on Riverside Drive, entering an Apple store, and attending a local gym. Even with these glimpses of her existence during her lost three weeks, her case history high-

lights one of the difficult aspects of diagnosing dissociative amnesia: with no recall of events during those three weeks, it is hard to know if there was any head injury, trauma, or other explanation for her mysterious disappearance.

It is believed that Hannah Upp's three-week disappearance from home and work in 2008 could have resulted from an episode of dissociative amnesia, fugue subtype.

Amnesia can occur after severe stress, such as marital discord, personal rejection, financial or occupational difficulties, war service, or a natural disaster. Nonetheless, not all amnesias immediately follow trauma (Hacking, 1998). In addition, dissociative amnesia and fugue are rare even among people who have experienced intense trauma, such as imprisonment in a concentration camp (Merckelbach, Dekkers, Wessel et al., 2003).

Dissociative amnesia raises fundamental questions about how memory works under stress. Psychodynamic theory suggests that in dissociative amnesia, traumatic events are repressed. In this model, memories are forgotten (i.e., dissociated) because they are so aversive. There is considerable debate about whether repression occurs. Cognitive scientists have questioned how repression could happen, because research shows that extreme stress usually enhances rather than impairs memory (Shobe & Kihlstrom, 1997). For example, children who go through very painful medical procedures have accurate, detailed memories of the experience. Among a sample of veterans, those with the most severe war experiences were most likely to provide consistent descriptions of combat memories over time (Krinsley, Gallagher, Weathers et al., 2003). Norepinephrine, a neurotransmitter associated with heightened arousal, enhances memory consolidation and retrieval (Sara, 2009).

The nature of attention and memory, however, does change during periods of intense stress. People under stress tend to focus on the central features of the threatening situation and to stop paying attention to peripheral features (McNally, 2003). As a consequence, people tend to remember emotionally relevant material more than the neutral details surrounding an event (Talmi, 2013). For example, people might remember every detail about a gun that was trained on them and yet be unable to remember the face of the person who held the gun.

Given that the usual response to trauma is enhanced memory of the central features of the threat, how can we explain the stress-related memory loss that seems to be evident in dissociative amnesia? One answer might be that dissociative amnesia involves unusual ways of responding to stress. For example, extremely high levels of stress hormones could interfere with memory formation (Andreano & Cahill, 2006). Chronic stress, such as repeated abuse, might have more detrimental effects on memory than acute stress (Reinhold & Markowitsch, 2009). Some theorists believe that severe dissociation could interfere with memory. That is, in the face of severe trauma, memories may be stored in such a way that they are not accessible to awareness later when the person has returned to a more normal state (Kihlstrom, Tataryn, & Holt, 1993). Dissociative amnesia is considered an extreme outcome of this process. Debate continues about how to understand memory loss in the context of trauma and dissociation (see Focus on Discovery 8.1).

FOCUS ON DISCOVERY 8.1

Debates About Repression: Recovered Memories of Abuse in Childhood

A history of severe abuse in childhood is thought to be an important cause of dissociative disorders. Many people diagnosed with dissociative identity disorder report a history of abuse. Clearly, abuse happens all too often and exerts important effects on mental health and well-being. About 19 percent of women and 5 percent of men report that they have experienced some form of childhood sexual abuse (CSA; Afifi, Enns, Cox et al., 2008), and more have experienced other forms of abuse.

Here we focus on recovered memories of childhood abuse—that is, on cases in which a person had no memory of being abused as a child but then "recovered" the memory. Few issues are more hotly debated in psychology than whether these recovered memories are real. On one side, some argue that these recovered memories provide evidence for repression. Repression, as initially defined by Freud, involved suppressing unacceptably painful memories from consciousness. In contrast to the idea that recovered memories provide evidence of repression, some question how valid the memories are.

What does the evidence say about repression? In laboratory studies of memory, researchers have asked people to forget information, such as a list of words, and have shown that people can do so (Anderson & Green, 2001). This demonstrates that people can deliberately forget material, but are people with recovered memories better at forgetting than are others? Apparently not—people with recovered memories of CSA do not show any superior ability to forget words related to their trauma (McNally, Ristuccia, & Perlman, 2005). The word lists used in these studies, though, may not be painful enough to inspire repression.

To understand more about memories for highly painful events, some researchers have studied memory for traumas that occurred outside of the laboratory setting. In one study of whether memories of abuse can be forgotten, 92 percent of people with documented childhood abuse still reported a memory of the abuse when they were asked about it almost 15 years later (Goodman, Ghetti, Quas et al., 2003). Those with more severe abuse memories were more likely to remember and disclose their abuse. On the other hand, 8 percent of people reported that they had no memory of abuse.

Even for those 8 percent, the lack of reported recall might reflect many processes other than repression. People might not want to disclose such distressing events to a researcher (Della Femina, Yeager, & Lewis, 1990). Some people might have been too young at the time of the abuse

to be able to remember the events: people were less likely to report the memory at the 15-year follow-up if they had been under age 5 at the time the abuse occurred. Some of the traumas may have caused brain injury that could explain the gaps in memory. Thus, a failure to describe a memory may not be the same thing as repression.

Beyond the debate about whether repression occurs, how should we interpret it when someone develops a new memory? Where could recovered memories come from, if not from actual experiences? A leading researcher suggests a couple of possibilities (Loftus, 1993):

1. **Popular writings.** *The Courage to Heal* (Bass & Davis, 2008) is an extremely popular guide for victims of CSA. It suggests to readers that they were probably abused and offers as signs of abuse low self-esteem, feeling different from others, substance abuse, sexual dysfunction, and depression. The problem is that symptoms such as these can result from many factors other than CSA.

2. **Therapists' suggestions.** By their own accounts (Poole, Lindsay, Memon et al., 1995), many therapists who genuinely believe that adult disorders result from abuse will suggest to their clients that they were probably sexually abused as children; sometimes the therapist does this with the assistance of hypnotic age regression and guided imagery (Legault & Laurence, 2007). Unfortunately, techniques such as hypnosis may actually create false memories (Lynn, Lock, Loftus et al., 2003). Guided imagery, in which a person closes his or her eyes and tries to imagine an event occurring, tends to increase confidence that a false memory actually occurred. One group of researchers found that with guided imagery, at least 55 percent of college students developed at least a partial memory for a childhood event that never occurred, such as getting lost or being hurt (Porter, Yuille, & Lehman, 1999). To examine the validity of memories recovered in therapy, one group of researchers studied three groups: persons who had continuous memories of CSA, those who had recovered memories without a therapist, and those who had recovered memories within the context of therapy. Striking differences emerged: whereas about half of the continuous memories or those recalled outside of therapy could be corroborated by another source, none of the 16 events recalled within therapy could be corroborated (Geraerts, Schooler, Merckelbach et al., 2007).

Not only do memory distortions occur, but once they do, they hold emotional power. In one study, researchers interviewed people who reported having been abducted by space aliens (a presumably false memory). While participants talked about the experience, the researchers recorded heart rate, sweating, and other signs of arousal. People describing their abduction demonstrated just as much arousal as others did when they recounted experiences of war or trauma (McNally, Lasko, Clancy et al., 2004). Even false memories, then, can be associated with a lot of pain!

There is no doubt that abuse occurs. But we must be wary of uncritically accepting reports of abuse. This is an important issue because recovered memories of abuse have been used in hundreds of court cases (Pope, 1998). In a typical scenario, a woman recovers a memory during psychotherapy, accuses one of her parents of having abused her during childhood, and brings

Studies of memory show that recall of even a major event such as the terrorist attacks on 9/11 can be considerably distorted.

© Robert Essel NYC/© Corbis

charges against the parent. For most crimes, plaintiffs must file suit within a certain number of years of a crime. In the 1980s, courts in more than 30 states increased the time allowed for filing suit in cases where plaintiffs claimed to have recovered memories of CSA (Brown, Scheflin, & Whitfield, 1999). By the late 1990s, however, the tide had turned, and many appellate courts refused to allow testimony based on recovered memories (Piper, Pope, & Borowiecki, 2000). More than 100 former patients have sued therapists for malpractice, claiming that the therapists implanted false memories of abuse (McNally, 2003).

Social scientists and the courts share a heavy responsibility in deciding whether a given recovered memory is an accurate reflection of a criminal event. Erring in either direction could result in an injustice to either the accused or the accuser.

Dissociative Identity Disorder

Consider what it would be like to have dissociative identity disorder (DID), as did Gina, the woman described at the opening of this chapter. People tell you about things you have done that seem out of character and interactions of which you have no memory. How can you explain these events?

Clinical Description of DID The diagnosis of **dissociative identity disorder (DID)**, formerly labeled multiple personality disorder, requires that a person have at least two separate personalities, or alters—different modes of being, thinking, feeling, and acting that exist independently of one another and that emerge at different times. Each determines the person's nature and activities when it is in command. The primary alter may be totally unaware that any other alter exists and may have no memory of what those other alters do and experience when they are in control.

Case reports suggest that there is typically one primary personality and that this is usually the alter that seeks treatment. Most commonly, two to four alters are identified when the diagnosis is made, but over the course of treatment others may emerge. Each alter may be quite complex, with its own behavior patterns, memories, and relationships. Usually, the personalities of the different alters are quite different from one another, even polar opposites. Case reports have described alters who have different handedness, wear glasses with different prescriptions, like different foods, and have allergies to different substances. The alters are aware of lost periods of time, and the voices of the others may sometimes echo in an alter's consciousness, even though the alter may not know to whom these voices belong. In some cultures, alters may be understood as spirits who take control of the person's body. When these experiences of possession are part of a broadly accepted spiritual or cultural practice, the diagnosis of DID is not appropriate.

DID is rarely diagnosed until adulthood, but often after their diagnosis, patients will recall symptoms dating back to childhood. It is more severe and extensive than the other dissociative disorders (Mueller-Pfeiffer, Rufibach, Perron et al., 2012). DID is much more common in women than in men. Other diagnoses are often present, including posttraumatic stress

DSM-5 Criteria for Dissociative Identity Disorder

- Disruption of identity characterized by two or more distinct personality states (alters) or an experience of possession. These disruptions lead to discontinuities in the sense of self or agency, as reflected in altered cognition, behavior, affect, perceptions, consciousness, memories, or sensory-motor functioning. This disruption may be observed by others or reported by the patient.

- Recurrent gaps in memory for events or important personal information that are beyond ordinary forgetting

- Symptoms are not part of a broadly accepted cultural or religious practice

- Symptoms are not due to drugs or a medical condition

- In children, symptoms are not better explained by an imaginary playmate or by fantasy play disorder, major depressive disorder, and somatic symptom disorders (Rodewald, Wilhelm-Goling, Emrich et al., 2011). Personality disorders are also common (Johnson, Cohen, Kasen et al., 2006). DID is commonly accompanied by other symptoms such as headaches, hallucinations, suicide attempts, and self-injurious behavior, as well as by other dissociative symptoms such as amnesia and depersonalization (Scroppo, Drob, Weinberger et al., 1998).

The inclusion of DID as a diagnosis in DSM is a matter of some controversy. For example, in a survey of psychiatrists, two-thirds reported reservations about the presence of DID in the DSM (Pope, Oliva, Hudson et al., 1999). Students and the public often ask, "Does DID exist?" Clinicians can describe DID reliably; it "exists" in this sense. As we will discuss later, though, controversy swirls about the reasons these symptoms occur.

Check Your Knowledge 8.1 (Answers are at the end of the chapter.)

Answer the questions.
1. The key feature of the fugue subtype of dissociative amnesia is:

2. In the context of dissociative identity disorder, *alter* refers to:

The Epidemiology of DID: Increases over Time Although descriptions of anxiety, depression, and psychosis have abounded in literature since ancient times, there were almost no identified reports of DID or dissociative amnesia before 1800 (Pope, Poliakoff, Parker et al., 2006). Reports of DID were relatively frequent between 1890 and 1920, with 77 case reports appearing in the literature during that time (Sutcliffe & Jones, 1962). After 1920, reports of DID declined until the 1970s, when they increased markedly, not only in the United States but also in countries such as Japan (Uchinuma & Sekine, 2000). As we described above, contemporary prevalence estimates have ranged from 1 to 3 percent (Ross, 1991; Sar et al., 2007). Even if one considers that these estimates could be inflated due to imprecise interview probes, these figures are quite high comparatively—prevalence was earlier thought to be about one in a million.

What has caused the ballooning rates of the DID diagnosis over time? It is possible that more people began to experience symptoms of DID. But there are other possible explanations for the surge. The case of Eve White, popularized in the book *The Three Faces of Eve* as well as a movie, provided a highly detailed report of DID in 1957. The popular 1973 book *Sybil* presented a dramatic case with 16 personalities (Schreiber, 1973). The book sold more than six million copies in the first four years in print, and more than a fifth of all Americans watched a television adaptation broadcast in 1976 (Nathan, 2011). A series of other case reports were published in the 1970s as well. DSM-III, which appeared in 1980, defined the diagnosis of DID for the first time (Putnam, 1996). The diagnostic criteria and growing literature may have increased detection and recognition of symptoms. Some critics hypothesize that the height-ened professional and media attention to this diagnosis led some therapists to suggest strongly to clients that they had DID, sometimes using hypnosis to probe for alters.

Etiology of DID Two major theories have been advanced for DID: the **posttraumatic model** and the **sociocognitive model**. Despite their confusing names, both theories actually suggest that severe physical or sexual abuse during childhood sets the stage for DID. Almost all patients in therapy for DID report severe childhood abuse (Dalenberg, Brand, Gleaves et al., 2012). Since few people who are abused develop DID, both models focus on why some people do develop DID after abuse. As we will see, considerable debate has arisen between the proponents of these two approaches.

The posttraumatic model The posttraumatic model proposes that some people are partic-ularly likely to use dissociation to cope with trauma, and this is seen as a key factor in causing people to develop alters after trauma (Gleaves, 1996). Research supports two important tenets of this model. First, there is evidence that children who are abused are at risk for developing dissociative symptoms (Chu, Frey, Ganzel et al., 2000). Second, there is evidence that chil-

In the film version of *Sybil,* about a famous case of dissociative identity disorder, the title role was played by Sally Field. Later review of case notes suggested that "Sybil's personalities had not popped up spontaneously, but were provoked over many years of rogue treatment" (Nathan, 2011, p. xviii).

NBC/Photofest © NBC

dren who dissociate are more likely to develop psychological symptoms after trauma (Kisiel & Lyons, 2001). But because DID is so rare, these studies have tended to focus on dissociative symptoms rather then diagnosable disorder, and no prospective studies have followed children from the time of trauma through the development of DID.

The sociocognitive model   According to the sociocognitive model, people who have been abused seek explanations for their symptoms and distress, and alters appear in response to suggestions by therapists, exposure to media reports of DID, or other cultural influences (Lilienfeld, Lynn, Kirsch et al., 1999; Spanos, 1994). This model, then, implies that DID could be **iatrogenic** (created within treatment) in that the person often learns to role-play these symptoms within treatment. This does not mean, however, that DID is viewed as conscious deception; the issue is not whether DID is real but how it develops.

Many of the treatment manuals for DID recommend therapeutic techniques that reinforce clients' identification of different alters, such as interviewing clients about their identities after administering hypnosis or sodium pentothal (Nathan, 2011; Ross, 1991). The reinforcement and suggestive techniques might promote false memories and DID symptoms in vulnerable people (Lilienfeld et al., 1999). The famous case of Sybil is now widely cited as an example of how a therapist might elicit and reinforce stories of alters. It has been claimed that in Sybil's case, the alters were created by a therapist who gave substance to Sybil's different emotional states by giving them names, and who helped Sybil elaborate on her early childhood experiences while administering sodium pentothal, a drug that has been shown to contribute to false memories (Borch-Jacobsen, 1997; Nathan, 2011). As another example of controversy, the Clinical Case of Elizabeth provides an extreme example of a therapist who unwittingly encourages her client to adopt a diagnosis of DID when it isn't justified by the symptoms. All of the symptoms that Elizabeth described are common experiences; indeed, none of the symptoms listed are actual diagnostic criteria for DID.

Consistent with the idea that some therapists may reinforce these symptoms in their clients, a small number of clinicians contribute most of the diagnoses of DID (Modestin, 1992). In many psychiatric centers, the diagnosis is not detected at all; for example, in one study of initial diagnostic interviews of more than 11,000 outpatients at a major psychiatric center, DID was not diagnosed in a single case (Mezzich et al., 1989). Therapists who diagnose more people with DID tend to use hypnosis, to urge clients to try to unbury unremembered abuse experiences, or to name different alters (Powell & Gee, 2000). Also consistent with the idea that treatment is evoking the DID symptoms, most patients are unaware of having alters until after they begin treatment, and as treatment progresses, they report a rapid increase in the number of alters they can identify.

We will never have experimental evidence for the sociocognitive model, since it would be unethical to intentionally reinforce dissociative symptoms. Given this reality, what kinds of evidence have been raised in support of the sociocognitive model?

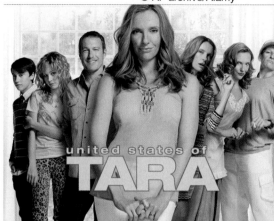

© AF archive/Alamy

In the TV show *United States of Tara,* family members struggle as the mother of the family shifts between different alters.

Clinical Case: Elizabeth, an Example of Unwarranted Diagnosis of DID

The book *Creating Hysteria: Women and Multiple Personality Disorder* provides a personal account of a person who received a false diagnosis of DID. Elizabeth Carlson, a 35-year-old married woman, was referred to a psychiatrist after being hospitalized for severe depression. Elizabeth reported that soon after treatment began, her psychiatrist suggested to her that perhaps her problem was the elusive, often undiagnosed condition of multiple personality disorder [MPD, now referred to as DID]. Her psychiatrist reviewed "certain telltale signs of MPD. Did Carlson ever 'zone out' while driving and arrive at her destination without remembering how she got there? Why yes, Carlson said. Well, that was an alter taking over the driving and then vanishing again, leaving her, the 'host' personality, to account for the blackout. Another sign of MPD [the psychiatrist said,] was 'voices in the head.' Did Carlson ever have internal arguments—for example, telling herself, 'Turn right' and then 'No, turn left'? Yes, Carlson replied, that happened sometimes. Well, that was the alters fighting with each other inside her head. Carlson was amazed and embarrassed. All these years, she had done these things, never realizing that they were symptoms of a severe mental disorder." (Acocella, 1999, p. 1)

DID Symptoms Can Be Role-Played Researchers have shown that people are capable of role-playing the symptoms of DID. Indeed, in one study, university students were hypnotized and instructed to let a second personality come forward. Most of the students endorsed having a second personality, and 81 percent of them even adopted a new name. Those who adopted a second personality were then asked to take personality tests twice—once for each personality. The personality test results of the two personalities differed considerably. These findings indicate that people can role-play DID.

Alters Share Memories, Even When They Report Amnesia One of the defining features of DID is the inability to recall information experienced by one alter when a different alter is present. One way to test whether alters share memory is to use implicit tests of memory (Huntjen, Postma, Peters et al., 2003). In **explicit memory** tests, researchers might ask a person to remember words. In **implicit memory** tests, experimenters determine if the word lists have subtler effects on performance. For example, if persons are first shown a word list that included the word *lullaby*, they might be quicker on a second task to identify *lullaby* as a word that fills in the puzzle l_l_a_y. People with DID were taught the initial word list and were then asked to complete the implicit memory test when they returned to the second session as a different alter. Twenty-one of the participants diagnosed with DID claimed at the second testing session that they had no memory of the first session. On tests of implicit memory, however, these 21 people performed comparably to people without DID. That is, memories seemed to be transferred between alters. This finding has been replicated in at least nine studies (Boysen & VanBergen, 2013). People with DID seem to demonstrate more accurate memory than they tend to acknowledge.

The famous actress and comedian, Roseanne Barr, talked about overcoming her history of dissociative identity disorder during an interview on *The Larry King Show* (March 2, 2006).

Physical or sexual abuse in childhood is regarded as a major factor in the development of dissociative disorders.

Ken Bianchi, a serial killer known as the Hillside strangler, unsuccessfully attempted an insanity defense, claiming that he suffered from DID. The jury decided that he was faking the symptoms of DID.

Check Your Knowledge 8.2

True or false?
1. DID was rarely diagnosed before the publication of *Sybil*.
2. Most patients with DID report childhood abuse.

Answer the question.
3. List the major sources of evidence for the sociocognitive model of DID.

Treatment of DID

There is widespread agreement on several principles in the treatment of dissociative identity disorder (Brand, Myrick, Loewenstein et al., 2012; International Society for the Study of Dissociation, 2011). These include the importance of an empathic and gentle stance, with the goal of helping the client function as one wholly integrated person. The goal of treatment should be to convince the person that splitting into different personalities is no longer necessary to deal with traumas. In addition, as DID is conceptualized as a means of escaping from severe stress, treatment can help teach the person more effective ways to cope with stress, such as emotion regulation strategies. Psychoeducation can help a person to understand why dissociation occurs and to begin to identify the triggers for dissociative responses in day-to-day life (Brand et al., 2012). Often, people with DID are hospitalized to help them avoid self-harm and to offer more intensive treatment.

Psychodynamic treatment is probably used more for DID and the other dissociative disorders than for any other psychological disorder. The goal of this treatment is to overcome repressions (MacGregor, 1996), as DID is believed to arise from traumatic events that the person is trying to block from consciousness. Unfortunately, some practitioners, particularly those who are drawing from a psychodynamic conceptualization, use hypnosis as a means of helping patients diagnosed with dissociative disorders to gain access to repressed material (International Society for the Study of Dissociation, 2011). Typically, the person is hypnotized and encouraged to go back in his or her mind to traumatic events in childhood—a technique called *age regression*. The hope is that accessing these traumatic memories will allow the person to realize that childhood threats are no longer present and that adult life need not be governed by these ghosts from the past (Grinker & Spiegel, 1944). Using hypnosis to promote age regression and recovered memories, though, can actually worsen DID symptoms (Fetkewicz, Sharma, & Merskey, 2000; Lilienfeld, 2007; Powell & Gee, 2000). More than 100 patients have sued therapists for harm caused by treatment of DID (Hanson, 1998).

No controlled studies have been done to assess the efficacy of psychotherapy for DID. Nine studies with no control group are available, covering a range from inpatient programs to outpatient individual therapies of different forms. Those studies show positive effects, but effects are difficult to interpret: notably, without a control group, the effects of time and support cannot be distinguished from the effect of the active treatment (Brand, Classen, McNary et al., 2009; Brand, McNary, Myrick et al., 2013).

DID is often comorbid with anxiety and depression, which can sometimes be lessened with antidepressant medications. These medications have no effect on the DID itself, however (Simon, 1998).

Quick Summary

Dissociative disorders are defined on the basis of disruptions in consciousness, in which memories, self-awareness, or other aspects of cognition become inaccessible to the conscious mind. In depersonalization/derealization disorder, the person's perception of the self and surroundings is altered; such people may feel detached from their body or may perceive the world as being unreal. Dissociative amnesia is defined by inability to recall important personal experience(s), usually of a traumatic nature. Dissociative fugue is a severe subtype of amnesia in which the person not only has an inability to recall important information but also leaves home and wanders without regard to work or social obligations. The person with dissociative identity disorder has two or more distinct personalities, each with unique memories, behavior patterns, and relationships.

Little research is available concerning the causes of these disorders. It is clear that DID is related to severe abuse, but considerable debate exists about the other causes of this disorder. The posttraumatic model suggests that DID is the result of using dissociation as a coping strategy to deal with the abuse. The sociocognitive model suggests that DID is caused by role-playing of symptoms among patients with a history of abuse. Proponents of the sociocognitive model note the dramatic shifts in diagnosis over time, the small proportion of clinicians who apply the diagnosis, the increases in number of alters recognized after treatment begins, and evidence that people can role-play symptoms of DID and that alters share more information than they acknowledge.

In the safe, supportive context of therapy, patients are encouraged to learn new strategies for coping with emotions, so as to gain better control over tendencies to rely on dissociation. Hypnosis and age regression techniques to recover memories are contraindicated for DID.

Somatic Symptom and Related Disorders

Somatic symptom and related disorders are defined by excessive concerns about physical symptoms or health. As shown in Table 8.2, the DSM-5 includes three major somatic symptom-related disorders: somatic symptom disorder, illness anxiety disorder, and conversion disorder. Many of us use the term *hypochondriasis* to describe chronic worries about developing a serious medical illness. Although hypochondriasis is not a DSM-5 diagnosis, both somatic symptom disorder and illness anxiety disorder overlap to some degree with hypochondriasis in that they involve distress and energy expenditure about a health concern. In somatic symptom disorder, the distress revolves around a somatic symptom that exists, whereas in illness anxiety disorder, the distress is about the potential for a medical illness in the absence of significant somatic symptoms. Conversion disorder involves neurological symptoms that are medically unexplained. Table 8.2 also lists malingering and factitious disorder, related disorders that we discuss in Focus on Discovery 8.2.

People with somatic symptom and related disorders tend to seek frequent medical treatment, sometimes at great expense. They often see several different physicians for a given health concern, and they may try many different medications. Hospitalization and even surgery are common experiences for them. It has been estimated that somatic symptom disorders lead to medical expenditures of $256 billion per year in the United States (Barsky, Orav, & Bates, 2005). In the UK, the average cost of medical care for patients with high levels of health anxiety was £2,796 (roughly $4,622) for a 6-month period in 2009-2010 (Barrett, Tyrer, Tyrer et al., 2012). Although people with these disorders are the most frequent consumers of medical care, they are often dissatisfied when no medical explanation or cure can be identified. They often view their physicians as incompetent and uncaring (Persing, Stuart, Noyes et al., 2000). Despite their negative assessment of the medical profession, they will often continue extensive treatment seeking, visiting new doctors and demanding new tests. Many patients become unable to work because of the severity of their concerns.

Even though these syndromes present a clear reason for concern, the diagnostic criteria for somatic symptom and related disorders have been criticized for several reasons:

- These conditions are remarkably varied. For example, some people develop somatic symptoms in the context of anxiety and depressive disorders, whereas others do not (Lieb, Meinlschmidt, & Araya, 2007). Some may have medical conditions that provoke the symptoms; others may not.
- Somatic symptom disorder and illness anxiety disorder are defined by health concerns that are a cause of excessive anxiety or involve too much expenditure of time and energy. These are very subjective criteria. What is the threshold for too much concern or too much energy expenditure? Some have argued that the subjective nature of these criteria may lead to overdiagnosis (Frances & Chapman, 2013).
- Patients often find the diagnosis of somatic symptom and related disorders to be stigmatizing. Perhaps because of these concerns, the DSM-IV-TR diagnoses related to somatic symptoms were rarely applied, even when the symptoms seemed to fit the diagnostic criteria. The DSM-IV-TR diagnostic criteria stipulated that symptoms had to be medically unexplained. In hopes of reducing the stigma associated with diagnosis, the DSM-5 committee removed the criterion that symptoms be medically unexplained from somatic symptom disorder. It is too soon to tell whether the DSM-5 diagnosis of somatic symptom disorder will be adopted in clinical practice.

Because these disorders are defined differently than they were In DSM-IV-TR (where they were labeled as somatoform disorders), we don't have data on the epidemiology or course of the somatic symptom-related disorders. Extrapolating from what we know about DSM-IV-TR diagnoses, however, concerns about somatic symptoms and illness anxiety tend to develop early in adulthood (Cloninger, Martin, Guze et al., 1986). Although many will experience these concerns throughout their lifetime, the symptoms may wax and wane, and for some, recovery occurs naturally. In one follow-up study, severe anxiety over health concerns persisted

Table 8.2 Diagnoses of Somatic Symptom and Related Disorders

DSM-5 Diagnosis	Description
Somatic symptom disorder	Excessive thought, distress, and behavior related to somatic symptoms
Illness anxiety disorder	Unwarranted fears about a serious illness in the absence of any significant somatic symptoms
Conversion disorder	Neurological symptom(s) that cannot be explained by medical disease or culturally sanctioned behavior
Malingering	Intentionally faking psychological or somatic symptoms to gain from those symptoms
Factitious disorder	Falsification of psychological or physical symptoms, without evidence of gains from those symptoms

for two-thirds of patients over a five-year period (Barsky, Fama, Bailey et al., 1998). Somatic symptom-related disorders tend to co-occur with anxiety disorders, mood disorders, substance use disorders, and personality disorders (Kirmayer, Robbins, & Paris, 1994). Somatic symptom-related disorders also appear to be more common in women than men (Demyttenaere, Bruffaerts, Posada-Villa et al., 2004).

Clinical Description of Somatic Symptom Disorder

The key feature of **somatic symptom disorder** is excessive anxiety, energy, or behavior focused on somatic symptoms. To be diagnosed, this preoccupation must persist for at least 6 months. The person with this disorder is typically quite worried about his or her health, and even small physical concerns can be taken as a sign of looming disease. The somatic symptoms can vary substantially. As illustrated by the Clinical Case of Maria, some might experience a multitude of symptoms from many different body systems. Others experience pain as the major concern.

Somatic symptom disorder can be diagnosed regardless of whether symptoms can be explained medically. It is nearly impossible to determine whether some symptoms are biologically caused. Doctors often disagree on whether a symptom has a medical cause (Rief & Broadbent, 2007). Indeed, most people experience at least one mild physical symptom at some point in their lifetime that cannot be explained medically (Simon, Von Korff, Piccinelli et al., 1999). Some people might have a condition that defies diagnosis because of limits in medical knowledge and technology. As technology has improved, some conditions that were historically difficult to explain have become better understood. As one example, complex regional pain syndrome was previously believed to be caused by psychological factors, but animal and human research now indicate that these symptoms result from inflammation secondary to autoimmune disorder (Cooper & Clark, 2013). Many common syndromes remain a focus for research because their etiology is not understood, including irritable bowel syndrome, fibromyalgia, chronic fatigue, nonulcer dyspepsia, and some forms of chronic pain (Cooper & Clark, 2013). The presence of these syndromes is not a reason to diagnose somatic symptom disorders. When psychological factors are the cause of symptoms, an alternative DSM diagnosis, labeled Psychological Factors Affecting Other Medical Conditions, may be appropriately considered.

Somatic symptoms may begin or intensify after some conflict or stress. To an outside observer, it may seem that the person is using the somatic symptom to avoid some unpleasant activity or to get attention and sympathy. People with somatic symptom disorder have no sense of this, however; they experience their symptoms as completely physical. Their distress over their symptoms is authentic.

For patients for whom pain is the central concern, dependency on painkillers is a risk. Understanding the psychological aspects of pain is important because millions of Americans experience chronic pain, accounting for billions of dollars of lost work time and incalculable personal and familial suffering (Turk, 2001).

DSM-5 Criteria for Somatic Symptom Disorder

- At least one somatic symptom that is distressing or disrupts daily life
- Excessive thought, distress, and behavior related to somatic symptom(s) or health concerns, as indicated by at least one of the following:
  - health-related anxiety
  - disproportionate and persistent concerns about the seriousness of symptoms
  - excessive time and energy devoted to health concerns
  - Duration of at least 6 months
- Specify if predominant pain

Clinical Case: Maria

Maria, a 32-year-old woman, was referred to a psychologist by her physician. Over a period of about 6 months, her physician had seen Maria 23 times for a range of complaints—general aches and pains, bouts of nausea, fatigue, irregular menstruation, and dizziness. But various tests, including complete blood workups, X-rays, and spinal taps, had not revealed any pathology.

On meeting her therapist, Maria immediately let him know that she was a somewhat reluctant client: "I'm here only because I trust my doctor, and she urged me to come. I'm physically sick and don't see how a psychologist is going to help." But when Maria was asked to describe the history of her physical problems, she quickly warmed to the task.

According to Maria, she had always been sick. As a child she had had episodes of high fever, frequent respiratory infections, convulsions, and her first two operations—an appendectomy and a tonsillectomy. During her 20s, Maria had gone from one physician to another. She had suffered with unbearable periods of vomiting. She had seen several gynecologists for her menstrual irregularity and for pain during intercourse, and she had undergone dilation and curettage (scraping the lining of the uterus). She had been referred to neurologists for her headaches, dizziness, and fainting spells, and they had performed EEGs, spinal taps, and even a CT scan. Other physicians had ordered EKGs for her chest pains. Maria seemed genuinely distressed by her health problems, and doctors responding to her desperate pleas for a cure had performed rectal and gallbladder surgery.

When the interview shifted away from Maria's medical history, it became apparent that she was highly anxious in many situations, particularly those in which she thought she might be evaluated by other people. Indeed, some of her physical symptoms were typical of those experienced by people diagnosed with anxiety disorders.

DSM-5 Criteria for Illness Anxiety Disorder

- Preoccupation with and high level of anxiety about having or acquiring a serious disease
- Excessive illness behavior (e.g., checking for signs of illness, seeking reassurance) or maladaptive avoidance (e.g., avoiding medical care)
- No more than mild somatic symptoms are present
- Not explained by other psychological disorders
- Preoccupation lasts at least 6 months

Clinical Description of Illness Anxiety Disorder

The main feature of **illness anxiety disorder** is a preoccupation with fears of having a serious disease despite having no significant somatic symptoms. To meet the DSM criteria for diagnosis, these fears must lead to excessive care seeking or maladaptive avoidance behaviors that persist for at least 6 months. People with this disorder are easily alarmed about their health, and they tend to worry about the possibility of cancer, heart attacks, AIDS, and strokes (Rachman, 2012). They may be haunted by powerful visual images of becoming ill or dying (Muse, McManus, Hackmann et al., 2010). They may react with anxiety when they hear about illnesses in their friends or in the broader community. These fears are not easily calmed, and others may become frustrated when attempts to soothe worries fail. Not surprisingly, illness anxiety disorder often co-occurs with anxiety and mood disorders (Noyes, 1999).

Somatic symptom disorder and illness anxiety disorder both involve health anxiety. When the fears about a serious disease are accompanied by somatic symptoms, the appropriate DSM-5 diagnosis is somatic symptom disorder. Because so few people with intense fears about their health are free of somatic symptoms, very few people are expected to meet the criteria for illness anxiety disorder. Somatic symptom disorder is expected to be three times as common as illness anxiety disorder (Heller et al., 2013).

Clinical Description of Conversion Disorder

In **conversion disorder**, the person suddenly develops neurological symptoms, such as blindness, seizures, or paralysis. The symptoms suggest an illness related to neurological damage, but medical tests indicate that the bodily organs and nervous system are fine. People may experience partial or complete paralysis of arms or legs; seizures and coordination disturbances; a sensation of prickling, tingling, or creeping on the skin; insensitivity to pain; or anesthesia—the loss of sensation. Vision may be seriously impaired; the person may become partially or completely blind or have *tunnel vision*, in which the visual field is constricted as it would be if the person were peering through a tube. *Aphonia*, loss of the voice other than whispered speech, can also occur. Many people with conversion disorder do not connect their symptoms with their stressful situations.

This disorder is described in the earliest writings on psychological disorders. *Hysteria* was the term originally used to describe the disorder, which the Greek physician Hippocrates considered to be an affliction limited to women and brought on by the wandering of the uterus through the body. (The Greek word *hystera* means "womb"; the wandering uterus symbolized the longing of the woman's body for the production of a child.) The term *conversion* originated with Sigmund Freud, who thought that anxiety and psychological conflict were converted into physical symptoms (see the Clinical Case of Anna O., an influential case for Freud's theory).

When a patient reports a neurological symptom, it is important to assess whether that symptom has a true neurological basis. Although some diagnostic distinctions are easy, the clinician still has to be careful in making this diagnosis. It is estimated that genuinely physical problems are misdiagnosed as conversion disorder about 4% of the time (Stone, Smyth, Carson et al., 2005). Sometimes behavioral tests can help make this distinction. For example, arm tremors might disappear when the person is asked to move the arm rhythmically. Leg weakness might not be consistent when tested with resistance (Stone, LaFrance, Levenson et al., 2010). In one form of conversion disorder, people report tunnel vision, which is incompatible with the biology of the visual system. In another example, people might show a seizure-like event at the same time that a normal EEG pattern is recorded (Stone et al., 2010).

Some symptoms that might seem medically implausible have been shown to have a biological basis. Consider, for instance, the classic example of "glove anesthesia," in which the person experiences little or no sensation in the part of the hand and lower arm that would be covered by a glove. For years this was considered a textbook illustration of anatomical nonsense because the nerves run continuously from the hand up the arm. Yet now it appears that carpal tunnel syndrome, a recognized medical condition, can produce symptoms similar to those of glove anesthesia. Nerves in the wrist run through a tunnel formed by the wrist bones and membranes. The tunnel can become swollen and may pinch the nerves, leading to tingling, numbness, and pain in the hand. People who use computer keyboards for many hours a day seem to be at risk for this condition. Beyond glove anesthesia, other symptoms that would intuitively seem difficult to explain medically, such as the perception of a burning sensation when touching a cold object, have clear medical explanations (in this case, ciguatera, a disease caused by eating certain reef fish). To enhance the reliability of conversion disorder, the DSM-5 provides guidance to clinicians about how to assess whether symptoms might be medically unexplained.

Symptoms of conversion disorder usually develop in adolescence or early adulthood, typically after a major life stressor. An episode may end abruptly, but sooner or later the disorder is likely to return, either in its original form or with a different symptom. The prevalence of conversion disorder is less than 1 percent, and more women than men are given the diagnosis (Faravelli, Salvatori, Galassi et al., 1997). The disorder is more common among patients visiting neurology clinics, where as many as 3 percent meet the criteria for conversion disorder (Fink, Hansen, & Sondergaard, 2005). Patients with conversion disorder are highly likely to meet criteria for another somatic symptom disorder (Brown, et al., 2007), and about half meet criteria for a dissociative disorder (Sar, Akyuz, Kundakci et al., 2004). Other common comorbid disorders include major depressive disorder, substance use disorders, and personality disorders (Brown et al., 2007).

DSM-5 Criteria for Conversion Disorder

- One or more symptoms affecting voluntary motor or sensory function
- The symptoms are incompatible with recognized medical disorder
- Symptoms cause significant distress or functional impairment or warrant medical evaluation

Clinical Case: Anna O.

As described in a case report, Anna O. was sitting at the bedside of her seriously ill father when she dropped off into a waking dream. She saw a black snake come toward her sick father to bite him. She tried to ward it off, but her arm had gone to sleep. When she looked at her hand, her fingers seemed to turn into little snakes with death's heads. The next day, when a bent branch recalled her hallucination of the snake, her right arm became rigidly extended. After that, whenever some object revived her hallucination, her arm responded in the same way—with rigid extension. Later, her symptoms extended to paralysis and anesthesia of her entire right side. [Drawn from Breuer & Freud (1982/1895)]

Etiology of Somatic Symptom-Related Disorders

Although one might expect somatic symptom-related disorders to be heritable, there is little concordance among twins for somatic symptom disorder (Torgersen, 1986) or conversion disorder (Slater, 1961). These disorders do not appear to be heritable.

In considering research on the etiology of somatic symptom-related disorders, one challenge is that the DSM-5 diagnoses differ from the DSM-IV-TR diagnoses that have been used in most studies. The major features of somatic symptom disorder and illness anxiety disorder, though, include excessive attention to somatic symptoms and disproportionate anxiety about one's health. Neurobiological and cognitive behavioral models have focused on understanding these two tendencies, and we describe those models here. After discussing that research, we consider a psychodynamic model of conversion disorder as well as social and cultural influences.

Neurobiological Factors That Increase Awareness of and Distress over Somatic Symptoms Everyone experiences occasional somatic symptoms. For example, we may feel muscle pain after a tough workout, small signs of an impending cold, or physiological responses of our body as we exercise. In understanding somatic symptom disorders, then, the key issue is not whether people have some bodily sensation, but rather why some people are more keenly aware of and distressed by these sensations.

Neurobiological models of somatic symptom-related disorders focus on brain regions activated by unpleasant body sensations. Pain and uncomfortable physical sensations, such as heat, increase activity in regions of the brain called the anterior insula and the anterior cingulate cortex (ACC) (Price, Craggs, Zhou et al., 2009). These regions have strong connections with the somatosensory cortex, a region of the brain involved with processing bodily sensations (see Figure 8.1). Heightened activity in these regions is related to greater propensity for somatic symptoms (Landgrebe, Barta, Rosengarth et al., 2008) and more intense pain ratings in response to a standardized stimulus (Mayer, Berman, Suyenobu et al., 2005). Some people, then, may have hyperactive brain regions that are involved in evaluating the unpleasantness of body sensations. This would help explain why they are more vulnerable to experiencing and noticing somatic symptoms and pain.

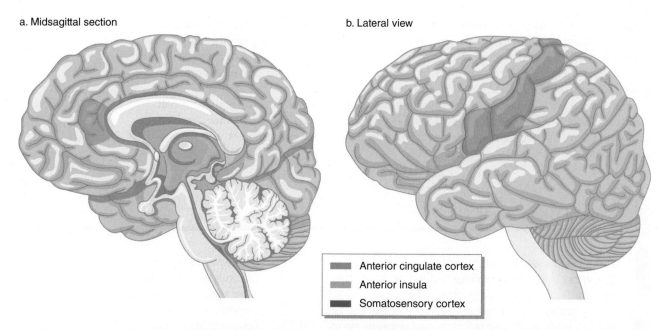

a. Midsagittal section   b. Lateral view

	Anterior cingulate cortex
	Anterior insula
	Somatosensory cortex

Figure 8.1 People with somatic symptom-related disorders appear to have increased activity in brain regions implicated in evaluating the unpleasantness of body sensations: the rostral anterior insula, the anterior cingulate, and the somatosensory cortex. The anterior cingulate is also involved in depression and anxiety.

It is well known that pain and somatic symptoms can be increased by anxiety, depression, and stress hormones (Gatchel, Peng, Peters et al., 2007). Depression and anxiety are also directly related to activity in the ACC (Wiech & Tracey, 2009). Experiences of emotional pain, such as remembering a relationship breakup, can also activate the ACC and the anterior insula. The involvement of these regions in experiences of physical and emotional pain may help explain why emotions and depression can intensify experiences of pain (Villemure & Bushnell, 2009).

In an interesting study, researchers studied whether learning to control ACC activity using real-time functional magnetic resonance imaging (fMRI) feedback could help reduce pain (deCharms, Maeda, Glover et al., 2005). Previous research suggested that specific regions of the ACC are particularly important in pain and emotion (Shackman, Salomons, Slagter et al., 2011). In a first study, healthy individuals with no somatic symptom-related disorder completed brain-scanning sessions in which they viewed graphs showing the changing level of activity in key regions of the ACC as they were exposed to uncomfortable sensations (a heat bar was attached to their hand, and pulses of 116–120 degree heat were sent to the bar). They were told various strategies for manipulating activity in their ACC, such as attending toward or away from the heat, changing their thoughts about their heat (e.g., to consider it as neutral vs. tissue-damaging), and trying to think of it as high or low intensity. Within three sessions, most individuals did learn to control the activity in their ACC. The more that people learned to control their ACC, the more they were able to reduce their experiences of pain. The fMRI feedback training was more powerful in reducing pain than control conditions of false fMRI feedback or no fMRI feedback. In a second study, ACC feedback training also was found to be helpful for people who suffered from chronic pain. These findings, then, support the idea that the ACC is important in experiences of pain.

Cognitive Behavioral Factors That Increase Awareness of and Distress over Somatic Symptoms Like the neurobiological models of somatic symptom-related disorders, cognitive behavioral models focus on the mechanisms that could contribute to the excessive focus on and anxiety over health concerns. Figure 8.2 illustrates one model of how these cognitive and behavioral risk factors could fit together. The orange boxes are relevant to understanding how a person might initially develop a somatic symptom. The blue boxes are relevant for understanding reactions to a somatic symptom. Once a somatic symptom develops, two cognitive variables appear important: attention to body sensations and interpretation of those sensations.

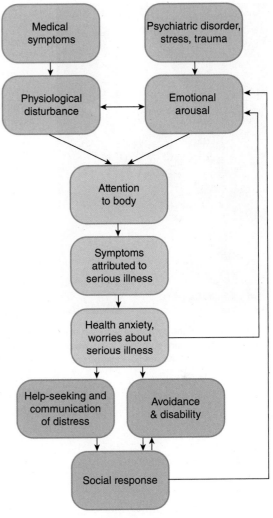

Figure 8.2 Mechanisms involved in somatic symptom-related disorders. [From Looper and Kirmayer (2002)]

Check Your Knowledge 8.3

Match the case description to the disorder. Assume that the symptoms cause significant distress or impairment.

1. Paula, a 24-year-old librarian, sought psychological help on the advice of her sister because of her deep fears about her health. In daily phone calls with her sister, she would describe worries that she had cancer or a brain tumor. She had no somatic symptoms or signs of these conditions, but every time she saw an Internet report, a TV program, or a newspaper article on some new serious condition, she became worried she might have it. She had seen doctors frequently for years, but when they identified no disease, she became annoyed with them, criticized the insensitivity of their medical tests, and sought a new consultant.

2. John, a 35-year-old man, was referred for psychological treatment by his surgeon because he seemed to be excessively nervous about his health. In the past 5 years, John had sought a stunning array of medical treatments and tests for stomach distress, itching, frequent urination, and

any number of other complaints. By the time he was referred, he had received 10 MRIs and too many X-rays to count, and he had seen 15 different specialists. Each test had been negative. He genuinely seemed to experience these symptoms, and there was no indication that he stood to gain from a medical diagnosis.

3. Thomas, a 50-year-old man, was referred for psychological treatment by an ophthalmologist. He reported that 2 weeks before, he had suddenly developed tunnel vision. Medical tests failed to reveal any reason for his tunnel vision, and there was no sign he was faking symptoms.

   a. somatic symptom disorder
   b. illness anxiety disorder
   c. malingering
   d. conversion disorder

Answer the question.

4. What is the major difference between somatic symptom disorder and illness anxiety disorder?

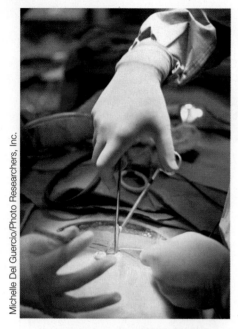

People with somatic symptom disorder may undergo unnecessary surgeries in hopes of finding a cure for their medical symptoms.

To study attention to health cues, researchers have used a version of the emotion Stroop task (see Chapter 2). Patients with the DSM-IV-TR diagnoses of somatic symptom-related disorders, major depressive disorder, or panic disorder were asked to name the color of words as quickly as possible, while ignoring the actual words (Lim & Kim, 2005). Many of the words were related to physical health and illness. Patients with somatic symptom-related disorders had more difficulty ignoring words that were related to physical health than other words, whereas other patients did not. Hence, people with excessive distress about their somatic symptoms may automatically focus on cues of physical health problems.

People prone to worries about their health also tend to interpret their physical symptoms in the worst possible way (Rief & Broadbent, 2007). A small physical sign is interpreted as a sign of impending catastrophe. For example, one person might interpret a red blotch on the skin as a sign of cancer (Marcus, Gurley, Marchi et al., 2007). Another person might overestimate the odds that a symptom is a sign of a disease (Rief, Buhlmann, Wilhelm et al., 2006). The exact form of the cognitive bias may vary, but once these negative thoughts begin, the resultant elevations of anxiety and cortisol may exacerbate somatic symptoms and distress over those symptoms (Rief & Auer, 2001). Focusing attention on the body may also increase awareness of unusual physical sensations that would otherwise have gone unnoticed. In Chapter 6, we described a very similar cognitive process as part of panic disorder. That is, people with panic disorder are likely to overreact to physiological symptoms. In panic disorder, the person often believes that the symptoms are a sign of an immediate threat (e.g., a heart attack), whereas in somatic symptom disorder, the person believes the symptoms are a sign of an underlying long-term disease (e.g., cancer or AIDS).

The tendency to be overly concerned about one's health may have evolved from early experiences of medical symptoms or from family attitudes to physical illness. Consistent with these childhood influences on cognitive biases, people with somatic symptom-related disorders report that as children they often missed school because of illness (Barsky, Brener, Coeytaux, et al., 1995).

Fear that a bodily sensation signifies illness is likely to have two behavioral consequences. First, the person may assume the role of being sick and avoid work, exercise, and social tasks (Martin & Jacobi, 2006), and these avoidant behaviors in turn can intensify symptoms by limiting other healthy behaviors. Second, the person may seek reassurance from doctors and from family members, and this help-seeking behavior may be reinforced if it results in the person getting attention or sympathy. Often, people with these disorders experience depression and interpersonal insecurity, so they may find attention and sympathy for health concerns particularly reinforcing (Rief & Broadbent, 2007). Beyond the attention, people may receive other types of behavioral reinforcers for somatic symptoms. For example, people receive disability payments based on how much symptoms interfere with their daily activities. Hence many different behavioral factors can maintain and intensify health anxiety.

Etiology of Conversion Disorder   Models of conversion disorder are distinct from the models that have developed for the other somatic symptom disorders. Although neuroimaging studies have been conducted, these are typically based on very small sample sizes and focus on different conversion symptoms, ranging from blindness to tremors to paralysis. Not surprisingly, then, the brain correlates of these conditions have not been consistent (Bell, Oakley, Halligan et al., 2011). In this section, then, we focus on psychodynamic views of conversion disorder and then consider sociocultural factors.

Psychodynamic Perspectives on Conversion Disorder   Conversion disorder occupies a central place in psychodynamic theories because the symptoms provide a clear example of the role of the unconscious. Consider trying to diagnose a woman who says that she awoke one morning with a paralyzed left arm. Assume that a series of neurological tests reveal no neurological disorder. Perhaps she has decided to fake paralysis to achieve some end—this would be an example of malingering (see Focus on Discovery 8.2). But what if you believe her? You would almost be forced to conclude that unconscious processes were operating. On a conscious level, she is telling the truth; she believes that her arm is paralyzed. On an unconscious level, some psychological factor is at work, making her unable to move her arm despite the absence of any physical cause. Psychodynamic theory suggests that the physical symptom is a response to an unconscious psychological conflict.

FOCUS ON DISCOVERY 8.2

Malingering and Factitious Disorder

In evaluating somatic symptoms, clinicians need to be aware of the potential for factitious disorder and malingering. Both can involve somatic symptoms. In **malingering**, a person intentionally fakes a symptom to avoid a responsibility, such as work or military duty, or to achieve some reward, such as being awarded an insurance settlement. This is in contrast to factitious disorder, where the sole goal often seems to be to adopt the patient role.

To distinguish between malingering and conversion disorder, clinicians try to determine whether the symptoms have been consciously or unconsciously adopted; in malingering, the symptoms are under voluntary control, which is not thought to be the case in conversion disorder. Insurance companies often go to great lengths to show that a person is faking symptoms and can actually function well outside of doctors' offices. When such detective work fails, though, it is often difficult, if not impossible, to know whether behavior is consciously or unconsciously motivated.

In **factitious disorder**, people intentionally produce physical symptoms (or sometimes psychological ones) to assume the role of a patient. They may make up symptoms—for example, reporting acute pain. Some will take extraordinary measures to make themselves ill. They may injure themselves, take damaging medications, or inject themselves with toxins.

In one of the most severe examples of factitious disorder that has been reported, a woman named Miss Scott described being hospitalized at more than 600 hospitals and having 42 operations, nearly all of which were not needed (Grady, 1999). Some days she would leave one hospital and be admitted to a different hospital by nightfall. One doctor who examined the scars on her abdomen reported that "she looked as if she had lost a duel with Zorro." When asked about her treatment seeking, she reported, "To begin with, it was just something I did when I needed someone to care about me. Then it became something I had to do. It was as if something took me over. I just had to be in the hospital. I had to."

She had grown up as an abused, lonely child, and one of her early positive memories was the care she received from a nurse after having her appendix removed. After that experience, she once walked into her local hospital feigning a stomachache, hoping that someone would care about her experience. She spent several days there appreciating the attention that she received. Over the course of the next year, she began to seek care at a series of different hospitals. "Soon she was spending all her time hitchhiking from town to town, trying to get into the hospital (Grady, 1999, p. D5). For Miss Scott, being a patient became her chief way of gaining support and nurturance.

Factitious disorder may also be diagnosed in a parent who creates physical illness in a child; in this case it is called *factitious disorder imposed on another* or *Munchausen syndrome by proxy*. In one extreme case, a 7-year-old girl was hospitalized over 300 times and experienced 40 surgeries at a cost of over $2 million. Her mother, Kathleen Bush, had caused her illnesses by administering drugs and even contaminating her feeding tube with fecal material (Toufexis, Blackman, & Drummond, 1996). The motivation in a case such as this appears to be a need to be regarded as an excellent parent who is tireless in seeing to the child's needs.

Alan Diaz/ASSOCIATED PRESS/© AP/Wide World Photos

Kathleen Bush was charged with child abuse and fraud for deliberately causing her child's illnesses.

Much of this theory has been developed based on case studies of people with conversion disorder involving unexplained blindness (Sackeim, Nordlie, & Gur, 1979). Psychodynamic theory suggests that this type of conversion disorder might involve two processes: (1) unconscious processing of perceptual stimuli and (2) motivation to be symptomatic.

Neuroscience supports the idea that much of our perceptual processing may operate outside of our conscious awareness. Take the example of unexplained blindness. The vision system consists of a set of modules within the brain. If these modules are not coordinated in an overarching conscious fashion, the brain may process some visual input such that the person can do well on certain visual tests, and yet the person could still lack a conscious sense of "seeing" certain types of stimuli. In one neuroimaging case study, a person with a conversion disorder involving blindness showed activity in brain regions involved with processing low levels of visual stimuli (such as lines and squares) but showed diminished activity in higher level visual cortex regions involved in integrating visual inputs into a consolidated whole (such as a house) (Becker, Scheele, Moessner et al., 2013). Because people may not be processing visual inputs at a higher level, they can truthfully claim that they cannot see, even when tests suggest that they can.

DSM-5 Criteria for Factitious Disorder

- Fabrication or induction of physical or psychological symptoms, injury or disease
- Deceptive behavior is present in the absence of obvious external rewards
- In Factitious Disorder Imposed on Self, the person presents himself or herself to others as ill, impaired, or injured
- In Factitious Disorder Imposed on Another, the person fabricates or induces symptoms in another person and then presents that person to others as ill, impaired, or injured

The second part of this model focuses on motivation— that is, some people are motivated to appear blind. This motivation for symptoms may be outside of conscious awareness. Support for the importance of motivation comes from a case study in which a man with a conversion disorder involving blindness had his vision tested over a large number of sessions. In each session, he was given different motivational instructions, and these instructions were found to influence performance (Bryant & McConkey, 1989). In sum, psychodynamic models of conversion disorder focus on the idea that people could be unconscious of certain perceptions and could be motivated to have certain symptoms. Unfortunately, despite the fact that case studies set the stage for further empirical work, this work has not yet been done.

Social and Cultural Factors in Conversion Disorder Social and cultural factors seem to shape the symptoms of conversion disorder. For example, symptoms of conversion disorder are more common among people from rural areas and people of lower socioeconomic status (Binzer & Kullgren, 1996). The influence of social factors is also supported by the many documented cases of "mass hysteria," in which a group of people with close contact, such as schoolmates or coworkers, develop inexplicable medical symptoms that would likely warrant a diagnosis of conversion disorder. Consider the following case example of one outbreak of seizure-type symptoms in a cotton processing facility, described in 1787. "A girl . . . put a mouse into the breast of another girl who had great dread of mice. She was immediately thrown into a fit and continued in it with the most violent convulsions for 24 hours. On the following day, three more girls were seized in the same manner, and the day after, six more." Within 3 days, 24 girls were affected. "The alarm was so great, that the whole work . . . was totally stopped" (Dr. St. Clare, 1787, *Gentleman's Magazine*, p. 268). Incidents like this suggest that modeling and social factors shape how conversion symptoms unfold.

Although many believe that vast changes have taken place in how frequently conversion disorder has occurred over time, there is reason to doubt this belief. It now appears more likely that treatment-seeking and diagnostic practices may be the factors that have changed over time (Stone, Hewett, Carson et al., 2008). That is, the level of interest in conversion disorder within psychiatry appears to have waxed and waned (Marlowe, 2001), with a peak occurring during the nineteenth century (Hare, 1969) and again during World War I (Ziegler, Imboden, & Meyer, 1960). Despite the strong social influences on this disorder, the prevalence of conversion disorder appears relatively stable over time in neurology clinics (Stone et al., 2008).

Quick Summary

The common feature of somatic symptom-related disorders is the excessive focus on physical symptoms. The nature of the concern, however, varies by disorder. The major somatic symptom-related disorders in the DSM-5 include somatic symptom disorder, illness anxiety disorder, and conversion disorder. Somatic symptom disorder is defined by excessive anxiety, worry, or behavior focused on somatic symptoms. Illness anxiety disorder is defined by fears of a severe disease in the absence of somatic symptoms. Conversion disorder is characterized by sensory and motor dysfunctions that cannot be explained by medical tests. Somatic symptom-related disorders may arise suddenly in stressful situations.

Neurobiological models suggest that some people may have a propensity toward hyperactivity in those regions of the brain involved in evaluating the unpleasantness of somatic sensations, including the anterior cingulate and the anterior insula. These brain regions are also implicated in negative emotions and depression. Cognitive behavioral models focus on attention to and interpretation of somatic symptoms as a way of understanding why some people experience such intense anxiety about their health. Behavioral responses to these health concerns can include disengagement and isolation, as well as excessive help-seeking behavior.

Psychodynamic theories of conversion disorder have focused on the idea that people can be unaware of their perceptions and may be motivated to have symptoms. Social influences on conversion disorder seem important, particularly given that sometimes cases cluster within small groups of co-workers or schoolmates. Nonetheless, the idea that the prevalence of conversion disorder has fluctuated substantially over time is controversial.

Check Your Knowledge 8.4

True or false?
1. Conversion disorder is highly heritable.
2. The two-stage psychodynamic model of conversion disorder emphasizes unconscious perceptions and motivation for having symptoms.

3. Somatic symptom disorder involves hyperactivation of the cerebellum.

Treatment of Somatic Symptom and Related Disorders

One of the major obstacles to treatment is that most people with somatic symptom-related disorders usually want medical care, not mental health care. Patients may resent mental health referrals from their physician because they interpret such a referral as a sign that the doctor thinks the illness is "all in their head." It is not a good idea for a provider to try to convince patients that their symptoms are caused by psychological factors. Most somatic and pain concerns have both physical and psychological components, and so it is unwise for the physician to debate the source of these symptoms with the patient. For many patients, a gentle reminder of the mind–body connection can enhance their willingness to consider psychological treatment approaches.

In the following sections, we will discuss a number of interventions that have been shown to be helpful in the treatment of somatic symptom-related disorders. There are no randomized controlled trials of treatments for conversion disorder, and so we focus on interventions designed to reduce distress and anxiety over one's health. One common approach has been to train primary care physicians to intervene. After discussing interventions offered through primary care, we discuss cognitive behavioral interventions that have been developed to address recurrent somatic symptoms and related distress. After describing cognitive behavioral treatment, we describe interventions to reduce pain within somatic symptom disorder.

Interventions in Primary Care Because most people with somatic symptom-related disorders will seek treatment through general practitioners, one important approach has been to teach primary care teams to tailor care for people with somatic symptom-related disorders. The goal is to establish a strong doctor–patient relationship that bolsters the patient's sense of trust and comfort, so that the patient will feel more reassured about his or her health. In one study, patients with distressing and medically unexplained gastrointestinal symptoms were randomly assigned to receive standard care or high levels of warmth, attention, and reassurance from doctors. Those who received high levels of support showed more improvement in symptoms and quality of life over the next 6 weeks compared to those who received standard care (Kaptchuk, Kelley, Conboy et al., 2008).

Other health care system interventions involve informing physicians when a patient appears to be an intensive user of health care services so that they can minimize the use of diagnostic tests and medications. These types of interventions with physicians can reduce the use of costly health care services (Konnopka, Schaefert, Heinrich et al., 2012).

Cognitive Behavioral Treatment Cognitive behavioral therapists have applied many different techniques to help people with somatic symptom-related disorders. As illustrated by our final Clinical Case, Louis, these techniques include helping people (1) identify and change the emotions that trigger their somatic concerns, (2) change their cognitions regarding their somatic symptoms, and (3) change their behaviors to stop playing the role of a sick person and to gain more reinforcement for engaging in other types of social interactions (Looper & Kirmayer, 2002).

The negative emotions that accompany anxiety and depressive disorders often trigger physiological symptoms and intensify the distress about those somatic symptoms (Simon, Gureje, & Fullerton, 2001). Indeed, as shown in Chapters 5 and 6, physical health concerns are common among people suffering from anxiety or depression. It should therefore come as no surprise that treating anxiety and depression often reduces somatic symptoms (Phillips, Li, & Zhang, 2002; Smith, 1992). Psychoeducation programs can help patients recognize links between their negative moods and somatic symptoms (Morley, 1997). Techniques such as relaxation training and various forms of cognitive behavioral treatment have proven useful in reducing depression and anxiety, and the reductions in depression and anxiety lead to reductions in somatic symptoms (Payne & Blanchard, 1995).

Many different cognitive strategies are used in the treatment of somatic symptom and related disorders. Some involve training people to pay less attention to their body. Alternatively, cognitive strategies might help people identify and challenge negative thoughts about their bodies (Warwick & Salkovskis, 2001). The person who struggles with thoughts about their pain and somatic symptoms such as "I cannot cope with this" might be taught to make more positive self-statements, such as "I've been able to manage bouts of pain on other days, and I'll get through this one as well."

Behavioral techniques might help people resume healthy activities and rebuild a lifestyle that has been damaged by too much focus on illness-related concerns (Warwick & Salkovskis, 2001). Maria, the woman described earlier, revealed that she was extremely anxious about her shaky marriage and about situations in which other people might judge her. Couples therapy, assertiveness training and social skills training—for example, coaching Maria in effective ways to approach and talk to people—could help her to develop healthier interpersonal interactions. In general, it is advisable to focus less on what patients cannot do because of their pain and somatic symptoms and more on encouraging them to reengage in satisfying activities and to gain a greater sense of control.

Behavioral and family approaches could help change Maria's reliance on playing the role of a sick person (Warwick & Salkovskis, 2001). If the people who live with Maria have adjusted to her illness by reinforcing her avoidance of normal adult responsibilities, family therapy might help. A therapist might teach family members about operant conditioning to reduce the amount of attention they give the person's somatic symptoms.

As a whole, these cognitive behavioral approaches have proven effective in reducing health concerns, depression, anxiety, and health care utilization compared to no treatment and to usual medical care (Thomson & Page, 2007). In one study, cognitive behavioral therapy (CBT) was as effective as an antidepressant in reducing illness anxiety symptoms (Greeven, van Balkom, Visser et al., 2007). CBT reduces somatic symptoms compared to control treatment, but these effects have tended to be small (Kleinstauber, Witthoft, & Hiller, 2011). That is, these interventions may do more to reduce the *distress* about somatic symptoms than they do to reduce the actual somatic symptoms.

Beyond addressing symptoms, CBT has been found to change key cognitive and brain mechanisms involved in somatic symptom-related disorders. For example, after treatment with CBT, people with health anxiety symptoms attend less to negative stimuli, as measured using the Emotion Stroop (Gropalis, Bleichhardt, Hiller et al., 2013). CBT treatment can also help reduce activity in regions of the brain that are involved in responding to pain stimuli (Flor, 2014).

Researchers have also examined several new approaches to treatment. One large-scale study found that Internet-based CBT was not potent enough to reduce health anxiety levels to a normative range (Tyrer, Tyrer, & Barrett, 2013). More positive effects were observed for a treatment in which people were taught to practice mindfulness meditation on a daily basis. Participants who learned mindfulness reported less health anxiety than control participants who took part in standard medical care (McManus, Surawy, Muse et al., 2012). The improvements associated with mindfulness practice were sustained at a one-year follow-up assessment.

Treatment for Somatic Symptom Disorder with Pain When the focus of somatic symptom disorder is on pain, several techniques can be helpful. CBT has fared well in research studies in this area (Ehde, Dillworth, & Turner, 2014). Hypnosis appears to help reduce pain levels and has been shown to influence brain regions involved in experiencing and interpreting pain (Jensen & Patterson, 2014). In acceptance and commitment therapy (ACT), a variant of cognitive behavioral treatment, the therapist encourages the client to adopt a more accepting attitude toward pain, suffering, and moments of depression and anxiety, and to view these as a natural part of life. The person might be coached not to struggle so intensely to avoid these difficult moments (McCracken & Vowles, 2014). Randomized controlled trials indicate that ACT appears to be as helpful as standard CBT

Clinical Case: Louis

Louis, a 66-year-old man, was referred to a psychiatrist by his cardiologist because of health anxiety. Although Louis acknowledged years of depressive and anxiety symptoms, he reported being much more concerned about his potential for heart problems. Several years before, he had developed intermittent symptoms of heart palpitations and chest pressure. Although extensive medical tests were within the normal range, he continued to seek additional tests and to monitor the results carefully. He had gathered a thick file of articles on cardiovascular conditions, had adopted strenuous diet and exercise routines, and had stopped all activities that might be too exciting and therefore challenging to his heart, such as travel and sex. He had even retired early from running his restaurant. By the time he sought treatment, he was measuring his blood pressure four times a day using two machines so that he could average the readings, and he was keeping extensive logs of his blood pressure readings.

Before treatment could begin, Louis had to understand that the way he was thinking about his physical symptoms was intensifying those physical symptoms as well as creating emotional distress. His therapist taught him a model of symptom amplification, in which initial physical symptoms are exacerbated by negative thoughts and emotions. The therapist used statements such as "A headache you believe is due to a brain tumor hurts much more than a headache you believe is due to eye strain." Once Louis understood that his thoughts and behavior might be increasing his medical concerns, treatment focused on four goals. First, Louis was coached to identify one doctor with whom to routinely discuss health concerns and to stop seeking multiple medical opinions. Second, Louis was taught to reduce the time spent engaging in excessive illness-related behaviors, such as logging his blood pressure. His therapist showed him that these behaviors were

actually increasing his anxiety rather than providing relief. Third, Louis was taught to consider the thoughts he had in response to his symptoms, which tended to be very negative and pessimistic. For example, the therapist and Louis identified ways in which he tended to catastrophize harmless physical sensations by viewing them as evidence for heart disease. Louis was taught to consider more benign reasons for his physical symptoms. Finally, Louis was encouraged to build other aspects of his life in order to diminish the focus on physical symptoms, and in response, he began to consult for restaurants. Taken together, these interventions helped Louis reduce his anxiety, diminish his focus on and concern about his health, and begin to lead a more enjoyable life. [Adapted from Barsky (2006)]

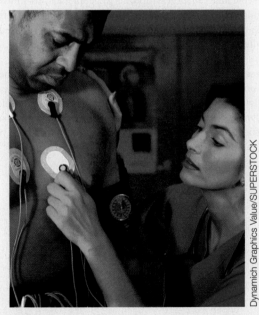

People with health anxiety are not easily reassured that they are well, even when extensive medical tests indicate no problems.

for somatic symptom-related disorders that involve pain (Veehof, Oskam, Schreurs et al., 2011). Hence, several psychological approaches may be helpful for somatic symptom disorders that involve a significant amount of pain.

Antidepressants can also be helpful when pain is a dominant symptom of somatic symptom disorder. Evidence from a number of double-blind randomized controlled trials indicates that low doses of antidepressant drugs can relieve pain and associated distress (Fishbain, Cutler, Rosomoff et al., 2000). Interestingly, antidepressants reduce pain even when given in dosages too low to alleviate the associated depression (Simon, 1998). Antidepressants are preferred over opioid medications, which are highly addictive (Streltzer & Johansen, 2006).

Summary

Dissociative Disorders

- Dissociative disorders are defined by disruptions in the conscious awareness of experience, memory, or identity.
- As described in Table 8.1, the DSM-5 dissociative disorders include depersonalization/derealization disorder, dissociative amnesia, and dissociative identity disorder.
- Most of the writing about the causes of dissociative disorders focuses on dissociative identity disorder. People with dissociative identity disorder very often report severe physical or sexual abuse during childhood. One model, the posttraumatic model, suggests that extensive reliance on dissociation to fend off overwhelming feelings from abuse puts people at risk for developing dissociative identity disorder. The sociocognitive model, though, proposes that these symptoms are elicited by treatment. Proponents of the sociocognitive model point out that that some therapists use strategies that suggest such symptoms to people, and that most people do not recognize the presence of any alters until after they see a therapist. Although one of the defining features of DID is the lack of shared memories among alters, evidence suggests that alters may share more memories than they report.
- Regardless of theoretical orientation, all clinicians focus their treatment efforts on helping clients cope with anxiety, face fears more directly, and operate in a manner that integrates their memory and consciousness.
- Psychodynamic treatment is perhaps the most commonly used treatment for dissociative disorders, but some of the techniques involved, such as hypnosis and age regression, may make symptoms worse.

Somatic Symptom and Related Disorders

- Somatic symptom and related disorders share a common focus on physical symptoms. As shown in Table 8.2, the major somatic symptom-related disorders include somatic symptom disorder, illness anxiety disorder, and conversion disorder.
- The somatic symptom-related disorders do not appear to be heritable.
- Neurobiological models suggest that key brain regions involved in processing the unpleasantness of bodily sensations may be hyperactive among people with somatic symptom-related disorders. These regions include the anterior cingulate and the anterior insula. Cognitive variables are also important: some people are overly attentive to physical concerns and make overly negative interpretations about these symptoms and their implications. Behavioral reinforcement may maintain help-seeking behavior.
- A psychodynamic model of conversion disorder focuses on lack of conscious awareness of perceptions as well as motivation for symptoms. Sociocultural factors also appear important in conversion disorder.
- People with somatic symptom-related disorders often resent being referred for mental health care. Programs that involve primary care physicians in addressing these symptoms by providing warmth and reassurance while limiting medical tests have been shown to be helpful. Cognitive behavioral treatments of somatic symptoms, which are efficacious approaches to addressing the distress over somatic symptoms, try to relieve depressive and anxious symptoms, to reduce the excessive attention to bodily cues, to address the overly negative interpretations of physical symptoms, and to reinforce behavior that is not consistent with the sick role. Meditation may also help patients reduce their health focus and anxiety. When pain is a primary concern in somatic symptom disorder, CBT, hypnosis, ACT, and low doses of antidepressant medication may be helpful.

Answers to Check Your Knowledge Questions

8.1 1. assumption of a new identity or bewildered wandering; 2. a distinct personality

8.2 1. T; 2. T; 3. Base rates of the disorder increased with media attention to the disorder; only a small proportion of therapists have ever seen DID cases, and the therapists who see the most DID cases rely on techniques like hypnosis that could produce alters; most clients are unaware of alters until after they receive psychotherapy; DID can be role-played; most people with DID do share memories among alters when sophisticated memory tests are used.

8.3 1. b; 2. a; 3. d; Somatic symptoms are present in somatic symptom disorder, but no significant somatic symptoms are present in illness anxiety disorder.

8.4 1. F; 2. T; 3. F

Key Terms

conversion disorder
depersonalization/derealization disorder
dissociative amnesia
dissociative disorders
dissociative identity disorder (DID)

explicit memory
factitious disorder
fugue subtype
iatrogenic
illness anxiety disorder

implicit memory
malingering
posttraumatic model of DID
sociocognitive model of DID
somatic symptom disorder

9 Schizophrenia

LEARNING GOALS

1. Be able to describe the clinical symptoms of schizophrenia, including positive, negative, and disorganized symptoms.
2. Be able to differentiate the genetic factors, both behavioral and molecular, in the etiology of schizophrenia.
3. Be able to describe how the brain has been implicated in schizophrenia.
4. Be able to describe the role of stress and other psychosocial factors in the etiology and relapse of schizophrenia.
5. Be able to distinguish the medication treatments and psychological treatments for schizophrenia.

Clinical Case: A Woman with Schizophrenia

All of a sudden things weren't going so well. I began to lose control of my life and, most of all, myself. I couldn't concentrate on my schoolwork, I couldn't sleep, and when I did sleep, I had dreams about dying. I was afraid to go to class, imagined that people were talking about me, and on top of that I heard voices. I called my mother in Pittsburgh and asked for her advice. She told me to move off campus into an apartment with my sister.

After I moved in with my sister, things got worse. I was afraid to go outside, and when I looked out of the window, it seemed that everyone outside was yelling, "Kill her, kill her." My sister forced me to go to school. I would go out of the house until I knew she had gone to work; then I would return home. Things continued to get worse. I imagined that I had a foul body odor, and I sometimes took up to 6 showers a day. I recall going to the grocery store one day, and I imagined that the people in the store were saying, "Get saved, Jesus is the answer." Things worsened—I couldn't remember a thing. I had a notebook full of reminders telling me what to do on that particular day. I couldn't remember my schoolwork, and I would study from 6:00 P.M. until

4:00 A.M. but never had the courage to go to class on the following day. I tried to tell my sister about it, but she didn't understand. She suggested that I see a psychiatrist, but I was afraid to go out of the house to see him.

One day I decided that I couldn't take this trauma anymore, so I took an overdose of 35 Darvon pills. At the same moment, a voice inside me said, "What did you do that for? Now you won't go to heaven." At that instant, I realized that I didn't really want to die. I wanted to live, and I was afraid. I got on the phone and called the psychiatrist whom my sister had recommended. I told him I had taken an overdose of Darvon and that I was afraid. He told me to take a taxi to the hospital. When I arrived at the hospital, I began vomiting, but I didn't pass out. Somehow, I just couldn't accept the fact that I was really going to see a psychiatrist. I thought that psychiatrists were only for crazy people, and I definitely didn't think I was crazy. As a result, I did not admit myself right away. As a matter of fact, I left the hospital and ended up meeting my sister on the way home. She told me to turn right back around because I was definitely going to be admitted. We then called my mother, and she said she would fly down the following day. (Quoted in O'Neal, 1984, pp. 109–110)

THE YOUNG WOMAN DESCRIBED in this clinical case was diagnosed with schizophrenia. **Schizophrenia** is a disorder characterized by disordered thinking, in which ideas are not logically related; faulty perception and attention; a lack of emotional expressiveness; and disturbances in behavior, such as a disheveled appearance. People with schizophrenia may withdraw from other people and from everyday reality, often into a life of odd beliefs (delusions) and hallucinations. Given that schizophrenia is associated with such widespread disruptions in a person's life, it has been difficult to uncover the causes of the disorder and develop effective methods to treat it. We still have a long way to go before we fully understand the multiple factors that trigger schizophrenia and develop treatments that are both effective and free of unpleasant side effects.

The symptoms of schizophrenia invade every aspect of a person: the way someone thinks, feels, and behaves. Not surprisingly then, these symptoms can interfere with maintaining stable employment, living independently, and having close relationships with other people. They can also provoke ridicule and persecution from other people. Substance use rates are high (Fowler, Carr, Carter et al., 1998), perhaps reflecting an attempt to achieve some relief from the symptoms (Blanchard, Squires, Henry et al., 1999). Moreover, the suicide rate among people with schizophrenia is high. Indeed, they are 12 times more likely to die of suicide than people in the general population. People with schizophrenia are also more likely to die from any cause than people in the general population (Saha, Chant, & McGrath, 2007), and their mortality rates are as high or higher than the rates for people who smoke (Chesney, Goodwin, & Fazel, 2014).

The lifetime prevalence of schizophrenia is around 1 percent, and it affects men slightly more often than women (Kirkbride, Fearon, Morgan et al., 2006; Walker, Kestler, Bollini et al., 2004). Schizophrenia is diagnosed more frequently among some groups, such as African Americans, though it remains unclear whether this reflects an actual difference among groups or bias among clinicians (Kirkbride et al., 2006; U.S. Department of Health and Human Services, 2001). Schizophrenia sometimes begins in childhood, but it usually appears in late adolescence or early adulthood, and usually somewhat earlier in men than in women. People with schizophrenia typically have a number of acute episodes of their symptoms and less severe but still debilitating symptoms between episodes.

Clinical Descriptions of Schizophrenia

DSM-5 Criteria for Schizophrenia

- Two or more of the following symptoms for at least 1 month; one symptom should be either 1, 2, or 3:
  (1) delusions
  (2) hallucinations
  (3) disorganized speech
  (4) disorganized (or catatonic) behavior
  (5) negative symptoms (diminished motivation or emotional expression)
- Functioning in work, relationships, or self-care has declined since onset
- Signs of disorder for at least 6 months; or, if during a prodromal or residual phase, negative symptoms or two or more of symptoms 1–4 in less severe form

Believing that others are taking special notice is a common paranoid delusion.

The range of symptoms in the diagnosis of schizophrenia is extensive, although people with the disorder typically have only some of these symptoms at any given time (see the DSM-5 criteria box). Schizophrenia symptoms are often described in three broad domains: positive, negative, and disorganization (Lenzenweger, Dworkin, & Wethington, 1991). The distinction among these domains has been very useful in research on etiology and treatment of schizophrenia; Table 9.1 shows the symptoms that comprise these domains.

In the following sections, we describe in some detail the individual symptoms that make up the positive, negative, and disorganized domains.

Positive Symptoms

Positive symptoms comprise excesses and distortions, and include hallucinations and delusions. For the most part, acute episodes of schizophrenia are characterized by positive symptoms.

Delusions No doubt all of us at one time or another have been concerned because we believed that others thought ill of us. Some of the time this belief may be justified. After all, who is universally loved? Consider, though, the anguish you would feel if you were firmly convinced that many people did not like you—indeed, that they disliked you so much that they were plotting against you. Imagine that your persecutors have sophisticated listening devices that let them tune in on your most private conversations and gather evidence in a plot to discredit you. Those around you, including your loved ones, are unable to reassure you that people are not spying on you. Even your closest friends are gradually joining forces with your tormentor. Anxious and angry, you begin taking counteractions against the persecutors. You carefully check any new room you enter for listening devices. When you meet people for the first time, you question them at great length to determine whether they are part of the plot against you.

Such **delusions**, which are beliefs contrary to reality and firmly held in spite of disconfirming evidence, are common positive symptoms of schizophrenia. Persecutory delusions such as those just described were found in 65 percent of a large, cross-national sample of people diagnosed with schizophrenia (Sartorius, Shapiro, & Jablonksy, 1974). Delusions may take several other forms as well, including the following:

- A person may believe that thoughts that are not his or her own have been placed in his or her mind by an external source; this is called *thought insertion*. For example, a woman may believe that the government has inserted a computer chip in her brain so that thoughts can be inserted into her head.

- A person may believe that his or her thoughts are broadcast or transmitted, so that others know what he or she is thinking; this is called *thought broadcasting*. When walking down the street, a man may look suspiciously at passersby, thinking that they are able to hear what he is thinking even though he is not saying anything out loud.

- A person may believe that an external force controls his or her feelings or behaviors. For example, a person may believe that his or her behavior is being controlled by the signals emitted from cell phone towers.

- A person may have **grandiose delusions**, an exaggerated sense of his or her own importance, power, knowledge, or identity. For example, a woman may believe that she can cause the wind to change direction just by moving her hands.

Table 9.1 Summary of the Major Symptom Domains in Schizophrenia

Positive Symptoms	Negative Symptoms	Disorganized Symptoms
Delusions, hallucinations	Avolition, alogia, anhedonia, blunted affect, asociality	Disorganized behavior, disorganized speech

James Lauritz/Getty Images, Inc.

- A person may have **ideas of reference**, incorporating unimportant events within a delusional framework and reading personal significance into the trivial activities of others. For instance, people with this symptom might think that overheard segments of conversations are about them, that the frequent appearance of the same person on a street where they customarily walk means that they are being watched, and that what they see on television or read in magazines somehow refers to them.

Although delusions are found among more than half of people with schizophrenia, they are also found among people with other diagnoses, including bipolar disorder, major depressive disorder with psychotic features, and delusional disorder.

Hallucinations and Other Disturbances of Perception People with schizophrenia frequently report that the world seems somehow different or even unreal to them. As in the Clinical Case at the beginning of this chapter, some people report difficulties in paying attention to what is happening around them:

> I can't concentrate on television because I can't watch the screen and listen to what is being said at the same time. I can't seem to take in two things like this at the same time especially when one of them means watching and the other means listening. On the other hand I seem to be always taking in too much at the one time, and then I can't handle it and can't make sense of it. (Quoted in McGhie & Chapman, 1961, p. 106)

The most dramatic distortions of perception are **hallucinations**—sensory experiences in the absence of any relevant stimulation from the environment. They are more often auditory than visual; 74 percent of one sample of people with schizophrenia reported having auditory hallucinations (Sartorius et al., 1974).

Some people with schizophrenia report hearing their own thoughts spoken by another voice. Other people may claim that they hear voices arguing, and others hear voices commenting on their behavior. Many people with schizophrenia experience their hallucinations as frightening or annoying. In one study of nearly 200 people with schizophrenia, those who had hallucinations that were longer, louder, more frequent, and experienced in the third person found them unpleasant. Hallucinations that were believed to come from a known person were experienced more positively (Copolov, Mackinnon, & Trauer, 2004).

Some theorists propose that people who have auditory hallucinations misattribute their own voice as being someone else's voice. Behavioral studies have shown that people with hallucinations are more likely to misattribute recordings of their own speech to a different source than are people without hallucinations or healthy controls (Allen, Johns, Fur et al., 2004). Neuroimaging studies have examined what happens in the brain during auditory hallucinations. These studies have found greater activity in Broca's area, an area of the frontal cortex that supports our ability to produce speech, and in Wernicke's area, an area of the temporal cortex that supports our ability to understand speech, when people with schizophrenia report hearing voices (Curcic-Blake, Liemburg, Vercammen et al., 2013). These data suggest that there is a problem in the connections between the frontal lobe areas that enable the production of speech and the temporal lobe areas that enable the understanding of speech (Ford, Mathalon, Whitfield et al., 2002). A meta-analysis of 10 neuroimaging studies found strongest activation in those areas of the brain associated with speech production (e.g., Broca's area), but it also found activation in areas associated with speech processing and understanding in the temporal lobes (Jardri, Pouchet, Pins et al., 2011).

Delusions and hallucinations are often considered the quintessential symptoms of schizophrenia. But as we have noted, they are not specific to schizophrenia and can occur in other psychological disorders, including bipolar disorder, major depressive disorder, and substance use disorders, to name just a few. Someone presenting with these symptoms may be incorrectly given a diagnosis of schizophrenia. In Focus on Discovery 9.1, we discuss the case of a young woman who had these symptoms but who most definitely did not have schizophrenia. This case points to the importance of conducting thorough assessments, as we discussed in Chapter 3.

FOCUS ON DISCOVERY 9.1

An Example of Misdiagnosis

A successful young woman who is a reporter for a major city newspaper begins to feel inklings of paranoia. At first, it doesn't seem like paranoia, but more like jealousy. She looks through her boyfriend's drawers for evidence he is cheating on her—something not atypical for new relationships.

But later, she begins to think people are taking special notice of her; that she is receiving special messages from TV; that her family is plotting against her. People are talking about her, whispering her name. People are spying on her and trying to hurt her. When others don't take her concerns seriously, she erupts into rages and becomes very agitated, and then without warning, begins sobbing uncontrollably.

She reports that she sees bright colors; then she reports having visions and seeing things that are most definitely not observed by others. In short, she begins to have visual hallucinations.

She begins to feel like she is having an out-of-body experience, like she is looking down on herself from above, watching her every move. She writes down random musings in a journal, but the thoughts are not connected and are very disorganized. Then, she has a seizure.

What can account for these symptoms, including hallucinations, paranoid delusions, disorganized thinking and behavior; and rapidly changing moods? Is it schizophrenia? Bipolar disorder with psychotic features? A substance use disorder? A seizure disorder? All of these are plausible diagnoses for the symptoms this young woman presented with. Yet none of them was correct.

In her beautifully written book, *Brain on Fire: My Month of Madness*, Susannah Cahalan writes about her experience with these symptoms over the course of a month. She did not remember many of these experiences and instead had to piece together what happened to her based on reports from family and friends who cared for her as well as her records that were collected once she was hospitalized because she was considered a danger to herself. She was evaluated for a seizure disorder in the hospital using standard procedures, which included continuous recording of her brain electrical activity via a cap of electroencephalogram (EEG) electrodes attached to her scalp and continuous videotaping of her behavior in her room. When Susannah later watched these videotapes of her disorganized and bizarre behavior and ramblings, she did not recognize herself.

She was under the care of neurologists in the hospital who were concerned she had a seizure disorder or some other neurological condition. Yet, they did not fully rule out a psychological disorder because her paranoia, hallucinations, and disorganization were so profound. And her MRIs and CT scans came back normal as did her blood tests, suggesting that she did not have an infection or a disease that had attacked the brain. The neurologists consulted psychiatrists who felt certain that she had some type of psychotic disorder. She was given antipsychotic medications. She began to develop motor symptoms that looked like catatonia. She wasn't getting any better.

Finally, the results of a second lumbar puncture (spinal tap) pointed to a possible clue. She had a very high number of white blood cells, or lymphocytes, in her cerebrospinal fluid (CSF). Recall from Chapter 2 that lymphocytes are a part of our immune system that fights infection by releasing cytokines. Cytokines promote inflammation to help fight infection.

Susannah's brain was quite literally inflamed or "on fire" as the title of her book describes. Further neuropsychological testing (see Chapter 3) revealed that she was experiencing left neglect, and this indicated that it was primarily the right side of her brain that was inflamed. Her immune system was not responding to an infection, instead it was attacking her healthy neurons as if they were infectious agents. Additional testing revealed that her immune system was attacking specific neurons with NMDA (N-methyl-D-aspartate acid) receptors. As we discuss later in the chapter, new treatments for schizophrenia are targeting NMDA receptors (if these receptors are blocked too much, psychotic symptoms can occur). Susannah was having what is called an "autoimmune" reaction, meaning the immune system was automatically going off for no identifiable reason and it was wreaking havoc on neurons with NMDA receptors, causing the paranoia, hallucinations, catatonia, and other symptoms. Her official diagnosis was "anti-NMDA-receptor-autoimmune encephalitis," an extremely rare condition that was only first identified in 2005 (Dalmau, Tüzün, Wu et al., 2007; Vitaliani, Mason, Ances et al., 2005).

At the time of her diagnosis, Susannah was just the 217th person to receive the diagnosis, and it took her doctors nearly a month to do so. Cahalan poignantly wonders, "If it took so long for one of the best hospitals in the world to get to this step, how many other people were going untreated, diagnosed with a mental illness or condemned to a life in a nursing home or a psychiatric ward?" (Cahalan, 2012, p. 151).

Given that anti-NMDA-receptor-autoimmune encephalitis is so rare, it is not likely that a huge number of people with schizophrenia are misdiagnosed. In fact, recent research has found that some people early in the course of schizophrenia have the NMDA antibodies but not anti-NMDA-receptor-autoimmune encephalitis (Steiner, Walter, Glanz et al., 2013), and there is new research on immune system dysfunction and schizophrenia (Carter, Bullmore, & Harrison, 2014). Still, Cahalan presents an important cautionary tale about diagnosis of psychological disorders. Since we do not yet have a blood or brain test for schizophrenia, the diagnosis is made based on the set of observed behavioral symptoms. Yet, as we have seen, these symptoms can occur in other disorders besides the psychological disorders we cover in this book. Thus, mental health professionals would do well not to be too quick to make a diagnosis of schizophrenia or bipolar disorder or any psychological disorder and instead consider that other factors might be contributing to the symptoms.

In Susannah's case, she was successfully treated over the course of several months with a combination of steroids to reduce the brain inflammation, plasma exchange (taking blood out of the body, treating the plasma to get rid of anti-NMDA antibodies, and returning the blood), and an intravenous immunoglobulin treatment. She also attended several cognitive rehabilitation sessions to help restore cognitive functions like planning, memory, and attention that were disrupted by the inflammation in her brain. She was able to return to work seven months after her hospitalization, and she wrote an article for the newspaper she worked for eight months after her diagnosis. Her book was published three years later.

Negative Symptoms

The **negative symptoms** of schizophrenia consist of behavioral deficits in motivation, pleasure, social closeness, and emotion expression (Kirkpatrick, Fenton, Carpenter et al., 2006). These symptoms tend to endure beyond an acute episode and have profound effects on the lives of people with schizophrenia. They are also important prognostically; the presence of many negative symptoms is a strong predictor of a poor quality of life (e.g., occupational impairment, few friends) 2 years following hospitalization (Ho, Nopoulos, Flaum et al., 1998; Milev, Ho, Arndt et al., 2005; Siegel, Irani, Brensinger et al., 2006).

Avolition Apathy, or **avolition,** refers to a lack of motivation and a seeming absence of interest in or an inability to persist in what are usually routine activities, including work or school, hobbies, or social activities. For example, people with avolition may not be motivated to watch TV or hang out with friends. They may have difficulty persisting at work, school, or household chores and may spend much of their time sitting around doing nothing. One recent study examined the types of motivation deficits in schizophrenia by interviewing people with and without schizophrenia four times a day for 7 days about their daily goals. The researchers found that people with schizophrenia were less motivated by goals about autonomy (self-expression), gaining new knowledge or skills, or praise by others compared to people without schizophrenia but were more motivated by goals that had to do with reducing boredom (Gard, Sanchez, Starr et al., 2014). However, people with schizophrenia were equally motivated by goals that had to do with relatedness to others and with avoiding a negative outcome (e.g., criticism). Thus, it appears that people with schizophrenia may have trouble with motivation for certain life areas, but not for others.

Asociality Some people with schizophrenia have severe impairments in social relationships, referred to as **asociality.** They may have few friends, poor social skills, and very little interest in being with other people. They may not desire close relationships with family, friends, or romantic partners. Instead, they may wish to spend much of their time alone. When around others, people with this symptom may interact only superficially and briefly and may appear aloof or indifferent to the social interaction.

Anhedonia A loss of interest in or a reported lessening of the experience of pleasure is called **anhedonia.** There are two types of pleasure experiences in the anhedonia construct. The first, called **consummatory pleasure,** refers to the amount of pleasure experienced in the moment or in the presence of something pleasurable. For example, the amount of pleasure you experience as you are eating a good meal is known as consummatory pleasure. The second type of pleasure, called **anticipatory pleasure,** refers to the amount of expected or anticipated pleasure from future events or activities. For example, the amount of pleasure you expect to receive after graduating from college is anticipatory pleasure. People with schizophrenia appear to have a deficit in anticipatory pleasure but not consummatory pleasure (Gard, Kring, Germans Gard, et al., 2007; Kring, 1999; Kring & Caponigro, 2010). That is, when asked about expected future situations or activities that are pleasurable for most people (e.g., good food, recreational activities, social interactions) on an anhedonia questionnaire, people with schizophrenia report that they derive less pleasure from these sorts of activities than do people without schizophrenia (Gard et al., 2007; Horan, Kring, & Blanchard, 2006). However, when presented with actual pleasant activities, such as amusing films or tasty beverages, people with schizophrenia report experiencing as much pleasure as do people without schizophrenia (Gard et al., 2007). Thus, the anhedonia deficit in schizophrenia appears to be in anticipating pleasure, not experiencing pleasure in the moment or in the presence of pleasurable things.

Blunted Affect **Blunted affect** refers to a lack of outward expression of emotion. A person with this symptom may stare vacantly, the muscles of the face motionless, the eyes lifeless. When spoken to, the person may answer in a flat and toneless voice and not look at his or her

People with schizophrenia who have blunted affect may not outwardly show happiness, but they will feel it as strongly as people who smile.

conversational partner. Blunted affect was found in 66 percent of a large sample of people with schizophrenia (Sartorius et al., 1974).

The concept of blunted affect refers only to the outward expression of emotion, not to the patient's inner experience, which is not impoverished at all. Over 20 different studies have shown that people with schizophrenia are much less facially expressive than are people without schizophrenia; this is true in daily life or in laboratory studies when emotionally evocative stimuli (films, pictures, foods) are presented. However, people with schizophrenia report experiencing the same amount or *even more* emotion than people without schizophrenia (Kring & Moran, 2008).

Alogia Alogia refers to a significant reduction in the amount of speech. Simply put, people with this symptom do not talk much. A person may answer a question with one or two words and will not be likely to elaborate on an answer with additional detail. For example, if you ask a person with alogia to describe a happy life experience, the person might respond "getting married" and then fail to elaborate even when asked for additional information.

Although we have just described five different negative symptoms, research suggests that these symptoms can be understood more simply as representing two domains (Blanchard & Cohen, 2006; Kring, Gur, Blanchard et al., 2013; Messinger, Tremeau, Antonius et al., 2011). The first domain, involving motivation, emotional experience, and sociality, is sometimes referred to as the *motivation and pleasure* domain. The second domain, involving outward expression of emotion and vocalization, is referred to as the *expression* domain.

Disorganized Symptoms

Disorganized symptoms include disorganized speech and disorganized behavior.

Disorganized Speech Also known as *formal thought disorder*, **disorganized speech** refers to problems in organizing ideas and in speaking so that a listener can understand. The following excerpt illustrates the incoherence sometimes found in the conversation of people with schizophrenia as an interviewer tries to ask John, a person with schizophrenia, several questions.

> *Interviewer: Have you been nervous or tense lately?*
> *John: No, I got a head of lettuce.*
> *Interviewer: You got a head of lettuce? I don't understand.*
> *John: Well, it's just a head of lettuce.*
> *Interviewer: Tell me about lettuce. What do you mean?*
> *John: Well . . . lettuce is a transformation of a dead cougar that suffered a relapse on the lion's toe. And he swallowed the lion and something happened. The . . . see, the. . . . Gloria and Tommy, they're two heads and they're not whales. But they escaped with herds of vomit, and things like that.*
> *Interviewer: Who are Tommy and Gloria?*
> *John: Uh, . . . there's Joe DiMaggio, Tommy Henrich, Bill Dickey, Phil Rizzuto, John Esclavera, Del Crandell, Ted Williams, Mickey Mantle, Roy Mande, Ray Mantle, Bob Chance . . .*
> *Interviewer: Who are they? Who are those people?*
> *John: Dead people . . . they want to be fucked . . . by this outlaw.*
> *Interviewer: What does all that mean?*
> *John: Well, you see, I have to leave the hospital. I'm supposed to have an operation on my legs, you know. And it comes to be pretty sickly that I don't want to keep my legs. That's why I wish I could have an operation.*
> *Interviewer: You want to have your legs taken off?*
> *John: It's possible, you know.*
> *Interviewer: Why would you want to do that?*
> *John: I didn't have any legs to begin with. So I would imagine that if I was a fast runner, I'd be scared to be a wife, because I had a splinter inside of my head of lettuce. (Neale & Oltmanns, 1980, pp. 103–104)*

Although John may make repeated references to central ideas or themes, the images and fragments of thought are not connected; it is difficult to understand what he is trying to tell the interviewer.

Speech may also be disorganized by what are called **loose associations,** or **derailment,** in which case the person may be more successful in communicating with a listener but has difficulty sticking to one topic. Steve Lopez, a reporter for the *Los Angeles Times,* befriended a man with schizophrenia named Nathaniel in the LA area who was a gifted musician (and also homeless). Lopez wrote about their friendship in the book *The Soloist* (Lopez, 2008). Nathaniel often exhibited loose associations. For example, in response to a question about Beethoven, Nathaniel replied:

> *Cleveland doesn't have the Beethoven statue. That's a military-oriented city, occupied, preoccupied, with all the military figures of American history, the great soldiers and generals, but you don't see the musicians on parade, although you do have Severance Hall, Cleveland Music School Settlement, Ohio University Bobcats, Buckeyes of Ohio State. All the great soldiers are there from the United States Military, World War Two, Korean War, whereas in Los Angeles you have the LAPD, Los Angeles County Jail, Los Angeles Times, Mr. Steve Lopez. That's an army, right? (Quoted in Lopez, 2008, pp. 23–24)*

Jamie Foxx played Nathaniel in the movie version of *The Soloist* (2009).

As this quote illustrates, a person with this symptom seems to drift off on a train of associations evoked by an idea from the past. People with schizophrenia have also described what it is like to experience disorganized speech.

> *My thoughts get all jumbled up. I start thinking or talking about something but I never get there. Instead, I wander off in the wrong direction and get caught up with all sorts of different things that may be connected with things I want to say but in a way I can't explain. People listening to me get more lost than I do. My trouble is that I've got too many thoughts. You might think about something, let's say that ashtray and just think, oh yes, that's for putting my cigarette in, but I would think of it and then I would think of a dozen different things connected with it at the same time. (Quoted in McGhie & Chapman, 1961, p. 108)*

It would seem logical to expect disorganized speech to be associated with problems in language production, but this does not appear to be the case. Instead, disorganized speech is associated with problems in what is called executive functioning—problem solving, planning, and making associations between thinking and feeling. Disorganized speech is also related to the ability to perceive semantic information (i.e., the meaning of words) (Kerns & Berenbaum, 2002, 2003).

Disorganized Behavior People with the symptom of **disorganized behavior** may go into inexplicable bouts of agitation, dress in unusual clothes, act in a silly manner, hoard food, or collect garbage. They seem to lose the ability to organize their behavior and make it conform to community standards. They also have difficulty performing the tasks of everyday living.

In DSM-5, one manifestation of disorganized behavior is called **catatonia.** People with this symptom may gesture repeatedly, using peculiar and sometimes complex sequences of finger, hand, and arm movements, which often seem to be purposeful. Some people manifest an unusual increase in their overall level of activity, including much excitement, flailing of the limbs, and great expenditure of energy similar to that seen in mania. At the other end of the spectrum is immobility: people adopt unusual postures and maintain them for very long periods of time. Catatonia can also involve waxy flexibility—another person can move the person's limbs into positions that the person will then maintain for long periods of time.

Catatonia is seldom seen today in people with schizophrenia, perhaps because medications work effectively on these disturbed movements or postures. Catatonia can be a symptom of other medical conditions as well. Boyle (1991) has argued that the apparent high prevalence of catatonia during the early part of the twentieth century reflected misdiagnosis of schizophrenia. Specifically, the similarities between encephalitis lethargica (sleeping sickness) and catatonia suggest that many cases of catatonia were misdiagnosed as schizophrenia. This idea was portrayed

FOCUS ON DISCOVERY 9.2

History of the Concept of Schizophrenia

Two European psychiatrists, Emil Kraepelin and Eugen Bleuler, initially formulated the concept of schizophrenia. Kraepelin first described **dementia praecox**, his term for what we now call schizophrenia, in 1898. Dementia praecox included several diagnostic subtypes—dementia paranoides, catatonia, and hebephrenia—that had been regarded as distinct entities by clinicians in the previous few decades. Although these disorders were symptomatically diverse, Kraepelin believed that they shared a common core. The term *dementia praecox* reflected what he believed was that core—an early-onset (praecox) and a progressive, inevitable intellectual deterioration (dementia). The dementia in dementia praecox is not the same as the dementias we discuss in the chapter on neurocognitive disorders (Chapter 14), which are defined principally by severe memory impairments. Kraepelin's term referred to a general "mental enfeeblement."

Bleuler broke with Kraepelin's description on two major points: he believed that the disorder did not necessarily have an early onset, and he believed that it did not inevitably progress toward dementia. Thus the label "dementia praecox" was no longer appropriate, and in 1908 Bleuler proposed his own term, *schizophrenia*, from the Greek words *schizein* ("to split") and *phren* ("mind"), capturing what he viewed as the essential nature of the condition.

With age of onset and deteriorating course no longer considered defining features of the disorder, Bleuler faced a conceptual problem. The symptoms of schizophrenia could vary widely among people, so he had to provide some justification for putting them into a single diagnostic category. That is, he needed to specify some common denominator, or essential property, that

Emil Kraepelin (1856–1926), a German psychiatrist, articulated descriptions of schizophrenia (then called dementia praecox) that have proved remarkably durable in the light of contemporary research.

would link the various disturbances. The metaphorical concept that he adopted for this purpose was the "breaking of associative threads."

For Bleuler, associative threads joined not only words but also thoughts. Thus, goal-directed, efficient thinking and communication were possible only when these hypothetical structures were intact. The notion that associative threads were disrupted in people with schizophrenia could then be used to account for the range of other disturbances. Bleuler viewed attentional difficulties, for example, as resulting from a loss of purposeful direction in thought, in turn causing passive responses to objects and people in the immediate surroundings.

Kraepelin had recognized that a small percentage of people with symptoms of dementia praecox did not deteriorate, but he preferred to limit this diagnostic category to people who had a poor prognosis. Bleuler's work, in contrast, led to a broader concept of the disorder. He diagnosed some people with a good prognosis as having schizophrenia, and he also diagnosed schizophrenia in many people who would have received different diagnoses from other clinicians.

Eugen Bleuler (1857–1939), a Swiss psychiatrist, contributed to our conceptions of schizophrenia and coined the term.

in the film *Awakenings,* which was based on the career and writings of Oliver Sacks. See Focus on Discovery 9.2 for more details on the history of schizophrenia and its symptoms.

Schizophrenia and the DSM-5

The DSM-5 criteria for schizophrenia are not too different from what they were in DSM-IV-TR. Like DSM-IV-TR, the DSM-5 requires that the symptoms last at least 6 months for the diagnosis. The 6-month period must include at least 1 month of an acute episode, or active phase, defined by the presence of at least two of the following symptoms: delusions, hallucinations, disorganized speech, disorganized behavior, and negative symptoms. The remaining time required for the diagnosis can occur either before or after the active phase. This time criterion eliminates people who have a brief psychotic episode and then recover quickly.

The biggest change in DSM-5 was the removal of the subtypes of schizophrenia (i.e., paranoid, disorganized, catatonic, undifferentiated). They were removed because they had questionable usefulness, poor reliability, and poor predictive validity; that is, the diagnosis of one or another subtype of schizophrenia provided little information helpful in either treating the disorder or predicting its course (Braff, Ryan, Rissling et al., 2013). Another change to DSM-5 was the addition of severity ratings for each of the five symptoms (see the DSM-5 criteria box) (Barch, Bustillo, Gaebel et al., 2013).

Schizophrenia is part of the DSM-5 chapter entitled "Schizophrenia Spectrum and Other Psychotic Disorders." Two other brief psychotic disorders appearing in this chapter are **schizophreniform disorder** and **brief psychotic disorder.** The symptoms of schizophreniform disorder are the same as those of schizophrenia but last only 1 to 6 months. Brief psychotic disorder lasts from 1 day to 1 month and is often brought on by extreme stress, such as bereavement. DSM-5 made only one change regarding these two disorders: the symptoms must include hallucinations, delusions, or disorganized speech. **Schizoaffective disorder** comprises a mixture of symptoms of schizophrenia and mood disorders. The DSM-5 requires either a depressive or manic episode rather than simply mood disorder symptoms, as in DSM-IV-TR.

A person with **delusional disorder** is troubled by persistent delusions. These can be delusions of persecution or jealousy, such as the unfounded conviction that a spouse or lover is unfaithful. Other delusions seen in this disorder include grandiose delusions, delusions of erotomania (believing that one is loved by some other person, usually a complete stranger with a higher social status), and somatic delusions (e.g., delusions about body functions).

The DSM-5 added a new category to the "Conditions for Further Study" part of Section III called *attenuated psychosis syndrome.* We discuss this disorer in more detail in Focus on Discovery 9.3.

FOCUS ON DISCOVERY 9.3

Attenuated Psychosis Syndrome

When DSM-5 first considered adding a new disorder to the "Schizophrenia Spectrum and Other Psychotic Disorders" chapter called attenuated psychosis syndrome (APS), the proposal generated a good deal of discussion and debate in the field. Ultimately, APS was placed in Section III of DSM-5 that covers conditions in need of further research before being included in the DSM.

The idea for APS came from research over the past two decades that has sought to identify young people who are at risk for developing schizophrenia. These types of studies are called **clinical high-risk studies**, and the starting point for these prospective, longitudinal studies is the reliable identification of youth who present with mild positive symptoms that might later develop into schizophrenia (Miller, McGlashan, Rosen et al., 2002). Research using the Structured Interview for Prodromal Syndromes (SIPS) has identified groups of young people who differ from people without these mild symptoms and from people who have a family history of schizophrenia (people studied in *familial high-risk* studies). Such people have been referred to as prodromal; the word *prodrome* refers to the early signs of a disease. Young people meeting prodromal criteria on the SIPS differ from young people who do not meet these criteria in a number of domains, including their everyday functioning and their rate of conversion to schizophrenia spectrum disorders (Woods, Addington, Cadenhead et al., 2009). Between 10 and 30 percent of people meeting prodromal criteria develop a schizophrenia spectrum disorder compared with only 0.2 percent of the general population (Carpenter & van Os, 2011; Yung, Woods, Ruhrman et al., 2012).

What were some of the arguments in favor of adding this new category to DSM-5? First, identifying APS may help people get treatment who otherwise would go unnoticed by mental health professionals. Unfortunately, under the current health insurance system in the United States, people often cannot get treatment unless they have an official diagnosis. Second, the hope is that the identification and treatment of people with APS might prevent them from developing schizophrenia or other schizophrenia spectrum disorders.

However, there were also a number of arguments against adding this new category (Yung, Woods, Ruhrmann et al., 2012). First, the category itself does not yet have enough reliability and validity to support its inclusion in the DSM. Second, there is a high level of comorbidity with prodromal symptoms: over 60 percent of young people meeting the prodromal criteria have a history of depression, raising the possibility that APS is really part of a mood disorder, not a schizophrenia spectrum disorder. Third, there is concern that applying a new diagnostic label, particularly to young people, might be stigmatizing or lead to discrimination. Because not all people with APS will develop schizophrenia, it may unnecessarily alarm young people and their families. Finally, while providing treatment for people with distressing or disabling attenuated positive symptoms is a laudable goal, there is concern that the treatment will too closely resemble that for schizophrenia, further blurring the line between the two conditions. Indeed, there is not yet an effective treatment for APS (Carpenter & van Os, 2011).

Quick Summary

Schizophrenia is a very heterogeneous disorder. It affects men slightly more than women and typically begins in late adolescence or early adulthood. Symptoms can be distinguished as positive, negative, and disorganized. Positive symptoms include hallucinations and delusions; negative symptoms include avolition, alogia, blunted affect, anhedonia, and asociality. Together, the negative symptoms represent two domains: motivation/pleasure and expression. Disorganized symptoms include disorganized speech and disorganized behavior. The DSM-5 no longer includes schizophrenia subtypes because they do not have a good deal of validity and are not very useful. Severity ratings for each of the schizophrenia symptoms were added in DSM-5. Other psychotic disorders include schizophreniform disorder and brief psychotic disorder, which differ from schizophrenia in duration. Schizoaffective disorder involves symptoms of both schizophrenia and either a depressive or manic episode. Delusional disorder involves delusions but no other symptoms of schizophrenia. The category attenuated psychosis syndrome, which involves positive symptoms in attenuated form that cause distress and have worsened in the past year, was not included in DSM-5 because the research to date is limited. Instead, it was added to the list of conditions in need of further study.

Check Your Knowledge 9.1 (Answers are at the end of the chapter.)

List the symptom that each clinical vignette describes.
1. Charlie enjoyed going to the movies. He particularly liked to see horror movies because they made him feel really scared. His sister was surprised to learn this, because when she went to the movies with Charlie, he didn't gasp out loud or show fear on his face.
2. Marlene was convinced that Christian Bale was sending her messages. In his movie *The Dark Knight,* his battles with the Joker were a signal that he was prepared to fight for them to be together. That he signed autographs at his movie opening also told her that he was trying to get in touch with her.
3. Sophia didn't want to go out to dinner with her family. She reasoned that these dinners were always the same food and conversation, so why bother? Later in the week, her mother mentioned that Sophia was not doing much around the house. Sophia said that nothing she could think of to do would be fun.
4. Jevon was talking with his doctor about the side effects of his medication. He talked about having dry mouth and then immediately began talking about cottonmouth snakes and jungle safaris and how hiking was good for your health but that Barack Obama was in better shape than George Bush.

Etiology of Schizophrenia

What can explain the scattering and disconnection of thoughts, delusions, hallucinations, and diminished emotion expression of people with schizophrenia? As we will see, a number of factors contribute to the cause of this complex disorder.

Genetic Factors

A good deal of research supports the idea that schizophrenia has a genetic component, as we discuss in the following sections on behavior genetics and molecular genetics research. The evidence is somewhat more convincing from behavior genetics studies, largely because they have been well replicated. Current evidence indicates that schizophrenia is genetically heterogeneous—that is, genetic factors may vary from case to case—mirroring the fact, noted earlier, that schizophrenia is symptomatically heterogeneous. As is the case for any gene or genes, they do their work via the environment, so gene–environment interaction studies are likely to help pinpoint the nature of the genetic contribution to schizophrenia (Walker & Tessner, 2008).

Behavior Genetics Research Family, twin, and adoption studies support the idea that genetic factors play a role in schizophrenia. Many behavior genetic studies of schizophrenia were conducted when the definition of schizophrenia was considerably broader than it is now. However, behavior genetics investigators collected extensive descriptive data on their samples, allowing the results to be reanalyzed later using newer diagnostic criteria.

Family Studies Table 9.2 presents a summary of the risk for schizophrenia in various relatives of index cases with schizophrenia. (In evaluating the figures, keep in mind that the risk for schizophrenia in the general population is a little less than 1 percent.) Quite clearly, relatives of people with schizophrenia are at increased risk, and the risk increases as the genetic relationship between proband (i.e., the person with schizophrenia) and relative becomes closer (Kendler, Karkowski-Shuman et al., 1996). Other studies have found that people with schizophrenia in their family histories have more negative symptoms than those whose families are free of schizophrenia (Malaspina, Goetz, Yale et al., 2000); this finding suggests that negative symptoms may have a stronger genetic component.

A family study examined over 2 million people from Denmark from the Danish Civil Registration System (Gottesman, Laursen, Bertelsen et al., 2010). This system records all inpatient and outpatient admissions for health-related issues, including psychological disorders. The researchers examined the cumulative incidence of schizophrenia and bipolar disorder among people with one, two, or no biological parents who had been admitted for treatment for schizophrenia or bipolar disorder. They also examined the incidence of these disorders among children who had one parent admitted for schizophrenia and one parent admitted for bipolar disorder. The findings are presented in Table 9.3. As you might expect, the incidence of schizophrenia was highest for children who had two parents admitted for schizophrenia. The incidence of schizophrenia was also higher for people with one parent admitted for schizophrenia and one parent admitted for bipolar disorder compared to those people who had just one parent admitted for schizophrenia. These findings suggest that there may be some shared genetic vulnerability between schizophrenia and bipolar disorder; molecular genetics studies, which we turn to shortly, also suggest this link.

Family studies show that genes likely play a role in schizophrenia, but of course the relatives of a person with schizophrenia share not only genes but also common experiences. Therefore, the influence of the environment cannot be discounted in explaining the higher risks among relatives.

Twin Studies Table 9.2 also shows the risk for identical (MZ) and fraternal (DZ) twins of people with schizophrenia. The risk for MZ twins (44.3 percent), though greater than that for DZ twins (12.08 percent), is still much less than 100 percent. Similar results have been obtained in more recent studies (Cannon, Kaprior, Lonnqvist et al., 1998; Cardno, Marshall, Coid et al., 1999). The less-than-100-percent concordance in MZ twins is important: if genetic transmission alone accounted for schizophrenia and one identical twin had schizophrenia, the other twin would also have schizophrenia. Twin study research also suggests that negative symptoms may have

Table 9.2 Summary of Major Family and Twin Studies of the Genetics of Schizophrenia

Relation to Proband	Percentage with Schizophrenia
Spouse	1.00
Grandchildren	2.84
Nieces/nephews	2.65
Children	9.35
Siblings	7.30
DZ twins	12.08
MZ twins	44.30

Source: After Gottesman, McGuffin, & Farmer (1987).

Behavior genetics studies often focus on twins or, more rarely, triplets and quadruplets. In one rare case, all of the Genain quadruplet girls (not pictured), born in 1930, developed schizophrenia. Two of the still surviving sisters were recently evaluated at age 81, and both were still taking antipsychotic medication (Mirsky, Bieliauskas, Duncan et al., 2013).

Table 9.3 Summary of Gottesman and Colleagues (2010) Family Study

Psychopathology in Parents	Incidence of Schizophrenia
Both parents with schizophrenia	27.3%
One parent with schizophrenia	7.0%
No parent with schizophrenia	0.86%
One parent with schizophrenia and one parent with bipolar disorder	15.6%

a stronger genetic component than do positive symptoms (Dworkin, Lenzenwenger, & Moldin, 1987; Dworkin & Lenzenwenger, 1984).

As with family studies, of course, there is a critical problem in interpreting the results of twin studies. Common shared (e.g., child-rearing practices) and nonshared (e.g., peer relationships) environmental factors rather than common genetic factors could account for some portion of the increased risk.

A clever analysis supporting a genetic interpretation of the high risk found for identical twins was performed by Fischer (1971). She reasoned that if these rates indeed reflected a genetic effect, the twins without schizophrenia would presumably carry risk genes for schizophrenia, even though it was not expressed behaviorally, and thus might pass along an increased risk for the disorder to their children. Indeed, the rate of schizophrenia and schizophrenia-like psychoses in the children of the MZ twins without schizophrenia was 9.4 percent, while the rate among the children of the twins with schizophrenia was only slightly and nonsignificantly higher, 12.3 percent. Both rates are substantially higher than the 1 percent prevalence found in the general population, which lends further support to the importance of genetic factors in schizophrenia.

Adoption Studies The study of children whose biological mothers had schizophrenia but who were reared from early infancy by adoptive parents without schizophrenia is another useful behavior genetics study method. Such studies eliminate the possible effects of being reared in an environment where a parent has schizophrenia.

In a now-classic study, Heston (1966) followed up 47 people born between 1915 and 1945 to women with schizophrenia who were raised by adoptive parents who did not have schizophrenia. Fifty control participants were selected from the same adoption agency that had placed the children of the women with schizophrenia. The follow-up assessment revealed that none of the controls was diagnosed with schizophrenia, versus 10.6 percent (five) of the offspring of women with schizophrenia.

Another large study of adopted offspring of mothers with schizophrenia found similar results. In this study, the risk for developing schizophrenia or a related diagnosis among the 164 adoptees who had a biological mother with schizophrenia was 8.1 percent; the risk for the 197 control adoptees who did not have a biological parent with schizophrenia was significantly lower at 2.3 percent (Tienari, Wynner, Moring et al., 2000).

Familial High-Risk Studies A different type of family study is called the **familial high-risk study**. This type of study begins with one or two biological parents with schizophrenia and follows their offspring longitudinally in order to identify how many of these children may develop schizophrenia and what types of childhood neurobiological and behavioral factors may predict the disorder's onset. The first familial high-risk study of schizophrenia was begun in the 1960s (Mednick & Schulsinger, 1968). The high-risk participants were 207 young people whose mothers had schizophrenia; the low-risk participants were similar in all respects to the high-risk group except that their mothers did not have schizophrenia. (The researchers decided that the mother should be the parent with the disorder because paternity is not always easy to determine.) In 1972, the now-grown men and women were followed up with a number of measures, including a battery of diagnostic tests. Fifteen of the high-risk participants were diagnosed with schizophrenia; none of the control participants were so diagnosed.

In the wake of this pioneering study, other familial high-risk investigations were undertaken. The New England Family Study found that children of a parent (mother or father) with a schizophrenia spectrum disorder were six times more likely to develop a schizophrenia spectrum disorder by age 40 than children without a parent with schizophrenia (Goldstein, Buka, Seidman et al., 2010). This study also included a group of parents who had what they called "affective psychosis," including bipolar disorder or major depressive disorder with psychotic features. Children of parents with affective psychosis were

Sarnoff Mednick, a psychologist at the University of Southern California, pioneered the use of the familial high-risk method for studying schizophrenia. He has also contributed to the hypothesis that a maternal viral infection is implicated in this disorder.

Courtesy Sarnoff A. Mednick

not at greater risk for developing a schizophrenia spectrum disorder, but they were 14 times more likely to develop an affective psychosis than children of parents without any psychosis.

A recent meta-analysis of 33 familial high-risk studies that included offspring of parents with schizophrenia, bipolar disorder, or major depressive disorder found that the risk of developing schizophrenia was highest for offspring of a parent with schizophrenia. However, offspring of a parent with schizophrenia were also at nearly two times greater risk of developing any severe psychological disorder compared to offspring of parents with no psychological disorders (Rasic, Hajek, Alda et al., 2014).

Molecular Genetics Research Knowing that schizophrenia has a genetic component is in many ways just the starting point for research. Understanding exactly what constitutes the genetic predisposition is the challenge faced by molecular genetics researchers. As with nearly all of the disorders we cover in this book, the predisposition for schizophrenia is not transmitted by a single gene. Furthermore, recent molecular genetics research has found that there are multiple common genes associated with both schizophrenia and bipolar disorder (Cross-Disorder Group of the Psychiatric Genomics Consortium, 2013).

Association studies try to narrow in on specific genes associated with schizophrenia by establishing how often specific genes and a particular trait or behavior (i.e., phenotype) co-occur. Three candidate genes have received some support from association studies. One of these genes has been associated with schizophrenia (*DTNBP1*), and two have been associated with the cognitive deficits associated with schizophrenia (*COMT* and *BDNF*). The gene called *DTNBP1* encodes a protein called dysbindin that is expressed throughout the brain, but the function of either the gene or the protein is not yet entirely clear. It appears to impact the dopamine and glutamate neurotransmitter systems throughout the brain (MacDonald & Chafee, 2006), and these systems are implicated in schizophrenia, as we discuss later on. In addition, a postmortem study has shown that compared to people without schizophrenia, the brains of people with schizophrenia had less dysbindin in a number of brain areas, including the frontal cortex, temporal cortex, hippocampus, and limbic system structures (Weickert, Straub, McClintock et al., 2004).

The gene called *COMT* is associated with cognitive control processes that rely on the **prefrontal cortex** (reviewed by Goldberg & Weinberger, 2004). A number of studies have demonstrated that people with schizophrenia have deficits in cognitive control processes, which include planning, working memory, and problem solving, and other studies have shown problems in the prefrontal cortex. A few association studies have implicated the *COMT* gene in schizophrenia (Harrison & Weinberger, 2004; Owen et al., 2004). The *BDNF* gene has been studied and linked with cognitive function in people with and without schizophrenia. This gene has a polymorphism called Val66Met, whereby a person can have two Val alleles (Val/Val), two Met alleles (Met/Met), or one Val and one Met allele (Val/Met). In a large study of people with and without schizophrenia, verbal memory was better in people who had two Val alleles (Val/Val) compared to people who had either one or two Met alleles (Val/Met or Met/Met) (Ho, Milev, O'Leary et al., 2006).

Although there have been some replications of studies with these four genes, other attempts to replicate the association between these genes and schizophrenia have failed. In addition, these four genes do not appear in genome-wide association studies. This may reflect the tremendous genetic heterogeneity associated with schizophrenia (Kim, Zerwas, Trace et al. 2011).

Genome-wide association studies (GWAS) have also been applied to the study of schizophrenia. Recall from Chapter 2 that this technique allows researchers to identify rare mutations, such as CNVs (copy number variations), in genes rather than just known gene loci. Mutations are changes in a gene that occur randomly and for unknown reasons. A CNV refers to an abnormal copy (a deletion or a duplication) of one or more sections of DNA in a gene. (see Chapter 2). As an example, one GWAS found over 50 rare CNV mutations that were three times more common among people with schizophrenia than in people without schizophrenia across two different samples of people (Walsh, McClellan, McCarthy et al., 2008). Some of the identified gene mutations are known to be associated with other presumed risk factors in the etiology of schizophrenia, including the neurotransmitter glutamate and proteins that promote the proper placement of neurons in the brain during brain development. Furthermore, even though the identified mutations were more common in people with schizophrenia than people without schizophrenia, they were identified in only about 20 percent of the people with schizophrenia. Thus, other genetic factors await discovery in future studies.

Reviews of GWAS studies in schizophrenia conducted in the past five years concluded that three CNV deletions (22ql1.21, 15q13.3, lq21.1; see Figure 9.1 for how to decode these tangles of letters and numbers) had met the stringent replication requirements of modern-day genetics research (Bassett, Scherer, & Brzustowicz, 2010; Kim et al., 2011). However, GWAS studies of the sequence of genes have also been conducted. These studies seek to identify single nucleotide polymorphisms (SNPs; see Chapter 2) that are associated with schizophrenia. The findings of these studies have not been as well replicated as the GWAS studies of CNVs, but one of the intriguing findings to emerge is that the SNPs associated with schizophrenia are also associated with bipolar disorder. SNP studies, like the familial high-risk studies, suggest that there may be a common genetic vulnerability for both of these disorders (Owen, Craddock, & O'Donovan, 2010; Ruderfer, Fanous, Ripke et al., 2013; Sullivan, Daly, & O'Donovan, 2012).

We can make three important points about these mutations: (1) they are all very rare; (2) only a small number of people with these rare mutations have schizophrenia; and (3) they are not specific to schizophrenia. Given that these are so rare, does this mean that these researchers are on the wrong track to finding genetic vulnerability to schizophrenia? Not necessarily. These findings confirm the genetic heterogeneity of schizophrenia and the idea that people with the same disorder (schizophrenia) may not necessarily have the same genetic factors contributing to the disorder. Current genetics research supports the idea that the genetic vulnerability to schizophrenia may be made up of many rare mutations.

The Role of Neurotransmitters

Present research is examining several different neurotransmitters, such as serotonin and glutamate, to see what role they might play in the etiology of schizophrenia. The first neurotransmitter to receive substantial research attention was dopamine. This research has both helped and hindered efforts to identify causes and treatments for schizophrenia.

Dopamine Theory The theory that schizophrenia is related to excess activity of the neurotransmitter dopamine is based principally on the knowledge that drugs effective in treating schizophrenia reduce dopamine activity. Researchers have noted that antipsychotic drugs, in addition to being useful in treating some symptoms of schizophrenia, produce side effects resembling the symptoms of Parkinson's disease. Parkinson's disease is caused in part by low levels of dopamine in a particular area of the brain. Antipsychotic drugs fit into and thereby

What do all the letters and numbers mean?

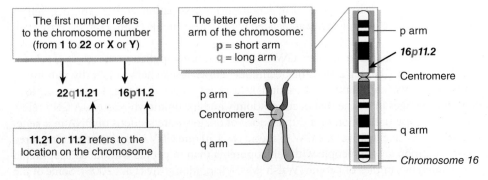

Figure 9.1 Decoding the language of genes.

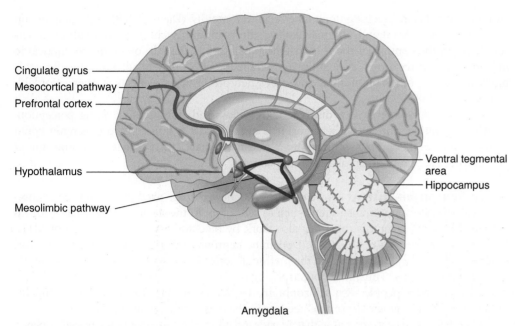

Cingulate gyrus
Mesocortical pathway
Prefrontal cortex

Hypothalamus

Mesolimbic pathway

Ventral tegmental area
Hippocampus

Amygdala

Figure 9.2 The brain and schizophrenia. The mesocortical pathway (in green) begins in the ventral tegmental area and projects to the prefrontal cortex. The mesolimbic pathway (in blue) also begins in the ventral tegmental area but projects to the hypothalamus, amygdala, hippocampus, and nucleus accumbens (not shown in the figure).

block a particular type of postsynaptic dopamine receptors, called D2 receptors. From this knowledge about the action of the drugs that help people with schizophrenia, it was natural to conjecture that schizophrenia resulted from excess activity in dopamine. Further indirect support for this dopamine theory of schizophrenia came from findings that amphetamines, which amplify dopamine activity, can produce a state that closely resembles schizophrenia in people who do not have the disorder; they can also exacerbate the symptoms of people with schizophrenia (Angrist, Lee, & Gershon, 1974).

But as other studies progressed, this assumption turned out to be too simple to account for schizophrenia's wide range of symptoms. For example, an excess of dopamine receptors appears to be related mainly to positive and disorganization symptoms, and antipsychotic medications help these symptoms by blocking dopamine receptors in the mesolimbic pathway (see Figure 9.2), thereby lowering dopamine activity. But what about the negative symptoms? Refinements to the dopamine theory have focused on the mesocortical pathway, another region of dopamine activity that projects to the prefrontal cortex (Davis, Kahn, Ko et al., 1991). The dopamine neurons in the prefrontal cortex may be underactive and thus fail to exert inhibitory control over the dopamine neurons in subcortical brain areas, such as the amygdala, with the result that there is dopamine overactivity in the pathways. Because the prefrontal cortex is thought to be especially relevant to the negative symptoms of schizophrenia, the underactivity of the dopamine neurons in this part of the brain may contribute to the negative symptoms of schizophrenia (see Figure 9.3). Furthermore, because antipsychotics do not have major effects on the dopamine neurons in the prefrontal cortex, we would expect them to be relatively ineffective as treatments for negative symptoms, and they are. When we examine research on structural abnormalities in the brains of people with schizophrenia, we will see some close connections between these two domains.

Despite the positive evidence we have reviewed, the dopamine theory is not a complete theory of schizophrenia. For example, it takes several weeks for antipsychotics to begin lessening the positive symptoms of schizophrenia,

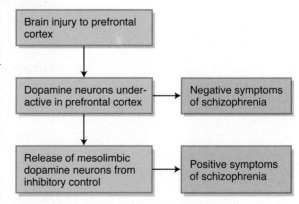

Brain injury to prefrontal cortex

Dopamine neurons under-active in prefrontal cortex

Negative symptoms of schizophrenia

Release of mesolimbic dopamine neurons from inhibitory control

Positive symptoms of schizophrenia

Figure 9.3 Dopamine theory of schizophrenia.

although they begin blocking dopamine receptors rapidly (Davis, 1978). This disjunction between the behavioral and pharmacological effects of antipsychotics is difficult to understand within the context of the theory. One possibility is that although antipsychotics do indeed block D2 receptors, their ultimate therapeutic effect may result from the effect this blockade has on other brain areas and other neurotransmitter systems (Cohen, Nordahl, Semple et al., 1997).

Because schizophrenia is a disorder with widespread symptoms covering perception, emotion, cognition, and social behavior, it is unlikely that a single neurotransmitter could account for all of them. Thus, schizophrenia researchers have cast a broader neurotransmitter net, moving away from an emphasis on dopamine.

Other Neurotransmitters As we discuss later, newer drugs used in treating schizophrenia implicate other neurotransmitters, such as serotonin, in the disorder. These newer drugs partially block D2 receptors, but they also work by blocking the serotonin receptor 5HT2 (e.g., Burris, Molski, Xu et al., 2002). Dopamine neurons generally modulate the activity of other neural systems; for example, in the prefrontal cortex they regulate gamma-aminobutyric acid (GABA) neurons. Thus, it is not surprising that GABA transmission is disrupted in the prefrontal cortex of people with schizophrenia (Volk, Austin, Pierri et al., 2000). Similarly, serotonin neurons regulate dopamine neurons in the mesolimbic pathway.

Glutamate, a neurotransmitter that is widespread in the human brain, may also play a role (Carlsson, Hanson, Waters et al., 1999). Low levels of glutamate have been found in the cerebrospinal fluid of people with schizophrenia (Faustman, Bardgett, Faull et al., 1999), and postmortem studies have revealed low levels of the enzyme needed to produce glutamate (Tsai, Parssani, Slusher et al., 1995). Studies have found elevated levels of the amino acid homocysteine, a substance that is known to interact with the NMDA receptor among people with schizophrenia and, during their third trimester, in the blood of pregnant women whose offspring developed schizophrenia as adults (Brown, Bottiglieri, Schaefer et al., 2007; Regland, Johansson, Grenfeldt et al., 1995). The illicit drug PCP can induce both positive and negative symptoms in people without schizophrenia by interfering with one of glutamate's receptors (O'Donnell & Grace, 1998). Furthermore, a decrease in glutamate inputs from either the prefrontal cortex or the hippocampus (both of these brain structures are implicated in schizophrenia) to the corpus striatum (a temporal lobe structure) could result in increased dopamine activity (O'Donnell & Grace, 1998). Additional evidence suggests that cognitive deficits in schizophrenia supported by the prefrontal cortex as well as symptoms of disorganization may be connected to deficits involving NMDA (MacDonald & Chafee, 2006).

Brain Structure and Function

Because schizophrenia affects so many domains (thought, emotion, and behavior), it makes sense that a single type of brain dysfunction cannot account for all of schizophrenia's symptoms. Among the most well-replicated findings of brain abnormalities in schizophrenia are enlargement of the ventricles and dysfunction in the prefrontal cortex and temporal cortex, as well as surrounding brain regions. Newer research has identified problems in how different areas of the brain are connected to one another.

Enlarged Ventricles Postmortem studies of the brains of people with schizophrenia consistently reveal enlarged ventricles. The brain has four ventricles, which are spaces in the brain filled with cerebrospinal fluid. Having larger fluid-filled spaces implies a loss of brain cells. Meta-analyses of several neuroimaging studies have revealed that some people with schizophrenia, even very early in the course of the illness and across the course of the illness, have enlarged ventricles (Kempton, Stahl, Williams et al., 2010; Olabi, Ellison-Wright, McIntosh et al., 2011; Wright, Rabe-Hesketh, Woodruff et al., 2000). Further evidence concerning enlarged ventricles comes from a meta-analysis of 69 studies that included over 2000 people with schizophrenia who had never taken antipsychotic medication (Haijma, Van Haren, Cahn et al., 2013). This is important because it helps to rule out the possibility that enlarged ventricles or other overall brain volume reductions may be due to the side effects of medications. Two MRI studies of MZ twin pairs, only one of whom had schizophrenia, assessed ventricle size (McNeil, Cantor-Graae, & Weinberger, 2000; Suddath, Christison, Torrey et al., 1990). In both studies the ill twins had larger ventricles than the well twins, and in one of the studies most of the twins with schizophrenia could be identified by simple visual inspection of the scan. Because the twins were nearly genetically identical in these studies, these results suggest that the origin of enlarged ventricles may not be genetic.

Large ventricles in people with schizophrenia are correlated with impaired performance on neuropsychological tests, poor functioning prior to the onset of the disorder, and poor response to medication treatment (Andreasen, Olsen, Dennert et al., 1982; Weinberger, Cannon-Spoor, Potkin et al., 1980). The extent to which the ventricles are enlarged, however, is modest, and many people with schizophrenia do not differ from people without schizophrenia in this respect. Furthermore, enlarged ventricles are not specific to schizophrenia, as they are also evident in the CT scans of people with other disorders, such as bipolar disorder with psychotic features (Rieder, Mann, Weinberger et al., 1983). People with these disorders can show ventricular enlargement almost as great as that seen in schizophrenia (Elkis, Friedman, Wise et al., 1995).[1]

Factors Involving the Prefrontal Cortex A variety of evidence suggests that the prefrontal cortex is of particular importance in schizophrenia.

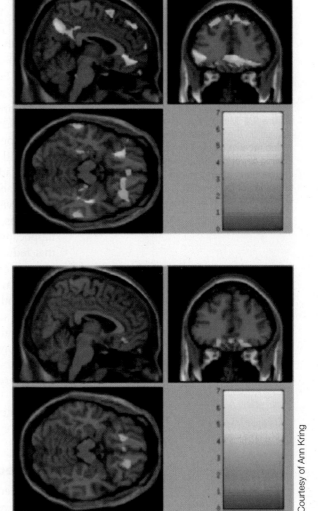

The pictures show brain activation from an fMRI study that involved maintaining pleasant emotional experience over a 12-second delay. The control group showed greater activation in areas of the frontal lobes compared to the schizophrenia group.

Courtesy of Ann Kring

- The prefrontal cortex is known to play a role in behaviors such as speech, decision making, emotion, and goal-directed behavior, which are disrupted in schizophrenia.

- MRI studies have shown reductions in gray matter and overall volume in the prefrontal cortex (Buchanan, Vladar, Barta et al., 1998; Ohtani et al., 2014; Sun et al., 2009).

- People with schizophrenia perform more poorly than people without schizophrenia on neuropsychological tests designed to tap functions supported by the prefrontal region, including working memory or the ability to hold bits of information in memory (Barch, Csernansky, Conturo et al., 2002, 2003; Heinrichs & Zakzanis, 1998), with some evidence that performance on some of these tests declines from before disorder onset to when people are in their late 30s (Meier, Caspi, Reichenberg et al., 2014).

- PET brain-imaging studies find that people with schizophrenia show lower glucose metabolism in the prefrontal cortex when performing neuropsychological tests tapping prefrontal function (Buchsbaum, Kessler, King et al., 1984). Because the tests place demands on the prefrontal cortex, glucose metabolism normally goes up as energy is used. People with schizophrenia, especially those with prominent negative symptoms, do poorly on the tests and also show less activation in the prefrontal region (Potkin, Alva, Fleming et al., 2002; Weinberger, Berman, & Illowsky, 1988). People with schizophrenia also show less blood flow to the brain as indicated with fMRI during performance of these same types of tests (Barch, Carter, Braver et al., 2001; MacDonald & Carter, 2003).

- Finally, failure to show frontal activation is related to the severity of negative symptoms (O'Donnell & Grace, 1998; Ohtani et al., 2014) and thus parallels the work on dopamine underactivity in the frontal cortex already discussed.

Despite the reduced volume of the gray matter in the prefrontal cortex (and also the temporal cortex), the number of neurons in this area does not appear to

---

[1]Other findings also suggest that perhaps the schizophrenia and psychotic mood disorders should not be totally separate diagnostic categories. The disorders share some symptoms (notably, delusions) and some possible etiological factors (e.g., genetic factors, increased dopamine activity), and they respond similarly to medications. Researchers would be well served to focus some of their efforts on psychotic symptoms in other disorders as well as in schizophrenia.

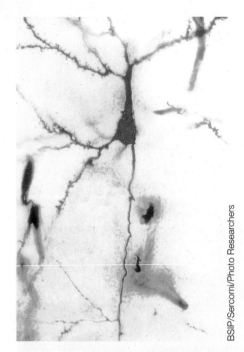

BSIP/Sercomi/Photo Researchers

Figure 9.4 Micrograph of a neuron. The bumps on the dendrites are dendritic spines, which receive inputs from other neurons. Having fewer dendritic spines may impair connections among neurons and may be a factor in schizophrenia.

be reduced. More detailed studies indicate that what is lost may be what are called "dendritic spines" (Glausier & Lewis, 2013; Goldman-Rakic & Selemon, 1997; McGlashan & Hoffman, 2000). Dendritic spines are small projections on the shafts of dendrites where nerve impulses are received from other neurons at the synapse (see Figure 9.4). The loss of these dendritic spines means that communication among neurons (i.e., functioning of the synapses) is disrupted, resulting in what some have termed a "disconnection syndrome." One possible result of the failure of neural systems to communicate could be the speech and behavioral disorganization seen in schizophrenia. Current research is linking these abnormalities in dendritic spines with the candidate genes and CNVs identified in schizophrenia, discussed in the earlier section on genetic factors (Pathania, Davenport, Muir et al., 2014; Penzes, Cahill, Jones et al., 2011).

Problems in the Temporal Cortex and Surrounding Regions Additional research has found that people with schizophrenia have structural and functional abnormalities in the temporal cortex, including areas such as the temporal gyrus, hippocampus, amygdala, and anterior cingulate. For example, research also shows a reduction in cortical gray matter in temporal as well as frontal brain regions (Gur, Turetsky, Cowell et al., 2000) and reduced volume in the basal ganglia (e.g., the caudate nucleus), hippocampus, and limbic structures (Keshavan, Rosenberg, Sweeney et al., 1998; Lim, Adalsteinssom, Spielman et al., 1998; Mathew, Gardin, Tandon et al., 2014; Nelson, Saykin, Flashman et al., 1998; Velakoulis, Pantelis, McGorry et al., 1999). A twin study found reduced hippocampus volume among twins with schizophrenia, but not among the twins without schizophrenia (van Erp, Saleh, Huttunen et al., 2004). A meta-analysis of MRI studies conducted with people during their first episode of schizophrenia concluded that the volume of the hippocampus was significantly reduced compared to people without schizophrenia (Steen, Mull, McClure et al., 2006).

An additional interesting piece of evidence regarding the hippocampus comes from a meta-analysis of nine studies assessing the brain volume of over 400 first-degree relatives of people with schizophrenia and over 600 first-degree relatives of people without schizophrenia (Boos, Aleman, Cahn et al., 2007). Relatives of people with schizophrenia had smaller hippocampal volumes than relatives of people without schizophrenia. These findings suggest that reduced hippocampal volume in people with schizophrenia may reflect a combination of genetic and environmental factors.

What makes these findings about the hippocampus all the more intriguing is the fact that the hypothalamic–pituitary–adrenal (HPA) axis is closely connected to this area of the brain. Chronic stress is associated with reductions in hippocampal volume in other disorders, such as posttraumatic stress disorder (see Chapter 7). Although people with schizophrenia do not necessarily experience more stress than people without schizophrenia, they are more reactive to stress. Other evidence indicates that the HPA axis is disrupted in schizophrenia, particularly very early in the course of the disorder (Walker, Mittal, Tessner et al., 2008; Walker, Trotman, Pearce et al., 2013). Taken together, stress reactivity and a disrupted HPA axis likely contribute to the reductions in hippocampal volume observed in people with schizophrenia (Walker et al., 2008).

Connectivity in the Brain

Recent neuroimaging methods measure how different areas of the brain are connected to each other. Given the widespread involvement of brain dysfunction in schizophrenia, it is perhaps not surprising that the connections between areas are also problematic (Rapoport, Giedd, & Gogtay, 2012).

Broadly speaking, there are three types of connectivity. *Structural (or anatomical) connectivity* refers to how different structures of the brain are connected via white matter (axon fibers). Studies have found that people with schizophrenia have less connectivity in brain white matter than people without schizophrenia in the frontal and temporal cortices (Ellison-Wright & Bullmore, 2009).

Functional connectivity refers to the connectivity between brain regions based on correlations between their blood oxygen level dependent (BOLD) signal measured with fMRI (see

Chapter 2). Several studies have found reduced functional connectivity in schizophrenia, particularly in the frontal cortex (Pettersson-Yeo, Allen, Benetti et al., 2011).

Effective connectivity combines both types of connectivity in that it not only reveals correlations between BOLD activations in different brain regions but also the direction and timing of those activations by showing, for example, that activation in the occipital cortex comes first, followed by activation on the frontal cortex when someone is viewing pictures of objects (Friston, 1994). Like the other types of connectivity, research has found diminished effective connectivity in schizophrenia (Deserno, Sterzer, Wustenberg et al., 2012).

These connectivity methods have revealed a number of what are called brain networks. Networks are clusters of brain regions that are connected to one another in that activation in these regions is reliably correlated when people perform certain types of tasks or are at rest. For example, the frontoparietal network involves activation of the frontal and parietal cortices, and this network is activated when people are doing cognitive tasks. The default-mode network involves areas of the prefrontal cortex and temporal cortex and is activated when people are daydreaming or thinking about the future and recalling memories.

Other brain connectivity research in schizophrenia has revealed that there is less connectivity between brain networks, including the frontoparietal and default-mode networks, and this diminished connectivity is correlated with poor performance on cognitive tests (Unschuld, Buchholz, Varvaris et al., 2014). Research has also found diminished connectivity among healthy relatives of people with schizophrenia, suggesting that diminished connectivity might be part of the genetic diathesis for schizophrenia (Collin, Kahn, de Reus et al., 2014; Unschuld et al., 2014).

Environmental Factors Influencing the Developing Brain

Several different environmental factors have been studied as possible contributing factors to schizophrenia (Brown, 2011; van Os, Kenis, & Rutten, 2010). A possible cause of some of the observed brain abnormalities in schizophrenia is damage during gestation or birth. Many studies have shown high rates of delivery complications in people with schizophrenia (Brown, 2011; Walker et al., 2004); such complications could have resulted in a reduced supply of oxygen to the brain, resulting in loss of cortical gray matter (Cannon, van Erp, Rosso et al., 2002). These obstetrical complications do not raise the risk for schizophrenia in everyone who experiences them. Rather, the risk for schizophrenia is increased in those who experience complications and have a genetic diathesis (Cannon & Mednick, 1993).

Additional research suggests that maternal infections during pregnancy are associated with greater risk of their children developing schizophrenia when they become adults (Brown & Derkits, 2010). For example, one study found that maternal exposure to the parasite toxoplasma gondii was associated with a nearly 2.5 times greater risk of schizophrenia among the mothers' children when they became adults (Brown, Schaefer, Quesenberry et al., 2005). This is a common parasite, carried by many people with no ill effects.

The most widely studied prenatal infection has been influenza. Studies have examined rates of schizophrenia among adults who had likely been exposed to the flu virus during their mothers' pregnancies (Mednick et al., 1988; Mednick, Huttonen, & Machon, 1994). During the 1957 Helsinki influenza epidemic, people who had been exposed to the flu virus during the second trimester of pregnancy had much higher rates of schizophrenia than those who had been exposed in either of the other trimesters and much higher rates than nonexposed control adults. This finding was replicated in only half of nearly 30 later studies, calling it into question. A more recent study found evidence that mothers' exposure to the flu during the *first* trimester of pregnancy, as directly measured by the presence of flu antibodies in the blood, was associated with a sevenfold increase in the risk for schizophrenia among their children (Brown, Begg, Gravenstein et al., 2004). Although the increase in risk sounds large, the difference from the control group was not quite statistically different, suggesting it is a small effect.

If, as the findings we have just reviewed suggest, the development of the brains of people with schizophrenia goes awry very early, why does the disorder begin many years later, in adolescence or early adulthood? The prefrontal cortex is a brain structure that matures late, typically in adolescence or early adulthood. Thus a problem in this area, even one that begins early in the course of development, may not show itself in the person's behavior until the period of development when the prefrontal cortex begins to play a larger role in behavior (Weinberger, 1987). Notably, dopamine activity also peaks in adolescence, which may further set the stage for the onset of schizophrenia symptoms (Walker et al., 2008). Adolescence is also typically a developmental period that is fraught with stress. Recall from our discussions in Chapter 2 that stress activates the HPA axis, causing cortisol to be secreted. Research in the past 10 years has demonstrated that cortisol increases dopamine activity, particularly in the mesolimbic pathway, perhaps increasing the likelihood of developing schizophrenia symptoms (Walker et al., 2008).

Another proposed explanation is that the development of symptoms in adolescence could reflect a loss of synapses due to excessive pruning, the elimination of synaptic connections. Pruning is a normal part of brain development that occurs at different rates in different areas of the brain. It is mostly complete in sensory areas by about 2 years of age but continues in the prefrontal cortex until mid-adolescence. If too extensive, pruning may result in the loss of necessary communication among neurons (McGlashan & Hoffman, 2000).

An additional environmental factor that has been studied as a risk factor for schizophrenia among adolescents is cannabis (marijuana) use. Among people already diagnosed with schizophrenia, cannabis use is associated with a worsening of symptoms (Foti, Kotov, Guey et al., 2010). But does cannabis use contribute to the onset of schizophrenia? A longitudinal study examining the prospective relationship between cannabis use in adolescence and the onset of schizophrenia in adolescence or adulthood indicated that the risk of developing schizophrenia symptoms was greater among those who used cannabis compared to those who did not (Arseneault, Cannon, Poulton et al., 2002), and a small meta-analysis of seven studies reported the same increased risk (Moore, Zammit, Lingford-Hughes et al., 2007). Furthermore, more frequent use and higher-potency cannabis are associated with greater risk (Di Forti, Sallis, Allegri, et al., 2013). However, recall from Chapter 4 that correlation does not mean causation. Other studies suggest that the linkage between cannabis use and risk of developing schizophrenia is observed only among those who are genetically vulnerable to schizophrenia. For example, Caspi and colleagues (2005) found a gene–environment interaction between a particular polymorphism in the *COMT* gene and cannabis use. The combination of cannabis use and one COMT polymorphism was associated with increased risk of schizophrenia, but neither alone was associated with increased risk for schizophrenia.

Psychological Factors

People with schizophrenia do not appear to experience more stress in daily life than people without schizophrenia (Phillips, Francey, Edwards et al., 2007; Walker et al., 2008). However, people with the disorder appear to be very reactive to the stressors we all encounter in daily living. In one study, people with psychotic disorders (92 percent with schizophrenia), their first-degree relatives, and people without any psychiatric disorder participated in a 6-day ecological momentary assessment study in which they recorded stress and mood several times each day. Daily life stress predicted greater decreases in positive moods in both people with schizophrenia and their relatives compared with controls. Stress also predicted greater increases in negative moods in the people with schizophrenia compared with both relatives and controls (Myin-Germeys, van Os, Schwartz et al., 2001). Thus, people with schizophrenia were particularly vulnerable to daily stress. Research also shows that, as with many of the disorders we have discussed in this book, increases in life stress increase the likelihood of a relapse (Ventura, Neuchterlein, Lukoff et al., 1989; Walker et al., 2008).

Additional research on psychological factors in the development and relapse of schizophrenia has focused on socioeconomic status and the family.

Socioeconomic Status For many years we have known that schizophrenia can be found at all levels of socioeconomic status (SES) in many countries, but that the highest rates of schizophrenia are found in people with the lowest SES (Hollingshead & Redlich, 1958; Kohn, 1968).

The correlation between SES and schizophrenia is consistent but difficult to interpret in causal terms. Is it that the stress associated with poverty, such as low education, limited opportunities, and stigma from others of high status contributes to the development of schizophrenia—the **sociogenic hypothesis?** Or is it the case that during the course of their developing illness, people with schizophrenia drift into poor neighborhoods because their illness impairs their earning power and they cannot afford to live elsewhere—the **social selection hypothesis?**

A study in Israel evaluated the two hypotheses by investigating both SES and ethnic background (Dohrenwend, Levav, Schwartz et al., 1992). The rates of schizophrenia were examined among Israeli Jews of European ethnic background and among more recent immigrants to Israel from North Africa and the Middle East. The latter group experienced considerable racial prejudice and discrimination in Israel. The sociogenic hypothesis would predict that because they experienced high levels of stress regardless of socioeconomic status, the members of the disadvantaged ethnic group should have consistently higher rates of schizophrenia regardless of status. However, this pattern did not emerge, supporting the social selection hypothesis. Thus, research results are more supportive of the social selection hypothesis than of the sociogenic hypothesis.

Family-Related Factors Early theorists regarded family relationships, especially those between a mother and her son, as crucial in the development of schizophrenia. At one time, the view was so prevalent that the terms *schizophrenogenic mother* was coined for the supposedly cold and dominant, conflict-inducing parent who was said to produce schizophrenia in her offspring (Fromm-Reichmann, 1948). Controlled studies evaluating the schizophrenogenic mother theory have not supported it. The damage done to families by this theory, however, was significant. For generations, parents blamed themselves for their child's illness, and until the 1970s, psychiatrists often joined in this blame game.

How Do Families Influence Schizophrenia? Other studies continued to explore the possibility that the family plays some role in the etiology of schizophrenia. For the most part, the findings are only suggestive, not conclusive. For example, a few studies of families of people with schizophrenia have found that they communicate more vaguely with one another and have higher levels of conflict than families of people without schizophrenia. It is plausible, though, that the conflict and unclear communication are a response to having a young family member with schizophrenia.

Families and Relapse A series of studies initiated in London found that the family can have an impact on the recovery of people with schizophrenia after they leave the hospital. In one study, investigators conducted a 9-month follow-up study of a sample of people with schizophrenia who returned to live with their families after being discharged from the hospital (Brown, Bone, Dalison et al., 1966). Interviews were conducted with parents or spouses before discharge and rated for the number of critical comments made about the family member with schizophrenia and for expressions of hostility toward and emotional overinvolvement with the ill relative. The following is an example of a critical comment made by a father remarking on his daughter's behavior, in which he is expressing the idea that his daughter is deliberately symptomatic to avoid housework: "My view is that Maria acts this way so my wife doesn't give her any responsibilities around the house" (quote in Weisman, Neuchterlein, Goldstein et al., 1998). Combining these three characteristics—critical comments, hostility, and emotional overinvolvement—led to the creation of the construct called **expressed emotion (EE).** Families in the original study were divided into two groups: those revealing a great deal of expressed emotion (high-EE families) and those revealing little (low-EE families). At the end of the follow-up period, only 10 percent of the people returning to low-EE homes had relapsed, but 58 percent of the people returning to high-EE homes had gone back to the hospital.

This research, which has since been replicated (see Butzlaff & Hooley, 1998, for a meta-analysis), indicates that the home environment of people with schizophrenia can influence how soon they relapse. Researchers have also found that negative symptoms of schizophrenia are most likely to elicit critical comments, as in the example presented in the previous para-

Lisette Le Bon/SUPERSTOCK

Expressed emotion, which includes hostility, critical comments, and emotional overinvolvement, has been linked with relapse in schizophrenia.

graph, and that the relatives who make the most critical comments are the most likely to view people with schizophrenia as being able to control their symptoms (Lopez, Nelson, Snyder et al., 1999; Weisman et al., 1998).

There are also important cultural differences in EE. Lopez and colleagues (2009) found that Anglo American caregivers were higher in EE than recently immigrated Mexican American caregivers, and this was true for all aspects of EE (i.e., critical comments, hostility, and emotional overinvolvement). Nearly three-quarters of Anglo American caregivers designated as high EE were so designated due to high hostility and critical comments; only 8 percent were designated as high EE based on emotional overinvolvement. By contrast, the Mexican American caregivers high in EE were fairly evenly divided between those who were high in hostility and critical comments and those who were high in emotional overinvolvement. These findings have important implications for developing and providing family interventions for schizophrenia, which we review a bit later in the chapter. Another study found that emotional overinvolvement specifically predicted relapse in Mexican Americans with schizophrenia, and that the linkage between EE and relapse was highest among Mexican Americans who had acculturated more to U.S. ways (Aguilera, Lopez, & Breitborde et al., 2010). However, the relationship between emotional overinvolvement and relapse in other European and Asian countries is not as robust as it is in North American countries (Singh, Harley, & Suhail, 2013). The different findings may be attributed either to the fact that emotional overinvolvement is measured differently across countries and cultures, or that emotional overinvolvement is more harmful in some cultures and countries than in others. This issue needs to be sorted out in future research.

What is not yet clear is exactly how to interpret the effects of EE. Is EE causal, or does it reflect a reaction to the ill relative's behavior? For example, if the condition of a person with schizophrenia begins to deteriorate, family concern and involvement may increase. Indeed, disorganized or dangerous behavior might seem to warrant familial efforts that could increase the level of EE. Research indicates that both interpretations of the operation of EE may be correct. In one study, people with schizophrenia and their high- or low-EE families were observed as they engaged in a discussion of a family problem. Two key findings emerged (Rosenfarb, Goldstein, Mintz et al., 1994).

1. The expression of unusual thoughts by the people with schizophrenia ("If that kid bites you, you'll get rabies") elicited a greater number of critical comments by family members who had previously been characterized as high in EE than by those characterized as low in EE.

2. In high-EE families, critical comments by family members led to increased expression of unusual thoughts by the people with schizophrenia.

Thus, this study found a bidirectional relationship in high-EE families: critical comments by family members elicited more unusual thoughts by relatives with schizophrenia, and unusual thoughts expressed by the relatives with schizophrenia led to increased critical comments.

How does stress, such as a high level of EE, increase the symptoms of schizophrenia and precipitate relapses? One answer to this question involves the effects of stress on the HPA axis and its link to dopamine (Walker et al., 2008). Stress activates the HPA axis, causing cortisol to be secreted, which can then increase dopamine activity (Walker et al., 2008). Furthermore, heightened dopamine activity itself can increase HPA activation, which may make a person overly sensitive to stress. Thus, there is a bidirectional relationship between HPA activation and dopamine activity.

Courtesy of Elaine F. Walker, Emory University

Elaine Walker has conducted many studies on the development of schizophrenia.

Developmental Factors

What are people who develop schizophrenia like before their symptoms begin? This question has been addressed using retrospective and prospective studies. The retrospective studies are sometimes referred to as "follow-back" studies because the starting point is a group of adults with schizophrenia that researchers then follow back to childhood to unearth records and tests from their early years.

Retrospective Studies In the 1960s, researchers found that children who later developed schizophrenia had lower IQs and were more often delinquent and withdrawn than members of various control groups, usually comprising siblings and neighborhood peers (Albee, Lane, & Reuter, 1964; Berry, 1967; Lane & Albee, 1965). Other studies found that boys who later developed schizophrenia were rated by teachers as disagreeable, whereas girls who later developed schizophrenia were rated as passive (Watt, 1974; Watt, Stolorow, Lubensky et al., 1970).

More recently, researchers have examined emotional and cognitive deficits that were present before the onset of schizophrenia. In one very clever study, Elaine Walker and colleagues analyzed the home movies of children who later developed schizophrenia. The movies were made as part of normal family life and were made before the onset of schizophrenia (Walker, Davis, & Savoie, 1994; Walker, Grimes, Davis et al., 1993). Compared with their siblings who did not later develop schizophrenia, the children who later developed schizophrenia as young adults showed poorer motor skills and more expressions of negative emotions. Other studies have examined past childhood assessments of the cognition and intellectual functioning of adults who had schizophrenia. These studies found that adults with schizophrenia scored lower on IQ and other cognitive tests as children compared to adults without schizophrenia (Davis, Malmberg, Brandt et al., 1997; Woodberry, Giuliano, & Seidman, 2008).

As intriguing as these findings are, these studies were not necessarily designed with the intention of predicting the development of schizophrenia from childhood behavior. Rather, they began with an adult sample of people with schizophrenia and then looked back at records and data collected from their childhoods to see if there were characteristics that distinguished them as young children.

Prospective Studies A more recent prospective study identified childhood characteristics that were associated with the development of schizophrenia in early adulthood (Reichenberg, Aushalom, Harrington et al., 2010). In this study, a large sample of people from Dunedin, New Zealand, were assessed several times between the ages of 7 and 32. IQ tests were administered at ages 7, 9, 11, and 13; diagnostic assessments were conducted at ages 21, 26, and 32. The researchers found that lower scores on the IQ test in childhood predicted the onset of schizophrenia in young adulthood, even after they controlled for low socioeconomic status (which is associated with lower IQ scores; see Chapter 3). Thus, children who developed schizophrenia as adults had signs of a cognitive deficit beginning at age 7 that remained stable through adolescence.

These findings are broadly consistent with the idea that something goes awry in development that is associated with the onset of schizophrenia in late adolescence or early adulthood. Nevertheless, more specific information is required if developmental histories are to provide clear evidence regarding the etiology of schizophrenia.

One of the difficulties with the familial high-risk studies that we discussed earlier has to do with the large sample sizes that are required. As shown in Table 9.2, around 10 percent of children with a biological parent who has schizophrenia go on to develop schizophrenia. If a study begins with 200 high-risk children, only about 20 of them may go on to develop schizophrenia. In addition, it is not particularly easy to locate a large sample of women or men with schizophrenia who have had their own children.

Because of these difficulties, the **clinical high-risk study** has been used in more recent research. A clinical high-risk study is a design that identifies people with early, attenuated signs of schizophrenia, most often milder forms of hallucinations, delusions, or disorganization that nonetheless cause impairment (see Focus on Discovery 9.3). One such study followed people between the ages of 14 and 30 in Australia who were referred to a mental health clinic in the mid-1990s (Yung, McGorry, McFarlane et al., 1995). None of the participants had schizophrenia when they entered the study, but many later exhibited varying degrees of schizophrenia symptoms and some, but not all, had a biological relative with a psychotic disorder. These participants were deemed to be at "ultra-high risk" of developing schizophrenia or psychotic disorders. Since the study began, 41 of the original 104 participants have developed some type of psychotic disorder (Yung, Phillips, Hok et al., 2004). An MRI study of 75 of the 104 participants found that those people who later developed a psychotic disorder had lower gray matter volumes than those who had not developed a psychotic disorder (Pantelis, Velakoulis, McGorry et al., 2003). Recall that reduced gray matter volume has been found in people with schizophrenia; the Pantelis et al. study suggests that this characteristic may predate the onset of schizophrenia and other psychotic disorders.

A similar longitudinal study, the North American Prodrome Longitudinal Study (NAPLS), is being carried out at eight different centers in the United States and Canada. Participants were identified as clinical high-risk based on the Structured Interview for Prodromal Syndromes (see Focus on Discovery 9.3). In this study, 82 of the 291 clinical high-risk (CHR) participants who also had a family history of schizophrenia (familial high risk, or FHR) had developed schizophrenia or some type of psychotic disorder (Cannon, Cadenhead, Cornblatt et al., 2008). The researchers identified a number of factors that predicted a greater likelihood of developing a psychotic disorder, including having a biological relative with schizophrenia, a recent decline in functioning, high levels of positive symptoms, and high levels of social impairment. Later analyses from the NAPLS sample are broadly consistent with the retrospective studies of 50 years ago: social and academic difficulties in childhood predicted conversion to a psychotic disorder (Tarbox, Addington, Cadenhead et al., 2013).

Quick Summary

Given its complexity, a number of causal factors are likely to contribute to schizophrenia. The genetic evidence is strong, with much of it coming from family, twin, and adoption studies. Familial high-risk studies have found that children with a biological parent with schizophrenia are more likely to develop adult psychopathology, including schizophrenia, and have difficulties with attention and motor control, among other things. Molecular genetics studies include association studies and GWAS studies. Promising genes from association studies include *DTNBP1*, *BDNF*, and *COMT*, but replication is also needed here. GWAS studies have pointed to copy number variations (CNVs) that are associated with genetic vulnerability to schizophrenia.

Neurotransmitters play a role in schizophrenia. For years, dopamine was the focus of study, but later findings led investigators to conclude that this one neurotransmitter could not fully account for schizophrenia. Other neurotransmitters are also the focus of study, such as serotonin, GABA, and glutamate. A number of different brain areas have been implicated in schizophrenia. One of the most widely replicated findings is that of enlarged ventricles. Other research supports the role of the prefrontal cortex, particularly reduced activation of this area, in schizophrenia. Dysfunction in the temporal cortex has also been documented.

Environmental factors, such as obstetric complications and prenatal infections, may impact the developing brain and increase the risk of schizophrenia. Cannabis use among adolescents has been associated with greater risk of schizophrenia, particularly among those who are genetically vulnerable to the disorder.

Research has examined the role of socioeconomic status in schizophrenia, and generally this work supports the social selection hypothesis more than the sociogenic hypothesis. Early theories blamed families, particularly mothers, for causing schizophrenia, but research does not support this view. Communication in families is important and could perhaps constitute the stress in the diathesis–stress theory of schizophrenia. Expressed emotion has also been found to predict relapse in schizophrenia, though there are important cultural differences in expressed emotion.

Retrospective developmental studies looked back at the childhood records of adults with schizophrenia and found that some adults with schizophrenia had lower IQs and were withdrawn and delinquent as children. Other studies found that adults who later developed schizophrenia expressed a lot of negative emotion and had poor motor skills. A prospective study confirmed that lower IQ in childhood is a predictor of the later onset of schizophrenia and that the IQ deficits are stable across childhood. Clinical high-risk studies identify people who are showing early signs of schizophrenia.

Check Your Knowledge 9.2

Fill in the blanks.

1. _____ and _____ studies do not do such a good job of teasing out genetic and environmental effects; _____ studies do a better job.
2. _____ and _____ are two genes that have been associated with schizophrenia; _____ and _____ are two genes that have been associated with cognitive deficits seen in schizophrenia.
3. Some studies showing the _____ area of the brain to be disrupted in schizophrenia also show that people with schizophrenia do poorly on tasks that rely on this area, such as planning and problem solving.
4. _____, _____, and _____ are the three components of expressed emotion.

Treatment of Schizophrenia

Treatments for schizophrenia most often include a combination of short-term hospital stays (during the acute phases of the illness), medication, and psychosocial treatment. A problem with any kind of treatment for schizophrenia is that some people with schizophrenia lack insight into their impaired condition and refuse any treatment at all (Amador, Flaum, Andreasen et al., 1994). Results from one study suggest that gender (female) and age (older) are predictors of better insight among people in their first episode of the illness (McEvoy, Johnson, Perkins et al., 2006), and this may help account for why women with schizophrenia tend to respond better to treatment than men (Salem & Kring, 1998). Those who lack insight, and thus don't believe they have an illness, don't see the need for professional help, particularly when it includes hospitalization or drugs. Family members therefore face a major challenge in getting their relatives into treatment.

Medications

In the 1950s, several medications collectively referred to as **antipsychotic drugs** (also referred to as *neuroleptics* because they produce side effects similar to the symptoms of a neurological disease), were found to help with some of the symptoms of schizophrenia. For the first time, many people with schizophrenia did not need to stay in a hospital for long periods of time and could instead go home with a prescription. Focus on Discovery 9.4 presents a brief history

FOCUS ON DISCOVERY 9.4

Stumbling toward a Cure: The Development of Antipsychotic Medications

One of the more frequently prescribed antipsychotic drugs, phenothiazine, was first produced by a German chemist in the late nineteenth century. But it was not until the discovery of the antihistamines, which have a phenothiazine nucleus, in the 1940s, that phenothiazines received much attention.

Reaching beyond their use to treat the common cold and asthma, the French surgeon Henri Laborit pioneered the use of antihistamines to reduce surgical shock. He noticed that they made his patients somewhat sleepy and less fearful about the impending operation. Laborit's work encouraged pharmaceutical companies to reexamine antihistamines in light of their tranquilizing effects. Shortly thereafter, the French chemist Paul Charpentier prepared a new phenothiazine derivative, which he called chlorpromazine. This drug proved very effective in calming people with schizophrenia. Phenothiazines derive their therapeutic properties by blocking dopamine receptors in the brain, thus reducing the influence of dopamine on thought, emotion, and behavior.

Chlorpromazine (trade name Thorazine) was first used therapeutically in the United States in 1954 and rapidly became the preferred treatment for schizophrenia. By 1970, more than 85 percent of all people in mental hospitals were receiving chlorpromazine or another phenothiazine.

of the development of these drugs. As we discussed in Chapter 1 and return to in Chapter 16, the zeal to discharge people with schizophrenia from hospitals did not match the needs of all people with the disorder. Some people did and still do need treatment in a hospital, even if for a short time. Unfortunately, it is difficult to receive such treatment today due to the cost and limited availability of hospital beds for people with schizophrenia and other severe mental disorders. Nevertheless, medications have made it possible for some people with schizophrenia to lead lives outside of a hospital. As we will see, however, medications have their own drawbacks.

First-Generation Antipsychotic Drugs and Their Side Effects The first generation antipsychotic drugs are those broad classes of medications that were the first to be discovered. See Table 9.4 for a summary of major drugs used to treat schizophrenia. These drugs can reduce the positive and disorganization symptoms of schizophrenia but have little or no effect on the negative symptoms, perhaps because their primary mechanism of action involves blocking dopamine D2 receptors. Despite the enthusiasm with which these drugs are prescribed, they are not a cure. About 30 percent of people with schizophrenia do not respond favorably to the first-generation antipsychotics, and about half the people who take any antipsychotic drug quit after 1 year and up to three-quarters quit before 2 years because the side effects are so unpleasant (Harvard Mental Health Letter, 1995; Lieberman et al., 2005).

People who respond positively to the antipsychotics are typically kept on so-called maintenance doses of the drug, just enough to continue the therapeutic effect. Results from a meta-analysis of over 60 randomized controlled clinical trials comparing either first- or second-generation drugs to placebo found that maintenance dosages of both were equally effective at reducing relapse compared to placebo (Leucht, Tardy, Komossa et al., 2009). Some people who are maintained on medication may still have difficulty with day-to-day functioning, however. For example, they may be unable to live independently or to hold down the kind of job for which they would otherwise be qualified, and their social relationships may be sparse. In short, some symptoms may go away, but lives are still not fulfilling for many people with schizophrenia.

The commonly reported side effects of all antipsychotics include sedation, dizziness, blurred vision, restlessness, and sexual dysfunction. In addition, some particularly disturbing side effects, termed *extrapyramidal side effects,* resemble the symptoms of Parkinson's disease. People taking antipsychotics may develop tremors of the fingers, a shuffling gait, and drooling. Other side effects can include dystonia, a state of muscular rigidity, and dyskinesia, an abnormal motion of voluntary and involuntary muscles, producing chewing movements as well as other movements of the lips, fingers, and legs. Another side effect is akasthesia, an inability to remain still; people on antipsychotics pace constantly and fidget.

In a rare muscular disturbance called *tardive dyskinesia,* the mouth muscles involuntarily make sucking, lip-smacking, and chin-wagging motions. In more severe cases, the whole body can be subject to involuntary motor movements. This syndrome is observed mainly in older people with schizophrenia who had been treated with first-generation medications before drugs were developed to prevent tardive dyskinesia. It affects about 10 to 20 percent of these older people treated with first-generation antipsychotics for a long period of time and is not responsive to any known treatment (Sweet, Mulsant, Gupta et al., 1995). Finally, a side effect called *neuroleptic malignant syndrome* occurs in about 1 percent of cases. In this condition, which can sometimes be fatal, severe muscular rigidity develops, accompanied by fever. The heart races, blood pressure increases, and the person may lapse into a coma.

Table 9.4 Summary of Major Drugs Used in Treating Schizophrenia		
Drug Category	**Generic Name**	**Trade Name**
First-generation drugs	Chlorpromazine	Thorazine
	Fluphenazine decanoate	Prolixin
	Haloperidol	Haldol
	Thiothixene	Navane
	Trifluoperazine	Stelazine
Second–generation drugs	Clozapine	Clozaril
	Aripiprazole	Abilify
	Olanzapine	Zyprexa
	Risperidone	Risperdal
	Ziprasidone	Geodon
	Quetiapine	Seroquel

Because of these serious side effects, some clinicians believe it is unwise to prescribe high doses of antipsychotics for extended periods of time. Current clinical practice guidelines from the American Psychiatric Association call for treating people with the smallest possible doses of drugs (APA, 2004). This situation puts the clinician in a bind: if medication is reduced, the chance of relapse increases, but if medication is continued, serious and untreatable side effects may develop.

Second-Generation Antipsychotic Drugs and Their Side Effects In the decades following the introduction of the first-generation antipsychotic drugs, there appeared to be little interest in developing new drugs to treat schizophrenia. This situation changed about 25 years ago, with the approval of clozapine (trade name Clozaril) in the United States. Early studies of this drug suggested that it could produce therapeutic gains in people with schizophrenia who did not respond well to first-generation antipsychotic drugs, produce fewer side effects, and lead to less relapse and treatment noncompliance (Conley, Love, Kelly et al., 1999; Kane, Honigfeld, Singer et al., 1988; Wahlbeck , Chelne, Essali et al., 1999).

Researchers and clinicians soon learned, however, that clozapine had its own set of serious side effects. It can impair the functioning of the immune system in a small percentage of people (about 1 percent) by lowering the number of white blood cells, a condition called agranulocytosis, which makes people vulnerable to infection and can even cause death. For this reason, people taking clozapine have to be carefully monitored with routine blood tests. It also can produce seizures and other side effects, such as dizziness, fatigue, drooling, and weight gain (Meltzer, Cola, & Way, 1993).

Nevertheless, the apparent success of clozapine stimulated drug companies to begin a more extensive search for other drugs that might be more effective than first-generation antipsychotics. These drugs, including clozapine, are referred to as the **second-generation antipsychotic drugs** because their mechanism of action is not like that of the typical or first-generation antipsychotic medications. Two second-generation antipsychotics developed after clozapine are olanzapine (trade name Zyprexa) and risperidone (trade name Risperdal). Early studies of these two drugs indicated that they produced fewer of the side effects seen with first-generation antipsychotics, suggesting that people were somewhat less likely to discontinue treatment (Dolder, Lacro, Dunn et al., 2002), but later studies have not always replicated this finding (Lieberman, 2006). One large randomized controlled trial found that people who were on maintenance doses of the drug risperidone for 1 year after beginning treatment had lower relapse rates than people who had dose reductions at either 4 or 26 weeks after the beginning of treatment (Wang, Xiang, Cai et al., 2010). According to a meta–analysis comparing the second-generation drugs with one another, all of them work about the same, with some advantage in reducing positive symptoms observed for clozapine and olanzapine (Leucht, Komossa, Rummel-Kluge et al., 2009).

The second-generation antipsychotics appear to be equally as effective as first-generation antipsychotics in reducing positive and disorganized symptoms (Conley & Mahmoud, 2001), particularly for people who have not responded to at least two other medications (Lewis, Barnes, Davies et al., 2006). A meta-analysis of 124 studies comparing first- and second-generation antipsychotic drugs found that some, but not all, second-generation drugs were modestly more effective than the first-generation drugs in reducing negative symptoms and improving cognitive deficits (Davis, Chen, & Glick, 2003). However, a recent study found no differences in relapse or adverse side effects between a long-acting (i.e., injectable) first- and second-generation drug (McEvoy, Byerly, Hamer et al., 2014).

Other research suggests that the second-generation antipsychotics are also effective in improving aspects of cognition, such as attention and memory, that are known to be deficient in many people with schizophrenia (Heinrichs & Zakzanis, 1998) and are associated with poor social functioning (Green, 1996). A number of studies suggest that these medications may be more effective than the first-generation drugs in improving cognitive functioning (Harvey, Green, Keefe et al., 2004; Harvey, Green, McGurk et al., 2003; Keefe,

Bilder, Davis et al., 2007). More generally, the second-generation antipsychotics may thus make possible more thoroughgoing changes in schizophrenia and its behavioral consequences than do drugs that do not help with these cognitive abilities. However, other evidence suggests that psychological treatments are also effective, perhaps more so, at alleviating cognitive deficits.

The news is not all good. A comprehensive randomized controlled clinical trial (called Clinical Antipsychotic Trials of Intervention Effectiveness, or CATIE) compared four second-generation drugs (olanzapine, risperidone, ziprasidone, and quetiapine) and one first-generation drug (perphenazine) to one another (Lieberman et al., 2005). Close to 1500 people from all over the United States were in the study. What set this study apart from others included in the meta-analyses mentioned earlier in this chapter was that it was not sponsored by one of the drug companies that makes the drugs. Among the many findings from this study, three stand out. First, the second-generation drugs were not more effective than the older, first-generation drugs. Second, the second-generation drugs did not produce fewer unpleasant side effects. And third, nearly three-quarters of the people stopped taking the medications before the 18 months of the study design had ended. Similar results have been found in another large study (Jones, Barnes, Davies et al., 2006). Despite the early promise of second-generation drugs, more work is needed to develop better treatments for schizophrenia.

In addition, other studies have revealed that second-generation antipsychotics have serious side effects of their own (Freedman, 2003). First, these drugs can and do also produce extrapyramidal side effects (Miller, Caroff, Davis et al., 2008; Rummel-Kluge, Komossa, Schwarz et al., 2010). Second, second-generation drugs cause weight gain (Rummel-Kluge et al., 2010), with one study finding that nearly half of the people taking these medications had significant weight gain (Young, Goey, Minassian et al., 2010). In addition to being unpleasant, weight gain is associated with other serious health problems, such as increased cholesterol and increases in blood glucose, which can cause type 2 diabetes. For example, clozapine and olanzapine have been related to the development of type 2 diabetes (Leslie & Rosenheck, 2004). However, it is not clear whether the medicine itself increases this risk, perhaps via the side effect of weight gain, or whether people taking the medications were predisposed to developing diabetes independent of their medication usage. In 2005, the drug company that produces olanzapine, Eli Lilly, agreed to settle a series of lawsuits, paying out over $700 million to people taking the drug. The company was sued for failing to adequately warn people of these serious side effects. The drug's label now contains warnings about possible side effects, including weight gain and elevated blood sugar and cholesterol levels.

Another disturbing aspect of the second-generation antipsychotic medications is that African Americans do not tend to receive them. Two different studies have found that African Americans were more likely to be prescribed first-generation than second-generation antipsychotic (Kreyenbuhl, Zito, Buchanan et al., 2003; Valenti , Narendran, & Pristach, 2003). This is unfortunate for a number of reasons, but particularly because African Americans may experience more side effects than whites in response to the first-generation medications (Frackiewicz, Sramek, Herrera et al., 1997). More broadly, these results echo the findings of the Surgeon General's supplement to his landmark report on mental health in 2001 that elucidated a number of disparities in mental health treatment among members of ethnic minority groups (USDHHS, 2001a). Compared with other disorders reviewed in this book, relatively less research has been done on schizophrenia across different ethnic groups. This must be a focus of future research.

Evaluation of Drug Treatments Antipsychotic drugs are an indispensable part of treatment for schizophrenia and will undoubtedly continue to be so. Furthermore, the mixed success of second-generation antipsychotic

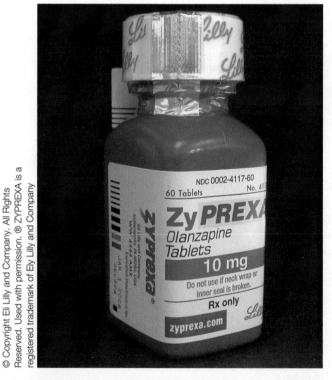

Second-generation antipsychotic drugs such as olanzapine may have different side effects than first-generation antipsychotic drugs, but they still have side effects.

drugs has stimulated a continued effort to find new and more effective drug therapies for schizophrenia. New drugs are currently being evaluated, but no significant breakthrough medications have yet been developed. Thus, the "third-generation" is a ways off.

Psychological Treatments

The limits of antipsychotic medications have spurred efforts to develop psychosocial treatments that can be used in addition to the medications. Indeed, the current treatment recommendations for schizophrenia as compiled by the schizophrenia Patient Outcomes Research Team (PORT) are medications plus psychosocial interventions (Kreyenbuhl, Buchanan, Dickerson et al., 2010). The 2009 updated PORT recommendations were based on extensive reviews of treatment research recommendations and were updated to include different types of psychosocial treatments. A number of psychosocial interventions, including skills training, cognitive behavior therapy, and family-based treatments, have a solid evidence base to support their use as an adjunctive treatment to medications (Dixon, Dickerson, Bellack et al., 2010). A review of 37 prospective studies of people after their first episode of schizophrenia found that the combination of medication and psychosocial treatment predicted the best outcome (Menezes, Arenovich, & Zipursky, 2006).

An example of the positive effects that come from combination treatments is found in a large (over 1200 people) randomized controlled trial conducted in China that compared medication alone with medication plus a comprehensive psychosocial intervention that included family therapy, cognitive behavior therapy, psychoeducation, and skills training. People in both groups had a similar reduction in schizophrenia symptoms. However, people who received the combined treatment had lower rates of relapse and treatment discontinuation, as well as greater improvements in functioning (Guo, Zhai, Liu et al., 2010). See Focus on Discovery 9.5 for another example of a successful combination treatment approach.

Other treatments, such as cognitive remediation approaches, have a growing evidence base and are the focus of much current research. We turn to these psychosocial treatments next.

Social Skills Training **Social skills training** is designed to teach people with schizophrenia how to successfully manage a wide variety of interpersonal situations—discussing their medications with their psychiatrist, ordering meals in a restaurant, filling out job applications, interviewing for jobs, saying no to drug dealers on the street, and reading bus schedules. Most of us take these skills for granted and give little thought to them in our daily lives, but people with schizophrenia cannot consider them a given—they need to work hard to acquire or reacquire such skills (Heinssen, Liberman, & Kopelowicz, 2000; Liberman, Eckman, Kopelowicz et al., 2000). Social skills training typically involves role-playing and other group exercises to practice skills, both in a therapy group and in actual social situations.

Research has shown that social skills training can help people with schizophrenia achieve fewer relapses, better social functioning, and a higher quality of life (Kopelowicz, Liberman, & Zarate, 2002). Some of the studies are noteworthy in demonstrating benefits over a 2-year period following treatment (Liberman, Wallace, Blackwell et al., 1998; Marder, Wirshing, Glynn et al., 1999), though not all results are positive (Pilling, Bebbington, Kuipers et al., 2002). Social skills training is usually a component of treatments for schizophrenia that go beyond the use of medications alone, including family therapies for lowering expressed emotion, which we discuss next. For example, social skills training that included family therapy was found to be more effective than treatment as usual (medication plus a 20-minute monthly meeting with a psychiatrist) in a randomized controlled trial conducted in Mexico (Valencia, Racon, Juarez et al., 2007). There is some evidence that social skills training may also be effective in reducing negative symptoms (Elis, Caponigro, & Kring, 2013).

FOCUS ON DISCOVERY 9.5

Living with Schizophrenia

A heartening example of one woman's struggles with and triumphs over schizophrenia is found in the 2007 book *The Center Cannot Hold: My Journey Through Madness.* This book was written by Elyn Saks, an endowed professor of law at the University of Southern California who also happens to have schizophrenia (Saks, 2007). In the book, she describes her lifelong experience with this illness. Prior to the publication of the book, only a few of Professor Saks's close friends even knew that she had schizophrenia. Why did she keep it a secret? Certainly, stigma is part of the reason. As we have discussed throughout this book, stigma toward people with psychological disorders is very much alive in the twenty-first century and can have seriously negative consequences for people with disorders such as schizophrenia.

What makes Professor Saks's life story particularly encouraging is that she has achieved exceptional professional and personal success in her life despite having such a serious psychological disorder. She grew up in a loving and supportive family, earned a bachelor's degree from Vanderbilt University, graduating as her class valedictorian, earned a prestigious Marshall fellowship to study philosophy at Oxford in the United Kingdom, graduated from Yale Law School as editor of the prestigious *Yale Law Review,* and is a tenured professor of law at a major university. How did she do it?

She believes that a combination of treatments (including psychoanalysis and medications), social support from family and friends, hard work, and acknowledgment of the seriousness of her illness have all helped her cope with schizophrenia and its sometimes unpredictable and frightening symptoms. Although psychoanalysis does not have a good deal of empirical support for its efficacy with schizophrenia, it was and remains a central part of Professor Saks's treatment regimen. Thus, even though some treatments may not be effective for a group of people, they can nonetheless be beneficial for individuals. One characteristic that appears to have been helpful for Professor Saks, from her early days in psychoanalysis as a Marshall scholar at Oxford University until the present, has been her ability to "be psychotic" when she is with her

Elyn Saks, a law professor at USC, has schizophrenia.

psychoanalyst. So much of her energy was spent trying to hide her symptoms and keep them from interfering with her life; psychoanalysis became a safe place for her to bring these symptoms more fully out into the open. The different analysts she has had over the years were also among the chief proponents of adding antipsychotic medication to her treatment, something that Professor Saks resisted for many years. Having the unwavering support of close friends and her husband has also been a tremendous help, particularly during her more symptomatic periods. Her loved ones would not turn and run the other way when she was psychotic. Instead, they would support her and help her get additional treatment if it was needed.

Professor Saks still experiences symptoms, sometimes every day. Her symptoms include paranoid delusions, which she describes as very frightening (e.g., believing that her thoughts have killed people). She also experiences disorganization symptoms, which she eloquently describes in the book:

Consciousness gradually loses its coherence. One's center gives way. The center cannot hold. The "me" becomes a haze, and the solid center from which one experiences reality breaks up like a bad radio signal. There is no longer a sturdy vantage point from which to look out, take things in, assess what's happening. No core holds things together, providing the lens through which to see the world, to make judgments and comprehend risk. (Saks, 2007, p. 13)

Even though she still experiences symptoms, she has come to terms with the fact that schizophrenia is a part of her life. Would she prefer not to have the illness? Sure. But she also recognizes that she has a wonderful life filled with friends, loved ones, and meaningful work. She is not defined by her illness, and she importantly notes that "the humanity we all share is more important than the mental illness we may not" (Saks, 2007, p. 336). Her life is an inspiration to all, not just those with psychological disorders. Her story reminds us that life is difficult, more so for some than others, but that it can be lived, and lived to the fullest.

Family Therapies Many people with schizophrenia live with their families. Earlier we discussed research showing that high levels of expressed emotion (EE) within the family, including being hostile, critical, and emotionally overinvolved, have been linked to relapse and rehospitalization. Based on this finding, a number of family therapies have been developed. These therapies may differ in length, setting, and specific techniques, but they have several features in common:

- *Education about schizophrenia—specifically about the genetic or neurobiological factors that predispose some people to the illness, the cognitive problems associated with schizophrenia, the symptoms of schizophrenia, and the signs of impending relapse.* High-EE families are typically not well informed about schizophrenia, and giving them some basic information helps them be less critical of the relative with schizophrenia. Knowing, for example, that neurobiology has a lot to do with having schizophrenia and that the illness involves problems in thinking clearly and rationally might help family members be more accepting and understanding of their relative's inappropriate or ineffectual actions. Therapists encourage family members to temper their expectations of their relative with schizophrenia, and they make clear to family and the person with schizophrenia alike that proper medication and therapy can reduce stress on the person and prevent deterioration.

- *Information about antipsychotic medication.* Therapists impress on both the family and the ill relative the importance of taking antipsychotic medication, becoming better informed about the intended effects and the side effects of the medication, taking responsibility for monitoring response to medication, and seeking medical consultation rather than just discontinuing the medication if adverse side effects occur.

- *Blame avoidance and reduction.* Therapists encourage family members to blame neither themselves nor their relative for the illness and for the difficulties all are having in coping with it.

- *Communication and problem-solving skills within the family.* Therapists focus on teaching the family ways to express both positive and negative feelings in a constructive, empathic, nondemanding manner rather than in a finger-pointing, critical, or overprotective manner. They also focus on making personal conflicts less stressful by teaching family members ways to work together to solve everyday problems.

- *Social network expansion.* Therapists encourage people with schizophrenia and their families to expand their social contacts, especially their support networks.

- *Hope.* Therapists instill hope that things can improve, including the hope that the person with schizophrenia may not have to return to the hospital.

Bruce Ayres/Stone/Getty Images

Family therapy can help educate people with schizophrenia and their families about schizophrenia and reduce expressed emotion.

Therapists use various techniques to implement these strategies. Examples include identifying stressors that could cause relapse, training families in communication skills and problem solving, and having high-EE family members watch videotapes of interactions of low-EE families (Penn & Mueser, 1996). Compared with standard treatments (usually just medication), family therapy plus medication has typically lowered relapse over periods of 1 to 2 years. This positive finding is evident particularly in studies in which the treatment lasted for at least 9 months (Falloon, Boyd, McGill et al., 1982, 1985; Hogarty, Anderson, Reiss et al., 1986, 1991; Kopelowicz & Liberman, 1998; McFarlane, Lukens, Link et al., 1995; Penn & Mueser, 1996).

Cognitive Behavior Therapy At one time, researchers assumed that it was futile to try to alter the cognitive distortions, including delusions, of people with schizophrenia. Now, however, a growing body of evidence demonstrates that the maladaptive beliefs of some people with schizophrenia can in fact benefit from cognitive behavior therapy (CBT) (Garety, Fowler, & Kuipers, 2000; Wykes, Steel, Everitt et al., 2008).

People with schizophrenia can be encouraged to test out their delusional beliefs in much the same way as people without schizophrenia do. Through collaborative discussions (and in the context of other modes of treatment, including antipsychotic drugs), some people with schizophrenia have been helped to attach a nonpsychotic meaning to paranoid symptoms and thereby reduce their intensity and aversive nature, similar to what is done for depression and panic disorder (Beck & Rector, 2000; Drury, Birchwood,

Cochrane et al., 1996; Haddock, Tarrier, Spaulding et al., 1998). Researchers have found that CBT can also reduce negative symptoms, for example, by challenging belief structures tied to low expectations for success (avolition) and low expectations for pleasure (anticipatory pleasure deficit in anhedonia) (Grant, Huh, Perivoliotis et al., 2012; Wykes et al., 2008).

Results from meta-analyses of over 50 studies of more than 2000 people with schizophrenia across eight countries found small to moderate effect sizes for positive symptoms, negative symptoms, mood, and general life functioning (Jauhar, McKenna, Radua et al., 2014; Wykes et al., 2008). The results are less encouraging for negative symptoms, but CBT is currently the most effective treatment for these symptoms (Elis et al., 2013). CBT has been used as an adjunctive treatment for schizophrenia in Great Britain for over 10 years, and the results have been positive, even in community settings (Sensky, Turkington, Kingdom et al., 2000; Turkington, Kingdom, & Turner, 2002; Wykes et al., 2008).

Cognitive Remediation Therapies Researchers and clinicians have been paying more attention to fundamental aspects of cognition that are disordered in schizophrenia in an attempt to improve these functions and thereby favorably affect behavior. The fact that positive clinical outcomes from risperidone are associated with improvements in certain kinds of memory (Green, Marshall, Wirshing et al., 1997) lends support to the more general notion that therapies directed at basic cognitive processes—the kind that nonclinical cognitive scientists study—hold promise for improving the social and emotional lives of people with schizophrenia. This general approach concentrates on trying to normalize such functions as attention and memory, which are known to be deficient in many people with schizophrenia and are associated with poor social adaptation (Green, Kern, Braff et al., 2000).

Treatments that seek to enhance basic cognitive functions such as verbal learning ability are referred to as **cognitive remediation training** or **cognitive enhancement therapy** (**CET**) or *cognitive training*. A 2-year randomized controlled clinical trial compared group-based CET with enriched supportive therapy (EST). CET consisted of nearly 80 hours of computer-based training in attention, memory, and problem solving. Groups also worked on such routine social-cognitive skills as reading and understanding newspaper editorials, solving social problems, and starting and maintaining conversations. EST included supportive and educational elements. All people were also taking medications. At the 1- and 2-year follow-up assessments, CET was more effective than EST in improving cognitive abilities in problem solving, attention, social cognition, and social adjustment, while symptom reduction was the same for both treatments (Hogarty, Flesher, Ulrich et al., 2004). People who received CET were also rated as being more ready for employment and, in fact, tended to be employed at the end of 2 years, largely driven by the fact that these people were more likely to be in volunteer positions than those in the EST group. A different study compared CET with supportive therapy and found that CET was associated with improvements in social functioning that remained 1 year after the treatment ended (Eack, Greenwald, Hogarty et al., 2010). Thus, CET appears to be effective in reducing symptoms and improving cognitive abilities, and it is linked to good functional outcomes, such as employment and social functioning.

Two meta-analyses of 26 (McGurk, Twamley, Sitzer et al., 2007) and 40 studies (Wykes, Huddy, Cellard et al., 2011) found small to medium effect sizes for overall cognitive functioning and specific cognitive domains, including attention, verbal memory, problem solving, verbal working memory, processing speed, and social cognition. Cognitive remediation was also associated with a reduction in symptoms and an improvement in everyday functioning, though the effect sizes for these two domains were small. Cognitive remediation was more likely to be associated with an improvement in functioning if another type of psychosocial treatment, such as social skills training, was added to the treatment program. As promising as these findings are, nearly all of the studies have been with white men; thus, their generalizability remains to be established.

A somewhat different cognitive remediation program has also shown promising results. This treatment also involves intensive (50 hours) computer training, but the task was developed based on neuroscience research showing that improving basic cognitive and perceptual processes (e.g., discriminating simple sounds) can then impact higher-order cognitive processes (e.g., memory and problem solving). The cognitive remediation task in this training is an auditory task that gets progressively more difficult as people get better at it. They perform a series of tasks that require them to discriminate between complex speech sounds. In a recent randomized controlled trial, people with schizophrenia who received the intensive auditory computer training showed greater improvement in overall cognition as well as in specific domains (memory, attention, processing speed, working memory, and problem solving) compared to participants who played computer games for the same amount of time (Fisher, Holland, Merzenich et al., 2009).

Psychoeducation As we discussed in Chapter 5 with regard to bipolar disorder, psychoeducation is an approach that seeks to educate people about their illness, including the symptoms of the disorder, the expected time course of symptoms, the biological and psychological triggers for symptoms, and treatment strategies. A recent meta-analysis of 44 studies of psychoeducation in schizophrenia found that, in combination with medication, it was effective in reducing relapse and rehospitalization and increasing medication compliance (Xia, Merinder, & Belgamwar, 2011).

Case Management After large numbers of people were discharged from hospitals (referred to as deinstitutionalization) in the 1960s, many people with schizophrenia no longer resided in hospitals and thus had to fend for themselves in securing needed services. Lacking the centralized hospital as the site where most services were delivered, the mental health system became more complex. In 1977, fearing that many people with schizophrenia were not accessing services, the National Institute of Mental Health established a grants program for the states to help people with schizophrenia cope with the mental health system. Out of this program, a new mental health specialty, the case manager, was created.

Initially, case managers were basically brokers of services; because they were familiar with the system, they were able to connect people with schizophrenia with providers of whatever services they required. As the years passed, different models of case management developed. The major innovation was the recognition that case managers often needed to provide direct clinical services and that services might best be delivered by a team rather than brokered out. The Assertive Community Treatment model (Stein & Test, 1980) and the Intensive Case Management model (Surles, Blanch, Shern et al., 1992) both entail a multidisciplinary team that provides services in the community, such as medication, treatment for substance abuse, help in dealing with stressors that people with schizophrenia face regularly (such as managing money), psychotherapy, vocational training, and assistance in obtaining housing and employment. Case managers hold together and coordinate the range of medical and psychological services that people with schizophrenia need to keep functioning outside of institutions with some degree of independence and peace of mind (Kopelowicz et al., 2002). Both of these models continue to be part of the PORT recommendations for psychosocial treatments, with established evidence of their effectiveness (Dixon et al., 2010).

This more intensive treatment has proven superior to less intensive methods in reducing time spent in the hospital, improving housing stability, and ameliorating symptoms (Mueser, Bond, Drake et al., 1998). However, more intensive case management has not shown positive effects in other domains, such as improvement in social functioning. In order for this approach to be effective, there have to be enough case managers for people with schizophrenia. Too often, the caseloads of these mental health professionals are much too large and so they are spread too thin.

Residential Treatment Residential treatment homes, or "halfway houses," are sometimes good alternatives for people who do not need to be in the hospital but are not quite well enough to live on their own or even with their family. These are protected living units, typically located in large, formerly private residences. Here people live, take their meals, and gradually return to ordinary community life by holding a part-time job or going to school. As part of what is called *vocational rehabilitation,* residents learn marketable skills that can help them secure employment and thereby increase their chances of remaining in the community. Living arrangements may be relatively unstructured; some houses set up moneymaking enterprises that help train and support the residents.

Depending on how well funded the residential treatment facility is, the staff may include psychiatrists or clinical psychologists, or both. The frontline staff members are often undergraduate psychology majors or graduate students in clinical psychology or social work, who live at the facility and act both as administrators and as friends to the residents. Group meetings, at which residents talk out their frustrations and learn to relate to others in honest and constructive ways, are often part of the routine. Many such programs across the United States have helped thousands of people with schizophrenia make enough of a social adaptation to be able to remain out of the hospital.

The need in the United States for effective residential treatment cannot be underestimated, especially in light of the deinstitutionalization that involved discharging tens of thousands of people from hospitals (Torrey, 2014). People with schizophrenia almost always need follow-up community-based services, and these services are scarce. Indeed, today a large percentage of homeless people in the United States are mentally ill, including many people with schizophrenia. Social Security benefits are available to those with schizophrenia, but if they do not have an address, they often do not receive all the benefits to which they are entitled. Although good residential treatment programs are available, there simply are not enough of them.

Integrating therapy with gainful employment is important in keeping people with schizophrenia out of hospitals (Kopelowicz & Liberman, 1998; Kopelowicz et al., 2002). For example, the U.S. government has begun to recognize the importance of employment by allowing people with schizophrenia to continue receiving Social Security disability benefits for up to 2 years while they are earning money from (low-paying) jobs that can increase their chances of living independently or at least outside of the hospital. This welcome change in policy (from one that terminated such benefits once the person began earning money) represents a recognition of the harmful effects of not working and will promote their ability to be reasonably independent.

Still, obtaining employment poses a major challenge because of the bias and stigma attached to people with schizophrenia. Although the Americans with Disabilities Act of 1990 prohibits employers from asking applicants if they have a history of serious psychological disorders, people with schizophrenia still have a difficult time obtaining regular employment. Their symptoms make negatively biased employers fearful of hiring them, and in addition, many employers are unwilling to give much leeway to people whose thinking, emotions, and behavior can be unconventional.

Given these difficulties, additional funding will be needed to create more residential treatment facilities, with the hope of reducing the number of people with schizophrenia in need of treatment.

Check Your Knowledge 9.3

True or false?

1. First-generation antipsychotics include medications like haldol or prolixin; second-generation antipsychotics include clozapine and olanzapine.
2. Second-generation antipsychotics produce more motor side effects than first-generation antipsychotics.
3. Cognitive behavior therapy, but not cognitive enhancement therapy, is effective for schizophrenia, if given along with medications.
4. One important focus of residential treatment programs is to help people with schizophrenia gain employment.

Summary

Clinical Description

- The symptoms of schizophrenia involve disturbances in several areas, including thought, perception, and attention; motor behavior; emotion; and life functioning. Symptoms are typically divided into positive, negative, and disorganized categories. Positive symptoms include excesses and distortions, such as delusions and hallucinations. Negative symptoms are behavioral deficits, which include avolition, asociality, anhedonia, blunted affect, and alogia. Disorganized symptoms include disorganized speech and behavior.
- The DSM-5 removed the subtypes of schizophrenia because they have little predictive validity and clinical usefulness.
- Other schizophrenia spectrum disorders in DSM-5 include schizophreniform disorder, brief psychotic disorder, schizoaffective disorder, and delusional disorder.

Etiology

- The evidence for genetic transmission of schizophrenia is impressive. Family and twin studies suggest a genetic component; adoption studies show a strong relationship between having a parent with schizophrenia and the likelihood of developing the disorder, typically in early adulthood. Familial high-risk studies have longitudinally studied the offspring of a parent with schizophrenia to determine if problems in childhood might predict the onset of the disorder. Association studies indicate that genes such as *DTNBP1*, *COMT*, and *BDNF* are associated with schizophrenia. Genome-wide association studies (GWAS) have found rare genetic mutations called copy number variations (CNVs) to be associated with schizophrenia.
- The genetic predisposition to develop schizophrenia may involve neurotransmitters. It appears that increased sensitivity of dopamine receptors in the brain is related to the positive symptoms of schizophrenia. The negative symptoms may be due to dopamine underactivity in the prefrontal cortex. Other neurotransmitters, such as serotonin, glutamate, and GABA, are also involved.
- The brains of some people with schizophrenia have enlarged ventricles as well as problems with the prefrontal cortex, the temporal cortex, and connectivity between brain regions. Some of these structural abnormalities could result from maternal viral infection during the first trimester of pregnancy or from damage sustained during a difficult birth. The combination of brain development during adolescence, stress, and the HPA axis is important for understanding why symptoms typically emerge during late adolescence, even if a brain disturbance has been in place since gestation. Cannabis use in adolescence has been linked to a higher risk for developing schizophrenia, primarily for those who are genetically vulnerable to schizophrenia.
- High levels of expressed emotion in families, as well as increases in general life stress, have been shown to be important determinants of relapse. Retrospective developmental studies have identified problems in childhood that existed prior to the onset of schizophrenia. Because these studies were not designed to predict schizophrenia, however, it is difficult to interpret the findings. Clinical high-risk studies have identified young people with mild symptoms who are at higher risk for developing schizophrenia spectrum disorders.

Treatment

- Antipsychotic drugs are widely used to treat schizophrenia. The first-generation drugs are somewhat effective, but they can also produce serious side effects. Second-generation antipsychotic drugs, such as clozapine and risperidone, are equally as effective as first-generation drugs, and they have their own set of side effects. Drugs alone are not a completely effective treatment, though, as people with schizophrenia need to be (re)taught ways of dealing with the challenges of everyday life.
- Family therapy aimed at reducing high levels of expressed emotion has been shown to be valuable in preventing relapse. In addition, social skills training and various cognitive behavioral therapies have helped people with schizophrenia meet the inevitable stresses of family and community living. Recent efforts to change the thinking of people with schizophrenia with cognitive behavior therapy are showing promise as well. Cognitive remediation therapies focus on improving cognitive skills. These therapies help promote memory, attention, and problem-solving skills and also improve daily functioning.

Answers to Check Your Knowledge Questions

9.1 1. blunted affect; 2. delusion or ideas of reference; 3. anhedonia (anticipatory); 4. disorganized thinking or derailment.

9.2 1. family, twin, adoption; 2. DTNBP1, NGRl, COMT, BDNF; 3. prefrontal; 4. hostility, critical comments, emotional overinvolvement

9.3 l. T; 2. F; 3. F; 4. T

Key Terms

alogia
anhedonia
anticipatory pleasure
antipsychotic drugs
asociality
avolition
blunted affect
brief psychotic disorder
catatonia
clinical high-risk study
cognitive enhancement therapy (CET)
 (cognitive remediation training)

consummatory pleasure
delusional disorder
delusions
dementia praecox
disorganized behavior
disorganized speech
disorganized symptoms
expressed emotion (EE)
familial high-risk study
grandiose delusions
hallucinations
ideas of reference

loose associations (derailment)
negative symptoms
positive symptoms
prefrontal cortex
schizoaffective disorder
schizophrenia
schizophreniform disorder
second-generation antipsychotic
 drugs
social selection hypothesis
social skills training
sociogenic hypothesis

10 Substance Use Disorders

PEOPLE HAVE USED VARIOUS substances in the hope of reducing pain, changing mood, or altering states of consciousness for centuries. Around the world, almost all people use one or more substances that affect the central nervous system, relieving physical and mental anguish or producing euphoria. Despite the often devastating consequences of taking such substances into the body, their initial effects are usually pleasing, a factor that is perhaps at the root of substance use disorders.

Clinical Descriptions, Prevalence, and Effects of Substance Use Disorders

The United States is a drug culture. Americans use drugs to wake up (coffee or tea), to stay alert throughout the day (cigarettes, soft drinks), to relax (alcohol), and to reduce pain (aspirin). The widespread availability and frequent use of drugs set the stage for the potential abuse of drugs, the topic of this chapter.

Table 10.1 Percentage of U.S. Population Reporting Drug Use in Past Month (2012)

Substance	Percentage Reporting Use
Alcohol	52.1
Cigarettes	22.1
Marijuana	7.3
Nonmedical psychotherapeutics	2.6
Cocaine	0.6
Heroin	0.1
Hallucinogens including PCP	0.4
Inhalants	0.2

Data are percentages of people in the United States age 12 and over. Nonmedical psychotherapeutics refers to the use of pain medicines (1.9%), tranquilizers (0.8%), stimulants (0.5%), or sedatives (0.1%) for a nonmedical, nonprescribed use.
Source: SAMHSA (2013).

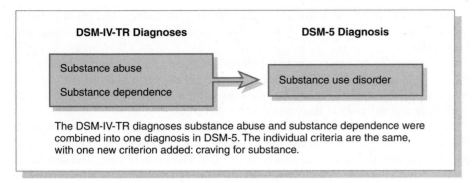

Figure 10.1 Diagnoses of substance use and addictive disorders.

In 2012, nearly 24 million people over the age of 12 in the United States reported having used an illicit drug in the past month [Substance Abuse and Mental Health Services Administration (SAMHSA, 2013)]. Of the currently illegal drugs, marijuana was the most frequently used, with nearly 19 million people over the age of 12 reporting using it in the past month. Alcohol remains the most used substance, with over 135 million Americans over the age of 12 reporting alcohol use of some kind, and 59.7 million Americans reported at least one episode of binge drinking (defined as having five or more drinks) in the last 30 days (SAMHSA, 2013). Recent data on the frequency of use of several drugs, legal and illegal, are presented in Table 10.1. These figures do not represent the frequency of substance use disorders but simply indicate the pervasiveness of drug and alcohol use in the United States.

The DSM-IV-TR included two broad categories: substance abuse and substance dependence. However, problems with these two categories, including low reliability and results of studies suggesting that the criteria fit better in one category rather than in two, led to revisions in DSM-5 (Hasin, O'Brien, Auriacombe et al., 2013). The DSM-5 has just one category: **substance use disorder**. The differences between DSM-IV-TR and DSM-5 are depicted in Figure 10.1.

The DSM-5 contains substance use disorder categories for specific substances, such as alcohol opioids, and tobacco. New to DSM-5 is the inclusion of gambling disorder in the chapter on Substance-Related and Addictive Disorders. The term **addiction** typically refers to a severe substance use disorder. Table 10.2 lists the DSM-5 severity ratings for substance use disorders. In the DSM-5, meeting six or more of the diagnostic criteria is considered severe substance use disorder.

Two symptoms that often are part of a severe substance use disorder are tolerance and withdrawal. **Tolerance** is indicated by either (1) larger doses of the substance being needed to produce the desired effect or (2) the effects of the drug becoming markedly less if the usual amount is taken. **Withdrawal** refers to the negative physical and psychological effects

DSM-5 Criteria for Substance Use Disorder

Problematic pattern of use that impairs functioning. Two or more symptoms within a 1-year period:
- Failure to meet obligations
- Repeated use in situations where it is physically dangerous
- Repeated relationship problems
- Continued use despite problems caused by the substance
- Tolerance
- Withdrawal
- Substance taken for a longer time or in greater amounts than intended
- Efforts to reduce or control use do not work
- Much time spent trying to obtain the substance
- Social, hobbies, or work activities given up or reduced
- Craving to use the substance is strong

Table 10.2 Severity Ratings for Substance Use Disorders in DSM-5

Rating	Number of Diagnostic Criteria Met
Mild	2–3 criteria
Moderate	4–5 criteria
Severe	6 or more criteria

Clinical Case: Alice

Alice was 54 years old and living alone when her family finally persuaded her to check into an alcohol rehabilitation clinic. She had taken a bad fall while drunk, and it may have been this event that finally got her to admit that something was wrong. Her drinking had been out of control for several years. She began each day with a drink, continued through the morning, and was totally intoxicated by the afternoon. She seldom had any memory for events after noon of any day. Since early adulthood she had drunk regularly, but rarely during the day and never to the point of drunkenness. The sudden death of her husband in an automobile accident 2 years earlier had triggered a quick increase in her drinking, and within 6 months she had slipped into a pattern of severe alcohol use. She had little desire to go out of her house and had cut back on social activities with family and friends. Repeated efforts by her family to get her to curtail her intake of alcohol had only led to angry confrontations.

that develop when a person stops taking the substance or reduces the amount. Substance withdrawal symptoms can include muscle pains and twitching, sweats, vomiting, diarrhea, and insomnia.

In 2012, over 22 million people in the United States met the diagnostic criteria for a substance use disorder. Of this large number of people, most (14.9 million) met the criteria for alcohol use disorder. Over 4 million met the criteria for a drug use disorder, and 2.8 million for both drug and alcohol use disorders (SAMHSA, 2013).

Drug and alcohol use disorders are among the most stigmatized of disorders. Terms such as *addict* or *alcoholic* are tossed about carelessly, as if these words capture the essence of people, not the disorder from which they suffer. Historically, drug and alcohol problems have been viewed as moral lapses rather than as conditions in need of treatment. Unfortunately, such attitudes persist today. True, people make decisions about whether or not to try alcohol or drugs, but the ways in which these decisions and the substances involved interact with an individual's neurobiology, social setting, culture, and other environmental factors all conspire to create a substance use disorder. Thus, it is a mistake to consider substance use disorders as somehow being solely the result of moral failing or personal choice.

We turn now to an overview of some of the major substance use disorders, those involving alcohol, tobacco, marijuana, opiates, stimulants, and hallucinogens.

Alcohol Use Disorder

People who are physiologically dependent on alcohol generally have more severe symptoms, such as tolerance or withdrawal, than do people without tolerance or withdrawal symptoms (Schuckit, Daeppen, Tipp et al., 1998). The effects of the abrupt withdrawal of alcohol in a heavy user may be rather dramatic because the body has become accustomed to alcohol. Specifically, a person may feel anxious, depressed, weak, restless, and unable to sleep. He or she may have muscle tremors, especially of the fingers, face, eyelids, lips, and tongue, and pulse, blood pressure, and temperature may be elevated.

In relatively rare cases, a person who has been drinking heavily for several years may also experience **delirium tremens (DTs)** when the level of alcohol in the blood drops suddenly. The person becomes delirious as well as tremulous and has hallucinations that are primarily visual but may be tactile as well. Unpleasant and very active creatures—snakes, cockroaches, spiders, and the like—may appear to be crawling up the wall or over the person's body or to be filling the room. Feverish, disoriented, and terrified, the person may claw frantically at his or her skin to get rid of the creatures.

Alcohol use disorder is often associated with other drug use. It is estimated, for example, that 80 to 85 percent of people who abuse alcohol are smokers. This very high comorbidity may occur because alcohol and nicotine are cross-tolerant; that is, nicotine can induce tolerance for the rewarding effects of alcohol and vice versa. Thus, consumption of both drugs may be increased to maintain their rewarding effects (Rose, Braner, Behm et al., 2004). Evidence from animal studies suggests that this may happen because nicotine influences the way alcohol works in the brain's dopamine pathways associated with reward (Doyon, Dong, Ostroumov et al., 2013), a topic we turn to later in the chapter.

Prevalence of Alcohol Use Disorder Because the diagnosis of alcohol use disorder in DSM-5 is new, we do not yet have prevalence estimates for this category. Results from the annual survey conducted by the Substance Abuse and Mental Health Services Administration (SAMHSA) indicates that 8.5 percent of the U.S. population met the criteria for the DSM-IV-TR categories of alcohol dependence or alcohol abuse in 2012.

Alcohol use is especially frequent among college-age adults. This is true for binge drinking, defined, as noted earlier, as having five drinks in a short period of time (e.g., within an hour), and heavy-use drinking, defined as having five drinks on the same occasion five or more times in a 30-day period. Among both male and female full-time college students, binge and

Alcohol and nicotine are a frequent combination, although most people who smoke and drink in social situations do not have problems with these substances.

heavy-use prevalence rates were 39.5 percent and 12.7 percent, respectively in 2012 (SAMHSA, 2013). Both of these numbers are lower than those reported in 2009 (43.5 and 16 percent).

Binge drinking can have serious consequences. Estimates suggest that as many as 1800 college students die from alcohol-related incidents (e.g., driving under the influence, toxicity) each year. Close to 700,000 are assaulted by other students who have been drinking, and as many as 97,000 students are sexually assaulted (Hingson, Edwards, Heeren, & Rosenbloom, 2009).

More men than women have problems with alcohol, though this varies a bit by age. In 2012, 16.7 percent of men ages 18-25 met the criteria for alcohol use disorders compared with 11.9 percent of women. However, 8.7 percent of men and 3.4 percent of women ages 26 and older met the criteria for these disorders (SAMHSA, 2013).

The prevalence of alcohol problems differs by ethnicity as well. European American and Hispanic adolescents and adults are more likely to binge drink than African American adolescents and adults. In fact, African American youth and adults are less likely to drink heavily than European Americans, perhaps due to cultural constraints on alcohol use in the African American community (Zapolski, Pedersen, McCarthy et al., 2014). Binge and heavy-use drinking are lowest among Asian and African Americans (SAMHSA, 2013). On the basis of DSM-IV-TR categories, alcohol dependence was most prevalent among Native Americans and Hispanics and least prevalent among Asian Americans and African Americans (SAMHSA, 2013).

Alcohol use disorders are comorbid with several personality disorders, mood disorders, schizophrenia, and anxiety disorders as well as with other drug use (Kessler et al., 1997; Morgenstern et al., 1997; Skinstad & Swain, 2001). In 2012, 6.8 percent of people ages 18–25 that met the criteria for a substance use disorder also had at least one other psychological disorder (SAMHSA, 2013).

Short-Term Effects of Alcohol How does alcohol produce its short-term effects? After being swallowed and reaching the stomach, alcohol begins to be metabolized by enzymes. Most of it goes into the small intestine and from there it is absorbed into the blood. It is then broken down, primarily in the liver, which can metabolize about 1 ounce of 100-proof (50 percent alcohol) liquor per hour.

Although Figure 10.2 shows mean blood alcohol levels based on a person's weight and amount of alcohol consumption, the effects of alcohol vary with its concentration in the bloodstream. Levels in the bloodstream depend on the amount ingested in a particular period of time, the presence of food in the stomach (food retains the alcohol and reduces its absorption rate), the weight and body fat of the person drinking, and the efficiency of the liver. Two ounces of alcohol will thus have a different effect on a 180-pound man who has just eaten than on a 110-pound woman with an empty stomach. However, women achieve higher blood alcohol concentrations even after adjustment for differences in body weight, perhaps due to differences in body water content between men and women.

It is also important to consider the question: what counts as a drink? A 12-ounce glass of beer, a 5-ounce glass of wine, and 1.5 ounces of "hard liquor" (like a shot of tequila) are all considered one drink. The size of the drink is not what matters. Rather, it is the alcohol content of the particular beverage (http://rethinkingdrinking.niaaa.nih.gov).

Alcohol produces its effects through its interactions with several neural systems in the brain. It stimulates gamma-aminobutyric acid (GABA) receptors, which may account for its ability to reduce tension. (GABA is a major inhibitory neurotransmitter; the benzodiazepines, such as Xanax, have an effect on GABA receptors similar to that of alcohol.) Alcohol also increases levels of serotonin and dopamine, which may be the source of its ability to produce pleasurable effects. Finally, alcohol inhibits glutamate receptors, which may cause the cognitive effects of alcohol intoxication, such as slowed thinking and memory loss.

A novel study examined the effects of alcohol on both the brain and behavior. Participants were given different doses of alcohol while in an fMRI scanner performing a simulated driving

Blood Alcohol Concentration Calculator									
# OF DRINKS CONSUMED/SEX		**WEIGHT**							
		100	120	140	160	180	200	220	240
1	Male	.04	.04	.03	.03	.02	.02	.02	.02
	Female	.05	.04	.04	.03	.03	.03	.02	.02
2	Male	.09	.07	.06	.05	.05	.04	.04	.04
	Female	.10	.08	.07	.06	.06	.05	.05	.04
3	Male	.13	.11	.09	.08	.07	.07	.06	.05
	Female	.15	.13	.11	.10	.08	.08	.07	.06
4	Male	.17	.15	.13	.11	.10	.09	.08	.07
	Female	.20	.17	.15	.13	.11	.10	.09	.09
5	Male	.22	.18	.16	.14	.12	.11	.10	.09
	Female	.25	.21	.18	.16	.14	.13	.12	.11
6	Male	.26	.22	.19	.16	.15	.13	.12	.11
	Female	.30	.26	.22	.19	.17	.15	.14	.13
7	Male	.30	.25	.22	.19	.17	.15	.14	.13
	Female	.36	.30	.26	.22	.20	.18	.16	.15
8	Male	.35	.29	.25	.22	.19	.17	.16	.15
	Female	.41	.33	.29	.26	.23	.20	.18	.16
9	Male	.39	.35	.28	.25	.22	.20	.18	.16
	Female	.46	.38	.33	.29	.26	.23	.21	.19
10	Male	.39	.35	.28	.25	.22	.20	.18	.16
	Female	.51	.42	.36	.32	.28	.25	.23	.21
11	Male	.48	.40	.34	.30	.26	.24	.22	.20
	Female	.56	.46	.40	.35	.31	.27	.25	.23
12	Male	.53	.43	.37	.32	.29	.26	.24	.21
	Female	.61	.50	.43	.37	.33	.30	.28	.25
13	Male	.57	.47	.40	.35	.31	.29	.26	.23
	Female	.66	.55	.47	.40	.36	.32	.30	.27
14	Male	.62	.50	.43	.37	.34	.31	.28	.25
	Female	.71	.59	.51	.43	.39	.35	.32	.29
15	Male	.66	.54	.47	.40	.36	.34	.30	.27
	Female	.76	.63	.55	.46	.42	.37	.35	.32

Figure 10.2 Blood alcohol concentration calculator. Note that values are just estimates. An actual BAC will vary depending on metabolism and amount of food in the stomach.

test (Calhoun, Pekar, & Pearlson, 2004). The low dose (.04 blood alcohol content) led to just a small impairment in motor functioning, but the high dose (.08 blood alcohol content) led to more significant motor impairment that interfered with driving ability. Furthermore, the effects of the alcohol in the brain were in areas associated with monitoring errors and making decisions (the anterior cingulate and orbitofrontal cortex). Based on this finding, the researchers suggested that people at the legal limit of alcohol may make poor decisions about driving and not realize they are making mistakes.

Long-Term Effects of Prolonged Alcohol Abuse Almost every tissue and organ of the body is adversely affected by prolonged consumption of alcohol. For example, alcohol impairs the digestion of food and absorption of vitamins. In older people who have chronically abused alcohol, a deficiency of B-complex vitamins can cause amnestic syndrome, a severe loss of memory for both recent and long-past events.

Prolonged alcohol use plus reduction in the intake of proteins contributes to the development of cirrhosis of the liver, a disease in which some liver cells become engorged with fat and protein, impeding their function. Some cells die, triggering an inflammatory process, and when scar tissue develops, blood flow is obstructed.

Other common changes to the body due to drinking include damage to the endocrine glands, brain, and pancreas, heart failure, erectile dysfunction, hypertension, stroke, and capillary hemorrhages, which are responsible for the swelling and redness in the face, especially the nose, of people who chronically abuse alcohol.

Heavy alcohol consumption by a woman during pregnancy is the leading known cause of intellectual disability among children. The growth of the fetus is slowed, and cranial, facial, and limb anomalies can be produced, a condition known as **fetal alcohol syndrome (FAS).** Even moderate drinking can produce undesirable, if less severe, effects on the fetus, leading the National Institute on Alcohol Abuse and Alcoholism to counsel total abstention during pregnancy as the safest course.

Although it is appropriate and accurate to pay attention to the negative effects of alcohol, other evidence points to the positive health benefits for some people. Light drinking has been related to lower risk for coronary heart disease and stroke (Kloner & Rezkalla, 2007; Sacco, Elkind, Beden-Albala et al., 1999; Theobald, Bygren, Carstensen et al., 2000). If alcohol does have a beneficial effect, it could be due to physiological (e.g., acetate, a metabolite of alcohol, increases coronary blood flow) or psychological (a less-driven lifestyle and diminished hostility) factors, or, most likely, the interaction between the two factors. Indirect evidence suggests that low to moderate consumption of red wine may lower the so-called bad cholesterol (i.e., LDL) and raise the so-called good cholesterol (HDL) levels (Kloner & Rezkalla, 2007; Powers, Saultz, & Hamilton, 2007).

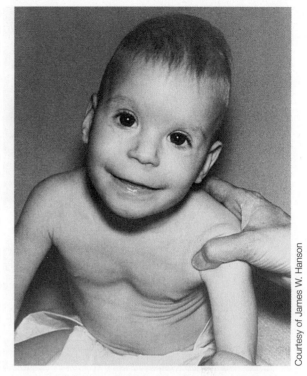

Courtesy of James W. Hanson

Heavy drinking during pregnancy can cause fetal alcohol syndrome. Children with this disorder can have facial abnormalities and intellectual developmental disorder.

Check Your Knowledge 10.1 (Answers are at the end of the chapter.)

True or false?

1. The diagnosis of a substance use disorder requires both tolerance and withdrawal.
2. Research suggests that nicotine can enhance the rewarding properties of alcohol.
3. Even moderate drinking by pregnant women can cause learning and attention problems in their children.

Tobacco Use Disorder

Nicotine is the addicting agent of tobacco. The neural pathways that become activated stimulate the dopamine neurons in the mesolimbic area that seem to be involved in producing the reinforcing effects of most drugs (Stein, Pankiewicz, Harsch et al., 1998).

Prevalence and Health Consequences of Smoking The threat to health posed by smoking has been documented convincingly by the Surgeon General of the United States in a series of reports published since 1964. In 2014, The Surgeon General released a new report commemorating the 50th anniversary of its first groundbreaking report on the health consequences of smoking (http://www.surgeongeneral.gov/library/reports/50-years-of-progress/). The report noted that the prevalence of smoking in 2014 was 18 percent, down from 43 percent in 1964. Although more than 20 million Americans have died from smoking over the past 50 years, another 45 million have quit smoking, no doubt saving many lives. Nevertheless, smoking remains the single most preventable cause of premature death in the United States as well as in other parts of the world. Unfortunately, the people most likely to smoke in the United States are people with a psychological disorder (Centers for Disease Control and Prevention (CDC), 2013).

Getty Images/Custom Medical Stock Photo RM/Getty Images, Inc.

Children of mothers who smoke are at increased risk for respiratory infections, bronchitis, and inner-ear infections.

WARNING: SMOKING CAUSES IMPOTENCE

California's Tobacco Education Media Campaign parodies tobacco ads to illustrate health risks associated with smoking and to attack pro-tobacco influences.

Parental smoking greatly increases the chances that children will begin to smoke.

Among the other medical problems associated with, and almost certainly caused or exacerbated by, long-term cigarette smoking are emphysema; cancers of the larynx and of the esophagus, pancreas, bladder, cervix, and stomach; complications during pregnancy; sudden infant death syndrome; periodontitis; and a number of cardiovascular disorders [U.S. Department of Health and Human Sources (USDHHS), 2014]. The most probable harmful components in the smoke from burning tobacco are nicotine, carbon monoxide, and tar, which consist primarily of certain hydrocarbons, many of which are known carcinogens (Jaffe, 1985).

In 2012, nearly 70 million people in the United States used a tobacco product (cigarette, cigar, smokeless tobacco, pipe), with over 57.5 million of these people smoking cigarettes. Cigarette smoking among youths age 12 to 17 has decreased from 15.2 percent of this age group in 2002 to just under 8.6 percent in 2012. Smoking is more prevalent among European American and Hispanic adolescents than among African American or Asian American adolescents. In general, more men than women smoke. However, prevalence among girls and boys between the ages of 12 and 17 is roughly the same (SAMHSA, 2013). Smoking is also more prevalent among people in the lower socioeconomic classes (Dwyer-Lindgren, Mokdad, Srebotnjak et al., 2014), likely adding to the disparity in health between rich and poor in the United States (see Focus on Discovery 2.2 in Chapter 2).

Research demonstrates the significance of ethnicity in nicotine addiction as well as the intricate interplay among behavioral, social, and neurobiological factors. It has been known for years that African American cigarette smokers are less likely to quit and are more likely, if they continue to smoke, to get lung cancer. Why? It turns out that they retain nicotine in their blood longer than do European Americans; that is, they metabolize it more slowly (Mustonen, Spencer, Hoskinson et al., 2005). Another reason has to do with the type of cigarette smoked. African Americans are more likely to smoke menthol cigarettes, largely due to extensive advertising of these types of cigarettes to this community beginning in the 1950s and continuing today (USDHHS, 2014). Research shows that people who smoke menthol inhale more deeply and hold the smoke in for a longer time, thus providing more opportunity for deleterious effects (Celebucki, Wayne, Connolly et al., 2005).

Research has found that Chinese Americans metabolize less nicotine from cigarettes than either European American or Latino smokers (Benowitz, Pérez-Stable, Herrera et al., 2002). In general, lung cancer rates are lower among Asians than among European Americans or Latinos. The relatively lower metabolism of nicotine among Chinese Americans may help explain why lung cancer rates are lower in this group.

Health Consequences of Secondhand Smoke As we have known for many years, the health hazards of smoking are not restricted to those who smoke. The smoke coming from the burning end of a cigarette, so-called **secondhand smoke**, or environmental tobacco smoke (ETS), contains higher concentrations of ammonia, carbon monoxide, nicotine, and tar than does the smoke actually inhaled by the smoker. In 2006, the Surgeon General issued a report detailing the health hazards of secondhand smoke and published an update in 2014. The National Institute of Health has classified ETS as a known carcinogen, indicating that evidence has established a cause–effect relationship between ETS and cancer. The effects of ETS include the following:

- Nonsmokers can suffer lung damage, possibly permanent, from extended exposure to cigarette smoke. Those living with smokers are at greatest risk. Precancerous lung abnormalities have been observed in those living with smokers, and nonsmokers are at greater risk for developing cardiovascular disease and lung cancer. In addition, some nonsmokers have allergic reactions to the smoke from burning tobacco.
- Babies of women exposed to secondhand smoke during pregnancy are more likely to be born prematurely, to have lower birth weights, and to have birth defects.
- Children of smokers are more likely to have upper respiratory infections, asthma, bronchitis, and inner-ear infections than are their peers whose parents do not smoke. Secondhand smoke can cause sudden infant death syndrome (SIDS).

The Surgeon General has stated that the best form of prevention for exposure to secondhand smoke is to promote smoke-free environments as there is really no safe level of exposure to secondhand smoke (USDHHS, 2006, 2014). As of 2014, 25 states[1] plus the District of Columbia received a grade of A from the American Lung Association for their strong smoke-free laws which ban smoking in nearly all public places, including restaurants and bars (http://www.stateoftobaccocontrol.org).

E-Cigarettes Electronic cigarettes or e-cigarettes look like cigarettes except that they are made of plastic or metal and are filled with liquid nicotine that is mixed with other chemicals and often with flavors. They are battery operated (hence the "e" for electronic) and work by heating up the nicotine liquid concoction so that people inhale and exhale the vapor. The term *vaping* has come to mean smoking an e-cigarette. Some models include a light at the end of the tube to mimic a lit cigarette. These are marketed as safe alternatives to cigarettes because they do not contain the tar and carbon monoxide that come from burning cigarettes. In fact, e-cigarettes are often not called cigarettes at all, but are instead called vape pipes, vaping pens, hookah pens, or e-hookahs. Although it is true that these devices do not have to contain nicotine (many are sold with flavored water vapor), they can all be used to deliver liquid nicotine to users.

E-cigarettes are becoming more popular even though we do not yet know about the safety of these products.

In a study of over 100,000 college students in the United States, researchers reported that 30 percent of them had tried an e-cigarette at least once (Primack, Shensa, Kim et al., 2013). In this large sample, twice as many students (16.8 percent) were using cigarettes than e-cigarettes (8.4 percent).

Some argue that e-cigarettes are safer alternatives to cigarettes containing tar and other carcinogens and that they may assist people who want to quit smoking actual cigarettes, a topic we return to later in the chapter. Others argue that nicotine is still an extremely addictive drug. Because they are so new, very little research has been done on the safety of these products, although several studies are currently underway. The Food and Drug Administration (FDA) proposed new regulations for e-cigarettes in 2014. These regulations would treat e-cigarettes like any other regulated tobacco product, thus making it illegal to sell them to children under the age of 18, requiring warning labels about nicotine's addictive properties, and calling for scientific evidence to support any claims about their safety relative to other tobacco products. A handful of states, counties, and cities have already imposed bans on e-cigarettes in the workplace, restaurants, and bars.

Marijuana

Marijuana consists of the dried and crushed leaves and flowering tops of the hemp plant, *Cannabis sativa*. It is most often smoked, but it may be chewed, prepared as a tea, or eaten in baked goods. **Hashish,** much stronger than marijuana, is produced by removing and drying the resin exudate of the tops of cannabis plants. In DSM-5, cannabis use disorder is the category name that includes marijuana.

Synthetic marijuana contains artificially created chemicals similar to those contained in cannabis. These chemicals are typically sprayed onto inert plant materials and placed in small packages and sold under names such as Spice or K2. Synthetic marijuana was made illegal in 2011, but its use among high school students has remained at about 11 percent (Johnston, O'Malley, Bachman et al., 2014). Little is known about these synthetic drugs because they are so new; they will be the focus

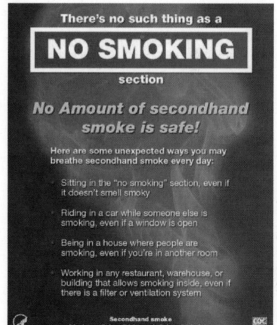

The Surgeon General's report from 2006 noted that no amount of secondhand smoke is safe.

[1]Arizona, California, Colorado, Delaware, Hawaii, Illinois, Iowa, Kansas, Maine, Maryland, Massachusetts, Minnesota, Montana, Nebraska, New Jersey, New Mexico, New York, Ohio, Oregon, Rhode Island, South Dakota, Utah, Vermont, Washington, and Wisconsin.

of much future research given their popularity among young people and concerns about their effects.

Prevalence of Marijuana Use Marijuana is the most frequently used illicit drug. In 2012, nearly 19 million people over the age of 12 reported using marijuana, and it is the most commonly used drug across all age groups (SAMHSA, 2013). (See Figure 10.3 for data on usage from 2003 to 2012 among young adults.) The prevalence is higher among men than women, with nearly twice as many men (11.8 percent) than women (6.6 percent) ages 18 and older reporting use in the past month in 2012. In 2012, marijuana use was roughly equivalent across racial and ethnic groups (SAMHSA, 2013). Daily use of marijuana increased from 5.1 million in 2007 to 7.6 million in 2012. This increase may reflect that fact that marijuana use is currently legal for all uses in adults over the age of 21 in two states (Colorado and Washington) and is approved for medical use in many more states, topics we return to later.

Effects of Marijuana As with most other drugs, legal or not, marijuana use has its risks. Generally, the more we learn about a drug, the less benign it turns out to be, at least for some people, and marijuana is no exception (see Focus on Discovery 10.1).

The major active chemical in marijuana is delta-9-tetrahydrocannabinol (THC). The amount of THC in marijuana is variable, but marijuana is more potent now than it was three decades ago (Zimmer & Morgan, 1995). In addition, users smoke more now than in the past (e.g., a "blunt" contains more cannabis than a joint).

Psychological Effects The intoxicating effects of marijuana, like those of most drugs, depend in part on the potency and size of the dose. Smokers of marijuana find that it makes them feel relaxed and sociable. Large doses have been reported to bring rapid shifts in emotion, to dull attention, to fragment thoughts, to impair memory, and to give the sense that time is moving more slowly. Extremely heavy doses have sometimes been found to induce hallucinations and other effects similar to those of hallucinogens, including extreme panic, sometimes arising from the belief that a frightening experience will never end. Dosage can be difficult to regulate because it may take up to half an hour after smoking marijuana for its effects to appear; many users thus get much higher than intended.

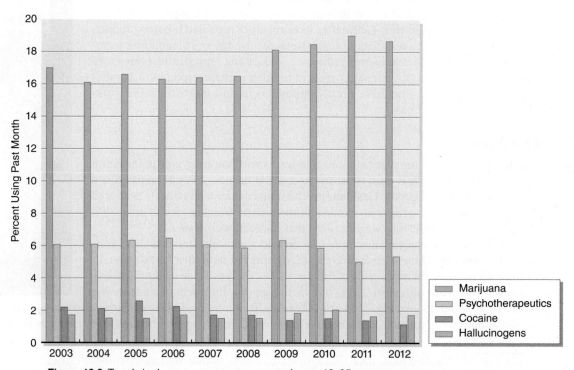

Figure 10.3 Trends in drug use among young people age 18–25. (SAMHSA, 2013.)

FOCUS ON DISCOVERY 10.1

Is Marijuana a Gateway Drug?

The so-called stepping-stone, or gateway, theory of marijuana use has been around for a long time. According to this view, marijuana is dangerous not only in itself but also because it is a first step for young people on the path to becoming addicted to other drugs, such as heroin.

Is there evidence that marijuana is indeed a gateway to more serious substance use? Overall, the evidence suggests that the answer to this question is no. For example, about 40 percent of regular marijuana users do *not* go on to use such drugs as heroin and cocaine (Stephens, Roffman, & Simpson, 1993). So if by *gateway* we mean that escalation to a more serious drug is inevitable, then marijuana is not a gateway drug. However, we do know that many, but far from all, who use heroin and cocaine began their drug experimentation with marijuana. And at least in the United States and New Zealand, users of marijuana are more likely

Most people who use marijuana do not go on to use heroin, but many heroin users do begin their drug use with marijuana.

© Bubbles Photolibrary/Alamy

than nonusers to experiment later with heroin and cocaine (Fergusson & Horwood, 2000; Kandel, 2002; Miller & Volk, 1996).

Thus, even though marijuana use often precedes other drug use, it does not appear to *cause* later drug use, as the term *gateway* implies. Rather, it may be that marijuana is the first drug to be tried because it is more socially acceptable than other drugs. Time will tell whether legalization of marijuana will increase the likelihood of other serious drug use, as some critics of legalization argue, or will instead be more like cigarettes and alcohol—legal drugs that are associated with other drug use but not necessarily the gateway to their use.

Accumulated scientific evidence indicates that marijuana can interfere with cognitive functioning, including areas such as planning, decision making, working memory, and problem solving (Crean, Crane, & Mason, 2011). Does chronic use of marijuana affect cognitive functioning even when the person is not using the drug? Unfortunately, not many well-controlled studies have been conducted to address this question. One large longitudinal study of people from New Zealand assessed marijuana use at five time points between the ages of 18 and 38. Neuropsychological functioning was assessed at age 13 prior to initiation of marijuana use and again at age 38. The researchers found that those people who persistently met the criteria for cannabis dependence (defined as the number of assessment periods out of five in which people met the diagnostic criteria for cannabis dependence) had decrements in IQ points and poorer performance on tests assessing working memory and processing compared to people who never used marijuana or did so less persistently (Meier, Caspi, Ambler et al., 2012). This was particularly true for those who began using marijuana chronically as adolescents. Those people in the study who used marijuana but not regularly showed no decline in IQ or impairment on the neuropsychological tests.

Studies have also demonstrated that being high on marijuana impairs complex psychomotor skills necessary for driving. Poor performance after smoking one or two marijuana cigarettes containing 2 percent THC can persist for up to 8 hours after a person believes he or she is no longer high. This creates the danger that people will drive when they are not functioning adequately.

Physical Consequences   The short-term effects of marijuana include bloodshot and itchy eyes, dry mouth and throat, increased appetite, reduced pressure within the eye, and somewhat raised blood pressure.

We know that the long-term use of marijuana can impair lung structure and function (Grinspoon & Bakalar, 1995). Even though marijuana users smoke far fewer cigarettes than do tobacco smokers, most inhale marijuana smoke more deeply and retain it in their lungs for much longer periods of time. Since marijuana has some of the same carcinogens found in tobacco, its harmful effects are greater than would be expected were only the absolute number of cigarettes or pipefuls considered. For example, one marijuana cigarette smoked in the typical way is the equivalent of five tobacco cigarettes in carbon monoxide intake, four in tar intake, and ten in terms of damage to cells lining the airways (Sussman, Stacy, Dent et al., 1996).

How does marijuana affect the brain? In the early 1990s, researchers identified two cannabinoid brain receptors, called CB1 and CB2 (Matsuda, Lolait, Brownstein et al., 1990; Munro, Thomas, Abu-Shaar et al., 1993). CB1 receptors are found throughout the body and the brain, with a particularly high number in the hippocampus, an important region of the brain for learning and memory. Based on accumulating evidence, researchers have concluded that the cognitive problems associated with marijuana use are linked to the effects of marijuana on these receptors in the hippocampus (e.g., Sullivan, 2000).

A brain imaging study using PET scanning (see Chapter 2) found that smoking marijuana was associated with increased blood flow to regions in the brain often associated with emotion, including the amygdala and the anterior cingulate. Decreased blood flow was observed in regions of the temporal lobe that have been associated with auditory attention, and participants in this study who were high on marijuana performed poorly on a listening task (O'Leary, Block, Flaum et al., 2000). These findings might help explain some of the psychological effects associated with marijuana use, including changes in emotion and attentional capabilities.

Demonstrators advocate the legalization of marijuana.

Is marijuana addictive? Here the evidence is mixed. Controlled observations have confirmed that habitual use of marijuana does produce tolerance (Compton, Dewey, & Martin, 1990). Whether long-term users experience withdrawal is less clear, though surveys and laboratory studies conducted in the past 10 years suggest that withdrawal symptoms, such as restlessness, anxiety, tension, stomach pains, and insomnia, can occur (Rey et al., 2004).

Therapeutic Effects and Legalization Research since the 1970s has established a number of therapeutic uses for marijuana. These include reduction in the nausea and loss of appetite that accompany chemotherapy for some people with cancer, glaucoma, chronic pain, muscle spasms, seizures, and discomfort from AIDS.

The potential benefits of smoking marijuana were confirmed in reports by a panel of experts to the National Institutes of Health (NIH, 1997) and a committee of the Institute of Medicine, a branch of the National Academy of Sciences (Institute of Medicine, 1999). The Institute of Medicine report recommended that people with "debilitating symptoms" or terminal illnesses be allowed to smoke marijuana under close medical supervision for up to 6 months; the rationale for smoking was based on findings that THC swallowed by mouth does not provide the same relief as does smoking. But the Institute of Medicine report also emphasized the dangers of smoking per se and urged the development of alternative delivery systems, such as inhalers.

California was the first state to pass a law making medical use of marijuana legal in 1996. Since then, 22 other states as well as the District of Columbia have approved the use of marijuana for medical purpose, and legislation is pending in three other states.[2] As noted earlier, in 2012, two states (Colorado and Washington) legalized all use of marijuana, and sales began in 2014 under strict state regulations. These state laws are currently in conflict with a federal law that makes marijuana use illegal. Thus, state officials in these states will not prosecute people for using medical marijuana, even though federal officials may do so. The debate on this issue will likely continue for years to come as more and more states are considering legalization of all uses of marijuana for adults over the age of 21.

---

[2]States that have approved medical marijuana use are Alaska, Arizona, California, Colorado, Connecticut, Delaware, Hawaii, Illinois, Maine, Maryland, Massachusetts, Michigan, Minnesota, Montana, Nevada, New Hampshire, New Jersey, New Mexico, New York, Oregon, Rhode Island, Vermont, and Washington. Legislation was pending in 2014 for Florida, Ohio, and Pennsylvania.

Quick Summary

Alcohol and drug use is common in the United States. The DSM-5 lists substance use disorders for alcohol and many other substances, with severity determined by the number of symptoms present.

Withdrawal from alcohol can involve hallucinations and delirium tremens. People who use or are addicted to alcohol may use other drugs, particularly nicotine. Alcohol use is particularly high among college students; men are more likely to drink alcohol than women, and differences in alcohol use disorder by ethnicity have been observed. Even moderate drinking during pregnancy can be problematic.

Smoking remains widespread, though it has been on the decline. Cigarette smoking causes a number of illnesses, including several cancers, heart disease, and other lung diseases. Although more men smoke than women, the rates are the same among adolescent boys and girls. The ill effects of tobacco are greater for African Americans. Secondhand smoke, also called environmental tobacco smoke, is also linked to a number of serious health problems. E-cigarettes are rapidly becoming popular, particularly among young people. The health effects of these products are not yet known, but studies are underway.

Marijuana makes people feel relaxed and sociable, but it can also interfere with cognitive functioning. In addition, it has been linked to lung-related problems. It remains the most prevalently used drug, particularly among younger people. Men use it more than women. Users can develop tolerance to marijuana; it is less clear whether withdrawal symptoms occur after users stop smoking it. Marijuana also has therapeutic benefits, including for those suffering from the side effects of chemotherapy and for those with AIDS, glaucoma, seizures, chronic pain, and muscle spasms.

Check Your Knowledge 10.2

Fill in the blanks.
1. List three types of cancer that are caused by smoking.
2. Marijuana can have ——— effects on learning and memory; it is less clear if there are ——— effects.
3. List three of the therapeutic benefits of marijuana.

Opiates

The **opiates** include opium and its derivatives morphine, **heroin**, and codeine. This group of addictive drugs can, in moderate doses, relieve pain and induce sleep. They are coded in DSM-5 as opioid use disorder.

Opiates that can be legally prescribed as pain medications, including **hydrocodone** and **oxycodone,** have become drugs of abuse. Hydrocodone is most often combined with other drugs, such as acetaminophen (the active agent in Tylenol), to create prescription pain medicines such as Vicodin, Zydone, or Lortab. Oxycodone is found in medicines such as Percodan, Tylox, and OxyContin. Vicodin is one of the most commonly abused drugs containing hydrocodone, and OxyContin is one of the most commonly abused drugs containing oxycodone.

Prevalence of Opiate Abuse and Dependence There are enormous difficulties in gathering data, but the considered opinion is that more than half a million people in the United States are addicted to heroin, with an estimated 156,000 new users in 2012, a significant increase over the prior 5 years (SAMHSA, 2013). Fifty years ago, heroin users were primarily young men living in urban areas whose first opiate was heroin. Today, however, both men and women in less urban areas are using heroin, most often after first taking prescription pain medicines (Cicero, Ellis, Surratt et al., 2014).

The most commonly abused opiates are prescription pain medications that are taken for nonmedical purposes. The rates of abuse of these drugs have remained relatively stable since 2002. However, the numbers are not small. In 2012, 6.8 million people in the United States used pain medicines for nonmedical uses. And the number of people seeking treatment for dependence on pain medications, continues to increase, more than doubling between 2002 and 2012. More men

National Library of Medicine/Photo Researchers, Inc.

Heroin was synthesized from opium in 1874 and was soon added to a variety of medicines that could be purchased without prescription. This ad shows a teething remedy containing heroin. It probably worked.

than women abuse prescription pain medicines, and abuse is highest among European Americans and Native Americans (SAMHSA, 2013).

The illicit supply comes from prescriptions that are forged, stolen, or diverted to dealers on the black market. Initially, OxyContin came in a pill format with polymer coating that made it easy to dissolve or crush into a form that could then be injected or snorted. In 2010, an extended-release formula that is not as susceptible to crushing for injection replaced the polymer-coated pills. This may have contributed to the decline in numbers of people abusing Oxycontin from 2010 (566,000) to 2012 (358,000). OxyContin's effects are quite similar to those of heroin, so health professionals are concerned that people dependent on OxyContin who can no longer afford its hefty street price will turn to heroin, which is less expensive. As shown in Figure 10.4, visits to hospital emergency rooms after overdoses of hydrocodone and oxycodone products continue to rise, tripling between 2004 and 2011 (SAMHSA, 2013).

Psychological and Physical Effects Opiates produce euphoria, drowsiness, and sometimes a lack of coordination. Heroin and OxyContin also produce a "rush," a feeling of warm, suffusing ecstasy immediately after an intravenous injection. The user sheds worries and fears and has great self-confidence for 4 to 6 hours. However, the user then experiences a severe letdown, bordering on stupor.

Opiates produce their effects by stimulating neural receptors of the body's own opioid system (the body naturally produces opioids, called endorphins and enkephalins). Heroin, for example, is converted into morphine in the brain and then binds to opioid receptors, which are located throughout the brain. Some evidence suggests that a link between these receptors and the dopamine system is responsible for opiates' pleasurable effects. However, evidence from animal studies suggests that opiates may achieve their pleasurable effects via their action in the area of the brain called the nucleus accumbens, perhaps independently from the dopamine system (Koob, Caine, Hyytia et al., 1999).

Opiates are clearly addicting, for users develop tolerance and show withdrawal symptoms. Withdrawal from heroin may begin within 8 hours of the last injection, at least after high tolerance has built up. During the next few hours after withdrawal begins, the person typically experiences muscle pain, sneezing, and sweating; becomes tearful; and yawns a great deal. The symptoms resemble those of influenza. Within 36 hours, the withdrawal symptoms become more severe. There may be uncontrollable muscle twitching, cramps, chills alternating with excessive flushing and sweating, and a rise in heart rate and blood pressure. The person is unable to sleep, vomits, and has diarrhea. These symptoms typically persist for about 72 hours and then diminish gradually over a 5- to 10-day period.

People who abuse opiates face serious problems. In a 29-year follow-up of 500 people addicted to heroin, about 28 percent had died by age 40; half of these deaths were from homicide, suicide, or accident, and one-third were from overdose (Hser, Anglin, & Powers, 1993). The social consequences of using an illegal drug are also serious. The drug itself and the process of obtaining it become the center of the person's existence, governing all activities and social relationships. The high cost of drugs—users

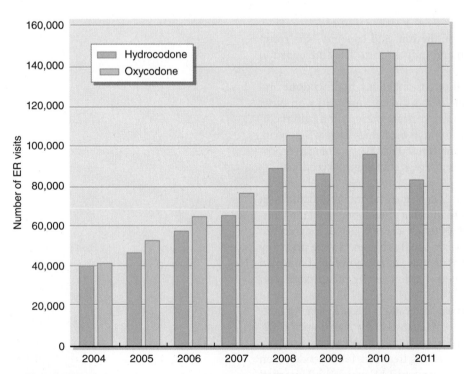

Figure 10.4 Emergency room visits after overdoses of hydrocodone and oxycodone continue to increase. In 2002, the numbers for hydrocodone and oxycodone were 25,000 and 21,000 respectively. (SAMHSA, 2013.)

Clinical Descriptions, Prevalence, and Effects of Substance Use Disorders **299**

Clinical Case: James

James was a 27-year-old man who had been addicted to heroin for 7 years. He first tried heroin during his time in the Marine Corps. Unable to control his habit, he was dishonorably discharged from the Marines a year later. He lived with his family for a short time, but after stealing money and valuables to support his habit, he was asked to leave the house. He then began living on the street, panhandling for money to support his habit. He also donated blood platelets when he was physically able. Over the years, James lost a tremendous amount of weight and became quite malnourished. He was over 6 feet tall, but he weighed only 150 pounds. Food wasn't a priority on most days, though he was usually able to gather a meal of scraps from the local diner. James tried to get into several rehabilitation programs, but they required that he remain free of heroin for at least a week before he could be admitted. James was able to resist for a day or two, but then withdrawal symptoms would begin, making it too painful to continue without the drug. A friend from the streets, formerly addicted to heroin, had recently helped James get to a methadone clinic. James tried methadone for a few weeks but was unable to tolerate the long waits outside the clinic each morning and the shame of being stared at by people passing on their way to work. Still, having been free of heroin for over a week, James gained admittance to a residential treatment program. One of the physicians at the program prescribed a newly approved medication called Suboxone that eased the discomfort of heroin withdrawal while also replacing the cravings for heroin. James no longer needed to go to the methadone clinic, and he was getting job training at the treatment program. He was hopeful that he would shake his habit for good.

must often spend upwards of $200 per day for opiates—often drives users into acquiring money through illegal activities, such as theft, prostitution, or selling drugs.

An additional problem associated with intravenous drug use is exposure, through sharing needles, to infectious agents such as the human immunodeficiency virus (HIV), which causes AIDS. Notably, there is good consensus among scientists that needle exchange programs reduce needle sharing and the spread of infectious agents associated with intravenous drug use (Gibson, 2001; Yoast, Williams, Deitchman et al., 2001). In 2009, the U.S. Congress lifted a 21-year ban on federal funding for needle exchange programs.

Stimulants

Stimulants act on the brain and the sympathetic nervous system to increase alertness and motor activity. Amphetamines are synthetic stimulants; cocaine is a natural stimulant extracted from the coca leaf. Focus on Discovery 10.2 discusses a less risky and more prevalently used stimulant, caffeine.

Amphetamines Amphetamines such as benzedrine, dexedrine, and methedrine produce their effects by causing the release of norepinephrine and dopamine and blocking the reuptake of these neurotransmitters. **Amphetamines** are taken orally or intravenously and can be addicting. Wakefulness is heightened, intestinal functions are inhibited, and appetite is reduced—hence their use in dieting. The heart rate quickens, and blood vessels in the skin and mucous membranes constrict. The person becomes alert, euphoric, and outgoing and is possessed of seemingly boundless energy and self-confidence. Larger doses can make a person nervous, agitated, and confused; other symptoms include palpitations, headaches, dizziness, and sleeplessness. Sometimes heavy users become extremely suspicious and hostile, to the extent that they can be dangerous to others.

Tolerance to amphetamines develops rapidly, so more and more of the drug is required to produce the stimulating effect. One study has demonstrated tolerance after just 6 days of repeated use (Comer, Hart, Ward et al., 2001).

FOCUS ON DISCOVERY 10.2

Our Tastiest Addiction—Caffeine

What may be the world's most popular drug is seldom viewed as a drug at all, and yet it has strong effects, produces tolerance in people, and even subjects habitual users to withdrawal (Hughes, Higgins, Bickel et al., 1991). Users and nonusers joke about it, and most readers of this book have probably had some this very day. We are, of course, referring to **caffeine**, a substance found in coffee, tea, cocoa, cola and other soft drinks, some cold remedies, and some diet pills.

Two cups of coffee, containing between 150 and 300 milligrams of caffeine, affect most people within half an hour. Metabolism, body temperature, and blood pressure all increase; urine production goes up, as most of us will attest; there may be hand tremors, appetite can diminish, and, most familiar of all, sleepiness is warded off. Extremely large doses of caffeine can cause headache, diarrhea, nervousness, severe agitation, even convulsions and death. Death, though, is virtually impossible unless the person grossly overuses tablets containing

The caffeine found in coffee, tea, and soft drinks is probably the world's favorite drug.

caffeine, because the drug is excreted by the kidneys without any appreciable accumulation.

Although it has long been recognized that drinkers of very large amounts of caffeinated coffee daily can experience withdrawal symptoms when consumption ceases, people who drink no more than two cups of coffee a day can suffer from headaches, fatigue, and anxiety if caffeine is withdrawn from their daily diet (Silverman, Evans, Strain et al., 1992), and these symptoms can interfere with social and occupational functioning. These findings are disturbing because more than three-quarters of Americans consume a little more than two cups of regular coffee a day (Roan, 1992). And although parents usually deny their children access to coffee and tea, they often do allow them to imbibe caffeine-laden soft drinks, hot chocolate, and cocoa, and to eat chocolate candy and chocolate and coffee ice cream. Thus, our addiction to caffeine can begin to develop as early as 6 months of age, the form of it changing as we move from childhood to adulthood.

Clinical Case: Anton

Anton, a 37-year-old man, had just been arrested for a parole violation: stealing a package of string cheese from a convenience store. He was also found to be under the influence of methamphetamine. Two months earlier, he had been released from prison after serving time for petty theft and for purchasing methamphetamine. He was determined to remain out of prison, but his cravings for meth were so intense that he was unable to abide by the terms of his parole. He had been using meth since he was 26 years old and had been arrested numerous times for drug-related offenses, including prostitution (to get money to support his habit).

Methamphetamine The most commonly abused stimulant drug is an amphetamine derivative called **methamphetamine.** Abuse of this drug skyrocketed in the 1990s. However, between 2006 and 2012, the number of people who reported using methamphetamine decreased from over 700,000 to 440,000 (SAMHSA, 2013).

Men tend to abuse methamphetamine more often than women in contrast with abuse of other amphetamines, where few gender differences occur. Methamphetamine is used (and manufactured) in small towns in the United States as much as, if not more than, in big cities. The loss of manufacturing jobs in rural towns along with consolidation of the American food business into a few big conglomerates instead of many smaller family farms may have contributed to a rise in methamphetamine use (Redding, 2009).

Like other amphetamines, methamphetamine can be taken orally, intravenously, or intranasally (i.e., by snorting). In a clear crystal form, the drug is often referred to as "crystal meth" or "ice." Craving for methamphetamine is particularly strong, often lasting several years after use is discontinued. Craving is also a reliable predictor of later use (Hartz, Frederick-Osborne, & Galloway, 2001). As with other amphetamines, users get an immediate high, or rush, that can last for hours. This includes feelings of euphoria as well as changes to the body, such as increases in blood flow to the heart and other organs and an increase in body temperature. The high eventually levels off (the "shoulder"), and then it comes crashing down ("tweaking"). Not only do the good feelings crash, but the person also becomes very agitated. Physiological dependence on methamphetamine often includes both tolerance and withdrawal.

Several animal studies have indicated that chronic use of methamphetamine causes damage to the brain, affecting both the dopamine and the serotonin systems (Frost & Cadet, 2000). Neuroimaging studies have found similar effects in the human brain, particularly in the dopamine system. For example, one study of chronic meth users found damage to the hippocampus (see Figure 10.5). The volume of the hippocampus was smaller among chronic meth users, which correlated with poorer performance on a memory test (Thompson, Hayashi, Simon et al., 2004).

In a different study, men who were in treatment for methamphetamine dependence participated in a laboratory task of decision making while having their brains scanned with fMRI (Paulus, Tapert, & Schuckit, 2005). The researchers found that lower activation in several brain areas (dorsolateral prefrontal cortex, insula, and areas of the temporal and parietal lobes) during the decision-making task predicted relapse to methamphetamine abuse 1 year after treatment. It seems obvious that poor decision making might put one at higher risk for relapse. This study also showed that the brain areas that contribute to sound decision making are disrupted in some people who are dependent on methamphetamine. What is less clear is whether the methamphetamine damaged these areas or whether these areas were damaged before methamphetamine use began.

A caveat should be noted here. One difficulty with conducting these types of studies is finding participants who use only the drug of interest (in this case, methamphetamine) so that any observed effects can be linked to that drug and not to others. However, it is difficult to find meth users who have not at some point used other substances, particularly alcohol and nicotine. For example, in one of the studies described earlier, the meth users did not differ from the control group in alcohol consumption, but they did smoke more (Thompson et al., 2004). Nevertheless, it seems clear that the deleterious effects of methamphetamine are many and serious.

Cocaine The drug **cocaine** comes from the leaves of the coca shrub. A form of cocaine, called **crack**, was developed in the mid-1980s and comes in a rock-crystal form that is then heated, melted, and smoked. The name *crack* comes from the crackling sound the rock makes when being heated. Crack is cheaper than cocaine and is used predominantly in urban areas.

Cocaine use in general soared in the 1970s and 1980s, increasing by more than 260 percent between 1974 and 1985. Today, use of cocaine is much less than it was 30 years ago. Use declined between 2002 and 2012, with the percentage of people over the age of 12 using cocaine dropping from 2 percent to 1.1 percent (see Figure 10.3). In 2012, 1.6 million people over the age of 12 reported using cocaine, down from 2.4 million in 2006 (SAMHSA, 2013). Use of crack is also declining. The number of people using crack for the first time decreased from 337,000 in 2002 to 84,000 in 2012 (SAMHSA, 2013). Men use cocaine and crack more often than women do.

Cocaine acts rapidly on the brain, blocking the reuptake of dopamine in mesolimbic areas. Cocaine yields pleasurable states because dopamine left in the synapse facilitates neural transmission. Self-reports of pleasure induced by cocaine are strongly related to the extent to which cocaine has blocked dopamine reuptake (Volkow, Wang, Fischman et al., 1997). Cocaine can increase sexual desire and produce feelings of self-confidence, well-being, and indefatigability. An overdose may bring on chills, nausea, and insomnia, as well as strong paranoid feelings

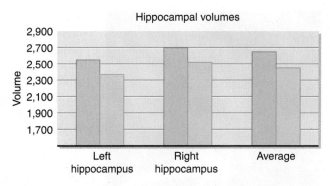

Figure 10.5 Results from an fMRI study showing that those who abused methamphetamine (green bars) had smaller hippocampal volume (size) than those in the control group (blue bars) who did not abuse methamphetamine. [Adapted from Thompson et al. (2004).]

A coca plant. The leaves contain about I percent cocaine.

Cocaine can be smoked, swallowed, injected, or snorted as shown here.

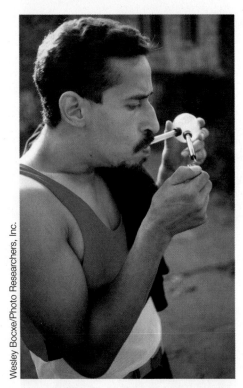

Crack use is highest in urban areas.

and terrifying hallucinations of insects crawling beneath the skin. Chronic use can lead to heightened irritability, impaired social relationships, paranoid thinking, and disturbances in eating and sleeping. Some, but not all, users develop tolerance to cocaine, requiring a larger dose to achieve the same effect. Other users may become more sensitive to cocaine's effects, which are believed to be a contributing factor in deaths after a fairly small dosage. Stopping cocaine use appears to cause severe withdrawal symptoms.

Cocaine is a vasoconstrictor, causing the blood vessels to narrow. As users take larger and larger doses of the purer forms of cocaine, they are more often rushed to emergency rooms and may die of an overdose, often from a heart attack. In 2011, there were over 500,000 cocaine-related visits to the emergency room (SAMHSA, 2013), nearly four times higher than the number of visits for prescription pain pills (see Figure 10.4). Cocaine also increases a person's risk for stroke and causes cognitive impairments, such as difficulty paying attention and remembering.

Because of its strong vasoconstricting properties, cocaine poses special dangers in pregnancy, for the blood supply to the developing fetus may be compromised. An MRI study compared the gray matter (i.e., neural tissue of the brain) volume of adolescents who were and were not exposed to cocaine prenatally. Adolescents who had been exposed to cocaine prenatally were found to have lower volumes in areas of the frontal cortex and nearby regions that aid in cognitive control and emotion regulation compared to adolescents who were not prenatally exposed to cocaine (Rando, Chaplin, Potenza et al., 2013). However, the prenatally exposed adolescents were also more likely to have initiated their own substance use, so it is impossible to tell if the different brain sizes were the result of prenatal cocaine exposure or their own substance use. It is likely that both contributed.

Cocaine can be sniffed (snorted), smoked in pipes or cigarettes, swallowed, or even injected into the veins; some heroin users mix the two drugs. In the 1970s, cocaine users in the United States began to separate, or free, a component of cocaine by heating it with ether. When purified by this chemical process, the cocaine base—or freebase—produces very powerful effects because it is absorbed so rapidly. Like most drugs, the faster it is absorbed, the quicker and more intense the high. Freebase is usually smoked in a water pipe or sprinkled on a tobacco or marijuana cigarette. It is rapidly absorbed into the lungs and carried to the brain in a few seconds, where it induces an intense 2-minute high, followed by restlessness and discomfort.

Hallucinogens, Ecstasy, and PCP

LSD and Other Hallucinogens The term **hallucinogen** refers to the main effects of such drugs, hallucinations. Unlike the hallucinations in schizophrenia, however, these are usually recognized by the person as being caused by the drug. More men than women use hallucinogens, and among youths between the ages of 12 and 17, African Americans and Asian Americans are less likely to use them than Native Americans, European Americans, or Hispanics (SAMHSA, 2013).

The use of one hallucinogen, **LSD** (lysergic acid diethylamide), peaked in the 1960s; by the 1980s, only 1 or 2 percent of people could be classified as regular users. In 2012, there were 421,000 new users (SAMHSA, 2013). There is no evidence of withdrawal symptoms during abstinence, but tolerance appears to develop rapidly (McKim, 1991).

In addition to hallucinations, LSD can alter a person's sense of time (it seems to go slowly). A person using LSD may have sharp mood swings but can also experience an expanded consciousness such that he or she seems to appreciate sights and sounds like never before.

Many users experience intense anxiety after taking LSD, in part because the perceptual experiences and hallucinations can provoke fears that they are "going crazy." For some, these anxieties unfold into full-blown panic attacks. The anxiety usually subsides as the drug is metabolized.

Flashbacks are visual recurrences of perceptual experiences after the physiological effects of the drug have worn off. In DSM-5, the category hallucinogen persisting perception disorder

Clinical Case: Tamara

Tamara tried Ecstasy (X) for the first time when she was a freshman in college. She went to her first rave, and a friend gave her a pill she thought was a Sweet Tart. Within a short period of time, she began to feel almost magical, as if she was seeing everything around her in a new light. She felt incredibly close to her friends and even to men and women she had just met. Hugging and close dancing were intensely pleasurable, in a completely new way. A few days

after the party, she asked her friend about the "Sweet Tart" and found out how she could obtain more. But the next time she tried X, she was unable to achieve the same pleasurable feelings. Instead, she felt more subdued, even anxious. After several more times using X, she noticed that despite her enthusiasm and even craving for the effects, she found instead that she felt a little depressed and anxious, even several days after taking the drug.

involves reexperiences of flashbacks and other perceptual symptoms that occurred during hallucinogen use, even though the drug is no longer used.

Ecstasy and PCP The hallucinogen-like substance **Ecstasy** is made from **MDMA** (methylenedioxymethamphetamine). Not until the 1970s were the psychoactive properties of MDMA reported in the scientific literature. Ecstasy became illegal in 1985.

Ecstasy contains compounds from both the hallucinogen and amphetamine families, but it is currently classified as "other hallucinogen use disorder" in DSM-5. Ecstasy remains popular on college campuses and in clubs. Focus on Discovery 10.3 discusses the use and effects of another club drug, nitrous oxide. It can be taken in pill form, but MDMA is often mixed with other substances (e.g., caffeine) or drugs (e.g., LSD, ketamine, talcum powder), making the effects vary dramatically. A purer powder version of Ecstasy is referred to as Molly. Whether it is actually purer requires a leap of faith, as powder can also be mixed

FOCUS ON DISCOVERY 10.3

Nitrous Oxide—Not a Laughing Matter

Nitrous oxide is a colorless gas that has been available since the nineteenth century. Within seconds, it induces light-headedness and a state of euphoria in most people; for some, important insights seem to flood the mind. Many people find otherwise mundane events and thoughts irresistibly funny, hence the nickname *laughing gas.*

Many people have received nitrous oxide at a dentist's office to facilitate relaxation and otherwise make a potentially uncomfortable and intimidating dental procedure more palatable. A major advantage of nitrous oxide over other analgesics and relaxants is that a person can return to a normal waking state within minutes of breathing enriched oxygen or normal air.

Nitrous oxide is no laughing matter.

Nitrous oxide fits in the broader category of inhalants and has been used recreationally since it first became available, although it has been illegal for many years in most states except as administered by appropriate health professionals. As with the other drugs examined in this chapter, illegality has not prevented unsupervised use. It is one of the most commonly used inhalants among teens (sniffing glue, gasoline, and paint are more prevalent), with rates of use as high as 22 percent among those who use inhalants (Wu, Pilowsky, & Schlenger, 2004). Sometimes called "hippie crack" or "whippets," nitrous oxide balloons are often combined with the use of Ecstasy and other drugs at parties with bright laser lights and loud dance music (i.e., at raves).

with other substances. Across all ages, use of Ecstasy was highest in 2001, with 1.8 million users. In 2012, 869,000 reported using in Ecstasy during the past year, down from 1.1 million in 2009 (SAMHSA, 2013). The average age of first use is around 20, a statistic that has remained stable since 2002.

Ecstasy acts primarily by contributing to both the release and the subsequent reuptake of serotonin (Huether, Zhou, & Ruther, 1997; Liechti, Baumann, Gamma et al., 2000; Morgan, 2000). Whether or not Ecstasy causes harm is still a topic of scientific debate. Some evidence suggests that it may have neurotoxic effects on the serotonin system (De Souza, Battaglia, & Insel, 1990; Gerra, Zaimovic, Ferri et al., 2000). It is difficult to say whether these toxic effects are directly due to drug use, since no studies in humans to date have assessed serotonin functioning both before and after Ecstasy use.

Users report that Ecstasy enhances intimacy and insight, improves interpersonal relationships, elevates mood and self-confidence, and promotes aesthetic awareness. It can also cause muscle tension, rapid eye movements, jaw clenching, nausea, faintness, chills or sweating, anxiety, depression, depersonalization, and confusion.

PCP, phencyclidine, often called *angel dust,* is coded as phencyclidine use disorder in DSM-5 and is in the chapter on hallucinogen-related disorders. The number of people trying PCP for the first time in 2012 was 90,000, down from 123,000 in 2002 but double the number in 2009 (SAMHSA, 2013).

PCP generally causes serious negative reactions, including severe paranoia and violence. Coma and death are also possible. PCP affects multiple neurotransmitters in the brain, and chronic use is associated with a variety of neuropsychological deficits. People who abuse PCP are likely to have used other drugs either before or concurrently with PCP, so it is difficult to sort out whether neuropsychological impairments are due solely to PCP, to other drugs, or to the combination.

David Seed Photography/Getty Images, Inc.

Ecstasy is a popular party drug but, like many drugs, is not free of ill effects.

Quick Summary

Opiates include heroin and other pain medications such as hydrocodone and oxycodone. Abuse of prescription pain medications has risen dramatically, and overdoses are common. Initial effects of opiates include euphoria; later, users experience a letdown. Death by overdose from opiates is a severe problem. Other problems include exposure to HIV and other infectious agents through the use of shared needles. Withdrawal is severe for opiates.

Amphetamines are stimulants that produce wakefulness, alertness, and euphoria. Men and women use these equally. Tolerance develops quickly. Methamphetamine is a synthesized amphetamine, and use increased dramatically after the 1990s but has leveled off in recent years. Methamphetamine can damage the brain, including

the hippocampus. Cocaine and crack remain serious problems. Cocaine can increase sexual desire, feelings of well-being, and alertness, but chronic use is associated with problems in relationships, paranoia, and trouble sleeping, among other things. The faster crack or cocaine is absorbed, the more quickly and intensely the person becomes high.

LSD was a popular hallucinogen in the 1960s and 1970s, often billed as a mind-expanding drug. The mind-expanding drug of the 1990s became Ecstasy. Although these drugs do not typically elicit withdrawal symptoms, tolerance can develop. Though Ecstasy use peaked in 2001, use of a purer form called Molly is on the rise. PCP remains a problem. This drug can cause severe paranoia and violence.

Check Your Knowledge 10.3

True or false?
1. Withdrawal from heroin begins slowly, days after use has been discontinued.
2. The use of OxyContin began in urban areas but quickly spread to rural areas.

3. Methamphetamine is a less potent form of amphetamine and so is less likely to be associated with brain impairment.
4. Ecstasy contains compounds associated with hallucinogens and amphetamines.

Etiology of Substance Use Disorders

Becoming physiologically dependent on a substance is a developmental process for some people. That is, some people begin with a positive attitude toward a substance, then start to experiment with using it, then begin using it regularly, then use it heavily, and finally become dependent on it (see Figure 10.6).

It appears that the factors that contribute to substance use disorders may depend on the point in the process that is being considered. For example, developing a positive attitude toward smoking and beginning to experiment with tobacco are strongly related to smoking by other family members (Robinson, Klesges, Zbikowski, et al., 1997). In contrast, becoming a regular smoker is more strongly related to smoking by peers and being able to acquire cigarettes readily (Robinson et al., 1997; Wang, Fitzhugh, Eddy, et al., 1997).

Although applicable in many cases, the developmental process approach does not account for all cases of substance use disorders. For example, some people have periods of heavy use of a substance—for example, alcohol—and then return to moderate use. Other people do not need a period of heavy use to become dependent on the substance, as in the case of methamphetamine. In the following sections, we discuss genetic, neurobiological, psychological, and sociocultural factors associated with substance use disorders. Keep in mind that these factors are likely to be differently related to different substances. Genetic factors, for example, may play a role in alcohol use disorder but may be less important in hallucinogen use disorder.

Genetic Factors

Much research has addressed the possibility that there is a genetic contribution to drug and alcohol use disorders. Several studies have shown that relatives and children of problem drinkers have higher-than-expected rates of alcohol use disorder (e.g., Chassin, Pitts, Delucia et al., 1999). Stronger evidence for genetic factors comes from twin studies, which have revealed greater concordance in identical twins than in fraternal twins for alcohol use disorder (McGue, Pickens, & Svikis, 1992), smoking (True, Xiam, Scherrer et al., 1999), heavy use of marijuana (Kendler & Prescott, 1998), and drug use disorders in general (Tsuang, Lyons, Meyer et al., 1998). Other behavioral genetics studies indicate that the genetic and shared environmental risk factors (see Chapter 2) for illicit drug use disorders may be rather nonspecific (Kendler, Jacobsen, Prescott et al., 2003). That is, genetic and shared environmental risk factors appear to be the same no matter what the drug (marijuana, cocaine, opiates, hallucinogens, sedatives, stimulants), and this appears to be true for both men and women (Kendler, Prescott, Myers et al., 2003).

Of course, genes do their work via the environment, and research has uncovered gene–environment relationships in alcohol and drug use disorders (Kendler, Chen, Dick et al., 2012). Among adolescents, peers appear to be particularly important environmental variables. For example, a large twin study in Finland found that heritability for alcohol problems among adolescents was higher among those teens who had a large number of peers who drank compared to those who had a smaller number of peers who drank (Dick, Pagan, Viken et al., 2007). The environment in this case was peer-group drinking behavior. Another study found that heritability for both alcohol and smoking among adolescents was higher for those teens whose best friend also smoked and drank (Harden, Hill, Turkheimer et al., 2008). In this case, the environment was best-friend behavior. Another study found that heritability for smoking was greater for teens who went to schools where the "popular crowd" smoked compared to schools where the popular students did not smoke (Boardman, Saint Onge, Haberstick et al., 2008).

The ability to tolerate large quantities of alcohol may be inherited for alcohol use disorder. That is, to become dependent on alcohol, a person usually has to be able to drink a lot. Some ethnic groups, such as Asians, may have a low rate of alcohol

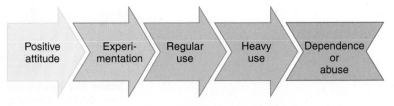

Figure 10.6 The process by which some people become dependent on a drug.

problems because of physiological intolerance, which is caused by an inherited deficiency in the enzymes involved in alcohol metabolism, called *alcohol dehydrogenases* or ADH. Mutations in genes called ADH2 and ADH3 code proteins for the ADH enzymes, and these genes have been linked with alcohol use disorders generally as well as among some Asian populations specifically (Edenberg, Xuie, Chen et al., 2006; Sher, Grekin, & Williams, 2005). About three-quarters of Asians experience unpleasant effects such as flushing (blood flow to the face) from small quantities of alcohol, which may protect them from becoming dependent on alcohol.

Research has also emerged on the mechanism through which genetics plays a role in smoking. Like most drugs, nicotine appears to stimulate dopamine release and inhibit its reuptake, and people who are more sensitive to these effects of nicotine are more likely to become regular smokers (Pomerleau, Collins, Shiffman et al., 1993). Research has examined a link between smoking and a gene that regulates the reuptake of dopamine called SLC6A3. One form of this gene has been related to a lower likelihood of smoking (Lerman, Caporaso, Audrain et al., 1999), a greater likelihood of quitting (Sabo, Nelson, Fisher et al., 1999), and greater sensitivity to smoking cues (e.g., cigarette pack) (Wetherill, Jagannathan, Lohoff et al., 2014). Research has also found that genes, such as *CYP2A6*, contribute to the body's ability to metabolize nicotine, with some people able to do this quickly and others more slowly. Slower nicotine metabolism means that nicotine stays in the brain longer. A longitudinal study of seventh graders showed that those adolescents who had genes linked with slower nicotine metabolism were more likely to become dependent on it 5 years later (O'Loughlin, Paradis, Kim et al., 2005). Other evidence has found that people with reduced activity in the *CYP2A6* gene smoke fewer cigarettes and are less likely to become dependent on nicotine (Audrain-McGovern & Tercyak, 2011). This is an interesting example of a gene polymorphism serving a protective function. More recent GWAS studies have identified SNPs (single nucleotide polymorphisms; see Chapter 2) that influence a certain nicotine receptor in the brain that are associated with nicotine dependence (Kendler et al., 2012).

Neurobiological Factors

You may have noticed that in our discussions of specific drugs, the neurotransmitter dopamine has almost always been mentioned. This is not surprising given that dopamine pathways in the brain are linked to pleasure and reward. Drug use typically results in rewarding or pleasurable feelings, and it is via the dopamine system that these feelings are produced. Research with both humans and animals shows that nearly all drugs, including alcohol, stimulate the dopamine systems in the brain (see Figure 10.7), particularly the mesolimbic pathway

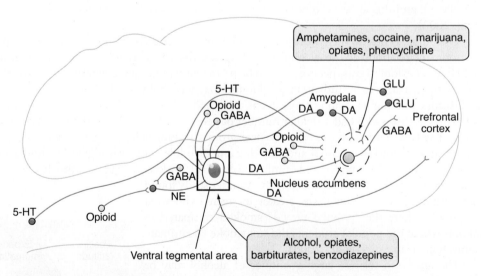

Figure 10.7 Reward pathways in the brain that are affected by different drugs. DA = dopamine; GABA = gamma-aminobutyric acid; GLU = glutamate; 5-HT = serotonin; NE = norepinephrine. [Adapted from Camí & Farré (2003).]

(Camí & Farré, 2003; Koob, 2008). Researchers have wondered, then, whether problems in the dopamine pathways in the brain might somehow account for why certain people become dependent on drugs.

One of the difficult issues to resolve is whether problems in the dopamine system may increase the vulnerability of some people to becoming dependent on a substance, sometimes called the "vulnerability model," or whether problems in the dopamine system are the consequence of taking substances (the "toxic effect model"). For drugs such as cocaine, there is currently research support for both views. Thus, this remains an important area to work out in future research.

Although people take drugs to feel good, they also take them to feel less bad. This is particularly true once a person becomes dependent on a substance, such as alcohol, methamphetamine, or heroin, whose withdrawal symptoms are excruciatingly unpleasant. In other words, people continue to take drugs to avoid the bad feelings associated with withdrawal. A substantial body of research with animals supports this motivation for drug-taking behavior (Koob & Le Moal, 2008); this research helps to explain why relapse is so common.

Cravings Investigators have proposed a neurobiological theory, referred to as the *incentive-sensitization theory,* which considers both the craving ("wanting") for drugs and the pleasure that comes with taking the drug ("liking") (Robinson & Berridge, 1993, 2003). According to this theory, the dopamine system linked to pleasure, or liking, becomes supersensitive not just to the direct effects of drugs but also to the cues associated with drugs (e.g., needles, spoons, rolling paper). This sensitivity to cues induces craving, or wanting, and people go to extreme lengths to seek out and obtain drugs. Over time, the liking for drugs decreases, but the wanting remains very intense. These investigators argue that the transition from liking to powerful wanting, accomplished by the drug's effects on brain pathways involving dopamine, is what maintains the addiction.

Many researchers study the neurobiology of wanting or craving. A number of laboratory studies have shown that cues for a particular drug can elicit responses not altogether unlike those associated with actual use of the drug. For example, those who were dependent on cocaine showed changes in physiological arousal, increases in cravings and "high" feelings, and increases in negative emotions in response to cues of cocaine, which consisted of audio- and videotapes of people preparing to inject or snort cocaine, compared to people not dependent on cocaine (e.g., Robbins, Kuncel, Shiner et al., 2000). Brain-imaging studies have shown that cues for a drug, such as a needle or a cigarette, activate the reward and pleasure areas of the brain implicated in drug use.

What about the psychology of craving? Do people who crave a substance more actually use it more, even if they are trying to quit? The answer appears to be yes. In a longitudinal study of heavy drinkers, the more participants reported wanting (craving) and liking samples of alcohol (carefully presented to reduce expectancies about alcohol) at a baseline assessment, the more alcohol use disorder symptoms they had six years later (King, McNamara, Hasin et al., 2014).

An experience sampling study of people who were trying to quit smoking showed that more craving was associated with more smoking (Berkman, Falk, & Lieberman, 2011). People who had just started a smoking-cessation program were given text messages 8 times a day for 21 consecutive days. At each text prompt, they reported how many cigarettes they had smoked, how much they were craving a cigarette, and how they were feeling. Reports of more craving predicted a greater likelihood of smoking when the participants received their next text. These investigators also examined participants' brain activation using fMRI during a task called the "go/no-go task." In this task, people are presented with letters one a time on a screen and are instructed to press a button when they see certain letters (e.g., L, V, T, N; the "go" part) but refrain from pressing the button when they see another letter (X; the "no-go" part). There are many more "go" trials than "no-go" trials, and thus it is challenging to keep from pressing the button during a "no-go" trial because people get into the habit of pressing the button many times in a row on the "go" trials. Areas of the brain that showed greater activation during "no-go" trials compared to "go" trials included the basal ganglia, inferofrontal gyrus, and pre-motor areas. People who showed greater activation in these areas during the task were better able to inhibit their button pressing; their brain was therefore likely doing a better job of providing the support for inhibiting a response when needed. In addition, greater activation in these brain regions was associated with less linkage between craving and smoking. That is, people who showed greater brain activation when inhibiting a button press were less likely to act on their cravings and begin to smoke again.

A large prospective study of heavy and light drinkers examined how wanting and liking during a lab session predicted actual drinking 2 years later. Heavy drinkers were people who had between 10 and 40 drinks a week and had more than one binge-drinking episode in most weeks; light drinkers were people who had between 1 and 5 drinks a week and had less than five binge-drinking episodes a year. The participants came to three lab sessions where they were given different amounts of alcohol and then rated wanting, liking, and sedation feelings. The researchers assessed participants' real-world drinking behavior 2 years later. Perhaps not surprisingly, they found that the heavy drinkers reported greater wanting and liking of alcohol during the laboratory sessions than did the light drinkers. By contrast, the light drinkers reported greater feelings of sedation than the heavy drinkers during the lab sessions. At follow-up, the heavy drinkers who reported greater wanting and liking for alcohol during the laboratory sessions were drinking more than the heavy drinkers who reported less liking and wanting during the lab sessions (King, de Wit, McNamara et al., 2011). Thus, even self-reports of wanting and liking are important for predicting drinking behavior.

Valuing the Short Term over the Long Term A related psychological and neurobiological model emphasizes the distinction between the value people place on short-term (immediate) versus long-term (delayed) rewards. People with a substance use disorder often value the immediate, even impulsive, pleasure and reward that comes from taking a drug more than delayed reward, such as a monthly paycheck from work.

Laboratory experiments to assess whether people value immediate or delayed rewards typically present people with choices of monetary rewards that are immediate but small (e.g., $1 now) or delayed but larger (e.g., $10 in a day). The extent to which people opt for the smaller, immediate reward can be calculated mathematically and is often called delay discounting. In other words, researchers can compute the extent to which people discount the value of larger, delayed rewards. People who are dependent on alcohol and drugs, such as opiates, nicotine, and cocaine, discount delayed rewards more steeply than do people not dependent on these substances (reviewed in Bickel, Koffarnus, Moody et al., 2014). One longitudinal study found that the extent of delay discounting predicted smoking initiation in adolescents that continued into early adulthood (Audrain-McGovern, Rodriguez, Epstein et al., 2009).

At the level of the brain, valuing immediate versus delayed rewards recruit different brain regions. Researchers have hypothesized that these brain regions compete with one another when people are faced with a decision of whether to take a drug. In fMRI studies, valuing the delayed reward is associated with activation of the prefrontal cortex; valuing the immediate reward is associated with activation in amygdala and nucleus accumbens (Bechara, 2005; Bickel, Miller, Yi et al., 2007).

Psychological Factors

In this section, we look at three other types of psychological factors that may contribute to the etiology of substance use disorders. First, we consider the effects of drugs (particularly alcohol and nicotine) on mood; we examine the situations in which a tension-reducing effect occurs and the role of cognition in this process. Second, we consider people's expectancies about the effects of substances on behavior, including beliefs about the prevalence with which a drug is used and about the health risks associated with using that drug. Third, we consider personality traits that may make it more likely for some people to use drugs heavily.

Mood Alteration It is generally assumed that one of the main psychological motives for using drugs is to alter mood—that is, drug use is reinforced because it enhances positive moods or diminishes negative ones. For example, most people believe that an increase in tension (e.g., because of a bad day at work) leads to increased alcohol consumption.

Laboratory studies have demonstrated that alcohol reduces self-reported and physiological indicators of anxiety, particularly when there is uncertainty about a negative event (e.g., having arrived home late after having drinks with friends, will you argue with your spouse?) (Bradford, Shapiro, & Curtin, 2013). In addition, research has found that alcohol lessens negative emotions such as stress and anxiety, but it also lessens positive emotions in response to anxiety-provoking situations (Curtin, Lang, Patrick et al., 1998; Stritzke, Patrick, & Lang, 1995). Longitudinal studies of stress and consumption have also provided support for this idea. For example, a longitudinal study of adolescent smokers found that increases in negative affect and negative life events were associated with increases in smoking (Wills, Sandy, & Yaeger, 2002). Other studies have found that life stress precedes alcohol-related relapses (e.g., Brown, Beck, Steer et al., 1990).

Studies of the tension-reducing properties of nicotine have yielded mixed findings, with some studies showing that nicotine reduces tension and others not finding this effect (Kassel, Stroud, & Paronis, 2003). The reasons for the mixed findings may have to do with a failure to consider where people are in their smoking behavior. Did they just start smoking? Are they regular smokers? Have they tried to quit and failed? Research suggests that people experience a greater reduction of tension and negative affect when starting to smoke than when regularly smoking or when in relapse after treatment (Kassel et al., 2003; Shiffman & Waters, 2004). Why might this be? A laboratory study examined the types of situations associated with a reduction in negative affect after smoking (Perkins, Karelitz, Conklin et al., 2010). Participants, who were regular smokers, had to give a speech, play a difficult computer game, abstain from smoking for 12 hours, and view disturbing pictures. The researchers found that people experienced the greatest reduction in negative affect after the abstinence condition. That is, smoking, after not being able to smoke, provided more relief from negative affect than it did after other stressful situations; thus, the situation is important to consider when thinking about whether smoking reduces negative affect.

Other studies suggest that it is the sensory aspect of smoking (i.e., inhaling), not nicotine, that is associated with tension reduction. In the study just described, participants experienced a reduction in negative affect regardless of whether they were smoking cigarettes with or without nicotine (Perkins et al., 2010). Another experimental study randomly assigned smokers to have cigarettes with or without nicotine (indistinguishable by participants) after a negative or positive mood was induced (Perkins, Ciccocioppo, Conklin et al., 2008). The researchers also manipulated smokers' expectancies. That is, some smokers expected and received a cigarette with nicotine; others expected nicotine but didn't get it; others expected no nicotine and didn't get it; and others expected no nicotine but received it anyway. Smoking reduced negative affect after both mood inductions, but this was true for smokers regardless of what they expected and actually received to smoke (i.e., a cigarette with or without nicotine). Instead, the effects of inhaling, whether or not there was nicotine, had the greatest association with reducing negative affect.

Subsequent research to examine why substances appear to reduce tension in some situations but not in others has focused on situations in which distraction is present. These studies find that tension reduction is more likely to occur when distractions are present (Curtin et al., 1998; Josephs & Steele, 1990; Steele & Josephs, 1988). Why might this be? Alcohol impairs cognitive processing and narrows our attention to the most immediately available cues, resulting in "alcohol myopia" (Steele & Josephs, 1990). In other words, an intoxicated person has less cognitive capacity and tends to use that capacity to focus on an immediate distraction, if available, rather than on tension-producing thoughts, with a resultant decrease in anxiety.

The benefits of distraction have also been documented for nicotine. Specifically, smokers who smoked in the midst of a distracting activity experienced a reduction in anxiety, whereas smokers who smoked without a distracting activity did not experience lessened anxiety (Kassel & Shiffman, 1997; Kassel & Unrod, 2000). However, alcohol and nicotine may increase tension when no distractions are present. For example, a person drinking alone may focus all his or her limited cognitive capacity on unpleasant thoughts, begin brooding, and become increasingly tense and anxious, a situation reflected in the expression "crying in one's beer."

Tension reduction is only one aspect of the possible effects of drugs on mood. Some people may use drugs to reduce negative affect, whereas others may use them to increase positive affect when they are bored (Cooper, Frone, Russell et al., 1995). In this case, increased drug use results from a high need for stimulation combined with expectancies that drugs will promote increased positive affect. These patterns have been confirmed among people who abuse alcohol and cocaine (Cooper et al., 1995; Hussong, Hicks, Levy et al., 2001).

Expectancies About Alcohol and Drug Effects If substances don't always reduce stress and tension, why do so many people who drink or take drugs believe that it helps them unwind? Expectation may play a role here—that is, people may drink after stress not because it actually reduces tension but because they expect it to do so. In support of this idea, studies have shown that people who expect alcohol to reduce stress and anxiety are more likely to be frequent users (Rather, Goldman, Roehrich et al., 1992; Sher, Walitzer, Wood et al., 1991; Tran, Haaga, & Chambless, 1997). Furthermore, the expectation that drinking will reduce anxiety increases drinking, which in turn makes the positive expectancies even stronger (Sher, Wood, Wood et al., 1996; Smith, Goldman, Greenbaum et al., 1995).

Expectations about alcohol influence whether people will drink.

Michael Blann/Getty Images, Inc.

Other research has shown that expectancies about a drug's effects—for example, the beliefs that a drug will stimulate aggression and increase sexual responsiveness—predict increased drug use in general (Stacy, Newcomb, & Bentler, 1991). Similarly, people who believe (falsely) that alcohol will make them seem more socially skilled are likely to drink more heavily than those who accurately perceive that alcohol can interfere with social interactions. In now-classic experiments demonstrating the power of expectancies, participants who believe they are consuming a quantity of alcohol when they are actually consuming an alcohol-free beverage subsequently become more aggressive (Lang, Goeckner, Adessor et al., 1975). Alcohol consumption is associated with increased aggression, but expectancies about alcohol's effects can also play a role (Bushman & Cooper, 1990; Ito, Miller, & Pollock, 1996). Thus, as we have seen in other contexts, cognitions can have a powerful effect on behavior.

The extent to which a person believes a drug is harmful and the perceived prevalence of use by others are also factors related to use. In general, the greater the perceived risk of a drug, the less likely it will be used. For example, the most commonly used illegal drug among high school students is marijuana; it is also the drug with the lowest perceived risk of harm in this age group (Johnston et al., 2014).

Personality Factors Personality factors that appear to be important in predicting the later onset of substance use disorders include high levels of negative affect, sometimes called *negative emotionality* or *neuroticism;* a persistent desire for arousal along with increased positive affect; and constraint, which refers to cautious behavior, harm avoidance, and conservative moral standards. One longitudinal study found that 18-year-olds who were low in constraint but high in negative emotionality were more likely to develop a substance use disorder as young adults (Krueger, 1999).

Another prospective longitudinal study investigated whether personality factors could predict the onset of substance use disorders in over 1000 male and female adolescents at age 17 and then again at age 20 (Elkins, King, McGue et al., 2006). Low constraint and high negative emotionality predicted the onset of alcohol, nicotine, and illicit drug use disorders for both men and women.

A large meta-analysis of both cross-sectional and prospective studies assessing personality traits and psychopathology, including substance use disorders, found strong associations with low levels of agreeableness and conscientiousness, and high levels of disinhibition (i.e., low constraint), as well as moderate associations with neuroticism (Kotov, Gamez, Schmidt et al., 2010). Current research is linking these personality factors with the neural circuits and genes that are associated with them (Belcher, Volkow, Moeller et al., 2014).

Sociocultural Factors

Sociocultural factors play a widely varying role in substance use disorders. People's interest in and access to drugs are influenced by peers, the media, and cultural norms about acceptable behavior.

At the broadest level, for example, we can look at great cross-national variation in substance consumption. Some research suggests that there are commonalities in substance use across countries. For example, a cross-national study of alcohol and drug use among high school students in 36 countries found that alcohol was the most common substance used across countries, despite great variation in the proportions of students who consumed alcohol, ranging from 32 percent in Zimbabwe to 99 percent in Wales (Smart & Ogburne, 2000). In all but two of the countries studied, marijuana was the next most commonly used drug. In those countries where marijuana was used most often (with more than 15 percent of high school students having ever used marijuana), there were also higher rates of use of amphetamines, Ecstasy, and cocaine.

Alcohol dependence is more prevalent in countries in which alcohol use is heavy.

Despite the commonalities across countries, other research documents cross-national differences in alcohol consumption. For example, high consumption rates have typically been found in wine-drinking societies, such as France, Spain, and Italy, where drinking alcohol regularly is widely accepted (deLint, 1978). Cultural attitudes and patterns of drinking thus influence the likelihood of drinking heavily and therefore of abusing alcohol. One finding that seems quite similar across different cultures is that men consume more alcohol than women. An analysis conducted by the International Research Group on Gender and Alcohol found that men drank more than women in Australia, Canada, the Czech Republic, Estonia, Finland, Israel, the Netherlands, Russia, Sweden, and the United States. Despite this consistency in gender differences, there was a large disparity across countries in the extent to which men drank more than women. For example, men drank three times more than women in Israel but only one and a half times more than women in the Netherlands (Wilsnack, Vogeltanz, Wilsnack et al., 2000). These findings suggest that cultural prescriptions about drinking by men and women are important to consider.

Ready availability of the substance is also a factor. For example, in wine-drinking societies, wine is present in many settings, even in university cafeterias. Also, rates of alcohol use disorder are high among bartenders and liquor store owners, people for whom alcohol is readily available (Fillmore & Caetano, 1980). Findings from the Monitoring the Future Study, an ongoing study begun in the 1960s that surveys over 50,000 high school students in the United States every year, indicate that the greater reported availability of particular drugs or alcohol corresponded to greater use of those drugs (Johnston et al., 2014). This is one of the reasons states raise taxes on alcohol and cigarettes so frequently. Of course, this tactic disproportionately affects the poor, which is not only unfair but does not necessarily target all who would benefit from substances being less available. Furthermore, it does not appear to work, at least for smoking, which is most prevalent among poorer people (Dwyer-Lindgren et al., 2014).

Family factors are important as well. For example, exposure to alcohol use by parents increases children's likelihood of drinking (Hawkins, Graham, Maguin et al., 1997). Unhappy marriages predicted the onset of alcohol use disorder in a study of nearly 2000 married couples (Whisman & Uebelacker, 2006). Acculturation into American society may interact with family factors for people of other cultural and ethnic backgrounds. For example, a study of middle school Hispanic students in New York found that children who spoke English with their parents were more likely to smoke marijuana than children who spoke Spanish (Epstein, Botvin, & Diaz, 2001). Longitudinal studies have shown that a lack of parental monitoring leads to increased association with drug-abusing peers and subsequent higher use of drugs (Chassin, Curran, Hussong et al., 1996; Thomas, Reifman, Barnes et al., 2000).

The social setting in which a person operates can also affect substance use. For example, studies of smokers in daily life show that they are more likely to smoke with other smokers than with nonsmokers. In addition, smoking was more likely to occur in or outside bars and restaurants, or at home, rather than in the workplace or in others' homes (Shiffman, Gwaltney, Balabanis et al., 2002; Shiffman, Paty, Gwaltney et al., 2004).

Other studies showed that having friends who smoke predicts smoking. In longitudinal studies, peer-group identification in the seventh grade predicted smoking in the eighth grade (Sussman, Dent, McAdams et al., 1994) and increased drug use over a 3-year period (Chassin et al., 1996). Peer influences are also important in promoting alcohol and marijuana use (Hussong et al., 2001; Stice, Barrera, & Chassin, 1998; Wills & Cleary, 1999).

These findings support the idea that social networks influence a person's drug or alcohol behavior. However, other evidence indicates that people who are inclined to develop substance use disorders may actually select social networks that conform to their own drinking or drug use patterns. Thus, we have two broad explanations for how the social environment is related to substance use disorders: a social influence model and a social selection model. A longitudinal study of over 1200 adults designed to test which model best accounted for drinking behavior found support for both models (Bullers, Cooper, & Russell, 2001). A person's social network predicted individual drinking, but individual drinking also predicted subsequent social network drinking. In fact, the social selection effects were stronger, indicating that people often choose social networks with drinking patterns similar to their own. No doubt the selected networks then support or reinforce their drinking.

Advertising is one way that expectancies develop.

Another variable to be considered is the media. Television commercials associate beer with athletic-looking males, bikini-clad women, and good times. Billboards equate cigarettes with excitement, relaxation, and being in style. A review of studies found that tobacco billboards were over two times more common in primarily African American neighborhoods than they were in primarily European American neighborhoods (Primack, Bost, Land et al., 2007).

Does advertising change substance use patterns among young people? Some evidence indicates that it does. In a longitudinal study of nonsmoking adolescents, those who had a favorite cigarette ad were twice as likely to begin smoking subsequently or to be willing to do so (Pierce, Choi, Gilpin, et al., 1998). The flipside also has support. That is, advertising about the ill-effects of smoking is associated with a lower likelihood of smoking (Emery, Kim, Choi et al., 2012).

As part of the 1998 settlement of a class-action lawsuit, which included 46 states that charged U.S. tobacco companies with manipulating nicotine levels to keep smokers addicted, several companies agreed to stop advertising and marketing efforts aimed at children.

Despite these promises by tobacco companies, an analysis of internal documents of several of these companies (made public thanks to the lawsuit mentioned above) by researchers at the Harvard School of Public Health revealed that they were still targeting their advertising toward young people (Kreslake, Wayne, Alpert et al., 2008). The tobacco companies' own research had found that cigarettes with mild menthol appealed more to young people, and thus they made efforts to market these milder menthol brands to young people. Between 2008 and 2010, over half of adolescent smokers chose menthol cigarettes (Giovino, Villanti, Mowery et al., 2013). Adolescents who begin smoking menthol cigarettes are more likely to continue smoking than those who do not begin with menthol cigarettes (Nonnemaker, Hersey, Homsi et al., 2013). The fact that menthol-flavored cigarettes appeal to young people will surely inform the debate over whether e-cigarettes with flavored liquid nicotine should be available to young people.

Quick Summary

A number of etiological factors have been proposed regarding substance use disorders, and some have more support than others. Genetic factors play a role in both alcohol and nicotine dependence. The ability to tolerate alcohol and metabolize nicotine may be what is heritable. Genes crucial to the operation of the dopamine system may be an important factor in explaining how genes influence substance dependence. Several studies show how genes interact with the environment for smoking and alcohol problems. The most-studied neurobiological factors are brain systems associated with dopamine pathways—the major reward pathways in the brain. The incentive-sensitization theory describes brain pathways involved in liking and wanting (i.e., craving) drugs. People with substance use problems also value immediate rewards more than delayed rewards.

Psychological factors have also been evaluated, and there is support for the idea that tension reduction plays a role, but only under certain circumstances, such as when distractions are present. Expectancies about the effects of drugs, such as reducing tension and increasing social skills, have been shown to predict drug and alcohol use. These expectancies are also powerful: the greater the perceived risk of a drug, the less likely it will be used. Studies of personality factors also help us understand why some people may be more prone to abuse drugs and alcohol.

Sociocultural factors play a role, including the culture, availability of a substance, family factors, social settings and networks, and advertising. Support exists for both a social influence model and a social selection model.

Check Your Knowledge 10.4

1. Which of the following is *not* one of the sociocultural factors implicated in the etiology of substance use disorders?
   a. the media
   b. gender
   c. availability of a substance
   d. social networks
2. Which of the following statements best captures the link between wanting, liking, and drinking according to a prospective study?
   a. Wanting, but not liking, predicted more drinking among heavy drinkers.
   b. Wanting predicted more drinking for heavy drinkers; liking predicted more drinking for light drinkers.
   c. Wanting and liking predicted more drinking among heavy drinkers.
   d. Sedation predicted less drinking for all types of drinking.
3. Genetic research on substance dependence indicates that:
   a. Genetic factors may be the same for many drugs.
   b. Additional studies need to be done to determine heritability.
   c. The dopamine receptor DRD1 may be faulty.
   d. Twin studies show that the environment is just as important as genes.

Treatment of Substance Use Disorders

> *The chronicity of addiction is really a kind of fatalism writ large. If an addict knows in his heart he is going to use again, why not today? But if a thin reed of hope appears, the possibility that it will not always be so, things change. You live another day and then get up and do it again. Hope is oxygen to someone who is suffocating on despair.* (Carr, 2008)

The challenges in treating people with substance use disorders are great, as illustrated by the quote above. Substance use disorders are typically chronic, and relapse occurs often. In view of these challenges, the field is constantly working to develop new and effective treatments, many of which we review in this section. The author of the quote, David Carr, was formerly addicted to cocaine, crack, and alcohol. Currently, he is a media columnist for the *New York Times*. For him, residential treatment was successful.

Many who work with those with alcohol or drug use disorders suggest that the first step to successful treatment is admitting there is a problem. To a certain extent, this makes sense. Why would someone get treatment for something that is not deemed a problem? Unfortunately, a number of treatment programs require people not only to admit a problem but also to demonstrate their commitment to treatment by stopping their use of alcohol or

Detoxification is often the first step in treatment for alcohol use disorder.

Alcoholics Anonymous is the largest self-help group in the world. At their regular meetings, newcomers rise to announce their addiction and receive advice and support from others.

drugs before beginning treatment. This requirement can exclude many who desire and need treatment. For example, James (in the Clinical Case presented earlier) might not have been admitted to a residential program had he not been free of heroin for a week before trying to gain admission. Imagine if people with lung cancer were told they had to demonstrate their commitment to treatment by stopping smoking before the cancer could be treated.

Treatment of Alcohol Use Disorder

In 2012, 14 million people over the age of 12 received treatment for alcohol use disorder (SAMHSA, 2013). Unfortunately, over 16.8 million people over the age of 12 were in need of treatment for alcohol problems in 2012 and did not receive it. A large epidemiological study found that only 24 percent of people who are physiologically dependent on alcohol ever receive treatment (Hasin, Stinson, Ogburn et al., 2007). We have far to go in developing and providing effective treatments and making sure that people who need treatment can get it.

Inpatient Hospital Treatment Often, the first step in treatment for substance use disorders is called **detoxification.** Withdrawal from substances including alcohol can be difficult, both physically and psychologically. Although detoxification does not have to occur in a hospital setting, it can be less unpleasant in such a supervised setting. Alice, the woman described in the earlier Clinical Case, would likely need hospital treatment, at least for detoxification.

Up until the mid-1990s, many people received treatment beyond detoxification in an inpatient hospital, in part because such treatment was covered by both private insurance companies and the federal government (Holder, Longabaugh, Miller et al., 1991). However, inpatient treatment is much more expensive than outpatient treatment, and the therapeutic results of inpatient treatment are not superior to those of outpatient treatment (Mundle, Bruegel, Urbaniak et al., 2001; Soyka, Horak, Morhart et al., 2001). But, inpatient treatment is probably necessary for people with few sources of social support who are living in environments that encourage heavy drinking, especially people with psychological disorders in addition to their alcohol problems (Finney & Moos, 1998). Nevertheless, outpatient treatment is more common these days than inpatient treatment, and this is true for alcohol and drug use disorders. In 2012, 2.5 million people received treatment for drug or alcohol use disorders at an outpatient facility, and 1.8 million received treatment in an inpatient rehabilitation or hospital setting (SAMHSA, 2013).

Alcoholics Anonymous The largest and most widely known self-help group in the world is Alcoholics Anonymous (AA), founded in 1935 by two recovering alcoholics. It has over 100,000 chapters and a membership numbering more than 2 million people around the world. In 2012, over half of the people who received treatment for alcohol or drug use disorders did so through a self-help program like AA (SAMHSA, 2013).

Each AA chapter runs regular and frequent meetings at which newcomers rise to announce that they are alcoholics and give testimonials, relating the stories of their problems with alcohol and indicating how their lives are better now. The group provides emotional support, understanding, and close counseling as well as a social network. Members are urged to call on one another around the clock when they need companionship and encouragement not to relapse. Programs modeled after AA are available for other substances, for example, Narcotics Anonymous, Cocaine Anonymous, and Marijuana Anonymous.

The AA program tries to instill in each member the belief that alcohol dependence is a disease that can never be cured and that continuing vigilance is necessary to resist taking even a single drink, lest uncontrollable drinking begin all over again. Even if the person has not consumed any alcohol for 15 years or more, the designation "alcoholic" is still necessary according to the tenets of AA, since the person is always an alcoholic, always carrying the disease, even if it is currently under control.

The spiritual aspect of AA is apparent in the 12 steps of AA, shown in Table 10.3, and there is evidence that belief in this philosophy is linked with achieving abstinence (Fiorentine & Hillhouse, 2000; Tonigan, Miller, & Connors, 2000). Other self-help groups do not have the religious overtones of AA, relying instead on social support, reassurance, encouragement, and suggestions for leading a life without alcohol. One such approach, termed *Rational Recovery*, focuses on promoting renewed self-reliance rather than reliance on a higher power (Trimpey, Velten, & Dain, 1993).

Uncontrolled trials show that AA provides significant benefit to participants (Moos & Moos, 2006; Ouimette, Finney, & Moos, 1997; Timko, Moos, Finney et al., 2001). A large prospective study of over 2,000 men with alcohol dependence found that participation in AA predicted a better outcome 2 years later (McKeller, Stewart, & Humphreys, 2003). A 16-year prospective study of over 400 people seeking treatment for the first time found that of the people who stayed in AA for at least 27 weeks of the first year in the program, two-thirds were abstinent at the 16-year follow-up. Of the people who stayed in AA for fewer than 27 weeks, only one-third were abstinent at follow-up (Moos & Moos, 2006). In addition, becoming an AA member early in treatment and staying involved for a longer period of time are associated with a better outcome 8 years after treatment began (Moos & Humphreys, 2004).

All of this sounds like good news for people participating in AA. However, a review of eight randomized controlled clinical trials found little benefit of AA over other types of treatment, including motivational enhancement, inpatient treatment, couples therapy, or cognitive behavior therapy (Ferri, Amato, & Davoli, 2008). In addition, AA has high dropout rates, and the dropouts are not always factored into the results of studies.

Couples Therapy Behaviorally oriented marital or couples therapy (O'Farrell & Fals-Stewart, 2000) has been found to achieve some reductions in problem drinking, even a year after treatment has stopped, as well as some improvement in couples' distress generally (McCrady & Epstein, 1995). This appears to be effective for straight, gay, and lesbian couples (Fals-Stewart, O'Farrell, & Lam, 2009). This treatment combines the skills covered in individual cognitive behavior therapy, with a focus on the couple's relationship and dealing with alcohol-related stressors together as a couple. A meta-analysis of 12 studies found that behaviorally oriented couples therapy was more effective than individual treatment approaches (Powers, Vedel, & Emmelkamp, 2008).

Table 10.3 The 12 Steps of Alcoholics Anonymous

1. We admitted we were powerless over alcohol—that our lives had become unmanageable.
2. Came to believe that a power greater than ourselves could restore us to sanity.
3. Made a decision to turn our will and our lives over to the care of God as we understood Him.
4. Made a searching and fearless moral inventory of ourselves.
5. Admitted to God, to ourselves, and to another human being the exact nature of our wrongs.
6. Were entirely ready to have God remove all these defects of character.
7. Humbly asked Him to remove our shortcomings.
8. Made a list of all persons we had harmed, and became willing to make amends to them all.
9. Made direct amends to such people wherever possible, except when to do so would injure them or others.
10. Continued to take personal inventory and, when we were wrong, promptly admitted it.
11. Sought through prayer and meditation to improve our conscious contact with God as we understood Him, praying only for knowledge of His will for us and the power to carry that out.
12. Having had a spiritual awakening as the result of these steps, we tried to carry this message to alcoholics and to practice these principles in all our affairs.

Source: The Twelve Steps and Twelve Traditions. Copyright © 1952 by Alcoholics Anonymous World Services, Inc. Reprinted with permission of Alcoholics Anonymous World Services, Inc.

Cognitive and Behavioral Treatments Contingency management therapy is a cognitive behavior treatment for alcohol and drug use disorders that involves teaching people and those close to them to reinforce behaviors inconsistent with drinking—for example, taking the drug Antabuse (discussed later in the chapter) and avoiding situations associated with drinking in the past. It is based on the belief that environmental contingencies can play an important role in encouraging or discouraging drinking. Vouchers are provided for not using a substance (alcohol, cocaine, heroin, marijuana; verified by urine samples), and the tokens are exchangeable for things that the person would like to have more of (Dallery, Silverman, Chutuape et al., 2001; Katz, Gruber, Chutuape et al., 2001; Silverman, Higgins, Brooner et al., 1996). This therapy also includes teaching job-hunting and social skills, as well as assertiveness training for refusing drinks. For socially isolated people, assistance and encouragement are provided to establish contacts with other people who are not associated with drinking.

Relapse prevention is another cognitive behavioral treatment that has been effective with alcohol and drug use disorders. It can be a stand-alone treatment or part of other interventions. Broadly, the goal is to help people avoid relapsing into drinking or drug use once they have stopped. Focus on Discovery 10.4 discusses this important treatment in more detail.

Motivational Interventions As we described earlier, heavy drinking is particularly common among college students. One team of investigators designed a brief intervention to try to curb such heavy drinking in college (Carey, Casey, Maisto et al., 2006). The intervention contained two parts: (1) a comprehensive assessment that included the Timeline Follow Back (TLFB) interview (Sobell & Sobell, 1996), which carefully assesses drinking in the past 3 months, and (2) a brief motivational treatment that included individualized feedback about a person's drinking in relation to community and national averages, education about the effects of alcohol, and tips for reducing harm and moderating drinking. Results from the study showed that the TLFB alone decreased drinking behavior, but that the combination of the TLFB and motivational intervention was associated with a longer-lasting reduction in drinking behavior, up to 1 year after the interview and intervention.

Moderation in Drinking At least since the advent of Alcoholics Anonymous, the popular belief has been that people with alcohol use disorder have to abstain completely if they are to be successfully treated, for they presumably have no control over drinking once they take that first drink. This continues to be the belief of Alcoholics Anonymous, but research mentioned earlier, indicating that drinkers' beliefs about themselves and alcohol may be as important as the addiction to the drug itself, has called this assumption into question. Considering the social difficulty of avoiding alcohol altogether, it may be preferable to teach a person who does not use alcohol in an extreme fashion to drink with moderation.

The term **controlled drinking** was introduced into the domain of alcohol treatment by Mark and Linda Sobell who developed the *guided self-change* approach to treatment (Sobell & Sobell, 1993). The basic assumption is that people have more potential control over their immoderate drinking than they typically believe and that heightened awareness of the costs of drinking to excess as well as of the benefits of abstaining or cutting down can help. For example, getting the person to delay 20 minutes before taking a second or third drink can help him or her reflect on the costs versus the benefits of drinking to excess. Evidence supports the effectiveness of this approach in helping people moderate their intake and otherwise improve their lives (Sobell & Sobell, 1993). A randomized controlled clinical trial demonstrated that guided self-change was just as effective as an individual or group treatment (Sobell, Sobell, & Agrawal, 2009).

Medications Some people who are in treatment for alcohol use disorder, inpatient or outpatient, take disulfiram, or **Antabuse,** a drug that discourages drinking by causing violent vomiting if alcohol is ingested. As one can imagine, adherence to an Antabuse regimen can be a problem. For it to be effective, a person must already be strongly committed to change.

Courtesy of Dr. Linda Sobell

Courtesy of Dr. Linda Sobell

Mark and Linda Sobell introduced controlled drinking approaches to the treatment of alcohol use disorder.

However, in a large, multicenter study, Antabuse was not shown to have any benefit, and dropout rates were as high as 80 percent (Fuller, 1988).

The FDA has approved the opiate antagonist naltrexone for alcohol use disorder. This drug blocks the activity of endorphins that are stimulated by alcohol, thus reducing the craving for it. Evidence is mixed regarding whether this drug is more effective than a placebo in reducing drinking when it is the only treatment (Krystal, Cramer, Krol et al., 2001). But it does appear to add to overall treatment effectiveness when combined with cognitive behavioral therapy (Pettinati, Oslin, Kampman et al., 2010; Streeton & Whelan, 2001; Volpicelli, Rhines, Rhines et al., 1997; Volpicelli, Watson, King et al., 1995).

Another drug shown to be effective is acamprosate. A review of data from all published double-blind, placebo-controlled clinical trials of acamprosate for people dependent on alcohol suggests that it is highly effective (Mason, 2001). A meta-analysis comparing the effectiveness of acamprosate and naltrexone found them to be equally effective (Kranzler & Van Kirk, 2001). Although its action is not completely understood, researchers believe that it impacts the glutamate and GABA neurotransmitter systems and thereby reduces the cravings associated with withdrawal. There is, of course, the more general question of whether treating a substance use disorder by giving another drug is necessarily a prudent strategy if one believes that some people come to rely on drugs in part because they are looking for a chemical solution to problems in their lives. Nevertheless, to the extent that medications are an effective treatment for alcohol use disorder, disallowing them due to a concern over substituting one drug for another seems misguided.

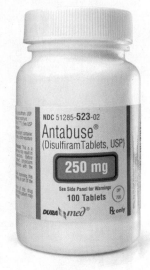

Courtesy of Teva Pharmaceuticals

Antabuse is used to treat alcohol dependence.

Quick Summary

Inpatient hospital treatment for alcohol dependence is not as common today as it was in earlier years, primarily due to the cost. Detoxification from alcohol does often take place in hospitals, but other treatment is more commonly done in outpatient settings.

Alcoholics Anonymous is the most common form of treatment for alcohol use disorder. This group-based self-help treatment instills the notion that alcohol dependence is a disease. Uncontrolled studies suggest that AA is effective, but randomized controlled trials do not. There is some evidence that behavioral couples therapy is an effective treatment. Contingency management therapy, which involves teaching people and those close to them to reinforce behaviors inconsistent

with drinking, has shown some promise. Controlled drinking refers to a pattern of alcohol consumption that is moderate, avoiding the extremes of total abstinence and inebriation. The guided self-change treatment approach emphasizes control over moderate drinking, the costs of drinking to excess, and the benefits of abstaining.

Medications for alcohol use disorder treatment include Antabuse, naltrexone, and acamprosate. Antabuse is not an effective treatment in the long run because noncompliance is a big problem. Some evidence suggests that other medications are effective on their own, but they seem more beneficial in combination with cognitive behavior therapy.

Treatments for Smoking

The numerous laws that currently prohibit smoking in almost all public places are part of a social context that provides incentives and support to stop smoking. In addition, people are more likely to quit smoking if other people around them quit. A longitudinal study of over 12,000 people demonstrated that if people in one's social network quit smoking (spouses, siblings, friends, co-workers), the odds that a person will quit smoking are much greater (Christakis & Fowler, 2008). For example, if a person's spouse stopped smoking, his or her chances of continued smoking decreased by nearly 70 percent. In short, peer pressure to quit smoking appears to be as effective as peer pressure to start smoking once was.

Some smokers who want to quit attend smoking clinics or consult with professionals for other specialized smoking-reduction programs. Even so, it is estimated that only about half of those who go through smoking-cessation programs succeed in abstaining by the time the program is over; only a very small percentage of those who have succeeded in the short term actually remain nonsmoking after a year (Brandon et al., 2007).

Laws that have banned smoking in many places have probably increased the quit rate.

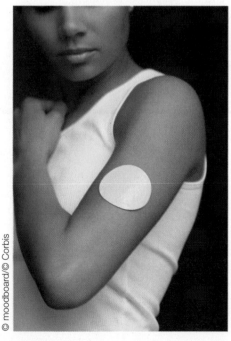

Nicotine patches are available over the counter to help relieve withdrawal symptoms.

Psychological Treatments Probably the most widespread psychological treatment consists of a physician telling the person to stop smoking. Each year millions of smokers are given this counsel—because of hypertension, heart disease, lung disease, or diabetes, or on general grounds of preserving or improving health. There is some evidence that a physician's advice can get some people to stop smoking, at least for a while, especially when the person also chews nicotine gum (Law & Tang, 1995). Motivational interviewing has been tried to help people quit smoking, but results from a meta-analysis indicate that it is only modestly effective (Hettema & Hendricks, 2010; Lai, Cahill, Qin et al., 2010).

One treatment approach that seems to work is called scheduled smoking (Compas, Haaga, Keefe et al., 1998). The strategy behind this approach is to reduce nicotine intake gradually over a period of a few weeks by getting smokers to agree to increase the time between cigarettes. For example, during the first week of treatment, a one-pack-a-day smoker would be put on a schedule allowing only 10 cigarettes per day; during the second week, only 5 cigarettes a day would be allowed; and during the third week, the person would taper off to zero. The cigarettes would have to be smoked on a schedule provided by the treatment team, not when the smoker feels an intense craving. In this way, the person's smoking behavior is controlled by the passage of time rather than by urges, mood states, or situations. Smokers who are able to stay with the agreed-upon schedule showed a 44 percent abstinence rate after 1 year (Cinciripini, Lapitsky, Wallfisch et al., 1994).

By age 18, about two-thirds of cigarette smokers regret having started smoking, one-half have already made an attempt to quit, and nearly 40 percent show interest in obtaining treatment to stop smoking (Henningfield, Michaelides, & Sussman, 2000). Thus, much effort has been directed at getting young people to stop smoking. Unfortunately, many efforts to date fail to show effectiveness beyond 6 months after treatment (Villanti, McKay, Abrams et al., 2010). One school-based program called Project EX includes training in coping skills and a psychoeducational component about the harmful effects of smoking. Two studies have found this program to be effective, both in the United States (Sussman, Dent, & Lichtman, 2001) and in China (Zheng, Sussman, Chen et al., 2004), where the program was adapted to fit Chinese culture and language. Cognitive behavioral approaches that focus on problem solving and coping skills show some promise (Curry, Mermelstein, & Sporer, 2009).

Nicotine Replacement Treatments and Medications Reducing a smoker's craving for nicotine by providing it in a different way is the goal of nicotine replacement treatments (NRT). Attention to nicotine dependence is clearly important because the more cigarettes people smoke daily, the less successful they are at quitting. Nicotine may be supplied in gum, patches, inhalers, or e-cigarettes. The idea is to help smokers endure the nicotine withdrawal that accompanies any effort to stop smoking. Although nicotine replacement alleviates withdrawal symptoms—which justifies its use in gum and in the nicotine patches to be described next—the severity of withdrawal is only minimally related to success in stopping smoking (Ferguson, Shiffman, & Gwaltney, 2006; Hughes, Higgins, Hatsukami et al., 1990).

Nicotine gum, available over the counter, is absorbed much more slowly and steadily than that in tobacco. The long-term goal is for the former smoker to be able to cut back on the use of the gum as well, eventually eliminating reliance on nicotine altogether. However, in doses that deliver an amount of nicotine equivalent to smoking one cigarette an hour, the gum causes cardiovascular changes, such as increased blood pressure, that can be dangerous to people with cardiovascular diseases. Nevertheless, some experts believe that even prolonged, continued use of the gum is healthier than obtaining nicotine by smoking, because the carcinogens are avoided (de Wit & Zacny, 2000).

Nicotine patches, also available over the counter, contain a polyethylene patch taped to the arm that slowly and steadily releases the drug into the bloodstream transdermally (through the skin) and then to the brain. An advantage of the patch over nicotine gum is that the person need only apply one patch each day and not remove it until applying the next patch, making compliance easier. Treatment can be effective after 8 weeks of use for most smokers (Stead, Perera, Bullen et al., 2008), with smaller and smaller patches used as treatment progresses. A drawback is that people who continue smoking while wearing the patch risk increasing the amount of nicotine in their body to dangerous levels.

Evidence suggests that the nicotine patch is superior to the placebo patch in terms of both abstinence and subjective craving (Hughes et al., 1990). A meta-analysis of 111 trials of all types of nicotine replacement treatments (patch, gum, nasal spray, inhaler, tablets) found that NRT was more effective than placebo in smoking cessation (Stead et al., 2008). People who begin to stop smoking after wearing the patch but before dedicated cessation efforts begin are more likely to remain abstinent from smoking at the end of NRT (Rose, Herskovic, Behm et al., 2009). However, NRT is not a panacea. Abstinence rates are only about 50 percent at 12-month follow-ups. The manufacturers state that the patch is to be used only as part of a psychological smoking-cessation program and then for not more than 3 months at a time. In addition, these types of nicotine replacement treatments are not effective with adolescents (Curry et al., 2009).

NRT plus medication or psychological treatment appears to be more effective than NRT alone (Hughes, 2009; Rose & Behm, 2014). For example, combining the antidepressant medication buproprion (trade name Wellbutrin) and nicotine patches yielded a 12-month abstinence rate of 35 percent in one study (Jorenby, Leischow, Nides et al., 1999) but less promising results in others (Hughes, Stead, & Lancaster, 2004; Killen, Fortmann, Murphy et al., 2006). Another drug, varenicline (trade name Chantix), may be effective in combination with behavioral treatment, and even more effective than buproprion (Cahill, Stead, & Lancaster, 2007; Tonstad, Tonnesen, Hajek et al., 2006).

There is a current debate about whether e-cigarettes are an effective form of NRT. Results from one longitudinal study found that only 10 percent of people using e-cigarettes had quit smoking 1 year later (Grana, Popova, & Ling, 2014). An Internet survey of over 400 people who used e-cigarettes found that 22 percent of people had stopped smoking after 1 month and 46 percent had stopped at the 1-year follow-up (Etter & Bullen, 2014). A randomized controlled clinical trial assigned people who wanted to quit smoking to either e-cigarettes, the nicotine patch, or placebo e-cigarettes. The numbers of people who quit smoking were very small in all three groups, so small in fact that the researchers did not have the statistical power to detect any significant differences between the groups (Bullen, Howe, Laugesen et al., 2013). Clearly, more research is needed, but thus far, e-cigarettes do not appear to be more effective than other forms of NRT.

Treatment of Drug Use Disorders

Central to the treatment of people who use drugs such as heroin and cocaine is detoxification—withdrawal from the drug itself. Heroin withdrawal reactions range from relatively mild bouts of anxiety, nausea, and restlessness for several days to more severe and frightening bouts of delirium and panic. The type of reaction depends primarily on the purity of the heroin that the person has been using. The cravings for the substance often remain even after the substance has been removed through detoxification.

Psychological Treatments   In the first direct comparison in a controlled study, the antidepressant medication desipramine (trade name Norpramine) and cognitive behavioral therapy (CBT) were both found to be somewhat effective in reducing cocaine use as well as in improving a person's family, social, and general psychological functioning (Carroll, Rounsaville, Gordon et al., 1994; Carroll, Rounsaville, Nich et al., 1995). In this 12-week study, desipramine was better than a placebo for people with a low degree of dependence on cocaine, whereas CBT was better for people with a high degree of dependence.

Group therapy in residential settings is frequently used to treat heroin addiction.

In this study, people receiving CBT learned how to avoid high-risk situations (e.g., being around people using cocaine), recognize the lure of the drug for them, and develop alternatives to using cocaine (e.g., recreational activities with nonusers). People also learned strategies for coping with the craving and for resisting the tendency to regard a slip as a catastrophe (relapse prevention training; see Focus on Discovery 10.4). A more recent study of computer-based CBT compared to standard substance abuse counseling found that CBT was more effective in helping people remain abstinent from cocaine (Carroll, Kiluk, & Nich et al., 2014) for up to 6 months after treatment. Despite this promise, we are still far short of developing more effective and longer lasting treatments.

Contingency management with vouchers has shown promise for cocaine, heroin, and marijuana use disorders (Dallery et al., 2001; Katz et al., 2001; Petry et al., 2005; Silverman et al., 1996). For example, a randomized treatment trial for people with marijuana use disorder compared a voucher treatment, CBT, and CBT plus vouchers (Budney, Moore, Rocha et al., 2006). During the treatment, people who received the voucher treatment were

FOCUS ON DISCOVERY 10.4

Relapse Prevention

Relapse prevention is an important part of any treatment for drug or alcohol use disorders. Mark Twain quipped that stopping smoking was easy—he'd done it hundreds of times! Marlatt and Gordon (1985) developed an approach to treatment called relapse prevention specifically to prevent relapse in substance use disorders. In this approach, people dependent on alcohol are encouraged to believe that a lapse will not inevitably precipitate a total relapse and should be regarded as a learning experience rather than as a sign that the battle is lost, a marked contrast from the AA perspective. This noncatastrophizing approach to relapse after therapy—falling off the wagon—is important because the overwhelming majority of people who are dependent on alcohol who become abstinent experience one or more relapses over a 4-year period (Polich, Armor, & Braiker, 1980). People dependent on alcohol examine sources of stress in their work, family, and relationships so that they can become active and responsible in anticipating and resisting situations that might lead them into excessive drinking (Marlatt, 1983; Sobell, Toneatto, & Sobell, 1990). The sources of stress that precipitate a relapse in alcohol use disorder may be different for men and women. For women, marital stress is a predictor of relapse. For men, however, marriage seems to protect them from relapse (Walitzer & Dearling, 2006).

Relapse prevention treatment appears to be more effective with some substances than with others. A meta-analysis of 26 randomized controlled clinical trials found that relapse prevention was most effective for alcohol and drug use disorders and least effective for nicotine use disorder (Irvin, Bowers, Dunn et al., 1999). Most smokers relapse within a year of stopping, regardless of the means used to stop. In a pattern we have already seen, people who smoked the most—and are presumably more addicted to nicotine—relapse more often and more quickly than moderate or light smokers. Frequent slips, intense cravings and withdrawal

symptoms, low tolerance for distress, younger age, physiological dependence on nicotine, low self-efficacy, stressful life events, observations of other smokers, weight concerns, and previous quitting attempts are all predictors of relapse (McCarthy, Piasecki, Fiore et al., 2006; Ockene, Mermelstein, Bonollo et al., 2000; Piasecki, 2006). One very detailed analysis, using experience sampling of smokers' thoughts, feelings, and symptoms both before and after they quit smoking, revealed that many smokers experience high levels of negative affect before their target quit day and that this anticipatory negative affect predicted a greater likelihood of relapse (McCarthy et al., 2006). Despite these difficulties, there is some encouraging evidence that self-help relapse prevention programs can be effective in reducing smoking relapse (Brandon, Vidrine, & Litvin, 2007). In these programs, smokers receive booklets in the mail describing the relapse prevention approach. These brochures appear to be effective up to 1 year after smoking was stopped.

What factors contribute to success? Research results (and common sense) tell us that ex-smokers who do not live with a smoker do better at follow-up than those who do live with a smoker (McIntyre-Kingsolver, Lichtenstein, & Mermelstein, 1986). So-called booster or maintenance sessions help, but in a very real sense they represent a continuation of treatment; when they stop, relapse is the rule (Brandon, Zelman, & Baker, 1987). Intensive interventions, such as telephone counseling (Brandon, Collins, Juliano et al., 2000), also help; however, they reach relatively few smokers. Brief relapse prevention interventions during medical visits are cost-effective and could potentially reach most smokers but are not consistently delivered (Ockene et al., 2000). On a positive note, there is considerably more social support for not smoking than there was 10 years ago, at least in the United States. Perhaps as time goes on, societal sanctions against smoking will help those who have succeeded in quitting to remain abstinent.

more likely to remain abstinent than those in the CBT treatment or in the CBT plus vouchers treatment. After treatment was over, however, people who received CBT plus vouchers were most likely to remain abstinent. Thus, vouchers appear to work in the short term, but CBT appears to be an effective component of treatment for marijuana use disorder in the long term with respect to maintaining abstinence after treatment is over.

Studies of contingency management for cocaine use disorder find that it is associated not only with a greater likelihood of abstinence but also with a better quality of life (Petry, Alessi, & Hanson, 2007). In an analysis that looked at four different studies of contingency management treatment for cocaine use disorder, the researchers found that people who received contingency management treatment were more likely to remain abstinent than people who received treatment as usual and that the duration of their abstinence during treatment was related to a higher quality of life after treatment. A meta-analysis of four randomized controlled clinical trials comparing contingency management, day treatment, or both treatments (combined condition) for cocaine use among homeless people found that the combined treatment and contingency management were both more effective than day treatment alone (Schumacher, Milby, Wallace et al., 2007).

Motivational enhancement therapy has also shown promise. This treatment involves a combination of CBT techniques and techniques associated with helping clients generate solutions that work for themselves. A meta-analysis of this treatment found that it was effective for both alcohol and drug use disorders (Burke, Arkowitz, & Menchola, 2003). Another study found that motivational enhancement combined with CBT and contingency management was an effective treatment package for young people (ages 18–25) who were dependent on marijuana (Carroll, Easton, Nich et al., 2006).

Self-help residential homes are another psychological approach to treating heroin and other types of drug use disorders. Daytop Village, Phoenix House, Odyssey House, and other drug-rehabilitation homes share the following features:

- Separation of people from previous social contacts, on the assumption that these relationships have been instrumental in maintaining the drug use disorder
- A comprehensive environment in which drugs are not available and continuing support is offered to ease the transition from regular drug use to a drug-free existence
- The presence of charismatic role models, people formerly dependent on drugs who appear to be meeting life's challenges without drugs
- Direct, often intense, confrontation in group therapy, in which people are goaded into accepting responsibility for their problems and for their drug habits and are urged to take charge of their lives
- A setting in which people are respected as human beings rather than stigmatized as failures or criminals

There are several obstacles to evaluating the efficacy of residential drug-treatment programs. Because the dropout rate is high, those who remain cannot be regarded as representative of the population of people addicted to illegal drugs; their motivation to stop using drugs is probably much stronger than that of people who don't volunteer for treatment or people who drop out. Any improvement participants in these programs make may reflect their strong motivation to quit more than the specific qualities of the treatment program. Such self-regulating residential communities do, however, appear to help a large number of those who remain in them for a year or so (Institute of Medicine, 1990; Jaffe, 1985).

In 2000, voters in California approved Proposition 36, enacted into law in 2001 as the Substance Abuse and Crime Prevention Act (SACPA). The act allows nonviolent drug offenders to be sent to drug treatment rather than prison. Participation in this program is voluntary—someone meeting the criteria of SACPA has the choice of treatment or prison. Researchers at UCLA studied the program, and findings from the first 7 years suggested that the program was working, at least with respect to treatment completion and reduced drug use. Just over one-third completed the treatment in year 4; 40 percent completed in year 7. These figures may seem low, but they are actually quite favorable in comparison to completion rates of other programs, particularly those to which offenders are referred by the criminal justice system (Longshore, Urada, Evans et al., 2003, 2005; Urada, Evans, Yang et al., 2009). Cost savings from this pro-

Methadone is a synthetic heroin substitute. People formerly addicted to heroin come to clinics each day and swallow their dose.

gram during its first 2 years were substantial. It would have cost as much as four times more had the participants been sent to prison (Longshore, Hawken, Urada et al., 2006). The news was not all good, however. Participants who went into treatment under SACPA were more likely to be rearrested for drug offenses than people who had similar offenses before the beginning of SACPA (Longshore et al., 2005; Urada et al., 2009).

Drug Replacement Treatments and Medications Two widely used programs for heroin use disorder involve the administration of *heroin substitutes,* drugs chemically similar to heroin that can replace the body's craving for it, or *opiate antagonists,* drugs that prevent the user from experiencing the heroin high. Recall from Chapter 2 that an antagonist is a drug that dampens the activity of neurotransmitters, and an agonist is a drug that stimulates neurotransmitters. The first category includes **methadone,** levomethadyl acetate, and bupreophine, synthetic narcotics designed to take the place of heroin. Since these drugs are themselves addicting, successful treatment essentially converts the person's dependence on heroin into dependence on a different substance. This conversion occurs because these synthetic narcotics are **cross-dependent** with heroin; that is, by acting on the same central nervous system receptors, they become a substitute for the original dependency. Abrupt discontinuation of methadone results in its own pattern of withdrawal reactions, but because these reactions are less severe than those of heroin, methadone has potential for weaning heroin users altogether from drug dependence (Strain, Bigelow, Liebson et al., 1999).

Treatment with the opiate antagonists involves a drug called naltrexone. First, people are gradually weaned from heroin. Then they receive increasing dosages of naltrexone, which prevents them from experiencing any high should they later take heroin. This drug works because it has great affinity for the receptors to which opiates usually bind; their molecules occupy the receptors without stimulating them. This leaves heroin molecules with no place to go, and so heroin does not have its usual effect on the user. As with methadone, however, treatment with naltrexone involves frequent (daily) and regular visits to a clinic, which requires motivation. In addition, people may not lose the craving for heroin for some time. Both clinical effectiveness and treatment compliance can be increased by adding a contingency management component to the therapy (Carroll, Ball, Nich et al., 2001). Giving people vouchers that they can exchange for food and clothing in return for taking naltrexone and having drug-free urine samples markedly improves effectiveness. One study compared two different naltrexone treatments: the daily pill naltrexone and surgically implanted naltrexone that was slowly released into the body over 30 days. People with implanted naltrexone used opioids less and reported less craving compared to those who received oral dose naltrexone (Hulse, Ngo, & Tait, 2010).

Treatment with a heroin substitute usually involves going to a drug-treatment clinic and swallowing the drug in the presence of a staff member, once a day for methadone and three times a week for levomethadyl acetate and bupreophine. There is some evidence that methadone maintenance can be carried out more simply and just as effectively by weekly visits to a physician (Fiellin, O'Connor, Chawarski et al., 2001). The effectiveness of methadone treatment is improved if a high (80- to 100-milligram) dose is used as opposed to the more typical 40- to 50-milligram dose (Strain et al., 1999) and if it is combined with regular psychological counseling (Ball & Ross, 1991). Drug treatment experts generally believe that treatment with heroin substitutes is best conducted in the context of a supportive social interaction, not merely as a medical encounter (Lilly, Quirk, Rhodes et al., 2000).

Since methadone does not provide a euphoric high, many people will return to heroin if it becomes available to them. In an effort to improve outcomes, researchers have tried adding contingency management to the usual treatment at methadone clinics. In one randomized controlled trial (Pierce, Petry, Stitzer et al., 2006), people receiving methadone from a clinic could draw for prizes each time they submitted a (carefully supervised and obtained) urine sample that had no trace of illegal drugs or alcohol. Prizes ranged from praise to televisions. People who were in the contingency management group were more likely to remain drug-free than those people who received only usual care from the methadone clinic. Of course, it remains to be seen whether such abstinence gains can be maintained after treatment ends and therapists are no longer providing such incentives.

Unfortunately, many people drop out of methadone programs, in part because of side effects such as insomnia, constipation, excessive sweating, and diminished sexual functioning. The stigma associated with going to methadone clinics is also linked to dropout rates, as illustrated in the Clinical Case of James described earlier.

Given the limitations of heroin substitutes such as methadone and other opiate antagonists, researchers have been searching for alternative medications. Buprenorphine (Suboxone) is a medication that actually contains two agents: buprenorphine and naloxone. Buprenorphine is a partial opiate agonist, which means it does not have the same powerfully addicting properties as heroin, which is a full agonist. Naloxone is an opiate antagonist, often used in emergency rooms for opiate or heroin overdoses. This unique combination in Suboxone does not produce an intense high, is only mildly addictive, and lasts for as long as 3 days. Heroin users do not need to go to a clinic to receive this medication since it can be prescribed to individuals. Thus, this treatment avoids the stigma associated with visiting methadone clinics. Suboxone is effective at relieving withdrawal symptoms, and because it lasts longer than methadone, researchers are hopeful that relapse will be less likely. Still, some users may miss the more euphoric high associated with heroin, thus hastening a relapse.

Drug replacement does not appear to be an effective treatment for cocaine use disorder. A meta-analysis of nine randomized controlled clinical trials of stimulant medication as a treatment for cocaine revealed little evidence that this type of medication is effective (Castells, Casas, Vidal et al., 2007).

Researchers were hopeful that a vaccine to prevent the high associated with cocaine use would be effective. The vaccine contains tiny amounts of cocaine attached to otherwise harmless pathogens. The body's immune system responds to this invasion by developing antibodies that then squelch the cocaine. It was hoped that with repeated exposure, the antibodies would be able to keep a good deal of the cocaine from reaching the brain. However, a randomized controlled clinical trial with over 100 people addicted to cocaine was not particularly promising (Martell, Orson, Poling et al., 2009). First, for the vaccine to be effective, people needed to receive five shots, and only half of the sample followed through. Second, just over a third of people receiving all shots developed enough antibodies to keep cocaine from reaching the brain. And finally, although about half of the sample used cocaine less, the vaccine did not help stave off cravings for cocaine. Clearly, additional work needs to be done in this area.

Developing effective treatments for methamphetamine dependence remains a challenge for the field. People like Anton, described in the Clinical Case earlier, do not have many places to turn for treatment. The largest effort to date is a randomized controlled clinical trial conducted across eight different sites referred to as the Methamphetamine Treatment Project (Rawson, Martinelli-Casey, Anglin et al., 2004). This study compared a multifaceted treatment called Matrix with treatment as usual. The Matrix treatment consisted of 16 CBT group sessions, 12 family education sessions, 4 individual therapy sessions, and 4 social support group sessions. Treatment as usual (TAU) consisted of the best available treatment currently offered at the eight outpatient clinics. This varied quite a bit across the sites, with some offering individual counseling and others offering group counseling; some offering 4 weeks of treatment and others offering 16 weeks. Results of the study are somewhat supportive of the Matrix treatment. Compared to those in TAU, those people receiving Matrix stayed in treatment longer and were less likely to use methamphetamine during treatment (confirmed with urine analysis). Unfortunately, at the end of treatment and at the 6-month follow-up, people who received Matrix were no less likely to have used methamphetamine than those in TAU. The good news is that all participants were less likely to use methamphetamine after 6 months, regardless of whether they received Matrix or TAU. Although these results are promising, additional work is clearly needed to develop effective treatments for methamphetamine problems.

Quick Summary

Psychological treatments have not been all that effective for smoking cessation. Scheduled smoking, which involves reducing nicotine intake gradually over a period of a few weeks, has shown some promise. Nicotine gum appears to be somewhat effective, though users can stop chewing the gum. Nicotine patches are more effective than placebo patches, but 9 months after the treatment, abstinence differences between these receiving the drug and those receiving a placebo disappear. Adding buproprion or therapy along with nicotine patches may be effective but not for adolescents. Early evidence about e-cigarettes as an effective treatment for stopping smoking is not promising but more work needs to be done.

Detoxification is usually the first step in treatment for drug use disorders. There is some evidence that CBT is an effective treatment for cocaine dependence. Motivational interviewing has shown promise for the treatment of alcohol and other drug use disorders. Residential treatment homes have not been adequately evaluated for their efficacy, though they are a common form of treatment.

The use of heroin substitutes, such as methadone or naltrexone, is an effective treatment for heroin use disorder. Methadone can only be administered in a special clinic, and there is stigma associated with this type of treatment. A prescription drug called buprenorphine can be taken at home. Treating methamphetamine dependence remains a challenge.

Check Your Knowledge 10.5

Match the treatment approach to the type of substance(s).

Treatment
1. Suboxone
2. AA
3. couples therapy
4. opiate antagonist
5. antidepressant
6. patch
7. Matrix

Substance
a. alcohol
b. heroin
c. cocaine
d. nicotine
e. methamphetamine

Prevention of Substance Use Disorders

Half of adult smokers began their habit before the age of 15, and nearly all before the age of 19 (U.S. Department of Health and Human Services, 2014). Thus, developing ways of discouraging young people from experimenting with tobacco has become a top priority among

Examples of the health warnings for cigarette packages proposed by the FDA. Tobacco companies sued to prevent the graphic images from being added to packages, and a federal judge and appeals panel ruled in their favor. The FDA began working on new health warnings in 2013.

health researchers and politicians, with encouragement from the Surgeon General and funding from the National Cancer Institute, one of the National Institutes of Health. The Legacy Foundation, an organization developed to prevent smoking among young people, was funded in part from the settlement that followed this class-action lawsuit against tobacco companies in 1998. It continues to this day, with many informative online resources (see more at www.legacyforhealth.org and www.mylegacystory.org)

The measures that hold promise for persuading young people to resist smoking may also be useful in dissuading them from trying other drugs and alcohol. Brief family interventions show such promise. In Iowa, the Iowa Strengthening Families Program and the five-session Preparing for the Drug Free Years Program have been found to forestall the onset of nicotine and alcohol use among teens (Spoth, Redmond, Shin et al., 2004). For adolescents, family treatments may also have preventative effects. Research has shown that two different brief family interventions were associated with less initiation of alcohol use among teens (Spoth, Guyll, & Day, 2002).

Statewide comprehensive tobacco control programs, which include increasing taxes on cigarettes, restricting tobacco advertising, conducting public education campaigns, and creating smoke-free environments, appear to be an effective strategy for reducing teenage smoking (Wakefield & Chaloupka, 2000). In 2011, the FDA proposed new health warnings for cigarette packages that contained graphic images of the ill effects on health that smoking can have. Several tobacco companies sued to prevent these graphic images from appearing on cigarette packages, and they prevailed, at least for now. This is unfortunate because research has found that graphic warning labels are effective in preventing smoking and helping people to quit, largely because they make clear the health consequences of smoking (Hammond, 2011; Huang, Chaloupka, & Fong, 2014). The FDA is currently working on new health warnings for cigarette packages.

In addition, scores of school-based programs aimed at preventing young people from starting to use tobacco have been implemented. By and large, such programs have succeeded in delaying the onset of smoking (Sussman, Dent, Simon et al., 1995). These programs share some common components, not all of them shown to be effective (Evans, 2001; Hansen, 1992; Sussman, 1996):

- *Peer-pressure resistance training*. Students learn about the nature of peer pressure and ways to say no. Overall, programs based on peer-pressure resistance training appear to be effective in reducing the onset and level of tobacco use, as well as illegal drug use, in young people (Tobler, Roona, Ochshorn et al., 2000).
- *Correction of beliefs and expectations*. Many young people believe that cigarette smoking is more prevalent (and by implication, more okay) than it actually is. Changing beliefs about the prevalence of smoking has been shown to be an effective strategy, perhaps because young people are so sensitive to what others their age do and believe. Establishing that it is not standard behavior to smoke cigarettes (or drink alcohol) appears to be significantly more effective than resistance training (Hansen & Graham, 1991).
- *Inoculation against mass media messages*. Some prevention programs try to counter the positive images of smokers that have been put forward in the media. Sophisticated mass media campaigns, similar to the ones that have made tobacco a profitable consumer product, can be successful in discouraging smoking. For example, the *truth* campaign, instituted by the Legacy Foundation, developed a website (www.thetruth.com) and radio and television ads to tell youth about the health and social consequences of smoking and the ways in which the tobacco industry targets them, so that they can make informed choices about whether to smoke. This campaign has been well received among young people, and one study found that awareness of and agreement with the *truth* messages were associated with less smoking among teens (Niederdeppe, Farrelly, & Haviland, 2004). These findings are particularly encouraging since we know that teenagers' receptivity to tobacco marketing is strongly related to whether or not they will actually smoke (Unger, Boley Cruz, Schuster et al., 2001).
- *Peer leadership*. Most smoking and other drug prevention programs involve peers of recognized status, which adds to the impact of the messages being conveyed.

Summary

Clinical Descriptions

• DSM-5 includes substance use disorder instead of separate categories for substance abuse and substance dependence. The number of symptoms present determines severity.

• Alcohol has a variety of short-term and long-term effects on individuals, ranging from poor judgment and impaired motor coordination to chronic health problems.

• People can become physiologically dependent on nicotine, most often via smoking cigarettes. Medical problems associated with long-term cigarette smoking include many cancers, emphysema, and cardiovascular disease. Moreover, the health hazards of smoking are not restricted to those who smoke, for secondhand (environmental) smoke can also cause lung damage and other problems. The health consequences of e-cigarettes are not yet well studied, but it seems clear that they will be addicting given that nicotine is their central ingredient.

• When used regularly, marijuana can damage the lungs and cardiovascular system and lead to cognitive impairments. Tolerance to marijuana may develop. However, marijuana also has therapeutic effects, easing the nausea of people undergoing chemotherapy and relieving the discomfort associated with AIDS, glaucoma, chronic pain, seizures, and muscle spasms.

• Opiates slow the activities of the body and, in moderate doses, are used to relieve pain and induce sleep. Heroin has been a focus of concern because usage is up and stronger varieties have become available. Dependence on prescription pain medication has skyrocketed in the past 20 years.

• Stimulants, which include amphetamines and cocaine, act on the brain and the sympathetic nervous system to increase alertness and motor activity. Tolerance and withdrawal are associated with all these drugs. Abuse of methamphetamine, a derivative of amphetamine, has declined since the 1990s but remains a problem.

• Hallucinogens such as LSD alter or expand consciousness. Use of the hallucinogen-like drug Ecstasy use is associated with positive feelings. PCP use often leads to violence.

Etiology

• Several factors are related to the etiology of substance use disorders. Genetic factors have been studied most often with alcohol and tobacco use disorders. Specific genes have been identified, but the interaction of these genes with the environment is key for understanding genetic contributions. Neurobiological factors involving the brain's reward pathways appear to play a role in the use of some substances. Many substances are used to alter mood (e.g., to reduce tension or increase positive affect), and people with certain personality traits, such as those high in negative affect or low in constraint, are especially likely to use drugs. Cognitive variables, such as the expectation that the drug will yield positive effects, are also important. Finally, sociocultural variables, such as attitudes toward the substance, peer pressure, and media portrayal of the substance, are all related to how frequently a substance is used.

Treatment

• Treatments of all kinds have been used to help people refrain from the use of both legal drugs (e.g., alcohol and tobacco) and illegal drugs (e.g., heroin and cocaine). Medications have attempted to release users from their dependency, often by substituting another drug. Some benefits have been observed for treatments using such drugs as naltrexone, suboxone, and methadone. Current medications seek to damp down cravings. Nicotine replacement via gum, patches, or inhalers has met with some success in reducing cigarette smoking. Less clear is whether e-cigarettes can help people stop smoking. None of these approaches appear to lead to enduring change, however, unless accompanied by psychological treatments, including cognitive behavior therapy, couples therapy, motivational interviewing, and contingency management. Controlled studies do not find that Alcoholics Anonymous is effective, but it is a standard part of many treatment programs.

• Since it is easier never to begin using drugs than to stop using them, considerable effort has been expended to prevent substance abuse by implementing educational and social programs to equip young people to develop their lives without a reliance on drugs.

Answers to Check Your Knowledge Questions

10.1 1. F; 2. T; 3. T

10.2 1. lung, larynx, esophagus, pancreas, bladder, cervix, stomach; 2. short-term, long-term; 3. pain relief, reduction of nausea, increased appetite, relief from the discomfort from AIDS

10.3 l. F; 2. F; 3. F; 4. T

10.4 l. b; 2. c; 3. a

10.5 1. b; 2. a; 3. a; 4. b; 5. a, c, d; 6. d; 7. e

Key Terms

addiction	delirium tremens (DTs)	hydrocodone	opiates
amphetamines	detoxification	LSD	oxycodone
Antabuse	Ecstasy	marijuana	PCP
caffeine	fetal alcohol syndrome (FAS)	MDMA	secondhand smoke
cocaine	flashback	methadone	stimulants
controlled drinking	hallucinogen	methamphetamine	substance use disorders
crack	hashish	nicotine	tolerance
cross-dependent	heroin	nitrous oxide	withdrawal

11 Eating Disorders

LEARNING GOALS

1. Be able to distinguish the symptoms associated with anorexia, bulimia, and binge eating disorder and be able to distinguish among the different eating disorders.
2. Be able to describe the neurobiological, sociocultural, and psychological factors implicated in the etiology of eating disorders.
3. Be able to discuss the issues surrounding the growing epidemic of obesity in the United States.
4. Be able to describe the treatments for eating disorders and the evidence supporting their effectiveness.

Clinical Case: Lynne

Lynne, a 24-year-old Caucasian woman, was admitted to the psychiatric ward of a general hospital for treatment of anorexia nervosa. Although she didn't really think anything was wrong with her, her parents had consulted with a psychiatrist, and the three of them had confronted her with a choice of admitting herself or being committed involuntarily.

At the time Lynne was 5 feet, 5 inches and weighed only 78 pounds. She hadn't menstruated for 3 years, and she had a variety of medical problems—hypotension, irregularities in her heartbeat, and abnormally low levels of potassium and calcium.

Lynne had experienced several episodes of dramatic weight loss, beginning at age 18 when she first left home for college. But none of the prior episodes had been this severe, and she had not sought treatment before. She had an intense fear of becoming fat, and although she had never really been overweight, she felt that her buttocks and abdomen were far too large. (This belief persisted even when she weighed 78 pounds.) During the periods of weight loss, she severely restricted food intake and used laxatives heavily. She had occasionally had episodes of binge eating, typically followed by self-induced vomiting so that she would not gain any weight.

MANY CULTURES ARE PREOCCUPIED with food. In the United States today, new restaurants abound, and numerous magazines, blogs, websites, and television shows are devoted to food and food preparation. Grocery stores in the United States are almost embarrassingly stocked with huge quantities of food, and food in the United States has never been cheaper. Perhaps not surprisingly, many people are overweight and obese. Dieting to lose weight is common, and the desire of many people, especially women, to be thinner has created a multibillion-dollar-a-year business. Given this intense interest in food and eating, it is not surprising that this aspect of human behavior is subject to disorder.

Although clinical descriptions of eating disorders can be traced back many years, even centuries for anorexia nervosa, these disorders appeared in the DSM for the first time in 1980 as one subcategory of disorders beginning in childhood or adolescence. Eating disorders became a distinct category in DSM-IV, reflecting the increased attention they had received from clinicians and researchers. In DSM-5, eating disorders are in a chapter called "Feeding and Eating Disorders" that also includes childhood disorders such as pica (eating nonfood substances for extended periods) and rumination disorders (repeated regurgitation of foods).

Unfortunately, eating disorders are also likely to be stigmatized. In one recent study, college students were presented vignettes depicting fictional women with different disorders and were then asked to rate these fictional women on a number of dimensions (Wingfield, Kelly, Serdar et al., 2011). Participants rated the women depicted with eating disorders as self-destructive and responsible for their conditions. Men in the study were particularly likely to believe that eating disorders were easy to overcome. In another study (Roehrig & McLean, 2010), participants were randomly assigned to read a vignette about a woman with an eating disorder or a woman with depression. Participants who read about the woman with the eating disorder viewed her as more responsible, more fragile, and more likely to be trying to get attention with her disorder compared to participants who read about the woman with depression. These types of attitudes and beliefs are not consistent with the current research on eating disorders.

Clinical Descriptions of Eating Disorders

We begin by describing anorexia nervosa and bulimia nervosa. The diagnoses of these two disorders share several clinical features. We then discuss binge eating disorder, which is a new diagnostic category in the DSM-5.

Anorexia Nervosa

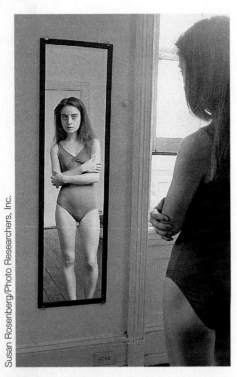

Susan Rosenberg/Photo Researchers, Inc.

Despite being thin, women with anorexia believe that parts of their bodies are too fat, and they spend a lot of time critically examining themselves in front of mirrors.

Lynne, the woman just described, had **anorexia nervosa.** The term *anorexia* refers to loss of appetite, and *nervosa* indicates that the loss is due to emotional reasons. The term is something of a misnomer because most people with anorexia nervosa actually do not lose their appetite or interest in food. On the contrary, while starving themselves, most people with the disorder become preoccupied with food; they may read cookbooks constantly and prepare gourmet meals for their families.

Lynne met all three features required for the diagnosis:

1. *Restriction of behaviors that promote healthy body weight.* This is usually taken to mean that the person weighs much less than is considered normal [e.g., **body mass index** (**BMI**; see Table 11.1) less than 18.5 for adults] for that person's age and height. Weight loss is typically achieved through dieting, although purging (self-induced vomiting, heavy use of laxatives or diuretics) and excessive exercise can also be part of the picture.

2. *Intense fear of gaining weight and being fat or behavior that interferes with gaining weight.* This fear is not reduced by weight loss. There is no such thing as "too thin."

3. *Distorted body image or sense of body shape.* Even when emaciated, those with anorexia nervosa maintain that they are overweight and that certain parts of their bodies, particularly the abdomen, hips, and thighs, are too fat. To check on their body size, they typically weigh themselves frequently, measure the size of different parts of the body, and gaze critically at their reflections in mirrors. Their self-esteem is closely linked to maintaining thinness.

Prior to DSM-5, *amenorrhea (loss of menstrual period)* was one of the diagnostic criteria for anorexia nervosa. It was removed, however, in DSM-5 because there are many reasons why women can stop having their menstrual period that do not have anything to do with weight loss. In addition, few differences have been found between women who have amenorrhea and the other three features of anorexia nervosa and those women who have the other three

Table 11.1 Computing Your Body Mass Index (BMI)

WEIGHT lbs	100	105	110	115	120	125	130	135	140	145	150	155	160	165	170	175	180	185	190	195	200	205	210	215
kgs	45.5	47.7	50.0	52.3	54.5	56.8	59.1	61.4	63.6	65.9	68.2	70.5	72.7	75.0	77.3	79.5	81.8	84.1	86.4	88.6	90.9	93.2	95.5	97.7
HEIGHT in/cm	Underweight				Healthy						Overweight				Obese				Extremely obese					
5'0" - 152.4	19	20	21	22	23	24	25	26	27	28	29	30	31	32	33	34	35	36	37	38	39	40	41	42
5'1" - 154.9	18	19	20	21	22	23	24	25	26	27	28	29	30	31	32	33	34	35	36	36	37	38	39	40
5'2" - 157.4	18	19	20	21	22	22	23	24	25	26	27	28	29	30	31	32	33	33	34	35	36	37	38	39
5'3" - 160.0	17	18	19	20	21	22	23	24	24	25	26	27	28	29	30	31	32	32	33	34	35	36	37	38
5'4" - 162.5	17	18	18	19	20	21	22	23	24	24	25	26	27	28	29	30	31	31	32	33	34	35	36	37
5'5" - 165.1	16	17	18	19	20	20	21	22	23	24	25	25	26	27	28	29	30	30	31	32	33	34	35	35
5'6" - 167.6	16	17	17	18	19	20	21	21	22	23	24	25	25	26	27	28	29	29	30	31	32	33	34	34
5'7" - 170.1	15	16	17	18	18	19	20	21	22	22	23	24	25	25	26	27	28	29	29	30	31	32	33	33
5'8" - 172.7	15	16	16	17	18	19	19	20	21	22	22	23	24	25	25	26	27	28	28	29	30	31	32	32
5'9" - 175.2	14	15	16	17	17	18	19	20	20	21	22	22	23	24	25	25	26	27	28	28	29	30	31	31
5'10" - 177.8	14	15	15	16	17	18	18	19	20	20	21	22	23	23	24	25	25	26	27	28	28	29	30	30
5'11" - 180.3	14	15	15	16	16	17	18	18	19	20	21	21	22	23	23	24	25	25	26	27	28	28	29	30
6'0" - 182.8	13	14	14	15	16	17	17	18	19	19	20	21	21	22	23	23	24	25	25	26	27	27	28	29
6'1" - 185.4	13	13	14	15	15	16	17	17	18	19	19	20	21	21	22	23	23	24	25	25	26	27	27	28
6'2" - 187.9	12	13	14	14	15	16	16	17	18	18	19	19	20	21	21	22	23	23	24	25	25	26	27	27
6'3" - 190.5	12	13	13	14	15	15	16	16	17	18	18	19	20	20	21	21	22	23	23	24	25	25	26	26
6'4" - 193.0	12	12	13	14	14	15	15	16	17	17	18	18	19	20	20	21	22	22	23	23	24	25	25	26

features but do not have amenorrhea (Attia & Roberto, 2009). Because some people do not report that they fear gaining weight, DSM-5 expanded this symptom by adding repeated or persistent behavior that interferes with gaining weight (Attia, Becker, Bryant-Waugh et al., 2013).

As discussed in Chapter 3, DSM-5 added severity ratings for nearly all disorders. For anorexia nervosa, the severity ratings (see Table 11.2) are based on BMI, which is consistent with the approach of the World Health Organization. The BMI is calculated by dividing weight in kilograms by height in meters squared and is considered a more valid estimate of body fat than many others. For women, a healthy weight BMI is between 20 and 25. To calculate your own BMI, see Table 11.1. The BMI is not a perfect measure. Many people may have a higher or lower BMI for reasons that do not have to do with body fat. For example, someone who is very muscular will likely have a high BMI but will not be overweight or obese. By contrast, an elite runner may be very lean and have a low BMI but not have anorexia.

The body image disturbance that accompanies anorexia nervosa has been assessed in several ways, most frequently by a questionnaire such as the Eating Disorders Inventory (Garner, Olmsted, & Polivy, 1983). Some of the items on this questionnaire are presented in Table 11.3. In another type of assessment, people with anorexia nervosa are shown line drawings of women with varying body weights and asked to pick the one closest to their own and the one that represents their ideal shape (see Figure 11.1). People with anorexia overestimate their own body size and choose a thin figure as their ideal. Despite this distortion in body size, people with anorexia nervosa are fairly accurate when reporting their actual weight (McCabe, McFarlane, Polivy et al., 2001), perhaps because they weigh themselves frequently.

One interesting study found a slightly different pattern for men with eating disorders. Men with eating disorders didn't differ from men without eating disorders when pointing to their ideal male body type. However, the men with eating disorders overestimated their own body size considerably, thus demonstrating a distortion in their own body images (Mangweth et al., 2004).

DSM-5 continues to include two subtypes of anorexia nervosa, even though research calls into question the validity of these types. In the *restricting type*, weight loss is achieved by severely limiting food intake; in the *binge-eating/purging type*, as illustrated in Lynne's case, the person has also regularly engaged in binge eating and purging. Longitudinal research, however, suggests that

DSM-5 Criteria for Anorexia Nervosa

- Restriction of food that leads to very low body weight; body weight is significantly below normal
- Intense fear of weight gain or repeated behaviors that interfere with weight gain
- Body image disturbance

Table 11.2 Severity Ratings for Anorexia Nervosa in DSM-5

Rating	BMI Range
Mild	≤17
Moderate	16–16.99
Severe	15–15.99
Extreme	<15

Table 11.3 Subscales and Illustrative Items from the Eating Disorders Inventory

Drive for thinness	I think about dieting.
	I feel extremely guilty after overeating.
	I am preoccupied with the desire to be thinner.
Bulimia	I stuff myself with food.
	I have gone on eating binges where I have felt that I could not stop.
	I have the thought of trying to vomit in order to lose weight.
Body dissatisfaction	I think that my thighs are too large.
	I think that my buttocks are too large.
	I think that my hips are too big.
Ineffectiveness	I feel inadequate.
	I have a low opinion of myself.
	I feel empty inside (emotionally).
Perfectionism	Only outstanding performance is good enough in my family.
	As a child, I tried hard to avoid disappointing my parents and teachers.
	I hate being less than best at things.
Interpersonal distrust	I have trouble expressing my emotions to others.
	I need to keep people at a certain distance (feel uncomfortable if someone tries to get too close).
Interoceptive awareness	I get confused about what emotion I am feeling.
	I don't know what's going on inside me.
	I get confused as to whether or not I am hungry.
Maturity fears	I wish that I could return to the security of childhood.
	I feel that people are happiest when they are children.
	The demands of adulthood are too great.

Source: From Garner, Olmsted, & Polivy (1983).
Note: Responses use a six-point scale ranging from "always" to "never."

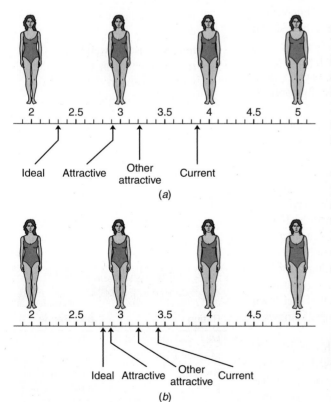

(a)

(b)

the distinction between subtypes may not be all that useful (Eddy et al., 2002). Nearly two-thirds of women who initially met criteria for the restricting subtype had switched over to the binge-eating/purging type 8 years later. A review of the subtype literature for the preparation of DSM-5 concluded that the subtypes had limited predictive validity even though clinicians found them useful (Peat, Mitchell, Hoek et al., 2009). Because one of the top priorities for the DSM-5 was to be useful to clinicians may explain why these subtypes were retained despite their limited validity.

Anorexia nervosa typically begins in the early to middle teenage years, often after an episode of dieting and the occurrence of a life stress. Lifetime prevalence of anorexia is less than 1 percent, and this rate has been stable for several decades. In short, the rates of anorexia are not rising or falling. Anorexia nervosa is at least 10 times more frequent in women than in men (Hoek & van Hoeken, 2003). When anorexia nervosa does occur in men, symptoms and other characteristics, such as reports of family difficulties, are generally similar to those reported by women with the disorder (Olivardia et al., 1995). As we

Figure 11.1 In this assessment of body image, respondents indicate their current shape, their ideal shape, and the shape they think is most attractive to the opposite sex. The figure actually rated as most attractive by members of the opposite sex is shown in both panels. Ratings of women who scored high on a measure of distorted attitudes toward eating are shown in (a); ratings of women who scored low are shown in (b). The high scorers overestimated their current size and ideally would be very thin. [Zellner, Harner, & Adler (1989).]

discuss more fully later, the gender difference in the prevalence of anorexia most likely reflects the greater cultural emphasis on women's beauty, which has promoted a thin shape as the ideal over the past several decades. Even though rare in men, one study found higher mortality from the disorder for men than women in France (Gueguen, Godart, Chambry et al., 2012).

For both men and women, anorexia nervosa is frequently comorbid with depression, obsessive-compulsive disorder, specific phobias, panic disorder, and various personality disorders (Baker, Mitchell, Neale et al., 2010; Godart, Flament, Lecrubier et al., 2000; Ivarsson, Råstam, Weitz et al., 2000; Root, Pinheiro, Thornton et al., 2010; Striegel-Moore, Garvin, Dohm et al., 1999). Suicide rates are quite high for people with anorexia, with as many as 5 percent completing suicide and 20 percent attempting suicide (Franko & Keel, 2006).

Physical Consequences of Anorexia Nervosa   Self-starvation and use of laxatives to lose weight produce numerous undesirable biological consequences in people with anorexia nervosa. Blood pressure often falls, heart rate slows, kidney and gastrointestinal problems develop, bone mass declines, the skin dries out, nails become brittle, hormone levels change, and mild anemia may occur. Some people lose hair from the scalp, and they may develop lanugo—a fine, soft hair—on their bodies. As in Lynne's case, levels of electrolytes, such as potassium and sodium, are altered. These ionized salts, present in various bodily fluids, are essential to neural transmission, and lowered levels can lead to tiredness, weakness, cardiac arrhythmias, and even sudden death.

Prognosis   Between 50 and 70 percent of people with anorexia eventually recover (Keel & Brown, 2010). However, recovery often takes 6 or 7 years, and relapses are common before a stable pattern of eating and weight maintenance is achieved (Strober, Freeman, & Morrell, 1997). As we discuss later, changing peoples' distorted views of themselves is very difficult, particularly in cultures that value thinness.

Anorexia nervosa is a life-threatening illness; death rates are 10 times higher among people with the disorder than among the general population and twice as high as among people with other psychological disorders. Mortality rates among women with anorexia range from 3 to 5 percent (Crow, Peterson, Swanson et al., 2009; Keel & Brown, 2010). Death most often results from physical complications of the illness—for example, congestive heart failure—and from suicide (Herzog, Greenwood, Dorer et al., 2000; Sullivan, 1995). A recent longitudinal study found that death was more likely to occur among those who had anorexia the longest (ranging from 7 to 25 years) (Franko, Keshaviah, Eddy et al., 2013).

Anorexia nervosa can be a life-threatening condition. It is especially prevalent among young women who are under intense pressure to keep their weight low. Brazilian model Ana Carolina Reston died from the condition in 2006 at age 21.

Clinical Case: Jill

Jill was the second child born to her parents. Both she and her brother became intensely involved in athletics at an early age, Jill in gymnastics and her brother in Little League baseball. At age 4 Jill was enrolled in gymnastics school, where she excelled. By the time she was 9, her mother had decided that Jill had outgrown the coaching abilities of the local instructors and began driving her to a nationally recognized coach several times a week. Over the next few years, Jill's trophy case swelled and her aspirations for a place on the Olympic team grew. As she reached puberty, though, her thin frame began to fill out, raising concerns about the effects of weight gain on her performance as a gymnast. She began to restrict her intake of food but found that after several days of semistarvation she would lose control and go on an eating binge. This pattern of dieting and bingeing lasted for several months, and Jill's fear of becoming fat seemed to increase during that time. At age 13, she hit on the solution of self-induced vomiting. She quickly fell into a pattern of episodes of bingeing and vomiting three or four times per week. Although she maintained this pattern in secret for a while, eventually her parents caught on and initiated treatment for her.

DSM-5 Criteria for Bulimia Nervosa

- Recurrent episodes of binge eating
- Recurrent compensatory behaviors to prevent weight gain, for example, vomiting
- Body shape and weight are extremely important for self-evaluation

Bulimia Nervosa

Jill's behavior illustrates the features of **bulimia nervosa**. *Bulimia* is from a Greek word meaning "ox hunger." This disorder involves episodes of rapid consumption of a large amount of food, followed by compensatory behavior, such as vomiting, fasting, or excessive exercise, to prevent weight gain. The DSM defines a *binge* as having two characteristics. First it involves eating an excessive amount of food, that is, much more than most people would eat, within a short period of time (e.g., 2 hours). Second, it involves a feeling of losing control over eating—as if one cannot stop. Bulimia nervosa is not diagnosed if the bingeing and purging occur only in the context of anorexia nervosa and its extreme weight loss; the diagnosis in such a case is anorexia nervosa, binge-eating/purging type. The key difference between anorexia and bulimia is weight loss: people with anorexia nervosa lose a tremendous amount of weight, whereas people with bulimia nervosa do not.

In bulimia, binges typically occur in secret; they may be triggered by stress and the negative emotions they arouse, and they continue until the person is uncomfortably full (Grilo, Shiffman, & Carter-Campbell, 1994). In the case of Jill, she was likely to binge after periods of stress associated with being an elite athlete. Foods that can be rapidly consumed, especially sweets such as ice cream and cake, are usually part of a binge. One study found that women with bulimia nervosa were more likely to binge while alone and during the morning or afternoon. In addition, avoiding a craved food on one day was associated with a binge episode with that food the next morning (Waters, Hill, & Waller, 2001). Other studies show that a binge is likely to occur after a negative social interaction—or at least the perception of a negative social exchange (Steiger et al., 1999).

Research suggests that although people with bulimia nervosa sometimes ingest enormous quantities of food during binges, often more than what a person eats in an entire day, there is wide variation in the caloric content consumed by people during binges (e.g., Rossiter & Agras, 1990). People report that they lose control during a binge, even to the point of experiencing something akin to what happens in addiction (Smith & Robbins, 2013), perhaps losing awareness of their behavior or feeling that it is not really they who are bingeing. They are usually ashamed of their binges and try to conceal them.

After the binge is over, feelings of discomfort, disgust, and fear of weight gain lead to the second step of bulimia nervosa—the inappropriate compensatory behavior (also known as purging) to attempt to undo the caloric effects of the binge. People with bulimia most often stick their fingers down their throats to cause gagging, but after a time many can induce vomiting at will without gagging themselves. Laxative and diuretic abuse (which do little to reduce body weight) as well as fasting and excessive exercise are also used to prevent weight gain.

Although many people binge occasionally and some people also purge, the DSM-5 diagnosis of bulimia nervosa requires that the episodes of bingeing and compensatory behavior occur at least once a week for 3 months. Is once a week a well-established cutoff point? Probably not. The frequency changed from twice a week in DSM-IV-TR to once a week in DSM-5 because few differences were found between people who binge twice a week and those who do so less frequently (Attia et al., 2013; MacDonald, McFarlane, & Olmsted, 2014; Wilson & Sysko, 2009).

Like those with anorexia nervosa, the self-esteem of people with bulimia nervosa depends heavily on maintaining normal weight. Whereas people without eating disorders typically underreport their weight and say they are taller than they actually are, people with bulimia nervosa are more accurate in their report (Doll & Fairburn, 1998; McCabe et al., 2001). Yet, people with bulimia nervosa are also likely to be highly dissatisfied with their bodies.

DSM-IV-TR included subtypes of bulimia nervosa, but because the subtypes did not have much validity or clinical utility, they were removed from DSM-5. New severity ratings in DSM-5 are based on the number of compensatory behaviors in a week (see Table 11.4).

Bulimia nervosa typically begins in late adolescence or early adulthood. About 90 percent of people with bulimia are women, and prevalence among women is thought to be about 1 to 2 percent of the population (Hoek & van Hoeken, 2003). Many people with bulimia nervosa were somewhat overweight before the onset of the disorder, and the binge eating often started during an episode of dieting. Although both anorexia nervosa and bulimia nervosa among women begin in adolescence, they can persist into adulthood and middle age (Keel, Gravener, Joiner et al., 2010; Slevec & Tiggemann, 2011).

Table 11.4 Severity Ratings for Bulimia Nervosa in DSM-5

Rating	Number of Compensatory Behaviors
Mild	1-3 compensatory behaviors/week
Moderate	4-7
Severe	8-13
Extreme	14 or more

Bulimia nervosa is comorbid with numerous other diagnoses, notably depression, personality disorders, anxiety disorders, substance use disorders, and conduct disorder (Baker et al., 2010; Gadalla & Piran, 2007; Godart et al., 2000; Godart, Flament, Perdereau et al., 2002; Root et al., 2010; Stice, Burton, & Shaw, 2004; Striegel-Moore et al., 1999). Suicide rates are higher among people with bulimia nervosa than in the general population (Favaro & Santonastaso, 1997) but substantially lower than among people with anorexia (Franko & Keel, 2006).

Which comes first, bulimia nervosa or the comorbid disorders? A prospective study examined the relationship between bulimia and depression symptoms among adolescent girls (Stice et al., 2004). This study found that bulimia symptoms predicted the onset of depression symptoms. However, the converse was also true: depression symptoms predicted the onset of bulimia symptoms. Thus, it appears each disorder increases the risk for the other. With respect to substance use disorders, another prospective study of over 1200 twin pairs found that bulimia symptoms came before substance use disorder symptoms (Baker et al., 2010).

Physical Consequences of Bulimia Nervosa Like anorexia, bulimia is associated with several physical side effects. Although less common than in anorexia, menstrual irregularities, including amenorrhea, can occur, even though people with bulimia typically have a normal BMI (Gendall et al., 2000).

Bulimia nervosa, like anorexia, is a serious disorder with many unfortunate medical consequences (Mehler, 2011). For example, frequent purging can cause potassium depletion. Heavy use of laxatives induces diarrhea, which can also lead to changes in electrolytes and cause irregularities in the heartbeat. Recurrent vomiting has been linked to menstrual problems and may lead to tearing of tissue in the stomach and throat and to loss of dental enamel as stomach acids eat away at the teeth, which become ragged. The salivary glands may become swollen. Death from bulimia nervosa was once thought to be less common than from anorexia nervosa (Herzog et al., 2000; Keel & Brown, 2010; Keel & Mitchell, 1997), but one study of nearly 1000 women with bulimia nervosa found the mortality rate to be nearly 4 percent (Crow et al., 2009).

Prognosis Long-term follow-ups of people with bulimia nervosa reveal that close to 75 percent recover, although about 10 to 20 percent remain fully symptomatic (Keel et al., 2010; Keel, Mitchell, Miller et al., 1999; Reas, Williamson, Martin et al., 2000; Steinhausen & Weber, 2009). Intervening soon after a diagnosis is made (i.e., within the first few years) is linked with an even better prognosis (Reas et al., 2000). People with bulimia nervosa who binge and vomit more and who have comorbid substance use or a history of depression have a poorer prognosis than people without these factors (Wilson, Loeb, Walsh et al., 1999).

Clinical Case: Amy

Amy, a 27-year-old African American woman, described a lifelong struggle with her weight. She was described as "chubby" as a child, and peers often called her "fatty." She went on several diets as a child, but none of them were successful. Currently, Amy is 5 feet, 4 inches tall and weighs 212 pounds (with a BMI of 35).

Amy had experienced several episodes of binge eating beginning at age 18, when she first left home for college. After being left out of a social group on campus, she retreated to her dorm room alone, where she ate two large pizzas and a bag of Doritos. After the binge, she felt very full and went to sleep.

After that first binge, she found herself doing this as often as twice a week throughout college. She was not always hungry when she binged, but even though she felt extremely full, she could not stop eating. Afterwards, she felt ashamed and angry at herself for having eaten so much. She gained 70 pounds during her college years.

Amy reported that she currently binges at least once a week, typically when she has had a very stressful day at work. She has recently confided in a friend about her troubled eating, and her friend recommended that she seek treatment at the local university mental health clinic.

Binge Eating Disorder

Binge eating disorder was first included as a diagnosis in DSM-5 (it was considered a diagnosis in need of further study in DSM-IV-TR). This disorder includes recurrent binges (one time per week for at least 3 months), lack of control during the bingeing episode, and distress about bingeing, as well as other characteristics, such as rapid eating and eating alone. It is distinguished from anorexia nervosa by the absence of weight loss and from bulimia nervosa by the absence of compensatory behaviors (purging, fasting, or excessive exercise). Most often, people with binge eating disorder are **obese**. A person with a BMI greater than 30 is considered obese. With the current explosion in the prevalence of obesity in the United States, it is perhaps not surprising that research on binge eating disorder continues to increase (Attia et al., 2013). It is important to point out, however, that not all obese people meet criteria for binge eating disorder. Indeed, only those who have binge episodes and report feeling a loss of control over their eating will qualify, which amounts to anywhere from 2 to 25 percent of obese people (Wonderlich, Gordon, Mitchell et al., 2009). For further discussion of obesity, see Focus on Discovery 11.1.

FOCUS ON DISCOVERY 11.1

Obesity: A Twenty-First Century Epidemic?

Obesity is not an eating disorder, though it is a serious public health problem, with estimated yearly health care costs of nearly $147 billion in the United States (Finkelstein, Trogdon, Cohen et al., 2009). The estimated lifetime health care costs for *each* 10-year-old child in the United States is $19,000, which added up among all 10-year-olds who are currently obese comes to $14 billion (Finkelstein, Graham, & Malhotra, 2014).

Why are the health care costs so high? Obesity is linked to many health problems, including diabetes, hypertension, cardiovascular disease, and several forms of cancer. Studies have found that blood pressure is rising among children, and this may be due in part to the increase in the number of children who are overweight or obese (Muntner et al., 2004). Recently, there was hopeful news about obesity in very young children ages 2 to 5, with one study finding that obesity rates declined from 14 percent in 2004 to 8 percent in 2012 (Ogden, Carroll, Kit et al., 2014). However, another team of researchers analyzed data all the way back to 1999 and found that obesity rates in children have remained consistent across the longer time period (Skinner & Skelton, 2014).

Not only are obesity rates not dropping among very young children, they are remaining steady and even growing among older children and adults. In 2012, over two-thirds of adults in the United States were overweight and over a third of adults were obese (Ogden et al., 2014). Furthermore, 20 percent of children in the United States were obese and one-third of children were overweight. Obesity rates are higher in some states than in others—the obesity rate was greater than 30 percent of adults in 13 states in 2012 (up from 8 states in 2009). Rates of obesity rate are much higher in the United States than in many other countries. Nevertheless, obesity is also increasing in other parts of the world, from Aborigines in Australia to children in Egypt, from Siberia to Peru (Ng, Fleming, Robinson et al., 2014). Why are so many people overweight?

A number of factors play a role, including the environment we live in. Two books published over the past 10 years both point to what psychologist Kelly Brownell calls our "toxic" environment with respect to the food and exercise options available to most people in the United States

(Brownell & Horgen, 2003; Cohen, 2014). The availability and amount of all food, not just fast food, have exponentially increased in the past decades. We pay far less for our food now, spending less than 10 percent of our income on food today compared to 25 percent of our income in the 1920s (Cohen, 2014). And, we can buy food at any time of day or night, with most grocery stores featuring unhealthy items (with higher profit margins) more prominently than healthy items. At the same time, many people, including children, have become more sedentary, spending more time working or playing at the computer or smartphones and watching TV than ever before. Furthermore, physical education programs for children in schools have been declining (Critser, 2003). People eat in restaurants more than ever before, calorie counts in cookbooks are higher, and portion sizes of foods, both in restaurants and in grocery stores, are larger than ever. In fact, most people do not know the portion size of most foods recommended by the U.S. Department of Agriculture. A 20-ounce bottle of soda is not one serving, but two and one-half servings. The recommended serving of cheese is 1½ ounces, about the size of a 9-volt battery. Americans eat an average of 2700 calories today compared with closer to 2200 calories a day 40 years ago. The ever-increasing portion sizes as well as the greater availability of unhealthy foods impact the amount we eat. Even our cookbooks can influence what we eat. In an analysis of 18 recipes that have been in *The Joy of Cooking* since 1936, Wansink and Payne (2009) found that the calories in these recipes increased by a third between 1936 and 2006. The limited availability and greater expense of healthy foods in poorer neighborhoods also contributes to obesity. Research has shown that poorer neighborhoods have fewer grocery stores, more fast-food restaurants, and fewer healthy food selections in their stores (Moreland et al., 2002). In addition, people in poorer neighborhoods may not have a means of transportation to and from grocery stores that carry more affordable, healthy food choices that are farther away.

We are all subject to the continuing impact of advertisements, especially those promoting alluring high-calorie products such as snack foods, desserts, and meals at fast-food restaurants. For example, the advertising budget for Coke and Pepsi combined was $3 billion in 2001 (Brownell & Horgen, 2003). Compare this to the $2 million advertising campaign by the National Cancer Institute to promote eating more fruits and vegetables (Nestle, 2002). A task force of the American Psychological Association concluded in 2004 that television advertisements of unhealthy foods (e.g., sugary cereals, soda) contribute to unhealthy eating habits of children under 8 years of age, largely because these children lack the requisite cognitive skills to discern truth from advertising (Kunkel et al., 2004). Showing the direct effects of TV marketing, one study provided snacks to children as they watched a TV cartoon containing commercials for snack foods or a TV cartoon containing commercials for other products. Children randomly assigned to watch the show with the snack food commercials ate more snacks than children assigned to watch the cartoon with nonfood advertising (Harris, Bargh, & Brownell, 2009).

Along with the environment, heredity plays a role in obesity. In behavior genetics terms, between 25 and 40 percent of the variance in obesity is attributed to genetic factors (Brownell & Horgen, 2003). Of course, these factors only have an impact when they interact with environmental factors. Heredity could produce its effects by regulating metabolic rate, impacting the hypothalamus, or influencing the production of enzymes that make it easier to store fat and gain weight. Molecular genetics studies have identified a number of possible genes that might contribute to obesity. A variation (polymorphism) of the *Insig2* gene has sparked interest among researchers. This gene is associated with regulating fatty acids and cholesterol and was found among 10 percent of people who are obese in a genome-wide association study (GWAS; Herbert et al., 2006), though later studies have not always found this association (Heid, Huth, Loos et al., 2009). Although genetic factors tell part of the story, they do not tell the whole of it. Clearly, the environment plays a critical role. For example, a recent study of over 500,000 women found that mothers' weight gain during pregnancy was more important in predicting high birth weight among babies than genetic factors (Ludwig & Currie, 2010).

In 2011, researchers published a study showing that many mammals, not just humans, have been gaining weight over the past decades (Klimentidis, Beasley, Lin et al., 2011). The researchers examined different kinds of monkeys, mice, rats, and marmosets that were raised in captivity and found that these animals have all become heavier over the decades even though they were fed highly controlled diets that have not markedly changed over the years in quantity or quality. Clearly, animals are not gaining weight based on advertising or access to fast food or even limited exercise. Yet the researchers suggested that their findings can provide important insights about changes in the environment that are influencing the obesity epidemic in humans, such as chemicals that disrupt the endocrine system, bacteria or other infectious agents, or stress.

Indeed, stress and its associated negative moods can induce eating in some people (Arnow, Kenardy, & Agras, 1992; Heatherton & Baumeister, 1991), and research in rats shows that foods rich in fat and sugar may actually reduce stress in the short term, giving new meaning to the term

Obesity has become quite prevalent, particularly in the United States, in the past 30 years.

Bourreau/Photo Researchers, Inc.

comfort food (Dallman et al., 2003; Kessler, 2009). Unfortunately, research also shows that negative moods usually get worse after eating, at least binge eating (Haedt-Matt & Keel, 2011). In addition, trying to suppress negative feelings is not effective in avoiding the tendency to eat when feeling bad. In one study, people who were asked to suppress their feelings of sadness after watching a sad film ate more ice cream than those who were asked to just watch the film (Vohs & Heatherton, 2000).

The stigma associated with being overweight remains a problem. There are a number of TV "reality" shows devoted to watching obese people struggle to lose weight such as *The Biggest Loser*, where participants are subjected to a tough exercise and eating regimen, or *Dance Your Ass Off*, where overweight people lose weight through dancing. Obese people now entertain us: this does not seem to be the most effective way to reduce stigma.

Stigma can also perpetuate the idea that obesity is simply a matter of personal responsibility—the belief that if people would just eat less and exercise more, obesity would not be a problem. But the science behind self-control tells another story. Given the multitude of factors contributing to obesity just noted, such a simple solution is not reasonable. Yet some members of the U.S. Congress subscribe to such beliefs. In 2004, the U.S. House of Representatives passed what became known as the "cheeseburger bill," which prevents people from suing fast-food companies for contributing to their obesity. Despite the evidence that environmental factors, including the availability and relatively unhealthy nature of a lot of fast food, contribute to obesity, some members of the House said that obesity was a matter of personal responsibility, not the responsibility of the fast-food industry. A number of states passed their own similar laws that protect food companies from lawsuits about obesity, but other states, such as Minnesota in 2011, have rejected such laws. Of course, personal responsibility is important. People can and should make better choices about what and how much they eat. Nevertheless, other environmental factors, such as availability, cost, and transportation can sometimes work against such choices.

In the past several years in the United States, a number of legislative and policy changes have been initiated to try to curb obesity. For example, First Lady Michelle Obama began the Let's Move! campaign in 2010 to target childhood obesity by focusing on getting young people to eat healthy foods and exercise. Many cities and states now require restaurants to post the calorie contents of their products, and the federal Food and Drug Administration (FDA) is finalizing a nationwide rule regarding the labeling of calorie content for chain restaurants with more than 20 locations. Food industry behavior is slowly changing, too. According to a 2011 report from the Domestic Policy Council and White House Taskforce on Childhood Obesity, 16 of the largest American food companies have pledged to reduce the calorie content of their products by 1.5 trillion calories by 2015 (http://www.letsmove.gov/sites/letsmove.gov/files/Obesity_update_report.pdf). Still, much work needs to be done to help halt the obesity epidemic.

● DSM-5 Criteria for Binge Eating Disorder

- Recurrent binge eating episodes
- Binge eating episodes include at least three of the following:
  - eating more quickly than usual
  - eating until over full
  - eating large amounts even if not hungry
  - eating alone due to embarrassment about large food quantity
  - feeling bad (e.g., disgusted, guilty, or depressed) after the binge
- No compensatory behavior is present

Table 11.5 Severity Ratings for Binge Eating Disorder in DSM-5

Rating	Number of Binges
Mild	1-3 binges/week
Moderate	4-7
Severe	8-13
Extreme	14 or more

Binge eating disorder was added to DSM-5 based on a growing body of research supporting its validity as a diagnostic category (Attia et al., 2013; Striegel-Moore & Franco, 2008; Wonderlich et al., 2009). Severity ratings for this disorder are shown in Table 11.5 and are based on the number of binges per week. Many people with binge eating disorder have a history of dieting (Kinzl, Traweger, Trefalt et al., 1999; Pike, Dohm, Striegel-Moore et al., 2001). Binge eating disorder is comorbid with several disorders, including mood disorders, anxiety disorders, ADHD, conduct disorder, and substance use disorders (Kessler, Berglund, Chiu et al., 2013; Wonderlich et al., 2009). Risk factors for developing binge eating disorder include childhood obesity, critical comments about being overweight, weight-loss attempts in childhood, low self-concept, depression, and childhood physical or sexual abuse (Fairburn, Doll, Welch et al., 1998; Rubinstein, McGinn, Wildman et al., 2010).

Binge eating disorder is more prevalent than either anorexia nervosa or bulimia nervosa (Hudson, Hiripi, Pope et al., 2007; Kessler et al., 2013) In a recent study of several countries, the lifetime prevalence ranged from 0.2 to 4.7 percent (Kessler et al., 2013). Binge eating disorder is more common in women than men, although the gender difference is not as great as it is in anorexia or bulimia (Kessler et al., 2013). Though only a few epidemiological studies have been done, binge eating disorder appears to be equally prevalent among European, African, Asian, and Hispanic Americans (Striegel-Moore & Franco, 2008).

Physical Consequences of Binge Eating Disorder Like the other eating disorders, binge eating disorder has physical consequences. Many of the physical consequences are likely a function of associated obesity, including increased risk of type 2 diabetes, cardiovascular problems, chronic back pain, and headaches even after controlling for the independent effects of other comorbid disorders (Kessler et al., 2013). Other research shows that a number of physical problems are present among people with binge eating disorder that are independent from co-occurring obesity, including sleep problems, anxiety, depression, irritable bowel syndrome, and, for women, early onset of menstruation (Bulik & Reichborn-Kjennerud, 2003).

Prognosis Perhaps because it is a relatively new diagnosis, fewer studies have assessed the prognosis of binge eating disorder. Research so far suggests that between 25 and 82 percent of people recover (Keel & Brown, 2010; Striegel-Moore & Franco, 2008). One retrospective study found that people reported having their binge eating disorder for an average of 14.4 years, which is much longer than is reported for people with anorexia or bulimia (Pope et al., 2006). However, another recent epidemiological study of binge eating disorder in several countries reported a duration of just over four years (Kessler et al., 2013).

Quick Summary

Anorexia nervosa has three characteristics: restriction of behaviors to promote a healthy body weight, an intense fear of gaining weight and being fat, and a distorted body image. Anorexia usually begins in the early teen years and is more common in women than men. Bodily changes that can occur after severe weight loss can be serious and life threatening. About 70 percent of women with anorexia eventually recover, but it can take many years.

Bulimia nervosa involves both bingeing and compensatory behavior. Bingeing often involves sweet foods and is more likely to occur when someone is alone, after a negative social encounter, and in the morning or afternoon. One striking difference between anorexia and bulimia is weight loss: people with anorexia nervosa lose a tremendous amount of weight, whereas people with bulimia nervosa do not lose weight. Bulimia typically begins in late adolescence and is more common in women than men.

Depression often co-occurs with bulimia, and each condition appears to be a risk factor for the other. Dangerous changes to the body can also occur as a result of bulimia, such as menstrual problems, tearing in the stomach and throat, and swelling of the salivary glands.

Binge eating disorder is characterized by several binges, and most (but not all) people who suffer from it are obese (defined as having a BMI greater than 30). Not all obese people meet the criteria for binge eating disorder—only those who have binge episodes and report feeling a loss of control over their eating qualify. Binge eating disorder is more common than anorexia and bulimia and is more common in women than men, though the gender difference is not as great as it is in anorexia and bulimia. About 60 percent of people with binge eating disorder recover, but it may take even longer than recovery for anorexia or bulimia.

Check Your Knowledge 11.1 (Answers are at the end of the chapter.)

Answer the questions.

1. All of the following are symptoms of anorexia *except:*
   a. fear of fat and gaining weight
   b. unwillingness to maintain normal weight
   c. perfectionism
   d. distorted body image
2. Which statement is true regarding binge eating disorder?
   a. It is more common in men than women.
   b. It was not an eating disorder category in DSM-IV-TR.

   c. It is synonymous with obesity.
   d. It includes binges and purges.
3. Which of the following are characteristics of both anorexia and bulimia?
   a. They involve a good deal of weight loss.
   b. They are more common in women than men.
   c. They have physical side effects (e.g., menstrual irregularities).
   d. All of the above but *a* are correct.
4. List three factors that contribute to obesity.

Etiology of Eating Disorders

As with other disorders, a single factor is unlikely to cause an eating disorder. Several areas of current research—genetics, neurobiology, sociocultural pressures to be thin, personality, the role of the family, and the role of environmental stress—suggest that eating disorders result when several influences converge in a person's life.

Genetic Factors

Eating disorders run in families. First-degree relatives of women with anorexia nervosa are more than 10 times more likely than average to have the disorder themselves (e.g., Strober et al., 2000) Similar results are found for bulimia nervosa, where first-degree relatives of women with bulimia nervosa are about four times more likely than average to have the disorder (e.g., Kassett et al., 1989; Strober et al., 2000). Furthermore, first-degree relatives of women with eating disorders appear to be at higher risk for anorexia or bulimia (Lilenfeld et al., 1998; Strober et al., 1990, 2000). Although eating disorders are quite rare among men, one study found that first-degree relatives of men with anorexia nervosa were at greater risk for having anorexia nervosa (though not bulimia) than relatives of men without anorexia (Strober et al., 2001). One behavior genetics study (Hudson, Lalonde, Berry et al., 2006) found that relatives of obese people with binge eating disorder were more likely to have binge eating disorder themselves (20 percent) than were relatives of obese people without binge eating disorder (9 percent).

Twin studies of eating disorders also suggest a genetic influence. Most studies of both anorexia and bulimia report higher MZ than DZ concordance rates (Bulik, Wade, & Kendler, 2000) and show that genes account for a portion of the variance among twins with eating disorders (Wade et al., 2000). On the other hand, research has shown that nonshared/unique environmental factors (see Chapter 2), such as different interactions with parents or different peer groups, also contribute to the development of eating disorders (Klump, McGue, & Iacono, 2002). For example, a study of more than 1200 twin pairs found that 42 percent of the variance in bulimia symptoms was attributable to genetic factors but 58 percent of the variance was attributable to unique environmental factors (Baker et al., 2010). Research also suggests that key features of the eating disorders, such as dissatisfaction with one's body, a strong desire to be thin, binge eating, and preoccupation with weight, are heritable (Klump, McGue, & Iacono, 2000). Additional evidence suggests that common genetic factors may account for the relationship between certain personality characteristics, such as negative emotionality and constraint with eating disorders (Klump, McGue, & Iacono, 2002). The largest GWAS study (see Chapter 4 for more information on this method) to date, which included nearly 3000 people with anorexia nervosa, identified a number of single nucleotide polymorphisms (SNPs; see Chapter 2) that were associated with anorexia (Boraska, Franklin, Floyd et al., 2014). Even though this sample size sounds large, it was not large enough for the findings to hold up during replication, something that GWAS researchers frequently do to avoid reporting findings that could be due to chance. The results of all the genetic studies are consistent with the possibility that genes play a role in eating disorders, but studies showing how genetic factors interact with the environment are needed.

Neurobiological Factors

The hypothalamus is a key brain center for regulating hunger and eating. Research on animals with lesions to the lateral hypothalamus indicates that they lose weight and have no appetite (Hoebel & Teitelbaum, 1966). Thus, it is not surprising that the hypothalamus has been proposed to play a role in anorexia. The level of some hormones regulated by the hypothalamus, such as cortisol, is indeed different in people with anorexia. Rather than causing the disorder, however, these hormonal differences occur as a result of self-starvation, and levels return to normal after weight gain (Doerr et al., 1980; Stoving et al., 1999). Furthermore, the weight loss of animals with hypothalamic lesions does not parallel what we know about anorexia. These animals appear to have no hunger and to become indifferent to food, whereas people with anorexia continue to starve themselves despite being hungry and having an interest in food. Nor does the hypothalamic model account for body-image disturbance or fear of becoming fat. Thus, a dysfunctional hypothalamus does not seem a likely factor in anorexia nervosa.

Endogenous opioids are substances produced by the body that reduce pain sensations, enhance mood, and suppress appetite. Opioids are released during starvation and have been hypothesized to play a role in anorexia, bulimia, and binge eating disorder. Starvation among people with anorexia may increase the levels of endogenous opioids, resulting in a positively reinforcing positive mood state (Marrazzi & Luby, 1986). Furthermore, the excessive exercise seen among some people with eating disorders would increase opioids and thus be reinforcing.

Some research supports the theory that endogenous opioids play a role in eating disorders. For example, two studies found low levels of the endogenous opioid beta-endorphin (see Figure 11.2) in people with bulimia (Brewerton, Lydiard, Laraia et al., 1992; Waller, Kiser, Hardy et al., 1986). In one of these studies, the researchers observed that the people with more severe cases of bulimia had the lowest levels of beta-endorphin (Waller et al., 1986). It is important to note, however, that these findings demonstrate that low levels of opioids are seen concurrently with bulimia, not that such levels are seen before the onset of the disorder. In other words, we don't know if the low levels of opioids are a cause of bulimia or an effect of changes in food intake or purging. The same thing is true for binge eating disorder. Animal studies have shown that bingeing leads to changes in the opioid system (e.g., Bello et al., 2011) but not that changes in the opioid system lead to more bingeing.

Finally, some research has focused on two neurotransmitters (Kaye, 2008): serotonin, which is related to eating and satiety (feeling full), and dopamine, which is related to the rewarding/pleasing aspects of food.

Animal research has shown that serotonin promotes satiety. Therefore, the binges of people with bulimia or binge eating disorder could result from a serotonin deficit that causes them not to feel full after they eat. Animal research has also shown that food restriction interferes with serotonin synthesis in the brain. Thus, among people with anorexia, the severe food intake restrictions could interfere with the serotonin system.

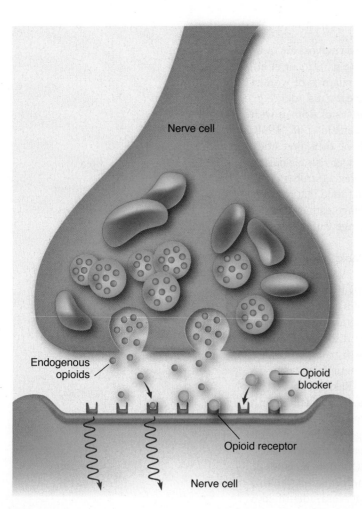

Figure 11.2 Endogenous opioid systems in the brain.

Researchers have examined levels of serotonin metabolites among people with anorexia and bulimia. Several studies have found low levels of serotonin metabolites among people with anorexia (e.g., Kaye et al., 1984) and bulimia (e.g., Carrasco et al., 2000; Jimerson et al., 1992; Kaye et al., 1998). Lower levels of a neurotransmitter's metabolites are one indicator that the neurotransmitter activity is underactive. In addition, people with anorexia who have not been restored to a healthy weight show a poorer response to serotonin agonists (i.e., drugs that stimulate serotonin receptors) than those people who have regained a good portion of their weight, again suggesting an underactive serotonin system (Attia et al., 1998; Ferguson et al., 1999). People with bulimia also show smaller responses to serotonin agonists (Jimerson et al., 1997; Levitan et al., 1997). The antidepressant drugs that can be effective treatments for some people with anorexia and bulimia (discussed later) are known to increase serotonin activity, adding to the possible importance of serotonin. Serotonin, though, more likely is linked to the comorbid depression often found in anorexia and bulimia.

Researchers have also examined the role of the dopamine in eating behavior. Studies with animals have shown that dopamine is linked to the pleasurable aspects of food that compel an animal to go after food (e.g., Szczypka et al., 2001), and brain-imaging studies in humans have shown how dopamine is linked to the motivation to obtain food and other pleasurable or rewarding things. In one study with healthy people, participants were presented with smells and tastes of food while undergoing a PET scan (Volkow et al., 2002). The participants also filled out a measure of dietary restraint (see Table 11.3). People who scored higher on dietary restraint exhibited greater dopamine activity in the dorsal striatum area of the brain during the presentation of food. This finding suggests that restrained eaters may be more sensitive to food cues, since one of the functions of dopamine is to signal the salience of particular stimuli. Whether or not these findings will be relevant to people with eating disorders remains to be seen.

A small fMRI study of 14 women with anorexia nervosa and 14 women without an eating disorder found that women with anorexia reported feeling more positively about pictures of underweight women compared to pictures of normal or overweight women (Fladung et al., 2010). The women without anorexia felt more positively when viewing pictures of normal-weight women. Brain activation matched these ratings of feelings: women with anorexia showed greater activation in the ventral striatum, an area of the brain linked to dopamine and reward (see also Chapter 5), than women without anorexia when viewing pictures of underweight women.

Another study found that women with either anorexia nervosa or bulimia nervosa had greater expression of the dopamine transporter gene *DAT* (Frieling, Romer, Scholz et al., 2010). Recall from Chapter 2 that a gene is "turned on," or expressed, as it interacts with

---

Table 11.3 The Restraint Scale

1. How often are you dieting? Never; rarely; sometimes; often; always.
2. What is the maximum amount of weight (in pounds) you have ever lost within 1 month? 0–4; 5–9; 10–14; 15–19; 20+.
3. What is your maximum weight gain within a week? 0–1; 1.1–2; 2.1–3; 3.1–5; 5.1+.
4. In a typical week, how much does your weight fluctuate? 0–1; 1.1–2; 2.1–3; 3.1–5; 5.1+.
5. Would a weight fluctuation of 5 pounds affect the way you live your life? Not at all; slightly; moderately; very much.
6. Do you eat sensibly in front of others and splurge alone? Never; rarely; often; always.
7. Do you give too much time and thought to food? Never; rarely; often; always.
8. Do you have feelings of guilt after overeating? Never; rarely; often; always.
9. How conscious are you of what you are eating? Not at all; slightly; moderately; extremely.
10. How many pounds over your desired weight were you at your maximum weight? 0–1; 1–5; 6–10; 11–20; 21+.

Source: From Polivy, Herman, & Howard (1980).

different aspects of the environment. The expression of DAT influences the release of a protein that regulates the reuptake of dopamine back into the synapse. This study also found that women with either eating disorder exhibited less expression of another dopamine gene called DRD_2. Other studies have found disturbances in the DRD_2 gene only among women with anorexia (Bergen et al., 2005). These findings point to the role of dopamine in eating disorders and will need to be replicated in future studies.

Animal studies of bingeing indicate that bingeing on sucrose (sugar) leads to increased release of dopamine in the striatum, and it has different effects on two dopamine receptors: more binding of D1 receptors in the ventral (bottom) part of the striatum but less binding of D2 receptors in the dorsal (top) part of the striatum (Avena & Bocarsly, 2012).

Although we can expect further neurotransmitter research in the future, keep in mind that much of this work focuses on brain mechanisms relevant to hunger, eating, and satiety (and a lot of it is in animals) but does little to account for other key features of eating disorders, in particular the intense fear of becoming fat. Furthermore, as suggested, the evidence so far does not show that brain changes predate the onset of eating disorders. Thus, we know that brain activity or gene expression of certain dopamine genes is correlated with eating disorders, not that these things cause eating disorders.

Cognitive Behavioral Factors

Cognitive behavioral theories of eating disorders focus on understanding the thoughts, feelings, and behaviors that contribute to distorted body image, fear of fat, and loss of control over eating. People with eating disorders may have maladaptive schemata that narrow their attention toward thoughts and images related to weight, body shape, and food (Fairburn, Shafran, & Cooper, 1999).

SERGIO MORAES/Reuters/Landov LLC

The fear of being fat, which is so important in eating disorders, is partly based on society's negative stereotypes of overweight people.

Anorexia Nervosa Cognitive behavioral theories of anorexia nervosa emphasize fear of fatness and body-image disturbance as the motivating factors that powerfully reinforce weight loss. Many who develop anorexia symptoms report that the onset followed a period of weight loss and dieting. Behaviors that achieve or maintain thinness are negatively reinforced by the reduction of anxiety about becoming fat as well as positively reinforced by comments from others (*Did you lose weight? You look great!*). Dieting and weight loss may also be positively reinforced by the sense of mastery or self-control they create (Fairburn et al., 1999; Garner, Vitousek, & Pike, 1997). Some theories also include personality and sociocultural variables in an attempt to explain how fear of fatness and body-image disturbances develop. For example, perfectionism and a sense of personal inadequacy may lead a person to become especially concerned with his or her appearance, making dieting a potent reinforcer. Similarly, seeing portrayals in the media of thinness as an ideal, being overweight, and tending to compare oneself with especially attractive others all contribute to dissatisfaction with one's body (Stormer & Thompson, 1996).

Another important factor in producing a strong drive for thinness and a disturbed body image is criticism from peers and parents about being overweight. In one study supporting this conclusion, adolescent girls aged 10 to 15 were evaluated twice, with a 3-year interval between assessments. Obesity at the first assessment was related to being teased by peers, and at the second assessment it was linked to dissatisfaction with their bodies. Dissatisfaction was in turn related to symptoms of an eating disorder (Paxton et al., 1999).

People often binge when diets are broken (Polivy & Herman, 1985). Thus, when a person with anorexia nervosa experiences a lapse in her strict dieting, the lapse is likely to escalate into a binge. The purging after an episode of binge eating can again be seen as motivated by the fear of weight gain elicited by the binge.

Research has also examined the role of emotion in anorexia nervosa. Not surprisingly, people with anorexia experience many negative emotions. Surprisingly, though, people with anorexia also experience positive emotion, even though they may not distinguish among different positive emotional states all that well (Selby, Wonderlich, Crosby et al., 2013). In other words, people with anorexia may experience a positive emotion such as pride very intensely after losing weight or by avoiding eating a piece of cake at a party. This may in turn be indistinguishable from happiness or success and is referred to as low positive emotion differentiation. One study found that low positive emotion differentiation prospectively predicted eating disorder behaviors such as vomiting, checking weight, exercising excessively, and using laxatives in a group of 118 women with anorexia (Selby et al., 2013). Feeling more strong negative emotions also predicted these behaviors.

Bulimia Nervosa and Binge Eating Disorder People with bulimia nervosa are also thought to be overconcerned with weight gain and body appearance; indeed, they often view their self-worth in terms of their weight and shape. They also have low self-esteem, and because weight and shape are somewhat more controllable than are other features of the self, they tend to focus on weight and shape, hoping their efforts in this area will make them feel better generally. They try to follow a very rigid pattern of restrictive eating, with strict rules regarding how much to eat, what kinds of food to eat, and when to eat. These strict rules are inevitably broken, and the lapse escalates into a binge. After the binge, feelings of disgust and fear of becoming fat build up, leading to compensatory actions such as vomiting (Fairburn, 1997). Although purging temporarily reduces the anxiety from having eaten too much, this cycle lowers the person's self-esteem, which triggers still more bingeing and purging—a vicious circle that maintains desired body weight but has serious medical consequences (see Figure 11.3 for a summary of this theory).

One group of researchers developed the Restraint Scale (see Table 11.3), a questionnaire measure of concerns about dieting and overeating (Polivy, Herman, & Howard, 1980). These researchers have conducted a series of laboratory studies, typically under the guise of being taste tests, with people who scored high on this measure. One such study was described as an assessment of the effects of temperature on taste (Polivy, Heatherton, & Herman, 1988). To achieve a "cold" condition, some participants first drank a 15-ounce chocolate milk shake (termed a *preload* by the investigators) and were then given three bowls of ice cream to taste and rate for flavor. Participants were told that once they had completed their ratings, they could eat as much of the ice cream as they wanted. The researchers then measured the amount of ice cream eaten.

In laboratory studies following this general design, people who scored high on the Restraint Scale ate more than nondieters after a fattening preload, even when the preload was perceived as fattening but was actually low in calories (Polivy, 1976) and even when the food was relatively unpalatable (Polivy, Herman, & McFarlane, 1994). Thus, people

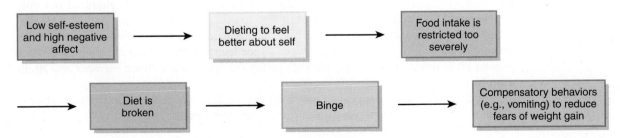

Figure 11.3 Schematic of cognitive behavioral theory of bulimia nervosa.

who score high on the Restraint Scale show a pattern similar to that of people with bulimia nervosa, albeit at a much less intense level.

Several additional conditions have been found to further increase the eating of restrained eaters after a preload, most notably various negative mood states, such as anxiety and depression (e.g., Herman et al., 1987). The increased consumption of restrained eaters is especially pronounced when their self-image is threatened (Heatherton, Herman, & Polivy, 1991) and if they have low self-esteem (Polivy et al., 1988). Finally, when restrained eaters are given false feedback indicating that their weight is high, they respond with increases in negative emotion and increased food consumption (McFarlane, Polivy, & Herman, 1998).

The eating pattern of people with bulimia or binge eating disorder is similar to, but more extreme than, the behavior highlighted in the studies of restrained eaters. People with bulimia nervosa or binge eating disorder typically binge when they encounter stress and experience negative emotions, as has been shown in several studies. In ecological momentary assessment (EMA; see Chapter 3), investigators are able to show how specific binge-and-purge events are linked to changes in emotions and stress in the course of daily life (Smyth et al., 2007). A meta-analysis of 82 EMA studies found that negative affect preceded the onset of a binge among people with bulimia or binge eating disorder, but the effect sizes (see Chapter 4) were stronger for binge eating disorder than for bulimia (Haedt-Matt & Keel, 2011). The binge may therefore function as a means of regulating negative affect (Smyth et al., 2007; Stice & Agras, 1999). However, the meta-analysis of EMA studies also showed that people with bulimia or binge eating disorder experienced *more* negative affect after the binge, so the use of bingeing as a way to regulate affect appears not to be very successful. Evidence also supports the idea that stress and negative affect are relieved by purging. That is, negative affect levels decline and positive affect levels increase after a purge event, supporting the idea that purging is reinforced by negative affect reduction (Haedt-Matt & Keel, 2011; Jarrell, Johnson, & Williamson, 1986; Smyth et al., 2007).

Given the similarities between people who score high on the Restraint Scale and people with bulimia nervosa, we might expect restrained eating to play a central role in bulimia. In fact, a study of the naturalistic course of bulimia (i.e., the course of bulimia left untreated) has found that the relationship between concern over shape and weight and binge eating was partially mediated by restrained eating (Fairburn et al., 2003). In other words, concerns about body shape and weight predicted restrained eating, which in turn predicted an increase in binge eating across 5 years of follow-up assessments. Other studies have failed to find this relationship (Burne & McLean, 2002), however, and thus additional research will need to sort out the ways in which restraint is linked with the symptoms of bulimia.

Research methods from cognitive science have been used to study how attention, memory, and problem solving are impacted in people with eating disorders. Using cognitive tasks such as the Stroop task (see Figure 2.13 in Chapter 2) and the dot probe test (see Figure 6.3 in Chapter 6), research shows that people with anorexia and bulimia focus their attention on food-related words or images more than other images (Brooks et al., 2011). People with anorexia nervosa and people who score high on restrained eating remember food words better when they are full but not when they are hungry (Brooks et al., 2011). Other studies have found that college women with eating disorder symptoms pay attention to and better remember images depicting other people's body size more than images depicting emotion (Treat & Viken, 2010). Thus, women with eating disorders pay greater attention not only to their own bodies, food, and weight but also to other women's bodies, food, and shapes. This bias toward food and body image may make it harder for women with eating disorders to change their thinking patterns. As we shall see later, cognitive behavior therapy devotes a good bit of time to teaching people with eating disorders to alter these memory and attention biases.

Sociocultural factors appear to play a role in the faulty perceptions and eating habits of those with eating disorders. We turn to these influences next.

Quick Summary

Genetic factors appear to play a role in both anorexia and bulimia. Both disorders tend to run in families, and twin studies support the role of genetics in the actual disorders and particular characteristics of the disorders, such as body dissatisfaction, preoccupation with thinness, and binge eating. The hypothalamus does not appear to be directly involved in eating disorders, and low levels of endogenous opioids are seen concurrently with bulimia, but not before the onset of the disorder. Thus, changes in food intake could affect the opioid system instead of changes in the opioid system affecting food intake. Research findings on the role of serotonin in anorexia are mixed. Serotonin may play a role in bulimia and binge eating disorders, with studies finding a decrease in serotonin metabolites and smaller responses to serotonin agonists. Other research suggests that dopamine may play a role in restrained eating, a characteristic that is found in people with eating disorders. Research linking dopamine to the brain's reward system can help account for how bingeing that is

part of bulimia and binge eating disorder influences the dopamine system. The neurobiological factors do not do a particularly good job of accounting for some key features of anorexia and bulimia, in particular the intense fear of becoming fat.

Cognitive behavioral theories focus on body dissatisfaction, preoccupation with thinness, and attention and memory. The Restraint Scale measures concerns about dieting and overeating, and high scores are linked to binge eating among people without eating disorders. The eating pattern of people with bulimia and binge eating disorder is similar to, but more extreme than, the behavior highlighted in the studies of restrained eaters. Studies have found that concerns about body shape and weight predicted restrained eating, which in turn predicted an increase in binge eating. People with eating disorders pay greater attention to food and body-image-related things, and they tend to remember these better as well, suggesting that their attention and memory may be biased toward food and body image.

Sociocultural Factors

Throughout history, the standards societies have set for the ideal body—especially the ideal female body—have varied greatly. Think of the famous nudes painted by Rubens in the seventeenth century: according to modern standards, these women are chubby. Over the past 55 years, the American cultural ideal has progressed steadily toward increasing thinness. *Playboy* centerfolds became thinner between 1959 and 1978, for example (Garner et al., 1980), and beauty pageant contestants also became thinner through 1988. A study that calculated the body mass index (BMI) of *Playboy* centerfolds from 1985 to 1997 (Owen & Laurel-Seller, 2000) found that all but one of the centerfolds had a BMI of less than 20, which is considered to be a low weight, and almost half of the centerfolds had a BMI of less than 18, which is considered to be underweight.

For men, the situation appears somewhat different. In a study parallel to the studies examining *Playboy* centerfolds, researchers analyzed the BMI of *Playgirl* male centerfolds from 1973 to 1997 (Leit, Pope, & Gray, 2001). They found that the centerfolds' BMI *increased* over the period and that their muscularity, assessed using a fat-to-muscle estimate, increased even more. Thus for men, magazines focus attention on the masculine ideal of normal body weight or on increased muscle mass (Mishkind et al., 1986).

Somewhat paradoxically, as cultural standards were moving in the direction of thinness over the latter part of the twentieth century, more and more people were becoming overweight. The prevalence of obesity has more than doubled since 1900 (see Focus on Discovery 11.1). Currently, over two-thirds of Americans are overweight (and over a third are obese), setting the stage for greater conflict between the cultural ideal and reality.

As society has become more health and fat conscious, dieting to lose weight has become more common; the number of dieters increased from 7 percent of men and 14 percent of women in 1950 to 29 percent of men and 44 percent of women in 1999 (Serdula et al., 1999). Results from a survey of over 4,000 women between the ages of 25 and 45 indicated that a third of the women reported spending over half of their lifetimes trying to lose weight (Reba-Harrelson, Von Holle, Hamer et al., 2009). Diet crazes come and go. For

Cultural standards regarding the ideal feminine shape have changed over time. Even in the 1950s and 1960s, the feminine ideal was considerably heavier than what it has become in the 1970s through today.

example, the number of low-carb diet books increased from 15 to 194 between 1999 and 2004; and 26 million people in the United States were on a diet that severely limited carbohydrate consumption in 2004 (Kadlic et al., 2004). Are some diets more effective than others? A study in the *New England Journal of Medicine* reported that diets were equally effective, whether carbs, fat, or protein is cut, as long as the total number of calories is reduced (Sacks et al., 2009). Surgeries such as liposuction (vacuuming out fat deposits just under the skin) and gastroplasty (surgically changing the stomach so that it cannot digest as much food) remain popular despite their risk (Brownell & Horgen, 2003).

The percentages above indicate that women are more likely than men to be dieters. The onset of eating disorders is typically preceded by dieting and other concerns about weight, supporting the idea that social standards stressing the importance of thinness play a role in the development of these disorders (Killen et al., 1994; Rubinstein et al., 2010; Stice, 2001).

It is likely that women who either are actually overweight or fear being fat are also dissatisfied with their bodies. Not surprisingly, studies have found that women and adolescents with both a high BMI and body dissatisfaction are at higher risk for developing eating disorders (Fairburn et al., 1997; Killen et al., 1996). Preoccupation with being thin or feeling pressure to be thin predicts an increase in body dissatisfaction among adolescent girls, which in turn predicts more dieting, eating pathology, and negative emotions (Stice, 2001); these factors were operating in the clinical case of Jill, presented earlier.

Finally, exposure to media portrayals of unrealistically thin models can influence reports of body dissatisfaction. One study reviewed results from 25 experiments that presented images of thin models to women and then asked the women to report on their body satisfaction. Perhaps not surprisingly, results from these studies showed that women reported a decline in body satisfaction after viewing these images (Groesz, Levine, & Murnen, 2002). Another study found that men's body dissatisfaction, as indexed by a greater discrepancy between the muscularity of the actual and ideal self, increased after viewing images of muscular men (Leit, Gray, & Pope, 2002).

The sociocultural ideal of thinness is a likely vehicle through which people learn to fear being or even feeling fat, and this was probably influential in the cases of both Lynne and Jill. In addition to creating an undesired physical shape, being fat has negative connotations, such as being unsuccessful and having little self-control. Obese people are viewed by others as less smart and are stereotyped as lonely, shy, and greedy for the affection of others (DeJong & Kleck, 1986). Even more disturbing, health professionals who specialize in obesity have also exhibited beliefs that obese people are lazy, stupid, or worthless (Schwartz et al., 2003). Reducing the stigma associated with being overweight will be beneficial to those with eating disorders as well as those who are obese.

Not only does the fear of being fat contribute to eating pathology, but the celebration of extreme thinness via websites, blogs, and magazines may also play a role. Websites that are "pro-ana" (short for anorexia) or "pro-mia" (short for bulimia) and other "thinsperation" websites and blogs have developed a following of women who seek support and encouragement for losing weight, often to a dangerously low level. These sites often post photos of female celebrities who are extremely thin as inspiration (hence, the term *thinsperation*). Some of these women have publicly discussed their struggles with eating disorders (e.g., the actress Jessica Alba), but others have not.

A recent review of the impact of these "pro–eating disorder" websites noted that women who visited these sites were more dissatisfied with their bodies, had more eating disorder symptoms, and experienced more prior hospitalizations for eating disorders (Rouleau & von Ranson, 2011). To tease apart causation from correlation, researchers have randomly assigned healthy women to view either pro–eating disorder, other health-related, or tourist websites (Jett, La Perte, & Wanchism, 2010), supposedly as part of a website evaluation survey. Women completed food diaries for one week before and one week after viewing these websites. Women assigned to the pro–eating disorder website condition restricted their eating more the following week than did the women assigned to the other website conditions. These results suggest that viewing these websites has the potential to cause unhealthful changes in eating behavior.

Gender Influences We have discussed the fact that eating disorders are more common in women than in men. One primary reason is likely the fact that Western cultural standards emphasize and reinforce the desirability of being thin more for women than for men. The risk for eating disorders among groups of women who might be expected to be particularly concerned with thinness and their weight—for example, models, dancers, and gymnasts, as in the case of Jill—appears to be especially high (Garner et al., 1980).

Another sociocultural factor, though, has remained remarkably resilient to change—namely, the objectification of women's bodies. Women's bodies are often viewed through a sexual lens; in effect, women are defined by their bodies, whereas men are esteemed more for their accomplishments. According to objectification theory (Fredrickson & Roberts, 1997), the prevalence of objectification messages in Western culture (in television, advertisements, and so forth) has led some women to "self-objectify," which means that they see their own bodies through the eyes of others. Research has shown that self-objectification causes women to feel more shame about their bodies. Shame is most often elicited in situations where an individual's ideal falls short of a cultural ideal or standard. Thus, women likely experience body shame when they observe a mismatch between their ideal self and the cultural (objectified) view of women. Research has also shown that both self-objectification and body shame are associated with disordered eating (Fredrickson et al., 1998; McKinley & Hyde, 1996; Noll & Fredrickson, 1998).

Do eating disorders and weight concerns go away as women get older? A large, 20-year prospective study of over 600 men and women reported important differences in dieting and other eating disorder risk factors for men and women (Keel et al., 2007). The men and women were first surveyed about dieting, BMI, weight, body image, and eating disorder symptoms when they were in college. Follow-up surveys were completed 10 and 20 years after college. Thus, the men and women were around age 40 at the 20-year follow-up assessment. The researchers found that after 20 years, women dieted less and were less concerned about their weight and body image than they were in college, even though they actually weighed more now. In addition, eating disorder symptoms decreased over the 20 years for women, as did the risk factors for eating disorders (concern about body image, frequency of dieting). Changes in life roles—having a life partner, having a child—were also associated with decreases in eating disorder symptoms for women. By contrast, men were more concerned about their weight and were dieting more. Like women, they weighed more in their early 40s than when they were in college. Decreases in risk factors such as concern about body image and dieting frequency were also associated with decreases in eating disorder symptoms for men.

Cross-Cultural Studies Evidence for eating disorders across cultures depends on the disorder. Anorexia has been observed in a number of cultures and countries besides the United States; for example, in Hong Kong, China, Taiwan, England, Korea, Japan, Denmark, Nigeria, South Africa, Zimbabwe, Ethiopia, Iran, Malaysia, India, Pakistan, Australia, the Netherlands, and Egypt (Keel & Klump, 2003). Furthermore, cases of anorexia have been documented in cultures with very little Western cultural influence. An important caveat must be made, however. The anorexia observed in these diverse cultures does not always include the intense fear of gaining weight or being fat that is part of the DSM criteria, at least initially. Thus, intense fear of fat likely reflects an ideal more widely espoused in more Westernized cultures.

Al Roker, the weatherperson on NBC's *Today* show, had gastric bypass surgery to accomplish weight loss.

Celebrities such as Christina Ricci have publicly discussed their struggles with eating disorders.

For example, Lee (1991) described a disorder similar to anorexia nervosa in Hong Kong that involved severe emaciation, food refusal, and amenorrhea, but not a fear of becoming fat. Is this a cultural variant of anorexia or a different disorder, such as depression? This question is but one of the challenges that face cross-cultural researchers (Lee et al., 2001). Indeed, in some other cultures, higher weight among women is especially valued and considered a sign of fertility and healthiness (Nasser, 1988). The variation in the clinical presentation of anorexia across cultures provides a window into the importance of culture in establishing realistic versus potentially disordered views of one's body. However, there is also evidence that cultural variation is diminishing when it comes to eating disorders. A 20-year study of eating disorders in Hong Kong found evidence of Western influence in both the prevalence and presentation of eating disorders (Lee et al., 2010). First, both anorexia and bulimia were twice as common in 2007 than they were in 1987. Second, 25 percent more women reported body dissatisfaction and fear of fat in 2007 than in 1987. Thus, in a fairly short period of time, eating disorders in Hong Kong appear to have become more Western.

Another feature of eating disorders that may be heavily influenced by Western ideals of beauty and thinness is body image. In a study supporting the notion of cross-cultural differences in body-image perception, Ugandan and British college students rated the attractiveness of drawings of nudes ranging from very emaciated to very obese (Furnham & Baguma, 1994). Ugandan students rated the obese females as more attractive than did the British students.

Bulimia nervosa appears to be more common in industrialized societies, such as the United States, Canada, Japan, Australia, and Europe, than in nonindustrialized nations. However, as cultures undergo social changes associated with adopting the practices of more Westernized cultures, particularly the United States (Watters, 2010), the incidence of bulimia appears to increase (Abou-Saleh, Younis, & Karim, 1998; Lee et al., 2010; Nasser, 1997). A comprehensive review of research on culture and eating disorders conducted nearly 10 years ago could not find evidence of bulimia outside of a Westernized culture (Keel & Klump, 2003). It will be interesting to see if this changes in the next 10 years.

Ethnic Differences There is a somewhat greater incidence of eating disturbances and body dissatisfaction among white women than black women (Grabe & Hyde, 2006; Perez & Joiner, 2003), but differences in actual eating disorders, particularly bulimia, do not appear to be as great (Wildes, Emery, & Simons, 2001). In addition, the greatest differences between white and black women in eating disorder pathology appear to be most pronounced in college student samples; fewer differences are observed in either high school or nonclinical community samples (Wildes et al., 2001). A meta-analysis found more similarities than differences in body dissatisfaction among ethnic groups in the United States (Grabe & Hyde, 2006). White women and Hispanic women reported greater body dissatisfaction than African American women, but no other ethnic differences were reliably found.

Differences have been observed in the United States in some areas, however. Studies show that white teenage girls diet more frequently than do African American teenage girls and are more likely to be dissatisfied with their bodies (Fitzgibbons et al., 1998; Striegel-Moore et al., 2000). The relationship between BMI and body dissatisfaction also differs by ethnicity. Compared with African American adolescents, white adolescents become more dissatisfied with their bodies as their BMI rises (Striegel-Moore et al., 2000). As already noted, both dieting and body dissatisfaction are related to an increased risk for developing an eating disorder. One study found that white women with binge eating disorder were more dissatisfied with their bodies than African American women with binge eating disorder, and that white women were more likely to have a history of bulimia nervosa than African American women (Pike et al., 2001).

In addition, acculturation, the extent to which someone assimilates their own culture with a new culture, may be another important variable to consider. This process can at times be quite stressful. A recent study found that the relationship between body dissatisfaction and bulimia symptoms was stronger for African American and Hispanic college students who reported higher levels of acculturative stress compared to those students who reported lower levels of this type of stress (Perez et al., 2002).

FilmMagic/Getty Images, Inc.

Jessica Alba has spoken openly about her eating disorder.

Little is known about the prevalence of eating disorders among Latina or Native American women, and this remains a much-needed research focus. Data from one epidemiological study of Latina women age 18 or older found that binge eating disorder was more prevalent than bulimia nervosa but that the prevalence rates for both disorders were comparable to prevalence rates in Caucasian women (Alegria et al., 2007). The diagnosis of bulimia was more likely for women who had lived in the United States for several years than for women who had recently immigrated, indicating that acculturation may play a role. In contrast to other eating disorders, anorexia nervosa was very rare among Latina women (only 2 out of over 2,500 women had a lifetime history of anorexia).

Beyond the racial or ethnic differences in eating disorders, stereotyped beliefs about race and eating disorders may play a role. For example, one study found that college students who read a fictional case study about a woman with eating disorder symptoms were more likely to ascribe an eating disorder to the woman if her race was presented as Caucasian rather than African American or Hispanic (Gordon, Perez, & Joiner, 2002). In other words, the symptoms were rated as clinically significant only for the white case presentation, not for the African American or Hispanic ones, even though the details were identical. Although it remains to be seen whether mental health professionals would exhibit the same stereotypes when making clinical judgments, it suggests that symptoms may be more easily overlooked among non-Caucasian women.

Socioeconomic status is also important to consider (Caldwell, Brownell, & Wilfley, 1997; French et al., 1997). The emphasis on thinness and dieting is found among all levels of socioeconomic status, as is the prevalence of eating disorder pathology (e.g., Story et al., 1995; Striegel-Moore et al., 2000).

Standards of beauty vary cross-culturally, as shown by Gauguin's painting of Tahitian women.

Other Factors Contributing to the Etiology of Eating Disorders

Personality Influences We have already seen that neurobiological changes occur as a result of an eating disorder. It is also important to keep in mind that an eating disorder itself can affect personality. A study of semistarvation in male conscientious objectors conducted in the late 1940s supports the idea that the personality of people with eating disorders, particularly those with anorexia, is affected by their weight loss (Keys, Brozek, Hsu et al., 1950). For a period of 6 weeks, the men were given two meals a day, totaling 1500 calories, to simulate the meals in a concentration camp. On average, the men lost 25 percent of their body weight. They all soon became preoccupied with food; they also reported increased fatigue, poor concentration, lack of sexual interest, irritability, moodiness, and insomnia. Four became depressed, and one developed bipolar disorder. This research shows vividly how severe restriction of food intake can have powerful effects on personality and behavior, which we need to consider when evaluating the personalities of people with anorexia and bulimia.

In part as a response to the findings just mentioned, some researchers have collected retrospective reports of personality before the onset of an eating disorder. This research describes people with anorexia as having been perfectionistic, shy, and compliant before the onset of the disorder. The description of people with bulimia includes the additional characteristics of histrionic features, affective instability, and an outgoing social disposition (Vitousek & Manke, 1994). It is important to remember, however, that retrospective reports in which people with an eating disorder and their families recall what the person was like before diagnosis can be inaccurate and biased by awareness of the person's current symptoms.

Prospective studies examine personality characteristics before an eating disorder is present. In one study, more than 2000 students in a suburban Minneapolis school district completed several tests, including measures of personality characteristics and the Eating Disorders Inventory, for 3 consecutive years. During year 1 of the study, cross-sectional predictors of disordered eating included body dissatisfaction; poor interoceptive awareness, which is the

Severe food restriction can have profound effects on behavior and personality, as illustrated by the study of male conscientious objectors in the 1940s.

extent to which people can distinguish different biological states of their bodies (see Table 11.3 for items that assess interoceptive awareness); and a propensity to experience negative emotions (Leon et al., 1995). At year 3, these same variables were found to have prospectively predicted disordered eating (Leon et al., 1999). A different prospective study found that perfectionism predicted the onset of anorexia in young adult women (Tyrka et al., 2002).

Additional research has taken a closer look at the link between perfectionism and anorexia. Perfectionism is multifaceted and may be self-oriented (setting high standards for oneself), other-oriented (setting high standards for others), or socially oriented (trying to conform to the high standards imposed by others). A recent review of many studies concludes that perfectionism, no matter how it is measured, is higher among girls with anorexia than among girls without anorexia and that perfectionism remains high even after successful treatment for anorexia (Bardone-Cone et al., 2007). A multinational study found that people with anorexia scored higher on self- and other-oriented types of perfectionism than people without anorexia (Halmi et al., 2000). Finally, mothers of girls with anorexia scored higher on perfectionism than mothers of girls without anorexia (Woodside et al., 2002). This intriguing finding needs to be replicated, but it suggests that what is genetically transmitted in anorexia could be a personality characteristic, such as perfectionism, that increases the vulnerability for the disorder rather than the disorder per se.

Characteristics of Families Studies of the characteristics of families of people with eating disorders have yielded variable results. Some of the variation stems, in part, from the different methods used to collect the data and from the sources of the information. For example, self-reports of people with eating disorders consistently reveal high levels of conflict in the family (e.g., Bulik, Sullivan, et al., 2000; Hodges, Cochrane, & Brewerton, 1998). Reports of parents, however, do not necessarily indicate high levels of family problems.

To better understand the role of family functioning, it is necessary to study these families directly by observational measures rather than by self-reports alone. Although an adolescent's perception of his or her family's characteristics is important, we also need to know how much of reported family discord is perceived and how much is consistent with others' perceptions. In one of the few observational studies conducted thus far, parents of children with eating disorders did not appear to be very different from parents of children with no eating disorders. The two groups did not differ in the frequency of positive and negative messages given to their children, and the parents of children with eating disorders were more self-disclosing. The parents of children with eating disorders did lack some communication skills, however, such as the ability to request clarification of vague statements (van den Broucke, Vandereycken, & Vertommen, 1995). Observational studies such as this, coupled with data on perceived family characteristics, would help determine whether actual or perceived family characteristics are related to eating disorders.

People with eating disorders consistently report that their family life was high in conflict.

Child Abuse and Eating Disorders Some studies have indicated that self-reports of childhood sexual abuse are higher among people with eating disorders than among people without eating disorders, especially those with bulimia nervosa (Deep et al., 1999; Webster & Palmer, 2000). Since, as discussed in Chapter 8, some memories of abuse may be created in therapy, it is notable that high rates of sexual abuse have been found among people with eating disorders who have not been in treatment as well as those who have (Romans et al., 2001; Wonderlich et al., 1996, 2001). Still, the role of childhood sexual abuse as a cause of eating disorders remains uncertain. Furthermore, high rates of childhood sexual abuse are found among people with different diagnoses, so if it plays some role, it is not likely to be highly specific to eating disorders (Fairburn, Cooper et al., 1999; Romans et al., 2001).

Quick Summary

Sociocultural factors, including society's preoccupation with thinness, may play a role in eating disorders. This preoccupation is linked to dieting efforts, and dieting precedes the development of eating disorders among many people. In addition, the preoccupation with thinness, as well as media portrayals of thin women, predicts an increase in body dissatisfaction, which also precedes the development of eating disorders. Stigma associated with being overweight also contributes. Women are more likely to have eating disorders than men, and the ways in which women's bodies are objectified may lead some women to see their bodies as others do (self-objectify), which in turn may increase body dissatisfaction and eating pathology. Anorexia appears to occur in many cultures, whereas bulimia appears to be more common in industrialized and Westernized societies. Eating disorders are slightly more common among white women than women of color, with the difference being most pronounced in college student samples. Eating disorders used to be more common among women of higher socioeconomic status, but this is less true today.

Research on personality characteristics finds that perfectionism may play a role. Other personality characteristics that predicted disordered eating across 3 years include body dissatisfaction, the extent to which people can distinguish different biological states of their bodies, and a propensity to experience negative emotions. Troubled family relationships are fairly common among people with eating disorders, but this could be a result of the eating disorder, not necessarily a cause of it. High rates of sexual and physical abuse are found among people with eating disorders, but these are not risk factors specific to the development of eating disorders.

Check Your Knowledge 11.2

True or false?
1. The brain structure linked to the cause of eating disorders is the hypothalamus.
2. Dopamine has been studied in all the eating disorders.
3. Prospective studies of personality and eating disorders indicate that the tendency to experience negative emotions is related to disordered eating.
4. Anorexia appears to be specific to Western culture; bulimia is seen all over the world and is thus not culture specific.
5. Cognitive behavioral views of bulimia suggest that women judge their self-worth by their weight and shape.
6. Child abuse appears to be a specific causal factor for eating disorders.

Treatment of Eating Disorders

Hospitalization is frequently required to treat people with anorexia so that their ingestion of food can be gradually increased and carefully monitored. This was necessary for Lynne. Weight loss can be so severe that intravenous feeding is necessary to save the person's life. The medical complications of anorexia, such as electrolyte imbalances, also require treatment. For both anorexia and bulimia, both medications and psychological treatments have been used.

Medications

Because bulimia nervosa is often comorbid with depression, it has been treated with various antidepressants. Findings from most studies, including double-blind randomized controlled trials with placebo controls, confirm the efficacy of a variety of antidepressants in reducing purging and binge eating, even among people who had not responded to prior psychological treatment (Walsh et al., 2000; Wilson & Fairburn, 1998; Wilson & Pike, 2001).

On the negative side, many people with bulimia drop out of drug treatment (Fairburn, Agras & Wilson, 1992). In contrast, in one study fewer than 5 percent of women dropped out of cognitive behavior therapy (Agras et al., 1992). Moreover, most people relapse when various kinds of antidepressant medications are withdrawn (Wilson & Pike, 2001), as is the case with many psychoactive drugs. There is some evidence that this tendency to relapse is reduced if antidepressants are given in the context of cognitive behavior therapy (Agras et al., 1994).

Medications have also been used to treat anorexia nervosa with little success in improving weight or other core features of anorexia (Attia et al., 1998; Johnson, Tsoh, & Varnado, 1996). Medication treatment for binge eating disorder has not been as well studied. Limited evidence suggests that antidepressant medications are not effective in reducing binges or weight loss (Grilo, 2007). Recent trials of antiobesity drugs, such as sibutramine and atomoxetine, show some promise in binge eating disorder, but additional clinical trials are needed. A randomized controlled trial compared the antidepressant medication Fluoxetine (Prozac) with CBT plus placebo, or CBT plus Fluoxetine and found that that CBT plus placebo was more effective in reducing binge episodes than either condition including Fluoxetine and this remained the case at a 12-month follow-up (Grilo et al., 2012).

Psychological Treatment of Anorexia Nervosa

Little in the way of controlled research exists on psychological treatments for anorexia nervosa, but we will present the most promising of the psychotherapeutic approaches to this life-threatening disorder.

Therapy for anorexia is generally believed to be a two-tiered process. The immediate goal is to help the person gain weight in order to avoid medical complications and the possibility of death. The person is often so weak and physiological functioning so disturbed that hospital treatment is medically imperative (in addition to being needed to ensure that the patient ingests some food). Operant conditioning behavior therapy programs (e.g., providing reinforcers for weight gain) have been somewhat successful in achieving weight gain in the short term (Hsu, 1990). However, the second goal of treatment—long-term maintenance of weight gain—remains a challenge for the field.

Beyond immediate weight gain, psychological treatment for anorexia can also involve CBT. One study that combined hospital treatment with CBT found that reductions in many anorexia symptoms persisted up to 1 year after treatment (Bowers & Ansher, 2008). Other studies have found that CBT is effective after hospitalization in reducing the risk for relapse (Pike, Walsh, Vitousek et al., 2003). A recent randomized controlled clinical trial compared CBT with supportive psychotherapy plus education about anorexia and found that both were equally effective for women with anorexia nervosa in reducing eating disorder symptoms and depression (Touyz, Le Grange, Lacey et al., 2013). Although BMI increased at the end of treatment and remained stable at the 12-month follow-up, the average BMIs for women in both treatment groups were still in the mild severity range (see Table 11.2). Additional analyses examined who might benefit the most from CBT, and the results indicated that women who were older and had more severe symptoms benefited the most from CBT (Le Grange, Fitzsimmons-Craft, Crosby et al., 2014).

Another randomized controlled clinical trial in Germany compared CBT to psychodynamic therapy and to "optimized treatment as usual," which included a good deal of support and referrals to psychotherapists (Zipfel, Wild, Gross et al., 2014). All three treatments were equally effective in increasing BMI, but the increase was modest: only about 0.7 points at the 10-month follow-up treatment and another 0.4 points at the 12-month follow-up.

Family therapy is another form of psychological treatment for anorexia and is based on the notion that interactions among members of the patient's family can play a role in treating the disorder (Le Grange & Lock, 2005). A family-based therapy (FBT) developed in England focuses on helping parents restore their daughter to a healthy weight while at the same time building up family functioning in the context of adolescent development (Lock & Le Grange, 2001; Lock, Le Grange, Agras et al., 2001; Loeb, Walsh, Lock et al., 2007). A randomized controlled clinical trial compared FBT with individual therapy and found that both treatments were equally effective at the end of the 24-session treatment. However, more girls receiving FBT were in full remission (49 percent) 1 year after treatment than girls receiving individual therapy (23 percent) (Lock, Le Grange, Agras et al., 2011). Another study of FBT found that the girls who had gained weight by session 4 were more likely to be in full remission at the end of treatment (Doyle, Le Grange, Loeb et al., 2010). Thus, early weight gain may be an important predictor of a good outcome. Although the findings are promising, additional work needs to be done to improve the outcomes for anorexia.

Family therapy is a main form of treatment for anorexia nervosa.

Psychological Treatment of Bulimia Nervosa

CBT is the best-validated and most current standard for the treatment of bulimia (Fairburn, 1985; Fairburn et al., 2009; Fairburn, Marcus, & Wilson, 1993). In CBT, people with bulimia are encouraged to question society's standards for physical attractiveness. People with bulimia must also uncover and then change beliefs that encourage them to starve themselves to avoid becoming overweight. They must be helped to see that normal body weight can be maintained without severe dieting and that unrealistic restriction of food intake can often trigger a binge. They are taught that all is not lost with just one bite of high-calorie food and that snacking need not trigger a binge, which will be followed by induced vomiting or taking laxatives, which in turn will lead to still lower self-esteem and depression. Altering this all-or-nothing thinking can help people begin to eat more moderately. They also learn assertiveness skills, which help them cope with unreasonable demands placed on them by others, as well as more satisfying ways of relating to people.

The overall goal of treatment in bulimia nervosa is to develop more typical eating patterns. People with bulimia need to learn to eat three meals a day and even some snacks between meals without sliding back into bingeing and purging. Regular meals control hunger and thereby, it is hoped, the urge to eat enormous amounts of food, the effects of which are counteracted by purging. To help people with bulimia develop less extreme beliefs about themselves, the cognitive behavior therapist gently but firmly challenges such beliefs as, "No one will respect me if I am a few pounds heavier than I am now" or "Eric loves me only because I weigh 112 pounds and would surely reject me if I ballooned to 120 pounds." Unrealistic demands and other cognitive distortions—such as the belief that eating a small amount of high-calorie food means that the person is an utter failure and doomed never to improve—are continually challenged. The therapist works collaboratively with the person to identify events, thoughts, and feelings that trigger an urge to binge and then to learn more adaptive ways to cope with these situations.

In the case of Jill, she and her therapist discovered that bingeing often took place after she was criticized by her coach. Therapy included the following:

- Encouraging Jill to assert herself if the criticism is unwarranted
- Desensitizing her to social evaluation and encouraging her to question society's standards for ideal weight and the pressures on women to be thin—not an easy task by any means
- Teaching her that it is not a catastrophe to make a mistake and it is not necessary to be perfect, even if the coach's criticism is valid

Findings from a number of studies indicate that CBT often results in less frequent bingeing and purging, with reductions ranging from 70 to more than 90 percent. For example, a recent randomized controlled clinical trial compared 5 months of CBT with 2 years of psychoanalytic therapy and found that those who received CBT had far fewer bingeing and purging episodes, both at the end of 5 months and at the end of 2 years (Poulsen, Lunn, Daniel et al., 2014). Extreme dietary restraint is also reduced significantly; attitudes toward body shape and weight improve (Compas et al., 1998; Richards et al., 2000); and therapeutic gains are maintained at 1-year follow-up (Agras et al., 2000), nearly 6 years later (Fairburn et al., 1995) and 10 years later (Keel, Mitchell, Davis et al., 2002). But there are limitations to these positive outcomes, as we will see.

Actress Mary-Kate Olsen has been treated for an eating disorder.

Peter Kramer/Getty Images News and Sport Services

CBT alone is more effective than any available drug treatment (Compas et al., 1998; Walsh et al., 1997), and a meta-analysis showed that CBT yielded better results than antidepressant medications (Whittal, Agras, & Gould, 1999). But are outcomes better when antidepressant medication is added to CBT? Evidence on this front is mixed. Adding antidepressant drugs, however, may be useful in helping to alleviate the depression that often occurs with bulimia (Keel et al., 2002; Wilson & Fairburn, 1998).

If, however, we focus on the people themselves rather than on the numbers of binges and purges across people, we find that at least half of those treated with CBT improve very little (Wilson & Pike, 2001). Clearly, while CBT may be the most effective treatment available for bulimia, it still has room for improvement.

Some studies have examined whether adding exposure and response prevention (ERP) to CBT for bulimia might boost the treatment effects of CBT (recall that ERP is an aspect of the cognitive behavioral treatment of obsessive-compulsive disorder in Chapter 7). This ERP component involves discouraging the person from purging after eating foods that usually elicit an urge to vomit. In one study, the combination of ERP and CBT was more effective than CBT without ERP, at least in the short term (e.g., Fairburn et al., 1995). ERP may not continue to be an advantage over the long term, however. One study examined outcome 3 years after treatment for people with bulimia who had received CBT either with or without ERP. It found similar outcomes for the two groups (Carter et al., 2003). That is, 85 percent of people with bulimia did not meet the criteria for bulimia 3 years after treatment, regardless of which treatment they had received.

Another form of CBT, called guided self-help CBT, has also shown promise for some people. In this type of treatment, people receive self-help books on topics such as perfectionism, body image, negative thinking, and food and health. Patients meet for a small number of sessions with a therapist who helps guide them through the self-help material. Preliminary results suggest that this is an effective treatment compared to a wait-list control group and to traditional CBT for bulimia. In addition, greater confidence in one's ability to change is associated with better outcomes (Steele, Bergin, & Wade, 2011).

Interpersonal therapy (IPT) has also been used for bulimia, and it fared well in comparisons with CBT, though it did not produce results as quickly (Fairburn et al., 1991; Fairburn, Jones et al., 1993). The two modes of intervention were equivalent at 1-year follow-up in effecting change across all four of the specific aspects of bulimia: bingeing, purging, dietary restraint, and maladaptive attitudes about body shape and weight (Wilson, 1995). This pattern—CBT superior to IPT immediately after treatment but IPT catching up at follow-up—was replicated in a later study (Agras et al., 2000).

Family therapy is also effective for bulimia, though it has been studied less frequently than either CBT or IPT. A randomized clinical trial demonstrated that family-based therapy was superior to supportive psychotherapy for adolescents with bulimia with respect to decreasing bingeing and purging up to 6 months after treatment was completed (Le Grange, Crosby, Rathouz et al., 2007).

Psychological Treatment of Binge Eating Disorder

Although not as extensively studied as with bulimia nervosa, cognitive behavior therapy has been shown to be effective for binge eating disorder in several studies (Grilo, 2007). CBT for binge eating disorder targets binges as well as restrained eating by emphasizing self-monitoring, self-control, and problem solving as regards eating. Gains from CBT appear to last up to 1 year after treatment. CBT also appears to be more effective than treatment with fluoxetine (Grilo, 2007). Randomized controlled clinical trials have shown that IPT is as effective as CBT and guided self-help CBT for binge eating disorder (Wilfley et al., 2002; Wilson et al., 2010). These three treatments are more effective than behavioral weight-loss programs, which are often used to treat obesity. More specifically, CBT and IPT reduce binge eating (but not necessarily weight), whereas behavioral weight-loss programs may promote weight loss but do not curb binge eating.

One study compared three treatments for binge eating disorder: (1) therapist-led group CBT, (2) therapist-assisted group CBT, and (3) structured self-help group CBT with no therapist. Results showed that people in the therapist-led group CBT had the greatest reduction in binge eating at 6-month and 12-month follow-ups but that all groups had a greater reduction in binges than a group of people assigned to a wait-list control group (Peterson, Mitchell, Crow et al., 2009). Fewer people dropped out of the therapist-led group as well. Thus, having a therapist lead a CBT group may help keep people in treatment and help reduce binges, but, importantly, people in the therapist-assisted and "therapist-free" groups also showed reductions in binges. Given that therapist cost and/or availability may limit treatment for some people, having options such as these available is promising.

Quick Summary

Antidepressant medications have shown some benefit in the treatment of bulimia, but not anorexia or binge eating disorder. However, people with bulimia are more likely to discontinue the medication than to discontinue therapy. Psychological treatment of anorexia must first focus on weight gain. CBT is effective, and although family therapy is common for anorexia, additional studies are needed to demonstrate its effectiveness. The most effective psychological treatment for bulimia is cognitive behavior therapy. CBT involves changing a patient's beliefs and thinking about thinness, being overweight, dieting, and restriction of food, with the overall goal being to reestablish normal eating patterns. CBT alone is more effective than medication treatment. CBT is also effective for binge eating disorder.

Preventive Interventions for Eating Disorders

A different approach to treating eating disorders involves prevention. Intervening with children or adolescents before the onset of eating disorders may help to prevent these disorders from ever developing. Broadly speaking, three different types of preventive interventions have been developed and implemented:

1. *Psychoeducational approaches.* The focus is on educating children and adolescents about eating disorders in order to prevent them from developing the symptoms.
2. *Deemphasizing sociocultural influences.* The focus here is on helping children and adolescents resist or reject sociocultural pressures to be thin.
3. *Risk factor approach.* The focus here is on identifying people with known risk factors for developing eating disorders (e.g., weight and body-image concern, dietary restraint) and intervening to alter these factors.

Stice, Shaw, and Marti (2007) conducted a meta-analysis of all such prevention studies conducted between 1980 and 2006, and they found modest support for some of these prevention approaches. The most effective prevention programs are those that are interactive rather than didactic, include adolescents age 15 or older, include girls only, and involve multiple sessions rather than just one session. Some effects appear to last as long as 2 years.

One randomized trial found that two types of preventive interventions show promise for

Prevention programs that are interactive have been effective for girls with eating disorders.

Tony Freeman/PhotoEdit

reducing eating disorder symptoms among adolescent girls (average age of 17). One program, called the Body Project, included a dissonance reduction intervention, focused on deemphasizing sociocultural influences; the other, called the Healthy Weight intervention, targeted risk factors (Stice, Marti, Spoor et al., 2008). Both programs included just one 3-hour session. Specifically, girls in the Body Project intervention talked, wrote, and role-played with one another to challenge society's notions of beauty (i.e., the thin-ideal). Girls in the Healthy Weight intervention worked together on developing healthy weight and exercise programs for themselves. Participation in either program was associated with less negative affect, less body dissatisfaction, lower thin-ideal internalization, and lower risk of developing eating disorder symptoms 2 to 3 years after the session compared to girls who did not participate in a session. These interventions have been successfully implemented with other high school samples and college women in a sorority, with some evidence suggesting that the Body Project may be more effective (Stice, Becker, & Yokum, 2013). An online version of the treatment (eBodyProject) also shows promise (Stice, Rohde, Shaw et al., 2013).

Check Your Knowledge 11.3

Fill in the blanks.
1. Research suggests that _____ therapy is an effective treatment for bulimia, both in the short and long term.
2. For anorexia, _____ may be required to get the patient to gain weight. There are not many _____ that have been shown to be effective. The most common type of therapy used to treat anorexia is _____.

3. Research on prevention programs has shown that two programs show promise up to 3 years after the intervention: _____ intervention and _____ intervention.

Summary

Clinical Descriptions

• Three DSM-5 eating disorders are anorexia nervosa, bulimia nervosa and binge eating disorder. The symptoms of anorexia nervosa include restriction of food to maintain healthy body weight, an intense fear of being fat, and a distorted sense of body shape. Anorexia typically begins in adolescence, is 10 times more frequent in women than in men, and is comorbid with several other disorders, notably depression. Its course is not favorable, and it can be life threatening. The symptoms of bulimia nervosa include episodes of binge eating followed by purging, fear of being fat, and a distorted body image. Like anorexia, bulimia begins in adolescence, is much more frequent in women than in men, and is comorbid with other diagnoses, such as depression. Prognosis for this disorder is somewhat more favorable than for anorexia. The symptoms of binge eating disorder include episodes of bingeing and a feeling of losing control over eating but no compensatory purging. People with binge eating disorder are often obese, but not all obese people have binge eating disorder.

Etiology

• Research on the eating disorders has examined genetics and brain mechanisms. Evidence is consistent with a possible genetic diathesis. Endogenous opioids and serotonin, both of which play a role in mediating hunger and satiety, have been examined in eating disorders. Low levels of both have been found in people with eating disorders, but evidence that these cause eating disorders is limited. Dopamine is also involved

with the rewarding aspects of eating, and studies show that the dopamine system may be altered as a consequence of eating disturbances but may not cause them.

• Cognitive behavioral theories of eating disorders propose that fear of being fat and body-image distortion make weight loss a powerful reinforcer. Among people with bulimia nervosa, negative affect and stress precipitate binges that create anxiety, which is then relieved by purging.

• As sociocultural standards changed to favor a thinner shape as the ideal for women, the frequency of eating disorders increased. The objectification of women's bodies also exerts pressure on women to see themselves through a sociocultural lens. The prevalence of eating disorders is higher in countries where the cultural pressure to be thin is strongest. White women tend to have more body dissatisfaction and general eating disturbances than African American women, though the prevalence rates for actual eating disorders are not markedly different between these two ethnic groups.

• Research on the characteristics of families has yielded different data depending on how the data were collected. Reports of people with eating disorders show high levels of conflict, but actual observations of the families do not find them especially troubled. Studies of personality have found that people with eating disorders are high in negative emotion and perfectionism and low in interoceptive awareness and positive emotion differentiation. Many women with eating disorders report being abused as children, but early abuse does not appear to be a specific risk factor for eating disorders.

Treatment

- The main neurobiological treatment for eating disorders is the use of antidepressants. Although they are somewhat effective for bulimia, they are not effective for anorexia or binge eating disorder. Dropout rates from drug-treatment programs are high and relapse is common when people stop taking the medication. Treatment of anorexia often requires hospitalization to reduce the medical complications of the disorder. CBT has been shown to be effective for anorexia, and family-based treatments show promise but need further study.

- Cognitive behavioral treatment for bulimia focuses on questioning beliefs about physical attractiveness and food restriction, and on developing normal eating patterns. Outcomes are good, both in the short and long term. Cognitive behavioral treatment for binge eating disorder focuses on reducing binges, and it also appears to be effective.

- Prevention programs are effective, particularly those programs that include girls age 15 or older, involve more than one session, and are interactive rather than didactic (i.e., lecture format).

Answers to Check Your Knowledge Questions

11.1 1. c; 2. b; 3. d; 4. Limited availability of healthy food; minimal awareness of portion size; abundance of food/cheap price; genetics; marketing/advertising

11.2 1. F; 2. T; 3, T; 4. F; 5. T; 6. F
11.3 1. cognitive behavior; 2. hospitalization, medications, family therapy; 3. dissonance reduction, healthy weight

Key Terms

anorexia nervosa
binge eating disorder

body mass index (BMI)
bulimia nervosa

obese

SEXUALITY IS ONE of the most personal areas of life. Each of us is a sexual being with preferences and fantasies that may surprise or even shock us from time to time. Usually, these are part of normal sexual functioning. But when our fantasies or desires begin to affect us or others in unwanted or harmful ways, they begin to qualify as abnormal.

For perspective, we begin by briefly describing norms and healthy sexual behavior. Then we consider two forms of sexual problems: sexual dysfunctions and paraphilic disorders. Sexual dysfunctions are defined as persistent disruptions in the ability to experience sexual arousal, desire, or orgasm, or as pain associated with intercourse. Paraphilic disorders are defined as persistent and troubling attractions to unusual sexual activities or objects.

Sexual Norms and Behavior

Definitions of what is normal or desirable in human sexual behavior vary with time and place. In contemporary Western worldviews, *inhibition* of sexual expression is seen as a problem. Contrast this with nineteenth- and early-twentieth-century views that *excess* was the culprit; in particular, excessive masturbation in childhood was widely believed to lead to sexual problems in adulthood. Von Krafft-Ebing (1902) postulated that early masturbation damaged the sexual organs and exhausted a finite reservoir of sexual energy, resulting in diminished ability to function sexually in adulthood. Even in adulthood, excessive sexual activity was thought to underlie problems such as erectile failure. The general Victorian view was that sexual appetite was dangerous and therefore had to be restrained. For example, to discourage children from handling their genitals, metal mittens were promoted; to distract adults from too much sex, outdoor exercise and a bland diet were recommended. In fact, Kellogg's Corn Flakes and graham crackers were developed as foods that would lessen sexual interest. They didn't.

Other historical changes have influenced people's attitudes and experiences of sexuality. For example, technology has changed sexual experiences, as the number of people accessing sexual content on the Internet increased dramatically over the past decade. Even as the accessibility of sexual content increased so

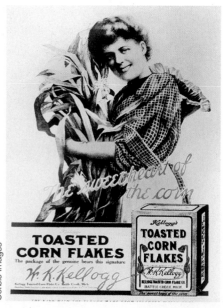

Corbis Images

Norms about sexuality have fluctuated a great deal over time. In the early twentieth century, corn flakes were promoted as part of a bland diet designed to reduce sexual desire.

dramatically, AIDS and other sexually transmitted diseases changed the risks associated with sexual behavior. In the United States more than 19 million sexually transmitted infections are estimated to occur each year (Centers for Disease Control and Prevention, 2009), and one in four women is affected with a sexually transmitted infection by age 19 (Forhan et al., 2009). See Figure 12.1 for recent HIV statistics. Other changes are influencing sexual norms as well. As the population of the United States ages, a newfound emphasis on the right to a good sex life until the day one dies has emerged, supported by an increasing array of medications (Tiefer, 2003).

Aside from changes over time and across generations, culture influences attitudes and beliefs about sexuality. In some cultures, sexuality is viewed as an important part of well-being and pleasure, whereas in others, sexuality is seen as relevant only for procreation (Bhugra, Popelyuk, & McMullen, 2010). Cultures also vary in their acceptance of variations in sexual behavior. For example, among Sambians living in Papua New Guinea, Herdt wrote in 1984 about rituals in which pubescent males engage in oral sex with older men as a way of learning about their sexuality. In other cultures it is common to stigmatize same-gender sexual behavior. Clearly, we must keep varying cultural norms in mind as we study human sexual behavior. See Focus on Discovery 12.1 for a look at the complicated path taken by health professionals in response to changing attitudes toward sexual orientation.

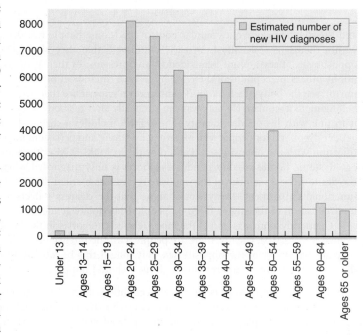

Figure 12.1 Estimated number of new diagnoses of HIV in the United States by age group in 2011. (Drawn from CDC, 2014)

FOCUS ON DISCOVERY 12.1

Learning from History

There has been a long history of debate over the DSM approach to sexual orientation (the preference for a male or female partner) and gender identity (the sense of self as male or female). Gender identity is distinct from sexual orientation. Many have argued that the DSM approach to both has fostered stigma.

Until 1973, homosexuality was listed in the DSM as one of the sexual disorders. In 1973, the Nomenclature Committee of the American Psychiatric Association, under pressure from professional and activist groups, recommended the elimination of the category "homosexuality" and the substitution of "sexual orientation disturbance." This new diagnosis was to be applied to gay men and women who are "disturbed by, in conflict with, or wish to change their sexual orientation." The change was approved, but not without vehement protests from several renowned psychiatrists who remained convinced that homosexuality reflects a fixation at an early stage of psychosexual development and is therefore inherently abnormal. Today, these protests would be considered misguided, prejudiced, and antiscientific.

Pathologizing homosexuality seems particularly odd when one considers how common such behavior is. For example, of men in their 40s and 50s, about 15 percent report that they have received oral

Jacquelyn Martin/AP Images

Martine Rothblatt, a founder of Sirius radio and the highest paid female CEO in the United States in 2012, was born as a male. In The Apartheid of Sex (Rothblatt, 1995), she wrote "There are five billion people in the world and five billion unique sexual identities. Genitals are as irrelevant to one's role in society as skin tone."

sex from men during their lifetime (Herbenick, et al., 2010b). In a different representative study that involved interviews with thousands of participants, about 30 percent of people reported that they would find a same-sex partner to be appealing (Laumann, Gagnon, Michael et al., 1994).

In the 1980 publication of the DSM-III, the Nomenclature Committee waffled by adding a new category called *ego-dystonic homosexuality*, which referred to a person who is homosexually aroused, is persistently distressed by this arousal, and wishes to become heterosexual. This category was dropped in later editions of the DSM. The DSM-IV and the DSM-IV-TR include the catchall category of "sexual disorder not otherwise specified," which refers to "persistent and marked distress about one's sexual orientation," which can be applied when a person is distressed over a heterosexual or homosexual orientation. The logic of this diagnosis is flawed. At the same time that the DSM has ceased labeling homosexuality as abnormal, a gay man or lesbian is considered abnormal if he or she has been persuaded by a prejudiced society that his or her sexual orientation is disordered.

Although homosexuality is no longer diagnosed, **gender dysphoria** remains in the DSM-5, and the diagnosis provokes similar controversy. Some people feel deep within themselves, usually from early childhood, that they are of the opposite sex. They are not persuaded by the presence of their genitals, nor by others' perceptions of their gender. A man can look at himself in a mirror, see the body of a biological man, and yet experience that body as belonging to a woman. He may want to surgically alter his body to bring it in line with his gender identity. The DSM-5 includes a diagnosis of gender dysphoria for people who experience a strong and persistent identification with the opposite sex. Parallel with the 1980 DSM criteria for ego-dystonic homosexuality, gender dysphoria is only diagnosed when the desire to be a member of the opposite sex causes marked distress or functional impairment. Many would argue that the distress reflects an internalization of the stigma faced by people who violate gender roles.

Gender dysphoria is one of the most debated categories in the DSM (Vance et al., 2010). Clearly, there are people with the intense belief that they are a member of the opposite sex. But should this be labeled as a disorder? There are several reasons to think it should not be.

- Cross-gender behavior is universal. In countless species, biologically male animals will adopt behavior, courtship rituals, and mating strategies that parallel those seen in female animals (Roughgarden, 2004). In humans, most children engage in some form of play that violates gender roles. It does not make sense to conceptualize such universal behavior as a disorder.

- The existence of this diagnosis implicitly contradicts the need for treatments to change the person's body to suit their gender identity. Some people who desire to change their gender identity pursue hormonal treatments to change secondary sexual characteristics and sex-reassignment surgery, in which the existing genitalia are altered to be more similar to those of the opposite sex. Surveys of hundreds of people one year after they have undergone such surgery indicate that more than 90 percent of people are satisfied and do not regret the surgery (Green & Fleming, 1990). Sex-reassignment surgery is related to improvements in partner relationships (De Cuypere et al., 2005) and sexual satisfaction (Lief & Hubschman, 1993). The psychological diagnosis of the desire to change one's gender is philosophically incongruent with the positive outcomes of sex-reassignment surgery.

- Rather than promoting mental health, diagnosing gender nonconformity might foster more stigma and social ostracism.

Because of these concerns, we have chosen not to include the diagnosis of gender dysphoria in this chapter.

What are the norms in our culture today? To answer this question, it is important to gather samples that are representative of the population in terms of age, gender, ethnicity, socioeconomic status, and other key characteristics. We will discuss various representative surveys involving thousands of participants throughout this chapter. See Table 12.1 for data from one of these large representative surveys. Sometimes participants in these studies are asked to respond to written questions, as people may feel more comfortable describing their behavior in writing than in discussion with an interviewer. In one recent large-scale representative study (Herbenick et al., 2010b), researchers gathered data over the Internet, as it seemed that participants might feel most comfortable with this format. Even with sensitivity to participant comfort, it remains difficult to gather data on how common certain sexual behaviors are. We will discuss this issue in more detail when we discuss paraphilic disorders later in this chapter.

Gender and Sexuality

Few topics raise as much political debate or personal turmoil as gender differences in sexuality. Across a wide range of indices, men report more engagement in sexual thought and behavior than do women. Of course, these are averages, there are going to be exceptions, and most of these differences are small (Andersen, Cyranowski, & Aarestad, 2000). But compared to women, men report thinking about sex, masturbating, and desiring sex more often, as well as desiring more sexual partners and having more partners (Baumeister, Catanese, & Vohs, 2001; Herbenick et al., 2010a).

Beyond these differences in sex drive, Peplau (2003) has described several other ways in which the genders tend to differ in sexuality. Women tend to be more ashamed of any flaws in their appearance than do men, and this shame can interfere with sexual satisfaction (Sanchez & Kiefer, 2007). For women, sexuality appears more closely tied to relationship status than for men (Baumeister, 2000). For example, women tend to report less sexual drive and masturbation when they are not in a relationship; men don't experience the same shift when a relationship ends. Some argue that the DSM pays too little attention to the relational components of human sexuality in describing sexual dysfunction, especially for women. Some propose that there should be a more women-centered definition that includes "discontent or dissatisfaction with any emotional, physical, or relational aspect of sexual experience" (Tiefer, Hall,

Table 12.1 Participation in Selected Sexual Behaviors in the Past Year by Gender

Behavior	Male (%)	Female (%)
Give oral sex		
Never	30.0	35.2
Occasionally	49.3	53.0
Always	20.7	11.8
Receive oral sex		
Never	30.5	33.2
Occasionally	50.5	52.2
Always	19.0	14.6
Number of sex partners		
0	9.9	13.6
1	66.7	74.7
2–4	18.3	10.0
5+	5.1	1.7
Frequency of sexual intercourse		
For unmarried participants		
None	22.2	30.6
< 3 × /month	38.9	36.6
At least 1 × /week	38.9	32.8
For married participants		
None	1.3	2.6
< 3 × /month	31.4	33.9
At least 1 × /week	67.3	63.5

Source: Laumann, Gagnon, Michael et al. (1994).

& Tavris, 2002, pp. 228–229). Among women with symptoms of sexual dysfunction, more than half believe their symptoms are caused by relationship problems (Nicholls, 2008). Men are more likely to think about their sexuality in terms of power than do women (Andersen, Cyranowski, & Espindle, 1999).

It is important to acknowledge commonalities as well as differences across genders. In one parallel to men's sexuality, in a survey of more than 1000 women, many reported that their primary motivation for having sex was sexual attraction and physical gratification (Meston & Buss, 2009). It would be an exaggeration to claim that the sole reason women are having sex is to promote relationship closeness.

Nonetheless, given that some gender differences are apparent, debate continues about the reasons for these gender differences. Are they based on cultural prohibitions regarding women's sexuality? Are they based on biological differences? Are they tied to women's greater investment in parenting? It is hard to design research to tease apart cultural and biological influences on sexuality. Intriguingly, though, at least some research suggests that some gender differences are remarkably consistent across cultures. In one study of more than 16,000 people (albeit mostly college students), men in 52 different countries reported that they wanted more partners over the course of a lifetime than did women (Schmitt et al., 2003). These findings suggest that biology may shape men's desire for many lifetime partners more than culture does. We know less about the basis for other gender differences in sexuality. There must be some reason for these differences, however. As Baumeister (2000) points out, in a perfect world, wouldn't men and women be well matched on their sexual preferences?

Throughout this chapter, we will see that gender shapes sexual disorders in a number of ways. Women are much more likely to report symptoms of sexual dysfunction than are men, but men are much more likely to meet diagnostic criteria for paraphilic disorder. Research on basic gender differences in sexuality is needed to understand why there are such major gender differences in sexual diagnoses.

Gamma-Keystone via Getty Images

As portrayed in the movie *Kinsey*, Alfred Kinsey (shown here) shocked people when he began to interview people to understand more about norms in sexual behavior.

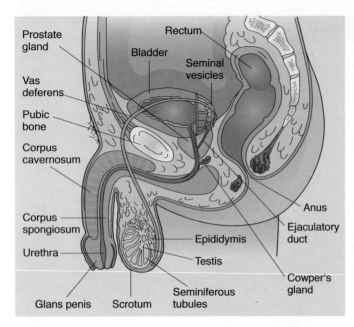

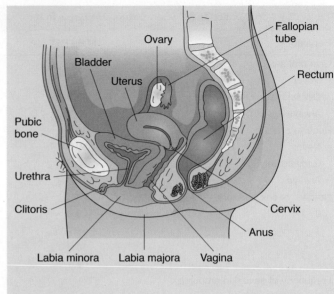

Figure 12.2 The male and female sexual anatomy.

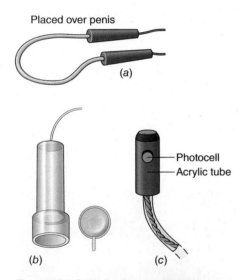

Figure 12.3 Behavioral researchers use genital devices for measuring biological sexual arousal. These devices are sensitive indicators of blood flow into the genitalia, a key physiological process in sexual arousal. For men, the penile plethysmograph measures changes in the size of the penis. (a) In one version of the penile plethysmograph, a very thin rubber tube is used. As the penis enlarges with blood, the tube stretches, changing its electrical resistance. (b) Less commonly, a rubber sheath is inserted over the penis, and then a chamber is placed over the penis. As the penis enlarges, the volume of air displaced is measured, providing a more accurate measure of change. (c) For women, biological sexual arousal can be measured by a vaginal plethysmograph. This tampon-shaped apparatus can be inserted into the vagina to measure increases in blood flow. Biological arousal may not be associated with subjective arousal or desire for women.

The Sexual Response Cycle

Many researchers have focused on understanding the **sexual response cycle.** The Kinsey group made breakthroughs in the 1940s by interviewing people about their sexuality (Kinsey, Pomeroy, & Martin, 1948). Masters and Johnson created another revolution in research on human sexuality 50 years ago when they began to gather direct observations and physiological measurements of people masturbating and having sexual intercourse. Most contemporary conceptualizations of the sexual response cycle draw from proposals by Masters and Johnson (1966), which were developed further by Kaplan (1974).

1. **Desire phase.** This phase, introduced by Kaplan (1974), refers to sexual interest or desire, often associated with sexually arousing fantasies or thoughts.

2. **Excitement phase.** During this phase, men and women experience increased blood flow to the genitalia (see Figure 12.2 for the sexual anatomy of men and women). In men, this flow of blood into tissues produces an erection of the penis. In women, blood flow creates enlargement of the breasts and changes in the vagina, such as increased lubrication.

3. **Orgasm phase.** In this phase, sexual pleasure peaks in ways that have fascinated poets and the rest of us ordinary people for thousands of years. In men, ejaculation feels inevitable and indeed almost always occurs (in rare instances, men have an orgasm without ejaculating, and vice versa). In women, the outer walls of the vagina contract. In both sexes, there is general muscle tension.

4. **Resolution phase.** This last phase refers to the relaxation and sense of well-being that usually follow an orgasm. In men there is an associated refractory period during which further erection is not possible. The duration of the refractory period varies across men and even in the same man across occasions. Women are often able to respond again with sexual excitement almost immediately, a capability that permits multiple orgasms.

Newer data calls into question the validity of distinguishing the desire and excitement phases for women. Although the model above suggests that desire would precede excitement, many women report that their desire and excitement co-occur and are not distinct (Graham, 2010), and about a third of women report that their desire follows (rather than precedes) physiological arousal (Carvalheira, Brotto, & Leal, 2010).

There is also some question about the way in which Kaplan defined the excitement phase by relying on biological changes. Subjective excitement may not mirror biological excitement for women. Some of the research on this topic has used a device called a **vaginal**

plethysmograph to measure women's physiological arousal (see Figure 12.3). When blood flow is measured by the vaginal plethysmograph, most women experience a rapid, automatic response to erotic stimuli. But the amount of blood flow to the vagina has little correlation with women's subjective level of desire or excitement (Basson, Brotto, Laan et al., 2005). Indeed, many women report little or no subjective excitement when those biological changes happen (Chivers, Seto, Lalumiere et al., 2010). Biological and subjective excitement need to be considered separately for women, even though they tend to be highly correlated for men.

Quick Summary

Sexuality is profoundly shaped by culture and experience, so it is important to be aware of subjective biases in thinking about diagnoses. Gender also shapes sexuality: for example, men report more frequent sexual thoughts and behaviors than do women.

Kaplan described four phases of the sexual response cycle: desire, excitement, orgasm, and resolution. Over time, researchers have learned that the Kaplan phases do not fit the data for women in two ways: the desire and excitement phase may not be distinct stages, and the Kaplan definition of the excitement phase may be overly biological.

Check Your Knowledge 12.1 (Answers are at the end of the chapter.)

Answer the questions.
1. Describe the most commonly documented gender differences in sexuality.
2. List Kaplan's four phases of the sexual response cycle.
3. Note one challenge to the validity of the Kaplan sexual response cycle phases as applied to women.

Sexual Dysfunctions

At its best, sexuality provides a forum for closeness, connection, and shared pleasure. For better or for worse, our sexuality shapes at least part of our self-concept. Do we please the people we love, or, more simply, are we able to enjoy fulfillment from a pleasurable sexual experience? When sexual problems emerge, they can wreak havoc on our self-esteem and relationships (Karney & Bradbury, 1995). Partnerships are likely to suffer if sexual dysfunctions become so severe that the intense satisfaction and tenderness of sexual activity are lost.

We turn now to sexual problems that interfere with sexual enjoyment for many people at some time during their life. We begin by describing the different types of sexual dysfunctions described in the DSM-5. Then we discuss etiology and treatments for these problems.

Clinical Descriptions of Sexual Dysfunctions

The DSM-5 divides **sexual dysfunctions** into three categories: those involving sexual desire, arousal, and interest; orgasmic disorders; and a disorder involving sexual pain (see Table 12.2). Separate diagnoses are provided for men and women. The diagnostic criteria for all sexual dysfunctions specify that dysfunction should be persistent and recurrent and should cause clinically significant distress or problems with functioning. A diagnosis of sexual dysfunction is not made if the problem is believed to be due entirely to a medical illness (such as advanced diabetes, which can cause erectile problems in men) or to another psychological disorder (such as major depression).

Table 12.2 Diagnoses of Sexual Dysfunction in the DSM-5

Category of Dysfunction	Diagnoses in Women	Diagnoses in Men
Sexual interest, desire, and arousal	Female sexual interest/arousal disorder	Male hypoactive sexual desire disorder
Orgasmic disorder	Female orgasmic disorder	Erectile disorder
Sexual pain	Genito-pelvic pain/penetration disorder	Premature ejaculation Delayed ejaculation

The pioneering work of the sex therapists William H. Masters and Virginia Johnson helped launch a candid and scientific appraisal of human sexuality.

One might not expect people to report problems as personal as sexual dysfunction in community surveys. But many people do report these symptoms—the prevalence of occasional symptoms of sexual dysfunctions is actually quite high. Table 12.3 presents data from a survey of more than 20,000 men and women who were asked whether they had experienced various symptoms of sexual dysfunction for at least 2 of the past 12 months (Laumann et al., 2005). More women (43 percent) than men (31 percent) reported symptoms of sexual dysfunction (Laumann, Paik, & Rosen, 1999). Other studies have reported a very similar percentage (about 44 percent) of women who reported symptoms of sexual dysfunction (cf. Bancroft, Loftus, & Long, 2003; Shifren, Monz, Russo et al., 2008). Although a lot of people acknowledged symptoms, clinical diagnoses are not made unless the symptoms cause distress or impairment. When asked whether they are distressed by these symptoms, only 11 to 23 percent of women report experiencing both sexual symptoms and distress over the symptoms.

Table 12.3 Self-Reported Rates of Experiencing Symptoms of Sexual Dysfunction for 2 of the Past 12 Months by Region among 20,000 Sexually Active Adults Ages 40 to 80

	Lacked Interest in Sex	Inability to Reach Orgasm	Orgasm Reached Too Quickly	Pain During Sex	Sex Not Pleasurable	Trouble Lubricating	Trouble Maintaining or Achieving an Erection
Women							
Northern Europe	25.6	17.7	7.7	9.0	17.1	18.4	NA
Southern Europe	29.6	24.2	11.5	11.9	22.1	16.1	NA
Non-European West	32.9	25.2	10.5	14.0	21.5	27.1	NA
Central/South America	28.1	22.4	18.3	16.6	19.5	22.5	NA
Middle East	43.4	23.0	10.0	21.0	31.0	23.0	NA
East Asia	34.8	32.3	17.6	31.6	29.7	37.9	NA
Southeast Asia	43.3	41.2	26.3	29.2	35.9	34.2	NA
Men							
Northern Europe	12.5	9.1	20.7	2.9	7.7	NA	13.3
Southern Europe	13.0	12.2	21.5	4.4	9.1	NA	12.9
Non-European West	17.6	14.5	27.4	3.6	12.1	NA	20.6
Central/South America	12.6	13.6	28.3	4.7	9.0	NA	13.7
Middle East	21.6	13.2	12.4	10.2	14.3	NA	14.1
East Asia	19.6	17.2	29.1	5.8	12.2	NA	27.1
Southeast Asia	28.0	21.1	30.5	12.0	17.4	NA	28.1

Note: Non-European West includes Australia, Canada, New Zealand, South Africa, and the United States.
Source: After Laumann et al. (2005).

DSM-5 Criteria for Female Sexual Interest/Arousal Disorder

Diminished, absent, or reduced frequency of at least three of the following:

- Interest in sexual activity
- Erotic thoughts or fantasies
- Initiation of sexual activity and responsiveness to partner's attempts to initiate
- Sexual excitement/pleasure during 75 percent of sexual encounters
- Sexual interest/arousal elicited by any internal or external erotic cues
- Genital or nongenital sensations during 75 percent of sexual encounters

DSM-5 Criteria for Male Hypoactive Sexual Desire Disorder

- Sexual fantasies and desires, as judged by the clinician, are deficient or absent

DSM-5 Criteria for Erectile Disorder

On at least 75 percent of sexual occasions:

- Inability to attain an erection, or
- Inability to maintain an erection for completion of sexual activity, or
- Marked decrease in erectile rigidity interferes with penetration or pleasure

Beyond a lack of attention to distress or impairment, these surveys typically do not assess how long symptoms have lasted. DSM-5 criteria for sexual dysfunction disorders specify that symptoms must last at least 6 months. It is pretty common for people to have sexual symptoms for a month. For more than three-quarters of people, these symptoms will remit naturally over time (Mercer et al., 2003).

Although the diagnostic system for sexual dysfunction reflects the stages in the sexual cycle, the problems often don't break out so cleanly in real life. Many people with problems in one phase of a sexual cycle will report problems in another phase. Some of this may just be a vicious circle. For example, men who develop premature ejaculation may begin to worry about sex and then experience problems with sexual desire or sexual arousal (Rowland, Cooper, & Slob, 1996). Beyond the consequences for the individual, sexual problems in one person may lead to sexual problems in the partner. Be aware of this potential for co-occurrence of diagnoses as we review the specific sexual dysfunction disorders defined in the DSM-5.

DSM-5 criteria for sexual dysfunctions include clear guidelines regarding relationship distress. Sexual concerns that arise as a consequence of severe relationship distress, such as partner abuse, should not be diagnosed as sexual dysfunctions. For women in particular, sexuality has strong links with relationship satisfaction (Tiefer, 2001).

Disorders Involving Sexual Interest, Desire, and Arousal The DSM-5 includes three disorders relevant to sexual interest, desire, and arousal. **Female sexual interest/arousal disorder** refers to persistent deficits in sexual interest (sexual fantasies or urges), biological arousal, or subjective arousal. For men, the DSM-5 diagnoses consider sexual interest and arousal separately. **Male hypoactive sexual desire disorder** refers to deficient or absent sexual fantasies and urges, and **erectile disorder** refers to failure to attain or maintain an erection through completion of the sexual activity. The Clinical Case of Paul and Petula illustrates erectile disorder, and the Clinical Case of Robert provides an illustration of hypoactive sexual desire disorder.

Clinical Case: Paul and Petula

When Paul and Petula sought treatment at a sex therapy clinic, they were a young couple who had been living together for 6 months and were engaged to be married. Petula reported that Paul "hasn't been able to keep his erection after he enters me" for the past 2 months. Paul would experience initial sexual arousal but then lose his erection almost immediately after entering Petula. Although they enjoyed sexual intercourse during the beginning of their relationship, the erectile problems started after they moved in together. During the interview, the psychiatrist learned that they had considerable conflict over the amount of time they spent together and over commitment, and at times Petula had been violent toward Paul. No medical problems appeared to be involved, nor was depression a concern for either Paul or Petula. (Drawn from Spitzer, Gibbon, Skodol, Williams, & First, 1994.)

DSM-5 Criteria for Female Orgasmic Disorder

On at least 75 percent of sexual occasions:

- Marked delay, infrequency, or absence of orgasm, or
- Markedly reduced intensity of orgasmic sensation

DSM-5 Criteria for Premature Ejaculation

- Tendency to ejaculate during partnered sexual activity within 1 minute of penile insertion on at least 75 percent of sexual occasions

DSM-5 Criteria for Delayed Ejaculation

- Marked delay, infrequency, or absence of orgasm on at least 75 percent of sexual occasions

Among people seeking treatment for sexual dysfunctions, more than half complain of low desire. As Table 12.3 shows, women are more likely than men to report at least occasional concerns about their level of sexual desire. Postmenopausal women are two to four times as likely as women in their 20s are to report low sexual desire. On the other hand, older women are less likely to be distressed over low sexual desire (Derogatis & Burnett, 2008).

DSM-5 criteria for sexual interest/arousal disorder in women include biologically or subjectively low arousal or desire. Women tend to be more concerned by a lack of subjective desire than by a lack of biological arousal (Basson et al., 2004). Most commonly, women with this disorder report that previously exciting stimuli, such as their partner's touch or a sensual dance, no longer trigger desire (Brotto & Luria, 2014). When laboratory studies are conducted using a vaginal plethysmograph, women who experience a subjective lack of desire often have normative levels of biological response to erotic stimuli (Graham, 2010). This again highlights the distinction between physiological and subjective measures of arousal in women.

Occasional symptoms of erectile disorder are the most common sexual concern among men, with rates ranging from 13 to 28 percent, depending on the country (Laumann et al., 2005). The prevalence of erectile disorder increases greatly with age, with as many as 50 percent of men ages 60 and older reporting at least occasional erectile dysfunction (Rosen, Miner, & Wincze, 2014).

Of all the DSM-5 diagnoses, the sexual interest, arousal and desire disorders, often colloquially referred to as low sex drive, seem the most subjective. How often should a person want sex? And with what intensity? Often, one partner will encourage the other partner to see a clinician. The hypoactive desire category may owe its existence to the high expectations some people have about being sexual. Data attest to the significance of subjective and cultural factors in defining low sex drive; for example, hypoactive sexual desire disorder is reported more often by American men than by British men despite similar levels of sexual activity across these cultures (Hawton et al., 1986). Cultural norms seem to influence perceptions of how much sex a person "should" want.

Orgasmic Disorders The DSM-5 includes separate diagnoses for problems in achieving orgasm for women and men. **Female orgasmic disorder** refers to the persistent absence or reduced intensity of orgasm after sexual excitement. Women differ in their thresholds for orgasm. Although some women have orgasms quickly and without much clitoral stimulation, others

Clinical Case: Robert

Robert, a very bright 25-year-old graduate student in physics at a leading university, sought treatment for what he called "sexual diffidence" toward his fiancée. He said he loved his fiancée very much and felt compatible with her in every conceivable way except in bed. There, try as he might, and with apparent understanding from his fiancée, he found himself uninterested in initiating or responding to sex. He and his fiancée had attributed these problems to the academic pressures he had faced for the past 2 years, but a discussion with the therapist revealed that Robert had had little interest in sex—either with men or with women—for as far back as he could remember, even when work pressures were not present. He asserted that he found his fiancée very attractive and appealing, but as with other women he had known, he did not feel passion for her.

He had masturbated very rarely in adolescence and did not begin dating until late in college, though he had had many female acquaintances. His general approach to life, including sex, was analytical and intellectual, and he described his problems in a very dispassionate and detached way to the therapist. He freely admitted that he would not have contacted a therapist at all were it not for the quietly stated wishes of his fiancée, who worried that his lack of interest in sex would interfere with their future relationship.

After a few individual sessions, the therapist asked the young man to invite his fiancée to a therapy session, which the client readily agreed to do. During a joint session, the couple appeared to be very much in love and looking forward to a life together, despite the woman's concern about Robert's lack of sexual interest.

Clinical Case: Anne

Anne was a 26-year-old, attractive woman who sought treatment after beginning her first "steady" sexual relationship. She reported that she and her partner, Colin, enjoyed their sexual life together. Nonetheless, Colin had begun to express concerns because she had been unable to achieve an orgasm. She sought therapy independently to talk about this concern. In therapy, she described that she had not really enjoyed sexual activities with her former partners and that she had rarely masturbated. Anne disclosed to the therapist that her brother had raped her when she was 12 years old, an event that she had not been able to disclose to anyone in the past. She described harboring fear about "letting herself go" after that incident. The therapist provided directed masturbation exercises (described as we review sex therapy interventions below) for Anne to begin to explore and enjoy her body independently, and in sessions they discussed her abuse history and her feelings about sexuality. With the use of a vibrator, Anne was able to begin to enjoy orgasms. As her comfort with her body and sexuality increased, Anne also learned to discuss her sexual preferences more openly with Colin.

[Adapted from Graham (2014).]

need prolonged clitoral stimulation. Therefore, it is not surprising that about one-third of women report that they do not consistently experience orgasms with their partners (Laumann et al., 2005). Female orgasmic disorder is not diagnosed unless the absence of orgasms is persistent and troubling. For many women, enjoying a sense of emotional closeness to their partner is more important than achieving an orgasm (Clark, Thompson, Graham et al., 2014). About two-thirds of women report that they have faked an orgasm, and most say that they did so to try to protect their partner's feelings (Muehlenhard & Shippee, 2010). Many men are unaware (or at least don't report) that their partners don't achieve orgasms (Herbenick et al., 2010a).

Women's problems reaching orgasm are distinct from problems with sexual arousal. As with the clinical case of Anne, many women with orgasmic disorder achieve sexual arousal and enjoy sexual contact, even though they have difficulty reaching orgasm. Indeed, laboratory research has shown that arousal levels while viewing erotic stimuli do not distinguish women with orgasmic disorder from those without orgasmic disorder (Meston & Gorzalka, 1995).

The DSM-5 includes two orgasmic disorders of men: **premature ejaculation,** defined by ejaculation that occurs too quickly, and **delayed ejaculation disorder,** defined by persistent difficulty in ejaculating. The DSM-5 defines "premature" as less than one minute after the penis is inserted. One minute was chosen based on cross-national studies showing that the median time to ejaculation is 5 minutes after penis insertion (Waldinger et al., 2005). As shown in Table 12.3, brief periods of symptoms are fairly common, but less than 3 percent of men report symptoms of premature ejaculation lasting 6 months or more (Segraves, 2010). Delayed ejaculation is the least common sexual dysfunction among men, reported by less than 1 percent of men (APA, 2013).

Sexual Pain Disorder The major symptom of **genito-pelvic pain/penetration disorder** is persistent or recurrent pain during intercourse. Although some men experience recurrent pain during sex, very few men seek treatment for it. For this reason, the DSM-5 criteria focus only on women. Sexual pain is a very common concern heard by gynecologists (Leiblum, 1997). Women with this disorder often experience vaginismus, defined by involuntary muscle spasms of the outer third of the vagina to a degree that makes intercourse impossible (Binik, 2010). A first step in diagnosing genito-pelvic/penetration disorder is ensuring that the pain is not caused by a medical problem, such as an infection, or by a lack of vaginal lubrication due to low desire or postmenopausal changes.

Most women diagnosed with this disorder experience sexual arousal and can have orgasms from manual or oral stimulation that does not involve penetration. Women who experience pain when attempting sexual intercourse show normative sexual arousal to films of oral sex, but, not surprisingly, their arousal declines when they watch a depiction of intercourse (Wouda et al., 1998).

DSM-5 Criteria for Genito-Pelvic Pain/Penetration Disorder

Persistent or recurrent difficulties with at least one of the following:
- Inability to have vaginal/penetration during intercourse
- Marked vulvar, vaginal or pelvic pain during vaginal penetration or intercourse attempts
- Marked fear or anxiety about pain or penetration
- Marked tensing of the pelvic floor muscles during attempted vaginal penetration

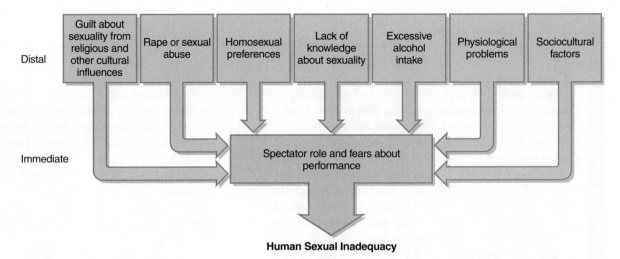

Figure 12.4 Distal and immediate causes of human sexual inadequacies, according to Masters and Johnson.

Etiology of Sexual Dysfunctions

In their widely acclaimed book *Human Sexual Inadequacy,* Masters and Johnson (1970) drew on their case studies to publish a theory of why sexual dysfunctions develop. Masters and Johnson differentiated immediate and distal causes of sexual dysfunction (see Figure 12.4). In their model, the two immediate causes are fears about performance and the adoption of a **spectator role.** Fears about performance involve concerns with how one is "performing" during sex. Spectator role refers to being an observer rather than a participant in a sexual experience. These two related concerns could both impede natural sexual responses. These immediate causes of sexual dysfunctions were hypothesized to have one or more historical antecedents, such as sociocultural influences, biological causes, or sexual abuse. Masters and Johnson emphasized that sexual functioning is complex and multifactorial, and set the stage for researchers to study these risk factors. We now turn to research on the causes of sexual dysfunctions. Figure 12.5 summarizes factors related to sexual dysfunctions.

	Successful sexual functioning	Poor sexual functioning
Psychological factors	Good emotional health Attraction toward partner Positive attitude toward partner Positive sexual attitude	Depression or anxiety disorders Focus on performance Too much routine Poor self-esteem Uncomfortable environment for sex Rigid, narrow attitude toward sex Negative thoughts about sex
Physical factors	Good physical health Regular appropriate exercise Good nutrition	Smoking Heavy drinking Cardiovascular problems Diabetes Neurological diseases Low physiological arousal SSRI medications Antihypertensive medication Other drugs
Social and sexual history factors	Positive sexual experiences in past Good relationship with partner Sexual knowledge and skills	Rape or sexual abuse Relationship problems, such as anger or poor communication Long periods of abstinence History of hurried sex

Figure 12.5 Predictors of sexual functioning. [Adapted from Wincze & Barlow (1997).]

Biological Factors As noted earlier, a first step in making a diagnosis of sexual dysfunction is to rule out medical diseases as the cause. The DSM-5 includes separate diagnoses for sexual dysfunctions that are caused by medical illnesses. Some have criticized this division in the diagnoses because sexual dysfunctions often have some biological and some psychological contributions. Biological causes of sexual dysfunctions can include diseases such as diabetes, multiple sclerosis, and spinal cord injury; heavy alcohol use before sex; chronic alcohol dependence; and heavy cigarette smoking (Bach, Wincze, & Barlow, 2001). Laboratory tests of hormone levels are a routine part of assessment of sexual dysfunctions for men and postmenopausal women (Bartlik & Goldberg, 2000; Buvat et al., 2010) because sexual dysfunctions can be caused by either low levels of testosterone or estrogen or by the high levels induced by chronic use of anabolic steroids or testosterone supplements. Certain medications, such as antihypertensive drugs and especially selective serotonin reuptake inhibitor (SSRI) antidepressant drugs (e.g., Prozac and Zoloft), have effects on sexual function, including delayed orgasm, decreased libido, and diminished lubrication (Segraves, 2003). Erectile symptoms are often related to an incipient vascular disorder (Wylie & MacInnes, 2005). Beyond these medical causes, some biological factors may be specific to certain sexual dysfunctions. As one example, some women who experience genito-pelvic pain/penetration disorder appear to have a neurologically based supersensitivity to pain (van Lankveld et al., 2010).

Psychosocial Factors Some sexual dysfunctions can be traced to rape or sexual abuse. Childhood sexual abuse is associated with diminished arousal and desire, and, among men, with double the rate of premature ejaculation (Laumann et al., 1999). See Focus on Discovery 12.3, later in this chapter, for a discussion of childhood sexual abuse and its repercussions. Beyond the role of traumatic experiences, it is important to consider the benefits of positive experiences—many people with sexual problems lack knowledge and skill because they have not had opportunities to learn about their sexuality.

Broader relationship problems often interfere with sexual arousal and pleasure (Burri & Spector, 2011). For women, concerns about a partner's affection appear particularly correlated with sexual satisfaction (Nobre & Pinto-Gouveia, 2008). For people who tend to be anxious about their relationships, sexual problems may exacerbate underlying worries about relationship security (Birnbaum, Reis, Mikulincer et al., 2006). As one might expect, people who are angry with their partners are less likely to want sex (Beck & Bozman, 1995). Even in couples who are satisfied with other realms of the relationship, poor communication can contribute to sexual dysfunction. For any number of reasons, including embarrassment, worry about the partner's feelings, or fear, one lover may not tell the other about preferences even if a partner is engaging in unstimulating or even aversive behaviors during sex.

Depression and anxiety increase the risk of sexual dysfunctions. People who are depressed are more than twice as likely as nondepressed people to have a sexual dysfunction (Angst, 1998). People with panic disorder, who are often fearful of physical sensations like rapid heart rate and sweating, are also at risk for sexual dysfunction (Sbrocco, Weisberg, Barlow et al., 1997). Anxiety and depression are particularly comorbid with sexual pain (Meana, Binik, Khalife et al., 1998) and with female sexual desire/arousal disorder (Forbes & Schniering, 2013).

Beyond the detrimental effects of depression and anxiety, several studies suggest that low general physiological arousal can interfere with specific sexual arousal. Meston and Gorzalka (1995) examined the role of arousal by assigning women to exercise or no-exercise conditions and then asking women to watch erotic films. Consistent with the positive role of higher arousal, exercise facilitated sexual arousal. No wonder, then, that exhausted couples, turning to sex after a full day of work, parenting, socializing, and other roles, can encounter problems with sexuality. Too much stress and exhaustion clearly impede sexual functioning (Morokoff & Gilliland, 1993).

Negative cognitions, such as worries about pregnancy or AIDS, negative attitudes about sex, or concerns about the partner, can interfere with sexual functioning (Reissing, Binik, & Khalife, 1999). Intrusive negative thoughts about their weight or appearance impinge on the enjoyment of sex for many women (Pujols, Seal, & Meston, 2010). But as Masters and Johnson first suggested, cognitions concerning sexual performance are particularly important for both men and women (Carvalho & Nobre, 2010). Consider the idea that variability in sexual performance is common; a stressful day, a distracting context, a relationship concern, or any number of other issues may diminish sexual responsiveness. The key issue may be how people think about their diminished physical response when it happens. One theory is that people who blame themselves for decreased sexual performance will be more likely to develop recurrent sexual problems.

In a test of the role of self-blame and erectile dysfunction, researchers asked 52 male participants to watch erotic videos (Weisberg, Brown, Wincze et al., 2001). During the videos, their sexual arousal (penile circumference) was measured using a **penile plethysmograph** (see Figure 12.3). Regardless of their actual arousal, the men were given false feedback that the size of their erection was smaller than that typically measured among aroused men. Men were randomly assigned to receive two different explanations for this false feedback. In the first, they were told that the films did not seem to be working for most men (external explanation). In the second, they were told that the pattern of their responses on questionnaires about sexuality might help explain the low arousal (internal explanation). After receiving this feedback, the men were asked to watch one more film. The men who were given an internal explanation reported less arousal and also showed less physiological arousal during this film than those given an external explanation. These results, then, support the idea that people who blame themselves when their body doesn't perform will experience diminished subsequent arousal. Needless to say, men in this study were carefully debriefed after the experiment!

In considering the source of negative cognitions, Masters and Johnson found that many of their sexually dysfunctional patients had learned negative views of sexuality from their social and cultural surroundings. For example, some religions and cultures may discourage sexuality for the sake of pleasure, particularly outside marriage. Other cultures may disapprove of sexual initiative or behavior among women, other than for the sake of procreation. One female patient suffering from a lack of sexual desire, for example, had been taught as she was growing up not to look at herself naked in the mirror and that intercourse was reserved for marriage and then only to be endured for purposes of having children. Guilt about engaging in sexual behavior varies by cultural group and can inhibit sexual desire (Woo, Brotto, & Gorzalka, 2011).

Quick Summary

In the DSM-5, the sexual dysfunction disorders are divided as follows:

- Sexual interest, desire, and arousal disorders (female sexual interest/arousal disorder, male hypoactive sexual desire disorder and erectile disorder)
- Orgasmic disorders (female orgasmic disorder, delayed ejaculation, and premature ejaculation)
- Sexual pain disorder (genito-pelvic pain/penetration disorder)

Although there are no good estimates of how many people meet full diagnostic criteria for sexual dysfunction disorders, in one major survey, 43 percent of women and 31 percent of men reported at least some symptoms of sexual dysfunction. People who experience one sexual dysfunction disorder often experience a comorbid sexual dysfunction disorder; for example, a man who is experiencing premature ejaculation may develop hypoactive sexual desire disorder.

Before diagnosing sexual dysfunction, it is important to rule out medical explanations for a symptom. The key etiological variables involved in sexual dysfunctions appear to be previous sexual abuse, lack of sexual knowledge, relationship problems, psychological disorders such as depression or anxiety, and negative cognitions and attitudes about sexuality.

Treatments of Sexual Dysfunctions

Given the complex matrix of factors that promote healthy sexual functioning, it is perhaps no surprise that sex therapists often draw on a rich array of strategies to help their clients. Sexual dysfunctions are often embedded in a distressed relationship, so that many therapists work from a systems perspective in which a sexual problem is viewed as one expression of relationship problems (Wylie, 1997). Troubled couples usually need training in nonsexual communication skills (Rosen, 2000). Some therapists focus on nonsexual issues, such as difficulties with in-laws or with child rearing—either in addition to or instead of interventions directly focused on sex. For some couples, planning romantic events together is recommended as a way to restore closeness and intimacy (Kaplan, 1997). For women with sexual dysfunctions occurring in the context of relationship distress, behavioral couples therapy has been found to improve many aspects of sexual functioning (Zimmer, 1987).

Beyond couples therapy, many techniques have been developed to target specific sexual concerns. The pioneering work of Masters and Johnson (1970) in the treatment of sexual dysfunctions is described in Focus on Discovery 12.2. Over the past decades, therapists and researchers have elaborated on this work, and now many different sex therapy interventions are available, several of which we will describe. A therapist may choose only one technique for a given case, but the multifaceted nature of sexual dysfunctions often requires the use of a combination of techniques. These approaches are generally suitable for treating sexual dysfunctions in homosexual as well as heterosexual clients. We will begin by considering different cognitive and behavioral interventions, which have been supported across 20 randomized controlled trials and appear particularly helpful for women with sexual interest/arousal disorder or orgasmic disorder (Frühauf, Gerger, Schmidt et al., 2013). After discussing cognitive behavioral approaches, we will turn to physical and medical treatments.

FOCUS ON DISCOVERY 12.2

Masters and Johnson's Therapy for Sexual Dysfunctions

In their book *Human Sexual Inadequacy,* Masters and Johnson (1970) reported the successful results of one of the first sex therapy programs, which they had offered to almost 800 clients. Each couple had traveled to St. Louis and spent 2 weeks participating in intensive therapy during the day and completing sexual homework in a hotel at night.

Couples were always seen by one male and one female therapist. For the first two days, couples completed an assessment of their medical, social, and sexual history. Sometimes the couple discussed sex for the first time at the clinic. During the assessment and first few days of treatment, sexual intercourse was forbidden.

On the third day, the therapists began to offer feedback about the sources of problems. If a person had negative attitudes toward sex, this issue would be addressed. But the basic emphasis was on relationship problems rather than the individual difficulties of either partner. Whatever the problem, the couple was encouraged to see it as their mutual responsibility. At the same time, the clients were introduced to the idea of the spectator role. They were told, for example, that a male with erectile problems—and often his partner as well—usually worries about how well he is doing and that this pattern of observing the state of the erection, though totally understandable, blocks his natural responses and interferes with sexual enjoyment.

At the end of the third day, the couple was asked to engage in sensate focus. The couple was instructed to choose a time when both partners felt a sense of warmth and compatibility. During sensate-focus exercises, the couple was instructed not to have intercourse. Indeed, initially they were instructed not to touch each other's genitalia.

Rather, they were instructed to undress and give each other pleasure by touching each other's bodies. The co-therapists appointed one marital partner to do the first pleasuring; the partner who was "getting" was simply allowed to enjoy being touched. The one being touched was not required to feel a sexual response and was responsible for immediately telling the partner if something became uncomfortable. Then the roles were switched. The sensate-focus assignment usually promoted contact, constituting a first step toward reestablishing sexual intimacy. Most of the time, partners began to realize that their physical encounters could be intimate and pleasurable without necessarily being a prelude to sexual intercourse.

On the next evening, the partner being pleasured was instructed to give specific direction by guiding his or her partner's hand to regulate pressure and rate of stroking. Touching of genitals and breasts was now allowed, but still no intercourse. After two days of sensate focus, treatment began to be tailored to specific problems. For example, guided masturbation exercises (covered below) might be introduced to address female orgasmic disorder.

Many therapists continue to use the Masters and Johnson techniques, although success rates have tended to be lower than those originally reported (Segraves & Althof, 1998). The lower success rates may be attributed to the couples who are seeking treatment these days rather than to the therapy itself. As sex therapy has become more popular and a broader range of couples have begun to sought treatment, treatment providers see couples today with poorer marital relationships than those who sought treatment in the early years of sex therapy.

Anxiety Reduction and Psychoeducation Many clients with sexual dysfunctions need gradual and systematic exposure to anxiety-provoking aspects of the sexual situation. Systematic desensitization and in vivo (real-life) desensitization have been employed with some success (Wolpe, 1958), especially when combined with skills training. For example, a woman with genito-pelvic pain/penetration disorder might first receive psychoeducation about her body, be trained in relaxation, and then practice inserting her fingers or dilators into her vagina, starting with inserting smaller dilators and working up to larger ones (Leiblum, 1997). Such programs have been shown to be helpful for many women with sexual pain disorder (ter Kuile & Reissing, 2014).

Psychoeducation programs about sexuality also do a great deal to reduce anxiety. Therapists often assign written materials and show clients explicit videos demonstrating sexual techniques. Several studies have now shown that psychoeducation can be as effective as systematic desensitization for male erectile disorder and for women with orgasmic disorder or low sexual arousal (Emmelkamp, 2004).

For the treatment of premature ejaculation, anxiety-reduction techniques sometimes have a different focus. Anxiety about ejaculating too soon may be a natural result of an overemphasis on intercourse as a sole focus of sexual behavior. Sex therapists advise couples to expand their repertoire of activities to include other ways to gratify the partner after the man has climaxed, such as oral or manual manipulation. When the exclusive focus on penile insertion is removed, anxieties about sex often diminish enough to enhance the man's control over ejaculation.

Procedures to Change Attitudes and Thoughts The sensate-focus exercises described in Focus on Discovery 12.2 are a way of helping the person focus on physical sensations as a counter to the destructive tendency to think about one's performance or attractiveness during sex. Other cognitive interventions are designed to challenge the self-demanding, perfectionistic thoughts that often cause problems for people with sexual dysfunctions. A therapist might try to reduce the pressure a man with erectile dysfunction feels by challenging his belief that intercourse is the only true form of sexual activity. Women who are hypercritical of their appearance might be coached to consider more positive ways of viewing their bodies and their sexuality.

Communication Training Encouraging partners to communicate their likes and dislikes to each other has been shown to be helpful for a range of sexual dysfunctions (Rosen, Leiblum, & Spector, 1994). Communication training also exposes partners to potentially anxiety-provoking material, such as expressing sexual preferences, which allows for a desensitizing effect. Skills and communication training is particularly warranted when sexual dysfunction is specific to a given relationship and was not a concern with previous partners.

Directed Masturbation Directed masturbation was devised by LoPiccolo and Lobitz (1972) to enhance women's comfort with and enjoyment of their sexuality. The first step is for the woman to carefully examine her nude body, including her genitals, and to identify various areas with the aid of diagrams. Next, she is instructed to touch her genitals and to find areas that produce pleasure. Then she increases the intensity of masturbation using erotic fantasies. If orgasm is not achieved, she is to use a vibrator in her masturbation. Finally, her partner enters the picture, first watching her masturbate, then doing for her what she has been doing for herself, and finally having intercourse in a position that allows him to stimulate the woman's genitals manually or with a vibrator. As illustrated in the Clinical Case of Anne, directed masturbation has been shown to be helpful in treating orgasmic disorder (O'Donohue, Dopke, & Swingen, 1997), particularly when women have a lifelong inability to experience orgasm, with 60–90 percent of that subgroup achieving orgasm post-treatment (ter Kuile, Both, & van Lankveld, 2012). It is also helpful in the treatment of low sexual desire (Renshaw, 2001).

Other Physical Treatments For the treatment of female orgasmic disorder, couples may be taught specific sexual positions that increase the amount of clitoral stimulation. For the treatment of premature ejaculation, the squeeze technique is often used, in which a partner is trained to squeeze the penis in the area where the head and shaft meet to rapidly reduce arousal. This technique is practiced without insertion, and then during insertion, the penis is withdrawn and the squeeze is repeated as needed. In a similar approach, men are taught to withdraw their penis as needed during intercourse, so as to reduce arousal. Initial success rates are high (60 to 90 percent), but some relapse takes place over time (Polonsky, 2000).

Medications There has been a huge increase in people taking medications to address sexual concerns. As one example, testosterone therapy is not approved by the FDA in the United States for treatment of female sexual interest/arousal disorder, and yet it is estimated that over 4 million off-label prescriptions are written per year for this purpose (Simes & Snabes, 2011). Many sexual problems are inherently interpersonal and psychological, though, and so adding psychological intervention to pharmacological approaches appears to produce better outcomes (Frühauf et al., 2013). For example, although premature ejaculation is often treated with medication alone, psychotherapy can help men regain confidence after experiences of these symptoms (Althof, 2014). Despite these caveats, medical treatments for sexual dysfunction, typically offered without psychotherapy, are popular.

Antidepressant Drugs Antidepressant drugs have been found to be helpful when depression appears to contribute to diminished sex drive. These drugs, particularly SSRIs, have also been found to be helpful in the treatment of premature ejaculation in a series of studies (Althof et al., 2010). A complicating factor, though, is that some antidepressants themselves interfere with sexual responsiveness. Sometimes a second medication is used to counteract the sexual side effects of the first; for example, buproprion (Wellbutrin) has been shown to help address the libido problems caused by SSRIs (Segraves, 2003).

PDE-5 inhibitors The most common intervention for erectile disorder is a phosphodiesterase type 5 (PDE-5) inhibitor, such as sildenafil (Viagra), tadafil (Cialis), or vardenafil (Levitra). PDE-5 inhibitors relax smooth muscles and thereby allow blood to flow into the penis, creating an erection during sexual stimulation but not in its absence (Eardley et al., 2010). PDE-5 inhibitors are taken 1 hour before sex, and the effects last about 4 hours. Although some men stop taking these medications due to side effects such as headaches and indigestion, most men will tolerate the side effects to gain relief from their sexual symptoms. Indeed, worldwide sales of PDE-5 medications reached $5 billion in 2010 (Wilson, 2011). PDE-5 inhibitors may be dangerous for men with cardiovascular disease, and this is a concern since erectile dysfunction is often comorbid with cardiovascular disease.

In a summary of 27 treatment studies, about 83 percent of men who took sildenafil were able to successfully have intercourse compared to about 45 percent of men who were assigned to a placebo condition (Fink, Mac Donald, Rutks et al., 2002). Some men continue to experience intermittent erectile dysfunction on PDE-5 inhibitors, and so sex therapy appears to be a helpful addition to medication treatment (Melnik, Soares, & Nasello, 2008). Several trials of PDE-5 inhibitors have been conducted for treatment of sexual dysfunction in women, but the results are not promising (Laan, Everaerd, & Both, 2005).

Quick Summary

Cognitive behavioral treatments for sexual dysfunction include couples therapy to improve the overall relationship and to build intimacy; techniques to reduce anxiety and increase knowledge; cognitive interventions; communication training; physical exercises to increase knowledge and awareness of the body; and the squeeze technique for the treatment of premature ejaculation. Medical treatments are increasingly popular, despite some criticism that such treatments do not address the interpersonal context in which sexual dysfunctions often emerge. PDE-5 inhibitors such as Viagra and Cialis are commonly used to treat erectile dysfunction, and antidepressant drugs can be helpful in the treatment of premature ejaculation.

Check Your Knowledge 12.2

True or false?
1. A person who experiences a brief problem with sexual arousal, orgasm, or desire is likely to meet the criteria for a sexual dysfunction.
2. The best treatment for premature ejaculation is Viagra.
3. Sex therapists may recommend that a woman who does not achieve orgasm practice masturbation without her partner present.
4. People with one sexual dysfunction tend to have other comorbid sexual dysfunctions.

The Paraphilic Disorders

The DSM-5 defines the **paraphilic disorders** as recurrent sexual attraction to unusual objects or sexual activities lasting at least 6 months. In other words, there is a deviation (*para*) in what the person is attracted to (*philia*). DSM differentiates the paraphilic disorders based on the source of arousal; for example, it provides one diagnostic category for people whose sexual attractions are focused on causing pain and another diagnostic category for people whose attractions are focused on children (see Table 12.4). Large surveys of people who volunteer for research on sexuality and health have shown that many people occasionally fantasize about some of the activities we will be describing. Voyeuristic attractions may be particularly common: about 50 percent of men report fantasies of watching unsuspecting naked women (Hanson & Harris, 1997). About 7.7 percent reported that they had been aroused by spying on others having sex, 7 percent reported that they had engaged in sadomasochistic sex at least once, and 3.1 percent reported that they had been aroused by exposing their genitalia to a stranger at least once during their lifetime (Långström & Seto, 2006; Vanwesenbeeck, Bakker, & Gesell, 2010). By April 2014, the website fetlife.com, a social network site for people interested in sadomasochistic and fetishistic sex, listed 2,806,416 members. *Fifty Shades of Gray*, a book describing a sadomasochistic relationship, became one of the best-selling books of all time, with 70 million copies sold in the United States by 2013 (Acuna, 2013).

As some of these behaviors become more common, considerable debate has emerged about whether it is appropriate to diagnose some of the paraphilias. In 2009, the Swedish National Board of Health and Welfare decided to remove some of the paraphilic diagnoses. Fetishistic disorder, sexual sadism disorder, sexual masochism disorder, and transvestic disorder are no longer included in their psychiatric classification system (Långström, 2010). The board reasoned that many people practice variant sexual behaviors safely with consenting adult partners and do not experience any distress or impairment as a result (Richters, de Visser, Rissel et al., 2008). The DSM-5 retains the labels, but the word *disorder* is added to the title of these diagnoses to emphasize that the diagnoses are to be considered only when the sexual attractions cause marked distress or impairment or when the person engages in sexual activities with a nonconsenting person.

Impairment and engagement of nonconsenting others are important boundaries between normative and problematic sexual behavior. For some sexual behaviors, though, these dimensions rarely apply. For example, transvestic disorder does not typically involve nonconsenting others, and it rarely leads to impairment; the diagnosis of this disorder typically rests on the presence of distress. In Focus on Discovery 12.1, we noted that the diagnostic criteria that rely on distress about sexual desires and behaviors are illogical. The person who cross-dresses for sexual gratification and accepts the behavior won't meet the diagnostic criteria. In contrast, the person who feels guilty and ashamed because he or she has internalized stigma about this behavior is diagnosable. Because transvestic behavior so rarely leads to impairment or involves nonconsenting others, we do not discuss transvestic disorder further here.

Table 12.4 Paraphilic Disorders Included in DSM

DSM-5 Diagnosis	Object of Sexual Attraction
Fetishistic disorder	An inanimate object or nongenital body part
Transvestic disorder	Cross-dressing
Pedophilic disorder	Children
Voyeuristic disorder	Watching unsuspecting others undress or have sex
Exhibitionistic disorder	Exposing one's genitals to an unwilling stranger
Frotteuristic disorder	Sexual touching of an unsuspecting person
Sexual sadism disorder	Inflicting pain
Sexual masochism disorder	Receiving pain

Clinical Case: William

William and Nancy sought marital therapy after Nancy learned that William had a long history of voyeurism. Nancy had been startled to walk into their guest room and find him viewing the neighbor with binoculars while masturbating. Upon confrontation, William shared with his wife that he had felt intense and uncontrollable urges to watch strangers undress since his early adolescence.

William and Nancy reported that they had been married for 20 years, and that throughout the duration of their relationship, neither had found their sexual life very satisfying. Nancy was concerned that he rarely initiated sexual contact with her, and indeed, in an individual session, William reported that he preferred watching strangers to having sex with his wife. He had never found sex with a consenting partner to be as exciting as the forbidden.

William had tried different strategies to gain control over his voyeuristic urges, including reading self-help books and attending a support group, with no success. He reported that he came from an extremely strict family and had been teased relentlessly by his father. Although his desire to watch strangers haunted him, he had felt too ashamed to discuss his sexual preferences with anyone in the past. His sense of sexual detachment appeared to be part of a broader pattern of emotional distance and lack of disclosure with others in his life. In therapy, he began to explore the sense of social rejection that he had experienced since early childhood. As his wife learned of his past, they achieved a stronger emotional bond, which freed them to discuss their sexuality more openly. As their sex life improved, William reported that his desire to watch others undress faded. [Adapted from Kleinplatz (2014).]

Accurate prevalence statistics are not available for the paraphilic disorders. Research is limited by the lack of structured diagnostic interviews to reliably assess these conditions (Krueger, 2010b) and even more by the reluctance of many people with paraphilias to reveal their proclivities. Because some persons with paraphilic disorders seek nonconsenting partners or otherwise violate people's rights in offensive ways (as we will see in exhibitionistic and pedophilic disorders), these disorders can have legal consequences. But statistics on arrests are likely to be underestimates because many crimes go unreported and some paraphilias (e.g., voyeuristic disorder) involve an unsuspecting victim. The data do indicate, however, that most people with paraphilic disorders are male and heterosexual; even with pedophilic disorder and sexual masochism disorder, which occur in noticeable numbers of women, men vastly outnumber women. Onset for many of the paraphilic disorders, including fetishistic disorder, voyeuristic disorder, and exhibitionistic disorder, typically occurs during adolescence. The onset of sexual sadism disorder and sexual masochism disorder tends to occur by early adulthood.

Most people with a paraphilic disorder meet the criteria for other paraphilic disorders. In samples of those arrested for their paraphilic behaviors, more than two-thirds meet the criteria for DSM mood disorders, and anxiety and substance abuse disorders are also common (Kafka & Hennen, 2002). Here we provide a clinical description of the paraphilic disorders. As we describe the symptoms, we briefly describe the epidemiology of these disorders.

Fetishistic Disorder

The key feature of **fetishistic disorder** is a reliance on an inanimate object or a nongenital part of the body for sexual arousal. A fetish refers to the object of these sexual urges, such as women's shoes or feet. The person with fetishistic disorder, almost always a man, has recurrent and intense sexual urges toward these fetishes, and the presence of the fetish is strongly preferred or even necessary for sexual arousal. Clothing (especially underwear), leather, and articles related to feet (stockings, women's shoes) are common fetishes. Beyond nonliving objects, some people focus on nonsexual body parts, such as hair, nails, hands, or feet, for sexual arousal. Because there is no evidence of a difference in the etiology or consequences of a boot fetish compared to a foot fetish, the DSM-5 includes a reliance on nonsexual body parts for sexual arousal under the diagnosis of fetishistic disorder.

DSM-5 Criteria for Fetishistic Disorder

- For at least 6 months, recurrent and intense sexually arousing fantasies, urges, or behaviors involving the use of nonliving objects or nongenital body parts
- Causes significant distress or impairment in functioning
- The sexually arousing objects are not limited to articles of clothing used in cross-dressing or to devices designed to provide tactile genital stimulation, such as a vibrator

Clinical Case: Ruben

Ruben, a single, 32-year-old male photographer, sought treatment for his concern that he was more attracted to women's underwear than to the women themselves. Ruben reported that he remembered being excited by pictures of women in their underwear at age 7. At age 13 he reached orgasm by masturbating while imagining women in their underwear. He began to steal underwear from his sister to use while masturbating. As he grew older, he would sneak into women's rooms and steal their underwear. He began

to have intercourse at age 18, and his preferred partner was a prostitute whom he asked to wear underwear with the crotch removed while they had sex. He found that he preferred masturbating into stolen underwear more than sexual intercourse. He avoided dating because he feared the scorn that his focus on underwear might provoke. He had begun to experience significant depression over the ways in which his sexual behavior was limiting his social life. [Adapted from Spitzer et al. (1994).]

The person with fetishistic disorder feels a compulsive attraction to the object; the attraction is experienced as involuntary and irresistible. The exclusive and very special status the object occupies as a sexual stimulant distinguishes fetishistic disorder from the ordinary attraction that, for example, high heels may hold for heterosexual men in Western cultures. The person with a boot fetish must see or touch a boot to become aroused, and the arousal is overwhelmingly strong when a boot is present. Some carry on their fetishism by themselves in secret by fondling, kissing, smelling, gazing at the adored object, or using the fetish as they masturbate. Others can only reach orgasm if a partner dons the fetish, and the resultant distress of the partner is one way that this syndrome reaches a diagnosable level.

Pedophilic Disorder and Incest

According to the DSM, **pedophilic disorder** (*pedes* is Greek for "child") is diagnosed when adults derive sexual gratification through sexual contact with prepubertal children, or when their recurrent and intense desires for sexual contact with prepubertal children cause distress either for themselves or others. DSM-5 criteria specify that the offender be at least 16 years old and at least 5 years older than the child. Some may meet diagnostic criteria in the absence of any actions, if their urges are provoking distress. As in most paraphilias, a strong attraction impels the behavior. Sometimes a man with pedophilic disorder is content to stroke the child's hair, but he may also manipulate the child's genitalia, encourage the child to manipulate his, and, less often, attempt penile insertion. The molestations may be repeated over a period of weeks, months, or years.

People with pedophilic disorder generally molest children whom they know, such as neighbors or friends of the family. Most with pedophilic disorder do not engage in violence other than the sexual act, although when they do become violent, it is often a focus of lurid stories in the media. Because overt physical force is seldom used in pedophilic disorder, the child molester often denies that he is actually forcing himself on his victim. Despite molesters' distorted beliefs, child sexual abuse inherently involves a betrayal of trust and other serious negative consequences (see Focus on Discovery 12.3 for a discussion of these consequences).

What are the demographic characteristics of people who meet the criteria for pedophilic disorder? Up to half are adolescent males (Morenz & Becker, 1995). People with pedophilic disorder can be straight or gay, though most are heterosexual. Most older heterosexual men with pedophilic disorder are or have been married.

Sexual arousal in response to pictures of young children can be measured by the penile plethysmograph, and in one meta-analysis of studies involving 28,972 sexual offenders, arousal as measured in this way was one of the strongest predictors of repeated sexual offenses

DSM-5 Criteria for Pedophilic Disorder

- For at least 6 months, recurrent and intense, sexually arousing fantasies, urges, or behaviors involving sexual contact with a prepubescent child
- Person has acted on these urges or the urges and fantasies cause marked distress or interpersonal problems
- Person is at least 16 years old and 5 years older than the child

FOCUS ON DISCOVERY 12.3

The Effects of Pedophilic Disorder: Outcomes After Childhood Sexual Abuse

In one major community survey, about 20 percent of women and 5 percent of men reported experiencing some form of childhood sexual abuse (CSA) (Afifi et al., 2008). A child abuser is usually not a stranger. He may be a father, an uncle, a brother, a teacher, a coach, a neighbor, or even a cleric. The abuser is often an adult whom the child knows and trusts. When the abuser is someone close to the child, the child is likely to be torn on the one hand by allegiance to the abuser and, on the other hand, by fear, revulsion, and the knowledge that what is happening is wrong. The betrayal of this trust makes the crime more abhorrent than it would be if no prior relationship existed between abuser and child. As with childhood incest, molestation or sexual harassment by an authority figure violates trust and respect. The victim, whatever his or her age, cannot give meaningful consent. The power differential is just too great.

Here, we consider two central questions. How does the all-too-common experience of CSA affect mental health during childhood and beyond? What can be done to help children heal from CSA?

Effects on the Child

About half of children who are exposed to CSA will develop symptoms, such as depression, low self-esteem, conduct disorder, and anxiety disorders like posttraumatic stress disorder (PTSD). On the other hand, almost half of children who are exposed to CSA do not appear to experience immediate symptoms (Kuehnle, 1998). What factors contribute to how CSA affects a child? The odds that CSA will produce clinically significant symptoms are increased when a perpetrator threatens the child, the child blames him- or herself, or the family is unsupportive (Kuehnle, 1998). Negative outcomes are more pronounced when the CSA involves sexual intercourse (Nelson et al., 2002). Symptoms also appear to be more likely when the CSA started at an earlier age (Kaplow & Widom, 2007).

In adulthood, CSA is related to higher risk of many different psychological disorders when assessed in representative community samples (Afifi et al., 2008). We have seen in previous chapters that a history of CSA is common among adults experiencing many different psychological disorders—notably, dissociative identity disorder, PTSD, eating disorders, borderline personality disorder, major depressive disorder, sexual dysfunctions, and substance abuse. CSA is also related to changes in the function of the HPA axis and the regulation of the stress hormone, cortisol, during adulthood (Stein, Yehuda, Koverola et al., 1997).

An issue in interpreting these correlations, though, is that families in which abuse occurs are often experiencing a broad array of problems, such as substance dependence in one or both parents, which may be entangled with other genetic and environmental risks for psychopathology. As a result, it is hard to isolate whether CSA is genuinely the factor that heightens the risk for a clinical disorder—most children who are exposed to child abuse also experience other forms of early

adversity (Green et al., 2010). Twin studies provide a way to disentangle these effects, particularly when one twin but not the other has been abused, because the twin who was not abused shares genetic, and at least some environmental, risk factors. In one study of almost 2000 twin pairs, adults with a history of CSA had substantially increased risk of depression, suicide, conduct disorder, alcohol dependence, social anxiety, rape, and divorce compared to their nonabused twins (Nelson et al., 2002).

Dealing with the Problem

When they suspect that something is awry, parents must raise the issue with their children; unfortunately, many adults are uncomfortable doing so. Physicians also need to be sensitive to signs of sexual abuse. Sexual and nonsexual forms of abuse are reportable offenses; professionals who suspect abuse are required by law to report their suspicions to the police or child protective agencies. For a child, reporting sexual abuse can be extremely difficult. We tend to forget how helpless and dependent the child feels, and it is difficult to imagine how frightening it would be to tell one's parents that one had been fondled by a brother or grandfather. Most cases of sexual abuse do not leave any physical evidence, such as torn vaginal tissue. Furthermore, there is no behavioral sign or emotional syndrome that unequivocally indicates that abuse has occurred (Kuehnle, 1998). Therefore, the child's own report is the primary source of information about whether CSA has occurred. The problem is that leading questions can produce some false reports. Great skill is required in questioning a child about possible sexual abuse to avoid biasing the youngster one way or the other. To reduce the stress on the child while protecting the rights of the accused adult, some jurisdictions use procedures such as videotaped testimony, closed-courtroom trials, closed-circuit televised testimony, and special coaching sessions to explain what to expect in the courtroom (Wolfe, 1990). Having the child play with anatomically correct dolls can be useful, but it should be only one part of an assessment because many nonabused children portray such dolls having sexual intercourse (Jampole & Weber, 1987). It is impossible to know what percentage of incest cases are not reported to the police, but it is safe to say that most are unreported, particularly if the offender is a family member (Finkelhor, 1983).

Many children need treatment (Litrownik & Castillo-Canez, 2000). As with adult survivors of rape, PTSD can be a consequence. Many interventions are similar to those used for PTSD in adults; the emphasis is on exposure to memories of the trauma through discussion in a safe and supportive therapeutic atmosphere. It is also important for children to learn that healthy human sexuality is not about power and fear (McCarthy, 1986). As with rape, it is important to change the person's attribution of responsibility from "I was bad" to "he/she was bad." Findings of a randomized controlled trial suggest that such treatments can help abused children find relief from their symptoms and can reduce their sense of shame (Cohen, Deblinger, Mannarino et al., 2004)

(Hanson & Bussiere, 1998). Penile plethysmograph indices may be helpful in predicting future offenses when sexual offenders deny an interest in young children (Blanchard, 2001). Nonetheless, arousal in response to pictures of children is not a perfect predictor of pedophilic disorder. Many men who are conventional in their sexual interests and behavior can be sexually aroused by erotic pictures of children. In a study using both self-report and penile plethysmography, one-quarter of men drawn from a community sample showed or reported arousal when viewing sexually provocative pictures of children (Hall, Hirschman, & Oliver, 1995). Indeed, across studies, 3 to 9 percent of men describe having experienced at least one sexual fantasy involving a child (Seto, 2009). Consider this quote from a man about recognizing that he held sexual attractions to children.

> That was the year when Father Smith hit the front page of every newspaper my parents brought home with them. A new evil was born from an inferno of horror and fear and its name was Pedophilia. I had never heard that word before. Father Smith was a pedophile and as the newspaper explained, a pedophile was a person who had an attraction to children. Father Smith had sex with young boys. The only people I seemed to be attracted to were boys. At first a wave of utter disbelief and confusion passed over me. There is no way on God's green earth I would do anything like the horror Father Smith perpetrated on those boys. (Goode, 2010, pp. 6–7)

Although the number of men who seem to experience a sexual attraction to children might seem disturbing (and perhaps even more disturbing for some of the men who experience the urges), the diagnosis of pedophilia is not made on the basis of sexual attraction alone. Pedophilic disorder is diagnosed only when adults act on their sexual urges toward children, or when the urges reach the frequency or intensity to be distressing to the person or those close to them.

Incest is listed as a subtype of pedophilic disorder. **Incest** refers to sexual relations between close relatives for whom marriage is forbidden. It is most common between brother and sister. The next most common form, which is considered more pathological, is between father and daughter.

The taboo against incest is virtually universal in human societies (Ford & Beach, 1951), with the notable exception of Egyptian pharaohs, who could marry their sisters or other females of their immediate families. In Egypt, it was believed that the royal blood should not be contaminated by that of outsiders. The incest taboo makes sense according to present-day scientific knowledge. The offspring from a father–daughter or a brother–sister union have a greater probability of inheriting a pair of recessive genes, one from each parent. Many recessive genes have negative biological effects, such as serious birth defects. The incest taboo, then, has adaptive evolutionary significance.

Men who commit incest usually abuse their pubescent daughters, whereas men with nonincestual pedophilic disorder are usually interested in prepubertal children. Consistent with this difference in the age of victims, men who molest children within their families show greater penile arousal (as measured by penile plethysmography) to adult heterosexual cues than do men who molest unrelated children (Marshall, Barbaree, & Christophe, 1986).

Voyeuristic Disorder

The central feature of **voyeuristic disorder** is an intense and recurrent desire to obtain sexual gratification by watching unsuspecting others in a state of undress or having sexual relations. Voyeuristic fantasies are quite common in men, but as with the other paraphilic disorders, fantasies alone do not warrant a diagnosis. For some men with this disorder, voyeurism is their only sexual activity; for others, it is preferred but not absolutely essential for sexual arousal (Kaplan & Kreuger, 1997). As in the case of William earlier in this chapter, the looking, sometimes called peeping, helps the person become sexually aroused and is sometimes essential for arousal. People with voyeuristic disorder achieve orgasm by masturbation, either while watching or later while remembering the peeping. Sometimes the person with voyeuristic disorder fantasizes about having sexual contact with the observed person, but it remains a fantasy; he or she seldom contacts the observed person. A true voyeur, almost always a man, does not find it particularly exciting to watch a woman who is undressing for his benefit.

DSM-5 Criteria for Voyeuristic Disorder

- For at least 6 months, recurrent and intense sexually arousing fantasies, urges, or behaviors involving the observation of unsuspecting others who are naked, disrobing, or engaged in sexual activity
- Person has acted on these urges with a nonconsenting person, or the urges and fantasies cause marked distress or interpersonal problems

DSM-5 Criteria for Exhibitionistic Disorder

- For at least 6 months, recurrent, intense, and sexually arousing fantasies, urges, or behaviors involving showing one's genitals to an unsuspecting person
- Person has acted on these urges to a nonconsenting person, or the urges and fantasies cause clinically significant distress or interpersonal problems

DSM-5 Criteria for Frotteuristic Disorder

- For at least 6 months, recurrent and intense and sexually arousing fantasies, urges, or behaviors involving touching or rubbing against a nonconsenting person
- Person has acted on these urges with a nonconsenting person, or the urges and fantasies cause clinically significant distress or problems

DSM-5 Criteria for Sexual Sadism Disorder

- For at least 6 months, recurrent, intense, and sexually arousing fantasies, urges, or behaviors involving the physical or psychological suffering of another person
- Causes clinically significant distress or impairment in functioning or the person has acted on these urges with a nonconsenting person

The element of risk seems important, for the voyeur is excited by the anticipation of how the woman would react if she knew he was watching.

Exhibitionistic Disorder

The focus of sexual desire in **exhibitionistic disorder** is on exposing one's genitals to an unwilling stranger, sometimes a child. As with voyeuristic disorder, there is seldom an attempt to have other contact with the stranger. Many exhibitionists masturbate during the exposure. In most cases, there is a desire to shock or embarrass the observer. The urge to expose seems overwhelming and virtually uncontrollable to the exhibitionist and is apparently triggered by anxiety and restlessness as well as by sexual arousal. In the tension of the moment, many describe symptoms of anxiety, including headaches, palpitations, and derealization. Because of the compulsive nature of the urge, the exposures may be repeated often and even in the same place and at the same time of day. At the time of the act, the social and legal consequences are far from exhibitionists' minds (Stevenson & Jones, 1972).. After exposing themselves, exhibitionists tend to flee and feel remorseful. In one study, persons diagnosed with exhibitionistic disorder reported that they had been arrested for only 1 out of every 150 incidents (Abel et al., 1987).

Frotteuristic Disorder

The focus of sexual desire and urges in **frotteuristic disorder** is on touching an unsuspecting person. The person with this disorder may rub his penis against a woman's thighs or buttocks or fondle her breasts or genitals. These attacks typically occur in places such as a crowded bus or sidewalk that provide an easy means of escape. Most men who engage in frotteurism report doing so dozens of times (Abel et al., 1987). Frotteuristic disorder has not been studied extensively.

Sexual Sadism and Masochism Disorders

The focus of desire in **sexual sadism disorder** is on inflicting pain or psychological suffering (such as humiliation) on another, and the focus of desire in **sexual masochism disorder** is on being subjected to pain or humiliation. Some sadists achieve orgasm by inflicting pain, and some masochists achieve orgasm by being subjected to pain. The manifestations of sexual masochism disorder are varied. Examples include physical bondage, blindfolding, spanking, whipping, electric shocks, cutting, humiliation (e.g., being urinated or defecated on, being forced to wear a collar and bark like a dog, or being put on display naked), and taking the role of slave and submitting to orders and commands. Most sadists establish relationships with masochists to derive mutual sexual gratification. Although many people are able to take both dominant and submissive roles, masochists outnumber sadists.

Sadistic and masochistic sexual behaviors have become more accepted over time: 5 to 10 percent of the population have tried some form of sadomasochistic activity, such as blindfolding or spanking one's partner (Baumeister & Butler, 1997). In major cities, clubs cater to members seeking sadomasochistic partnerships. Most people who engage in sadomasochistic behaviors are relatively comfortable with their sexual practices and would not meet the diagnostic criteria requiring that the desires lead to distress or impairment (Spengler, 1977).

Because these disorders have become more common and are typically not related to impairment or distress, there was debate about whether these diagnoses should be retained in DSM-5 (Krueger, 2010b). These diagnostic labels were retained because some sadistic and masochistic practices can be dangerous. One particularly dangerous form of masochism, called

Many people experiment with sadomasochism and fetishes. Paraphilias are not diagnosed unless the sexual interests cause marked distress or impairment.

Cindy Charles/PhotoEdit

DSM-5 Criteria for Sexual Masochism Disorder

- For at least 6 months, recurrent, intense, and sexually arousing fantasies, urges, or behaviors involving the act of being humiliated, beaten, bound, or made to suffer
- Causes marked distress or impairment in functioning

asphyxiophilia, can result in death or brain damage; it involves sexual arousal by restricting breathing, which can be achieved using a noose, a plastic bag, or chest compression. More commonly, the diagnosis is applicable when the sadomasochistic urges and preferences lead to either personal or relationship distress.

There is also some concern that the diagnosis of sexual sadism disorder is rarely applied in clinical settings. In an unpublished review of over 500 million visits to psychiatrists, gynecologists, urologists, and other physicians, no doctor recorded a diagnosis of sexual sadism disorder (Narrow, 2008, cited in Krueger, 2010a). Doctors in clinical settings may not use the diagnosis even when symptoms are present because of worries over stigma. The diagnosis, then, seems to be applied almost entirely within forensic settings (Krueger, 2010a).

Both of these disorders are found in straight and gay relationships. Surveys have found that 20 to 30 percent of the members of sadomasochistic clubs are female (Moser & Levitt, 1987), and it has been assumed that a similar gender ratio might be true of diagnoses of sexual sadism and masochism. Most sadists and masochists lead otherwise conventional lives, and there is some evidence that they are above average in income and educational status (Moser & Levitt, 1987). Alcohol abuse is common among sadists (Allnutt, Bradford, Greenberg et al., 1996).

Check Your Knowledge 12.3

Choose the diagnostic category that best fits each vignette. If not diagnosable, state so.

1. Joe is able to obtain sexual arousal only by rubbing his body against strangers. He has worked out a set of rituals to engage in this behavior; he knows which bus routes and times will be most crowded, chooses a bus that tends to have many women, and times his attacks so that he can leave the bus at a stop along with many other people.
2. Sam and Terry enjoy a good sexual relationship. They have mutually satisfying sex at least weekly. Occasionally, Terry likes to be tied down before sex, but she is able to enjoy sex without bondage as well. Most of their sex life involves no hint of pain or bondage.

3. Matt feels aroused only when he is able to cause pain to someone as part of engaging in sex. Most of the time, he indulges in these activities at a sadomasochism club. He has not been able to sustain a relationship with any of the women he has met in clubs. He is deeply distressed by his inability to enjoy other forms of sexuality.
4. Barry is a 40-year-old single man who has never had a sustained dating relationship or sexual partnership. Several times a week, Barry parks his car at the beach, masturbates, and then finds a way to lure a woman to his car, usually by asking for directions. He is unable to have an orgasm unless the woman notices his erection. He has been arrested three times for this behavior.

Etiology of the Paraphilic Disorders

Here, we will discuss the etiology of the paraphilic disorders, including the role of neurobiological factors, early abuse, and psychological variables. Because many people do not want to talk about their paraphilias, researchers have few opportunities to understand their causes. Indeed, most studies rely on small samples. As an example, only four studies were published between 1990 and 2009 that included more than 25 participants diagnosed with fetishistic disorder (Kafka, 2010). Beyond the lack of research and the small sample sizes, most of the research focuses on men who are arrested for their sexual behavior; little is known about those whose sexual behavior does not lead to arrest. Hence, much of this literature is most relevant for understanding sexual offenders, who represent a more severe subset of those with paraphilic disorders.

Neurobiological Factors   Because the overwhelming majority of people with paraphilic disorders are men, there has been speculation that androgens (hormones like testosterone) play a role. Androgens regulate sexual desire, and sexual desire appears to be atypically high among sexual offenders with paraphilic disorders (Kafka, 1997). Nonetheless, men with paraphilic disorders do not appear to have high levels of testosterone or other androgens (Thibaut, De La Barra, Gordon et al., 2010).

Childhood Sexual Abuse   Across multiple studies of adult offenders, about two-thirds of sexual offenders reported a history of sexual abuse, a rate that is more than threefold higher than the rate among those charged with nonsexual offenses (Jespersen, Lalumiere, & Seto, 2009).

But this cannot be the whole story—several large-scale follow-up studies of boys with confirmed sexual abuse have shown that fewer than 5 percent were charged with any type of sexual offense as adults (Ogloff, Cutajar, Mann et al., 2012; Salter et al., 2003).

Psychological Factors Psychological research tends to consider the immediate triggers of sexual behavior and the more distal personality and cognitive risk factors for paraphilic disorders. We'll cover triggers and then the broader risk factors, and then we will discuss specific models of pedophilia.

For some of the paraphilias, succumbing to the sexual urge can be thought of as an impulsive act, in which the person loses control over his behavior. Alcohol decreases the ability to inhibit impulses, and accordingly, incidents of pedophilic disorder, voyeuristic disorder, and exhibitionistic disorder often occur in the context of alcohol use. Others report that their sexual behaviors are most likely to happen in the context of negative moods, suggesting that sexual activity is being used as a means to escape from negative affect.

If the immediate act can be triggered by negative emotions and by a loss of impulse control, then it should not be surprising that personality traits relevant to those triggers are often observed in those with paraphilic disorder. People with paraphilic disorders do tend to show heightened impulsivity and poor emotion regulation (Ward & Beech, 2006).

Cognitive distortions and attitudes also play a role in the paraphilic disorders. Men who engage in paraphilias that involve nonconsenting women may have hostile attitudes and a lack of empathy toward women. Others may have distortions in the ways they think about their sexual behavior. For example, a voyeur may believe that a woman who left her blinds up while undressing wanted someone to look at her (Kaplan & Kreuger, 1997). A person with pedophilic disorder may believe that children want to have sex with adults (Marshall, 1997) or may think of himself as innocently teaching a child about sex (Maletzky, 2002). Men who engage in rape may blame the woman, saying that she "deserved a lesson" or that her dress was provocative. See Focus on Discovery 12.4 for a discussion of rape.

A separate line of work focuses on the psychological traits associated with pedophilia. On average, men with pedophilic disorder have a slightly lower IQ and higher rates of neurocognitive problems than the general population (Cantor, Blanchard, Robichaud et al., 2005; Suchy, Eastvold, Strassberg et al., 2014). Academic problems are common, as are other criminal behaviors (Becker & Hunter, 1997). Beyond the cognitive deficits related to pedophilia, it is important to understand that there may be more than one psychological pathway to pedophilia (Knight & King, 2012). Some pedophiles show an intense preoccupation with sex, a sense of emotional compatibility with children, and a specific sexual preference for children. Other pedophiles demonstrate a general profile of elevated impulsivity and psychopathy compared to the general population (Mann, Hanson, & Thornton, 2010).

Quick Summary

Paraphilic disorders are defined as a sexual attraction to an unusual sexual object or activity that lasts at least 6 months and causes significant distress or impairment. The DSM diagnostic criteria for paraphilic disorders are distinguished based on the object of sexual attraction. The major DSM-5 diagnoses of paraphilias include fetishistic disorder, pedophilic disorder, voyeuristic disorder, exhibitionistic disorder, frotteuristic disorder, sexual sadism disorder, sexual masochism disorder, and transvestic disorder. (The last-named diagnosis was not discussed here.)

Researchers do not know the prevalence of these disorders. Few major studies have been done on the etiology of paraphilic disorders, and the available studies largely focus on sexual offenders. Neurobiological theory has focused on excessively high levels of male hormones (testosterone), but the theory has not received strong support. Sexual offenders do appear to have higher rates of sexual abuse than do other offenders, but very few children who are abused grow up to engage in sexual offenses against others. Psychological theories focus on impulsivity, poor emotion regulation, and distorted cognitions. Alcohol use and negative affect are often immediate triggers of inappropriate sexual behaviors. For pedophilia, there may be more than one pathway: some men seem sexually preoccupied with children and experience a sense of emotional compatibility with children; other men have a profile of more general impulsive, psychopathic traits. Neurocognitive deficits and lower IQ are often observed in men diagnosed with pedophilic disorder.

FOCUS ON DISCOVERY 12.4

The Rapist

Is the rapist primarily someone who seeks the thrill of dominating and humiliating a woman through intimidation and assault? Is he an ordinarily unassertive man with a fragile ego who, feeling inadequate after disappointment and rejection in work or love, takes out his frustrations on an unwilling stranger? What types of characteristics distinguish rapists? Can treatment reduce the risk of recidivism?

Understanding the Etiology of Rape

There is no DSM diagnosis to capture a tendency to rape. Several traits appear to be elevated among rapists. Sexually aggressive men tend to show antisocial and impulsive personality traits (Knight, 2010) and unusually high hostility toward women (Malamuth, 1998). More specific to sexual interactions, rapists appear to have a high sex drive (as measured by frequency of sexual outlets) (Kafka, 1997) and may also have cognitive distortions that lead them to minimize the consequences of their behavior. Some rapists seem to have problems distinguishing friendliness from seductiveness and in accurately reading cues from a woman indicating that she wants intimacies to cease (Malamuth & Brown, 1994). In one major community survey, men who had assaulted women sexually were 3.5 times more likely to report erectile dysfunction than those who had not committed assaults (Laumann, et al., 1999). It is also likely that there may be different subgroups of rapists, who show a different cluster of traits: some may show more prominent sadistic traits, some may show more hypersexuality, and some may show more impulsive traits (Knight, 2010).

Data also suggests that exposure to violence may increase the likelihood of rape. That is, rapists are more likely than nonrapists to have been the victim of sexual and physical abuse (Knight & Sims-Knight, 2011).

Even watching violence against women in films can lead men to view violence as more acceptable. In a controlled experiment, undergraduate men who stated that they regarded rape as unacceptable were aroused by video portrayals of rape if the woman was depicted as having an orgasm during the assault (Malamuth & Check, 1983). Since the time this study was conducted, eight experiments have been conducted in which men are asked to watch videos that contain either sexual activities with violence or sexual activities without violence. A meta-analysis of these studies suggested that after watching the videos that contained violence, men were significantly more likely to report that violence toward women was acceptable (Allen, D'Alessio, & Brezgel, 1995). This research suggests that rape may be encouraged by pornography that depicts women enjoying violent sexual relations and more broadly highlights the importance of social factors.

Psychological Treatment for Rapists

Treatment programs for rapists rely on the general approaches we describe for paraphilic disorders: motivational strategies, a range of cognitive behavioral techniques, and pharmacological treatments. As with the research on treatment for paraphilic disorders, the evidence regarding the effectiveness of these approaches is remarkably slim. Only one study has randomly assigned men who are sexual offenders to cognitive behavioral treatment or to no treatment (Marques, Wiederanders, Day et al., 2005). Examination of the outcomes for the 24 rapists who took part in that study suggested that 20 percent of men in the treatment group committed an offense during the 5-year follow-up period, compared to 29 percent in the no-treatment group. Although this may seem like a small gain from treatment, any gain is important with such a difficult problem.

Everett Collection, Inc.

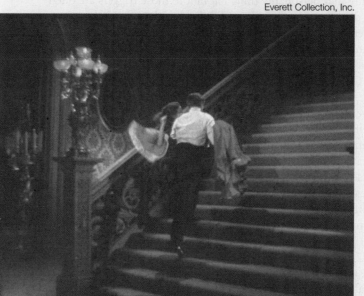

This famous scene from *Gone with the Wind* illustrates one of the myths about rape—that despite initial resistance, women like to be "taken."

Treatments for the Paraphilic Disorders

Findings on the treatment of paraphilic disorders are hard to interpret for several reasons. Most of the available research on treatment focuses on men who have been charged with sexual offenses, and even on those who are court-ordered into treatment. Beyond the lack of representative samples, outcomes in this area are highly variable; perhaps this is not surprising given that researchers have varied in their focus on adolescent or adult offenders, or on the most or least severe offenders. In a meta-analysis of 12 studies of men arrested for sexual offenses, those who received treatment of some form—either biological or psychological—were about a third less likely to have repeat offenses than those who did not receive treatment (Hall et al., 1995). Caution is warranted in interpreting this finding, for two reasons. First, because many researchers consider it unethical to withhold treatment when the consequences of sexual offenses are so severe, most studies have not randomly assigned people into control groups. Rather, outcomes for those who complete treatment are typically compared to outcomes for men who were not offered treatment or who refused treatment. Second, most studies have not included long-term follow-up, even though recidivism increases as the years go by (Maletzky, 2002). With these issues as background, we now describe cognitive behavioral and biological treatments for the paraphilic disorders.

Strategies to Enhance Motivation Sex offenders often lack the motivation to change their illegal behavior. They may deny their problem, minimize the seriousness of their problem, and feel confident that they can control their behavior without professional assistance. Some blame the victim, even a child, for being overly seductive. Many refuse to take part in treatment, and even among those who begin treatment, many will drop out. To enhance motivation for treatment, a therapist can bolster the client's hope that he can gain control over his urges through treatment, highlight the potential legal and other consequences of continued engagement in the same sexual behavior, and note that plethysmograph assessments will make it hard to "fake" a recovery (Miller & Rollnick, 1991).

Cognitive Behavioral Treatment In the earliest years of behavioral treatment, paraphilic disorders were narrowly viewed as attractions to inappropriate objects and activities. Looking to behavioral psychology for ways to reduce these attractions, researchers fixed on aversion therapy. Thus, a person with a boot fetish would be given a shock on the hands or a drug that produces nausea when looking at a boot, a person with pedophilic disorder when gazing at a photograph of a nude child, and so on. In the form of aversion therapy called satiation, men are coached to pair their paraphilic fantasies with another aversive stimulus: masturbating for 55 minutes after orgasm (Kaplan & Krueger, 2012). Another variation of aversion therapy is covert sensitization, in which the person imagines situations he finds inappropriately arousing and also imagines feeling sick or ashamed for feeling and acting this way. Studies of covert sensitization have shown that it reduces deviant arousal, but little evidence is available that these techniques alone actually change the behavior (Maletzky, 2000).

Cognitive procedures are often used to counter the distorted thinking of people with paraphilic disorders. For example, an exhibitionist might claim that the girls he exposes himself to are too young to be harmed by it. The therapist would counter this distortion by pointing out that the younger the victim, the worse the harm will be (Maletzky, 1997).

In general, cognitive and behavioral approaches have become more sophisticated and broader in scope since the 1960s, when the paraphilic disorders were addressed almost exclusively through aversive conditioning and cognitive interventions. Current approaches supplement these traditional approaches with techniques such as social skills training and sexual impulse control training (Maletzky, 2002). Training in empathy toward others is another increasingly common cognitive technique; teaching the sex offender to consider how his or her behavior would affect someone else may lessen the tendency to engage in such activities. Relapse prevention, modeled after the work on substance abuse described in Chapter 10, is also an important component of many broader treatment programs. A therapist who uses relapse prevention techniques would help a person identify situations and emotions that might trigger symptomatic behavior. Interventions that combine cognitive interventions with behavioral interventions appear to be more successful than those that are strictly behavioral (Hall et al., 1995).

As with the treatment literature on the whole, most of the available evidence for cognitive behavioral interventions is based on studies with no adequate control group. Without a control group, it seemed that psychological interventions were helping relieve symptoms—many people reported diminished paraphilic symptoms after treatment (Maletzky, 2002). Unfortunately, when compared to a control group that did not receive treatment, cognitive behavioral therapy did not appear to reduce legal recidivism (Marques et al., 2005). Although these findings are discouraging, this remains an important area for ongoing research.

Biological Treatments A variety of biological interventions have been tried on sex offenders. Castration, or removal of the testes, was used a great deal until hormonal treatments (described next) became available (Wille & Boulanger, 1984). Surgical castration is not a common treatment today due to major ethical concerns.

On the other hand, several medications have been used to treat paraphilic disorders, particularly among sex offenders. Typically, these medications are used as a supplement to psychological treatment. Among men, sexual drive and functioning are regulated by androgens (such as testosterone). Hence, hormonal agents that reduce androgens have been used to treat paraphilic disorders, including medroxyprogesterone acetate (MPA, trade name Depo-Provera) and cyproterone acetate (CPA, Gyrostat). Randomized controlled trials show that these agents reduce arousal to deviant objects, as measured using the penile plethysmograph (Thibaut et al., 2010). Despite the promising findings, ethical issues are raised about the indefinite use of hormonal agents. Long-term use of hormonal agents is associated with a number of negative side effects, including infertility, liver problems, osteoporosis, and diabetes. Informed consent concerning these risks must be obtained, and many patients will not agree to use these drugs long term (Hill, Briken, Kraus et al., 2003).

Beyond drugs that influence hormones, SSRI antidepressants are commonly used. Although pre–post measures suggest that SSRIs reduce arousal to deviant objects, researchers have not conducted randomized controlled trials of SSRIs compared to a control condition, and so the quality of the research evidence is poor (Thibaut et al., 2010).

Balancing Efforts to Protect the Public Against Civil Liberties for Those with Paraphilias Most people are frightened by sexual offenses, so balancing the protection of the public against civil liberties of sexual offenders is not easy. Issues arise in multiple aspects of the legal process and outcome, including how diagnoses of paraphilic disorders can influence institutionalization, but also with laws concerning the public's "right to know" when a sex offender is released.

In the United States, it is generally unconstitutional to detain a person on the basis of his or her potential for future crimes. Nonetheless, the Supreme Court has ruled that a person deemed at high risk for a sex crime can be detained if the risk is related to a psychological disorder that diminishes the person's ability to control his or her sexual behavior. The diagnosis of paraphilia, then, has significant implications for civil liberties: receipt of this diagnosis can lead to placement in a psychiatric facility. In this context, it has been argued that particular care should be taken to ensure that this set of diagnoses has validity (Wakefield, 2011).

Legal statutes referred to as Megan's law allow police to publicize the whereabouts of registered sex offenders if they are considered to be a potential danger. Citizens can then use computerized police records to determine whether sex offenders are living in their neighborhoods. Megan's law and related statutes arose from public outrage at the brutal murder of a second grader in New Jersey who was kidnapped while walking home from school. The person convicted of this crime was a twice-convicted child molester. Sadly, some have committed violent crimes toward sex offenders in their neighborhoods (Younglove & Vitello, 2003). It should come as no surprise that civil liberties groups are challenging these laws. The tension between protecting the public and civil liberties for offenders is an ongoing process.

Check Your Knowledge 12.4

Answer the questions.

1. Which of the following has not been related to paraphilic disorders?
   a. childhood abuse
   b. cognitive distortions
   c. negative affect
   d. all of the above have been related to paraphilic disorders
2. The most commonly used biological treatments to reduce sexual desire and paraphilic behaviors are:

   a. surgical castration
   b. hormonal agents and antidepressants
   c. anti-anxiety medications
   d. none of the above
3. Name three cognitive behavioral strategies used in the treatment of paraphilic disorders: _____, _____, _____.

Summary

Sexual Norms

- Sexual behavior and attitudes are heavily influenced by culture, so any discussion of disorders in sexuality must be sensitive to the idea that norms are likely to change across time and place. Currently, a great deal of research is focused on gender differences in sexuality.

- Kaplan identified four phases in the sexual response cycle: desire, excitement, orgasm, and resolution. The validity of the Kaplan model for women has been criticized.

Sexual Dysfunctions

- The DSM-5 includes the following sexual dysfunction diagnoses: female sexual interest/arousal disorder, male hypoactive sexual desire disorder, erectile disorder, female orgasmic disorder, premature ejaculation, delayed ejaculation, and genito-pelvic pain/penetration disorder. Many people experience brief sexual symptoms, but these are not diagnosable unless they are recurrent, cause either distress or impairment, and are not explained by medical conditions.

- Research on the etiology of sexual dysfunctions is difficult to conduct, as surveys may be inaccurate and laboratory measures may be difficult to gather. Researchers have identified many different variables that can contribute to sexual dysfunctions, including biological variables, previous sexual experiences, relationship issues, psychopathology, negative affect, low arousal, and negative cognitions.

- Many effective cognitive behavioral interventions for sexual dysfunctions are available. Sex therapy, aimed at reversing old habits and teaching new skills, was propelled into public consciousness by the Masters and Johnson work. Their method hinges on gradual, non-threatening exposure to increasingly intimate sexual encounters. Sex therapists also aim to educate patients in sexual anatomy and physiology, reduce anxiety, teach communication skills, and improve attitudes and thoughts about sexuality. Couples therapy is sometimes appropriate as well. Biological treatments such as Viagra may be used for the treatment of erectile dysfunction.

Paraphilic Disorders

- The paraphilic disorders are defined by attractions and urges toward unusual sexual objects or behaviors that are persistent and lead to distress or impairment. The principal DSM-5 paraphilic disorders are fetishistic disorder, pedophilic disorder, voyeuristic disorder, exhibitionistic disorder, frotteuristic disorder, sexual sadism disorder, sexual masochism disorder, and transvestic disorder. (We do not discuss transvestic disorder because there is no evidence that the behavior causes impairment.)

- Exposure to childhood sexual abuse may be a risk factor for paraphilic disorders. Alcohol use may increase the odds of acting on sexual urges. Impulsivity, emotion dysregulation, and distorted cognitions appear to be involved.

- Pedophilia has been related to neurocognitive deficits and lower IQ. It has been argued that some men with pedophilia are obsessed with sex and strongly attracted to children both emotionally and sexually; other men with pedophilia seem to act out of a more general cluster of impulsive and antisocial traits.

- The research evidence regarding treatments for paraphilic disorders is limited. Treatment approaches must begin by engaging and motivating the client, which is often difficult to do. Early cognitive behavioral approaches focused on aversion therapy and cognitive techniques to challenge distorted beliefs about the consequences of sexual behaviors. Over time, cognitive behavioral therapists have also begun to use techniques to improve social skills, to help people control impulses, to increase empathy for potential victims, and to identify potential high-risk situations for the return of symptoms. Studies suggest that psychological treatments do not significantly reduce rates of legal offenses. Drugs that reduce testosterone levels have been found to reduce both sex drive and deviant sexual behaviors, but because of the side effects, there are ethical issues involved in the long-term use of these drugs. SSRI antidepressants are commonly prescribed to reduce the sexual drive of men with paraphilic disorders, but the quality of the research evidence is poor.

- A diagnosis of paraphilic disorder has relevance for whether a person can be detained in a psychiatric facility for possible future crimes. Laws have been passed that allow the public to access information about where sexual offenders live, but civil liberties groups are opposed to some aspects of these laws.

Answers to Check Your Knowledge Questions

12.1 1. Men report higher frequency of sexual thought, desire, and behavior than do women, and women's sexuality tends to be more influenced by their perceptions of their attractiveness and by relationship status, and less related to perceptions of power than is men's sexuality. 2. desire phase, excitement phase, orgasm phase, resolution phase; 3. Desire and excitement phases are not distinct stages for women, and although Kaplan relied on biological changes to define the excitement phase, biological changes do not closely mirror subjective arousal for women.

12.2 1. F (unless the problem is recurrent and leads to distress or impairment, it cannot be diagnosed); 2. F; 3. T; 4. T

12.3 1. frotteuristic disorder; 2. not a diagnosable disorder (because there is no evidence of distress or impairment); 3. sexual sadism disorder; 4. exhibitionistic disorder

12.4 1. d; 2. b; 3. any three of the following: cognitive interventions to reduce distorted thinking, aversion therapy (including covert sensitization), social skills training, interventions to improve sexual impulse control, empathy training, relapse prevention

Key Terms

delayed ejaculation
desire phase
erectile disorder
excitement phase
exhibitionistic disorder
female orgasmic disorder
female sexual interest/arousal disorder
fetishistic disorder
frotteuristic disorder

gender dysphoria
genito-pelvic pain/penetration disorder
incest
male hypoactive sexual desire disorder
orgasm phase
paraphilic disorders
pedophilic disorders
penile plethysmograph
premature ejaculation

resolution phase
sexual dysfunctions
sexual masochism disorder
sexual response cycle
sexual sadism disorder
spectator role
vaginal plethysmograph
voyeuristic disorder

13 Disorders of Childhood

LEARNING GOALS

1. Be able to describe the issues in the diagnosis of psychopathology in children.
2. Be able to discuss the description, etiology, and treatments for externalizing problems, including ADHD and conduct disorder, and for internalizing problems, including depression and anxiety disorders.
3. Be able to understand the learning disorders dyslexia and dyscalculia as well as learn the causes and treatments for dyslexia.
4. Be able to describe the description and diagnosis of intellectual disability and the current research on causes and treatments.
5. Be able to describe the symptoms, causes, and treatments for autism spectrum disorders.

Clinical Case: Eric

"Eric. Eric? Eric!!" His teacher's voice and the laughter of his classmates roused the boy from his reverie. Glancing at the book of the girl sitting next to him, he noticed that the class was pages ahead of him. He was supposed to be answering a question about the Declaration of Independence, but he had been lost in thought, wondering about what seats he and his father would have for the baseball game they'd be attending that evening. A tall, lanky 12-year-old, Eric had just begun seventh grade. His history teacher had already warned him about being late to class and not paying attention, but Eric just couldn't seem to get from one class to the next without stopping for drinks of water or to investigate an altercation between classmates. In class, he was rarely prepared to answer when the teacher called on him, and he usually forgot to write down the homework assignment. He already had a reputation among his peers as an "airhead."

Eric's relief at the sound of the bell was quickly replaced by anxiety as he reached the playground for physical education. Despite his speed and physical strength, Eric was always picked last for baseball teams. His team was up to bat first, and Eric sat down to wait his turn. Absorbed in studying a pile of pebbles at his feet, he failed to notice his team's third out and missed the change of innings. The other team had already come in from the outfield before Eric noticed that his team was out in the field—too late to avoid the irate yells of his P.E. teacher to take his place at third base. Resolved to watch for his chance to field the ball, Eric nonetheless found himself without his glove on when a sharply hit ball rocketed his way; he had taken it off to toss it in the air in the middle of the pitch.

At home, Eric's father told him he had to finish his homework before they could go to the Giants game. He had only one page of math problems and was determined to finish them quickly. Thirty minutes later, his father emerged from the shower to find Eric building an elaborate Lego structure on the floor of his room; the math homework was only half done. In exasperation, Eric's father left for the game without him.

At bedtime, frustrated and discouraged, Eric was unable to sleep. He often lay awake for what seemed like hours, reviewing the disappointments of the day and berating himself for his failures. On this night, he ruminated about his lack of friends, the frustration of his teachers, and his parents' exhortations to pay attention and "get it together." Feeling hopeless about doing better, despite his daily resolve, Eric often found his thoughts turning to suicide. Tonight he reviewed his fantasy of wandering out into the street in front of a passing car. Although Eric had never acted on his suicidal thoughts, he frequently replayed in his mind his parents' sorrow and remorse, his classmates' irritation with him, and the concern of his teachers.

CHILDHOOD DISORDERS, LIKE ADULT disorders, involve a combination of behavioral, cognitive, genetic, neurobiological, and social factors in their etiology and treatment. The number of children diagnosed with and treated for different psychological disorders has dramatically increased in recent years, but not without controversy (see Focus on Discovery 13.3 later in the chapter). For example, the number of people ever receiving a diagnosis of ADHD (attention-deficit/hyperactivity disorder) in the United States increased 41 percent between 2003 and 2012 (Hinshaw & Scheffler, 2014)! Also controversial is the tremendous increase in the number of medication prescriptions given to children. In fact, most antipsychotics prescribed for children are for disorders or symptoms, such as ADHD and oppositional defiant disorder, that have not been approved by the FDA (called "off label" use) (Harrison, Cluxton-Keller, & Gross, 2012; Olfson, Blanco, Liu et al., 2012).

In this chapter we discuss several of the disorders that are most likely to arise in childhood and adolescence. We first consider disorders involving inattention, impulsivity, and disruptive behavior, followed by depression and anxiety disorders. Finally, we discuss disorders in which the acquisition of cognitive, language, motor, or social skills is disturbed. These include learning disorders as well as the most severe of developmental disorders, intellectual disability and autism spectrum disorder, which are usually chronic, persisting into adulthood.

Classification and Diagnosis of Childhood Disorders

Before making a diagnosis of a particular disorder in children, clinicians must first consider what is typical for a particular age. The children who lie on the floor kicking and screaming when they don't get their way would be assessed differently at age 2 than at age 7. The field of **developmental psychopathology** focuses on the disorders of childhood within the context of life-span development, enabling us to identify behaviors that are considered appropriate at one stage but not at another.

The childhood disorders are shown in Figure 13.1. In DSM-5, most of the childhood disorders are presented in two chapters: "Neurodevelopmental

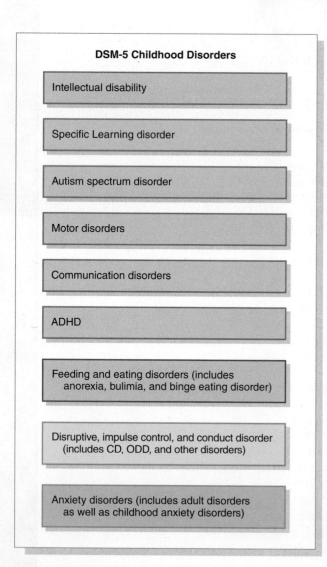

DSM-5 Childhood Disorders

Intellectual disability

Specific Learning disorder

Autism spectrum disorder

Motor disorders

Communication disorders

ADHD

Feeding and eating disorders (includes anorexia, bulimia, and binge eating disorder)

Disruptive, impulse control, and conduct disorder (includes CD, ODD, and other disorders)

Anxiety disorders (includes adult disorders as well as childhood anxiety disorders)

Figure 13.1 DSM-5 childhood disorders.

FOCUS ON DISCOVERY 13.1

The Role of Culture in Internalizing and Externalizing Behavior Problems

The values of a culture may play a role in whether a certain pattern of child behavior develops or is considered a problem. One study found that in Thailand, children with internalizing behavior problems, such as fearfulness, were the ones most likely to be seen in clinics, whereas in the United States, those with externalizing behavior problems, such as aggressiveness and hyperactivity, were more commonly seen (Weisz et al., 1987). The researchers attributed these differences to the fact that Buddhism, which disapproves of and discourages aggression, is widely practiced in Thailand. In other words, cultural sanctions against acting out in aggressive ways may have kept these behaviors from developing at the rate that they do in the United States. One of the issues in this study was that the researchers only used assessment measures that were normed on U.S. samples, leaving open the possibility that behavior differences between the two cultures were missed because they were not validly assessed for both cultures (see Chapter 3 for more discussion of culture and assessment).

Indeed, findings from a follow-up study suggest that the behavior problems described in the same terms may not really be exactly the same across Thai and U.S. cultures (Weisz, Weiss, Suwanlert et al., 2003). The researchers compared specific behavior problems (e.g., somatic complaints, aggressive behavior) and broad domains (internalizing, externalizing) using U.S. and Thai assessment measures. The broad domains of internalizing and externalizing behaviors were found to be the same in Thai and U.S. children, but more specific categories within those domains were not. Among boys, somatic complaints were seen consistently across cultures, but shyness was seen less consistently. Among girls, shyness was seen consistently across cultures but verbal aggressive behavior was not.

These studies point to the importance of studying psychopathology across cultures. It is dangerous to assume that the measures we develop to assess psychopathology in the United States will work equally well across cultures. As the investigators cited above point out, our theories about the causes of psychopathology need to be able to take into account cultural variation in such factors as parenting practices, beliefs and values, and the ways in which parents report on their child's behavior problems. This remains an urgent and important challenge for our field.

Thai teenagers serving as novices in a Buddhist temple. Buddhist culture may contribute to the relatively low prevalence of externalizing disorders in Thailand.

Disorders" and "Disruptive, Impulse-Control, and Conduct Disorders." Eating disorders (which we cover separately in Chapter 11) are in their own chapter in DSM-5. Other disorders, such as separation anxiety disorder, are in the DSM-5 chapter on anxiety disorders.

The more prevalent childhood disorders are often divided into two broad domains, externalizing disorders and internalizing disorders. **Externalizing disorders** are characterized by more outward-directed behaviors, such as aggressiveness, noncompliance, overactivity, and impulsiveness; the category includes attention-deficit/hyperactivity disorder, conduct disorder, and oppositional defiant disorder. **Internalizing disorders** are characterized by more inward-focused experiences and behaviors, such as depression, social withdrawal, and anxiety; the category includes childhood anxiety and mood disorders. Children and adolescents may exhibit symptoms from both domains, as described in the Clinical Case of Eric.

The behaviors that comprise externalizing and internalizing disorders are prevalent across many countries and cultures (Polanczyk, de Lima, Horta et al., 2007), such as Switzerland (Steinhausen & Metzke, 1998), Australia (Achenbach, Hensley et al., 1990), Puerto Rico (Achenbach, Hensley et al., 1990), Kenya (Weisz et al., 1993), and Greece (MacDonald et al., 1995). Focus on Discovery 13.1 discusses the possible role of culture in the prevalence of these problem behaviors in children.

Attention-Deficit/Hyperactivity Disorder

The term *hyperactive* is familiar to most people, especially parents and teachers. The child who is constantly in motion—tapping fingers, jiggling legs, poking others for no apparent reason, talking out of turn, and fidgeting—is often called hyperactive. Often, these children also have difficulty concentrating on the task at hand for an appropriate period of time. When such problems are severe and persistent enough, these children may meet the criteria for diagnosis of **attention-deficit/hyperactivity disorder (ADHD)**.

Clinical Descriptions, Prevalence, and Prognosis of ADHD

Clinical Descriptions What distinguishes the typical range of hyperactive behaviors from a diagnosable disorder? When these behaviors are extreme for a particular developmental period, persistent across different situations, and linked to significant impairments in functioning, the diagnosis of ADHD may be appropriate (Hinshaw & Scheffler, 2014). The DSM-5 criteria are presented in the margin.

Children with ADHD seem to have particular difficulty controlling their activity in situations that call for sitting still, such as in the classroom or at mealtimes. When asked to be quiet, they appear unable to stop moving or talking. Their activities and movements may seem haphazard. They may quickly wear out their shoes and clothing, smash their toys, and exhaust their families and teachers.

Many children with ADHD have inordinate difficulty getting along with peers and establishing friendships (Blachman & Hinshaw, 2002; Hinshaw & Melnick, 1995), perhaps because their behavior is often aggressive and intrusive. Although these children are usually friendly and talkative, they often miss subtle social cues, such as noticing when other children are tiring of their constant jiggling. Unfortunately, children with ADHD often overestimate their ability to navigate social situations with peers (Hoza, Murray-Close, Arnold et al., 2010). A longitudinal study of children with and without ADHD who were followed up every year for 6 years found that poor social skills, aggressive behavior, and self-overestimation of performance in social situations all predicted problems with peers up to 6 years later. The researchers also found what they called "vicious cycles" with these three domains—poor social skills, aggressive behavior, and overestimation of one's social abilities—all in turn predicted a decline in these abilities at the next follow-up, which in turn predicted greater problems with peers at the next follow-up (Murray-Close, Hoza, Hinshaw et al., 2010).

In another study, children were asked to instant-message (IM) other children in what appeared to be an online chat room (Mikami, Huang-Pollack, Pfiffner et al., 2007). Actually, children were interacting with four simulated peers on the computer, and thus all children got the same IMs from the simulated peers. The researchers coded the messages and the participants' reported experiences of the chat elicited in subsequent interviews. Children with ADHD were more likely to IM statements that were hostile and off the topic than were children without ADHD, and children's chat room experiences were related to other measures of social skills difficulties, suggesting that this common way of "interacting" with peers, even though not face-to-face, is also impaired among children with ADHD.

Children with ADHD are often singled out very quickly and rejected or neglected by their peers. For example, in a study of previously unacquainted boys at a summer camp, boys with ADHD who exhibited a number of externalizing behaviors, such as overt aggression and noncompliance, were regarded quite negatively by their peers during the first day of camp, and these impressions remained unchanged throughout the 6-week camp period (Erhardt & Hinshaw, 1994; Hinshaw et al., 1997).

ADHD in the DSM-5 and Comorbidities Two changes in the DSM-5 criteria for ADHD may result in more children and adults receiving the diagnosis. First, the age of onset was changed from under age 7 to under age 12. This means that children who begin to show symptoms after age 7 can now meet the diagnosis for ADHD. Second, adults only need to show symptoms in five domains instead of the six required for children.

● DSM-5 Criteria for Attention-Deficit/ Hyperactivity Disorder

- Either A or B:
  A. Six or more manifestations of inattention present for at least 6 months to a maladaptive degree and greater than what would be expected given a person's developmental level, e.g., careless mistakes, not listening well, not following instructions, easily distracted, forgetful in daily activities
  B. Six or more manifestations of hyperactivity-impulsivity present for at least 6 months to a maladaptive degree and greater than what would be expected given a person's developmental level, e.g., fidgeting, running about inappropriately (in adults, restlessness), acting as if "driven by a motor," interrupting or intruding, incessant talking

- Several of the above present before age 12

- Present in two or more settings, e.g., at home, school, or, work

- Significant impairment in social, academic, or occupational functioning

- For people age 17 or older, only five signs of inattention and/ or five signs of hyperactivity-impulsivity are needed to meet the diagnosis

The DSM-5 includes three specifiers to indicate which symptoms predominate:

1. Predominantly inattentive: children whose problems are primarily those of poor attention
2. Predominantly hyperactive-impulsive: children whose difficulties result primarily from hyperactive/impulsive behavior
3. Combined: children who have both sets of problems

The combined specifier comprises the majority of children with ADHD. These children are more likely than those with other subtypes to develop conduct problems and oppositional behavior, to be placed in special classes for children with behavior problems, and to have difficulties interacting with their peers (Faraone, Biederman, Weber et al., 1998). Children with the predominantly inattentive specifier have more difficulties with focused attention or speed of information processing (Barkley, Grodzinsky, & DuPaul, 1992), perhaps associated with problems involving dopamine and the prefrontal cortex (Volkow, Wang, Kollins et al., 2009).

ADHD and conduct disorder (discussed later in the chapter) frequently co-occur and share some features in common (Beauchaine, Hinshaw, & Pang, 2010). There are some differences, however. ADHD is associated more with off-task behavior in school, cognitive and achievement deficits, and a better long-term prognosis.

When these two disorders occur in the same child, the worst features of each are manifest. Such children exhibit the most serious antisocial behavior, are most likely to be rejected by their peers, have the worst academic achievement, and have the poorest prognosis (Hinshaw & Lee, 2003). Girls with both ADHD and conduct disorder exhibit more antisocial behavior, other psychopathology, and risky sexual behavior than girls with only ADHD (Monuteaux, Faraone, Gross et al., 2007).

Internalizing disorders, such as anxiety and depression, also frequently co-occur with ADHD. Estimates suggest that as many as 30 percent of children with ADHD may have comorbid internalizing disorders (e.g., Jensen et al., 1997; MTA Cooperative Group, 1999b). In addition, about 15 to 30 percent of children with ADHD have a learning disorder (Barkley, DuPaul, & McMurray, 1990; Casey, Rourke, & Del Dotto, 1996).

Although having both ADHD and conduct disorder is associated with substance use, a prospective study found that the hyperactive symptoms of ADHD predicted subsequent substance use (nicotine, alcohol, illicit drugs) at age 14 and substance use disorder at age 18 even after controlling for symptoms of conduct disorder, and this was equally true for boys and girls (Elkins, McGue, & Iacono, 2007).

Prevalence By some accounts, the prevalence of ADHD has risen dramatically in the past decade, ranging from 8 to 11 percent compared to older estimates of 3 to 7 percent (Merikangas, He, Brody et al., 2010). A nationally representative study conducted by the Centers for Disease Control and Prevention reported a prevalence rate of 11 percent in 2011 (Visser, Danielson, Bitsko et al., 2014). By contrast, a study from one large health care system in California reported a prevalence rate of just over 3 percent (Getahun, Jacobsen, Fassett et al., 2013). Why the difference in rates? Several explanations are possible, suggesting that the increase is due to factors other than an actual increase in the disorder. For example, most children receive a diagnosis after a brief visit with a pediatrician, but correct diagnoses require careful and thorough assessments (Hinshaw & Scheffler, 2014). Thus, many children may be getting the diagnosis when it is not warranted.

Second, children in some states, such as North Carolina, are far more likely to get the diagnosis than children in other states, such as California, and this appears to be largely due to the education policies in the states (Hinshaw & Scheffler, 2014). Specifically, states like North Carolina that had school accountability standards in place prior to the national standards enacted in 2001 had strong incentives to remove children from the classroom (and thereby classroom test score averages) that were disruptive and inattentive. Indeed, many children with ADHD are placed in special educational programs because of their difficulty in adjusting to a typical classroom environment (Barkley et al., 1990). Thus these children's test scores would be counted as part of the overall school's performance statistics. As Hinshaw and Scheffler (2014) noted, "labels that produce mandated services tend to get used" (p. 77).

Courtesy of Dr. Stephen Hinshaw

Stephen Hinshaw, a renowned developmental psychopathology researcher and expert on mental illness stigma, is conducting one of the largest ongoing studies of girls with ADHD.

Aggression is not uncommon among boys with ADHD, and it contributes to their being rejected by peers.

Sex Differences Despite the controversy over the increasing prevalence rates of ADHD, much evidence indicates that ADHD is three times more common in boys than in girls (Merikangas et al., 2010). Until recently, very few carefully controlled studies of girls with ADHD were conducted. Two groups of researchers have conducted large, careful studies of ADHD in girls (Biederman & Faraone, 2004; Hinshaw, 2002). Here are some of the key findings at the initial assessment and then again 5 years later (Hinshaw, Carte, Sami et al., 2002; Hinshaw, Owens, Sami et al., 2006) and 10 to 11 years later (Biederman, Petty, Monuteaux et al., 2010; Hinshaw, Owens, Zalecki et al., 2012):

- Girls with the DSM-IV-TR combined subtype (now a specifier in DSM-5) were more likely to have a comorbid diagnosis of conduct disorder or oppositional defiant disorder than girls without ADHD, and this difference remained 5 years after initial diagnosis.
- Girls with ADHD were viewed more negatively by peers than girls without ADHD.
- Girls with ADHD were likely to be more anxious and depressed than were girls without ADHD, and this remained true 5 years after initial diagnosis and into early adulthood.
- Girls with ADHD exhibited a number of neuropsychological deficits, particularly in executive functioning (e.g., planning, solving problems), compared with girls without ADHD.
- By adolescence, girls with ADHD were more likely to have symptoms of an eating disorder and substance abuse than girls without ADHD (Mikami, Hinshaw, Arnold et al., 2010), but not by early adulthood.

ADHD in Adulthood At one time it was thought that ADHD simply went away by adolescence. However, this belief has been challenged by numerous longitudinal studies (Barkley, Fischer, Smallish et al., 2002; Hinshaw et al., 2006; Lee, Lahey, Owens et al., 2008; Weiss & Hechtman, 1993). Although some children show reduced severity of symptoms in adolescence and early adulthood, 65 to 80 percent of children with ADHD still have symptoms associated with impairments in adolescence (Biederman, Monuteasu, Mick et al., 2006; Hart, Lahey, Loeber et al., 1995; Hinshaw et al., 2006). Table 13.1 provides a catalogue of behaviors that are found more often among adolescents with ADHD than among adolescents without it. Many children with ADHD do not appear to take a "hit" with respect to academic achievement, however—many studies indicate that achievement is within the average range for both adolescent boys (Lee et al., 2008) and girls (Hinshaw et al., 2006).

In adulthood, most people with ADHD are employed and financially independent, but some studies have found that adults with ADHD are generally at a lower socioeconomic

Table 13.1 Behaviors in Adolescents With and Without ADHD

Behavior	Percentage of Adolescents Who Show This Behavior	
	With ADHD	**Without ADHD**
Blurts out answers	65.0	10.6
Is easily distracted	82.1	15.2
Doesn't complete tasks before moving to another	77.2	16.7
Doesn't sustain attention	79.7	16.7
Doesn't follow instructions	83.7	12.1
Doesn't listen to others well	80.5	15.2
Engages in physically dangerous activities	37.4	3.0
Fidgets	73.2	10.6
Finds it hard to play quietly	39.8	7.6
Gets out of seat often	60.2	3.0
Interrupts others	65.9	10.6
Loses things needed for tasks	62.6	12.1
Talks a lot	43.9	6.1

Source: Adapted from Barkley, Du Paul, & McMurray (1990).

level and change jobs more frequently than is typical (Mannuzza, Klein, Bonagura et al., 1991; Weiss & Hechtman, 1993). Findings from a review of the studies that have assessed ADHD longitudinally into adulthood indicate that up to 15 percent of people continued to meet DSM criteria as 25-year-old adults. Even more people—close to 60 percent—continue to exhibit symptoms that are associated with impairment in several domains (Faraone, Biederman, & Mick, 2005; Hinshaw et al., 2012). Thus, ADHD symptoms may decline with age, but they do not entirely go away for many people.

Etiology of ADHD

Genetic Factors Substantial evidence indicates that genetic factors play a role in ADHD (Thapar, Langley, Owen et al., 2007). Adoption studies (e.g., Sprich, Biederman, Crawford et al., 2000) and numerous large-scale twin studies (e.g., Levy, Hay, McStephen et al., 1997; Sherman, Iacono, & McGue, 1997) indicate that ADHD has a genetic component, with heritability estimates as high as 70 to 80 percent (Sullivan, Daly, & O'Donovan, 2012). Molecular genetics studies that seek to discover the multiple genes linked to ADHD have revealed a number of candidate genes. Most notable are those genes associated with the neurotransmitter dopamine. Specifically, three different dopamine genes have been implicated in ADHD and have modest effect sizes in meta-analyses: dopamine receptor genes called *DRD4* and *DRD5*, and a dopamine transporter gene called *DAT1* (Gizer, Ficks, & Waldman, 2009). An additional gene, *SNAP-25*, that codes for a protein that promotes plasticity (i.e., adaptability) of neuron synapses has also been associated with ADHD (Forero, Arboleda, Vasquez et al., 2009; Gizer et al., 2009). Even with these promising findings, most investigators agree that a single gene will not ultimately be found to account for ADHD (Nigg, 2013). Rather, several genes interacting with each other and with environmental factors will provide the most complete picture of the role of genes in ADHD. For example, studies have found that the *DRD4* or *DAT1* genes are associated with increased risk of ADHD only among those who also had particular environmental factors—namely, prenatal maternal nicotine or alcohol use (Brookes, Mill, Guindalini et al., 2006; Neuman, Lobos, Reich et al., 2007). In addition, polygene (i.e., multiple genes; see Chapter 2) scores derived from meta-analyses of genetic factors are higher in those with ADHD compared to those without ADHD (Hamshere, Langley, Martin et al., 2013).

Neurobiological Factors Studies suggest that brain structure, function, and connectivity differ in children with and without ADHD, particularly in areas of the brain linked to the neurotransmitter dopamine. For example, studies of brain structure have found that dopaminergic areas of the brain, such as the caudate nucleus, globus pallidus, and frontal lobes, are smaller in children with ADHD than in children without ADHD (Castellanos, Lee, Sharp et al., 2002; Swanson, Kinsbourne, Nigg et al., 2007). A meta-analysis of 55 brain-imaging studies found that children with ADHD exhibit less activation in frontal areas of the brain (Cortese, Kelly, Chabernaud et al., 2012). Moreover, children with ADHD perform poorly on neuropsychological tests that rely on the frontal lobes (such as inhibiting behavioral responses), providing further support for the theory that a basic deficit in this part of the brain may be related to the disorder (Nigg & Casey, 2005).

Perinatal and Prenatal Factors Other neurobiological risk factors for ADHD include a number of perinatal and prenatal complications. Low birth weight, for example, is a predictor of the development of ADHD (e.g., Bhutta, Cleves, Casey et al., 2002; Breslau, Brown, Del Dotto et al., 1996; Whitaker, van Rossen, Feldman et al., 1997). However, the impact of low birth weight on later symptoms of ADHD can be mitigated by greater maternal warmth (Tully, Arseneault, Caspi et al., 2004).

Environmental Toxins Early theories of ADHD in the 1970s involved the role of environmental toxins. Feingold (1973) proposed that additives and artificial colors in foods upset the central nervous systems of children who were hyperactive, and he prescribed a diet free of them. However, well-controlled studies of the so-called Feingold diet have found that very

Michael Phelps, who won eight gold medals in swimming at the 2008 Olympics, also struggled with ADHD as a child.

few children with ADHD respond positively to it. More recent and better-designed studies have found that elements of the diet, particularly additives, may influence ADHD symptoms for a subset of children. Two meta-analyses reported small effect sizes for artificial food coloring on hyperactive behavior among children with ADHD (Nigg, Lewis, Edinger et al., 2012; Schnab & Trinh, 2004). Thus, there is limited evidence that food additives impact hyperactive behavior. The popular view that refined sugar can cause ADHD has not been supported by careful research (Wolraich, Wilson, & White, 1995).

Lead is another environmental toxin that has been studied. Some evidence suggests that higher blood levels of lead may be associated to a small degree with symptoms of hyperactivity and attentional problems (Braun, Kehn, Froelich et al., 2006), as well as with the diagnosis of ADHD. However, most children with higher blood levels of lead do not develop ADHD, and most children with ADHD do not show such elevated blood levels. Nevertheless, given the unfortunate frequency with which children are exposed to low levels of lead, investigators continue to examine how lead exposure might play a role, perhaps by influencing other cognitive abilities.

Nicotine—specifically, maternal smoking—is an environmental toxin that may play a role in the development of ADHD. A review of 24 studies examining the association between maternal smoking and ADHD found that exposure to tobacco in utero was associated with ADHD symptoms (Linnet, Dalsgaard , Obel et al., 2003). However, an interesting study calls this linkage into question. Thapar and colleagues (2009) examined ADHD symptoms in the offspring of two groups of mothers who were regular smokers when pregnant. One group of smoking mothers delivered babies that were not genetically related to them (e.g., surrogate mother delivering a genetically unrelated baby for another family); the other group of mothers delivered babies that were genetically related. The researchers reasoned that if maternal smoking during pregnancy was an important factor in ADHD, smoking ought to be related to ADHD symptoms in the offspring from both groups of mothers. By contrast, if genetic factors were important, then the association between smoking and ADHD symptoms ought to be higher in the offspring of genetically related mothers. They found that ADHD symptoms were related to maternal smoking in both groups, but the association was significantly higher in children whose genetically related mothers smoked during pregnancy. These findings suggest that smoking might not be a causal factor by itself but that it is related to other maternal behavior and psychopathology that might increase the risk of ADHD.

Family Factors in ADHD Family factors are also important in ADHD, particularly in their interaction with neurobiological factors. For example, the parent–child relationship interacts with neurobiological factors in a complex way to contribute to ADHD symptom expression (Hinshaw et al., 1997). Just as parents of children with ADHD may give them more commands and have negative interactions with them (Anderson, Hinshaw, & Simmel, 1994; Heller et al., 1996), so these children have been found to be less compliant and more negative in interactions with their parents (Barkley, Karlsson, & Pollard, 1985; Tallmadge & Barkley, 1983). Certainly, it must be difficult to parent a child who is impulsive, aggressive, noncompliant, and unable to follow instructions. As we will discuss shortly, children with ADHD take stimulant medication, either alone or in combination with behavioral treatment, parents' commands, negative behavior, and ineffective parenting decrease (Barkley, 1990; Wells, Epstein, Hinshaw et al., 2000), suggesting that the child's behavior has at least some negative effect on the parents' behavior.

It is also important to consider a parent's own history of ADHD. As noted earlier, ADHD appears to have a substantial genetic component. Thus, it is not surprising that many parents of children with ADHD have ADHD themselves. In one study that examined couples' parenting practices with their ADHD children, fathers who had a diagnosis of ADHD were less effective parents, suggesting that parental psychopathology may make parenting all the more difficult (Arnold, O'Leary, & Edwards, 1997). Family characteristics thus may well contribute to maintaining or exacerbating the symptoms and consequences of ADHD; however, there is little evidence to suggest that families actually cause ADHD (Johnston & Marsh, 2001).

Children born to mothers who smoked cigarettes during pregnancy have an increased risk for ADHD.

Treatment of ADHD

We now turn to treatments. ADHD is typically treated with medication and with behavioral therapies based on operant conditioning.

Stimulant Medications Stimulant medications, such as methylphenidate, or Ritalin, have been prescribed for ADHD since the early 1960s. Other medications approved by the Food and Drug Administration (FDA) to treat ADHD include Adderall, Concerta, and Strattera. A recent report from a company that managed 90 million prescriptions in the United States found that more than 80 percent of children with ADHD had been given a prescription for stimulant medications, including almost 10 percent of all adolescent boys (Express Scripts Lab, 2014). The prescription of these medications often continues into adolescence and adulthood in light of the accumulating evidence that the symptoms of ADHD do not usually disappear with the passage of time. The number of adults taking stimulant medication increased more than 50 percent between 2008 and 2012 (Express Scripts Lab, 2014).

The drugs used to treat ADHD reduce disruptive behavior and impulsivity and improve ability to focus attention (Hinshaw & Scheffler, 2014). Numerous controlled studies comparing stimulants with placebos in double-blind designs have shown short-term improvements in concentration, goal-directed activity, classroom behavior, and social interactions with parents, teachers, and peers, as well as reductions in aggressiveness and impulsivity in about 75 percent of children with ADHD (Spencer, Biederman, Wilens et al., 1996; Swanson, McBurnett, Christian et al., 1995). These drugs appear to help in these domains by interacting with the dopamine system in the brain (Volkow, Wang, Newcorn et al., 2011).

The best designed randomized controlled trial of treatments for ADHD was the Multimodal Treatment of Children with ADHD (MTA) study. Conducted at six different sites for 14 months with nearly 600 children with ADHD, the study compared standard community-based care and three other treatments: (1) medication alone, (2) medication plus intensive behavioral treatment, involving both parents and teachers, and (3) intensive behavioral treatment alone. Across the 14-month period, children receiving medication alone had fewer ADHD symptoms than children receiving intensive behavioral treatment alone. The combined treatment was slightly superior to the medication alone and had the advantage of not requiring as high a dosage of Ritalin to reduce ADHD symptoms. In addition, the combined treatment yielded improved functioning in areas such as social skills more than did the medication alone. The medication alone and the combined treatment were superior to community-based care, though the behavioral treatment alone was not (MTA Cooperative Group, 1999a, 1999b).

Despite the initially promising findings from the MTA study, additional follow-ups from this study have not been quite as encouraging, at least where medication is concerned. Importantly, all the children maintained the gains made during the 14-month treatment, even as they all returned to receiving standard community care, and this was true at the 3-, 6-, and 8-year follow-ups. However, children in the medication alone or the combined treatment groups were no longer doing better than children who received the intensive behavioral treatment or standard community care at the 3-year follow-up (Jensen, Arnold, Swanson et al., 2007) or the 6- and 8-year follow-ups (Molina, Hinshaw, Swanson et el., 2009). In other words, the relatively superior effects of medication that were observed in the combined treatment and medication alone groups did not persist beyond the study, at least for some of the children (Swanson, Hinshaw, Arnold et al., 2007).

Does this mean that medication does not work? Not necessarily. The MTA study demonstrated that carefully prescribed and managed stimulant medication is effective for children with ADHD. However, medication as it is administered in the community does not appear to offer any benefits above and beyond other forms of treatment, according to these MTA follow-up studies.

These findings are important in light of the side effects that stimulant medication can have, such as transient loss of appetite, weight loss, stomach pain, and sleep problems. In 2006 and again in 2011, the FDA recommended but did not mandate that a "black box" warning, the strongest possible safety warning the FDA can issue for medications, about cardiovascular risks (e.g., heart attack) be added to stimulant medications.

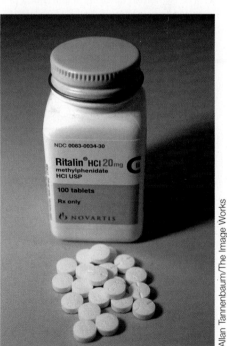

Ritalin is a commonly prescribed and effective drug treatment for ADHD.

Point systems and star charts, which are common in classrooms, are particularly useful in the treatment of ADHD.

Psychological Treatment Other promising treatments for ADHD involve parent training and changes in classroom management (Chronis, Jones, & Raggi, 2006). These programs have demonstrated at least short-term success in improving both social and academic behavior. In these treatments, children's behavior is monitored at home and in school, and they are reinforced for behaving appropriately—for example, for remaining in their seats and working on assignments. Point systems and daily report cards (DRCs) are typical components of these programs. Children earn points or stars for behaving in certain ways; the children can then spend their earnings for rewards. The DRC also allows parents to see how their child is doing in school. The focus of these programs is on improving academic work, completing household tasks, or learning specific social skills, rather than on reducing ADHD symptoms. Parent-training programs are also effective, although it is unclear whether they improve children's behavior beyond the effects of treatment with medication (MTA Cooperative Group, 1999a, 1999b).

Findings from the MTA study indicate that intensive behavioral therapies can be very helpful to children with ADHD. In that study, some of the children participated in an intensive 8-week summer program that included a number of validated behavioral treatments. At the end of the summer program, children receiving the combined treatment had very few significant improvements over children receiving the intensive behavioral treatment alone (Arnold et al., 2003; Pelham, Gnagy, Greiner et al., 2000). This finding suggests that intensive behavioral therapy may be as effective as Ritalin combined with a less intensive behavioral therapy.

Check Your Knowledge 13.1 (Answers are at the end of the chapter.)

True or false?
1. The two broad domains of childhood psychopathology are internalizing disorders and externalizing disorders.
2. Adolescent girls with ADHD are more likely to have symptoms of an eating disorder and substance abuse than girls without ADHD.
3. Dopamine has been investigated in ADHD, with respect to both genes and the brain.
4. The most effective treatment for ADHD is behavioral treatment without medication.

Conduct Disorder

Conduct disorder is another externalizing disorder. Before discussing this disorder, however, we briefly discuss two other related but less well-understood disorders.

Intermittent explosive disorder (IED) involves recurrent verbal or physical aggressive outbursts that are far out of proportion to the circumstances. What distinguishes IED from conduct disorder is that the aggression is impulsive and not preplanned toward other people (American Psychiatric Association, 2013). For example, a child with IED may have an aggressive outburst after not getting his or her way but would not plan aggressive retaliation.

There is some debate as to whether another DSM disorder, *oppositional defiant disorder* (ODD), is distinct from conduct disorder, a precursor to it, or an earlier and milder manifestation of it (Hinshaw & Lee, 2003; Lahey, McBurnett, & Loeber, 2000). ODD is diagnosed if a child does not meet the criteria for conduct disorder—most especially, extreme physical aggressiveness—but exhibits such behaviors as losing his or her temper, arguing with adults, repeatedly refusing to comply with requests from adults, deliberately doing things to annoy others, and being angry, spiteful, touchy, or vindictive.

Lew Merrim/Photo Researchers, Inc.

ODD and ADHD frequently occur together, but ODD is different from ADHD in that the defiant behavior is not thought to arise from attentional deficits or impulsiveness. One manifestation of difference is that children with ODD are more deliberate in their unruly behavior than children with ADHD. Although conduct disorder is three to four times more common among boys than among girls, research suggests that boys are only slightly more likely to have ODD, and some studies find no difference in prevalence rates for ODD between boys and girls (Loeber, Burke, Lahey et al., 2000; Merikangas et al., 2010). Because less is known about IED and ODD, we will focus here on the more serious diagnosis of conduct disorder.

Clinical Description, Prevalence, and Prognosis of Conduct Disorder

Perhaps more than any other childhood disorder, conduct disorder is defined by the impact of the child's behavior on people and surroundings.

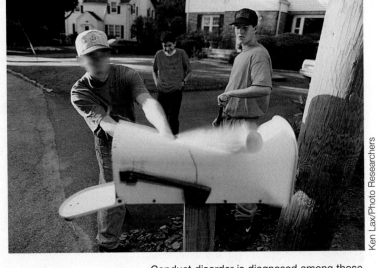

Conduct disorder is diagnosed among those who are aggressive, steal, lie, and vandalize property.

Conduct Disorder in DSM-5   The DSM-5 criteria for conduct disorder (see margin box) focus on aggressive behaviors (e.g., physical cruelty to people or animals, serious rule violations (e.g., truancy), property destruction, and deceitfulness. Often the behavior is marked by callousness, viciousness, and lack of remorse.

DSM-5 includes a "limited prosocial emotions" diagnostic specifier for children who have what are referred to as callous and unemotional traits. These traits refer to characteristics such as a lack of remorse, empathy, and guilt, and shallow emotions. A longitudinal study found that children with high levels of conduct problems and high levels of callous and unemotional traits had more problems with symptoms, peers, and families compared to children with conduct problems but low levels of callous and unemotional traits (Fontaine, McCrory, Boivin et al., 2011). A comprehensive review of callous and unemotional traits in children and adolescence revealed that these traits are associated with a more severe course, more cognitive deficits, more antisocial behavior, poorer response to treatment, and perhaps distinct etiologies (Frick, Ray, Thornton et al., 2014).

Comorbidities and Longitudinal Course   Many children with conduct disorder display other problems, such as substance abuse and internalizing disorders. Some research suggests that conduct disorder precedes substance use problems (Nock, Kazdin, Hiripi et al., 2006), but other findings suggest that conduct disorder and substance use occur concomitantly, with the two conditions exacerbating each other (Loeber et al., 2000).

Anxiety and depression are common among children with conduct disorder, with comorbidity estimates varying from 15 to 45 percent (Loeber & Keenan, 1994; Loeber et al., 2000). Evidence suggests that conduct disorder precedes depression and most anxiety disorders, with the exceptions of specific phobias and social anxiety, which appear to precede conduct disorder (Nock et al., 2006).

How early does conduct disorder begin? Studies estimate that as many as 7 percent of preschool children exhibit the symptoms of conduct disorder (Egger & Angold, 2006). One longitudinal study assessed a group of preschool children at age 3 and again at age 6 (Rolon-Arroyo, Arnold, & Harvey, 2013). Parents were interviewed using diagnostic interviews at the two time points. The researchers found that conduct disorder symptoms at age 3 predicted conduct disorder symptoms at age 6, even when controlling for symptoms of ADHD and ODD. These findings suggest that assessing conduct disorder early is important because these symptoms are not just manifestations of typical developmentally disruptive behaviors.

Moffitt (1993) theorized that two different courses of conduct problems should be distinguished. Some people seem to show a life-course-persistent pattern of antisocial

DSM-5 Criteria for Conduct Disorder

- Repetitive and persistent behavior pattern that violates the basic rights of others or conventional social norms as manifested by the presence of three or more of the following in the previous 12 months and at least one of them in the previous 6 months:
  A. Aggression to people and animals, e.g., bullying, initiating physical fights, physical cruelty to people or animals, forcing someone into sexual activity
  B. Destruction of property, e.g., fire-setting, vandalism
  C. Deceitfulness or theft, e.g., breaking into another's house or car, conning, shoplifting
  D. Serious violation of rules, e.g., staying out at night before age 13 in defiance of parental rules, truancy before age 13
- Significant impairment in social, academic, or occupational functioning

The Image Works

Children with the life-course-persistent type of conduct disorder continue to have trouble with the law into their mid-20s.

behavior, beginning to show conduct problems by age 3 and continuing to commit serious transgressions into adulthood. Others are adolescence-limited—they have typical childhoods, engage in high levels of anti-social behavior during adolescence, and have typical, nonproblematic adulthoods. Moffitt proposed that the adolescence-limited form of antisocial behavior is the result of a maturity gap between the adolescent's physical maturation and his or her opportunity to assume adult responsibilities and obtain the rewards usually accorded such behavior.

Cumulative evidence supports this distinction (Moffitt, 2007). The original sample from which Moffitt and colleagues made the life-course-persistent and adolescence-limited distinction was a sample of over 1000 people from Dunedin, New Zealand, who were assessed every 2 or 3 years from age 3 to 32. Both boys and girls with the life-course-persistent form of conduct disorder had an early onset of antisocial behavior that persisted through adolescence and into adulthood. As children they had a number of other problems, such as academic underachievement, neuropsychological deficits, and comorbid ADHD (Moffitt & Caspi, 2001). Other evidence supports the notion that children with the life-course-persistent type have more severe neuropsychological deficits and family psychopathology, and these findings have been replicated across cultures (Hinshaw & Lee, 2003).

Those who were classified as life-course-persistent continued to have the most severe problems, including psychopathology, poorer physical health, lower socioeconomic status, lower levels of education, partner and child abuse, and violent behavior at age 32; this was true for men and women (Odgers, Moffitt, Broadbent et al., 2008).

Interestingly, those classified as adolescence-limited, who were expected to "grow out" of their aggressive and antisocial behavior, continued to have troubles with substance use, impulsivity, crime, and overall mental health in their mid-20s (Moffitt, Caspi, Harrington et al., 2002). Moffitt and colleagues have since suggested that *adolescent onset* is the more appropriate term for this group of people, as the conduct problems are not entirely limited to adolescence (Odgers, Caspi, Broadbent et al., 2007). By age 32, women with the adolescent-onset type were not having difficulties with violent behavior, but men still were. However, both men and women continued to have substance use problems, economic problems, and physical health problems (Odgers et al., 2008).

Prevalence Estimates suggest that conduct disorder is fairly common, with prevalence rates ranging from 6 to 9.5 percent (Merikangas et al., 2010; Nock, Kazdin, Hiripi et al., 2006). Like ADHD, conduct disorder is more common in boys than in girls. As shown in Figure 13.2, both the incidence and the prevalence of serious law breaking peak sharply at around age 17 and drop precipitously in young adulthood (Moffitt, 1993). Not all the criminal acts represented in Figure 13.2 are marked by the viciousness and callousness that are often a part of conduct disorder, but the figure illustrates the problem of antisocial behavior in children and adolescents. The life-course-persistent type is more common among boys (10.5 percent) than girls (7.5 percent); the adolescence-limited type is also more common among boys (19.6 percent) than girls (17.4 percent) (Odgers et al., 2008).

Prognosis The prognosis for children diagnosed as having conduct disorder is mixed. The results just described show that men and women with the life-course-persistent type of conduct disorder will likely continue to have all

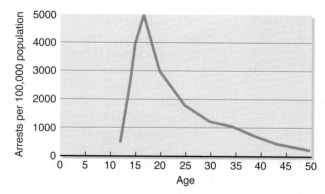

Figure 13.2 Arrest rates across ages for the crimes of homicide, rape, robbery, aggravated assault, and auto theft. Adapted from Blumstein, Cohen, & Farrington (1988). Copyright © 1988. The American Society of Criminology.

sorts of problems in adulthood, including violent and antisocial behavior. However, conduct disorder in childhood does not inevitably lead to antisocial behavior in adulthood. For example, another longitudinal study indicated that although about half of boys with conduct disorder did not fully meet the criteria for the diagnosis at a later assessment (1 to 4 years later), almost all of them continued to demonstrate some conduct problems (Lahey, Loeber, Burker et al., 1995).

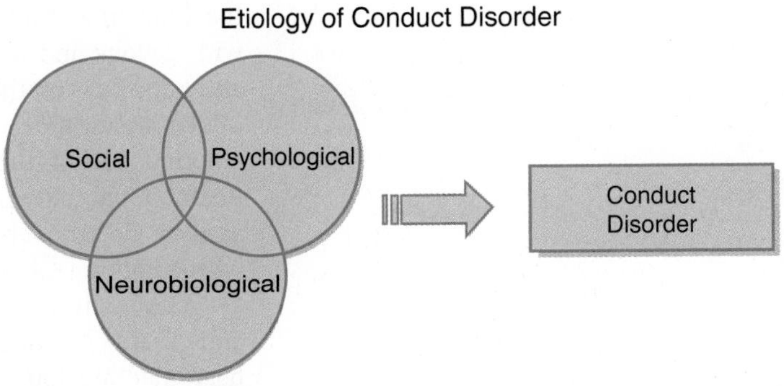

Etiology of Conduct Disorder

Multiple factors are involved in the etiology of conduct disorder, including genetic, neurobiological, psychological, and social factors that interact in a complex manner (Figure 13.3). A review concluded that the evidence favors an etiology that includes heritable temperamental characteristics that interact with other neurobiological difficulties (e.g., neuropsychological deficits) as well as with a whole host of environmental factors (e.g., parenting, school performance, peer influences) (Hinshaw & Lee, 2003).

Genetic Factors The evidence for genetic influences in conduct disorder is mixed, although heritability likely plays a part. Part of the reason for the mixed findings is that some of the genetic influences for conduct disorder are shared with other disorders, including ADHD and depression, and some of the genetic influences are specific to conduct disorder (Lahey, Van Hulle, Singh et al., 2011; Lahey & Waldman, 2012).

Three large-scale adoption studies, in Sweden, Denmark, and the United States, have been conducted, but two of them focused on the heritability of criminal behavior rather than conduct disorder (Simonoff, 2001). As with most traits, these studies indicate that criminal and antisocial behavior is accounted for by both genetic and environmental factors. Interestingly, despite different prevalence rates for boys and girls, the evidence favoring genetic and environmental contributions to conduct disorder and antisocial behavior does not differ between boys and girls. A meta-analysis of twin and adoption studies of antisocial behavior indicated that 40 to 50 percent of antisocial behavior was heritable (Rhee & Waldman, 2002).

Distinguishing types of conduct problems may help to clarify findings on the heritability of conduct disorder. Evidence from twin studies indicates that aggressive behavior (e.g., cruelty to animals, fighting, destroying property) is more heritable than other delinquent behavior (e.g., stealing, running away, truancy) (Burt, 2009). Other evidence suggests that the age when antisocial and aggressive behavior problems begin is related to heritability. For example, aggressive and antisocial behaviors that begin in childhood, as in the case of Moffitt's life-course-persistent type, are more heritable than similar behaviors that begin in adolescence (Taylor, Iacono, & McGue, 2000).

One elegant study examined the interaction between genetic and environmental factors in predicting later adult antisocial behavior (Caspi, McClay, Moffitt et al., 2002). It examined the *MAOA* gene, which is located on the X chromosome and releases an MAO enzyme, which metabolizes a number of neurotransmitters, including dopamine, serotonin, and norepinephrine. This gene varies in its activity, with some people having high and others low MAOA activity. Using a large sample of over 1000 children from Dunedin, New Zealand, the researchers measured MAOA activity and assessed the extent to which the children had been maltreated. Being maltreated as a child was not enough to predict later conduct disorder, nor was the presence of low MAOA activity. Rather, those children who were both maltreated and had low MAOA activity were more likely to develop conduct disorder than either children who were maltreated but had high MAOA activity or children who were not maltreated but had low MAOA activity. Thus, both environment and genes mattered. A meta-analysis of several such studies confirms these findings: being maltreated was linked to later antisocial behavior only via genetics (Taylor & Kim-Cohen, 2007).

Brain Function, Autonomic Nervous System, and Neuropsychological Factors
Neuroimaging studies of children with conduct disorder have revealed deficits in regions of

Figure 13.3 Neurobiological, psychological, and social factors all play a role in conduct disorder.

the brain that support emotion, particularly empathetic responses. For example, children with callous and unemotional traits have difficulty perceiving distress (fear, sadness, pain) and happiness on the face of others, but do not have trouble perceiving anger (Marsh & Blair, 2008). In addition, these children show reduced activation in brain regions associated with emotion, such as the amygdala and prefrontal cortex (Blair, 2013). Children with callous and unemotional traits also do not learn to associate their behavior with reward or punishment as easily as do other children, and this is associated with dysfunction in brain regions associated with emotion (e.g., amygdala) and reward (e.g., ventral striatum) (Blair, 2013).

Other studies indicate that autonomic nervous system abnormalities are associated with antisocial behavior in adolescents. Specifically, lower levels of resting skin conductance and heart rate are found among adolescents with conduct disorder, suggesting that they have lower arousal levels than adolescents without conduct disorder (Ortiz & Raine, 2004; Raine, Venebales, & Williams, 1990). Why does low arousal matter? Like the neuroimaging studies just discussed, these findings suggest that adolescents who exhibit antisocial behavior may not fear punishment as much as adolescents who don't exhibit such behavior. Thus, these children may be more likely to behave in antisocial ways without the fear that they will get caught.

Neuropsychological deficits have also been observed in children with conduct disorder (Lynam & Henry, 2001; Moffitt, Lynam, & Silvia, 1994). These deficits include poor verbal skills, difficulty with executive functioning (the ability to anticipate, plan, use self-control, and solve problems), and problems with memory. In addition, children who develop conduct disorder at an earlier age (i.e., life-course-persistent type) have an IQ score of 1 standard deviation below age-matched peers without conduct disorder, and this IQ deficit is apparently not attributable to lower socioeconomic status or school failure (Lynam, Moffitt, & Stouthamer-Loeber, 1993; Moffitt & Silvia, 1988).

Psychological Factors An important part of typical child development is the growth of social emotions and moral awareness—the acquisition of a sense of what is right and wrong and the ability, even desire, to abide by rules and norms. Most people refrain from hurting others not only because it is illegal but also because it would make them feel guilty. Children with conduct disorder, particularly those with callous and unemotional traits, seem to be deficient in this moral awareness, lacking remorse for their wrongdoing (Cimbora & McIntosh, Blair, 2013; Frick et al., 2014). In adulthood, these traits figure prominently in antisocial personality disorder and psychopathy (discussed in Chapter 15).

A social-cognitive perspective on aggressive behavior (and, by extension, conduct disorder) comes from the work of Kenneth Dodge and associates. In one of his early studies (Dodge & Frame, 1982), Dodge found that the social information processing of aggressive children had a particular bias; these children interpreted ambiguous acts, such as being bumped in line, as evidence of hostile intent. Such perceptions may lead these children to retaliate aggressively for actions that may not have been intended as provocative. This can create a vicious cycle: their peers, remembering these aggressive behaviors, may tend to be aggressive more often against them, further angering the already aggressive children (see Figure 13.4). More recently, Dodge and colleagues have linked deficits in social information processing to heart rate among adolescents who exhibit antisocial behavior. Specifically, low heart rate predicted antisocial behavior for male adolescents independent from social information processing deficits, a finding consistent with studies reviewed earlier on low arousal and conduct problems. However, the link between low heart rate and antisocial behavior was accounted for by social information processing deficits for both male and female adolescents (Crozier, Dodge, Griffith et al., 2008).

Peer Influences Investigations of how peers influence aggressive and antisocial behavior in children have focused on two broad areas: (1) acceptance or rejection by peers and (2) affiliation with deviant peers. Studies have shown that being rejected by peers is causally related to aggressive behavior, particularly in combination with ADHD (Hinshaw & Melnick, 1995). Other studies have shown that being rejected by peers can predict later aggressive behavior, even after controlling

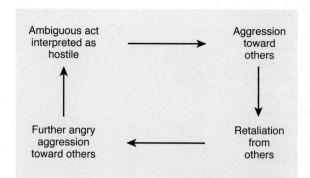

Figure 13.4 Dodge's cognitive theory of aggression. The interpretation of ambiguous acts as hostile is part of a vicious cycle that includes aggression toward and from others.

for prior levels of aggressive behavior (Coie & Dodge, 1998). Associating with other deviant peers also increases the likelihood of delinquent behavior (Capaldi & Patterson, 1994).

Do children with conduct disorder choose to associate with like-minded peers, thus continuing on their path of antisocial behavior (i.e., a social selection view), or does simply being around deviant peers help initiate antisocial behavior (i.e., a social influence view)? Studies examining gene–environment interactions have shed light on this question, and the answer appears to be that both views are correct. That is, as we reviewed earlier, we know that genetic factors are at play in conduct disorder, and these factors in turn play a role in encouraging children with conduct disorder to select more deviant peers to associate with. However, environmental influence, particularly neighborhood (e.g., poverty in the neighborhood) and family (e.g., parental monitoring) factors play a role in whether children associate with deviant peers, and this in turns influences and exacerbates conduct disorder (Kendler, Jacobson, Myers, et al., 2008).

Treatment of Conduct Disorder

The treatment of conduct disorder appears to be most effective when it addresses the multiple systems involved in the life of a child (family, peers, school, neighborhood).

Family Interventions Some of the most promising approaches to treating conduct disorder involve intervening with the parents and families of the child. In addition, evidence suggests that intervening early, if even just briefly, can make an impact. In a randomized controlled trial (Shaw, Dishion, Supplee et al., 2006), researchers compared what is called the family checkup (FCU) treatment to no treatment. FCU involves three meetings to get to know, assess, and provide feedback to parents regarding their children and parenting practices. In this study, FCU was offered to families with toddlers who were at high risk of developing conduct problems (based on the presence of conduct or substance abuse problems in parents or early signs of conduct behavior in the children). This brief, three-session intervention was associated with less disruptive behavior compared to no treatment, even 2 years after the intervention.

Gerald Patterson and colleagues have worked for over four decades developing and testing a behavioral program called **parent management training (PMT)**, in which parents are taught to modify their responses to their children so that prosocial rather than antisocial behavior is consistently rewarded. Parents are taught to use techniques such as positive reinforcement when the child exhibits positive behaviors and time-out and loss of privileges for aggressive or antisocial behaviors.

This treatment has been modified by others, but, in general, it is the most efficacious intervention for children with conduct disorder and oppositional defiant disorder. Both parents' and teachers' reports of children's behavior and direct observation of behavior at home and at school support the program's effectiveness (Kazdin, 2005; Patterson, 1982). PMT has been shown to alter parent–child interactions, which in turn is associated with a decrease in antisocial and aggressive (Dishion & Andrews, 1995; Dishion, Patterson, & Kavanagh, 1992). PMT has been adapted for Latino families and has been shown to be effective in modifying parent and child behaviors (Martinez & Eddy, 2005).

Parent and teacher training approaches have been incorporated into larger community-based programs such as Head Start and have been shown to reduce childhood conduct problems and increase positive parenting behaviors (Webster-Stratton, 1998; Webster-Stratton, Reid, & Hammond, 2001). (See Focus on Discovery 13.2 for more information on Head Start.)

Multisystemic Treatment Another promising treatment for serious juvenile offenders is **multisystemic treatment (MST)** (Borduin,

Michael Newman/PhotoEdit

Parent management training can be effective in treating conduct disorder.

FOCUS ON DISCOVERY 13.2

Head Start: A Community-Based Prevention Program

Head Start is a federally funded program whose goal is to prepare children from low-income families to succeed in the regular school setting. The core of the Head Start program is community-based preschool education, focusing on the early development of cognitive and social skills. Head Start contracts with professionals in the community to provide children with health and dental services, including vaccinations, hearing and vision testing, medical treatment, parent training, and nutrition information (Office of Head Start: http://www.acf.hhs.gov/programs/ohs). Mental health services are another important component of the Head Start program.

The National Head Start Impact study, mandated by Congress in 1998, was a randomized, controlled clinical trial of Head Start that included close to 5000 children in Head Start programs across the country. Data collection for the study occurred between 2002 and 2006, and the study sought to address how Head Start impacts school readiness and what types of children benefit the most from Head Start. The final results found that children reaped many intellectual, social, and behavioral benefits while in Head Start. Unfortunately, many of these gains did not seem to hold once children completed first grade (U.S. Department of Health and Human Services, Administration for Children and Families, 2010) and third grade (Puma, Bell, Cook et al., 2012). Given the overall disappointing results, many changes to Head Start have been made, including more teacher and staff training as well as removal of programs that are not helping children as well as other programs. Does this mean Head Start does not work? Not necessarily. That the children in Head Start were doing better than the children not in Head Start during preschool is encouraging. The challenge now is to help these positive effects last longer as the children go off to a variety of different school settings.

Mann, Cone et al., 1995). MST involves delivering intensive and comprehensive therapy services in the community, targeting the adolescent, the family, the school, and, in some cases, the peer group (Figure 13.5). The treatment is based on the view that conduct problems are influenced by multiple factors within the family as well as between the family and other social systems.

The strategies used by MST therapists are varied, incorporating behavioral, cognitive, family-systems, and case-management techniques. The therapy's uniqueness lies in emphasizing individual and family strengths, identifying the social context for the conduct problems, using present-focused and action-oriented interventions, and using interventions that require daily or weekly efforts by family members. Treatment is provided in "ecologically valid" settings, such as the home, school, or local recreational center, to maximize the chances that improvement will carry through into the regular daily lives of children and their families. MST has been shown to be effective in a number of studies (Henggeler, Schoenwald, Borduin et al., 1998; Ogden & Halliday-Boykins, 2004).

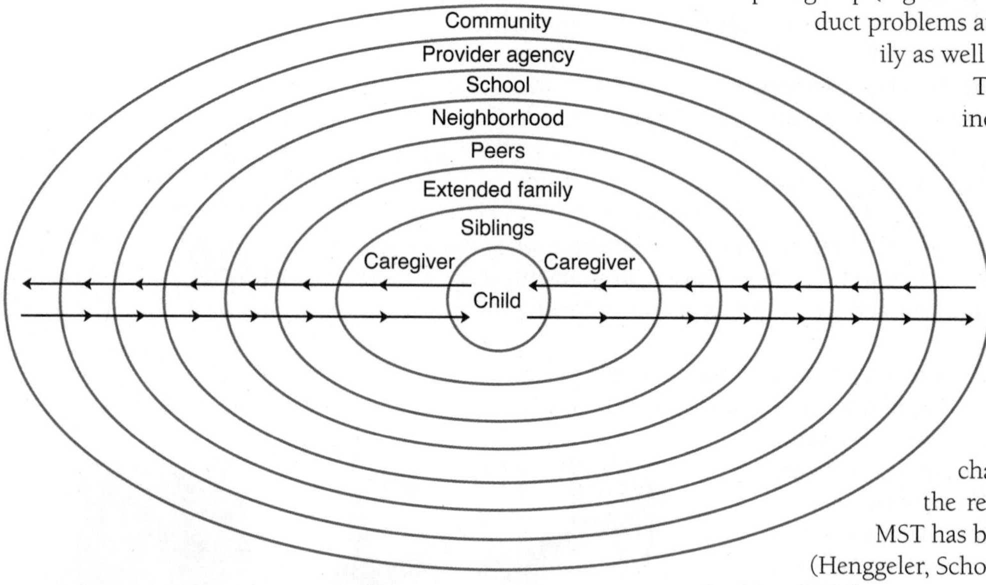

Figure 13.5 Multisystemic treatment (MST) includes consideration of many different factors when developing a child's treatment, including family, school, community, and peers.

Prevention Programs It would be ideal if we could prevent conduct disorder from ever developing (see Focus on Discovery 13.2 for another type of prevention program, Head Start). Can this be done? One such prevention program that has been studied for 20 years is called Fast Track. Findings from the Conduct Problems Prevention Research Group (CPRG), the group of researchers who developed, implemented, and evaluated Fast Track, point to just how difficult it is to prevent something as complex as conduct disorder.

In this study, nearly 10,000 kindergarten children from four poor, high-crime regions in the United States were evaluated. From this large group, nearly 900 children who were exhibiting conduct problems were randomly assigned to either the Fast Track intervention or a control intervention. The Fast Track intervention was designed to help children academically, socially, and behaviorally, focusing on areas that are problematic in conduct disorder, including peer relationships, aggressive and disruptive behavior, social information processing, and parent–child relationships. The intervention was delivered over the course of 10 years in groups and at individual families' homes, with a more intensive treatment in years 1 to 5 and less intensive in years 6 to 10.

Results from the study showed that children who received the Fast Track intervention benefited. However, the benefits appeared to dwindle as the children got older. For example, children who received Fast Track displayed fewer behavior problems and better social information processing skills than children in the control condition at the end of first grade, but by third grade some of the gains in social information processing were no longer evident, and even fewer gains were apparent by fourth and fifth grade (Conduct Problems Prevention Research Group, 2010a).

However, the news is not all bad. The intervention was still making a difference in some domains. By ninth grade, the children who had the most severe problem behaviors at the baseline assessment in kindergarten and who received Fast Track exhibited fewer delinquent behaviors and were less likely to have a diagnosis of conduct disorder or any externalizing disorder compared to children in the control group (Conduct Problems Prevention Research Group, 2010a, 2011). Results from an additional analysis of outcomes in ninth grade revealed that the impact of Fast Track on reducing behavior problems was due, in part, to a decrease in the hostile attribution bias discussed earlier (Dodge & Godwin, 2013). By the end of high school, a full two years after the intervention ended, children who received Fast Track were less likely to have been arrested (Conduct Problems Prevention Research Group, 2010b) and receive a diagnosis of any externalizing disorder (Conduct Problems Prevention Research Group, 2011).

Quick Summary

ADHD and conduct disorder are referred to as externalizing disorders. They appear across cultures, although there are also differences in the manifestation of externalizing symptoms in different cultures. Both disorders are more common in boys than girls. A number of factors work together to cause ADHD and conduct disorder. Genetic factors play a particularly important role in ADHD but are also implicated in conduct disorder. Neurobiological research has implicated areas of the brain and neurotransmitters such as dopamine in ADHD and amygdala in conduct disorder; neuropsychological deficits are seen in both disorders. Other risk factors for ADHD include low birth weight and maternal smoking. Family and peer variables are also important factors to consider, especially in how they interact with genetic and neurobiological vulnerabilities. The most effective treatment for ADHD is a combination of stimulant medication and behavioral therapy. For conduct disorder, family-based treatments, such as PMT, are effective, as are treatments that include multiple points for intervention, as in MST. Prevention approaches, such as Fast Track, can also be helpful.

Check Your Knowledge 13.2

Fill in the blanks.

1. Moffitt and colleagues have provided a good deal of evidence for two types of conduct disorder. The _____ type is associated with an early age of onset and continued problems into adolescence and adulthood. The _____ type begins in the teenage years and is hypothesized to remit by adulthood, though a recent follow-up study has not supported the idea that this type remits.

2. Comorbidity is common in conduct disorder. Other problems that co-occur with conduct disorder include: _____, _____, _____, and _____.

3. A successful treatment for conduct disorder that involves the family is called _____. Another successful community-focused treatment that works with the child, parents, peers, and schools is _____.

Depression and Anxiety in Children and Adolescents

So far, we have discussed disorders that are specific to children. The internalizing disorders, which include depression and anxiety disorders, first begin in childhood or adolescence but are quite common in adults as well. Much richer descriptions of these disorders are presented in Chapter 5 (mood disorders) and Chapters 6 and 7 (anxiety disorders, obsessive-compulsive and trauma-related disorders). Here, we describe the ways in which the symptoms, etiology, and treatment of these disorders differ in children as compared to adults.

Depression

Clinical Descriptions, Prevalence, and Comorbidities of Depression in Childhood and Adolescence There are both similarities and differences in the symptomatology of children and adults with major depressive disorder (Garber & Flynn, 2001). Children and adolescents ages 7 to 17 and adults show the following symptoms: depressed mood, inability to experience pleasure, fatigue, concentration problems, and suicidal ideation. Children and adolescents differ from adults in showing more guilt but lower rates of early-morning wakefulness, early-morning depression, loss of appetite, and weight loss. As in adults, depression in children is recurrent. Longitudinal studies have demonstrated that both children and adolescents with major depression are likely to continue to exhibit significant depressive symptoms when assessed even 4 to 8 years later (Garber, Kelly, & Martin, 2002; Lewinsohn, Rohde, Seeley et al., 2000).

Depression occurs in 2 to 3 percent of school-age children under age 13 (Costello, Erkanli, & Angold, 2006). By adolescence, rates of depression range from 6 to 16 percent for girls and 4 to 7 percent for boys (Costello et al., 2006; Merikangas et al., 2010).

The prevalence among adolescent girls is almost twice that among adolescent boys, just as we have seen with adult depression (see Focus on Discovery 5.1). Although adolescent girls experience depression more often than adolescent boys, there are few differences in the types of symptoms they experience (Lewinsohn, Petit, Joiner et al., 2003). Interestingly, the gender difference does not occur before age 12; the full gender difference does not emerge until adolescence (Hankin, Abramson, Moffitt et al., 1998).

As with adults, depression is comorbid with anxiety, particularly in adolescents (Cummings, Caporino, & Kendall, 2014). There is recent evidence that comorbidity between depression and anxiety in adolescence may be caused in part by shared genetic vulnerabilities (Waszczuk, Zavos, Gregory et al., 2014).

Etiology of Depression in Childhood and Adolescence What causes a young person to become depressed? As with adults, evidence suggests that genetic factors play a role (Klein, Lewinsohn, Seeley et al., 2001). Indeed, the results of genetic studies with adults (see Chapter 5) apply to children and adolescents also, since genetic influences are present from birth, though they may not be expressed right away. A child with a depressed parent has four times the risk of developing depression as a child without a depressed parent (Hammen & Brennan, 2001). Of course, having a depressed parent likely confers risk via both genes and environment.

As has been found with older adults (see Chapter 5), gene–environment interactions predict the onset of depression in late adolescence and early adulthood. Results from the Northwestern-UCLA Youth Emotion Project, a large prospective study beginning with adolescents in their junior year of high school, are informative with respect to such interactions. In this study, those individuals who had a short allele of the serotonin transporter gene (short-short or short-long; see Chapter 2) *and* had experienced significant interpersonal stressful life events were more likely to have a major depressive disorder episode than either those people who had a short allele but no such stress or those people who experienced interpersonal stressful life events but had the long-long allele combination of the gene (Vrshek-Schallhorn, Mineka, Zinbarg et al., 2013). Other research shows that interpersonal factors seem to be

Christian JACQUET/Getty Images

Many of the symptoms of childhood depression are the same as adult depression, including sad mood.

particularly important in predicting the development of depression among adolescent girls (Hammen, 2009).

As with adults, other types of early adversity and negative life events also play a role (Garber, 2006). For example, one study found that early adversity (e.g., financial hardship, maternal depression, chronic illness as a child) predicted depression between ages 15 and 20, particularly among adolescents who had experienced a number of negative life events by age 15 (Hazel, Hamman, Brennan et al., 2008). Rejection by parents is modestly associated with depression in childhood, as confirmed by a meta-analysis of 45 studies (McLeod, Wood, & Weisz, 2007). The effect size for parental rejection was considered small across the studies, suggesting that factors other than parental rejection play a larger role in causing depression in childhood.

As we learned in Chapter 2, our bodies respond to stress via the HPA axis and the release of cortisol. Additional results from the Youth Emotion Project study indicate that cortisol taken first thing in the morning prospectively predicted the onset of a major depressive episode up to 2.5 years later (Vrshek-Schallhorn, Doane, Mineka et al., 2013). These results are consistent with findings from adults (reviewed in Chapter 5).

Recall from discussions in Chapters 5 that cortisol in people with depression is associated with smaller volumes (size) of the hippocampus. This may also be true for adolescents. A longitudinal study of adolescents at risk for developing depression found that the volume of the hippocampus grew more slowly between early and middle adolescence for those who developed an episode of depression compared to those who did not develop an episode (Whittle, Lichter, Dennison et al., 2014). Although these researchers did not measure stressful life events or cortisol, the evidence from the different studies reviewed here suggests that genes, stressful life events, cortisol, and the brain are all important when considering depression in adolescence.

Consistent with both Beck's theory and the hopelessness theory of depression (see Chapter 5), cognitive distortions and negative attributional styles are associated with depression in children and adolescents in ways similar to what has been found with adults (Garber et al., 2002; Lewinsohn et al., 2000). For example, research with children with depression indicates that their outlooks are more negative than are those of children without depression and resemble those of adults with depression (Prieto, Cole, & Tageson, 1992). Negative thoughts and hopelessness also predict a slower time to recovery from depression among adolescents (Rhode, Seeley, Kaufman et al., 2006). Of course, depression can make children think more negatively (Cole, Martin, Peeke et al., 1998). Hence, it is important to consider longitudinal research.

A key question in the study of children with depression is: when do children actually develop stable attributional styles? That is, can young children have a stable way of thinking about themselves in the midst of such profound cognitive development? A longitudinal study examined the development of attributional style in children (Cole, Ciesla, Dallaire et al., 2008). Specifically, the researchers prospectively studied three groups of children for 4 years each. At year 1 of the study, the three groups were (1) children in second grade, (2) children in fourth grade, and (3) children in sixth grade. These three groups were followed yearly until the children were in grades 5, 7, and 9, respectively. The researchers found that attributional style didn't appear to be a stable style until children were early adolescents. In addition, attributional style did not interact with negative life events to predict depression (i.e., it was not a cognitive diathesis) for young children. It wasn't until the children were in eighth or ninth grade that support for attributional style as a cognitive diathesis emerged. Thus, results of this study suggest that attributional style becomes style-like by early adolescence and serves as a cognitive diathesis for depression by the middle school years.

Treatment of Childhood and Adolescent Depression Results from a large randomized controlled trial called the Treatment for Adolescents with Depression Study (TADS) provide some support for the efficacy of antidepressants. In the TADS study, adolescents were randomized to receive either Prozac, cognitive behavioral therapy (CBT), or both combined.

Results indicated that the combined treatment was the most effective through 12 weeks and that Prozac had modest advantages compared to CBT (March, Silva, Petrycki et al., 2004), a pattern that remained true after 36 weeks (TADS team, 2007). A meta-analysis of 27 randomized controlled trials of antidepressant medication treatment for depression and anxiety disorders in children found that the medications were most effective for anxiety disorders other than obsessive compulsive disorder (OCD) and less effective for OCD and depression (Bridge, Iyengar, Salary et al., 2007).

However, several concerns have been raised about antidepressants (see Focus on Discovery 13.3). The side effects experienced by some children taking antidepressants include diarrhea, nausea, sleep problems, and agitation (Barber, 2008). More importantly, concerns with respect to suicidality prompted a series of hearings in the United States and the United Kingdom about the safety of antidepressants for children. In the study cited above (March et al., 2004), 7 out of 439 adolescents attempted suicide, of whom 6 were in the Prozac group and 1 was in the CBT group. (See Focus on Discovery 13.3 for more discussion of this complex issue.) In the meta-analysis by Bridge and colleagues (2007), the researchers looked at suicidality rates in the studies of depression. The risk of suicidal ideation was 3 percent for those children taking antidepressants and 2 percent for those taking placebo. It is important to note that this analysis shows that children taking medication were at risk for suicidal ideation, not that medication caused the suicide thoughts or attempts. There were no completed suicides in any of the 27 studies reviewed.

Another issue has to do with how long the treatment effects last. A naturalistic follow-up of just under half the adolescents in the TADS study found that although most (96 percent) had recovered 2 years after the study, close to half of those who recovered by the end of treatment had a recurrent episode of depression 5 years later (Curry, Silva, Rohde et al., 2011). Girls were more likely to have a recurrence than boys, as were adolescents who had a comorbid anxiety disorder. However, the rate of recurrence did not differ depending on the kind of treatment the adolescents received during the TADS study. In other words, the modest benefits of Prozac over cognitive behavior therapy reported in the TADS study did not seem to protect this group of adolescents from having a future episode of depression 5 years later.

Cognitive behavioral therapy (CBT) in school settings appears to be effective and is associated with more rapid reduction of symptoms than family or supportive therapy (Curry, 2001). About 63 percent of adolescents with depression treated with CBT show significant improvement at the end of treatment (Lewinsohn & Clarke, 1999). However, other evidence

Clinical Case: Sharon

When initially seen, Sharon was extremely dysphoric, experienced recurrent suicidal ideation, and displayed a number of vegetative signs of depression. . . . [After being] placed on antidepressant medication . . . she was introduced to a cognitive behavioral approach to depression. . . . She was able to understand how her mood was affected by her thoughts and behavior and was able to engage in behavioral planning to increase the occurrence of pleasurable and mastery-oriented events. Sharon manifested extremely high standards for evaluating her performance in a number of areas, and it became clear that her parents also subcribed to these standards, so that family therapy sessions were held to encourage Sharon and her parents to reevaluate their standards.

Sharon had difficulty with the notion of changing her standards and noted that when she was not depressed she actually valued her perfectionism. At that point she resisted the therapy because she perceived it as trying to change something she valued in herself. With this in mind, we began to explore and identify those situations or domains in which her perfectionism worked for her and when and how it might work against her. She became increasingly comfortable with this perspective and decided she wanted to continue to set high standards regarding her performance in mathematical course work (which was a clear area of strength), but she did not need to be so demanding of herself regarding art or physical education. [Adapted from Braswell & Kendall (1988), p. 194.]

suggests that the benefits of CBT may not last long for young people (Weisz, McCarty, & Valeri, 2006). Some evidence shows that CBT is most beneficial for Caucasian adolescents, those adolescents with good coping skills at pretreatment, and adolescents with recurrent depression (Rhode et al., 2006). The Clinical Case of Sharon illustrates CBT techniques with an adolescent.

A good deal of work has focused on how to prevent the onset of depression in adolescents and children. A meta-analysis examined two types of preventive interventions for depression: selective and universal (Horowitz & Garber, 2006). Selective prevention programs target particular youth based on family risk factors (e.g., parents with depression), environmental factors (e.g., poverty), or personal factors (e.g., hopelessness). Universal programs are targeted toward large groups, typically in schools, and seek to provide education and information about depression. Results of the meta-analysis indicated that selective prevention programs were more effective than universal programs in preventing depression symptoms among adolescents.

A large randomized control clinical trial of a selective prevention program for at-risk adolescents, defined as having at least one parent with depression, showed promising results (Garber, Clarke, Weersing et al., 2009). Adolescents were randomly assigned to a group CBT intervention that focused on problem-solving skills and changing negative thoughts or to a usual care group (i.e., any mental health care they sought out on their own). The incidence of depression episodes was lower for adolescents in the CBT group than for those in the usual care group; therefore, the treatment may have had an effective preventative effect.

Anxiety

Just about every child experiences fears and worries as part of the normal course of development. Common fears, most of which are outgrown, include fear of the dark and of imaginary creatures and fear of being separated from parents. In general, as with adults, fears are reported more often for girls than for boys (Lichenstein & Annas, 2000),though this sex difference may be due at least in part to social pressures on boys that make them reluctant to admit that they are afraid of things.

The seriousness of some childhood anxiety problems should not be underestimated. Not only do children suffer, as do adults, from the aversiveness of being anxious—simply put, anxiety doesn't feel good—but their anxiety may also work against their acquisition of skills appropriate to various stages of their development. For example, a child who is painfully shy and finds interacting with peers virtually intolerable is unlikely to learn important social skills. This deficit may persist as the child grows into adolescence and will form the foundation of still further social difficulties. Then, whether in the workplace or at college, the adolescent's worst fear—"people will dislike and reject me"—is likely to be realized as his or her awkward, even off-putting, behavior toward others may produce rejecting and avoiding responses.

VOISIN/PHANIE/Photo Researchers, Inc.

Anxiety disorders in childhood and adolescence can interfere with other aspects of development.

Clinical Descriptions and Prevalence of Anxiety in Childhood and Adolescence For fears and worries to be classified as disorders according to DSM criteria, children's functioning must be impaired; unlike adults, however, children need not regard their fear as excessive or unreasonable, because children sometimes are unable to make such judgments. Based on these criteria, about 3 to 5 percent of children and adolescents would be diagnosed as having an anxiety disorder (Rapee, Schniering, & Hudson, 2009). Using data from the National Comorbidity Replication study, researchers found that over 30 percent of the 10,000 adolescents ages 13 to 18 who were interviewed had a lifetime occurrence of an anxiety disorder. Specific phobias (19.3 percent) and social anxiety disorder (9.1 percent) were the most common.

Separation anxiety disorder in childhood is characterized by constant worry that some harm will befall their parents or themselves when they are away from their parents. When at home, such children shadow one or both of their parents. Since the beginning of school is often the first circumstance that requires lengthy and frequent separations of children from their parents, separation anxiety is often first observed when children begin school.

FOCUS ON DISCOVERY 13.3

Controversies in the Diagnosis and Treatment of Children with Psychopathology

The number of children diagnosed with psychological disorders continues to rise, sometimes dramatically, as has the number of children taking psychoactive medications. These increases raise several questions:

Has there truly been an increase in the number of children with psychological disorders?

Have our diagnostic system and assessment measures improved enough to identify children once overlooked?

Are children being misdiagnosed and then treated for problems they do not have?

Are medications safe for children?

Will medication use lead to later drug use or abuse among children?

Here we briefly discuss some of the controversies and current evidence accumulated to address these questions.

Bipolar Disorder in Children

For years, professionals thought bipolar disorders were very rare or even nonexistent among children. Today, however, diagnoses of bipolar disorders in children have increased dramatically. Has bipolar disorder among children increased? Probably not. In fact, bipolar disorder in children is much higher in the United States than in other countries, suggesting that the increase is specific to the United States (James, Hoang, Seagroatt et al., 2014; Van Meter, Moreira, & Youngstrom, 2011)

One of the difficult diagnostic issues facing mental health professionals is distinguishing bipolar disorders from ADHD. Agitated behavior can be a sign of both, and only through careful and thorough assessments can the distinction be made. An early controversy was whether the diagnostic criteria for bipolar disorders in children should be the same as the criteria for bipolar disorders in adults. Some argued that the criteria for children should include explosive but brief outbursts of emotion and behavioral dysregulation (e.g., Biederman, Mick, Faraone et al., 2000), but these are fundamentally different from the current DSM criteria for bipolar I disorder (see Chapter 5), and emotion dysregulation is also present in ADHD (Carlson & Meyer, 2006; Dickstein & Leibenluft, 2006). Later research has confirmed that the adult criteria are applicable to children and adolescents (Youngstrom, Freeman, & Jenkins, 2009). The American Academy of Child and Adolescent Psychiatry recommends using the adult DSM-5 criteria for diagnosing bipolar disorder in children and adolescents (McClellan, Kowatch, Findling, 2007). These guidelines also recommend that impairment be identified in two different settings (e.g., home, school), a requirement not found in the DSM.

The DSM-5 added a new category called *disruptive mood dysregulation disorder* (DMDD) in the hopes that this will help clinicians distinguish emotion dysregulation that is part of bipolar disorder from severe irritability, thus reducing the number of children receiving a diagnosis of bipolar disorder. The criteria for DMDD include severe temper outbursts that tend to happen three times a week and in two different settings (e.g., home, school). The diagnosis is only for children between the ages of 6 and 18, and it must be diagnosed prior to age 10. The symptoms need to have been present for at least a year.

Because this category was only introduced in 2013, not much research has been done yet. In fact, it was added to DSM-5 without much research support to warrant its inclusion, and this has rightly been controversial (Axelson, Birmaher, Findling et al., 2011). Research on severe mood dysregulation, a category not in DSM-IV but developed by researchers to capture children who exhibited irritability and not mania, showed that children with such extreme irritability were also highly likely to meet the diagnostic criteria for ADHD or ODD. However, over the course of more than 2 years, only 1 out of 84 children with severe mood dysregulation developed a manic episode (Leibenluft, 2011). These findings support the inclusion of DMDD in DSM-5, at least with respect to distinguishing it from bipolar disorder. Unfortunately, the new disorder may be problematic with respect to its reliability: the DSM-5 field trials (see Chapter 3) found that the reliability of the DMDD criteria was poor (Regier, Narrow, Clarke et al., 2013). This does not bode well for the new category.

One study sought to assess the DMDD criteria using data from three ongoing longitudinal studies of childhood psychopathology (Copeland, Angold, Costello et al., 2013). Even though these studies began before the DMDD criteria were released in May 2013, the researchers were able to test the DMDD criteria in these samples because "its criteria overlap entirely with those of other common disorders" (p. 174). Such overlap in criteria suggests that the new diagnosis will be comorbid with other conditions. Indeed, this study found significant comorbidity between DMDD and depression, anxiety, ODD, and ADHD. Although many childhood disorders are comorbid with one another, the comorbidity between DMDD and ODD was very high, suggesting that these might not be distinct categories. One of the seven children who had a manic episode also met the criteria for DMDD. Additional research in the coming years will reveal whether or not DMDD is a category that should remain in the DSM.

Antidepressant Medications

Can antidepressant medications increase the likelihood of suicide in adolescents? This question was the focus of intense debate 10 years ago, and the issue is still not fully resolved.

Findings from the TADS (Treatment of Adolescent Depression Study) study indicated that the most effective treatment was a combination of Prozac and cognitive behavioral therapy (March et al., 2004). However, the authors also reported that six adolescents taking Prozac attempted suicide (1.5 percent of the sample), whereas only one receiving CBT attempted suicide. The participants in the study were randomly assigned to treatment conditions, so it is less likely that the adolescents taking Prozac were more seriously ill or suicidal than the ones receiving CBT.

Antidepressants can take as long as 3–4 weeks to start working (see Chapter 5), and one analysis of adolescent suicide attempts and antidepressant use found that the risk for suicide was highest in the first 3–4 weeks of treatment. Thus, it could be the case that the medications did not have sufficient time to begin working in the adolescents who attempted suicide. It may also be true that the combined treatment in the TADS study was most effective because CBT began working earlier in the course of treatment.

These findings prompted the FDA to hold a series of hearings on the safety of treating children and adolescents with antidepressant medications. The United Kingdom had already made a strong statement that the benefits of antidepressants for the treatment of adolescent depression were not greater than the risks. At the end of the FDA hearings, the panel mandated a "black box" warning to accompany information sent to physicians on the use of antidepressants with adolescents. This is the strongest safety warning the FDA can issue with medications. In the United Kingdom, the equivalent regulatory agency, the Medicines and Healthcare Products Regulatory Agency (MHRA), also recommended warnings for antidepressant labels. Since then, the numbers of prescriptions for antidepressants have declined, in the United States and in the United Kingdom (Kurian, Ray, Arbogast et al., 2007). Although suicides among youths have decreased at the same time, too many other variables have changed during this time to know whether the reduction in antidepressant use explains the decline in suicide rates.

Stimulant Medications

As reviewed earlier, the number of children taking stimulant medications has risen dramatically. Does the use of stimulant medications lead to increases in illicit drug use among children? Three prospective, longitudinal studies suggest that the answer to this question is no. In one study, two groups of children with ADHD were studied for 13 years (Barkley, Fischer, Smallish et al., 2003). One group of children had been treated with stimulant medication for 3 ½ years on average and the other group had never received stimulant medication. At follow-up in young adulthood, those who had taken stimulant medication were not more likely to have used illicit drugs than those who had not been treated, with one exception—those who had taken stimulant medication were at greater risk for having tried cocaine. However, after controlling for the severity of conduct disorder symptoms, the relationship between stimulant medication use and trying cocaine disappeared. This suggests that having severe conduct disorder symptoms accounts for the link between stimulant medication and trying cocaine, not the use of stimulant medication per se.

The second study followed into adulthood a group of children with reading disorders who had been treated with stimulant medications for 12 to 18 weeks and compared them to a group of children with reading disorders who had not received stimulant medication. Sixteen years after the medication treatment, the two groups did not differ in their use of illicit drugs (Mannuzza, Klein, & Moulton, 2003).

The third study followed up children 8 years after they participated in the MTA treatment study (discussed earlier) when they were in middle to late adolescence (Molina, Hinshaw, Eugene Arnold et al., 2013). Children with ADHD, regardless of treatment type, were more likely to have used alcohol, tobacco, marijuana and other drugs in adolescence than the children without ADHD, a finding that is consistent with studies showing comorbidity between ADHD and substance use. However, there was no relationship between stimulant medication use and later drug use. Neither the total amount of medication taken, the dosage of medication, or initial MTA treatment group (medication alone, combined treatment), or continued use of medication after the MTA study was associated with later drug or alcohol use. Thus, children with ADHD are at a higher risk for substance use, but it is not because they have taken stimulant medication.

Autism Spectrum Disorder: Diagnosis and Causes

The number of cases of autism spectrum disorder (ASD) has increased dramatically over the past 15 years. As reported by the Centers for Disease Control and Prevention (CDC), the prevalence rate of ASD in the United States has risen from 1 in 150 children to 1 in 110 children to 1 in 68 children (CDC, 2009, 2014). A large study in Korea found the prevalence rate to be even higher—over 2 percent (1 in every 38 children; Kim, Young, Leventhal et al., 2011). Why has there been such an increase? Are there that many more children with autism, or have mental health professionals gotten better at making a diagnosis?

Autism wasn't formally recognized in the DSM until 1980, and the diagnostic criteria broadened quite a bit between the publication of DSM-III in 1980 and the release of DSM-IV in 1994. (Asperger's disorder was first formally recognized in DSM-IV; this is now combined with autism in DSM-5.) More children met the criteria for a diagnosis of autism under the broader criteria of DSM-IV than they did under the narrower criteria of DSM-III (Gernsbacher, Dawson, & Goldsmith, 2005). Additionally, there is greater public awareness of ASD, and this may spur families to seek out mental health professionals for a formal psychological assessment. Indeed, the delay in or lack of language acquisition has become a widely recognized warning sign among parents and mental health professionals that ASD may be a consideration. In addition, public schools are mandated by law to provide services for children with ASD, and this may have helped families to seek a formal diagnosis. Indeed, the number of children classified as having ASD and thus qualifying for special education services increased between 2000 and 2011 by over 300,000 (U. S. Department of Education, 2013). However, the latest increases in ASD rates appear to be driven by children with ASD but no intellectual disability (CDC, 2014).

Although the rise in autism diagnoses may be accounted for in part by better diagnosis, awareness, and mandated services, most experts agree that there are actually more cases today than there were 30 years ago.

With the increase in ASD have come concerns over what might be causing this increase. Based largely on celebrity proclamations, parents became particularly worried that vaccines routinely given to toddlers may cause ASD. The MMR vaccine (for measles, mumps, and rubella) is given to children right around the age when autism signs and symptoms begin to appear. A related concern is that the product used to preserve these vaccines—a substance called thimerosal, which contains mercury—may be responsible for autism.

There is no evidence, however, linking autism with either the MMR vaccine or thimerosal. Vaccines have not been stored in thimerosal for the last several years, and even those vaccines that were stored in thimerosal contained very small amounts of mercury. One study examined the number of ASD diagnoses reported to the California Department of Developmental Services between 1995 and 2007 (Schecter & Grether, 2008). By 2001, all but the smallest trace of thimerosal had been removed from childhood vaccines. If thimerosal was causing autism, the decline in its use in vaccines might correspond to a decrease in the number of new cases of autism. However, the study found no such association. In fact, the number of new cases of autism increased. In May 2004, the Institute of Medicine published the results of its comprehensive review of available evidence on the link between MMR and autism. This report concluded that the MMR vaccines are not responsible for autism (Institute of Medicine, 2004).

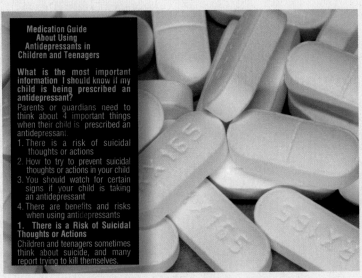

FDA required that black-box warnings be put on antidepressants for use with adolescents.

DSM-5 Criteria for Separation Anxiety Disorder

Excessive anxiety that is not developmentally appropriate about being away from people to whom one is attached, with at least three symptoms that last for at least 4 weeks (for adults symptoms must last for 6 months or more).

- Repeated and excessive distress when separated
- Excessive worry that something bad will happen to an attachment figure
- Refusal or reluctance to go to school, work, or elsewhere
- Refusal or reluctance to sleep away from home
- Nightmares about separation from attachment figure
- Repeated physical complaints (e.g., headache, stomachache) when separated from attachment figure

Two changes happened with DSM-5. First, the category was moved into the Anxiety Disorders chapter, and second, the age of onset prior to age 18 requirement was removed. Thus, adults can now receive a diagnosis of separation anxiety disorder. For adults, the anxiety stems from separation from an attachment figure that is not necessarily a parent (e.g., spouse).

Another anxiety disorder among children and adolescents is social anxiety disorder. Most classrooms include at least one or two children who are extremely quiet and shy. Often these children will play only with family members or familiar peers, avoiding strangers both young and old. Their social anxiety may prevent them from acquiring skills and participating in a variety of activities enjoyed by most of their peers, for they avoid playgrounds and stay out of games played by other children. Extremely shy children may refuse to speak at all in unfamiliar social circumstances, a condition called *selective mutism*.

Prevalence estimates for social anxiety disorder among children and adolescents range from 1 to 7 percent (Merikangas et al., 2010; Rapee et al., 2009). Higher prevalence rates are observed with adolescents, who have a more acute concern about the opinions of others than younger children do.

Children who are exposed to traumas such as chronic abuse, community violence, and natural disasters may experience symptoms of posttraumatic stress disorder (PTSD) similar to those experienced by adults. As many as 5 percent of children meet criteria for PTSD (Merikangas et al., 2010). For children older than age 6, these symptoms are organized into the same four broad categories discussed in Chapter 7: (1) intrusively reexperiencing the traumatic event, as in nightmares, flashbacks, or intrusive thoughts; (2) avoiding trauma-related situations or information and experiencing a general numbing of responses, as in feelings of detachment or anhedonia; (3) negative changes in cognitions or mood related to the traumatic event; and (4) increased arousal and reactivity, which can include irritability, sleep problems, and hypervigilance.

DSM-5 added separate criteria for PTSD in children age 6 and younger. The symptoms for these younger children fall into the same four broad categories just described, but they are presented in ways that are more developmentally appropriate for younger children. For example, extreme temper tantrums are an example of an increased reactivity symptom; intrusive thoughts about the trauma may be experienced as reenactment play. In addition, some of the symptom descriptors that don't apply to young children are removed from these criteria. For example, holding negative beliefs about oneself is part of the negative changes in cognitions or mood symptom cluster that does not apply to very young children.

Obsessive compulsive disorder (OCD) is also found among children and adolescents, with prevalence estimates ranging from less than 1 to 4 percent (Rapee et al., 2009). The symptoms in childhood are similar to symptoms in adulthood: both obsessions and compulsions are involved. The most common obsessions in childhood involve dirt or contamination as well as aggression; recurrent thoughts about sex or religion become more common in adolescence (Turner, 2006). OCD in children is more common in boys than girls, but by adulthood, OCD is slightly more common in women than men.

Etiology of Anxiety Disorders in Childhood and Adolescence
As with adults, genetics plays a role in anxiety among children, with heritability estimates ranging from 29 to 50 percent in one study (Lau, Gregory, Goldwin et al., 2007). However, genes do their work via the environment, with genetics playing a role in separation anxiety in the context of more negative life events experienced by a child (Lau et al., 2007).

Parenting practices play a small role in childhood anxiety. Specifically, parental control and overprotectiveness, more than parental rejection, is associated with childhood anxiety. However, parental control accounted for only 4 percent of the variance in childhood anxiety according to a meta-analysis of 47 studies (McCleod, Weisz, & Wood, 2007). Thus, 96 percent of the variance is accounted for by other factors. Other psychological factors that predict anxiety symptoms among children and adolescents include emotion-regulation problems and insecure attachment in infancy (Bosquet & Egeland, 2006).

Theories of the etiology of social anxiety in children are generally similar to theories of social anxiety in adults. For example, research has shown that children with anxiety disorders overestimate the danger in many situations and underestimate their ability to cope with them (Boegels & Zigterman, 2000). The anxiety created by these cognitions then interferes with social interaction, causing the child to avoid social situations and thus not to get much practice at social skills. In adolescence, peer relationships are important. Specifically, a longitudinal study found that adolescents who perceived that their peers did not accept them were more likely to be socially anxious (Teachman & Allen, 2007). Other research points to behavioral inhibition as an important risk factor for developing social anxiety (also discussed in Chapter 6). Children who had high levels of behavioral inhibition at age 4 were 10 times as likely as children with lower levels to have social anxiety disorder by age 9 (Essex et al., 2010).

Theories about the causes of PTSD are similar for children and adults. For both, there must be exposure to a trauma, either experienced or witnessed. Like adults, children who have a propensity to experience anxiety may be at more risk for developing PTSD after exposure to trauma. Specific risk factors for children may include level of family stress, coping styles of the family, and past experiences with trauma (Martini, Ryan, Nakayama et al., 1990). Some theorists suggest that parental reactions to trauma can help to lessen children's distress; specifically, if parents appear to be in control and are calm in the face of stress, a child's reaction may be less severe (Davis & Siegal, 2000).

Separation anxiety disorder involves an intense fear of being away from parents or other attachment figures.

Treatment of Anxiety in Childhood and Adolescence For the most part, treatment of anxiety is similar to that employed with adults, with suitable modifications to accommodate the different abilities and circumstances of childhood. The major focus of these treatments is on exposure. Compared to exposure treatments for adults, treatments may be modified for children by including more modeling (seeing an adult approach the feared object) and more reinforcement.

Evidence from a meta-analysis of 48 randomized controlled trials indicates that cognitive behavior therapy can be helpful to many children with anxiety disorders (Reynolds, Wilson, Austin et al., 2012). One of the more widely used treatments is called the Coping Cat (Kendall, Aschenbrand, & Hudson, 2003). This treatment focuses on confrontation of fears, development of new ways to think about fears, exposure to feared situations, and relapse prevention. Parents are also included in a couple of sessions. Data from randomized controlled clinical trials have shown this treatment to be effective in the short term, 7 years later (Kendall, Flannery-Schroeder, Panichelli-Mindel et al., 1997; Kendall, Safford, Flannery-Schroeder et al., 2004), and 19 years later (Benjamin, Harrison, Settipani et al., 2013).

Another randomized controlled trial compared individual CBT, family CBT, and family psychoeducation for the treatment of childhood anxiety. Both individual and family CBT included the Coping Cat workbook, both were more effective than family psychoeducation at reducing anxiety (Kendall, Hudson, Gosch, et al., 2008), and the effects persisted at a 1-year and 7-year follow-up (Benjamin et al., 2013). The family CBT was more effective than individual CBT when both parents had an anxiety disorder. This study points to the importance of considering not only the child's anxiety but also levels of parental anxiety when deciding on a treatment for childhood anxiety.

Another study examined the Coping Cat treatment alone and in combination with sertraline (Zoloft) for children with separation anxiety, general anxiety, and social anxiety and found that the combination treatment was more effective than either the Coping Cat or medication alone (Walkup, Albano, Piacentini et al., 2008). Two- and three-year follow-up studies of these children found that children assigned to the Coping Cat alone or medication alone conditions continued to get better, such that these two conditions were as effective in reducing anxiety as the combination treatment (Piacentini, Bennett, Compton et al., 2014). Thus, the combination treatment appears to provide the most immediate improvement, but over time the Coping Cat CBT treatment (and medication alone) yielded the same benefits.

Behavior therapy and group cognitive behavior therapy have been found to be effective for social anxiety disorder in children (Davis & Whiting, 2011). Only a few studies have examined the efficacy of cognitive behavior therapy for OCD in children and adolescents. In one study, CBT was equally as effective as medication, but CBT plus medication was more effective than medication alone but not more than CBT alone (O'Kearney, Anstey, & von Sanden, 2006). However, for children and adolescents with severe OCD, a combination of CBT and sertraline (Zoloft) was more effective than CBT alone (Pediatric OCD Treatment Study (POTS) team, 2004). In another study, CBT plus medication was more effective than medication alone or medication plus generic instructions about what CBT involves (Franklin, Sapyta, Freeman et al., 2011). Results from a recent randomized controlled trial suggest that CBT is also effective for young children (i.e., ages 5 to 8). In this study, participants were randomly assigned to receive either family-based CBT, which included exposure plus response prevention (see Chapter 7), or family-based relaxation therapy. At the end of the 14-week treatment, children who received CBT had fewer symptoms and better functioning compared to the children who received the relaxation training (Freeman, Sapyta, Garcia et al., 2014).

Other methods of providing treatment, including "bibliotherapy" and computer-assisted therapy, have shown promise as well. In bibliotherapy, parents are given written materials and are the "therapist" with their children. Although this approach is effective in reducing childhood anxiety, it does not appear to be as effective as CBT group treatments (Rapee, Abbott, & Lyneham, 2006). Nevertheless, it will be important to develop these types of mobile treatments for people who live in areas where CBT therapists are not available or are too expensive.

Only a few studies have evaluated the efficacy of treatment of PTSD among children and adolescents, but the available research suggests that cognitive behavioral treatments, whether individual or group, are effective for children and adolescents with PTSD (Davis & Whiting, 2011).

Quick Summary

Anxiety disorders and depression in children are referred to as internalizing disorders. Depression in childhood and adolescence appears to be similar to depression in adulthood, although there are notable differences. In childhood, depression affects boys and girls equally, but in adolescence girls are affected almost twice as often as boys. Genetics and stressful life events play a role in depression in childhood. Research on cognitive factors in childhood depression supports the notion that attributional style also plays a role; however, this work must consider the developmental stage of the child. A randomized controlled trial found that a combination of medication and CBT was the most effective treatment for depression, but concerns about the effect of medications on suicide risk need to be addressed.

Anxiety and fear are typical in childhood. When fears interfere with functioning, such as keeping a child from school, intervention is warranted. Theories about the causes of anxiety disorders in children are similar to theories about their causes in adulthood, though less research has been done with children on, for example, cognitive factors. Cognitive behavioral therapy is an effective intervention for a number of different anxiety disorders in childhood. Other problems, such as PTSD in childhood, require additional study.

Specific Learning Disorder

Clinical Case: Marcus

Marcus was excited about his psychology major and dreamed of becoming a clinical psychologist. He eagerly signed up for as many courses as would fit into his schedule and as had open seats. He sat in the front of the large lecture courses, raising his hand and contributing to the discussion whenever possible. When it came time to take the first exam, he carefully reviewed his notes and textbook. He also experienced that creeping anxiety that came whenever he took written exams. Even though he thought he studied as much if not more than the other students, he just did not do well on the exams. "He didn't test well" was what he told himself. But when he thought about it, he realized that when he was reading the textbook, the words and letters sometimes got scrambled in a way that made it difficult to remember the material.

When he received his grade on the first midterm, he was worried. It contained all sorts of marks from the grader indicating that his writing was indecipherable and that he had not covered all the concepts required for the correct answers. His graduate student instructor suggested that he go for testing at the campus clinic in charge of assessments for learning disorders.

After a comprehensive assessment from the campus clinic, Marcus received a diagnosis of specific learning disorder with the dyslexia specifier. Marcus was now going to get extra time for his exams and papers, and not just in his psychology classes but in all of his classes. The following semester, Tim's grade point average went up to a 3.8, and he felt confident that he was closer to achieving his goal of attending graduate school in clinical psychology.

A **specific learning disorder** is a condition in which a person shows a problem in a specific area of academic, language, speech, or motor skills that is not due to intellectual disability or deficient educational opportunities. Children with a specific learning disorder are usually of average or above-average intelligence but have difficulty learning some specific skill in the affected area (e.g., arithmetic or reading), and thus their progress in school is impeded.

Clinical Descriptions

The term *learning disabilities* is not used in DSM-5 but is used by mental health professionals to group together three categories that do appear in the DSM: specific learning disorder, communication disorders, and motor disorders. These disorders are described briefly in Table 13.2. Any of these disorders may apply to a child who fails to develop to the degree appropriate to his or her developmental level in a specific academic, language, or motor skill area. These disorders are often identified and treated within the school system rather than through mental health clinics. An analysis of four large epidemiological samples indicates that a specific learning disorder involving reading is far more common in boys than in girls (Rutter, Caspi, Fergusson et al., 2004). The prevalence rates for specific learning disorders involving reading or math (i.e., dyslexia and dyscalculia) are about the same, ranging from 4 to 7 percent of children (Landerl, Fussenegger, Moll et al., 2009).

Etiology of Specific Learning Disorder

Most research on specific learning disorder concerns dyslexia, perhaps because it is the most prevalent of this group of disorders: it affects 5 to 15 percent of school-age children. In DSM-5, neither dyslexia nor dyscalculia is named as a distinct disorder. Instead, dyslexia and dyscalculia are specifiers for the DSM-5 category specific learning disorder. Because more research has been done on dyslexia than on dyscalculia, we consider dyslexia here in some detail.

DSM-5 Criteria for Specific Learning Disorder

- Difficulties in learning basic academic skills (reading, mathematics, or writing) inconsistent with person's age, schooling, and intelligence persisting for at least 6 months
- Significant interference with academic achievement or activities of daily living

DAVE M. BENETT/Getty Images, Inc.

Keira Knightley, a highly successful actress, suffers from dyslexia.

Table 13.2 Specific Learning, Communication, and Motor Disorders in DSM-5

Specific Learning disorder includes specifiers:

- **Dyslexia** (formerly called reading disorder) involves significant difficulty with word recognition, reading comprehension, and typically written spelling as well.
- **Dyscalculia** (formerly called mathematics disorder) involves difficulty in producing or understanding numbers, quantities, or basic arithmetic operations.

Communication disorders include:

- **Speech sound disorder** (formerly called phonological disorder) involves correct comprehension and sufficient vocabulary use, but unclear speech and improper articulation. For example, *blue* comes out *bu*, and *rabbit* sounds like *wabbit*. With speech therapy, complete recovery occurs in almost all cases, and milder cases may recover spontaneously by age 8.
- **Childhood onset fluency disorder** (stuttering) is a disturbance in verbal fluency that is characterized by one or more of the following speech patterns: frequent repetitions or prolongations of sounds, long pauses between words, substituting easy words for those that are difficult to articulate (e.g., words beginning with certain consonants), and repeating whole words (e.g., saying "go-go-go-go" instead of just a single "go"). DSM-IV-TR estimates that up to 80 percent of people with stuttering recover, most of them without professional intervention, before the age of 16.
- **Language disorder** (combines expressive and mixed receptive expressive language disorders from DSM-IV).
- **Social (pragmatic) communication disorder** (new in DSM-5).
- **Motor disorders** include:
- **Tourette's disorder** involves one or more vocal and multiple motor tics (sudden, rapid movement or vocalization) that start before the age of 18.
- **Developmental coordination disorder** (formerly called motor skills disorder) involves marked impairment in the development of motor coordination that is not explainable by intellectual disability or a disorder such as cerebral palsy.
- **Stereotypic movement disorder** involves seemingly purposeless movements repeated over and over that interfere with functioning and could even cause self-injury.

Etiology of Dyslexia Family and twin studies confirm that there is a heritable component to dyslexia (Pennington, 1995; Raskind, 2001). Furthermore, the genes that are associated with dyslexia are the same genes associated with typical reading abilities (Plomin & Kovas, 2005). These so-called generalist genes are thus important for understanding normal as well as abnormal reading abilities. Research has also examined gene–environment interactions in dyslexia, and here the evidence so far suggests that the heritability of reading problems varies depending on parental education. Genes play a bigger role in dyslexia among children whose parents have more education compared to children whose parents have less education (Friend, DeFries, Olson et al., 2009; Kremen, Jacobson, Xian et al., 2005). Homes with high parental education likely emphasize reading and provide a lot of opportunity for children to read. In this type of environment, then, a child's risk for developing dyslexia is more driven by heritable combinations of genes than by environment.

Evidence from psychological, neuropsychological, and neuroimaging studies suggests that dyslexia involves problems in language processing. These problems include perception of speech and analysis of the sounds of spoken language and their relation to printed words (Mann & Brady, 1988), difficulty recognizing rhyme and alliteration (Mann & Brady, 1988), problems with rapidly naming familiar objects (Scarborough, 1990; Wolf, Bally, & Morris, 1986), and delays in learning syntactic rules (Scarborough, 1990). Many of these processes fall under what is called *phonological awareness*, which is believed to be critical to the development of reading skills (Anthony & Lonigan, 2004).

Early fMRI studies supported the idea that children with dyslexia have a problem in phonological awareness. These studies show that areas in the left temporal, parietal, and occipital regions of the brain are important for phonological awareness, and these same regions are centrally involved in dyslexia (see Figure 13.6).

For example, a study using fMRI found that, compared to children without dyslexia, children with dyslexia showed less activation in the left temporoparietal and occipitotemporal areas while doing a number of reading-relevant tasks, such as identifying letters and sounding out words (Shaywitz, Shaywitz, Pugh et al., 2002). A treatment study showed that after a year of intensive treatment for reading problems, children with dyslexia were better readers and also showed greater activation in the left temporoparietal and occipitotemporal areas while completing a reading task, compared to a group of children who received a less intensive treatment (Shaywitz, Shaywitz, Blachman et al., 2004).

More recent fMRI studies suggest that the problem might not be in areas of the brain that support phonological awareness per se, but in their connections to other areas of the brain that support the ability to produce speech, including Broca's area (Boets, Op de Beeck, Vandermosten et al., 2013; Vandermosten, Boets, Poelmans et al., 2012). These findings suggest the interesting possibility that children with dyslexia may not have problems with phonological awareness but with integrating this awareness with generating the ability to read (Ramus, 2014).

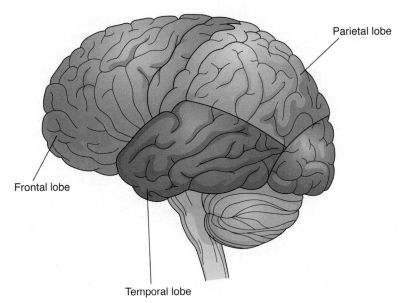

Figure 13.6 Areas of the brain implicated in dyslexia include parts of the frontal, parietal, and temporal lobes, at least for Western languages.

Future studies will need with be conducted to connect these recent fMRI studies with well-replicated neuropsychological studies revealing deficits in phonological awareness.

The fMRI studies discussed above involved participants in the United States who spoke English. A study examining Chinese children with dyslexia failed to find a problem with the temporoparietal area of the brain during reading tasks; instead, the left middle frontal gyrus showed less activation (Siok, Perfetti, Lin et al., 2004). The investigators speculate that the differences between the English and Chinese written languages may account for the different brain regions involved. Reading English requires putting together letters that represent sounds. Reading Chinese, in contrast, requires putting together symbols that represent meanings. Indeed, reading Chinese requires mastery of nearly 6000 different symbols. Thus, Chinese relies more on visual processing, while English relies more on sound processing.

Etiology of Dyscalculia There is evidence of some genetic influence on individual variations in math skills. In particular, the type of math disability that involves poor semantic memory is most likely to be heritable. Furthermore, the evidence suggests that any genes associated with dyscalculia are also associated with mathematics ability (Plomin & Kovas, 2005).

fMRI studies of people with dyscalculia suggest that areas of the parietal lobe are less active during tasks requiring mathematics. Specifically, an area called the intraparietal sulcus has been implicated in dyscalculia (Wilson & Dehane, 2007).

Researchers have investigated whether dyscalculia might be linked to dyslexia in terms of the cognitive deficits that are associated with both of these types of specific learning disorders. That is, children who have problems with phonological awareness might have problems not only with reading but also with the symbols and numbers in mathematics. The evidence suggests, however, that these two learning disorders are somewhat independent (Jordan, 2007). Children with both dyslexia and dyscalculia have deficits in phonological awareness, but children with only dyscalculia do not. Children with dyscalculia have trouble with tasks requiring manipulation of numbers, whether with actual numbers or with the use of calculations, as in estimating size, but children with dyslexia do not (Landerl et al., 2009).

Treatment of Specific Learning Disorder

Several strategies are used to treat specific learning disorder, both in school programs and in private tutoring. Traditional linguistic approaches, used primarily in cases of reading and writing difficulties, focus on instruction in listening, speaking, reading, and writing skills in a logi-

Interventions for dyslexia have improved children's reading.

cal, sequential, and multisensory manner, such as reading out loud under close supervision. In young children, readiness skills, such as letter discrimination, phonetic analysis, and learning letter–sound correspondences, may need to be taught before explicit instruction in reading is attempted. Phonics instruction involves helping children master the task of converting sounds to words. Findings from the National Reading Panel, a comprehensive review of the research on teaching children to read, indicate that phonics instruction is beneficial for children with reading difficulties (National Institute of Child Health and Human Development, 2000). As in the Clinical Case of Marcus described earlier, people with dyslexia can often succeed in college with the aid of instructional supports, such as podcast or webcast lectures that can be re-reviewed, tutors, and untimed tests. Colleges are required by law to provide special services to help such students, and public schools are now required to provide transitional vocational and career planning for older adolescents with learning disorders.

Despite early promise in uncontrolled trials (Tallal, Miller, Bedi et al., 1996) a commercially available computer-based learning treatment called Fast ForWord does not appear to be effective in improving speech, language, and auditory processing skills. A meta-analysis of six randomized controlled trials found that Fast ForWord was not effective (Strong, Torgerson, Torgerson et al., 2011).

Intellectual Disability

In DSM-IV-TR, mental retardation was the name of the disorder that was renamed **intellectual disabilty** in DSM-5. Why the change? After all, many people are familiar with the term *mental retardation*. However, this is not the term that most mental health professionals use or prefer, perhaps due to the stigma associated with this older term. Most mental health professionals follow the guidelines of the American Association on Intellectual and Developmental Disabilities (AAIDD).

The AAIDD is an organization whose mission is to "promote progressive policies, sound research, effective practices, and universal human rights for people with intellectual and developmental disabilities" (www.aaidd.org). This group changed its own name in 2006 (it was formerly known as the American Association of Mental Retardation) in large part to acknowledge that *intellectual disability* is now the preferred term over *mental retardation* (Schalock, Luckasson, & Shogren, 2007). The current AAIDD guidelines are summarized in Table 13.3.

Diagnosis and Assessment of Intellectual Disability

The DSM-5 diagnostic criteria for intellectual disability include three criteria: (1) deficits in intellectual functioning, (2) deficits in adaptive functioning, and (3) an onset during development (i.e., as a child).

DSM-5 Criteria for Intellectual Disability

- Intellectual deficits (e.g., in solving problems, reasoning, abstract thinking) determined by intelligence testing and broader clinical assessment
- Significant deficits in adaptive functioning relative to the person's age and cultural group in one or more of the following areas: communication, social participation, work or school, independence at home or in the community, requiring the need for support at school, work, or independent life
- Onset during child development

Table 13.3 The AAIDD Definition of Intellectual Disability

Intellectual disability is characterized by significant limitations both in intellectual functioning and in adaptive behavior as expressed in conceptual, social, and practical adaptive skills.

This disability begins before age 18.

Five Assumptions Essential to the Application of the Definition

1. Limitations in present functioning must be considered within the context of community environments typical of the individual's age, peers, and culture.
2. Valid assessment considers cultural and linguistic diversity as well as differences in communication, sensory, motor, and behavioral factors.
3. Within an individual, limitations often coexist with strengths.
4. An important purpose of describing limitations is to develop a profile of needed supports.
5. With appropriate personalized supports over a sustained period, the life functioning of the person with intellectual disability generally will improve.

Source: © 2002 American Association on Intellectual and Developmental Disabilities, from http://aaidd.org/publications/bookstore-home/product-listing/2013/06/24/intellectual-disability-definition-classification-and-systems-of-supports-(11th-edition)#.U-KIA4BdXsQ

The first two criteria make the DSM-5 consistent with the approach of the AAIDD. First, there is explicit recognition that an IQ score must be considered within the context of a more thorough assessment. Second, adaptive functioning must be assessed across a broad range of domains. Finally, the DSM-5 no longer distinguishes among mild, moderate, and severe intellectual disability based on IQ scores alone, as was done in DSM-IV-TR. The severity of intellectual disability is assessed in three domains: conceptual (which includes intellectual and other cognitive functioning), social, and practical.

The AAIDD approach encourages the identification of an individual's strengths and weaknesses on psychological, physical, and environmental dimensions with a view toward determining the kinds and degrees of support needed to enhance the person's functioning in different domains. Consider Roger, a 24-year-old man with an IQ of 45 who has attended a special program for people with intellectual disability since he was 6. The AAIDD approach would emphasize what is needed to maximize Roger's functioning. Thus, a clinician might discover that Roger can use the bus system if he takes a route familiar to him, and thus he might be able to go to a movie by himself from time to time. And although he cannot prepare complicated meals, he might be able to learn to prepare frozen entrées in a microwave oven. The assumption is that by building on what he can do, Roger will make more progress. We hope that the DSM-5 approach will also work like this.

In the schools, an individualized educational program (IEP) is based on the person's strengths and weaknesses and on the amount of instruction needed. Students are identified by the classroom environment they are judged to need. This approach can lessen the stigmatizing effects of having intellectual disability and may also encourage a focus on what can be done to improve the student's learning.

When assessing adaptive behavior, the cultural environment must be considered. A person living in a rural community may not need the same skills as those needed by someone living in New York City, and vice versa.

Etiology of Intellectual Disability

At this time, the primary cause of intellectual disability can be identified in only 25 percent of the people affected. The causes that can be identified are typically neurobiological.

Genetic or Chromosomal Abnormalities

One chromosomal abnormality that has been linked with intellectual disability is *trisomy 21*, which refers to having an extra copy (i.e., three instead of two) of chromosome 21. This is also known as **Down syndrome**. It has been estimated that it occurs in about 1 out of every 850 live births in the United States (Shin, Besser, Kucik et al., 2009).

People with Down syndrome may have intellectual disability as well as some distinctive physical signs, such as short and stocky stature; oval, upward-slanting eyes; a prolongation of the fold of the upper eyelid over the inner corner of the eye; sparse, fine, straight hair; a wide and flat nasal bridge; square-shaped ears; a large, furrowed tongue, which may protrude because the mouth is small and its roof low; and short, broad hands.

Another chromosomal abnormality that can cause intellectual disability is **fragile X syndrome**, which involves a mutation in the *fMR1* gene on the X chromosome (National Fragile X Foundation: www.fragilex.org). Physical symptoms associated with fragile X include large, underdeveloped ears and a long, thin face. Many people with fragile X syndrome have intellectual disability. Others may not have intellectual disability but may have a specific learning disorder, difficulties on neuropsychological tests, and mood swings. About a third of children

Child with Down syndrome.

with fragile X syndrome also exhibit autism spectrum behaviors, suggesting that the *fMR1* gene may be one of the many genes that contribute to autism (Hagerman, 2006).

Recessive-Gene Diseases Several hundred recessive-gene diseases have been identified, and many of them can cause intellectual disability. Here we discuss one recessive-gene disease, phenylketonuria.

In **phenylketonuria (PKU),** the infant, born without obvious signs of difficulty, soon begins to suffer from a deficiency of a liver enzyme, phenylalanine hydroxylase. Because of this enzyme deficiency, phenylalanine and its derivative, phenylpyruvic acid, are not broken down and instead build up in the body's fluids. This buildup can damage the brain because the unmetabolized amino acid interferes with the process of myelination, the sheathing of neuron axons, which is essential for neuronal function. Myelination supports the rapid transmittal of neuronal impulses. If not properly treated, intellectual disabilities can be profound.

Although PKU is rare, with an incidence of about 1 in 15,000 live births, it is estimated that 1 person in 70 is a carrier of the recessive gene. A blood test is available for prospective parents who have reason to suspect that they might be carriers. Pregnant women who carry the recessive gene must monitor their diet closely so that the fetus will not be exposed to toxic levels of phenylalanine. State laws require testing newborns for PKU. If the test is positive, the parents are taught to provide the infant a diet low in phenylalanine.

Parents are encouraged to introduce the special diet as early as possible and to maintain it indefinitely. Studies have indicated that children whose dietary restrictions stop at age 5–7 begin to show subtle declines in functioning, particularly in IQ, reading, and spelling (Fishler, Azen, Henderson et al., 1987). Even among children with PKU who maintain the diet, however, deficits in perceptual, memory, and attentional abilities have been observed (Banich , Passarotti, White et al., 2000; Huijbregts, de Sonneville, Licht et al., 2002).

Infectious Diseases While in utero the fetus is at increased risk of intellectual disabilities resulting from maternal infectious diseases, such as rubella, cytomegalovirus, toxoplasmosis,

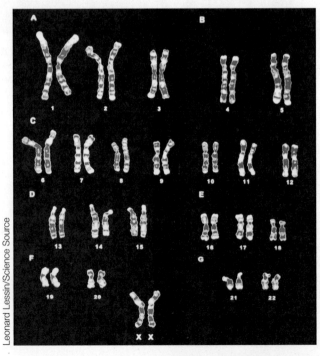
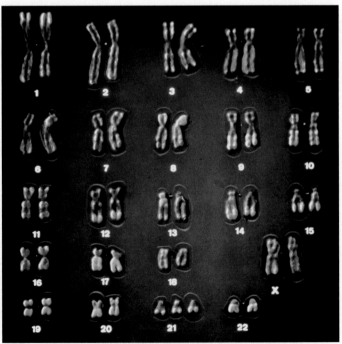

The normal complement of chromosomes is 23 pairs (figure on the left). In Down syndrome, there are three copies (a trisomy) of chromosome 21 (figure on the right).

herpes simplex, and HIV. The consequences of these diseases are most serious during the first trimester of pregnancy, when the fetus has no detectable immunological response, that is, its immune system is not developed enough to ward off infection. The mother may experience slight or no symptoms from the infection, but the effects on the developing fetus can be devastating.

Infectious diseases can also affect a child's developing brain after birth. Encephalitis and meningococcal meningitis may cause brain damage and even death if contracted in infancy or early childhood. In adulthood, these infections are usually far less serious. There are several forms of childhood meningitis, a disease in which the protective membranes of the brain are acutely inflamed and fever is very high.

Environmental Hazards   Several environmental pollutants are implicated in intellectual disability. One such pollutant is mercury, which may be ingested by eating affected fish. Another is lead, which is found in lead-based paints, smog, and the exhaust from automobiles that burn leaded gasoline. Lead poisoning can cause kidney and brain damage as well as anemia, intellectual disabilities, seizures, and death. Lead-based paint is now prohibited in the United States, but it is still found in older homes, where children may eat pieces that flake off.

Treatment of Intellectual Disability

Residential Treatment   Since the 1960s, serious and systematic attempts have been made to educate children with intellectual disability as fully as possible. Although many people can acquire the competence needed to function effectively in the community, some people need the extra support of a residential treatment program.

Ideally, adults with intellectual disability in need of such support live in small to medium-sized residences that are integrated into the community. Medical care is provided, and trained, live-in supervisors and aides help with residents' special needs around the clock. Residents are encouraged to participate in household routines to the best of their abilities. Many adults with intellectual disability have jobs and are able to live independently in their own apartments. Others live semi-independently in apartments housing three to four adults; generally, a counselor provides aid in the evening.

Behavioral Treatments   Early-intervention programs using behavioral techniques have been developed to improve the level of functioning of people with intellectual disability. Specific behavioral objectives are defined, and children are taught skills in small, sequential steps (Reid, Wilson, & Faw, 1991).

To teach a child a particular routine, the therapist usually begins by dividing the targeted behavior, such as eating, into smaller components: pick up spoon, scoop food from plate onto spoon, bring spoon to mouth, remove food with lips, chew, and swallow food. Operant conditioning principles are then applied to teach the child these components of eating. For example, the child may be reinforced for successive approximations to picking up the spoon until he or she is able to do so. This operant approach, sometimes called *applied behavior analysis*, is also used to reduce inappropriate and self-injurious behavior. Reinforcing substitute behaviors can often reduce these behaviors.

Cognitive Treatments   Many children with intellectual disability have difficulty using strategies in solving problems, and when they do use strategies, they often do not use them effectively. Self-instructional training teaches these children to guide their problem-solving efforts through speech.

For example, one group of researchers taught high school students with intellectual disability to make their own buttered toast and clean up after themselves (Hughes, Hugo, & Blatt, 1996). A teacher would demonstrate and verbalize the steps involved in solving a problem, such as the toaster's being upside down or unplugged. The young people learned to talk themselves through the steps using simple verbal or signed instructions. For example, when the toaster was presented upside down, the person would be taught to first state the problem ("Won't go in"), then to state the response ("Turn it"), self-evaluate ("Fixed it"), and

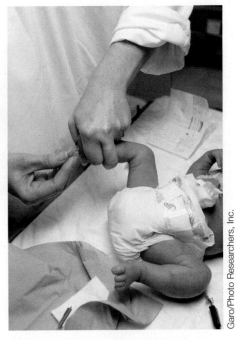

States require that newborns be tested for PKU. If excess phenylalanine is found in the blood, a special diet is recommended for the baby.

Although lead-based paint is now illegal, it can still be found in older homes. Eating these paint chips can cause lead poisoning, which can cause intellectual disability.

Robin Nelson/PhotoEdit

Computer-assisted instruction is well suited for applications in the treatment of intellectual disabiity.

self-reinforce ("Good"). They were rewarded with praise and high-fives when they verbalized and solved the problem correctly. Several studies have demonstrated that even people with severe intellectual disability can learn self-instructional approaches to problem solving and then generalize the strategy to new tasks, including taking lunch orders at a cafeteria and performing janitorial duties (Hughes & Agran, 1993).

Computer-Assisted Instruction Computer-assisted instruction is increasingly found in educational and treatment settings of all kinds; it may be especially well suited to the education of people with intellectual disability. The visual and auditory components of computers can help to maintain the attention of distractible students; the level of the material can be geared to the individual, ensuring successful experiences; and the computer can meet the need for numerous repetitions of material without becoming bored or impatient, as a human teacher might. For example, computers have been used to help people with intellectual disability learn to use an ATM (Davies, Stock, & Wehmeyer, 2003). Smartphones can be enormously helpful by serving as aids for reminders, directions, instructions, and daily tasks.

Quick Summary

Mental health professionals often refer to specific learning disorders, communication disorders, and motor disorders as learning disabilities, Children with dyslexia have significant difficulty with word recognition, reading comprehension, and, typically, written spelling as well. Research has uncovered how the brain is involved in dyslexia, particularly areas of the brain that support language, including the temporoparietal and occipitotemporal areas. However, important cultural differences have been noted, suggesting that there may not be one universal mechanism to account for dyslexia. Interventions for dyslexia involve intensive work on reading and language skills.

The DSM-5 uses the term *intellectual disability* rather than *mental retardation* and emphasizes the importance of assessing intellectual ability and adaptive functioning within a person's cultural group, consistent with the approach of the AAIDD. Categories based on IQ scores will no longer be used. Instead, like the AAIDD, the DSM-5 stresses the importance of identifying an individual's strengths and weaknesses. There are a number of known causes of intellectual disability, including genetic abnormalities, infections, and toxins.

Check Your Knowledge 13.3

Answer the questions.

1. Which of the following is *not* considered a learning disability?
   a. dyscalculia
   b. dyslexia
   c. intellectual disability
   d. developmental coordination disorder
2. A study examining children with dyslexia who spoke either Chinese or English found:
   a. The left middle frontal gyrus showed less activation during reading among Chinese-speaking children with dyslexia.
   b. The left temporoparietal cortex showed less activation during reading among Chinese-speaking children with dyslexia.
   c. The left middle frontal gyrus showed less activation during reading among English-speaking children with dyslexia.

   d. The left temporoparietal cortex showed more activation during reading among English-speaking children with dyslexia.
3. Which of the following has not been established as a cause for intellectual disability?
   a. chromosomal abnormalities such as trisomy 21
   b. PKU
   c. lead poisoning
   d. All the above have been found to cause intellectual disability.
4. Which of the following has been studied as possible causes for dyscalculia?
   a. gene–environment interactions
   b. the frontal lobes of the brain
   c. dyslexia
   d. All the above have been found to cause dyscalculia.

Autism Spectrum Disorder

Although autism was first described about 70 years ago (see Focus on Discovery 13.4 for the history of autism), it was not formally included in the DSM until the third edition, published in 1980. As discussed in Focus on Discovery 13.3, the rates of autism spectrum disorder have been rising over the past 20 years. With this increase in prevalence has come an increase in research on the causes of this disorder.

Clinical Descriptions, Prevalence, and Prognosis of Autism Spectrum Disorder

In DSM-5, four diagnostic categories from DSM-IV-TR—autistic disorder, Asperger's disorder, pervasive developmental disorder not otherwise specified, and childhood disintegrative disorder—were combined into one category called **autism spectrum disorder.** Why the change? Research conducted on the different DSM-IV-TR categories did not support the distinct categories. In other words, these disorders all share similar clinical features and etiologies and seem to vary only in severity. Thus, DSM-5 has one disorder category, autism spectrum disorder (ASD), which includes different clinical specifiers relating to severity and the extent of language impairment.

The DSM-5 criteria for ASD are presented in the nearby box. In the next sections, we describe the clinical features, focusing on problems in social and emotional interactions and in communication as well as on repetitive or ritualistic behaviors.

Social and Emotional Disturbances   Children with ASD can have profound problems with the social world (Dawson, Toth, Abbott et al., 2004). They may rarely approach others and may look through or past people or turn their backs on them. For example, one study found that children with ASD rarely offered a spontaneous greeting or farewell (either verbally or through smiling, making eye contact, or gesturing) when meeting or departing from an adult (Hobson & Lee, 1998). Few children with ASD initiate play with other children, and they are usually unresponsive to anyone who approaches them.

FOCUS ON DISCOVERY 13.4

A Brief History of Autism Spectrum Disorder

Autism was identified in 1943 by a psychiatrist at Johns Hopkins, Leo Kanner, who, in the course of his clinical work, noted 11 disturbed children who behaved in ways that were not common in children with intellectual disability or schizophrenia. He named the syndrome *early infantile autism* because he observed that "there is from the start an extreme autistic aloneness that, whenever possible, disregards, ignores, shuts out anything that comes to the child from the outside" (Kanner, 1943).

Kanner considered autistic aloneness to be the most fundamental symptom. He also learned that these 11 children had been unable from the beginning of life to relate to people in the ordinary way. They were severely limited in language and had a strong, obsessive desire for everything about them to remain unchanged. Despite its early description by Kanner and others (Rimland, 1964), the disorder was not accepted into official diagnostic nomenclature until the publication of DSM-III in 1980, where it was called autistic disorder.

Asperger's disorder was named after Hans Asperger, who in 1944 described the syndrome as being less severe and having fewer communication deficits than autism. It was first introduced to the DSM in 1994 in DSM-IV. Social relationships are poor and stereotyped behavior is intense and rigid, but language and intelligence are intact. Because research suggests that Asperger's disorder does not differ qualitatively from autistic disorder, these two categories will likely be combined in DSM-5. Nevertheless, more research has been conducted in the last 10 years on Asperger's disorder, perhaps due to the recognition of this condition among adults who for years wondered why they were different from others. Adults with the DSM-IV-TR diagnosis Asperger's disorder are now more frequently recognized and treated by mental health professionals (Gaus, 2007).

People formerly in the Asperger's disorder category but now under the broader domain of ASD will likely continue to seek and receive the support and help they need. Researchers, clinicians, and families have referred to the "autism spectrum" for years, so, in some ways, this change might not be so difficult to accommodate, at least in terms of the name. However, some worry that the stigma associated with the name *autism* might keep people from seeking help (see Focus on Discovery 3.3 on the underreporting of stigmatized behavior). On the other hand, some states, such as California and Texas, mandate services for children with autism but not Asperger's, and thus more people might get help.

Circe Hamilton/Camera Press/Redux

Heather Kuzmich, a finalist on the television show *America's Next Top Model,* has what was called Asperger's disorder in DSM-IV-TR but is called autism spectrum disorder in DSM-5.

Children with ASD sometimes make eye contact, but their gaze may have an unusual quality. Typically, children gaze to gain someone's attention or to direct the other person's attention to an object; children with ASD generally do not (Dawson et al., 2004). This is often referred to as a problem in **joint attention**. That is, interactions that require two people to pay attention to each other, whether speaking or communicating emotion nonverbally, are impaired in children with autism.

More fine-grained analyses of gaze involve measuring eye movements and looking time. In one study, 6-month old infants later diagnosed with ASD spent less time looking at videos of dynamic speaking faces, particularly in the eyes and mouth regions, compared to typically developing children (Shic, Macari, & Chawarska, 2014). A different study measured the eye movements of infants several different times between the ages of 2 months and 24 months (Jones & Klin, 2013). At 2 months, the eye movements of infants who later were diagnosed with ASD did not differ from typically developing infants, suggesting that children with ASD are not born with gaze deficits. However, between 2 months and 24 months, the pattern of gaze between the two groups of infants began to diverge. Overall, the time spent looking at faces declined in the group of infants with ASD, so much so that by 2 years of age, these children were looking at the faces 50 percent less than children without ASD. Infants who showed a faster decline in looking time, particularly in the eyes region, were the ones who later had more social deficits.

Consistent with the findings showing that children with ASD spend less time looking at other people's faces, fMRI studies have found that people with ASD do not show activation in the fusiform gyrus, other regions in the temporal lobes, and the amygdala, the areas of the brain most often associated with identifying faces and emotion, when completing face perception or identity tasks (Critchley, Daly, Bullmore et al., 2001; Pierce, Haist, Sedaghadt et al., 2004; Pierce, Muller, Ambrose et al., 2001). Instead, other areas of the brain show activation during these tasks, suggesting perhaps a less efficient system for identifying faces.

Some researchers have proposed that children with ASD have a deficient "theory of mind" that is at the core of the kinds of social dysfunctions we have described here (Gopnik, Capps, & Meltzoff, 2000; Sigman, 1994). *Theory of mind* refers to a person's understanding that other people have desires, beliefs, intentions, and emotions that may be different from one's

⬤ DSM-5 Criteria for Autism Spectrum Disorder

A. Deficits in social communication and social interactions as exhibited by the following:

- Deficits in social or emotional reciprocity such as not approaching others, not having a back-and-forth conversation, reduced sharing of interests and emotions
- Deficits in nonverbal behaviors such as eye contact, facial expression, body language
- Deficit in development of peer relationships appropriate to developmental level
B. Restricted, repetitive behavior patterns, interests, or activities exhibited by at least two of the following:
- Stereotyped or repetitive speech, motor movements, or use of objects
- Excessive adherence to routines, rituals in verbal or nonverbal behavior, or extreme resistance to change
- Very restricted interests that are abnormal in focus, such as preoccupation with parts of objects
- Hyper- or hyporeactivity to sensory input or unusual interest in sensory environment, such as fascination with lights or spinning objects
C. Onset in early childhood
D. Symptoms limit and impair functioning

own. This ability is crucial for understanding and successfully engaging in social interactions. Theory of mind typically develops between 2½ and 5 years of age. Children with ASD seem not to undergo this developmental milestone and thus seem unable to understand others' perspectives and emotional reactions.

Although some children with ASD can learn to understand emotional experiences, they "answer questions about . . . emotional experiences like normal children answer difficult arithmetic questions" (Sigman, 1994, p. 151), with concentrated effort. Laboratory studies of children with ASD have found that they may recognize others' emotions without really understanding them (Capps , Rasco, Losh et al., 1999; Capps, Yirmiya, & Sigman, 1992). For example, when asked to explain why someone was angry, a child with ASD responded "because he was yelling" (Capps, Losh, & Thurber, 2000).

Communication Deficits   Even before they acquire language, some children with ASD show deficits in communication. Babbling, a term describing the utterances of infants before they begin to use words, is less frequent in infants with ASD and conveys less information than it does in other infants (Ricks, 1972). By 2 years of age, most typically developing children use words to represent objects in their surroundings and construct one- and two-word sentences to express more complex thoughts, such as "Mommy go" or "Me juice." In contrast, children with ASD lag well behind in these abilities and often show other language disturbances.

One such feature associated with ASD is echolalia, in which the child echoes, usually with remarkable fidelity, what he or she has heard another person say. The teacher may ask a child with ASD, "Do you want a cookie?" The child's response may be, "Do you want a cookie?" This is immediate echolalia. In delayed echolalia, the child may be in a room with the television on and appear to be completely uninterested. Several hours later or even the next day, the child may echo a word or phrase from the television program.

Another language abnormality common in the speech of children with ASD is **pronoun reversal**, in which children refer to themselves as "he," "she," or "you" (or even by their own name). For example:

> *Parent: What are you doing, Johnny?*
> *Child: He's here.*
> *Parent: Are you having a good time?*
> *Child: He knows it.*

Pronoun reversal is closely linked to echolalia—when children with ASD use echolalic speech, they refer to themselves as they have heard others speak of them and misapply pronouns. Children with ASD are very literal in their use of words. If a father provided positive reinforcement by putting his daughter on his shoulders when she learned to say the word *yes*, then the child might say *yes* to mean she wants to be lifted onto her father's shoulders. Or a child may say "do not drop the cat" to mean "no," because a parent had used these emphatic words when the child was about to drop the family feline.

Repetitive and Ritualistic Acts   Children with ASD can become extremely upset over changes in their daily routines and surroundings. An offer of milk in a different drinking cup or a rearrangement of furniture may make them cry or may precipitate a temper tantrum.

An obsessional quality may pervade the behavior of children with ASD. In their play, they may continually line up toys or construct intricate patterns with household objects. As they grow older, they may become preoccupied with train schedules, subway routes, and number sequences. Children with ASD are also likely to perform a more limited number of behaviors than children without ASD and are less likely to explore new surroundings.

Children with ASD may also display stereotypical behavior, peculiar ritualistic hand movements, and other rhythmic movements, such as endless body rocking, hand flapping, and walking on tiptoe. They may spin and twirl string, crayons, sticks, and plates, twiddle their fingers in front of their eyes, and stare at fans and

Ruth Jenkinson/Getty Images

Children with ASD do not often play or socially interact with other children.

other spinning things. Researchers often describe these as self-stimulatory activities. The children may become preoccupied with manipulating an object and may become very upset when interrupted.

Some children with ASD can become preoccupied with and form strong attachments to simple inanimate objects (e.g., keys, rocks, a wire-mesh basket, light switches, a large blanket) and to more complex mechanical objects (e.g., refrigerators and vacuum cleaners). If the object is something they can carry, they may walk around with it in their hands, and this may interfere with their learning to do more useful things.

Comorbidity and ASD Many children with ASD also have intellectual disability. However, sensorimotor development is the area of greatest relative strength among these children. These children, who may show severe and profound deficits in cognitive abilities, can be quite graceful and adept at swinging, climbing, or balancing, whereas children with intellectual disability have far more difficulty in areas of gross motor development, such as learning to walk. Sometimes children with ASD may have isolated skills that reflect great talent, such as the ability to multiply two four-digit numbers rapidly in their heads. They may also have exceptional long-term memory, being able to recall the exact words of a song heard years earlier.

One study found that over a third of the children with ASD also have a specific learning disorder (Lichtenstein, Carlstrom, Ramstam et al., 2010). In addition, ASD is also frequently comorbid with anxiety, including separation anxiety, social anxiety, general anxiety, and specific phobias (White, Oswald, Ollendick et al., 2009).

Prevalence of Autism Spectrum Disorder ASD begins in early childhood and can be evident in the first months of life. It affects about 1 of every 68 children (CDC, 2014). About five times more boys than girls have ASD (CDC, 2014). There has been a large increase in the number of ASD diagnoses over the past 25 years (see Focus on Discovery 13.3 for more on this). It is found in all socioeconomic, ethnic, and racial groups. The diagnosis of ASD is remarkably stable. In one study, only 1 out of 84 children diagnosed with ASD at age 2 no longer met the diagnostic criteria at age 9 (Lord, Risi, DiLavore et al., 2006).

Prognosis for Autism Spectrum Disorder What happens to children with ASD when they reach adulthood? Generally, children with higher IQs who learn to speak before age 6 have the best outcomes. For example, one longitudinal study of children with ASD from preschool to early adulthood found that IQs over 70 predicted more strengths and fewer weaknesses in adaptive functioning as they grew older (McGovern & Sigman, 2005), and outcomes were better for those who had interacted and engaged more with their peers. Other studies of people with ASD who have higher IQ scores have indicated that most do not require residential care and some are able to attend college and support themselves through employment (Yirmiya & Sigman, 1991). Still, many independently functioning adults with ASD continue to show impairment in social relationships (Howlin, Goode, Hutton et al., 2004; Howlin, Mawhood, & Rutter, 2000). Focus on Discovery 13.5 describes a woman with ASD whose adult life is remarkable for its professional distinction blended with the social and emotional deficits that are part of ASD.

Etiology of Autism Spectrum Disorder

The earliest theory about the etiology of ASD was that psychological factors such as bad parenting were responsible for its development. This narrow and faulty perspective has been replaced by theories based on evidence that genetic and neurological factors are important in the etiology. Despite the lack of empirical support for early psychological theories, they gained enough recognition to place a tremendous emotional burden on parents who were told that they were at fault for their child's ASD.

Genetic Factors Evidence suggests a genetic component for ASD, with heritability estimates of around .80 (Lichtenstein et al., 2010; Sullivan et al., 2012). The risk of ASD or

People with ASD may engage in stereotyped behavior, such as ritualistic hand movements.

language delay among siblings of people with the disorder is much higher than it is among siblings of people who do not have ASD (Constantino, Zhang, Frazier et al., 2010). Evidence for genetic transmission of ASD comes from twin studies, which have found between 47 and 90 percent concordance for ASD between identical twins, compared with concordance rates of 0 to 20 percent between fraternal twins (Bailey, LeCouteur, Gottesman et al., 1995; Le Couteur, Bailey, Goode et al., 1996; Lichtenstein et al., 2010).

Even though genes play a big role in ASD, remember that genes do their work via the environment. Another twin study used the most current and well-validated method for diagnosing ASD rather than relying solely on medical records or parental reports as other studies have done. This study found that shared environmental factors (e.g., common experiences in a family; see Chapter 2) accounted for over half of the risk for developed autism (Hallmayer, Cleveland, Torres et al., 2011).

Studies of twins and families with a member with ASD suggest that ASD is linked genetically to a broader spectrum of deficits in communication and social interaction. In families where more than one child had ASD or language delay, unaffected siblings also exhibited deficits in social communication and interactions (Constantino et al., 2010).

Molecular genetics studies try to pinpoint areas of the genome that may confer risk for ASD. Recall from Chapter 2 that genome-wide association studies (GWAS) look for differences in gene sequence (single nucleotide polymorphisms—SNPs) and gene structure (copy number variations—CNVs). One research group studying CNVs found that a deletion on chromosome 16 was associated with ASD in three different samples (Weiss, Shen, Korn et al., 2008). The deletion represents a genetic flaw—it was not supposed to be deleted—and the researchers suggest that, although it is not clear why the flaw occurs, it is nonetheless associated with an increased risk of developing ASD. Other GWAS studies have identified SNPs between two genes on chromosome 5 that have been replicated in two independent samples of people with ASD (Wang, Zhang, Ma et al., 2009) and one sample of people without ASD but who had communication and social-emotional difficulties (St. Pourcain, Wang, Glessner et al., 2010).

Neurobiological Factors   More and more research is linking the language, social, and emotional deficits in ASD to the brain. A number of studies examining the brain in ASD have been well replicated, allowing for a clearer picture of what may go wrong in the brain among people with ASD. What remains to be figured out is why the brain goes awry early in development.

Studies using magnetic resonance imaging (MRI) found that, overall, the brains of adults and children with ASD are larger than the brains of adults and children without ASD (Courchesne, Carnes, & Davis, 2001; Piven, Arndt, Bailey et al., 1995, 1996). This same finding has been supported by studies using the measurement of head circumference as an indicator of brain size (Courchesne, Carper, & Akshoomoff, 2003), but studies using this measure don't always find support for larger brain size in ASD (Raznahan, Wallace, Antezana et al., 2013). What makes these findings more interesting and puzzling is that most children with ASD are born with brains of a relatively normal size; however, between the ages of 2 and 4, the brains of children with ASD become significantly larger (Courchesne, 2004). One longitudinal study assessed brain size using MRI when children with and without autism were 2 years old and again when they were 4 or 5 years old. The researchers found that the children with autism had larger brain size at age 2 but that it did not continue to increase at ages 4 or 5, thus suggesting that brain growth does not continue past the first few years of life (Hazlett, Poe, Gerig et al., 2011).

Having a larger-than-normal brain is not necessarily a good thing, as it might indicate that neurons are not being pruned correctly. The pruning of neurons is an important part of brain maturation; older children have fewer connections between neurons than do babies. Adding further to this puzzle, brain growth in ASD appears to slow abnormally in later childhood. We do not yet know how this pattern of brain growth is linked to the signs and symptoms of ASD. It is worth noting that the areas of the brain that are "overgrown" in ASD include the frontal, temporal, and cerebellar, which have been linked with language, social, and emotional functions.

FOCUS ON DISCOVERY 13.5

The Story of a Woman Living with Autism Spectrum Disorder

Temple Grandin is a woman with autism spectrum disorder. She also has a Ph.D. in animal science, runs her own business designing machinery for use with farm animals, and is on the faculty at Colorado State University. Four autobiographical books (Grandin 1986, 1995, 2008, 2013) and a profile by neurologist Oliver Sacks (1995) provide a moving and revealing portrait of the mysteries of ASD. A highly acclaimed and awarded HBO movie based on Grandin's 1995 book *Thinking in Pictures* was released in 2010 and starred Clare Danes as Temple. Grandin has also written other books about her professional work with animals.

Lacking understanding of the complexities and subtleties of human social discourse, and deficient in the ability to empathize with others, Grandin sums up her relationship to the nonautistic world by saying, "Much of the time I feel like an anthropologist on Mars" (Sacks, 1995, p. 259).

Grandin was diagnosed with autism in 1950 at age 3. She had no speech at all, and doctors predicted that institutionalization would be her fate. However, with the help of a therapeutic nursery school, speech therapy, and the support of her family, she learned to speak by age 6 and began to make more contact with others. Still, as an adolescent observing other children interact, Grandin "sometimes wondered if they were all telepathic" (Sacks, 1995, p. 272), so mysterious did she find the ability of normal children to understand each other's needs and wishes, to empathize, to communicate.

In her own writings, Grandin points out that many people with ASD are great fans of *Star Trek*, especially the characters of Spock and Data, the former a member of the Vulcan race, purely intellectual, logical beings who eschew any consideration of the emotional side of life, and the latter an android, a highly sophisticated computer housed in a human body and, like Spock, lacking in emotion. (One of the dramatic themes involv-

ing both characters was, of course, their flirtation with the experience of human emotion, portrayed with particular poignancy by Data. This is a theme in Grandin's life as well.) As Grandin (1995) wrote at age 47:

All my life I have been an observer, and I have always felt like someone who watches from the outside. I could not participate in the social interactions of high school life.

Even today, personal relationships are something I don't really understand. I've remained celibate because doing so helps me avoid the many complicated situations that are too difficult for me to handle. [M]en who want to date often don't understand how to relate to a woman. They [and I myself] remind me of Data, the android on Star Trek. In one episode, Data's attempts at dating were a disaster. When he tried to be romantic [by effecting a change in a subroutine of his computer program], he complimented his date by using scientific terminology. Even very able adults with autism have such problems. (pp. 132–133)

Some of the difficulties of people with ASD make them charmingly honest and trustworthy. "Lying," wrote Grandin, "is very anxiety-provoking because it requires rapid interpretations of subtle social cues [of which I am incapable] to determine whether the other person is really being deceived" (Grandin, 1995, p. 135).

Grandin's professional career is impressive. She uses her remarkable powers of visualization and her empathy for farm animals to design machines such as a chute leading cows to slaughter that takes them on a circular route, protecting them from awareness of their fate until the moment of death. She has also designed and built a "squeeze machine," a device that provides comforting hugs without the need for human contact. It has "two heavy, slanting wooden sides, perhaps four by three feet each, pleasantly upholstered with a thick, soft padding. They [are]

Other areas of the brain are implicated in ASD as well. A meta-analysis of 46 studies found a large effect size for enlarged cerebellum (Stanfield, McIntosh, Spencer et al., 2008). Another study found that the commonly observed tendency of children with ASD to explore their surroundings less than other children do is correlated with a larger-than-normal cerebellum (Pierce & Courchesne, 2001).

Given that ASD is associated with social and emotional difficulties, and that the amygdalae are associated with social and emotional behavior, it stands to reason that the amygdalae might be involved in ASD. One study found that the amygdalae were larger among children with ASD (Munson, Dawson, Abbott et al., 2006) and that larger amygdalae at ages 3 or 4 predicted more difficulties in social behavior and communication at age 6. This finding is consistent with studies showing overgrowth of other brain areas. However, the other study found that *small* amygdalae size in ASD was correlated with difficulties in emotional face perception and less gaze in the eye region of faces during the perception task (Nacewicz, Dalton, Johnstone et al., 2006). How can we make sense of these seemingly different findings? Participants in the study by Nacewicz and colleagues were older, suggesting that the brain changes that continue throughout in development may be differentially related to social and emotional impairments. A later meta-analysis confirmed that amygdala size was related to age, with older age being associated with smaller amygdala size (Stanfield et al., 2008).

joined by hinges to a long, narrow bottom board to create a V-shaped, body-sized trough. There [is] a complex control box at one end, with heavy-duty tubes leading off to another device, in a closet. [An] industrial compressor exerts a firm but comfortable pressure on the body, from the shoulders to the knees" (Sacks, 1995, pp. 262–263). Her explanation of the rationale behind this contraption is that as a little girl she longed to be hugged but was also very fearful of physical contact with another person. When a favorite, large-bodied aunt hugged her, she felt both overwhelmed and comforted. Terror commingled with pleasure.

> She started to have daydreams—she was just five at the time—of a magic machine that could squeeze her powerfully but gently, in a huglike way, and in a way entirely commanded and controlled by her. Years later, as an adolescent, she had seen a picture of a squeeze chute designed to hold or restrain calves and realized that that was it: a little modification to make it suitable for human use, and it could be her magic machine. (Sacks, 1995, p. 263)

After watching her demonstrate the machine and trying it himself, Sacks observed:

> It is not just pleasure or relaxation that Temple gets from the machine but, she maintains, a feeling for others. As she lies in her machine, she says, her thoughts often turn to her mother, her favorite aunt, her teachers. She feels their love for her, and hers for them. She feels that the machine opens a door into an otherwise closed emotional world and allows her, almost teaches her, to feel empathy for others. (Sacks, 1995, p. 264)

Accounts such as those of Grandin and Sacks can provide insight into how people adapt to their own idiosyncrasies, using the sometimes peculiar gifts they have been given and working around the difficulties they experience. "Autism, while it may be pathologized as a syndrome, must also be seen as a whole mode of being, a deeply different mode or identity, one that needs to be conscious (and proud) of itself," wrote Sacks (1995, p. 277). "At a public lecture, Temple ended by saying, 'If I could snap my fingers and be nonautistic, I would not—because then I wouldn't be me. Autism is part of who I am'" (Sacks, 1995, p. 291).

This type of sentiment was emphasized in Grandin's most recent book (2013) where she stated that there are many things *right* with the autistic brain. In other words, some of the difficulties experienced by people with autism can actually be strengths. For example, one of the reasons that that social interactions are difficult for her to decipher is that it requires an integration of many things happening all at once (e.g., words, facial expressions, gestures, tone of voice). However, she is quite good at focusing on one thing at a time, and this means she is really good at paying attention to small details. She believes that this is why she has been so successful with animals; she is able to see a small detail that might scare an animal that other people would ignore.

JOHN EPPERSON/ASSOCIATED PRESS/AP/Wide World Photos

Temple Grandin, Ph.D., was diagnosed with autism in early childhood but has had a successful academic career.

Treatment of Autism Spectrum Disorder

Even though genetic and neurological factors in the etiology of ASD have much more empirical support than psychological factors, it is the psychological treatments that currently show the most promise, not medications. The lesson is that a neurological problem may well be treatable psychologically.

Treatments for children with ASD are usually aimed at reducing their unusual behavior and improving their communication and social skills. In most cases, the earlier the intervention begins, the better the outcome. In a promising longitudinal study, children at high risk for developing ASD (parent or sibling with an ASD) were studied beginning at age 14 months. Even though these children did not yet have language, the researchers were able to identify deficits in joint attention and communication that allowed for an early provisional diagnosis of ASD (Landa, Holman, & Garrett-Mayer, 2007).

Behavioral Treatment   In the late 1980s, Ivar Lovaas conducted an intensive operant conditioning–based program of behavioral treatment with young (under 4 years old) children with ASD (Lovaas, 1987). Therapy encompassed all aspects of the children's lives for more than 40 hours a week over more than 2 years. Parents were trained extensively so that treatment could continue during almost all the children's waking hours. Nineteen children

Ivar Lovaas, a behavior therapist, was noted for his operant conditioning treatment of children with autism.

receiving this intensive treatment were compared with 40 children who received a similar treatment for less than 10 hours per week. Both groups of children were rewarded for being less aggressive, more compliant, and more socially appropriate—for example, talking and playing with other children.

The results of this landmark study were dramatic and encouraging: a larger increase in IQ scores was shown for children in the intensive-therapy group in first grade (after about 2 years in the intensive therapy) compared to the other group. Furthermore, 9 of the 19 in the intensive-therapy group were promoted to second grade in a regular public school, whereas only 1 of the much larger group achieved this level of functioning. A follow-up of these children 4 years later indicated that the intensive-treatment group maintained their gains in IQ, adaptive behavior, and grade promotions in school (McEachin , Smith, & Lovaas, 1993). Although critics rightly pointed out weaknesses in the study's methodology and outcome measures (Schopler, Short, & Mesibov, 1989), this ambitious program demonstrated the benefits of intensive therapy with the heavy involvement of both professionals and parents in dealing with the challenges of ASD.

A randomized controlled clinical trial examined the efficacy of intensive behavioral treatment on a broader scale. This study compared an intensive behavioral treatment (about 25 hours a week, instead of 40) to a treatment that consisted of parent training only (Smith, Groen, & Wynn, 2000). Although the behavioral treatment was more effective than parent training alone, the children in this study did not show the same gains as in the study discussed above, perhaps because the treatment was implemented for fewer hours.

A meta-analysis of 22 studies using other types of intensive behavioral treatments, either in a clinic setting or with parents as the primary point of intervention, reported a number of noteworthy results. First, the average quality of these studies, rated on a 1 to 5 scale with 5 being the best, was only 2.5. Few were randomized clinical trials, and many had very small sample sizes. With these limitations in mind, the overall effect sizes were large for changes in IQ, language skills, overall communication, socialization, and daily living skills (Virués-Ortega, 2010). These results are encouraging, but it remains important to conduct more rigorous studies of these types of treatments.

Other interventions seek to improve children's problems in joint attention and communication. In a randomized controlled clinical trial, children ages 3 and 4 with ASD were randomly assigned to a joint attention (JA) intervention, a symbolic play (SP) intervention, or a control group (Kasari, Freeman, & Paparella, 2006). All children were already part of an early-intervention program; the JA and SP interventions were additional interventions provided to the children in 30-minute daily blocks for 6 weeks. Children in the JA and SP treatments showed more improvement than children in the control group, and at 6 and 12 months after the treatment, children in the JA and SP groups had greater expressive language skills than children in the control group (Kasari, Paparella, Freeman et al., 2008).

Drug Treatment Drug treatment of ASD is, at this point, less effective than behavioral treatment. The most commonly used medication for treating problem behaviors in children with ASD is haloperidol (trade name Haldol), an antipsychotic medication used in the treatment of schizophrenia. Some controlled studies have shown that this drug reduces social withdrawal, stereotyped motor behavior, and such maladaptive behaviors as self-mutilation and aggression (Anderson, Campbell, Adams et al., 1989; Perry, Campbell, Adams et al., 1989). Many children do not respond positively to the drug, however, and it has not shown any positive effects on other aspects of ASD, such as social functioning and language impairments (Holm & Varley, 1989). Haloperidol also has serious side effects (Posey & McDougle, 2000). In a longitudinal study, over 30 percent of children with ASD developed drug-related dyskinesias, or jerky muscle disturbances, although most such effects went away after the drug was withdrawn (Campbell, Armenteros, Malone et al., 1997).

Researchers have also studied naltrexone, an opioid receptor antagonist, and found that this drug reduces hyperactivity in children with ASD and produces a moderate improvement in the initiation of social interactions (Aman & Langworthy, 2000; Willemsen-Swinkels, Buitelaar et al., 1996; Williams, Allard, Spears et al., 2001). The drug does not appear to affect the core symptoms of ASD, and some evidence suggests that at some doses it may increase self-injurious behavior (Anderson, Hanson, Malecha et al., 1997).

Check Your Knowledge 13.4

True or false?
1. All children with ASD also have intellectual disability.
2. Children with ASD have difficulty recognizing emotions in others.

3. Medication is an effective treatment for ASD.

Summary

Clinical Descriptions

- Childhood disorders are often organized into two domains: externalizing disorders and internalizing disorders. Externalizing disorders are characterized by such behaviors as aggressiveness, noncompliance, overactivity, and impulsiveness; they include attention-deficit/hyperactivity disorder, conduct disorder, and oppositional defiant disorder. Internalizing disorders are characterized by such behaviors as depression, social withdrawal, and anxiety; they include childhood anxiety and mood disorders.

- Attention-deficit/hyperactivity disorder (ADHD) is a persistent pattern of inattention and/or hyperactivity and impulsivity that is more frequent and more severe than what is typically observed in children of a given age. Conduct disorder is characterized by high and widespread levels of aggression, lying, theft, vandalism, cruelty to other people and to animals, and other acts that violate laws and social norms.

- Mood and anxiety disorders in children share similarities with the adult forms of these disorders. However, differences that reflect different stages of development are also important.

- Learning disorders are diagnosed when a child fails to develop to the degree expected for his or her intellectual level in a specific academic, communication, or motor skill area. These disorders are often identified and treated within the school system rather than through mental health clinics. Phonological awareness appears to be a key deficit in dyslexia.

- The DSM-5 diagnostic criteria for intellectual disability include deficits in intellectual functioning and adaptive behavior, with onset during the course of development. Most professionals focus more on the strengths of people with intellectual disability. This shift in emphasis is associated with increased efforts to design psychological and educational interventions that make the most of individuals' abilities. The term *mental retardation* is no longer used in DSM-5.

- Autism spectrum disorder begins early in life, and the number of children with this diagnosis has risen in recent years. The major symptoms are a failure to relate to other people; communication problems, consisting of either a failure to learn any language or speech irregularities, such as echolalia and pronoun reversal; and theory of mind problems.

Etiology

- There is strong evidence for genetic and neurobiological factors in the etiology of ADHD. Low birth weight and maternal smoking are also risk factors. Family factors interact with these genetic vulnerabilities.

- Among the apparent etiological and risk factors for conduct disorder are genes, inadequate learning of moral awareness and social emotions, dysfunction in brain areas including amygdala and prefrontal cortex, and negative peer influences.

- Etiological factors for mood and anxiety disorders in children are believed to be largely the same as in adulthood, though additional research is needed.

- There is mounting evidence that dyslexia has genetic and other neurobiological components. fMRI studies point to different areas of the brain impacted in dyslexia and dyscalculia.

- Some forms of intellectual disability have a neurological basis, such as the chromosomal trisomy that causes Down syndrome. Certain infectious diseases in a pregnant mother, such as toxoplasmosis, HIV, and rubella, as well as illnesses that affect the child directly, such as encephalitis, can interfere with cognitive and social development. Environmental factors such as lead paint can also cause intellectual disability.

- Family, twin, and GWAS studies give compelling evidence for genetic factors in ASD. Abnormalities have been found in the brains of children with ASD, including an overgrowth of the brain by age 2 and abnormalities in the cerebellum.

Treatment

- A combined treatment including stimulant drugs, such as Adderall or Ritalin, and intensive behavioral treatment has shown effectiveness in reducing the symptoms of ADHD.

- The most promising approach to treating young people with conduct disorder involves intensive intervention in multiple systems, including the family, school, and peer systems. Preventive interventions like Fast Track also show promise.

- Cognitive behavior therapy is effective for mood and anxiety disorders. Medication is effective for depression among adolescents, though its use is not without controversy. Medication is also effective for anxiety when combined with cognitive behavior therapy.

- The most widespread interventions for dyslexia and dyscalculia are educational.

- Behavioral treatments and self-instructional training have been used to successfully treat many of the behavioral problems of people with intellectual disability and to improve their problem-solving skills.

- The most promising treatments for ASD are psychological, involving intensive behavioral interventions and work with parents. Various drug treatments have been used but have proved less effective than behavioral interventions.

Answers to Check Your Knowledge Questions

13.1 1. T; 2. T; 3. T; 4. F

13.2 1. life-course-persistent, adolescent-onset; 2. ADHD, substance abuse, depression, anxiety; 3. parent management training, multisystemic treatment.

13.3 1. c; 2. a; 3. d; 4. a

13.4 1. F; 2. T; 3. F

Key Terms

attention-deficit/hyperactivity disorder (ADHD)

autism spectrum disorder

childhood onset fluency disorder (stuttering)

communication disorders

conduct disorder

developmental psychopathology

Down syndrome

dyscalculia

dyslexia

externalizing disorders

fragile X syndrome

intellectual disability

internalizing disorders

joint attention

motor disorders

multisystemic treatment (MST)

parent management training (PMT)

phenylketonuria (PKU)

pronoun reversal

separation anxiety disorder

specific learning disorder

speech sound disorder

14 Late Life and Neurocognitive Disorders

LEARNING GOALS

1. Be able to differentiate common misconceptions from established findings about age-related changes.
2. Be able to discuss issues involved in conducting research on aging.
3. Be able to describe the prevalence of psychological disorders in the elderly and issues involved in estimating the prevalence.
4. Be able to explain the symptoms, etiology, and treatment of the major forms of dementia.
5. Be able to discuss the symptoms, causes, and treatment of delirium.

Clinical Case: Henry

Henry, a 56-year-old businessman, was hospitalized for cervical disk surgery. Because he was busy as well as anxious about the surgery, he had canceled two previous admissions. Henry drank heavily but did not appear to have problems from his drinking. Surgery went well, and in the first couple of days recovery seemed normal. The third night after his operation, though, Henry could not sleep and became restless. The next day he appeared severely fatigued. The next night his restlessness worsened, and he became fearful. Later that night, he thought that he saw people hiding in his room, and just before dawn, he thought he saw strange little animals running around the room. By morning rounds, the patient was very frightened, lethargic, and incoherent. He knew who he was and where he was but did not know the date, or how many days it had been since his surgery. During that day his mental status fluctuated, but by nightfall he had become grossly disoriented and agitated.

A psychiatric consultant diagnosed Henry with delirium, probably due to several factors: alcohol withdrawal, use of strong analgesics, and the stress of the operation. The treatment consisted of a reduction in pain medications, the presence of a family member at all times, and administration of 50 mg of chlorpromazine (Thorazine) three times daily and 500 mg of chloral hydrate at bedtime. Treatment reversed his confusion within 2 days, and he was able to return home in a week with no symptoms. (Strub & Black, 1981, pp. 89–90.)

I N THIS CHAPTER, we focus on psychological disorders in late life. The elderly are vulnerable to the neurocognitive disorders of dementia and delirium, and we consider these topics in detail. We begin by reviewing some general topics relevant to understanding late life. We describe common myths about aging, challenges faced by the elderly, and some remarkable strengths that come with growing older. Conducting research on psychological health and aging though, is complicated by a few key methodological issues, and we describe some of the ways these issues can influence findings. We discuss evidence that the prevalence of psychological disorders such as depression, anxiety, and substance abuse in the elderly is quite low. With this information as backdrop, we turn to dementia and delirium, the main topics of this chapter.

Aging: Issues and Methods

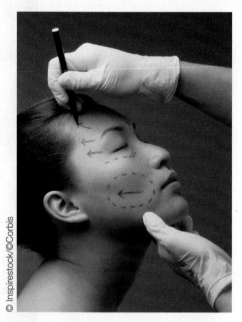

People spend billions of dollars per year on cosmetics and plastic surgery to reduce signs of aging.

As we age, physiological changes are inevitable, and there may be emotional and mental changes as well. Many of these changes will influence social interactions. The social problems of aging may be especially severe for women. Even with the consciousness-raising of the past decades, our society does not readily accept women with wrinkles and sagging bodies. Although men with gray hair at the temples are often seen as distinguished, signs of aging in women are not valued in the United States and many other countries. The cosmetics and plastic surgery industries make billions of dollars each year exploiting the fear inculcated in women about looking their age.[1] According to some experts, however, being female confers certain mental health benefits as people age.

The old are usually defined as those over the age of 65, an arbitrary point set largely by social policies rather than any physiological process. To have some rough demarcation points, gerontologists usually divide people over age 65 into three groups: the young-old, those aged 65 to 74; the old-old, those aged 75 to 84; and the oldest-old, those over age 85.

At the time of the last census, people 65 and older comprised 12.4 percent (35 million) of the U.S. population. Figure 14.1 shows the dramatic increase in the number of older

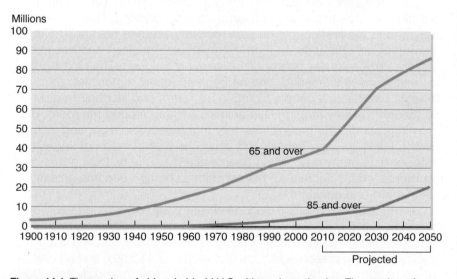

Figure 14.1 The number of old and old-old U.S. citizens is on the rise. The number of people age 65 and over, by decade of birth, 1900–2000, and projected, 2010–2050. From U.S. Census Bureau, Decennial Census and Projections.

[1]We should point out that increasing numbers of men are also undergoing plastic surgery and other treatments in an effort to look younger than their years.

Americans over time. As of 2009, there were 50,000 Americans at least 100 years old; by 2050, that number is expected to grow more than tenfold to over 800,000 (U.S. Bureau of the Census, 2010).

Given these statistics, it is not surprising that 69 percent of practicing psychologists conduct clinical work with older adults (Qualls, Segal, Norman et al., 2002). A major concern, though, is that fewer than 30 percent of psychologists report receiving any formal training about late-life issues (Qualls et al., 2002).

Myths About Late Life

The ethical principles of the American Psychological Association state that it is important for psychologists working with the elderly to examine their stereotypes about late life (APA, 2004). Most people in the United States cling to certain assumptions about old age. Common myths include the idea that we will become doddering and befuddled. We worry that we will be unhappy, cope poorly with troubles, become focused on our poor health, and lead a lonely life.

Each of these myths has been debunked. As we will see, severe cognitive problems do not occur for most people in late life, though a mild decline in cognitive functioning is common (Langa, Larson, Karlawish et al., 2008). Elderly people (age 60 and older in this study) actually experience less negative emotion than do young people (age 18–30 years) (Lawton, Kleban, & Dean, 1993). Although some might suspect that these findings are artifacts of a reluctance of older individuals to describe negative feelings to researchers, laboratory studies verify that the elderly are actually more skilled at regulating their emotions. For example, when shown positive and negative images, older people tend to pay more attention to the positive images (Isaacowitz, 2012) and to display less psychophysiological response to the negative images than do younger people (Kisley, Wood, & Burrows, 2007; Levenson, Carstensen, & Gottman, 1994). When viewing positive images, they show more robust brain activation in key emotion regions than do younger people (Mather, Canli, English et al., 2004). Many older people underreport somatic symptoms, perhaps because of beliefs that aches and pains are an inevitable part of late life. People in late life are no more likely to meet criteria for somatic symptom disorders than are the young (Regier, Boyd, Burke et al., 1988; Siegler & Costa, 1985).

Another myth, that older people are lonely, has received considerable attention. The truth is that the number of social activities that older people engage in is unrelated to their psychological well-being (Carstensen, 1996). As we age, our interests shift away from seeking new social interactions to cultivating a few social relationships that really matter to us, such as those with family and close friends. This phenomenon has been called **social selectivity.**

When we have less time ahead of us, we tend to place a higher value on emotional intimacy than on exploring the world. This preference applies not just to older people but also to younger people who see themselves as having limited time, such as those who are preparing to move far away from their home or who have a life-threatening illness (Frederickson & Carstensen, 1990). When we can't see a future without end, we prefer to spend our limited time with our closest ties rather than with casual acquaintances. Older people do not tend to report that they want more social contacts (York Cornwell & Waite, 2009). To those unfamiliar with these age-related changes, social selectivity could be misinterpreted as harmful social withdrawal. This body of research highlights some of the many strengths that come with aging.

Many stereotypes we hold about the elderly are false, but considerable research suggests that the negative attitudes about the elderly learned early in life persist and become negative self-perceptions as people move into their later years (Levy, 2003). These negative self-perceptions have serious consequences. For example, in one experiment, researchers randomly assigned elderly people to a condition in which they were reminded of negative stereotypes of aging (like memory loss or slower walking speed) or to a control condition without such reminders (Hausdorff, Levy, & Wei, 1999). Participants who were reminded of the negative stereotypes did worse on a memory test than did the control group (Levy, 1996). In a second experimental study, reminders of *positive* stereotypes about aging led participants to walk

The quality of sleep diminishes as people age.

As illustrated by John Glenn's space flight at age 77, advancing age need not lead to a curtailment of activities.

more quickly compared to a control condition with no reminders (Hausdorff et al., 1999). Of much more concern than how stereotypes might influence memory and walking speed, researchers have also shown that negative self-views about aging can predict earlier death, even controlling for baseline health status and many other potential confounds (Levy, Slade, & Kasl, 2002). Not only do we need to challenge our own negative stereotypes, but we also need to help older adults challenge those views.

The Problems Experienced in Late Life

We know that mental health is tied to the physical and social problems in a person's life. As a group, no other people have more of these problems than the elderly. They have them all—physical decline and disabilities, sensory acuity deficits, loss of loved ones, the social stress of stigmatizing attitudes toward the elderly, and the cumulative effects of a lifetime of unfortunate experiences. Eighty percent of elderly people have at least one major medical condition (National Academy on an Aging Society, 1999). As described by one author, "Late life would qualify as the Olympics of coping" (Fisher, 2011, p. 145).

One facet of aging deserves particular attention. As people age, the quality and depth of sleep decline (Fetveit, 2009). Rates of sleep apnea, a disorder in which a person stops breathing for seconds to minutes during the night, also increase with age (Prechter & Shepard, 1990). Untreated and chronic sleep deficits can worsen physical, psychological, and cognitive problems and can even increase the risk of mortality (Ancoli, Kripke, Klauber et al., 1996). Fortunately, psychological treatment has been shown to reduce insomnia among the elderly (Fetveit, 2009).

Several problems complicate medical treatment for elderly people. One of the main difficulties is that the chronic health problems of older people seldom diminish; physicians focused on identifying cures can become frustrated when none are available (Zarit, 1980). Other problems result from the time pressure of the health care system. All too often, doctors do not check to see if the person is taking other medications or seeing other doctors. *Polypharmacy,* the prescribing of multiple drugs to a person, can result. About one-third of elderly persons are prescribed at least five medications (Qato, Alexander, Conti et al., 2008). This increases the risk of adverse drug reactions such as side effects and toxicity. Often, physicians prescribe more medications to combat the side effects, thus continuing the vicious circle.

Further complicating the picture is the fact that most psychoactive drugs are tested on younger people. Gauging the appropriate dose for the less efficient metabolism of the kidneys and liver of the older person represents a challenge for the medical practitioner—side effects and toxicity are much more likely as people age (Gallo & Lebowitz, 1999). The increased sensitivity to side effects is a particular problem with psychiatric medications. One review of medical charts of more than 750,000 elderly patients found that more than one-fifth had filled a prescription for a medication deemed inappropriate for people over the age of 65 due to serious side effects (Curtis, Ostbye, Sendersky et al., 2004). Therefore, it is important that the primary care physician of elderly people keep track of all prescribed medications taken, discontinue nonessential drugs, and prescribe only the minimum dosages needed.

Research Methods in the Study of Aging

Research on aging requires an understanding of several special issues. Chronological age is not as simple a variable in psychological research as it might seem. Because other factors associated with age may influence findings, we must be cautious when we attribute differences between age groups solely to the effects of aging. In the field of aging, as in studies of childhood development, a distinction is made among three kinds of effects (see Table 14.1):

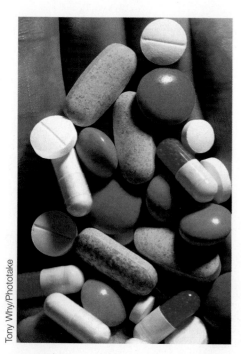

Polypharmacy is all too common in late life.

- **Age effects** are the consequences of being a certain chronological age.
- **Cohort effects** are the consequences of growing up during a particular time period with its unique challenges and opportunities. For example, experiences like the Great Depression, a world war, or 9/11 shape experiences and attitudes. Similarly, the expectations for marriage have changed drastically in the past century, at least in Western societies, from a focus on stability to a focus on happiness and personal fulfillment.

Table 14.1 Age, Cohort, and Time-of-Measurement Effects

Age Effects	Cohort Effects	Time-of-Measurement Effects
The effects of being a certain age; e.g., being old enough to receive Social Security	The effects of having grown up during a particular time period; e.g., frugality may be increased among those who lived through the Great Depression of the 1930s	The effects of testing people at a particular time in history; e.g., people became more frank during the 1990s in their responses to surveys about their sexual behavior, as media discussion of sexuality increased

- **Time-of-measurement effects** are confounds that arise because events at a particular point in time can have a specific effect on a variable that is being studied (Schaie & Hertzog, 1982). For example, people tested right after experiencing the 2005 earthquake in Haiti might demonstrate elevated levels of anxiety.

Two major research designs are used to assess developmental change: cross-sectional and longitudinal. In cross-sectional studies, the investigator compares different age groups at the same moment in time on the variable of interest. Suppose that in 1995 we took a poll in the United States and found that many interviewees over age 80 spoke with a European accent, whereas those in their 40s and 50s did not. Could we conclude that as people grow older, they develop European accents? Hardly! Cross-sectional studies do not examine the same people over time; consequently, they do not provide clear information about how people change as they age.

In longitudinal studies, the researcher periodically retests one group of people using the same measure over a number of years or decades. For example, the Baltimore Longitudinal Study of Aging is one of the longest-running studies of aging. Since 1958, researchers have been following 1400 men and women to see how their lifestyles, medical conditions, and psychological health change over time. In this study, a great deal has been learned about mental

Liaison/Getty Images, Inc.

Marc Romanelli/Getty Images

Cohort effects refer to the fact that people of the same chronological age may differ considerably depending on when they were born.

health and aging. For example, researchers were able to combat myths that people become unhappier over time. Rather, people who were happy at age 30 tended to be happy as they moved into late life (Costa, Metter, & McCrae, 1994). In general, longitudinal designs allow us to trace individual patterns of consistency or change over time. Although longitudinal studies offer fundamental advantages, results can be biased by attrition, in which participants drop out of the study due to death, immobility, or lack of interest. When people are no longer available for follow-up because of death, this is called **selective mortality.** Selective mortality results in a particular form of bias, in that results obtained with the remaining sample are more relevant to drawing conclusions about relatively healthy people than about unhealthy people. Beyond attrition due to death, people with the most problems are likely to drop out from a study, whereas the people who remain are usually healthier than the general population. Later in this chapter, we will discuss how these issues of cohort effects and selective mortality might influence estimates of the prevalence of psychological disorder (Kiecolt-Glaser & Glaser, 2002).

Check Your Knowledge 14.1 (Answers are at the end of the chapter.)

True or false?
1. The key to happiness in late life is to have many different types of social activities.

Answer the question.

2. How do emotions and responses to emotion-relevant stimuli change as people age?
3. How do values about social relationships change as people age?

Psychological Disorders in Late Life

The DSM criteria are the same for older and younger adults. The process of diagnosis, however, must be considered with care. DSM criteria specify that a psychological disorder should not be diagnosed if the symptoms can be accounted for by a medical condition or medication side effects. Because medical conditions are more common in the elderly, it is particularly important to rule out such explanations. Medical problems such as thyroid problems, Addison's disease, Cushing's disease, Parkinson's disease, Alzheimer's disease, hypoglycemia, anemia, testosterone deficits, and vitamin deficiencies can produce symptoms that mimic schizophrenia, depression, or anxiety. Medical problems can also worsen the course of depression. Angina, congestive heart failure, and excessive caffeine consumption may all cause a faster heart rate, which can be mistaken as a symptom of anxiety (Fisher & Noll, 1996). Age-related deterioration in the vestibular system (inner-ear control of one's sense of balance) can account for panic symptoms such as severe dizziness. Depression is also common after strokes or heart attacks (Teper & O'Brien, 2008). Antihypertensive medication, corticosteroids, and antiparkinson medications may contribute to depression or anxiety. Cardiovascular problems can cause erectile problems. Clinicians must be extremely careful to consider the interactions between physical and psychological health. With this consideration in mind, we next examine how common it is for older people to have psychological disorders.

Estimating the Prevalence of Psychological Disorders in Late Life

The prevalence estimates for psychological disorders defy stereotypes of unhappiness and anxiety in late life. Findings indicate that persons over age 65 have the lowest prevalence of psychological disorders of all age groups. Table 14.2 provides 12-month estimates from the National Comorbidity Survey–Replication (NCS–R) study, which involved a community representative sample of 9282 people living in the United States who completed extensive diagnostic interviews (Gum, King-Kallimanis, & Kohn, 2009). As shown, every single disorder was less common in the elderly than in younger adults. None of those aged 65 and older

Table 14.2 One-Year Prevalence Estimates for Psychological Disorders by Age Group

	18–44 Years	60–64 Years	65 Years and Older
Anxiety disorders			
Panic disorder	3.2 (0.3)	2.8 (0.4)	0.7 (0.2)
Agoraphobia without panic	0.8 (0.2)	1.1 (0.3)	0.4 (0.2)
Specific phobia	9.7 (0.5)	9.2 (0.7)	4.7 (0.6)
Social phobia	8.6 (0.5)	6.1 (0.5)	2.3 (0.4)
Generalized anxiety	2.8 (0.2)	3.2 (0.3)	1.2 (0.3)
Posttraumatic stress[a]	3.7 (0.4)	5.1 (0.6)	0.4 (0.1)
Any anxiety disorder[a]	20.7 (0.7)	18.7 (1.3)	7.0 (0.8)
Mood disorders			
Major depressive disorders	8.2 (0.4)	6.5 (0.5)	2.3 (0.3)
Dysthymia	1.5 (0.2)	1.9 (0.4)	0.5 (0.2)
Bipolar I and bipolar II disorders	1.9 (0.2)	1.2 (0.3)	0.2 (0.1)
Any mood disorder	10.2 (0.4)	8.0 (0.6)	2.6 (0.4)
Substance disorders[a]			
Alcohol abuse	2.6 (0.2)	0.9 (0.2)	0
Drug abuse	1.5 (0.2)	0.2 (0.01)	0
Any substance disorder	3.6 (0.3)	1.0 (0.2)	0
Any disorder[a]			
At least one disorder	27.6 (0.8)	22.4 (1.5)	8.5 (0.9)

[a]5692 people completed interviews regarding these diagnoses.
Drawn from the NCS–R study Gum, King-Kallimanis; & Kohn (2009).

met criteria for a drug abuse or dependency disorder. Although not covered in the NCS–R study, rates of schizophrenia are also low among the elderly (Howard, Rabins, Seeman et al., 2000). Overall, only about 8.5 percent of elderly people who took part in the NCS-R survey reported symptoms that were severe enough to be diagnosed. The elderly also are less likely to meet criteria for personality disorders compared to younger individuals (Balsis, Gleason et al., 2007). Most people 65 years of age and older are free from serious psychopathology.

Beyond examining the prevalence rates of disorder, it is important to consider the incidence rates, or how many people are experiencing the onset of a new disorder. Most people who have an episode of a psychological disorder late in life are experiencing a recurrence of a disorder that started earlier in life rather than an initial onset. For example, 97 percent of older adults with generalized anxiety disorder report that their symptoms began before the age of 65 (Alwahhabi, 2003), and more than 90 percent of older adults with major depressive or agoraphobia report that their symptoms began earlier in life (Norton, Skoog, Toone et al., 2006; Ritchie, Norton, Mann et al., 2013). Late onset is also extremely rare for schizophrenia (Karon & VandenBos, 1998). In contrast, late onset is more common for alcohol dependence among older adults with drinking problems (Zarit & Zarit, 2011). It appears, though, that most people with psychological disorders in late life are experiencing a continuation of symptoms that began earlier.

Why are rates of psychopathology so low in late life? There are several completely different answers to this question. Above, we described some of the ways that aging relates to more positive emotionality and more close-knit social circles. Changes like these might enhance mental health as people age. In contrast, some have argued that methodological issues might be leading us to underestimate the prevalence of psychological disorders in late life. We turn to some of these methodological issues next.

Methodological Issues in Estimating the Prevalence of Psychopathology

Methodologically, older adults may be more uncomfortable acknowledging and discussing mental health or drug use problems compared to younger people. In one study, researchers interviewed elderly people about depressive symptoms and then interviewed a family member about whether that elderly person was experiencing depressive symptoms. Among those elderly whom family members described as meeting the criteria for major depressive disorder, about one-quarter did not disclose depressive symptoms to the interviewer (Davison, McCabe, & Mellor, 2009). Discomfort discussing symptoms may minimize prevalence estimates.

In addition to reporting bias, there may be cohort effects. For example, many people who reached adulthood during the drug-oriented era of the 1960s continue to use drugs as they age (Zarit & Zarit, 2011). Their generation is more likely to have problems with substance abuse in late life than previous generations had. Although the 50-and-older age group accounted for only 6.6 percent of substance abuse admissions in the United States in 1992, by 2008 the same age group accounted for 12.2 percent of such admissions.

Beyond these explanations, people with psychological disorders are at risk for dying earlier—before age 65—for several different reasons. Among heavy drinkers, the peak years for death from cirrhosis are between 55 and 64 years of age, and cardiovascular disease is also common (Balsis, Gleason, Woods et al., 2007; Shaper, 1990). Cardiovascular disease is also more common among people with a history of anxiety disorders, depressive disorders, and bipolar disorder (Kubzansky, 2007). Even milder psychological disorders compromise immune function, and as people age, they become particularly sensitive to these immune effects (Kiecolt-Glaser & Glaser, 2001). This may lead to worse outcomes for many medical conditions that are more common as people age. Psychological disorders are associated with increased mortality (Angst, Stassen, Clayton et al., 2002). For example, Frojdh and colleagues (2003) conducted surveys with over 1200 elderly people living in Sweden. Compared to those with low scores, those who obtained high scores on a self-report measure of depression were 2.5 times as likely to die within the next 6 years. Because people with psychological disorders may die earlier, studies on aging may suffer from the issue of selective mortality.

These three methodological issues—response biases, cohort effects, and selective mortality—could help explain the low rates of psychological disorders in late life. Most researchers, however, believe that aging is also genuinely related to better mental health. Above, we noted that emotional coping improves as people age. This should translate into a decrease in psychological disorders. Some longitudinal studies suggest that many people who experience psychological disorders early in life seem to grow out of those symptoms. For example, longitudinal studies indicate that heavy drinkers tend to drink less as they enter late life (Fillmore, 1987). Findings like these suggest that enhanced coping abilities developed across the life course may help protect people from psychological disorders during late life.

Quick Summary

As the number of older people in the United States burgeons, more and more mental health professionals are working with this population. Unfortunately, even mental health professionals tend to hold certain stereotypes about late life. It is important to recognize that, as they age, most people tend to become more effective at regulating emotions, to downplay medical symptoms, and to focus on core relationships over superficial social acquaintances and activities. Negative stereotypes are often held even by those who are older, and the effects of such negative self-beliefs can be quite damaging. The challenges of late life do include insomnia and declining health for many people. As increasing numbers of chronic health problems emerge, polypharmacy becomes an issue for many. Compounding the hazards of polypharmacy, people become more sensitive to medication side effects and toxicity as they age.

In research on aging, it is difficult to disentangle age effects, cohort effects, and time-of-measurement effects. Cross-sectional studies do not help distinguish age and cohort effects. Longitudinal studies provide more clarity about age and cohort effects, but the validity of findings can be challenged by attrition. One form of attrition, selective mortality, is particularly important to consider in studies of aging.

When the elderly present with psychological disorders, it is critically important to evaluate potential medical causes. The elderly are particularly susceptible to the negative effects of medical conditions and medications, and these effects may mimic psychological conditions.

Studies suggest lower rates of psychological disorders among the elderly compared to other age groups. Although some methodological issues (cohort effects, selective mortality, and lack of disclosure) might explain part of this effect, it is also possible that some people become more psychologically healthy as they age.

Neurocognitive Disorders in Late Life

Most elderly people do not have cognitive disorders. Indeed, the prevalence of cognitive impairment has declined among people over the age of 70 in the United States in the last 15 years, perhaps because of improvements in diet, medical care, and education levels over time (Langa et al., 2008). Nonetheless, cognitive disorders account for more medical costs than any other geriatric condition (Zarit & Zarit, 2011). We will examine two principal types of cognitive disorders: dementia, a deterioration of cognitive abilities, and delirium, a state of mental confusion. For each, we will consider the clinical description as well as causal factors and treatment.

Dementia

Dementia is a descriptive term for the deterioration of cognitive abilities to the point that functioning becomes impaired. As we will discuss, there are many different causes for dementia, and the nature of symptoms depends on the type of dementia. Difficulty remembering things, especially recent events, is the most common symptom of dementia. People with dementia may lose control of their impulses; they may use coarse language, tell inappropriate jokes, shoplift, and make sexually inappropriate remarks. The ability to deal with abstract ideas deteriorates, and disturbances in emotions are common, including symptoms of depression, flatness of affect, and sporadic emotional outbursts. Delusions and hallucinations can occur (APA, 2013). People with dementia are likely to show language disturbances as well, such as vague patterns of speech. Many people with progressive dementia eventually become withdrawn and apathetic.

The course of dementia may be progressive, static, or remitting, depending on the cause. Most dementias develop very slowly over a period of years; subtle cognitive and behavioral deficits can be detected well before the person shows any noticeable impairment (Small, Fratiglioni, Viitanen et al., 2000). The early signs of decline noted before functional impairment is present have been labeled as **mild cognitive impairment**.

Diagnostic criteria for dementia and mild cognitive impairment have been developed by a consensus panel of leading experts with support from the National Institute of Aging and the Alzheimer's Association (Albert, Dekosky, Dickson et al., 2011; McKhann, Knopman, Chertkow et al., 2011). The DSM-5 system also provides parallel diagnoses like those for dementia and for mild cognitive impairment. See Table 14.3 for an overview of the DSM-5 diagnoses. DSM mild neurocognitive disorders are similar to mild cognitive impairment, whereas DSM major neurocognitive disorders are similar to a diagnosis of dementia.

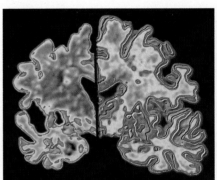

Alfred Pasieka/Science Photo Library/Photo Researchers

Computer-generated images of a brain of a person with Alzheimer's disease and a healthy brain. Note that the diseased brain (left) has shrunk considerably owing to the loss of nerve cells.

Table 14.3 DSM-5 Neurocognitive Disorders

Delirium

Neurocognitive disorder: Specify mild or major

    Neurocognitive disorder associated with Alzheimer's disease

    Neurocognitive disorder associated with frontotemporal lobar degeneration

    Neurocognitive disorder associated with vascular disease

    Neurocognitive disorder associated with traumatic brain injury

    Neurocognitive disorder associated with Lewy body disease

    Neurocognitive disorder associated with Parkinson's disease

    Neurocognitive disorder associated with HIV infection

    Neurocognitive disorder associated with substance/medication use

    Neurocognitive disorder associated with Huntington's disease

    Neurocognitive disorder associated with prion disease

    Neurocognitive disorder due to another medical condition

    Neurocognitive disorder due to multiple etiologies

DSM-5 Criteria for Mild Neurocognitive Disorder

- Modest cognitive decline from previous levels in one or more domains based on both of the following:
  - Concerns of the patient, a close other, or a clinician
  - Modest neurocognitive decline (i.e., between the 3rd and 16th percentile) on formal testing or equivalent clinical evaluation
- The cognitive deficits do not interfere with independence in everyday activities (e.g., paying bills or managing medications), even though greater effort, compensatory strategies, or accommodation may be required to maintain independence
- The cognitive deficits do not occur exclusively in the context of delirium and are not due to another psychological disorder

DSM-5 Criteria for Major Neurocognitive Disorder

- Significant cognitive decline from previous levels in one or more domains based on both of the following:
  - Concerns of the patient, a close other, or a clinician
  - Substantial neurocognitive impairment (i.e., below the 3rd percentile on formal testing) or equivalent clinical evaluation
- The cognitive deficits interfere with independence in everyday activities
- The cognitive deficits do not occur exclusively in the context of delirium and are not due to another psychological disorder

Throughout this chapter, we use the terms *dementia* (rather than *major neurocognitive disorder*) and *mild cognitive impairment* (rather than *mild neurocognitive disorder*).

There is some debate about where to draw the line between mild cognitive impairment and dementia, as well as how early to diagnose mild cognitive impairment. The DSM-5 distinguishes between mild and major neurocognitive disorder based on whether symptoms interfere with the ability to live independently. The DSM-5 criteria for mild neurocognitive disorder require a low score on only one cognitive test. This may lead to an artificially high rate of diagnosis for mild neurocognitive disorder; requiring low scores on at least two different cognitive tests could drastically decrease the rates of diagnosis (Jak, Bondi, Delano-Wood et al., 2009).

Caution is warranted in diagnosing these early signs of decline. Not all people with mild cognitive symptoms develop dementia. Among adults with mild cognitive impairment, about 10 percent per year will develop dementia; among adults without mild cognitive impairment, about 1 percent per year will develop dementia (Bischkopf, Busse, & Angermeyer, 2002). It is important to provide careful psychoeducation regarding these diagnoses so that patients and family members do not assume that symptoms will necessarily progress.

Clinical Case: Ellen

"I am so glad you came," Ellen says when I greet her. She is sitting at the dining room table sipping juice, a slender, almost frail woman. But Ellen has presence. She has the posture of a dancer: shoulders back, neck elongated, head up, and the gaunt face of a once beautiful woman, with large milky hazel eyes and high patrician cheekbones. She smiles and reaches for my hand. "It is so nice of you to visit," she says.

Ellen is gracious and polite, but the truth is, she doesn't remember me. She doesn't remember that we've visited a half dozen times before, that a few days ago we had tea together, that just yesterday I sat on her bed for a half hour massaging her hands with rosemary mint lotion. Ellen, like the 43 others living at this residential care facility, has Alzheimer's disease. Her short-term memory is shot, and her long-term memory is quirky and dreamlike, with images that are sometimes bright and lucid, and other times so out of focus that she can hardly make them out. Her life is like a puzzle someone took apart when she wasn't looking. She can see some of the pieces, but she can no longer see how they fit together. (Kessler, August 22, 2004, p.1)

Worldwide prevalence estimates of dementia in 2000 were over 25 million, which represented about 0.4 percent of the population (Wimo, Winblad, Aguero-Torres et al., 2003). The prevalence of dementia increases with advancing age. Across international studies, the prevalence of dementia has been found to be 1 to 2 percent in people aged 60 to 69 but increases progressively to more than 20 percent in those 85 or older (Ferri, Prince, Brayne et al., 2005).

There are many different types of dementia. Here we discuss four types of dementia: Alzheimer's disease, the most researched form; frontotemporal dementia, defined by the areas of the brain that are most affected; vascular dementia, caused by cerebrovascular disease; and dementia with Lewy bodies, defined by the presence of Lewy bodies (a type of abnormal deposit that forms on neurons). After discussing these four types of dementia, we briefly describe other causes of dementia. By far, the most common form of dementia is Alzheimer's disease, which accounts for about 80 percent of dementias (Terry, 2006).

Alzheimer's Disease   In **Alzheimer's disease**, initially described by the German neurologist Alois Alzheimer in 1906, the brain tissue irreversibly deteriorates, and death usually occurs within 12 years after the onset of symptoms. Over 50,000 Americans die each year from this disease, and in 2010, it was the sixth leading cause of death in the United States (Murphy, Xu, & Kochanek, 2013).

The most common symptom of Alzheimer's disease is memory loss. The illness may begin with absentmindedness and gaps in memory for new material, as described in the Clinical Case of Mary Ann. The person may leave tasks unfinished and forgotten if interrupted. The person who had started to fill a teapot at the sink leaves the water running. It may be hard to find words. These shortcomings may be overlooked for several years but eventually interfere with daily living.

Memory loss is not the only symptom of Alzheimer's disease. Apathy is common even before the cognitive symptoms become noticeable (Balsis, Carpenter, & Storandt, 2005), and about a third of people develop full-blown depression as the illness worsens (Vinkers, Gussekloo, Stek et al., 2004). As the disease develops, problems with language skills and word finding intensify. Visual-spatial abilities decline, which can be manifested in **disorientation** (confusion with respect to time, place, or identity). The person may easily become lost, even in familiar surroundings.

As the brain deterioration progresses, the range and severity of behavioral symptoms increase. People with the disorder are typically unaware of their cognitive problems initially, and they may blame others for lost objects even to the point of developing delusions of being persecuted. Memory continues to deteriorate, and the person becomes

---

Clinical Case: Mary Ann

Mary Ellen was a 62-year-old family therapist who loved her career in end-stage hospice work when she was first diagnosed with early-stage Alzheimer's disease. "All of a sudden—but it wasn't all of a sudden, of course—I began to realize that I wasn't the gal I used to be. It was different inside my head.

"It was the very simple things. I would be talking with someone on the telephone, then hang up and ask myself, 'Who was that? What did we talk about?' My husband John says he knew something serious was going on when we returned from a vacation together and I told him, 'I really had a great time in California. I'm so sorry you couldn't make it.'

"My message to people with Alzheimer's is this: Be gentle with yourself. This disease requires that you lower your expectations of yourself. That's a hard thing for most of us to do. The fear is losing yourself, knowing that you won't bring this self to the end stage of your life."

(Quoted from Mary Ellen Becklenberg, *Time* magazine, October 2010, p. 59.)

increasingly disoriented and agitated. As the dementia progresses, a parent is unable to remember the name of a daughter or son and later may not even recall that he or she has children or recognize them when they come to visit. The person may forget to bathe or dress adequately. Judgment may become faulty, and the person may have difficulty comprehending situations and making plans or decisions. In the terminal phase of the illness, personality loses its sparkle and integrity. Relatives and friends say that the person is just not himself or herself anymore. Social involvement with others keeps narrowing. Finally, the person is oblivious to his or her surroundings.

People with Alzheimer's disease have more **plaques** (small, round beta-amyloid protein deposits that are outside the neurons) and **neurofibrillary tangles** (twisted protein filaments composed largely of the protein tau in the axons of neurons) than would be expected for the person's age. Some people produce excessive amounts of beta-amyloid, whereas others seem to have deficiencies in the mechanisms for clearing beta-amyloid from the brain (Jack, Albert, Knopman et al., 2011). The beta-amyloid plaques are most densely present in the frontal cortex (Klunk, Engler, Nordberg et al., 2004), and they may be present for 10 to 20 years before the cognitive symptoms become noticeable. Plaques can be measured using a specialized type of PET scan. Tangles are most often measured in cerebrospinal fluid, although they can be measured using a PET scan as well. Tangles are most densely present in the hippocampus, an area that is important for memory. Over time, as the disease progresses, plaques and tangles spread through more of the brain (Klunk et al., 2004; Sperling, Aisen, Beckett et al., 2011).

Immune responses to plaques lead to inflammation (Gorelick, 2010), which then trigger a series of brain changes over time, as shown in Figure 14.2. At early stages, there seems to be a loss of synapses for acetylcholinergic (ACh) and glutamatergic neurons (Selkoe, 2002).

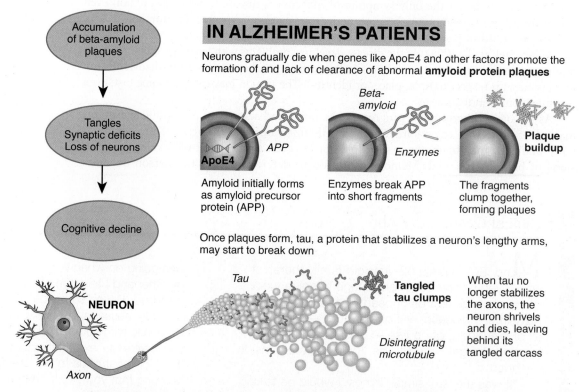

Figure 14.2 In Alzheimer's disease, risk factors such as the gene *ApoE-4* lead to an increased deposition of beta-amyloid plaques. These plaques build up outside of the neurons for 10 to 20 years before the cognitive symptoms are noticeable. Neurofibrillary tangles of tau form, and the neurons die. To prevent the death of neurons, researchers hope to develop treatments that will address as many of the genetic amyloid and tau targets as possible.

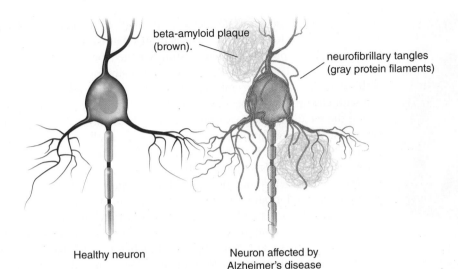

beta-amyloid plaque (brown).

neurofibrillary tangles (gray protein filaments)

Healthy neuron

Neuron affected by Alzheimer's disease

Figure 14.3 Alzheimer's disease have more **plaques** (small, round beta-amyloid protein deposits that are outside the neurons) and **neurofibrillary tangles** (twisted protein filaments composed largely of the protein tau in the axons of neurons) than would be expected for the person's age.

Neurons also begin to die. As neurons die, the entorhinal cortex (see Figure 14.3) and then the hippocampus (see Figure 2.11) and other regions of the cerebral cortex shrink, and later the frontal, temporal, and parietal lobes shrink. As this happens, the ventricles become enlarged. The cerebellum, spinal cord, and motor and sensory areas of the cortex are less affected, which is why people with Alzheimer's do not appear to have anything physically wrong with them until late in the disease process. For some time people with Alzheimer's are able to walk around normally, and their overlearned habits, such as making small talk, remain intact, so that in short encounters strangers may not notice anything amiss. About 25 percent of people with Alzheimer's disease eventually develop brain deterioration that leads to motor deficits.

In the largest twin study of Alzheimer's disease, a heritability estimate of 79 percent was reported. That is, about 79 percent of the variance in onset of Alzheimer's disease appears related to genes, and about 21 percent of the variance appears related to environmental factors (Gatz, Reynolds, Fratiglioni et al., 2006).

Considerable progress has been made in understanding the molecular genetics of Alzheimer's disease. As we discuss these findings, though, it is important to be aware that the effects of specific genetic polymorphisms on Alzheimer's disease risk may vary by ethnicity (Froehlich, 2001). In GWAS studies, researchers have identified a set of 10 specific genes that explain about 20 percent of the risk for Alzheimer's disease among white non-Hispanic samples (Sullivan, Daly, & O'Donovan, 2012).

By far, the genetic polymorphism with the largest contribution to Alzheimer's disease is a polymorphism of a gene on chromosome 19, called the apolipoprotein ε4 or ApoE-4 allele.

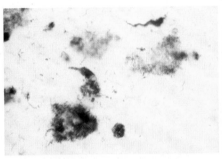

Dr. M. Goedert/Science Source

Light micrograph of a section of entorhinal cortex brain tissue affected by Alzheimer's disease showing amyloid plaques in brown and neurofibrillary tangles in grey. In Alzheimer's disease, neurons die in the entorhinal cortex, and then the loss of neurons begins to occur in other regions of the brain.

Alzheimer's Disease

Normal Control

Courtesy of Dr. Claudia Prada and Dr. Brian Bacskai

Positron emission tomography (PET) images of the brain after administration of Pittsburgh Compound B (Dugger, Ritchie, Ball et al.) in a woman with Alzheimer's disease shows high levels of amyloid plaque (upper series). In contrast, low levels of amyloid plaque are seen in the PET images of a woman with no Alzheimer's symptoms (lower series).

Exercise programs are of some help in reducing the risk and severity of Alzheimer's disease.

Whereas having one ε4 allele increases the risk of Alzheimer's disease to about 20 percent, having two ε4 alleles brings the risk substantially higher. Some companies now sell genetic testing for the ApoE-4 allele (and other genes) directly to consumers. Researchers are beginning to understand some of the ways that the ε4 may increase risk of the disorder. ε4 appears to interfere with clearing excess beta-amyloid peptide from the brain. People with two of the ε4 alleles show overproduction of beta-amyloid plaques, loss of neurons in the hippocampus, and low glucose metabolism in several regions of the cerebral cortex even before they develop symptoms of Alzheimer's disease (Bookheimer & Burggren, 2009).

Many of the genes that increase risk for Alzheimer's disease are related to immune function and cholesterol metabolism. Immune processes and excessively high cholesterol can trigger inflammation, and accordingly conditions that involve immune and inflammatory processes also appear related to a greater risk of Alzheimer's disease. For example, type II diabetes, which has been tied to immune and inflammatory changes, is related to greater risk of developing Alzheimer's disease (Ferreira, Clarke, Bomfim et al., 2014). Similarly, brain traumas from accidents or injuries can also increase the risk of Alzheimer's disease later in life.

Beyond genes, lifestyle variables may play a role in Alzheimer's. For example, smoking, being single, obesity, depression, and low social support are related to a greater risk of Alzheimer's disease, while a Mediterranean diet, exercise, education, and engagement in cognitive activities are related to a lower risk (Lieb, Beiser, Vasan et al., 2009; Williams, Plassman, Burke et al., 2010). In one study, lifestyle effects were studied in 2509 elderly who were enrolled in the study during their 70s and followed for 8 years. Those with a high school education who exercised at least once a week, remained socially active, and did not smoke sustained their cognitive functioning without decline throughout the 8 years (Yaffe, Fiocco, Lindquist et al., 2009). Of the various lifestyle factors, the effects for exercise, cognitive engagement, and depression have received a good deal of study, and so we focus on those here.

Several studies suggest that exercise may predict fewer memory problems. Regular exercise predicts less decline in cognitive functions (Sofi, Valecchi, Bacci et al., 2011), and as shown in a meta-analysis of 163,797 participants, it also strongly predicts decreased risk of developing Alzheimer's disease over time (Hamer & Chida, 2009). Exercise levels at midlife seem important, but so does sustaining exercise as one enters late life. Exercise has been related to lower levels of plaques in the brain, and particularly so for those with the APOE-4 polymorphism (Head, Bugg, Goate et al., 2012).

Engagement in intellectual activities also appears helpful, with some proposing a "use it or lose it" model of Alzheimer's. For example, regular reading of a newspaper is related to lower risk (Wilson, Scherr, Schneider et al., 2007). Findings of a meta-analysis including 29,000 persons drawn from 22 representative community samples suggested that frequent cognitive activity (for example, reading and puzzle solving) is related to a 46 percent decrease in risk of Alzheimer's disease compared to infrequent cognitive activity (Valenzuela & Sachdev, 2006). Parallel with the findings for exercise, engagement in intellectual activities protects against cognitive decline for those with the APOE-4 polymorphism (Vemuri, Lesnick, Przybelski et al., 2014).

Intriguingly, among people with similar levels of plaques and tangles in their brain, those with higher levels of intellectual activity show fewer cognitive symptoms. That is, intellectual activity seems to protect against the expression of underlying neurobiological disease (Wilson, et al., 2007). This type of work has led to the concept of **cognitive reserve,** or the idea that some people may be able to compensate for the disease by using alternative brain networks or cognitive strategies such that cognitive symptoms are less pronounced.

One concern is that naturalistic studies cannot disentangle whether the people who choose to engage in exercise or cognitive activities differ in some important way (on characteristics relevant to disease) from those who do not engage in these activities. We know that biological changes in the brain begin 20 years before the symptoms of Alzheimer's disease first emerge; it is plausible that those brain changes influence motivation to take part in exercise or cognitive activities. Intervention studies, described below, that randomly assign people to take part in exercise or cognitive training can help address this methodological issue.

The complexity of trying to identify the direction of effects is illustrated by considering the relationship of depression and Alzheimer's disease. We mentioned above that depression can be a consequence of dementia. The opposite direction of effects seems to occur as well: A lifetime history of depression predicts more decline in cognitive functioning (Ganguli, Du, Dodge et al., 2006), greater risk for Alzheimer's disease and other forms of dementia (Diniz, Butters, Albert et al., 2013), and, among those who develop Alzheimer's disease, a faster progression of the illness (Rapp, Schnaider-Beeri, Grossman et al., 2006). These effects seem to be present even when baseline cognitive impairment and other medical issues are controlled (Goveas, Espeland, Woods et al., 2011).

Frontotemporal Dementia As suggested by the name, **frontotemporal dementia (FTD)** is caused by a loss of neurons in frontal and temporal regions of the brain. The neuronal deterioration of FTD occurs predominantly in the anterior temporal lobes and prefrontal cortex (Miller, Ikonte, Ponton et al., 1997). FTD typically begins in the mid- to late 50s, and it progresses rapidly; death usually occurs within 5–10 years of the diagnosis (Hu, Seelaar, Josephs et al., 2009). FTD is rare, affecting less than 1 percent of the population (Pressman & Miller, 2014).

Unlike Alzheimer's disease, memory is not severely impaired in FTD. There are multiple subtypes of FTD. The diagnostic criteria for the most common variant of FTD (called behavioral variant FTD) recently developed by an international consortium include deterioration in at least three of the following areas at a level that leads to functional impairment: empathy, executive function (cognitive capacity to plan and organize), ability to inhibit behavior, compulsive or perseverative behavior, hyperorality (tendencies to put nonfood objects in the mouth), and apathy (Rascovsky, Hodges, Knopman et al., 2011). In early stages, significant others may notice changes in personality and judgment. For example, the successful and savvy businessman may begin to make terrible investments (Levenson & Miller, 2007). Because a person affected by this disorder might suddenly start to overeat, chain smoke, drink alcohol, or demonstrate other behavioral symptoms, FTD is often misdiagnosed as a midlife crisis or as a psychological disorder such as depression, bipolar disorder, or schizophrenia (Zhou & Seeley, 2014).

FTD strikes emotional processes more profoundly than Alzheimer's disease does, and in doing so, it can damage social relationships. Particular deficits seem to emerge in the ability to regulate emotions (Goodkind, Gyurak, McCarthy et al., 2010). This may lead the person to violate social conventions (Mendez, Lauterbach, & Sampson, 2008). Persons with FTD do not seem to notice that they have made a social mistake, and so they do not experience embarrassment in contexts where others might. As you might imagine, the changes in personality and emotion, together with a lack of insight, influence relationships (Mendez et al., 2008). Marital satisfaction is more affected by FTD than by Alzheimer's disease (Ascher, Sturm, Seider et al., 2010).

FTD can be caused by many different molecular processes (Mackenzie, Neumann, Bigio et al., 2009). One of these is Pick's disease, characterized by the presence of Pick bodies (spherical inclusions) within neurons, but many other diseases or pathological processes can result in FTD. Some people with FTD show high levels of tau, the protein filaments that contribute to the neurofibrillary tangles observed in Alzheimer's disease, but others do not (Josephs, 2008). FTD has a strong genetic component, (Cruts, Gijselinck, van der Zee et al., 2006).

Vascular Dementia By definition, **vascular dementia** is caused by cerebrovascular disease. Most commonly, strokes cause a blood clot, which then impairs circulation and results in the death of neurons. About 7 percent of people will develop dementia in the year after a

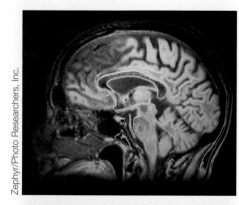

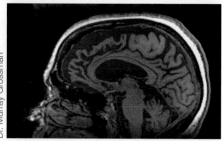

Frontotemporal dementia. The photo on the top is a colored magnetic resonance imaging (MRI) scan of the brain of a 50-year-old with Frontotemporal dementia. The front of the brain is at left. The frontal (left) and temporal (center) lobes have atrophied (shrunk). The photo on the bottom is a MRI scan of a healthy brain.

first stroke, and the risk of dementia increases with recurrent strokes (Pendlebury & Rothwell, 2009). Risk for vascular dementia involves the same risk factors as those for cardiovascular disease in general—for example, a high level of "bad" (LDL) cholesterol, cigarette smoking, and elevated blood pressure (Moroney, Tang, Berglund et al., 1999). Strokes and vascular dementias are more common in African Americans than in Caucasians (Froehlich, Bogardus, & Inouye, 2001). Because strokes and cardiovascular disease can strike different regions of the brain, the symptoms of vascular dementia vary a good deal. The onset of symptoms is usually more rapid in vascular dementia than in other forms of dementia. Vascular dementia can co-occur with Alzheimer's disorder.

Dementia with Lewy Bodies In **dementia with Lewy bodies (DLB)**, protein deposits called Lewy bodies form in the brain and cause the cognitive decline. DLB can be divided into two subtypes, depending on whether or not it occurs in the context of Parkinson's disease (True, Rice, Eisen et al., 1993). About 80 percent of people with Parkinson's disease will develop DLB, but some people without Parkinson's will develop DLB as well.

The symptoms associated with this type of dementia are often hard to distinguish from the symptoms of Parkinson's (such as the shuffling gait) and Alzheimer's disease (such as loss of memory). DLB is more likely than Alzheimer's disease to include prominent visual hallucinations and fluctuating cognitive symptoms (APA, 2013). People with DLB are often extremely sensitive to the physical side effects of antipsychotic medications. Another distinct symptom of DLB is that people often experience intense dreams accompanied by levels of movement and vocalizing that may make them seem as though they are "acting out their dreams" (McKeith, Dickson, Lowe et al., 2005).

Dementias Caused by Disease and Injury A number of other medical conditions can produce dementia. Encephalitis, a term for any inflammation of brain tissue, is caused by viruses that enter the brain. Meningitis, an inflammation of the membranes covering the outer brain, is usually caused by a bacterial infection. Both encephalitis and meningitis can cause dementia. The organism that produces the venereal disease syphilis can invade the brain and cause dementia. HIV, head traumas, brain tumors, nutritional deficiencies (especially of B-complex vitamins), kidney or liver failure, and endocrine problems such as hyperthyroidism can result in dementia. Exposure to toxins (such as lead or mercury) and chronic substance use are both additional causes.

Treatments for Dementia Sadly, despite intensive research in this area, there is no cure for dementia (Williams et al., 2010), although some medications are used to treat it and related syndromes. There are also some psychological and lifestyle approaches to treatment.

Medications Because no medications have been shown to help address the cognitive symptoms of FTD (Caselli & Yaari, 2008), we focus on interventions for dementias other than FTD. Much of the treatment research has focused on Alzheimer's disease and on memory decline. Medications help slow decline, but they do not restore memory function to previous levels. The most commonly used medications for dementia are the cholinesterase inhibitors (drugs that interfere with the breakdown of acetylcholine), including donepezil (Aricept) and rivastigmine (Exelon). Cholinesterase inhibitors have a slight effect in slowing memory decline compared to placebo for those with

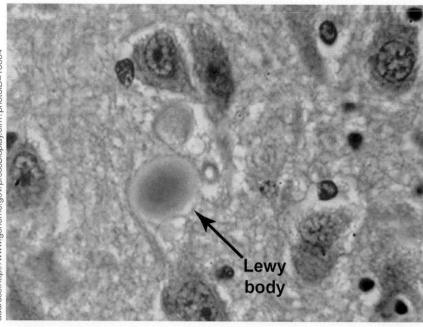

Dementia with Lewy bodies is defined by the presence of abnormal deposits called Lewy bodies. The Lewy bodies are found throughout the brain.

Alzheimer's (Birks, 2006; Howard, McShane, Lindesay et al., 2012) and dementia with Lewy bodies (Maidment, Fox, & Boustani, 2006). In addition to cholinesterase inhibitors, memantine (Namenda), a drug that affects glutamate receptors involved in memory, has shown small effects in placebo-controlled trials for Alzheimer's disease. Unfortunately, many people discontinue these drugs due to aversive side effects such as nausea (Maidment et al., 2006).

Medical treatments are commonly used to address psychological symptoms, such as depression and agitation that commonly co-occur with dementia. For example, antidepressants can help relieve comorbid depressive symptoms in Alzheimer's disease (Modrego, 2010) and FTD (Mendez & Shapira, 2008). Because depression produces more cognitive impairment in the elderly than it does in younger people (Lockwood, Alexopoulos, Kakuma et al., 2000), treating depressive symptoms can often lead to improvements in cognitive symptoms. Although antipsychotic medications can provide modest relief for aggressive agitation (Lonergan, Britton, & Luxenberg, 2007), they also increase the risk of death among elderly people with dementia (Food and Drug Administration, 2005).

Some of the disappointments in developing treatments have led to new ways of thinking about these disorders. For example, for some time, researchers were striving to find ways to remove plaques from the brains of people with Alzheimer's disease. Surprisingly, when researchers developed a medication that removed beta-amyloid plaques, they found that cognitive deficits continued and even worsened after the plaques were removed (Holmes, Boche, Wilkinson et al., 2008). Remember, though, that beta-amyloid plaques accumulate in the brain for years before symptoms are observable among people with Alzheimer's disease. By the time people had been diagnosed and had begun to receive the intervention, biological disease processes had already been occurring for years. Findings like these have led researchers to focus more on prevention. One way to do this is to study factors that reduce the chances that mild cognitive impairment will develop into full-blown dementia. Another way is to study people who have early biological markers indicating risk for Alzheimer's disease, such as signs of plaques, tangles, and neuronal death (Sperling et al., 2011). Researchers are testing a host of interventions to target the development of plaques and tangles, as well as the associated immune processes (Gandy, 2014). Current thinking is that the best hope for future treatments may be treating the biological processes before symptoms emerge (Sutphen, Fagan, & Holtzman, 2014).

Psychological and Lifestyle Treatments Supportive psychotherapy can help families and patients deal with the effects of the disease. Generally, the therapist allows opportunities for the person with dementia and the family to discuss the illness. The therapist also provides accurate information about the illness, helps family members care for the person in the home, and encourages a realistic rather than a catastrophic attitude in dealing with the many specific challenges that this cognitive disorder presents (Knight, 1996). See Focus on Discovery 14.1 for more detail on treatments offered to support caregivers.

Interventions to increase exercise also have modest benefits in improving cognitive function. In a meta-analysis of studies including 824 people, exercise programs were shown to improve cognitive functioning for those with mild to moderate cognitive deficits (Heyn, Abreu, & Ottenbacher, 2004). Exercise programs have also been shown to improve cognitive functioning among those already diagnosed with Alzheimer's disease (Forbes, Thiessen, Blake et al., 2013).

Cognitive training programs that focus on improving memory, reasoning, or cognitive processing speed have been shown to have modest benefits for elderly persons. For example, the effects of 14 sessions of 60- to 75-minute reasoning and cognitive processing speed training were shown to have positive benefits at a 10-year follow-up. These benefits seem to be specific to the area involved in the training—for example, memory training might help enhance memory but doesn't seem to help reasoning abilities (Rebok, Ball, Guey et al., 2014). To help skills generalize more, several researchers have begun to focus on how to teach "meta-cognitive" skills—that is, ways to think about thinking. As an example of the success of these meta-cognitive programs, teaching people strategies for enhancing memory seems

Former president Ronald Reagan died from Alzheimer's disease. His daughter wrote the following about his disease: "The past is like the rudder of a ship. It keeps you moving through the present, steers you into the future. Without it, without memory, you are unmoored, a wind-tossed boat with no anchor. You learn this by watching someone you love drift away" (Davis, 2002).

Computerized training programs have been developed with the aim of enhancing cognitive skills. Companies producing these training programs report tens of millions of users.

Providing memory aids is one way of compensating for memory loss.

to improve performance across a range of tasks (Hertzog, Kramer, Wilson et al., 2009). Similarly, training in multitasking appeared to improve not just ability to multitask, but also ability to hold items in memory and to sustain attention to a task (Anguera, Boccanfuso, Rintoul et al., 2013).

Behavioral approaches have been shown to help compensate for memory loss and to reduce depression and disruptive behavior among people with early stages of Alzheimer's disease. For example, external memory aids such as shopping lists, calendars, phone lists, and labels can help when placed prominently as visual reminders (Buchanan, Christenson, Houlihan et al., 2011). Pleasant and engaging activities can be increased as a way of diminishing depression (Logsdon, McCurry, & Teri, 2007). Triggers for disruptive behavior can be identified and changed. Music may help reduce agitation and disruptive behavior while it is being played (Livingston, Johnston, Katona et al., 2005). These behavioral interventions can provide important alternatives to medication approaches.

FOCUS ON DISCOVERY 14.1

Support for Caregivers

For every person with a severe dementia who is living in an institution, there are at least two living in the community, usually supported by a family (typically by wives and daughters). Caregiving for dementia requires much more time than caregiving for most other disorders (Ory, Hoffman, Yee et al., 1999) and has been shown to be extremely stressful across a number of cultures (Torti, Gwyther, Reed et al., 2004). Caregivers are at heightened risk for clinical depression and anxiety (Dura, Stukenberg, & Kiecolt-Glaser, 1991), physical illness (Vitaliano, Zhang, & Scanlan, 2003), and decreased immune functioning (Kiecolt-Glaser, Dura, Speicher et al., 1991) compared to noncaregivers.

Families can be helped to cope better with the daily stress of caregiving. For example, because people with Alzheimer's have difficulty placing new information into memory, they can engage in a reasonable conversation but forget the discussion within a few minutes. A caregiver may become impatient unless he or she understands that this impairment is an expected consequence of the brain damage. Family members can learn communication strategies to adapt to the memory loss. For example, families can ask questions that embed the answer. It is much easier to respond to "Was the person you just spoke to on the phone Harry or Tom?" than to "Who just called?"

It is also useful for caregivers to understand that patients do not always recognize their limitations and may try to engage in activities

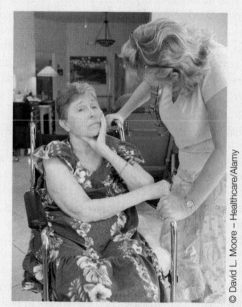

Caring for a relative with Alzheimer's disease is a source of severe stress.

beyond their abilities. Caregivers must set limits regarding dangerous activities. For example, caregivers often need to tell a relative with Alzheimer's disease that driving is off-limits (and then remove the car keys, as the relative is likely to forget the new rule).

Programs that teach coping strategies for the caregivers (e.g., increasing pleasant activities, exercise, or social support) as well as individual behavioral therapy programs have been shown to relieve caregiver burden (Selwood, Johnson, Katona et al., 2007) and depression (Mittelman, Brodaty, Wallen et al., 2008). Programs lasting at least 6 weeks (Selwood et al., 2007) or offering multiple components (e.g., psychoeducation about dementia, case-management services, and cognitive behavioral strategies) more consistently reduce caregivers' distress (Acton & Kang, 2001). Because caregivers are so powerfully affected, it is recommended that they be given respites from their task. To give the caretaker a break, sometimes the person with dementia is admitted to a hospital briefly or enrolled in an adult day-care center; sometimes a health care worker takes over long enough for the family to take a holiday. Caregiver support programs have been found to improve the immune function of caregivers (Garand, Buckwalter, Lubaroff et al., 2002), decrease the medical costs of the person with dementia, and slow the timing of institutionalization (Teri, Gibbons, McCurry et al., 2003).

Quick Summary

Dementia is a broad term to capture cognitive decline, most commonly a decline in memory for recent events. As cognitive deficits become more widespread and profound, social and occupational functioning becomes more and more disturbed. Dementia affects approximately 1 to 2 percent of people in their 60s but more than 20 percent of people over the age of 85.

There are many types of dementia, including Alzheimer's, frontotemporal, vascular, dementia with Lewy bodies, and dementia from other medical causes. Alzheimer's disease is characterized by plaques and tangles in the brain. Memory loss is a key symptom of Alzheimer's disease, but apathy may be present long before cognitive symptoms are observable. Risk of developing the disease is higher among those with at least one ApoE-4 allele. Immune and inflammation processes may increase vulnerability to Alzheimer's disease. Lifestyle and psychological factors, such as depression, exercise, and cognitive engagement, appear to be involved as well. Frontotemporal dementia (FTD) is characterized by neuronal deterioration in the frontal and temporal lobes. Pick's disease is one form of FTD. The primary symptoms of FTD include marked changes in social and emotional behavior, including problems with empathy, executive function, disinhibition, compulsive behavior, hyperorality,

and apathy. Vascular dementia often occurs after a stroke. The symptoms of vascular dementia depend on the brain regions that are influenced by the cerebrovascular disease. Dementia with Lewy bodies is characterized by visual hallucinations, fluctuations in cognitive functioning, supersensitivity to side effects of antipsychotic medications, and intense dreams during which the person moves and talks. It is common among people diagnosed with Parkinson's disease.

The cholinesterase inhibitors and memantine are the major medical treatments for dementia, but these medications offer modest effects. Exercise appears to improve cognitive functioning for people with mild cognitive impairment as well as those with Alzheimer's disease. Cognitive training programs are increasingly popular, and those that teach meta-cognitive skills, such as general strategies for enhancing memory, may generalize across tasks. Antidepressants and behavioral treatments can help relieve comorbid symptoms of depression. Antipsychotic medications can reduce agitation for those with dementia but also increase the risk of death; behavioral treatments can be used safely to reduce agitation. Many types of programs are available to support caregivers of people with Alzheimer's disease.

Check Your Knowledge 14.2

Choose the best answer.
1. A plaque is:
   a. a small, round beta-amyloid protein deposit
   b. a filament composed of the protein tau
   c. a buildup of the myelin sheath surrounding neurons in the hippocampus
   d. a small white spot on a brain scan
2. A neurofibrillary tangle is:
   a. a small, round beta-amyloid protein deposit
   b. a filament composed of the protein tau
   c. a buildup of the myelin sheath surrounding neurons in the hippocampus
   d. a small white spot on a brain scan
3. FTD involves profound changes in:
   a. memory
   b. social and emotional behavior
   c. motor control
   d. attention

Answer the questions.
4. Which neurotransmitter is most involved in Alzheimer's disease?
5. Describe the efficacy of current medical treatments for dementia.

Delirium

The term **delirium** is derived from the Latin words *de,* meaning "out of," and *lira,* meaning "track." The term implies being off-track or deviating from the usual state (Wells & Duncan, 1980). As illustrated in the Clinical Case of Henry at the beginning of this chapter, delirium is typically described as a clouded state of consciousness. The two most common symptoms are extreme trouble focusing attention and profound disturbances in the sleep/wake cycle (Meagher, 2007). Patients, sometimes rather suddenly, have so much trouble focusing attention that they cannot maintain a coherent stream of thought. They may have trouble answering questions because their mind wanders. As the sleep/wake cycle becomes disturbed, patients become drowsy during the day, yet awake and agitated at night. Vivid dreams and nightmares are common. People with delirium may be impossible to engage in conversation because of their wandering attention and fragmented thinking. In severe delirium, speech is rambling and

DSM-5 Criteria for Delirium

- Disturbance in attention and awareness
- A change in cognition, such as disturbance in orientation, language, memory, perception, or visuospatial ability, not better accounted for by a dementia
- Rapid onset (usually within hours or days) and fluctuation during the course of a day
- Symptoms are caused by a medical condition, substance intoxication or withdrawal, or toxin

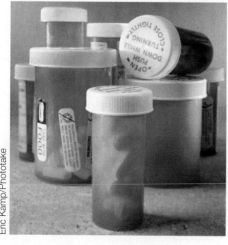

Medication misuse, whether deliberate or inadvertent, can be a serious problem among older people and can cause delirium.

incoherent. Bewildered and confused, some people with delirium may become so disoriented that they are unclear about what day it is, where they are, and even who they are. Memory impairment, especially for recent events, is common.

Perceptual disturbances are frequent in delirium. People mistake the unfamiliar for the familiar; for example, they may state that they are at home instead of in a hospital. Although visual hallucinations are common, they are not always present. Delusions—beliefs contrary to reality—have been noted in about 25 percent of older adults with delirium (Camus, Burtin, Simeone et al., 2000). These delusions tend to be poorly worked out, fleeting, and changeable.

Swings in activity and mood accompany these disordered thoughts and perceptions. People with delirium can be erratic, ripping their clothes one moment and sitting lethargically the next. They may also shift rapidly from one emotion to another, fluctuating between depression, anxiety, fright, anger, euphoria, and irritability. Fever, flushed face, dilated pupils, tremors, rapid heartbeat, elevated blood pressure, and incontinence of urine and feces are common. If delirium worsens, the person may become lethargic and even unresponsive (Webster & Holroyd, 2000). In the course of a 24-hour period, people with delirium have lucid intervals in which they become alert and coherent. Symptoms are usually worse during sleepless nights. These daily fluctuations help distinguish delirium from other syndromes, especially Alzheimer's disease.

People of any age are subject to delirium, but it is more common among children and older adults. Among older adults, it is particularly common in nursing homes and hospitals. One study found that 6 to 12 percent of nursing home residents developed delirium in the course of 1 year (Katz, Parmelee, & Brubaker, 1991), and rates much higher than this have been found in elderly hospital patients (Meagher, 2001).

Unfortunately, delirium is often misdiagnosed (Knight, 1996). For example, among 77 hospitalized older adults with clear symptoms of delirium, about 60 percent had no notation of delirium in their hospital chart (Lauril, Pitkala, Strandberg et al., 2004). Physicians are particularly unlikely to detect delirium when lethargy is present (Cole, 2004). Delirium is also often misdiagnosed when a person has dementia. Table 14.4 compares the features of dementia and delirium. Consider this suggestion for distinguishing delirium from dementia:

> The clinical "feel" of talking with a person with delirium is rather like talking to someone who is acutely intoxicated or in an acute psychotic episode. Whereas the demented patient may not remember the name of the place where she or he is, the delirious patient may believe it is a different sort of place altogether, perhaps mistaking a psychiatric ward for a used car lot. (Knight, 1996, pp. 96–97)

Detecting and treating delirium is of fundamental importance. Untreated, the mortality rate for delirium is high; more than one-third of people with the condition die within a year (McCusker, Cole, & Abrahamowicz, 2002). Beyond the risk of death, elderly adults who develop delirium in the hospital are at an increased risk of further cognitive decline (Jackson, Gordon, Hart et al., 2004) and of being transferred to a nursing home (Witlox, Eurelings, de Jonghe et al., 2010). It is not clear why delirium predicts such bad outcomes; some believe that delirium may be an indicator of an underlying frailty that becomes apparent in the face of medical conditions.

Etiology of Delirium As noted in the diagnostic criteria, delirium is caused by medical conditions. Several causes of delirium have been identified: drug intoxications and drug-withdrawal reactions, metabolic and nutritional imbalances (as in uncontrolled diabetes, thyroid dysfunction, kidney or liver failure, congestive heart failure, or malnutrition), dehydration, infections or fevers (like pneumonia or urinary tract infections), neurological disorders (like dementia, head trauma, or seizures), and the stress of major surgery (Zarit & Zarit, 2011). One of the most common triggers of delirium is hip surgery (Marcantonio, Flacker, Wright et al., 2001). As in the case of Henry at the start of this chapter, however, delirium usually has more than one cause.

Why are older adults so vulnerable to delirium? Many explanations have been offered: notably, the physical declines of late life, the increased susceptibility to chronic diseases, the many medications prescribed for older people, and the greater sensitivity to drugs.

Table 14.4 Comparative Features of Dementia and Delirium

Dementia	Delirium
Gradual deterioration of abilities	Rapid onset
Most commonly, deficits in memory for recent events	Trouble concentrating and staying with a train of thought
Caused by disease processes that are directly influencing the brain	Secondary to another medical condition
Usually progressive and nonreversible	Symptoms fluctuate over the course of a day
Treatment offers only minimal benefit	Usually reversible by treating underlying condition but potentially fatal if cause—e g., infection or malnutrition—not treated
Prevalence increases with age	Prevalence is highest in the very young as well as the old

Treatment of Delirium Complete recovery from delirium is possible if the underlying cause is treated promptly and effectively. Physicians must consider all possible reversible causes of the disorder and then treat any of the conditions identified. Beyond treating underlying medical conditions, the most common treatment is atypical antipsychotic medication (Lonergan et al., 2007). It usually takes 1 to 4 weeks for the condition to clear; it takes longer in older people than in younger people.

Because of the high rates of delirium in hospitalized older adults, preventive strategies are recommended to keep delirium from starting. It may help patients to stay oriented if clocks are placed within their field of vision, shades are open during the day and lights are turned off at night, and disruptions to sleep are minimized. In one study of such strategies, researchers randomly assigned 852 elderly hospitalized patients to receive either standard medical care alone or along with an intervention designed to prevent delirium. This intervention addressed common risk factors for delirium within the hospital setting, such as sleep deprivation, immobility, dehydration, and visual and hearing impairment. Among other strategies, medical tests and rounds were scheduled later in the morning to avoid waking patients, patients were helped to resume walking soon after surgery, nursing staff made sure that patients stayed hydrated and consumed enough calories, and patients' glasses and hearing aids were returned as soon as possible after medical procedures. Patients who received the intervention were less likely to develop delirium, and those who did develop delirium recovered more quickly compared to patients who received standard medical care (Inouye, Bogardus, Charpentier et al., 1999).

The high risk of delirium among people with dementia raises another set of prevention issues. The family of a person with dementia should learn the symptoms of delirium and know about its reversible nature so that they do not interpret the onset of delirium as a new stage of a progressive dementia. With proper diagnosis and treatment, the person can usually return to the earlier state.

Check Your Knowledge 14.3

Answer the questions.

1. What is the most prominent symptom of Alzheimer's disease?
2. What is the most common symptom of delirium?
   a. anxiety
   b. memory loss
   c. frank disorganization
   d. sad mood
3. Mary, a 70-year-old woman, was hospitalized for hip surgery. Although there were no immediate complications from the surgery, her son became concerned when he visited her that night because she was not making any sense. She thanked him for checking her into the Ritz Carlton and laughed giddily when he told her that she was in the hospital. Half an hour later, she began sobbing. Although she seemed fine the next morning, symptoms of acute confusion reemerged by lunchtime. Which diagnosis is most likely for Mary?
   a. Alzheimer's disease
   b. frontotemporal dementia
   c. mania
   d. delirium

Summary

Aging: Issues and Methods

- As life expectancy continues to improve, it will become even more important to learn about the disorders suffered by some older people and the most effective means of treating them.

- Several stereotypes about aging are false. Generally, people in late life report low levels of negative emotion, are not inappropriately concerned with their health, and are not lonely. On the other hand, stigma, bereavement, physical disease, polypharmacy, medication sensitivity, and sleep disruption, are common challenges for people as they age.

- In research studies, differences between a younger and an older group could reflect either cohort effects or effects of chronological age. Longitudinal studies are more helpful for making this distinction than cross-sectional studies are.

Psychological Disorders in Late Life

- Data indicate that persons over age 65 have the lowest overall rates of psychological disorders of all age groups. When older people do experience psychological disorders, the symptoms are often a recurrence of a disorder that first emerged earlier in life. It is important to rule out medical causes of psychological symptoms occurring during late life.

Neurocognitive Disorders in Late Life

- Serious cognitive disorders affect a small minority of older people. Two principal disorders have been distinguished: dementia and delirium.

- In dementia, the person's intellectual functioning declines and memory, abstract thinking, and judgment deteriorate. As the dementia progresses, the person may become oblivious to his or her surroundings. A variety of diseases can cause this deterioration. The most common is Alzheimer's disease. Genes play a major role in the etiology of Alzheimer's disease. A history of depression is a risk factor, and exercise and cognitive engagement appear to be protective.

- Other forms of dementia include frontotemporal dementia, vascular dementia, dementia with Lewy bodies, and dementia due to other medical conditions.

- Dementia usually responds only minimally to medication treatment, but the person and the family affected by the disease can be counseled on how to make the remaining time manageable and even rewarding. Exercise programs for people with dementia may help improve cognitive functioning.

- Delirium is defined by a sudden onset of difficulties with attention and awareness. The person may show a sudden clouding of consciousness, as well as other symptoms such as fragmented and undirected thought, incoherent speech, inability to sustain attention, hallucinations, illusions, disorientation, lethargy or hyperactivity, and mood swings. Symptoms tend to come on acutely and vary throughout the day. Delirium is most likely to affect children and older adults. The condition is reversible, provided that the underlying cause is adequately treated. Causes include overmedication, infection of brain tissue, high fevers, malnutrition, dehydration, endocrine disorders, head trauma, cerebrovascular problems, and surgery. Delirium is often not detected.

Answers to Check Your Knowledge Questions

14.1 1. F; 2. People report less negative emotion, tend to attend and react more to positive information, and are less reactive to negative information.; 3. People place more emphasis on close ties rather than broader social networks

14.2 1. a; 2. b; 3. b; 4. acetylcholine; 5. Medications might slow decline, but do not cure dementia.

14.3 l. memory loss; 2. c; 3. d

Key Terms

age effects
Alzheimer's disease
cognitive reserve
cohort effects
delirium
dementia

dementia with Lewy bodies
disorientation
frontotemporal dementia (FTD)
mild cognitive impairment
neurofibrillary tangles
plaques

selective mortality
social selectivity
time-of-measurement effects
vascular dementia

15 Personality Disorders

Clinical Case: Mary

Mary was single and 26 years old when she was first admitted to a psychiatric hospital. She had been in outpatient treatment with a psychologist for several months when her persistent thoughts of cutting, burning, and killing herself led her therapist to conclude that she needed more than outpatient treatment.

Mary's first experience with psychotherapy occurred when she was an adolescent. Her grades declined sharply in the eleventh grade, and her parents suspected she was using drugs. She began to miss curfews and, occasionally, to stay out all night. She often skipped school. Family therapy was started, and it seemed to go well at first. Mary was enthusiastic about the therapist and asked for additional private sessions with him.

During individual sessions, Mary revealed she had used drugs extensively and had prostituted herself several times to get drug money. Her relationships with her peers were in chronic turmoil. There was a constant parade of new friends, whom Mary at first thought to be the greatest ever but who soon disappointed her and were cast aside, often in very unpleasant ways.

After several weeks of family therapy, Mary's parents noticed that Mary was angry and abusive toward the therapist. After a few more weeks had passed, Mary refused to attend any more sessions. In a subsequent conversation with the therapist, Mary's father learned that she had behaved seductively toward the therapist during their private sessions and that her changed attitude coincided with his rejection of her advances despite the therapist's attempt to mix firmness with warmth and empathy.

Mary managed to graduate from high school and enrolled in a local community college, but the old patterns returned. Poor grades, continuing drug use, and lack of interest in her studies finally led her to quit college in the middle of the first semester of her second year. After leaving school,

Mary held a series of low-paying jobs. Most of them didn't last long, as her relationships with co-workers paralleled her relationships with her peers in high school. When Mary started a new job, she would find someone she really liked, but something would come between them, and the relationship would end angrily. She was often suspicious of her co-workers and reported that she heard them plotting how to prevent her from getting ahead on the job. She was quick to find hidden meanings in their behavior, as when she interpreted being the last person asked to sign a birthday card to mean that she was the least-liked person in the office. She indicated that she "received vibrations" from others and could tell when they really didn't like her even in the absence of any direct evidence.

Mary's frequent mood swings, with periods of depression and extreme irritability, led her to seek therapy several times. But after initial enthusiasm, her relationships with therapists always deteriorated, resulting in premature termination of therapy. By the time of her hospitalization, she had seen six therapists.

THE PERSONALITY DISORDERS ARE defined by enduring problems with forming a stably positive identity and with sustaining close and constructive relationships. Although these disorders are all defined by extreme and inflexible traits, the 10 **personality disorders** cover a broad range of symptom profiles. As examples of that heterogeneity, paranoid personality disorder is defined by chronic tendencies to be mistrustful and suspicious, antisocial personality disorder by patterns of irresponsibility and callous disregard for the rights of others, and dependent personality disorder by an overreliance on others. From time to time, we all behave, think, and feel in ways that are similar to symptoms of personality disorders, but an actual personality disorder is defined by the persistent, pervasive, and maladaptive ways in which these traits are expressed.

Our personalities shape almost every domain of our lives—our career choices, the quality of our relationships, the size of our social network, our favorite activities and preferred level of activity, our approach to tackling everyday problems, our willingness to break rules, and our typical level of well-being (Ozer & Benet-Martinez, 2006). Given how many areas of our life are shaped by personality traits, it stands to reason that the extreme and inflexible traits found in personality disorders create problems in multiple domains. People with personality disorders experience difficulties with their identity and their relationships, and these problems are sustained for years.

In this chapter we begin by considering the DSM-5 approach to classifying personality disorders and the assessment of the personality disorders. We will note some concerns about the DSM-5 approach to personality disorders, and we will then discuss an alternative system of classification that has been placed in the DSM-5 appendix. After considering these broad issues in the classification of personality disorders, we describe factors that increase the risk of personality disorders in general. Then, we discuss the specific personality disorders, including the clinical description and risk factors. We conclude with discussion of treatment of the personality disorders.

The DSM-5 Approach to Classification

In DSM-5, the 10 different personality disorders are classified in three clusters, reflecting the idea that these disorders are characterized by odd or eccentric behavior (cluster A); dramatic, emotional, or erratic behavior (cluster B); or anxious or fearful behavior (cluster C). These clusters form a useful organizational framework for our discussions in this chapter. Table 15.1 presents the personality disorders, their key features, and their grouping in clusters.

Table 15.1 Key Features of the DSM-5 Personality Disorders

	Key Features	Included in the Alternative DSM-5 Model for Personality Disorders?
Cluster A (odd/eccentric)		
Paranoid	Distrust and suspiciousness of others	No
Schizoid	Detachment from social relationships and restricted range of emotional expression	No
Schizotypal	Lack of capacity for close relationships, cognitive distortions, and eccentric behavior	Yes
Cluster B (dramatic/erratic)		
Antisocial	Disregard for and violation of the rights of others	Yes
Borderline	Instability of interpersonal relationships, self-image, and affect, as well as marked impulsivity	Yes
Histrionic	Excessive emotionally and attention seeking	No
Narcissistic	Grandiosity, need for admiration, and lack of empathy	Yes
Cluster C (anxious/fearful)		
Avoidant	Social inhibition, feelings of inadequacy, and hypersensitivity to negative evaluation	Yes
Dependent	Excessive need to be taken care of, submissive behavior, and fears of separation	No
Obsessive-compulsive	Preoccupation with order, perfection, and control	Yes

About 1 out of every 10 people meet the diagnostic criteria for a personality disorder (Sansone & Sansone, 2011). With rates this high, it is likely you know people who would meet the diagnostic criteria for a personality disorder.

Personality disorders tend to be more common among people with a psychological disorder such as major depressive disorder or an anxiety disorder. In one study, it was estimated that people with a personality disorder were seven times more likely to have an anxiety disorder or mood disorder than were those with no personality disorder, and four times as likely to have a substance use disorder (Lenzenweger, Lane, Loranger et al., 2007). The links of personality disorder with anxiety, mood, and substance are particularly pronounced for the cluster B personality disorders. As a result, personality disorders are commonly encountered in treatment settings, with as many as 40 percent of outpatients meeting the diagnostic criteria for a personality disorder (Newton-Howes, Tyrer, Anagnostakis et al., 2010). See Figure 15.1 for rates of specific personality disorders in the general community as compared to treatment settings.

When comorbid personality disorders are present, they are associated with more severe symptoms, poorer social functioning, and worse treatment outcome for many psychological disorders. For example, findings of a meta-analysis of 24 studies indicate that a comorbid personality disorder doubles the risk of poor outcomes in depressive disorders (Newton-Howes, Tyrer, & Johnson, 2006). Comorbid personality disorders also predict worse outcomes for anxiety disorders (Ansell, Pinto, Edelen et al., 2011).

Assessment of DSM-5 Personality Disorders

DSM-5 provides a list of criteria for each of the personality disorders, and structured interviews have been developed to cover these criteria. Table 15.2 shows interrater reliabilities of the personality disorders, as assessed using a structured diagnostic interview administered by experts (Zanarini, Skodol, Bender et al., 2000). Although diagnoses of most personality disorders have adequate or good reliability when structured interviews are used, schizoid personality disorder is still characterized by relatively low interrater reliability.

Of concern, most clinicians do not use structured interviews to assess personality. To examine the reliability of diagnoses for the three most common personality disorders when assessed with an unstructured clinical interview, the DSM-5 field trials involved clinicians from seven different major psychiatric centers. Clinicians were encouraged to use their typical

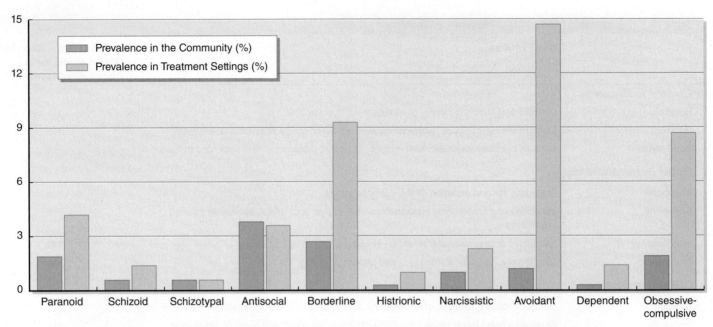

Figure 15.1 Rates of DSM personality disorders in the community and in treatment settings. *Source:* Prevalence estimates for community settings are drawn from Trull, Jahng, Tomko, et al., (2010); Samuels et al. (2002). Prevalence estimates for treatment settings are drawn from Zimmerman, Rothschild, & Chelminski (2005).

Table 15.2 Interrater Reliability for the Personality Disorders as Assessed by Structured Interview

Diagnosis	Interrater reliability (correlation)
Paranoid	.86
Schizoid	.69
Schizotypal	.91
Antisocial	.97
Borderline	.90
Histrionic	.83
Narcissistic	.88
Avoidant	.79
Dependent	.87
Obsessive-compulsive	.85

Source: Structured interview estimates from Zanarini et al. (2000)

clinical interviews, but two simple techniques were used to enhance those interviews. First, all patients completed a self-rating of their symptoms that was shared with the clinicians before the interview. Second, after the clinical interview, the interviewers completed a computerized checklist of symptoms to help organize their diagnostic decisions. Although the interrater reliability for borderline personality disorder was adequate, the reliability estimates of antisocial and obsessive-compulsive personality disorders were not adequate—clinicians who had relied on an unstructured interview frequently disagreed about whether the personality disorder was present (Regier, Kuhl, & Kupfer, 2013).

Beyond the relatively low agreement rates, clinicians using unstructured clinical interviews often miss personality disorder diagnoses (Zimmerman & Mattia, 1999). In one study, researchers conducted structured diagnostic interviews to assess borderline personality disorder with more than 400 patients, and then compared the results to the clinical diagnoses that those patients had received. Among patients who met the criteria for borderline personality disorder according to the structured clinical interviews, less than half had received that clinical diagnosis from their treatment provider (Zimmerman & Mattia, 1999).

Despite this strong evidence that structured diagnostic interviews can enhance diagnostic accuracy and reliability, many clinicians still prefer to use their own unstructured assessments rather than a structured interview. They often argue that a well-trained clinician might have a refined notion of personality disorders, and that we should rely on their judgments before those based on a structured interview. Research does not support this idea. Diagnoses based on structured interviews do a better job of predicting functioning and symptoms 5 years later than do those based on unstructured clinical interviews (Samuel, Sanislow, Hopwood et al., 2013).

Beyond decisions about whether to use a structured diagnostic interview, diagnosticians need to decide whether to interview someone who knows the patient. The diagnostic criteria specify that people with personality disorders tend to see themselves in distorted ways (Thomas, Turkheimer, & Oltmanns, 2003), and so it should not be surprising that clients' reports of their personality disorder symptoms tend to differ from the reports of their friends and families (Klonsky, Oltmanns, & Turkheimer, 2002). Interviews with people who know the patient well improve the accuracy of diagnosis (Bernstein, Kasapis, Bergman et al., 1997) and enhance the ability to predict social outcomes across a several-year follow-up (Klein,

2003). However, fewer than 10 percent of published studies of personality disorders gather data from people other than the person being diagnosed (Bornstein, 2003).

Problems with the DSM-5 Approach to Personality Disorders

There are some major concerns about the DSM-5 approach to personality disorders. For example, a growing body of research suggests that these disorders are not as stable as the definition implies, and there are extremely high rates of comorbidity among the personality disorders..

Personality Disorders Are Not Stable over Time

Although the very definition of personality disorders suggests that they should be stable over time, Figure 15.2 shows that about half of the people diagnosed with a personality disorder at one point in time had achieved remission (i.e., did not meet the criteria for the same diagnosis) when they were interviewed two years later (McGlashan, Grilo, Sanislow et al., 2005). When patients diagnosed with personality disorder were followed for 16 years, 99 percent of personality disorder diagnoses remitted (Zanarini, Frankenburg, Reich et al., 2011). Personality disorder symptoms appear to be most common during adolescence and then decline into the 20s (Johnson, Cohen, Kasen et al., 2000), with even more declines by late life (Balsis, Gleason, Woods et al., 2007). These results, then, indicate that many of the personality disorders may not be as enduring as the DSM asserts.

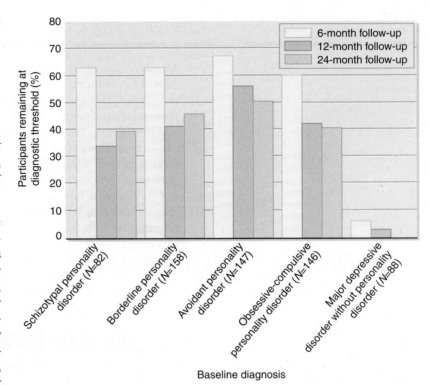

Figure 15.2 Test–retest stability for personality disorders and major depressive disorder across 6-, 12-, and 24-month follow-up interviews. [Drawn from Grilo, Shea, Sanislow et al. (2004); Shea, Stout, Gunderson et al. (2002).]

Even though these symptoms are not as persistent as the definition of personality disorder implies, these diagnoses do seem important for predicting long-term outcomes. First, many people still have some symptoms after remission, just not at the levels required for diagnosis. Second, even after remission, many problems with functioning persist. Baseline diagnoses of personality disorders predict lower functioning and more depression even 10 to 15 years later (Hong, Samuels, Bienvenu et al., 2005; Morey, Hopwood, Markowitz et al., 2012). Third, even years after remission, the risk of relapse remains high—symptoms of personality disorders often wax and wane over time (Zanarini et al., 2011). Hence, even after remission, a diagnosis of personality disorder can predict ongoing difficulty in achieving a truly satisfying lifestyle.

Personality Disorders Are Highly Comorbid A second major problem in classifying personality disorders arises from their comorbidity with each other. The Clinical Case of Mary illustrates this issue: Mary met the diagnostic criteria not only for borderline personality disorder but also for paranoid personality disorder. More than 50 percent of people diagnosed with a personality disorder meet the diagnostic criteria for another personality disorder (Lenzenweger et al., 2007). Some of the personality disorders involve similar types of concerns. For example, as we will see, the diagnostic criteria for schizotypal, avoidant, and paranoid personality disorders all emphasize difficulty in forming close relationships, and so it is not surprising that these diagnoses often co-occur. The high rates of overlap among the personality disorders is discouraging when we try to interpret the results of research that compares people who have a specific personality disorder with some control group. If, for example, we find that people with borderline personality disorder differ from healthy people, is our finding related to borderline personality disorder or to personality disorders in general?

In sum, the DSM system might not be ideal for classifying personality disorders, because of the lack of test–retest stability and the high rates of comorbidity. These types of concerns led the DSM-5 Committee on Personality and Personality Disorders to recommend a fundamentally revised approach to personality disorders. We turn to this system next.

Alternative DSM-5 Model for Personality Disorders

To address issues with the traditional approach to diagnosing personality disorders, the DSM-5 Committee on Personality and Personality Disorders suggested a bold overhaul. They recommended reducing the number of personality disorders, incorporating personality trait dimensions, and diagnosing personality disorders on the basis of extreme scores on personality trait dimensions. The APA Board of Trustees decided to retain the personality disorder system that was in place in DSM-IV-TR but included the alternative approach in the appendix of the DSM-5 manual. Although the approach to personality disorders that appears in the main text dominates clinical practice, it is worth considering the merits of the alternative approach.

As shown in Table 15.1, the alternative DSM-5 Model for Personality Disorders includes only 6 of the 10 DSM-5 personality disorders. Schizoid, histrionic, and dependent personality disorders are excluded from the alternative system because they rarely occur. Paranoid personality disorder, which frequently overlapped with other personality disorders in its occurrence, is also excluded from the alternative system. As shown in Table 15.2, interrater reliability is adequate for each of the six personality disorders included in the alternative system when assessed with a structured diagnostic interview.

Table 15.3 The 5 Personality Trait Domains and 25 Facets in the DSM-5

I. Negative Affectivity (vs. Emotional Stability)

Facet
1. Anxiousness
2. Emotional lability
3. Hostility
4. Perseveration
5. Separation insecurity
6. Submissiveness

II. Detachment (vs. Extraversion)

7. Anhedonia
8. Depressivity
9. Intimacy avoidance
10. Suspiciousness
11. Withdrawal
12. Restricted affectivity

III. Antagonism (vs. Agreeableness)

13. Attention seeking
14. Callousness
15. Deceitfulness
16. Grandiosity
17. Manipulativeness

IV. Disinhibition (vs. Conscientiousness)

18. Distractibility
19. Impulsivity
20. Irresponsibility
21. (Lack of) rigid perfectionism
22. Risk taking

V. Psychoticism

23. Eccentricity
24. Cognitive perceptual dysregulation
25. Unusual beliefs and experiences

In the alternative DSM-5 model, diagnoses are based on personality traits. The system includes two types of dimensional scores: 5 **personality trait domains** and 25 more specific **personality trait facets**, as shown in Table 15.3. Each dimension can be rated using self-report items (Krueger, et al., 2012). For example, the Anxiousness facet is assessed with items like "I worry a lot about terrible things that might happen." These personality trait domains and facets are closely related to a very influential model of personality called the five-factor model (McCrae & Costa, 1990).

Extreme scores on these dimensions have been shown to distinguish people with personality disorders from those in the general population (Clark & Livesley, 2002; Samuel & Widiger, 2008). In the alternative DSM-5 model, personality disorders are to be diagnosed when a person shows persistent and pervasive impairments in self and interpersonal aspects of functioning from early adulthood. If a personality disorder is to be diagnosed, the clinician uses the person's profile of personality domain and facet scores to decide which personality disorder might best fit. For example, obsessive-compulsive personality disorder is defined by high scores on rigid perfectionism, along with high scores on at least two of the three dimensions of perseveration, intimacy avoidance, and restricted affectivity.

The focus on personality traits has several advantages. Some of the key strengths include the following.

- Those who meet the criteria for a given personality disorder can vary a good deal from one another in their personality traits and the severity of their symptoms. By using the personality trait dimension system, clinicians can specify which personality traits are of most concern for a given client. The 25 dimensional scores provide richer detail than do the personality disorder diagnoses.
- Personality trait ratings tend to be more stable over time than are personality disorder diagnoses (McGlashan, et al., 2005).
- Personality trait dimensions are related to many aspects of psychological adjustment and even physical outcomes. For example, many psychological disorders such as anxiety, depression, and somatic symptom disorder can be related to elevations of personality traits such as negative affectivity (Kotov, Gamez, Schmidt et al., 2010). Personality dimensions also robustly predict important interpersonal outcomes such as the quality of friendships and partnerships, performance in one's career, health behaviors, and happiness, and they even predict life expectancy (Hopwood & Zanarini, 2010; Ozer & Benet-Martinez, 2006; Roberts, Kuncel, Shiner et al., 2007). A system based on personality traits helps link the DSM with a broad research literature on personality (Tyrer, 2013).

Despite the strengths of the alternative DSM-5 model for personality disorders, we focus on the approach to personality disorders that appears in the main body of the DSM-5. Debate about the best classification systems should not lead us to underestimate the importance of identifying personality disorders. Personality disorders are prevalent, and they cause severe impairments.

Quick Summary

Personality disorders are defined by long-standing and pervasive ways of being that cause distress and impairment through their influence on forming and sustaining a positive self-identity and constructive relationships. Many people with personality disorders also meet the diagnostic criteria for comorbid conditions such as depressive, anxiety, and substance use disorders as well as other personality disorders. In DSM-5, personality disorders are classified in three clusters: cluster A personality disorders are characterized by odd or eccentric behavior; cluster B by dramatic, emotional, or erratic behavior; and cluster C by anxious or fearful behavior. Most personality disorders can be reliably assessed with structured clinical interviews, but unstructured clinical interviews tend to be unreliable and have less predictive validity.

Two concerns have emerged about the DSM-5 personality disorder approach: the personality disorders are not stable over time, and they overlap substantially. An alternative DSM-5 model was developed to address these concerns. The alternative model includes only six personality disorders and also includes a dimensional system for evaluating five personality trait domains and 25 more specific personality facets. The alternative model is placed in the appendix of the DSM-5.

Check Your Knowledge 15.1 (Answers are at the end of the chapter.)

Answer the following questions.
1. Describe the level of interrater reliability obtained for the DSM-5 personality disorders with structured diagnostic interviews and with unstructured diagnostic interviews.

2. List two primary concerns about the DSM-5 approach to personality disorders.
3. List two ways in which the alternative DSM-5 approach to personality differs from the approach that appears in the main body of the DSM manual.

Common Risk Factors Across the Personality Disorders

Theorists over the past 100 years have tried to understand why the chronic, wide-ranging symptoms of personality disorders develop. Although psychoanalytic and behavioral theory placed emphasis on parenting and early developmental influences, more recent work provides evidence for a strong biological component to these syndromes as well. To provide some background on how nature and nurture could be related to the personality disorders, we will focus on two major studies. Both studies examined all 10 DSM-5 personality disorders. Although much of the research on personality disorders has focused on patient samples (and so might be most relevant for those with severe personality disorders), both of these studies relied on large community samples.

Let's begin with the Children in the Community Study, designed to assess the links between childhood adversity and personality disorders. In this study, researchers recruited a representative sample of 639 families with children between ages 1 and 11. Families and children were first interviewed in 1975, again in 1983–1985, for a third time between 1991 and 1993, and then the offspring were interviewed when they reached age 33. Records from child protective services documented childhood maltreatment for 31 of the children, and another 50 cases of abuse were identified through self-report. In the assessments conducted in the 1970s and 1980s, researchers conducted interviews with the parents and children to assess two aspects of parenting style: aversive parental behavior (e.g., harsh punishment, loud arguments) and lack of parental affection (e.g., little time together, poor supervision, poor communication). At the third and fourth interviews, the researchers conducted structured diagnostic interviews to assess personality disorders, and the young adults were interviewed about experiences of childhood neglect. Offspring who experienced childhood abuse or neglect were compared with a control group matched on age, parental education, and parental psychiatric disorders (Johnson, Cohen, Brown et al., 1999).

Findings of this study suggested that personality disorders were strongly related to early adversity. Childhood abuse or neglect was related to significantly higher risk of six of the personality disorders: paranoid, antisocial, borderline, narcissistic, dependent, and obsessive-compulsive personality disorders. Some of the personality disorders were particularly related to childhood abuse or neglect. For example, children who experienced abuse or neglect were 18 times as likely to develop narcissistic personality disorder and more than 6 times as likely to develop paranoid, borderline, or dependent personality disorder, as were those with no history of abuse or neglect. Parenting style also predicted six of the DSM-5 personality disorders after controlling for childhood behavioral problems and parental psychopathology. Offspring who had experienced aversive or unaffectionate parental styles were several times more likely to develop a personality disorder than were those who had not experienced those parental styles (Johnson, Cohen, Chen et al., 2006). Clearly, many people with personality disorders have had difficult experiences during their childhood.

Let's now consider a study designed to estimate the heritability of personality disorders. Researchers used the Norwegian birth registry to recruit a representative sample of twins. To improve diagnostic reliability, the researchers combined self-ratings with interview-based ratings of personality disorder severity. As shown in Table 15.4, heritability estimates for all of the personality disorders were at least moderately high. These statistics indicate that we need to consider the biological as well as the social roots of personality disorders.

The magnitude of the genetic influence on personality disorders suggests that we should be cautious throughout this chapter as we think about parenting and early environment—many parents of those with personality disorders are likely to experience at least mild

Table 15.4 Estimated Heritability of the Personality Disorders

Disorder	Estimated Heritability
Paranoid	.66
Schizoid	.55
Schizotypal	.72
Antisocial	.69
Borderline	.67
Histrionic	.63
Narcissistic	.71
Avoidant	.64
Dependent	.66
Obsessive-compulsive	.77

Heritability estimates from Kendler, Myers et al. (2007); Gjerde et al. (2012); Torgersen, Myers et al. (2012); Torgersen, Lygren, Øien et al. (2000).

personality problems themselves. We will discuss the idea that correlation may not mean causation later in the chapter, as we consider studies that have tried to fit together the genetic and environmental contributions to personality disorders.

We now turn to the clinical description of the personality disorders and to the risk factors that shape their development more specifically than the general influences described here. As we do so, our coverage of etiology will depend on the depth of research available. There is a vast literature on borderline personality disorder and antisocial personality disorder, but for other disorders, little is known beyond the genetic vulnerability and early adversity factors described here. Because so little is known about the etiology of paranoid, schizoid, or histrionic personality disorders, we will not discuss the etiology of these three disorders further.

Clinical Description and Etiology of the Odd/Eccentric Cluster

The odd/eccentric cluster of personality disorders includes paranoid personality disorder, schizoid personality disorder, and schizotypal personality disorder. The symptoms of these three disorders bear some similarity to the types of bizarre thinking and experiences seen in schizophrenia. In the cluster A personality disorders, though, the bizarre thinking and experiences are less severe than they are in schizophrenia.

DSM-5 Criteria for Paranoid Personality Disorder

Presence of 4 or more of the following signs of distrust and suspiciousness from early adulthood across many contexts:

- Unjustified suspiciousness of being harmed, deceived, or exploited
- Unwarranted doubts about the loyalty or trustworthiness of friends or associates
- Reluctance to confide in others because of suspiciousness
- The tendency to read hidden meanings into the benign actions of others
- Bears grudges for perceived wrongs
- Angry reactions to perceived attacks on character or reputation
- Unwarranted suspiciousness of the partner's fidelity

DSM-5 Criteria for Schizoid Personality Disorder

Presence of 4 or more of the following signs of aloofness and flat affect from early adulthood across many contexts:

- Lack of desire for or enjoyment of close relationships
- Almost always prefers solitude to companionship
- Little interest in sex
- Few or no pleasurable activities
- Lack of friends
- Indifference to praise or criticism
- Flat affect, emotional detachment, or coldness

Clinical Case: Danielle

Danielle and her partner sought marital therapy because their day-to-day life was filled with acrimonious quarrels. During the course of the interview, it became clear that Danielle was often angry and hostile toward her partner over small daily incidents. For instance, she thought that he chewed loudly as a way of upsetting her and that he rolled over in bed to deliberately wake her up at night. At a deeper level, they had experienced several periods in which she became deeply fearful that he was having an affair, and despite his protestations to the contrary, her fears were very difficult to calm.

In an individual interview, it became clear that her husband was only one of many sources of worry and annoyance for Danielle. Danielle worried that that the neighbors played their stereo loudly just to get at her and that her boss assigned her challenging jobs because he wanted to see her squirm. She had long since stopped using banks as she felt that the management might scheme to keep her money, and she refused to use email because she was concerned that the government would monitor her computer transactions. Although bright and witty, she was unable to identify women whom she could trust, leaving her friendless. Indeed, every relationship in her life seemed to be colored by the sense that the other person could harm her or take her resources. Although Danielle felt extremely stressed by her social troubles, she did not believe that she had contributed to any of the conflicts, and she felt highly victimized by these difficult interpersonal circumstances.

2

2

DSM-5 Criteria for Schizotypal Personality Disorder

Presence of 5 or more of the following signs of unusual thinking, eccentric behavior, and interpersonal deficits from early adulthood across many contexts:

- Ideas of reference
- Odd beliefs or magical thinking, e.g., belief in extrasensory perception
- Unusual perceptions
- Odd thought and speech
- Suspiciousness or paranoia
- Inappropriate or restricted affect
- Odd or eccentric behavior or appearance
- Lack of close friends
- Social anxiety and interpersonal fears that do not diminish with familiarity

Paranoid Personality Disorder

People with **paranoid personality disorder** (see the Clinical Case of Danielle) are suspicious of others, including strangers, casual acquaintances, and even family members. They expect to be mistreated or exploited and thus are secretive and continually on the lookout for signs of trickery and abuse. They are often hostile and angry in response to perceived insults. Co-workers tend to see them as difficult and critical. Their lives tend to be filled with conflict, and those conflicts can be quite long-lasting. Sadly, the conflicts tend to perpetuate their paranoia—their frequent battles provide evidence that people just cannot be trusted.

This disorder is different from paranoid schizophrenia because other symptoms of schizophrenia, such as hallucinations, are not present and there is less impairment in social and occupational functioning. Also absent is the cognitive disorganization that is characteristic of schizophrenia. It differs from delusional disorder because full-blown delusions are not present. Paranoid personality disorder co-occurs most often with schizotypal, borderline, and avoidant personality disorders.

Schizoid Personality Disorder

Like Joe (see Clinical Case), people with **schizoid personality disorder** do not desire or enjoy social relationships, and they usually have no close friends. They appear dull, bland, and aloof and have no warm, tender feelings for other people. They rarely experience strong emotions, are not interested in sex, and have few pleasurable activities. Indifferent to praise or criticism, people with this disorder are loners who pursue solitary interests.

Schizotypal Personality Disorder

The defining features of **schizotypal personality disorder** include eccentric thoughts and behavior, interpersonal detachment, and suspiciousness. People with this disorder might have odd beliefs or magical thinking—for instance, the belief that they can read other people's minds and see into the future. It is also common for them to have ideas of reference (the belief that events have a particular and unusual meaning for them personally). For example, they might feel that a TV program conveys a special message designed for them. They are often suspicious of others and concerned that others might hurt them. They might also have recurrent illusions (inaccurate sensory perceptions), such as sensing the presence of a force or a person that is not actually there. In their speech, they might use words in an unusual and unclear fashion—for example, they might say "not a very talkable person" to mean a person who is not easy to talk to. Their behavior and appearance might also be eccentric—for example, they might talk to themselves or wear dirty and disheveled clothing. Their affect appears constricted and flat, and they tend to be aloof from others. A study of the relative

Clinical Case: Joe

Joe, a 53-year-old unmarried Vietnam veteran, was referred for therapy by his general practitioner due to concerns about Joe's disconnection from most aspects of the social world. Joe reluctantly agreed to see a therapist. He had not worked in several years and survived on a small disability pension from the Veterans Administration. He said that he found it unpleasant to shop for groceries because he didn't like having other people around him. The landlady at his boarding house persisted in trying to introduce him to women, even though he had declared his lack of interest in each and every one of the 10 women she had pestered him to meet. He stated that he did not like talking, and in therapy sessions, he was often silent for long periods. He did talk about his sense that he had no real interpersonal ties and that he experienced little emotion other than mild irritability. Indeed, he was unable to describe a single person or activity that made him happy. After six weeks of therapy, Joe announced that he didn't think that he was the type of person who would feel any better from talking about things and that he had decided to spend his remaining savings to purchase a small cabin in a remote section of Maine. He seemed content with his decision, stating that by living there, he could successfully escape from almost all social interaction. He moved the next week.

importance of these symptoms for diagnosis found that suspiciousness, ideas of reference, and illusions were most telling (Widiger, Frances, & Trull, 1987). Although most do not develop delusions (convictions in patently absurd beliefs) or schizophrenia, some people diagnosed with schizotypal personality disorder develop more severe psychotic symptoms over time, and a small proportion do develop schizophrenia over time (Raine, 2006).

A fair amount of research has focused on the causes of the odd thinking, bizarre behavior, and interpersonal difficulties that appear in schizotypal personality disorder. As noted above, genetic factors and childhood adversity are likely both involved. Beyond this, the biological vulnerability for schizotypal personality disorder appears to overlap with the genetic vulnerability for schizophrenia (Siever & Davis, 2004). That is, family studies and adoption studies have shown that the relatives of people with schizophrenia are at increased risk for schizotypal personality disorder (Nigg & Goldsmith, 1994; Tienari, Wynne, Laksy et al., 2003). Studies also have consistently shown that people with schizotypal personality disorder have deficits in cognitive and neuropsychological functioning that are similar to but milder than those seen in schizophrenia (McClure, Barch, Flory et al., 2008; Raine, 2006). Furthermore, and again paralleling findings from schizophrenia research, people with schizotypal personality disorder have enlarged ventricles and less temporal lobe gray matter (Dickey, McCarley, & Shenton, 2002).

Clinical Description and Etiology of the Dramatic/Erratic Cluster

The disorders in the dramatic/erratic cluster—antisocial personality disorder, borderline personality disorder, histrionic personality disorder, and narcissistic personality disorder—are characterized by symptoms that range from highly inconsistent behavior to inflated self-esteem, rule-breaking behavior, and exaggerated emotional displays, including anger outbursts. More is known about the etiology of personality disorders in the dramatic/erratic cluster than those in the other clusters.

Antisocial Personality Disorder and Psychopathy

Informally, the lay public often uses the terms *antisocial personality disorder* and *psychopathy* interchangeably. Antisocial behavior, such as law breaking, is a core component of both, but the two syndromes differ in important ways. One difference is that antisocial personality disorder is included in the DSM, whereas psychopathy is not.

Antisocial Personality Disorder: Clinical Description The core feature of **antisocial personality disorder** (APD) is a pervasive pattern of disregard for the rights of others (as described in the Clinical Case of Alec). The person with APD is distinguished by aggressive, impulsive, and callous traits. DSM-5 criteria specify the presence of conduct disorder: People with APD often report a history of such symptoms as truancy, running away from home, frequent lying, theft, arson, and deliberate destruction of property by early adolescence. As adults, people with APD show irresponsible behavior such as working inconsistently, breaking laws, being irritable and physically aggressive, defaulting on debts, being reckless and impulsive, and neglecting to plan ahead. They show little regard for truth and little remorse for their misdeeds, even when those actions hurt family and friends.

Men are about five times more likely than are women to meet criteria for APD (Oltmanns & Powers, 2012). About three-quarters of people with APD meet the diagnostic criteria for another disorder, with substance abuse being very common (Lenzenweger et al., 2007). Not surprisingly, then, high rates of APD are observed in drug and alcohol rehabilitation facilities (Sutker & Adams, 2001). About three-quarters of convicted felons meet the diagnostic criteria for APD.

Psychopathy: Clinical Description The concept of **psychopathy** predates the DSM diagnosis of antisocial personality disorder. In his book *The Mask of Sanity*, Hervey Cleckley (1976) drew on his clinical experience to formulate diagnostic criteria for psychopathy. The criteria for psychopathy focus on the person's thoughts and feelings. One of the key characteristics of psychopathy is poverty of emotions, both positive and negative: Psychopathic people

---

DSM-5 Criteria for Antisocial Personality Disorder

- Age at least 18
- Evidence of conduct disorder before age 15
- Pervasive pattern of disregard for the rights of others since the age of 15 as shown by at least three of the following:

  1. Repeated law breaking
  2. Deceitfulness, lying
  3. Impulsivity
  4. Irritability and aggressiveness
  5. Reckless disregard for own safety and that of others
  6. Irresponsibility as seen in unreliable employment or financial history
  7. Lack of remorse

Clinical Case: Alec

Alec, a 40-year-old man, was court-ordered to take part in a psychological assessment after being charged with manufacturing counterfeit bills. He described his history of three divorces with no remorse. His first marriage had ended in a rancorous divorce after he was discovered having two simultaneous extramarital affairs. His second marriage ended within three months, and he bragged about emptying her large savings account, stating, "A fool and her money are easily parted." His third wife divorced him after discovering that he had been trafficking in stolen furniture. He had a long history of petty financial and drug-related crimes, and despite his frequent drug dealing, he was deeply in debt. He was estranged from all family members, and his friends seemed to consist of the regulars at his neighborhood bar.

have no sense of shame, and their seemingly positive feelings for others are merely an act. They are superficially charming and use that charm to manipulate others for personal gain. Their lack of anxiety might make it impossible for them to learn from their mistakes, and their lack of remorse leads them to behave irresponsibly and often cruelly toward others. The rule-breaking behavior of a person with psychopathy is performed impulsively, as much for thrills as for financial gain. Researchers have argued that three core traits underpin these different symptoms: boldness, meanness, and impulsivity (Patrick, Fowles, & Krueger, 2009). The most commonly used scale to assess psychopathy is the Psychopathy Checklist–Revised (PCL-R; Hare, 2003). Ratings on this 20-item scale are made based on an interview and review of criminal records and mental health charts.

There are two chief differences between the criteria for APD and the definition of psychopathy as reflected on the PCL-R. First, even though the PCL-R covers many of the criteria for APD, the scale differs from the DSM-5 criteria for APD in including more affective symptoms, such as shallow affect and lack of empathy (Hare & Neumann, 2006). Second, the DSM-5 criteria for antisocial personality disorder differ from psychopathy criteria in the requirement that a person develop symptoms before age 15. The differences in definition lead to considerable divergence between the two syndromes; many people diagnosed with DSM APD will not obtain high scores on the Psychopathy Checklist (Rutherford, Cacciola, & Alterman, 1999).

FOCUS ON DISCOVERY 15.1

Media Images of Psychopathy: Will the Real Psychopath Please Stand Up?

Media images of psychopathy vary considerably, ranging from portrayals of ruthless murderers to charming business tycoons to white-collar criminals. The media is quick to label psychopathy in mass murderers and other ruthless, violent offenders. At the same time, the idea that people with psychopathy use their charm, boldness, and lack of empathy to climb their way into the board room, where they are influencing the culture of current business practice, also has become quite widespread in the media. Stories abound like the one portrayed in the film *The Wolf of Wall Street* of remorseless capitalists who bilk their customers of money through white-collar crime (Smith & Lilienfeld, 2013).

Data is available regarding each of these stereotypes. Some, but certainly not all, people with high levels of psychopathy engage in violence as a means of achieving their goals (Reidy, Shelley-Tremblay, & Lilienfeld, 2011). Regarding corporate success, a widely cited study did suggest that employees in a large corporate management training program obtained PCL-R scores that were somewhat higher than the general population, but only 3 percent of the employees scored above the PCL-R threshold for psychopathy (Babiak, Neumann, & Hare, 2010). Moreover, psychopathy scores were not elevated in one sample of white-collar criminals (Ragatz, Fremouw, & Baker, 2012). It is not safe to presume that someone is psychopathic just because he or she engages in violent or unethical behavior, or is highly ambitious and successful. Careful diagnosis depends on evaluating whether an entire syndrome is present.

Etiology of Antisocial Personality Disorder and Psychopathy As we review research on the etiology of ASP and psychopathy, keep in mind two issues that make findings a little hard to integrate. First, research has been conducted on persons diagnosed in different ways—some with APD and some with psychopathy. Second, most research on APD and psychopathy has been conducted on persons who have been convicted as criminals. Thus, the results of this research might not be applicable to those with APD who are not criminals or who avoid arrest. Indeed, among people with high psychopathy levels, cognitive and psychophysiological deficits are more likely among people who have been convicted than those who have not been caught (Ishikawa, Raine, Lencz et al., 2001).

Three-quarters of convicted felons meet the DSM criteria for antisocial personality disorder.

More than any other area of personality disorder research, the work on APD often conjointly considers biology with social and psychological risk factors. In this section, we will see this in two ways. First, in considering the social correlates of APD, we will describe how genes and social risk factors work together. Second, as we discuss psychological models of APD, we will note several studies that have used brain imaging to test these models. To capture these integrated models, we will deviate from our organizational approach in other sections of the book, where we tend to separate neurobiological and psychological models.

Interactions of Genes and the Social Environment Major studies support the role of the social environment as a key factor in APD. Parenting qualities of negativity, inconsistency, and low warmth predict antisocial behavior (Marshall & Cooke, 1999; Reiss, Heatherington, Plomin et al., 1995). Substantial prospective research also shows that broader social factors, including poverty and exposure to violence, predict antisocial behavior (Loeber & Hay, 1997). For example, among adolescents with conduct disorder, those who are impoverished are twice as likely to develop APD as are those from higher socioeconomic status backgrounds (Lahey, Loeber, Burke et al., 2005). There is little question that childhood adversity can set the stage for the development of APD.

The effects of early adversity might be particularly negative for those who are genetically vulnerable to APD. Across multiple studies, a polymorphism of the *MAO-A* gene has been found to predict psychopathy among males who had experienced childhood physical or sexual abuse or maternal rejection (Byrd & Manuck, 2014; Caspi, McClay, Moffitt et al., 2002). The effects of growing up in a difficult environment on APD may be amplified by genetic factors.

Adoption research has also shown that genetic, behavioral, and family influences are very hard to disentangle (Ge, Conger, Cadoret et al., 1996). That is, the genetically influenced antisocial behavior of the child can provoke harsh discipline and lack of warmth, even in adoptive parents, and these parental characteristics in turn exacerbate the child's antisocial tendencies. Nonetheless, the findings of many studies indicate that social influences such as harsh discipline and poverty robustly predict APD even after controlling for genetic risk (Jaffee, Strait, & Odgers, 2012).

Psychological Risk: Insensitivity to Threat and to Others' Emotions People with psychopathy seem unable to learn from experience; they often repeat misconduct that has been harshly punished, even if it resulted in jail time. They seem immune to the anxiety that keeps most of us from breaking the law, lying, or injuring others. Cleckley argued that people with psychopathy do not learn to avoid trouble because they are insensitive to threats.

A large body of work relates psychopathy to deficits in the experience of fear and threat. At rest, people with psychopathy have lower-than-normal levels of skin conductance, and their skin conductance is less reactive when they are confronted with or anticipate an aversive stimulus

(Lorber, 2004). This low skin conductance reactivity to aversive stimuli (loud tones) at age 3 was found to predict psychopathy scores at age 28 (Glenn, Raine, Venables et al., 2007).

The behavioral model draws from this idea to suggest that the rule breaking observed in psychopathy stems from deficits in developing conditioned fear responses. In an interesting test of this theory, researchers used brain activity as a way to examine what happens with classical conditioning in which an unconditioned stimulus (painful pressure) was repeatedly paired with neutral pictures (the conditioned stimuli). To measure responses to the conditioned stimulus after these repeated pairings, the researchers measured the activity of the amygdala and other brain regions involved in emotion (Birbaumer, Veit, Lotze et al., 2005). The amygdala is a brain region that is strongly implicated in emotion reactivity (see Figure 6.3), and activity of this region has been found to be heightened in several disorders that involve intense emotionality, including mood disorders and anxiety disorders. After conditioning, healthy control participants showed increases in amygdala activity when viewing the neutral pictures. People with high psychopathy scores, though, did not show this expected increase in amygdala activity. These findings suggest that people with psychopathy show weakened classical conditioning to aversive stimuli.

Beyond their general lack of response to threat, the person with psychopathy might become even more unresponsive to threats when trying to gain a reward, such as money or other resources. In a study demonstrating this phenomenon, participants played a computerized card game in which they earned 5¢ for each face card that appeared; if a nonface card appeared, the participant lost 5¢ (Newman, Patterson, & Kosson, 1987). Participants could quit the game anytime they wanted. The game was rigged so that over time, the probability of losing increased. People with high psychopathy scores continued to play the game much longer than did people with low psychopathy, even when they were being punished. Findings like these suggest that psychopathy is related to inattentiveness to threats when pursuing a goal (Zeier & Newman, 2013). Consistent with these findings, antisocial behavior is associated with deficits in regions of the prefrontal cortex that are involved in attending to negative information during goal pursuit (Ermer, Cope, Nyalakanti et al., 2012; Yang & Raine, 2009).

In contrast to a general insensitivity to threat, some researchers believe that a lack of empathy, defined as the capacity to share the emotional reactions of others, could be the central deficit driving the callous exploitation of others observed in psychopathy (Blair, 2005). Several types of research provide support for this theory. When asked to identify the emotion conveyed in videos of strangers, men with psychopathy do very poorly in recognizing others' fear, even though they recognize other emotions well (Brook & Kosson, 2013). To test whether their lack of empathy extends to insensitivity toward others' victimization, researchers have studied responses to pictures of victimization events (e.g., a break-in, a physical attack). People with high psychopathy levels show less psychophysiological or neural response to viewing pictures of victimization than do those with low psychopathy levels (Harenski, Harenski, Shane et al., 2010; Levenston, Patrick, Bradley et al., 2000).

Borderline Personality Disorder

Borderline personality disorder (BPD) has been a major focus of interest for several reasons: it is very common in clinical settings, very hard to treat, and associated with recurrent periods of suicidality. The core features of **borderline personality disorder** are impulsivity and instability in relationships and mood. For example, people with this disorder may shift from blissful happiness to outraged explosions in the blink of an eye. Attitudes and feelings toward other people can also change drastically, inexplicably, and very quickly, particularly from passionate idealization to contemptuous anger (Trull, Solhan, Tragesser et al., 2008). As in the Clinical Case of Mary, which opened this chapter, the intense anger of people with BPD often damages relationships. People with BPD are overly sensitive to small signs of emotions in others (Lynch, Rosenthal, Kosson et al., 2006). Their unpredictable, impulsive, and potentially self-damaging behavior might include gambling, reckless spending, indiscriminate sexual activity, and substance abuse. People with BPD often have not developed a clear and coherent sense of self—they sometimes experience major swings in such basic aspects of identity as their values, loyalties, and career choices. One month, they might consider a career in the business world, complete with the wardrobe and polished demeanor of a professional salesperson; the next month, they might decide to try acting, trading in their business apparel for colorful artistic garb, accompanied by a new set of interests in the arts. They cannot bear to be alone, have fears of abandonment, and experience chronic feelings of depression and emptiness. They may experience transient psychotic and dissociative symptoms when stressed.

Suicidal behavior is all too common in BPD. Many people with this disorder make multiple suicide attempts during their lifetime (Boisseau, Yen, Markowitz et al., 2013). In one 20-year follow-up study, about 7.5 percent of people with BPD died from suicide (Linehan & Heard, 1999). People with BPD are also particularly likely to engage in nonsuicidal self-injury (see Focus on Discovery 5.7). For example, they might slice their legs with a razor blade or burn their arms with cigarettes—behaviors that are harmful but unlikely to cause death. At least two-thirds of people with BPD will engage in self-mutilation at some point during their lives (Stone, 1993).

People with BPD are very likely to have comorbid posttraumatic stress disorder, and mood disorders, substance-related disorders, and eating disorders (McGlashan, Grilo, Skodol et al., 2000). When present, comorbid conditions predict greater likelihood that BPD symptoms will be sustained over several years (Zanarini, Frankenburg, Hennen et al., 2004).

A colorful account by Jonathan Kellerman, a clinical psychologist and successful mystery writer, gives a good sense of what people with BPD are like.

After he was diagnosed with borderline personality disorder in 2010, Brandon Marshall, the highly successful wide receiver for the Chicago Bears, created the Brandon Marshall Foundation to help improve awareness of mental health, to reduce stigma, and to provide funding for treatment.

They're the chronically depressed, the determinedly addictive, the compulsively divorced, living from one emotional disaster to the next. Bed hoppers, stomach pumpers, freeway jumpers, and sad-eyed bench-sitters with arms stitched up like footballs and psychic wounds that can never be sutured. Their egos are as fragile as spun sugar, their psyches irretrievably fragmented, like a jigsaw puzzle with crucial pieces missing. They play roles with alacrity, excel at being anyone but themselves, crave intimacy but repel it when they find it. Some of them gravitate toward stage or screen; others do their acting in more subtle ways. . . . Borderlines go from therapist to therapist, hoping to find a magic bullet for the crushing feelings of emptiness. They turn to chemical bullets, gobble tranquilizers and antidepressants, alcohol and cocaine. (Kellerman, 1989, pp. 113–114)

Fortunately, research on new treatments for BPD, discussed later in the chapter, supports a more positive outlook than Kellerman offers.

Etiology of Borderline Personality Disorder Many different risk factors may contribute to the development of BPD. We discuss neurobiological factors, research that conjointly considers genetic vulnerability and social factors, and Linehan's diathesis–stress theory, which integrates neurobiological and social factors.

Neurobiological Factors Some neurobiological factors are thought to increase risk for the full syndrome of BPD, whereas others are thought to help explain only the intense emotionality or impulsivity of those with the disorder (Siever, 2000). Relevant to a general dysregulation, people with BPD demonstrate lower serotonin function than do controls (Soloff, Meltzer, Greer et al., 2000). Relevant to the emotion dysregulation, people with BPD show increased activation of the amygdala to emotional pictures (Hazlett, Zhang, New et al., 2012; Silbersweig, Clarkin, Goldstein et al., 2007), in contrast to the diminished amygdala activity shown among fearless psychopaths. Deficits in the prefrontal cortex are thought to contribute to impulsivity, and people with BPD show deficits in the prefrontal cortex (Minzenberg, Fan, New et al., 2008; van Elst, 2003) and disrupted connectivity between the prefrontal cortex and the

DSM-5 Criteria for Borderline Personality Disorder

Presence of five or more of the following signs of instability in relationships, self-image, and impulsivity from early adulthood across many contexts:

- Frantic efforts to avoid abandonment
- Unstable interpersonal relationships in which others are either idealized or devalued
- Unstable sense of self
- Self-damaging, impulsive behaviors in at least two areas, such as spending, sex, substance abuse, reckless driving, and binge eating
- Recurrent suicidal behavior, gestures, or self-injurious behavior (e.g., cutting self)
- Marked mood reactivity
- Chronic feelings of emptiness
- Recurrent bouts of intense or poorly controlled anger
- During stress, a tendency to experience transient paranoid thoughts and dissociative symptoms

People with borderline personality disorder often engage in self-injurious behavior.

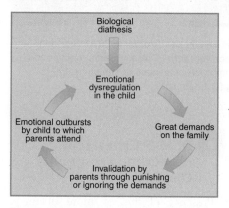

Figure 15.3 Marsha Linehan's diathesis–stress theory of borderline personality disorder.

● DSM-5 Criteria for Histrionic Personality Disorder

Presence of five or more of the following signs of excessive emotionality and attention seeking from early adulthood across many contexts:

- Strong need to be the center of attention
- Inappropriate sexually seductive behavior
- Rapidly shifting and shallow expression of emotions
- Use of physical appearance to draw attention to self
- Speech that is excessively impressionistic and lacking in detail
- Exaggerated, theatrical emotional expression
- Overly suggestible
- Misreads relationships as more intimate than they are

amygdala (New, Hazlett, Buchsbaum et al., 2007). Taken together, findings suggest that multiple facets of neurobiology may converge to create the complex array of symptoms that comprise BPD.

Social Factors: Childhood Abuse in the Context of Genetic Vulnerability In our earlier discussion of risk factors common across personality disorders, we noted that BPD has been tied to extremely high rates of childhood abuse or neglect, as well as to high estimates of heritability. How can we fit these two risk factors together? To consider this question, researchers studied 197 MZ twin pairs in which one twin, but not the other, reported childhood abuse (Bornovalova, Huibregtse, Hicks et al., 2013). If abuse, rather than genetic vulnerability, is driving BPD, twins who experienced abuse should have a higher rate of BPD than their co-twins who were not abused. This was not the case. The twin pairs had similar levels of BPD. That is, childhood abuse did not predict BPD after genetic risk was controlled. In a second twin study, childhood traumatic experiences accounted for less than 1 percent in the variance in who developed BPD after accounting for family characteristics (Berenz, Amstadter, Aggen et al., 2013).

Even though a history of abuse is common for those with BPD, these findings indicate that abuse may not be the driving force that sets this personality disorder in motion. How can we make sense of the high rates of abuse among those with BPD, then? Researchers are still working on this puzzle, but it is important to consider the idea that abuse often happens in a context of many different problems. Genetically driven impulsivity, emotionality, or risk-seeking in the parents could increase the risk that both abuse and BPD will occur. Findings highlight the complexity of abuse, as it often occurs within a matrix of risk factors. Although much remains unknown, it is worth noting that common sense still holds—child abuse has many deleterious effects. These have been shown in other studies and even in other studies of twins discordant for abuse (Nelson, Heath, Madden et al., 2002).

Linehan's Diathesis–Stress Theory Marsha Linehan proposes that BPD develops when people who have difficulty controlling their emotions because of a biological diathesis (possibly genetic) are raised in a family environment that is invalidating. That is, a diathesis of emotional dysregulation interacts with experiences of invalidation to promote the development of BPD. In an invalidating environment, the person's feelings are discounted and disrespected— that is, the person's efforts to communicate feelings are disregarded or even punished.

The two main hypothesized factors—emotional dysregulation and invalidation—interact with each other in a dynamic fashion (see Figure 15.3). For example, the emotionally dysregulated child makes enormous demands on his or her family. The exasperated parents ignore or even punish the child's outbursts, which leads the child to suppress his or her emotions. The suppressed emotions build up to an explosion, which then gets the attention of the parents. Thus, the parents end up reinforcing the very behaviors that they find aversive. Many other patterns are possible, of course, but what they have in common is a vicious circle, a constant back-and-forth between dysregulation and invalidation.

Histrionic Personality Disorder

The key feature of **histrionic personality disorder** is overly dramatic and attention-seeking behavior. People with this disorder often use their physical appearance, such as unusual clothes, makeup, or hair color, to draw attention to themselves. Despite their expressions of extravagant and intense emotions, they are thought to be emotionally shallow. For example, someone with this disorder might gush about and call a person his or her best friend, only to have trouble remembering a conversation with that person the next day. They are self-centered, overly concerned with their physical attractiveness, and uncomfortable when not the center of attention. They can be inappropriately sexually provocative and seductive and are easily influenced by others. Their speech is often impressionistic and lacking in detail. For example, they might

Clinical Case: Bob

Bob, a 50-year-old college professor, sought treatment only after urging from his wife. During the interview, Bob's wife noted that he seemed so focused on himself and his own advancement that he often belittled others. Bob was dismissive of these concerns, stating that he had never been the sort of person to tolerate idiots, and he could see no reason why he should begin offering such tolerance now—in rapid fire, he described his supervisor, his students,

his parents, and a set of former friends as lacking the intelligence to merit his friendship. He willingly acknowledged working long hours but stated that his research had the potential to change life for people and that other activities could not be allowed to interfere with his success. The therapist's gentle questioning of whether his expressions of superiority might provoke some interpersonal tension was met with a scathing rebuke.

state a strong opinion, yet be completely unable to support it. (Patient: "She was absolutely the greatest." Interviewer: "What did you like best about her?" Patient: "Gosh, I'm not sure I could describe that.").

Narcissistic Personality Disorder

People with **narcissistic personality disorder** have a grandiose view of their qualities and are preoccupied with fantasies of great success (as demonstrated by Bob in the Clinical Case). They are more than a little self-centered—they require almost constant attention. Their interpersonal relationships are disturbed by their lack of empathy, by their arrogance coupled with feelings of envy, by their habit of taking advantage of others, and by their feelings of entitlement and expectations that others will do special favors for them. Partnerships are often challenged by their excessive need to be in charge. They tend to seek out high-status partners whom they idealize and proudly show off, only to change partners if given an opportunity to be with a person of higher status. Fame and wealth are often overly valued as a way to gain the admiration of others. With their focus on gaining admiration, appearance matters—in one study, independent observers were able to make snap judgments of narcissism from photographs with some accuracy, most typically by noticing the expensive clothes and overinvestment in appearance of those with narcissistic traits (Vazire, Naumann, Rentfrow et al., 2008). At the same time that they exude overconfidence, an underlying vulnerability is apparent in their envy and need to be admired (Miller, Hoffman, Campbell et al., 2008). Just as they will bask in compliments and praise, they also tend to be overly reactive to criticism. They are highly likely to be vindictive and aggressive when faced with a competitive threat or a put-down (Bushman & Thomaes, 2011).

Frank Lloyd Wright, one of the most influential American architects, displayed at least some narcissistic traits. He is quoted as saying "Early in life, I had to choose between honest arrogance and hypocritical humility. I chose honest arrogance and have seen no reason to change."

DSM-5 Criteria for Narcissistic Personality Disorder

Presence of five or more of the following signs of grandiosity, need for admiration, and lack of empathy from early adulthood across many contexts:

- Grandiose view of one's importance
- Preoccupation with one's success, brilliance, beauty
- Belief that one is special and can be understood only by other high-status people
- Extreme need for admiration
- Strong sense of entitlement
- Tendency to exploit others
- Lack of empathy
- Envious of others
- Arrogant behavior or attitudes

FOCUS ON DISCOVERY 15.2

Have College Students Become More Narcissistic Over Time?

In recent years, debate has unfolded about whether young people are becoming more narcissistic. To look at this puzzle, Drs. Twenge and Foster (2010) accumulated the data from 107 studies conducted between 1984 and 2008 in which 49,818 university students had taken the Narcissistic Personality Inventory (NPI), a self-report scale designed to assess risk for narcissistic personality disorder. Questions on the NPI cover self-perceptions of authority, self-sufficiency, exhibitionism, exploitativeness, vanity, and entitlement. When controlling for which college the students were attending, NPI scores have increased over time, as shown in Figure 15.4. Although the effect size is statistically significant, one question is whether the increase of a couple of points out of a possible score of 40 is really meaningful.

A second question, though, is what the increase means. Twenge and Foster (2010) argue that parents of today's college students, more than those of previous generations, imbue their children with a deeper sense of specialness. To them, this shift in parenting might be driving an increase in narcissism. Others suggest that the changed responses on the NPI reflect more superficial changes in how people describe themselves that are not so likely to have maladaptive consequences. For example, it has become more socially acceptable, if not socially expected, for people to describe themselves as special and as having high self-esteem than it was in previous generations, and this is reflected in those higher scores. Facebook and other social media websites are relatively recent innova-

tions, and these might be changing how people learn to present themselves. Undergraduates today are also more comfortable "showing off their body," an item that is part of the assessment of vanity. One part of this debate then, is whether changing scores reflect harmless shifts in self-presentation or more worrisome changes in pathological narcissism.

Much of the data being considered in this debate comes from the self-report NPI inventory, which does not assess functional impairment or diagnosis. To assess diagnoses of narcissistic personality disorder, one study involved thousands of diagnostic interviews with a representative sample of adults in the United States. In this study, younger adults were more likely to endorse the symptoms of narcissistic personality disorder than were older adults (Stinson, Dawson, Goldstein et al., 2008). But as we've discussed earlier in this chapter, the rates of most personality disorders fall as people age (Grant, Hasin, Stinson et al., 2004).

To truly answer the question of whether narcissistic personality disorder is becoming more common, we need to conduct longitudinal interviews of representative community samples of people born in different years. Because we don't have this type of data, some have argued that the evidence marshaled is dubious, and that the measures and study designs are just too poor to reach conclusions that narcissism is on the rise (Arnett, Trzesniewski, & Donnellan, 2013). Either way, recent data suggests that NPI scores in college students have fallen since 2008; even if narcissism was on the rise until 2008, entering the job market during a difficult economic period might be related to lowered narcissism scores (Bianchi, 2014).

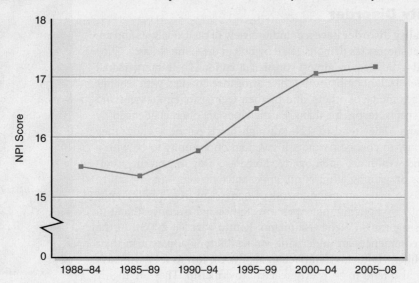

Figure 15.4 Mean Narcissistic Personality Inventory (NPI) scores across five time periods for university students. Data shown exclude samples from UC Davis. Adapted from Twenge & Foster, 2010.

Given the associated tendencies toward confidence and ambition, could a small amount of narcissism be adaptive? In one study, 121 scholars with expertise in American leaders rated the relative (subclinical) narcissism of the U.S. presidents. Presidents who were rated as relatively more narcissistic were more likely to be seen as persuasive, able to win the popular vote and to initiate legislation. On the other hand, they were also likely to get in trouble for unethical behavior (Watts, Lilienfeld, Smith et al., 2013). Those with clinical diagnoses of narcissism would be expected, however, to have more troubles than those with these more subtle elevations of narcissistic traits.

Etiology of Narcissistic Personality Disorder In this section, we begin by discussing a theory of how parenting could contribute to narcissistic personality traits.

Parenting Several different models have been developed for how parenting might contribute to narcissism. In one prominent account, Millon (1986) hypothesized that parents who are overly indulgent foster children's belief that they are special (and even more special than other children), and that behavioral expressions of their specialness will be tolerated by others. Several recent studies indicate that people with high self-reported levels of narcissism do report experiencing overindulgence from their parents (Horton, 2011). In Focus on Discovery 15.2, we discuss whether changes in parenting practices over time could be increasing the prevalence of narcissism in our culture.

Self-Psychology In his two books, *The Analysis of the Self* (1971) and *The Restoration of the Self* (1977), Heinz Kohut developed a model of narcissism based on self-psychology, a variant of psychodynamic theory. He started from the clinical observation that the person with narcissistic personality disorder projects self-importance, self-absorption, and fantasies of limitless success on the surface. Kohut theorized that these characteristics mask a very fragile self-esteem. People with narcissistic personality disorder strive to bolster their sense of self-worth through unending quests for respect from others. Inflated self-worth and denigration of others, then, are seen as defenses against feelings of shame. Research studies do support the hypothesis that people diagnosed with narcissistic personality disorder experience shame more frequently than do those without personality disorder (Ritter, Vater, Rusch et al., 2014).

Social-Cognitive Model A model of narcissistic personality disorder developed by Carolyn Morf and Frederick Rhodewalt (2001) is built around two basic ideas: (1) people with this disorder have fragile self-esteem, in part because they are trying to maintain the belief that they are special, and (2) interpersonal interactions are important to them for bolstering self-esteem rather than for gaining closeness or warmth. In other words, they are captive to the goal of maintaining a grand vision of themselves, and this goal pervades their experiences. Like the self-psychology model, this model focuses on the fragile self-esteem of the narcissist but places greater emphasis on social and cognitive mechanisms driving this syndrome.

To assess the idea that people with narcissistic personality disorder are trying to maintain grandiose beliefs about themselves, Morf and Rhodewalt have examined biases in how people with this disorder rate themselves in various settings. For example, in laboratory studies, people with narcissistic personality disorder overestimate their attractiveness to others and their contributions to group activities. ("Others must be jealous of me; I've been responsible for the lion's share of our progress here today.") In some studies, researchers have provided people with feedback that they were successful on a task (regardless of their actual performance) and then asked participants to rate the reasons why they were successful. In these types of studies, people with narcissistic personality disorder attribute successes to their abilities rather than to chance or luck to a greater extant than do those without personality disorder. So a set of studies suggest that people with narcissistic personality disorder show cognitive biases that would help maintain grandiose beliefs about the self.

To assess whether people with narcissistic personality disorder have fragile self-esteem, Morf and Rhodewalt (2001) have reviewed studies of how much self-esteem depends on external feedback. For example, when falsely told they have done poorly on an IQ test, they show much more reactivity than others do; similarly, they show more reactivity to being told they have succeeded at something.

According to this theory, when people with narcissistic personality disorder interact with others, their primary goal is to bolster their own self-esteem. This goal influences how they act toward others in several ways. First, they tend to brag a lot; this often works well initially, but over time, repeated bragging comes to be perceived negatively by others (Paulhus, 1998). Second, when someone else performs better than they do on a task that is relevant to self-esteem, they will denigrate the other person, even to that person's face. This framework makes it easy to understand why people with narcissistic personality disorder engage in behaviors that alienate others; their sense of self depends on being admired, not in gaining or maintaining closeness (Campbell, Bosson, Goheen et al., 2007).

Narcissistic personality disorder draws its name from the Greek mythological figure Narcissus, who fell in love with his own reflection, was consumed by his own desire, and was transformed into a flower. Narcissus Peter Paul Rubens (1577-1640/Flemish) Museum Bojimans Van Beuningen, Rotterdam, Netherlands.

Quick Summary

All personality disorders are at least moderately heritable. Childhood abuse or neglect is significantly correlated with 6 of the 10 personality disorders.

The odd/eccentric cluster of personality disorders (cluster A) includes paranoid personality disorder, schizoid personality disorder, and schizotypal personality disorder. People with paranoid personality disorder are suspicious of others, people with schizoid personality disorder are socially aloof, and people with schizotypal personality disorder are eccentric in their thoughts and behavior. Biological studies indicate that schizotypal personality disorder and schizophrenia are related.

The dramatic/erratic cluster (cluster B) includes antisocial personality disorder (APD), borderline personality disorder (BPD), histrionic personality disorder, and narcissistic personality disorder. The key features of APD include violation of rules and a disregard for others' feeling and social norms. Psychopathy is related to antisocial personality disorder but is not defined in the DSM. Psychopathy criteria focus on internal experiences (such as a poverty of emotion) as well as observable behavior. BPD is defined by intense emotionality, unstable sense of identity, and impulsivity. Histrionic personality disorder is characterized by exaggerated emotional displays. Narcissistic personality disorder is characterized by highly inflated self-esteem but a deep need for admiration.

A harsh family environment and poverty play a role in the development of APD, and these social risk factors may be particularly important for those who are at higher genetic risk for the disorder. Psychopathy is related to blunted responses to threat and, as a consequence, to difficulty learning from punishment. This insensitivity to threat may be especially present during goal pursuit. The callous treatment of others might also be linked to a lack of empathy. This lack of anxiety and empathy may drive misconduct without regret.

BPD is related to serotonergic dysfunction and to biological risk factors for emotion dysregulation and impulsivity. Consistent with the greater emotionality, people with BPD demonstrate the increased activity of the amygdala to emotion stimuli. Consistent with the impulsivity, research indicates diminished activity in the prefrontal cortex among people with BPD. People with BPD report elevated rates of abuse, but some of the abuse may be tied to parental genetic vulnerability. Linehan's model integrates the high rates of parental invalidation reported by people with BPD with the biological diathesis for emotional dysregulation.

Across studies, those with narcissistic personality disorder report that their parents were overly indulgent. According to self-psychology theory, those with narcissistic personality disorder inflate their own self-worth to combat feelings of shame. Social-cognitive theory proposes that the behavior of the person with narcissistic personality disorder is shaped by the goal of maintaining specialness and the belief that the purpose of interpersonal interactions is to bolster self-esteem.

Check Your Knowledge 15.2

Answer the questions.
1. Which personality disorder is most related to schizophrenia in family history studies?
2. What is the level of heritability for the personality disorders?
3. Which of these personality disorders is most common in clinical settings?

a. obsessive-compulsive
b. schizotypal
c. antisocial
d. borderline

4. Which personality disorders have been related to impulsivity?

Clinical Description and Etiology of the Anxious/Fearful Cluster

The anxious/fearful cluster includes avoidant personality disorder, dependent personality disorder, and obsessive-compulsive personality disorder. People with these disorders are prone to worry and distress.

Avoidant Personality Disorder

People with **avoidant personality disorder** are so fearful of criticism, rejection, and disapproval that they will avoid jobs or relationships to protect themselves from negative feedback. In social situations, they are restrained and timid because of an extreme fear of saying some-

© F1 online digitale Bildagentur GmbH/Alamy

People with avoidant personality disorder often avoid interpersonal interactions, as they find them to be so stressful.

thing foolish, being embarrassed, blushing, or showing other signs of anxiety. They believe they are incompetent and inferior to others, and they are reluctant to take risks or try new activities. Even though they would like to form close relationships, their fears often make it difficult for them to do so.

Avoidant personality disorder often co-occurs with social anxiety disorder (see Chapter 6), probably because the diagnostic criteria for these two disorders are so similar (Skodol, Oldham, Hyler et al., 1995). The genetic vulnerability for avoidant personality disorder and social anxiety disorder appears to overlap (Reichborn-Kjennerud, Czajkowski, Torgersen et al., 2007). Some have argued that avoidant personality disorder might actually be a more chronic variant of social anxiety disorder (Alden, Laposa, Taylor et al., 2002). Etiological variables, then, might overlap with those of social anxiety, discussed in Chapter 6.

As is true for social anxiety disorders, several other types of disorders are often comorbid with avoidant personality disorder. About 80 percent of people with avoidant personality disorder, like Leon in the Clinical Case, have comorbid major depression. Alcohol abuse is also common among people with this disorder (McGlashan et al., 2000).

Dependent Personality Disorder

The core feature of **dependent personality disorder** is an excessive reliance on others. People with dependent personality disorder have an intense need to be taken care of, which often leads them to feel uncomfortable with being alone. They subordinate their own needs to ensure that they do not threaten the protective relationships they have established. When a

● DSM-5 Criteria for Avoidant Personality Disorder

A pervasive pattern of social inhibition, feelings of inadequacy, and hypersensitivity to criticism as shown by four or more of the following from early adulthood across many contexts:

- Avoidance of occupational activities that involve significant interpersonal contact, because of fears of criticism or disapproval
- Unwilling to get involved with people unless certain of being liked
- Restrained in intimate relationships because of the fear of being shamed or ridiculed
- Preoccupation with being criticized or rejected
- Inhibited in new interpersonal situations because of feelings of inadequacy
- Views self as socially inept, unappealing or inferior
- Unusually reluctant to try new activities because they may prove embarrassing

---

Clinical Case: Leon

Leon, a 45-year-old man, sought treatment for depression. During the interview, Leon described feeling depressed and uncomfortable socially for as long as he could remember. By age 5, he would experience intense anxiety when he was with other children, and his mind would "go blank" if he had to speak in front of others. He grew up dreading birthday parties, teachers' classroom questions, and meeting new children. Although he was able to play with some of the children in his neighborhood, he had never asked a woman out on a date or developed a "best friend." He took a job at the post office after graduation because it involved little social interaction. [Adapted from Spitzer, Gibbon, Skodol et al. (1994).]

Clinical Case: Matthew

Matthew, a 34-year-old man, sought treatment after breaking up with a girlfriend. His mother, with whom he lived, had disapproved of his marriage plans because his girlfriend came from a different religious background. Matthew felt that he could not marry his girlfriend without his mother's approval.

Although he canceled the engagement, he was angry with his mother and feared that she would never approve of anyone he wanted to marry. He said that he feared disagreeing with his mother because he did not want to have to fend for himself. [Adapted from Spitzer (2002).]

DSM-5 Criteria for Dependent Personality Disorder

An excessive need to be taken care of, as shown by the presence of at least five of the following from early adulthood across many contexts:

- Difficulty making decisions without excessive advice and reassurance from others
- Need for others to take responsibility for most major areas of life
- Difficulty disagreeing with others for fear of losing their support
- Difficulty doing things on own or starting projects because of lack of self-confidence
- Doing unpleasant things as a way to obtain the approval and support of others
- Feelings of helplessness when alone because of fears of being unable to care for self
- Urgently seeking new relationship when one ends
- Preoccupation with fears of having to take care of self

close relationship ends, they urgently seek another relationship to replace it. They see themselves as weak, and they turn to others for support and decision making. The Clinical Case of Matthew provides an example of dependent personality disorder. People with this disorder particularly fear being alone.

The DSM diagnostic criteria portray people with dependent personality disorder as being very passive (e.g., having difficulty initiating projects or doing things on their own, allowing others to make decisions for them). Research indicates, however, that people with dependent personality disorder actually can do what is necessary to maintain a close relationship; this might involve being very deferential and passive, but it might involve taking active steps to preserve the relationship (Bornstein, 1997). Also contrary to the idea that this disorder is characterized by passivity, men with higher levels of dependency, perhaps because of their insecurity when their partnerships are threatened, are at elevated risk of perpetrating domestic violence (Bornstein, 2006).

People with dependent personality disorder are likely to develop depression after interpersonal losses (Hammen, Burge, Daley et al., 1995), and when they are depressed, they show more suicidality than do other depressed patients (Bolton, Belik, Enns et al., 2008). They are also at elevated risk for developing anxiety disorders and bulimia (Bornstein, 2012).

In addition to the genetic and early adversity findings described above, theorists argue that overprotective parents may reinforce children for dependency, while authoritarian discipline may limit the opportunities for children to develop feelings of self-efficacy (Bornstein, 1992). Findings of several studies support the idea that dependent personality traits are related to overprotective and authoritarian parenting (Bornstein, 1992).

Obsessive-Compulsive Personality Disorder

The person with **obsessive-compulsive personality disorder** is a perfectionist, preoccupied with details, rules, and schedules. Although order and perfectionism have their adaptive sides, particularly in fostering success in complex occupational goals, people with this disorder often pay so much attention to detail that they fail to finish projects (as illustrated in the Clinical Case of Sarah). They are more oriented toward work than pleasure, and social relationships often suffer as the pursuit of perfection in the workplace takes time away from family and friends. They have inordinate difficulty making decisions (lest they err) and allocating time (lest they focus on the wrong thing). Their interpersonal relationships are often troubled because they demand that everything be done the right way—their way. Generally, they are serious, rigid, formal, and inflexible, especially regarding moral issues. They are unable to discard worn-out and useless objects, even those with no sentimental value, and they are likely to be excessively frugal to a level that causes concern among those around them.

Obsessive-compulsive personality disorder is distinct from obsessive-compulsive disorder, despite the similarity in names. The personality disorder does not include the obsessions and compulsions that define the latter. Nonetheless, the two conditions often co-occur (Skodol et al., 1995) and seem to have some overlapping genetic vulnerability (Taylor, Asmundson, & Jang, 2011).

For the person with obsessive-compulsive personality disorder, the overly perfectionistic quest for order may interfere with being productive.

DSM-5 Criteria for Obsessive-Compulsive Personality Disorder

Intense need for order, perfection, and control, as shown by the presence of at least four of the following from early adulthood across many contexts:

- Preoccupation with rules, details, and organization to the extent that the point of an activity is lost
- Extreme perfectionism interferes with task completion
- Excessive devotion to work to the exclusion of leisure and friendships
- Inflexibility about morals and values
- Difficulty discarding worthless items
- Reluctance to delegate unless others conform to one's standards
- Miserliness
- Rigidity and stubbornness

Clinical Case: Sarah

Sarah, a 22-year-old woman, was ecstatic to attain a research assistant position with a highly accomplished scientist just after graduation. She was planning to pursue a career in science, and the position fit perfectly with her long-held interests. Despite Sarah's initial enthusiasm, things soon soured with her new boss. When asked to collect data using methods that she already knew well, she began by creating large spreadsheets of the planned process, and then shifted gears and invested in elaborate software for project management. No matter how hard she tried, she could not move from project planning into actual data collection. When faced with the idea of writing up a project description for the University ethics board review, she became buried as she wrote over 50 pages of detailed notes on potentially relevant issues but then could not find a way to describe the study in the one page allowed on the form. When asked to manage eight undergraduate volunteers who worked with the team, she found it difficult to delegate any tasks to them, instead redoing any of the work that they finished to quell her anxiety about what might happen if they were to make a mistake. Even though she worked 15-hour days, her boss asked her to resign at the end of the 3-month probation period because she had accomplished less than her predecessor who had worked only 20 hours a week. She was deeply disillusioned by the experience, and she sought therapy with a sense that this was just one in a series of events in which she had gotten herself into trouble by losing sight of the forest for the trees.

Quick Summary

The anxious or fearful cluster of personality disorders (cluster C) includes avoidant personality disorder, dependent personality disorder, and obsessive-compulsive personality disorder. People with avoidant personality disorder are timid and often feel inadequate. Those with dependent personality disorder are overly reliant on others, to the extent that they are vulnerable to depression after interpersonal losses. Those with obsessive-compulsive disorder are intensely focused on the details of maintaining order, perfection, and control.

Avoidant personality disorder may be a more chronic variant of social anxiety disorder. People with dependent personality disorder often describe their parents as both overprotective and authoritarian. Although the two conditions have distinct symptom profiles, obsessive-compulsive personality disorder and obsessive-compulsive disorder are often comorbid and may have overlapping genetic vulnerability.

Check Your Knowledge 15.3

You are the director of human resources for a large corporation. You are asked to review a set of situations in which employees had interpersonal and task-focused problems that were severe and persistent enough to raise concerns in the workplace. Name the most likely personality disorder for each of the following.

1. Mariana refuses to meet with customers. She states that she is terrified that they will see that she does not know much. It turns out that she has called in sick the last three times her boss scheduled an appointment with her, and her colleagues barely know her name. When asked, she says that meeting with any of these people makes her feel horribly nervous about potential rejection of her ideas. She asks for a position that would involve little social contact.

2. Sheila has had three subordinate employees request transfers from her department. They each stated that she was too controlling, picked on small mistakes, and would not listen to any new ideas for solving problems. At the interview, she brought in a typed, 15-page chart of the goals she would like to execute for the company. Despite having an inordinate number of goals, she has failed to complete a single project during her first year with the company.

3. Police contact you to let you know that they have arrested Sam, one of your employees. He was caught at a bank trying to cash a $10,000 company check on which he had forged the signature. You learn that Sam had previously defrauded three other companies. When you meet with Sam, he does not seem the least bit sorry.

Treatment of Personality Disorders

Many people with personality disorders enter treatment for a condition other than their personality disorder. For example, a person with antisocial personality disorder might seek treatment of substance abuse; a person with avoidant personality disorder might seek treatment for social anxiety disorder; and a patient with obsessive-compulsive personality disorder might seek help for depression. Clinicians are encouraged to consider whether personality disorders are present because their presence predicts slower improvement in psychotherapy (Crits-Christoph & Barber, 2002; Hollon & DeRubeis, 2003).

Here we consider treatments to address the symptoms of personality disorders. We begin by describing approaches that are relevant across the various personality disorders and then discuss treatments designed for specific personality disorders.

General Approaches to the Treatment of Personality Disorders

Psychotherapy is considered the treatment of choice for personality disorders. In one meta-analysis, psychotherapy was shown to provide small but positive effects compared to treatment as usual across 22 studies of borderline personality disorder and 8 of other personality disorders (Budge, Moore, Del Re et al., 2013). Psychotherapy is often supplemented with medications. For example, antidepressants are used to quell some of the depressive or impulsive symptoms that accompany personality disorders (Tyrer & Bateman, 2004).

People with serious symptoms of personality disorders might attend weekly psychotherapy sessions, or they might attend a day treatment program that offers psychotherapy, in both group and individual formats, for several hours per day. Many day treatment programs also provide occupational therapy. The length of day treatment programs varies, but some last several months.

Psychodynamic theory suggests that childhood problems are at the root of personality disorders, and so the aim of psychodynamic therapy is to help the patient reconsider those early experiences, become more aware of how those experiences drive their current behaviors, and then reconsider their beliefs and responses to those early events. For example, a psychodynamic therapist might guide a man with obsessive-compulsive personality disorder to the realization that his need to be perfect is based on a childhood quest to win his parents' love, and that this quest does not need be carried into adulthood—that he does not need to be perfect to win the approval of others and that mistakes might not lead his loved ones to abandon him. Studies of psychodynamic treatment often include a broad range of different personality disorders.

Cognitive theory suggests that negative cognitive beliefs, such as those shown in Table 15.5, are at the heart of the personality disorders (Beck & Freeman, 1990). The aim of cognitive therapy, then, is to help a person become more aware of those beliefs and then to challenge maladaptive cognitions. For example, cognitive therapy for a perfectionistic person with obsessive-compulsive personality disorder entails first persuading the patient to accept the essence of the cognitive model—that feelings and behaviors are primarily a function of thoughts. Biases in thinking are then explored, such as when the patient concludes that he or she cannot do anything right because of a small failure in one particular endeavor. The therapist also looks for dysfunctional assumptions or schemas that might underlie the person's thoughts and feelings—for example, the belief that it is critical for every decision to be correct. Beyond challenging cognitions, Beck's approach to personality disorders incorporates a variety of other cognitive behavioral techniques.

The traits that characterize the personality disorders are probably too ingrained to change thoroughly. Instead, the therapist—regardless of theoretical orientation—might find it more realistic to change a disorder into a style or a more adaptive way of approaching life (Millon, 1996). Because relatively little is known, we focus on only three personality disorders in the next sections.

Table 15.5 Examples of Maladaptive Cognitions Hypothesized to Be Associated with Each Personality Disorder

Personality Disorder	Maladaptive Cognitions
Avoidant	If people get to know the real me, they will reject me.
Dependent	I am not capable of making a decision without reassurance.
Obsessive-compulsive	I know what's best. If things get disorganized, horrible mistakes will happen.
Paranoid	It is foolish to trust anyone.
Antisocial	People ask for exploitation—they let down their guard.
Narcissistic	I am better than others, and people who can't understand that don't deserve my time.
Histrionic	People are there to admire me.
Schizoid	Relationships are more hassle than reward.

Source: Adapted from Beck & Freeman (1990).

Treatment of Schizotypal Personality Disorder and Avoidant Personality Disorder

Treatments for schizotypal personality disorder draw on the links of this disorder with schizophrenia. More specifically, antipsychotic drugs (e.g., risperidone, trade name Risperdal) have shown effectiveness with schizotypal personality disorder (Raine, 2006). These medications seem particularly helpful for reducing the unusual thinking. Little research is available on psychological approaches to the treatment of schizotypal personality disorder.

Avoidant personality disorder appears to respond to the same treatments that are effective for those with social anxiety disorder: that is, antidepressant medications as well as cognitive behavioral treatment (Reich, 2000). Cognitive behavioral treatment might involve helping a person challenge his or her negative beliefs about social interactions by teaching behavioral strategies for dealing with difficult social situations and by exposure treatment, in which the person gradually takes part in feared social situations. Cognitive behavioral treatment lasting 20 sessions has been found to be more helpful than psychodynamic treatment for avoidant personality disorder (Emmelkamp, Benner, Kuipers et al., 2006). Group versions of cognitive behavioral treatment have been found to be helpful and may offer chances to practice constructive social interactions in a safe environment (Alden, 1989).

Treatment of Borderline Personality Disorder

Few clients pose a greater challenge to treat than do those with borderline personality disorder (BPD), regardless of the type of treatment being used. Clients with BPD tend to show their interpersonal problems in the therapeutic relationship as much as they do in other relationships. Because these clients find it inordinately difficult to trust others, therapists find it challenging to develop and maintain the therapeutic relationship. Patients alternately idealize and vilify the therapist, demanding special attention and consideration one moment—such as therapy sessions at odd hours and countless phone calls during crisis periods— and refusing to keep appointments the next; they beg the therapist for understanding and support but insist that certain topics are off-limits.

Suicide is always a serious risk , but it is often difficult for the therapist to judge whether a frantic phone call at 2:00 A.M. from a BPD patient is a call for help or a manipulative gesture designed to test how special the patient is to the therapist and to what lengths the therapist will go to meet the patient's needs at the moment. As in the case of Mary (see the Clinical Case at the beginning of this chapter), hospitalization is often necessary to protect against the threat of suicide. Seeing such clients is so stressful for therapists that many of them regularly consult with another therapist for advice and for support in dealing with their own emotions as they cope with the extraordinary challenges of helping these clients.

We will focus on dialectical behavior therapy because the benefits of this approach have been demonstrated in more than a dozen research studies. A small set of studies have provided support for psychodynamic therapy (Clarkin, Levy, Lenzenweger et al., 2007) and for a longer-term version of cognitive therapy for BPD (Blum, John, Pfohl et al., 2008; Giesen-Bloo, van Dyck, Spinhoven et al., 2006).

Dialectical behavior therapy (DBT) combines client-centered empathy and acceptance with cognitive behavioral problem solving, emotion-regulation techniques, and social skills training (Linehan, 1987). The concept of dialectics comes from German philosopher Georg Wilhelm Friedrich Hegel (1770–1831). It refers to a constant tension between any phenomenon (any idea, event, etc., called the *thesis*) and its opposite (the *antithesis*), which is resolved by creating a new phenomenon (the *synthesis*). In DBT, the term *dialectical* is used in two main ways:

1. In one sense, it refers to the seemingly opposite strategies that the therapist must use when treating people with BPD—accepting them as they are and yet helping them change. (For a closer look at the dialectic between acceptance and change, see Focus on Discovery 15.3.)

2. In the other sense, it refers to the patient's realization that splitting the world into good and bad is not necessary; instead, one can achieve a synthesis of these apparent opposites. For example, instead of seeing a friend as either all bad (thesis) or all good (antithesis), the friend can be seen as having both kinds of qualities (synthesis).

FOCUS ON DISCOVERY 15.3

Drawing from Personal Experience to Promote Acceptance and Change

As described earlier, Marsha Linehan developed dialectical behavior therapy, the best validated approach for BPD. In a brave move, Linehan decided to speak publicly about her own experiences of BPD (Carey, 2011). Hospitalized at age 17 for her severe suicidality, she found ways to injure herself even when the staff confined her to a seclusion chamber—left alone with no objects, she banged her head against the wall and floor. She remained hospitalized for 26 months. Failed treatments continued for several years, until she found a way out of the struggles on her own—through radical acceptance. She earned a Ph.D. in clinical psychology, and she drew on her own personal experiences to help others, in the process becoming one of the most productive researchers in the field of clinical psychology.

Linehan (1987) argues that a therapist treating clients with BPD has to adopt a posture that might seem inconsistent to the Western mind. The therapist must work for change while at the same time accepting the real possibility that no changes are going to occur. Linehan's notions of acceptance are drawn from Zen philosophy and from Rogerian approaches to psychotherapy. Linehan's reasoning is that people with BPD are so sensitive to rejection and criticism that even gentle encouragement to behave or think differently can be misinterpreted as a serious rebuke, leading to extreme emotional reactions. When this happens, the therapist, who may have been revered a moment earlier, is suddenly vilified. Thus, while observing

Marsha Linehan created dialectical behavior therapy, which combines cognitive behavioral therapy with acceptance.

Courtesy of Marsha M. Linehan

limits—"I would be very sad if you killed yourself, so I hope very much that you won't"—the therapist must convey to the patient that he or she is fully accepted. This is hard to do if the patient is threatening suicide, showing uncontrolled anger, or railing against imagined rebukes from the therapist.

Completely accepting the patient does not mean approving of everything the patient does; rather, it means that the therapist must accept the situation for what it is. And this acceptance, argues Linehan, must be real: the therapist must truly accept clients as they are; acceptance should not be in the service of change, an indirect way of encouraging clients to behave differently. "Acceptance can transform but if you accept in order to transform, it is not acceptance. It is like loving. Love seeks no reward but when given freely comes back a hundredfold. He who loses his life finds it. He who accepts, changes" (Linehan, personal communication, November 16, 1992). Full acceptance does not, in Linehan's view, preclude change. Indeed, she proposes the opposite—that it is the refusal to accept that precludes change.

Linehan's approach also emphasizes that clients, too, must accept who they are and what they have been through. Clients are asked to accept that their childhood is now unchangeable, that their behaviors might have caused relationships to end, and that they feel emotions more intensely than others do. This approach, it is hoped, will provide a basis for understanding the self and promoting growth.

Hence, both the therapist and the client in DBT are encouraged to adopt a dialectical view of the world.

The cognitive behavioral aspect of DBT, conducted both individually and in groups, involves four stages. In the first stage, dangerously impulsive behaviors such as suicidal actions are addressed, with the goal of promoting greater control. The client is taught to identify triggers for these behaviors and to apply coping strategies when the triggers are present. In the second stage, the focus is on learning to modulate the extreme emotionality. This phase might involve coaching to help a person learn to tolerate emotional distress. In this stage, clients are taught to mindfully notice their emotions in a nonjudgmental manner, without rushing into impulsive actions. Stage three focuses on improving relationships and self-esteem. Stage four is designed to promote connectedness and happiness. Throughout, clients learn more effective and socially acceptable ways of handling their day-to-day problems. Basically, DBT involves cognitive behavioral therapy combined with interventions to provide validation and acceptance to the client.

Linehan and colleagues conducted a trial in which clients were randomly assigned either to DBT or to treatment as usual, meaning any therapy available in the community. After 1 year of treatment and again 6 and 12 months later, clients in the two groups were compared on a variety of measures (Linehan, Heard, & Armstrong, 1993). The findings immediately after treatment revealed that DBT was superior to treatment as usual—clients engaged in less intentional self-injurious behavior, including fewer suicide attempts; dropped out of treatment less; spent fewer days in the hospital; and reported better adjustment and work records. There were, however, no differences in self-reported depression between the two treatment groups, underscoring the extreme difficulty of treating these clients. At the follow-up assessments, the superiority of DBT was sustained. In a meta-analysis of 16 studies conducted since that time, DBT was found to have moderate positive effects in reducing self-injury and suicidality compared to control conditions (Kliem, Kröger, & Kosfelder, 2010).

Summary

- Personality disorders are defined as enduring patterns of behavior and inner experience that disrupt functioning.
- The DSM-5 model includes 10 personality disorders; the alternative DSM-5 includes 6 personality disorders, along with dimensional personality domain and facet ratings.
- Personality disorders are usually comorbid with other disorders such as depression and anxiety disorders, and they predict poorer outcomes for these disorders.
- Most personality disorders appear to be at least moderately heritable when careful research methods are used. High rates of child abuse/neglect, aversive parental behavior, and lack of parental affection are observed across many of the personality disorders.

Odd/Eccentric Cluster

- Specific diagnoses in the odd/eccentric cluster include paranoid, schizoid, and schizotypal personality disorders.
- The major symptom of paranoid personality disorder is suspiciousness and mistrust; that of schizoid personality disorder, interpersonal detachment; and that of schizotypal personality disorder, unusual thought and behavior.
- Genetic, neurobiological, and cognitive research supports the idea that schizotypal personality disorder is related to schizophrenia.

Dramatic/Erratic Cluster

- The dramatic/erratic cluster includes antisocial, borderline, histrionic, and narcissistic personality disorders.
- Antisocial personality disorder and psychopathy overlap a great deal but are not equivalent. The diagnosis of antisocial personality focuses on behavior, whereas that of psychopathy emphasizes emotional deficits. The major symptom of borderline personality disorder (BPD) is unstable, highly changeable emotion and behavior; that of histrionic personality disorder, exaggerated emotional displays; and that of narcissistic personality disorder, highly inflated self-esteem.
- Psychopathy and antisocial behavior are related to family environment and poverty, and genes may amplify the effects of these social variables.
- Psychopathy is related to lack of response to punishment and poor empathy.

- BPD is related to serotonin dysfunction and to greater amygdala activation in response to emotion stimuli, and potentially relevant to the impulsive symptoms, to diminished function of the prefrontal cortex.
- People with BPD report extremely high rates of child abuse compared to the general population, but the genetic vulnerability to the disorder may increase the risk of abuse.
- Linehan's cognitive behavioral theory of BPD proposes an interaction between emotional dysregulation and an invalidating family environment.
- Narcissism appears to be related to overindulgent parenting. The psychodynamic model and the social-cognitive model of narcissistic personality disorder both focus on how the need for admiration develops and shapes behavior.

Anxious/Fearful Cluster

- The anxious/fearful cluster includes avoidant, dependent, and obsessive-compulsive personality disorders.
- The major symptom of avoidant personality disorder is fear of rejection or criticism; that of dependent personality disorder, excessive reliance on others; and that of obsessive-compulsive personality disorder, a perfectionistic, detail-oriented style.
- Avoidant personality disorder might be a more severe variant of social anxiety disorder. Dependent personality might be caused by parental overprotectiveness and authoritarian styles. Obsessive-compulsive personality disorder may be genetically related to obsessive compulsive disorder.

Treatment of Personality Disorders

- Psychodynamic, cognitive behavioral, and pharmacological treatments are all used for personality disorders. Relatively little research has been conducted regarding the treatment of some personality disorders.
- Treatment of schizotypal personality disorder is parallel with the treatment of schizophrenia; antipsychotic medication can be helpful.
- Treatment of avoidant personality disorder is parallel with the treatment of social anxiety disorder; antidepressants and cognitive behavioral treatment can be helpful.
- Dialectical behavior therapy has been well-validated, and psychodynamic therapy and a longer-term version of cognitive therapy have also received some support as treatments for BPD.

Answers to Check Your Knowledge Questions

15.1 1. Most personality disorders can be reliably assessed when structured diagnostic interviews are used: Interrater reliability correlations have been .79 or higher with the exception of schizoid personality disorder, where agreement is more modest. Interrater reliability when clinicians use unstructured interviews is adequate for borderline personality disorder but is not adequate for two other common personality disorders; 2. personality disorders are not as stable as the definition implies, and they are highly comorbid with each other; 3. 6 personality disorders instead of 10, and the inclusion of personality trait domains and facets (dimensional scores)

15.2 1. schizotypal; 2. More than half (55–72 percent); 3. d; 4. antisocial personality disorder and borderline personality disorder

15.3 1. avoidant personality disorder; 2. obsessive-compulsive personality disorder; 3. antisocial personality disorder

Key Terms

antisocial personality disorder
avoidant personality disorder
borderline personality disorder
dependent personality disorder
dialectical behavior therapy

histrionic personality disorder
narcissistic personality disorder
obsessive-compulsive personality disorder
paranoid personality disorder
personality disorder

personality trait domains
personality trait facets
psychopathy
schizoid personality disorder
schizotypal personality disorder

16 Legal and Ethical Issues

LEARNING GOALS

1. Be able to differentiate the legal concepts of insanity and the various standards for the insanity defense.
2. Be able to describe the issues surrounding competency to stand trial.
3. Be able to delineate the conditions under which a person can be committed to a hospital under civil law.
4. Be able to discuss the difficulties associated with predicting dangerousness and the issues surrounding the rights to receive and refuse treatment.
5. Be able to describe the ethics surrounding psychological research and therapy.

Amendment I   Congress shall make no law respecting an establishment of religion, or prohibiting the free exercise thereof; or abridging the freedom of speech, or of the press; or the right of the people peaceably to assemble, and to petition the Government for a redress of grievances.

Amendment IV   The right of the people to be secure in their persons, houses, papers, and effects, against unreasonable searches and seizures, shall not be violated . ...

Amendment V   No person ... shall be compelled in any criminal case to be a witness against himself, nor be deprived of life, liberty, or property, without due process of law . ...

Amendment VI   In all criminal prosecutions, the accused shall enjoy the right to a speedy and public trial ... to be confronted with the witnesses against him; to have compulsory process for obtaining witnesses in his favor, and to have the Assistance of Counsel for his defense.

Amendment VIII   Excessive bail shall not be required, nor excessive fines imposed, nor cruel and unusual punishment inflicted.

Amendment XIII   ... Neither slavery nor involuntary servitude, except as a punishment for crime whereof the party shall have been duly convicted, shall exist within the United States, or any place subject to their jurisdiction

Amendment XIV   ... No State shall ... deprive any person of life, liberty, or property, without due process of law; nor deny to any person within its jurisdiction the equal protection of the laws.

Amendment XV   ... The right of citizens of the United States to vote shall not be denied or abridged by the United States or by any State on account of race, color, or previous condition of servitude.

THESE ELOQUENT STATEMENTS DESCRIBE and protect some of the rights of U.S. citizens and others residing in the United States. Against what are these rights being protected? Be mindful of the circumstances under which most of these statements were issued. After the Constitutional Convention had delineated the powers of government in 1787, the first Congress saw fit in 1789 to amend what had been framed and to set specific limits on the federal government. This was accomplished with what came to be called the Bill of Rights,

Clinical Case: David

David had been hearing voices for several days. Unable to drown them out with music or talking, he became more and more troubled. The voices were telling him that he was the one chosen by God to rid the world of evil. David went to the emergency room of the local hospital seeking relief. Instead of being admitted, David was given a prescription for Haldol and sent on his way. Two days later, David took a loaded gun into a busy train station and began shooting. He killed two people and injured four others. When he was arrested, David told the police he was answering to God. His speaking was disorganized and hard to follow, and he expressed a number of paranoid beliefs.

David was found competent to stand trial because he understood that he was charged with murder and he was able to help his attorney with his defense. At trial, David entered a plea of "not guilty by reason of insanity." His defense lawyer arranged for David to be evaluated by a psychologist. The psychologist concluded that David had schizophrenia and that at the time of the crime he was unable to discern right from wrong (he thought his behavior was the right thing to do since God was directing him) and unable to conform his behavior to the requirements of the law. The prosecution did not dispute these findings, and the case was settled before going to trial. David was committed to the local forensic hospital for an indeterminate period of time. He was to remain there until he was no longer dangerous and mentally ill. Periodic evaluations would be conducted to see if David could be transferred to a less secure hospital.

After 7 years in the hospital, David had done very well. He took his prescribed medication (Zyprexa), was never in a physical altercation with other peoples, participated in individual and group therapy, worked in the hospital machine shop, and served as a team leader for the unit he was living in. David felt horribly remorseful for the crimes he had committed, and he recognized that he had schizophrenia that would require treatment for the rest of his life. The treatment team on the unit all agreed that David was no longer dangerous and that his schizophrenia was under control with the medication. They recommended that he be transferred to a less secure psychiatric hospital. David's attorney presented the case before a judge in the courtroom that was part of the hospital. The attorneys for the state objected to David's release, arguing that David could stop taking his medications and become violent again. The judge agreed that release was premature at this time and ordered that David remain in the forensic hospital for another year before being evaluated again.

which are the first 10 amendments to the Constitution. The philosophical ideal of the U.S. government is to allow citizens the maximum degree of liberty consistent with preserving order in the community at large.

We open our final chapter in this way because the legal and mental health systems collaborate continually, although often subtly, to deny a substantial proportion of the U.S. population their basic civil rights. With the best of intentions, judges, governing boards of hospitals, legal associations, and professional mental health groups have worked over the years to protect society at large from the actions of people regarded as mentally ill and considered dangerous to themselves or to others. But in so doing they have denied many thousands of people their basic civil rights.

People with a psychological disorder who have broken the law or who are alleged to have done so are subject to **criminal commitment,** a procedure that confines a person in a mental or forensic hospital (see Focus on Discovery 1.2 for discussion of types of hospitals) either for determination of competency to stand trial or after acquittal by reason of insanity, as in the Clinical Case of David. **Civil commitment** is a set of procedures by which a person who is deemed mentally ill and dangerous but who has not broken a law can be deprived of liberty and placed in a hospital. In this chapter we look at these legal procedures in depth. Then we turn to an examination of some important ethical issues as they relate to treatment and research.

Criminal Commitment

We examine first the role of psychiatry and psychology in the criminal justice system. Almost as early as the concept of mens rea, or "guilty mind," and the rule "No crime without an evil intent" had begun to be accepted in English common law, the concept of *insanity* was taken into consideration. Broadly speaking, insanity refers to a disordered mind, and a disordered mind may be regarded as unable to formulate and carry out a criminal purpose (Morse, 1992). In other words, a disordered mind cannot be a guilty mind, and only a guilty mind can engender culpable actions.

It is important to note that insanity is a legal concept, not a psychological one. As such, its definition comes from court proceedings. In today's courts, judges and lawyers call on psychiatrists and clinical psychologists for assistance in dealing with criminal acts thought to result from the accused person's disordered mental state. Although the insanity defense was developed to protect people's rights, in practice, it often results in a greater denial of liberties than they would otherwise experience.

The Insanity Defense

The **insanity defense** is the legal argument that a defendant should not be held responsible for an illegal act if it is attributable to a psychological disorder or intellectual disability that interferes with rationality or that results from some other excusing circumstance, such as not knowing right from wrong. A staggering amount of material has been written on the insanity defense, even though it is pleaded in less than 1 percent of all cases that reach trial, and even when pleaded is rarely successful (Steadman 1979; Steadman, Mulvey, Monahan et al., 1993). In New York, for example, only 7 people were successful with an insanity plea out of over 5000 murders tried during the past 10 years.

Because an insanity defense is based on the accused's mental condition at the time the crime was committed, retrospective, often speculative, judgment on the part of attorneys, judges, jurors, and mental health professionals is required. And disagreement between defense and prosecution psychiatrists and psychologists is the rule.

It is critically important to understand that psychological disorders and crime do not go hand in hand. That is, a person can have a diagnosis of a psychological disorder and be held fully responsible for a crime. For example, David Tarloff, a New York man with a confirmed diagnosis of schizophrenia, killed his psychologist in 2008 and was found guilty of this crime in 2014 and sentenced to life in prison without parole (his insanity defense was unsuccessful). However, someone who has no psychological disorder at all can commit the most heinous or bizarre crime, despite our tendency to think someone must have been "crazy" to commit such an act. Indeed, decades of social psychological research tell us that otherwise healthy people can commit horrendous, criminal acts in the right circumstances or contexts (Aronson, 2012).

Where did the insanity defense come from? Some type of insanity defense, loosely defined, has been around since the seventh century BCE (Robinson, 1996). However, we will consider more recent legal precedents that set the stage for our current definitions of insanity and have shaped the development of the two main insanity pleas used today.

Landmark Cases and Laws

Several court rulings and established principles bear on the problems of legal responsibility and psychological disorders. Table 16.1 summarizes these rulings and principles (for more on these issues, see Frederick, Mrad, & DeMier, 2007).

Irresistible Impulse The **irresistible-impulse** concept was formulated in 1834 in a case in Ohio. According to this concept, if a pathological impulse or uncontrollable drive compelled the person to commit the criminal act, an insanity defense is legitimate. The irresistible-impulse test was confirmed in two subsequent court cases, *Parsons v. State* and *Davis v. United States*.[1]

---

[1]*Parsons v. State*, 2 So. 854, 866–67 (Ala.1887); *Davis v. United States*, 165 U.S. 373, 378 (1897).

Table 16.1 Landmark Cases and Laws Regarding the Insanity Defense

Irresistible impulse (1834)	A pathological impulse or drive that the person could not control compelled that person to commit a criminal act.
M'Naghten rule (1843)	The person did not know the nature and quality of the criminal act in which he or she engaged, or, if the person did know it, the person did not know what he or she was doing was wrong.
Durham test (1954)	The person's criminal act is the product of mental disease or defect.
American Law Institute guidelines (1962)	1. The person's criminal act is a result of "mental disease or defect" that results in the person's not appreciating the wrongfulness of the act or in the person's inability to behave according to the law (combination of M'Naghten rule and irresistible impulse).
	2. "[T]he terms 'mental disease or defect' do not include an abnormality manifested only by repeated criminal or otherwise antisocial conduct" (American Law Institute, 1962).
Insanity Defense Reform Act (1984)	1. The person's criminal act is a result of severe mental illness or defect that prevents the person from understanding the nature of his or her crime.
	2. The burden of proof is shifted from the prosecution to the defense. The defense has to prove that the person is insane.
	3. The person is released from the forensic or prison hospital only after being judged to be no longer dangerous and to have recovered from mental illness. This could be longer than he or she would have been imprisoned if convicted.
Guilty but mentally ill (1975)	The person can be found legally guilty of a crime—thus maximizing the chances of incarceration—and the person's mental illness plays a role in how he or she is dealt with. Thus, even a seriously ill person can be held morally and legally responsible but can then be committed to a prison hospital or other suitable facility for psychiatric treatment rather than to a regular prison for punishment.

The M'Naghten Rule The **M'Naghten rule** was formulated in the aftermath of a murder trial in England in 1843. The defendant, Daniel M'Naghten, had set out to kill the British prime minister, Sir Robert Peel, but had mistaken Peel's secretary for Peel. M'Naghten claimed that he had been instructed to kill Lord Peel by the "voice of God." The judges ruled that

> to establish a defense of insanity, it must be clearly proved that, at the time of the committing of the act, the party accused was labouring under such a defect of reason, from disease of the mind, as not to know the nature and quality of the act he was doing; or if he did know it, that he did not know he was doing what was wrong.

The Durham Test A 1954 ruling (*Durham v. United States*[2]) established that a person is not responsible for a crime if it was the "the product of mental disease or mental defect." The definition of what constitutes a mental disease or defect was left open to jurisdictions and mental health professionals to decide. The only state using the Durham standard for its insanity defense today is New Hampshire, likely because the defense is so vague. Yet, concepts of mental disease or defect remain in later insanity defense standards, albeit more clearly defined.

American Law Institute Guidelines In 1962, the American Law Institute (ALI) proposed its own guidelines, which were intended to be more specific and informative to lay jurors than were other tests. The **American Law Institute guidelines**, sometimes referred to as the "model penal code", state the following:

Daniel M'Naghten had a mental disorder when he tried to kill the prime minister. His case helped to establish a legal definition for the insanity defense.

---

[2] *Durham v. United States, 214 F.2d 862, 876 (D.C. Cir. 1954).*

John Hinckley, President Reagan's assailant, was found not guilty by reason of insanity.

1. A person is not responsible for criminal conduct if at the time of such conduct as a result of mental disease or defect he lacks substantial capacity either to appreciate the criminality (wrongfulness) of his conduct or conform his conduct to the requirements of law.

2. As used in the article, the terms "mental disease or defect" do not include an abnormality manifested only by repeated criminal or otherwise antisocial conduct (American Law Institute, 1962, p. 66).

The first ALI guideline combines the M'Naghten rule and the concept of irresistible impulse. The phrase "substantial capacity" in the first guideline is designed to limit an insanity defense to those with the most serious mental disorders. The second guideline concerns those who are repeatedly in trouble with the law; repetitive criminal behavior and psychopathy are not evidence for insanity.

Insanity Defense Reform Act In a highly publicized trial in March 1981, John Hinckley Jr. was found not guilty by reason of insanity (NGRI) for his assassination attempt against President Ronald Reagan. After the verdict, the court received a flood of mail from citizens outraged that a would-be assassin of a U.S. president had not been held criminally responsible and had only been committed to an indefinite stay in a mental hospital until deemed mentally healthy enough for release. The outrage reflects the public's misperceptions about the insanity defense. The public often believes that a person is "getting away" with a crime when found not guilty by reason of insanity and that he or she will be released from the hospital in short order. In reality, many people who are committed to a mental hospital stay there longer than they would have stayed in prison had they been given a sentence (as vividly illustrated in the Clinical Case of Michael Jones). With respect to John Hinckley, he has been committed to St. Elizabeth's Hospital, a public mental hospital in Washington, D.C., for over three decades. Although he can be released whenever his mental health is deemed adequate and he is no longer considered dangerous, this has not yet happened. He has slowly won more freedoms over the past decade. Most recently, in December, 2013, a judge ruled that Hinckley can have eight 17-day visits at his mother's home in Virginia, but he must carry a GPS-enabled mobile phone.

Because of the publicity surrounding the trial and the public outrage at the Hinckley verdict, the insanity defense became a target of vigorous criticism from many quarters. As Judge Parker, who presided at the trial, put it: "For many, the [Hinckley] defense was a clear manifestation of the failure of our criminal justice system to punish people who have clearly violated the law" (quoted in Simon & Aaronson, 1988, p. vii).

As a consequence of political pressures to "get tough" on criminals, Congress enacted the Insanity Defense Reform Act in October 1984, addressing the insanity defense for the first time at the federal level. This law, which has been adopted in all federal courts, contains several provisions designed to make it more difficult to enter an insanity plea.

- It eliminates the irresistible-impulse component of the ALI rules. This volitional and behavioral aspect of the ALI guidelines had been strongly criticized because one could regard any criminal act as arising from an inability to stay within the limits of the law.

- It changes the ALI's "lacks substantial capacity . . . to appreciate" to "unable to appreciate." This alteration in the cognitive component of the law was intended to tighten the grounds for an insanity defense by making the criterion for impaired judgment more stringent.

- The act also stipulates that the mental disease or defect must be "severe," the intent being to exclude insanity defenses on the basis of disorders such as antisocial personality disorder. Also abolished by the act were defenses relying on "diminished capacity" or "diminished responsibility," based on such mitigating circumstances as extreme passion or "temporary insanity." Again, the purpose was to make it harder to mount an insanity defense.

- It shifts the burden of proof from the prosecution to the defense. Instead of the prosecution's having to prove that the person was sane beyond a reasonable doubt at the time of the crime (the most stringent criterion, consistent with the constitutional requirement that people are considered innocent until proved guilty), the defense must prove that the defendant was not sane and must do so with "clear and convincing evidence" (a less stringent but still demanding standard of proof). Table 16.2 shows the different standards of proof used in U.S. courts. The heavier burden now placed on the defense is, like the other provisions, designed to make it more difficult to relieve a defendant of moral and legal responsibility.[3]

- Finally, the person may remain committed longer than the ordinary sentence. A person is released only when deemed by professionals to be no longer dangerous and no longer mentally ill.

Current Insanity Pleas The two most common insanity pleas used in state and federal courts in the United States have been crafted from the legal definitions and precedents just reviewed. With the **not guilty by reason of insanity (NGRI)** plea, there is no dispute over whether the person actually committed the crime—both sides agree that the person committed the crime. However, due to the person's insanity at the time of the crime, the defense attorney argues that the person should not be held responsible for and thus should be acquitted of the crime. A successful NGRI plea means the person is not held responsible for the crime due to his or her psychological disorder. People acquitted with the NGRI plea are committed indefinitely to a forensic hospital. That is, they are released from forensic hospitals only if they are deemed no longer dangerous and no longer mentally ill (we discuss the difficulties in making these determinations later in the chapter).

Table 16.2 Standards of Proof

Standard	Certainty Needed to Convict (%)
Beyond a reasonable doubt	95
Clear and convincing evidence	75
Beyond a preponderance of the evidence	51

Clinical Case: Michael Jones

To illustrate the predicament that a person can get into by raising insanity as a condition for a criminal act, we consider a celebrated—some would call it infamous—Supreme Court case.[4]

Michael Jones was arrested, unarmed, on September 19, 1975, for attempting to steal a jacket from a department store in Washington, D.C. He was charged the next day with attempted petty larceny, a misdemeanor punishable by a maximum prison sentence of 1 year. The court ordered that he be committed to St. Elizabeth's Hospital for a determination of his competency to stand trial.

On March 2, 1976, almost 6 months after the alleged crime, a hospital psychologist reported to the court that Jones was competent to stand trial, although he had "schizophrenia, paranoid type."

The psychologist also reported that the alleged crime resulted from Jones's condition, his paranoid schizophrenia. This comment is noteworthy because the psychologist was not asked to offer an opinion on Jones's state of mind during the crime, only on whether Jones was competent to stand trial. Jones then pleaded not guilty by reason of insanity. Ten days later, on March 12, the court found him NGRI and formally committed him to St. Elizabeth's Hospital for treatment of his mental disorder.

On May 25, 1976, a customary 50-day hearing was held to determine whether Jones should remain in the hospital any longer. A psychologist from the hospital testified that Jones still suffered from paranoid schizophrenia and was a danger to himself and

---

[3]According to Simon and Aaronson (1988), this provision arose in large measure from the inability of the prosecution to prove John Hinckley's sanity when he shot Reagan and three others. Several members of the jury testified after the trial to a subcommittee of the Senate Judiciary Committee that the judge's instructions on the burden of proof played a role in their verdict of NGRI. Even before the act, almost half the states required that the defendant must prove insanity, but only one, Arizona, had the "clear and convincing" standard. A majority of the states now place the burden of proof on the defense, albeit with the least exacting of legal standards of proof, "by a preponderance of the evidence."

[4]*Jones v. United States,* 463 U.S. 354 (1983).

to others. A second hearing was held on February 22, 1977, 17 months after Jones's commitment to St. Elizabeth's, for determination of competency. The defendant demanded release since he had already been hospitalized longer than the 1-year maximum sentence he would have served had he been found guilty of the theft of the jacket. The court denied the request and returned him to St. Elizabeth's.

In response to an appeal, the District of Columbia Court of Appeals agreed with the original court. Ultimately, in November 1982, more than 7 years after his hospitalization, Jones's appeal to the Supreme Court was heard. On June 29, 1983, by a five-to-four decision, the Court affirmed the earlier decision: Jones was to remain at St. Elizabeth's. Jones was fully released from St. Elizabeth's in August 2004, 28 years after the crime!

A forensic hospital looks very much like a regular hospital except that the perimeter of the grounds is secured with gates, barbed wires, or electric fences. Inside the hospital, doors to the different units may be locked, and bars may be placed on windows on the lower floors. Peoples do not stay in jail cells, however, but in either individual or shared rooms. Security professionals are on hand to keep people safe. They typically do not carry weapons of any sort, and they may be dressed in regular clothing rather than uniforms.

In the case of Michael Jones, the court considered whether someone who was found NGRI could be kept in a hospital longer than the person might have spent in prison had he or she been found guilty of the crime. Jones argued that he should be released; the Supreme Court disagreed. According to the Court ruling, Jones could not be punished for the crime because his insanity left him legally blameless—this is the logic of the insanity defense. Jones would have been released from prison sooner had he pleaded guilty.

The Court was also concerned about Jones's dangerousness. Jones argued in his petition to the Supreme Court that his theft of the jacket was not dangerous because it was not a violent crime. The Court stated, however, that for there to be violence in a criminal act, the act itself need not be dangerous. It cited a previous decision that a nonviolent theft of an article such as a watch may frequently result in violence through the efforts of the criminal to escape, or of the victim to protect his or her property, or of the police to apprehend the fleeing thief.[5]

The dissenting justices of the Court commented that the longer someone such as Jones had to remain in the hospital, the harder it would be for him to demonstrate that he was no longer a dangerous person or mentally ill. Extended institutionalization would likely make it more difficult for him to afford medical experts other than those associated with the hospital and to behave like someone who was not mentally ill. Given that Jones remained in the hospital for 28 years, it would seem that the dissenting justices were correct.

In a later case in 1992, the Supreme Court ruled that someone found NGRI could not remain committed if no longer mentally ill, even if that person was still considered dangerous.[6]

The second insanity plea is **guilty but mentally ill (GBMI).** A GBMI plea allows an accused person to be found legally guilty of a crime—thus maximizing the chances of incarceration—but also allows for psychiatric judgment on how to deal with the convicted person if he or she is considered to have been mentally ill when the act was committed. Thus, even a seriously ill person can be held morally and legally responsible for a crime but can then, in theory, be committed to a prison hospital or other suitable facility for psychiatric treatment rather than to a regular prison for punishment. In reality, however, people judged GBMI are usually put in the general prison population, where they may or may not receive treatment. If the person is still considered to be dangerous or mentally ill after serving the imposed prison sentence, he or she may be committed to a mental hospital under civil law proceedings.

One of the more famous cases involving something like the GBMI verdict was the 1992 conviction of Jeffrey Dahmer in Milwaukee, Wisconsin. He had been accused of and had admitted to butchering, cannibalizing, and having sex with the corpses of 15 boys and young men. Dahmer entered a plea of guilty but then his attorneys argued that his psychological

---

[5]*Overholser v. O'Beirne,* 302 F.2d 85, 861, (D.C. Cir. 1961).
[6]*Foucha v. Louisiana,* 504 U.S. 71 (1992).

Table 16.3 Comparing NGRI and GBMI

	NGRI	GBMI
Responsibility for crime	Not responsible	Responsible
Where committed	Forensic hospital	Prison
Given sentence?	No	Yes
When released	When no longer dangerous and mentally ill	End of sentence, but could then be committed civilly if dangerous and mentally ill
Treatment given?	Yes	Possibly

disorder be considered when it came time to imposing a sentence. His sanity was the sole focus of an unusual trial that had jurors listening to conflicting testimony from mental health experts about the defendant's state of mind during the serial killings to which he had confessed. They had to decide whether he had had a mental disease that prevented him from knowing right from wrong or from being able to control his actions. Even though there was no disagreement that he was mentally ill, with a diagnosis of a type of paraphilia (see Chapter 14), Dahmer was deemed sane and therefore legally responsible for the grisly murders. The judge sentenced him to 15 consecutive life terms. Later, another inmate in prison killed him.

Critics of the GBMI verdict argue that it does not benefit criminal defendants with psychological disorders and does not result in appropriate treatment for those convicted (Woodmansee, 1996). A 1997 South Carolina Supreme Court case[7] found that South Carolina's GBMI statute did provide some benefit because it mandated that convicted people with psychological disorders receive mental health evaluations before being placed in the general prison population. Unfortunately, these assessments have not been shown to lead to better treatment. Other critics of the GBMI verdict note that the verdict is confusing and even deceiving to jurors. Jurors believe that GBMI is not as "tough" as a guilty verdict, but in reality people receiving a GBMI verdict often spend more time incarcerated than if they had been found guilty (Melville & Naimark, 2002).

Table 16.3 compares these two insanity pleas. Only a few states allow for some or all of the GBMI provisions. Four states—Idaho, Montana, Kansas, and Utah—do not allow for any

Quick Summary

Insanity is a legal term, not a mental health term. Meeting the legal definition is not necessarily the same thing as having a diagnosable psychological disorder. The insanity defense is the legal argument that a defendant should not be held responsible for an illegal act if it is attributable to a psychological disorder that interferes with rationality or that results from some other excusing circumstance, such as not knowing right from wrong.

The irresistible-impulse standard suggested that an impulse or drive that the person could not control compelled that person to commit the criminal act. The M'Naghten rule specified that a person could not distinguish right from wrong at the time of the crime because of the person's psychological disorder. The Durham test specified that a person not be held responsible if the crime was the product of a mental disease or defect. The first part of the American Law Institute guidelines combines the M'Naghten rule and

the concept of irresistible impulse. The second concerns those who are repeatedly in trouble with the law; they are not to be deemed mentally ill only because they keep committing crimes. The Insanity Defense Reform Act shifted the burden of proof from the prosecution to the defense, removed the irresistible impulse component, changed wording regarding substantial capacity, and specified that the psychological disorder must be severe. The Jones case illustrates a number of the complexities associated with the insanity defense.

The not guilty by reason of insanity (NGRI) plea means that an accused person should not be held responsible for the crime due to his or her psychological disorder. The guilty but mentally ill (GBMI) plea means that an accused person is legally guilty of a crime but can then, in theory, be committed to a prison hospital or other suitable facility for psychiatric treatment rather than to a regular prison for punishment.

[7]*South Carolina v. Hornsby,* 484 S.E.2d 869 (S.C. Sup. Ct. 1997).

insanity defense, though three of them (Idaho, Montana, Utah) will consider mental state at the time of the crime in some form or fashion. The remaining states have some version of NGRI available. Taking a cue from the Insanity Defense Reform Act, 39 states require that the burden of proof rests with the defendant.

Check Your Knowledge 16.1 (Answers are at the end of the chapter.)

Match the statement with the correct insanity standard.

1. can't control behavior
2. found guilty
3. doesn't know right from wrong
4. affirmative defense

a. GBMI
b. NGRI
c. irresistible impulse
d. M'Naghten rule

Other cases have considered the impact of medication on a person entering the NGRI plea. If a defendant wishes, the effects of the medication must be explained to the jury, lest the jury conclude from the defendant's relatively rational drug-produced demeanor that he or she could not have been insane at the time of the crime.[8] This requirement acknowledges that juries form their judgments of legal responsibility or insanity at least in part based on how the defendant appears during the trial. If the defendant appears healthy, the jury may be less likely to believe that the crime was the result of a disturbed mental state rather than of free will—even though an insanity defense has to do with the defendant's state of mind during the crime, not his or her psychological state during the trial.

Competency to Stand Trial

The insanity defense concerns the accused person's mental state at the time of the crime. An important consideration before deciding what kind of defense to adopt is whether the accused person is competent to stand trial at all. In the U.S. criminal justice system, **competency to stand trial** must be decided before it can be determined whether a person is responsible for the crime of which he or she is accused. It is possible for a person to be judged competent to stand trial and then be judged not guilty by reason of insanity.

The legal standard for being competent to stand trial has not changed since it was articulated by a 1960 U.S. Supreme Court decision:[9] "The test [is] whether [the defendant] has sufficient present ability to consult with his lawyer with a reasonable degree of rational understanding, and whether he has a rational as well as a factual understanding of the proceedings against him."

With the 1966 Supreme Court case *Pate v. Robinson*[10] as precedent, the defense attorney, prosecutor, or judge may raise the question of psychological disorder whenever there is reason to believe that the accused person's mental condition might interfere with his or her upcoming trial. Another way to look at competency is that the courts do not want a person to be brought to trial **in absentia** ("not present"), which is a centuries-old principle of English common law that refers here to the person's mental state, not his or her physical presence. If, after examination, the person is deemed too mentally ill to participate meaningfully in a trial, the trial is delayed, and the accused person is placed in a hospital with the hope that the means of restoring adequate mental functioning can be found.

If a court fails to order a hearing when there is evidence that raises a reasonable doubt about competency to stand trial, or if it convicts a legally incompetent defendant, there is a violation of due process.[11] Once competency is questioned, there must be a preponderance

---

[8]*State v. Jojola*, 553 F.2d 1296 (N.M. Ct. App. 1976).
[9]*Dusky v. United States*, 362 U.S. 402 (1960).
[10]*Pate v. Robinson*, 383 U.S. 375 (1996).
[11]*United States v. White*, 887 F.2d 705 (6th Cir. 1989); *Wright v. Lockhart*, 914 F.2d 1093, cert, denied, 111 S.Ct. 1089(1991).

of evidence (see Table 16.2) showing that the defendant is competent to stand trial.[12] As just indicated, the test to be applied is whether the defendant is able to consult adequately with his or her lawyer and whether he or she can understand the proceedings.[13] The court has to consider evidence such as irrational behavior as well as any medical or psychological data that might bear on the defendant's competency.[14] However, analogous to the insanity defense, being deemed mentally ill does not necessarily mean that the person is incompetent to stand trial; a person with schizophrenia, for example, may still understand legal proceedings and be able to assist in his or her defense. In Focus on Discovery 16.1, we consider the case of Andrea Yates, who was found competent to stand trial despite clear agreement that she was mentally ill.

Being judged incompetent to stand trial can have severe consequences for the individual. Bail is automatically denied, even if it would be routinely granted had the question of incompetency not been raised. The person is usually kept in a hospital for the pretrial examination. During this period the accused person is supposed to receive treatment to render him or her competent to stand trial.[15] In the meantime, the person may lose employment and undergo the trauma of being separated from family and friends and from familiar surroundings for months or even years, perhaps making his or her psychological state even worse and thus making it all the more difficult to show competency to stand trial. Until the 1970s, some people languished in hospitals for many years waiting to be found competent to stand trial.

Clinical Case: Yolanda

Yolanda, a 51-year-old African American woman, was arrested after taking a box of doughnuts from the local QuickMart. At the time of her arrest, she claimed she needed the doughnuts to feed the seven babies growing inside her. She said that Malcolm X was the father of her soon-to-be-born children and that she would soon assume the position of Queen of the New Cities. When asked what the New Cities were, she responded this was a new world order that would be in place following the alignment of the clouds with the planets Jupiter, Saturn, and Venus. Yolanda's public defender immediately realized that Yolanda was not ready for trial; she asked for a competency hearing and arranged for a psychologist to conduct an evaluation. Yolanda was diagnosed with schizophrenia, and her thought disturbance was found to be so profound that she was not able to understand that she had been charged with a crime. Furthermore, she was unable to help her attorney prepare a defense. Instead, Yolanda viewed her attorney as a threat to her unborn babies (she was not pregnant) and feared the attorney would keep her from assuming her rightful position as queen. At her competency hearing, the judge declared that Yolanda was not competent to stand trial and that she be committed to the local forensic hospital for a period of 3 months, after which another competency evaluation would be held.

At the hospital, Yolanda was prescribed Olanzapine, and her thinking became more coherent and organized after 2 months. One of the unit's psychologists worked with Yolanda, teaching her about the criminal justice system. She worked to help Yolanda understand what the charge of theft meant and what a defense attorney, prosecuting attorney, judge, and jury were. At the end of 3 months, a different psychologist evaluated Yolanda and recommended that she now be considered competent to stand trial. Yolanda's public defender came to the hospital and met with her to discuss the case. Yolanda was able to help her attorney by telling her about her past hospitalizations and treatment history for schizophrenia. Yolanda realized she was not pregnant but still held onto beliefs about the New Cities. Still, Yolanda understood that she had stolen the doughnuts and this was why she had to go to court. At her next competency hearing, Yolanda was deemed competent to stand trial. Two months later, she went to court again. This time, she entered a plea of NGRI. After a short trial, the judge accepted her NGRI plea and she returned to the forensic hospital. The treatment goals were now focused on helping Yolanda recover from schizophrenia, not on restoring her competency to stand trial.

---

[12]United States v. Frank, 956 F.2d 872, cert, denied, 113 S.Ct. 363 (1992); United States v. Blohm, 579 F.Supp. 495 (1983).
[13]Frank, 956 F.2d at 872; Wright v. Lockhart, 914 F.2d 1093 (8th Cir. 1990).
[14]*United States v Hemsi*, 901 F.2d 293 (2d Cir. 1990); Balfour v Haws, 892 F.2d 556 (7th Cir. 1989).
[15]United States v. Sherman, 912 F.2d 907 (7th Cir. 1990).

FOCUS ON DISCOVERY 16.1

Another Look at Insanity versus Psychological disorder

On June 20, 2001, believing that her five children, ranging in age from 6 months to 7 years, were condemned to eternal damnation, 37-year-old Andrea Yates, who lived with her husband and children in Houston, Texas, systematically drowned each child in a bathtub. As recounted on the CNN website:

> when the police reached [the] modest brick home on Beachcomber Lane in suburban Houston, they found Andrea drenched with bathwater, her flowery blouse and brown leather sandals soaking wet. She had turned on the bathroom faucet to fill the porcelain tub and moved aside the shaggy mat to give herself traction for kneeling on the floor. It took a bit of work for her to chase down the last of the children; toward the end, she had a scuffle in the family room, sliding around on wet tile. ... She dripped watery footprints from the tub to her bedroom, where she straightened the blankets around the kids in their pajamas once she was done with them. She called 911 and then her husband. "It's time. I finally did it," she said before telling him to come home and hanging up.

The nation was horrified by her actions, and in the months following the murders, information became known about Yates's frequent bouts of depression, especially after giving birth, as well as her several suicide attempts and hospitalizations for severe depression.

Eight months later her trial was held. The defense argued that she was mentally ill at the time of the murders—and for many periods of time preceding the events—and that she was unable to distinguish right from wrong when she put her children to death. The prosecution argued that she had known right from wrong and therefore should be found guilty. On two things the defense and the prosecution agreed: (1) she had murdered her children, and (2) she was mentally ill at the time of the murder. Where they disagreed was on the crucial question as to whether her psychological disorder entailed not being able to distinguish right or wrong, the familiar M'Naghten principle of criminal responsibility.

This trial shows the difficulty of making a successful insanity defense and is a vivid example of the critical difference between a psychological disorder and insanity. No one disagreed that she was severely depressed, probably psy-

chotic, when she killed her five small children. But, as we have seen, a psychological disorder is not the same as legal insanity. Employing the right–wrong principle, the jury deliberated for only 3 hours and 40 minutes on March 12, 2002, and delivered a verdict of guilty. They had rejected the defense's contention that Ms. Yates could not distinguish right from wrong at the time of the crime. On March 15, the jury decided to spare her life and recommended to the presiding judge that she get life in prison, not being eligible for parole for 40 years.

The trial and the guilty verdict occasioned impassioned discussion in the media and among thousands of people. How could the jury *not* have considered her insane? If such a person is not insane, who could be judged to be so? Should the right–wrong M'Naghten principle be dropped from the laws of half the states in the United States? Didn't her phoning 911 to report what she had done prove that she knew she had done something very wrong? Didn't the careful and systematic way she killed her children reflect a mind that, despite her deep depression and delusional thinking, could formulate a complex plan and execute it successfully? Had she received proper treatment from psychiatrists, especially from the one who had recently taken her off the antidepressant medication that had been helping her and had sent her home without adequate follow-up?

Andrea Yates, who drowned her five children, pled NGRI. Although she was suffering from a psychological disorder, her initial plea was unsuccessful because she was judged capable of knowing right from wrong. After the initial verdict was thrown out, her NGRI plea was successful in the second trial.

As it turns out, these questions were addressed in the Yates case after all. In January 2005, an appeals court overturned Yates's murder conviction because the jury had heard false testimony from one of the expert witnesses that may have unduly influenced their decision. A prosecution witness testified that Yates's behavior may have been influenced by an episode of the television show *Law and Order* that showed a woman with depression drowning her children, suggesting she knew right from wrong. However, there had been no such episode on this television show, so Yates could not have been so influenced. A new trial was conducted, and on July 26, 2006, after 3 days of deliberations, the new jury found Yates not guilty by reason of insanity. She was placed in a maximum-security forensic hospital in Texas. In 2007, she was transferred to a minimum-security hospital in Texas. In 2012, she was denied the opportunity to leave the hospital for two hours a week to attend church services.

A 1972 Supreme Court case, *Jackson v. Indiana*,[16] forced the states to a speedier determination of incompetency. The case concerned a deaf and mute man with intellectual disability who was deemed not only incompetent to stand trial but unlikely ever to become competent. The Court ruled that the length of pretrial confinement must be limited to the time it takes to determine whether treatment during this detainment is likely to render the defendant competent to stand trial. If the defendant is unlikely ever to become competent, the state must, after this period, either institute civil commitment proceedings or release the defendant. Federal and most state laws define more precisely the minimal requirements for competency to stand trial, ending the latitude that has deprived thousands of people of their rights to due process (Fourteenth Amendment) and a speedy trial (Sixth Amendment). Defendants cannot be committed for determination of competency for a period longer than the maximum possible sentence they face.[17] Most people are deemed competent to stand trial in about 6 months. As illustrated in the Clinical Case of Yolanda, she was able to understand the charges against her and assist her attorney in her defense after about 5 months of treatment. People who have intellectual disabilities or a serious psychological disorder such as schizophrenia that has required longer hospitalization are least likely to ever be deemed competent to stand trial (Zapf & Roesch, 2011).

Medication has had an impact on the competency issue. On the one hand, the concept of "synthetic sanity" (Schwitzgebel & Schwitzgebel, 1980) has been used to argue that if a drug, such as Zyprexa, temporarily produces a bit of rationality in an otherwise incompetent defendant, the trial may proceed. The likelihood that the defendant will again become incompetent to stand trial if the drug is withdrawn does not disqualify the person from going to court.[18] On the other hand, the individual rights of the defendant should be protected against forced medication, because there is no guarantee that such treatment would render the person competent to stand trial, and there is a chance that it might cause harm. Supreme Court rulings[19] in the 1980s and 1990s held that a criminal defendant generally couldn't be forced to take medication in an effort to render him or her competent to stand trial and that the defendant's civil rights are protected, even when a drug might restore legal competency to stand trial.[20]

In 2003, the Supreme Court issued a new ruling that limited the circumstances under which forced medication to restore competency could be used.[21] In this case, St. Louis dentist Charles Sell had been charged with two different counts of fraud and with conspiring to kill a former employee and an FBI agent who had arrested him. Sell was later diagnosed with delusional disorder and was found incompetent to stand trial. This was in essence a nonviolent crime, and the Supreme Court did not see that forced medication was justified in this case. The Court ruled that forced medication could be used only if alternative treatments had failed, medication is likely to be effective, medication won't interfere with a person's right to defend him- or herself at trial, and there is an important government interest in trying the defendant for a serious crime.

It turns out, however, the medications are often the most effective means of restoring competency. Research has shown that the more medications reduce a person's symptoms, the more likely they are to be able to be deemed competent. Though more research is needed, education about the legal proceedings seems to help competency restoration, but it appears that education without medication is not as effective (Zapf & Roesch, 2011).

Even if a person with a psychological disorder is found competent to stand trial, that person may not be able to serve as his or her own defense attorney. A 2008 U.S. Supreme Court decision[22] held that a judge may deny the right of self-representation if it is clear that

---

[16]*Jackson v. Indiana*, 406 U.S. 715 (1972).

[17]*United States v. DeBellis* 649 F.2d 1 (1st Cir. 1981); *State v. Moore*, 467 N.W. 2d 201 (Wis. Ct. App. 1991).

[18]*State v. Hampton*, 218 So.2d 311 (La. 1969); *State v. Stacy,* no. 446 (Crim. App., Knoxville, Tenn., August 4, 1977); *United States v. Hayes*, 589 F.2d 811 (1979).

[19]*Riggins v. Nevada*, 504 U.S. 127 (1992).

[20]*United States v. Waddell*, 687 F. Supp. 208 (1988).

[21]*Sell v. United States*, 539 U.S. 02-5664 (2003).

[22]*Indiana v. Edwards,* 554 U.S. 164 (2008).

FOCUS ON DISCOVERY 16.2

Dissociative Identity Disorder and the Insanity Defense

Imagine that as you are having a cup of coffee one morning, you hear pounding at the front door. You hurry to answer and find two police officers staring grimly at you. One of them asks, "Are you Jane Smith?" "Yes," you reply. "Well, ma'am, you are under arrest for grand theft and for the murder of John Doe." The officer then reads you your Miranda rights against self-incrimination, handcuffs you, and takes you to the police station, where you are allowed to call your lawyer.

This would be a scary situation for anybody. What is particularly frightening and puzzling to you and your lawyer is that you have absolutely no recollection of having committed the crime that a detective later describes to you. You are horrified that you cannot account for the time period when the murder was committed—in fact, your memory is startlingly blank for that entire time. And, as if this were not bizarre enough, the detective then shows you a tape in which you are clearly firing a gun at a bank teller during a holdup. "Is that you in the videotape?" asks the detective. You confer with your lawyer, saying that it certainly looks like you, including the clothes, but you are advised not to admit anything one way or the other.

Let's move forward in time now to your trial some months later. Witnesses have come forward and identified you beyond a reasonable doubt. There is no one you know who can testify that you were somewhere other than at the bank on the afternoon of the robbery and the murder. But did you murder the teller in the bank? You are able to assert honestly to yourself and to the jury that you did not. And yet even you have been persuaded that the person in the videotape is you—and that that person committed the robbery and the murder.

Because of the strange nature of the case, your lawyer arranged prior to the trial to have you interviewed by a psychiatrist and a clinical psychologist, both of them well-known experts in forensics. Through extensive questioning, they have decided that you have dissociative identity disorder (DID, formerly called multiple personality disorder) and that the crimes were committed not by you, Jane Smith, but by your rather violent alter, Laura. Indeed, during one of the interviews, Laura emerged and boasted about the crime, even chuckling over the fact that you, Jane, would be imprisoned for it.

Can DID be an excusing condition for a criminal act? Should Jane Smith be held responsible for a crime committed by her alter, Laura?

In reviews of the DID literature and of its forensic implications, Elyn Saks (1997) of the University of Southern California Law Center argued that DID should be regarded as a special case in mental health law and that a new legal principle should be established. Her argument takes issue with legal practice that would hold a person with DID

responsible for a crime as long as the personality acting at the time of the crime intended to commit it.

What is intriguing about Saks's argument is that she devotes a major portion of it to defining personhood. What is a person? Is a person the body we inhabit? Well, most of the time our sense of who we are as persons does not conflict with the bodies we have come to know as our own or, rather, as us. But in DID there is a discrepancy. The body that committed the crimes at the bank was Jane Smith. But it was her alter, Laura, who committed the crimes. Saks argues that, peculiar as it may sound, the law should be interested in the body only as a container for the person. It is the person who may or may not be blameworthy, not the body. Nearly all the time they are one and the same, but in the case of DID they are not. In a sense, Laura committed the murder by using Jane's body.

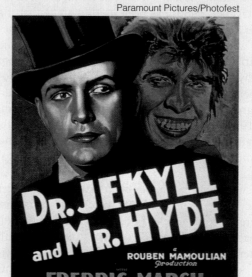

Paramount Pictures/Photofest

Poster for the classic film about Jekyll and Hyde.

Then is Jane blameworthy? The person Jane did not commit the crime; she did not even know about it. For the judge to sentence Jane—or, more specifically, the body in the courtroom who usually goes by that name—would be unjust, argues Saks, for Jane is descriptively innocent. To be sure, sending Jane to prison would punish Laura, for whenever Laura would emerge, she would find herself imprisoned. But what of Jane? Saks concludes that it is unjust to imprison Jane because she is not blameworthy. Rather, we must find her not guilty by reason of dissociative identity disorder and remand her for treatment of the disorder.

Dissociative identity disorder would not, however, be a justification for a verdict of NGRI if the alter that did not commit the crime was aware of the other alter's criminal intent and did not do anything to prevent the criminal act. Under these circumstances, argues Saks, the first alter would be complicit in the crime and would therefore be somewhat blameworthy. A comparison Saks draws is to Robert Louis Stevenson's fictional character of Dr. Jekyll and Mr. Hyde. Jekyll made the potion that caused the emergence of Mr. Hyde, his alter, with the foreknowledge that Hyde would do evil. So even though Jekyll was not present when Hyde was in charge, he would nonetheless be blameworthy because of his prior knowledge of what Hyde would do—not to mention that he, Jekyll, had concocted the potion that created his alter, Hyde.

Saks is optimistic about the effectiveness of therapy for DID and believes that people like Jane/Laura can be integrated into one personality and then released to rejoin society. Saks goes so far as to argue that people with DID who are judged dangerous but who have not committed a crime should be subject to civil commitment, even though this would be tantamount to preventive detention. In this way, she suggests, future crimes might be avoided.

the defendant would not receive a fair trial. Focus on Discovery 16.2 discusses the unusual challenge posed by dissociative identity disorder in criminal commitments.

Insanity, Intellectual Disability, and Capital Punishment

As we have just seen, an accused person's mental state can be taken into consideration to determine whether he or she is competent to stand trial and/or should be held legally responsible for a criminal act. On very rare occasions, the sanity or mental capacity of a person also becomes an issue after a conviction. The question is, should a person who is sentenced to be put to death (i.e., capital punishment) by the state have to be legally sane at the time of the execution? Furthermore, what if the person has intellectual disability (formerly called mental retardation) and thus does not understand what is about to happen to him or her? The Clinical Cases of Horace Kelly and Scott Panetti illustrate the difficulties with capital punishment cases that involve a person with a psychological disorder.

Clinical Cases: Horace Kelly and Scott Panetti

The question of insanity and capital punishment arose in the case of Horace Kelly, a 39-year-old man who had been found guilty of the rapes and murders of two women and the slaying of an 11-year-old boy in 1984. Although Kelly's mental state had not been an issue at the time of his trial, his lawyers argued—12 years later and just days before his scheduled execution by lethal injection—that his mental health had deteriorated during his imprisonment on death row to such an extent that one of his defense attorneys referred to him as a "walking vegetable." They made reference to a 1986 Supreme Court ruling[23] stating that it is a violation of the Eighth Amendment (which prohibits cruel and unusual punishment) for an insane individual to be executed.

Evidence of a psychological disorder during Kelly's imprisonment included psychiatrists' reports of delusions, hallucinations, and inappropriate affect. He was also described by fellow inmates and by guards as hoarding his feces and smearing them on the walls of his prison cell. By 1995, after 10 years

David Bauman/Associated Press/AP/Wide World Photo

Horace Kelly was sentenced to death, but this sentence was not carried out because the courts ruled that the insane cannot be executed.

on death row, one court-appointed psychiatrist had concluded that Kelly was legally insane. On the other hand, another psychiatrist reported that when asked what being executed would mean for him, Kelly had given the rational reply that he would not be able to have a family; he was also able to name two of his victims and beat the psychiatrist in several games of tic-tac-toe. A federal judge decided in June 1998 and the U.S. Supreme Court concurred in April 1999 to stay (delay) Kelly's execution and allow his lawyers to argue, among other things, that he should not be put to death because he was insane. After these arguments, Kelly's execution was permanently stayed.

In 2007, the U.S. Supreme Court overturned another death sentence in the case of Scott Panetti.[24] Panetti shot and killed his estranged wife's parents in 1992. He had been diagnosed with schizophrenia and had been hospitalized numerous times prior to the murders. At his trial, Panetti

---

[23] *Ford v. Wainright,* 477 U.S. 399 (1986).
[24] *Panetti v. Quarterman,* 551 U.S. (2007).

served as his own attorney, dressed up as a cowboy (he had narrowly been deemed competent to stand trial). The court transcripts are filled with incoherent ramblings from him. For example, he tried to subpoena Jesus Christ. In his closing arguments, he said:

The ability to reason correctly. Common sense, the common sense, the horse sense. This is Texas and we're not talking loopholes and if we're talking—well, let's talk a lariat. Let's talk a catch rope . . .

A Texas court sentenced him to death, and an appeals court upheld this sentence. The U.S. Supreme Court ruled, however, that Panetti could not understand why he was to be put to death given his mental state and returned the case for further evaluation of insanity by a Texas lower court. That court ruled in 2013 that Panetti was competent to be executed; his case may well be returned to the Supreme Court.

The question of intellectual disability and capital punishment arose in the case of Daryl Atkins who in 1996 was convicted and sentenced to death in Virginia for a kidnapping and murder. His IQ was rated at 59, which would likely place him in the category of what is today called intellectual disability but was then called moderate mental retardation. His defense attorney argued that his intellectual limitations rendered capital punishment unconstitutional because he lacked understanding of the consequences of his actions and was therefore not as morally culpable for his acts as a person of normal intelligence.

In 2002, the United States Supreme Court ruled in a six-to-three decision in the case of *Atkins v. Virginia*[25] that capital punishment of those with intellectual disability constitutes cruel and unusual punishment, which is prohibited by the Eighth Amendment. The Supreme Court left open the question of what constitutes intellectual disability, however, leaving it up to the states to decide how to remain within the requirements of the Eighth Amendment.

The state of Virginia subsequently defined intellectual disability as consisting of an IQ score of 70 or less along with difficulties in self-care and social interaction. In Virginia, a defendant must convince the jury of intellectual disability using the standard "beyond a preponderance of the evidence" (see Table 16.2). Since 1998, Atkins had been given an IQ test at least four times. He scored below 70 on two testing occasions (scores of 59 and 67) and above 70 on two other testing occasions (scores of 74 and 76). In August 2005, a Virginia jury decided that Daryl Atkins did not meet Virginia's definition of intellectual disability. Thus, even though the *Atkins* case effectively abolished the practice of executing people with intellectual disabilities, Daryl Atkins could have been put to death in Virginia because the state jury's decision paved the way for the original death sentence to be carried out. However, in January 2008 a Virginia judge changed Atkins's death sentence to life imprisonment. The reason for this change was not due to any rethinking of Atkins's mental capacity. Rather, it was due to prosecutorial misconduct (improper witness coaching) that was revealed by one of the attorneys.

Following the 2002 Supreme Court ruling, the definitions of intellectual disability varied quite a bit from state to state. In 2012, for example, Texas executed Marvin Wilson, a man with an IQ of 61 who was convicted of murder in 1994. Texas officials argued that Wilson's criminal activities showed him to be savvy and not suffering from an intellectual disability despite the IQ score.

In 2014, the Supreme Court revised its decision to leave determination of what constitutes intellectual disability up to the states with the case of Freddie Lee Hall, a Florida man with an IQ score of around 70 who was convicted of murder and sentenced to death. The court ruled that intellectual disability cannot be determined solely on the basis of an IQ score (which can vary from testing occasion to testing occasion) but must also include assessments of adaptive functioning over the lifetime.[26] The case was returned to Florida courts for a new, broader assessment. It remains to be seen how Florida will respond to this new ruling.

---

[25]*Atkins v. Virgina*, 536 U.S. 304 (2002).
[26]*Hall v. Florica*, 572 U.S. (2014).

If a person should not be executed due to insanity or intellectual disability, what are the ethics of providing medications to improve a person's mental state? Increasing attention is being paid to this issue. In 2002, for example, the Georgia Board of Pardons and Paroles threw out the death sentence of a convicted rapist and murderer on the grounds that he was delusional (note that he had not been found NGRI and that he had been on death row for nearly 16 years). What makes this case significant is that the person had been forced to take psychoactive medication that improved his mental condition enough to meet the federal standard that only a person who is legally sane can be executed (Weinstein, 2002).

Check Your Knowledge 16.2

True or false?
1. The *Jackson* case established that people who will not be restored to competency should be found NGRI.
2. To be competent to stand trial, a person must be able to understand the charges and assist his or her attorney.

3. The Supreme Court ruled that executing prisoners with a psychological disorder constitutes cruel and unusual punishment.

Civil Commitment

Historically, governments have had a duty to protect their citizens from harm. We take for granted the right and duty of government to set limits on our freedom for the sake of protecting us. Few drivers, for example, question the legitimacy of the state's imposing limits on them by requiring seat belts or by providing traffic signals that often make them stop when they would rather go. Government has a long-established right as well as an obligation to protect us both from ourselves—the *parens patriae*, "power of the state"—and from others—the police power of the state. Civil commitment is one further exercise of these powers.

In virtually all states, a person can be committed to a hospital against his or her will if a judgment is made that he or she is (1) mentally ill and (2) a danger to self—that is, the person is suicidal or unable to provide for the basic physical needs of food, clothing, and shelter—or to others (Perlin, 1994). At present, dangerousness to others is more often the principal criterion in court rulings that point to imminent dangerousness (e.g., the person is right on the verge of committing a violent act).[27] In some states, a finding of imminent dangerousness must be evidenced by a recent overt act, attempt, or threat; however, some states do not require an overt act. Civil commitment is supposed to last only as long as the person remains dangerous.[28]

Specific commitment procedures generally fit into one of two categories, formal and informal. Formal (or judicial) commitment is by order of a court. Any responsible citizen—usually the police, a relative, or a friend—can request it. If a judge believes that there is a good reason to pursue the matter, he or she will order a mental health examination. The person has the right to object to these attempts to "certify" him or her, and a court hearing can be scheduled to allow the person to present evidence against commitment.

---

[27]*Suzuki v. Yuen*, 617 F.2d 173 (9th Cir. 1980).
[28]*United States v. Debellis*, 649 F.2d 1 (1st Cir. 1981).

Informal, emergency commitment of people with a psychological disorder can be accomplished without initially involving the courts. For example, if a hospital administrative board believes that a person requesting discharge is too mentally ill and dangerous to be released, it is able to detain the person with a temporary, informal commitment order.

The police may take any person acting in an out-of-control or dangerous manner immediately to a psychiatric hospital. Perhaps the most common informal commitment procedure is the PC, or physician's certificate. In most states, a physician, not necessarily a psychiatrist, can sign a certificate that allows a person to be hospitalized for some period of time, ranging from 24 hours to as long as 20 days. Detainment beyond this period requires formal judicial commitment.

Civil commitment affects far more people than criminal commitment. It is beyond the scope of this book to examine in detail the variety of state civil commitment laws and regulations; each state has its own, and they are in almost constant flux. Our aim is to present an overview that will provide a basic understanding of the issues and of current directions of change.

Preventive Detention and Problems in the Prediction of Dangerousness

The perception is widespread that people with psychological disorders account for a significant proportion of the violence that besets contemporary society, but this is not the case (Bonta, Law, & Hanson, 1998; Monahan, 1992). Only about 3 percent of the violence in the United States is clearly linked to psychological disorders (Swanson et al., 1990). Moreover, about 90 percent of people diagnosed with psychotic disorders (primarily schizophrenia) are not violent (Swanson et al., 1990). People with disorders such as schizophrenia or bipolar disorder—even allowing for their relatively small numbers—do not account for a large proportion of violent offenses, especially when compared with people who abuse drugs or alcohol and people who are in their teens and 20s, are male, and are poor (Corrigan & Watson, 2005; Douglas, Guy, & Hart, 2009; Fazel et al., 2009). The MacArthur Violence Risk Assessment Study, a large prospective study of violent behavior among persons recently discharged from psychiatric hospitals, found that people with psychological disorders who did not also abuse substances were no more likely to engage in violence than are people without psychological disorders and substance abuse (Steadman, Mulvey, Monahan et al., 1998).

When people with psychological disorders do act aggressively, it is usually against family members or friends, and the incidents tend to occur at home (Steadman et al., 1998). Indeed, stranger homicide by people with a psychological disorder is extremely rare (Nielssen, Bourget, Laajasalo et al., 2011). Another analysis from the MacArthur study found that people with psychological disorders reported more violent thoughts while in the hospital compared to people not in the hospital However, these people were not necessarily more likely to actually be violent once they left the hospital (Grisso, Davis, Vesselinov et al., 2000). Actual violent behavior was found only among a subsample of people (e.g., those with a diagnosis of substance use disorder or those who had severe symptoms and persistent violent thoughts). Two recent meta-analyses of violence and psychological disorders focusing mostly on disorders that involve psychosis (schizophrenia spectrum disorders, bipolar disorder, depression with psychotic features) found that people with some type of psychotic disorder were slightly more likely to be aggressive, but this was particularly true when a person had the positive or disorganization symptoms of schizophrenia (see Chapter 9) or was also abusing drugs (Douglas, Guy, & Hart, 2009; Fazel et al., 2009). Importantly, the increased risk for violence in people who also had a comorbid substance use disorder was similar to that found in people with a substance use disorder and no psychotic disorder. This suggests that issues of substance abuse rather than psychotic disorders are the main contributory factors to violence. By and large, then, the general public is seldom affected

People with a psychological disorder are not necessarily more likely to be violent than people without a psychological disorder, contrary to the way movies often portray people with a psychological disorder.

by violence from people with psychological disorders, even though certain people with certain disorders can and will be violent.

The Prediction of Dangerousness The likelihood of committing a dangerous act is central to civil commitment, but is dangerousness easily predicted? Early studies examining the accuracy of predictions that a person would commit a dangerous act found that mental health professionals were poor at making this judgment (e.g., Kozol, Boucher, & Garofalo, 1972; Monahan, 1973, 1976).

However, newer, empirically supported methods for assessing and predicting violence have been developed that identify and measure violence risk factors based on clinical judgment (e.g., Historical-Clinical-Risk Management-20, or HCR-20; Webster, Douglas, Eaves et al., 1997) or a combination of clinical judgment and statistical algorithms (e.g., Violence Risk Appraisal Guide (VRAG); Quinsey, Harris, Rice et al., 2006). These measures seem to work equally well, but even with these improved measures it remains a challenge to accurately predict future dangerousness (Skeem & Monahan, 2011).

John Monahan is an expert on predicting dangerousness.

Courtesy of John Monahan, University of Virginia School of Law

Research suggests that violence prediction is most accurate under the following conditions (Campbell, Stefan, & Loder, 1994; Monahan, 1984; Monahan & Steadman, 1994; Steadman et al., 1998):

- If a person has been repeatedly violent in the recent past, it is reasonable to predict that he or she will be violent in the near future unless there have been major changes in the person's attitudes or environment.

- If violence is in the person's distant past, and if it was a single but very serious act, and if that person has been incarcerated for a period of time, then violence can be expected on release if there is reason to believe that the person's predetention personality and physical abilities have not changed and if the person is going to return to the same environment in which he or she was previously violent.

- Even with no history of violence, violence can be predicted if the person is judged to be on the brink of a violent act, for example, if the person is pointing a loaded gun at an occupied building.

Violence among people with a psychological disorder is more likely when they do not receive treatment, whether due to lack of availability or noncompliance (Monahan, 1992; Keers, Ullrich, DeStavola et al., 2014; Steadman et al., 1998). Outpatient commitment or **assisted outpatient treatment** (AOT) is one way of increasing medication compliance. It is an arrangement whereby a person is mandated by the court to receive treatment on an outpatient basis (i.e., not in the hospital); 45 states have laws covering this type of treatment (Torrey, 2014). To the extent that AOT increases compliance with medication regimens and other mental health treatment—and evidence indicates that it does (Munetz, Grande, Kleist et al., 1996; Torrey, 2014)—we can expect violence to be reduced. Indeed, support services can markedly reduce the chance that a person who might otherwise be prone to committing a violent act will actually commit one (Dvoskin & Steadman, 1994). For a discussion of mental health professionals' responsibilities to predict dangerousness, see Focus on Discovery 16.3.

Protection of the Rights of People with Psychological Disorders

The U.S. Constitution is a remarkable document. It lays down the basic duties of elected federal officials and guarantees a set of civil rights. But there is often some distance between the abstract delineation of a civil right and its day-to-day implementation. Moreover, judges must interpret the Constitution as it bears on specific contemporary problems. Since nowhere in this cornerstone of U.S. democracy is there specific mention of people with psychological disorders, lawyers and judges interpret various sections of the document to justify what they consider necessary in society's treatment of people whose mental health is in question.

FOCUS ON DISCOVERY 16.3

The *Tarasoff* Case—The Duty to Warn and to Protect

The client's right to privileged communication—the legal right of a client to require that what goes on in therapy remain confidential—is an important protection, but it is not absolute. Society has long stipulated certain conditions in which confidentiality in a relationship should not be maintained because of the harm that can befall others. A famous California court ruling in 1974[a] described circumstances in which a therapist not only may but also *must* breach the sanctity of a client's communication. First, we describe the facts of the case.

Clinical Case

In the fall of 1968, Prosenjit Poddar, a graduate student from India studying at the University of California at Berkeley, met Tatiana (Tanya) Tarasoff at a folk dancing class. They saw each other weekly during the fall, and on New Year's Eve she kissed him. Poddar interpreted this act as a sign of formal engagement (as it might have been in India, where he was a member of the Harijan, or "untouchable," caste). But Tanya told him that she was involved with other men and indicated that she did not wish to have an intimate relationship with him.

Poddar was depressed as a result of the rebuff, but he saw Tanya a few times during the spring (occasionally tape-recording their conversations in an effort to understand why she did not love him). Tanya left for Brazil in the summer, and Poddar, at the urging of a friend, went to the student health facility, where a psychiatrist referred him to a psychologist for psychotherapy. When Tanya returned in October 1969, Poddar discontinued therapy. Based in part on Poddar's stated intention to purchase a gun, the psychologist notified the campus police, both orally and in writing, that Poddar was dangerous and should be taken to a community mental health center for psychiatric commitment.

The campus police interviewed Poddar, who seemed rational and promised to stay away from Tanya. They released him and notified the health service. No further efforts at commitment were made because the supervising psychiatrist apparently decided that there was no need and, as a matter of confidentiality, requested that the letter to the police as well as certain therapy records be destroyed.

On October 27, Poddar went to Tanya's home armed with a pellet gun and a kitchen knife. She refused to speak to him. He shot her with the pellet gun. She ran from the house; he pursued, caught, and repeatedly and fatally stabbed her. Poddar was found guilty of voluntary manslaughter rather than first- or second-degree murder. The defense established with the aid of the expert testimony of three psychiatrists that Poddar's diminished mental capacity, schizophrenia, precluded the malice necessary for first- or second-degree murder. After his prison term, he returned to India, where, according to his own report, he is happily married (Schwitzgebel & Schwitzgebel, 1980, p. 205).

Under the privileged communication statute of California, the counseling center psychologist properly breached the confidentiality of the professional relationship and took steps to have Poddar civilly committed, for he judged Poddar to be an imminent danger. Poddar had stated that he intended to purchase a gun, and by his other words and actions he had convinced the therapist that he was desperate enough to harm Tarasoff. What the psychologist did not do, and what the court decided he should have done, was to warn the likely victim, Tanya Tarasoff, that her former friend had bought a gun and might use it against her. As stated by the California Supreme Court in *Tarasoff*: "Once a therapist does in fact determine, or under applicable professional standards reasonably should have determined, that a patient poses a serious danger of violence to others, he bears a duty to exercise reasonable care to protect the foreseeable victims of that danger." The *Tarasoff* ruling requires clinicians, in deciding when to violate confidentiality, to use the very imperfect skill of predicting dangerousness. Since the original ruling, it has been extended in several ways.

Extending Protection to Foreseeable Victims

A subsequent California court ruling[b] held by a bare majority that foreseeable victims include those in close relationship to the identifiable victim. In this instance, a mother was hurt by a shotgun fired by the dangerous person, and her 7-year-old son was present when the shooting took place. The boy later sued the psychologists for damages brought on by emotional trauma. Since a young child is likely to be in the company of his or her mother, the court concluded in *Hedlund* that the *Tarasoff* ruling extended to the boy.

Extending Protection Further to Potential Victims

A 1983 decision of a federal circuit court in California[c] ruled that Veterans Administration psychiatrists should earlier have warned the

---

[a]*Tarasoff v. Regents of the University of California*, 529 P.2d 553 (Cal. 1974), vacated, reheard in bank, and affirmed, 131 Cal. Rptr. 14, 551 P.2d 334 (1976). The 1976 California Supreme Court ruling was by a four-to-three majority.
[b]*Hedlund v. Superior Court*, 34 Cal.3d 695 (1983).
[c]*Jablonski by Pahls v. United States*, 712 F.2d 391 (1983).

Beginning in the 1970s, a number of court decisions were rendered to protect people from being involuntarily hospitalized unless absolutely necessary. For example, a 1979 Supreme Court decision, *Addington v. Texas*,[29] further provides that the state must produce clear and convincing evidence that a person is mentally ill and dangerous before he or she can be involuntarily committed to a psychiatric hospital. In 1980, the Ninth Circuit Court of Appeals ruled that this danger must be imminent.[30] Beyond hospitalization, many rights of people with a

---

[29]*Addington v. Texas*, 441 U.S. 418 (1979).
[30]*Susiki v. Yuen*, 617 F. 2d at 173.

murdered lover of an outpatient, Phillip Jablonski, that she was a foreseeable victim, even though the person had never made an explicit threat against her to the therapists. The reasoning was that Jablonski, having previously raped and otherwise harmed his wife, would likely direct his continuing "violence . . . against women very close to him" (p. 392).

The court also found the hospital psychiatrists negligent in not obtaining Jablonski's earlier medical records. These records showed a history of harmful violent behavior, which, together with the threats his lover was complaining about, should have moved the hospital to institute emergency civil commitment. The court ruled that the failure to warn was a proximate or immediate cause of the woman's murder. Proper consideration of the medical records, said the judge, would have convinced the psychiatrists that Jablonski was a real danger to others and should be committed.

This broadening of the duty to warn and protect has placed mental health professionals in California in an even more difficult predicament, for the potentially violent person need not even mention the specific person he or she may harm. It is up to the therapist to deduce who are possible victims, based on what he or she can learn of the person's past and present circumstances.

Extending Protection to Potential Victims as Yet Unknown

Many courts have augmented the duty to warn and protect to foreseeable victims of child abuse and even to possible victims as yet unknown. In one such case,[d] a medical student underwent his own psychoanalysis as one of the requirements to become a psychoanalyst. During the therapy, he admitted that he was a pedophile. Later in his training, he saw a male child as a patient as part of his psychiatric residency and sexually assaulted the boy. The court decided that the training analyst, who was not only the student's therapist but also an instructor in the school, had reason to know that his patient–student "posed a specific threat to a specific group of persons, namely future minor patients, with whom [the stu-

© AP/Wide World Photos

© AP/Wide World Photos

Prosenjit Poddar was convicted of manslaughter in the death of Tatiana Tarasoff. The court ruled that his therapist, who had become convinced Poddar might harm Tarasoff, should have warned her of the impending danger.

dent] would necessarily interact as part of his training" (p. 8). Even though the student did not have child patients at the time he revealed his pedophilia (and thus there were no specific people whom the instructor could warn and take steps to protect), the supervisor—as his instructor, not just his therapist—was judged to have sufficient control over the student's professional training and activities (specifically, the power to keep the student from pursuing his interests in working with children) for the *Tarasoff* ruling to be relevant.

Extending Protection Based on Families' Reports

In 2004, a California appeals court ruled that therapists have a duty to warn a possible victim if the threat is reported by a member of the patient's family.[e] In this case, a therapist learned about a threat not from his patient but from a family member of his patient. His patient revealed to his parents that he had thoughts of killing his ex-girlfriend's new boyfriend. The parents contacted the therapist about this threat. The therapist did not contact the new boyfriend, who was later killed by his patient. The parents of the boyfriend sued for wrongful death, saying the therapist should have warned their son. The court agreed and ruled that a close family member is in essence a part of the patient, and thus a therapist does have a duty to warn potential victims if notified by a close family member of a patient.

Extending Protection to Property

Tarasoff was further extended by a Vermont State Supreme Court ruling, *Peck v. Counseling Service of Addison County*,[f] which held that a mental health practitioner has a duty to warn a third party if there is a danger of damage to property. The case involved a 29-year-old male person who, after a heated argument with his father, told his therapist that he wanted to get back at his father and indicated that he might do so by burning down his father's barn. He proceeded to do just that. No people or animals were harmed in the fire; the barn housed no animals and was located 130 feet away from the parents' home. The court's conclusion that the therapist had a duty to warn was based on reasoning that arson is a violent act and therefore a lethal threat to people who may be in the vicinity of the fire.

[d]Almonte v. *New York Medical College*, 851 F. Supp. 34, 40 (D. Conn. 1994) (denying motion for summary judgment).

[e]Ewing v. Goldstein, Cal. App. 4th B163112.2d. (2004).

[f]Peck v. *Counseling Service of Addison County*, 499 A.2d 422 (Vt. 1985).

psychological disorder are still curtailed. An analysis of mental health–related bills introduced in state legislatures in 2002 (Corrigan, Watson, Heyrman et al., 2005) found that 75 percent of these bills took away liberties of people with a psychological disorder (e.g., allowing involuntary medication) and 33 percent took away privacy rights (e.g., sharing mental health records in the interest of public safety) (see also Focus on Discovery 1.1 in Chapter 1).

Being hospitalized against one's wishes is less likely today, in large part due to changes in health care that emphasize outpatient over inpatient care. In fact, today it is increasingly difficult to hospitalize a person who is in real need of at least a short hospital stay, and this is also problematic. People with a psychological disorder such as schizophrenia or bipolar disorder may need to spend time in a hospital when symptoms become severe. Yet, people in need of hospitalization are more likely to be sent to a nursing home or board and care facility, which may offer little or substandard care. Worse, people with psychological disorders in need of a hospital stay are now more likely to be sent to jails and prisons than to a hospital, a topic we return to later.

We turn now to a discussion of several issues and trends that revolve around the protections provided to those with psychological disorders: the principle of the least restrictive alternative; the right to treatment; the right to refuse treatment; and, finally, the way in which these several themes conflict in efforts to provide humane mental health treatment while respecting individual rights.

Least Restrictive Alternative As noted earlier, civil commitment in most states rests on presumed dangerousness, a condition that may vary depending on the circumstances. A person may be deemed dangerous if living in an apartment by himself or herself, but not dangerous if living in a residential treatment home and taking prescribed medications every day under medical supervision. The **least restrictive alternative** to freedom is to be provided when treating people with psychological disorders and protecting them from harming themselves and others. A number of court rulings require that only those people who cannot be adequately looked after in less restrictive settings be placed in hospitals.[31] In general terms, mental health professionals have to provide the treatment that restricts the person's liberty to the least possible degree while remaining workable.[32] It is unconstitutional to confine a person with a psychological disorder who is nondangerous and who is capable of living on his or her own or with the help of willing and responsible family or friends.[33] Of course, this principle has meaning only if society provides suitable residences and treatments, which unfortunately does not happen as much as it needs to.

Right to Treatment Another aspect of civil commitment that has come to the attention of the courts is the so-called right to treatment. If a person is deprived of liberty because he or she is mentally ill and is a danger to self or others, is the state not required to provide treatment to alleviate these problems?

The right to treatment was extended to all people committed under civil law in a landmark 1972 case, *Wyatt v. Stickney*.[34] In that case, an Alabama federal court ruled that treatment is the only justification for the civil commitment of people with a psychological disorder to a psychiatric hospital. This ruling, upheld on appeal, is frequently cited as ensuring the protection of people confined by civil commitment, at least to the extent that the state cannot simply "put them away" without meeting minimal standards of care. In fact, when people with intellectual disability (as opposed to those deemed to be mentally ill) are released from an institution, health officials are not relieved of their constitutional duty to provide reasonable care and safety as well as appropriate training.[35]

The *Wyatt* ruling was significant because previously the courts had asserted that it was beyond their competence to pass judgment on the care given to people with psychological disorders, and they had assumed that mental health professionals possessed special and exclusive knowledge about psychopathology and its treatment. Repeated reports of abuses, however, gradually prodded the judicial system to rule on what went on within the walls of psychiatric hospitals. The *Wyatt* decision set forth very specific requirements for psychiatric hospitals—for example, dayrooms of at least 40 square feet, curtains or screens for privacy in multiperson bedrooms, and no physical restraints except in emergency situations. The ruling also specified how many mental health professionals ought to be working in the hospital. When the *Wyatt* action was taken, Alabama state psychiatric hospitals averaged one physician per 2000 patients, an extreme situation. After *Wyatt*, there were to be at least two psychiatrists for every 250 patients.

[31]*Lake v. Cameron*, 267 F. Supp 155 (D.C. Cir. 1967); *Lessard*, 349 F. Supp. at 1078.
[32]*In Re: Tarpley*, 556 N.E.2d, superseded by 581 N.E.2d 1251 (1991).
[33]*Project Release v. Prevost*, 722 F.2d 960 (2d Cir. 1983).
[34]*Wyatt v. Stickney*, 325 F.Supp. 781 (M.D. Ala. 1971), enforced in 334 F.Supp. 1341 (M.D. Ala. 1971), 344 F.Supp. 373, 379 (M.D. Ala.1972), *aff'd sub nom Wyatt v. Anderholt*, 503 F.2d 1305 (5th Cir. 1974).
[35] *Thomas S. v. Flaherty*, 902 F.2d 250, cert. denied, 111 S.Ct. 373 (1990).

In a celebrated case, *O'Connor v. Donaldson*,[36] a civilly committed man sued two state hospital doctors for his release and for monetary damages on the grounds that he had been kept against his will for 14 years without being treated and without being dangerous to himself or to others. In January 1957, at the age of 49, Kenneth Donaldson was committed to the Chattahoochee state hospital in Florida on petition of his father, who felt that his son was delusional. At a brief court hearing, a county judge found that Donaldson had schizophrenia and committed him for "care, maintenance, and treatment."

In 1971, Donaldson sued Dr. O'Connor, the hospital superintendent, and Dr. Gumanis, a hospital psychiatrist, for release. Testimony at the trial in a U.S. District Court in Florida made it clear that at no time during his hospitalization had Donaldson's conduct posed any real danger to others or to himself. Furthermore, just before his commitment in 1957 he had been earning a living and taking adequate care of himself. Nonetheless, O'Connor had repeatedly refused Donaldson's requests for release, feeling it was his duty to determine whether he could adapt successfully outside the hospital. His judgment was that Donaldson could not. In deciding the question of dangerousness on the basis of how well the person could live outside the institution, O'Connor was applying a more restrictive standard than that required by most state laws.

The evidence indicated that Donaldson received only custodial care during his hospitalization. No treatment that could conceivably alleviate his assumed psychological disorder was undertaken. The therapy that O'Connor claimed Donaldson was undergoing consisted of being kept in a large room with 60 other people. Donaldson had been denied privileges to stroll around the hospital grounds or even to discuss his case with Dr. O'Connor. O'Connor also regarded as delusional Donaldson's expressed desire to write a book about his hospital experiences (which Donaldson did after his release; the book sold well).

The Supreme Court[37] ruled on June 26, 1975, that "a State cannot constitutionally confine . . . a nondangerous individual who is capable of surviving safely in freedom by himself or with the help of willing and responsible family members or friends." In 1977, Donaldson settled for $20,000 from Dr. Gumanis and from the estate of Dr. O'Connor, who had died during the appeals process.

Because of this decision, a civilly committed person's status must be periodically reviewed, for the grounds on which the person was committed cannot be assumed to continue to be in effect forever.

Right to Refuse Treatment Does a person committed under civil law have the right to refuse treatment or a particular kind of treatment? The answer is yes, but with qualifications.

The right of committed people to refuse medication is hotly debated. Psychiatrist E. Fuller Torrey (1996) asserts that because many people with a psychological disorder have no insight into their condition, they believe they do not need any treatment and thus subject themselves and their loved ones to sometimes desperate and frightening situations by refusing medication or other modes of therapy, most of which involve hospitalization. Torrey's arguments plead for consideration of the costs of untreated psychological disorders, which are substantial (Torrey, 2014).

On the other hand, there are many arguments against forcing a person to take medications. The side effects of most antipsychotic drugs are often aversive and are sometimes harmful and irreversible in the long run. Notably, as many as one-third of people who take medications do not benefit from them.

Although there is inconsistency across jurisdictions, there is a trend toward granting even involuntarily committed people certain rights to refuse medication, based on the constitutional protections of freedom from physi-

Kenneth Donaldson, displaying a copy of the Supreme Court opinion stating that nondangerous people with psychological disorders cannot be confined against their will under civil commitment.

[36] *O'Connor v. Donaldson*, 95 S.Ct. 2486 (1975).
[37] *O'Connor v. Donaldson*, 422, U.S. 563 (1975).

Civil commitment supposedly requires that the person be dangerous. But in actual practice, the decision to commit can be based on a judgment of severe disability, as in the case of some people who are homeless.

cal invasion, freedom of thought, and the right to privacy. In an extension of the least-restrictive-treatment principle, the Court ruled that the government cannot force antipsychotic drugs on a person only on the supposition that at some future time he or she might become dangerous.[38] The threat to the public safety has to be clear and imminent to justify the risks and restrictions that such medications pose, and it must be shown that less intrusive intervention will not likely reduce impending danger to others. In other words, forcible medication necessarily restricts liberty in addition to whatever physical risks it could bring; there has to be a very good reason to deprive a person of liberty and privacy via such intrusive measures. For example, a ruling in favor of forcible medication was made in a case of a person who had been threatening to assassinate the president of the United States. He posed a threat to his own safety, and he could be shown by clear and convincing evidence to be seriously mentally impaired.[39]

Deinstitutionalization, Civil Liberties, and Mental Health

Court rulings such as *Wyatt v. Stickney* and *O'Connor v. Donaldson* put mental health professionals on notice to be careful about keeping people in psychiatric hospitals against their will and to attend more to the specific treatment needs of people with psychological disorders. Pressure was placed on state governments to upgrade the quality of care in hospitals. But the picture is not all that rosy. For judges to declare that health care must meet certain minimal standards does not automatically translate into realization of that praiseworthy goal. Money is not in unlimited supply, and the care of people with psychological disorders has not been one of government's high priorities.

Beginning in the 1950s, many states embarked on a policy referred to as *deinstitutionalization*, discharging as many peoples as possible from hospitals and discouraging admissions. Indeed, civil commitment is more difficult to achieve now than it was in the 1950s and 1960s, despite the fact that some people with psychological disorders very much need short stays in a hospital.

The population of state mental hospitals peaked in the 1950s at more than half a million people. By 2000, these numbers had dropped to around 50,000. The number of hospitals continues to decline: as of 2010, there were approximately 14 psychiatric hospital beds for every 100,000 people in the United States; in 1955 there were 350 psychiatric hospital beds for every 100,000 people (Torrey, 2014). By some estimates, we need at least 50 hospital beds for every 100,000 people in the United States to meet the needs of people with psychological disorders—nearly four times more than what we currently have (Torrey, 2014). The maxim "Treat them in the community" has been in place for over 50 years, with the (incorrect) assumption being that virtually anything is preferable to institutionalization.

Unfortunately, there are woefully inadequate resources for such treatment in the community. Some effective programs were described in Chapter 9, but these are very much the exception, not the rule. The state of affairs in cities is an unrelenting crisis for the hundreds of thousands of people with psychological disorders who have been released from hospitals without adequate community services to help them. Many people discharged from hospitals are eligible for benefits from the Veterans Administration and for Social Security Disability Insurance, but a large number are not receiving this assistance. Rates of homelessness have soared among those with psychological disorders, and homeless persons do not have fixed addresses and need help in establishing eligibility and residency for the purpose of receiving benefits. The state of homelessness undoubtedly exacerbates the suffering of people with psychological disorders.

---

[38]*United States v. Charters*, 863, F.2d 302.
[39]*Dautremont v. Broadlawns Hospital*, 827 F.2d 291 (8th Cir. 1987).

Corbis Images

Deinstitutionalization may be a misnomer. *Trans*institutionalization may be more apt, for declines in the number of psychiatric hospital beds have occasioned increases in the presence of people with psychological disorders in nursing homes, the mental health departments of nonpsychiatric hospitals, and most sadly prisons (Kiesler, 1991; Torrey, 2014). These settings are by and large not equipped to handle the particular needs of people with psychological disorders.

Indeed, jails and prisons have become the new "hospitals" for people with psychological disorders in the twenty-first century. In the 1970s, about 5 percent of people in prisons had a serious psychological disorder; by 2007, between 17 and 30 percent of people in prisons had a serious psychological disorder (Steadman, Osher, Robbins et al., 2009; Torrey, 2014). A 2014 report by the Treatment Advocacy Center notes that 44 of the 50 states have more people with psychological disorders in prison than in the remaining psychiatric hospitals in those states (Torrey, Zdanowicz, Kennard et al., 2014). In a cruel twist, some states are investigating whether shuttered former mental hospitals can be reopened and repurposed to house prisoners who have a serious psychological disorder (Torrey, 2014). Other states are repurposing closed hospitals as tourist attractions for people interested in ghost hunting (Searles, 2013). Have we come that far from the days of the abysmal institutions that we discussed in Chapter 1? Clearly, we must do more.

> It is deplorable and outrageous that this state's prisons appear to have become a repository for a great number of its mentally ill citizens. Persons who, with psychiatric care, could fit well into society, are instead locked away, to become wards of the state's penal system. Then, in a tragically ironic twist, they may be confined in conditions that nurture, rather than abate, their psychoses. [Judge William Wayne Justice, Ruiz. v. Johnson, 37 F. Supp.2d 855 (S.D. Texas, 1999)].

Police officers are now called on to do the work of mental health professionals. They are often the first to come in contact with a person with a psychological disorder and can make decisions as to whether a person should be taken to a hospital or jail. In several cities, mental health professionals have teamed up with police officers to form mobile crisis units (Lamb, Weinberger, & DeCuir, 2002). These units consist of trained mental health professionals who work in conjunction with local police to find the best option for a person with a psychological disorder in the community. Because police officers are increasingly called on to work with people with psychological disorders, communities are recognizing the need for the police to receive proper training. New laws passed in the past 15 years—including America's Law Enforcement and Mental Health Project Act (2000) and the later extension of this law, called the Mentally Ill Offender Treatment and Crime Reduction Act (2004)—provide funding for such training. These laws also provide funds to set up so-called mental health courts in local communities. The idea is that people with psychological disorders who commit crimes may be better served by courts that can monitor treatment availability and adherence. So far, the evidence suggests that this is the case. A longitudinal study of people in San Francisco found that those people with a psychological disorder who went through a mental health court instead of traditional court went for a longer period of time after release without reoffending or committing a violent act (McNiel & Binder, 2007).

The approach of building partnerships between mental health professionals and law enforcement led to the creation of the Consensus Project (www.consensusproject.org). The Council of State Governments coordinated collaboration among criminal justice, mental health, and local and national lawmakers. A report entitled *Criminal Justice/Mental Health Consensus Project*, released in 2002, has been influential in increasing awareness of the large numbers of people with psychological disorders who are now housed in jails rather than in treatment facilities. The report outlines a number of policy ideas, all aimed at increasing cooperation between mental health and criminal justice and ultimately benefiting those with psychological disorders who are in the criminal justice system or who are at risk of becoming involved (e.g., sent to jail rather than treatment following a public outburst that reflects an exacerbation of illness). Over a decade later, however, few of these policy recommendations have been able to reduce the number of people with psychological disorders in prison even as they have helped to better the chances of receiving treatment while in prison.

Quick Summary

The legal standard for competency to stand trial requires that the accused understand the charges against him or her and be able to assist his or her attorney in the defense. Someone who is judged incompetent to stand trial receives treatment to restore competence and then returns to face the charges. The *Jackson* case specified that the pretrial period could be no longer than it takes to determine whether a person will ever become competent to stand trial. The use of medication to restore competency to stand trial can be used in limited circumstances.

The U.S. Supreme Court has ruled that it is unconstitutional (a violation of the Eighth Amendment, which prohibits cruel and unusual punishment) to execute people who are deemed legally insane or have intellectual disabilities. Individual states can determine what constitutes intellectual disability and insanity.

A person can be civilly committed to a hospital against his or her wishes if the person is mentally ill and a danger to self or others. Formal commitment requires a court order; informal commitment does not. People with psychological disorders who do not abuse substances are not necessarily more likely to engage in violence than are non-mentally ill people who do not abuse substances.

Early studies on the prediction of dangerousness had a number of flaws. Later research has shown that violence can be more accurately predicted if any of these conditions apply: repeated acts of violence, a single serious violent act, being on the brink of violence, or medication noncompliance.

Court cases have tried to balance a person's rights with the rights of society to be protected. The least restrictive alternative to freedom is to be provided when treating people with mental disorders and protecting them from harming themselves and others. A series of court cases have generally supported the notion that those people committed to a hospital have the right to receive treatment. People with psychological disorders have the right to refuse treatment as well, except when doing so poses a danger to self or others.

Beginning in the 1960s, large numbers of people were released from mental hospitals in what has been called deinstitutionalization. Unfortunately, not enough treatment options are available in the community. Jails and prisons are now the new "hospitals" for people with psychological disorders. Police officers are called on to do the work once reserved for mental health professionals. Partnerships among police, courts, and community mental health providers are promising for helping people with psychological disorders.

Check Your Knowledge 16.3

True or false?
1. People with schizophrenia who have negative symptoms are more likely to be violent than those without negative symptoms.
2. Past violence is a predictor of future violence.
3. Court decisions have determined that hospitalized peoples do not have a right to treatment unless they are dangerous.
4. People with psychological disorders can refuse treatment if they are found incompetent to stand trial after being charged with a nonviolent offense.

Ethical Dilemmas in Therapy and Research

The issues reviewed thus far place legal limits on the activities of mental health professionals. These legal constraints are important, for laws are one of society's strongest means of encouraging all of us to behave in certain ways. Mental health professionals also have ethical constraints. Ethics statements are designed to provide an ideal, to review moral issues of right and wrong that may or may not be reflected in the law. All professional groups promulgate "shoulds." These ethics guidelines describe what therapists and researchers should do with their patients, clients, and research participants. Courts have also ruled on some of these questions. Most of the time what we believe is unethical is also illegal, but sometimes existing laws are in conflict with our moral sense of right and wrong. The American Psychological Association publishes a *Code of Ethics* that includes the ethical standards that constrain research and practice in psychology (APA, 2002; http://www.apa.org/ethics). We now examine the ethics of making psychological inquiries into and interventions in the lives of other human beings.

Ethical Restraints on Research

The training of scientists equips them to pose interesting questions, sometimes even important ones, and to design research that is as free of confounds as possible. Scientists have no special qualifications, however, for deciding whether a particular line of research with people should be followed. Society needs knowledge, and a scientist has a right in a democracy to seek that knowledge. However, the ordinary citizens who participate in experiments must be protected from unnecessary harm, risk, humiliation, and invasion of privacy.

Perhaps the most reprehensible ethical insensitivity was evidenced in the brutal experiments conducted by German physicians on concentration camp prisoners during World War II. One experiment, for example, investigated how long people lived when their heads were bashed repeatedly with a heavy stick. Clearly, such actions violate our sense of decency and morality. The Nuremberg Trials, conducted by the Allies following the war, brought these and other barbarisms to light and meted out severe punishment

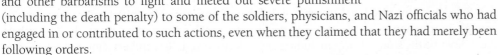
Defendants at the Nuremberg Trials.

(including the death penalty) to some of the soldiers, physicians, and Nazi officials who had engaged in or contributed to such actions, even when they claimed that they had merely been following orders.

It would be reassuring to be able to say that such gross violations of human decency take place only during incredible and cruel epochs such as the Third Reich, but unfortunately this is not the case. Spurred on by a blind enthusiasm for their work, researchers in the United States and other countries have sometimes dealt with human participants in reproachable ways.

For example, one experiment conducted after World War II compared penicillin with a placebo as a treatment to prevent rheumatic fever. Even though penicillin had already been acknowledged as the drug of choice for people with a streptococcal respiratory infection in order to protect them from later contracting rheumatic fever, placebos were administered to 109 service personnel without their knowledge or permission. More participants received penicillin than received the placebo, but three members of the control group contracted serious illnesses—two had rheumatic fever and one had acute nephritis, a kidney disease. None of those who had received penicillin contracted such illnesses (Beecher, 1966).

Half a century later, in January 1994, spurred on by Eileen Welsome, a journalist who won a Pulitzer Prize for her investigative reporting on the issue, the United States Energy Department began to publicize numerous experiments conducted in the 1950s through the 1970s that had exposed hundreds of people—usually without their informed consent or prior knowledge—to harmful doses of radiation. Particular concern was expressed because the overwhelming majority were people of low socioeconomic status, members of ethnic minorities, people with intellectual disabilities, nursing home patients, or prisoners. The scientists, for the most part supported in their research with federal funds, understood that the risks were great, even though relatively little was known about the harmful effects of radiation at the time. Some of these experiments involved giving women in the third trimester of pregnancy a radioactive tonic to determine safe levels of exposure and irradiating the testicles of prisoners to find out the degree of radiation that service personnel could endure without negative effects on sperm production.

Responding to the many instances of harm inflicted on research participants, several international codes of ethics for the conduct of scientific research have been developed—the Nuremberg Code formulated in 1947 in the aftermath of the Nazi war-crime trials, the 1964 Declaration of Helsinki, and statements from the British Medical Research Council. In 1974, the U.S. Department of Health, Education, and Welfare began to issue guidelines and regulations governing scientific research that employs human and animal participants. In addition, a blue-ribbon panel, the National Commission for the Protection of Human Subjects of Biomedical and Behavioral Research, issued a report in 1978 that arose from hearings and inquiries into restrictions that the U.S. government might impose on research performed with prisoners, children, and peoples in psychiatric hospitals. These various codes and principles are continually being reevaluated and revised as new challenges are posed to the research community.

For more than four decades, the proposals of behavioral researchers, many of whom conduct experiments related to psychopathology, have been reviewed for safety and general ethical propriety by institutional review boards in hospitals, universities, and research institutes. Such committees—and this is significant—comprise not only behavioral scientists but also citizens from the community. They are able to block any research proposal, and they can require questionable aspects to be modified if in their collective judgment the research would put participants at too great a risk. Such committees now also pass judgment on the scientific merits of proposals, the rationale being that it is not ethical to recruit participants for studies that will not yield valid data (Capron, 1999). Beginning in 2000, universities and other research institutions have been required to certify researchers on the basis of special coursework and examinations concerning research ethics. Researchers who receive funds from federal agencies, such as the National Institute of Mental Health, are also required to receive specialized training in research ethics.

Informed Consent

A core component of ethical research is **informed consent.** The investigator must provide enough information to enable people to decide whether they want to be in a study. Researchers must describe the study clearly, including any risks involved. Researchers should disclose even minor risks that could occur from a study, including emotional distress from answering personal questions or side effects from drugs. There must be no coercion in obtaining informed consent. Participants must understand that they have every right not to take part in the study or to withdraw from the study at any point, without any fear of penalty. For example, a psychologist might want to determine whether imagery helps students to associate one word with another. One group of students might be asked to associate pairs of words in their minds by generating a wacky image connecting the two, such as a cat riding on a bicycle. Current procedure allows prospective participants to decide that the experiment is likely to be boring and to decline to participate.

A central issue is that potential participants must be able to understand the study and associated risks. What if the prospective participant is a child with intellectual disability, unable to understand fully what is being asked? In clinical and research settings, researchers must ascertain that people are not having trouble understanding the study. A report from the National Bioethics Advisory Commission pointed to many published experiments involving people with psychological disorders in which no effort had been made to determine whether the research participants had the decision-making capacity to give informed consent (Capron, 1999). Instead of simply allowing a guardian or family member to make the decision for a person, the commission proposed that a health professional who has nothing to do with the particular study make a judgment on whether a given person can give informed consent. The commission also recommended that if a guardian is allowed to give consent on behalf of a person who is unable to give consent for him- or herself, the guardian's own ability to give consent should also be evaluated (Capron, 1999).

Still, as with the right to refuse treatment, there is recognition that people with a psychological disorder are not necessarily incapable of giving informed consent (Appelbaum & Gutheil, 1991). For example, although people with schizophrenia may do more poorly than people without schizophrenia on tests designed to assess decision-making skills, people with schizophrenia can give informed consent if a more detailed procedure describing a study is included—for example, one that describes what they will be asked to do and what they will see and explains that their participation is voluntary and that it in no way will impact their treatment (Carpenter, Gold, Lahti et al., 2000; Wirshing, Wirshing, Marder et al., 1998).

Joselito Briones/Getty Images, Inc.

Informed consent must be obtained for research.

The issue of informed consent is also of concern to researchers and clinicians who work with people with Alzheimer's disease. As with schizophrenia, having an Alzheimer's diagnosis does not necessarily mean a person cannot provide informed consent (Marson, Huthwaite, & Hebert, 2004). Measures have been developed to assess capacity for consent in this population; as the number of people over age 65 continues to increase, this will continue to be an area of active research (Marson, 2001).

These results point to the importance of examining each person individually for ability to give informed consent, rather than assuming that a person hospitalized for schizophrenia or Alzheimer's disease is unable to do so.

What people tell their therapist is confidential, although in certain situations confidentiality may be broken.

Confidentiality and Privileged Communication

When people consult a psychiatrist or clinical psychologist, they are assured by professional ethics codes that what goes on in the session will remain confidential. **Confidentiality** means that nothing will be revealed to a third party except for other professionals and those intimately involved in the treatment, such as a nurse or medical secretary.

A **privileged communication** goes even further. It is communication between parties in a confidential relationship that is protected by law. The recipient of such a communication cannot legally be compelled to disclose it as a witness. The right of privileged communication is a major exception to the courts' access to evidence in judicial proceedings. Society believes that in the long term the interests of people are best served if communications to a spouse and to certain professionals remain off-limits to the prying eyes and ears of the police, judges, and prosecutors. The privilege applies to such relationships as those between husband and wife, physician and patient, pastor and penitent, attorney and client, and psychologist and patient. The legal expression is that the patient or client "holds the privilege," which means that only he or she may release the other person to disclose confidential information in a legal proceeding.

There are important limits to a person's right of privileged communication, however. For example, this right is eliminated for any of the following reasons in some states:

- A person has accused the therapist of malpractice. In such a case, the therapist can divulge information about the therapy in order to defend himself or herself in any legal action initiated by the person.
- The person is less than 16 years old, and the therapist has reason to believe that the child has been a victim of a crime such as child abuse. In fact, the psychologist is required to report to the police or to a child welfare agency within 36 hours any suspicion he or she has that the child has been physically or sexually abused.
- The person initiated therapy in hopes of evading the law for having committed a crime or for planning to do so.
- The therapist judges that the person is a danger to self or others and disclosure of information is necessary to ward off such danger (recall Focus on Discovery 16.3 on *Tarasoff*).

Quick Summary

Ethical restraints on research are necessary to avoid the abuses that have occurred in the past. Since the Nuremberg Codes of 1947, a number of ethical codes regarding psychological research have been developed. Research must be approved for safety and ethics by an institutional review board. Universities and other research institutions, as well as federal grant-funding agencies, require that researchers receive specialized training and certification in research

ethics, on the basis of special coursework and examinations, to make it less likely that research participants will be put at risk.

Special precautions must be taken to ensure that research participants with psychological disorders fully understand the risks and benefits of any research they are asked to participate in. In addition, particular care must be taken to make certain that they can decline or withdraw from research without feeling coerced.

Informed consent procedures must include enough information about the research so that participants know about the risks and feel free to withdraw without penalty.

In therapy sessions, people have the right to have what is discussed kept confidential (can't be disclosed to a third party), and this discussion is considered a privileged communication (information in confidential relationship protected by law). However, confidentiality and the privileged communication can be broken if a person is a danger to self or others, is suing a therapist for malpractice, is a child under 16 who has been the victim of a crime or abuse, or is trying to evade the law for a crime committed or planned.

Summary

• Some civil liberties are rather routinely set aside when mental health professionals and the courts judge that a psychological disorder has played a decisive role in determining an individual's behavior. This may occur through criminal or civil commitment.

• There is an important difference between a psychological disorder and insanity. Insanity is a legal concept. A person can be diagnosed as mentally ill and yet be deemed sane enough both to stand trial and to be found guilty of a crime.

• Criminal commitment sends a person to a hospital either before a trial for an alleged crime, because the person is deemed incompetent to stand trial, or after an acquittal by reason of insanity.

• A person who is considered mentally ill and dangerous to self and to others, although he or she has not broken a law, can be civilly committed to a hospital or be allowed to live outside of a hospital, but only under supervision and with restrictions placed on his or her activities.

• Several landmark cases and principles in law address the conditions under which a person who has committed a crime might be excused from legal responsibility for it—that is, not guilty by reason of insanity.

These involve the presence of an irresistible impulse and the notion that some people may not be able to distinguish between right and wrong (the M'Naghten rule). The Insanity Defense Reform Act of 1984 made it harder for accused criminals to argue insanity as a defense.

• Two insanity pleas used today are not guilty by reason of insanity and guilty but mentally ill. They differ in terms of whether a person is responsible for his or her criminal actions, where the person receives treatment, and how long the person remains committed.

• Court rulings have provided greater protection to all people with psychological disorders, particularly those under civil commitment. They have the right to the least restrictive treatment setting; the right to be treated; and, in most circumstances, the right to refuse treatment, particularly any procedure that entails considerable risk.

• Ethical issues concerning research include restraints on what kinds of research are allowable and the duty of scientists to obtain informed consent from prospective human participants.

• In the area of therapy, ethical issues concern the right of people to confidentiality.

Answers to Check Your Knowledge Questions

16.1 1. c; 2. a; 3. d; 4. b
16.2 1. F; 2. T; 3. T

16.3 1. F; 2. T; 3. F; 4. T

Key Terms

American Law Institute guidelines
assisted outpatient treatment
civil commitment
competency to stand trial
confidentiality

criminal commitment
guilty but mentally ill (GBMI)
in absentia
informed consent
insanity defense

irresistible impulse
least restrictive alternative
M'Naghten rule
not guilty by reason of insanity (NGRI)
privileged communication

Glossary

ABAB design. An experimental design in which behavior is measured during a baseline period (A), during a period when a treatment is introduced (B), during the reinstatement of the conditions that prevailed in the baseline period (A), and finally during a reintroduction of the treatment (B); commonly used in operant research to isolate cause–effect relationships.

acute stress disorder. A short-lived anxiety reaction to a traumatic event; if it lasts more than a month, it is diagnosed as posttraumatic stress disorder.

addiction. Use of a drug that is accompanied by a physiological dependence on it, made evident by tolerance and withdrawal symptoms.

adoptees method. Research method that studies children who were adopted and reared completely apart from their parents, thereby eliminating the influence of being raised by disordered parents.

advanced directive. Legal document in which an individual—before becoming incapable of making such decisions—prescribes and proscribes certain courses of action to be taken to preserve his or her health or terminate life support.

age effects. The consequences of being a given chronological age. Compare *cohort effects.*

agonist. A drug that stimulates receptors normally specific to a particular neurotransmitter.

agoraphobia. Literally, fear of the marketplace. Anxiety disorder in which the person fears situations in which it would be embarrassing or difficult to escape if panic symptoms occurred; most commonly diagnosed in some individuals with panic disorder.

allele. Any of the various forms of a particular gene.

alogia. A negative symptom in schizophrenia, marked by poverty of speech.

alternate-form reliability. See *reliability.*

Alzheimer's disease. A dementia involving a progressive atrophy of cortical tissue and marked by memory impairment, intellectual deterioration, and loss of motivation. See also *plaques* and *neurofibrillary tangles.*

American Law Institute guidelines. Rules proposing that insanity is a legitimate defense plea if, during criminal conduct, an individual could not judge right from wrong or control his or her behavior as required by law. Repetitive criminal acts are disavowed as a sole criterion. Compare *M'Naghten rule* and *irresistible impulse.*

amphetamines. A group of stimulating drugs that produce heightened levels of energy and, in large doses, nervousness, sleeplessness, and paranoid delusions.

amygdala. A subcortical structure of the temporal lobe involved in attention to emotionally salient stimuli and memory of emotionally relevant events.

anal stage. In psychoanalytic theory, the second psychosexual stage, which occurs during the second year of life when the anus is considered the principal erogenous zone.

analogue experiment. An experimental study of a phenomenon different from but related to the actual interests of the investigator; for example, animal research used to study human disorders or research on mild symptoms used as a bridge to clinical disorders.

anhedonia. A negative symptom in schizophrenia or a symptom in depression in which the individual experiences a loss of interest and pleasure. See also *anticipatory pleasure* and *consummatory pleasure.*

anorexia nervosa. A disorder in which a person refuses to maintain normal weight, has an intense fear of becoming obese, and feels fat even when emaciated.

Antabuse. A drug that makes the drinking of alcohol produce nausea and other unpleasant effects; trade name for disulfiram.

antagonist. A drug that dampens the effect of a neurotransmitter on its receptors; for example, many dopamine antagonists block dopamine receptors.

anterior cingulate. In the subcortical region of the brain, the anterior portion of the cingulate gyrus, stretching about the corpus callosum.

anterior insula. A region of the cerebral cortex involved in processing bodily sensations. Believed to be hyperactive to somatic sensations among people with somatic symptom disorders.

anticipatory pleasure. Expected or anticipated pleasure for events, people, or activities in the future. See also *consummatory pleasure.*

antidepressant. Any drug that alleviates depression; also widely used to treat anxiety disorders.

antipsychotic drugs. Psychoactive drugs, such as Thorazine, that reduce psychotic symptoms but have long-term side effects resembling symptoms of neurological diseases.

antisocial personality disorder. Personality disorder defined by the absence of concern for others' feelings or social norms and a pervasive pattern of rule breaking.

anxiety. An unpleasant feeling of fear and apprehension accompanied by increased physiological arousal. Anxiety can be assessed by self-report, by measuring physiological arousal, and by observing overt behavior.

anxiety disorders. Disorders in which fear or anxiety is overriding and the primary disturbance; include phobic disorders, social anxiety disorder, panic disorder, generalized anxiety disorder, and agoraphobia.

Anxiety Sensitivity Index (ASI). A test that measures the extent to which people respond fearfully to their bodily sensations; predicts the degree to which unexplained physiological arousal leads to panic attacks.

anxiolytics. Minor tranquilizers or benzodiazepines used to treat anxiety disorders.

asociality. A negative symptom of schizophrenia marked by an inability to form close relationships and to feel intimacy.

Asperger's disorder. A former DSM-IV-TR disorder believed to be a mild form of autism in which social relationships are poor and stereotyped behavior is intense and rigid, but language and intelligence are intact. Combined with autism in autism spectrum disorder category in DSM-5.

assisted outpatient commitment. A form of civil commitment consistent with the principle of least restrictive alternative, whereby the person is not hospitalized but rather is allowed to remain free in the community under legal/medical constraints that ensure, for example, that prescribed medication is taken and other measures are observed.

association study. A type of molecular genetics study where researchers examine the relationship between a specific allele of a gene and a trait or behavior in the population

asthma. A disorder characterized by narrowing of the airways and increased secretion of mucus, often causing extremely labored and wheezy breathing.

asylums. Refuges established in western Europe in the fifteenth century to confine and provide for the mentally ill; forerunners of the mental hospital.

attachment theory. The type or style of an infant's attachment to his or her caregivers can set the stage for psychological health or problems later in development

attention-deficit/hyperactivity disorder (ADHD). A disorder in children marked by difficulties in focusing adaptively on the task at hand, inappropriate fidgeting and antisocial behavior, and excessive non-goal-directed behavior.

attribution. The explanation a person has for why an event or behavior has occurred.

autism spectrum disorder. A disorder beginning in childhood that involves deficits in social communication and social interactions, restricted and repetitive behaviors, and in some cases severe deficits in speech. DSM-5 combined Asperger's disorder, pervasive developmental disorder not otherwise specified, and childhood disintegrative disorder into the category autism spectrum disorder.

autonomic nervous system (ANS). The division of the nervous system that regulates involuntary functions; innervates endocrine glands, smooth muscle, and heart muscle; and initiates the physiological changes that are part of the expression of emotion. See also *sympathetic* and *parasympathetic nervous systems;* compare *somatic nervous system.*

avoidant personality disorder. Personality disorder defined by aloofness and extreme sensitivity to potential rejection, despite an intense desire for affiliation and affection.

avolition. A negative symptom in schizophrenia in which the individual lacks interest and drive.

behavior genetics. The study of individual differences in behavior that are attributable to differences in genetic makeup.

behavior therapy. A branch of psychotherapy conceived narrowly as the application of classical and operant conditioning to the alteration of clinical problems but more broadly as applied experimental psychology in a clinical context.

behavioral activation (BA) therapy. Clinical approach to depression that seeks to increase participation in positively reinforcing activities.

behavioral assessment. A sampling of ongoing cognitions, feelings, and overt behavior in their situational context. Compare *projective test* and *personality inventory*.

behavioral couples therapy. Clinical approach to depression in which a couple works to improve communication and satisfaction; more likely to relieve relationship distress than individual cognitive therapy.

behavioral inhibition. The tendency to exhibit anxiety or to freeze when facing threat. In infants, it manifests as a tendency to become agitated and cry when faced with novel stimuli and may be a heritable predisposition for the development of anxiety disorders.

behavioral medicine. An interdisciplinary field concerned with integrating knowledge from medicine and behavioral science to understand health and illness and to prevent as well as treat psychophysiological disorders and other illnesses in which a person's psyche plays a role. See also *health psychology*.

behaviorism. The school of psychology originally associated with John B. Watson, who proposed that observable behavior, not consciousness, is the proper subject matter of psychology. Contemporary behaviorists do use mediational concepts, provided they are firmly anchored to observables.

benzodiazepines. Any of several drugs commonly used to treat anxiety, such as Valium and Xanax.

binge eating disorder. Included as a disorder in DSM-5; includes recurrent episodes of unrestrained eating.

bipolar I disorder. A diagnosis defined on the basis of at least one lifetime episode of mania. Most people with this disorder also experience episodes of major depression.

bipolar II disorder. A form of bipolar disorder, diagnosed in those who have experienced at least one major depressive episode and at least one episode of hypomania.

blunted affect. A negative symptom of schizophrenia that involves a lack of outward expression of emotion.

body dysmorphic disorder. A disorder marked by preoccupation with an imagined or exaggerated defect in appearance—for example, facial wrinkles or excess facial or body hair.

body mass index (BMI). Measure of body fat calculated by dividing weight in kilograms by height in meters squared; considered a more valid estimate of body fat than many others.

BOLD (blood oxygenation level dependent). The signal detected by functional MRI studies of the brain; measures blood flow and thus neural activity in particular regions.

borderline personality disorder. Personality disorder defined by impulsiveness and unpredictability, an uncertain self-image, intense and unstable social relationships, and extreme swings of mood.

brain stem. The part of the brain connecting the spinal cord with the cerebrum; contains the pons and medulla oblongata and functions as a neural relay station.

brief psychotic disorder. A disorder in which a person has a sudden onset of psychotic symptoms— incoherence, loose associations, delusions,

hallucinations—immediately after a severely disturbing event; the symptoms last more than 1 day but no more than 1 month. Compare *schizophreniform disorder*.

brief therapy. Time-limited psychotherapy, usually ego-analytic in orientation and lasting no more than 25 sessions.

bulimia nervosa. A disorder characterized by episodic, uncontrollable eating binges followed by purging either by vomiting or by taking laxatives.

caffeine. Perhaps the world's most popular drug; a generalized stimulant of body systems, including the sympathetic nervous system. Though seldom viewed as a drug, caffeine is addictive, produces tolerance, and subjects habitual users to withdrawal.

cardiovascular disease. Medical problems involving the heart and the blood circulation system, such as hypertension or coronary heart disease.

case study. The collection of historical or biographical information on a single individual, often including experiences in therapy.

catatonia. Constellation of schizophrenia symptoms including repetitive, peculiar, complex gestures and, in some cases, an almost manic increase in overall activity level. It can also manifest itself as immobility, with a fixity of posture maintained for long periods, with accompanying muscular rigidity, trancelike state of consciousness, and waxy flexibility.

categorical classification. An approach to assessment in which a person is or is not a member of a discrete grouping. Compare *dimensional classification*.

cathartic method. A therapeutic procedure to relieve emotional suffering introduced by Breuer and developed further by Freud in the late nineteenth century, whereby a patient recalls and relives an earlier emotional catastrophe and reexperiences the tension and unhappiness.

caudate nucleus. A nucleus within the basal ganglia involved in learning and memory that is implicated in body dysmorphic disorder and obsessive-compulsive disorder.

central nervous system. The part of the nervous system that in vertebrates consists of the brain and spinal cord, to which all sensory impulses are transmitted and from which motor impulses pass out; supervises and coordinates the activities of the entire nervous system.

cerebellum. An area of the hindbrain concerned with balance, posture, and motor coordination.

cerebral cortex. The thin outer covering of each of the cerebral hemispheres; highly convoluted and composed of nerve cell bodies that constitute the gray matter of the brain.

cerebrum. The two-lobed structure extending from the brain stem and constituting the anterior (frontal) part of the brain; the largest and most recently developed portion of the brain, responsible for coordinating sensory and motor activities and performing higher cognitive processes.

childhood onset fluency disorder (stuttering). Communication disorder of childhood marked by frequent and pronounced verbal dysfluencies, such as repetitions of certain sounds.

chromosomes. The threadlike bodies within the nucleus of the cell, composed primarily of DNA and bearing the genetic information of the organism.

civil commitment. A procedure whereby a person can be legally certified as mentally ill and hospitalized, even against his or her will. Compare *criminal commitment* and *assisted outpatient commitment*.

classical conditioning. A basic form of learning, sometimes referred to as Pavlovian conditioning, in which a neutral stimulus is repeatedly paired with another stimulus (called the unconditioned stimulus, UCS) that naturally elicits a certain desired response (called the unconditioned response, UCR). After repeated trials, the neutral stimulus becomes a conditioned stimulus (CS) and evokes the same or a similar response, now called the conditioned response (CR). Compare *operant conditioning*.

clinical high-risk study. A study that identifies people who show subtle or early clinical signs of a disorder, such as schizophrenia, and then follows them over time to determine who might be at risk for developing the disorder.

clinical interview. General term for conversation between a clinician and a patient that is aimed at determining diagnosis, history, causes of problems, and possible treatment options.

clinical psychologist. An individual who has earned a Ph.D. degree in psychology or a Psy. D. and whose training has included an internship in a mental hospital or clinic.

clinical significance. The degree to which effect size is large enough to be meaningful in predicting or treating a clinical disorder. Compare *statistical significance*.

cocaine. A pain-reducing, stimulating, and addictive alkaloid obtained from coca leaves that increases mental powers, produces euphoria, heightens sexual desire, and in large doses causes paranoia and hallucinations.

cognition. The process of knowing; the thinking, judging, reasoning, and planning activities of the human mind. Behavior is now often explained as depending on these processes.

cognitive behavior therapy (CBT). Behavior therapy that incorporates theory and research on cognitive processes such as thoughts, perceptions, judgments, self-statements, and tacit assumptions; a blend of both the cognitive and behavioral paradigms.

cognitive behavioral paradigm. General view that people can best be understood by studying how they perceive and structure their experiences and how this influences behavior.

cognitive biases. Tendencies to perceive events in a negative manner, for example, by attending to or remembering negative information more than positive information; hypothesized to be driven by underlying negative schemas.

cognitive enhancement therapy (CET). Also known as cognitive training, treatment that seeks to improve basic cognitive functions such as verbal learning ability in people with schizophrenia, meanwhile reducing symptoms as well.

cognitive restructuring. Any behavior therapy procedure that attempts to alter the manner in which a client thinks about life so that he or she changes overt behavior and emotions.

cognitive therapy. See *cognitive restructuring*. See also *cognitive behavior therapy*.

cohort effects. The consequences of having been born in a given year and having grown up during a particular time period with its own unique pressures, problems, challenges, and opportunities. Compare *age effects*.

collective unconscious. Jung's concept that every human being carries within the wisdom, ideas, and strivings of those who have come before.

communication disorders. Learning disorders in a child who fails to develop to the degree expected by his or her intellectual level in a specific language skill area; include speech sounds disorder and child onset fluency disorder.

comorbidity. The co-occurrence of two disorders, as when a person has depression and social phobia.

competency to stand trial. A legal decision as to whether a person can participate meaningfully in his or her own defense.

compulsion. The irresistible impulse to repeat an irrational act or thought over and over again. Compare *obsession*.

concordance. As applied in behavior genetics, the similarity in psychiatric diagnosis or in other traits within a pair of twins.

concurrent validity. See *validity*.

conditioned response (CR). See *classical conditioning*.

conditioned stimulus (CS). See *classical conditioning*.

conduct disorder. Pattern of extreme disobedience in youngsters, including theft, vandalism, lying, and early drug use.

confidentiality. A principle observed by lawyers, doctors, pastors, psychologists, and psychiatrists which dictates that the contents of a professional and private relationship not be divulged to anyone else. See also *privileged communication*.

construct validity. The extent to which scores or ratings on an assessment instrument relate to other variables or behaviors according to some theory or hypothesis.

consummatory pleasure. Pleasure experienced in-the-moment or in the presence of a pleasurable stimulus. See also *anticipatory pleasure*.

content validity. See *validity*.

control group. Those for whom the active condition of the independent variable is not administered, thus forming a baseline against which the effects of the active condition of the independent variable can be evaluated.

controlled drinking. A pattern of alcohol consumption that is moderate, avoiding the extremes of total abstinence and of inebriation.

conversion disorder. A disorder in which sensory or motor function is impaired, even though there is no detectable neurological explanation for the deficits.

copy number variation (CNV). Refers to variation in gene structure involving copy number changes in a defined chromosomal region; could be in the form of a deletion where a copy is deleted or an addition (duplication) where an extra copy is added.

corpus callosum. The large band of nerve fibers connecting the two cerebral hemispheres.

correlation. The tendency for two variables, such as height and weight, to covary.

correlation coefficient. A statistic ranging in value from −1.00 to +1.00 that measures the degree to which two variables are related. The sign indicates whether the relationship is positive or negative, and the magnitude indicates the strength of the relationship.

correlational method. The research strategy used to establish whether two or more variables are related without manipulating the independent variable. Relationships may be positive—as values for one variable increase, those for the other do also—or negative—as values for one variable increase, those for the other decrease. Compare *experiment*.

cortisol. A "stress hormone" secreted by the adrenal cortices; helps the body prepare to face threats.

counseling psychologist. A doctoral-level mental health professional whose training is similar to that of a clinical psychologist, though usually with less emphasis on research and serious psychopathology.

crack. A rock-crystal form of cocaine that is heated, melted, and smoked; more often used in poorer urban areas than conventional cocaine.

criminal commitment. A procedure whereby a person is confined in a mental hospital either for determination of competency to stand trial or after acquittal by reason of insanity. Compare *civil commitment*.

criterion validity. See *validity*.

cross-dependent. Acting on the same neurotransmitter receptors, as methadone does with heroin.

cross-fostering. Research method that studies offspring who were adopted and reared completely apart from their biological parents, where the adoptive parent has a particular disorder but the biological parent does not, thereby introducing the influence of being raised by disordered parents.

cross-sectional design. Studies in which different age groups are compared at the same time. Compare *longitudinal design*.

CT or CAT scan. Refers to computerized axial tomography, a method of diagnosis in which X-rays are taken from different angles and then analyzed by computer to produce a representation of the part of the body in cross section.

cultural competence. The capacity of a therapist to understand the patient's cultural framework and its implications for therapeutic work.

Cushing's syndrome. An endocrine disorder usually affecting young women, produced by oversecretion of cortisone and marked by mood swings, irritability, agitation, and physical disfigurement.

cyclothymic disorder. A form of bipolar disorder characterized by swings between elation and depression over at least a 2-year period, but with moods not so severe as manic or major depressive episodes.

cytokines. Immune system molecules, released by activated macrophages, which help initiate such bodily responses to infection as fatigue, fever, and activation of the HPA axis.

D-cycloserine (DCS). A medication that enhances learning which has been found to enhance the effects of exposure therapy for several of the anxiety disorders.

deep brain stimulation. A neurosurgical treatment in which electrodes are implanted into specific brain regions.

defense mechanisms. In psychoanalytic theory, reality-distorting strategies unconsciously adopted to protect the ego from anxiety.

delayed ejaculation. A disorder in men involving delay in reaching orgasm or inability to reach orgasm.

delirium. A state of great mental confusion in which consciousness is clouded, attention cannot be sustained, and the stream of thought and speech is incoherent. The person is probably disoriented, emotionally erratic, restless or lethargic, and often has illusions, delusions, and hallucinations.

delirium tremens (DTs). One of the withdrawal symptoms that sometimes occurs when a period of heavy alcohol consumption is terminated; marked by fever, sweating, trembling, cognitive impairment, and hallucinations.

delusional disorder. A disorder in which the individual has persistent delusions and is very often contentious but has no disorganized thinking or hallucinations.

delusions. Beliefs contrary to reality, firmly held in spite of evidence to the contrary and common in paranoid disorders: of control, belief that one is being manipulated by some external force such as radar, television, or a creature from outer space; of grandeur, belief that one is an especially important or powerful person; of persecution, belief that one is being plotted against or oppressed by others.

dementia. Deterioration of mental faculties—memory, judgment, abstract thought, control of impulses, intellectual ability—that impairs social and occupational functioning and eventually changes the personality. See *Alzheimer's disease*.

dementia praecox. An older term for schizophrenia, believed then to be an incurable and progressive deterioration of mental functioning beginning in adolescence.

dementia with Lewy bodies (DLB). Form of dementia that often co-occurs with Parkinson's disease; characterized by shuffling gait, memory loss, and hallucinations and delusions.

demonology. The doctrine that a person's abnormal behavior is caused by an autonomous evil spirit.

dependent personality disorder. A personality disorder in which people are overly concerned about maintaining relationships. People with this disorder often allow others to make decisions for them and are reluctant to make demands that could challenge relationships.

dependent variable. In a psychological experiment, the behavior that is measured and is expected to change with manipulation of the independent variable.

depersonalization. An alteration in perception of the self in which the individual loses a sense of reality and feels estranged from the self and perhaps separated from the body; may be a temporary reaction to stress and fatigue or part of panic disorder, depersonalization disorder, or schizophrenia.

depersonalization/derealization disorder. A dissociative disorder in which the individual feels unreal and estranged from the self and surroundings enough to disrupt functioning. People with this disorder may feel that their extremities have changed in size or that they are watching themselves from a distance.

derealization. Loss of the sense that the surroundings are real; present in several psychological disorders, such as panic disorder, depersonalization disorder, and schizophrenia.

desire phase. The first stage of the sexual response cycle, characterized by sexual interest or desire, often associated with sexually arousing fantasies.

detoxification. The initial stage in weaning an addicted person from a drug; involves medical supervision of the sometimes painful withdrawal.

developmental psychopathology. The field that studies disorders of childhood within the context of normal life-span development.

diagnosis. The determination that the set of symptoms or problems of a patient indicates a particular disorder.

Diagnostic and Statistical Manual of Mental Disorders. See *DSM-5*.

dialectical behavior therapy. A therapeutic approach to borderline personality disorder that combines client-centered empathy and acceptance with behavioral problem solving, social skills training, and limit setting.

diathesis. Predisposition toward a disease or abnormality.

diathesis–stress. As applied in psychopathology, a view that assumes that individuals predisposed toward a particular psychological disorder will be particularly affected by stress and will then manifest abnormal behavior.

dimensional classification. An approach to assessment in which a person is placed on a continuum. Compare *categorical classification.*

directionality problem. A difficulty that arises in the correlational method of research when it is known that two variables are related but it is unclear which is causing the other.

disorganized behavior. Symptom of schizophrenia that is marked by odd behaviors that do not appear organized, such as bouts of agitation, unusual dress, or childlike, silly behavior.

disorganized speech. Speech found in schizophrenia patients that is marked by poorly organized ideas and speech that is difficult for others to understand; also known as formal thought disorder.

disorganized symptoms. Broad category of symptoms in schizophrenia that includes disorganized speech, disorganized thinking, and disorganized behavior.

disorientation. A state of mental confusion with respect to time; place; and identity of self, other persons, and objects.

disruptive mood dysregulation disorder. A DSM-5 disorder defined by severe temper outbursts and observably irritable mood between outbursts in youth older than age 6.

dissemination. The process of facilitating adoption of efficacious treatments in the community, most typically by offering clinicians guidelines about the best available treatments along with training on how to conduct those treatments.

dissociation. A process whereby a group of mental processes is split off from the main stream of consciousness or behavior loses its relationship with the rest of the personality.

dissociative amnesia. A dissociative disorder in which the person suddenly becomes unable to recall important personal information to an extent that cannot be explained by ordinary forgetfulness.

dissociative disorders. Disorders in which the normal integration of consciousness, memory, or identity is suddenly and temporarily altered; include dissociative amnesia, dissociative identity disorder (multiple personality), and depersonalization/derealization disorder.

dissociative fugue. See *fugue subtype.*

dissociative identity disorder (DID). A rare dissociative disorder (formerly called multiple personality disorder, or MPD) in which two or more distinct and separate personalities are present within the same individual, each with his or her own memories, relationships, and behavior patterns, with only one of them dominant at any given time.

dizygotic (DZ) twins. Birth partners who developed from separate fertilized eggs and who are only 50 percent alike genetically, just as siblings born from different pregnancies involving the same father; also called fraternal twins. Compare *monozygotic twins.*

dopamine. Central nervous system neurotransmitter, a catecholamine that is also a precursor of norepinephrine and apparently figures in schizophrenia and Parkinson's disease.

dorsolateral prefrontal cortex. A region of the prefrontal cortex involved in working memory, motor planning, organization, and regulation and implicated in many psychopathologies.

double-blind procedure. A method for reducing the biasing effects of the expectations of research participant and experimenter; neither is allowed to know whether the independent variable of the experiment is being applied to the participant.

Down syndrome (trisomy 21). A form of intellectual disability caused by a third copy of a particular chromosome; involves an IQ usually less than 50 as well as distinctive physical characteristics.

DSM-5. The current *Diagnostic and Statistical Manual of Mental Disorders* of the American Psychiatric Association.

dyscalculia. Learning disorder characterized by difficulty recalling arithmetic facts, counting objects, and aligning numbers in columns.

dyslexia. A learning disorder involving significant difficulty with word recognition, reading comprehension, and (typically) spelling.

ecological momentary assessment (EMA). Form of self-observation involving collection of data in real time (e.g., diaries) regarding thoughts, moods, and stressors.

Ecstasy. A relatively new hallucinogen, chemically similar to mescaline and the amphetamines.

effectiveness. How well a therapeutic treatment works in the real world in the hands of broader samples of nonacademic, less supervised therapists. Compare *efficacy.*

efficacy. How well a therapeutic treatment works under rarified, academic research conditions. Compare *effectiveness.*

ego. In psychoanalytic theory, the predominantly conscious part of the personality, responsible for decision making and for dealing with reality.

electrocardiogram (EKG). A recording of the electrical activity of the heart, made with an electrocardiograph.

electroconvulsive therapy (ECT). A treatment that produces a convulsion by passing electric current through the brain; despite public concerns about this treatment, it can be useful in alleviating profound depression.

electrodermal responding. A recording of the minute electrical activity of the sweat glands on the skin, allowing inference of an emotional state.

electroencephalogram (EEG). A graphic recording of electrical activity of the brain, usually of the cerebral cortex, but sometimes of lower areas.

emotion. The expression, experience, and physiology that guide responses to problems and challenges in the environment.

empirically supported treatments (ESTs). Approaches whose efficacy has been demonstrated and documented through research that meets the APA's standards for research on psychotherapy.

endorphins. Opiates produced within the body; may have an important role in the processes by which the body builds up tolerance to drugs and is distressed by their withdrawal.

enzyme. A complex protein that acts as a catalyst in regulating metabolic activities.

epidemiology. The study of the frequency and distribution of illness in a population.

epigenetics. The study of changes in gene expression that are caused by something other than changes in the DNA (gene) sequence or structure, such as DNA methylation.

episodic disorder. A condition, such as major depressive disorder, whose symptoms dissipate but that tends to recur.

erectile disorder. A recurrent and persistent inability to attain an erection or maintain it until completion of sexual activity.

etiology. All the factors that contribute to the development of an illness or disorder.

excitement phase. As applied by Masters and Johnson, the second stage of the sexual response cycle, characterized by pleasure associated with increased blood flow to the genitalia.

excoriation. A DSM-5 disorder defined by skin picking.

executive functioning. The cognitive capacity to plan how to do a task, how to devise strategies, and how to monitor one's performance.

exhibitionistic disorder (exhibitionism). Marked preference for obtaining sexual gratification by exposing one's genitals to an unwilling observer.

exorcism. The casting out of evil spirits by ritualistic chanting or torture.

experiment. The most powerful research technique for determining causal relationships; involves the manipulation of an independent variable, the measurement of a dependent variable, and the random assignment of participants to the several different conditions being investigated. Compare *correlational method.*

experimental effect. A statistically significant difference between two groups experiencing different manipulations of the independent variable.

explicit memory. Memory involving the conscious recall of experiences; the area of deficits typically seen in dissociative amnesia. Compare *implicit memory.*

exposure. Real-life (in vivo) or imaginal confrontation of a feared object or situation, especially as a component of systematic desensitization. See also *imaginal exposure.*

exposure and response prevention (ERP). The most widely used and accepted treatment of obsessive-compulsive disorder, in which the sufferer is prevented from engaging in compulsive ritual activity and instead faces the anxiety provoked by the stimulus, leading eventually to extinction of the conditioned response (anxiety).

expressed emotion (EE). Hostility, criticism, and emotional overinvolvement directed from other people toward the patient, usually within a family.

external validity. The extent to which the results of a study can be considered generalizable.

externalizing disorders. Domain of childhood disorders characterized by outward-directed behaviors, such as aggressiveness, noncompliance, overactivity, and impulsiveness; the category includes attention-deficit/hyperactivity disorder, conduct disorder, and oppositional defiant disorder. Compare *internalizing disorders.*

extinction. The elimination of a classically conditioned response by the omission of the unconditioned stimulus. In operant conditioning, the elimination of the conditioned response by the omission of reinforcement.

extraversion. Personality trait associated with frequent experiences of positive affect and social engagement.

factitious disorder. Disorder in which the individual's physical or psychological symptoms appear under voluntary control and are adopted merely to assume the role of a sick person; called factitious disorder by proxy or Munchausen syndrome when a parent produces a physical illness in a child.

falsifiability. The extent to which a scientific assertion is amenable to systematic probes, any one of which could negate the scientist's expectations.

familial high-risk study. A study involving the offspring of people with a disorder, such as schizophrenia, who have a high probability of later developing a disorder.

family method. A research strategy in behavior genetics in which the frequency of a trait or of abnormal behavior is determined in relatives who have varying percentages of shared genetic background.

family-focused treatment (FFT). With the goal of reducing the likelihood of relapse of bipolar disorder or schizophrenia, treatment that aims to educate the person's family about illness, enhance communication, and develop problem-solving skills.

fear. A reaction to real or perceived immediate danger in the present; can involve arousal, or sympathetic nervous system activity.

fear circuit. Set of brain structures, including the amygdala, that tend to be activated when the individual is feeling anxious or fearful; especially active among people with anxiety disorders.

fear-of-fear hypothesis. A cognitive model for the etiology of agoraphobia; suggests the condition is driven by negative thoughts about the consequences of having a panic attack in public.

female orgasmic disorder. A recurrent and persistent delay or absence of orgasm in a woman during sexual activity adequate in focus, intensity, and duration; in many instances the woman may experience considerable sexual excitement.

female sexual arousal disorder. Formerly called frigidity, the inability of a female to reach or maintain the lubrication–swelling stage of sexual excitement or to enjoy a subjective sense of pleasure or excitement during sexual activity.

female sexual interest/arousal disorder. A sexual dysfunction characterized by a loss of sexual interest (urges, fantasies, or desires) or lack of physiological or subjective arousal to sexual cues.

fetal alcohol syndrome (FAS). Retarded growth of the developing fetus and infant involving cranial, facial, and limb anomalies as well as intellectual disabilities; caused by heavy consumption of alcohol by the mother during pregnancy.

fetishistic disorder. A paraphilic disorder that involves reliance on an inanimate object for sexual arousal.

fixation. In psychoanalytic theory, the arrest of psychosexual development at a particular stage through too much or too little gratification at that stage.

flashback. An unpredictable recurrence of experiences from an earlier drug high.

flight of ideas. A symptom of mania that involves a rapid shift in conversation from one subject to another with only superficial associative connections.

fragile X syndrome. Malformation (or even breakage) of the X chromosome, associated with intellectual disability; symptoms include large, underdeveloped ears; a long, thin face; a broad nasal root; enlarged testicles in males; and, in many cases, attention deficits and hyperactivity.

frontal lobe. The anterior portion of each cerebral hemisphere, in front of the central sulcus; active in reasoning and other higher mental processes.

frontal-subcortical dementias. Dementias that involve impairment of both cognitive and motor functions; include Huntington's chorea, Parkinson's disease, normal-pressure hydrocephalus, and vascular dementia.

frontotemporal dementia (FTD). Dementia that begins typically in the mid- to late 50s, characterized by deficits in executive functions such as planning, problem solving, and goal-directed behavior as well as recognition and comprehension of emotions in others. Compare *Alzheimer's disease.*

frotteuristic disorder. A disorder in which the chief concern involves the sexually oriented touching of an unsuspecting person, typically in public places that provide an easy means of escape.

fugue subtype. Subtype of dissociative amnesia disorder in which the person experiences total amnesia, moves, and establishes a new identity.

functional magnetic resonance imaging (fMRI). Modification of magnetic resonance imaging (MRI) that allows researchers to take pictures of the brain so quickly that metabolic changes can be measured, resulting in a picture of the brain at work rather than of its structure alone.

gamma-aminobutyric acid (GABA). Inhibitory neurotransmitter that may be involved in the anxiety disorders.

gender identity. The ingrained sense a person has of being either a man or a woman.

gene. The smallest portion of DNA within a chromosome that functions as a piece of functional hereditary information.

gene expression. The switching on and off of the reading (transcription and translation) of genes into their products (usually proteins) and thus their associated phenotypes.

gene–environment interaction. The influence of genetics on an individual's sensitivity or reaction to an environmental event. Compare *reciprocal gene–environment interaction.*

general adaptation syndrome (GAS). Hans Selye's model to describe the biological reaction of an organism to sustained and unrelenting stress; the several stages culminate in death in extreme circumstances.

generalized anxiety disorder (GAD). Disorder characterized by chronic, persistent anxiety and worry.

genetic paradigm. The approach to human behavior that focuses on both heritability of traits and complex interactions between genes and environment.

genital stage. In psychoanalytic theory, the final psychosexual stage, reached in adulthood, in which heterosexual interests predominate.

genito-pelvic pain/penetration disorder. A disorder in which the woman persistently experiences pain or vaginal muscle spasms when intercourse is attempted.

genome-wide association studies (GWAS). Studies of variations in the entire human genome to identify associations between variations in genes and particular behaviors, traits, or disorders. Large sample sizes are needed for these types of studies.

genotype. An individual's unobservable, genetic constitution, that is, the totality of genes present in the cells of an individual; often applied to the genes contributing to a single trait. Compare *phenotype.*

glial cell. Cells in the brain that are not neurons. They support and protect neurons.

G-proteins. Guanine nucleotide-binding proteins that serve to modulate activity within the postsynaptic cell, are implicated in mania and depression, and are possibly the intracellular target of lithium.

grandiose delusions. Found in paranoid schizophrenia, delusional disorder, and mania, an exaggerated sense of one's importance, power, knowledge, or identity. See also *delusions.*

gray matter. The neural tissue—made up largely of nerve cell bodies—that constitutes the cortex covering the cerebral hemisphere, the nuclei in lower brain areas, columns of the spinal cord, and the ganglia of the autonomic nervous system. Compare *white matter.*

guilty but mentally ill (GBMI). Insanity plea in which a mentally ill person can be held morally and legally responsible for a crime but can then, in theory, be sent to a prison hospital or other suitable facility for psychiatric treatment rather than to a regular prison for punishment. In reality, however, people judged GBMI are usually put in the general prison population, where they may or may not receive treatment. Compare *not guilty by reason of insanity.*

hallucinations. Perceptions in any sensory modality without relevant and adequate external stimuli.

hallucinogen. A drug or chemical, such as LSD, psilocybin, or mescaline, whose effects include hallucinations; often called a psychedelic.

harmful dysfunction. Proposed definition of psychological disorder that contains both a value judgment (harmful) and a putatively objective scientific component (dysfunction).

hashish. The dried resin of the cannabis plant, stronger in its effects than the dried leaves and stems that constitute marijuana.

health psychology. A branch of psychology dealing with the role of psychological factors in health and illness. See also *behavioral medicine.*

heritability. The extent to which variability in a particular behavior/disorder within a population can be attributed to genetic factors.

heroin. An extremely addictive narcotic drug derived from morphine.

high-risk method. A research technique involving the intensive examination of people, such as the offspring of people with schizophrenia, who have a high probability of later developing a disorder.

hippocampus. In the subcortical region of the brain, the long, tubelike structure that stretches from the septal area into the temporal lobe.

histrionic personality disorder. A personality disorder defined by overly dramatic behavior, emotional excess, and sexually provocative behavior.

hoarding disorder. A disorder in which the person has a compulsive need to acquire objects and extreme difficulty in disposing of those objects.

hopelessness theory. Cognitive theory of depression that began with learned helplessness theory, was modified to incorporate attributions, and has been modified again to emphasize hopelessness—an expectation that desirable outcomes will not occur and that no available responses can change the situation.

HPA axis. The neuroendocrine connections among hypothalamus, pituitary gland, and adrenal cortex, central to the body's response to stress.

hydrocodone. An opiate combined with other drugs such as acetaminophen to produce prescription pain medications, including the commonly abused drug Vicodin. See also *oxycodone.*

hypnosis. A trancelike state or behavior resembling sleep, induced by suggestion, characterized primarily by increased suggestibility.

hypomania. An extremely happy or irritable mood accompanied by symptoms such as increased energy and decreased need for sleep, but without the significant functional impairment associated with mania.

hypothalamus. In the subcortical region of the brain, the structure that regulates many visceral processes, including metabolism, temperature, perspiration, blood pressure, sleeping, and appetite.

hypothesis. Specific expectation or prediction about what should occur or be found if a theory is true or valid.

iatrogenic. Inadvertently induced by treatment.

id. In psychoanalytic theory, that part of the personality present at birth, comprising all the energy of the psyche and expressed as biological urges that strive continually for gratification.

ideas of reference. Delusional thinking that reads personal significance into seemingly trivial remarks or activities of others and completely unrelated events.

illness anxiety disorder. A disorder defined by excessive concern and help seeking about health concerns in the absence of major physical symptoms.

imaginal exposure. Treatment for anxiety disorders that involves visualizing feared scenes for extended periods of time. Frequently used in the treatment of posttraumatic stress disorder when in vivo exposure to the initial trauma cannot be conducted.

implicit memory. Memory that underlies behavior but is based on experiences that cannot be consciously recalled; typically not compromised in cases of dissociative amnesia. Compare *explicit memory*.

in absentia. Literally, "in one's absence." Courts are concerned that a person be able to participate personally and meaningfully in his or her own trial and not be tried in absentia because of a distracting psychological disorder.

in vivo. As applied in psychology, taking place in a real-life situation.

inappropriate affect. Emotional responses that are out of context, such as laughter when hearing sad news.

incest. Sexual relations between close relatives, most often between daughter and father or between brother and sister.

incidence. In epidemiological studies of a particular disorder, the rate at which new cases occur in a given place at a given time. Compare *prevalence*.

independent variable. In a psychological experiment, the factor, experience, or treatment that is under the control of the experimenter and that is expected to have an effect on participants as assessed by changes in the dependent variable.

index case (proband). The person who in a genetic investigation bears the diagnosis or trait in which the investigator is interested.

informed consent. The agreement of a person to serve as a research participant or to enter therapy after being told the possible outcomes, both benefits and risks.

insanity defense. The legal argument that a defendant should not be held responsible for an illegal act if the conduct is attributable to mental illness. See also *not guilty by reason of insanity* and *guilty but mentally ill*.

intellectual disability. A disorder characterized by below-average intellectual functioning associated with impairment in adaptive behavior and identified at an early age.

intelligence quotient (IQ). A standardized measure indicating how far an individual's raw score on an intelligence test is from the average raw score of his or her chronological age group.

intelligence test. A standardized means of assessing a person's current mental ability, for example, the Stanford–Binet test or the Wechsler Adult Intelligence Scale.

interleukin-6 (IL-6). A proinflammatory cytokine; elevated levels can result from stress as well as infection and have been linked to numerous diseases in older adults.

internal consistency reliability. See *reliability*.

internal validity. See *validity*.

internalizing disorders. Domain of childhood disorders characterized by inward-focused experiences and behaviors, such as depression, social withdrawal, and anxiety; the category includes childhood anxiety and mood disorders. Compare *externalizing disorders*.

interoceptive conditioning. Classical conditioning of panic attacks in response to internal bodily sensations of arousal (as opposed to the external situations that trigger anxiety).

interpersonal psychotherapy (IPT). A short-term, here-and-now focused psychological treatment initially developed for depression and influenced by the psychodynamic emphasis on relationships.

interrater reliability. See *reliability*.

irresistible impulse. The term used in an 1834 Ohio court ruling on criminal responsibility which determined that an insanity defense can be established by proving that the accused had an uncontrollable urge to perform the act.

joint attention. Interactions between two people require paying attention to each other, whether speaking or communicating emotion nonverbally. This is impaired in children with autism spectrum disorder.

latency period. In psychoanalytic theory, the years between ages 6 and 12, during which id impulses play a minor role in motivation.

law of effect. A principle of learning that holds that behavior is acquired by virtue of its consequences.

learning disabilities. General term for learning disorders, communication disorders, and motor skills disorder.

least restrictive alternative. The legal principle according to which a hospitalized patient must be treated in a setting that imposes as few restrictions as possible on his or her freedom.

libido. Freudian term for the life-integrating instinct or force of the id; sometimes equated with sexual drive.

lithium. A drug useful in treating both mania and depression in bipolar disorder.

locus ceruleus. The brain region in the fear circuit that is especially important in panic disorder; the major source in the brain of norepinephrine, which helps trigger sympathetic nervous system activity.

longitudinal design. Investigation that collects information on the same individuals repeatedly over time, perhaps over many years, in an effort to determine how phenomena change. Compare *cross-sectional design*.

loose associations (derailment). In schizophrenia, an aspect of disorganized thinking wherein the patient has difficulty sticking to one topic and drifts off on a train of associations evoked by an idea from the past.

LSD. *d*-lysergic acid diethylamide, a drug synthesized in 1938 and discovered by accident to be a hallucinogen in 1943.

magnetic resonance imaging (MRI). A technique for measuring the structure (or, in the case of functional magnetic resonance imaging, the activity) of the living brain. The person is placed inside a large circular magnet that causes hydrogen atoms to move; the return of the atoms to their original positions when the current to the magnet is turned off is translated by a computer into pictures of brain tissue.

major depressive disorder (MDD). A disorder of individuals who have experienced episodes of depression but not of mania. Depression episodes are marked by sadness or loss of pleasure, accompanied by symptoms such as feelings of worthlessness and guilt; withdrawal from others; loss of sleep, appetite, or sexual desire; and either lethargy or agitation.

male hypoactive sexual desire disorder. A sexual dysfunction disorder defined by absence of or deficiency in sexual fantasies and urges in men; for women, see *female sexual interest/arousal disorder*.

male orgasmic disorder. A recurrent and persistent delay or absence of ejaculation after an adequate phase of sexual excitement.

malingering. Faking a physical or psychological incapacity in order to avoid a responsibility or gain an end, where the goal is readily recognized from the individual's circumstances; distinct from conversion disorder, in which the incapacity is assumed to be beyond voluntary control.

mania. Intense elation or irritability, accompanied by symptoms such as excessive talkativeness, rapid thoughts, distractibility, grandiose plans, heightened activity, and insensitivity to the negative consequences of actions.

marijuana. A drug derived from the dried and ground leaves and stems of the female hemp plant *Cannabis sativa*.

marriage and family therapist. A mental health professional who specializes in treating couples and families and in how these relationships impact mental health. Training can be at the master's or Ph.D. level, and some M.S.W. programs offer training in marriage and family therapy.

MDMA. Methylenedioxymethamphetamine, a chemical component of Ecstasy; initially used as an appetite suppressant for World War I soldiers and derived from precursors found in nutmeg, dill, saffron, and sassafras.

medial prefrontal cortex. A region of the cortex in the anterior frontal lobes involved in executive function and emotion regulation that is implicated in mood and anxiety disorders.

melancholic. Subtype of major depressive disorder in which the individual is unable to feel better even momentarily when something good happens, regularly feels worse in the morning and awakens early, and suffers a deepening of other symptoms of depression.

mental retardation. Former DSM-IV-TR disorder characterized by below-average intellectual functioning associated with impairment in adaptive behavior and identified at an early age. Changed in name and criteria to intellectual disability in DSM-5.

mescaline. A hallucinogen and alkaloid that is the active ingredient of peyote.

mesmerize. The first term for *hypnotize*, after Franz Anton Mesmer, an Austrian physician who in the late eighteenth century treated and cured hysterical or conversion disorders with what he considered the animal magnetism emanating from his body and permeating the universe.

meta-analysis. A quantitative method of analyzing the results of a set of studies on a topic, by standardizing the results.

metabolite. A chemical breakdown product of an endogenous molecule, such as a neurotransmitter, or of an exogenous drug; used to gauge current or recent level of its precursor.

metacognition. The knowledge people have about the way they know and learn about their world, for example, recognizing the usefulness of a map in finding their way in a new city.

methadone. A synthetic addictive heroin substitute for treating those addicted to heroin that eliminates its effects and the cravings.

methamphetamine. An amphetamine derivative whose abuse skyrocketed in the 1990s.

mindfulness-based cognitive therapy (MBCT). Recent adaptation of cognitive therapy/restructuring that focuses on relapse prevention after successful treatment for recurrent episodes of major depression; aims to "decenter" the person's perspective in order to break the cycle between sadness and thinking patterns.

Minnesota Multiphasic Personality Inventory (MMPI). A lengthy personality inventory that identifies individuals with states such as anxiety, depression, masculinity–femininity, and paranoia, through their true–false replies to groups of statements.

M'Naghten rule. An 1843 British court decision stating that an insanity defense can be established by proving that the defendant did not know what he or she was doing or did not realize that it was wrong.

modeling. Learning by observing and imitating the behavior of others or teaching by demonstrating and providing opportunities for imitation.

molecular genetics. Studies that seek to determine the components of a trait that are heritable by identifying relevant genes and their functions.

monoamine oxidase inhibitors (MAOIs). A group of antidepressant drugs that prevent the enzyme monoamine oxidase from deactivating catecholamines and indolamines.

monozygotic (MZ) twins. Genetically identical twins who have developed from a single fertilized egg. Compare *dizygotic twins.*

mood disorders. Disorders, such as depressive disorders or mania, in which there are disabling disturbances in emotion.

moral treatment. A therapeutic regimen, introduced by Philippe Pinel during the French Revolution, whereby mentally ill patients were released from their restraints and were treated with compassion and dignity rather than with contempt and denigration.

morphine. An addictive narcotic alkaloid extracted from opium, used primarily as an analgesic and as a sedative.

motor disorder. A learning disorder characterized by marked impairment in the development of motor coordination that is not accounted for by a physical disorder such as cerebral palsy.

Mowrer's two-factor model. Mowrer's theory of avoidance learning according to which (1) fear is attached to a neutral stimulus by pairing it with a noxious unconditioned stimulus, and (2) a person learns to escape the fear elicited by the conditioned stimulus, thereby avoiding the unconditioned stimulus.

multisystemic treatment (MST). Treatment for serious juvenile offenders that involves delivering intensive and comprehensive therapy services in the community, targeting the adolescent, the family, the school, and, in some cases, the peer group, in ecologically valid settings and using varied techniques.

narcissistic personality disorder. Personality disorder defined by extreme selfishness and self-centeredness; a grandiose view of one's uniqueness, achievements, and talents; an insatiable craving for admiration and approval from others; willingness to exploit others to achieve goals; and expectation of much more from others than one is willing to give in return.

negative reinforcement. The strengthening of a tendency to exhibit desired behavior by rewarding responses in that situation with the removal of an aversive stimulus.

negative symptoms. Behavioral deficits in schizophrenia, which include flat affect, anhedonia, asociality, alogia, and avolition. Compare *positive symptoms.*

negative triad. In Beck's theory of depression, a person's negative views of the self, the world, and the future, in a reciprocal causal relationship with pessimistic assumptions (schemas) and cognitive biases such as selective abstraction.

neurofibrillary tangles. Abnormal protein filaments present in the cell bodies of brain cells in patients with Alzheimer's disease.

neurologist. A physician who specializes in medical diseases that affect the nervous system, such as muscular dystrophy, cerebral palsy, or Alzheimer's disease.

neuron. A single nerve cell.

neuropsychological tests. Psychological tests, such as the Luria–Nebraska, which can detect impairment in different parts of the brain.

neuropsychologist. A psychologist who studies how brain dysfunction affects cognition, emotion, and behavior.

neuroscience paradigm. A broad theoretical view that holds that psychological disorders are caused in part by some aberrant process directed by the brain.

neuroticism. The tendency to react to events with greater-than-average negative affect; a strong predictor of onset of anxiety disorders and depression.

neurotransmitters. Chemical substances important in transferring a nerve impulse from one neuron to another, for example, serotonin and norepinephrine.

nicotine. The principal alkaloid of tobacco (an addicting agent).

nitrous oxide. A gas that, when inhaled, produces euphoria and sometimes giddiness.

nonshared environment. Factors distinct among family members, such as relationships with friends or specific experiences unique to a person. Compare *shared environment.*

nonsuicidal self-injury (NSSI). Behaviors that are meant to cause immediate bodily harm but are not intended to cause death.

norepinephrine. A catecholamine neurotransmitter, disturbances of which have been related to mania, depression, and particularly to anxiety disorders.. It is also a sympathetic nervous system neurotransmitter, a hormone released in addition to epinephrine and similar in action, and a strong vasoconstrictor.

not guilty by reason of insanity (NGRI). Insanity plea that specifies an individual is not to be held legally responsible for the crime because the person had a mental illness at the time of the crime. Different states and federal law have different standards for defining mental illness and what must be demonstrated by the defense. In most cases, the defense must show that because of the mental illness, the accused person could not conform his or her behavior to the law and did not know right from wrong when the crime was committed. Compare *guilty but mentally ill.*

obese. Currently defined as exhibiting a body mass index (BMI) of greater than 30.

object relations theory. Variant of psychoanalytic theory that focuses on the way children internalize (*introject*) images of the people who are important to them (e.g., their parents), such that these internalized images (*object representations*) become part of the ego and influence how the person reacts to the world.

obsession. An intrusive and recurring thought that seems irrational and uncontrollable to the person experiencing it. Compare *compulsion.*

obsessive-compulsive disorder (OCD). An anxiety disorder in which the mind is flooded with persistent and uncontrollable thoughts or the individual is compelled to repeat certain acts again and again, causing significant distress and interference with everyday functioning.

obsessive-compulsive personality disorder. Personality disorder defined by inordinate difficulty making decisions, hyperconcern with details and efficiency, and poor relations with others due to demands that things be done just so, as well as the person's unduly conventional, serious, formal, and stingy emotions.

occipital lobe. The posterior portion of each cerebral hemisphere, situated behind the parietal lobe and above the temporal lobes; responsible for reception and analysis of visual information and for some visual memory.

operant conditioning. The acquisition or elimination of a response as a function of the environmental contingencies of reinforcement and punishment. Compare *classical conditioning.*

opiates. A group of addictive sedatives that in moderate doses relieve pain and induce sleep.

opium. One of the opiates, the dried, milky juice obtained from the immature fruit of the opium poppy; an addictive narcotic that produces euphoria and drowsiness while reducing pain.

oppositional defiant disorder. An externalizing disorder of children marked by high levels of disobedience to authority but lacking the extremes of conduct disorder.

oral stage. In psychoanalytic theory, the first psychosexual stage, which extends into the second year; during this stage the mouth is the principal erogenous zone.

orbitofrontal cortex. The portion of the frontal lobe located just above the eyes; one of three closely related brain regions that are unusually active in individuals with obsessive-compulsive disorder.

orgasm phase. The third stage of the sexual response cycle, characterized by a peak of sexual pleasure, generally including ejaculation in men and contraction of the outer vaginal walls in women.

outcome research. Research on the efficacy of psychotherapy.

outpatient commitment. A form of civil commitment consistent with the principle of least restrictive alternative, whereby the person is not hospitalized but rather is allowed to remain free in the community under legal/medical constraints that ensure, for example, that prescribed medication is taken and other measures are observed.

oxycodone. An opiate combined with other drugs to produce prescription pain medications, including the commonly abused drug OxyContin. See also *hydrocodone.*

pain disorder. A somatoform disorder in which the person complains of severe and prolonged pain that is not fully explainable by organic pathology and is thus assumed to be caused or intensified by psychological factors.

panic attack. A sudden attack of intense apprehension, terror, and impending doom, accompanied by symptoms such as labored breathing, nausea, chest pain, feelings of choking and smothering, heart palpitations, dizziness, sweating, and trembling.

panic control therapy (PCT). A cognitive behavior treatment, based on the tendency of individuals with panic disorder to overreact to bodily stimuli, in which sensations are induced physically and coped with under safe conditions.

panic disorder. An anxiety disorder in which the individual has sudden, inexplicable, and frequent panic attacks. See also *panic attack*.

paradigm. A set of basic assumptions that outlines the universe of scientific inquiry, specifying both the concepts regarded as legitimate and the methods to be used in collecting and interpreting data.

paranoia. The general term for delusions of persecution, of grandiosity, or both; found in several pathological conditions, delusional disorders, paranoid schizophrenia, and paranoid personality disorder but can also be produced by large doses of certain drugs, such as cocaine or alcohol.

paranoid personality disorder. A personality disorder defined by expectation of mistreatment at the hands of others, suspicion, secretiveness, jealousy, argumentativeness, unwillingness to accept blame, and cold and unemotional affect.

paraphilic disorder. Sexual attraction to unusual objects or unusual sexual activities that leads to social difficulties or distress.

parasympathetic nervous system. The division of the autonomic nervous system that is involved with maintenance; controls many of the internal organs and is active primarily when the organism is not aroused. Compare *sympathetic nervous system*.

parent management training (PMT). Behavioral program in which parents are taught to modify their responses to their children so that prosocial rather than antisocial behavior is consistently rewarded.

parietal lobe. The middle division of each cerebral hemisphere, situated behind the central sulcus and above the lateral sulcus; the receiving center for sensations of the skin and of bodily positions.

PCP. Phencyclidine, also known by street names such as angel dust, and zombie; this very powerful and hazardous drug causes profound disorientation, agitated and often violent behavior, and even seizures, coma, and death.

pedophilia. A paraphilia defined by a marked preference for obtaining sexual gratification through contact with people defined legally as underage.

penile plethysmograph. A device for detecting blood flow and thus for recording changes in the size of the penis.

peripartum onset. Onset during pregnancy or within 4 weeks postpartum, characterizing a subtype of episodes of major depressive disorder or mania.

persistent depressive disorder (dysthymia). A DSM-5 disorder defined by depressive symptoms that last at least two years.

personality disorder. A group of disorders involving long-standing, inflexible, and maladaptive personality traits that impair social and occupational functioning.

personality inventory. A self-report questionnaire comprised of statements assessing habitual behavioral and affective tendencies.

personality trait domains. Five personality dimensions included in the appendix of DSM-5 to help supplement diagnoses of personality disorders: negative affectivity, detachment, antagonism, disinhibition, and psychoticism.

personality trait facets. Twenty-five specific personality dimensions included in the appendix of DSM-5 to provide greater detail on the personality trait domains.

PET scan. Computer-generated picture of the living brain, created by analysis of emissions from radioactive isotopes injected into the bloodstream.

phallic stage. In psychoanalytic theory, the third psychosexual stage, extending from ages 3 to 5 or 6, during which maximal gratification is obtained from genital stimulation.

phenotype. The totality of physical characteristics and behavioral traits of an individual or a particular trait exhibited by an individual; the product of interactions between genetics and the environment over the course of development. Compare *genotype*.

phenylketonuria (PKU). A genetic deficiency in a liver enzyme, phenylalanine hydroxylase, that causes severe intellectual disability unless phenylalanine can be largely restricted from the diet.

phobia. An anxiety disorder in which there is intense fear and avoidance of specific objects and situations, recognized as irrational by the individual.

phonological disorder. DSM-IV-TR communication disorder in childhood in which some words sound like baby talk because the person is not able to make certain speech sounds. Renamed speech sound disorder in DSM-5.

placebo. Any inactive therapy or chemical agent, or any attribute or component of such a therapy or chemical, that affects a person's behavior for reasons related to his or her expectation of change.

placebo effect. The action of a drug or psychological treatment that is not attributable to any specific operations of the agent. For example, a tranquilizer can reduce anxiety both because of its special biochemical action and because the recipient expects relief. See also *placebo*.

plaques. Small, round areas composed of remnants of lost neurons and beta-amyloid, a waxy protein deposit; present in the brains of patients with Alzheimer's disease.

pleasure principle. In psychoanalytic theory, the demanding manner by which the id operates, seeking immediate gratification of its needs.

polygenic. As applied to psychopathology or any other trait, caused by multiple genes contributing their effects, typically during multiple stages of development.

polymorphism. Any specific difference in DNA sequence that exists within a population.

positive reinforcement. The strengthening of a tendency to exhibit desired behavior by rewarding responses in that situation with a desired reward.

positive symptoms. Behavioral excesses in schizophrenia, such as hallucinations and delusions. Compare *negative symptoms*.

posttraumatic model (of DID). Etiological model of dissociative identity disorder that assumes the condition begins in childhood as a result of severe physical or sexual abuse. Compare *sociocognitive model (of DID)*.

posttraumatic stress disorder (PTSD). An anxiety disorder in which a particularly stressful event, such as military combat, rape, or a natural disaster, brings in its aftermath intrusive reexperiencing of the trauma, a numbing of responsiveness to the outside world, estrangement from others, and a tendency to be easily startled, as well as nightmares, recurrent dreams, and otherwise disturbed sleep.

predictive validity. See *validity*.

predisposition. An inclination or diathesis to respond in a certain way, either inborn or acquired; in abnormal psychology, a factor that lowers the ability to withstand stress and inclines the individual toward pathology.

prefrontal cortex. The region of the frontal lobe of the brain that helps maintain an image of threats and rewards faced, as well as maintain focus and plan relevant to those threats and rewards.

premature (early) ejaculation. Inability of the male to inhibit his orgasm long enough for mutually satisfying sexual relations.

premenstrual dysphoric disorder. A DSM-5 disorder defined by mood and physical symptoms that consistently emerge in the week before menses and clear within a week after menses.

prepared learning. In classical conditioning theory, a biological predisposition to associate particular stimuli readily with the unconditioned stimulus.

prevalence. In epidemiological studies of a disorder, the percentage of a population that has the disorder at a given time. Compare *incidence*.

privileged communication. The communication between parties in a confidential relationship that is protected by statute, which a spouse, doctor, lawyer, pastor, psychologist, or psychiatrist thus cannot be forced to disclose, except under unusual circumstances.

probands. The sample of people who in a genetic investigation bears the diagnosis or trait in which the investigator is interested.

prognosis. A prediction of the likely course and outcome of an illness. Compare *diagnosis*.

projective hypothesis. The notion that standard but highly unstructured stimuli, as found in the Rorschach assessment's series of inkblots, are necessary to bypass defenses in order to reveal unconscious motives and conflicts.

projective test. A psychological assessment device, such as the Rorschach series of inkblots, employing a set of standard but vague stimuli, on the assumption that unstructured material will allow unconscious motivations and fears to be uncovered.

pronoun reversal. A speech problem in which the child refers to himself or herself as "he," "she," or "you" and uses "I" or "me" in referring to others; often found in the speech of children with autistic disorder.

pruning. In neural development, the selective loss of synaptic connections, especially in the fine-tuning of brain regions devoted to sensory processing.

psilocybin. A psychedelic drug extracted from the mushroom *Psilocybe mexicana*.

psyche. In psychoanalytic theory, the totality of the id, ego, and superego, including both conscious and unconscious components.

psychiatric nurse. A nurse, typically with a bachelor's degree, who receives specialized training in mental illness. A nurse practitioner may prescribe psychiatric medications.

psychiatrist. A physician (M.D.) who has taken specialized postdoctoral training, called a residency, in the diagnosis, treatment, and prevention of psychological disorders.

psychoactive medications. Prescribed chemical compounds—for example, Prozac—having a psychological effect that alters mood or thought process.

psychoanalysis. Primarily the therapy procedures pioneered by Freud, entailing free association, dream analysis, and working through the transference neurosis. More recently the term has come to encompass the numerous variations on basic Freudian therapy.

psychoanalytic theory. Theory originating with Freud that psychopathology results from unconscious conflicts in the individual.

psychoeducational approaches. Especially with bipolar disorder and schizophrenia, the component of treatment that helps people learn about symptoms, expected time course, triggers for symptoms, and treatment strategies.

psychological disorder. The DSM defines psychological disorder as a clinically significant behavioral or psychological syndrome or patterns. The definition includes a number of key features, including distress, disability or impaired functioning, violation of social norms, and dysfunction.

psychological tests. Standardized procedures designed to measure performance on a particular task or to assess personality.

psychomotor agitation. A symptom characterized by pacing, restlessness, and inability to sit still.

psychomotor retardation. A symptom commonly observed in major depressive disorder in which the person moves his or her limbs and body slowly.

psychoneuroimmunology. Field that studies how psychological factors (especially stressors) impact the immune system (adversely).

psychopathology. The field concerned with the nature and development of psychological disorders.

psychopathy. A personality syndrome related to antisocial personality disorder but defined by an absence of emotion, impulsivity, manipulativeness, and irresponsibility.

psychophysiology. The discipline concerned with the bodily changes that accompany psychological events.

psychotherapy. A primarily verbal means of helping troubled individuals change their thoughts, feelings, and behavior to reduce distress and to achieve greater life satisfaction.

psychotic features. Delusions or hallucinations characterizing a subtype of episodes of major depressive disorder or mania. Also used to refer to positive symptoms of schizophrenia.

random assignment. A method of assigning people to groups by chance (e.g., using a flip of a coin). The procedure helps to ensure that groups are comparable before the experimental manipulation begins.

randomized controlled trials (RCTs). Studies in which clients are randomly assigned to receive either active treatment or a comparison (a placebo condition involving no treatment or an active-treatment control group that receives another treatment); experimental treatment studies, where the independent variable is the treatment type and the dependent variable is client outcome.

rapid cycling. Term applied to bipolar disorders if the person has experienced at least four episodes within the past year.

reactivity. The phenomenon wherein behavior changes because it is being observed.

reality principle. In psychoanalytic theory, the manner in which the ego delays gratification and otherwise deals with the environment in a planned, rational fashion.

receptor. A protein embedded in a neural cell membrane that interacts with one or more neurotransmitters. Nonneural receptor proteins include hormone receptors.

reliability. The extent to which a test, measurement, or classification system produces the same scientific observation each time it is applied. Reliability types include test–retest, the relationship between the scores that a person achieves when he or she takes the same test twice; interrater, the relationship between the judgments that at least two raters make independently about a phenomenon; split-half, the relationship between two halves of an assessment instrument that have been determined to be equivalent; alternate-form, the relationship between scores achieved by people when they complete two versions of a test that are judged to be equivalent; and internal consistency, the degree to which different items of an assessment are related to one another.

research domain criteria (RDoc). A long-term project by the National Institute of Mental Health to develop new ways of classifying psychological disorders based on dimensions of observable behavior and neurobiological measures.

resolution phase. The fourth and final stage of the sexual response cycle, characterized by an abatement of muscle tension, relaxation, and a sense of well-being.

reuptake. Cellular process by which released neurotransmitters are taken back into the presynaptic cell, terminating their present postsynaptic effect but making them available for subsequent modulation of nerve impulse transmission.

reversal (ABAB) designs. See ABAB designs.

reward system. System of brain structures involved in the motivation to pursue rewards. Believed to be involved in depression, mania, schizophrenia, and substance use disorders.

risk factor. A condition or variable that increases the likelihood of developing a disorder.

Rorschach Inkblot Test. A projective test in which the examinee is instructed to interpret a series of 10 inkblots reproduced on cards.

rumination. Repetitive thought about why a person is experiencing a negative mood.

safety behaviors. Behaviors used to avoid experiencing anxiety in feared situations, such as the tendency of people with social phobia to avoid looking at other people (so as to avoid perceiving negative feedback) or the tendency of people with panic disorder to avoid exercise (so as to avoid somatic arousal that could trigger a panic attack).

schema. A mental structure for organizing information about the world.

schizoaffective disorder. Diagnosis applied when a patient has symptoms of both mood disorder and either schizophreniform disorder or schizophrenia.

schizoid personality disorder. A personality disorder defined by emotional aloofness; indifference to the praise, criticism, and feelings of others; maintenance of few, if any, close friendships; and solitary interests.

schizophrenia. A disorder characterized by disturbances in thought, emotion, and behavior; disordered thinking in which ideas are not logically related; delusional beliefs; faulty perception, such as hallucinations; disturbances in attention; disturbances in motor activity; blunted expression of emotion; reduced desire for interpersonal relations and withdrawal from people; diminished motivation and anticipatory pleasure. See also *schizoaffective disorder*, *schizophreniform disorder*, and *brief psychotic disorder*.

schizophreniform disorder. Diagnosis given to people who have all the symptoms of schizophrenia for more than 2 weeks but less than 6 months. Compare *brief psychotic disorder*.

schizotypal personality disorder. Personality disorder defined by eccentricity, oddities of thought and perception (magical thinking, illusions, depersonalization, derealization), digressive speech involving overelaborations, and social isolation; under stress, behavior may appear psychotic.

seasonal affective disorder. A subtype of mood disorders in which episodes consistently occur at the same time of year; in the most common form, major depressive episodes consistently occur in the winter.

second-generation antipsychotic drugs. Any of several drugs, such as clozapine, used to treat schizophrenia that produce fewer motor side effects than traditional antipsychotics while reducing positive and disorganized symptoms at least as effectively; may, however, be associated with increased and serious side effects of other varieties.

secondhand smoke. Also referred to as environmental tobacco smoke (ETS), the smoke from the burning end of a cigarette; contains higher concentrations of ammonia, carbon monoxide, nicotine, and tar than the smoke inhaled by the smoker.

sedatives. Drugs that slow bodily activities, especially those of the central nervous system; used to reduce pain and tension and to induce relaxation and sleep.

selective mortality. The tendency for less healthy individuals to die more quickly, which leads to biased samples in long-term follow-up studies.

selective serotonin reuptake inhibitors (SSRIs). A specific form of serotonin reuptake inhibitors (SRIs) with less effect on dopamine and norepinephrine levels; SSRIs inhibit the reuptake of serotonin into the presynaptic neuron, so that serotonin levels in the cleft are sustained for a longer period of time.

self-monitoring. In behavioral assessment, a procedure whereby the individual observes and reports certain aspects of his or her own behavior, thoughts, or emotions.

sensate focus. A term applied to exercises prescribed at the beginning of the Masters and Johnson sex therapy program, in which partners are instructed to fondle each other to give pleasure but to refrain from intercourse, thus reducing anxiety about sexual performance.

separation anxiety disorder. A disorder in which the child feels intense fear and distress when away from someone on whom he or she is very dependent.

septal area. In the subcortical region of the brain, the area anterior to the thalamus.

serotonin. A neurotransmitter of the central nervous system whose disturbances apparently figure in depression.

serotonin reuptake inhibitors (SRIs). Any of various drugs that inhibit the presynaptic reuptake of the neurotransmitter serotonin, thereby prolonging its effects on postsynaptic neurons.

serotonin transporter gene. A particular gene critical to the gene–environment interactions that apparently contribute to the development of depression.

serotonin–norepinephrine reuptake inhibitors (SNRIs). Any of various drugs that inhibit the presynaptic reuptake of serotonin and norepinephrine, such that both neurotransmitters will have more prolonged effects on postsynaptic neurons.

sex-reassignment surgery. An operation removing existing genitalia and constructing a substitute for the genitals of the opposite sex.

sexual dysfunctions. Dysfunctions in which the appetitive or psychophysiological changes of the normal sexual response cycle are inhibited. Compare *hypoactive sexual desire disorder.*

sexual masochism disorder. A paraphilic disorder defined by a marked preference for obtaining or increasing sexual gratification through subjection to pain or humiliation.

sexual orientation. An individual's emotional, romantic, or sexual attraction toward other people that is stable and enduring.

sexual response cycle. The general pattern of sexual physical processes and feelings, made up of four phases: appetitive interest, excitement, orgasm, and resolution.

sexual sadism disorder. A paraphilic disorder defined by a marked preference for obtaining or increasing sexual gratification by inflicting pain or humiliation on another person.

shared environment. Factors that family members have in common, such as income level, child-rearing practices, and parental marital status and quality. Compare *nonshared environment.*

single nucleotide polymorphism (SNP). A variation in gene sequence. Specifically, differences between people in a single nucleotide (A, T, G, or C) in the DNA sequence of a particular gene.

single-case experimental design. A design for an experiment conducted with a single subject. Typically, behavior is measured within a baseline condition, then during an experimental or treatment condition, and finally within the baseline condition again.

social anxiety disorder (social phobia). A collection of fears linked to the presence of other people.

social selection hypothesis. An attempt to explain the correlation between social class and schizophrenia by arguing that people with schizophrenia tend to move downward in socioeconomic status. Compare *sociogenic hypothesis.*

social selectivity. The late-life shift in interest away from seeking new social interactions and toward cultivating those few social relationships that matter most, such as with family and close friends.

social skills training. Behavior therapy procedures, such as modeling and behavior rehearsal, for teaching individuals how to meet others, talk to them and maintain eye contact, give and receive criticism, offer and accept compliments, make requests and express feelings, and otherwise improve their relations with other people.

social worker. A mental health professional who holds a master of social work (M.S.W.) degree.

sociocognitive model (of DID). Etiological model of dissociative identity disorder that considers the condition to be the result of learning to enact social roles, though not through conscious deception, but in response to suggestion. Compare *posttraumatic model (of DID).*

sociogenic hypothesis. An idea that seeks causes in social conditions, for example, that being in a low social class can cause one to develop schizophrenia. Compare *social selection hypothesis.*

somatic nervous system. The division of the nervous system that controls muscles under voluntary control. Compare *autonomic nervous system.*

somatic symptom disorder. A DSM-5 diagnosis defined by excessive concern and help seeking regarding physical symptoms.

somatic symptom and related disorders. A group of disorders defined by anxiety about health and excessive focus on physical symptoms.

somatosensory cortex. A region of the cortex along the lateral postcentral gyrus that is key in processing the sensation of touch.

specific learning disorders. A set of developmental disorders encompassing dyslexia and dyscalculia; characterized by failure to develop in a specific academic area to the degree expected by the child's intellectual level.

specific phobia. An unwarranted fear and avoidance of a specific object or circumstance, for example, fear of nonpoisonous snakes or fear of heights.

spectator role. As applied by Masters and Johnson, a pattern of behavior in which the individual's focus on and concern with sexual performance causes him or her to be an observer rather than a participant and thus impedes natural sexual responses.

speech sounds disorder. Communication disorder in childhood in which some words sound like baby talk because the person is not able to make certain speech sounds.

standardization. The process of constructing a normed assessment procedure that meets the various psychometric criteria for reliability and validity.

statistical significance. A result that has a low probability of having occurred by chance alone and is by convention regarded as important. Compare *clinical significance.*

stigma. The pernicious beliefs and attitudes held by a society, ascribed to groups considered deviant in some manner, such as people with mental illness.

stimulant. A drug, such as cocaine, that increases alertness and motor activity and at the same time reduces fatigue, allowing an individual to remain awake for an extended period of time.

stress. State of an organism subjected to a stressor; can take the form of increased autonomic activity and in the long term can cause breakdown of an organ or development of a psychological disorder.

structured interview. An interview in which the questions are set out in a prescribed fashion for the interviewer; assists professionals in making diagnostic decisions based on standardized criteria.

stuttering. DSM-IV-TR communication disorder of childhood marked by frequent and pronounced verbal dysfluencies, such as repetitions of certain sounds. See also *childhood onset fluency disorder.*

subgenual anterior cingulate. A region in the anterior cortex that is part of a network of structures involved in emotion processing; believed to be overly active in major depressive disorder.

substance use disorders. Disorders in which drugs such as alcohol and cocaine are abused to such an extent that behavior becomes maladaptive, social and occupational functioning are impaired, and control or abstinence becomes impossible. Dependence on the drug may be physiological and produce tolerance and withdrawal.

subthreshold symptoms. Symptoms of a disorder that are clinically significant but do not meet full diagnostic criteria.

suicide. The intentional taking of one's own life.

superego. In psychoanalytic theory, the part of the personality that acts as the conscience and reflects society's moral standards as learned from parents and teachers.

sympathetic nervous system. The division of the autonomic nervous system that acts on bodily systems—for example, contracting the blood vessels, reducing activity of the intestines, and increasing the heartbeat—to prepare the organism for exertion, emotional stress, or extreme cold. Compare *parasympathetic nervous system.*

symptom. An observable physiological or psychological manifestation of a disease.

synapse. Small gap between two neurons where the nerve signal passes electrically or chemically from the axon of the first to the dendrites, cell body, or axon of the second.

systematic desensitization. A major behavior therapy procedure that has a fearful person, while deeply relaxed, imagine a series of progressively more fearsome situations, such that fear is dispelled as a response incompatible with relaxation; useful for treating psychological problems in which anxiety is the principal difficulty.

tardive dyskinesia. A muscular disturbance of patients who have taken phenothiazines for a very long time, marked by involuntary motor movements such as lip smacking and chin wagging.

temporal lobe. A large region of each cerebral hemisphere situated below the lateral sulcus and in front of the occipital lobe; contains primary auditory and general association areas.

test–retest reliability. See *reliability.*

thalamus. A major brain relay station consisting of two egg-shaped lobes; receives impulses from all sensory areas except the olfactory and transmits them to the cerebrum for higher processing.

Thematic Apperception Test (TAT). A projective test consisting of black-and-white pictures, each depicting a potentially emotion-laden situation, about each of which the examinee is instructed to make up a story. See also *projective hypothesis.*

theory. A formally stated and coherent set of propositions that explain and logically order a range of phenomena, generating testable predictions or hypotheses.

third-variable problem. The difficulty in the correlational method of research whereby the relationship between two variables may be attributable to a third factor.

thought suppression. Key feature of obsessive-compulsive disorder; has the paradoxical effect of inducing preoccupation with the object of thought.

time-of-measurement effects. A possible confound in longitudinal studies whereby conditions at a particular point in time can have a specific effect on a variable that is being studied over time.

time-out. An operant conditioning procedure in which, after bad behavior, the person is temporarily removed from a setting where reinforcers can be obtained and placed in a less desirable setting, for example, in a boring room.

token economy. A behavior therapy procedure, based on operant conditioning principles, in which hospitalized patients are given scrip rewards, such as poker chips, for socially constructive behavior. The tokens can be exchanged for desirable items and activities such as cigarettes and extra time away from the ward.

tolerance. A physiological process in which greater and greater amounts of an addictive drug are required to produce the same effect. See also *addiction.*

transcranial magnetic stimulation. A noninvasive technique in which pulsing magnets are used to intensify or diminish brain activity in a given region.

transcription. In genetics, the first step in gene expression. A section of DNA sequence is transcribed to RNA; a sequence of DNA synthesizes a copy of RNA.

transference. The venting of the analysand's emotions, either positive or negative, by treating the psychoanalyst as the symbolic representative of someone important in the past.

transvestic fetishism. The practice of dressing in the clothing of the opposite sex, for the purpose of sexual arousal.

treatment outcome research. Studies designed to assess whether medical or psychological approaches are efficacious in relieving symptoms of a disorder. See also *randomized controlled trials 5.*

trichotillomania. A DSM-5 disorder defined by repeated pulling of one's hair that results in hair loss.

tricyclic antidepressants. A group of antidepressants with molecular structures characterized by three fused rings; they interfere with the reuptake of norepinephrine and serotonin.

tryptophan. Amino acid that is the major precursor of serotonin; experimental depletion has found that a lowered serotonin level causes temporary depressive symptoms in people with a personal or family history of depression.

twin method. Research strategy in behavior genetics in which concordance rates of monozygotic and dizygotic twins are compared.

unconditioned response (UCR). See *classical conditioning.*

unconditioned stimulus (UCS). See *classical conditioning.*

unconscious. A state of unawareness without sensation or thought; in psychoanalytic theory, the part of the personality, in particular the id impulses or energy, of which the ego is unaware.

vaginal plethysmograph. A device for measuring physiological signs of sexual arousal in women; the device is shaped like a tampon and is inserted into the vagina to measure increases in blood flow.

vaginismus. Painful, spasmodic contractions of the outer third of the vagina, making penetration impossible or extremely difficult.

validity. In research, includes internal, the extent to which results can be confidently attributed to the manipulation of the independent variable, and external, the extent to which results can be generalized to other populations and settings. Validity as applied to psychiatric diagnoses includes concurrent, the extent to which previously undiscovered features are found among patients with the same diagnosis, and predictive, the extent to which predictions can be made about the future behavior of patients with the same diagnosis. Validity as applied to psychological and psychiatric measures includes content validity, the extent to which a measure adequately samples the domain of interest, and criterion, the extent to which a measure is associated in an expected way with some other measure (the criterion). See also *construct validity.*

vascular dementia. A form of dementia caused by cerebrovascular disease, most commonly occurring after strokes. Because the areas of the brain affected by disease can vary, the symptoms of vascular dementia vary as well.

ventricles. Cavities deep within the brain, filled with cerebrospinal fluid, that connect to the spinal cord.

voyeuristic disorder. A disorder defined by a marked preference for obtaining sexual gratification by watching others in a state of undress or having sexual relations.

white matter. Neural tissue, particularly of the brain and spinal cord, consisting of tracts or bundles of myelinated (sheathed) nerve fibers. Compare *gray matter.*

withdrawal. Negative physiological and psychological reactions evidenced when a person suddenly stops taking an addictive drug; reactions include cramps, restlessness, and even death. See also *addiction.*

yedasentience. The subjective sense of knowing that one has achieved closure on an action or thought; theorized to be deficient among persons with obsessive-compulsive disorder.

References

Abbey, S. E., & Stewart, D. E. (2000). Gender and psychosomatic aspects of ischemic disease. *Journal of Psychosomatic Research, 48*, 417–423.

Abel, G. G., Becker, J. V., Mittelman, M., Cunningham-Rathner, J., Rouleau, J. L., & Murphy, W. D. (1987). Self-reported sex crimes of nonincarcerated paraphiliacs. *Journal of Interpersonal Violence, 2*, 3–25.

Abou-Saleh, M. T., Younis, Y., & Karim, L. (1998). Anorexia nervosa in an Arab culture. *International Journal of Eating Disorders, 23*, 207–212.

Abramowitz, J. S., & Braddock, A. E. (2008). *Psychological treatment of health anxiety and hypochondriasis: A biopsychosocial approach.* Boston, MA: Hogrefe & Huber Publishing.

Abramowitz, J. S., Franklin, M. E., Schwartz, S. A., & Furr, J. M. (2003). Symptom presentation and outcome of cognitive-behavioral therapy for obsessive-compulsive disorder. *Journal of Consulting and Clinical Psychology, 71*, 1049–1057.

Abramson, L. Y., Metalsky, G. I., & Alloy, L. B. (1989). Hopelessness depression: A theory-based subtype of depression. *Psychological Review, 96*, 358–372.

Acarturk, C., de Graaf, R., van Straten, A., Have, M. T., & Cuijpers, P. (2008). Social phobia and number of social fears, and their association with comorbidity, health-related quality of life and help seeking: A population-based study. *Social Psychiatry and Psychiatric Epidemiology, 43*, 273–279.

Achenbach, T. M., Hensley, V. R., Phares, V., & Grayson, D. (1990). Problems and competencies reported by parents of Australian and American children. *Journal of Child Psychology and Psychiatry, 31*, 265–286.

Acocella, J. (1999). *Creating hysteria: Women and multiple personality disorder.* San Francisco: Jossey-Bass.

Acton, G. J., & Kang, J. (2001). Interventions to reduce the burden of caregiving for an adult with dementia: A meta-analysis. *Research in Nursing and Health, 24*, 349–360.

Acuna, K. (2013). By the numbers: The "Fifty Shades of Grey" phenomenon. *Business Insider.*

Adler, A. (1930). *Guiding the child on the principles of individual psychology.* New York: Greenberg.

Afifi, T. O., Enns, M. W., Cox, B. J., Asmundson, G. J. G., Stein, M. B., & Sareen, J. (2008). Population attributable fractions of psychiatric disorders and suicide ideation and attempts associated with adverse childhood experiences. *American Journal of Public Health, 98*, 946–952.

Agras, W. S., Crow, S. J., Halmi, K. A., Mitchell, J. E., Wilson, G. T., & Kraemer, H. C. (2000). Outcome predictors for the cognitive-behavioral treatment of bulimia nervosa: Data from a multisite study. *American Journal of Psychiatry, 157*, 1302–1308.

Agras, W. S., Rossiter, E. M., Arnow, B., et al. (1994). One-year follow-up of psychosocial and pharmacologic treatments for bulimia nervosa. *Journal of Clinical Psychiatry, 55*, 179–183.

Agras, W. S., Rossiter, E. M., Arnow, B., Schneider, J. A., Telch, C. F., Raeburn, S. D., Bruce, B., Perl, M., & Koran, L. M. (1992). Pharmacologic and cognitive-behavioral treatment for bulimia nervosa: A controlled comparison. *American Journal of Psychiatry, 149*, 82–87.

Aguilera, A., Lopez, S. R., Breitborde, N. J., Kopelowicz, A., & Zarate, R. (2010). Expressed emotion and sociocultural moderation in the course of schizophrenia. *Journal of Abnormal Psychology, 119*, 875–885.

Ainsworth, M. S., Blehar, M. C., Waters, E., & Wall, S. (1978). *Patterns of attachment: A psychological study of the strange situation.* Oxford, UK: Erlbaum.

Alarcon, R. D., Becker, A. E., Lewis-Fernandez, R., Like, R. C., Desai, P., Foulks, E., et al. for the Cultural Psychiatry Committee of the Group for the Advancement of Psychiatry. (2009). Issues for DSM-V: The role of culture in psychiatric diagnosis. *Journal of Nervous and Mental Disease, 197*, 559–560.

Albee, G. W., Lane, E. A., & Reuter, J. M. (1964). Childhood intelligence of future schizophrenics and neighborhood peers. *Journal of Psychology, 58*, 141–144.

Albert, M. S., Dekosky, S. T., Dickson, D., Dubois, B., Feldman, H. H., Fox, N. C., et al. (2011). The diagnosis of mild cognitive impairment due to Alzheimer's disease: Recommendations from the National Institute on Aging-Alzheimer's Association workgroups on diagnostic guidelines for Alzheimer's disease. *Alzheimer's and Dementia: The Journal of the Alzheimer's Association, 7*, 270–279.

Alden, L. E. (1989). Short-term structured treatment for avoidant personality disorder. *Journal of Consulting and Clinical Psychology, 57*, 756–764.

Alden, L. E., Laposa, J. M., Taylor, C. T., & Ryder, A. G. (2002). Avoidant personality disorder: Current status and future directions. *Journal of Personality Disorders, 16*, 1–29.

Alegria, M., Canino, G., Shrout, P. E., Woo, M., Duan, N., & Vila, D. (2008). Prevalence of mental illness in immigrant and non-immigrant U.S. Latino groups. *American Journal of Psychiatry, 165*, 359–369.

Alegria, M., Woo, M., Cao, Z., Torres, M., Meng, X-L., & Striegel-Moore, R. (2007). Prevalence and correlates of eating disorders among Latinos in the United States. *International Journal of Eating Disorders, 40*, s15–s21.

Allderidge, P. (1979). Hospitals, mad houses, and asylums: Cycles in the care of the insane. *British Journal of Psychiatry, 134*, 321–324.

Allen, J. G. (2001). *Traumatic relationships and serious mental disorders.* New York: John Wiley & Sons.

Allen, J. J., Iacono, W. G., Depue, R. A., & Arbisi, P. (1993). Regional electroencephalographic asymmetries in bipolar seasonal affective disorder before and after exposure to bright light. *Biological Psychiatry, 33*, 642–646.

Allen, M., D'Alessio, D., & Brezgel, K. (1995). A meta-analysis summarizing the effects of pornography: II. aggression after exposure. *Human Communication Research, 22*, 258–283.

Allen, P., Johns, L. C., Fu, C. H. Y., Broome, M. R., Vythelingum, G. N., & McGuire, P. K. (2004). Misattribution of external speech in patients with hallucinations and delusions. *Schizophrenia Research, 69*, 277–287.

Allnutt, S. H., Bradford, J. M., Greenberg, D. M., & Curry, S. (1996). Co-morbidity of alcoholism and the paraphilias. *Journal of Forensic Science, 41*, 234–239.

Alloy, L. B., Abramson, L. Y., Smith, J. M., Gibb, B. E., & Neeren, A. M. (2006). Role of parenting and maltreatment histories in unipolar and bipolar mood disorders: Mediation by cognitive vulnerability to depression. *Clinical Child and Family Psychology Review, 9*, 23–64.

Alloy, L. B., Abramson, L. Y., Walshaw, P. D., Cogswell, A., Grandin, L. D., Hughes, M. E., et al. (2008). Behavioral approach system and behavioral inhibition system sensitivities and bipolar spectrum disorders: Prospective prediction of bipolar mood episodes. *Bipolar Disorders, 10*, 310–322.

Alonso, J., Petukhova, M., Vilagut, G., Chatterji, S., Heeringa, S., Ustun, T. B., et al. (2011). Days out of role due to common physical and mental conditions: Results from the WHO World Mental Health surveys. *Molecular Psychiatry, 16*, 1234–1246.

Althof, S. E. (2014). Treatment of premature ejaculation: Psychotherapy, pharmacotherapy, and combined therapy. In Y. M. Binik & K. S. K. Hall (Eds.), *Principles and practice of sex therapy* (5 ed., pp. 112–137). New York: Guilford Press.

Althof, S. E., Abdo, C. H., Dean, J., Hackett, G., McCabe, M., McMahon, C. G., et al. (2010). International Society for Sexual Medicine's guidelines for the diagnosis and treatment of premature ejaculation. *Journal of Sexual Medicine, 7*, 2947–2969.

Altshuler, L. L., Kupka, R. W., Hellemann, G., Frye, M. A., Sugar, C. A., McElroy, S. L., et al. (2010). Gender and depressive symptoms in 711 patients with bipolar disorder evaluated prospectively in the Stanley Foundation Bipolar Treatment Outcome Network. *American Journal of Psychiatry, 167*, 708–715.

Alwahhabi, F. (2003). Anxiety symptoms and generalized anxiety disorder in the elderly: A review. *Harvard Review of Psychiatry, 11*, 180–193.

Amador, X. F., Flaum, M., Andreasen, N. C., Strauss, D. H., Yale, S. A., et al. (1994). Awareness of illness in schizophrenia and schizoaffective and mood disorder. *Archives of General Psychiatry, 51*, 826–836.

Aman, M. G., & Langworthy, K. (2000). Pharmacotherapy for hyperactivity in children with autism and other pervasive developmental disorders. *Journal of Autism and Developmental Disorders, 30*, 451–459.

American Law Institute. (1962). *Model penal code: Proposed official draft.* Philadelphia: Author.

American Psychiatric Association. (2004). Practice guidelines for the treatment of patients with schizophrenia (2nd ed.) Available online at http://www.psych.org.

American Psychiatric Association. (2013). *Diagnostic and Statistical Manual of Mental Disorders 5th edition (DSM-5)* (5th ed.).

American Psychological Association. (2002). Ethical principles of psychologists and code of conduct. *American Psychologist, 57*, 1060–1073.

American Psychological Association. (2004). Guidelines for psychological practice with older adults. *American Psychologist, 59*, 236–260.

Amir, N., Beard, C., Burns, M., & Bomyea, J. (2009). Attention modification program in individuals with generalized anxiety disorder. *Journal of Abnormal Psychology, 118*, 28–33.

Amir, N., Cashman, L., & Foa, E. B. (1997). Strategies of thought control in obsessive-compulsive disorder. *Behaviour Research and Therapy, 35*, 775–777.

Amir, N., Foa, E. B. & Coles, M. E. (1998). Negative interpretation bias in social phobia. *Behaviour Research and Therapy, 36*, 945–957.

Anand, A., Verhoeff, P., Seneca, N., Zoghbi, S. S., Seibyl, J. P., Charney, D. S., et al. (2000). Brain SPECT imaging of amphetamine-induced dopamine release in euthymic bipolar disorder patients. *American Journal of Psychiatry, 157*, 1109–1114.

Ancoli, I., S., Kripke, D. F., Klauber, M. R., Fell, R., Stepnowsky, C., Estline, E., et al. (1996). Morbidity, mortality and sleep-disordered breathing in community dwelling elderly. *Sleep: Journal of Sleep Research and Sleep Medicine, 19*, 277–282.

Andersen, B. L., Cyranowski, J. M., & Aarestad, S. (2000). Beyond artificial, sex-linked distinctions to conceptualize female sexuality: Comment on Baumeister (2000). *Psychological Bulletin, 126*(3), 380–384.

Andersen, B. L., Cyranowski, J. M., & Espindle, D. (1999). Men's sexual self-schema. *Journal of Personality and Social Psychology, 76*, 645–661.

Andersen, S. M., Reznik, I., & Manzella, L. M. (1996). Eliciting transient affect, motivation, and expectancies in transference: Significant-other representations and the self in social relations. *Journal of Personality and Social Psychology, 71*, 1108–1129.

Anderson, C. A., Hinshaw, S. P., & Simmel, C. (1994). Mother–child interactions in ADHD and comparison boys: Relationships to overt and covert externalizing behavior. *Journal of Abnormal Child Psychology, 22*, 247–265.

Anderson, L. T., Campbell, M., Adams, P., Small, A. M., Perry, R., & Shell, J. (1989). The effects of haloperidol on discrimination learning and behavioral symptoms in autistic children. *Journal of Autism and Developmental Disorders, 19*, 227–239.

Anderson, M. C., & Green, C. (2001). Suppressing unwanted memories by executive control. *Nature, 410*, 366–369.

Anderson, S., Hanson, R., Malecha, M., Oftelie, A., Erickson, C., & Clark, J. M. (1997). The effectiveness of naltrexone in treating task attending, aggression, self-injury, and stereotypic mannerisms of six young males with autism or pervasive developmental disorders. *Journal of Developmental and Physical Disabilities, 9*, 211–221.

Andreano, J. M., & Cahill, L. (2006). Glucocorticoid release and memory consolidation men and women. *Psychological Science, 17*, 466-470.

Andreasen, N. C., Olsen, S. A., Dennert, J. W., & Smith, M. R. (1982). Ventricular enlargement in schizophrenia: Relationship to positive and negative symptoms. *American Journal of Psychiatry, 139*, 297–302.

Andrews, G., Charney, D. S., Sirovatka, P. J., & Regier, D. A. (Eds.). (2009). *Stress-induced and fear circuitry disorders*. Arlington, VA: American Psychiatric Association.

Andrews, G., Cuijpers, P., Craske, M. G., McEvoy, P., & Titov, N. (2010). Computer therapy for the anxiety and depressive disorders is effective, acceptable and practical health care: A meta-analysis. *PloS One, 5*, e13196.

Andrews, P. W., & Thomson, J. A. (2009). The bright side of being blue: Depression as an adaptation for analyzing complex problems. *Psychological Review, 116*, 620–654.

Angrist, B., Lee, H. K., & Gershon, S. (1974). The antagonism of amphetamine-induced symptomatology by a neuroleptic. *American Journal of Psychiatry, 131*, 817–819.

Angst, F., Stassen, H. H., Clayton, P. J., & Angst, J. (2002). Mortality of patients with mood disorders: Follow-up over 34–38 years. *Journal of Affective Disorders, 68*, 167–181.

Angst, J. (1998). Sexual problems in healthy and depressed persons. *International Clinical Psychopharmacology, 13*, S1–S4.

Anguera, J. A., Boccanfuso, J., Rintoul, J. L., Al-Hashimi, O., Faraji, F., Janowich, J., et al. (2013). Video game training enhances cognitive control in older adults. *Nature, 501*, 97–101.

Ansell, E. B., Pinto, A., Edelen, M. O., Markowitz, J. C., Sanislow, C. A., Yen, S., et al. (2011). The association of personality disorders with the prospective 7-year course of anxiety disorders. *Psychological Medicine, 41*, 1019–1028.

Anthony, J. L., & Lonigan, C. L. (2004). The nature of phonological awareness: Converging evidence from four studies of preschool and early grade school children. *Journal of Educational Psychology, 96*, 43–55.

Appelbaum, P. S., & Gutheil, T. (1991). *Clinical handbook of psychiatry and the law*. Baltimore: Williams & Wilkins.

Appignannesi, L. (2008). *Mad, bad, and sad: Women and the mind doctors*. New York: W. W. Norton.

Arbisi, P. A., Ben-Porath, Y. S., & McNulty, J. (2002). A comparison of MMPI-2 validity in African American and Caucasian psychiatric patients. *Psychological Assessment, 14*, 3–15.

Arias, E., Anderson, R. N., Kung, H. C., Murphy, S. L., & Kochanek, K. D. (2003). *Deaths: Final Reports, 52*. Hyattsville, MD: National Center for Health Statistics. DHHS Publication No. 2003–1120.

Arnett, J. J. (2008). The neglected 95%: Why American psychology needs to become less American. *American Psychologist, 63*, 602–614.

Arnett, J. J., Trzesniewski, K. H., & Donnellan, M. B. (2013). The dangers of generational myth-making: Rejoinder to Twenge. *Emerging Adulthood, 1*, 17–20.

Arnold, E. H., O'Leary, S. G., & Edwards, G. H. (1997). Father involvement and self-reported parenting of children with attention deficit hyperactivity disorder. *Journal of Consulting and Clinical Psychology, 65*, 337–342.

Arnold, L. E., Elliott, M., Sachs, L., et al. (2003). Effects of ethnicity on treatment attendance, stimulant response/dose, and 14-month outcome in ADHD. *Journal of Consulting and Clinical Psychology, 71*, 713–727.

Arnold, L. M., Keck, P. E., Jr., Collins J., Wilson, R., Fleck, D. E., Corey, K. B., Amicone, J., Adebimpe, V. R., & Strakowski, S. M. (2004). Ethnicity and first-rank symptoms in patients with psychosis. *Schizophrenia Research, 67*, 207–212.

Arnow, B., Kenardy, J., & Agras, W. S. (1992). Binge eating among the obese. *Journal of Behavioral Medicine, 15*, 155–170.

Aronson, E. (2012). *The social animal* (11th ed.). New York: Worth.

Arseneault, L., Cannon, M., Poulton, R., Murray, R., Caspi, A., & Moffitt, T. E. (2002). *Cannabis* use in adolescence and risk for adult psychosis: longitudinal prospective study. *British Medical Journal, 325*, 1212–1213.

Artiles, A. J., & Trent, S. C. (1994). Overrepresentation of minority students in special education: A continuing debate. *Journal of Special Education, 27*, 410–437.

Ascher, E. A., Sturm, V. E., Seider, B. H., Holley, S. R., Miller, B. L., & Levenson, R. W. (2010). Relationship satisfaction and emotional language in frontotemporal dementia and Alzheimer's disease patients and spousal caregivers. *Alzheimer's Disease and Associated Disorders, 24*, 49–55.

Ashbaugh, A. R., Antony, M. M., McCabe, R. E., Schmidt, L. A., & Swinson, R. P. (2005). Self-evaluative biases in social anxiety. *Cognitive Therapy and Research, 29*, 387–398.

Asmundson, G. J., Larsen, D. K., & Stein, M. B. (1998). Panic disorder and vestibular disturbance: An overview of empirical findings and clinical implications. *Journal of Psychosomatic Research, 44*, 107–120.

Association, A. P. (2013). *Diagnostic and Statistical Manual of Mental Disorders Fifth Edition (DSM-5)* (Vol. 5). First edition, 1952; second edition, 1968; third edition, 1980; revised, 1987; fourth edition, 1994; revised 2000; 5th edition, 2013. Washington, DC: American Psychiatric Association.

Attia, E., & Roberto, C. A. (2009). Should amenorrhea be a diagnostic criterion for anorexia nervosa? *International Journal of Eating Disorders, 42*, 581–589.

Attia, E., Becker, A. E., Bryant-Waugh, R., Hoek, H. W., Kreipe, R. E., Marcus, M. D., et al. (2013). Feeding and eating disorders in DSM-5. *American Journal of Psychiatry, 170*(11), 1237–1239.

Attia, E., Haiman, C., Walsh, B. T., & Flater, S. R. (1998). Does fluoxetine augment the inpatient treatment of anorexia nervosa? *American Journal of Psychiatry, 155*, 548–551.

Aubry, J., Gervasoni, N., Osiek, C., Perret, G., Rossier, M. F., Bertschy, G., et al. (2007). The DEX/CRH neuroendocrine test and the prediction of depressive relapse in remitted depressed outpatients. *Journal of Psychiatric Research, 41*, 290–294.

Audrain-McGovern, J., Rodriguez, D., Epstein, L. H., Cuevas, J., Rodgers, K., & Wileyto, E. P. (2009). Does delay discounting play an etiological role in smoking or is it a consequence of smoking? *Drug and Alcohol Dependence, 103*(3), 99–106.

Audrain-McGovern, J., & Tercyak, K. P. (2011). Genes, enviroment, and adolesent smoking: Implications for prevention. In K. S. Kendler, S. R. Jaffee & D. Romer (Eds.), *The dynamic genome and mental health* (pp. 294–321). New York: Oxford University Press.

Avena, N. M., & Bocarsly, M. E. (2012). Dysregulation of brain reward systems in eating disorders: Neurochemical information from animal models of binge eating, bulimia nervosa, and anorexia nervosa. *Neuropharmacology, 63*(1), 87–96.

Axelson, D. A., Birmaher, B., Findling, R. L., Fristad, M. A., Kowatch, R. A., Youngstrom, E. A., et al. (2011). Concerns regarding the inclusion of temper dysregulation disorder with dysphoria in the Diagnostic and Statistical Manual of Mental Disorders, Fifth Edition. *Journal of Clinical Psychiatry, 72*(9), 1257–1262.

Babiak, P., Neumann, C. S., & Hare, R. D. (2010). Corporate psychopathy: Talking the walk. *Behavioral Sciences and the Law, 28*, 174–193.

Bach, A. K., Wincze, J. P., & Barlow, D. H. (2001). Sexual dysfunction. In D. H. Barlow (Ed.), *Clinical handbook of psychological disorders* (pp. 562–608). New York: Guilford Press.

Baer, R. A., & Sekirnjak, G. (1997). Detection of under-reporting on the MMPI-II in a clinical population. Effects of information about validity scales. *Journal of Personality Assessment, 69*, 555–567.

Bagby, M. R., Nicholson, R. A., Bacchionchi, J. R., et al.(2002). The predictive capacity of the MMPI-2 and PAI validity scales and indexes to detect coached and uncoached feigning. *Journal of Personality Assessment, 78*, 69–86.

Bailey, A., LeCouteur, A., Gottesman, I., Bolton, P., Simonoff, E., Yuzda, E., & Rutter, M. (1995). Autism as a strongly genetic disorder: Evidence from a British twin study. *Psychological Medicine, 25*, 63–77.

Baillargeon, J., Binswanger, I. A., Penn, J. V., Williams, B. A., & Murray, O. J. (2009). Psychiatric disorders and repeat incarcerations: The revolving prison door. *American Journal of Psychiatry, 166*(1), 103–109.

Baker, J. H., Mitchell, K. S., Neale, M. C., & Kendler, K. S. (2010). Eating disorder symptomatology and substance use disorders: Prevalence and shared risk in a population based twin sample. *International Journal of Eating Disorders, 43*, 648–658.

Ball, J. C., & Ross, A. (1991). *The effectiveness of methadone maintenance treatment*. New York: Springer-Verlag.

Balsis, S., Carpenter, B. D., & Storandt, M. (2005). Personality change precedes clinical diagnosis of dementia of the Alzheimer type. *Journal of Gerontology, 60B*, 98–101.

Balsis, S., Gleason, M. E., Woods, C. M., & Oltmanns, T. F. (2007). An item response theory analysis of DSM-IV personality disorder criteria across younger and older age groups. *Psychology and Aging, 22*, 171–185.

Bancroft, J., Loftus, J., & Long, J. S. (2003). Distress about sex: A national survey of women in heterosexual relationships. *Archives of Sexual Behavior, 32*, 193–208.

Bandelow, B., Zohar, J., Hollander, E., Kasper, S., Möller, H. J., & WFSBP Task Force on Treatment Guide. (2008). World Federation of Societies of Biological Psychiatry (WFSBP) Guidelines for the pharmacological treatment of anxiety, obsessive-compulsive and post-traumatic stress disorders—First Revision. *World Journal of Biological Psychiatry, 9*, 248–312.

Bandura, A., Blanchard, E. B., & Ritter, B. (1969). Relative efficacy of desensitization and modeling approaches for inducing behavioral, affective, and attitudinal changes. *Journal of Personality and Social Psychology, 13*, 173–199.

Bandura, A., & Menlove, F. L. (1968). Factors determining vicarious extinction of avoidance behavior through symbolic modeling. *Journal of Personality and Social Psychology, 8*, 99–108.

Banich, M. T., Passarotti, A. M., White, D. A., Nortz, M. J., & Steiner, R. D. (2000). Interhemispheric interaction during childhood: II. Children with early-treated phenylketonuria. *Developmental Neuropsychology, 18*, 53–71.

Barbato, A., & D'Avanzo, B. (2008). Efficacy of couple therapy as a treatment for depression: A meta-analysis. *Psychiatric Quarterly, 79*, 121–132.

Barber, C. (2008). *Comfortably numb*. New York: Pantheon Books.

Barbini, B., Benedetti, F., Colombo, C., Dotoli, D., Bernasconi, A., Cigala-Fulgosi, M., et al. (2005). Dark therapy for mania: A pilot study. *Bipolar Disorders, 7*, 98–101.

Barch, D. M., Bustillo, J., Gaebel, W., Gur, R., Heckers, S., Malaspina, D., et al. (2013). Logic and justification for dimensional assessment of symptoms and related clinical phenomena in psychosis: Relevance to DSM-5. *Schizophrenia Research, 150*(1), 15–20.

Barch, D. M., Carter, C. S., Braver, T. S., et al. (2001). Selective deficits in prefrontal cortex function in medication naïve patients with schizophrenia. *Archives of General Psychiatry, 58*, 280–288.

Barch, D. M., Carter, C. S., MacDonald, A. W., Braver, T. S., & Cohen, J. D. (2003). Context processing deficits in schizophrenia: Diagnostic specificity, four-week course, and relationship to clinical symptoms. *Journal of Abnormal Psychology, 112*, 132–143.

Barch, D. M., Csernansky, J. G., Conturo, T., & Snyder, A. Z. (2002). Working and long-term memory deficits in schizophrenia: Is there a common prefrontal mechanism? *Journal of Abnormal Psychology, 111*, 478–494.

Bardone-Cone, A. M., Wonderlich, S. A., Frost, R. O., Bulik, C. M., Mitchell, J., et al. (2007). Perfectionism and eating disorders: Current status and future directions. *Clinical Psychology Review*, 384–405.

Bar-Haim, Y., Lamy, D., Pergamin, L., Bakermans-Kranenburg, M. J., & van, I. M. H. (2007). Threat-related attentional bias in anxious and nonanxious individuals: A meta-analytic study. *Psychological Bulletin, 133*, 1–24.

Barkley, R. A. (1981). *Hyperactive children: A handbook for diagnosis and treatment*. New York: Guilford Press.

Barkley, R. A. (1990). *Attention-deficit hyperactivity disorder: A handbook for diagnosis and treatment*. New York: Guilford Press.

Barkley, R. A., DuPaul, G. J., & McMurray, M. B. (1990). A comprehensive evaluation of attention deficit disorder with and without hyperactivity defined by research criteria. *Journal of Consulting and Clinical Psychology, 58*, 775–789.

Barkley, R. A., Fischer, M., Smallish, L., & Fletcher, K. (2002). The persistence of attention-deficit hyperactivity disorder into young adulthood as a function of reporting source and definition of disorder. *Journal of Abnormal Psychology, 111*, 279–289.

Barkley, R. A., Fischer, M., Smallish, L., & Fletcher, K. (2003). Does the treatment of attention-deficit/hyperactivity disorder with stimulants contribute to drug use/abuse? A 13 year prospective study. *Pediatrics, 111*, 97–109.

Barkley, R. A., Grodzinsky, G., & DuPaul, G. J. (1992). Frontal lobe functions in attention deficit disorder with and without hyperactivity: A review and research report. *Journal of Abnormal Child Psychology, 20*, 163–188.

Barkley, R. A., Karlsson, J., & Pollard, S. (1985). Effects of age on the mother-child interactions of hyperactive children. *Journal of Abnormal Child Psychology, 13*, 631–638.

Barlow, D. H. (2004). *Anxiety and its disorders: The nature and treatment of anxiety and panic*. New York: Guilford Press.

Barlow, D. H., Blanchard, E. B., Vermilyea, J. A., Vermilyea, B. B., & DiNardo, P. A. (1986). Generalized anxiety and generalized anxiety disorder: Description and reconceptualization. *American Journal of Psychiatry, 143*, 40–44.

Barrett, B., Tyrer, P., Tyrer, H., Cooper, S., Crawford, M. J., & Byford, S. (2012). An examination of the factors that influence costs in medical patients with health anxiety. *Journal of Psychosomatic Research, 73*, 59-62.

Barsky, A. (2006). "Doctor, are you sure my heart is okay?" Cognitive-behavioral treatment of hypochondriasis. In R. L. Spitzer, M. B. W. First, J. B. Williams & M. Gibbon (Eds.), *DSM-IV-TR® casebook, volume 2: Experts tell how they treated their own patients* (pp. 251–261). Washington, DC: American Psychiatric Association.

Barsky, A. J., Brener, J., Coeytaux, R. R., & Cleary, P. D. (1995). Accurate awareness of heartbeat in hypochondriacal and non-hypochondriacal patients. *Journal of Psychosomatic Research, 39*, 489–497.

Barsky, A. J., Fama, J. M., Bailey, E. D., & Ahern, D. K. (1998). A prospective 4- to 5-year study of DSM-III-R hypochondriasis. *Archives of General Psychiatry, 55*, 737–744.

Barsky, A. J., Orav, E. J., & Bates, D. W. (2005). Somatization increases medical utilization and costs independent of psychiatric and medical comorbidity. *Archives of General Psychiatry, 62*, 903–910.

Barth, J., Schumacher, M., & Herrmann-Lingen, C. (2004). Depression as a risk factor for mortality in patients with coronary heart disease: A meta-analysis. *Psychosomatic Medicine, 66*, 802–813.

Bartlik, B., & Goldberg, J. (2000). Female sexual arousal disorder. In S. R. Lieblum & R. C. Rosen (Eds.), *Principles and practice of sex therapy* (3rd ed., pp. 85–117). New York: Guilford Press.

Bass, E., & Davis, L. (2008). *The courage to heal: A guide for women survivors of child sexual abuse* (4th ed.). New York: HarperCollins.

Bassett, A. S., Scherer, S. W., & Brzustowicz, L. M. (2010). Copy number variations in schizophrenia: Critical review and new perspectives on concepts genetics and disease. *American Journal of Psychiatry, 167*, 899–914.

Basson, R., Althof, S. A., Davis, S., Fugl-Meyer, K., Goldstein, I., Leiblum, S., et al. (2004). Summary of the recommendations on sexual dysfunctions in women. *Journal of Sexual Medicine, 1*, 24–34.

Basson, R., Brotto, L. A., Laan, E., Redmond, G., & Utian, W. H. (2005). Assessment and management of women's sexual dysfunctions: Problematic desire and arousal. *Journal of Sexual Medicine, 2*, 291–300.

Bates, G. W., Campbell, I. M., & Burgess, P. M. (1990). Assessment of articulated thoughts in social anxiety: Modification of the ATSS procedure. *British Journal of Clinical Psychology, 29* (Pt 1), 91-98.

Baumeister, R. F. (2000). Gender differences in erotic plasticity: The female sex drive as socially flexible and responsive. *Psychological Bulletin, 126*(3), 347–374.

Baumeister, R. F., & Butler, J. L. (1997). Sexual masochism: Deviance without pathology. In D. R. Laws & W. O'Donohue (Eds.), *Sexual deviance* (pp. 225–239). New York: Guilford Press.

Baumeister, R. F., Catanese, K. R., & Vohs, K. (2001). Is there a gender difference in strength of sex drive? Theoretical views, conceptual distinctions, and a review of relevant evidence. *Personality and Social Psychology Review, 5*(3), 242–273.

Baxter, L. R., Ackermann, R. F., Swerdlow, N. R., Brody, A., Saxena, S., Schwartz, J. M., . . . Phelps, M. E. (2000). Specific brain system mediation of obsessive-compulsive disorder responsive to either medication or behavior therapy. In W. K. Goodman, M. V. Rudorfer & J. D. Maser (Eds.), *Obsessive-compulsive disorder: Contemporary issues in treatment* (pp. 573–610). Mahwah, NJ: Lawrence Erlbaum.

Beauchaine, T. P., Hinshaw, S. P., & Pang, K. L. (2010). Comorbidity of attention-deficit/hyperactivity disorder and early-onset conduct disorder: Biological, environmental, and developmental mechanisms. *Clinical Psychology: Science and Practice, 17*, 327–336.

Beautrais, A. L., Gibb, S. J., Fergusson, D., Horwood, L. J., & Larkin, G. L. (2009). Removing bridge barriers stimulates suicides: An unfortunate natural experiment. *Australian and New Zealand Journal of Psychiatry, 43*, 495–497.

Bechara, A. (2005). Decision making, impulse control and loss of willpower to resist drugs: A neurocognitive perspective. *Nature Neuroscience, 8*(11), 1458–1463.

Beck, A. T. (1967). *Depression: Clinical, experimental and theoretical aspects*. New York: Harper & Row.

Beck, A. T. (1976). *Cognitive therapy and the emotional disorders*. New York: International Universities Press.

Beck, A. T., & Freeman, A. (1990). *Cognitive therapy for personality disorders*. New York: Guilford Press.

Beck, A. T., Kovacs, M., & Weissman, A. (1975). Hopelessness and suicidal behavior: An overview. *Journal of the American Medical Association, 234*, 1146–1149.

Beck, A. T., & Rector, N. A. (2000). Cognitive therapy of schizophrenia: A new therapy for the new millennium. *American Journal of Psychotherapy, 54*, 291–300.

Beck, J. G., & Bozman, A. (1995). Gender differences in sexual desire: The effects of anger and anxiety. *Archives of Sexual Behavior, 24*, 595–612.

Becker, B., Scheele, D., Moessner, R., Maier, W., & Hurlemann, R. (2013). Deciphering the neural signature of conversion blindness. *American Journal of Psychiatry, 170*, 121–122.

Becker, J. V., & Hunter, J. A. (1997). Understanding and treating child and adolescent sexual offenders. In T. H. Ollendick & R. J. Prinz (Eds.), *Advances in clinical child psychology* (pp. 177–196). New York: Plenum.

Beecher, H. K. (1966). Ethics and clinical research. *New England Journal of Medicine, 274*, 1354–1360.

Beevers, C. G., Lee, H. J., Wells, T. T., Ellis, A. J., & Telch, M. J. (2011). Association of predeployment gaze bias for emotion stimuli with later symptoms of PTSD and depression in soldiers deployed in Iraq. *American Journal of Psychiatry, 168*, 735–741.

Belcher, A. M., Volkow, N. D., Moeller, F. G., & Ferre, S. (2014). Personality traits and vulnerability or resilience to substance use disorders. *Trends in Cognitve Sciences, 18*(4), 211–217.

Bell, V., Oakley, D. A., Halligan, P. W., & Deeley, Q. (2011). Dissociation in hysteria and hypnosis: Evidence from cognitive neuroscience. *Journal of Neurology, Neurosurgery, and Psychiatry, 82*, 332–339.

Bellack, A. S., & Hersen, M. (1998). *Behavioral assessment: A practical handbook* (4th ed.). Boston: Allyn & Bacon.

Bello, N. T., Patinkin, Z. W., & Moran, T. H. (2011). Opioidergic consequences of dietary-induced binge eating. *Physiology and Behavior, 104*(1), 98–104.

Belluck, P. (2014, June 15). Thinking of ways to harm her: New findings on timing and range of maternal mental illness, *New York Times*.

Benjamin, C. L., Harrison, J. P., Settipani, C. A., Brodman, D. M., & Kendall, P. C. (2013). Anxiety and related outcomes in young adults 7 to 19 years after receiving treatment for child anxiety. *Journal of Consulting and Clinical Psychology, 81*(5), 865–876.

Benkelfat, C., Ellenbogen, M. A., Dean, P., Palmour, R. M., & Young, S. N. (1994). Mood-lowering effect of tryptophan depletion: Enhanced susceptibility in young men at genetic risk for major affective disorders. *Archives of General Psychiatry, 51*, 687–700.

Benowitz, N., Pérez-Stable, E., Herrera, B., & Jacob, P. (2002). Slower metabolism and reduced intake of nicotine from cigarette smoking in Chinese-Americans. *Journal of the National Cancer Institute, 94*, 108–115.

Berenz, E. C., Amstadter, A. B., Aggen, S. H., Knudsen, G. P., Reichborn-Kjennerud, T., Gardner, C. O., et al. (2013). Childhood trauma and personality disorder criterion counts: A co-twin control analysis. *Journal of Abnormal Psychology, 122*, 1070–1076.

Bergen, A. W., Yeager, M., Welch, R. A., Haque, K., Ganjei, J. K., van den Bree, M. B. M., . . . Kaye, W. H. (2005). Association of multiple DRD2 polymorphisms with anorexia nervosa. *Neuropsychopharmacology, 30*, 1703–1710.

Berkman, E. T., Falk, E. M., & Lieberman, M. D. (2011). In the trenches of real-world self-control: Neural correlates of breaking the link between craving and smoking. *Psychological Science, 22*, 498–506.

Bernal, M., Haro, J. M., Bernert, S., Brugha, T., de Graaf, R., Bruffaerts, R., et al. (2007). Risk factors for suicidality in Europe: Results from the ESEMED study. *Journal of Affective Disorders, 101*, 27–34.

Bernstein, D. P., Kasapis, C., Bergman, A., Weld, E., Mitropoulou, V., et al. (1997). Assessing Axis II disorders by informant interview. *Journal of Personality Disorders, 11*, 158–167.

Berry, J. C. (1967). *Antecedents of schizophrenia, impulsive character and alcoholism in males*. Paper presented at the 75th Annual Convention of the American Psychological Association, Washington, DC.

Bewernick, B. H., Hurlemann, R., Matusch, A., Kayser, S., Grubert, C., Hadrysiewicz, B., et al. (2010). Nucleus accumbens deep brain stimulation decreases ratings of depression and anxiety in treatment-resistant depression. *Biological Psychiatry, 67*, 110–116.

Bhugra, D., Popelyuk, D., & McMullen, I. (2010). Paraphilias across cultures: contexts and controversies. *Journal of Sex Research, 47*, 242–256.

Bhutta, A. T., Cleves, M. A., Casey, P. H., Cradock, M. M., & Anand, K. J. (2002). Cognitive and behavioral outcomes of school-aged children who were born preterm: A meta-analysis. *Journal of the American Medical Association, 288*, 728–737.

Bianchi, E. C. (2014, in press). Entering adulthood in a recession tempers later narcissism. *Psychological Science*.

Bickel, W. K., Koffarnus, M. N., Moody, L., & Wilson, A. G. (2014). The behavioral- and neuro-economic process of temporal discounting: A candidate behavioral marker of addiction. *Neuropharmacology, 76, Part B*(0), 518–527.

Bickel, W. K., Miller, M. L., Yi, R., Kowal, B. P., Lindquist, D. M., & Pitcock, J. A. (2007). Behavioral and neuroeconomics of drug addiction: Competing neural systems and temporal discounting processes. *Drug and Alcohol Dependence, 90* (Suppl. 1), S85–S91.

Biederman, J., & Faraone, S. (2004). The Massachusetts General Hospital studies of gender influences on attention-deficit/hyperactivity disorder in youth and relatives. *Psychiatric Clinics of North America, 27*, 215–224.

Biederman, J., Mick, E., Faraone, S. V., & al., e. (2000). Pediatric mania: A developmental subtype of bipolar disorder? *Biological Psychiatry, 48*, 458–466.

Biederman, J., Monuteasu, M. C., Mick, E., Spencer, T., Wilens, T. E., Silva, J. M., et al. (2006). Young adult outcome of attention deficit hyperactivity disorder: a controlled 10-year follow-up study. *Psychological Medicine, 36*, 167–179.

Biederman, J., Petty, C. R., Monuteaux, M. C., Fried, R., Byrne, D., Mirto, T., et al. (2010). Adult psychiatric outcomes of girls with attention deficit hyperactivity disorder: 11-year follow-up in a longitudinal case-control study. *American Journal of Psychiatry, 167*, 409–417.

Biglan, A., Hops, H., & Sherman, L. (1988). Coercive family processes and maternal depression. In R. J. McMahon & R. D. Peter (Eds.), *Marriages and Families: Behavioral Treatments and Processes* (pp. 72–103). New York: Brunner/Mazel.

Binik, Y. M. (2010). The DSM diagnostic criteria for vaginismus. *Archives of Sexual Behavior, 39*, 278–291.

Binzer, M., & Kullgren, G. (1996). Conversion symptoms: What can we learn from previous studies? *Nordic Journal of Psychiatry, 50*, 143–152.

Birbaumer, N., Veit, R., Lotze, M., Erb, M., Hermann, C., Grodd, W., et al. (2005). Deficient fear conditioning in psychopathy: A functional magnetic resonance imaging study. *Archives of General Psychiatry, 62*, 799–805.

Birks, J. (2006). Cholinesterase inhibitors for Alzheimer's disease. *Cochrane Database of Systematic Reviews* CD005593.

Birnbaum, G. E., Reis, H. T., Mikulincer, M., Gillath, O., & Orpaz, A. (2006). When sex is more than just sex: Attachment orientations, sexual experience, and relationship quality. *Journal of Personality and Social Psychology, 91*, 929–943.

Bischkopf, J., Busse, A., & Angermeyer, M. C. (2002). Mild cognitive impairment: A review of prevalence, incidence and outcome according to current approaches. *Acta Psychiatrica Scandinavica, 106*, 403–414.

Bishop, T. F., Press, M. J., Keyhani, S., & Pincus, H. (2014). Acceptance of insurance by psychiatrists and the implications for access to mental health care. *Journal of the American Medical Association Psychiatry, 71*(2), 176–181.

Blachman, D. R., & Hinshaw, S. P. (2002). Patterns of friendship among girls with and without attention-deficit/hyperactivity disorder. *Journal of Abnormal Child Psychology, 30*, 625–640.

Blair, K. S., Shaywitz, J., Smith, B. W., Rhodes, R., Geraci, M., Jones, M., et al. (2008). Response to emotional expressions in generalized social phobia and generalized anxiety disorder: Evidence for separate disorders. *American Journal of Psychiatry, 165*, 1193–1202.

Blair, R. J. (2013). The neurobiology of psychopathic traits in youths. *Nature Reviews Neuroscience, 14*(11), 786–799.

Blair, R. J. R. (2005). Responding to the emotions of others: Dissociating forms of empathy through the study of typical and psychiatric populations. *Consciousness and Cognition, 14*, 698–718.

Blanchard, R. (2010). The specificity of victim count as a diagnostic indicator of pedohebephilia. *Archives of sexual behavior, 39*, 1245–1252.

Blanchard, J. J., & Brown, S. B. (1998). Structured diagnostic interviews. In C. R. Reynolds (Ed.), *Comprehensive clinical psychology, Volume 3, assessment* (pp. 97–130). New York: Elsevier.

Blanchard, J. J., & Cohen, A. S. (2006). The structure of negative symptoms within schizophrenia: implications for assessment. *Schizophrenia Bulletin, 32*, 238–245.

Blanchard, J. J., Squires, D., Henry, T., Horan, W. P., Bogenschutz, M., et al. (1999). Examining an affect regulation model of substance abuse in schizophrenia: The role of traits and coping. *Journal of Nervous and Mental Disease, 187*, 72–79.

Bloch, M. H., Landeros-Weisenberger, A., Sen, S., Dombrowski, P., Kelmendi, B., Coric, V., et al. (2008). Association of the serotonin transporter polymorphism and obsessive-compulsive disorder: Systematic review. *American Journal of Medical Genetics Part B, Neuropsychiatric Genetics, 147B*, 850–858.

Blum, N., John, D. S., Pfohl, B., Stuart, S., McCormick, B., Allen, J. J., et al. (2008). Systems training for emotional predictability and problem solving (STEPPS) for outpatients with borderline personality disorder: A randomized controlled trial and 1-year follow-up. *American Journal of Psychiatry, 165*, 468–478.

Blumstein, A., Cohen, J., & Farrington, D. P. (1988). Criminal career research: Its value for criminology *Criminology, 26*, 11.

Boardman, J. D., Saint Onge, J. M., Haberstick, B. C., Timberlake, D. S., & Hewitt, J. K. (2008). Do schools moderate the genetic determinants of smoking? *Behavioral Genetics, 28*, 234–246.

Bockhoven, J. (1963). *Moral treatment in American psychiatry*. New York: Springer-Verlag.

Boegels, S. M., & Zigterman, D. (2000). Dysfunctional cognitions in children with social phobia, separation anxiety disorder, and generalized anxiety disorder. *Journal of Abnormal Child Psychology, 28*, 205–211.

Boets, B., Op de Beeck, H. P., Vandermosten, M., Scott, S. K., Gillebert, C. R., Mantini, D., et al. (2013). Intact but less accessible phonetic representations in adults with dyslexia. *Science, 342*(6163), 1251–1254.

Bohne, A., Keuthen, N. J., Wilhelm, S., Deckersback, T., & Jenike, M. A. (2002). Prevalence of symptoms of body dysmorphic disorder and its correlates: A cross-cultural comparison. *Psychosomatics, 43*, 486–490.

Boiger, M., & Mesquita, B. (2012). The construction of emotion in interactions, relationships, and cultures. *Emotion Review, 4*, 221–229.

Boisseau, C. L., Yen, S., Markowitz, J. C., Grilo, C. M., Sanislow, C. A., Shea, M. T., et al. (2013). Individuals with single versus multiple suicide attempts over 10 years of prospective follow-up. *Comprehensive Psychiatry, 54*, 238–242.

Bolton, J. M., Belik, S. L., Enns, M. W., Cox, B. J., & Sareen, J. (2008). Exploring the correlates of suicide attempts among individuals with major depressive disorder: Findings from the National Epidemiologic Survey on Alcohol and Related Conditions. *Journal of Clinical Psychiatry, 69*, 1139–1149.

Bolton, P., Bass, J., Neugebauer, R., Verdeli, H., Clougherty, K. F., Wickramaratne, P., et al. (2003). Group interpersonal psychotherapy for depression in rural Uganda: A randomized controlled trial. *Journal of the American Medical Association, 289*, 3117–3124.

Bonanno, G. A. (2004). Loss, trauma, and human resilience: Have we underestimated the human capacity to thrive after extremely aversive events? *American Psychologist, 59*, 20–28.

Bonanno, G. A., Wortman, C. B., Lehman, D. R., Tweed, R. G., Haring, M., Sonnega, J., et al. (2002). Resilience to loss and chronic grief: A prospective study from preloss to 18-months postloss. *Journal of Personality and Social Psychology, 83*, 1150–1164.

Bonta, J., Law, M., & Hanson, K. (1998). The prediction of criminal and violent recidivism among mentally disordered offenders. *Psychological Bulletin, 123*, 123–142.

Bookheimer, S., & Burggren, A. (2009). APOE-4 genotype and neurophysiological vulnerability to Alzheimer's and cognitive aging. *Annual Review of Clinical Psychology, 5*, 343–362.

Boos, H. B., Aleman, A., Cahn, W., Hulshoff, H., & Kahn, R. S. (2007). Brain volumes in relatives of patients with schizophrenia: A meta-analysis. *Archives of General Psychiatry, 64*, 297–304.

Boraska, V., Franklin, C. S., Floyd, J. A., Thornton, L. M., Huckins, L. M., Southam, L., et al. (2014). A genome-wide association study of anorexia nervosa. *Molecular Psychiatry.*

Borch-Jacobsen, M. (1997, April 24). Sybil: The making of a disease? An interview with Dr. Herbert Spiegel. *New York Review of Books, 44*(7), 60.

Borduin, C. M., Mann, B. J., Cone, L. T., Henggeler, S. W., Fucci, B. R., Blaske, D. M., & Williams, R. A. (1995). Multisystemic treatment of serious juvenile offenders: Long-term prevention of criminality and violence. *Journal of Consulting and Clinical Psychology, 63*, 569–578.

Borkovec, T. D., Alcaine, O. M., & Behar, E. (2004). Clinical presentation and diagnostic features. In R. G. Heimberg, C. L. Turk & D. S. Mennin (Eds.), *Generalized anxiety disorder* (pp. 77–108). New York: Guilford Press.

Borkovec, T. D., & Newman, M. G. (1998). Worry and generalized anxiety disorder. In P. Salkovskis (Ed.), *Comprehensive clinical psychology* (Vol. 6, 439–459). Oxford, UK: Elsevier.

Bornovalova, M. A., Huibregtse, B. M., Hicks, B. M., Keyes, M., McGue, M., & Iacono, W. (2013). Tests of a direct effect of childhood abuse on adult borderline personality disorder traits: A longitudinal discordant twin design. *Journal of Abnormal Psychology, 122*, 180–194.

Bornstein, R. F. (1992). The dependent personality: Developmental, social, and clinical perspectives. *Psychological Bulletin, 112*, 3–23.

Bornstein, R. F. (1997). Dependent personality disorder in the DSM-IV and beyond. *Clinical Psychology: Science and Practice, 4*, 175–187.

Bornstein, R. F. (2003). Behaviorally referenced experimentation and symptom validation: A paradigm for 21st century personality disorder research. *Journal of Personality Disorders, 17*, 1–18.

Bornstein, R. F. (2006). The complex relationship between dependency and domestic violence: Converging psychological factors and social forces. *American Psychologist, 61*, 595-606.

Bornstein, R. F. (2012). Dependent personality disorders. In T. A. Widiger (Ed.), *The Oxford Handbook of Personality Disorders*. New York: Oxford University Press.

Boscarino, J. A. (2006). Posttraumatic stress disorder and mortality among U.S. Army veterans 30 years after military service. *Annals of Epidemiology, 16*, 248–256.

Bosquet, M., & Egeland, B. (2006). The development and maintenance of anxiety symptoms from infancy through adolescence in a longitudinal sample. *Development and Psychopathology, 18*, 517–550.

Bouton, M. E., Mineka, S., & Barlow, D. H. (2001). A modern learning theory perspective on the etiology of panic disorder. *Psychological Review, 108*, 4–32.

Bouton, M. E., & Waddell, J. (2007). Some biobehavioral insights into persistent effects of emotional trauma. In L. J. Kirmayer, R. Lemelson & M. Barad (Eds.), *Understanding trauma: Integrating biological, clinical, and cultural perspectives* (pp. 41–59). New York: Cambridge University Press.

Bowers, W. A., & Ansher, L. S. (2008). The effectiveness of cognitive behavioral therapy on changing eating disorder symptoms and psychopathy of 32 anorexia nervosa patients at hospital discharge and one year follow-up. *Annals of Clinical Psychiatry, 20*, 79–86.

Boyle, M. (1991). *Schizophrenia: A scientific delusion?* New York: Routledge.

Boysen, G. A., & VanBergen, A. (2013). A review of published research on adult dissociative identity disorder: 2000–2010. *Journal of Nervous and Mental Disease, 201*, 5–11.

Bradford, D. E., Shapiro, B. L., & Curtin, J. J. (2013). How bad could it be? Alcohol dampens stress responses to threat of uncertain intensity. *Psychological Science, 24*(12), 2541–2549.

Bradley, R., Greene, J., Russ, E., Dutra, L., & Westen, D. (2005). A multidimensional meta-analysis of psychotherapy for PTSD. *American Journal of Psychiatry, 162*, 214–227.

Braff, D. L., Ryan, J., Rissling, A. J., & Carpenter, W. T. (2013). Lack of use in the literature from the last 20 years supports dropping traditional schizophrenia subtypes from DSM-5 and ICD-11. *Schizophrenia Bulletin, 39*(4), 751–753.

Brakoulias, V., Starcevic, V., Sammut, P., Berle, D., Milicevic, D., Moses, K., et al. (2011). Obsessive-compulsive spectrum disorders: A comorbidity and family history perspective. *Australasian Psychiatry, 19*, 151–155.

Brand, B. L., Classen, C. C., McNary, S. W., & Zaveri, P. (2009). A review of dissociative disorders treatment studies. *Journal of Nervous and Mental Disease, 197*, 646–654.

Brand, B. L., McNary, S. W., Myrick, A. C., Classen, C., Lanius, R., Loewenstein, R. J., et al. (2013). Supplemental material for a longitudinal naturalistic study of patients with dissociative disorders treated by community clinicians. *Psychological Trauma: Theory, Research, Practice, and Policy*. Advance online publication.

Brand, B. L., Myrick, A. C., Loewenstein, R. J., Classen, C. C., Lanius, R., McNary, S. W., et al. (2012). A survey of practices and recommended treatment interventions among expert therapists treating patients with dissociative identity disorder and dissociative disorder not otherwise specified. *Psychological Trauma: Theory, Research, Practice, and Policy, 4*, 490–500.

Brandon, T. H., Collins, B. N., Juliano, L. M., & Lazev, A. B. (2000). Preventing relapse among former smokers: A comparison of minimal interventions through telephone and mail. *Journal of Consulting and Clinical Psychology, 68*, 103–113.

Brandon, T. H., Vidrine, J. I., & Litvin, E. B. (2007). Relapse and relapse prevention. *Annual Review of Clinical Psychology, 3*, 257–284.

Brandon, Y. H., Zelman, D. C., & Baker, T. B. (1987). Effects of maintenance sessions on smoking relapse: Delaying the inevitable? *Journal of Consulting and Clinical Psychology, 55*, 780–782.

Bransford, J. D., & Johnson, M. K. (1973). Considerations of some problems of comprehension. In W. G. Chase (Ed.), *Visual Information Processing*. New York: Academic Press.

Braswell, L., & Kendall, P. C. (1988). Cognitive-behavioral methods with children. In K. S. Dobson (Ed.), *Handbook of Cognitive-Behavioral Therapies*. New York: Guilford.

Braun, J. M., Kahn, R. S., Froehlich, T., Auinger, P., Lanphear, B. (2006). Exposures to environmental toxicants and attention deficit hyperactivity disorder in U.S. children. *Environmental Health Perspectives, 114*, 1904–1909.

Bremner, J. D., Vythilingam, M., Vermetten, E., Southwick, S. M., McGlashan, T., Nazeer, A., et al. (2003). MRI and PET study of deficits in hippocampal structure and function in women with childhood sexual abuse and posttraumatic stress disorder. *American Journal of Psychiatry, 160*, 924–932.

Brems, C. (1995). Women and depression: A comprehensive analysis. In E. E. Beckham & W. Leber (Eds.), *Handbook of depression* (2nd ed., pp. 539–566). New York: Guilford Press.

Breslau, J., Aguilar-Gaxiola, A., Kendler, K. S., Su, M., Williams, D., & Kessler, R. (2006). Specifying race-ethnic differences in risk for psychiatric disorder in a USA national sample. *Psychological Medicine, 36*, 57–68.

Breslau, N., Brown, G. G., Del Dotto, J. E., Kumar, S., Ezhuthachan, S., Andreski, P., & Hufnagle, K. G. (1996). Psychiatric sequalae of low birth weight at 6 years of age. *Journal of Abnormal Child Psychology, 24*, 385–400.

Breslau, N., Chilcoat, H. D., Kessler, R. C., & Davis, G. C. (1999). Previous exposure to trauma and PTSD effects of subsequent trauma: Results from the Detroit Area Survey of Trauma. *American Journal of Psychiatry, 156*, 902–907.

Breslau, N., Davis, G. C., & Andreski, P. (1995). Risk factors for PTSD-related traumatic events: A prospective analysis. *American Journal of Psychiatry, 152*, 529–535.

Breslau, N., Lucia, V., & Alvarado, G. F. (2006). Intelligence and other predisposing factors in exposure to trauma and protramatic stress disorder: A follow-up study at age 17 years. *Archives of General Psychiatry, 63*, 1238–1245.

Breuer, J., & Freud, S. (1982). *Studies in hysteria.* (J. Strachey, Trans. and Ed., with the collaboration of

A. Freud). New York: Basic Books. (Original work published 1895).

Brewerton, T. D., Lydiard, B. R., Laraia, M. T., Shook, J. E., & Ballenger, J. C. (1992). CSF Beta-endorphin and dynorphin in bulimia nervosa. *American Journal of Psychiatry, 149,* 1086–1090.

Brewin, C. R. (2014). Episodic memory, perceptual memory, and their interaction: Foundations for a theory of posttraumatic stress disorder. *Psychological Bulletin, 140,* 69–97.

Brewin, C. R., Andrews, B., & Valentine, J. D. (2000). Metaanalysis of risk factors for posttraumatic stress disorder in trauma-exposed adults. *Journal of Consulting and Clinical Psychology, 68,* 748–766.

Brewin, C. R., & Holmes, E. A. (2003). Psychological theories of posttraumatic stress disorder. *Clinical Psychology Review, 23,* 339–376.

Brewin, C. R., Kleiner, J. S., Vasterling, J. J., & Field, A. P. (2007). Memory for emotionally neutral information in posttraumatic stress disorder: A meta-analytic investigation. *Journal of Abnormal Psychology, 116,* 448–463.

Brezo, J., Paris, J., & Turecki, G. (2006). Personality traits as correlates of suicidal ideation, suicide attempts, and suicide completions: A systematic review. *Acta Psychiatrica Scandinavica, 113,* 180–206.

Brickman, A. S., McManus, M., Grapentine, W. L., & Alessi, N. (1984). Neuropsychological assessment of seriously delinquent adolescents. *Journal of the American Academy of Child Psychiatry, 23,* 453–457.

Bridge, J. A., Iyengar, S., Salary, C. B., et al. (2007). Clinical response and risk for reported suicidal ideation and suicide attempts in pediatric antidepressant treatment: A meta-analysis of randomized controlled trials. *Journal of the American Medical Association, 297,* 1683–1696.

Briere, J., Scott, C., & Weathers, F. (2005). Peritraumatic and persistent dissociation in the presumed etiology of PTSD. *American Journal of Psychiatry, 162,* 2295–2301.

Britton, J., Grillon, C., Lissek, S., Norcross, M. A., Szuhany, K. L., Chen, G., et al. (2013). Response to learned threat: An fMRI study in adolescent and adult anxiety. *American Journal of Psychiatry, 170.*

Bromet, E., Andrade, L. H., Hwang, I., Sampson, N. A., Alonso, J., de Girolamo, G., et al. (2011). Cross-national epidemiology of DSM-IV major depressive episode. *BMC Medicine, 9,* 90.

Brook, M., & Kosson, D. S. (2013). Impaired cognitive empathy in criminal psychopathy: Evidence from a laboratory measure of empathic accuracy. *Journal of Abnormal Psychology, 122,* 156–166.

Brookes, K., Mill, J., Guindalini, C., Curran, S., Xu, X., Knight, J., Chen, C. K., Huang, Y. S., Sentha, V., Taylor, E., Chen, W., Breen, G., & Asherson, P. (2006). A common haplotype of the dopamine transporter gene associated with attention-deficit/hyperactivity disorder and interacting with maternal use of alcohol during pregnancy. *Archives of General Psychiatry, 63,* 74–81.

Brooks, M. (2004). *Extreme measures: The dark visions and bright ideas of Francis Galton.* London: Bloomsbury.

Brooks, S., Prince, A., Stahl, D., Campbell, I. C., & Treasure, J. (2011). A systematic review and meta-analysis of cognitive bias to food stimuli in people with disordered eating behaviour. *Clinical Psychology Review, 31,* 37–51.

Brosh, A. (2013). *Hyperbole and a half: Unfortunate situations, flawed coping mechanisms, mayhem, and other things that happened.* New York: Simon and Schuster.

Brotto, L. A., & Luria, M. (2014). Sexual interest/arousal disorder in women. In Y. M. Binik & K. S. K. Hall (Eds.), *Principles and practice of sex therapy* (5th ed., pp. 17–41). New York: Guilford Press.

Brown, A. S. (2011). The environment and susceptibility to schizophrenia. *Progress in Neurobiology, 93,* 23–58.

Brown, A. S., & Derkits, E. J. (2010). Prenatal infections and schizophrenia: A review of epidemiologic and translational Studies. *American Journal of Psychiatry, 167,* 261–280.

Brown, A. S., Begg, M. D., Gravenstein, S., Schaefer, C. A., Wyatt, R. J., Bresnahan, M., Babulas, V. P., & Susser, E. S. (2004). Serologic evidence of prenatal influenza in the etiology of schizophrenia. *Archives of General Psychiatry, 61,* 774–780.

Brown, A. S., Bottiglieri, T., Schaefer, C. A., Quesenberry, C. P., Jr., Liu, L., Bresnahan, M., & Susser, E. S. (2007). Elevated prenatal homocysteine levels as a risk factor for schizophrenia. *Archives of General Psychiatry, 64,* 31–39.

Brown, A. S., Schaefer, C. A., Quesenberry, C. P., Jr., Liu, L., Babulas, V. P., & Susser, E. S. (2005). Maternal exposure to toxoplasmosis and risk of schizophrenia in adult offspring. *American Journal of Psychiatry, 162,* 767–773.

Brown, D., Scheflin, A. W., & Whitfield, C. L. (1999). Recovered memories: The current weight of the evidence in science and in the courts. *Journal of Psychiatry and the Law, 27,* 5–156.

Brown, G. K., Beck, A. T., Steer, R. A., & Grisham, J. R. (2000). Risk factors for suicide in psychiatric outpatients: A 20-year prospective study. *Journal of Consulting and Clinical Psychology, 68,* 371–377.

Brown, G. K., Henriques, G. R., Ratto, C., & Beck, A. T. (2002). *Cognitive therapy treatment manual for suicide attempters.* Philadelphia: University of Pennsylvania.

Brown, G. K., Ten Have, T., Henriques, G. R., Xie, S. X., Hollander, J. E., & Beck, A. T. (2005). Cognitive therapy for the prevention of suicide attempts. *Journal of the American Medical Association, 294,* 563–570.

Brown, G. W., & Andrews, B. (1986). Social support and depression. In R. Trumbull & M. H. Appley (Eds.), *Dynamics of stress: Physiological, psychological, and Social perspectives* (pp. 257–282). New York: Plenum.

Brown, G. W., & Harris, T. O. (1978). *The Bedford College lifeevents and difficulty schedule: directory of contextual threat of events.* London: Bedford College University of London.

Brown, G. W., & Harris, T. O. (1989). Depression. In T. O. Harris & G. W. Brown (Eds.), *Life events and illness* (pp. 49–93). New York: Guilford Press.

Brown, G. W., & Harris, T. O. (1989). *Life events and illness.* New York: Guilford Press.

Brown, G. W., Bone, M., Dalison, B., & Wing, J. K. (1966). *Schizophrenia and social care.* London: Oxford University Press.

Brown, R. J., Cardena, E., Nijenhuis, E., Sar, V., & Van der Hart, O. (2007). Should conversion disorder be reclassified as dissociative disorder in DSM-5? *Psychosomatics, 48,* 369–378.

Brown, S. A., Vik, P. W., McQuaid, J. R., Patterson, T. L., Irwin, M. R., et al. (1990). Severity of psychosocial stress and outcome of alcoholism treatment. *Journal of Abnormal Psychology, 99,* 344–348.

Brown, T. A. (2007). Temporal course and structural relationships among dimensions of temperament and DSM-IV anxiety and mood disorder constructs. *Journal of Abnormal Psychology, 116,* 313-328.

Brown, T. A., Campbell, L. A., Lehman, C. L., Grisham, J. R., & Mancill, R. B. (2001). Current and lifetime comorbidity of the DSM-IV anxiety and mood disorders in a large clinical sample. *Journal of Abnormal Psychology, 110,* 585–599.

Brownell, K. D., & Horgen, K. B. (2003). *Food fight: The inside story of the food industry, America's obesity crisis, and what we can do about it.* Chicago: Contemporary Books.

Bruce, M. L., Ten Have, T. R., Reynolds III, C. F., Katz, I. I., Schulberg, H. C., Mulsant, B. H., et al. (2004). Reducing suicidal ideation and depressive symptoms in depressed older primary care patients. *Journal of the American Medical Association, 291,* 1081–1091.

Brugha, T. S., & Cragg, D. (1990). The list of threatening experiences: The reliability and validity of a brief life events questionnaire. *Acta Psychiatrica Scandinavica, 82,* 77-81.

Bryant, R. A. (2011). Acute stress disorder as a predictor of posttraumatic stress disorder: A systematic review. *Journal of Clinical Psychiatry, 72,* 233–239.

Bryant, R. A., Creamer, M., O'Donnell, M. L., Silove, D., & McFarlane, A. C. (2008). A multisite study of the capacity of acute stress disorder diagnosis to predict posttraumatic stress disorder. *Journal of Clinical Psychiatry, 69,* 923–929.

Bryant, R. A., Mastrodomenico, J., Felmingham, K. L., Hopwood, S., Kenny, L., Kandris, E., et al. (2008). Treatment of acute stress disorder: A randomized controlled trial. *Archives of General Psychiatry, 65,* 659–667.

Bryant, R. A., & McConkey, K. M. (1989). Visual conversion disorder: A case analysis of the influence of visual information. *Journal of Abnormal Psychology, 98,* 326–329.

Bryant, R. A., Sackville, T., Dang, S. T., Moulds, M., & Guthrie, R. (1999). Treating acute stress disorder: An evaluation of cognitive behavior therapy and supporting counseling techniques. *American Journal of Psychiatry, 156,* 1780–1786.

Buchanan, J. A., Christenson, A., Houlihan, D., & Ostrom, C. (2011). The role of behavior analysis in the rehabilitation of persons with dementia. *Behavior Therapy, 42,* 9–21.

Buchanan, R. W., Vladar, K., Barta, P. E., & Pearlson, G. D. (1998). Structural evaluation of the prefrontal cortex in schizophrenia. *American Journal of Psychiatry, 155,* 1049–1055.

Buchsbaum, M. S., Kessler, R., King, A., Johnson, J., & Cappelletti, J. (1984). Simultaneous cerebral glucography with positron emission tomography and topographic electroencephalography. In G. Pfurtscheller, E. J. Jonkman & F. H. L. d. Silva (Eds.), *Brain ischemia: Quantitative EEG and imaging techniques.* Amsterdam: Elsevier.

Budge, S. L., Moore, J. T., Del Re, A. C., Wampold, B. E., Baardseth, T. P., & Nienhuis, J. B. (2013). The effectiveness of evidence-based treatments for personality disorders when comparing treatment-as-usual and bona fide treatments. *Clinical Psychology Review, 33,* 1057–1066.

Budney, A. J., Moore, B. A., Rocha, H. L., & Higgens, S. T. (2006). Clinical trial of abstinence-based vouchers and cognitive behavior therapy for *Cannabis* dependence. *Journal of Consulting and Clinical Psychology, 74,* 307–316.

Buhlmann, U., Glaesmer, H., Mewes, R., Fama, J. M., Wilhelm, S., Brähler, E., et al. (2010). Updates on the prevalence of body dysmorphic disorder: A population-based survey. *Psychiatry Research, 178,* 171–175.

Bukalo, O., Pinard, C., & Holmes, A. (2014, in press). Mechanisms to medicines: Elucidating neural and molecular substrates of fear extinction to identify novel treatments for anxiety disorders. *British Journal of Pharmacology.*

Bulik, C. M., & Reichborn-Kjennerud, T. (2003). *Medical morbidity in binge eating disorder.* Published online in Wiley InterScience (http://www.interscience.wiley.com).

Bulik, C. M., Sullivan, P. F., Wade, T. D., & Kendler, K. S. (2000). Twin studies of eating disorders: A review. *International Journal of Eating Disorders, 27,* 1–20.

Bulik, C. M., Wade, T. D., & Kendler, K. S. (2000). Characteristics of monozygotic twins discordant for bulimia nervosa. *International Journal of Eating Disorders, 29,* 1–10.

Bullen, C., Howe, C., Laugesen, M., McRobbie, H., Parag, V., Williman, J., & Walker, N. (2013). Electronic cigarettes for smoking cessation: a randomised controlled trial. *The Lancet, 382*(9905), 1629–1637.

Bullers, S., Cooper, M. L., & Russell, M. (2001). Social network drinking and adult alcohol involvement: A longitudinal exploration of the direction of influence. *Addictive Behaviors, 26,* 181–199.

Burke, B. L., Arkowitz, H., & Menchola, M. (2003). The efficacy of motivational interviewing: A meta-analysis of controlled clinical trials. *Journal of Consulting and Clinical Psychology, 71,* 843–861.

Burne, S. M., & McLean, N. J. (2002). The cognitive behavioral model of bulimia nervosa: A direct evaluation. *International Journal of Eating Disorders, 31,* 17–31.

Burri, A., & Spector, T. (2011). Recent and lifelong sexual dysfunction in a female UK population sample: Prevalence and risk factors. *Journal of Sexual Medicine, 8,* 2420–2430.

Burris, K. D., Molski T. F., Xu, C., Ryan, E., Tottori, K., Kikuchi, T., Yocca F. D., & Molinoff, P. B. (2002). Aripiprazole, a novel antipsychotic, is a high-affinity partial agonist at human dopamine D2 receptors. *Journal of Pharmacology and Experimental Therapeutics, 302,* 381–389.

Burt, S. A. (2009). Are there meaningful etiological differences within antisocial behavior? Results of a meta-analysis. *Clinical Psychology Review, 29*(2), 163–178.

Bushman, B. J., & Cooper, H. M. (1990). Effects of alcohol on human aggression: An integrative research review. *Psychological Bulletin, 107,* 341–354.

Bushman, B. J., & Thomaes, S. (2011). When the narcissistic ego deflates, narcissistic aggression inflates. In W. K. Campbell & J. D. Miller (Eds.), *The handbook of narcissism and narcissistic personality disorder: Theoretical approaches, empirical findings, and treatments* (pp. 319-329). Hoboken, NJ: Wiley Press.

Butcher, J. N., Dahlstrom, W. G., Graham, J. R., Tellegen, A., & Kraemer, B. (1989). *Minnesota Multiphasic Personality Inventory-2: Manual for administration and scoring.* Minneapolis: University of Minnesota Press.

Butzlaff, R. L., & Hooley, J. M. (1998). Expressed emotion and psychiatric relapse: A meta-analysis. *Archives of General Psychiatry, 55,* 547–553.

Buvat, J., Maggi, M., Gooren, L., Guay, A. T., Kaufman, J., Morgentaler, A., et al. (2010). Endocrine aspects of male sexual dysfunctions. *Journal of Sexual Medicine, 7,* 1627–1656.

Byrd, A. L., & Manuck, S. B. (2014). MAOA, childhood maltreatment, and antisocial behavior: Meta-analysis of a gene-environment interaction. *Biological Psychiatry, 75,* 9–17.

Cadoret, R. J., Yates, W. R., Troughton, E., Woodworth, G., & Stewart, M. A. (1995). Adoption study demonstrating two genetic pathways to drug abuse. *Archives of General Psychiatry, 52,* 42–52.

Cahalan, S. (2012). *Brain on fire: My month of madness.* New York: Free Press.

Cahill, K., Stead, L., & Lancaster, T. (2007). Nicotine receptor partial agonists for smoking cessation. *Cochrane Database of Systematic Reviews,* CD006103.

Caldwell, M. B., Brownell, K. D., & Wilfley, D. (1997). Relationship of weight, body dissatisfaction, and self-esteem in African American and white female dieters. *International Journal of Eating Disorders, 22,* 127–130.

Calhoun, V. D., Pekar, J. J., & Pearlson, G. D. (2004). Alcohol intoxication effects on simulated driving: Exploring alcohol-dose effects on brain activation using functional MRI. *Neuropsychopharmacology, 29,* 2197–2107.

Calvin, C. M., Deary, I. J., Fenton, C., Roberts, B. A., Der, G., Leckenby, N., & Batty, G. D. (2010). Intelligence in youth and all-cause-mortality: systematic review with meta-analysis. *International Journal of Epidemiology, 40,* 626–644.

Camí, J., & Farré, M. (2003). Drug addiction. *New England Journal of Medicine, 349,* 975–986.

Campbell, J., Stefan, S., & Loder, A. (1994). Putting violence in context. *Hospital and Community Psychiatry, 45,* 633.

Campbell, M., Armenteros, J. L., Malone, R. P., Adams, P. B., Eisenberg, Z. W., & Overall, J. E. (1997). Neurolepticrelated dyskinesias in autistic children: A prospective, longitudinal study. *Journal of the American Academy of Child and Adolescent Psychiatry, 36,* 835–843.

Campbell, W. K., Bosson, J. K., Goheen, T. W., Lakey, C. E., & , & Kernis, M. H. (2007). Do narcissists dislike themselves "deep down inside"? *Psychological Science, 18,* 227–229.

Camus, V., Burtin, B., Simeone, I., Schwed, P., Gonthier, R., & Dubos, G. (2000). Factor analysis supports the evidence of existing hyperactive and hypoactive subtypes of delirium. *International Journal of Geriatric Psychiatry, 15,* 313–316.

Canivez, G. L., & Watkins, M. W. (1998). Long-term stability of the Wechsler Intelligence Scale for Children (3rd ed.). *Psychological Assessment, 10,* 285–291.

Cannon, T. D., Cadenhead, K., Cornblatt, B., Woods, S. W., Addington, J., Walker, E. F, Seidman, L. J., Perkins, D., Tsuang, M., McGlashan, T., & Heinssen, R. (2008). Prediction of psychosis in youth at high clinical risk: a multisite longitudinal study in North America. *Archives of General Psychiatry, 65,* 28–37.

Cannon, T. D., Kaprio, J., Lonnqvist, J., Huttunen, M., & Koskenvuo, M. (1998). The genetic epidemiology of schizophrenia in a Finnish twin cohort: A population-based modeling study. *Archives of General Psychiatry, 55,* 67–74.

Cannon, T. D., & Mednick, S. A. (1993). The schizophrenia high-risk project in Copenhagen: Three decades of progress. *Acta Psychiatrica Scandanavica, 87,* 33–47.

Cannon, T. D., van Erp, T. G., Rosso, I. M., et al. (2002). Fetal hypoxia and structural brain abnormalities in schizophrenic patients, their siblings, and controls. *Archives of General Psychiatry, 59,* 35–42.

Cantor, J. M., Blanchard, R., Robichaud, L. K., & Christensen, B. K. (2005). Quantitative reanalysis of aggregate data on IQ in sexual offenders. *Psychological Bulletin, 131,* 555–568.

Capaldi, D. M., & Patterson, G. R. (1994). Interrelated influences of contextual factors on antisocial behavior in childhood and adolescence for males. In D. C. Fowles, P. Sutker & S. H. Goodman (Eds.), *Progress in experimental personality and psychopathology research* (pp. 165–198). New York: Springer-Verlag.

Capps, L., Losh, M., & Thurber, C. (2000). "The frog ate the bug and made his mouth sad": Narrative competence in children with autism. *Journal of Abnormal Child Psychology, 28,* 193–204.

Capps, L., Rasco, L., Losh, M., & Heerey, E. (1999). *Understanding of self-conscious emotions in high-functioning children with autism.* Paper presented at the Biennial Meeting of the Society for Research In Child Development, Albuquerque, NM.

Capps, L., Yirmiya, N., & Sigman, M. (1992). Understanding of simple and complex emotion in high-functioning children with autism. *Journal of Child Psychology and Psychiatry, 33,* 1169–1182.

Capron, A. M. (1999). Ethical and human rights issues in research on mental disorders that may affect decision-making capacity. *New England Journal of Medicine, 340,* 1430–1434.

Cardno, A. G., Marshall, E. J., Coid, B., Macdonald, A. M., Ribchester, T. R., et al. (1999). Heritability estimates for psychotic disorders: The Maudsley Twin Psychosis Series. *Archives of General Psychiatry, 56,* 162–170.

Carey, B. (2011, June 23). Expert on mental illness reveals her own fight, *New York Times.*

Carey, K. B., Carey, M. P., Maisto, S. A., & Henson, J. M. (2006). Brief motivational interventions for heavy college drinkers: A randomized controlled trial. *Journal of Consulting and Clinical Psychology, 74,* 943–954.

Carlsson, A., Hanson, L. O., Waters, N., & Carlsson, M. L. (1999). A glutamatergic deficiency model of schizophrenia. *British Journal of Psychiatry, 174,* 2–6.

Carlson, G. A., & Meyer, S. E. (2006). Phenomenology and diagnosis of bipolar disorder in children, adolescents, and adults: Complexities and developmental issues. *Development and Psychopathology 18,* 939–969.

Carpenter, W. T., Gold, J. M., Lahti, A. C., Queern, C. A., Conley, R. R., Bartko, J. J., Kovnick, J., & Appelbaum, P. S. (2000). Decisional capacity for informed consent in schizophrenia research. *Archives of General Psychiatry, 57,* 533–538.

Carpenter, W. T., & van Os, J. (2011). Should attenuated psychosis syndrome be a DSM-5 diagnosis? *American Journal of Psychiatry, 168,* 460–463.

Carr, D. (2008). *The night of the gun: A reporter investigates the darkest story of his life. His own.* New York: Simon & Schuster Adult Publishing Group.

Carr, E. G., Levin, L., McConnachie, G., Carlson, J. I., Kemp, D. C., & Smith, C. E. (1994). *Communication based intervention for problem behavior.* Baltimore: Paul H. Brookes.

Carrasco, J. L., Dyaz-Marsa, M., Hollander, E., Cesar, J., & Saiz-Ruiz, J. (2000). Decreased monoamine oxidase activity in female bulimia. *European Neuropsychopharmacology, 10,* 113–117.

Carroll, K. M., Ball, S. A., Nich, C., et al. (2001). Targeting behavioral therapies to enhance naltrexone treatment of opioid dependence: Efficacy of contingency management and significant other involvement. *Archives of General Psychiatry, 58,* 755–761.

Carroll, K. M., Easton, C. J., Nich, C., Hunkele, K. A., Neavins, T. M. et al. (2006). The use of contingency management and motivational/skills-building therapy to treat young adults with marijuana dependence. *Journal of Consulting and Clinical Psychology, 74,* 955–966.

Carroll, K. M., Kiluk, B. D., Nich, C., Gordon, M. A., Portnoy, G. A., Marino, D. R., & Ball, S. A. (2014). Computer-assisted delivery of cognitive-behavioral therapy: efficacy and durability of CBT4CBT among cocaine-dependent individuals maintained on methadone. *American Journal of Psychiatry, 171*(4), 436–444.

Carroll, K. M., Rounsaville, B. J., Gordon, L. T., Nich, C., Jatlow, P., Bisighini, R. M., & Gawin, F. H. (1994). Psychotherapy and pharmacotherapy for ambulatory cocaine abusers. *Archives of General Psychiatry, 51,* 177–187.

Carroll, K. M., Rounsaville, B. J., Nich, C., Gordon, L. T., & Gawin, F. (1995). Integrating psychotherapy and pharmacotherapy for cocaine dependence: Results from a randomized clinical trial. In L. S. Onken, J. D. Blaine & J. J. Boren (Eds.), *Integrating behavioral therapies with medications in the treatment of drug dependence* (pp. 19–36). Rockville, MD: National Institute on Drug Abuse.

Carstensen, L. L. (1996). Evidence for a life-span theory of socioemotional selectivity. *Current Directions in Psychological Science, 4,* 151–156.

Carter, C. S., Bullmore, E. T., & Harrison, P. (2014). Is there a flame in the brain in psychosis? *Biological Psychiatry, 75*(4), 258–259.

Carter, F. A., McIntosh, V. V. W., Joyce, P. R., Sullivan, P. F., & Bulik, C. M. (2003). Role of exposure with response prevention in cognitive-behavioral therapy for bulimia nervosa: Three-year follow-up results. *International Journal of Eating Disorders, 33,* 127–135.

Carter, J. S., & Garber, J. (2011). Predictors of the first onset of a major depressive episode and changes in depressive symptoms across adolescence: stress and negative cognitions. *Journal of Abnormal Psychology, 120,* 779–796.

Carvalheira, A. A., Brotto, L. A., & Leal, I. (2010). Women's motivations for sex: Exploring the Diagnostic and Statistical Manual, fourth edition, text revision criteria for hypoactive sexual desire and female sexual arousal disorders. *Journal of Sexual Medicine, 7,* 1454–1463.

Carvalho, J., & Nobre, P. (2010). Biopsychosocial determinants of men's sexual desire: Testing an integrative model. *Journal of Sexual Medicine, 8,* 754-763.

Carver, C. S., Johnson, S. L., & Joormann, J. (2008). Serotonergic function, two-mode models of self-regulation, and vulnerability to depression: What depression has in common with impulsive aggression. *Psychological Bulletin, 134,* 912–943.

Caselli, R. J., & Yaari, R. (2008). Medical management of frontotemporal dementia. *American Journal of Alzheimer's Disease and Other Dementias, 22,* 489–498.

Casey, J. E., Rourke, B. P., & Del Dotto, J. E. (1996). Learning disabilities in children with attention deficit disorder with and without hyperactivity. *Child Neuropsychology, 2,* 83–98.

Caspi, A., Hariri, A. R., Holmes, A., Uher, R., & Moffitt, T. E. (2010). Genetic sensitivity to the environment:The case of the serotonin transporter gene and its implications for studying complex diseases and traits. *American Journal of Psychiatry, 167,* 509–527.

Caspi, A., Houts, R. M., Belsky, D. W., et al. (2014). The p factor: One general psychopathology factor in the structure of psychiatric disorders? *Clinical Psychological Science, 2*(2), 119–137.

Caspi, A., McClay, J., Moffitt, T. E., Mill, J., Martin, J., Craig, I. W., Taylor, A., & Poulton, R. (2002). Role of genotype in the cycle of violence in maltreated children. *Science, 297,* 851–854.

Caspi, A., Moffitt, T. E., Cannon, M., McClay, J., Murray, R., Harrington, H., Taylor, A., Arseneault, L., Williams, B., Braithwaite, A., Pulton, R., & Craig, I. W. (2005). Moderation of the effect of adolescent-onset *Cannabis* use on adult psychosis by a functional polymorphism in the catechol-O-methyltransferase gene: Longitudinal evidence of a gene–environment interaction. *Biological Psychiatry, 57,* 1117–1127.

Caspi, A., Sugden, K., Moffitt, T. E., Taylor, A., Craig, I. W., Harrington, H., et al. (2003). Influence of life stress on depression: Moderation by a polymorphism in the 5-HTT gene. *Science, 301,* 386–389.

Castellanos, F. X., Lee, P. P., Sharp, W., Jeffries, N. O., Greenstein, D. K., et al. (2002). Developmental trajectories of brain volume abnormalities in children and adolescents with attention-deficit/hyperactivity disorder. *Journal of the American Medical Association, 288,* 1740–1748.

Castells, X., Casas, M., Vidal, X., Bosch, R., Roncero, C., Ramos-Quiroga, J. A., et al. (2007). Efficacy of CNS stimulant treatment for cocaine dependence. A systematic review and meta-analysis of randomized controlled clinical trials. *Addiction, 102,* 1871–1887.

Celebucki, C. C., Wayne, G. F., Connolly, G. N., Pankow, J. F., & Chang, E. I. (2005). Characterization of measured menthol in 48 U.S. cigarette sub-brands. *Nicotine and Tobacco Research, 7,* 523–531.

Centers for Disease Control and Prevention. (2006). Homicides and suicides—National violent death reporting system, United States, 2003–2004. *American Journal of Medicine, 296,* 506–510.

Centers for Disease Control and Prevention (CDC). (2009). Prevalence of autism spectrum disorders—Autism and developmental disabilities monitoring network, 2006. *MMWR, 58,* 1–20.

Centers for Disease Control and Prevention. (2009). *Sexually transmitted disease surveillance, 2008.* Atlanta, GA.

Centers for Disease Control and Prevention. (2014). *HIV Surveillance Report: Diagnoses of HIV infection and AIDS in the United States and dependent areas, 2011.* Atlanta: CDC Retrieved from http://www.cdc.gov/hiv/surveillance/resources/reports.

Centers for Disease Control and Prevention (CDC). (2013). Vital Signs: Current cigarette smoking among adults aged ≥18 years with mental illness—United States, 2009–2011. *MMWR, 62,* 81–87.

Centers for Disease Control and Prevention (CDC). (2014). Prevalence of autism spectrum disorder among children aged 8 Years—Autism and developmental disabilities monitoring network, 11 sites, United States, 2010. *MMWR, 63*(SS02), 1–21.

Cerny, J. A., Barlow, D. H., Craske, M. G., & Himadi, W. G. (1987). Couples treatment of agoraphobia: A two year follow-up. *Behavior Therapy, 18,* 401–415.

Chabris, C. F., Lee, J. J., Benjamin, D. J., Beauchamp, J. P., Glaeser, E. L., Borst, G., et al. (2013). Why it is hard to find genes associated with social science traits: Theoretical and empirical considerations. *American Journal of Public Health, 103 Suppl 1,* S152–166.

Chaffin, M., Silovsky, J. F., & Vaughn, C. (2005). Temporal concordance of anxiety disorders and child sexual abuse: implications for direct versus artifactual effeects of sexual abuse. *Journal of Clinical Child and Adolescent Psychology, 34,* 210–222.

Chambless, D. L., Caputo, G. C., Bright, P., & Gallagher, R. (1984). Assessment of fear of fear in agoraphobics: The body sensations questionnaire and the agoraphobic cognitions questionnaire. *Journal of Consulting and Clinical Psychology, 52,* 1090–1097.

Chambless, D. L., & Ollendick, T. H. (2001). Empirically supported psychological interventions: Controversies and evidence. *Annual Review of Psychology, 52,* 685–716.

Chang, S. M., Hahm, B., Lee, J., Shin, M. S., Jeon, H. J., Hong, J., et al. (2008). Cross-national difference in the prevalence of depression caused by the diagnostic threshold. *Journal of Affective Disorders, 106,* 159–167.

Chard, K. M. (2005). An evaluation of cognitive processing therapy for the treatment of posttraumatic stress disorder related to childhood sexual abuse. *Journal of Consulting and Clinical Psychology, 73,* 965–971.

Charuvastra, A., & Cloitre, M. (2008). Social bonds and posttraumatic stress disorder. *Annual Review of Psychology, 59,* 301–328.

Chase, A. (1980). *The legacy of Malthus.* Urbana: University of Illinois Press.

Chassin, L., Curran, P. J., Hussong, A. M., & Colder, C. R. (1996). The relation of parent alcoholism to adolescent substance abuse: A longitudinal follow-up. *Journal of Abnormal Psychology, 105,* 70–80.

Chassin, L., Pitts, S. C., DeLucia, C., & Todd, M. (1999). A longitudinal study of children of alcoholics: Predicting young adult substance use disorders, anxiety, and depression. *Journal of Abnormal Psychology, 108,* 106–119.

Chavira, D. A., Stein, M. B., & Malcarne, V. L. (2002). Scrutinizing the relationship between shyness and social phobia. *Journal of Anxiety Disorders, 16,* 585–598.

Chen, C. H., Suckling, J., Lennox, B. R., Ooi, C., & Bullmore, E. T. (2011). A quantitative meta-analysis of fMRI studies in bipolar disorder. *Bipolar Disorders, 13,* 1–15.

Chen, S., Boucher, H. C., Andersen, S. M., & Saribay, S. A. (2013). *Transference and the relational self.* New York: Oxford University Press.

Chen, S., Boucher, H. C., & Parker Tapias, M. (2006). The relational self revealed: Integrative conceptualization and implications for interpersonal life. *Psychological Bulletin, 132,* 151–179.

Chesney, E., Goodwin, G. M., & Fazel, S. (2014). Risks of all-cause and suicide mortality in mental disorders: a meta review. *World Psychiatry, 13,* 153–160.

Chiao, J. Y., & Blizinsky, K. D. (2010). Culture-gene coevolution of individualism-collectivism and the serotonin transporter gene. *Proceedings of the Royal Society B, 277,* 529–537.

Chiao, J. Y., & Blizinsky, K. D. (2013). Population disparities in mental health: Insights from cultural neuroscience. *American Journal of Public Health, 103*(S1), S122–S132.

Chivers, M. L., Seto, M. C., Lalumiere, M. L., Laan, E., & Grimbos, T. (2010). Agreement of self-reported and genital measures of sexual arousal in men and women: A meta-analysis. *Archives of Sexual Behavior, 39,* 5–56.

Chorpita, B. F., Brown, T. A., & Barlow, D. H. (1998). Perceived control as a mediator of family environment in etiological models of childhood anxiety. *Behavior Therapy, 29,* 457–476.

Chorpita, B. F., Vitali, A. E., & Barlow, D. H. (1997). Behavioral treatment of choking phobia in an adolescent: An experimental analysis. *Journal of Behavior Therapy and Experimental Psychiatry, 28,* 307–315.

Christakis, N., & Fowler, J. (2008). The collective dynamics of smoking in a large social network. *New England Journal of Medicine, 358,* 2249–2258.

Chronis, A. M., Jones, H. A., & Raggi, V. L. (2006). Evidence-based psychosocial treatments for children and adolescents with attention-deficit/hyperactivity disorder. *Clinical Psychology Review, 26,* 486–502.

Chronis-Tuscano, A., Degnan, K. A., Pine, D. S., Perez-Edgar, K., Henderson, H. A., Diaz, Y., et al. (2009). Stable early maternal report of behavioral inhibition predicts lifetime social anxiety disorder in adolescence. *Journal of the American Academy of Child and Adolescent Psychiatry, 48,* 928–935.

Chu, J. A., Frey, L. M., Ganzel, B. L., & Matthews, J. A. (2000). Memories of childhood abuse: Dissociation, amnesia, and corroboration. *American Journal of Psychiatry, 156,* 749–755.

Cicero, T. J., Ellis, M. S., Surratt, H. L., & Kurtz, S. P. (2014). The changing face of heroin use in the United States: A retrospective analysis of the past 50 years. *Journal of the American Medical Association, Psychiatry, 71,* 821-826

Cimbora, D. M., & McIntosh, D. N. (2003). Emotional responses to antisocial acts in adolescent males with conduct disorder: A link to affective morality. *Journal of Clinical Child and Adolescent Psychology, 32,* 296–301.

Cinciripini, P. M., Lapitsky, L. G., Wallfisch, A., Mace, R., Nezami, E., & Van Vunakis, H. (1994). An evaluation of a multicomponent treatment program involving scheduled smoking and relapse prevention procedures: Initial findings. *Addictive Behaviors, 19,* 13–22.

Cipriani, A., Pretty, H., Hawton, K., & Geddes, J. R. (2005). Lithium in the prevention of suicidal behavior and all-cause mortality in patients with mood disorders: A systematic review of randomized trials. *American Journal of Psychiatry, 162,* 1805–1819.

Cisler, J. M., & Koster, E. H. (2010). Mechanisms of attentional biases towards threat in anxiety disorders: An integrative review. *Clinical Psychology Review, 30,* 203–216.

Clark, A. W., Thompson, D. G., Graham, D., & Cooper, J. M. (2014). Engineering DNA binding sites to assemble and tune plasmonic nanostructures. *Advanced materials, 26,*4286-4292.

Clark, D. A. (1997). Twenty years of cognitive assessment: Current status and future directions. *Journal of Consulting and Clinical Psychology, 65,* 996–1000.

Clark, D. A. (2006). *Cognitive-Behavioral Therapy for OCD.* New York: Guilford Press.

Clark, D. M. (1996). Panic disorder: From theory to therapy. In P. M. Salkovskis (Ed.), *Frontiers of Cognitive Therapy* (pp. 318–344). New York: Guilford Press.

Clark, D. M. (1997). Panic disorder and social phobia. In D. M. Clark & C. G. Fairburn (Eds.), *Science and practice of cognitive behaviour Therapy* (pp. 121–153). Oxford, UK: Oxford University Press.

Clark, D. M., Ehlers, A., Hackmann, A., McManus, F., Fennell, M., Grey, N., et al. (2006). Cognitive therapy versus exposure and applied relaxation in social phobia: A randomized controlled trial. *Journal of Consulting and Clinical Psychology, 74,* 568–578.

Clark, D. M., Ehlers, A., McManus, F., Hackmann, A., Fennell, M., Campbell, H., et al. (2003). Cognitive therapy versus fluoxetine in generalized social phobia: A randomized control trial. *Journal of Consulting and Clinical Psychology, 71,* 1058–1067.

Clark, D. M., Salkovskis, P. M., Hackmann, A., Wells, A., Ludgate, J., & Gelder, M. (1999). Brief cognitive therapy for panic disorder: A randomized controlled trial. *Journal of Consulting and Clinical Psychology, 67,* 583–589.

Clark, D. M., & Wells, A. (1995). A cognitive model of social phobia. In R. Heimberg, M. R. Liebowitz, D. A. Hope & F. R. Schneier (Eds.), *Social phobia: Diagnosis, assessment and treatment* (pp. 69–93). New York: Guilford Press.

Clark, L. A., & Livesley, W. J. (2002). Two approaches to identifying the dimensions of personality disorder: Convergence on the five-factor model. In T. A. Widiger & P. T. J. Costa (Eds.), *Personality disorders and the five factor model of personality* (pp. 161–176). Washington, DC: American Psychological Association.

Clarkin, J. F., Levy, K. N., Lenzenweger, M. F., & Kernberg, O. F. (2007). Evaluating three treatments for borderline personality disorder: A multiwave study. *American Journal of Psychiatry, 164,* 922–928.

Cleckley, H. (1976). *The mask of sanity* (5th ed.). St. Louis: Mosby.

Cloitre, M., Courtois, C. A., Charuvastra, A., Carapezza, R., Stolbach, B. C., & Green, B. L. (2011). Treatment of complex PTSD: Results of the ISTSS expert clinician survey on best practices. *Journal of Traumatic Stress, 24,* 615–627.

Cloitre, M., Stovall-McClough, K. C., Nooner, K., Zorbas, P., Cherry, S., Jackson, C. L., et al. (2010). Treatment for PTSD related to childhood abuse: A randomized controlled trial. *American Journal of Psychiatry, 167,* 915–924.

Cloninger, R. C., Martin, R. L., Guze, S. B., & Clayton, P. L. (1986). A prospective follow-up and family study of somatization in men and women. *American Journal of Psychiatry, 143,* 713–714.

Coe, C. L., Kramer, M., Kirschbaum, C., Netter, P., & Fuchs, E. (2002). Prenatal stress diminishes cytokine production after an endotoxin challenge and induces glucocorticoid resistance in juvenile rhesus monkeys. *Journal of Clinical Endocrinology and Metabolism, 87,* 675–681.

Coe, C. L., & Lubach, G. R. (2005). Prenatal origins of individual variation in behavior and immunity. *Neuroscience and Biobehavioral Reviews, 25,* 39–49.

Coe, C. L., Lubach, G. R., & Schneider, M. L. (1999). Neuromotor and socioemotional behavior in the young monkey is presaged by prenatal conditions. In M. Lewis & D. Ramsay (Eds.), *Soothing and stress* (pp. 19–38). Mahwah, NJ: Lawrence Erlbaum Associates.

Cohen, D. (2014). *A big fat crisis: The hidden forces behind the obesity epidemic and how we can end it.* New York: Nation Books.

Cohen, J. A., Deblinger, E., Mannarino, A. P., & Steer, R. (2004). A multi-site, randomized controlled trial for children with abuse-related PTSD symptoms. *Journal of the American Academy of Child and Adolescent Psychiatry, 43,* 393–402.

Cohen, P. (2008, February 21). Midlife suicide rises, puzzling researchers, *New York Times,* pp. 1–4.

Cohen, R. M., Nordahl, T. E., Semple, W. E., Andreason, P., et al. (1997). The brain metabolic patterns of clozapine and fluphenazine-treated patients with schizophrenia during a continuous performance task. *Archives of General Psychiatry, 54,* 481–486.

Cohen, S., Frank, E., Doyle, W. J., Rabin, B. S., et al. (1998). Types of stressors that increase susceptibility to the common cold in healthy adults. *Health Psychology, 17,* 214–223.

Coie, J. D., & Dodge, K. A. (1998). Aggression and antisocial behavior. In W. Damon & N. Eisenberg (Eds.), *Handbook of child psychology: Volume 3: Social, emotional and personality development* (pp. 779–862). New York: John Wiley & Sons.

Cole, D. A., Ciesla, J. A., Dallaire, D. H. et al. (2008). Emergence of attributional style and its relations to depressive symptoms. *Journal of Abnormal Psychology, 117,* 16–31.

Cole, D. A., Martin, J. M., Peeke, L. G., Seroczynski, A. D., & Hoffman, K. (1998). Are cognitive errors of underestimation predictive or reflective of depressive symptoms in children? A longitudinal study. *Journal of Abnormal Psychology, 107,* 481–496.

Cole, D. A., Martin, J. M., Powers, B., & Truglio, R. (1990). Modeling causal relations between academic and social competence and depression: A multitrait-multimethod longitudinal study of children. *Journal of Abnormal Psychology, 105,* 258–270.

Cole, M. G. (2004). Delirium in elderly patients. *American Journal of Geriatric Psychiatry, 12,* 7–21.

Collin, G., Kahn, R. S., de Reus, M. A., Cahn, W., & van den Heuvel, M. P. (2014). Impaired rich club connectivity in unaffected siblings of schizophrenia patients. *Schizophrenia Bulletin, 40*(2), 438–448.

Colom, F., Vieta, E., Reinares, M., Martinez-Aran, A., Torrent, C., Goikolea, J. M., & Gasto, C. (2003). Psychoeducation efficacy in bipolar disorders: Beyond compliance enhancement. *Journal of Clinical Psychiatry, 64,* 1101–1105.

Colombo, C., Benedetti, F., Barbini, B., Campori, E. et al. (1999). Rate of switch from depression into mania after therapeutic sleep deprivation in bipolar depression. *Psychiatry Research, 86,* 267–270.

Colombo, C., Benedetti, F., Barbini, B., Campori, E., & Smeraldi, E. (1999). Rate of switch from depression into mania after therapeutic sleep deprivation in bipolar depression. *Psychiatry Research, 86,* 267–270.

Comer, S. D., Hart, C. L., Ward, A. S., Haney, M., Foltin, R. W., & Fischman, M. W. (2001). Effects of repeated oral methamphetamine administration in humans. *Psychopharmacology, 155,* 397–404.

Compas, B. E., Haaga, D. A. F., Keefe, F. J., Leitenberg, H., & Williams, D. A. (1998). Sampling of empirically supported psychological treatments from health psychology: Smoking, chronic pain, cancer, and bulimia nervosa. *Journal of Consulting and Clinical Psychology, 66,* 89–112.

Compton, D. R., Dewey, W. L., & Martin, B. R. (1990). *Cannabis* dependence and tolerance production. *Advances in Alcohol and Substance Abuse, 9,* 129–147.

Conceicao do Rosario-Campos, M., Leckman, J. F., Mercadante, M. T., Shavitt, R. G., Prado, H. S., Sada, P., et al. (2001). Adults with early-onset obsessive-compulsive disorder. *American Journal of Psychiatry, 158,* 1899–1903.

Conduct Problems Prevention Research Group. (2010a). The difficulty of maintaining positive intervention effects: A look at disruptive behavior, deviant peer relations, and social skills during the middle school years. *Journal of Early Adolescence, 30*(4).

Conduct Problems Prevention Research Group. (2010b). Fast track intervention effects on youth arrests and delinquency. *Journal of Experimental Criminology, 6*(2), 131–157.

Conduct Problems Prevention Research Group. (2011). The effects of the fast track preventive intervention on the development of conduct disorder across childhood. *Child Development, 82*(1), 331–345.

Conley, R. R., Love, R. C., Kelly, D. L., & Bartko, J. J. (1999). Rehospitalization rates of patients recently discharged on a regimen of risperidone or clozapine. *American Journal of Psychiatry, 156,* 863–868.

Conley, R. R., & Mahmoud, R. (2001). A randomized double-blind study of risperidone and olanzapine in the treatment of schizophrenia or schizoaffective disorder. *American Journal of Psychiatry, 158,* 765–774.

Constantino, J. N., Zhang, Z., Frazier, T., Abbachi, A. M., & Law, P. (2010). Sibling recurrence and the genetic epidemiology of autism. *American Journal of Psychiatry, 167,* 1349–1356.

Cook, M., & Mineka, S. (1989). Observational conditioning of fear to fear-relevant versus fear-irrelevant stimuli in rhesus monkeys. *Journal of Abnormal Psychology, 98,* 448–459.

Cooper, M. L., Frone, M. R., Russell, M., & Mudar, P. (1995). Drinking to regulate positive and negative emotion: A motivational model of alcoholism. *Journal of Personality and Social Psychology, 69,* 961–974.

Cooper, M. S., & Clark, V. P. (2013). Neuroinflammation, neuroautoimmunity, and the co-morbidities of complex regional pain syndrome. *Journal of Neuroimmune Pharmacology, 8,* 452–469.

Copeland, W. E., Angold, A., Costello, E. J., & Egger, H. (2013). Prevalence, comorbidity, and correlates of DSM-5 proposed disruptive mood dysregulation disorder. *American Journal of Psychiatry, 170*(2), 173–179.

Copolov, D. L., Mackinnon, A., & Trauer, T. (2004). Correlates of the affective impact of auditory hallucinations in psychotic disorders. *Schizophrenia Bulletin, 30,* 163–171.

Corrigan, P. W., & Watson, A. C. (2005). Findings from the National Comorbidity Survey on the frequency of violent behavior in individuals with psychiatric disorders. *Psychiatry Research, 136,* 153–162.

Corrigan, P. W., Watson, A. C., Heyrman, J. D., Warpinski, A., Gracia, G., Slopen, N., & Hall, L. L. (2005). Structural stigma in state legislatures. *Psychiatric Services, 56,* 557–563.

Cortese, S., Kelly, C., Chabernaud, C., Proal, E., Di Martino, A., Milham, M. P., & Castellanos, F. X. (2012). Toward systems neuroscience of ADHD: a meta-analysis of 55 fMRI studies. *American Journal of Psychiatry, 169*(10), 1038–1055.

Coryell, W., & Schlesser, M. (2001). The dexamethasone suppression test and suicide prevention. *Archives of General Psychiatry, 158,* 748–753.

Costa, P. T., Metter, E. J., & McCrae, R. R. (1994). Personality stability and its contribution to successful aging. *Journal of Geriatric Psychiatry, 27,* 41–59.

Costello, J. E., Erkanli, A., & Angold, A. (2006). Is there an epidemic of child or adolescent depression? *Journal of Child Psychology and Psychiatry, 47*(12), 1263–1271.

Courchesne, E. (2004). Brain development in autism: Early overgrowth followed by premature arrests of growth. *Mental Retardation and Developmental Disabilities Research Reviews, 10,* 106–111.

Courchesne, E., Carnes, B. S., & Davis, H. R. (2001). Unusual brain growth patterns in early life in patients with autistic disorder: An MRI study. *Neurology, 57,* 245–254.

Courchesne, E., Carper, R., & Akshoomoff, N. (2003). Evidence of brain overgrowth in the first year of life in autism. *Journal of the American Medical Association, 290,* 337–344.

Cox, B. J., Clara, I. P., & Enns, M. W. (2002). Posttraumatic stress disorder and the structure of common mental disorders. *Depression and Anxiety, 15,* 168–171.

Coyne, J. C. (1976). Depression and the response of others. *Journal of Abnormal Psychology, 85,* 186–193.

Coyne, J. C. (1994). Self-reported distress: Analog or ersatz depression? *Psychological Bulletin, 116,* 29–45.

Craske, M. G., & Barlow, D. H. (2001). Panic disorder and agoraphobia. In D. H. Barlow (Ed.), *Clinical Handbook of Psychological Disorders* (pp. 1–59). New York: Guilford Press.

Craske, M. G., Kircanski, K., Zelikowsky, M., Mystkowski, J., Chowdhury, N., & Baker, A. (2008). Optimizing inhibitory learning during exposure therapy. *Behaviour Research and Therapy, 46,* 5–27.

Craske, M. G., Maidenberg, E., & Bystritsky, A. (1995). Brief cognitive-behavioral versus nondirective therapy for panic disorder. *Journal of Behavior Therapy and Experimental Psychiatry, 26,* 113–120.

Craske, M. G., & Mystkowski, J. (2006). Exposure therapy and extinction: Clinical studies. In M. G. Craske, D. Hermans & D. Vansteenwegen (Eds.), *Fear and learning from basic processes to clinical implications* (pp. 217–233). Washington DC: American Psychological Association.

Craske, M. G., Rauch, S. L., Ursano, R., Prenoveau, J., Pine, D. S., & Zinbarg, R. E. (2009). What is an anxiety disorder? *Depression and Anxiety, 26,* 1066–1085.

Creamer, M., Burgess, P., & McFarlane, A. C. (2001). Posttraumatic stress disorder: Findings from the Aus-tralian national survey of mental health and well-being. *Psychological Medicine, 31,* 1237–1247.

Crean, R. D., Crane, N. A., & Mason, B. J. (2011). An evidence based review of acute and long-term effects of *Cannabis* use on executive cognitive functions. *Journal of Addictive Medicines, 5*(1), 1–8.

Critchley, H. D., Daly, E. M., Bullmore, E. T., Williams, S. C. R., Van Amelsvoort, T., Robertson, D. M., Rowe, A., Phillips, M., McAlonan, G., Howlin, P., & Murphy, D. G. M. (2001). The functional neuroanatomy of social behaviour: Changes in cerebral blood flow when people with autistic disorder process facial expressions. *Brain, 123,* 2203–2212.

Crits-Christoph, P., & Barber, J. P. (2002). Psychological treatments for personality disorders. In P. E. Nathan & J. M. Gorman (Eds.), *A guide to treatments that work.* New York: Oxford University Press.

Crits-Christoph, P., Chambless, D. L., Frank, E., Brody, C., et al. (1995). Training in empirically validated treatments: What are clinical psychology students learning? *Professional Psychology: Research and Practice, 26,* 514–522.

Critser, G. (2003). *Fatland: How Americans became the fattest people in the world.* Boston: Houghton Mifflin.

Cronbach, L. J., & Meehl, P. E. (1955). Construct validity in psychological tests. *Psychological Bulletin, 52,* 281–302.

Cross-Disorder Group of the Psychiatric Genomics Consortium. (2013). Identification of risk loci with shared effects on five major psychiatric disorders: a genome-wide analysis. *The Lancet, 381*(9875), 1371–1379.

Cross-Disorder Group of the Psychiatric Genomics Consortium. (2013). Identification of risk loci with shared effects on five major psychiatric disorders: A genome-wide analysis. *The Lancet, 381,* 1371–1379.

Crow, S. J., Peterson, C. B., Swanson, S. A., Raymond, N. C., Specker, S., Eckert, E. D., & Mitchell, J. E. (2009). Increased mortality in bulimia nervosa and other eating disorders. *American Journal of Psychiatry, 166,* 1342–1346.

Crozier, J. C., Dodge, K. A., Griffith, R. et al. (2008). Social information processing and cardiac predictors of adolescent antisocial behavior. *Journal of Abnormal Psychology, 117,* 253–267.

Cruts, M., Gijselinck, I., van der Zee, J., Engelborghs, S., Wils, H., Pirici, D., et al. (2006). Null mutations in progranulin cause ubiquitin-positive frontotemporal dementia linked to chromosome 17q21. *Nature, 442,* 920–924.

Cuellar, A. K., Johnson, S. L., & Winters, R. (2005). Distinctions between bipolar and unipolar depression. *Clinical Psychology Review, 25,* 307–339.

Cuijpers, P., Sijbrandij, M., Koole, S. L., Andersson, G., Beekman, A. T., & Reynolds, C. F. (2013). The efficacy of psychotherapy and pharmacotherapy in treating depressive and anxiety disorders: a meta-analysis of direct comparisons. *World Psychiatry, 12,* 137–148.

Cummings, C. M., Caporino, N. E., & Kendall, P. C. (2014). Comorbidity of anxiety and depression in children and adolescents: 20 years after. *Psychological Bulletin, 140*(3), 816–845.

Curcic-Blake, B., Liemburg, E., Vercammen, A., Swart, M., Knegtering, H., Bruggeman, R., & Aleman, A. (2013). When Broca goes uninformed: reduced information flow to Broca's area in schizophrenia patients with auditory hallucinations. *Schizophrenia Bulletin, 39*(5), 1087–1095.

Curry, J. F. (2001). Specific psychotherapies for childhood and adolescent depression. *Biological Psychiatry, 49,* 1091–1100.

Curry, J., Silva, S., Rohde, P., Ginsburg, G., Kratochvil, C., Simons, A., Kirchner, J., May, D., Kennard, B., et al. (2011). Recovery and recurrence following treatment for adolescent major depression. *Archives of General Psychiatry, 68,* 263–270.

Curry, S. J., Mermelstein, R. J., & Sporer, A. K. (2009). Therapy for specific problems: youth tobacco cessation. *Annual Review of Psychology, 60,* 229–255.

Curtin, J. J., Lang, A. R., Patrick, C. J., & Strizke, W. G. K. (1998). Alcohol and fear-potentiated startle: The role of competing cognitive demands in the stress-reducing effects of intoxication. *Journal of Abnormal Psychology, 107,* 547–557.

Curtis, L. H., Ostbye, T., Sendersky, V., Hutchison, S., Dans, P. E., Wright, A., et al. (2004). Inappropriate prescribing for elderly Americans in a large outpatient population. *Archives of Internal Medicine, 164,* 1621–1625.

Dalenberg, C. J., Brand, B. L., Gleaves, D. H., Dorahy, M. J., Loewenstein, R. J., Cardena, E., et al. (2012). Evaluation of the evidence for the trauma and fantasy models of dissociation. *Psychological Bulletin, 138,* 550–588.

Daley, S. E., Hammen, C., & Rao, U. (2000). Predictors of first onset and recurrence of major depression in young women during the 5 years following high school graduation. *Journal of Abnormal Psychology 109,* 525–533.

Dallery, J., Silverman, K., Chutuape, M. A., Bigelow, G. E., & Stitzer, M. (2001). Voucher-based reinforcement of opiate plus cocaine abstinence in treatment-resistant methadone patients: Effects of reinforcer magnitude. *Experimental and Clinical Psychopharmacology, 9,* 317–325.

Dallman, M. F., Pecoraro, N., Akana, S. F., La Fleur, S. E., Gomez, F., Houshyar, H., Bell, M. E., Bhatnagar, S., Laugero, K. D., & Manalo, S. (2003). Chronic stress and obesity: A new view of comfort food. *Proceedings of the National Academy of Sciences, 100,* 11696–11701.

Dalmau, J., Tüzün, E., Wu, H. Y., Masjuan, J., Rossi, J. E., Voloschin, A., et al. (2007). Paraneoplastic anti-N-methyl-D-aspartate receptor encephalitis associated with ovarian teratoma. *Annals of Neurology, 61*(1), 25–36.

Dandeneau, S. D., Baldwin, M. W., Baccus, J. R., Sakellaropoulo, M., & Pruessner, J. C. (2007). Cutting stress off at the pass: Reducing vigilance and responsiveness to social threat by manipulating attention. *Journal of Personality and Social Psychology, 93,* 651–666.

Dannlowski, U., Kugel, H., Franke, F., Stuhrmann, A., Hohoff, C., Zwanzger, P., et al. (2011). Neuropeptide-S (NPS) receptor genotype modulates basolateral amygdala responsiveness to aversive stimuli. *Neuropsychopharmacology, 36,* 1879–1885.

Dantzer, R., O'Connor, J. C., Freund, G. G., Johnson, R. W., & Kelley, K. W. (2008). From inflammation to sickness and depression: when the immune system subjugates the brain. *Nature Reviews Neuroscience, 9,* 46–56.

Davidson, R. J., Pizzagalli, D., & Nitschke, J. B. (2002). The representation and regulation of emotion in depression: Perspectives from affective neuroscience. In C. L. Hammen & I. H. Gotlib (Eds.), *Handbook of Depression* (pp. 219–244). New York: Guilford Press.

Davies, D. K., Stock, S. E., & Wehmeyer, M. (2003). Application of computer simulation to teach ATM access to individuals with intellectual disabilities. *Education and Training in Developmental Disabilities, 38,* 451–456.

Davila, J., Hammen, C. L., Burge, D., Paley, B., & Daley, S. E. (1995). Poor interpersonal problem solving as a mechanism of stress generation in depression among adolescent women. *Journal of Abnormal Psychology, 104,* 592–600.

Davis A. S., Malmberg, A., Brandt, L., Allebeck, P., & & Lewis, G. (1997). IQ and risk for schizophrenia: A population-based cohort study. *Psychological Medicine, 27*, 1311–1323.

Davis, J. M. (1978). Dopamine theory of schizophrenia: A two-factor theory. In L. C. Wynne, R. L. Cromwell & S. Matthysse (Eds.), *The nature of schizophrenia*. New York: John Wiley & Sons.

Davis, J. M., Chen, N., & Glick, I. D. (2003). A meta-analysis of the efficacy of second-generation antipsychotics. *Archives of General Psychiatry, 60*, 553–564.

Davis, K. L., Kahn, R. S., Ko, G., & Davidson, M. (1991). Dopamine and schizophrenia: A review and reconceptualization. *American Journal of Psychiatry, 148*, 1474–1486.

Davis, L., & Siegel, L. J. (2000). Posttraumatic stress disorder in children and adolescents: A review and analysis. *Clinical Child and Family Psychology Review, 3*, 135–153.

Davis, M. C., Matthews, K. A., & Twamley, E. W. (1999). Is life more difficult on Mars or Venus? A meta-analytic review of sex differences in major and minor life events. *Annals of Behavioral Medicine, 21*, 83–97.

Davis, P. (2002, August 18, 2002). The faces of Alzheimer's. *Time Magazine*.

Davis, T. E., May, A., & Whiting, S. E. (2011). Evidence-based treatment of anxiety and phobia in children and adolescents: Current status and effects on the emotional response. *Clinical Psychology Review, 31*, 592–602.

Davison, T. E., McCabe, M., & Mellor, D. (2009). An examination of the "gold standard" diagnosis of major depression in aged-care settings. *American Journal of Geriatric Psychiatry, 17*, 359–367.

Dawson, G., Toth, K., Abbott, R., Osterling, J., Munson, J., Estes, A., & Liaw, J. (2004). Early social attention impairments in autism: Social orienting, joint attention, and attention to distress. *Developmental Psychology, 40*, 271–283.

Dawson, M. E., Schell, A. M., & Banis, H. T. (1986). Greater resistance to extinction of electrodermal responses conditioned to potentially phobic CSs: A noncognitive process? *Psychophysiology, 23*, 552–561.

De Cuypere, G., Tsjoen, G., Beerten, R., Selvaggi, G., De Sutter, P., Hoebeke, P., et al. (2005). Sexual and physical health after sex reassignment surgery. *Archives of Sexual Behavior, 34*, 679–690.

de Graaf, R., Bijl, R. V., Ravelli, A., Smit, F., & Vollenbergh, W. A. M. (2002). Predictors of first incidence of DSM-III-R psychiatric disorders in the general population: Findings from the Netherlands mental health survey and incidence study. *Acta Psychiatrica Scandinavica, 106*, 303–313.

De Souza, E. B., Battaglia, G., & Insel, T. L. (1990). Neurotoxic effect of MDMA on brain serotonin neurons: Evidence from neurochemical and radioligand binding studies. *Annual Proceedings of the New York Academy of Science, 600*, 682–697.

de Wit, H., & Zacny, J. (2000). Abuse potential of nicotine replacement therapies. In K. J. Palmer (Ed.), *Smoking Ccessation* (pp. 79–92). Kwai Chung, Hong Kong: Adis International Publications.

Deacon, B. J., & Abramowitz, J. S. (2004). Cognitive and behavioral treatments for anxiety disorders: A review of meta-analytic findings. *Journal of Clinical Psychology, 60*, 429–441.

Deary, I. J., & Johnson, W. (2010). Intelligence and education: Causal perceptions drive analytic processes and therefore conclusions. *International Journal of Epidemiology, 39*, 1362–1369.

deCharms, R. C., Maeda, F., Glover, G. H., Ludlow, D., Pauly, J. M., Soneji, D., et al. (2005). Control over brain activation and pain learned by using real-time functional MRI. *Proceedings of the National Academy of Sciences of the United States of America, 102*, 18626–18631.

Deep, A. L., Lilenfeld, L. R., Plotnicov, K. H., Pollice, C., & Kaye, W. H. (1999). Sexual abuse in eating disorder subtypes and control women: The role of cormorbid substance dependence in bulimia nervosa. *International Journal of Eating Disorders, 25*, 1–10.

DeJong, W., & Kleck, R. E. (1986). The social psychological effects of overweight. In C. P. Herman, M. P. Zanna & E. T. Higgins (Eds.), *Physical Appearance, Stigma, and Social Behavior*. Hillside, NJ: Lawrence Erlbaum.

deLint, J. (1978). Alcohol consumption and alcohol problems from an epidemiological perspective. *British Journal of Alcohol and Alcoholism, 17*, 109–116.

Dell, P. F. (2006). A new model of dissociative identity disorder. *Psychiatric Clinics of North America, 29*, 1–26, vii.

Della Femina, D., Yeager, C. A., & Lewis, D. O. (1990). Child abuse: adolescent records vs. adult recall. *Child Abuse and Neglect, 14*, 227–231.

Demyttenaere, K., Bruffaerts, R., Posada-Villa, J., Gasquet, I., Kovess, V., Lepine, J. P., et al. (2004). Prevalence, severity, and unmet need for treatment of mental disorders in the World Health Organization World Mental Health Surveys. *Journal of the American Medical Association, 291*, 2581–2590.

Depression Guidelines Panel. (1993). Depression in primary care: Treatment of major depression. Clinical practice guideline No. 5. (Vol. 2). Rockville, MD: U.S. Department of Health and Human Services, Public Health Service, Agency for Health Care Policy and Research.

Depue, R. A., Collins, P. F., & Luciano, M. (1996). A model of neurobiology: Environment interaction in developmental psychopathology. In M. F. Lenzenweger & J. J. Haugaard (Eds.), *Frontiers of Developmental Psychopathology* (pp. 44–76). New York: Oxford University Press.

Depue, R. A., & Iacono, W. G. (1989). Neurobehavioral aspects of affective disorders. *Annual Review of Psychology, 40*, 457–492.

Derogatis, L. R., & Burnett, A. L. (2008). The epidemiology of sexual dysfunctions. *Journal of Sexual Medicine, 5*, 289–300.

DeRubeis, R. J., & Crits-Christoph, P. (1998). Empirically supported individual and group psychological treatments for adult mental disorders. *Journal of Consulting and Clinical Psychology, 66*, 37–52.

Deserno, L., Sterzer, P., Wustenberg, T., Heinz, A., & Schlagenhauf, F. (2012). Reduced prefrontal-parietal effective connectivity and working memory deficits in schizophrenia. *Journal of Neuroscience, 32*(1), 12–20.

Di Forti, M., Sallis H., Allegri, F., Trotta, A., Ferraro L., Stilo, S. A., et al. (2013). Daily use, especially of high-potency *Cannabis*, drives the earlier onset of psychosis in *Cannabis* users. *Schizophrenia Bulletin*, doi: 10.1093/schbul/sbt181

Dick, D. M., Pagan, J. L., Viken, R., Purcell, S., Kaprio, J., Pulkinnen, L., et al. (2007). Changing environmental influencec on substance use across development. *Twin Research and Human Genetics, 10*, 315–326.

Dickerson, S. S., Gruenewald, T. L., & Kemeny, M. E. (2009). Psychobiological responses to social self threat: Functional or detrimental? *Self and Identity, 8*, 270–285.

Dickerson, S. S., & Kemeny, M. E. (2004). Acute stressors and cortisol responses: A theoretical integration and synthesis of laboratory research. *Psychological Bulletin, 130*, 355–391.

Dickey, C. C., McCarley, R. W., & Shenton, M. E. (2002). The brain in schizotypal personality disorder: A review of structural MRI and CT findings. *Harvard Review of Psychiatry, 10*, 1–15.

Dickstein, D. P., & Leibenluft, E. (2006). Emotion regulation in children and adolescents: Boundaries between normalcy and bipolar disorder. *Development and Psychopathology, 18*, 1105–1131.

Didie, E. R., Menard, W., Stern, A. P., & Phillips, K. A. (2008). Occupational functioning and impairment in adults with body dysmorphic disorder. *Comprehensive Psychiatry, 49*, 561–569.

Dieserud, G., Roysamb, E., Braverman, M. T., Dalgard, O. S., & Ekeberg, O. (2003). Predicating repetition of suicide attempt: A prospective study of 50 suicide attempters. *Archives of Suicide Research, 7*, 1–15.

DiLillo, D., Giuffre, D., Tremblay, G. C., & Peterson, L. (2001). A closer look at the nature of intimate partner violence reported by women with a history of child sexual abuse. *Journal of Interpersonal Violence, 16*, 116–132.

Dimidjian, S., Barrera, M., Martell, C., Muñoz, R. F., & Lewinsohn, P. M. (2011). The origins and current status of behavioral activation treatments for depression. *Annual Review of Clinical Psychology, 7*, 1–38.

Diniz, B. S., Butters, M. A., Albert, S. M., Dew, M. A., & Reynolds, C. F., III. (2013). Late-life depression and risk of vascular dementia and Alzheimer's disease: Systematic review and meta-analysis of community-based cohort studies. *The British Journal of Psychiatry: The Journal of Mental Science, 202*, 329–335.

Dishion, T. J., & Andrews, D. W. (1995). Preventing escalation in problem behaviors with high-risk young adolescents: Immediate and 1-year outcomes. *Journal of Consulting and Clinical Psychology, 63*, 538–548.

Dishion, T. J., Patterson, G. R., & Kavanagh, K. A. (1992). An experimental test of the coercion model: Linking theory, measurement, and intervention. In J. McCord & R. E. Tremblay (Eds.), *Preventing Antisocial Behavior* (pp. 253–282). New York: Guilford Press.

Disner, S. G., Beevers, C. G., Lee, H.-J., Ferrell, R. E., Hariri, A. R., & Telch, M. J. (2013). War zone stress interacts with the 5-HTTLPR polymorphism to predict the development of sustained attention for negative emotion stimuli in soldiers returning from Iraq. *Clinical Psychological Science, 1*, 413–425.

Dixon, L. B., Dickerson, F., Bellack, A. S., Bennett, M., Dickinson, D., Goldberg, R. W., et al. (2010). The 2009 schizophrenia PORT psychosocial treatment recommendations and summary statements. *Schizophrenia Bulletin, 36*, 48–70.

Dobson, K. S., Hollon, S. D., Dimidjian, S., Schmaling, K. B., Kohlenberg, R. J., Gallop, R., et al. (2008). Randomized trial of behavioral activation, cognitive therapy, and antidepressant medication in the prevention of relapse and recurrence in major depression. *Journal of Consulting and Clinical Psychology, 76*, 468–477.

Dodge, K. A., & Frame, C. L. (1982). Social cognitive biases and deficits in aggressive boys. *Child Development, 53*, 620–635.

Dodge, K. A., & Godwin, J. (2013). Social-information-processing patterns mediate the impact of preventive intervention on adolescent antisocial behavior. *Psychological Science, 24*(4), 456–465.

Doerr, P., Fichter, M., Pirke, K. M., & Lund, R. (1980). Relationship between weight gain and hypothalamic-pituitary-adrenal function in patients with anorexia nervosa. *Journal of Steroid Biochemistry, 13*, 529–537.

Dohrenwend, B. P. (2006). Inventorying stressful life events as risk factors for psychopathology: Toward resolution of the problem of intracategory variability. *Psychological Bulletin, 132,* 477–495.

Dohrenwend, B. P., & Dohrenwend, B. S. (1974). Social and cultural influences on psychopathology. *Annual Review of Psychology, 25,* 417–452.

Dohrenwend, B. P., Levav, P. E., Schwartz, S., Naveh, G., Link, B. G., Skodol, A. E., & Stueve, A. (1992). Socioeconomic status and psychiatric disorders: The causation–selection issue. *Science, 255,* 946–952.

Dohrenwend, B. S., Krasnoff, L., Askenasy, A. R., & Dohrenwend, B. P. (1978). Exemplification of method for scaling life events: The PERI life events scale. *Journal of Health and Social Behavior, 19,* 205–229.

Dolder, C. R., Lacro, J. P., Dunn, L. B., & Jeste, D. V. (2002). Antipsychotic medication adherence: Is there a difference between typical and atypical agents? *American Journal of Psychiatry, 159,* 103–108.

Doll, H. A., & Fairburn, C. G. (1998). Heightened accuracy of self-reported weight in bulimia nervosa: A useful cognitive "distortion". *International Journal of Eating Disorders, 24,* 267–273.

Domschke, K., Reif, A., Weber, H., Richter, J., Hohoff, C., Ohrmann, P., et al. (2011). Neuropeptide S receptor gene—Converging evidence for a role in panic disorder. *Molecular Psychiatry, 16,* 938–948.

Domschke, K., Stevens, S., Pfleiderer, B., & Gerlach, A. L. (2010). Interoceptive sensitivity in anxiety and anxiety disorders: An overview and integration of neurobiological findings. *Clinical Psychology Review, 30,* 1–11.

Donner, J., Haapakoski, R., Ezer, S., Melen, E., Pirkola, S., Gratacos, M., et al. (2010). Assessment of the neuropeptide S system in anxiety disorders. *Biological Psychiatry, 68,* 474–483.

Douglas, K. S., Guy, L. S., & Hart, S. D. (2009). Psychosis as a risk factor for violence to others: a meta-analysis. *Psychological Bulletin, 135,* 679–706.

Doyle, P. M., Le Grange, D., Loeb, K., Doyle, A. C., & Crosby, R. D. (2010). Early response to family-based treatment for adolescent anorexia nervosa. *International Journal of Eating Disorders, 43,* 659–662.

Doyon, W. M., Dong, Y., Ostroumov, A., Thomas, A. M., Zhang, T. A., & Dani, J. A. (2013). Nicotine decreases ethanol-induced dopamine signaling and increases self-administration via stress hormones. *Neuron, 79*(3), 530–540.

Draguns, J. G. (1989). Normal and abnormal behavior in cross-cultural perspective: Specifying the nature of their relationships. In J. J. Berman (Ed.), *Nebraska Symposium on Motivation, 1989: Cross-cultural perspectives. Current theory and research in motivation, Vol. 37* (pp. 235-277). Lincoln: University of Nebraska Press.

Drury, V., Birchwood, M., Cochrane, R., & Macmillan, R. (1996). Cognitive therapy and recovery from acute psychosis: A controlled trial. *British Journal of Psychiatry, 169,* 593–601.

Duffy, F. F., West, J. C., Wilk, J., Narrow, W. E., Hales, D., Thompson, J., et al. (2004). Mental health practitioners and trainees. In R. W. Manderscheid & M. J. Henderson (Eds.), *Mental Health, United States, 2002.* Rockville, MD: Substance Abuse and Mental Health Services Administration DHHS Pub No.

Dugas, M. J., Brillon, P., Savard, P., Turcotte, J., Gaudet, A., Ladouceur, R., et al. (2010). A randomized clinical trial of cognitive-behavioral therapy and applied relaxation for adults with generalized anxiety disorder. *Behavior Therapy, 41,* 46–58.

Dugas, M. J., Marchand, A., & Ladouceur, R. (2005). Further validation of a cognitive-behavioral model of generalized anxiety disorder: Diagnostic and symptom specificity. *Journal of Anxiety Disorders, 19,* 329–343.

Dugger, M., Ritchie, B. G., Ball, J., Pasyuk, E., Adams, G., Anciant, E., et al. (2002). Eta photoproduction on the proton for photon energies from 0.75 to 1.95 GeV. *Physical Review Letters, 89,* 222002.

Duncan, L. E., & Keller, M. C. (2011). A critical review of the first 10 years of candidate gene-by-environment interaction research in psychiatry. *American Journal of Psychiatry, 168*(10), 1041–1049.

Dura, J. R., Stukenberg, K. W., & Kiecolt-Glaser, J. K. (1991). Anxiety and depressive disorders in adult children caring for demented parents. *Psychology and Aging, 6,* 467–473.

Dvoskin, J. A., & Steadman, H. J. (1994). Using intensive case management to reduce violence by mentally ill persons in the community. *Hospital and Community Psychiatry, 45,* 679–684.

Dworkin, R. H., & Lenzenwenger, M. F. (1984). Symptoms and the genetics of schizophrenia: Implications for diagnosis. *American Journal of Psychiatry, 141,* 1541–1546.

Dworkin, R. H., Lenzenwenger, M. F., & Moldin, S. O. (1987). Genetics and the phenomenology of schizophrenia. In P. D. Harvey & E. F. Walker (Eds.), *Positive and negative symptoms of psychosis.* Hillsdale, NJ: Lawrence Erlbaum.

Dwyer-Lindgren, L., Mokdad, A. H., Srebotnjak, T., Flaxman, A. D., Hansen, G. M., & Murray, C. J. (2014). Cigarette smoking prevalence in US counties: 1996–2012. *Population Health Metrics, 12*(1), 5.

Eack, S. M., Greenwald, D. P., Hogarty, S. S., & Keshavan, M. S. (2010). One-year durability of the effects of cognitive enhancement therapy on functional outcome in early schizophrenia. *Schizophrenia Research, 120,* 210–216.

Eardley, I., Donatucci, C., Corbin, J., El-Meliegy, A., Hatzimouratidis, K., McVary, K., et al. (2010). Pharmacotherapy for erectile dysfunction. *Journal of Sexual Medicine, 7,* 524–540.

Eastwood, M. R., & Peter, A. M. (1989). Prospective studies: Infradian mood rhythms and seasonal affective disorder. In C. Thompson & T. Silverstone (Eds.), *Seasonal affective disorder* (pp. 29-36). London: CNS Publishers.

Eddy, K. T., Keel, P. K., Dorer, D. J., Delinksy, S. S., Franko, D. L., & Herzog, D. B. (2002). Longitudinal comparison of anorexia nervosa subtypes. *International Journal of Eating Disorders, 31,* 191–201.

Edenberg, H. J., Xuie, X., Chen, H-J., Tian, H., Weatherill, L. F., Dick, D. M., et al. (2006). Association of alcohol dehydrogenase genes with alcohol dependence: A comprehensive analysis. *Human Molecular Genetics, 15,* 1539–1549.

Edvardsen, J., Torgersen, S., Roysamb, E., Lygren, S., Skre, I., Onstad, S., & Oien, P. A. (2008). Heritability of bipolar spectrum disorders. Unity or heterogeneity? *Journal of Affective Disorders, 106,* 229–240.

Egger, H. L., & Angold, A. (2006). Common emotional and behavioral disorders in preschool children: presentation, nosology, and epidemiology. *Journal of Child Psychology and Psychiatry, 47*(3–4), 313–337.

Ehde, D. M., Dillworth, T. M., & Turner, J. A. (2014). Cognitive-behavioral therapy for individuals with chronic pain: efficacy, innovations, and directions for research. *American Psychologist, 69,* 153–166.

Ehlers, A., Mayou, R. A., & Bryant, B. (1998). Psychological predictors of chronic posttraumatic stress disorder after motor vehicle accidents. *Journal of Abnormal Psychology, 107,* 508–519.

Eisen, J. L., Sibrava, N. J., Boisseau, C. L., Mancebo, M. C., Stout, R. L., Pinto, A., et al. (2013). Five-year course of obsessive-compulsive disorder: Predictors of remission and relapse. *Journal of Clinical Psychiatry, 74,* 233–239.

Elis, O., Caponigro, J. M., & Kring, A. M. (2013). Psychosocial treatments for negative symptoms in schizophrenia: Current practices and future directions. *Clinical Psychology Review, 33*(8), 914–928.

Elkin, I., Shea, M. T., Watkins, J. T., Imber, S. D., Sotsky, S. M., Collins, J. F., et al. (1989). National Institute of Mental Health Treatment of Depression Collaborative Research Program. General effectiveness of treatments. *Archives of General Psychiatry, 46,* 971–982; discussion 983.

Elkins, I., McGue, M., & Iacono, W. (2007). Prospective effects of attention-deficit/hyperactivity disorder, conduct disorder, and sex on adolescent substance use and abuse. *Archives of General Psychiatry, 64,* 1145–1152.

Elkis, H., Friedman, L., Wise, A., & Meltzer, H. T. (1995). Meta-analysis of studies of ventricular enlargement and cortical sulcal prominence in mood disorders. *Archives of General Psychiatry, 52,* 735–746.

Ellenberger, H. F. (1972). The story of "Anna O": A critical review with new data. *Journal of the History of the Behavioral Sciences, 8,* 267–279.

Ellis, A. (1991). The revised ABC's of rational-emotive therapy (RET). *Journal of Rational-Emotive and Cognitive Behavior Therapy, 9,* 139–172.

Ellis, A. (1993). Changing rational-emotive therapy (RET) to rational emotive behavior therapy (REBT). *The Behavior Therapist, 16,* 257–258.

Ellis, A. (1995). Changing rational-emotive therapy (RET) to rational emotive behavior therapy (REBT). *Journal of Rational-Emotive and Cognitive Behavior Therapy, 13,* 85–89.

Ellison-Wright, I., & Bullmore, E. (2009). Meta-analysis of diffusion tensor imaging studies in schizophrenia. *Schizophrenia Research, 108*(1–3), 3–10.

Emery, S., Kim, Y., Choi, Y. K., Szczypka, G., Wakefield, M., & Chaloupka, F. J. (2012). The effects of smoking-related television advertising on smoking and intentions to quit among adults in the United States: 1999–2007. *American Journal of Public Health, 102*(4), 751–757.

Emmelkamp, P. M. G. (2004). Behavior therapy with adults. In M. J. Lambert (Ed.), *Bergin and Garfield's handbook of psychotherapy and behavior change* (5th ed., pp. 393–446). New York: John Wiley & Sons.

Emmelkamp, P. M. G., Benner, A., Kuipers, A., Feiertag, G. A., Koster, H. C., & van Apeldoorn, F. J. (2006). Comparison of brief dynamic and cognitive-behavioural therapies in avoidant personality disorder. *British Journal of Psychiatry, 189,* 60–64.

Engdahl, B., Dikel, T. N., Eberly, R., & Blank, A. (1997). Posttraumatic stress disorder in a community group of former prisoners of war: A normative response to severe trauma. *American Journal of Psychiatry, 154,* 1576–1581.

Enserink, M. (1999). Drug therapies for depression: From MAO inhibitors to substance. *Science, 284,* 239.

Epstein, J. A., Botvin, G. J., & Diaz, T. (2001). Linguistic acculturation associated with higher marijuana and polydrug use among Hispanic adolescents. *Substance Use and Misuse, 36,* 477–499.

Erdberg, P., & Exner, J. E., Jr. (1984). Rorschach assessment. In G. Goldstein & M. Hersen (Eds.), *Handbook of Psychological Assessment.* New York: Pergamon Press.

Erhardt, D., & Hinshaw, S. P. (1994). Initial sociometric impressions of attention-deficit hyperactivity disorder and comparison boys: Predictions from social behaviors and nonverbal behaviors. *Journal of Consulting and Clinical Psychology, 62,* 833–842.

Ermer, E., Cope, L. M., Nyalakanti, P. K., Calhoun, V. D., & Kiehl, K. A. (2012). Aberrant paralimbic gray matter in criminal psychopathy. *Journal of Abnormal Psychology, 121*, 649–658.

Essex, M. J., Klein, M. H., Slattey, M. J., Goldsmith, H. H., & Kalin, N. H. (2010). Early risk factors and developmental pathways to chronic high inhibition and social anxiety disorder in adolescence. *American Journal of Psychiatry, 167*, 40–46.

Etter, J. F., & Bullen, C. (2014). A longitudinal study of electronic cigarette users. *Addictive Behaviors, 39*(2), 491–494.

Evans, R. J. (2001). Social influences in etiology and prevention of smoking and other health threatening behaviors in children and adolescents. In A. Baum, T. A. Revenson & J. E. Singer (Eds.), *Handbook of Health Psychology* (pp. 459–468). Mahwah, NJ: Lawrence Erlbaum.

Everett, F., Proctor, N., & Cartmell, B. (1989). Providing psychological services to American Indian children and families. In D. R. Atkinson, G. Morten & D. W. Sue (Eds.), *Counseling American minorities* (3rd ed.). Dubuque, IA: W. C. Brown.

Exner, J. E. (1978). *The Rorschach: A comprehensive system: Volume 2.* Current research and advanced interpretation. New York: John Wiley & Sons.

Exner, J. E. (1986). *The Rorschach: A comprehensive system: Volume 1. Basic foundations* (2nd ed.). New York: John Wiley & Sons.

Express Scripts Lab. (2014). Turning Attention to ADHD Report:An Express Scripts Report on U.S. Medication Trends for Attention Deficit Hyperactivity Disorder.

Fabrega, H., Jr. (2002). Evolutionary theory, culture and psychiatric diagnosis. In M. Maj & W. Gaebel (Eds.), *Psychiatric diagnosis and classification* (pp. 107–135). New York: John Wiley & Sons.

Fairburn, C. G. (1985). Cognitive-behavioral treatment for bulimia. In D. M. Garner & P. E. Garfinkel (Eds.), *Handbook of psychotherapy for anorexia nervosa and bulimia* (pp. 160-192). New York: Guilford Press.

Fairburn, C. G. (1997). Eating disorders. In D. M. Clark & C. G. Fairburn (Eds.), *Science and practice of cognitive behavior therapy* (pp. 209–243). New York: Oxford University Press.

Fairburn, C. G., Agras, W. S., & Wilson, G. T. (1992). The research on the treatment of bulimia nervosa: Practical and theoretical implications. In G. H. Anderson & S. H. Kennedy (Eds.), *The biology of feast and famine: Relevance to eating disorders* (pp. 317-340). New York: Academic Press.

Fairburn, C. G., Cooper, A., Doll, H. A., O'Connor, M. E., Bohn, K., Hawker, D. M., Wales, J. A., & Palmer, R. L. (2009). Transdiagnostic cognitive-behavioral therapy for patients with eating disorders: A two-site trial with 60-week follow-up. *American Journal of Psychiatry, 166*, 311–319.

Fairburn, C. G., Cooper, Z., Doll, H. A., & Welch, S. L. (1999). Risk factors for anorexia nervosa: Three integrated case-control comparisons. *Archives of General Psychiatry, 56*, 468–478.

Fairburn, C. G., Doll, H. A., Welch, S. L., Hay, P. J., Davies, B. A., & O'Connor, M. E. (1998). Risk factors for binge eating disorder. *Archives of General Psychiatry, 55*, 425–432.

Fairburn, C. G., Jones, R., Peveler, R. C., Carr, S. J., Solomon, R. A., O'Connor, M. E., Burton, J., & Hope, R. A. (1991). Three psychological treatments for bulimia nervosa. *Archives of General Psychiatry, 48*, 463–469.

Fairburn, C. G., Jones, R., Peveler, R. C., Hope, R. A., & O'Connor, M. E. (1993). Psychotherapy and bulimia nervosa: The longer-term effects of interpersonal psychotherapy, behavior therapy, and cognitive therapy. *Archives of General Psychiatry, 50*, 419–428.

Fairburn, C. G., Marcus, M. D., & Wilson, G. T. (1993). Cognitive behaviour therapy for binge eating and bulimia nervosa: A comprehensive treatment manual. In C. G. Fairburn & G. T. Wilson (Eds.), *Binge eating: Nature, assessment, and treatment.* New York: Guilford Press.

Fairburn, C. G., Norman, P. A., Welch, S. L., O'Connor, M. E., Doll, H. A., & Peveler, R. C. (1995). A prospective study of outcome in bulimia nervosa and the long-term effects of three psychological treatments. *Archives of General Psychiatry, 52*, 304–312.

Fairburn, C. G., Shafran, R., & Cooper, Z. (1999). A cognitive behavioural theory of anorexia nervosa. *Behaviour Research and Therapy, 37*, 1–13.

Fairburn, C. G., Stice, E., Cooper, Z., Doll, H. A., Norman, P. A., & O'Connor, M. E. (2003). Understanding persistence in bulimia nervosa: A 5-year naturalistic study. *Journal of Consulting and Clinical Psychology, 71*, 103–109.

Fairburn, C. G., Welch, S. L., Doll, H. A., Davies, B. A., & O'Connor, M. E. (1997). Risk factors for bulimia nervosa: A community-based case-control study. *Archives of General Psychiatry, 54*, 509–517.

Falloon, I. R. H., Boyd, J. L., McGill, C. W., Razani, J., Moss, H. B., & Gilderman, A. N. (1982). Family management in the prevention of exacerbation of schizophrenia: A controlled study. *New England Journal of Medicine, 306*, 1437–1440.

Fals-Stewart, W., O'Farrell, T. J., & Lam, W. K. K. (2009). Behavioral couple therapy for gay and lesbian couples with alcohol use disorders. *Journal of Substance Abuse Treatment, 37*(4), 379–387.

Fanous, A. H., Prescott, C. A., & Kendler, K. S. (2004). The prediction of thoughts of death or self-harm in a population-based sample of female twins. *Psychological Medicine, 34*, 301–312.

Faraone, S. V., Biederman, J., & Mick, E. (2005). The age-dependent decline of attention deficit hyperactivity disorder: A meta-analysis of follow-up studies. *Psychological Medicine, 36*, 159–165.

Faraone, S. V., Biederman, J., Weber, W., & Russell, R. L. (1998). Psychiatric, neuropsychological, and psychosocial features of DSM-IV subtypes of attention-deficit/hyperactivity disorder: Results from a clinically referred sample. *Journal of the American Academy of Child and Adolescent Psychiatry, 37*, 185–193.

Faravelli, C., Salvatori, S., Galassi, F., & Aiazzi, L. (1997). Epidemiology of somatoform disorders: A community survey in Florence. *Social Psychiatry and Psychiatric Epidemiology, 32*, 24–29.

Farina, A. (1976). *Abnormal psychology.* Englewood Cliffs, NJ: Prentice-Hall.

Faustman, W. O., Bardgett, M., Faull, K. F., Pfefferman, A., & Cseransky, J. G. (1999). Cerebrospinal fluid glutamate inversely correlates with positive symptom severity in unmedicated male schizophrenic/schizoaffective patients. *Biological Psychiatry, 45*, 68–75.

Favaro, A., & Santonastaso, P. (1997). Suicidality in eating disorders: Clinical and psychological correlates. *Acta Psychiatrica Scandanavica, 95*, 508–514.

Fazel, S., Gulati, G., Linsell, L., Geddes, J. R., & Grann, M. (2009). Schizophrenia and violence: Systematic review and meta-analysis. *PLoS Medicine,* http://www.plosmedicine.org/article/info%3A-doi%2F10.1371%2Fjournal.pmed.1000120.

Febbraro, G. A. R., & Clum, G. A. (1998). Meta-analytic investigation of the effectiveness of self-regulatory components in the treatment of adult behavior problems. *Clinical Psychology Review, 18*, 143–161.

Feingold, B. F. (1973). *Introduction to clinical allergy.* Springfield, IL: Charles C. Thomas.

Feldman Barrett, L. (2003). So you want to be a social neuroscientist? *APS Observer, 16*, 5–7.

Ferguson, C. P., La Via, M. C., Crossan, P. J., & Kaye, W. H. (1999). Are SSRI's effective in underweight anorexia nervosa? *International Journal of Eating Disorders, 25*, 11–17.

Ferguson, S. B., Shiffman, S., & Gwaltney, C. J. (2006). Does reducing withdrawal severity mediate nicotine patch efficacy? A randomized clinical trial. *Journal of Consulting and Clinical Psychology, 74*, 1153–1161.

Fergusson, D. M., & Horwood, L. J. (2000). Does *Cannabis* use encourage other forms of illicit drug use? *Addiction, 95*, 505–520.

Ferreira, S. T., Clarke, J. R., Bomfim, T. R., & De Felice, F. G. (2014). Inflammation, defective insulin signaling, and neuronal dysfunction in Alzheimer's disease. *Alzheimer's and Dementia: The Journal of the Alzheimer's Association, 10*, S76–83.

Ferri, C. P., Prince, M., Brayne, C., Brodaty, H., & Lyketsos, C. G. (2005). Global prevalence of dementia: A delphi consensus study. *The Lancet, 366*, 2112–2117.

Ferri, M., Amato, L., & Davoli, M. (2008). Alcoholics anonymous and other 12 step programmes for alcohol dependence (review). *Cochrane Database of Systematic Reviews*, Issue 3. Art. No.: CD005032.

Fetkewicz, J., Sharma, V., & Merskey, H. (2000). A note on suicidal deterioration with recovered memory treatment. *Journal of Affective Disorders, 58*, 155–159.

Fetveit, A. (2009). Late-life insomnia: A review. *Geriatrics and Gerontology International, 9*, 220–234.

Feusner, J. D., Phillips, K. A., & Stein, D. J. (2010). Olfactory reference syndrome: Issues for DSM-V. *Depression and Anxiety, 27*, 592–599.

Fiellin, D. A., O'Connor, P. G., Chawarski, M., Pakes, J. P., Pantalon, M. V., & Schottenfeld, R. S. (2001). Methadone maintenance in primary care: A randomized controlled trial. *Journal of the American Medical Association, 286*, 1724–1731.

Fillmore, K. M. (1987). Prevalence, incidence and chronicity of drinking patterns and problems among men as a function of age: A longitudinal and cohort analysis. *British Journal of Addiction, 82*, 77–83.

Fink, H. A., Mac Donald, R., Rutks, I. R., Nelson, D. B., & Wilt, T. J. (2002). Sildenafil for male erectile dysfunction: A systematic review and meta-analysis. *Archives of Internal Medicine, 162*, 1349–1360.

Fink, P., Hansen, M. S., & Sondergaard, L. (2005). Somatoform disorders among first-time referrals to a neurology service. *Psychosomatics, 46*, 540–548.

Finkelhor, D. (1983). Removing the child—prosecuting the offender in cases of sexual abuse: Evidence from the national reporting system for child abuse and neglect. *Child Abuse and Neglect, 7*, 195–205.

Finkelstein, E. A., Graham, W. C., & Malhotra, R. (2014). Lifetime direct medical costs of childhood obesity. *Pediatrics.* doi: 10.1542/peds.2014-0063

Finkelstein, E. A., Trogdon, J. G., Cohen, J. W., & Dietz, W. (2009). Annual medical spending attributable to obesity: Payer- and service-specific estimates. *Health Affairs, 28*, w822–w831.

Finlay-Jones, R. (1989). Anxiety. In G. W. Brown & T. O. Harris (Eds.), *Life events and illness* (pp. 95–112). New York: Guilford Press.

Finney, J. W., & Moos, R. H. (1998). Psychosocial treatments for alcohol use disorders. In P. E. Nathan & J. M. Gorman (Eds.), *A guide to treatments that work* (pp. 156–166). New York: Oxford University Press.

Fiorentine, R., & Hillhouse, M. P. (2000). Exploring the additive effects of drug misuse treatment and Twelve Step involvement: Does Twelve-Step ideology matter? *Substance Use and Misuse, 35*, 367–397.

Fischer, M. (1971). Psychoses in the offspring of schizophrenic monozygotic twins and their normal cotwins. *British Journal of Psychiatry, 118*, 43–52.

Fishbain, D. A., Cutler, R., Rosomoff, H. L., & Rosomoff, R. S. (2000). Evidence-based data from animal and human experimental studies on pain relief with antidepressants: A structured review. *Pain Medicine, 1*, 310–316.

Fisher, J. E. (2011). Understanding behavioral health in late life: Why age matters. *Behavior Therapy, 42*, 143–149.

Fisher, J. E., & Noll, J. P. (1996). Anxiety disorders. In L. L. Carstensen, B. A. Edelstein & L. Dornbrand (Eds.), *The Practical Handbook of Clinical Gerontology* (pp. 304–323). Thousand Oaks, CA: Sage.

Fisher, M., Holland, C., Merzenich, M. M., & Vinogradov, S. (2009). Using neuroplasticity-based auditory training to improve verbal memory in schizophrenia. *American Journal of Psychiatry, 166*, 805–811.

Fishler, K., Azen, C. G., Henderson, R., Friedman, E. G., & Koch, R. (1987). Psychoeducational findings among children treated for phenylketonuria. *American Journal of Mental Deficiency, 92*, 65–73.

Fitzgibbons, M. L., Spring, B., Avellone, M. E., Blackman, L. R., Pingitore, R., & Stolley, M. R. (1998). Correlates of binge eating in Hispanic, black, and white women. *International Journal of Eating Disorders, 24*, 43–52.

Fladung, A., Gron, G., Grammer, K., Herrnberger, B., Schilly, E., Grasteit, S., Wolf, R. C., Walter, H., & von Wietersheim, J. (2010). A neural signature of anorexia nervosa in the ventral striatal reward system. *American Journal of Psychiatry, 167*, 206–212.

Flor, H. (2014). Psychological pain interventions and neurophysiology: implications for a mechanism-based approach. *American Psychologist, 69*, 188–196.

Foa, E. B., & Franklin, M. E. (2001). Obsessive-compulsive disorder. In D. H. Barlow (Ed.), *Clinical handbook of psychological disorders* (pp. 209–263). New York: Guilford Press.

Foa, E. B., Libowitz, M. R., Kozak, M. J., Davies, S., Campeas, R., Franklin, M. E., et al. (2005). Randomized, placebo-controlled trail of exposure and ritual prevention, clomipramine, and their combination in the treatment of obsessive-compulsive disorder. *American Journal of Psychiatry, 162*, 151–161.

Foa, E. B., & Meadows, E. A. (1997). Psychosocial treatments for posttraumatic stress disorder: A critical review. *Annual Review of Psychology, 48*, 449–480.

Foa, E. B., Riggs, D. S., Marsie, E. D., & Yarczower, M. (1995). The impact of fear activation and anger on the efficacy of exposure treatment for posttraumatic stress disorder. *Behavior Therapy, 26*, 487–499.

Fontaine, N. M. G., McCrory, E. J. P., Boivin, M., Moffitt, T. E., & Viding, E. (2011). Predictors and outcomes of joint trajectories of callous-unemotional traits and conduct problems in childhood. *Journal of Abnormal Psychology, 120,*730-742.

Food and Drug Administration. (2005). Deaths with antipsychotics in elderly patients with behavioral disturbances. Public Health Advisory.

Food and Drug Administration. (2008, January 31). Serious health risks with antiepileptic drugs. Public Health Advisory. Available by Web at www.fda.gov/consumer/updates/antiepileptic020508.html.

Forbes, D., Thiessen, E. J., Blake, C. M., Forbes, S. C., & Forbes, S. (2013). Exercise programs for people with dementia. *The Cochrane Database of Systematic Reviews, 12*, CD006489.

Forbes, M. K., & Schniering, C. A. (2013). Are sexual problems a form of internalizing psychopathology? A structural equation modeling analysis. *Archives of Sexual Behavior, 42*, 23–34.

Ford, C. S., & Beach, F. A. (1951). *Patterns of sexual behavior.* New York: Harper and Brothers.

Ford, J. M., Mathalon, D. H., Whitfield, S., Faustman, W. O., & Roth, W. T. (2002). Reduced communication between frontal and temporal lobes during talking in schizophrenia. *Biological Psychiatry, 51*, 485–492.

Forero, D. A., Arboleda, G. H., Vasquez, R., & Arboleda, H. (2009). Candidate genes involved in neural plasticity and the risk for attention-deficit hyperactivity disorder: a meta-analysis of 8 common variants. *Journal of Psychiatry and Neuroscience, 34*(5), 361–366.

Forhan, S. E., Gottlieb, S. L., Sternberg, M. R., Xu, F., Datta, S. D., McQuillan, G. M., et al. (2009). Prevalence of sexually transmitted infections among female adolescents aged 14 to 19 in the United States. *Pediatrics, 124*, 1505–1512.

Foti, D. J., Kotov, R., Guey, L. T., & Bromet, E. J. (2010). *Cannabis* use and the course of schizophrenia: 10-year follow-up after first hospitalization. *American Journal of Psychiatry, 167*, 987–993.

Fournier, J. C., DeRubeis, R. J., Hollon, S. D., Dimidjian, S., Amsterdam, J. D., Shelton, R. C., & Fawcett, J. (2010). Antidepressant drug effects and depression severity: A patient-level meta-analysis. *Journal of the American Medical Association, 303*, 47–53.

Fowler, I. L., Carr, V. J., Carter, N. T., & Lewin, T. J. (1998). Patterns of current and lifetime substance use in schizophrenia. *Schizophrenia Bulletin, 24*, 443–455.

Frackiewicz, E. J., Sramek, J. J., Herrera, J. M., Kurtz, N. M., & Cutler, N. R. (1997). Ethnicity and antipsychotic response. *Annals of Pharmacotherapy, 31*, 1360–1369.

Fraley, R. C., & Shaver, P. R. (2000). Adult romantic attachment: Theoretical developments, emerging controversies, and unanswered questions. *Review of General Psychology, 4*, 132–154.

Frances, A., & Chapman, S. (2013). DSM-5 somatic symptom disorder mislabels medical illness as mental disorder. *Australian and New Zealand Journal of Psychiatry, 47*, 483–484.

Francis, D., Diorio, J., Liu, D., & Meaney, M. J. (1999). Nongenomic transmission across generations of maternal behavior and stress responses in the rat. *Science, 286*, 1155–1158.

Frank, E., Kupfer, D. J., Perel, J. M., Cornes, C., Jarrett, D. B., Mallinger, A. G., et al. (1990). Three-year outcomes for maintenance therapies in recurrent depression. *Archives of General Psychiatry, 47*, 1093–1099.

Frank, E., Kupfer, D. J., Thase, M. E., Mallinger, A. G., Swartz, H. A., Fagiolini, A. M., et al. (2005). Two-year outcomes for interpersonal and social rhythm therapy in individuals with bipolar I disorder. *Archives of General Psychiatry, 62*, 996–1004.

Franklin, J. C., Hessel, E. T., Aaron, R. V., Arthur, M. S., Heilbron, N., & Prinstein, M. J. (2010). The functions of nonsuicidal self-injury: Support for cognitive-affective regulation and opponent processes from a novel psychophysiological paradigm. *Journal of Abnormal Psychology, 119*, 850–862.

Franklin, M. E., & Foa, E. B. (2011). Treatment of obsessive compulsive disorder. *Annual Review of Clinical Psychology, 7*, 229–243.

Franklin, M. E., Sapyta, J., Freeman, J. B., Khanna, M., Compton, S., Almirall, D., et al. (2011). Cognitive behavior therapy augmentation of pharmacotherapy in pediatric obsessive-compulsive disorder: The Pediatric OCD Treatment Study II (POTS II) randomized controlled trial. *Journal of the American Medical Association, 306*(11), 1224–1232.

Franko, D. L., & Keel, P. K. (2006). Suicidality in eating disorders: Occurrence, correlates, and clinical implications. *Clinical Psychology Review, 26*, 769–782.

Franko, D. L., Keshaviah, A., Eddy, K. T., Krishna, M., Davis, M. C., Keel, P. K., & Herzog, D. B. (2013). A longitudinal investigation of mortality in anorexia nervosa and bulimia nervosa. *American Journal of Psychiatry, 170*(8), 917–925.

Frederick, R. I., Mrad, D. F., & DeMier, R. L. (2007). *Examinations of criminal responsibility: Foundations in mental health case law.* Sarasota, FL: Professional Resource Press.

Frederickson, B. L., & Carstensen, L. L. (1990). Choosing social partners: How old age and anticipated endings make people more selective. *Psychology and Aging, 5*, 335–347.

Fredrickson, B. L., & Levenson, R. W. (1998). Positive emotions speed recovery from the cardiovascular sequelae of negative emotions. *Cognition and Emotion, 12*, 191–200.

Fredrickson, B. L., & Roberts, T. A. (1997). Objectification theory: Toward understanding women's lived experience and mental health risks. *Psychology of Women Quarterly, 21*, 173–206.

Freedman, R. (2003). Schizophrenia. *New England Journal of Medicine, 349*, 1738-1749.

Freeman, J., Sapyta, J., Garcia, A., & et al. (2014). Family-based treatment of early childhood obsessive-compulsive disorder: The pediatric obsessive-compulsive disorder treatment study for young children (POTS jr)—a randomized clinical trial. *Journal of the American Medical Association, Psychiatry, 71*(6), 689–698.

Freeston, M. H., Dugas, M. J., & Ladoceur, R. (1996). Thoughts, images worry, and anxiety. *Cognitive Therapy and Research, 20*, 265–273.

Fremouw, W. J., De Perczel, M., & Ellis, T. E. (1990). *Suicide risk: Assessment and response guidelines.* New York: Pergamon Press.

French, S. A., Story, M., Neumark-Sztainer, D., Downes, B., Resnick, M., et al. (1997). Ethnic differences in psychosocial and health behavior correlates of dieting, purging, and binge eating in a population-based sample of adolescent females. *International Journal of Eating Disorders, 22*, 315–322.

Freud, A. (1946/1966). *The ego and mechanisms of defense.* New York: International Universities Press.

Freud, S. (1917/1950). Mourning and melancholia. *Collected papers* (Vol. 4). London: Hogarth and the Institute of Psychoanalysis, 1950.

Frick, P. J., Ray, J. V., Thornton, L. C., & Kahn, R. E. (2014). Can callous-unemotional traits enhance the understanding, diagnosis, and treatment of serious conduct problems in children and adolescents? A comprehensive review. *Psychological Bulletin, 140*(1), 1–57.

Fried, P., Watkinson, B., James, D., & Gray, R. (2002). Current and former marijuana use: Preliminary findings of a longitudinal study of effects on IQ in young adults. *CMAJ, 166*, 887–891.

Frieling, H., Romer, K. D., Scholz, S., Mittelbach, F., Wilhelm, J., De Zwaan, M., et al. (2010). Epigenetic dysregulation of dopaminergic genes in eating disorders. *International Journal of Eating Disorders, 43*, 577–583.

Friend, A., DeFries, J. C., Olson, R. K., & Penningon, B. F. (2009). Heritability of high reading ability and its interaction with parental education. *Behavior Genetics, 39*, 427-436.

Friston, K. J. (1994). Functional and effective connectivity in neuroimaging: A synthesis. *Human Brain Mapping, 2*, 56–78.

Froehlich, T. E., Bogardus, S. T., & Inouye, S. K. (2001). Dementia and race: Are there differences between African Americans and Caucasians? *Journal of the American Gerontological Society, 49*, 477–484.

Frojdh, K., Hakansson, A., Karlsson, I., & Molarius, A. (2003). Deceased, disabled or depressed—A population-based 6-year followup study of elderly people with depression. *Social Psychiatry and Psychiatric Epidemiology, 38*, 557–562.

Fromm-Reichmann, F. (1948). Notes on the development of treatment of schizophrenics by psychoanalytic psychotherapy. *Psychiatry, 11*, 263–273.

Frost, D. O., & Cadet, J.-L. (2000). Effects of methamphetamine-induced toxicity on the development of neural circuitry: A hypothesis. *Brain Research Reviews, 34*, 103–118.

Frost, R. O., & Steketee, G. (2010). *Stuff: Compulsive Hoarding and the Meaning of Things.* New York: Houghton Mifflin Harcourt.

Frost, R. O., Steketee, G., & Greene, K. A. I. (2003). Cognitive and behavioral treatment of compulsive hoarding. *Brief Treatment and Crisis Intervention, 3*, 323–337.

Frost, R. O., Steketee, G., & Tolin, D. F. (2011). Comorbidity in hoarding disorder. *Depression and Anxiety, 28*, 876–884.

Frost, R. O., Steketee, G., & Tolin, D. F. (2012). Diagnosis and assessment of hoarding disorder. *Annual Review of Clinical Psychology, 8*, 219–242.

Frost, R. O., Tolin, D. F., Steketee, G., Fitch, K., & Selbo-Bruns, A. (2009). Excessive acquisition in hoarding. *Journal of Anxiety Disorders, 23*, 632–639.

Frühauf, S., Gerger, H., Schmidt, H. M., Munder, T., & Barth, J. (2013). Efficacy of psychological interventions for sexual dysfunction: A systematic review and meta-analysis. *Archives of Sexual Behavior, 42*, 915–933.

Fuller, R. K. (1988). Disulfiram treatment of alcoholism. In R. M. Rose & J. E. Barrett (Eds.), *Alcoholism: Origins and outcome* (pp. 237–250). New York: Raven Press.

Furnham, A., & Baguma, P. (1994). Cross-cultural differences in the evaluation of male and female body shapes. *International Journal of Eating Disorders, 15*, 81–89.

Gadalla, T., & Piran, N. (2007). Co-occurrence of eating disorders and alcohol use disorders in women: a meta analysis. *Archives of Womens Mental Health, 10*(4), 133–140.

Gale, A., & Edwards, J. A. (Eds.). (1983). *Physiological correlates of human behaviour* (Vol. 3). London: Academic Press.

Gale, C. R., Batty, G. D., Tynelius, P., Deary, I. J., & Rasmussen, F. (2010). Intelligence in early adulthood and subsequent hospitalization for mental disorders. *Epidemiology, 21*, 70–77.

Galea, S., Ahern, J., Resnick, H., Kilpatrick, D., Bucuvalas, M., Gold, J., et al. (2002). Psychological sequelae of the September 11 terrorist attacks in New York City. *New England Journal of Medicine, 346*, 982–987.

Galea, S., Tracy, M., Hoggatt, K. J., Dimaggio, C., & Karpati, A. (2011). Estimated deaths attributable to social factors in the United States. *American Journal of Public Health, 101*, 1456–1465.

Gallo, C. L., & Pfeffer, C. R. (2003). Children and adolescents bereaved by a suicidal death: Implications for psychosocial outcomes and interventions. In A. Apter & R. A. King (Eds.), *Suicide in children and adolescents* (pp. 294–312). New York: Cambridge University Press.

Gallo, J. J., & Lebowitz, B. D. (1999). The epidemiology of common late-life mental disorders in the community: Themes for the new century. *Psychiatric Services, 50*, 1158–1166.

Gandy, S. (2014). Alzheimer's disease: new data highlight nonneuronal cell types and the necessity for presymptomatic prevention strategies. *Biological Psychiatry, 75*, 553–557.

Ganguli, M., Du, Y., Dodge, H. H., Ratcliff, G. G., & Chang, C.-C. H. (2006). Depressive symptoms and cognitive decline in late life: A prospective epidemiological study. *Archives of General Psychiatry, 63*, 153–160.

Garand, L., Buckwalter, K. C., Lubaroff, D., Tripp-Reimer, T., Frantz, R. A., & Ansley, T. N. (2002). A pilot study of immune and mood outcomes of a community-based intervention for dementia caregivers: The PLST intervention. *Archives of Psychiatric Nursing, 16*, 156–167.

Garb, H. N. (2005). Clinical judgment and decision making. *Annual Review of Clinical Psychology, 1*, 67–89.

Garber, J. (2006). Depression in children and adolescents: Linking risk research and prevention. *American Journal of Preventative Medicine, 31*, S104–S125.

Garber, J., Clarke, G. N., Weersing, V. R., Beardslee, W. R., Brent, D. A., Gladstone, T. R., et al. (2009). Prevention of depression in at-risk adolescents: A randomized controlled trial. *Journal of the American Medical Association, 301*, 2215–2224.

Garber, J., & Flynn, C. (2001). Vulnerability to depression in childhood and adolescence. In R. M. Ingram & J. M. Price (Eds.), *Vulnerability to psychopathology: Risk across the lifespan* (pp. 175–225). New York: Guilford Press.

Garber, J., Kelly, M. K., & Martin, N. C. (2002). Developmental trajectories of adolescents' depressive symptoms: Predictors of change. *Journal of Consulting and Clinical Psychology, 70*, 79–95.

Gard, D. E., Kring, A. M., Germans Gard, M., Horan, W. P., & Green, M. F. (2007). Anhedonia in schizophrenia: Distinctions between anticipatory and consummatory pleasure. *Schizophrenia Research, 93*, 253–260.

Gard, D. E., Sanchez, A. H., Starr, J., Cooper, S., Fisher, M., Rowlands, A., & Vinogradov, S. (2014). Using self-determination theory to understand motivation deficits in schizophrenia: The "why" of motivated behavior. *Schizophrenia Research, 156*(2–3), 217–222.

Garety, P. A., Fowler, D., & Kuipers, E. (2000). Cognitive behavioral therapy for medication-resistant symptoms. *Schizophrenia Bulletin, 26*, 73–86.

Garfield, R. L., Zuvekas, S.H., Lave, J.R., & Donohue, J.M. (2011). The impact of national health care reform on adults with several mental disorders. *American Journal of Psychiatry, 168*, 486–494.

Garner, D. M., Garfinkel, P. E., Schwartz, D., & Thompson, M. (1980). Cultural expectation of thinness in women. *Psychological Reports, 47*, 483–491.

Garner, D. M., Olmsted, M. P., & Polivy, J. (1983). Development and validation of a multi-dimensional eating disorder inventory for anorexia nervosa and bulimia. *International Journal of Eating Disorders, 2*, 15–34.

Garner, D. M., Vitousek, K. M., & Pike, K. M. (1997). Cognitive-behavioral therapy for anorexia nervosa. In D. M. Garner & P. E. Garfinkel (Eds.), *Handbook of Treatment for Eating Disorders* (pp. 94–144). New York: Guilford Press.

Gatchel, R. J., Peng, Y. B., Peters, M. L., Fuchs, P. N., & Turk, D. C. (2007). The biopsychosocial approach to chronic pain: Scientific advances and future directions. *Psychological Bulletin, 133*, 581–624.

Gatz, M., Reynolds, C. A., Fratiglioni, L., Johansson, B., Mortimer, J. A., Berg, S., et al. (2006). Roles of genes and environments for explaining Alzheimer disease. *Archives of General Psychiatry, 63*, 168–174.

Gaus, V. L. (2007). *Cognitive behavior therapy for adults with Asperger's syndrome.* New York: Guilford Press.

Gaw, A. C. (2001). *Concise guide to cross-cultural psychiatry.* Washington, DC: American Psychiatric Association.

Ge, X., Conger, R. D., Cadoret, R. J., Neiderhiser, J. M., Yates, W., Troughton, E., et al. (1996). The developmental interface between nature and nurture: A mutual influence model of child antisocial behavior and parent behaviors. *Developmental Psychology, 32*, 574–589.

Geddes, J. R., Burgess, S., Hawton, K., Jamison, K., & Goodwin, G. M. (2004). Long-term lithium therapy for bipolar disorder: Systematic review and meta-analysis of randomized controlled trials. *American Journal of Psychiatry, 161*, 217–222.

Geddes, J. R., Carney, S. M., Davies, C., Furukawa, T. A., Frank, E., Kupfer, D. J., et al. (2003). Relapse prevention with antidepressant drug treatment in depressive disorders: A systematic review. *The Lancet, 361*, 653–661.

Geller, J. L. (2006). A history of private psychiatric hospitals in the USA: From start to almost finished. *Psychiatric Quarterly, 77*, 1–41.

Gendall, K. A., Bulik, C. M., Joyce, P. R., McIntosh, V. V., & Carter, F. A. (2000). Menstrual cycle irregularity in bulimia nervosa: Associated factors and changes with treatment. *Journal of Psychosomatic Research, 49*, 409–415.

Gentes, E. L., & Ruscio, A. M. (2011). A meta-analysis of the relation of intolerance of uncertainty to symptoms of generalized anxiety disorder, major depressive disorder, and obsessive-compulsive disorder. *Clinical Psychology Review, 31*, 923–933.

Geraerts, E., Schooler, J. W., Merckelbach, H., Jelicic, M., Hauer, B. J. A., & Ambadar, Z. (2007). The reality of recovered memories: Corroborating continuous and discontinuous memories of childhood sexual abuse. *Psychological Science, 18*, 564–568.

Gerlach, A. L., Wilhelm, F. H., Gruber, K., & Roth, W. T. (2001). Blushing and physiological arousability in social phobia. *Journal of Abnormal Psychology, 110*, 247–258.

Gernsbacher, M. A., Dawson, M., & Goldsmith, H. H. (2005). Three reasons not to believe in an autism epidemic. *Current Directions in Psychological Science, 14*, 55–58.

Gerra, G., Zaimovic, A., Ferri, M., Zambelli, U., Timpano, M., Neri, E., Marzocchi, G. F., Delsignore, R., & Brambilla, F. (2000). Long-lasting effects of (6)3, 4methylenedioxymethamphetamine (Ecstasy) on serotonin system function in humans. *Biological Psychiatry, 47*, 127–136.

Getahun, D., Jacobsen, S. J., Fassett, M. J., Chen, W., Demissie, K., & Rhoads, G. G. (2013). Recent trends in childhood attention-deficit/hyperactivity disorder. *Journal of the American Medical Association, Pediatrics, 167*(3), 282–288.

Ghaemi, S. N., & Goodwin, F. K. (2003). Introduction to special issue on antidepressant use in bipolar disorder. *Bipolar Disorders, 5*, 385–387.

Ghanem, K. G., Hutton, H. E., Zenilman, J. M., Zimba, R., & Erbelding, E. J. (2005). Audio computer assisted self interview and face to face interview modes in assessing response bias among STD clinic patients. *Sexually Transmitted Infections, 81*(5), 421–425.

Gibson, D. R. (2001). Effectiveness of syringe exchange programs in reducing HIV risk behavior and seroconversion among injecting drug users. *AIDS, 15*, 1329–1341.

Giesbrecht, T., Smeets, T., Leppink, J., Jelicic, M., & Merckelbach, H. (2013). Acute dissociation after 1 night of sleep loss. *Psychology of Consciousness: Theory, Research, and Practice, 1,* 150–159.

Giesen-Bloo, J., van Dyck, R., Spinhoven, P., van Tilburg, W., Dirksen, C., van Asselt, T., et al. (2006). Outpatient psychotherapy for borderline personality disorder: Randomized trial of schema-focused therapy vs transference-focused psychotherapy. *Archives of General Psychiatry, 63,* 649–658.

Gilbertson, M. W., Shenton, M. E., Ciszewski, A., Kasai, K., Lasko, N. B., Orr, S. P., et al. (2002). Smaller hippocampal volume predicts pathologic vulnerability to psychological trauma. *Nature Neuroscience, 5,* 1242–1247.

Gillan, C. M., Morein-Zamir, S., Urcelay, G. P., Sule, A., Voon, V., Apergis-Schoute, A. M., et al. (2014). Enhanced avoidance habits in obsessive-compulsive disorder. *Biological Psychiatry, 75,* 631–638.

Giovino, G. A., Villanti, A. C., Mowery, P. D., Sevilimedu, V., Niaura, R. S., Vallone, D. M., & Abrams, D. B. (2013). Differential trends in cigarette smoking in the USA: is menthol slowing progress? *Tobacco Control.* doi: 10.1136/tobaccocontrol-2013-051159

Gizer, I. R., Ficks, C., & Waldman, I. D. (2009). Candidate gene studies of ADHD: a meta-analytic review. *Human Genetics, 126*(1), 51–90.

Gjerde, L. C., Czajkowski, N., Roysamb, E., Orstavik, R. E., Knudsen, G. P., Ostby, K., et al. (2012). The heritability of avoidant and dependent personality disorder assessed by personal interview and questionnaire. *Acta Psychiatrica Scandinavica, 126,* 448–457.

Glass, C. R., & Arnkoff, D. B. (1997). Questionnaire methods of cognitive self-statement assessment. *Journal of Consulting and Clinical Psychology, 65,* 911–927.

Glausier, J. R., & Lewis, D. A. (2013). Dendritic spine pathology in schizophrenia. *Neuroscience, 251*(0), 90–107.

Gleaves, D. H. (1996). The sociocognitive model of dissociative identity disorder: A reexamination of the evidence. *Psychological Bulletin, 120,* 42–59.

Glenn, A. L., Raine, A., Venables, P. H., & Mednick, S. A. (2007). Early temperamental and psychophysiological precursors of adult psychopathic personality. *Journal of Abnormal Psychology, 116,* 508–518.

Gloaguen, V., Cottraux, J., Cucherat, M., & Blackburn, I. M. (1998). A meta-analysis of the effects of cognitive therapy in depressed patients. *Journal of Affective Disorders, 49,* 59–72.

Godart, N. T., Flament, M. F., Lecrubier, Y., & Jeammet, P. (2000). Anxiety disorders in anorexia nervosa and bulimia nervosa: Co-morbidity and chronology of appearance. *European Psychiatry, 15,* 38–45.

Godart, N. T., Flament, M., Perdereau, F., & Jeammet, P. (2002). Comorbidity between eating disorders and anxiety disorders: A review. *International Journal of Eating Disorders, 32,* 253–270.

Goenjian, A. K., Walling, D., Steinberg, A. M., Karayan, I., Najarian, L. M., & Pynoos, R. (2005). A prospective study of posttraumatic stress and depressive reactions among treated and untreated adolescents 5 years after a catastrophic disaster. *American Journal of Psychiatry, 162,* 2302–2308.

Goldapple, K., Segal, Z., Garson, C., Lau, M., Bieling, P., Kennedy, S., et al. (2004). Modulation of cortical-limbic pathways in major depression. *Archives of General Psychiatry, 61,* 34–41.

Goldberg, T. E., & Weinberger, D. R. (2004). Genes and the parsing of cognitive processes. *Trends in Cognitive Sciences, 8,* 325–335.

Golden, C. J. (1981a). The Luria-Nebraska Children's Battery: Theory and formulation. In G. W. Hynd & J.

E. Obrzut (Eds.), *Neuropsychological assessment and the school-age child: Issues and procedures.* New York: Grune & Stratton.

Golden, C. J. (1981b). A standardized version of Luria's neuropsychological tests: A quantitative and qualitative approach to neuropsychological evaluation. In S. B. Filskov & T. J. Boil (Eds.), *Handbook of clinical neuropsychology.* New York: John Wiley & Sons.

Golden, C. J., Hammeke, T., & Purisch, A. (1978). Diagnostic validity of a standardized neuropsychological battery derived from Luria's neuropsychological tests. *Journal of Consulting and Clinical Psychology, 46,* 1258–1265.

Golden, R. N., Gaynes, B. N., Ekstrom, R. D., Hamer, R. M., Jacobsen, F. M., Suppes, et al. (2005). The efficacy of light therapy in the treatment of mood disorders: A review and meta-analysis of the evidence. *American Journal of Psychiatry, 162,* 656–662.

Goldin, P. (2014). A grand gender convergence: its last chapter. *American Economic Review, 104*(4), 1–30.

Goldin, P. R., Manber-Ball, T., Werner, K., Heimberg, R., & Gross, J. J. (2009). Neural mechanisms of cognitive reappraisal of negative self-beliefs in social anxiety disorder. *Biological Psychiatry, 66,* 1091–1099.

Goldman-Rakic, P. S., & Selemon, L. D. (1997). Functional and anatomical aspects of prefrontal pathology in schizophrenia. *Schizophrenia Bulletin, 23,* 437–458.

Goldstein, A. J., & Chambless, D. L. (1978). A reanalysis of agoraphobic behavior. *Behavior Therapy, 9,* 47–59.

Goldstein, A. J., de Beurs, E., Chambless, D. L., & Wilson, K. A. (2000). EMDR for panic disorder with agoraphobia: Comparison with waiting list and credible attention-placebo control conditions. *Journal of Consulting and Clinical Psychology, 68,* 947–956.

Goldstein, J. M., Buka, S. L., Seidman, L. J., & Tsuang, M. T. (2010). Specificity of familial transmission of schizophrenia psychosis spectrum and affective psychoses in the New England Family Study's high-risk design. *Archives of General Psychiatry, 67,* 458–467.

Gomez, F. C., Piedmont, R. L., & Fleming, M. Z. (1992). Factor analysis of the Spanish version of the WAIS: The Escala de Inteligencia Wechsler para Adultos (EIWA). *Psychological Assessment, 4,* 317–321.

Gonzalez, H. M., Vega, W. A., Williams, D. R., Tarraf, W., West, B. T., & Neighbors, H. W. (2010). Depression care in the United States: Too little for too few. *Archives of General Psychiatry, 67,* 37–46.

Goode, S. D. (2010). *Understanding and addressing adult sexual attraction to children: A study of paedophiles in contemporary society.* London: Routledge.

Goodkind, M. S., Gyurak, A., McCarthy, M., Miller, B. L., & Levenson, R. W. (2010). Emotion regulation deficits in frontotemporal lobar degeneration and Alzheimer's disease. *Psychological Aging, 25,* 30–37.

Goodman, G. S., Ghetti, S., Quas, J. A., Edelstein, R. S., Alexander, K. W., Redlich, A. D., et al. (2003). A prospective study of memory for child sexual abuse: New findings relevant to the repressed-memory controversy. *Psychological Science, 14,* 113–118.

Goodwin, D. K. (2003, Feb. 17). The man in our memory. NY Times.

Goodwin, F., & Jamison, K. (2007). *Manic-depressive illness: Bipolar disorders and recurrent depression* (2nd ed.). New York: Oxford University Press.

Gopnik, A., Capps, L., & Meltzoff, A. N. (2000). Early theories of mind: What the theory theory can tell us about autism. In S. Baren-Cohen, H. Tager-Flusberg & D. Cohen (Eds.), *Understanding Other Minds* (2nd ed., pp. 50–72). Oxford, UK: Oxford University Press.

Gordon, K. H., Perez, M., & Joiner, T. E. (2002). The impact of racial stereotypes on eating disorder recognition. *International Journal of Eating Disorders, 32,* 219–224.

Gorelick, P. B. (2010). Role of inflammation in cognitive impairment: results of observational epidemiological studies and clinical trials. *Annals of the New York Academy of Sciences, 1207,* 155–162.

Gotlib, H., & Joormann, J. (2010). Cognition and depression: Current status and future directions. *Annual Review of Clinical Psychology, 6,* 285–312.

Gottesman, I. I., Laursen, T. M., Bertelsen, A., & Mortensen, P. B. (2010). Severe mental disorders in offspring with 2 psychiatrically ill parents. *Archives of General Psychiatry, 67,* 252–257.

Gottesman, I. I., McGuffin, P., & Farmer, A. E. (1987). Clinical genetics as clues to the "real" genetics of schizophrenia. *Schizophrenia Bulletin, 13,* 23–47.

Goveas, J. S., Espeland, M. A., Woods, N. F., Wassertheil-Smoller, S., & Kotchen, J. M. (2011). Depressive symptoms and incidence of mild cognitive impairment and probable dementia in elderly women: The Women's Health Initiative memory study. *Journal of the American Geriatrics Society, 59,* 57–66.

Grabe, S., & Hyde, J. S. (2006). Ethnicity and body dissatisfaction among women in the United States: A meta-analyis. *Psychological Bulletin, 132,* 622–640.

Grady, D. (1999). A great pretender now faces the truth of illness, *The New York Times.*

Graham, C. A. (2010). The DSM diagnostic criteria for female sexual arousal disorder. *Archives of Sexual Behavior, 39,* 240–255.

Graham, C. A. (2014). Orgasm disorders in women. In Y. M. Binik & K. S. K. Hall (Eds.), *Principles and practice of sex therapy* (5th ed., pp. 89–111). New York: Guilford Press.

Graham, J. (2011). *MMPI-2: Assessing personality and psychopathology,* (5th ed.). New York: Oxford University Press.

Grana, R. A., Popova, L., & Ling, P. M. (2014). A longitudinal analysis of electronic cigarette use and smoking cessation. *Journal of the American Medical Association, Internal Medicine, 174*(5), 812–813.

Grandin, T. (1986). *Emergence: Labeled autistic.* Novato, CA: Arena Press.

Grandin, T. (1995). *Thinking in pictures.* New York: Doubleday.

Grandin, T. (2008). *The way I see it: A personal look at autism and Asperger's.* Arlington, TX: Future Horizons.

Grandin, T. (2013). *The autistic brain.* New York: Houghton Mifflin Harcourt.

Grant, B. F., Hasin, D. S., Stinson, F. S., Dawson, D. A., Chou, S. P., Ruan, W. J., et al. (2004). Prevalence, correlates, and disability of personality disorders in the United States: Results from the national epidemiologic survey on alcohol and related conditions. *Journal of Clinical Psychiatry, 65,* 948–958.

Grant, J. E., Odlaug, B. L., & Schreiber, L. R. N. (2014). Pharmacotherapy for obsessive-compulsive and related disorders among adults. In E. A. Storch & D. McKay (Eds.), *Obsessive-Compulsive Disorder and Its Spectrum: A Life-Span Approach.* Wasington DC: American Psychological Association.

Grant, P. M., Huh, G., Perivoliotis, D., Stolar, N., & Beck, A. T. (2012). Randomized trial to evaluate the efficacy of cognitive therapy for low-functioning patients with schizophrenia. *Archives of General Psychiatry, 69*(121–127).

Gravel, S., Henn, B. M., Gutenkunst, R. N., Indap, A. R., Marth, G. T., Clark, A. G., et al. (2011). Demographic history and rare allele sharing among human populations. *Proceedings of the National Academy of Sciences. 108*, 11983-11988.

Green, J. G., McLaughlin, K. A., Berglund, P. A., Gruber, M. J., Sampson, N. A., Zaslavsky, A. M., et al. (2010). Childhood adversities and adult psychiatric disorders in the National Comorbidity Survey Replication: Associations with first onset of DSM-IV Disorders. *Archives of General Psychiatry, 67,* 113-123.

Green, M. F. (1996). What are the functional consequences of neurocognitive deficits in schizophrenia? *American Journal of Psychiatry, 153,* 321–330.

Green, M. F., Kern, R. S., Braff, D. L., & Mintz, J. (2000). Neurocognitive deficits and functional outcome in schizophrenia: Are we measuring the "right stuff"? *Schizophrenia Bulletin, 26,* 119–136.

Green, M. F., Marshall, B. D., Wirshing, W. C., Ames, D., Marder, S. R., McGurk, S., Kern, R. S., & Mintz, J. (1997). Does risperidone improve verbal working memory in treatment-resistant schizophrenia? *American Journal of Psychiatry, 154,* 799–804.

Green, R., & Fleming, D. T. (1990). Transsexual surgery follow-up: Status in the 1990s. In J. Bancroft, C. Davis & D. Weinstein (Eds.), *Annual Review of Sex Research* (pp. 163-174).

Greenberg, B. D., Rauch, S. L., & Haber, S. N. (2010). Invasive circuitry-based neurotherapeutics: Stereotactic ablation and deep brain stimulation for OCD. *Neuropsychopharmacology, 35,* 317–336.

Greeven, A., van Balkom, A. J. L. M., Visser, S., Merkelbach, J. W., van Rood, Y. R., van Dyck, R., et al. (2007). Cognitive behavior therapy and paroxetine in the treatment of hypochondriasis: A randomized controlled trial. *American Journal of Psychiatry, 164,* 91–99.

Grillon, C. (2002). Startle reactivity and anxiety disorders: Aversive conditioning, context, and neurobiology. *Biological Psychiatry, 52,* 958–975.

Grilo, C. M. (2007). Treatment of binge eating disorder. In S. Wonderlich, J. E. Mitchell, M. d. Zwaan & H. Steiger (Eds.), *Annual Review of Eating Disorders* (pp. 23–34). Oxford, UK: Radcliffe.

Grilo, C. M., Crosby, R. D., Wilson, G. T., & Masheb, R. M. (2012). 12-month follow-up of fluoxetine and cognitive behavioral therapy for binge eating disorder. *Journal of Consulting and Clinical Psychology, 80*(6), 1108–1113.

Grilo, C. M., Shea, M. T., Sanislow, C. A., Skodol, A. E., Gunderson, J. G., Stout, R. L., et al. (2004). Two-year stability and change of schizotypal, borderline, avoidant, and obsessive-compulsive personality disorders. *Journal of Consulting and Clinical Psychology, 72,* 767–775.

Grilo, C. M., Shiffman, S., & Carter-Campbell, J. T. (1994). Binge eating antecedents in normal weight nonpurging females: Is there consistency? *International Journal of Eating Disorders, 16,* 239–249.

Griner, D., & Smith, T. B. (2006). Culturally adapted mental health intervention: A meta-analytic review. *Psychotherapy, 43,* 531–548.

Grinker, R. R., & Spiegel, J. P. (1944). *Management of neuropsychiatric casualties in the zone of combat: Manual of military neuropsychiatry.* Philadelphia: W.B. Saunders.

Grinspoon, L., & Bakalar, J. B. (1995). Marijuana as medicine: A plea for reconsideration. *Journal of the American Medical Association, 273,* 1875–1876.

Grisham, J. R., Frost, R. O., Steketee, G., Kim, H. J., & Hood, S. (2006). Age of onset of compulsive hoarding. *Journal of Anxiety Disorders, 20,* 675–686.

Grisso, T., Davis, J., Vesselinov, R. Appelbaum, P. S. & Monahan, J. (2000). Violent thoughts and violent behavior following hospitalization for mental disorder. *Journal of Consulting and Clinical Psychology, 68,* 388–398.

Groesz, L. M., Levine, M. P., & Murnen, S. K. (2002). The effect of experimental presentation of thin media images on body dissatisfaction: A meta-analytic review. *International Journal of Eating Disorders, 31,* 1–16.

Gropalis, M., Bleichhardt, G., Hiller, W., & Witthoft, M. (2013). Specificity and modifiability of cognitive biases in hypochondriasis. *Journal of Consulting and Clinical Psychology, 81,* 558–565.

Gross, C., Zhuang, X., Stark, K., Ramboz, S., Oosting, R., Kirby, L., Santarelli, L., Beck, S. & Hen, R. (2002). Serotonin 1A receptor acts during development to establish normal anxiety-like behaviour in the adult. *Nature, 416,* 396–400.

Grossman, D. (1995). *On killing: The psychological cost of learning to kill in war and society.* Boston: Little, Brown.

Gueguen, J., Godart, N., Chambry, J., Brun-Eberentz, A., Foulon, C., Divac, S. M., . . . Huas, C. (2012). Severe anorexia nervosa in men: Comparison with severe an in women and analysis of mortality. *International Journal of Eating Disorders, 45*(4), 537–545.

Gum, A. M., King-Kallimanis, B., & Kohn, R. (2009). Prevalence of mood, anxiety, and substance-abuse disorders for older Americans in the National Comorbidity Survey-Replication. *American Journal of Psychiatry, 17,* 769–781.

Gump, B. S., Matthews, K. A., & Räikkönen, K. (1999). Modeling relationships among socioeconomic status, hostility, cardiovascular reactivity, and left ventricular mass in African American and White children. *Health Psychology, 18,* 140–150.

Guo, X., Zhai, J., Liu, Z., Fang, M., Wang, B., Wang, C., Hu, B., Sun, X., et al. (2010). Effect of antipsychotic medication alone vs combined with psychosocial intervention on outcomes of early-stage schizophrenia. *Archives of General Psychiatry, 67,* 895–904.

Gur, R. E., Turetsky, B. I., Cowell, P. E., et al. (2000). Temporolimbic volume reductions in schizophrenia. *Archives of General Psychiatry, 57,* 769–776.

Gustad, J., & Phillips, K. A. (2003). Axis I comorbidity in body dysmorphic disorder. *Comprehensive Psychiatry, 44,* 270–276.

Gutman, D. A., & Nemeroff, C. B. (2003). Persistent central nervous system effects of an adverse early environment: Clinical and preclinical studies. *Physiology and Behavior, 79,* 471–478.

Guyll, M., Matthews, K. A., & Bromberger, J. T. (2001). Discrimination and unfair treatment: Relationship to cardiovascular reactivity among African American and European American women. *Health Psychology, 20,* 315–325.

Haaga, D. A. F., Dyck, M. J., & Ernst, D. (1991). Empirical status of cognitive theory of depression. *Psychological Bulletin, 110,* 215–236.

Haaga, D. A. F., & Stiles, W. B. (2000). Randomized clinical trials in psychotherapy research: Methodology, design and evaluation. In R. E. Ingram & C. Snyder (Eds.), *Handbook of psychological change: Psychotherapy processes & practices for the 21st century* (pp. 14-39). New York: John Wiley & Sons, Inc.

Hacking, I. (1998). *Mad travelers: Reflections on the reality of transient mental illness.* Charlottesville, VA: University Press of Virginia.

Haddock, G., Tarrier, N., Spaulding, W., Yusupoff, L. K., & McCarthy, E. (1998). Individual cognitive-behavior therapy in the treatment of hallucinations and delusions: A review. *Clinical Psychology Review, 18,* 821–838.

Haedt-Matt, A. A., & Keel, P. K. (2011). Revisiting the affect regulation model of binge eating: A meta-analysis of studies using ecological momentary assessment. *Psychological Bulletin, 137,* 660–681.

Hagerman, R. (2006). Lessons from fragile x regarding neurobiology, autism, and neurodegeneration. *Developmental and Behavioral Pediatrics, 27,* 63–74.

Haijma, S. V., Van Haren, N., Cahn, W., Koolschijn, P. C., Hulshoff Pol, H. E., & Kahn, R. S. (2013). Brain volumes in schizophrenia: a meta-analysis in over 18 000 subjects. *Schizophrenia Bulletin, 39*(5), 1129–1138.

Hall, G. C. (2001). Psychotherapy research with ethnic minorities: Empirical, ethical, and conceptual issues. *Journal of Consulting and Clinical Psychology, 69*(3), 502–510.

Hall, G. C., Hirschman, R., & Oliver, L. L. (1995). Sexual arousal and arousability to pedophilic stimuli in a community sample of normal men. *Behavior Therapy, 26,* 681–694.

Hallmayer, J., Cleveland, S., Torres, A., Phillips, J., Cohen, B., Torigoe, T., Miller, J., Fedele, A., et al. (2011). Genetic heritability and shared environmental factors among twin pairs with autism. *Archives of General Psychiatry, 68,* 1095-1102

Halmi, K. A., Sunday, S. R., Strober, M., Kaplan, A., Woodside, D. B., Fichter, N., Treasure, J., Berrettini, W. H., & Kaye, W. (2000). Perfectionism in anorexia nervosa: Variation by clinical subtype, obsessionality, and pathological eating behavior. *American Journal of Psychiatry, 157,* 1799–1805.

Hamer, M., & Chida, Y. (2009). Physical activity and risk of neurodegenerative disease: a systematic review of prospective evidence. *Psychological Medicine, 39,* 3–11.

Hamilton, J. P., Etkin, A., Furman, D. J., Lemus, M. G., Johnson, R. F., & Gotlib, I. H. (2012). Functional neuroimaging of major depressive disorder: A meta-analysis and new integration of base line activation and neural response data. *American Journal of Psychiatry, 169,* 693–703.

Hammen, C. (2009). Adolescent depression: Stressful interpersonal contexts and risk for recurrence. *Current Directions in Psychological Science, 18,* 200–204.

Hammen, C. L., Burge, D., Daley, S. E., Davila, J., Paley, B., & Rudolph, K. D. (1995). Interpersonal attachment cognitions and prediction of symptomatic responses to interpersonal stress. *Journal of Abnormal Psychology, 104,* 436–443.

Hammen, C., & Brennan, P. (2001). Depressed adolescents of depressed and nondepressed mothers: Tests of an interpersonal impairment hypothesis. *Journal of Consulting and Clinical Psychology, 69,* 284–294.

Hammen, C., Hazel, N. A., Brennan, P. A., & Najman, J. (2012). Intergenerational transmission and continuity of stress and depression: Depressed women and their offspring in 20 years of follow-up. *Psychological Medicine, 42,* 931–942.

Hammond, D. (2011). Health warning messages on tobacco products: Review. *Tobacco Control, 20*(5), 327–337.

Hamshere, M. L., Langley, K., Martin, J., Agha, S. S., Stergiakouli, E., Anney, R. J., et al. (2013). High loading of polygenic risk for ADHD in children with comorbid aggression. *American Journal of Psychiatry, 170*(8), 909–916.

Hankin, B. J., Abramson, L. Y., Moffitt, T. E., Silva, P. A., McGee, R., et al. (1998). Development of depression from preadolescence to young adulthood: Emerging gender differences in a 10-year longitudinal study. *Journal of Abnormal Psychology, 107,* 128–140.

Hankin, B. L., & Abramson, L. Y. (2001). Development of gender differences in depression: An elaborated cognitive vulnerability-transactional stress theory. *Psychological Bulletin, 127,* 773–796.

Hankin, B. L., Mermelstein, R., & Roesch, L. (2007). Sex differences in adolescent depression: Stress exposure and reactivity models. *Child Development, 78,* 279–295.

Hansen, W. B. (1992). School-based substance abuse prevention: A review of the state of the art in curriculum, 1980–1990. *Health Education Research: Theory and Practice, 7,* 403–430.

Hansen, W. B., & Graham, J. W. (1991). Preventing alcohol, marijuana, and cigarette use among adolescents: Peer pressure resistance training versus establishing conservative norms. *Preventive Medicine, 20,* 414–430.

Hanson, C. (1998, November 30). *Dangerous therapy: The story of Patricia Burgus and multiple personality disorder.* Chicago Magaine. Downloaded from http://www.chicagomag.com/Chicago-Magazine/June-1998/Dangerous-Therapy-The-Story-of-Patricia-Burgus-and-Multiple-Personality-Disorder/

Hanson, J. L., Adluru, N., Chung, M. K., Alexander, A. L., Davidson, R. J., & Pollak, S. D. (2013). Early neglect is associated with alterations in white matter integrity and cognitive functioning. *Child Development, 84,* 1566–1578.

Hanson, R. K., & Bussiere, M. T. (1998). Predicting relapse: A meta-analysis of sexual offender recidivism studies. *Journal of Consulting and Clinical Psychology, 66,* 348–362.

Hanson, R. K., & Harris, A. J. R. (1997). Voyeurism: Assessment and treatment. In D. R. Laws & W. O'Donohue (Eds.), *Sexual deviance* (pp. 311–331). New York: Guilford Press.

Hanson, R. K., Hunsley, J., & Parker, K. C. (1988). The relationship between WAIS subtest reliability, "g" loadings, and meta-analytically derived validity estimates. *Journal of Clinical Psychology, 44*(4), 557–563.

Harden, K. P., Hill, J. E., Turkheimer, E., & Emery, R. E. (2008). Gene–environment correlation and interaction in peer effects on adolescent alcohol and tobacco use. *Behavior Genetics, 38,* 339–347.

Hare, E. (1969). *Triennial statistical report of the Royal Maudsley and Bethlem Hospitals.* London: Bethlem and Maudsley Hospitals.

Hare, R. D. (2003). *The Hare Psychopathy Checklist* (Rev. ed.). Toronto, Canada: Multi-Health System.

Hare, R. D., & Neumann, C. N. (2006). The PCL-R assessment of psychopathy: Development, structural properties, and new directions. In C. Patrick (Ed.), *Handbook of psychopathy* (pp. 58–88). New York: Guilford Press.

Harenski, C. L., Harenski, K. A., Shane, M. S., & Kiehl, K. A. (2010). Aberrant neural processing of moral violations in criminal psychopaths. *Journal of Abnormal Psychology, 119,* 863–874.

Harkness, K. L., Bagby, R. M., & Kennedy, S. H. (2012). Childhood maltreatment and differential treatment response and recurrence in adult major depressive disorder. *Journal of Consulting and Clinical Psychology, 80,* 342–353.

Harmer, C. J., Goodwin, G. M., & Cowen, P. J. (2009). Why do antidepressants take so long to work? A cognitive neuropsychological model of antidepressant drug action. *British Journal of Psychiatry, 195,* 102–108.

Harrington, A. (2008). *The cure within: A history of mindbody medicine.* New York: W. W. Norton.

Harris, J. L., Bargh, J. A., & Brownell, K. D. (2009). Priming effects of television food advertising on eating behavior. *Health Psychology, 28*(4), 404–413.

Harris, V. L. (2000). Insanity acquittees and rearrest: The past 24 years. *Journal of the American Academy of Psychiatry and the Law, 28*(2), 225–231.

Harrison, J. N., Cluxton-Keller, F., & Gross, D. (2012). Antipsychotic medication prescribing trends in children and adolescents. *Journal of Pediatric Health Care, 26*(2), 139–145.

Harrison, P. J., & Weinberger, D. R. (2004). Schizophrenia genes, gene expression, and neuropathology: On the matter of their convergence. *Molecular Psychiatry,* 1–29.

Harrow, M., Goldberg, J. F., Grossman, L. S., & Meltzer, H. Y. (1990). Outcome in manic disorders: A naturalistic follow-up study. *Archives of General Psychiatry, 47,* 665–671.

Hart, E. L., Lahey, B. B., Loeber, R., Applegate, B., & Frick, P. J. (1995). Developmental changes in attention-deficit hyperactivity disorder in boys: A four-year longitudinal study. *Journal of Abnormal Child Psychology, 23,* 729–750.

Hartz, D. T., Fredrick-Osborne, S. L., & Galloway, G. P. (2001). Craving predicts use during treatment for methamphetamine dependence: A prospective repeated measures, within-subjects analysis. *Drug and Alcohol Dependence, 63,* 269–276.

Harvard Mental Health Letter. (1995, July). *Schizophrenia update-Part II, 12,* 1–5.

Harvey, A. G., & Bryant, R. A. (2002). Acute stress disorder: A synthesis and critique. *Psychological Bulletin, 128,* 886–902.

Harvey, A. G., Watkins, E., Mansell, W., & Shafran, R. (2004). *Cognitive behavioural processes across psychological disorders: A transdiagnostic approach to research and treatment.* Oxford, UK: Oxford University Press.

Harvey, P. D., Green, M. F., Keefe, R. S. I., & Velligan, D. (2004). Changes in cognitive functioning with risperidone and olanzapine treatment: A large-scale, doubleblind, randomized study. *Journal of Clinical Psychiatry, 65,* 361–372.

Harvey, P. D., Green, M. F., McGurk, S., & Meltzer, H. Y. (2003). Changes in cognitive functioning with risperidone and olanzapine treatment: A large-scale, doubleblind, randomized study. *Psychopharmacology, 169,* 404–411.

Hasin, D. S., O'Brien, C. P., Auriacombe, M., Borges, G., Bucholz, K., Budney, A., et al. (2013). DSM-5 criteria for substance use disorders: Recommendations and rationale. *American Journal of Psychiatry, 170*(8), 834–851.

Hasin, D. S., Stinson, F. S., Ogburn, E., & Grant, B. F. (2007). Prevalence, correlates, disability, and comorbidity of DSM-IV alcohol abuse and dependence in the United States: Results from the National Epidemiologic Survey on Alcohol and Related Conditions. *Archives of General Psychiatry, 64,* 830–842.

Hathaway, S. R., & McKinley, J. C. (1943). *MMPI manual.* New York: Psychological Corporation.

Hausdorff, J. M., Levy, B. R., & Wei, J. Y. (1999). The power of ageism on physical function of older persons: Reversibility of age-related gait changes. *Journal of the American Geriatrics Society, 47,* 1346–1349.

Hawton, K., Catalan, J., Martin, P., & Fagg, J. (1986). Longterm outcome of sex therapy. *Behaviour Research and Therapy, 24,* 665–675.

Hayes, S. C. (2005). *Get out of your mind and into your life: The new acceptance and commitment therapy.* Oakland, CA: New Harbinger Publications.

Haynes, S. N., & Horn, W. F. (1982). Reactivity in behavioral observation: A review. *Behavioral Assessment, 4,* 369–385.

Hawkins, J. D., Graham, J. W., Maguin, E., Abbott, R., et al. (1997). Exploring the effects of age of alcohol use initiation and psychosocial risk factors on subsequent alcohol misuse. *Journal of Studies on Alcohol, 58,* 280–290.

Hazel, N. A., Hamman, C., Brennan, P. A., Najman, J. (2008). Early childhood adversity and adolescent depression: The mediating role of continued stress. *Psychological Medicine, 38,* 581–589.

Hazlett, E. A., Zhang, J., New, A. S., Zelmanova, Y., Goldstein, K. E., Haznedar, M. M., et al. (2012). Potentiated amygdala response to repeated emotional pictures in borderline personality disorder. *Biological Psychiatry, 72,* 448–456.

Hazlett, H. C., Poe, M. D., Gerig, G., Styner, M., Chappell, C., Smith, R. G., Vachet, C., & Priven, J. (2011). Early brain overgrowth in autism associated with an increase in cortical surface area before age 2 years. *Archives of General Psychiatry, 68,* 467–476.

Head, D., Bugg, J. M., Goate, A. M., Fagan, A. M., Mintun, M. A., Benzinger, T., et al. (2012). Exercise engagement as a moderator of the effects of APOE genotype on amyloid deposition. *Archives of neurology, 69,* 636–643.

Heatherton, T. F., & Baumeister, R. F. (1991). Binge eating as escape from self-awareness. *Psychological Bulletin, 110,* 86–108.

Heatherton, T. F., Herman, C. P., & Polivy, J. (1991). Effects of physical threat and ego threat on eating behavior. *Journal of Personality and Social Psychology, 60,* 138–143.

Heid, I. M., Huth, C., Loos, R. J., Kronenberg, F., Adamkova, V., Anand, S. S., et al. (2009). Meta-analysis of the INSIG2 association with obesity including 74,345 individuals: Does heterogeneity of estimates relate to study design? *PLoS Genetics, 5*(10), e1000694.

Heinrichs, R. W., & Zakzanis, K. K. (1998). Neurocognitive deficits in schizophrenia: A quantitative review of the evidence. *Neuropsychology, 12,* 426–445.

Heinssen, R. K., Liberman, R. P., & Kopelowicz, A. (2000). Psychosocial skills training for schizophrenia: Lessons from the laboratory. *Schizophrenia Bulletin, 26,* 21–46.

Heiss, G., Wallace, R., Anderson, G. L., Aragaki, A., Beresford, S. A. A., et al. (2008). Health risks and benefits 3 years after stopping randomized treatment with estrogen and progestin. *Journal of the American Medical Association, 299,* 1036–1045.

Heller, A. S., van Reekum, C. M., Schaefer, S. M., Lapate, R. C., Radler, B. T., Ryff, C. D., et al. (2013). Sustained striatal activity predicts eudaimonic well–being and cortisol output. *Psychological Science, 24,* 2191–2200.

Heller, T. L., Baker, B. L., Henker, B., & Hinshaw, S. P. (1996). Externalizing behavior and cognitive functioning from preschool to first grade: Stability and predictors. *Journal of Clinical Child Psychology, 25,* 376–387.

Helmuth, L. (2003). In sickness or in health? *Science, 302,* 808–810.

Henggeler, S. W., Schoenwald, S. D., Borduin, C. M., Rowland, M. D., & Cunningham, P. B. (1998). *Multisystemic treatment of antisocial behavior in children and adolescents.* New York: Guilford Press.

Henningfield, J. E., Michaelides, T., & Sussman, S. (2000). Developing treatment for tobacco addicted youth—issues and challenges. *Journal of Child and Adolescent Substance Abuse, 9,* 5–26.

Henriques, G., Wenzel, A., Brown, G. K., & Beck, A. T. (2005). Suicide attempter's reaction to survival as a risk factor for eventual suicide. *American Journal of Psychiatry, 162,* 2180–2182.

Herbenick, D., Reece, M., Schick, V., Sanders, S. A., Dodge, B., & Fortenberry, J. D. (2010a). Sexual behaviors, relationships, and perceived health status among adult women in the United States: Results from a national probability sample. *Journal of Sexual Medicine, 7 Suppl 5,* 277–290.

Herbenick, D., Reece, M., Schick, V., Sanders, S. A., Dodge, B., & Fortenberry, J. D. (2010b). An event-level analysis of the sexual characteristics and composition among adults ages 18 to 59: Results from a national probability sample in the United States. *Journal of Sexual Medicine, 7 Suppl 5,* 346–361.

Herbert, M. A., Gerry, N. P., McQueen, I. M., Heid, A. P., Illig, T., et al. (2006). Common genetic variant is associated with adult and childhood obesity. *Science, 312,* 279–312.

Herdt, G. H. (Ed.). (1984). *Ritualized homosexuality in Melanesia.* Berkeley: University of California Press.

Herman, C. P., Polivy, J., Lank, C., & Heatherton, T. F. (1987). Anxiety, hunger, and eating. *Journal of Abnormal Psychology, 96,* 264–269.

Herman, J. L. (1992). *Trauma and recovery.* New York: Basic Books.

Hersen, M., & Barlow, D. H. (1976). *Single case experimental designs: Strategies for studying behavior change.* New York: Pergamon Press.

Hertzog, C., Kramer, A., Wilson, R. S., & Lindenberger, U. (2009). Enrichment effects on adult cognitive development: Can the functional capacity of older adults be preserved and enhanced? *Psychological Science in the Public Interest, 9.*

Herzog, D. B., Greenwood, D. N., Dorer, D. J., Flores, A. T., Ekeblad, E. R., Richards, A., et al. (2000). Mortality in eating disorders: A descriptive study. *International Journal of Eating Disorders, 28,* 20–26.

Heston, L. L. (1966). Psychiatric disorders in foster home reared children of schizophrenic mothers. *British Journal of Psychiatry, 112,* 819–825.

Hettema, J. E., & Hendricks, P. S. (2010). Motivational interviewing for smoking cessation: A meta-analytic review. *Journal of Consulting and Clinical Psychology, 78*(6), 868–884.

Hettema, J. M., Neale, M. C., & Kendler, K. S. (2001). A review and meta-analysis of the genetic epidemiology of the anxiety disorders. *American Journal of Psychiatry, 158,* 1568–1578.

Hettema, J. M., Prescott, C. A., Myers, J. M., Neale, M. C., & Kendler, K. S. (2005). The structure of genetic and environmental risk factors for anxiety disorders in men and women. *Archives of General Psychiatry, 62,* 182–189.

Heuser, I., Yassouridis, A., & Holsboer, F. (1994). The combined dexamethasone CRH test: A refined laboratory test for psychiatric disorders. *Journal of Psychiatric Research, 28,* 341–346.

Heyn, P., Abreu, B. C., & Ottenbacher, K. J. (2004). Meta-analysis: The effects of exercise training on elderly persons with cognitive impairment and dementia: A meta-analysis. *Archives of Physical Medicine and Rehabilitation, 85,* 1694–1704.

Hibbeln, J. R., Nieminen, L. R. G., Blasbalg, T. L., Riggs, J. A., & Lands, W. E. M. (2006). Healthy intakes of n-3 and n-6 fatty acids: Estimations considering worldwide diversity. *Journal of Clinical Nutrition, 83,* 1483S–1493S.

Hill, A., Briken, P., Kraus, C., Strohm, K., & Berner, W. (2003). Differential pharmacological treatment of paraphilias and sex offenders. *International Journal of Offender Therapy and Comparative Criminology, 47,* 407–421.

Hingson, R. W., Edwards, E. M., Heeren, T., & Rosenbloom, D. (2009). Age of drinking onset and injuries, motor vehicle crashes, and physical fights after drinking and when not drinking. *Alcoholism, Clinical and Experimental Research, 33,* 783–790.

Hinshaw, S. P. (2002). Preadolescent girls with attention-deficit/hyperactivity disorder: I. Background characteristics, comorbidity, cognitive and social functioning, and parenting practices. *Journal of Consulting and Clinical Psychology, 70,* 1086–1098.

Hinshaw, S. P. (2007). *The mark of shame: The stigma of mental illness and an agenda for change.* New York: Oxford University Press.

Hinshaw, S. P., Carte, E. T., Sami, N., Treuting, J. J., & Zupan, B. A. (2002). Preadolescent girls with attention-deficit/hyperactivity disorder: II. Neuropsychological performance in relation to subtypes and individual classification. *Journal of Consulting and Clinical Psychology, 70,* 1099–1111.

Hinshaw, S. P., & Lee, S. S. (2003). Oppositional defiant and conduct disorders. In E. J. Mash & R. A. Barkley (Eds.), *Child Psychopathology* (2nd ed., pp. 144–198). New York: Guilford Press.

Hinshaw, S. P., & Melnick, S. M. (1995). Peer relationships in boys with attention-deficit hyperactivity disorder with and without comorbid aggression. *Development and Psychopathology, 7,* 627–647.

Hinshaw, S. P., Owens, E. B., Sami, N., & Fargeon, S. (2006). Prospective follow-up of girls with attention-deficit/hyperactivity disorder into adolescence: Evidence for continuing cross-domain impairment. *Journal of Consulting and Clinical Psychology, 74,* 489–499.

Hinshaw, S. P., Owens, E. B., Zalecki, C., Huggins, S. P., Montenegro-Nevado, A. J., Schrodek, E., & Swanson, E. N. (2012). Prospective follow-up of girls with attention-deficit/hyperactivity disorder into early adulthood: Continuing impairment includes elevated risk for suicide attempts and self-injury. *Journal of Consulting and Clinical Psychology, 80*(6), 1041–1051.

Hinshaw, S. P., & Scheffler, R. M. (2014). *The ADHD explosion: myths, medication, money, and today's push for performance.* New York: Oxford University Press.

Hinshaw, S. P., Zupan, B. A., Simmel, C., Nigg, J. T., & Melnick, S. (1997). Peer status in boys with and without attention-deficit hyperactivity disorder: Predictions from overt and covert antisocial behavior, social isolation, and authoritative parenting beliefs. *Child Development, 68,* 880–896.

Hinton, D., Ba, P., Peou, S., & Um, K. (2000). Panic disorder among Cambodian refugees attending a psychiatric clinic. *General Hospital Psychiatry, 22,* 437–444.

Hinton, E., Um, K., & Ba, P. (2001). Kyol Goeu ('Wind Overload') Part II: Prevalence, characteristics, and mechanisms of Kyol Goeu and near Kyol Goeu episodes of Khmer patients attending a psychiatric clinic. *Transcultural Psychiatry, 38,* 433–460.

Hirsch, C. R., & Clark, D. M. (2004). Mental imagery and social phobia. In J. Yiend (Ed.), *Cognition, emotion and psychopathology: Theoretical, empirical and clinical directions* (pp. 232–250). Cambridge, UK: Cambridge University Press.

Ho, B. C., Milev, P., O'Leary, D. S., Librant, A., Flaum, M., Andreasen, N. C., & Wassink, T. (2006). Cognitive and magnetic resonance imaging brain morphometric correlates of brain-derived neurotrophic factor Val66Met gene polymorphism in patients with schizophrenia and healthy volunteers. *Archives of General Psychiatry, 63,* 731–740.

Ho, B. C., Nopoulos, P., Flaum, M., Arndt, S., & Andreasen, N. C. (1998). Two-year outcome in first-episode schizophrenia: Predictive value of symptoms for quality of life. *American Journal of Psychiatry, 155,* 1196–1201.

Hobson, R. P., & Lee, A. (1998). Hello and goodbye: A study of social engagement in autism. *Journal of Autism and Developmental Disorders, 28,* 117–127.

Hodges, E. L., Cochrane, C. E., & Brewerton, T. D. (1998). Family characteristics of binge-eating disorder patients. *International Journal of Eating Disorders, 23,* 145–151.

Hoebel, B. G., & Teitelbaum, P. (1966). Weight regulation in normal and hypothalamic hyperphagic rats. *Journal of Comparative and Physiological Psychology, 61,* 189–193.

Hoek, H. W., & van Hoeken, D. (2003). Review of the prevalence and incidence of eating disorders. *International Journal of Eating Disorders, 34,* 383–396.

Hoffart, A., & Torgensen, S. (1991). Causal attributions in first-degree relatives of depressed and agoraphobic inpatients. *Comprehensive Psychiatry, 32,* 458–464.

Hoffman, E. J., & Mathew, S. J. (2008). Anxiety disorders: A comprehensive review of pharmacotherapies. *Mount Sinai Journal of Medicine, 75,* 248–262.

Hofmann, S. G., Sawyer, A. T., Witt, A. A., & Oh, D. (2010). The effect of mindfulness-based therapy on anxiety and depression: A meta-analytic review. *Journal of Consulting and Clinical Psychology, 78,* 169–183.

Hofmann, S. G., & Smits, J. A. (2008). Cognitive-behavioral therapy for adult anxiety disorders: A meta-analysis of randomized placebo-controlled trials. *The Journal of Clinical Psychiatry, 69,* 621–632.

Hogarty, G. E., Anderson, C. M., Reiss, D. J., Kornblith, S. J., Greenwald, D. P., et al. (1986). Family psychoeducation, social skills training, and maintenance chemotherapy in the aftercare treatment of schizophrenia: 1. One-year effects of a controlled study on relapse and expressed emotion. *Archives of General Psychiatry, 43,* 633–642.

Hogarty, G. E., Anderson, C. M., Reiss, D. J., Kornblith, S. J., Greenwald, D. P., Ulrich, R. F., Carter, M., et al. The Environmental-Personal Indicators in the Course of Schizophrenia (EPICS) Research Group. (1991). Family psychoeducation, social skills training, and maintenance chemotherapy in the aftercare treatment of schizophrenia. *Archives of General Psychiatry, 48,* 340–347.

Hogarty, G. E., Flesher, S., Ulrich, R., et al. (2004). Cognitive enhancement therapy for schizophrenia: Effects of a 2-year randomized trial on cognition and behavior. *Archives of General Psychiatry, 61,* 866–876.

Holder, H. D., Longabaugh, R., Miller, W. R., & Rubonis, A. V. (1991). The cost effectiveness of treatment for alcoholism: A first approximation. *Journal of Studies on Alcohol, 52,* 517–540.

Hollingshead, A. B., & Redlich, F. C. (1958). *Social class and mental illness: A community study.* New York: John Wiley & Sons.

Hollon, S. D., & DeRubeis, R. J. (2003). *Cognitive therapy for depression.* Paper presented at the Annual Conference of the American Psychiatric Association, Philadelphia, PA.

Hollon, S. D., DeRubeis, R. J., Shelton, R. C., Amsterdam, J. D., Salomon, R. M., & O'Reardon, J. P. (2005).

Prevention of relapse following cognitive therapy vs medications in moderate to severe depression. *Archives of General Psychiatry, 62*, 417–422.

Hollon, S. D., Stewart, M. O., & Strunk, D. (2006). Enduring effects for cognitive behavior therapy in the treatment of depression and anxiety. *Annual Review of Psychology, 57*, 285–315.

Hollon, S. D., Thase, M. E., & Markowitz, J. C. (2002). Treatment and prevention of depression. *Psychological Science in the Public Interest, 3*, 39–77.

Holm, V. A., & Varley, C. K. (1989). Pharmacological treatment of autistic children. In G. Dawson (Ed.), *Autism: Nature, diagnosis, and treatment* (pp. 386–404). New York: Guilford Press.

Holmes, C., Boche, D., Wilkinson, D., Yadegarfar, G., Hopkins, V., Bayer, A., et al. (2008). Long-term effects of Abeta42 immunization in Alzheimer's disease: Follow-up of a randomised, placebo-controlled phase I trial. *The Lancet, 372*, 216–223.

Holmes, E. A., Brown, R. J., Mansell, W., Fearon, R. P., Hunter, E. C., Frasquilho, F., et al. (2005). Are there two qualitatively distinct forms of dissociation? A review and some clinical implications. *Clinical Psychology Review, 25*, 1–23.

Holtzheimer, P. E., & Mayberg, H. S. (2011). Deep brain stimulation for psychiatric disorders. *Annual Review of Neuroscience, 34*, 289–307.

Hong, J. P., Samuels, J., Bienvenu, O. J., Hsu, F. C., Eaton, W. W., Costa, P. T., Jr., et al. (2005). The longitudinal relationship between personality disorder dimensions and global functioning in a community-residing population. *Psychological Medicine, 35*, 891–895.

Hope, D. A., Heimberg, R. G., & Bruch, M. A. (1995). Dismantling cognitive-behavioral group therapy for social phobia. *Behaviour Research and Therapy, 33*, 637–650.

Hopwood, C. J., & Zanarini, M. C. (2010). Borderline personality traits and disorder: Predicting prospective patient functioning. *Journal of Consulting and Clinical Psychology, 78*, 585–589.

Horan, W. P., Kring, A. M., & Blanchard, J. J. (2006). Anhedonia in schizophrenia: A review of assessment strategies. *Schizophrenia Bulletin, 32*, 259–273.

Horowitz, J. L., & Garber, J. (2006). The prevention of depressive symptoms in children and adolescents: A meta-analytic review. *Journal of Consulting and Clinical Psychology, 74*, 401–415.

Horton, A. M. J. (2008). The Halstead-Reitan Neuropsychological Test Battery: Past, present, and future. In A. M. Horton & D. Wedding (Eds.), *The Neuropsychology Handbook* (3rd ed.) (pp. 251–278). New York: Springer Publishing.

Horton, R. S. (2011). Parenting as a cause of narcissism: Empirical support for psychodynamic and social learning theories. In W. K. Campbell & J. D. Miller (Eds.), *The handbook of narcissism and narcissistic personality disorder: Theoretical approaches, empirical findings, and treatments* (pp. 181–190). Hoboken, NJ: John Wiley & Sons.

Houenou, J., Frommberger, J., Carde, S., Glasbrenner, M., Diener, C., Leboyer, M., & Wessa, M. (2011). Neuroimaging-based markers of bipolar disorder: Evidence from two meta-analyses. *Journal of Affective Disorders, 132*, 344–355.

Houts, A. C. (2001). Harmful dysfunction and the search for value neutrality in the definition of mental disorder: Response to Wakefield, Part 2. *Behaviour Research and Therapy, 39*, 1099–1132.

Howard, R., McShane, R., Lindesay, J., Ritchie, C., Baldwin, A., Barber, R., et al. (2012). Donepezil and memantine for moderate-to-severe Alzheimer's disease. *New England Journal of Medicine, 366*, 893–903.

Howard, R., Rabins, P. V., Seeman, M. V., & Jeste, D. V. (2000). Late-onset schizophrenia and very-late-onset schizophrenia-like psychosis: an international consensus. The International Late-Onset Schizophrenia Group. *American Journal of Psychiatry, 157*, 172–178.

Howlin, P., Goode, S., Hutton, J., & Rutter, M. (2004). Adult outcome or children with autism. *Journal of Child Psychology and Psychiatry, 45*, 212–229.

Howlin, P., Mawhood, L., & Rutter, M. (2000). Autism and developmental receptive language disorder—A follow-up comparison in early adult life. II. Social, behavioral, and psychiatric outcomes. *Journal of Child Psychiatry and Psychology, 41*, 561–578.

Hoza, B., Murray-Close, D., Arnold, L. E., Hinshaw, S. P., Hechtmen, L., & The MTA Cooperative Group. (2010). Time-dependent changes in positive illusory self-perceptions of children with attention-deficit/hyperactivity disorder: A developmental psychopathology perspective. *Developmental and Psychopathology, 22*, 375–390.

Hser, Y., Anglin, M. D., & Powers, K. (1993). A 24-year follow-up of California narcotics addicts. *Archives of General Psychiatry, 50*, 577–584.

Hsu, L. K. G. (1990). *Eating disorders*. New York: Guilford Press.

Hu, W. T., Seelaar, H., Josephs, K. A., Knopman, D. S., Boeve, B. F., Sorenson, E. J., et al. (2009). Survival profiles of patients with frontotemporal dementia and motor neuron disease. *Archives of Neurology, 66*, 1359–1364.

Huang, J., Chaloupka, F. J., & Fong, G. T. (2014). Cigarette graphic warning labels and smoking prevalence in Canada: A critical examination and reformulation of the FDA regulatory impact analysis. *Tobacco Control, 23 Suppl 1*, i7–12.

Hudson, J. I., Hiripi, E., Pope, H. G., & Kessler, R. C. (2007). The prevalence and correlates of eating disorders in the National Comorbidity Survey Replication. *Biological Psychology, 61*, 348–358.

Hudson, J. I., Lalonde, J. K., Berry, J. M., Pindyck, L. J., & Bulick, C. (2006). Binge-eating disorder as a distinct familial phenotype in obese individuals. *Archives of General Psychology, 63*, 3138–3319.

Huether, G., Zhou, D., & Ruther, E. (1997). Causes and consequences of the loss of serotonergic presynapses elicited by the consumption of 3, 4methylenedioxymethamphetamine (MDMA, "ecstasy") and its congeners. *Journal of Neural Transmission, 104*, 771–794.

Hughes, C., & Agran, M. (1993). Teaching persons with severe disabilities to use self-instruction in community settings: An analysis of applications. *Journal of the Association for Persons with Severe Handicaps, 18*, 261–274.

Hughes, C., Hugo, K., & Blatt, J. (1996). Self-instructional intervention for teaching generalized problem-solving within a functional task sequence. *American Journal on Mental Retardation, 100*, 565–579.

Hughes, J. R. (2009). How confident should we be that smoking cessation treatments work? *Addiction, 104*(10), 1637–1640.

Hughes, J. R., Higgins, S. T., & Hatsukami, D. K. (1990). Effects of abstinence from tobacco: A critical review. In L. T. Kozlowski, H. Annis, H. D. Cappell, F. Glaser, M. Goodstadt, Y. Israel, H. Kalant, E. M. Sellers & J. Vingilis (Eds.), *Research advances in alcohol and drug problems*. New York: Plenum.

Hughes, J. R., Higgins, S. T., Bickel, W. K., Hunt, W. K., & Fenwick, J. W. (1991). Caffeine self-adminstration, withdrawal, and adverse effects among coffee drinkers. *Archives of General Psychiatry, 48*, 611–617.

Hughes, J., Stead, L., & Lancaster, T. (2004). Antidepressants for smoking cessation. *Cochrane Database of Systematic Reviews*, CD000031.

Huijbregts, S. C. J., de Sonneville, L. M. J., Licht, R., van Spronsen, F. J., Verkerk, P. H., & Sergeant, J. A. (2002). Sustained attention and inhibition of cognitive interference in treated phenylketonuria: Associations with concurrent and lifetime phenylalanine concentrations. *Neuropsychologia, 40*, 7–15.

Hulley, S., Grady, D., Bush, T., Furberg, C., Herrington, D., Riggs, B., & Vittinghoff, E. (1998). Randomized trial of estrogen plus progestin for secondary prevention of coronary heart disease in postmenopausal women. Heart and Estrogen/progestin Replacement Study (HERS) Research Group. *Journal of the American Medical Association, 280*, 605–613.

Hulse, G. K., Ngo, H. T., & Tait, R. J. (2010). Risk factors for craving and relapse in heroin users treated with oral or implant naltrexone. *Biological Psychiatry, 68*, 296–302.

Human Genome Project. (2008). How many genes are in the human genome? Accessed online at http://www.ornl.gov/sci/techresources/Human_Genome/faq/gene-number.shtml.

Hunsley, J., & Bailey, J. M. (1999). The clinical utility of the Rorschach: Unfulfilled promises and an uncertain future. *Psychological Assessment, 11*, 266–277.

Hunter, E. C., Sierra, M., & David, A. S. (2004). The epidemiology of depersonalisation and derealisation. A systematic review. *Social Psychiatry and Psychiatric Epidemiology, 39*, 9–18.

Hunter, R., & Macalpine, I. (1963). *Three hundred years of psychiatry 1535–1860*. Oxford, UK: Oxford University Press.

Huntjen, R. J. C., Postma, A., Peters, M. L., Woertman, L., & van der Hart, O. (2003). Interidentity amnesia for neutral, episodic information in dissociative identity disorder. *Journal of Abnormal Psychology, 112*, 290–297.

Hurlburt, R. T. (1979). Random sampling of cognitions and behavior. *Journal of Research on Personality, 13*, 103–111.

Hussong, A. M., Hicks, R. E., Levy, S. A., & Curran, P. J. (2001). Specifying the relations between affect and heavy alcohol use among young adults. *Journal of Abnormal Psychology, 110*, 449–461.

Hustvedt, A. (2011). *Medical muses: Hysteria in nineteenth-century Paris*. New York: W. W. Norton.

Hyman, S. E. (2002). Neuroscience, genetics, and the future of psychiatric diagnosis. *Psychopathology, 35*, 139–144.

Hyman, S. E. (2010). The diagnosis of mental disorders: The problem of reification. *Annual Review of Clinical Psychology, 6*, 155–179.

Iarovici, D. (2014). *Mental health issues and the university student*. Baltimore: Johns Hopkins University Press.

Iervolino, A. C., Perroud, N., Fullana, M. A., Guipponi, M., Cherkas, L., Collier, D. A., et al. (2009). Prevalence and heritability of compulsive hoarding: A twin study. *American Journal of Psychiatry, 166*, 1156–1161.

IMS Health. (2012). IMS national prescription audit PlusTM. (2011). Downloaded June 2014 from http://www.imshealth.com/portal/site/imshealth.

IMS Health. (2014). Medicine use and shifting costs of healthcare: A review of the use of medicines in the United States in 2013. Retrieved April 28, 2014, at http://www.imshealth.com/cds/imshealth/Global/Content/Corporate/IMS Health Institute/Reports/Secure/IIHI_US_Use_of_Meds_for_2013.pdf.

Indovina, I., Robbins, T. W., Nunez-Elizalde, A. O., Dunn, B. D., & Bishop, S. J. (2011). Fear-conditioning mechanisms associated with trait vulnerability to anxiety in humans. *Neuron, 69*, 563–571.

Inouye, S. K., Bogardus, S. T., Jr., Charpentier, P. A., Leo-Summers, L., Acampora, D., Holford, T. R., et al. (1999). A multicomponent intervention to prevent delirium in hospitalized older patients. *New England Journal of Medicine, 340*, 669–676.

Insel, T. R. (2014). The NIMH Research Domain Criteria (RDoC) Project: Precision Medicine for Psychiatry. *American Journal of Psychiatry, 171*(4), 395–397.

Insel, T. R., Scanlan, J., Champoux, M., & Suomi, S. J. (1988). Rearing paradigm in a nonhuman primate affects response to B-CCE challenge. *Psychopharmacology, 96*, 81–86.

Institute of Medicine. (1990). *Treating drug problems.* Washington, DC: National Academy Press.

Institute of Medicine. (1999). *Marijuana and medicine: Assessing the science base.* Washington, DC: National Academy Press.

Institute of Medicine. (2004). *Immunization safety review: Vaccines and autism.* Immunization Safety Review Board on Health Promotion and Disease Prevention. Washington, DC: National Academies Press.

International Society for the Study of Dissociation. (2011). Guidelines for treating dissociative identity disorder in adults, third revision: Summary version. *Journal of Trauma and Dissociation 12*, 188–212.

Ipser, J. C., Sander, C., & Stein, D. J. (2009). Pharmacotherapy and psychotherapy for body dysmorphic disorder. *Cochrane Database of Systematic Reviews* CD005332.

Irvin, J. E., Bowers, C.A., Dunn, M.E., & Wang, M.C. (1999). Efficacy of relapse prevention: A meta-analytic review. *Journal of Consulting and Clinical Psychology, 67*, 563–570.

Isaacowitz, D. M. (2012). Mood regulation in real time: Age differences in the role of looking. *Current Directions in Psychological Science, 21*, 237–242.

Ishikawa, S. S., Raine, A., Lencz, T., Bihrle, S., & Lacasse, L. (2001). Autonomic stress reactivity and executive functions in successful and unsuccessful criminal psychopaths from the community. *Journal of Abnormal Psychology, 110*, 423–432.

Ito, T., Miller, N. & Pollock, V. (1996). Alcohol and agression: A meta-analysis on the moderating effects of inhibitory cues, triggering events, and self-focused attention. *Psychological Bulletin, 120*, 60–82.

Ivanoff, A., Jang, S. J., Smyth, N. J., & Linehan, M. M. (1994). Fewer reasons for staying alive when you are thinking of killing yourself: The Brief Reasons for Living Inventory. *Journal of Psychopathology and Behavioral Assessment, 16*, 1–13.

Ivarsson, T., Råstam, M., Weitz, E., Gilberg, I. C., & Gilberg, G. (2000). Depressive disorders in teen-age-onset anorexia nervosa: A controlled longitudinal, partly community-based study. *Comprehensive Psychiatry, 41*, 398–403.

Jack, C. R., Jr., Albert, M. S., Knopman, D. S., McKhann, G. M., Sperling, R. A., Carrillo, M. C., et al. (2011). Introduction to the recommendations from the National Institute on Aging-Alzheimer's Association workgroups on diagnostic guidelines for Alzheimer's disease. *Alzheimer's and Dementia : The Journal of the Alzheimer's Association, 7*, 257–262.

Jackson, J. C., Gordon, S. M., Hart, R. P., Hopkins, R. O., & Ely, E. W. (2004). The association between delirium and cognitive decline: A review of the empirical literature. *Neuropsychology Review, 14*, 87–98.

Jacobi, E. A. (2004). Prevalence, co-morbidity and correlates of mental disorders in the general population: Results from the German Health Interview and Examination Survey. *Psychological Medicine, 34*, 597–611.

Jacobsen, L. K., Southwick, S. M., & Kosten, T. R. (2001). Substance use disorders in patients with posttraumatic stress disorder: A review of the literature. *American Journal of Psychiatry, 158*, 1184–1190.

Jacobson, N. S., Dobson, K. S., Fruzzetti, A. E., & Schmaling, K. B. (1991). Marital therapy as a treatment for depression. *Journal of Consulting and Clinical Psychology, 59*, 547–557.

Jacobson, N. S., & Gortner, E. T. (2000). Can depression be de-medicalized in the 21st century?: Scientific revolutions, counter-revolutions and the magnetic field of normal science. *Behaviour Research and Therapy, 38*, 103–117.

Jacobson, N. S., Roberts, L. J., Berns, S. B., & McGlinchey, J. B. (1999). Methods for defining and determining the clinical significance of treatment effects: Description, application, and alternatives. *Journal of Consulting and Clinical Psychology, 67*, 300–307.

Jaffe, J. H. (1985). Drug addiction and drug abuse. In Goodman, A. G. & Gilman, A. (Eds.), *Goodman and Gilman's The pharmacological basis of therapeutic behavior.* New York: Macmillan.

Jaffee, S. R., Strait, L. B., & Odgers, C. L. (2012). From correlates to causes: Can quasi-experimental studies and statistical innovations bring us closer to identifying the causes of antisocial behavior? *Psychological Bulletin, 138*, 272–295.

Jak, A. J., Bondi, M. W., Delano-Wood, L., Wierenga, C., Corey-Bloom, J., Salmon, D., et al. (2009). Quantification of five neuropsychological approaches to defining mild cognitive impairment. *American Journal of Geriatric Psychiatry, 17*, 368–375.

James, A., Hoang, U., Seagroatt, V., Clacey, J., Goldacre, M., & Leibenluft, E. (2014). A comparison of American and English hospital discharge rates for pediatric bipolar disorder, 2000 to 2010. *Journal of the American Academy of Child and Adolescent Psychiatry, 53*(6), 614-624.

James, D. J., & Glaze, L. E. (2006). Mental health problems of prison and jail inmates. *NCJ 213600.* Retrieved from http://www.bjs.gov/content/pub/pdf/mhppji.pdf website: http://www.bjs.gov/content/pub/pdf/mhppji.pdf.

Jamison, K. R. (1993). *Touched with fire: Manic-depressive illness and the artistic temperament.* New York: Simon & Schuster.

Jamison, K. R. (1995). *The unquiet mind: A memoir of moods and madness.* New York: Vintage Books.

Jampole, L., & Weber, M. K. (1987). An assessment of the behavior of sexually abused and nonsexually abused children with anatomically correct dolls. *Child Abuse and Neglect, 11*, 187–192.

Jardri, R., Pouchet, A., Pins, D., & Thomas, P. (2011). Cortical activation during auditory verbal hallucinations in schizophrenia: a coordinate-based meta-analysis. *American Journal of Psychiatry, 168*, 73–81.

Jarrell, M. P., Johnson, W. G., & Williamson, D. A. (1986). *Insulin and glucose response in the binge purge episode of bulimic women.* Paper presented at the annual convention of the Association for Advancement of Behavior Therapy, Chicago.

Jauhar, S., McKenna, P., Radua, J., E., F., R., S., & Laws, K. R. (2014). Cognitive-behavioural therapy for the symptoms of schizophrenia: Systematic review and meta-analysis with examination of potential bias. *British Journal of Psychiatry, 204*, 20–29.

Jeans, R. F. I. (1976). An independently validated case of multiple personality. *Journal of Abnormal Psychology, 85*, 249–255.

Jensen, M. P., & Patterson, D. R. (2014). Hypnotic approaches for chronic pain management: clinical implications of recent research findings. *American Psychologist, 69*, 167–177.

Jensen, P. S., Arnold, L. E., Swanson, J. M. et al. (2007). 3-year follow-up of the NIMH MTA study. *Journal of the American Academy of Child and Adolescent Psychiatry, 46*, 989–1002.

Jensen, P. S., Martin, D., & Cantwell, D. P. (1997). Comorbidity in ADHD: Implications for research, practice, and DSM-V. *Journal of the American Academy of Child and Adolescent Psychiatry, 36*, 1065–1079.

Jespersen, A. F., Lalumiere, M. L., & Seto, M. C. (2009). Sexual abuse history among adult sex offenders and non-sex offenders: a meta-analysis. *Child Abuse and Neglect, 33*, 179–192.

Jett, D., LaPorte, D. J., & Wanchism, J. (2010). Impact of exposure to pro-eating disorder websites on eating behaviour in college women. *European Eating Disorders Review, 18*, 410–416.

Jimerson, D. C., Lesem, M. D., Kate, W. H., & Brewerton, T. D. (1992). Low serotonin and dopamine metabolite concentrations in cerebrospinal fluid from bulimic patients with frequent binge episodes. *Archives of General Psychiatry, 49*, 132–138.

Jimerson, D. C., Wolfe, B. E., Metzger, E. D., Finkelstein, D. M., Cooper, T. B., et al. (1997). Decreased serotonin function in bulimia nervosa. *Archives of General Psychiatry, 54*, 529–536.

Johnson, J. G., Cohen, P., Brown, J., Smailes, E. M., & Bernstein, D. P. (1999). Childhood maltreatment increases risk for personality disorders during early adulthood. *Archives of General Psychiatry, 56*, 600–606.

Johnson, J. G., Cohen, P., Chen, H., Kasen, S., & Brook, J. S. (2006). Parenting behaviors associated with risk for offspring personality disorder during adulthood. *Archives of General Psychiatry, 63*, 579–583.

Johnson, J. G., Cohen, P., Kasen, S., & Brook, J. S. (2006). Dissociative disorders among adults in the community, impaired functioning, and axis I and II comorbidity. *Journal of Psychiatric Research, 40*, 131–140.

Johnson, J. G., Cohen, P., Kasen, S., Skodol, A. E., Hamagami, F., & Brook, J. S. (2000). Age-related change in personality disorder trait levels between early adolescence and adulthood: A community-based longitudinal investigation. *Acta Psychiatrica Scandinavica, 2*, 263–275.

Johnson, J., Weissman, M. M., & Klerman, G. L. (1992). Service utilization and social morbidity associated with depressive symptoms in the community. *Journal of the American Medical Association, 267*, 1478–1483.

Johnson, S. L., Cuellar, A. K., & Peckham, A. D. (Eds.). (2014). *Risk factors for bipolar disorder* (3rd ed.). New York: Guilford Press.

Johnson, S. L., Edge, M. D., Holmes, M. K., & Carver, C. S. (2012). The behavioral activation system and mania. *Annual Review of Clinical Psychology, 8*, 243–267.

Johnson, W. G., Tsoh, J. Y., & Varnado, P. J. (1996). Eating disorders: Efficacy of pharmacological and psychological interventions. *Clinical Psychology Review, 16*, 457–478.

Johnston, C., & Marsh, E. J. (2001). Families of children with attention-deficit/hyperactivity disorder: Review and recommendations for future research. *Clinical Child and Family Psychology Review, 4*, 183–207.

Johnston, L. D., O'Malley, P. M., Bachman, J. G., Schulenberg, J. E., & Miech, R. A. (2014). Monitoring the future national survey results on drug use, 1975–2013: Volume I, Secondary school. Ann Arbor: Institute for Social Research, The University of Michigan

Joiner, T. E. (1995). The price of soliciting and receiving negative feedback: Self-verification theory as a vulnerability to depression theory. *Journal of Abnormal Psychology, 104*, 364–372.

Joiner, T. E., & Metalsky, G. I. (2001). Excessive reassurance-seeking: delineating a risk factor involved in the development of depressive symptoms. *Psychological Science, 12*, 371–378.

Joiner, T. E., Alfano, M. S., & Metalsky, G. I. (1992). When depression breeds contempt: Reassurance seeking, selfesteem, and rejection of depressed college students by their roommates. *Journal of Abnormal Psychology, 101*, 165–173.

Joiner, T. E., Brown, J. S., & Wingate, L. R. (2005). The psychology and neurobiology of suicidal behavior. *Annual Review of Psychology, 56*, 287–314.

Joiner, T. E., Voelz, Z. R., & Rudd, M. D. (2001). For suicidal young adults with comorbid depressive and anxiety disorders, problem-solving treatment may be better than treatment as usual. *Professional Psychology: Research and Practice, 32*, 278–282.

Jonas, B. S., Gu, Q., & Albertorio-Diaz, J. R. (2013). Psychotropic medication use among adolescents: United States, 2005–2010. *NCHS Data Brief,* no 135.

Jones, P. B., Barnes, T. R. E., Davies, L., Dunn, G., Lloyd, H., et al. (2006). Randomized controlled trial of the effect on quality of life of second- vs first-generation antipsychotic drugs in schizophrenia: Cost utility of the latest antipsychotic drugs in schizophrenia study (CUtLASS 1). *Archives of General Psychiatry, 63*, 1079–1087.

Jones, W., & Klin, A. (2013). Attention to eyes is present but in decline in 2-6-month-old infants later diagnosed with autism. *Nature, 504*(7480), 427–431.

Jones, E., & Wessely, S. (2001). Psychiatric battle casualties: An intra-and interwar comparision. *British Journal of Psychiatry, 178*, 242–247.

Jordan, N. C. (2007). Do words count? Connections between mathematics and reading difficulties. In D. B. Berch & M. M. M. Mazzocco (Eds.), *Why is math so hard for some children?* (pp. 107–120). Baltimore: Brooks.

Jorenby, D. E., Leischow, S. J., Nides, M. A., Rennard, S. I., Johnston, J. A., et al. (1999). A controlled trial of sustained-release buproprion, a nicotine patch, or both for smoking cessation. *New England Journal of Medicine, 340*, 685–691.

Jorm, A. F., Christensen, H., Henderson, A. S., Jacomb, P. A., Korten, A. E., & Rodgers, B. (2000). Predicting anxiety and depression from personality: Is there a synergistic effect of neuroticism and extraversion? *Journal of Abnormal Psychology, 109*, 145-149.

Josephs, K. A. (2008). Frontotemporal dementia and related disorders: Deciphering the enigma. *Annals of Neurology, 64*, 4–14.

Josephs, R. A., & Steele, C. M. (1990). The two faces of alcohol myopia: attentional mediation of psychological stress. *Journal of Abnormal Psychology, 99*, 115–126.

Judd, L. L. (1997). The clinical course of unipolar major depressive disorders. *Archives of General Psychiatry, 54*, 989–991.

Judd, L. L., Akiskal, H. S., Maser, J. D., Zeller, P. J., Endicott, J., Coryell, W., et al. (1998). A prospective 12-year study of subsyndromal and syndromal depressive symptoms in unipolar major depressive disorders. *Archives of General Psychiatry, 55*, 694–701.

Just, N., & Alloy, L. B. (1997). The response styles theory of depression: Tests and an extension of the theory. *Journal of Abnormal Psychology, 106*, 221–229.

Kadlec, D., Rawe, J., Park, A., Fonda, D., Cole, W., et al. (2004, May 3). The low carb frenzy. *Time Magazine,* 46.

Kafka, M. P. (1997). Hypersexual desire in males: An operational definition and clinical implications for males with paraphilias and paraphilia-related disorders. *Archives of Sexual Behavior, 26*(5), 505–526.

Kafka, M. P. (2010). The DSM diagnostic criteria for fetishism. *Archives of Sexual Behavior, 39*, 357–362.

Kafka, M. P., & Hennen, J. (2002). A DSM-IV Axis I comorbidity study of males (*n* = 120) with paraphilias and paraphilia-related disorders. *Sexual Abuse: A Journal of Research and Treatment, 14*, 349–366.

Kagan, J., & Snidman, N. (1999). Early childhood predictors of adult anxiety disorders. *Biological Psychiatry, 46*, 1536–1541.

Kandel, D. B. (2002). *Stages and pathways of drug involvement: examining the gateway hypothesis.* New York: Cambridge University Press.

Kane, J., Honigfeld, G., Singer, J., Meltzer, H., and the Clozapine Collaborative Study Group. (1988). Clozapine for treatment resistant schizophrenics. *Archives of General Psychiatry, 45*, 789–796.

Kanner, L. (1943). Autistic disturbances of affective contact. *Nervous Child, 2*, 217–250.

Kapczinski, F., Lima, M. S., Souza, J. S., Cunha, A., & Schmitt, R. (2002). Antidepressants for generalized anxiety disorder. *Cochrane Database of Systematic Reviews, Issue 2,* CD003592.

Kaplan, H. S. (1974). *The new sex therapy.* New York: Brunner/Mazel.

Kaplan, H. S. (1997). Sexual desire disorders (hypoactive sexual desire and sexual aversion). In G. O. Gabbard & S. D. Atkinson (Eds.), *Synopsis of treatments of psychiatric disorders* (2nd ed., pp. 771–780). Washington, DC: American Psychiatric Press.

Kaplan, M. S., & Kreuger, R. B. (1997). Voyeurism: Psychopathology and theory. In D. R. Laws & W. O'Donohue (Eds.), *Sexual deviance* (pp. 297–310). New York: Guilford Press.

Kaplan, M. S., & Krueger, R. B. (2012). Cognitive-behavioral treatment of the paraphilias. *Israel Journal of Psychiatry Related Sciences, 49*, 291–296.

Kaplow, J. B., & Widom, C. S. (2007). Age of onset of child maltreatment predicts long-term mental health outcomes. *Journal of Abnormal Psychology, 116*, 176–187.

Kaptchuk, T. J., Kelley, J. M., Conboy, L. A., Davis, R. B., Kerr, C. E., Jacobson, E. E., et al. (2008). Components of placebo effect: Randomised controlled trial in patients with irritable bowel syndrome. *British Medical Journal, 336*, 999–1003.

Karg, K. (2011). The serotonin transporter promoter variant (5-HTTLPR), stress, and depression meta-analysis revisited: Evidence of genetic moderation. *Archives of General Psychiatry, 68*, 444.

Karg, K., Burmeister, M., Shedden, K., & Sen, S. (2011). The serotonin transporter promoter variant (5-HTTLPR), stress, and depression meta-analysis revisited: evidence of genetic moderation. *Archives of General Psychiatry, 68*, 444–454.

Karney, B. R., & Bradbury, T. N. (1995). The longitudinal course of marital quality and stability: A review of theory, method, and research. *Psychological Bulletin, 118*, 3–34.

Karon, B. P., & VandenBos, G. R. (1998). Schizophrenia and psychosis in elderly populations. In I. H. Nordhus, G. R. VandenBos, S. Berg & P. Fromholt (Eds.), *Clinical Geropsychology* (pp. 219–227). Washington, DC: American Psychological Association.

Kasahara, T. (1995). [Diagnosis of Taijin-Kyofu and social phobia]. *Seishin shinkeigaku zasshi. Psychiatria et neurologia Japonica, 97*, 357–366.

Kasari, C., Freeman, S., & Paparella, T. (2006). Joint attention and symbolic play in young children with autism: A randomized controlled intervention study. *Journal of Child Psychology and Psychiatry, 47*, 611–620.

Kasari, C., Paparella, T., Freeman, S., & Jahromi, L. B. (2008). Language outcome in autism: randomized comparison of joint attention and play interventions. *Journal of Consulting and Clinical Psychology, 76*, 125–137.

Kashdan, T. B., & McKnight, P. E. (2010). The darker side of social anxiety: When aggressive impulsivity prevails over shy inhibition. *Current Directions in Psychological Science, 19*, 47–50.

Kashden, J., & Franzen, M. D. (1996). An interrater reliability study of the Luria-Nebraska Neuropsychological Battery Form-II quantitative scoring system. *Archives of Clinical Neuropsychology, 11*, 155–163.

Kassel, J. D., & Shiffman, S. (1997). Attentional mediation of cigarette smoking's effect on anxiety. *Health Psychology, 16*, 359–368.

Kassel, J. D., & Unrod, M. (2000). Smoking, anxiety, and attention: Support for the role of nicotine in attentionally mediated anxiolysis. *Journal of Abnormal Psychology, 109*, 161–166.

Kassel, J. D., Stroud, L. R., & Paronis, C. A. (2003). Smoking, stress, and negative affect: Correlation, causation, and context across stages of smoking. *Psychological Bulletin, 129*, 270–304.

Kassett, J. A., Gershon, E. S., Maxwell, M. E., et al. (1989). Psychiatric disorders in the first-degree relatives of probands with bulimia nervosa. *American Journal of Psychiatry, 146*, 1468–1471.

Katz, E. C., Gruber, K., Chutuape, M. A., & Stitzer, M. L. (2001). Reinforcement-based outpatient treatment for opiate and cocaine abusers. *Journal of Substance Abuse Treatment, 20*, 93–98.

Katz, I. R., Parmelee, P., & Brubaker, K. (1991). Toxic and metabolic encephalopathies in long-term care patients. *International Psychogeriatrics, 3*, 337–347.

Kawakami, N., Shimizu, H., Haratani, T., Iwata, N., & Kitamura, T. (2004). Lifetime and 6-month prevalence of DSM-III-R psychiatric disorders in an urban community in Japan. *Psychiatry Research, 121*, 293–301.

Kaye, W. H. (2008). Neurobiology of anorexia and bulimia nervosa. *Physiology and Behavior, 94*, 121–135.

Kaye, W. H., Greeno, C. G., Moss, H., Fernstrom, J., Lilenfeld, L. R., Wahlund, B., et al. (1998). Alterations in serotonin activity and platelet monoamine oxidase and psychiatric symptoms after recovery from bulimia nervosa. *Archives of General Psychiatry, 55*, 927–935.

Kaye, W. H., Ebert, M. H., Raleigh, M., & Lake, R. (1984). Abnormalities in CNS monoamine metabolism in anorexia nervosa. *Archives of General Psychiatry, 41*, 350–355.

Kazdin, A. E. (2005). *Parent management training: Treatment for oppositional, aggressive, and antisocial behavior in children and adolescents.* New York: Oxford University Press.

Kazdin, A. E., & Weisz, J. R. (1998). Identifying and developing empirically supported child and adolescent treatments. *Journal of Consulting and Clinical Psychology, 66*, 19–36.

Keane, T. M., Fairbank, J. A., Caddell, J. M., & Zimering, R. T. (1989). Implosive (flooding) therapy reduces symptoms of PTSD in Vietnam combat veterans. *Behavior Therapy, 20*, 245–260.

Keane, T. M., Gerardi, R. J., Quinn, S. J., & Litz, B. T. (1992). Behavioral treatment of post-traumatic stress disorder. In S. M. Turner, K. S. Calhoun & H. E. Adams (Eds.), *Handbook of Clinical Behavior Therapy* (2nd ed., pp. 87–97). New York: John Wiley & Sons.

Keane, T. M., Marshall, A. D., & Taft, C. T. (2006). Posttraumatic stress disorder: Etiology, epidemiology, and treatment outcome. *Annual Review of Clinical Psychology, 2,* 161–197.

Keane, T. M., Zimering, R. T., & Caddell, J. (1985). A behavioral formulation of posttraumatic stress disorder in Vietnam veterans. *The Behavior Therapist, 8,* 9–12.

Keefe, R. S. E., Bilder, R. M., Davis, S.M., Harvey, P.D., Palmer, B. W. et al. (2007). Neurocognitive effects of antipsychotic medications in patients with chronic schizophrenia in the CATIE trial. *Archives of General Psychiatry, 64,* 633–647.

Keel, P. K., Baxter, M. G., Heatherton, T. F., & Joiner, T. E. (2007). A 20-year longitudinal study of body weight, dieting, and eating disorder symptoms. *Journal of Abnormal Psychology, 116,* 422–432.

Keel, P. K., & Brown, T. A. (2010). Update on course and outcome in eating disorders. *International Journal of Eating Disorders, 43,* 195–204.

Keel, P. K., Gravener, J. A., Joiner, T. E., Jr., & Haedt, A. A. (2010). Twenty-year follow-up of bulimia nervosa and related eating disorders not otherwise specified. *International Journal of Eating Disorders, 43,* 492–497.

Keel, P. K., & Klump, K. L. (2003). Are eating disorders culture-bound syndromes? Implications for conceptualizing their etiology. *Psychological Bulletin, 129,* 747–769.

Keel, P. K., & Mitchell, J. E. (1997). Outcome in bulimia nervosa. *American Journal of Psychiatry, 154,* 313–321.

Keel, P. K., Mitchell, J. E., Davis, T. L., & Crow, S. J. (2002). Long-term impact of treatment in women diagnosed with bulimia nervosa. *International Journal of Eating Disorders, 31,* 151–158.

Keel, P. K., Mitchell, J. E., Miller, K. B., Davis, T. L., & Crowe, S. J. (1999). Long-term outcome of bulimia nervosa. *Archives of General Psychiatry, 56,* 63–69.

Keers, R., Ullrich, S., DeStavola, B. L., & Coid, J. W. (2014). Association of violence with emergence of persecutory delusions in untreated schizophrenia. *American Journal of Psychiatry, 171,* 332–339.

Keilp, J. G., Sackeim, H. A., Brodsky, B. S., Oquendo, M. A., Malone, K. M., & Mann, J. J. (2001). Neuropsychological dysfunction in depressed suicide attempters. *Archives of General Psychiatry, 158,* 735–741. .

Keller, M. B., McCullough, J. P., Klein, D. N., Arnow, B., Dunner, D. L., Gelenberg, A. J., et al. (2000). A comparison of nefazodone, the cognitive behavioral-analysis system of psychotherapy, and their combination for the treatment of chronic depression. *The New England Journal of Medicine, 342,* 1462–1470.

Kellerman, J. (1989). *Silent partner.* New York: Bantam Books.

Kellner, C. H., Fink, M., Knapp, R., Petrides, G., Husain, M., Rummans, T., et al. (2005). Relief of expressed suicidal intent by ECT: A consortium for research in ECT study. *American Journal of Psychiatry, 162,* 977–982.

Keltner, D., & Kring, A. M. (1998). Emotion, social function, and psychopathology. *Review of General Psychology, 2,* 320–342.

Kempster, N. (August 25, 1996). Clinton orders tracking of sex offenders, *Los Angeles Times,* p. A20.

Kempton, M. J., Stahl, D., Williams, S. C., & DeLisi, L. E. (2010). Progressive lateral ventricular enlargement in schizophrenia: A meta-analysis of longitudinal MRI studies. *Schizophrenia Research, 120,* 54-62.

Kenardy, J., & Taylor, C. B. (1999). Expected versus unexpected panic attacks: A naturalistic prospective study. *Journal of Anxiety Disorders, 13,* 435–445.

Kendall, P. C., Aschenbrand, S. G., & Hudson, J. L. (2003). Child-focused treatment of anxiety. In A. E. Kazdin & J. R. Weisz (Eds.), *Evidence-based psychotherapies for children and adolescents* (pp. 81–100). New York: Guilford Press.

Kendall, P. C., & Beidas, R. S. (2007). Trail for dissemination of evidence-based practices for youth: Flexibility within fidelity. *Professional Psychology: Research and Practice, 38,* 13–20.

Kendall, P. C., Flannery-Schroeder, E. C., Panichelli-Mindel, S., Southam-Gerow, M., Henin, A., & Warman, M. (1997). Therapy for youths with anxiety disorders: A second randomized clinical trial. *Journal of Consulting and Clinical Psychology, 65,* 366–380.

Kendall, P. C., Haaga, D. A. F., Ellis, A., Bernard, M., DiGiuseppe, R., & Kassinove, H. (1995). Rationalemotive therapy in the 1990s and beyond: Current status, recent revisions, and research questions. *Clinical Psychology Review, 15,* 169–185.

Kendall, P. C., Hudson, J. L. Gosch, E., Flannery-Schroeder, E., & Suveg, C. (2008). Cognitive–behavioral therapy for anxiety disordered youth: A randomized clinical trial evaluating child and family modalities. *Journal of Consulting and Clinical Psychology, 76,* 282–297.

Kendall, P. C., & Ingram, R. E. (1989). Cognitive-behavioral perspectives: Theory and research on depression and anxiety. In D. Watson & P. C. Kendall (Eds.), *Personality, psychopathology, and psychotherapy* (pp. 27–53). San Diego, CA: Academic Press.

Kendall, P. C., Safford, S., Flannery-Schroeder, E., & Webb, A. (2004). Child anxiety treatment: Outcomes in adolescence and impact on substance use and depression at 7.4-year follow-up. *Journal of Consulting and Clinical Psychology, 72,* 276–287.

Kendler, K. S. (1997). The diagnostic validity of melancholic major depression in a population-based sample of female twins. *Archives of General Psychiatry, 54,* 299–304.

Kendler, K. S., Chen, X., Dick, D., Maes, H., Gillespie, N., Neale, M. C., & Riley, B. (2012). Recent advances in the genetic epidemiology and molecular genetics of substance use disorders. *Nature Neuroscience, 15*(2), 181–189.

Kendler, K. S., Hettema, J. M., Butera, F., Gardner, C. O., & Prescott, C. A. (2003). Life event dimensions of loss, humiliation, entrapment, and danger in the prediction of onsets of major depression and generalized anxiety. *Archives of General Psychiatry, 60,* 789–796.

Kendler, K. S., Jacobson, K., Myers, J. M., & Eaves L. J. (2008). A genetically informative developmental study of the relationship between conduct disorder and peer deviance in males. *Psychological Medicine, 38,* 1001–1011.

Kendler, K. S., Jacobson, K. C., Prescott, C. A., & Neale, M. C. (2003). Specificity of genetic and environmental risk factors for use and abuse/dependence of *Cannabis,* cocaine, hallucinogens, sedatives, stimulants, and opiates in male twins. *American Journal of Psychiatry, 160,* 687–695.

Kendler, K. S., Karkowski-Shuman, L., & Walsh, D. (1996). Age of onset in schizophrenia and risk of illness in relatives. *British Journal of Psychiatry, 169,* 213–218.

Kendler, K. S., Myers, J., & Prescott, C. A. (2002). The etiology of phobias: An evaluation of the stress-diathesis model. *Archives of General Psychiatry, 59,* 242–249.

Kendler, K. S., Myers, J., & Zisook, S. (2008). Does bereavement-related major depression differ from major depression associated with other stressful life events? *American Journal of Psychiatry, 165,* 1449–1455.

Kendler, K. S., Myers, J., Prescott, C. A., & Neale, M. C. (2001). The genetic epidemiology of irrational fears and phobias in men. *Archives of General Psychiatry, 58,* 257–267.

Kendler, K. S., Myers, J., Torgersen, S., Neale, M. C., & Reichborn-Kjennerud, T. (2007). The heritability of cluster A personality disorders assessed by both personal interview and questionnaire. *Psychological Medicine, 37,* 655–665.

Kendler, K. S., & Prescott, C. A. (1998). *Cannabis* use, abuse, and dependence in a population-based sample of female twins. *American Journal of Psychiatry, 155,* 1016–1022.

Kendler, K. S., Prescott, C. A., Myers, J., & Neale, M. C. (2003). The structure of genetic and environmental risk factors for common psychiatric and substance use disorders in men and women. *Archives of General Psychiatry, 60,* 929–937.

Kerns, J. G., & Berenbaum, H. (2002). Cognitive impairments associated with formal thought disorder in people with schizophrenia. *Journal of Abnormal Psychology, 111,* 211–224.

Kerns, J. G., & Berenbaum, H. (2003). The relationship between formal thought disorder and executive functioning component processes. *Journal of Abnormal Psychology, 112,* 339–352.

Keshavan, M. S., Rosenberg, D., Sweeney, J. A., & Pettegrew, J. W. (1998). Decreased caudate volume in neuroleptic-naive psychotic patients. *American Journal of Psychiatry, 155,* 774–778.

Kessler, D. A. (2009). *The end of overeating.* Emmaus, PA: Rodale.

Kessler, L. (August 22, 2004). Dancing with Rose: A strangely beautiful encounter with Alzheimer's patients provides insights that challenge the way we view the disease. *Los Angeles Times Magazine.*

Kessler, R. C. (2003). Epidemiology of women and depression. *Journal of Affective Disorders, 74,* 5–13.

Kessler, R. C., Akiskal, H. S., Angst, J., Guyer, M., Hirschfeld, R. M. A., Merikangas, K. R., & Stang, P. E. (2006). Validity of the assessment of bipolar spectrum disorders in the WHO CIDI 3.0. *Journal of Affective Disorders, 96,* 259–269.

Kessler, R. C., Angermeyer, M., Anthony, J. C., de Graaf, R., Demyttenaere, K., Gasquet, I., et al. (2007). Lifetime prevalence and age-of-onset distributions of mental disorders in the World Health Organization's World Mental Health Survey Initiative. *World Psychiatry, 6.*

Kessler, R. C., Berglund, P. A., Chiu, W. T., Deitz, A. C., Hudson, J. I., Shahly, V., . . . Xavier, M. (2013). The Prevalence and Correlates of Binge Eating Disorder in the World Health Organization World Mental Health Surveys. *Biological Psychiatry, 73*(9), 904–914.

Kessler, R. C., Berglund, P., Borges, G., Nock, M., & Wang, P. S. (2005). Trends in suicide ideation, plans, gestures, and attempts in the United States, 1990–1992 to 2001-2003. *Journal of the American Medical Association, 293,* 2487–2495.

Kessler, R. C., Berglund, P., Demler, O., Jin, R., Koretz, D., Merikangas, K. R., et al. (2003). The epidemiology of major depressive disorder: Results from the National Comorbidity Survey Replication (NCS-R). *Journal of the American Medical Association, 289,* 3095–3105.

Kessler, R. C., Berglund, P., Demler, O., Jin, R., Merikangas, K. R., & Walters, E. E. (2005). Lifetime prevalence and age-of-onset distributions of DSM-IV disorders in the national comorbidity survey replication. *Archives of General Psychiatry, 62,* 593–602.

Kessler, R. C., Birnbaum, H. G., Shahly, V., Bromet, E., Hwang, I., McLaughlin, K. A., et al. (2010). Age differences in the prevalence and co-morbidity of DSM-IV major depressive episodes: results from the WHO World Mental Health Survey Initiative. *Depression and Anxiety, 27*, 351–364.

Kessler, R. C., Chiu, W. T., Demler, O., & Walters, E. E. (2005). Prevalence, severity, and comorbidity of 12 month DSM-IV disorders in the National Comorbidity Survey Replication. *Archives of General Psychiatry, 62*, 617–627.

Kessler, R. C., Chiu, W. T., Jin, R., Ruscio, A. M., Shear, K., & Walters, E. E. (2006). The epidemiology of panic attacks, panic disorder, and agoraphobia in the national comorbidity survey replication. *Archives of General Psychiatry, 63*, 415–424.

Kessler, R. C., Crum, R. M., Warner, L. A., Nelson, C. B., et al. (1997). Lifetime co-occurrence of DSM-IIIR alcohol dependence with other psychiatric disorders in the National Comorbidity Study. *Archives of General Psychiatry, 54*, 313–321.

Kessler, R. C., Crum, R. M., Warner, L. A., Nelson, C. B., Schulenberg, J., & Anthony, J. C. (1997). Lifetime co-occurrence of DSM-IIIR alcohol dependence with other psychiatric disorders in the National Comorbidity Study. *Archives of General Psychiatry, 54*, 313–321.

Kessler, R. C., Heeringa, S., & Lakoma, M. D., et al. (2008). Individual and society effects of mental disorders on earnings in the United States: Results from the National Comorbidity Survey Replication. *American Journal of Psychiatry, 165*, 703–711.

Kessler, R. C., McLaughlin, K. A., Green, J. G., Gruber, M. J., Sampson, N. A., Zaslavsky, A. M., et al. (2010). Childhood adversities and adult psychopathology in the WHO World Mental Health Surveys. *British Journal of Psychiatry, 197*, 378–385.

Kessler, R. C., Petukhova, M., Sampson, N. A., Zaslavsky, A. M., & Wittchen, H. U. (2012). Twelve-month and lifetime prevalence and lifetime morbid risk of anxiety and mood disorders in the United States. *International Journal of Methods in Psychiatric Research, 21*, 169–184.

Keys, A., Brozek, J., Hsu, L. K. G., McConoha, C. E., & Bolton, B. (1950). *The biology of human starvation.* Minneapolis: University of Minnesota Press.

Kiecolt-Glaser, J. K., Dura, J. R., Speicher, C. E., & Trask, O. (1991). Spousal caregivers of dementia victims: Longitudinal changes in immunity and health. *Psychosomatic Medicine, 54*, 345–362.

Kiecolt-Glaser, J. K., & Glaser, R. (2001). Stress and immunity: Age enhances the risks. *Current Directions in Psychological Science, 10*, 18–21.

Kiecolt-Glaser, J. K., & Glaser, R. (2002). Depression and immune function: Central pathways to morbidity and mortality. *Journal of Psychosomatic Research, 53*, 873–876.

Kieseppa, T., Partonen, T., Haukka, J., Kaprio, J., & Lonnqvist, J. (2004). High concordance of bipolar I disorder in a nationwide sample of twins. *American Journal of Psychiatry, 161*, 1814–1821.

Kiesler, C. A. (1991). Changes in general hospital psychiatric care. *American Psychologist, 46*, 416–421.

Kihlstrom, J. F., Tataryn, D. J., & Holt, I. P. (1993). Dissociative disorders. In P. B. Sutker & H. E. Adams (Eds.), *Comprehensive handbook of psychopathology* (pp. 203–234). New York: Plenum.

Killen, J. D., Fortmann, S. P., Murphy Jr., G. M., Hayward, C., Arredondo, C. et al. (2006). Extended treatment with bupropion SR for cigarette smoking cessation. *Journal of Consulting and Clinical Psychology, 74*, 286–294.

Killen, J. D., Taylor, C. B., Hayward, C., Haydel, K. F., Wilson, D. M., Hammer, L., Kraemer, H., Blair-Grein-er, A., & Strachowski, D. (1996). Weight concerns influence the development of eating disorders: A 4-year prospective study. *Journal of Consulting and Clinical Psychology, 64*, 936–940.

Killen, J. D., Taylor, C. B., Hayward, C., Wilson, D. M., Haydel, K. F., et al. (1994). Pursuit of thinness and onset of eating disorders in a community sample of adolescent girls. *International Journal of Eating Disorders, 16*, 227–238.

Kim, E. (2005). The effect of the decreased safety behaviors on anxiety and negative thoughts in social phobics. *Journal of Anxiety Disorders, 19*, 69–86.

Kim, E. D., & Lipshultz, L. I. (1997). Advances in the evaluation and treatment of the infertile man. *World Journal of Urology, 15*, 378–393.

Kim, H. J., Steketee, G., & Frost, R. O. (2001). Hoarding by elderly people. *Health and Social Work, 26*, 176–184.

Kim, M. J., Loucks, R. A., Palmer, A. L., Brown, A. C., Solomon, K. M., Marchante, A. N., et al. (2011). The structural and functional connectivity of the amygdala: From normal emotion to pathological anxiety. *Behavioural Brain Research, 223*, 403-410.

Kim, Y. S., Leventhal, B. L., Koh, Y-J., Fombonne, E., Laska, E., Lim, E-C., Cheon, K-A., Kim, S-J., Kim, Y-K., Lee, H., Song, D-H., & Grinker, R. R. (2011). Prevalence of autism spectrum disorders in a total population sample. *American Journal of Psychiatry in Advance,* 1–9.

Kim, Y., Zerwas, S., Trace, S. E., & Sullivan, P. F. (2011). Schizophrenia genetics: where next? *Schizophrenia Bulletin, 37*, 456–463.

King, A. C., de Wit, H., McNamara, P. J., & Cao, D. (2011). Rewarding, stimulant, and sedative alcohol responses and relationship to future binge drinking. *Archives of General Psychiatry, 68*, 389–399.

King, A. C., McNamara, P. J., Hasin, D. S., & Cao, D. (2014). Alcohol challenge responses predict future alcohol use disorder symptoms: A 6-year prospective study. *Biological Psychiatry, 75*(10), 798–806.

Kinsey, A. C., Pomeroy, W. B., & Martin, C. E. (1948). *Sexual behavior in the human male.* Philadelphia: Saunders.

Kinzl, J. F., Traweger, C., Trefalt, E., Mangweth, B., & Biebl, W. (1999). Binge eating disorder in females: A population based investigation. *International Journal of Eating Disorders, 25*, 287–292.

Kirkbride, J. B., Fearon, P., Morgan, C., Dazzon, P., Morgan, K. et al. (2006). Heterogeneity in the incidence of schizophrenia and other psychotic illnesses: Results from the 3-center Aesop study. *Archives of General Psychiatry, 63*, 250–258.

Kirkpatrick, B., Fenton, W., Carpenter, W.T., & Marder, S.R. (2006). The NIMH-MATRICS consensus statement on negative symptoms. *Schizophrenia Bulletin, 32*, 296–303.

Kirmayer, L. J. (2001). Cultural variations in the clinical presentation of depression and anxiety: Implications for diagnosis and treatment. *Journal of Clinical Psychiatry, 62* (Suppl. 13), 22–28.

Kirmayer, L. J., Robbins, J. M., & Paris, J. (1994). Somatoform disorders: Personality and social matrix of somatic distress. *Journal of Abnormal Psychology, 103*, 125–136.

Kirsch, I. (2000). Are drug and placebo effects in depression additive? *Biological Psychiatry, 47*, 733–735.

Kisiel, C. L., & Lyons, J. S. (2001). Dissociation as a mediator of psychopathology among sexually abused children and adolescents. *American Journal of Psychiatry, 158*, 1034–1039.

Kisley, M. A., Wood, S., & Burrows, C. L. (2007). Looking at the sunny side of life: Age-related change in an event-related potential measure of the negativity bias. *Psychological Science, 18*, 838.

Kitayama, S., & Uskul, A. K. (2011). Culture, mind, and the brain: Current evidence and future directions. *Annual Review of Psychology, 62*, 419–449.

Klein, D. N. (2003). Patients' versus informants' reports of personality disorders in predicting 7 1/2-year outcome in outpatients with depressive disorders. *Psychological Assessment, 15*, 216–222.

Klein, D. N., Arnow, B. A., Barkin, J. L., Dowling, F., Kocsis, J. H., Leon, A. C., et al. (2009). Early adversity in chronic depression: Clinical correlates and response to pharmacotherapy. *Depression and Anxiety, 26*, 701–710.

Klein, D. N., Lewinsohn, P. M., Seeley, J. R., & Rohde, P. A. (2001). A family study of major depressive disorder in a community sample of adolescents. *Archives of General Psychiatry, 58*, 13–20.

Klein, D. N., Schwartz, J. E., Rose, S., & Leader, J. B. (2000). Five-year course and outcome of dysthymic disorder: A prospective, naturalistic follow-up study. *American Journal of Psychiatry, 157*, 931–939.

Klein, D. N., Shankman, S. A. M. A., & Rose, S. M. A. (2006). Ten-year prospective follow-up study of the naturalistic course of dysthymic disorder and double depression. *American Journal of Psychiatry, 163*, 872–880.

Kleinman, A. (1986). *Social origins of distress and disease: Depression, neurasthenia, and pain in modern China.* New Haven, CT: Yale University Press.

Kleinplatz, P. J. (2014). The paraphilias: An experiential approach to "dangerous" desires. In Y. M. Binik & K. S. K. Hall (Eds.), *Principles and practice of sex therapy* (5th ed.). New York: Guilford Press.

Kleinstauber, M., Witthoft, M., & Hiller, W. (2011). Efficacy of short-term psychotherapy for multiple medically unexplained physical symptoms: a meta-analysis. *Clinical Psychology Review, 31*, 146–160.

Klerman, G. L. (1988). Depression and related disorders of mood (affective disorders). In A. M. Nicholi, Jr. (Ed.), *The new Harvard guide to psychiatry.* Cambridge, MA: Harvard University Press.

Klerman, G. L., Weissman, M. M., Rounsaville, B. J., & Chevron, E. S. (1984). *Interpersonal psychotherapy of depression.* New York: Basic Books.

Kliem, S., Kröger, C., & Kosfelder, J. (2010). Dialectical behavior therapy for borderline personality disorder: A meta-analysis using mixed-effects modeling. *Journal of Consulting and Clinical Psychology, 78*, 936–951.

Klimentidis, Y. C., Beasley, T. M., Lin, H. Y., Murati, G., Glass, G. E., Guyton, M., et al. (2011). Canaries in the coal mine: a cross-species analysis of the plurality of obesity epidemics. *Proceedings of the Royal Society B: Biological Sciences, 278*(1712), 1626–1632.

Klinger, E., Bouchard, S., Legeron, P., Roy, S., Lauer, F., Chemin, I., et al. (2005). Virtual reality therapy versus cognitive behavior therapy for social phobia: A preliminary controlled study. *CyberPsychology & Behvaior, 8*, 76–88.

Kloner, R. A., & Rezkalla, S. H. (2007). To drink or not to drink? That is the question. *Circulation, 116*, 1306–1317.

Klonsky, E. D., Oltmanns, T. F., & Turkheimer, E. (2002). Informant-reports of personality disorder: Relations to self-reports and future research directions. *Clinical Psychology: Science and Practice, 9*, 300–311.

Klump, K. L., McGue, M., & Iacono, W. G. (2000). Age differences in genetic and environmental influences on eating attitudes and behaviors in preadolescent and adolescent female twins. *Journal of Abnormal Psychology, 109*, 239–251.

Klump, K. L., McGue, M., & Iacono, W. G. (2002). Genetic relationships between personality and eating attitudes and behaviors. *Journal of Abnormal Psychology, 111*, 380–389.

Klunk, W. E., Engler, H., Nordberg, A., Wang, Y., Blomqvist, G., & Holt, D. P. (2004). Imaging brain amyloid in Alzheimer's disease with Pittsburgh Compound-B. *Annals of Neurology, 55*, 306–319.

Knight, B. G. (1996). *Psychotherapy with older adults* (2nd ed.). Thousand Oaks, CA: Sage.

Knight, R. A., & King, M. (2012). Typologies for child molesters: The generation of a new structural model. In B. K. Schwartz (Ed.), *The sexual offender*. Kingston, NJ: Civic Research Institute.

Knight, R. A., & Sims-Knight, J. (2011). Risk factors for sexual violence. In J. White, M. Koss & A. E. Kazdin (Eds.), *Violence against women and children, Volume 1: Mapping the terrain*. Washington DC: American Psychological Association.

Knox, K. L., Pflanz, S., Talcott, G. W., Campise, R. L., Lavigne, J. E., Bajorska, A., et al. (2010). The US Air Force suicide prevention program: Implications for public health policy. *American Journal of Public Health, 100*, 2457–2463.

Koenen, K. C., Moffitt, T. E., Poulton, R., Martin, J., & Caspi, A. (2007). Early childhood factors associated with the development of post-traumatic stress disorder: Results from a longitudinal birth cohort. *Psychological Medicine, 37*, 181–192.

Kohn, L. P., Oden, T., Munoz, R. F., Robinson, A., & Leavitt, D. (2002). Adapted cognitive behavioral group therapy for depressed low-income African American women. *Community Mental Health Journal, 38*(6), 497–504.

Kohn, M. L. (1968). Social class and schizophrenia: A critical review. In D. Rosenthal & S. S. Kety (Eds.), *The transmission of schizophrenia*. Elmsford, NY: Pergamon Press.

Kohut, H. (1971). *The analysis of the self*. New York: International Universities Press.

Kohut, H. (1977). *The restoration of the self*. New York: International Universities Press.

Konnopka, A., Schaefert, R., Heinrich, S., Kaufmann, C., Luppa, M., Herzog, W., et al. (2012). Economics of medically unexplained symptoms: A systematic review of the literature. *Psychotherapy and Psychosomatics, 81*, 265–275.

Koob, G. F. (2008). A role for brain systems in addiction. *Neuron, 59*, 11–34.

Koob, G. F., Caine, B., Hyytia, P., Markou, A., Parsons, L. H., Roberts, A. J., et al. (1999). Neurobiology of drug addiction. In M. D. Glantz & C. R. Hartel (Eds.), *Drug abuse: Origins and interventions* (pp. 161–190). Washington, DC: American Psychological Association.

Koob, G. F., & Le Moal. (2008). Addiction and the brain antireward system. *Annual Review of Psychology, 59*, 29–53.

Kopelowicz, A., & Liberman, R. P. (1998). Psychosocial treatments for schizophrenia. In P. E. Nathan & J. M. Gorman (Eds.), *A guide to treatments that work* (pp. 190–211). New York: Oxford University Press.

Kopelowicz, A., Liberman, R. P., & Zarate, R. (2002). Psychosocial treatments for schizophrenia. In P. E. Nathan & J. M. Gorman (Eds.), *A guide to treatments that Work*, 2nd Edition (pp. 201–229). New York: Oxford University Press.

Kornør, H., Winje, D., Ekeberg, Ø., Weisæth, L., Kirkehei, I., Johansen, K., et al. (2008). Early trauma-focused cognitive-behavioural therapy to prevent chronic post-traumatic stress disorder and related symptoms: A

systematic review and meta-analysis. *Biological Medical Central Psychiatry, 8*, 1–8.

Kotov, R., Gamez, W., Schmidt, F., & Watson, D. (2010). Linking "big" personality traits to anxiety, depressive, and substance use disorders: A meta-analysis. *Psychological Bulletin, 136*(5), 768–821.

Kozol, H., Boucher, R., & Garofalo, R. (1972). The diagnosis and treatment of dangerousness. *Crime and Delinquency, 18*, 37–92.

Kraemer, H., Kupfer, D. J., Clarke, D. E., Narrow, W. E., & Regier, D. A. (2012). DSM-5: How reliable is reliable enough? *American Journal of Psychiatry, 169*, 13–15.

Kranzler, H. R., & van Kirk, J. (2001). Efficacy of naltrexone and acamprosate for alcoholism treatment: A metaanalysis. *Alcoholism: Clinical and Experimental Research, 25*, 1335–1341.

Kremen, W. S., Jacobson, K. C., Xian, H., Eisen, S. A., Waterman, B., Toomey, R., et al. (2005). Heritability of word recognition in middle-aged men varies as a function of parental education. *Behavior Genetics, 35*, 417-433.

Kremen, W. S., Koenen, K. C., Boake, C., Purcell, S., Eisen, S. A., Franz, C. E., et al. (2007). Pretrauma cognitive ability and risk for posttramatic stress disorder. *Archives of General Psychiatry, 64*, 361–368.

Kreslake, J. M., Wayne, G. F., Alpert, H. R., Koh, H. K., & Connolly, G. N. (2008). Tobacco industry control of menthol in cigarettes and targeting of adolescents and young adults. *American Journal of Public Health, 98*, 1685–1692.

Kreyenbuhl, J., Buchanan, R. W., Dickerson, F. B., & Dixon, L. B. (2010). The schizophrenia patient outcomes research team (PORT): Updated treatment recommendations 2009. *Schizophrenia Bulletin, 36*, 94–103.

Kreyenbuhl, J., Zito, J. M., Buchanan, R. W., Soeken, K. L., & Lehman, A. F. (2003). Racial disparity in the pharmacological management of schizophrenia. *Schizophrenia Bulletin, 29*, 183–193.

Kring, A. M. (1999). Emotion in schizophrenia: Old mystery, new understanding. *Current Directions in Psychological Science, 8*, 160–163.

Kring, A. M. (2000). Gender and anger. In A. H. Fischer (Ed.), *Gender and Emotion* (pp. 211–231). Cambridge, UK: Cambridge University Press.

Kring, A. M., & Caponigro, J. M. (2010). Emotion in schizophrenia: Where feeling meets thinking. *Current Directions in Psychological Science, 19*, 255–259.

Kring, A. M., & Moran, E. K. (2008). Emotional response deficits in schizophrenia: Insights from affective science. *Schizophrenia Bulletin, 38*, 819-834.

Kring, A. M., Gur, R. E., Blanchard, J. J., Horan, W. P., & Reise, S. P. (2013). The Clinical Assessment Interview for Negative Symptoms (CAINS): Final development and validation. *American Journal of Psychiatry, 170*(2), 165–172.

Krinsley, K. E., Gallagher, J., Weathers, F. W., Kutter, C. J., & Kaloupek, D. G. (2003). Consistency of retrospective reporting about exposure to traumatic events. *Journal of Traumatic Stress, 16*, 399–409.

Krishnan, V., & Nestler, E. J. (2010). Linking molecules to mood: New insight into the biology of depression. *American Journal of Psychiatry, 167*, 1305–1320.

Krueger, R. B. (2010a). The DSM diagnostic criteria for sexual masochism. *Archives of Sexual Behavior, 39*, 346–356.

Krueger, R. B. (2010b). The DSM diagnostic criteria for sexual sadism. *Archives of Sexual Behavior, 39*, 325–345.

Krueger, R. F., Derringer, J., Markon, K. E., Watson, D., & Skodol, A. E. (2012). Initial construction of a maladap-

tive personality trait model and inventory for DSM-5. *Psychological Medicine, 42*, 1879–1890.

Krueger, R. F., Markon, K. E., Patrick, C. J., & Iacono, W. G. (2005). Externalizing psychopathology in adulthood: A dimensional-spectrum conceptualization and its implications for DSM-V. *Journal of Abnormal Psychology, 114*, 537–550.

Krystal, J. H., Cramer, J. A., Krol, W. F., et al. (2001). Naltrexone in the treatment of alcohol dependence. *New England Journal of Medicine, 345*, 1734–1739.

Kubzansky, L. D. (2007). Sick at heart: The pathophysiology of negative emotions. *Cleveland Clinic Journal of Medicine, 74 Suppl 1*, S67–72.

Kuehnle, K. (1998). Child sexual abuse evaluations: The scientist-practitioner model. *Behavioral Sciences and the Law, 16*, 5–20.

Kuhn, T. S. (1962/1970). *The structure of scientific revolutions*. Chicago: University of Chicago Press.

Kumsta, R., Chen, F. S., Pape, H. C., & Heinrichs, M. (2013). Neuropeptide S receptor gene is associated with cortisol responses to social stress in humans. *Biological Psychology, 93*, 304–307.

Kunkel, D., Wilcox, B. L., Cantor, J., Palmer, E., Linn, S., & Dowrick, P. (2004, February 20). Report of the APA Task Force on advertising and children. Washington DC: American Psychological Association.

Kunst-Wilson, W. R., & Zajonc, R. B. (1980). Affective discrimination of stimuli that cannot be recognized. *Science, 207*, 557–558.

Kupfer, D. J. (2005). The increasing medical burden in bipolar disorder. *Journal of the American Medical Association , 293*, 2528–2530.

Kurian, B. T., Ray, W. A., Arbogast, P. G., Fuchs, D. C., Dudley, J. A., & Cooper, W. O. (2007). Effect of regulatory warnings on antidepressant prescribing for children and adolescents. *Archives of General Psychiatry, 161*, 690–696.

Kwok, W. (2014, in press). Is there evidence that social class at birth increases risk of psychosis? A systematic review. *International Journal of Social Psychiatry*.

Kyaga, S., Lichtenstein, P., Boman, M., Hultman, C., Langstrom, N., & Landen, M. (2011). Creativity and mental disorder: Family study of 300,000 people with severe mental disorder. *British Journal of Psychiatry, 199*, 373–379.

Laan, E., Everaerd, W., & Both, S. (2005). Female sexual arousal. In R. Balon & R. T. Segraves (Eds.), *Handbook of sexual dysfunctions and paraphilias*. Boca Raton, Fl: Taylor and Francis Group.

Ladoceur, R., Dugas, M. J., Freeston, M. H., Leger, E., Gagnon, F., & Thibodeau, N. (2000). Efficacy of a new cognitive-behavioral treatment for generalized anxiety disorder: Evaluation in a controlled clinical trial. *Journal of Consulting and Clinical Psychology, 68*, 957–996.

Lahey, B. B., & Waldman, I. D. (2012). Phenotypic and causal structure of conduct disorder in the broader context of prevalent forms of psychopathology. *Journal of Child Psychology and Psychiatry, 53*, 536–557.

Lahey, B. B., Loeber, R., Burke, J. D., & Applegate, B. (2005). Predicting future antisocial personality disorder in males from a clinical assessment in childhood. *Journal of Consulting and Clinical Psychology, 73*, 389–399.

Lahey, B. B., Loeber, R., Hart, E. L., Frick, P. J., Applegate, B., Zhang, Q., et al. (1995). Four year longitudinal study of conduct disorder in boys: Patterns and predictors of persistence. *Journal of Abnormal Psychology, 104*, 83–93.

Lahey, B. B., McBurnett, K., & Loeber, R. (2000). Are attention-deficit/hyperactivity disorder and oppositional defiant disorder developmental precursors to conduct disorder? In A. J. Sameroff & M. Lewis, et al. (Eds.), *Handbook of developmental psychology* (2nd ed., pp. 431–446). New York: Kluwer Academic/Plenum.

Lahey, B. B., Van Hulle, C. A., Singh, A. L., Waldman, I. D., & Rathouz, P. J. (2011). Higher-order genetic and environmental structure of prevalent forms of child and adolescent psychopathology. *Archives of General Psychiatry, 68*(2), 181–189.

Lai, D. T., Cahill, K., Qin, Y., & Tang, J. L. (2010). Motivational interviewing for smoking cessation. *Cochrane Database of Systematic Reviews*(1), CD006936.

Lam, D. H., Bright, J., Jones, S., Hayward, P., Schuck, N., Chisholm, D., et al. (2000). Cognitive therapy for bipolar illness—a pilot study of relapse prevention. *Cognitive Therapy and Research, 24*, 503–520.

Lam, D. H., Jones, S. H., Hayward, P., & Bright, J. A. (1999). *Cognitive therapy for bipolar disorder: A therapist's guide to concepts, methods and practice.* New York: John Wiley & Sons.

Lam, R. W., Levitt, A. J., Levitan, R. D., Enns, M. W., Morehouse, R., Michalak, E. E., et al. (2006). The Can-SAD study: A randomized controlled trial of the effectiveness of light therapy and fluoxetine in patients with winter seasonal affective disorder. *American Journal of Psychiatry, 163*, 805–812.

Lamb, H. R., Weinberger, L. E., DeCuir, W. J. (2002). The police and mental health. *Psychiatry Services, 53*, 1266–1271.

Lambert, M. J. (2004). Psychotherapeutically speaking—updates from the Division of Psychotherapy (29). Washington, DC: APA Division 29 Newsletter.

Lambert, M. J., & Ogles, B. M. (2004). The efficacy and effectiveness of psychotherapy. In M. J. Lambert (Ed.), *Bergin and Garfield's handbook of psychotherapy and behavior change* (5th ed., pp. 139–193). Hoboken, NJ: John Wiley & Sons.

Lambrou, C., Veale, D., & Wilson, G. (2011). The role of aesthetic sensitivity in body dysmorphic disorder. *Journal of Abnormal Psychology, 120*, 443–453.

Landa, R. J., Holman, K. C., Garrett-Mayer, E. (2007). Social and communication development in toddlers with early and later diagnosis of autism spectrum disorders. *Archives of General Psychiatry, 64*, 853–864.

Landerl, K., Fussenegger, B., Moll, K., & Willburger, E. (2009). Dyslexia and dyscalculia: Two learning disorders with different cognitive profiles. *Journal of Experimental Child Psychology, 103*, 309–324.

Landgrebe, M., Barta, W., Rosengarth, K., Frick, U., Hauser, S., Langguth, B., et al. (2008). Neuronal correlates of symptom formation in functional somatic syndromes: A fMRI study. *NeuroImage, 41*, 1336–1344.

Lane, E. A., & Albee, G. W. (1965). Childhood intellectual differences between schizophrenic adults and their siblings. *American Journal of Orthopsychiatry, 35*, 747–753.

Lang, A. R., Goeckner, D. J., Adessor, V. J., & Marlatt, G. A. (1975). Effects of alcohol on aggression in male social drinkers. *Journal of Abnormal Psychology, 84*, 508–518.

Langa, K. M., Larson, E. B., Karlawish, J. H., Cutler, D. M., Kabeto, M. U., Kim, S. Y., et al. (2008). Trends in the prevalence and mortality of cognitive impairment in the United States: Is there evidence of a compression of cognitive morbidity? *Alzheimer's and Dementia: The Journal of the Alzheimer's Association, 4*, 134–144.

Långström, N. (2010). The DSM diagnostic criteria for exhibitionism, voyeurism, and frotteurism. *Archives of Sexual Behavior, 39*, 317–324.

Långström, N., & Seto, M. C. (2006). Exhibitionistic and voyeuristic behavior in a Swedish national population survey. *Archives of Sexual Behavior, 35*, 427–435.

Lantz, P. M., House, J. S., Lepkowski, J. M., Williams, D. R., et al. (1998). Socioeconomic factors, health behaviors, and mortality. *Journal of the American Medical Association, 279*, 1703–1708.

Lau, J. Y. F., Gregory, A. M., Goldwin, M. A., Pine, D. S., & Eley, T. C. (2007). Assessing gene–environment interactions on anxiety symptom subtypes across childhood and adolescence. *Development and Psychopathology, 19*, 1129–1146.

Laugesen, N., Dugas, M. J., & Bukowski, W. M. (2003). Understanding adolescent worry: The application of a cognitive model. *Journal of Abnormal Child Psychology, 31*, 55–64.

Laumann, E. O., Gagnon, J. H., Michael, R. T., & Michaels, S. (1994). *The social organization of sexuality.* Chicago: University of Chicago Press.

Laumann, E. O., Nicolosi, A., Glasser, D. B., Paik, A., Gingell, C., Moreira, E., et al. (2005). Sexual problems among women and men aged 40–80 years: Prevalence and correlates identified in the global study of sexual attitudes and behaviors. *International Journal of Impotence Research, 17*, 39–57.

Laumann, E. O., Paik, A., & Rosen, R. C. (1999). Sexual dysfunction in the United States: Prevalence and predictors. *Journal of the American Medical Association, 281*, 537–544.

Lauril, J. V., Pitkala, K. H., Strandberg, T. E., & Tilvis, R. S. (2004). Detection and documentation of dementia and delirium in acute geriatric wards. *General Hospital Psychiatry, 26*, 31–35.

Lavoie, K. L., Miller, S. B., Conway, M., & Fleet, R. P. (2001). Anger, negative emotions, and cardiovascular reactivity during interpersonal conflict in women. *Journal of Psychosomatic Research, 15*, 503–512.

Law, M., & Tang, J. L. (1995). An analysis of the effectiveness of interventions intended to help people stop smoking. *Archives of Internal Medicine, 155*, 1933–1941.

Lawton, M. P., Kleban, M. H., & Dean, J. (1993). Affect and age: Cross-sectional comparisons of structure and prevalence. *Psychology and aging, 8*, 165–175.

Le Couteur, A., Bailey, A., Goode, S., Pickles, A., Robertson, S., Gottesman, I., & Rutter, M. (1996). A broader phenotype of autism: The clinical spectrum in twins. *Journal of Child Psychology and Psychiatry and Allied Disciplines, 37*, 785–801.

Le Grange, D., Crosby, R. D., Rathouz, P. J., & Leventhal, B. L. (2007). A randomized controlled comparison of family-based treatment and supportive psychotherapy for adolescent bulimia nervosa. *Archives of General Psychiatry, 64*, 1049–1056.

Le Grange, D., Fitzsimmons-Craft, E. E., Crosby, R. D., Hay, P., Lacey, H., Bamford, B., et al. (2014). Predictors and moderators of outcome for severe and enduring anorexia nervosa. *Behaviour Research and Therapy, 56*(0), 91–98.

Leahy, R. L. (2003). *Cognitive therapy techniques: A practitioner's guide.* New York: Guilford Press.

Le Grange, D., & Lock, J. A. (2005). The dearth of psychological treatment studies for anorexia nervosa. *International Journal of Eating Disorders, 37*, 79–91.

LeBeau, R. T., Glenn, D., Liao, B., Wittchen, H. U., Beesdo-Baum, K., Ollendick, T., et al. (2010). Specific phobia: A review of DSM-IV specific phobia and preliminary recommendations for DSM-V. *Depression and Anxiety, 27*, 148–167.

Lee, S. (1991). Anorexia nervosa in Hong Kong: A Chinese perspective. *Psychological Medicine*, 703–711.

Lee, S. S., Lahey, B., Owens, E. B., & Hinshaw, S. P. (2008). Few preschool boys and girls with ADHD are well-adjusted during adolescence. *Journal of Abnormal Child Psychology, 36*, 373–383.

Lee, S., Lee, A. M., Ngai, E., Lee, D. T. S., & Wing, Y. K. (2001). Rationale for food refusal in Chinese patients with anorexia nervosa. *International Journal of Eating Disorders, 29*, 224–229.

Lee, S., Ng, K. L., Kwok, K., & Fung, C. (2010). The changing profile of eating disorders at a tertiary psychiatric clinic in Hong Kong (1987–2007). *International Journal of Eating Disorders, 43*, 307–314.

Legault, E., & Laurence, J. P. (2007). Recovered memories of childhood sexual abuse: Social worker, psychologist, and psychiatrist reports of beliefs, practices, and cases. *Australian Journal of Clinical and Experimental Hypnosis, 35*, 111–133.

Leibenluft, E. (2011). Severe mood dysregulation, irritability, and the diagnostic boundaries of bipolar disorder in youths. *American Journal of Psychiatry, 168*(2), 129–142.

Leiblum, S. R. (1997). Sexual pain disorders. In G. O. Gabbard & S. D. Atkinson (Eds.), *Synopsis of treatments of psychiatric disorders* (2nd ed., pp. 805–810). Washington, DC: American Psychiatric Press.

Leit, R. A., Gray, J. J., & Pope, H. G. (2002). The media's presentation of the ideal male body: A cause for muscle dysmorphia? *International Journal of Eating Disorders, 31*, 334–338.

Leit, R. A., Pope, H. G., & Gray, J. J. (2001). Cultural expectations of muscularity in men: The evolution of playgirl centerfolds. *International Journal of Eating Disorders, 29*, 90–93.

Lenzenweger, M. F., Dworkin, R. H., & Wethington, E. (1991). Examining the underlying structure of schizophrenic phenomenology: Evidence for a 3-process model. *Schizophrenia Bulletin, 17*, 515–524.

Lenzenweger, M. F., Lane, M. C., Loranger, A. W., & Kessler, R. C. (2007). DSM-IV personality disorders in the National Comorbidity Survey Replication. *Biological Psychiatry, 62*, 553–564.

Leon, A. C., Portera, L., & Weissman, M. M. (1995). The social costs of anxiety disorders. *British Journal of Psychiatry, 166* (Suppl. 27), 19–22.

Leon, G. R., Fulkerson, J. A., Perry, C. L., & Early-Zald, M. B. (1995). Prospective analysis of personality and behavioral vulnerabilities and gender influences in the later development of disordered eating. *Journal of Abnormal Psychology, 104*, 140–149.

Leon, G. R., Fulkerson, J. A., Perry, C. L., Peel, P. K., & Klump, K. L. (1999). Three to four year prospective evaluation of personality and behavioral risk factors for later disordered eating in adolescent girls and boys. *Journal of Youth and Adolescence, 28*, 181–196.

Lerman, C., Caporaso, N. E., Audrain, J., Main, D., Bowman, E. D., et al. (1999). Evidence suggesting the role of specific genetic factors in cigarette smoking. *Health Psychology, 18*, 14–20.

Leslie, D. L., & Rosenheck, R. A. (2004). Incidence of newly diagnosed diabetes attributable to atypical antipsychotic medications. *American Journal of Psychiatry, 161*, 1709–1711.

Leucht, S., Komossa, K., Rummel-Kluge, C., Corves, C., Hunger, H., Schmid, F., Lobos, C. A., Schwarz, S., & Davis, J. M. (2009). A meta-analysis of head-to-head comparisons of second-generation antipsychotics in the treatment of schizophrenia *American Journal of Psychiatry, 166*, 152–163.

Leucht, S., Tardy, M., Komossa, K., Heres, S., Kissling, W., & Davis, J. M. (2009). Maintenance treatment with antipsychotic drugs for schizophrenia. (1469-493X (Electronic)).

Levav, I., Kohn, R., Golding, J. M., & Weissman, M. M. (1997). Vulnerability of Jews to major depression. *American Journal of Psychiatry, 154*, 941–947.

Levenson, R. W., Carstensen, L. L., & Gottman, J. M. (1994). Influence of age and gender on affect, physiology, and their interrelations: A study of long-term marriages. *Journal of Personality and Social Psychology, 67*, 56–68.

Levenson, R. W., & Miller, B. L. (2007). Loss of cells—Loss of self: Frontotemporal lobar degeneration and human emotion. *Current Directions in Psychological Science, 16*, 289–294.

Levenston, G. K., Patrick, C. J., Bradley, M. M., & Lang, P. J. (2000). The psychopath as observer: Emotion and attention in picture processing. *Journal of Abnormal Psychology, 109*, 373–385.

Levitan, R. D., Kaplan, A. S., Joffe, R. T., Levitt, A. J., & Brown, G. M. (1997). Hormonal and subjective responses to intravenous meta-chlorophenylpiperazine in bulimia nervosa. *Archives of General Psychiatry, 54*, 521–528.

Levy, B. R. (1996). Improving memory in old age through implicit self-stereotyping. *Journal of Personality and Social Psychology, 71*, 1092–1107.

Levy, B. R. (2003). Mind matters: Cognitive and physical effects of aging self-stereotypes. *Journal of Gerontology: Psychological Sciences, 58B*, 203–211.

Levy, B. R., Slade, M. D., & Kasl, S. V. (2002). Longitudinal benefit of positive self-perceptions of aging on functional health. *Journal of Gerontology: Psychological Sciences, 57B*, 409–417.

Levy, F., Hay, D. A., McStephen, M., Wood, C., & Waldman, I. (1997). Attention-deficit hyperactivity disorder: A category or a continuum? Genetic analysis of a large-scale twin study. *Journal of the American Academy of Child and Adolescent Psychiatry, 36*, 737–744.

Lewinsohn, P. M. (Ed.). (1974). *A behavioral approach to depression.* New York: Springer Publishing.

Lewinsohn, P. M., & Clarke, G. N. (1999). Psychosocial treatments for adolescent depression. *Clinical Psychology Review, 19*, 329–342.

Lewinsohn, P. M., Joiner, T. E., & Rohde, P. (2001). Evaluation of cognitive diathesis-stress models in predicting major depressive disorder. *Journal of Abnormal Psychology, 110*, 203–215.

Lewinsohn, P. M., Petit, J. W., Joiner, T. E., & Seeley, J. R. (2003). The symptomatic expression of major depressive disorder in adolescents and young adults. *Journal of Abnormal Psychology, 112*, 244–252.

Lewinsohn, P. M., Rohde, P., Seeley, J. R., Klein, D. N., & Gotlib, I. H. (2000). Natural course of adolescent major depressive disorder in a community sample: Predictors of recurrence in young adults. *American Journal of Psychiatry, 157*, 1584–1591.

Lewis, S. W., Barnes, T. R. E., Davies, L., Murray, R. M., Dunn, G., et al. (2006). Randomized controlled trial of effect of quality of life of prescription of clozapine vs other second generation antipsychotic drugs in resistant schizophrenia. *Schizophrenia Bulletin, 32*, 715–723.

Lewis-Fernandez, R., Gorritz, M., Raggio, G. A., Pelaez, C., Chen, H., & Guarnaccia, P. J. (2010). Association of trauma-related disorders and dissociation with four idioms of distress among Latino psychiatric outpatients. *Cultural and Medical Psychiatry, 34*(2), 219–243.

Liberman, R. P., Eckman, T. A., Kopelowicz, A., & Stolar, D. (2000). *Friendship and intimacy module.* Camarillo, CA: Psychiatric Rehabilitation Consultants PO Box 2867 Camarillo CA 93011.

Liberman, R. P., Wallace, C. J., Blackwell, G., Kopelowicz, J. V., et al. (1998). Skills training versus psychosocial occupational therapy for persons with persistent schizophrenia. *American Journal of Psychiatry, 155*, 1087–1091.

Lichenstein, P., & Annas, P. (2000). Heritability and prevalence of specific fears and phobias in childhood. *Journal of Child Psychology and Psychiatry and Allied Disciplines, 41*, 927–937.

Lichtenstein, P., Carlstrom, E., Ramstam, M., Gillberg, C., & Anckarsater, H. (2010). The genetics of autism spectrum disorders and related neuropsychiatric disorders in childhood. *American Journal of Psychiatry, 167*, 1357–1363.

Lieb, R., Meinlschmidt, G., & Araya, R. (2007). Epidemiology of the association between somatoform disorders and anxiety and depressive disorders: An update. *Psychosomatic Medicine, 69*, 860–863.

Lieb, W., Beiser, A. S., Vasan, R. S., Tan, Z. S., Au, R., Harris, T. B., et al. (2009). Association of plasma leptin levels with incident Alzheimer disease and MRI measures of brain aging. *Journal of the American Medical Association, 302*, 2565–2572.

Lieberman, J. A. (2006). Comparing effectiveness of antipsychotic drugs. *Archives of General Psychiatry, 63*, 1069–1072.

Lieberman, J. A., Stroup, T. S., et al. (2005). Effectiveness of antipsychotic drugs in patients with chronic schizophrenia. *New England Journal of Medicine, 353*, 1209–1223.

Liebowitz, M. R., Heimberg, R. G., Fresco, D. M., Travers, J., & Stein, M. B. (2000). Social phobia or social anxiety disorder: What's in a name? *Archives of General Psychiatry, 57*, 191–192.

Liechti, M. E., Baumann, C., Gamma, A., & Vollenweider, F. X. (2000). Acute psychological effects of 3, 4methylenedioxymethamphetamine (MDMA, "Ecstasy") are attenuated by the serotonin uptake inhibitor citalopram. *Neuropsychopharmacology, 22*, 513–521.

Lief, H. I., & Hubschman, L. (1993). Orgasm in the postoperative transsexual. *Archives of Sexual Behavior, 22*, 145–155.

Lieverse, R., Van Someren, E. J. W., Nielen, M. M. A., Uitdehaag, B. M. J., Smit, J. H., & Hoogendijk, W. J. (2011). Bright light treatment in elderly patients with nonseasonal major depressive disorder: A randomized placebo-controlled trial. *Archives of General Psychiatry, 68*, 61–70.

Lilenfeld, L. R., Kaye, W. H., Greeno, C. G., Merikangas, K. R., Plotnicov, K., et al. (1998). A controlled family study of anorexia nervosa and bulimia nervosa: Psychiatric disorders in first-degree relatives and effects of proband comorbidity. *Archives of General Psychiatry, 55*, 603–610.

Lilienfeld, S. O. (2007). Psychological treatments that cause harm. *Perspectives on Psychological Science, 2*, 53–70.

Lilienfeld, S. O., Lynn, S. J., Kirsch, I., Chaves, J. F., Sarbin, T. R., & Ganaway, G. K. (1999). Dissociative identity disorder and the sociogenic model: Recalling lessons from the past. *Psychological Bulletin, 125*, 507–523.

Lilienfeld, S. O., Lynn, S. J., Ruscio, J., & Beyerstein, B. L. (2010). Sad, mad, and bad: Myths about mental illness. In S. O. Lilienfeld, S. J. Lynn, J. Ruscio & B. L. Beyerstein (Eds.), *50 great myths of popular psychology: Shattering widespread misconceptions about human behavior* (pp. 181–208). Hoboken, NJ: John Wiley & Sons.

Lilienfeld, S. O., & Marino, L. (1999). Essentialism revisited: Evolutionary theory and the concept of mental disorder. *Journal of Abnormal Psychology, 108*, 400–411.

Lilienfeld, S. O., Wood, J. M., & Garb, H. N. (2000). The scientific status of projective techniques. *Psychological Science in the Public Interest, 1*, 27–66.

Lilly, R., Quirk, A., Rhodes, T., & Stimson, G. V. (2000). Sociality in methadone treatment: Understanding methadone treatment and service delivery as a social process. *Drugs: Education, Prevention and Policy, 7*, 163–178.

Lim, K. O., Adalsteinssom, E., Spielman, D., Sullivan, E. V., Rosenbloom, M. J., & Pfefferman, A. (1998). Proton magnetic resonance spectroscopic imaging of cortical gray and white matter in schizophrenia. *Archives of General Psychiatry, 55*, 346–353.

Lim, S., & Kim, J. (2005). Cognitive processing of emotional information in depression, panic, and somatoform disorder. *Journal of Abnormal Psychology, 114*, 50–61.

Lindemann, E., & Finesinger, I. E. (1938). The effect of adrenalin and mecholyl in states of anxiety in psychoneurotic patients. *American Journal of Psychiatry, 95*, 353–370.

Linehan, M. M. (1987). Dialectical behavior therapy for borderline personality disorder. *Bulletin of the Menninger Clinic, 51*, 261–276.

Linehan, M. M. (1997). Behavioral treatments of suicidal behaviors: Definitional obfuscation and treatment outcomes. In D. M. Stoff & J. J. Mann (Eds.), *Neurobiology of suicide* (pp. 302–327). New York: Annals of the New York Academy of Sciences.

Linehan, M. M., Goodstein, J. L., Nielsen, S. L., & Chiles, J. A. (1983). Reasons for staying alive when you are thinking of killing yourself. *Journal of Consulting and Clinical Psychology, 51*, 276–286.

Linehan, M. M., & Heard, H. L. (1999). Borderline personality disorder: Costs, course, and treatment outcomes. In N. E. Miller & K. M. Magruder (Eds.), *Cost-effectiveness of psychotherapy: A guide for practitioners, researchers, and policymakers* (pp. 291–305). London: Oxford Univeristy Press.

Linehan, M. M., Heard, H. L., & Armstrong, H. E. (1993). Naturalistic follow-up of a behavioral treatment for chronically parasuicidal borderline patients. *Archives of General Psychiatry, 50*, 971–974.

Linehan, M. M., & Shearin, E. N. (1988). Lethal stress: A social-behavioral model of suicidal behavior. In S. Fisher & J. Reason (Eds.), *Handbook of life stress, cognition, and health.* New York: John Wiley & Sons.

Linnet, K. M., Dalsgaard, S., Obel, C., et al. (2003). Maternal lifestyle factors in pregnancy risk of attention deficit hyperactivity disorder and associated behaviors: Review of the current evidence. *American Journal of Psychiatry, 160*, 1028–1040.

Lipsitz, J. D., Mannuzza, S., Klein, D. F., Ross, D. C., & Fyer, A. J. (1999). Specific phobia 10–16 years after treatment. *Depression and Anxiety, 10*, 105–111.

Lissek, S., Powers, A. S., McClure, E. B., Phelps, E. A., Woldehawariat, G., Grillon, C., et al. (2005). Classical fear conditioning in the anxiety disorders: A meta-analysis. *Behaviour Research and Therapy, 43*, 1391–1424.

Litrownik, A. F., & Castillo-Canez, I. (2000). Childhood maltreatment: Treatment of abuse and incest survivors. In C. R. Snyder & R. E. Ingram (Eds.), *Handbook of psychological change* (pp. 520–545). New York: John Wiley & Sons.

Litz, B. T., Gray, M. J., Bryant, R. A., & Adler, A. B. (2002). Early intervention for trauma: Current status and future directions. *Clinical Psychology: Science and Practice, 9*, 112–134.

Livingston, G., Johnston, K., Katona, C., Paton, J., & Lyketsos, C. G. (2005). Systematic review of psychological approaches to the management of neuropsychiatric symptoms of dementia. *American Journal of Psychiatry, 162*, 1996–2021.

Lock, J., & Le Grange, D. (2001). Can family-based treatment of anorexia nervosa be manualized? *Journal of Psychotherapy Practice and Research, 10*, 253–261.

Lock, J., Le Grange, D., Agras, S., Moye, A., Bryson, S. W., & Jo, B. (2011). Randomized clinical trial comparing family-based treatment with adolescent-focused individual therapy for adolescents with anorexia nervosa. *Archives of General Psychiatry, 67*, 1025–1032.

Lock, J., Le Grange, D., Agras, W. S., & Dare, C. (2001). *Treatment manual for anorexia nervosa: A family-based approach*. New York: Guilford Press.

Lockwood, K. A., Alexopoulos, G. S., Kakuma, T., & van Gorp, W. G. (2000). Subtypes of cognitive impairment in depressed older adults. *American Journal of Geriatric Psychiatry, 8*, 201–208.

Loeb, K. L., Walsh, B. T., Lock, J., le Grange, D., Jones, J., Marcus, S., et al. (2007). Open trial of family-based treatment for full and partial anorexia nervosa in adolescence: Evidence of successful dissemination. *Journal of the American Academy of Child and Adolescent Psychiatry, 46*, 792–800.

Loeber, R., Burke, J. D., Lahey, B. B., Winters, A., & Zera, M. (2000). Oppositional defiant and conduct disorder: A review of the past 10 years, Part I. *Journal of the American Academy of Child and Adolescent Psychiatry, 39*, 1468–1484.

Loeber, R., & Hay, D. (1997). Key issues in the development of aggression and violence from childhood to early adulthood. *Annual Review of Psychology, 48*, 371–410.

Loeber, R., & Keenan, K. (1994). Interaction between conduct disorder and its comorbid conditions: Effects of age and gender. *Clinical Psychology Review, 14*, 497–523.

Loftus, E. F. (1993). The reality of repressed memories. *American Psychologist, 48*, 518–537.

Logsdon, R. G., McCurry, S. M., & Teri, L. (2007). Evidence-based psychological treatments for disruptive behaviors in individuals with dementia. *Psychology and Aging, 22*, 28–36.

Lohr, J., Tolin, D. F., & Lilienfeld, S. O. (1998). Efficacy of eye movement desensitization and reprocessing: Implications for behavior therapy. *Behavior Therapy, 29*, 123–156.

London, P. (1964). *The modes and morals of psychotherapy*. New York: Holt Rinehart & Winston.

Lonergan, E., Britton, A. M., & Luxenberg, J. (2007). Antipsychotics for delirium. *Cochrane Database of Systematic Reviews, Issue 2*, CD005594.

Longshore, D., Hawken, A., Urada, D., & Anglin, M. (2006). Evaluation of the Substance Abuse and Crime Prevention Act: SACPA Cost-Analysis Report (First and Second Years). Online at http://www.uclaisap.org/prop36/html/reports.html.

Longshore, D., Urada, D., Evans, E., Hser, Y. I., Prendergast, M., & Hawken, A. (2005). Evaluation of the Substance Abuse and Crime Prevention Act: 2004 report. Sacramento, CA: Department of Alcohol and Drug Programs, California Health and Human Services Agency.

Longshore, D., Urada, D., Evans, E., Hser, Y. I., Prendergast, M., Hawken, A., Bunch, T., & Ettner, S. (2003). *Evaluation of the Substance Abuse and Crime Prevention Act*. Online at http://www.uclaisap.org/prop36/html/reports.html.

Looper, K. J., & Kirmayer, L. J. (2002). Behavioral medicine approaches to somatoform disorders. *Journal of Consulting and Clinical Psychology, 70*, 810–827.

Lopez, S. (2008). *The soloist: A lost dream, an unlikely friendship, and the redemptive power of music*. New York: Putnam.

Lopez, S. R. (1989). Patient variable biases in clinical judgment: Conceptual overview and methodological considerations. *Psychological Bulletin, 106*, 184–203.

Lopez, S. R. (1994). Latinos and the expression of psychopathology: A call for direct assessment of cultural influences. In C. Telles & M. Karno (Eds.), *Latino mental health: Current research and policy perspectives*. Los Angeles: UCLA.

Lopez, S. R. (1996). Testing ethnic minority children. In B. B. Wolman (Ed.), *The encyclopedia of psychology, psychiatry, and psychoanalysis*. New York: Holt.

Lopez, S. R. (2002). Teaching culturally informed psychological assessment: Conceptual issues and demonstrations. *Journal of Personality Assessment, 79*, 226–234.

Lopez, S. R., Barrio, C., Kopelowicz, A., & Vega, W. A. (2012). From documenting to eliminating disparities in mental health care for Latinos. *American Psychologist, 67*, 511–523.

Lopez, S. R., Lopez, A. A., & Fong, K. T. (1991). Mexican Americans' initial preferences for counselors: The role of ethnic factors. *Journal of Counseling Psychology, 38*, 487–496.

Lopez, S. R., Nelson, K. A., Snyder, K. S., & Mintz, J. (1999). Attributions and affective reactions of family members and course of schizophrenia. *Journal of Abnormal Psychology, 108*, 307–314.

Lopez-Ibor, J. J., Jr. (2003). Cultural adaptations of current psychiatric classifications: Are they the solution? *Psychopathology, 36*, 114–119.

LoPiccolo, J., & Lobitz, W. C. (1972). The role of masturbaton in the treatment of orgasmic dysfunction. *Archives of Sexual Behavior, 2*, 163–171.

Lorber, M. F. (2004). Psychophysiology of aggression, psychopathy, and conduct problems: A meta-analysis. *Psychological Bulletin, 130*, 531–552.

Lord, C., Risi, S., DiLavore, P. S., Shulman, C. Thurm, A., & Pickles, A. (2006). Autism from 2 to 9 years of age. *Archives of General Psychiatry, 63*, 694–701.

Lovaas, O. I. (1987). Behavioral treatment and normal educational and intellectual functioning in young autistic children. *Journal of Consulting and Clinical Psychology, 55*, 3–9.

Ludwig, D. S., & Currie, J. (2010). The association between pregnancy weight gain and birthweight: A within-family comparison. *The Lancet, 376*, 984–990.

Lumley, M. N., & Harkness, K. L. (2007). Specificity in the relations among childhood adversity, early maladaptive schemas, and symptom profiles in adolescent depression. *Cognitive Therapy and Research, 31*, 639–657.

Luo, F., Florence, C. S., Quispe-Agnoli, M., Ouyang, L., & Crosby, A. E. (2011). Impact of business cycles on US suicide rates, 1928–2007. *American Journal of Public Health, 101*, 1139–1146.

Lynam, D., & Henry, B. (2001). The role of neuropsychological deficits in conduct disorders. In J. Hill & B. Maughan (Eds.), *Conduct disorders in childhood and adolescence* (pp. 235–263). New York: Cambridge University Press.

Lynam, D., Moffitt, T. E., & Stouthamer-Loeber, M. (1993). Explaining the relation between IQ and delinquency: Race, class, test motivation, school failure, or self-control. *Journal of Abnormal Psychology, 102*, 187–196.

Lynch, T. R., Rosenthal, M. Z., Kosson, D. S., Cheavens, J. S., Lejuez, C. W., & Blair, R. J. R. (2006). Heightened sensitivity to facial expressions of emotion in borderline personality disorder. *Emotion, 6*, 647–655.

Lynn, S. J., Lock, T., Loftus, E. F., Krackow, E., & Lilienfeld, S. O. (2003). The remembrance of things past: Problematic memory recovery techniques in psychotherapy. In S. J. Lynn & S. O. Lilienfeld (Eds.), *Science and pseudoscience in clinical psychology* (pp. 205–239). New York: Guilford Press.

Ma, S. H., & Teasdale, J. D. (2004). Mindfulness-based cognitive therapy for depression: Replication and exploration of differential relapse prevention effects. *Journal of Consulting and Clinical Psychology, 72*, 31–40.

MacDonald, A. W., III, & Carter, C. S. (2003). Event-related fMRI study of context processing in dorsolateral prefrontal cortex of patients with schizophrenia. *Journal of Abnormal Psychology, 112*, 689–697.

MacDonald, A. W., III, & Chafee, D. (2006). Translational and developmental perspective on N-methyl-D-aspartate synaptic deficits in schizophrenia. *Development and Psychopathology, 18*, 853–876.

MacDonald, D. E., McFarlane, T. L., & Olmsted, M. P. (2014). "Diagnostic shift" from eating disorder not otherwise specified to bulimia nervosa using DSM-5 criteria: A clinical comparison with DSM-IV bulimia. *Eating Behaviors, 15*(1), 60–62. MacDonald, V. M., Tsiantis, J., Achenbach, T. M., Motti-Stefanidi, F., & Richardson, C. (1995). Competencies and problems reported by parents of Greek and American children, ages 6–11. *European Child and Adolescent Psychiatry, 4*, 1–13.

MacDonald, V. M., Tsiantis, J., Achenbach, T. M., Motti-Stefanidi, F., & Richardson, C. (1995). Competencies and problems reported by parents of Greek and American children, ages 6–11. *European Child and Adolescent Psychiatry, 4*, 1–13.

MacGregor, M. W. (1996). Multiple personality disorder: Etiology, treatment, and techniques from a psychodynamic perspective. *Psychoanalytic Psychology, 13*, 389–402.

Mackenzie, I. R., Neumann, M., Bigio, E. H., Cairns, N. J., Alafuzoff, I., Kril, J., et al. (2009). Nomenclature for neuropathologic subtypes of frontotemporal lobar degeneration: consensus recommendations. *Acta Neuropathologica, 117*, 15–18.

MacLeod, C., & Mathews, A. (2012). Cognitive bias modification approaches to anxiety. *Annual Review of Clinical Psychology, 8*, 189–217.

Maidment, I., Fox, C., & Boustani, M. (2006). Cholinesterase inhibitors for Parkinson's disease dementia. *Cochrane Database of Systematic Reviews, Issue 1*, CD004747.

Maier, S. F., & Watkins, L. R. (1998). Cytokines for psychologists: Implications of bidirectional immune-to-brain communication for understanding behavior, mood, and cognition. *Psychological Review, 105*, 83–107.

Main, M., Kaplan, K., & Cassidy, J. (1985). Security in infancy, childhood, and adulthood: A move to the level of representation. *Monographs of the Society for Research in Child Development, 50*, (1–2, Serial No. 209).

Maj, M., Pirozzi, R., Magliano, L., & Bartoli, L. (1998). Long-term outcome of lithium prophylaxis in bipolar disorder: A 5-year prospective study of 402 patients at a lithium clinic. *American Journal of Psychiatry, 155*, 30–35.

Malamuth, N. M. (1998). An evolutionary-based model integrating research on the characteristics of sexually coercive men. In J. G. A. a. D. Belanger (Ed.), *Advances in psychological science, Volume 1: Social, personal, and cultural aspects* (pp. 151–184). Hove, UK: Psychology Press/Erlbaum.

Malamuth, N. M., & Brown, L. M. (1994). Sexually aggresive men's perceptions of women's communications: Testing three explanations. *Journal of Personality and Social Psychology, 67,* 699–712.

Malamuth, N. M., & Check, J. V. P. (1983). Sexual arousal to rape depictions: Individual differences. *Journal of Abnormal Psychology, 92,* 55–67.

Malaspina, D., Goetz, R. R., Yale, S., et al. (2000). Relation of familial schizophrenia to negative symptoms but not to the deficit syndrome. *American Journal of Psychiatry, 157,* 994–1003.

Maldonado, J. R., Butler, L. D., & Spiegel, D. (1998). Treatments for dissociative disorders. In P. E. Nathan & J. M. Gorman (Eds.), *A guide to treatments that work* (pp. 423–446). New York: Oxford University Press.

Maletzky, B. M. (1997). Exhibitionism: Assessment and treatment. In D. R. Laws & W. O'Donohue (Eds.), *Sexual deviance* (pp. 40–74). New York: Guilford Press.

Maletzky, B. M. (2000). Exhibitionism. In M. Hersen & M. Biaggio (Eds.), *Effective brief therapy: A clinician's guide* (pp. 235–257). New York: Plenum.

Maletzky, B. M. (2002). The paraphilias: research and treatment. In P. E. Nathan & J. M. Gorman (Eds.), *A guide to treatments that work* (pp. 525–558). New York: Oxford University Press.

Malizia, A. L. (2003). Brain imaging and anxiety disorders. In D. Nutt & J. Ballenger (Eds.), *Anxiety Disorders* (pp. 201–228). Malden, MA: Blackwell.

Malkoff-Schwartz, S., Frank, E., Anderson, B. P., Hlastala, S. A., Luther, J. F., Sherrill, J. T., et al. (2000). Social rhythm disruption and stressful life events in the onset of bipolar and unipolar episodes. *Psychological Medicine, 30,* 1005–1016.

Malone, K. M., Oquendo, M. A., Haas, G. L., Ellis, S. P., Li, S., & Mann, J. J. (2000). Protective factors against suicidal acts in major depression: Reasons for living. *American Journal of Psychiatry, 157,* 1084–1088.

Malvezzi, M., Bertuccio, P., Levi, F., La Vecchia, C., & Negri, E. (2014). European cancer mortality predictions for the year 2014. *Annals of Oncology, 25,* 1650-1656.

Mancebo, M. C., Eisen, J. L., Sibrava, N. J., Dyck, I. R., & Rasmussen, S. A. (2011). Patient utilization of cognitive-behavioral therapy for OCD. *Behavior Therapy, 42,* 399–412.

Mangweth, B., Hausmann, A., Walch, T., Hotter, A., Rupp, C. I., Biebl, W. et al. (2004). Body-fat perception in men with eating disorders. *International Journal of Eating Disorders, 35,* 102–108.

Mann, J. J., Huang, Y. Y., Underwood, M. D., Kassir, S. A., Oppenheim, S., & Kelly, T. M. (2000). A serotonin transporter gene promoter polymorphism (5-HTTLPR) and prefrontal cortical binding in major depression and suicide. *Archives of General Psychiatry, 57,* 729–738.

Mann, R. E., Hanson, R. K., & Thornton, D. (2010). Assessing risk for sexual recidivism: Some proposals on the nature of psychologically meaningful risk factors. *Sexual Abuse: A Journal of Research and Treatment, 22,* 191–217.

Mann, V. A., & Brady, S. (1988). Reading disability: The role of language deficiencies. *Journal of Consulting and Clinical Psychology, 56,* 811–816.

Mannuzza, S., Klein, R. G., & Moulton, J. L. (2003). Does stimulant medication place children at risk for adult substance abuse? A controlled, prospective follow-up study. *Journal of Child and Adolescent Psychopharmacology, 13,* 273–282.

Manson, J. E., Chlebowski, R. T., Stefanick, M. L., Aragaki, A. K., Rossouw, J. E., Prentice, R. L., et al. (2013). Menopausal hormone therapy and health outcomes during the intervention and extended poststopping phases of the Women's Health Initiative randomized trials. *Journal of the American Medical Association, 310*(13), 1353–1368.

Maramba, G. G., & Nagayama-Hall, G. C. (2002). Metaanalyses of ethnic match as a predictor of dropout, utilization, and level of functioning. *Cultural Diversity and Ethnic Minority Psychology, 8,* 290–297.

Marcantonio, E. R., Flacker, J. M., Wright, R. J., & Resnick, N. M. (2001). Reducing delirium after hip fracture: A randomized trial. *Journal of the American Geriatrics Society, 49,* 516–522.

March, J., Silva, S., Petrycki, S., et al. (2004). Fluoxetine, cognitive-behavioral therapy, and their combination for adolescents with depression: Treatment for adolescents with depression study (TADS) randomized controlled trial. *Journal of the American Medical Association, 292,* 807–820.

Marcus, D. K., Gurley, J. R., Marchi, M. M., & Bauer, C. (2007). Cognitive and perceptual variables in hypolchondriasis and health anxiety: A systematic review. *Clinical Psychology Review, 27,* 127–139.

Marcus, S. C., & Olfson, M. (2010). National trends in the treatment for depression from 1998 to 2007. *Archives of General Psychiatry, 67,* 1265–1273.

Marder, S. R., Wirshing, W. C., Glynn, S. M., Wirshing, D. A., Mintz, J., & Liberman, R. P. (1999). Risperidone and haloperidol in maintenance treatment: Interactions with psychosocial treatments. *Schizophrenia Research, 36,* 288.

Maren, S., Phan, K. L., & Liberzon, I. (2013). The contextual brain: Implications for fear conditioning, extinction and psychopathology. *Nature Reviews Neuroscience, 14,* 417–428.

Margraf, J., Ehlers, A., & Roth, W. T. (1986). Sodium lactate infusions and panic attacks: A review and critique. *Psychosomatic Medicine, 48,* 23–51.

Marks, I. (1995). Advances in behavioral-cognitive therapy of social phobia. *Journal of Clinical Psychiatry, 56,* 25–31.

Marks, I. M., & Cavanagh, K. (2009). Computer-aided psychological treatments: Evolving issues. *Annual Review of Clinical Psychology, 5,* 121–141.

Marlatt, G. A. (1983). The controlled drinking controversy: A commentary. *American Psychologist, 38,* 1097–1110.

Marlatt, G. A., & Gordon, J. R. (Eds.). (1985). *Relapse prevention: Maintenance strategies in the treatment of addictive behaviors.* New York: Guilford Press.

Marlowe, D. H. (2001). *Psychological and psychosocial consequences of combat and deployment: With special emphasis on the Gulf War.* Santa Monica, CA: RAND.

Marques, J. K., Wiederanders, M., Day, D. M., Nelson, C., & van Ommeren, A. (2005). Effects of a relapse prevention program on sexual recidivism: Final results from California's Sex Offender Treatment and Evaluation Project (SOTEP). *Sexual Abuse: A Journal of Research and Treatment, 17,* 79–107.

Marquez, M., Segui, J., Garcia, L., Canet, J., & Ortiz, M. (2001). Is panic disorder with psychosensorial symptoms (depersonalization-derealization) a more severe clinical subtype? *Journal of Nervous and Mental Disease, 189,* 332–335.

Marrazzi, M. A., & Luby, E. D. (1986). An auto-addiction model of chronic anorexia nervosa. *International Journal of Eating Disorders, 5,* 191–208.

Marsh, A. A., & Blair, R. J. (2008). Deficits in facial affect recognition among antisocial populations: a meta-analysis. *Neuroscience and Biobehavioral Reviews, 32*(3), 454–465.

Marshall, L. A., & Cooke, D. J. (1999). The childhood experiences of psychopaths: A retrospective study of familial and societal factors. *Journal of Personality Disorders, 13,* 211–225.

Marshall, W. L. (1997). Pedophilia: Psychopathology and theory. In D. R. Laws & W. O'Donohue (Eds.), *Sexual deviance* (pp. 152–174). New York: Guilford Press.

Marshall, W. L., Barbaree, H. E., & Christophe, D. (1986). Sexual offenders against female children: Sexual preferences for age of victims and type of behaviour. *Canadian Journal of Behavioural Science, 18,* 424–439.

Marson, D. C. (2001). Loss of competency in Alzheimer's disease: Conceptual and psychometric approaches. *International Journal of Law and Psychiatry, 24,* 267–283.

Marson, D. C., Huthwaite, J. S., & Hebert, K. (2004). Testamentary capacity and undue influence in the elderly: A jurisprudent therapy perspective. *Law and Psychology Review, 28,* 71–96.

Martell, B. A., Orson, F. M., Poling, J., Mitchell, E., Rossen, R. D., Gardner, T., & Kosten, T. R. (2009). Cocaine vaccine for the treatment of cocaine dependence in methadone-maintained patients: A randomized, double-blind, placebo-controlled efficacy trial. *Archives of General Psychiatry, 66,* 1116–1123.

Martell, C. R., Addis, M. E., & Jacobson, N. S. (2001). *Ending depression one step at a time: The new behavioral activation approach to getting your life back.* New York: Oxford University Press.

Martin, A., & Jacobi, F. (2006). Features of hypochondriasis and illness worry in the general population in Germany. *Psychosomatic Medicine, 68,* 770–777.

Martin, J. H. (1996). *Neuroanatomy: Text and atlas* (4th ed.). New York: McGraw-Hill Medical.

Martinez, C., & Eddy, M. (2005). Effects of culturally adapted parent management training on Latino youth behavioral health outcomes. *Journal of Consulting and Clinical Psychology, 73,* 841–851.

Martini, D. R., Ryan, C., Nakayama, D., & Ramenofsky, M. (1990). Psychiatric sequelae after traumatic injury: The Pittsburgh regatta accident. *Journal of the American Academy of Child and Adolescent Psychiatry, 29,* 70–75.

Marx, R. F., & Didziulis, V. (2009, February 27). A life, interrupted, *The New York Times.*

Mason, B. J. (2001). Treatment of alcohol-dependent outpatients with acamprosate: A clinical review. *Journal of Clinical Psychiatry, 62,* 42–48.

Masters, W. H., & Johnson, V. E. (1966). *Human sexual response.* Boston: Little, Brown.

Masters, W. H., & Johnson, V. E. (1970). *Human sexual inadequacy.* Boston: Little, Brown.

Mataix-Cols, D., Marks, I. M., Greist, J. H., Kobak, K. A., & Baer, L. (2002). Obsessive-compulsive symptom dimensions as predictors of compliance with and response to behaviour therapy: Results from a controlled trial. *Psychotherapy and Psychosomatics, 71,* 255–262.

Mather, M., Canli, T., English, T., Whitfield, S., Wais, P., Ochsner, K., et al. (2004). Amygdala responses to emotionally valenced stimuli in older and younger adults. *Psychological Science, 15,* 259–263.

Mathew, I., Gardin, T. M., Tandon, N., Eack, S., Francis, A. N., Seidman, L. J., et al. (2014). Medial temporal lobe structures and hippocampal subfields in psychotic disorders: Findings from the Bipolar-Schizophrenia Network on Intermediate Phenotypes (B-SNIP) study. *Journal of the American Medical Association, Psychiatry, 71,* 769-777.

Mathews, A., & MacLeod, C. (2002). Induced processing biases have causal effects on anxiety. *Cognition and Emotion, 16,* 331–354.

Matsuda, L. A., Lolait, S. J., Brownstein, M. J., Young, A. C., & Bonner, T. I. (1990). Structure of a cannabinoid receptor and functional expression of the cloned cDNA. *Nature, 346,* 561–564.

Matthews, K. A., Owens, J. F., Kuller, L. H., Sutton-Tyrrell, K., & Jansen-McWilliams, L. (1998). Are hostility and anxiety associated with carotid atherosclerosis in health postmenopausal women? *Psychosomatic Medicine, 60,* 633–638.

Mayberg, H. S., Lozano, A. M., Voon, V., McNeely, H. E., Seminowicz, D., Hamani, C., et al. (2005). Deep brain stimulation for treatment-resistent depression. *Neuron, 45,* 651–660.

Mayer, E. A., Berman, S., Suyenobu, B., Labus, J., Mandelkern, M. A., Naliboff, B. D., et al. (2005). Differences in brain responses to visceral pain between patients with irritable bowel syndrome and ulcerative colitis. *Pain, 115,* 398–409.

Mayes, V., Cochran, S., & Barnes, N. W. (2007). Race, race-based discrimination, and health outcomes among African Americans. *Annual Review of Psychology, 58,* 201–225.

McCabe, R. E., McFarlane, T., Polivy, J., & Olmsted, M. (2001). Eating disorders, dieting, and the accuracy of self-reported weight. *International Journal of Eating Disorders, 29,* 59–64.

McCall, W. V., Reboussin, D. M., Weiner, R. D., & Sackeim, H. A. (2000). Titrated moderately suprathreshold vs fixed high-dose right unilateral electroconvulsive therapy: Acute antidepressant and cognitive effects. *Archives of General Psychiatry, 57,* 438–444.

McCarthy, B. W. (1986). A cognitive-behavioral approach to understanding and treating sexual trauma. *Journal of Sex and Marital Therapy, 12,* 322–329.

McCarthy, D. E., Piasecki, T. M., Fiore, M. C., & Baker, T. (2006). Life before and after quitting smoking: An electronic diary study. *Journal of Abnormal Psychology, 115,* 454–466.

McClellan, J., Kowatch, R., & Findling, R. L. (2007). Practice parameter for the assessment and treatment of children and adolescents with bipolar disorder. *Journal of the American Academy of Child and Adolescent Psychiatry, 46,* 107–125.

McCleod, B. D., Weisz, J. R., & Wood, J. J. (2007). Examining the association between parenting and childhood anxiety: A meta-analysis. *Clinical Psychology Review, 27,* 155–172.

McClure, M. M., Barch, D. M., Flory, J. D., Harvey, P. D., & Siever, L. J. (2008). Context processing in schizotypal personality disorder: Evidence of specificity of impairment to the schizophrenia spectrum. *Journal of Abnormal Psychology, 117,* 342–354.

McCracken, L. M., & Vowles, K. E. (2014). Acceptance and commitment therapy and mindfulness for chronic pain: model, process, and progress. *American Psychologist, 69,* 178–187.

McCrady, B. S., & Epstein, E. E. (1995). Directions for research on alcoholic relationships: Marital and individual-based models of heterogeneity. *Psychology of Addictive Behaviors, 9,* 157–166.

McCrae, R. R., & Costa, P. T., Jr. (1990). *Personality in adulthood.* New York: Guilford Press.

McCullough, J. P., Klein, D. N., Keller, M. B., Holzer, C. E., Davis, S. M., Korenstein, S. G., et al. (2000). Comparison of DSM-III major depression and major depression superimposed on dysthymia (double depression): Validity of the distinction. *Journal of Abnormal Psychology, 109,* 419–427.

McCusker, J., Cole, M., & Abrahamowicz, M. (2002). Delirium predicts 12-month mortality. *Archives of Internal Medicine, 162,* 457–463.

McDonough, M., & Kennedy, N. (2002). Pharmacological management of obsessive-compulsive disorder: A review for clinicians. *Harvard Review of Psychiatry, 10,* 127–137.

McEachin, J. J., Smith, T., & Lovaas, O. I. (1993). Longterm outcome for children with autism who received early intensive behavioral treatment. *American Journal on Mental Retardation, 97,* 359–372.

McEvoy, J. P., Byerly, M., Hamer, R. M., Dominik, R., Swartz, M. S., Rosenheck, R. A., et al. (2014). Effectiveness of paliperidone palmitate vs haloperidol decanoate for maintenance treatment of schizophrenia: a randomized clinical trial. *Journal of the American Medical Association, 311*(19), 1978–1987.

McEvoy, J. P., Johnson, J., Perkins, D., Lieberman, J. A., Hamer, R. M., Keefe, R. S. E., et al. (2006). Insight in first episode psychosis. *Psychological Medicine, 36,* 1385–1393.

McFall, R. M., & Hammen, C. L. (1971). Motivation, structure, and self-monitoring: Role of nonspecific factors in smoking reduction. *Journal of Consulting and Clinical Psychology, 37,* 80–86.

McFarlane, T., Polivy, J., & Herman, C. P. (1998). Effects of false weight feedback on mood, self-evaluation, and food intake in restrained and unrestrained eaters. *Journal of Abnormal Psychology, 107,* 312–318.

McFarlane, W. R., Lukens, E., Link, B., Dushay, R., Deakins, S., Newmark, M., Dunne, E. J., Horen, B., & Toran, J. (1995). Multiple-family groups and psychoeducation in the treatment of schizophrenia. *Archives of General Psychiatry, 52,* 679–687.

McGhie, A., & Chapman, I. S. (1961). Disorders of attention and perception in early schizophrenia. *British Journal of Medical Psychology, 34,* 103–116.

McGlashan, T. H., Grilo, C. M., Sanislow, C. A., Ralevski, E., Morey, L. C., Gunderson, J. G., et al. (2005). Two-year prevalence and stability of individual criteria for schizotypal, borderline, avoidant, and obsessive-compulsive personality disorders. *American Journal of Psychiatry, 162,* 883–889.

McGlashan, T. H., Grilo, C. M., Skodol, A. E., Gunderson, J. G., Shea, M. T., Morey, L. C., et al. (2000). The collaborative longitudinal personality disorders study: Baseline axis I/II and II/II diagnostic co-occurrence. *Acta Psychiatrica Scandinavica, 102,* 256–264.

McGlashan, T. H., & Hoffman, R. E. (2000). Schizophrenia as a disorder of developmentally reduced synaptic connectivity. *Archives of General Psychiatry, 57,* 637–648.

McGovern, C. W., & Sigman, M. (2005). Continuity and change from early childhood to adolescence in autism. *Journal of Child Psychology and Psychiatry, 46,* 401–408.

McGue, M., Pickens, R. W., & Svikis, D. S. (1992). Sex and age effects on the inheritance of alcohol problems: A twin study. *Journal of Abnormal Psychology, 101,* 3–17.

McGuire, P. K., Bench, C. J., Frith, C. D., & Marks, I. M. (1994). Functional anatomy of obsessive-compulsive phenomena. *British Journal of Psychiatry, 164,* 459–468.

McGurk, S. R., Twamley, E. W., Sitzer, D. I., McHugo, G. J., & Mueser, K. T. (2007). A meta-analysis of cognitive remediation in schizophrenia. *American Journal of Psychiatry, 164,* 1791–1802.

McHugh, R. K., & Barlow, D. H. (2010). The dissemination and implementation of evidence-based psychological treatments. A review of current efforts. *American Psychologist, 65,* 73–84.

McIntyre-Kingsolver, K., Lichtenstein, E., & Mermelstein, R. J. (1986). Spouse training in a multicomponent smoking-cessation program. *Behavior Therapy, 17,* 67–74.

McKeith, I. G., Dickson, D. W., Lowe, J., Emre, M., O'Brien, J. T., Feldman, H., et al. (2005). Diagnosis and management of dementia with Lewy bodies; third report of the DLB consortium. *Neurology, 65,* 1863–1872.

McKeller, J., Stewart, E., & Humphreys, K. (2003). Alcoholics anonymous involvement and positive alcohol related outcomes: Cause, consequence, or just a correlate? A prospective 2-year study of 2,319 alcohol dependent men. *Journal of Consulting and Clinical Psychology, 71,* 302–308.

McKhann, G. M., Knopman, D. S., Chertkow, H., Hyman, B. T., Jack, C. R., Jr., Kawas, C. H., et al. (2011). The diagnosis of dementia due to Alzheimer's disease: Recommendations from the National Institute on Aging–Alzheimer's Association workgroups on diagnostic guidelines for Alzheimer's disease. *Alzheimer's & Dementia: The Journal of the Alzheimer's Association, 7,* 263–269.

McKim, W. A. (1991). *Drugs and behavior: An introduction to behavioral pharmacology.* Englewood Cliffs, NJ: Prentice-Hall.

McKinley, N. M., & Hyde, J. S. (1996). The objectified body consciousness scale: Development and validation. *Psychology of Women Quarterly, 20,* 181–216.

McKown, C., & Weinstein, R. S. (2003). The development and consequences of stereotype consciousness in middle childhood. *Child Development, 74,* 498–515.

McLeod, B. D., Wood, J. J., & Weisz, J. R. (2007). Examining the association between parenting and childhood anxiety: A meta-analysis. *Clinical Psychology Review, 27,* 155–172.

McManus, F., Surawy, C., Muse, K., Vazquez-Montes, M., & Williams, J. M. (2012). A randomized clinical trial of mindfulness-based cognitive therapy versus unrestricted services for health anxiety (hypochondriasis). *Journal of Consulting and Clinical Psychology, 80,* 817–828.

McNally, R. J. (1987). Preparedness and phobias: A review. *Psychological Bulletin, 101,* 283–303.

McNally, R. J. (1997). Atypical phobias. In G. C. L. Davey (Ed.), *Phobias: A handbook of theory, research and treatment* (pp. 183–199). Chichester, UK: John Wiley & Sons.

McNally, R. J. (2003). *Remembering trauma.* Cambridge, MA: Belknap Press of Harvard University Press.

McNally, R. J., Caspi, S. P., Riemann, B. C., & Zeitlin, S. B. (1990). Selective processing of threat cues in posttraumatic stress disorder. *Journal of Abnormal Psychology, 99,* 398–402.

McNally, R. J., Lasko, N. B., Clancy, S. A., Macklin, M. L., Pitman, R. K., & Orr, S. P. (2004). Psychophysiological responding during script-driven imagery in people reporting abduction by space aliens. *Psychological Science, 15,* 493–497.

McNally, R. J., Ristuccia, C. S., & Perlman, C. A. (2005). Forgetting trauma cues in adults reporting continuous or recovered memories of childhood sexual abuse. *Psychological Science, 16,* 336–340.

McNeil, T. F., Cantor-Graae, E., & Weinberger, D. R. (2000). Relationship of obstetric complications and differences in size of brain structures in monozygotic twin pairs discordant for schizophrenia. *American Journal of Psychiatry, 157,* 203–212.

McNiel, D. E., & Binder, R. L. (2007). Effectiveness of a mental health court in reducing criminal recidivism and violence. *American Journal of Psychiatry, 164,* 1395–1403.

McQuaid, J. R., Monroe, S. M., Roberts, J. R., & Johnson, S. L., et al. (1992). Toward the standardization of life stress assessment: Definitional discrepancies and inconsistencies in methods. *Stress Medicine, 8,* 47–56.

McTeague, L. M., & Lang, P. J. (2012). The anxiety spectrum and the reflex physiology of defense: From circumscribed fear to broad distress. *Depression and Anxiety, 29,* 264–281.

Meagher, D. J. (2001). Delirium: Optimizing management. *British Medical Journal, 322,* 144–149.

Meagher, D. J. (2007). Phenomenology of delirium: Assessment of 100 adult cases using standardised measures. *British Journal of Psychiatry, 190,* 135–141.

Meana, M., Binik, I., Khalife, S., & Cohen, D. (1998). Affect and marital adjustment in women's ratings of dyspareunic pain. *Canadian Journal of Psychiatry, 43,* 381–385.

Mednick, S. A., Huttonen, M. O., & Machon, R. A. (1994). Prenatal influenza infections and adult schizophrenia. *Schizophrenia Bulletin, 20,* 263–268.

Mednick, S. A., Machon, R., Hottunen, M. O., & Bonett, D. (1988). Fetal viral infection and adult schizophrenia. *Archives of General Psychiatry, 45,* 189–192.

Mednick, S. A., & Schulsinger, F. (1968). Some premorbid characteristics related to breakdown in children with schizophrenic mothers. In D. Rosenthal & S. S. Kety (Eds.), *The transmission of schizophrenia.* Elmsford, NY: Pergamon Press.

Mehler, P. S. (2011). Medical complications of bulimia nervosa and their treatments. *International Journal of Eating Disorders, 44,* 95–104.

Meier, M. H., Caspi, A., Ambler, A., Harrington, H., Houts, R., Keefe, R. S. E., et al. (2012). Persistent cannabis users show neuropsychological decline from childhood to midlife. *Proceedings of the National Academy of Sciences, 109*(40), E2657–E2664.

Meier, M. H., Caspi, A., Reichenberg, A., Keefe, R. S., Fisher, H. L., Harrington, H., et al. (2014). Neuropsychological decline in schizophrenia from the premorbid to the postonset period: Evidence from a population-representative longitudinal study. *American Journal of Psychiatry, 171*(1), 91–101.

Melamed, B. G., & Siegel, L. J. (1975). Reduction of anxiety in children facing hospitalization and surgery by use of filmed modeling. *Journal of Consulting and Clinical Psychology, 43,* 511–521.

Melnik, T., Soares, B. G. O., & Nasello, A. G. (2008). The effectiveness of psychological interventions for the treatment of erectile dysfunction: Systematic review and meta-analysis, including comparisons to sildenafil treatment, intracavernosal injection, and vacuum devices. *Journal of Sexual Medicine, 5,* 2562–2574.

Meltzer, H. Y. (2003). Suicide in schizophrenia. *Journal of Clinical Psychiatry, 64,* 1122–1125.

Meltzer, H. Y., Cola, P., & Way, L. E. (1993). Cost effectiveness of clozapine in neuroleptic-resistant schizophrenia. *American Journal of Psychiatry, 150,* 1630–1638.

Melville, J. D., & Naimark, D. (2002). Punishing the insane: The verdict of guilty but mentally ill. *Journal of the American Academy of Psychiatry and the Law, 30,* 553–555.

Mendez, M. F., Lauterbach, E. C., & Sampson, S. M. (2008). An evidence-based review of the psychopathology of frontotemporal dementia: A report of the ANPA Committee on Research. *Journal of Neuropsychiatry and Clinical Neurosciences, 20,* 130–149.

Mendez, M. F., & Shapira, J. S. (2008). The spectrum of recurrent thoughts and behaviors in frontotemporal dementia. *CNS Spectrums, 13,* 202–208.

Menezes, N. M., Arenovich, T., & Zipursky, R. B. (2006). A systematic review of longitudinal outcome studies of first-episode psychosis. *Psychological Medicine, 36,* 1349–1362.

Mennin, D. S., Heimberg, R. G., & Turk, C. L. (2004). Clinical presentation and diagnostic features. In R. G. Heimberg, C. L. Turk & D. S. Mennin (Eds.), *Generalized anxiety disorder* (pp. 3–28). New York: Guilford Press.

Mennin, D. S., Heimberg, R. G., Turk, C. L., & Fresco, D. M. (2002). Applying an emotion regulation framework to integrative approaches to generalized anxiety disorder. *Clinical Psychology: Science and Practice, 9,* 135–141.

Menzies, L., Chamberlain, S. R., Laird, A. R., Thelen, S. M., Sahakian, B. J., & Bullmore, E. T. (2008). Integrating evidence from neuroimaging and neuropsychological studies of obsessive-compulsive disorder: The orbitofronto-striatal model revisited. *Neuroscience and Biobehavioral Reviews, 32,* 525–549.

Mercer, C. H., Fenton, K. A., Johnson, A. M., Wellings, K., Macdowall, W., McManus, S., et al. (2003). Sexual function problems and help seeking behaviour in Britain: national probability sample survey. *British Medical Journal, 327,* 426–427.

Merckelbach, H., Dekkers, T., Wessel, I., & Roefs, A. (2003). Dissociative symptoms and amnesia in Dutch concentration camp survivors. *Comprehensive Psychiatry, 44,* 65–69.

Merikangas, K. R., Akiskal, H. S., Angst, J., Greenberg, P. E., Hirschfeld, R. M. A., Petukhova, M., et al. (2007). Lifetime and 12-month prevalence of bipolar spectrum disorder in the National Comorbidity Survey Replication. *Archives of General Psychiatry, 64,* 543–552.

Merikangas, K. R., He, J. P., Brody, D., Fisher, P. W., Bourdon, K., & Koretz, D. S. (2010). Prevalence and treatment of mental disorders among US children in the 2001–2004 NHANES. *Pediatrics, 125*(1), 75–81.

Merikangas, K. R., Jin, R., He, J., Kessler, R. C., Lee, S., Sampson, N. A., et al. (2011). Prevalence and correlates of bipolar spectrum disorder in the World Mental Health Survey Initiative. *Archives of General Psychiatry, 68,* 241–251.

Messinger, J. W., Tremeau, F., Antonius, D., Mendelsohn, E., Prudent, V., Stanfore, A. D., & Malaspina, D. (2011). Avolition and expressive deficits capture negative symptom phenomoenology: Implications for the DSM-5 and schizophrenia research. *Clinical Psychology Review, 31,* 161–168.

Meston, C. M., & Buss, D. (2009). *Why women have sex: Women reveal the truth about their sex lives, from adventure to revenge (and everything in between).* New York: St. Martin's Press.

Meston, C. M., & Gorzalka, B. B. (1995). The effects of sympathetic activation on physiological and subjective sexual arousal in women. *Behaviour Research and Therapy, 33,* 651–664.

Metalsky, G. I., Joiner, T. E., Hardin, T. S., & Abramson, L. Y. (1993). Depressive reactions to failure in a natural setting: A test of the hopelessness and self-esteem theories of depression. *Journal of Abnormal Psychology, 102,* 101–109.

Meyer, B., Johnson, S. L., & Winters, R. (2001). Responsiveness to threat and incentive in bipolar disorder: Relations of the BIS/BAS scales with symptoms. *Journal of Psychopathology and Behavioral Assessment, 23,* 133–143.

Meyer, G. J., & Archer, R. P. (2001). The hard science of Rorschach research: "What do we know and where do we go?" *Psychological Assessment, 13,* 486–502.

Meyer, V. (1966). Modification of expectations in cases with obsessional rituals. *Behaviour Research and Therapy, 4,* 273–280.

Mezzich, J. E., Fabrega, H., Jr., Coffman, G. A., & Haley, R. (1989). DSM-III disorders in a large sample of psychiatric patients: Frequency and specificity of diagnoses. *American Journal of Psychiatry, 146,* 212–219.

Michael, T., Blechert, J., Vriends, N., Margraf, J., & Wilhelm, F. H. (2007). Fear conditioning in panic disorder: Enhanced resistance to extinction. *Journal of Abnormal Psychology, 116,* 612–617.

Mikami, A. Y., Hinshaw, S. P., Arnold, L. E., Hoza, B., Hechtman, L., Newcorn, J. H., & Abikoff, H. B. (2010). Bulimia nervosa symptoms in the multimodal treatment study of children with ADHD. *International Journal of Eating Disorders, 43,* 248–259.

Mikami, A. Y., Huang-Pollack, C. L., Pfiffner, L. J., McBurnett, K., & Hangai, D. (2007). Social skills differences among attention-deficit/hyperactivity disorder types in a chat room assessment task. *Journal of Abnormal Child Psychology, 35,* 509–521.

Miklowitz, D. J., & Goldstein, M. J. (1997). *Bipolar disorder: A family-focused treatment approach.* New York: Guilford Press.

Miklowitz, D. J., & Taylor, D.O. (2005). Family-focused treatment of the suicidal bipolar patient. Unpublished manuscript.

Miklowitz, D. J., George, E. L., Richards, J. A., Simoneau, T. L., & Suddath, R. L. (2003). A randomized study of family-focused psychoeducation and pharmacotherapy in the outpatient management of bipolar disorder. *Archives of General Psychiatry, 60,* 904–912.

Miklowitz, D. J., Otto, M. W., Frank, E., Reilly-Harrington, N. A., Kogan, J. N., Sachs, G. S., et al. (2007). Intensive psychosocial intervention enhances functioning in patients with bipolar depression: Results from a 9-month randomized controlled trial. *American Journal of Psychiatry, 164,* 1340–1347.

Miklowitz, D. J., Otto, M. W., Frank, E., Reilly-Harrington, N. A., Wisniewski, S. R., Kogan, J. N., et al. (2007). Psychosocial treatments for bipolar depression: A 1-year randomized trial from the systematic treatment enhancement program. *Archives of General Psychiatry, 64,* 419–427.

Miklowitz, D. J., Simoneau, T. L., Sachs-Ericsson, N., Warner, R., & Suddath, R. (1996). Family risk indicators in the course of bipolar affective disorder. In E. Mundt et al. (Ed.), *Interpersonal factors in the origin and course of affective disorders* (pp. 204–217). London: Gaskell.

Milev, P., Ho, B. C., Arndt, S., & Andreasen, N. C. (2005). Predictive values of neurocognition and negative symptoms on functional outcome in schizophrenia: A longitudinal first-episode study with 7-year follow-up. *American Journal of Psychiatry, 162*(3), 495–506.

Miller, B. L., Ikonte, C., Ponton, M., & Levy, M. (1997). A study of the Lund Manchester research criteria for frontotemporal dementia: Clinical and single-photon emission CT correlations. *Neurology, 48,* 937–942.

Miller, D. D., Caroff, S. N., Davis, S. M., et al. (2008). Extrapyramidal side-effects of antipsychotics in a randomised trial. *British Journal of Psychiatry, 193,* 279–288.

Miller, J. D., Hoffman, B. J., Campbell, W. K., & Pilkonis, P. A. (2008). An examination of the factor structure of Diagnostic and Statistical Manual of Mental Disorders, Fourth Edition, narcissistic personality disorder criteria: One or two factors? *Comprehensive Psychiatry, 49,* 141–145.

Miller, M., & Hemenway, D. (1999). The relationship between firearms and suicide: A review of the literature. *Aggression and Violent Behavior, 4,* 59–75.

Miller, T. J., McGlashan, T. H., Rosen, J. L., et al. (2002). Prospective diagnosis of the initial prodrome for schizophrenia based on the Structured Interview for Prodromal Syndromes: Preliminary evidence of interrater reliability and predictive validity. *American Journal of Psychiatry, 159,* 863–865.

Miller, T. Q., & Volk, R. J. (1996). Weekly marijuana use as a risk factor for initial cocaine use: Results from a six wave national survey. *Journal of Child and Adolescent Substance Abuse, 5,* 55–78.

Miller, W. R., & Rollnick, S. (Eds.). (1991). *Motivational interviewing: Preparing people to change addictive behavior.* New York: Guilford Press.

Millon, T. (1996). *Disorders of personality: DSM-IV and beyond* (2nd ed.). New York: John Wiley & Sons.

Milrod, B., Leon, A. C., Busch, F., Rudden, M., Schwalberg, M., Clarkin, J., et al. (2007). A randomized controlled clinical trial of psychoanalytic psychotherapy for panic disorder. *American Journal of Psychiatry, 164,* 265–272.

Mineka, S., & Öhman, A. (2002). Born to fear: Nonassociative vs. associative factors in the etiology of phobias. *Behaviour Research and Therapy, 40,* 173–184.

Mineka, S., & Sutton, J. (2006). Contemporary learning theory perspectives on the etology of fear and phobias. In M. G. Craske, D. Hermans & D. Vansteenwegen (Eds.), *Fear and learning: From basic processes to Clinical implications* (pp. 75–97). Washington DC: American Psychological Association.

Mineka, S., & Zinbarg, R. (1998). Experimental approaches to the anxiety and mood disorders. In J. G. Adair, D. Belanger & K. L. Dion (Eds.), *Advances in psychological science, Volume 1: Social personal and cultural aspects* (pp. 429-454). Hove, UK: Psychology Press.

Mineka, S., & Zinbarg, R. (2006). A contemporary learning theory perspective on the etiology of anxiety disorders: It's not what you thought it was. *The American Psychologist, 61,* 10–26.

Minzenberg, M. J., Fan, J., New, A. S., Tang, C. Y., & Siever, L. J. (2008). Frontolimbic structural changes in borderline personality disorder. *Journal of Psychiatric Research, 42,* 727–733.

Miranda, J., Bernal, G., Lau, A., Kohn, L., Hwang, W., & LaFromboise, T. (2005). State of the science on psychosocial interventions for ethnic minorities. *Annual Review of Psychology, 1,* 113–142.

Miranda, J., Green, B. L., Krupnick, J. L., Chung, J., Siddique, J., Belin, T., et al. (2006). One-year outcomes of a randomized clinical trail treating depression in low-income minority women. *Journal of Consulting and Clinical Psychology, 74,* 99–111.

Mirsky, A. F., Bieliauskas, L. A., Duncan, C. C., & French, L. M. (2013). Letter to the editor. *Schizophrenia Research, 148*(1–3), 186–187.

Mishkind, M. E., Rodin, J., Silberstein, L. R., & Striegel-Moore, R. H. (1986). The embodiment of masculinity: Cultural, psychological, and behavioral dimensions. *American Behavioral Scientist, 29,* 545–562.

Mitchell, J. T., & Everly, G. S., Jr. (2000). Critical incident stress management and critical incident stress debriefings: Evolutions, effects and outcomes. In J. P. Wilson & B. Raphael (Eds.), *Psychological debriefing: Theory, practice and evidence* (pp. 71–90). New York: Cambridge University Press.

Mitte, K. (2005). Meta-analysis of cognitive-behavioral treatments for generalized anxiety disorder: A comparison with pharmacotherapy. *Psychological Bulletin, 131,* 785–795.

Mittelman, M. S., Brodaty, H., Wallen, A. S., & Burns, A. (2008). A three-country randomized controlled trial of a psychosocial intervention for caregivers combined with pharmacological treatment for patients with Alzheimer disease: Effects on caregiver depression. *American Journal of Geriatric Psychiatry, 16,* 893–904.

Modestin, J. (1992). Multiple personality disorder in Switzerland. *American Journal of Psychiatry, 149,* 88–92.

Modrego, P. J. (2010). Depression in Alzheimer's disease: Pathophysiology, diagnosis, and treatment. *Journal of Alzheimer's Disease, 21,* 1077–1087.

Moffitt, T. E. (1993). Adolescence-limited and life-course-persistent antisocial behavior: A developmental taxonomy. *Psychological Review, 100,* 674–701.

Moffitt, T. E. (2007). A review of research on the taxonomy of life-course persistent versus adolescence-limited antisocial behavior. In D. J. Flannery, A. T. Vazsonyi, & I. D. Waldman (Eds.), *The Cambridge handbook of violent behavior and aggression* (pp. 49–74). New York: Cambridge University Press.

Moffitt, T. E., Caspi, A., Harrington, H., & Milne, B. J. (2002). Males on the life-course persistent and adolescence-limited antisocial pathways: Follow-up at age 26. *Development and Psychopathology 14,* 179–207.

Moffitt, T. E., Caspi, A., Harrington, H., Milne, B. J., Melchior, M., Goldberg, D., et al. (2007). Generalized anxiety disorder and depression: childhood risk factors in a birth cohort followed to age 32. *Psychological Medicine, 37,* 441–452.

Moffitt, T. E., Lynam, D., & Silva, P. A. (1994). Neuropsychological tests predict persistent male delinquency. *Criminology, 32,* 101–124.

Moffitt, T. E., & Silvia, P. A. (1988). IQ and delinquency: A direct test of the differential detection hypothesis. *Journal of Abnormal Psychology, 97,* 330–333.

Molina, B. S. G., Hinshaw, S. P., Swanson, J. M., Arnold, L. E., Vitiello, B., Jensen, P. S., et al. (2009). The MTA at 8 years: Prospective follow-up of children treated for combined-type ADHD in a multisite study. *Journal of the American Academy of Child and Adolescent Psychiatry, 48,* 484–500.

Molina, B. S., Hinshaw, S. P., Eugene Arnold, L., Swanson, J. M., Pelham, W. E., Hechtman, L., et al. (2013). Adolescent substance use in the multimodal treatment study of attention-deficit/hyperactivity disorder (ADHD) (MTA) as a function of childhood ADHD, random assignment to childhood treatments, and subsequent medication. *Journal of the American Academy of Child and Adolescent Psychiatry, 52*(3), 250–263.

Monahan, J. (1973). The psychiatrization of criminal behavior. *Hospital and Community Psychiatry, 24,* 105–107.

Monahan, J. (1976). The prevention of violence. In J. Monahan (Ed.), *Community mental health and the criminal justice system.* Elmsford, NY: Pergamon Press.

Monahan, J. (1984). The prediction of violent behavior: Toward a second generation of theory and policy. *American Journal of Psychiatry, 141,* 10–15.

Monahan, J. (1992). Mental disorder and violent behavior: Perceptions and evidence. *American Psychologist, 47,* 511–521.

Monahan, J., & Steadman, H. (1994). Toward a rejuvenation of risk assessment research. In J. Monahan & H. Steadman (Eds.), *Violence and mental disorder: Developments in risk assessment.* Chicago: University of Chicago Press.

Moniz, E. (1936). *Tentatives operatoires dans le traitement de certaines psychoses.* Paris: Mason.

Monk, C. S., Nelson, E. E., McClure, E. B., Mogg, K., Bradley, B. P., Leibenluft, E., et al. (2006). Ventrolateral prefrontal cortex activation and attentional bias in response to angry faces in adolescents with generalized anxiety disorder. *American Journal of Psychiatry, 163,* 1091–1097.

Monuteaux, M., Faraone, S. V., Gross, L., & Biederman, J. (2007). Predictors, clinical characteristics, and outcome of conduct disorder in girls with attention-deficit/hyperactivity disorder: a longitudinal study. *Psychological Medicine, 37,* 1731–1741.

Monzani, B., Rijsdijk, F., Iervolino, A. C., Anson, M., Cherkas, L., & Mataix-Cols, D. (2012). Evidence for a genetic overlap between body dysmorphic concerns and obsessive-compulsive symptoms in an adult female community twin sample. *American Journal of Medical Genetics Part B, Neuropsychiatric genetics, 159B,* 376–382.

Moore, T. H. M., Zammit, S., Lingford-Hughes, A., Barnes, T. R. E., Jones, P. B., Burke, M., & Lewis, G. (2007). Cannabis use and risk of psychotic or affective mental health outcomes: a systematic review. *The Lancet, 370*(9584), 319–328.

Moos, R. H., & Humphreys, K. (2004). Long-term influence of duration and frequency of participation in Alcoholics Anonymous on individuals with alcohol use disorders. *Journal of Consulting and Clinical Psychology, 72,* 81–90.

Moos, R. H., & Moos, B. S. (2006). Participation in treatment and Alcoholics Anonymous: A 16-year follow-up of initially untreated individuals. *Journal of Clinical Psychology, 62,* 735–750.

Mora, S., Redberg, R. F., Cui, Y., Whiteman, M. K., Flaws, J. A., Sharrett, A. R., & Blumenthal, R. S. (2003). Ability of exercise testing to predict cardiovascular and all-cause death in asymptomatic women: A 20-year follow-up of the lipid research clinics prevalence study. *Journal of the American Medical Association, 290,* 1600–1607.

Moreland, K., Wing, S., Diez Roux, A., & Poole, C. (2002). Neighborhood characteristics associated with the location of food stores and food services places. *American Journal of Preventive Medicine, 22,* 23–29.

Morenz, B., & Becker, J. V. (1995). The treatment of youthful sexual offenders. *Applied and Preventive Psychology, 4,* 247–256.

Morey, L. C., Hopwood, C. J., Markowitz, J. C., Gunderson, J. G., Grilo, C. M., McGlashan, T. H., et al. (2012). Comparison of alternative models for personality disorders, II: 6-, 8- and 10-year follow-up. *Psychological Medicine, 42,* 1705–1713.

Morf, C. C., & Rhodewalt, F. (2001). Unraveling the paradoxes of narcissism: A dynamic self-regulatory processing model. *Psychological Inquiry, 12,* 177–196.

Morgan, C. A. I., Hazlett, G., Wang, S., Richardson, E. G. J., Schnurr, P., & Southwick, S. M. (2001). Symptoms of dissociation in humans experiencing acute, uncontrollable stress: A prospective investigation. *American Journal of Psychiatry, 158,* 1239–1247.

Morgan, M. J. (2000). Ecstasy (MDMA): A review of its possible persistent psychological effects. *Psychopharmacology, 152,* 230–248.

Morgenstern, J., Langenbucher, J., Labouvie, E., & Miller, K. J. (1997). The comorbidity of alcoholism and personality disorders in a clinical population; Prevalence rates and relation to alcohol typology variables. *Journal of Abnormal Psychology, 106,* 74–84.

Morley, S. (1997). Pain management. In A. Baum, S. Newman, J. Weinman, R. West & C. McManus (Eds.), *Cambridge handbook of psychology, health and medicine* (pp. 234–237). Cambridge, UK: Cambridge University Press.

Morokoff, P. J., & Gilliland, R. (1993). Stress, sexual functioning, and marital satisfaction. *Journal of Sex Research, 30,* 43–53.

Moroney, J. T., Tang, M. X., Berglund, L., Small, S., Merchant, C., Bell, K., et al. (1999). Low-density lipoprotein cholesterol and the risk of dementia with stroke. *Journal of American Medical Association, 282,* 254–260.

Morriss, R. K., Faizal, M. A., Jones, A. P., Williamson, P. R., Bolton, C., & McCarthy, J. P. (2007). Interventions for helping people recognise early signs of recurrence in bipolar disorder. *Cochrane Database of Systematic Reviews, Issue 1*, CD004854.

Morrow, J., & Nolen-Hoeksema, S. (1990). Effects of responses to depression on the remediation of depressive affect. *Journal of Personality and Social Psychology, 58*, 519–527.

Morse, S. J. (1992). The "guilty mind": Mens rea. In D. K. Kagehiro & W. S. Laufer (Eds.), *Handbook of psychology and law* (pp. 207–229). New York: Springer-Verlag.

Mortberg, E., Clark, D. M., & Bejerot, S. (2011). Intensive group cognitive therapy and individual cognitive therapy for social phobia: Sustained improvement at 5-year follow-up. *Journal of Anxiety Disorders, 25*, 994–1000.

Moser, C., & Levitt, E. E. (1987). An exploratory descriptive study of a sadomasochistically oriented sample. *Journal of Sex Research, 23*, 322–337.

Moses, J. A., & Purisch, A. D. (1997). The evolution of the Luria-Nebraska Battery. In G. Goldstein & T. Incagnoli (Eds.), *Contemporary approaches to neuropsychological assessment* (pp. 131–170). New York: Plenum.

Moses, J. A., Schefft, B. A., Wong, J. L., & Berg, R. A. (1992). Interrater reliability analyses of the Luria-Nebraska neuropsychological battery, form II. *Archives of Clinical Neurology, 7*, 251–269.

Mowrer, O. H. (1947). On the dual nature of learning: A reinterpretation of "conditioning" and "problem-solving." *Harvard Educational Review, 17*, 102–148.

Moylan, S., Staples, J., Ward, S. A., Rogerson, J., Stein, D. J., & Berk, M. (2011). The efficacy and safety of alprazolam versus other benzodiazepines in the treatment of panic disorder. *Journal of Clinical Psychopharmacology, 31*, 647–652.

MTA Cooperative Group. (1999a). A 14-month randomized clinical trial of treatment strategies for attention-deficit/hyperactivity disorder. *Archives of General Psychiatry, 56*, 1073–1086.

MTA Cooperative Group. (1999b). Moderators and mediators of treatment response for children with attention-deficit/hyperactivity disorder. *Archives of General Psychiatry, 56*, 1088–1096.

Mudd, S. H., Cerone, R., Schiaffino, M. C., Fantasia, A. R., Minniti, G., Caruso, U., et al. (2001). Glycine N-methyltransferase deficiency: A novel inborn error causing persistent isolated hypermethioninaemia. *Journal of Inherited Metabolic Disease, 24*, 448–464.

Muehlenhard, C. L., & Shippee, S. K. (2010). Men's and women's reports of pretending orgasm. *Journal of Sex Research, 47*, 552–567.

Mueller-Pfeiffer, C., Rufibach, K., Perron, N., Wyss, D., Kuenzler, C., Prezewowsky, C., et al. (2012). Global functioning and disability in dissociative disorders. *Psychiatry Research, 200*, 475–481.

Mueser, K. T., Bond, G. R., Drake, R. E., & Resnick, S. G. (1998). Models of community care for severe mental illness: A review of research on case management. *Schizophrenia Bulletin, 24*, 37–74.

Multon, K. D., Kivlighan, D. M., & Gold, P. B. (1996). Changes in counselor adherence over the course of training. *Journal of Counseling Psychology, 43*, 356–363.

Mundle, G., Bruegel, R., Urbaniak, H., Laengle, G., Buchkremer, G., & Mann, K. (2001). Kurzund mittelfristige Erfolgsraten ambulanter Entwoehnungsbehandlungen fuer alkoholabhaengige Patienten. *Fortschritte der Neurologie Psychiatrie, 69*, 374–378.

Mundo, E., Maina, G., & Uslenghi, C. (2000). Multi-centre, double-blind comparison of fluvoxamine and clomipramine in the treatment of obsessive-compulsive disorder. *International Clinical Psychopharmacology, 15*, 69–76.

Munetz, M. R., Grande, T., Kleist, J., & Peterson, G. A. (1996). The effectiveness of outpatient civil commitment. *Psychiatric Services, 47*, 1251–1253.

Munro, S., Thomas, K. L., & Abu-Shaar, M. (1993). Molecular characterization of a peripheral receptor for cannabinoids. *Nature, 365*, 61–65.

Munson, J., Dawson, G., Abbott, R., et al. (2006). Amygdalar volume and behavioral development in autism. *Archives of General Psychiatry, 63*, 686–693.

Muntner, P., He, J., Cutler, J. A., Wildman, R. P., & Whelton, P. K. (2004). Trends in blood pressure among adolescents and children. *JAMA, 291*, 2107–2113.

Muroff, J., Levis, M. E., & Bratiotis, C. (2014). Hoarding disorder. In E. A. Storch & D. McKay (Eds.), *Obsessive-compulsive disorder and its spectrum: A life-span approach* (pp. 117–140). Washington, DC: American Psychological Association.

Murphy, J. (1976). Psychiatric labeling in cross-cultural perspective. *Science, 191*, 1019–1028.

Murphy, S. L., Xu, J., & Kochanek, K. D. (2013). Deaths: Final data for 2010. In N. C. F. H. Statistics (Ed.), *National Vital Statistics Reports* (Vol. 61). Hyattsville, MD.

Murray, C. J. L., & Lopez, A. D. (1996). *The global burden of disease: A comprehensive assessment of disease, injuries, and risk factors in 1990 and projected to 2020*. Cambridge, MA: Harvard University Press.

Murray, G., & Harvey, A. (2010). Circadian rhythms and sleep in bipolar disorder. In L. N. Yatham & M. Maj (Eds.), *Bipolar disorder: Clinical and neurobiological foundations* (pp. 263–274). New York: John Wiley & Sons.

Murray-Close, D., Hoza, B., Hinshaw, S. P., Arnold, L. E., Swanson, J., Jensen, P. S., Hechtman, L., & Wells, K. (2010). Developmental processes in peer problems of children with attention-deficit/hyperactivity disorder in The Multimodal Treatment Study of Children with ADHD: Developmental cascades and vicious cycles. *Developmental and Psychopathology, 22*, 785–802.

Muse, K., McManus, F., Hackmann, A., & Williams, M. (2010). Intrusive imagery in severe health anxiety: Prevalence, nature and links with memories and maintenance cycles. *Behaviour Research and Therapy, 48*, 792–798.

Mustonen, T. K., Spencer, S. M., Hoskinson, R. A., Sachs, D. P. L., & Garvey, A. J. (2005). The influence of gender, rance, and menthol content on tobacco exposure measures. *Nicotine and Tobacco Research, 7*, 581–590.

Myin-Germeys, I., van Os, J., Schwartz, J. E., et al. (2001). Emotional reactivity to daily life stress in schizophrenia. *Archives of General Psychiatry, 58*, 1137–1144.

Mykletun, A., Bjerkeset, O., Overland, S., Prince, M., Dewey, M., & Stewart, R. (2009). Levels of anxiety and depression as predictors of mortality: The HUNT study. *British Journal of Psychiatry, 195*, 118–125.

Nacewicz, B. M., Dalton, K. M., Johnstone, T. et al. (2006). Amygdala volume and nonverbal social impairment in adolescent and adult males with autism. *Archives of General Psychiatry, 63*, 1417–1448.

Naranjo, C. A., Tremblay, L. K., & Busto, U. E. (2001). The role of the brain reward system in depression. *Progress in Neuro-Psychopharmacology and Biological Psychiatry, 25*, 781–823.

Narrow, W. E., Clarke, D. E., Kuramoto, S. J., Kraemer, H. C., Kupfer, D. J., Greiner, L., & Regier, D. A. (2013). DSM-5 field trials in the United States and Canada, Part III: development and reliability testing of a cross-cutting symptom assessment for DSM-5. *American Journal of Psychiatry, 170*(1), 71–82.

Nasser, M. (1988). Eating disorders: The cultural dimension. *Social Psychiatry and Psychiatric Epidemiology, 23*, 184–187.

Nathan, D. (2011). *Sybil exposed: The extraordinary story behind the famous multiple personalty case*. New York: Free Press.

Nathan, P. E., & Gorman, J. M. (2002). Efficacy, effectiveness, and the clinical utility of psychotherapy research. In P. E. Nathan & J. M. Gorman (Eds.), *A Guide to Treatments that Work* (2nd ed., pp. 643–654). New York: Oxford University Press.

National Academy on an Aging Society. (1999). Challenges for the 21st century: Chronic and disabling conditions. Retrieved from http://www.agingsociety.org/agingsociety/publications/chronic/index.html.

National Center for Justice. (2003). *National Crime Victimization Survey*. National Center for Justice, Document NCJ 206348.

National Institute of Child Health and Human Development. (2000). Report of the National Reading Panel. Teaching children to read: An evidence-based assessment of the scientific research literature on reading and its implications for reading instruction. Available at http://www.nichd.nih.gov/publications/nrp/smallbook.htm.

National Institutes of Health. (1997, August). The Ad Hoc Group of Experts. *Workshop on the Medical Utility of Marijuana: Report to the Director*.

Nay, W., Brown, R., & Roberson-Nay, R. (2013). Longitudinal course of panic disorder with and without agoraphobia using the National Epidemiologic Survey on Alcohol and Related Conditions (NESARC). *Psychiatry Research, 208*, 54–61.

Neale, J. M., & Liebert, R. M. (1986). *Science and behavior: An introduction to methods of research* (3rd ed.). Englewood Cliffs, NJ: Prentice-Hall.

Neale, J. M., & Oltmanns, T. (1980). *Schizophrenia*. New York: John Wiley & Sons.

Neisser, U. (1976). *Cognition and reality*. San Francisco: Freeman.

Nelson, E. C., Heath, A. C., Madden, P. A. F., Cooper, M. L., Dinwiddie, S. H., Bucholz, K. K., et al. (2002). Association between self-reported childhood sexual abuse and adverse psychosocial outcomes: Results from a twin study. *Archives of General Psychiatry, 59*, 139–145.

Nelson, J. C. (2006). The STAR*D study: A four-course meal that leaves us wanting more. *American Journal of Psychiatry, 163*, 1864–1866.

Nelson, M. D., Saykin, A. J., Flashman, L. A., & Riordin, H. J. (1998). Hippocampal volume reduction in schizophrenia as assessed by magnetic resonance imaging: A meta analytic study. *Archives of General Psychiatry, 55*, 433–440.

Nelson, R. O., Lipinski, D. P., & Black, J. L. (1976). The reactivity of adult retardates' self-monitoring: A comparison among behaviors of different valences, and a comparison with token reinforcement. *Psychological Record, 26*, 189–201.

Nemeroff, C. B., & Schatzberg, A. F. (1998). Pharmacological treatment of unipolar depression. In P. E. Nathan & J. M. Gorman (Eds.), *A guide to treatments that work* (pp. 212–225). New York: Oxford University Press.

Nestle, M. (2002). *Food politics: How the food industry influences nutrition and health*. Berkeley: University of California Press.

Neugebauer, R. (1979). Mediaeval and early modern theories of mental illness. *Archives of General Psychiatry, 36*, 477–484.

Neuman, R. J., Lobos, E., Reich, W., Henderson, C. A., Sun, L. W., & Todd, R. D. (2007). Prenatal smoking exposure and dopaminergic genotypes interact to cause a severe ADHD subtype. *Biological Psychiatry, 61*, 1320–1328.

Neumeister, A., Daher, R. J., & Charney, D. S. (2005). Anxiety disorders: noradrenergic neurotransmission. *Handbook of Experimental Pharmacology, 169*, 205–223.

Neumeister, A., Konstantinidis, A., Stastny, J., Schwarz, M. J., Vitouch, O., Willeit, M., et al. (2002). Association between the serotonin transporter gene promoter polymorphism (5-HTTLPR) and behavioral responses to tryptophan depletion in healthy women with and without family history of depression. *Archives of General Psychiatry, 59*, 613–620.

New, A. S., Hazlett, E. A., Buchsbaum, M. S., Goodman, M., Mitelman, S. A., Newmark, R., et al. (2007). Amygdala-prefrontal disconnection in borderline personality disorder. *Neuropsychopharmacology 32*, 1629–1640.

Newman, D. L., Moffitt, T. E., Caspi, A., & Silva, P. A. (1998). Comorbid mental disorders: Implications for treatment and sample selection. *Journal of Abnormal Psychology, 107*, 305–311.

Newman, J. P., Patterson, C. M., & Kosson, D. S. (1987). Response perseveration in psychopaths. *Journal of Abnormal Psychology, 96*, 145–149.

Newman, J. P., Schmitt, W. A., & Voss, W. D. (1997). The impact of motivationally neutral cues on psychopathic individuals: Assessing the generality of the response modulation hypothesis. *Journal of Abnormal Psychology, 196*, 563–575.

Newton-Howes, G., Tyrer, P., Anagnostakis, K., Cooper, S., Bowden-Jones, O., & Weaver, T. (2010). The prevalence of personality disorder, its comorbidity with mental state disorders, and its clinical significance in community mental health teams. *Social Psychiatry and Psychiatric Epidemiology, 45*, 453–460.

Newton-Howes, G., Tyrer, P., & Johnson, T. (2006). Personality disorder and the outcome of depression: Meta-analysis of published studies. *British Journal of Psychiatry, 188*, 13–20.

Ng, M., Fleming, T., Robinson, M., Thomson, B., Graetz, N., Margono, C., et al. (2014). Global, regional, and national prevalence of overweight and obesity in children and adults during 1980–2013: A systematic analysis for the Global Burden of Disease Study 2013. *The Lancet*. doi: http://dx.doi.org/10.1016/S0140-6736(14)60460-8

Nicholls, L. (2008). Putting the New View Classification Scheme to an empirical test. *Feminism and Psychology, 18*, 515–526.

Nicholson, A., Kuper, H., & Hemingway, H. (2006). Depression as an aetiologic and prognostic factor in coronary heart disease: A meta-analysis of 6362 events among 146538 participants in 54 observational studies. *European Heart Journal, 27*, 2763–2774.

Niederdeppe, J., Farrelly, M. C., & Haviland, M. L. (2004). Confirming "truth": More evidence of a successful tobacco countermarketing campaign in Florida. *American Journal of Public Health, 94*, 255–257.

Nielssen, O., Bourget, D., Laajasalo, T., Liem, M., Labelle, A., Hakkanen-Nyholm, H., et al. (2011). Homicide of strangers by people with a psychotic illness. *Schizophrenia Bulletin, 37*, 572–579.

Nietzel, M. T., & Harris, M. J. (1990). Relationship of dependency and achievement/autonomy to depression. *Clinical Psychology Review, 10*, 279–297.

Nigg, J. T. (2013). Attention deficits and hyperactivity-impulsivity: What have we learned, what next? *Development and Psychopathology, 25*(4 Pt 2), 1489–1503.

Nigg, J. T., & Casey, B. J. (2005). An integrative theory of attention-deficit/ hyperactivity disorder based on the cognitive and affective neurosciences. *Development and Psychopathology, 17*, 785–806.

Nigg, J. T., & Goldsmith, H. H. (1994). Genetics of personality disorders: Perspectives from personality and psychopathology research. *Psychological Bulletin, 115*, 346–380.

Nigg, J. T., Lewis, K., Edinger, T., & Falk, M. (2012). Meta-analysis of attention-deficit/hyperactivity disorder or attention-deficit/hyperactivity disorder symptoms, restriction diet, and synthetic food color additives. *Journal of the American Academy of Child and Adolescent Psychiatry, 51*(1), 86–97.e88.

Nikolaus, S., Antke, C., Beu, M., & Muller, H. W. (2010). Cortical GABA, striatal dopamine and midbrain serotonin as the key players in compulsive and anxiety disorders—Results from in vivo imaging studies. *Reviews Neuroscience, 21*, 119–139.

Nobler, M. S., Oquendo, M. A., Kegeles, L. S., Malone, K. M., Campbell, C., Sackheim, H. A., et al. (2001). Decreased regional brain metabolism after ECT. *American Journal of Psychiatry, 158*, 305–308.

Nobre, P. J., & Pinto-Gouveia, J. (2008). Cognitions, emotions, and sexual response: Analysis of the relationship among automatic thoughts, emotional responses, and sexual arousal. *Archives of Sexual Behavior, 37*, 652–661.

Nock, M. K. (2009). Why do people hurt themselves? New insights into the nature and function of self-injury. *Current Directions in Psychological Science, 18*, 78–83.

Nock, M. K. (2010). Self-injury. *Annual Review of Clinical Psychology, 6*, 339–363.

Nock, M. K., Kazdin, A. E., Hiripi, E., & Kessler, R. C. (2006). Prevalence, subtypes, and correlates of DSM-IV conduct disorder in the National Comorbidity Survey Replication. *Psychological Medicine, 36*, 699–710.

Nock, M. K., & Mendes, W. B. (2008). Physiological arousal, distress tolerance, and social problem-solving deficits among adolescent self-injurers. *Journal of Consulting and Clinical Psychology, 76*, 28–38.

Nock, M. K., & Prinstein, M. J. (2004). A functional approach to the assessment of self-mutilative behavior. *Journal of Consulting and Clinical Psychology, 72*, 885–890.

Nock, M. K., Prinstein, M. J., & Sterba, S. K. (2009). Revealing the form and functions of self-injurious thoughts and behaviors: A real-time ecological assessment study among adolescents and young adults. *Journal of Abnormal Psychology, 118*, 816–827.

Nolen-Hoeksema, S. (1991). Responses to depression and their effects on the duration of depressive episodes. *Journal of Abnormal Psychology, 100*, 569–582.

Nolen-Hoeksema, S. (2000). The role of rumination in depressive disorders and mixed anxiety/depressive symptoms. *Journal of Abnormal Psychology, 109*, 504–511.

Nolen-Hoeksema, S. (2001). Gender differences in depression. *Current Directions in Psychological Science, 10*, 173–176.

Noll, S. M., & Fredrickson, B. L. (1998). A mediational model linking self-objectification, body shame, and disordered eating. *Psychology of Women Quarterly, 22*, 623–636.

Nonnemaker, J., Hersey, J., Homsi, G., Busey, A., Allen, J., & Vallone, D. (2013). Initiation with menthol cigarettes and youth smoking uptake. *Addiction, 108*(1), 171–178.

Norberg, M. M., Krystal, J. H., & Tolin, D. F. (2008). A meta-analysis of D-cycloserine and the facilitation of fear extinction and exposure therapy. *Biological Psychiatry, 63*, 1118–1126.

Nordsletten, A. E., Reichenberg, A., Hatch, S. L., de la Cruz, L. F., Pertusa, A., Hotopf, M., et al. (2013). Epidemiology of hoarding disorder. *British Journal of Psychiatry, 203*, 445–452.

Norton, M. C., Skoog, I., Toone, L., Corcoran, C., Tschanz, J. T., Lisota, R. D., et al. (2006). Three-year incidence of first-onset depressive syndrome in a population sample of older adults: The Cache County Study. *American Journal of Geriatric Psychiatry, 14*, 237–245.

Norton, P. J., & Price, E. C. (2007). A meta-analytic review of adult cognitive-behavioral treatment outcome across the anxiety disorders. *Journal of Nervous and Mental Disease, 195*, 521–531.

Noyes, R. (1999). The relationship of hypochondriasis to anxiety disorders. *General Hospital Psychiatry, 21*, 8–17.

O'Brien, W. H., & Haynes, S. N. (1995). Behavioral assessment. In L. A. Heiden & M. Hersen (Eds.), *Introduction to clinical psychology* (pp. 103–139). New York: Plenum.

O'Brien, J. T., Sahakian, B. J., & Checkley, S. A. (1993). Cognitive impairments in patients with seasonal affective disorder. *British Journal of Psychiatry, 163*, 338–343.

O'Donnell, P., & Grace, A. A. (1998). Dysfunctions in multiple interrelated systems as the neurobiological bases of schizophrenic symptom clusters. *Schizophrenia Bulletin, 24*, 267–283.

O'Donohue, W. (1993). The spell of Kuhn on psychology: An exegetical elixir. *Philosophical Psychology, 6*, 267–287.

O'Donohue, W., Dopke, C. A., & Swingen, D. N. (1997). Psychotherapy for female sexual dysfunction: A review. *Clinical Psychology Review, 17*, 537–566.

O'Farrell, T. J., & Fals-Stewart, W. (2000). Behavioral couples therapy for alcoholism and drug abuse. *Journal of Substance Abuse Treatment, 18*, 51–54.

O'Kearney, R. T., Anstey, K. J., & von Sanden, C. (2006). Behavioural and cognitive behavioural therapy for obsessive compulsive disorder in children and adolescents. *Cochrane Database of Systematic Reviews 2006*, Issue 4.

O'Leary, D. S., Block, R. I., Flaum, M., Schultz, S. K., Ponto, L. L., Boles, Watkins, G. L., Hurtig, R. R., Andreasen, N. C., & Hichwa, R. D. (2000). Acute marijuana effects on rCBF and cognition: A PET study. *Neuroreport, 11*, 3835–3841.

O'Leary, K. D., & Wilson, G. T. (1987). *Behavior therapy: Application and outcome*. Englewood Cliffs, NJ: Prentice-Hall.

O'Loughlin, J. O., Paradis, G., Kim, W., DiFranza, J., Meshefedjian, G., McMillan-Davey, E., Wong, S., Hanley, J., & Tyndale, R. F. (2005). Genetically decreased CYP2A6 and the risk of tobacco dependence: A prospective study of novice smokers. *Tobacco Control, 13*, 422–428.

O'Neal, J. M. (1984). First person account: Finding myself and loving it. *Schizophrenia Bulletin, 10*, 109–110.

Ockene, J. K., Mermelstein, R. J., Bonollo, D. S., Emmons, K. M., Perkins, K. A., Voorhees, C. C., & Hollis, J. F. (2000). Relapse and maintenance issues for smoking cessation. *Health Psychology, 19*, 17–31.

Odgers, C. L., Caspi, A., Broadbent, J. M., Dickson, N., Hancox, R. J., Harrington, H., Poulton, R., Sears, M. R., Thomson, W. M., & Moffitt, T. E. (2007). Prediction of differential adult health burden by conduct problem subtypes in males. *Archives of General Psychiatry, 64*, 476–484.

Odgers, C. L., Moffitt, T. E., Broadbent, J. M., Dickson, N., Hancox, R. J., Harrington, H., Poulton, R., Sears, M. R., Thomson, W. M., & Caspi, A. (2008). Female and male antisocial trajectories: From childhood origins to adult outcomes. *Developmental and Psychopathology, 20,* 673–716.

Oei, T. P. S., & Dingle, G. (2008). The effectiveness of group cognitive behaviour therapy for unipolar depressive disorders. *Journal of Affective Disorders, 107,* 5–21.

Ogden, C. L., Carroll, M. D., Kit, B. K., & Flegal, K. M. (2014). Prevalence of childhood and adult obesity in the United States, 2011–2012. *Journal of the American Medical Association, 311*(8), 806–814.

Ogden, T., & Halliday-Boykins, C. A. (2004). Multisystemic treatment of antisocial adolescents in Norway: Replication of clinical outcomes outside the U.S. *Child and Adolescent Mental Health Volume, 9,* 77–83.

Ogloff, J. R. P., Cutajar, M. C., Mann, E., & Mullen, P. (2012). Child sexual abuse and subsequent offending and victimisation: A 45 year follow-up study. *Trends and Issues in Crime and Criminal Justice, 440.*

Öhman, A., Flykt, A., & Esteves, F. (2001). Emotion drives attention: Detecting the snake in the grass. *Journal of Experimental Psychology: General, 137,* 466–478.

Öhman, A., & Mineka, A. (2003). The malicious serpent: Snakes as a prototypical stimulus for an evolved module of fear. *Current Directions in Psychological Science, 12,* 5–9.

Öhman, A., & Soares, J. J. F. (1994). "Unconscious anxiety": Phobic responses to masked stimuli. *Journal of Abnormal Psychology, 103,* 231–240.

Ohtani, T., Levitt, J. J., Nestor, P. G., Kawashima, T., Asami, T., Shenton, M. E., et al. (2014). Prefrontal cortex volume deficit in schizophrenia: A new look using 3T MRI with manual parcellation. *Schizophrenia Research, 152*(1), 184–190.

Olabi, B., Ellison-Wright, I., McIntosh, A. M., Wood, S. J., Bullmore, E., & Lawrie, S. M. (2011). Are there progressive brain changes in schizophrenia? A meta-analysis of structural magnetic resonance imaging studies. *Biological Psychiatry, 70,* 88–96.

Olatunji, B. O., Cisler, J. M., & Tolin, D. F. (2007). Quality of life in the anxiety disorders: A meta-analytic review. *Clinical Psychology Review, 27,* 572–581.

Olatunji, B. O., Etzel, E. N., Tomarken, A. J., Ciesielski, B. G., & Deacon, B. (2011). The effects of safety behaviors on health anxiety: An experimental investigation. *Behaviour Research and Therapy, 49,* 719–728.

Olatunji, B. O., Moretz, M. W., & Zlomke, K. R. (2010). Linking cognitive avoidance and GAD symptoms: The mediating role of fear of emotion. *Behaviour Research and Therapy, 48,* 435–441.

Olff, M., Langeland, W. L., Draijer, N., & Gersons, B. P. R. (2007). Gender differences in posttraumatic stress disorder. *Psychological Bulletin, 133,* 183–204.

Olfson, M., Blanco, C., Liu, L., Moreno, C., & Laje, G. (2006). National trends in the outpatient treatment of children and adolescents with antipsychotic drugs. *Archives of General Psychiatry, 63,* 679–687.

Olfson, M., Blanco, C., Liu, S., Wang, S., & Correll, C. U. (2012). National trends in the office-based treatment of children, adolescents, and adults with antipsychotics. *Archives of General Psychiatry, 69*(12), 1247–1256.

Olfson, M., & Marcus, S. C. (2010). National trends in outpatient psychotherapy. *American Journal of Psychiatry, 167,* 1456–1463.

Olivardia, R., Pope, H. G., Mangweth, B., & Hudson, J. I. (1995). Eating disorders in college men. *American Journal of Psychiatry, 152,* 1279–1284.

Oltmanns, T. F., & Powers, A. D. (2012). Gender and personality disorder. In T. A. Widiger (Ed.), *The Oxford handbook of personality disorders* (1st ed.). New York: Oxford University Press.

O'Neal, J. M. (1984). First person account: Finding myself and loving it. *Schizophrenia Bulletin, 10,* 109–110.

Orr, S. P., Metzger, L. J., Lasko, N. B., Macklin, M. L., Hu, F. B., Shalev, A. Y., et al. (2003). Physiologic responses to sudden, loud tones in monozygotic twins discordant for combat exposure: Association with posttraumatic stress disorder. *Archives of General Psychiatry, 60,* 283–288.

Ortiz, J., & Raine, A. (2004). Heart rate level and antisocial behavior in children and adolescents: A meta-analysis. *Journal of the American Academy of Child and Adolescent Psychiatry, 43,* 154–162.

Ory, M., Hoffman, R. R., Yee, J. L., Tennstedt, S., & Schulz, R. (1999). Prevalence and impact of caregiving: A detailed comparison between dementia and nondementia caregivers. *The Gerontologist, 39,* 177–185.

Osby, U., Brandt, L., Correia, N., Ekbom, A., & Sparen, P. (2001). Excess mortality in bipolar and unipolar disorder in Sweden. *Archives of General Psychiatry, 58,* 844–850.

Osgood, C. E., Luria, Z., Jeans, R. F., Smith, S. W. (1976). The three faces of Evelyn: A case report. *Journal of Abnormal Psychology, 85,* 47-248.

Ouimette, P. C., Finney, J. W., & Moos, R. H. (1997). Twelve-step and cognitive-behavioral treatment for substance abuse: A comparison of treatment effectiveness. *Journal of Consulting and Clinical Psychology, 65,* 230–240.

Owen, M. J., Craddock, N., & O'Donovan, M. C. (2010). Suggestion of roles for both common and rare risk variants in genome-wide studies of schizophrenia. *Archives of General Psychiatry, 67,* 667-673.

Owen, M. J., Williams, N. M., & O'Donovan, M. C. (2004). The molecular genetics of schizophrenia: New findings promise new insights. *Molecular Psychiatry, 9,* 14–27.

Owen, P. P., & Laurel-Seller, E. (2000). Weight and shape ideals: Thin is dangerously in. *Journal of Applied Social Psychology, 54,* 682–687.

Ozer, D. J., & Benet-Martinez, V. (2006). Personality and the prediction of consequential outcomes. *Annual Review of Psychology, 57,* 401–421.

Ozer, E. J., Best, S. R., Lipsey, T. L., & Weiss, D. S. (2003). Predictors of posttraumatic stress disorder and symptoms in adults: A meta-analysis. *Psychological Bulletin, 129,* 52–73.

Pacchiarotti, I., Bond, D. J., Baldessarini, R. J., Nolen, W. A., Grunze, H., Licht, R. W., et al. (2013). The International Society for Bipolar Disorders (ISBD) task force report on antidepressant use in bipolar disorders. *American Journal of Psychiatry, 170,* 1249–1262.

Palmer, B. A., Pankratz, V., & Bostwick, J. (2005). The lifetime risk of suicide in schizophrenia: A reexamination. *Archives of General Psychiatry, 62,* 247–253.

Pantelis, C., Velakoulis, D., McGorry, P. D., et al. (2003). Neuroanatomical abnormalities before and after onset of psychosis: A cross-sectional and longitudinal MRI comparison. *The Lancet, 361,* 281–288.

Parsons, T. D., & Rizzo, A. A. (2008). Affective outcomes of virtual reality exposure therapy for anxiety and specific phobias: A meta-analysis. *Journal of Behavior Therapy and Experimental Psychiatry, 39,* 250–261.

Pathania, M., Davenport, E. C., Muir, J., Sheehan, D. F., Lopez-Domenech, G., & Kittler, J. T. (2014). The autism and schizophrenia associated gene CYFIP1 is critical for the maintenance of dendritic complexity and the stabilization of mature spines. *Translational Psychiatry, 4,* e374.

Patient Protection and Affordable Care Act, 42 U.S.C § 18001. (2010).

Patrick, C. J., Fowles, D. C., & Krueger, R. F. (2009). Triarchic conceptualization of psychopathy: Developmental origins of disinhibition, boldness, and meanness. *Development and Psychopathology, 21,* 913–938.

Patronek, G. J., & Nathanson, J. N. (2009). A theoretical perspective to inform assessment and treatment strategies for animal hoarders. *Clinical Psychology Review, 29,* 274–281.

Patterson, G. R. (1982). *Coercive family process.* Eugene, OR: Castilia.

Paulhus, D. L. (1998). Interpersonal and intrapsychic adaptiveness of trait self-enhancement: A mixed blessing? *Journal of Personality and Social Psychology, 74,* 1197–1208.

Paulus, M. P., Tapert, S. F., & Schuckit, M. A. (2005). Neural activation patterns of methamphetamine-dependent subjects during decision making predict relapse. *Archives of General Psychiatry, 62,* 761–768.

Paxton, S. J., Schutz, H. K., Wertheim, E. H., & Muir, S. L. (1999). Friendship clique and peer influences on body image concerns, dietary restraint, extreme weight-loss behaviors, and binge eating in adolescent girls. *Journal of Abnormal Psychology, 108,* 255–264.

Payne, A., & Blanchard, E. B. (1995). A controlled comparison of cognitive therapy and self-help support groups in the treatment of irritable bowel syndrome. *Journal of Consulting and Clinical Psychology, 63,* 779–786.

Peat, C., Mitchell, J. E., Hoek, H. W., & Wonderlich, S. A. (2009). Validity and utility of subtyping anorexia nervosa. *International Journal of Eating Disorders, 42,* 590–594.

Pediatric OCD treatment study (POTS) team. (2004). Cognitive-behavior therapy, setraline, and their combination for children and adolescents with obsessive-compulsive disorder: The pediatric OCD treatment study (POTS) randomized controlled trial. *Journal of the American Medical Association, 292,* 1969–1976.

Pelham, W. E., Gnagy, E. M., Greiner, A. R., Hoza, B., Hinshaw, S. P., Swanson, J. M., Simpson, S., Shapiro, C., Bukstein, O., Baron-Myak, C., & McBurnett, K. (2000). Behavioral versus behavioral plus pharmacological treatment for ADHD children attending a summer treatment program. *Journal of Abnormal Child Psychology, 28,* 507–525.

Pendlebury, S. T., & Rothwell, P. M. (2009). Risk of recurrent stroke, other vascular events and dementia after transient ischaemic attack and stroke. *Cerebrovascular Diseases, 27 Suppl 3,* 1–11.

Penn, D. L., Chamberlin, C., & Mueser, K. T. (2003). The effects of a documentary film about schizophrenia on psychiatric stigma. *Schizophrenia Bulletin, 29,* 383–391.

Penn, D. L., & Mueser, K. T. (1996). Research update on the psychosocial treatment of schizophrenia. *American Journal of Psychiatry, 153,* 607–617.

Pennebaker, J. W., Kiecolt-Glaser, J. K., & Glaser, R. (1988). Disclosure of traumas and immune function: Health implications for psychotherapy. *Journal of Consulting and Clinical Psychology, 56,* 239–245.

Pennington, B. F. (1995). Genetics of learning disabilities. *Journal of Child Neurology, 10,* S69–S77.

Penzes, P., Cahill, M. E., Jones, K. A., VanLeeuwen, J. E., & Woolfrey, K. M. (2011). Dendritic spine pathology in neuropsychiatric disorders. *Nature Neuroscience, 14,* 285–293.

Peplau, L. A. (2003). Human sexuality: How do men and women differ? *Current Directions in Psychological Science, 12,* 37–40.

Perez, M., & Joiner, T. E. (2003). Body image dissatisfaction and disordered eating in black and white women. *International Journal of Eating Disorders, 33,* 342–350.

Perez, M., Voelz, Z. R., Pettit, J. W., & Joiner, T. E. (2002). The role of acculturative stress and body dissatisfaction in predicting bulimic symptomatology across ethnic groups. *International Journal of Eating Disorders, 31,* 442–454.

Perkins, K. A., Ciccocioppo, M., Conklin, C. A., Milanek, M. E., Grottenthaler, A., & Sayette, M. A. (2008). Mood influences on acute smoking responses are independent of nicotine intake and dose expectancy. *Journal of Abnormal Psychology, 117,* 79–93.

Perkins, K. A., Karelitz, J. L., Conklin, C. A., Sayette, M. A., & Giedgowd, G. E. (2010). Acute negative affect relief from smoking depends on the affect situation and measure but not on nicotine. *Biological Psychiatry, 67,* 707–714.

Perkonigg, A., Pfister, H., Stein, M. B., Hofler, M., Lieb, R., Maercker, A., et al. (2005). Longitudinal course of posttraumatic stress disorder and posttramatic stress. *American Journal of Psychiatry, 162,* 1320–1327.

Perlin, M. L. (1994). *Law and mental disability.* Charlottesville, VA: The Michie Company.

Perry, R., Campbell, M., Adams, P., Lynch, N., Spencer, E. K., Curren, E. L., & Overall, J. E. (1989). Longterm efficacy of haloperidol in autistic children: Continuous versus discontinuous administration. *Journal of the American Academy of Child and Adolescent Psychiatry, 28,* 87–92.

Persing, J. S., Stuart, S. P., Noyes, R., & Happel, R. L. (2000). Hypochondriasis: The patient's perspective. *International Journal of Psychiatry in Medicine, 30,* 329–342.

Persons, J. B., Bostrom, A., & Bertagnolli, A. (1999). Results of randomized controlled trials of cognitive therapy for depression generalize to private practice. *Cognitive Therapy Research, 23,* 535–548.

Perugi, G., Akiskal, H. S., Giannotti, D., Frare, F., Di Vaio, S., & Cassano, G. B. (1997). Gender-related differences in body dysmorphic disorder. *Journal of Nervous and Mental Disease, 185,* 578–582.

Pescosolido, B. A., Martin, J. K., Long, J. S., Medina, T. R., Phelan, J. C., & Link, B. G. (2010). "A disease like any other?" A decade of change in public relations to schizophrenia, depression and alcohol dependence. *American Journal of Psychiatry, 167,* 1321–1330.

Peterson, C. B., Mitchell, J. E., Crow, S. J., Crosby, R. D., & Wonderlich, S. A. (2009). The efficacy of self-help group treament and therapist-led group treatment for binge eating disorder. *American Journal of Psychiatry, 166,* 1347–1354.

Petry, N. M., Alessi, S. M., & Hanson. (2007). Contingency management improves abstinence and quality of life in cocaine abusers. *Journal of Consulting and Clinical Psychology, 75,* 307–315.

Petry, N. M., Alessi, S. M., Marx, J., Austin, M., & Tardif, M. (2005). Vouchers versus prizes: Contingency management treatment of substance abusers in community settings. *Journal of Consulting and Clinical Psychology, 73,* 1005–1014.

Pettersson-Yeo, W., Allen, P., Benetti, S., McGuire, P., & Mechelli, A. (2011). Dysconnectivity in schizophrenia: where are we now? *Neuroscience Biobehavoral Reviews, 35*(5), 1110–1124.

Pettinati, H. M., Oslin, D. W., Kampman, K. M., Dundon, W. D., Xie, H., Gallis, T. L., et al. (2010). A double-blind, placebo-controlled trial combining sertraline and naltrexone for treating co-occuring depression and alcohol dependence. *American Journal of Psychiatry, 167,* 668–675.

Phillips, D. P. (1974). The influence of suggestion on suicide: Substantive and theoretical implications of the Werther effect. *American Sociological Review, 39,* 340–354.

Phillips, D. P. (1985). The Werther effect. *The Sciences, 25,* 33–39.

Phillips, K. A. (2005). *The broken mirror: Understanding and treating body dysmorphic disorder.* New York: Oxford University Press.

Phillips, K. A. (2006). "I look like a monster": Pharmacotherapy and cognitive-behavioral therapy for body dysmorphic disorder. In R. L. Spitzer, M. B. First, J. B. W. Williams & M. Gibbon (Eds.), *DSM-IV-TR Case Book* (Vol. 2) *Experts tell how they treated their own patients* (pp. 263–276). Washington, DC: American Psychiatric Publishing.

Phillips, K. A., Menard, W., Quinn, E., Didie, E. R., & Stout, R. L. (2013). A 4-year prospective observational follow-up study of course and predictors of course in body dysmorphic disorder. *Psychological Medicine, 43,* 1109–1117.

Phillips, K. A., Pinto, A., Hart, A. S., Coles, M. E., Eisen, J. L., Menard, W., et al. (2012). A comparison of insight in body dysmorphic disorder and obsessive–compulsive disorder. *Journal of Psychiatric Research, 46,* 1293–1299.

Phillips, K. A., Stein, D. J., Rauch, S. L., Hollander, E., Fallon, B. A., Barsky, A., et al. (2010). Should an obsessive-compulsive spectrum grouping of disorders be included in DSM-V? *Depression and Anxiety, 27,* 528–555.

Phillips, K. A., Wilhelm, S., Koran, L. M., Didie, E. R., Fallon, B. A., Feusner, J., et al. (2010). Body dysmorphic disorder: Some key issues for DSM-V. *Depression and Anxiety, 27,* 573–591.

Phillips, L. J., Francey, S.M., Edwards, J., & McMurray, N. (2007). Stress and psychosis: towards the development of new models of investigation. *Clinical Psychology Review, 27,* 307–317.

Phillips, M. L., Ladouceur, C. D., & Drevets, W. C. (2008). A neural model of voluntary and automatic emotion regulation: Implications for understanding the pathophysiology and neurodevelopment of bipolar disorder. *Molecular Psychiatry, 13,* 833–857.

Phillips, M. R., Li, X., & Zhang, Y. (2002). Suicide rates in China, 1995–99. *The Lancet, 359,* 835–840.

Piasecki, T. M. (2006). Relapse to smoking. *Clinical Psychology Review, 26,* 196–125.

Piacentini, J., Bennett, S., Compton, S. N., Kendall, P. C., Birmaher, B., Albano, A. M., et al. (2014). 24- and 36-week outcomes for the Child/Adolescent Anxiety Multimodal Study (CAMS). *Journal of the American Academy of Child and Adolescent Psychiatry, 53*(3), 297–310.

Pierce, J. M., Petry, N. M., Stitzer, M. L., Blaine, J., Kellog, S., et al. (2006). Effects of lower-cost incentives on stimulant abstinence in methadone maintenance treatment. *Archives of General Psychiatry, 63,* 201–208.

Pierce, J. P., Choi, W. S., Gilpin, E. A., Farkas, A. J., & Berry, C. C. (1998). Tobacco ads, promotional items linked with teen smoking. *Journal of the American Medical Association, 279,* 511–515.

Pierce, K., & Courchesne, E. (2001). Evidence for a cerebellar role in reduced exploration and stereotyped behavior in autism. *Biological Psychiatry, 49,* 655–664.

Pierce, K., Haist, F., Sedaghadt, F., & Corchesne, E. (2004). The brain response to personally familiar faces in autism: Findings of fusiform activity and beyond. *Brain, 127,* 1–14.

Pierce, K., Muller, R. A., Ambrose, J., Allen, G., & Courchesne, E. (2001). Face processing occurs outside the fusiform "face area" in autism: Evidence from functional MRI. *Brain, 124,* 2059–2073.

Pietromonaco, P. R., & Barrett, L. F. (1997). Working models of attachment and daily social interactions. *Journal of Personality and Social Psychology, 73,* 1409–1423.

Pike, K. M., Dohm, F., Striegel-Moore, R. H., Wilfley, D. E., & Fairburn, C. M. (2001). A comparison of black and white women with binge eating disorder. *American Journal of Psychiatry, 158,* 1455–1460.

Pike, K. M., Walsh, B. T., Vitousek, K., Wilson, G. T., & Bauer, J. (2003). Cognitive behavior therapy in the posthospitalization treatment of anorexia nervosa. *American Journal of Psychiatry, 160*(11), 2046–2049.

Pilhatsch, M., Vetter, N. C., Hubner, T., Ripke, S., Muller, K. U., Marxen, M., et al. (2014). Amygdala-function perturbations in healthy mid-adolescents with familial liability for depression. *Journal of the American Academy of Child & Adolescent Psychiatry, 53,* 559–558.

Pilling, S., Bebbington, P., Kuipers, E., Garety, P., Geddes, L., Martindale, B., Orbach, G., & Morgan, C. (2002). Psychological treatments in schizophrenia: II. Meta-analyses of randomized controlled trials of social skills training and cognitive remediation. *Psychological Medicine, 32,* 783–791.

Pineles, S. L., & Mineka, S. (2005). Attentional biases to internal and external sources of potential threat in social anxiety. *Journal of Abnormal Psychology, 114,* 314–318.

Piper, A., Jr., Pope, H. G., Jr., & Borowiecki, J. J. I. (2000). Custer's last stand: Brown, Schefln, and Whitfiled's latest attempt to salvage "dissociative amnesia." *Journal of Psychiatry and the Law, 28,* 149–213.

Piven, J., Arndt, S., Bailey, J., & Andreasen, N. (1996). Regional brain enlargement in autism: A magnetic resonance imaging study. *Journal of the American Academy of Child and Adolescent Psychiatry, 35,* 530–536.

Piven, J., Arndt, S., Bailey, J., Havercamp, S., Andreasen, N. C., & Palmer, P. (1995). An MRI study of brain size in autism. *American Journal of Psychiatry, 152,* 1145–1149.

Pizzagalli, D. A., Goetz, E., Ostacher, M., Iosifescu, D. V., & Perlis, R. H. (2008). Euthymic patients with bipolar disorder show decreased reward learning in a probabilistic reward task. *Biological Psychiatry, 64,* 162–168.

Plomin, R. (1999). Genetics and general cognitive ability. *Nature, 402,* C25–C29.

Plomin, R., DeFries, J. C., Craig, I. W., & McGuffin, P. (2003). *Behavioral genetics in the postgenomic rra.* Washington, DC: APA Books.

Plomin, R., & Kovas, Y. (2005). Generalist genes and learning disabilities. *Psychological Bulletin, 131,* 592–617.

Polanczyk, G., de Lima, M. S., Horta, B. L., Biederman, J., & Rohde, L. A. (2007). The worldwide prevalence of ADHD: A systematic review and metaregression analysis. *American Journal of Psychiatry, 164*(6), 942–948.

Pole, N., Neylan, T. C., Otte, C., Henn-Hasse, C., Metzler, T. J., & Marmar, C. R. (2009). Prospective prediction of posttraumatic stress disorder symptoms using fear potentiated auditory startle responses. *Biological Psychiatry, 65,* 235–240.

Polich, J. M., Armor, D. J., & Braiker, H. B. (1980). Patterns of alcoholism over four years. *Journal of Studies on Alcohol, 41,* 397–415.

Polivy, J. (1976). Perception of calories and regulation of intake in restrained and unrestrained eaters. *Addictive Behaviors, 1,* 237–244.

Polivy, J., Heatherton, T. F., & Herman, C. P. (1988). Self esteem, restraint and eating behavior. *Journal of Abnormal Psychology, 97,* 354–356.

Polivy, J., & Herman, C. P. (1985). Dieting and binging: A causal analysis. *American Psychologist, 40*, 193–201.

Polivy, J., Herman, C. P., & Howard, K. (1988). The Restraint Scale: Assessment of dieting. In M. Hersen & A. S. Bellack (Eds.), *Dictionary of behavioral assessment techiniques* (pp. 377-380). Elmsford, NY: Pergamon Press..

Polivy, J., Herman, C. P., & McFarlane, T. (1994). Effects of anxiety on eating: Does palatability moderate distress-induced overeating in dieters? *Journal of Abnormal Psychology, 103*, 505–510.

Polonsky, D. C. (2000). Premature ejaculation. In R. C. Rosen & S. R. Leiblum (Eds.), *Principles and practice of sex therapy* (3rd ed., pp. 305–332). New York: Guilford Press.

Pomerleau, O. F., Collins, A. C., Shiffman, S., & Pomerleau, C. S. (1993). Why some people smoke and others do not: New perspectives. *Journal of Consulting and Clinical Psychology, 61*, 723–731.

Poole, D. A., Lindsay, D. S., Memon, A., & Bull, R. (1995). Psychotherapy and the recovery of memories of childhood sexual abuse: U.S. and British practitioners' opinions, practices and experiences. *Journal of Consulting and Clinical Psychology, 63*, 426–437.

Pope, H. G. J., Lalonde, J. K., Pindyck, L. J., Walsh, B. T., Bulik, C. M., et al. (2006). Binge eating disorder: A stable syndrome. *American Journal of Psychology, 163*, 2181–2183.

Pope, H. G. J., Oliva, P. S., Hudson, J. I., Bodkin, J. A., & Gruber, A. J. (1999). Attitudes toward DSM-IV dissociative disorders diagnoses among board-certified American psychiatrists. *American Journal of Psychiatry, 156*, 321–323.

Pope, H. G. J., Poliakoff, M. B., Parker, M. P., Boynes, M., & Hudson, J. J. (2006). Is dissociative amnesia a culture-bound syndrome? Findings from a survey of historical literature. *Psychological Medicine, 37*, 1067–1068.

Pope, K. S. (1998). Pseudoscience, cross-examination, and scientific evidence in the recovered memory controversy. *Psychology, Public Policy, and Law, 4*, 1160–1181.

Porter, S., Yuille, J. C., & Lehman, D. R. (1999). The nature of real, implanted, and fabricated memories for emotional childhood events: Implications for the recovered memory debate. *Law and Human Behavior, 23*, 415–537.

Posey, M. J., & McDougle, C. M. (2000). The pharmacotherapy of target symptoms associated with autistic disorder and other pervasive developmental disorders. *Harvard Review of Psychiatry, 8*, 45–63.

Potkin, S. G., Alva, G., Fleming, K., et al. (2002). A PET study of the pathophysiology of negative symptoms in schizophrenia. *American Journal of Psychiatry, 159*, 227–237.

Poulsen, S., Lunn, S., Daniel, S. I., Folke, S., Mathiesen, B. B., Katznelson, H., & Fairburn, C. G. (2014). A randomized controlled trial of psychoanalytic psychotherapy or cognitive-behavioral therapy for bulimia nervosa. *American Journal of Psychiatry, 171*(1), 109–116.

Powell, R. A., & Gee, T. L. (2000). "The effects of hypnosis on dissociative identity disorder: A reexamination of the evidence": Reply. *Canadian Journal of Psychiatry, 45*, 848–849.

Powers, E., Saultz, J., & Hamilton, A. (2007). Which lifestyle interventions effectively lower LDL cholesterol? *Journal of Family Practice, 56*, 483–485.

Powers, M. B., Halpern, J. M., Ferenschak, M. P., Gillihan, S. J., & Foa, E. B. (2010). A meta-analytic review of prolonged exposure for posttraumatic stress disorder. *Clinical Psychology Review, 30*, 635–641.

Powers, M. B., Vedel, E., & Emmelkamp, P. M. G. (2008). Behavioral couples therapy (BCT) for alcohol and drug use disorders: A meta-analysis. *Clinical Psychology Review, 28*(6), 952–962.

Pratt , L. A., Brody, D. J., & Gu, Q. (2011). Antidepressant use in personsaged 12 and over: United States, 2005–2008. *NCHS data brief, no 76.*

Prechter, G. C., & Shepard, J. W. J. (1990). Sleep and sleep disorders in the elderly. In R. J. Martin (Ed.), *Cardiorespiratory disorders during sleep* (pp. 365–386). Armonk, NY: Futura Publishing Co.

Pressman, P. S., & Miller, B. L. (2014). Diagnosis and management of behavioral variant frontotemporal dementia. *Biological Psychiatry, 75*, 574–581.

Price, D. D., Craggs, J. G., Zhou, Q., Verne, G. N., Perlstein, W. M., & Robinson, M. E. (2009). Widespread hyperalgesia in irritable bowel syndrome is dynamically maintained by tonic visceral impulse input and placebo/nocebo factors: Evidence from human psychophysics, animal models, and neuroimaging. *NeuroImage, 47*, 995–1001.

Prien, R. F., & Potter, W. Z. (1993). Maintenance treatment for mood disorders. In D. L. Dunner (Ed.), *Current psychiatric therapy*. Philadelphia: Saunders.

Prieto, S. L., Cole, D. A., & Tageson, C. W. (1992). Depressive self-schemas in clinic and nonclinic children. *Cognitive Therapy and Research, 16*, 521–534.

Primack, B. A., Bost, J. E., Land, S. R., & Fine, M. J. (2007). Volume of tobacco advertising in African American markets: Systematic review and meta-analysis. *Public Health Reports, 122*, 607–615.

Primack, B. A., Shensa, A., Kim, K. H., Carroll, M. V., Hoban, M. T., Leino, E. V., et al. (2013). Waterpipe smoking among U.S. university students. *Nicotine and Tobacco Research, 15*(1), 29–35.

Przeworski, A., & Newman, M. G. (2006). Efficacy and utility of computer-assisted cognitive behavioural therapy for anxiety disorders. *The Clinical Psychologist, 10*, 43–53.

Pujols, Y., Seal, B. N., & Meston, C. M. (2010). The association between sexual satisfaction and body image in women. *Journal of Sexual Medicine, 7*, 905–916.

Puma, M., Bell, S., Cook, R., Heid, C., Broene, P., Jenkins, F., et al. (2012). Third grade follow-up to the Head Start Impact Study Final Report *OPRE Report # 2012-45*. Washington, DC: U.S. Department of Health and Human Services.

Putnam, F. W. (1996). A brief history of multiple personality disorder. *Child and Adolescent Psychiatric Clinics of North America, 5*, 263–271.

Qualls, S. H., Segal, D. L., Norman, S., Niederehe, G., & Gallagher-Thompson, D. (2002). Psychologists in practice with older adults: Current patterns, sources of training, and need for continuing education. *Professional Psychology: Research and Practice, 33*, 435–442.

Quart, A. (2013). *Republic of outsiders: The power of amatuers, dreamers, and rebels*. New York: The New Press.

Qato, D. M., Alexander, G. C., Conti, R. M., Johnson, M., Schumm, P., & Lindau, S. T. (2008). Use of prescription and over-the-counter medications and dietary supplements among older adults in the United States. *Journal of the American Medical Association, 300*, 2867–2878.

Quinsey, V. L., Harris, G. T., Rice, M. E., & Cormier, C. A. (2006). *Violent offenders: Appraising and managing risk* (2nd ed.). Washington, DC: American Psychological Association.

Rachman, S. (2012). Health anxiety disorders: a cognitive construal. *Behaviour Research and Therapy, 50*, 502–512.

Rachman, S. J. (1977). The conditioning theory of fear acquisition: A critical examination. *Behaviour Research and Therapy, 15*, 375–387.

Rachman, S. J., & DeSilva, P. (1978). Abnormal and normal obsessions. *Behaviour Research and Therapy, 16*, 233–248.

Rachman, S. J., & Wilson, G. T. (1980). *The effects of psychological therapy* (2nd ed.). Elmsford, NY: Pergamon Press

Rademaker, A. R., van Zuiden, M., Vermetten, E., & Geuze, E. (2011). Type D personality and the development of PTSD symptoms: A prospective study. *Journal of Abnormal Psychology, 120*, 299–307.

Ragatz, L. L., Fremouw, W., & Baker, E. (2012). The psychological profile of white-collar offenders: Demographics, criminal thinking, psychopathic traits, and psychopathology. *Criminal Justice and Behavior, 39*, 978–997.

Raine, A. (2006). Schizotypal personality: Neurodevelopmental and psychosocial trajectories. *Annual Review of Clinical Psychology, 2*, 291–326.

Raine, A., Venables, P. H., & Williams, M. (1990). Relationships between central and autonomic measures of arousal at age 15 years and criminality at age 24 years. *Archives of General Psychiatry, 47*, 1003–1007.

Raison, C. L., Capuron, L., & Miller, A. H. (2006). Cytokines sing the blues: Inflammation and the pathogenesis of depression. *Trends in Immunology, 27*, 24–31.

Ramus, F. (2014). Neuroimaging sheds new light on the phonological deficit in dyslexia. *Trends in Cognitive Sciences, 18*(6), 274–275.

Rando, K., Chaplin, T. M., Potenza, M. N., Mayes, L., & Sinha, R. (2013). Prenatal cocaine exposure and gray matter volume in adolescent boys and girls: Relationship to substance use initiation. *Biological Psychiatry, 74*(7), 482–489.

Rapee, R. M., Abbott, M., & Lyneham, H. (2006). Bibliotherapy for children with anxiety disorders using written materials for parents: A randomized controlled trial. *Journal of Consulting and Clinical Psychology, 74*, 436–444.

Rapee, R., Mattick, R., & Murrell, E. (1986). Cognitive mediation in the affective component of spontaneous panic attacks. *Journal of Behavior Therapy and Experimental Psychiatry, 17*, 245–253.

Rapee, R. M., Schniering, C. A., & Hudson, J. L. (2009). Anxiety disorders during childhood adolescence: Origins and treatment. *Annual Review of Clinical Psychology, 5*, 311–341.

Rapoport, J. L., Giedd, J., & Gogtay, N. (2012). Neurodevelopmental model of schizophrenia: Update 2012. *Molecular Psychiatry, 17*, 1228–1238.

Rapoport, J. L., Swedo, S. E., & Leonard, H. L. (1992). Childhood obsessive compulsive disorder. *Journal of Clinical Psychiatry, 53*, 11–16.

Rapoport, M. J., Lanctot, K. L., Streiner, D. L., Bedard, M., Vingilis, E., Murray, B., et al. (2009). Benzodiazepine use and driving: A meta-analysis. *Journal of Clinical Psychiatry, 70*, 663–673.

Rapp, M. A., Schnaider-Beeri, M., Grossman, H. T., Sano, M., Perl, D. P., Purohit, D. P., Gorman, J. M., et al. (2006). Increased hippocampal plaqyes and tangles in patients with Alzheimer disease with a lifetime history of major depression. *Archives of General Psychiatry, 63*, 161–167.

Rascovsky, K., Hodges, J. R., Knopman, D., Mendez, M. F., Kramer, J. H., Neuhaus, J., et al. (2011). Sensitivity of revised diagnostic criteria for the behavioural variant of frontotemporal dementia. *Brain: A Journal of Neurology, 134*, 2456–2477.

Rasic, D., Hajek, T., Alda, M., & Uher, R. (2014). Risk of mental illness in offspring of parents with schizophrenia, bipolar disorder, and major depressive disorder: A meta-analysis of family high-risk studies. *Schizophrenia Bulletin, 40*(1), 28–38.

Raskind, W. H. (2001). Current understanding of the genetic basis of reading and spelling disability. *Learning Disability Quarterly, 24*, 141–157.

Rather, B. C., Goldman, M. S., Roehrich, L., & Brannick, M. (1992). Empirical modeling of an alcohol expectancy memory network using multidimensional scaling. *Journal of Abnormal Psychology, 101*, 174–183.

Rauch, S. L., Whalen, P. J., Shin, L. M., McInerney, S. C., Macklin, M. L., Lasko, N. B., et al. (2000). Exaggerated amygdala response to masked facial stimuli in posttraumatic stress disorder: A functional MRI study. *Biological Psychiatry, 47*, 769–776.

Rawson, R. A., Martinelli-Casey, P., Anglin, M. D., et al. (2004). A multi-site comparison of psychosocial approaches for the treatment of methamphetamine dependence. *Addiction, 99*, 708–717.

Raznahan, A., Wallace, G. L., Antezana, L., Greenstein, D., Lenroot, R., Thurm, A., et al. (2013). Compared to what? Early brain overgrowth in autism and the perils of population norms. *Biological Psychiatry, 74*(8), 563–575.

Reas, D. L., Williamson, D. A., Martin, C. K., & Zucker, N. L. (2000). Duration of illness predicts outcome for bulimia nervosa: A long-term follow-up study. *International Journal of Eating Disorders, 27*, 428–434.

Reba-Harrelson, L., Von Holle, A., Hamer, R. M., Swann, R., Reyes, M. L., & Bulik, C. M. (2009). Patterns and prevalence of disordered eating and weight control behaviors in women ages 25–45. *Eating and Weight Disorders, 14*(4), e190–198.

Rebok, G. W., Ball, K., Guey, L. T., Jones, R. N., Kim, H.-Y., King, J. W., et al. (2014). Ten-year effects of the advanced cognitive training for Independent and Vital Elderly Cognitive Training Trial on cognition and everyday functioning in older adults. *Journal of the American Geriatrics Society, 62*, 16–24.

Redding, N. (2009). *Methland: The death and life of an American small town.* New York: Bloomsbury USA.

Regeer, E. J., ten Have, M., Rosso, M. L., van Roijen, L. H., Vollebergh, W., & Nolen, W. A. (2004). Prevalence of bipolar disorder in the general population: A reappraisal study of the Netherlands Mental Health Survey and incidence study. *Acta Psychiatrica Scandinavica, 110*, 374–382.

Regier, D. A., Boyd, J. H., Burke, J. D., & Rae, D. S. (1988). One-month prevalence of mental disorders in the United States: Based on five epidemiologic catchment area sites. *Archives of General Psychiatry, 45*, 977–986.

Regier, D. A., Kuhl, E. A., & Kupfer, D. J. (2013). The DSM-5: Classification and criteria changes. *World Psychiatry, 12*, 92–98.

Regier, D. A., Narrow, W. E., Clarke, D. E., Kraemer, H. C., Kuramoto, S. J., Kuhl, E. A., & Kupfer, D. J. (2013). DSM-5 field trials in the United States and Canada, Part II: Test-retest reliability of selected categorical diagnoses. *American Journal of Psychiatry, 170*, 59–70.

Regier, D. A., Narrow, W. E., Rae, D. S., & Manderscheid, R. W. (1993). The de facto US mental and addictive disorders service system: Epidemiologic catchment area prospective 1-year prevalence rates of disorders and services. *Archives of General Psychiatry, 50*, 85–94.

Regland, B., Johansson, B.V., Grenfeldt, B., Hjelmgren, L.T., & Medhus, M. (1995). Homocysteinemia is a common feature of schizophrenia. *Journal of Neural Transmission: General Section, 100*, 165–169.

Reich, J. (2000). The relationship of social phobia to avoidant personality disorder: A proposal to reclassify avoidant personality disorder based on clinical empirical findings. *European Psychiatry, 15*, 151–159.

Reichborn-Kjennerud, T., Czajkowski, N., Neale, M. C., Ørstavik, R. E., Torgersen, S., Tambs, K., et al. (2007). Genetic and environmental influences on dimensional representations of DSM-IV cluster C personality disorders: A population-based multivariate twin study. *Psychological Medicine, 37*, 645–653.

Reichborn-Kjennerud, T., Czajkowski, N., Torgersen, S., Neale, M. C., Orstavik, R. E., Tambs, K., et al. (2007). The relationship between avoidant personality disorder and social phobia; A population-base twin study. *American Journal of Psychiatry, 164*, 1722–1728.

Reichenberg, A., Avshalom, C., Harrington, H, Houts, R., Keefe, R. S. E., Murray, R. M., Poulton, R., & Moffitt, T. E. (2010). Static and dynamic cognitive deficits in childhood preceding adult schizophrenia: A 30-year study. *American Journal of Psychiatry, 167*, 160–169.

Reid, D. H., Wilson, P. G., & Faw, G. D. (1991). Teaching self-help skills. In J. L. Matson & J. A. Mulick (Eds.), *Handbook of Mental Retardation.* New York: Pergamon Press.

Reidy, D. E., Shelley-Tremblay, J. F., & Lilienfeld, S. O. (2011). Psychopathy, reactive aggression, and precarious proclamations: A review of behavioral, cognitive, and biological research. *Aggression and Violent Behavior, 16*, 512–524.

Reilly-Harrington, N. A., Alloy, L. B., Fresco, D. M., & Whitehouse, W. G. (1999). Cognitive styles and life events interact to predict bipolar and unipolar symptomatology. *Journal of Abnormal Psychology, 108*, 567–578.

Reinhold, N., & Markowitsch, H. J. (2009). Retrograde episodic memory and emotion: a perspective from patients with dissociative amnesia. *Neuropsychologia, 47*, 2197–2206.

Reiss, D., Heatherington, E. M., Plomin, R., Howe, G. W., Simmens, S. J., et al. (1995). Genetic questions for environmental studies: Differential parenting and psychopathology in adolescence. *Archives of General Psychiatry, 52*, 925–936.

Reissing, E. D., Binik, Y. M., & Khalife, S. (1999). Does vaginismus exist? A critical review of the literature. *Journal of Nervous and Mental Disease, 187*, 261–274.

Renshaw, D. C. (2001). Women coping with a partner's sexual avoidance. *Family Journal—Counseling & Therapy for Couples and Families, 9*, 11–16.

Resick, P. A., Bovin, M. J., Calloway, A. L., Dick, A. M., King, M. W., Mitchell, K. S., et al. (2012). A critical evaluation of the complex PTSD literature: Implications for DSM-5. *Journal of Traumatic Stress, 25*, 241–251.

Resick, P. A., Nishith, P., & Griffin, M. G. (2003). How well does cognitive-behavioral therapy treat symptoms of complex PTSD? An examination of child sexual abuse survivors within a clinical trial. *CNS Spectrums, 8*, 351–355.

Resick, P. A., Nishith, P., Weaver, T. L., Astin, M. C., & Feuer, C. A. (2002). A comparison of cognitive-processing therapy with prolonged exposure and a waiting condition for the treatment of chronic posttraumatic stress disorder in female rape victims. *Journal of Consulting and Clinical Psychology, 70*, 867–879.

Resick, P. A., Suvak, M. K., Johnides, B. D., Mitchell, K. S., & Iverson, K. M. (2012). The impact of dissociation on PTSD treatment with cognitive processing therapy. *Depression and Anxiety, 29*, 718–730.

Ressler, K. J., Rothbaum, B. O., Tannenbaum, L., Anderson, P., Graap, K., Zimand, E., et al. (2004). Cognitive enhancers as adjuncts to psychotherapy: Use of D-cycloserine in phobic individuals to facilitate extinction of fear. *Archives of General Psychiatry, 61*, 1136–1144.

Rey, J. M., Martin, A., & Krabman, P. (2004). Is the party over? Cannabis and juvenille psychiatric disorder: The past 10 years. *Journal of the American Academy of Child and Adolescent Psychiatry, 43*, 1194–1205.

Reynolds, C. R., Chastain, R. L., Kaufman, A. S., & McLean, J. E. (1997). Demographic characteristics and IQ among adults: Analysis of the WAIS-R standardization sample as a function of the stratification variables. *Journal of School Psychology, 25*, 323–342.

Reynolds, S., Wilson, C., Austin, J., & Hooper, L. (2012). Effects of psychotherapy for anxiety in children and adolescents: A meta-analytic review. *Clinical Psychology Review, 32*(4), 251–262.

Rhee, S. H., & Waldman, I. D. (2002). Genetic and environmental influences on antisocial behavior: A meta-analysis of twin and adoption studies. *Psychological Bulletin, 128*, 490–529.

Rhode, P., Seeley, J. R., Kaufman, N. K, Clarke, G. N., & Stice, E. (2006). Predicting time to recovery among depressed adolescents treated in two psychosocial group interventions. *Journal of Consulting and Clinical Psychology, 74*, 80–88.

Richards, P. S., Baldwin, B. M., Frost, H. A., Clark-Sly, J. B., Berrett, M. E., & Hardman, R. K. (2000). What works for treating eating disorders? Conclusions of 28 outcome reviews. *Eating Disorders, 8*, 189–206.

Richards, R. L., Kinney, D. K., Lunde, I., Benet, M., & Merzel, A. (1988). Creativity in manic-depressives, cyclothymes, their normal relatives, and control subjects. *Journal of Abnormal Psychology, 97*, 281–288.

Richters, J., de Visser, R. O., Rissel, C. E., Grulich, A. E., & Smith, A. M. (2008). Demographic and psychosocial features of participants in bondage and discipline, "sadomasochism"or dominance and submission (BDSM): Data from a national survey. *Journal of Sexual Medicine, 7*, 1660–1668.

Ricks, D. M. (1972). *The beginning of vocal communication in infants and autistic children.* Doctoral dissertation, University of London.

Ridker, P. M., Cook, N. R., Lee, I.-M., Gordon, D., Gaziano, J. M., Manson, J. E., Hennekens, C. H., & Buring, J. E. (2005). A randomized trial of low-dose aspirin in the primary prevention of cardiovascular disease in women. *Journal of the American Medical Association, 352*, 1293–1304.

Ridley, M. (2003). *Nature via nurture: Genes, experience, and what makes us human.* Great Britain: HarperCollins.

Rieder, R. O., Mann, L. S., Weinberger, D. R., van Kammen, D. P., & Post, R. M. (1983). Computer tomographic scans in patients with schizophrenia, schizoaffective, and bipolar affective disorder. *Archives of General Psychiatry, 40*, 735–739.

Rief, W., & Auer, C. (2001). Is somatization a habituation disorder? Physiological reactivity in somatization syndrome. *Psychiatry Research, 101*, 63–74.

Rief, W., & Broadbent, E. (2007). Explaining medically unexplained symptoms-models and mechanisms. *Clinical Psychology Review, 27*, 821–841.

Rief, W., Buhlmann, U., Wilhelm, S., Borkenhagen, A., & Brähler, E. (2006). The prevalence of body dysmorphic disorder: A population-based survey. *Psychological Medicine, 36*, 877–885.

Rimland, B. (1964). *Infantile autism.* New York: Appleton-Century-Crofts.

Ritchie, K., Norton, J., Mann, A., Carriere, I., & Ancelin, M. L. (2013). Late-onset agoraphobia: General population incidence and evidence for a clinical subtype. *American Journal of Psychiatry, 170*, 790–798.

Ritsher, J. B., Struening, E. L., Hellman, F., & Guardino, M. (2002). Internal validity of an anxiety disorder screening instrument across five ethnic groups. *Psychiatry Research, 111*, 199–213.

Ritter, K., Vater, A., Rusch, N., Schroder-Abe, M., Schutz, A., Fydrich, T., et al. (2014). Shame in patients with narcissistic personality disorder. *Psychiatry Research, 215*, 429–437.

Roan, S. (1992, October 15). Giving up coffee tied to withdrawal symptoms. *Los Angeles Times*, p. A26.

Robbins, S. J., Ehrman, R. N., Childress, A. R., Cornish, J. W., & O'Brien, C. P. (2000). Mood state and recent cocaine use are not associated with levels of cocaine cue reactivity. *Drug and Alcohol Dependence, 59*, 33–42.

Roberts, B. W., Kuncel, N. R., Shiner, R., Caspi, A., & Goldberg, L. R. (2007). The power of personality: The comparative validity of personality traits, socioeconomic status, and cognitive ability for predicting important life outcomes. *Perspectives on Psychological Science, 2*, 313–345.

Robiner, W. N. (2006). The mental health professions: Workforce supply and demand, issues, and challenges. *Clinical Psychology Review, 26*, 600–625.

Robinson, D. N. (1996). *Wild beasts and idle humours: The insanity defense from antiquity to the present*. Cambridge, Massachusetts: Harvard University Press.

Robinson, L. A., Klesges, R. C., Zbikowski, S. M., & Glaser, R. (1997). Predictors of risk for different stages of adolescent smoking in a biracial sample. *Journal of Consulting and Clinical Psychology, 65*, 653–662.

Robinson, N. S., Garber, J., & Hillsman, R. (1995). Cognitions and stress: Direct and moderating effects on depression versus externalizing symptoms during the junior high school transition. *Journal of Abnormal Psychology, 104*, 453–463.

Robinson, T. E., & Berridge, K. C. (1993). The neural basis of drug craving: An incentive sensitization theory of addiction. *Brain Research Reviews, 18*, 247–191.

Robinson, T. E., & Berridge, K. C. (2003). Addiction. *Annual Review of Psychology, 54*, 25–53.

Rodewald, F., Wilhelm-Goling, C., Emrich, H. M., Reddemann, L., & Gast, U. (2011). Axis-I comorbidity in female patients with dissociative identity disorder and dissociative identity disorder not otherwise specified. *Journal of Nervous and Mental Disease, 199*, 122–131.

Roecklein, K., Wong, P., Ernecoff, N., Miller, M., Donofry, S., Kamarck, M., Wood-Vasey, W. M., & Franzen, P. (2013). The post illumination pupil response is reduced in seasonal affective disorder. *Psychiatry Research, 210*, 150–158.

Roehrig, J. P., & McLean, C. P. (2010). A comparison of stigma toward eating disorders versus depression. *International Journal of Eating Disorders, 43*, 671–674.

Roemer, L., Lee, J. K., Salters-Pedneault, K., Erisman, S. M., Orsillo, S. M., & Mennin, D. S. (2009). Mindfulness and emotion regulation difficulties in generalized anxiety disorder: Preliminary evidence for independent and overlapping contributions. *Behavior Therapy, 40*, 142–154.

Roemer, L., Molina, S., & Borkovec, T. D. (1997). An investigation of worry content among generally anxious individuals. *Journal of Nervous and Mental Disease, 185*, 314–319.

Roemer, L., Orsillo, S. M., & Barlow, D. H. (2004). Generalized anxiety disorder. In D. H. Barlow (Ed.), *Anxiety and its disorders: The nature and treatment of anxiety and panic* (pp. 477-515). New York: Guilford Press.

Roest, A. M., Martens, E. J., de Jonge, P., & Denollet, J. (2010). Anxiety and risk of incident coronary heart disease: A meta-analysis. *Journal of the American College of Cardiology, 56*, 38–46.

Rogler, L. H., & Hollingshead, A. B. (1985). *Trapped: Families and schizophrenia* (3rd ed.). Maplewood, NJ: Waterfront Press.

Rohan, K. J., Roecklein, K. A., Tierney Lindsey, K., Johnson, L. G., Lippy, R. D., Lacy, T. J., et al. (2007). A randomized controlled trial of cognitive-behavioral therapy, light therapy, and their combination for seasonal affective disorder. *Journal of Consulting and Clinical Psychology, 75*, 489–500.

Rolon-Arroyo, B., Arnold, D. H., & Harvey, E. A. (2013). The predictive utility of conduct disorder symptoms in preschool children: A 3-year follow-up study. *Child Psychiatry and Human Development*.

Romans, S. E., Gendall, K. A., Martin, J. L., & Mullen, P. E. (2001). Child sexual abuse and later disordered eating: A New Zealand epidemiological study. *International Journal of Eating Disorders, 29*, 380–392.

Root, T. L., Pinheiro, A. P., Thornton, L., Strober, M., Fernandez-Aranda, F., Brandt, H., et al. (2010). Substance use disorders in women with anorexia nervosa. *International Journal of Eating Disorders, 43*, 14–21.

Rorschach, H. (1921). *Psychodiagnostik: methodik und ergebnisse eines warhrnehmungsdiagnostischen experiments*. Berlin: Dritte aufl. Hrsg. von W. Morgenthaler.

Rosa-Alcazar, A. I., Sanchez-Meca, J., Gomez-Conesa, A., & Marin-Martinez, F. (2008). Psychological treatment of obsessive-compulsive disorder: A meta-analysis. *Clinical Psychology Review, 28*, 1310–1325.

Rose, J. E., & Behm, F. M. (2014). Combination Treatment With Varenicline and Bupropion in an Adaptive Smoking Cessation Paradigm. *American Journal of Psychiatry*.

Rose, J., E., Brauer, L. H., Behm, F. M., Cramblett, M. Calkins, K., & Lawhon, D. (2004). Psychopharmacological interactions between nicotine and ethanol. *Nicotine & Tobacco Research, 6*, 133–144. ARosen, 2000, 369

Rose, J. E., Herskovic, J. E., Behm, F. M., & Westman, E. C. (2009). Precessation treatment with nicotine patch significantly increases abstinence rates relative to conventional treatment. *Nicotine and Tobacco Research, 11*(9), 1067–1075.

Rosen, G. M., & Davison, G. C. (2003). Psychology should list empirically supported principles of change (ESPs) and not credential trademarked therapies or other treatment packages. *Behavior Modification, 27*, 300–312.

Rosen, L. N., Targum, S. D., Terman, M., Bryant, M. J., Hoffman, H., Kasper, S. F., et al. (1990). Prevalence of seasonal affective disorder at four latitudes. *Psychiatry Research, 31*, 131–144.

Rosen, R. C., Leiblum, S. R., & Spector, I. (1994). Psychologically based treatment for male erectile disorder: A cognitive-interpersonal model. *Journal of Sex and Marital Therapy, 20*, 67–85.

Rosen, R. C., Miner, M. M., & Wincze, J. P. (2014). Erectile dysfunction: Integration of medical and psychological approaches. In Y. M. Binik & K. S. K. Hall (Eds.), *Principles and Practice of Sex Therapy* (5 ed., pp. 61–88). New York: Guilford Press.

Rosenfarb, I. S., Goldstein, M. J., Mintz, J., & Neuchterlein, K. H. (1994). Expressed emotion and subclinical psychopathology observable within transactions between schizophrenics and their family members. *Journal of Abnormal Psychology, 104*, 259–267.

Ross, C. A. (1989). *Multiple personality disorder: Diagnosis, clinical features, and treatment*. New York: John Wiley & Sons.

Ross, C. A. (1991). Epidemiology of multiple personality disorder and dissociation. *Psychiatric Clinics of North America, 14*, 503–517.

Ross, C. A., Duffy, C. M. M., & Ellason, J. W. (2002). Prevalence, reliability and validity of dissociative disorders in an inpatient setting. *Journal of Trauma and Dissociation, 3*, 7–17.

Rossello, J., Bernal, G., & , & Rivera-Medina, C. (2008). Individual and group CBT and IPT for puerto rican adolescents with depressive symptoms. *Cultural Diversity and Ethnic Minority Psychology, 14*, 234–245.

Rossiter, E. M., & Agras, W. S. (1990). An empirical test of the DSM-IIIR definition of binge. *International Journal of Eating Disorders, 9*, 513–518.

Rotge, J. Y., Guehl, D., Dilharreguy, B., Tignol, J., Bioulac, B., Allard, M., et al. (2009). Meta-analysis of brain volume changes in obsessive-compulsive disorder. *Biological Psychiatry, 65*, 75–83.

Rothbaum, B. O., Anderson, P., Zimand, E., Hodges, L., Lang, D., & Wilson, J. (2006). Virtual reality exposure therapy and standard (in vivo) exposure therapy in the treatment of fear of flying. *Behavior Therapy, 37*, 80–90.

Rothbaum, B. O., Foa, E. B., Murdock, T., Riggs, D. S., & Walsh, W. (1992). A prospective examination of posttraumatic stress disorder in rape victims. *Journal of Traumatic Stress, 5*, 455–475.

Rothbaum, B. O., Hodges, L., Alarcon, R., Ready, D., Shahar, F., Graap, K., et al. (1999). Virtual reality exposure therapy for PTSD Vietnam veterans: A case study. *Journal of Traumatic Stress, 12*, 263–271.

Rothblatt, M. (1995). *The apartheid of sex*. Chicago, IL: Rivers Oram and Pandora Press.

Roughgarden, J. (2004). *Evolution's rainbow: Diversity, gender and sexuality in nature and people*. Oakland, CA: University of California Press.

Roughton, E. C., Schneider, M. L., Bromley, L. J., & Coe, C. L. (1998). Maternal activation during pregnancy alters neurobehavioral state in primate infants. *American Journal of Occupational Therapy, 52*, 90–98.

Rouleau, C. R., & von Ranson, K. M. (2011). Potential risks of pro-eating disorder websites. *Clinical Psychology Review, 31*, 525–531.

Rowland, D. L., Cooper, S. E., & Slob, A. K. (1996). Genital and psychoaffective responses to erotic stimulation in sexually functional and dysfunctional men. *Journal of Abnormal Psychology, 105*, 194–203.

Roy, A. (1994). Recent biologic studies on suicide. *Suicide and life threatening behaviors, 24*, 10–24.

Roy, A. (1995). Suicide. In H. I. Kaplan & B. J. Sadock (Eds.), *Comprehensive textbook of psychiatry* (pp. 1739–1752). Baltimore: Williams & Wilkins.

Rubin, D. C., Berntsen, D., & Bohni, M. K. (2008). A memory-based model of posttraumatic stress disorder: Evaluating basic assumptions underlying the PTSD diagnosis. *Psychological Review, 115*, 985–1011.

Rubinstein, T. B., McGinn, A. P., Wildman, R. P., & Wylie-Rosett, J. (2010). Disordered eating in adulthood is associated with reported weight loss attempts in childhood. *International Journal of Eating Disorders, 43*, 663–666.

Ruderfer, D. M., Fanous, A. H., Ripke, S., McQuillin, A., Amdur, R. L., Gejman, P. V., et al. (2013). Polygenic dissection of diagnosis and clinical dimensions of bipolar disorder and schizophrenia. *Molecular Psychiatry*. doi: 10.1038/mp.2013.138

Rummel-Kluge, C., Komossa, K., Schwarz, S., Hunger, H., Schmid, F., Lobos, C. A., . . . Leucht, S. (2010).

Head-to-head comparisons of metabolic side effects of second generation antipsychotics in the treatment of schizophrenia: A systematic review and meta-analysis. *Schizophrenia Research, 123*, 225–233.

Ruscio, A. M., Brown, T. A., Chiu, W. T., Sareen, J., Stein, M. B., & Kessler, R. C. (2008). Social fears and social phobia in the USA: Results from the National Comorbidity Survey Replication. *Psychological Medicine, 38*, 15–28.

Ruscio, A. M., Stein, D. J., Chiu, W. T., & Kessler, R. C. (2010). The epidemiology of obsessive-compulsive disorder in the National Comorbidity Survey Replication. *Molecular Psychiatry, 15*, 53–63.

Rush, A. J., Trivedi, M., Wisniewski, S. R., Nierenberg, A. A., Stewart, J. W., Warden, D., et al. (2006). Acute and longer-term outcomes in depressed outpatients requiring one or several treatment steps: A STARD report. *American Journal of Psychiatry, 163*, 1905–1917.

Rutherford, M. J., Cacciola, J. S., & Alterman, A. I. (1999). Antisocial personality disorder and psychopathy in cocaine-dependent women. *American Journal of Psychiatry, 156*, 849–856.

Rutledge, T., Reis, S. E., Olson, M., Owens, J., Kelsey, S. F., Pepine, C. J., . . . al., e. (2001). Psychosocial variables are associated with atherosclerosis risk factors among women with chest pain: The WISE study. *Psychosomatic Medicine, 63*, 282–288.

Rutter, M., Caspi, A., Fergusson, D., Horwood, L. J., Goodman, R., Maughan, B., Moffitt, T. E., Meltzer, H., & Carroll, J. (2004). Sex differences in developmental reading disability: New findings from 4 epidemiological studies. *Journal of the American Medical Association, 291*, 2007–2012.

Rutter, M., & Silberg, J. (2002). Gene-environment interplay in relation to emotional and behavioral disturbance. *Annual Review of Psychology, 53*, 463–490.

Sabo, S. Z., Nelson, M. L., Fisher, C., Gunzerath, L., Brody, C. L., et al. (1999). A genetic association for cigarette smoking behavior. *Health Psychology, 18*, 7–13.

Sacco, R. L., Elkind, M., Boden-Albala, B., Lin, I., Kargman, D. E., et al. (1999). The protective effect of moderate alcohol consumption on ischemic stroke. *Journal of the American Medical Association, 281*, 53–60.

Sachs, G. S., & Thase, M. E. (2000). Bipolar disorder therapeutics: Maintenance treatment. *Biological Psychiatry, 48*, 573–581.

Sackeim, H. A., & Lisanby, S. H. (Eds.). (2001). *Physical treatments in psychiatry: Advances in electroconvulsive therapy, transcranial magenetic stimulation, and vagus nerve stimulation*. Washington, D. C.: American Psychiatric Publishing.

Sackeim, H. A., Nordlie, J. W., & Gur, R. C. (1979). A model of hysterical and hypnotic blindness: Cognition, motivation and awareness. *Journal of Abnormal Psychology, 88*, 474–489.

Sackeim, H. A., Prudic, J., Fuller, R., Keilp, J., Lavori, P. W., & Olfson, M. (2007). The cognitive effects of electroconvulstive therapy in community settings. *Neuropsychopharmacology, 32*, 244–254.

Sacks, F. M., Bray, G. A., Carey, V. J., Smith, S. R., Ryan, D. H., Anton, S. D., McManus, K., Champagne, C. M., Bishop, L. M., Laranjo, N., Leboff, M. S., Rood, J. C., de Jonge, L., Greenway, F. L., Loria, C. M., Obarzanek, E., & Williamson, D. A. (2009). Comparison of weight-loss diets with different compositions of fat, protein, and carbohydrates. *New England Journal of Medicine, 360*, 859–873.

Sacks, O. (1995). *An anthropologist on Mars*. New York: Knopf.

Saha, S., Chant, D., & McGrath, J. (2007). A systematic review of mortality in schizophrenia: Is the differential mortality gap worsening over time? *Archives of General Psychiatry, 64*, 1123–1131.

Sakel, M. (1938). The pharmacological shock treatment of schizophrenia. *Nervous and Mental Disease Monograph, 62*.

Saks, E. R. (1997). *Jekyll on trial: Multiple personality disorder and criminal law*. New York: New York University Press.

Saks, E. R. (2007). *The center cannot hold: My journey through madness*. New York: Hyperion.

Salamone, J. D. (2000). A critique of recent studies on placebo effects of antidepressants: Importance of research on active placebos. *Psychopharmacology, 152*, 1–6.

Salamone, J. D., & Correa, M. (2012). The mysterious motivational functions of mesolimbic dopamine: *Neuron, 76*, 470–485.

Salem, J. E., & Kring, A. M. (1998). The role of gender differences in the reduction of etiologic heterogeneity in schizophrenia. *Clinical Psychology Review, 18*, 795–819.

Salkovskis, P. M. (1996). Cognitive-behavioral approaches to understanding obsessional problems. In R. M. Rapee (Ed.), *Current controversies in anxiety disorders*. New York: Guilford Press.

Salter, D., McMillan, D., Richards, M., Talbot, T., Hodges, J., Bentovim, A., et al. (2003). Development of sexually abusive behaviour in sexually victimised males: A longitudinal study. *The Lancet, 361*, 471–476.

Samuel, D. B., Sanislow, C. A., Hopwood, C. J., Shea, M. T., Skodol, A. E., Morey, L. C., et al. (2013). Convergent and incremental predictive validity of clinician, self-report, and structured interview diagnoses for personality disorders over 5 years. *Journal of Consulting and Clinical Psychology, 81*, 650–659.

Samuel, D. B., & Widiger, T. A. (2008). A meta-analytic review of the relationships between the five-factor model and DSM-IV-TR personality disorders: A facet level analysis. *Clinical Psychology Review, 28*, 1326–1342.

Samuels, J., Eaton, W. W., Bienvenu, O. J., 3rd, Brown, C. H., Costa, P. T., Jr., & Nestadt, G. (2002). Prevalence and correlates of personality disorders in a community sample. *The British Journal of Psychiatry, 180*, 536–542.

Samuels, J. F. (2009). Recent advances in the genetics of obsessive-compulsive disorder. *Current Psychiatry Reports, 11*, 277–282.

Samuels, J. F., Bienvenu, O. J., 3rd, Pinto, A., Fyer, A. J., McCracken, J. T., Rauch, S. L., et al. (2007). Hoarding in obsessive-compulsive disorder: Results from the OCD Collaborative Genetics Study. *Behaviour Research and Therapy, 45*, 673–686.

Sanchez, D. T., & Kiefer, A. K. (2007). Body concerns in and out of the bedroom: Implications for sexual pleasure and problems. *Archives of Sexual Behavior, 36*, 808–820.

Sansone, R. A., & Sansone, L. A. (2011). Personality disorders: A nation-based perspective on prevalence. *Innovations in Clinical Neuroscience, 8*, 13–18.

Sar, V., Akyuz, G., & Dogan, O. (2007). Prevalence of dissociative disorders among women in the general population. *Psychiatry Research, 149*, 169–176.

Sar, V., Akyuz, G., Kundakci, T., Kiziltan, E., & Dogan, O. (2004). Childhood trauma, dissociation, and psychiatric comorbidity in patients with conversion disorder. *American Journal of Psychiatry, 161*, 2271–2276.

Sara, S. J. (2009). The locus coeruleus and noradrenergic modulation of cognition. *Nature Reviews Neuroscience, 10*, 211–223.

Sareen, J., Cox, B. J., Afifi, T. O., de Graaf, R., Asmundson, G. J. G., ten Have, M., et al. (2005). Anxiety disorders and risk for suicidal ideation and suicide attempts: A population-based longitudinal study of adults. *Archives of General Psychiatry, 62*, 1249–1257.

Sartorius, N., Jablensky, A., Korten, A., Ernberg, G., et al. (1986). Early manifestations and first-contact incidence of schizophrenia in different cultures: A preliminary report on the initial evaluation phase of the WHO Collaborative Study on Determinants of Outcome of Severe Mental Disorders. *Psychological Medicine, 16*, 909–928.

Sartorius, N., Shapiro, R., & Jablonsky, A. (1974). The international pilot study of schizophrenia. *Schizophrenia Bulletin, 2*, 21–35.

Saxena, S., Brody, A. L., Maidment, K. M., & Baxter, L. R. J. (2007). Paroxetine treatment of compulsive hoarding. *Journal of Psychiatric Research, 41*, 481–487.

Sbrocco, T., Weisberg, R. B., Barlow, D. H., & Carter, M. M. (1997). The conceptual relationship between panic disorder and male erectile dysfunction. *Journal of Sex and Marital Therapy, 23*, 212–220.

Scarborough, H. S. (1990). Very early language deficits in dyslexic children. *Child Development, 61*, 128–174.

Schaefer, H. S., Putnam, K. M., Benca, R. M., & Davidson, R. J. (2006). Event-related functional magnetic resonance imaging measures of neural activity to positive social stimuli in pre- and post-treatment depression. *Biological Psychiatry, 60*, 974–986.

Schaie, K. W., & Hertzog, C. (1982). Longitudinal methods. In B. B. Wolman (Ed.), *Handbook of developmental Ppsychology*. Englewood Cliffs, NJ: Prentice-Hall.

Schalock, R. L., Luckasson, R. A., & Shogren, K. A., et al. (2007). The renaming of mental retardation: Understanding the change to the term intellectual disability. *Intellectual and Developmental Disabilities, 45*, 116–124.

Schecter, R., & Grether, J. K. (2008). Continuing increases in autism reported to California's Developmental Services System. *Archives of General Psychiatry, 65*, 19–24.

Scherk, H., Pajonk, F. G., & Leucht, S. (2007). Second-generation antipsychotic agents in the treatment of acute mania: A systematic review and meta-analysis of randomized controlled trials. *Archives of General Psychiatry, 64*, 442–455.

Schilder, P. (1953). *Medical psychology*. New York: International Universities Press.

Schmidt, N. B., Lerew, D. R., & Jackson, R. J. (1999). Prospective evaluation of anxiety sensitivity in the pathogenesis of panic: Prospective evaluation of spontaneous panic attacks during acute stress. *Journal of Abnormal Psychology, 106*, 355–364.

Schmidt, N. B., Richey, J. A., Buckner, J. D., & Timpano, K. R. (2009). Attention training for generalized social anxiety disorder. *Journal of Abnormal Psychology, 118*, 5–14.

Schmidt, N. B., Woolaway-Bickel, K., & Bates, M. (2000). Suicide and panic disorder: Integration of the literature and new findings. In M. D. Rudd & T. E. Joiner (Eds.), *Suicide science: Expanding the boundaries* (pp. 117–136). New York: Kluwer Academic/Plenum.

Schmitt, D. P., Alcalay, L., Allik, J., Ault, L., Austers, I., Bennett, K. L., et al. (2003). Universal sex differences in the desire for sexual variety: Tests from 52 nations, 6 continents and 13 islands. *Journal of Personality and Social Psychology, 85*, 85–104.

Schnab, D. W., & Trinh, N. G. (2004). Do artificial food colors promote hyperactivity in children with hyperactive syndromes? A meta-analysis of double-blind placebo-controlled trials. *Journal of Developmental and Behavioral Pediatrics, 25,* 425–434.

Schneck, C. D., Miklowitz, D. J., Miyahara, S., Araga, M., Wisniewski, S. R., Gyulai, L., et al. (2008). The prospective course of rapid-cycling bipolar disorder: Findings from the STEP-BD. *American Journal of Psychiatry, 165,* 370–376.

Schoeneman, T. J. (1977). The role of mental illness in the European witch-hunts of the sixteenth and seventeenth centuries: An assessment. *Journal of the History of the Behavioral Sciences, 13,* 337–351.

Schopler, E., Short, A., & Mesibov, G. (1989). Relation of behavioral treatment to "normal functioning": Comment on Lovaas. *Journal of Consulting and Clinical Psychology, 57,* 162–164.

Schreiber, F. L. (1973). *Sybil.* Chicago: Regnery.

Schuckit, M. A., Daeppen, J. B., Tipp, J. E., Hesselbrock, M., & Bucholz, K. K. (1998). The clinical course of alcohol-related problems in alcohol dependent and nonalcohol dependent drinking women and men. *Journal of Studies on Alcohol, 59,* 581–590.

Schumacher, J. E., Milby, J. B., Wallace, D., Meehan, D. C., Kertesz, S. et al. (2007). Meta-analysis of day treatment and contingency-management dismantling research: Birmingham homeless cocaine studies (1990–2005). *Journal of Consulting and Clinical Psychology, 75,* 823–828.

Schwartz, M. B., Chambliss, O. H., Brownell, K. D., Blair, S., & Billington, C. (2003). Weight bias among health professionals specializing in obesity. *Obesity Research, 11,* 1033–1039.

Schweizer, E., Rickels, K., Case, G., & Greenblatt, D. J. (1990). Long-term therapeutic use of benzodiazapines: Effects of gradual taper. *Archives of General Psychiatry, 47,* 908–915.

Schwitzgebel, R. L., & Schwitzgebel, R. K. (1980). *Law and psychological practice.* New York: John Wiley & Sons.

Scroppo, J. C., Drob, S. L., Weinberger, J. L., & Eagle, P. (1998). Identifying dissociative identity disorder: A selfreport and projective study. *Journal of Abnormal Psychology, 107,* 272–284.

Searles, J. (2013, October 10). Getting into the spirit. *New York Times, travel section.,* p. TR10.

Seedat, S., & Matsunaga, H. (2007). Cross-national and ethnic issues in OC spectrum disorders. *CNS Spectrums, 12,* 392-400.

Seedat, S., Scott, K. M., Angermeyer, M., Berglund, P., Bromet, E., Brugha, T., et al. (2009). Cross-national associations between gender and mental disorders in the world health organization world mental health surveys. *Archives of General Psychiatry, 66,* 785–795.

Segal, Z. V., Kennedy, S., Gemar, M., Hood, K., Pedersen, R., & Buis, T. (2006). Cognitive reactivity to sad mood provocation and the prediction of depressive relapse. *Archives of General Psychiatry, 63,* 749–755.

Segal, Z. V., Williams, J. M. G., & Teasdale, J. D. (2003). Mindfulness-based cognitive therapy for depression: A new approach to preventing relapse. *Psychotherapy Research, 13,* 123–125.

Segal, Z. V., Williams, J. M., & Teasdale, J. D. (2001). *Mindfulness-based cognitive therapy for depression.* New York: Guilford Press.

Segerstrom, S. C., & Miller, G. E. (2004). Psychological stress and the immune system: A meta-analytic study of 30 years of inquiry. *Psychological Bulletin, 130,* 601–630.

Segraves, R. T. (2003). Recognizing and reversing sexual side effects of medications. In S. B. Levine, C. B. Candace, et al. (Eds.), *Handbook of clinical sexuality for mental health professionals* (pp. 377-391). New York: Brunner-Routledge.

Segraves, R. T. (2010). Considerations for an evidence-based definition of premature ejaculation in the DSM-V. *Journal of Sexual Medicine, 7,* 672–679.

Segraves, R. T., & Althof, S. (1998). Psychotherapy and pharmacotherapy of sexual dysfunctions. In P. E. Nathan & J. M. Gorman (Eds.), *A guide to treatments that work.* New York: Oxford University Press.

Seidler, G. H., & Wagner, F. E. (2006). Comparing the efficacy of EMDR and trauma-focused cognitive-behavioral therapy in the treatment of PTSD: A meta-analytic study. *Psychological Medicine, 36,* 1515-1522.

Selby, E. A., Wonderlich, S. A., Crosby, R. D., Engel, S. G., Panza, E., Mitchell, J. E., et al. (2013). Nothing tastes as good as thin feels: Low positive emotion differentiation and weight-loss activities in anorexia nervosa. *Clinical Psychological Science.*

Seligman, M. E. P. (1971). Phobias and preparedness. *Behavior Therapy, 2,* 307–320.

Seligman, M. E., Maier, S. F., & Geer, J. H. (1968). Alleviation of learned helplessness in the dog. *Journal of Abnormal Psychology, 73,* 256–262.

Selkoe, D. J. (2002). Alzheimer's disease is a synaptic failure. *Science, 298,* 789–791.

Selling, L. S. (1940). *Men against madness.* New York: Greenberg.

Selwood, A., Johnson, K., Katona, C., llyketsos, C., & Livingson, G. (2007). Systematic review of the effect of psychological interventions on family caregivers of people with dementia. *Journal of Affective Disorders, 101,* 75–89.

Selye, H. (1950). *The physiology and pathology of exposure to stress.* Montreal: Acta.

Sensky, T., Turkington, D., Kingdon, D., et al. (2000). A randomized controlled trial of cognitive-behavioural therapy for persistent symptoms in schizophrenia resistant to medication. *Archives of General Psychiatry, 57,* 165–172.

Serdula, M. K., Mokdad, A. H., Williamson, D. F., Galuska, D. A., et al. (1999). Prevalence of attempting weight loss and strategies for controlling weight. *Journal of the American Medical Association, 282,* 1353–1358.

Seto, M. C. (2009). Pedophilia. *Annual Review of Clinical Psychology, 5,* 391-407.

Shackman, A. J., Salomons, T. V., Slagter, H. A., Fox, A. S., Winter, J. J., & Davidson, R. J. (2011). The integration of negative affect, pain and cognitive control in the cingulate cortex. *Nature Reviews Neuroscience, 12,* 154–167.

Shaper, A. G. (1990). Alcohol and mortality: A review of prospective studies. *British Journal of Addiction, 85,* 837–847.

Shapiro, F. (1999). Eye movement desensitization and reprocessing (EMDR) and the anxiety disorders: Clinical and research implications of an integrated psychotherapy treatment. *Journal of Anxiety Disorders, 13,* 35–67.

Shaw, D. S., Dishion, T. J., Supplee, L., Gardner, F., & Arnds, K. (2006). Randomized trial of a family-centered approach to the prevention of early conduct problems: 2-year effects of the family check-up in early childhood. *Journal of Consulting and Clinical Psychology, 74,* 1–9.

Shaw, L. J., Bairy Merz, C. N., Pepine. C. J., Reis, S. E., Bittner, V. E., et al. (2006). Insights from the NHL-BI-sponsored Women's Ischemia Syndrome Evaluation (WISE) study. Part I: Gender differences in tradition-al and novel risk factors symptom evaluation and gender-optimized diagnostic strategies. *Journal of the American College of Cardiology, 47,* 4S–20S.

Shaywitz, B. A., Shaywitz, S. E., Blachman, B. A., et al. (2004). Development of left occipitotemporal systems for skilled reading in children after a phonologically-based intervention. *Biological Psychiatry, 55,* 926–933.

Shaywitz, B. A., Shaywitz, S. E., Pugh, K. R., et al. (2002). Disruption of posterior brain systems for reading in children with developmental dyslexia. *Biological Psychiatry, 52,* 101–110.

Shea, M. T., Stout, R., Gunderson, J., Morey, L. C., Grilo, C. M., McGlashan, T., et al. (2002). Short-term diagnostic stability of schizotypal, borderline, avoidant, and obsessive-compulsive personality disorders. *American Journal of Psychiatry, 159,* 2036–2041.

Sheline, Y., Barch, D., Donnelly, J. M., Ollinger, J. M., Snyder, A. Z., & Mintun, M. A. (2001). Increased amygdala response to masked emotional faces in depressed subjects resolves with antidepressant treatment: An fMRI study. *Biological Psychiatry, 50,* 651–658.

Shen, G. H. C., Sylvia, L. G., Alloy, L. B., Barrett, F., Kohner, M., Iacoviello, B., et al. (2008). Lifestyle regularity and cyclothymic symptomatology. *Journal of Clinical Psychology, 64,* 482–500.

Shenk, D. (2010). *The genius is in all of us: Why everything you've been told about genetics, talent, and IQ is wrong.* New York: Doubleday.

Sher, K. J., Grekin, E. R., & Williams, N. A. (2005). The development of alcohol use disorders. *Annual Review of Clinical Psychology, 1,* 493–523.

Sher, K. J., Walitzer, K. S., Wood, P. K., & Brent, E. F. (1991). Characteristics of children of alcoholics: Putative risk factors, substance use and abuse, and psychopathology. *Journal of Abnormal Psychology, 100,* 427–448.

Sher, K. J., Wood, M. D., Wood, P. K., & Raskin, G. (1996). Alcohol outcome expectancies and alcohol use: A latent variable cross-lagged panel study. *Journal of Abnormal Psychology, 105,* 561–574.

Sherman, D. K., Iacono, W. G., & McGue, M. K. (1997). Attention-deficit hyperactivity disorder dimensions: A twin study of inattention and impulsivity-hyperactivity. *Journal of the American Academy of Child and Adolescent Psychiatry, 36,* 745–753.

Shic, F., Macari, S., & Chawarska, K. (2014). Speech disturbs face scanning in 6-month-old infants who develop autism spectrum disorder. *Biological Psychiatry, 75*(3), 231–237.

Shiffman, S., Gwaltney, C. J., Balabanis, M. H., Liu, K. S., Paty, J. A., Kassel, J. D., Hickcox, M., & Gnys, M. (2002). Immediate antecedents of cigarette smoking: An analysis from ecological momentary assessment. *Journal of Abnormal Psychology, 111,* 531–545.

Shiffman, S., Paty, J. A., Gwaltney, C. J., & Dang, Q. (2004). Immediate antecedents of cigarette smoking: An analysis of unrestricted smoking patterns. *Journal of Abnormal Psychology, 113,* 166–171.

Shiffman, S., & Waters, A. J. (2004). Negative affect and smoking lapses: A prospective analysis. *Journal of Consulting and Clinical Psychology, 72,* 192–201.

Shifren, J. L., Monz, B. U., Russo, P. A., Segreti, A., & Johannes, C. B. (2008). Sexual problems and distress in United States women: Prevalence and correlates. *Obstetrics and Gynecology, 112,* 970–978.

Shin, L. M., & Liberzon, I. (2010). The neurocircuitry of fear, stress, and anxiety disorders. *Neuropsychopharmacology, 35,* 169–191.

Shin, M., Besser, L. M., Kucik, J. E., Lu, C., Siffel, C., & Correa, A. (2009). Prevalence of Down syndrome among children and adolescents in 10 regions of the United States. *Pediatrics, 124,* 1565–1571.

Shneidman, E. S. (1987). A psychological approach to suicide. In G. R. VandenBos & B. K. Bryant (Eds.), *Cataclysms, crises, and catastrophes: Psychology in action.* Washington, DC: American Psychological Association.

Shobe, K. K., & Kihlstrom, J. F. (1997). Is traumatic memory special? *Current Directions in Psychological Science, 6,* 70–74.

Siegel, S. J., Irani, F., Brensinger, C. M., Kohler, C. G., Bilker, W. B., Ragland, J. D., et al. (2006). Prognostic variables at intake and long-term level of function in schizophrenia. *American Journal of Psychiatry, 163*(3), 433–441.

Siegler, I. C., & Costa, P. T., Jr. (1985). Health behavior relationships. In J. E. Birren & K. W. Schaie (Eds.), *Handbook of the psychology of aging* (2nd ed.). New York: Van Nostrand-Reinhold.

Siever, L. J. (2000). S6.Genetics and neurobiology of personality disorders. *European Psychiatry, 15,* 54–57.

Siever, L. J., & Davis, K. L. (2004). The pathophysiology of schizophrenia disorders: Perspectives from the spectrum. *American Journal of Psychiatry, 161,* 398–413.

Sigman, M. (1994). What are the core deficits in autism? In S. H. Broman & J. Grafman (Eds.), *Atypical cognitive deficits in developmental disorders: Implications for brain function* (pp. 139–157). Hillsdale, NJ: Erlbaum.

Silbersweig, D., Clarkin, J. F., Goldstein, M., Kernberg, O. F., Tuescher, O., Levy, K. N., et al. (2007). Failure of frontolimbic inhibitory function in the context of negative emotion in borderline personality disorder. *American Journal of Psychiatry, 164,* 1832–1841.

Silverman, K., Evans, S. M., Strain, E. C., & Griffiths, R. R. (1992). Withdrawal syndrome after the double-blind cessation of caffeine consumption. *New England Journal of Medicine, 327,* 1109–1114.

Silverman, K., Higgins, S. T., Brooner, R. K., Montoya, I. D., Cone, E. J., Schuster, C. R., & Preston, K. I. (1996). Sustained cocaine abstinence in methadone maintenance patients through voucher-based reinforcement therapy. *Archives of General Psychiatry, 53,* 409–413.

Simeon, D. (2009). Depersonalization disorder. In P. F. Dell & J. A. O'Neil (Eds.), *Dissociation and dissociative disorders: DSM-5 and beyond* (pp. 441–442). New York: Routledge.

Simeon, D., Gross, S., Guralnik, O., Stein, D. J., Schmeidler, J., & Hollander, E. (1997). Feeling unreal: 30 cases of DSM-III-R depersonalization disorder. *American Journal of Psychiatry, 154,* 1107–1112.

Simeon, D., Guralnik, O., Schmeidler, J., Sirof, B., & Knutelska, M. (2001). The role of childhood interpersonal trauma in depersonalization disorder. *American Journal of Psychiatry, 158,* 1027–1033.

Simeon, D., Knutelska, M., Nelson, D., & Guralnik, O. (2003). Feeling unreal: Depersonalization disorder update of 117 cases. *Journal of Clinical Psychiatry, 64,* 990-997.

Simes, S. M., & Snabes, M. C. (2011). Reaction to the recent publication by Rosemary Basson entitled "Testosterone therapy for reduced libido in women." *Therapeutic Advances in Endocrinology and Metabolism, 2,* 95–96.

Simon, G. E. (1998). Management of somatoform and factitious disorders. In P. E. Nathan & J. M. Gorman (Eds.), *A guide to treatments that work* (pp. 408–422). New York: Oxford University Press.

Simon, G. E., Goldberg, D. P., Von Korff, M., & Ustun, T. B. (2002). Understanding cross-national differences in depression prevalence. *Psychological Medicine, 32,* 585–594.

Simon, G. E., Gureje, O., & Fullerton, C. (2001). Course of hypochondriasis in an international primary care study. *General Hospital Psychiatry, 23,* 51–55.

Simon, G. E., Von Korff, M., Piccinelli, M., Fullerton, C., & Ormel, J. (1999). An international study of the relation between somatic symptoms and depression. *New England Journal of Medicine, 341,* 1329–1335.

Simon, G., Ormel, J., VonKroff, M., & Barlow, W. (1995). Health care costs associated with depressive and anxiety disorders in primary care. *American Journal of Psychiatry, 152,* 352–357.

Simon, R. J., & Aaronson, D. E. (1988). *The insanity defense: A critical assessment of law and policy in the post-Hinckley era.* New York: Praeger.

Simon, W. (2009). Follow-up psychotherapy outcome of patients with dependent, avoidant and obsessive-compulsive personality disorders: A meta-analytic review. *International Journal of Psychiatry in Clinical Practice, 13,* 153–165.

Simonoff, E. (2001). Genetic influences on conduct disorder. In J. Hill & B. Maughan (Eds.), *Conduct disorders in childhood and adolescence* (pp. 202–234). Cambridge, UK: Cambridge University Press.

Singh, S. P., Harley, K., & Suhail, K. (2013). Cultural specificity of emotional overinvolvement: A systematic review. *Schizophrenia Bulletin, 39*(2), 449–463.

Sinha, S. S., Mohlman, J., & Gorman, J. M. (2004). Neurobiology. In R. G. Heimberg, C. L. Turk & D. S. Mennin (Eds.), *Generalized anxiety disorder* (pp. 187–218). New York: Guilford Press.

Siok, W. T., Perfetti, C. A., Lin, Z., & Tan, L. H. (2004). Biological abnormality of impaired reading is constrained by culture. *Nature, 431,* 71–76.

Skeem, J. L., & Monahan, J. (2011). Current directions in violence risk assessment. *Current Directions in Psychological Science, 20,* 38–42.

Skinner, A. C., & Skelton, J. A. (2014). Prevalence and trends in obesity and severe obesity among children in the United States, 1999–2012. *Journal of the American Medical Association, Pediatrics.*

Skinstad, A. H., & Swain, A. (2001). Comorbidity in a clinical sample of substance abusers. *American Journal of Drug and Alcohol Abuse, 27,* 45–64.

Skodol, A. E., Oldham, J. M., Hyler, S. E., Stein, D. J., Hollander, E., Gallaher, P. E., et al. (1995). Patterns of anxiety and personality disorder comorbidity. *Journal of Psychiatric Research, 29,* 361–374.

Slater, E. (1961). The thirty-fifth Maudsley lecture: Hysteria 311. *Journal of Mental Science, 107,* 358–381.

Slavich, G. M., & Irwin, M. R. (2014). From stress to inflammation and major depressive disorder: A social signal transduction theory of depression. *Psychological Bulletin, 140,* 774–815.

Slevec, J. H., & Tiggemann, M. (2011). Predictors of body dissatisfaction and disordered eating in middle-aged women. *Clinical Psychology Review, 31,* 515–524.

Slotema, C. W., Blom, J. D., Hoek, H. W., & Sommer, I. E. (2010). Should we expand the toolbox of psychiatric treatment methods to include repetitive transcranial magnetic stimulation (rTMS)? A meta-analysis of the efficacy of rTMS in psychiatric disorders. *Journal of Clinical Psychiatry, 71,* 873–884.

Small, B. J., Fratiglioni, L., Viitanen, M., Winblad, B., & Backman, L. (2000). The course of cognitive impairment in preclinical Alzheimer disease. *Archives of Neurology, 57,* 839–844.

Smart, R. G., & Ogburne, A. C. (2000). Drug use and drinking among students in 36 countries. *Addictive Behaviors, 25,* 455–460.

Smith, D. (2012). *Monkey mind.* New York: Simon & Schuster.

Smith, D. G., & Robbins, T. W. (2013). The neurobiological underpinnings of obesity and binge eating: A rationale for adopting the Food Addiction Model. *Biological Psychiatry, 73*(9), 804–810.

Smith, G. (1992). The epidemiology and treatment of depression when it coincides with somatoform disorders, somatization, or panic. *General Hospital Psychiatry, 14,* 265–272.

Smith, G. T., Goldman, M. S., Greenbaum, P. E., & Christiansen, B. A. (1995). Expectancy for social facilitation from drinking: The divergent paths of high expectancy and low expectancy adolescents. *Journal of Abnormal Psychology, 104,* 32–40.

Smith, M. L., Glass, G. V., & Miller, T. I. (1980). *The benefits of psychotherapy.* Baltimore: Johns Hopkins University Press.

Smith, S. F., & Lilienfeld, S. O. (2013). Psychopathy in the workplace: The knowns and unknowns. *Aggression and Violent Behavior, 18,* 204–218.

Smith, T., Groen, A., & Wynn, J. W. (2000). Randomized trial of intensive early intervention for children with pervasive developmental disorder. *Research in Developmental Disabilities, 21,* 297–309.

Smyth, J., Wonderlich, S. A., Heron, K. E., Sliwinski, M. J., Crosby, R. D., et al. (2007). Daily and momentary mood and stress are associated with binge eating and vomiting in bulimia nervosa patients in the natural environment. *Journal of Consulting and Clinical Psychology, 75,* 629-638.

Snowden, L. R. (2012). Health and mental health policies' role in better understanding and closing African American-White American disparities in treatment access and quality of care. *American Psychologist, 67,* 524–531.

Snyder, D. K., Castellani, A. M., & Whisman, M. A. (2006). Current status and future directions in couple therapy. *Annual Review of Psychology, 57,* 317–344.

Snyder, S. H. (1996). *Drugs and the brain.* New York: Freeman.

Sobczak, S., Honig, A., Nicolson, N. A., & Riedel, W. J. (2002). Effects of acute tryptophan depletion on mood and cortisol release in first-degree relatives of type I and type II bipolar patients and healthy matched controls. *Neuropsychopharmacology, 27,* 834–842.

Sobell, L. C., & Sobell, M. B. (1996). *Timeline Followback user's guide: A calendar method for assessing alcohol and drug use.* Toronto, Canada: Addiction Research Foundation.

Sobell, L. C., Sobell, M. B., & Agrawal, S. (2009). Randomized controlled trial of a cognitive-behavioral motivational intervention in a group versus individual format for substance use disorders. *Psychology of Addictive Behaviors: Journal of the Society of Psychologists in Addictive Behaviors, 23,* 672–683.

Sobell, L. C., Toneatto, A., & Sobell, M. B. (1990). Behavior therapy. In A. S. Bellack & M. Hersen (Eds.), *Handbook of comparative treatments for adult disorders* (pp. 479–505). New York: John Wiley & Sons.

Sobell, M. B., & Sobell, L. C. (1993). *Problem drinkers: Guided self-change treatment.* New York: Guilford Press.

Sofi, F., Valecchi, D., Bacci, D., Abbate, R., Gensini, G. F., Casini, A., et al. (2011). Physical activity and risk of cognitive decline: A meta-analysis of prospective studies. *Journal of Internal Medicine, 269,* 107–117.

Soloff, P. H., Meltzer, C. C., Greer, P. J., Constantine, D., & Kelly, T. M. (2000). A fenfluramine-activated FDG-

PET study of borderline personality disorder. *Biological Psychiatry, 47,* 540–547.

Solomon, D. A., Keller, M. B., Leon, A. C., Mueller, T. I., Lavori, P. W., Shea, M. T., et al. (2000). Multiple recurrences of major depressive disorder. *American Journal of Psychiatry, 157,* 229–233.

Soyka, M., Horak, M., Morhart, V., & Moeller, H. J. (2001). Modellprojekt "Qualifizierte ambulante Entgiftung"/Qualified outpatient detoxification. *Nervenarzt, 72,* 565–569.

Spanos, N. P. (1994). Multiple identity enactments and multiple personality disorder: A sociocognitive perspective. *Psychological Bulletin, 116,* 143–165.

Spek, V., Cuijpers, P., Nyklicek, I., Riper, H., Keyzer, J., & Pop, V. (2007). Internet-based cognitive behaviour therapy for symptoms of depression and anxiety: A meta-analysis. *Psychological Medicine, 37,* 319–328.

Spencer, S. J., Steele, C. M., & Quinn, D. M. (1999). Stereotype threat and women's math performance. *Journal of Experimental Social Psychology, 35,* 4–28.

Spencer, T., Biederman, J., Wilens, T., Harding, M., O'Donnell, D., & Griffin, S. (1996). Pharmacotherapy of attention-deficit hyperactivity disorder across the life cycle. *Journal of the American Academy of Child and Adolescent Psychiatry, 35,* 409–432.

Spengler, A. (1977). Manifest sadomasochism of males: Results of an empirical study. *Archives of Sexual Behavior, 6,* 441–456.

Sperling, R. A., Aisen, P. S., Beckett, L. A., Bennett, D. A., Craft, S., Fagan, A. M., et al. (2011). Toward defining the preclinical stages of Alzheimer's disease: Recommendations from the National Institute on Aging-Alzheimer's Association workgroups on diagnostic guidelines for Alzheimer's disease. *Alzheimer's and Dementia : The Journal of the Alzheimer's Association, 7,* 280–292.

Spitzer, R. L. (2002). *DSM-IV-TR casebook: A learning companion to the Diagnostic and Statistical Manual of Mental Disorders, Fourth Edition, Text Revision.* Washington, D.C.: American Psychiatric Association.

Spitzer, R. L., Gibbon, M., Skodol, A. E., Williams, J. B. W., & First, M. B. (Eds.). (1994). *DSM-IV casebook: A learning companion to the Diagnostic and Statistical Manual of Mental Disorders* (4th ed.). Washington, DC: American Psychiatric Press.

Spitzer, R. L., Gibbon, M., & Williams, J. B. W. (1996). *Structured clinical interview of DSM-IV Axis I disorders.* New York: N. Y. State Psychiatric Institute, Biometrics Research Department.

Spoth, R. A., Guyll, M., & Day, S. X. (2002). Universal family-focused interventions in alcohol-use prevention: Cost-benefit analyses of two interventions. *Journal of Studies on Alcohol, 63,* 219–228.

Spoth, R. A., Redmond, C., Shin, C., & Azevedo, K. (2004). Brief family intervention effects on adolescent substance initiation: School-level growth curve analyses 6 years following baseline. *Journal of Consulting and Clinical Psychology, 72,* 535–542.

Sprich, S., Biederman, J., Crawford, M. H., Mundy, E., & Faraone, S. V. (2000). Adoptive and biological families of children and adolescents with ADHD. *Journal of the American Academy of Child and Adolescent Psychiatry, 39,* 1432–1437.

St. Pourcain, B., Wang, K., Glessner, J. T., Golding, J., Steer, C., Ring, S. M., Skuse, D. H., Grant, S. F. A., Hakonarson, H., & Smith, G. D. (2010). Association between a high-risk autism locus on 5p14 and social communication spectrum phenotypes in the general population. *American Journal of Psychiatry, 167,* 1364–1372.

Stack, S. (2000). Media impacts on suicide: A quantitative review of 293 findings. *Social Science Quarterly, 81,* 957–971.

Stacy, A. W., Newcomb, M. D., & Bentler, P. M. (1991). Cognitive motivation and drug use: A 9-year longitudinal study. *Journal of Abnormal Psychology, 100,* 502–515.

Stanfield, A. C., McIntosh, A. M., Spencer, M. D., Philip, R., Gaur, S., & Lawrie, S. M. (2008). Towards a neuroanatomy of autism: A systematic review and meta-analysis of structural magnetic resonance imaging studies. *European Psychiatry, 23*(4), 289–299.

Staugaard, S. R. (2010). Threatening faces and social anxiety: A literature review. *Clinical Psychology Review, 30,* 669–690.

Stead, L. F., Perera, R., Bullen, C., Mant, D., & Lancaster, T. (2008). Nicotine replacement therapy for smoking cessation. *Cochrane Database of Systematic Reviews,* No.: CD000146.

Steadman, H. J. (1979). *Beating a rap: Defendants found incompetent to stand trial.* Chicago: University of Chicago Press.

Steadman, H. J., McGreevy, M. A., Morrissey, J. P., Callahan, L. A., Robbins, P. C., & Cirincione, C. (1993). *Before and after Hinckley: Evaluating insanity defense reform.* New York: Guilford Press.

Steadman, H. J., Mulvey, E. P., Monahan, J., Robbins, P. C., Appelbaum, P. S., Grisso, T., Roth, L. H., & Silver, E. (1998). Violence by people discharged from acute psychiatric inpatient facilities and by others in the same neighborhoods. *Archives of General Psychiatry, 55,* 393–401.

Steadman, H. J., Osher, F. C., Robbins, P. C., Case, B., & Samuels, S. (2009). Prevalence of serious mental illness among jail inmates. *Psychiatric Services, 60,* 761–765.

Steele, A. L., Bergin, J., & Wade, T. D. (2011). Self-efficacy as a robust predictor of outcome in guided self-help treatment for broadly defined bulimia nervosa. *International Journal of Eating Disorders, 44,* 389–396.

Steele, C. M., & Josephs, R. A. (1988). Drinking your troubles away: 2. An attention-allocation model of alcohol's effects on psychological stress. *Journal of Abnormal Psychology, 97,* 196–205.

Steele, C. M., & Josephs, R. A. (1990). Alcohol myopia: Its prized and dangerous effects. *American Psychologist, 45*(8), 921–933.

Steen, R. G., Mull, C., McClure, R., Hamer, R. M.,& Lieberman, J. A. (2006). Brain volume in first-episode schizophrenia: Systematic review and meta-analysis of magnetic resonance imaging studies. *British Journal of Psychiatry, 188,* 510–518.

Steiger, H., Gauvin, L., Jabalpurwala, S., & Séguin, J. R. (1999). Hypersenstivity to social interactions in bulimic syndromes: Relationship to binge eating. *Journal of Consulting and Clinical Psychology, 67,* 765–775.

Stein, D. J., Aguilar-Gaxiola, S., Alonso, J., Bruffaerts, R., De Jonge, P., Liu, Z., et al. (2014). Associations between mental disorders and subsequent onset of hypertension. *General Hospital Psychiatry, 36,* 142–149.

Stein, D. J., Ipser, J. C., & Balkom, A. J. (2004). Pharmacotherapy for social anxiety disorder. *Cochrane Database of Systematic Reviews, Issue 4,* CD001206.

Stein, D. J., Ipser, J. C., & Seedat, S. (2000). Pharmacotherapy for post traumatic stress disorder (PTSD). *Cochrane Database of Systematic Reviews, Issue 4,* CD002795.

Stein, D. J., Koenen, K. C., Friedman, M. J., Hill, E., McLaughlin, K. A., Petukhova, M., et al. (2013). Dissociation in posttraumatic stress disorder: Evidence from the World Mental Health surveys. *Biological Psychiatry, 73,* 302–312.

Stein, D. J., Phillips, K. A., Bolton, D., Fulford, K. W., Sadler, J. Z., & Kendler, K. S. (2010). What is a mental/psychiatric disorder? From DSM-IV to DSM-V. *Psychological Medicine, 40,* 1759–1765.

Stein, E. A., Pankiewicz, J., Harsch, H. H., Cho, J. K., Fuller, S. A., et al. (1998). Nicotine-induced limbic cortical activation in the human brain: A functional MRI study. *American Journal of Psychiatry, 155,* 1009–1015.

Stein, L. I., & Test, M. A. (1980). Alternative to mental hospital treatment: I. Conceptual model, treatment program, and clinical evaluation. *Archives of General Psychiatry, 37,* 392–397.

Stein, M. B., Yehuda, R., Koverola, C., & Hanna, C. (1997). Enhanced dexamethasone suppression of plasma cortisol in adult women traumatized by childhood sexual abuse. *Biological Psychiatry, 42,* 680–686.

Steiner, J., Walter, M., Glanz, W., Sarnyai, Z., Bernstein, H. G., Vielhaber, S., et al. (2013). Increased prevalence of diverse N-methyl-D-aspartate glutamate receptor antibodies in patients with an initial diagnosis of schizophrenia: Specific relevance of IgG NR1a antibodies for distinction from N-methyl-D-aspartate glutamate receptor encephalitis. *Journal of the American Medical Association Psychiatry, 70*(3), 271–278.

Steinhausen, H. C., & Metzke, C. W. (1998). Youth self-report of behavioral and emotional problems in a Swiss epidemiological study. *Journal of Youth and Adolescence, 27,* 429–441.

Steinhausen, H., & Weber, S. (2009). The outcome of bulimia nervosa: Findings from one-quarter century of research. *American Journal of Psychiatry, 166,* 1331–1341.

Steketee, G., & Barlow, D. H. (Eds.). (2004). *Obsessive-compulsive disorder.* New York: Guilford Press.

Steketee, G., & Frost, R. O. (2003). Compulsive hoarding: Current status of the research. *Clinical Psychology Review, 23,* 905–927.

Steketee, G., Frost, R. O., Tolin, D. F., Rasmussen, J., & Brown, T. A. (2010). Waitlist-controlled trial of cognitive behavior therapy for hoarding disorder. *Depression and Anxiety, 27,* 476–484.

Stephen, 1900, 203.

Stephens, R. S., Roffman, R. A., & Simpson, E. E. (1993). Adult marijuana users seeking treatment. *Journal of Consulting and Clinical Psychology, 61,* 1100–1104.

Stern, R. S., & Cobb, J. P. (1978). Phenomenology of obsessive-compulsive neurosis. *British Journal of Psychiatry, 132,* 233–234.

Stevenson, J., & Jones, I. H. (1972). Behavior therapy technique for exhibitionism: A preliminary report. *Archives of General Psychiatry, 27,* 839–841.

Stewart, W. F., Ricci, J. A., Chee, E., Hahn, S. R., & Morganstein, D. (2003). Cost of lost productive work time among US workers with depression. *Journal of the American Medical Association, 289,* 3135–3144.

Stice, E. (2001). A prospective test of the dual-pathway model of bulimic pathology: Mediating effects of dieting and negative affect. *Journal of Abnormal Psychology, 110,* 124–135.

Stice, E., & Agras, W. S. (1999). Subtyping bulimics along dietary restraint and negative affect dimensions. *Journal of Consulting and Clinical Psychology, 67,* 460–469.

Stice, E., Barrera, M., & Chasin, L. (1998). Prospective differential prediction of adolescent alcohol use and problem use: Examining the mechanisms of effect. *Journal of Abnormal Psychology, 107,* 616–628.

Stice, E., Becker, C. B., & Yokum, S. (2013). Eating disorder prevention: Current evidence-base and future directions. *International Journal of Eating Disorders, 46*(5), 478–485.

Stice, E., Burton, E. M., & Shaw, H. (2004). Prospective relations between bulimic pathology, depression, and substance abuse: Unpacking comorbidity in adolescent girls. *Journal of Consulting and Clinical Psychology, 72,* 62–71.

Stice, E., Marti, C. N., Spoor, S., Presnell, K., & Shaw, H. (2008). Dissonance and healthy weight eating disorder prevention programs: Long-term effects from a randomized efficacy trial. *Journal of Consulting and Clinical Psychology, 76,* 329–240.

Stice, E., Rohde, P., Shaw, H., & Marti, C. N. (2013). Efficacy trial of a selective prevention program targeting both eating disorders and obesity among female college students: 1- and 2-year follow-up effects. *Journal of Consulting and Clinical Psychology, 81*(1), 183–189.

Stice, E., Shaw, H., & Marti, C. N. (2007). A meta-analytic review of eating disorder prevention programs: Encouraging findings. *Annual Review of Clinical Psychology, 3,* 207–231.

Stinson, F. S., Dawson, D. A., Goldstein, R. B., Chou, S. P., Huang, B., Smith, S. M., et al. (2008). Prevalence, correlates, disability, and comorbidity of DSM-IV narcissistic personality disorder: Results from the Wave 2 National Epidemiologic Survey on Alcohol and Related Conditions. *Journal of Clinical Psychiatry, 69,* 1033–1045.

Stone, A. A., Schwartz, J., Neale, J. M., Shiffman, S., Marco, C. A., et al. (1998). A comparison of coping assessed by ecological momentary assessment and retrospective recall. *Journal of Personality and Social Psychology, 74,* 1670–1680.

Stone, A. A., & Shiffman, S. (1994). Ecological momentary assessment (EMA) in behavioral medicine. *Annals of Behavioral Medicine, 16,* 199–202.

Stone, J., Hewett, R., Carson, A., Warlow, C., & Sharpe, M. (2008). The "disappearance" of hysteria: Historical mystery or illusion? *Journal of the Royal Society of Medicine, 101,* 12–18.

Stone, J., LaFrance, W. C., Jr., Levenson, J. L., & Sharpe, M. (2010). Issues for DSM-5: Conversion disorder. *American Journal of Psychiatry, 167,* 626–627.

Stone, J., Smyth, R., Carson, A., Lewis, S., Prescott, R., Warlow, C., et al. (2005). Systematic review of misdiagnosis of conversion symptoms and "hysteria". *British Medical Journal, 331,* 989.

Stone, M. H. (1993). *Abnormalities of personality. Within and beyond the realm of treatment.* New York: W. W. Norton.

Stopa, L., & Clark, D. M. (2000). Social phobia and interpretation of social events. *Behaviour Research and Therapy, 38,* 273–283.

Stormer, S. M., & Thompson, J. K. (1996). Explanations of body image disturbance: A test of maturational status, negative verbal commentary, and sociological hypotheses. *International Journal of Eating Disorders, 19,* 193–202.

Story, M., French, S. A., Resnick, M. D., & Blum, R. W. (1995). Ethnic/racial and socioeconomic differences in dieting behaviors and body image perceptions in adolescents. *International Journal of Eating Disorders, 18,* 173–179.

Stossel, S. (2014, January/February). Surviving anxiety. *Atlantic Monthly,* 1–6.

Stoving, R. K., Hangaard, J., Hansen-Nord, M., & Hagen, C. (1999). A review of endocrine changes in anorexia nervosa. *Journal of Psychiatric Research, 33,* 139–152.

Strain, E. C., Bigelow, G. E., Liebson, I. A., & Stitzer, M. L. (1999). Moderate- vs low-dose methadone in the treatment of opioid dependence. *Journal of the American Medical Association, 281,* 1000–1005.

Streeton, C., & Whelan, G. (2001). Naltrexone, a relapse prevention maintenance treatment of alcohol dependence: A meta-analysis of randomized controlled trials. *Alcohol and Alcoholism, 36,* 544–552.

Streltzer, J., & Johansen, L. G. (2006). Prescription drug dependence and evolving beliefs about chronic pain management. *American Journal of Psychiatry, 163,* 594–598.

Striegel-Moore, R. H., & Franco, D. L. (2008). Should binge eating disorder be included in the DSM-V? A critical review of the state of the evidence. *Annual Review of Clinical Psychology, 4,* 305–324.

Striegel-Moore, R. H., Garvin, V., Dohm, F. A., & Rosenheck, R. (1999). Psychiatric comorbidity of eating disorders in men: A national study of hospitalized veterans. *International Journal of Eating Disorders, 25,* 399–404.

Striegel-Moore, R. H., Schreiber, G. B., Lo, A., Crawford, P., Obarzanek, E., & Rodin, J. (2000). Eating disorder symptoms in a cohort of 11 to 16-year-old black and white girls: The NHLBI growth and health study. *International Journal of Eating Disorders, 27,* 49–66.

Stritzke, W. G. K., Patrick, C. J., & Lang, P. J. (1995). Alcohol and emotion: A multidimensional approach incorporating startle probe methodology. *Journal of Abnormal Psychology, 104,* 114–122.

Strober, M., Freeman, R., Lampert, C., Diamond, J., & Kaye, W. (2000). Controlled family study of anorexia nervosa and bulimia nervosa: Evidence of shared liability and transmission of partial syndromes. *American Journal of Psychiatry, 157,* 393–401.

Strober, M., Freeman, R., Lampert, C., Diamond, J., & Kaye, W. (2001). Males with anorexia nervosa: A controlled study of eating disorders in first-degree relatives. *International Journal of Eating Disorders, 29,* 264–269.

Strober, M., Freeman, R., & Morrell, W. (1997). The longterm course of severe anorexia nervosa in adolescents: Survival analysis of recovery, relapse, and outcome predictors over 10–15 years in a prospective study. *International Journal of Eating Disorders, 22,* 339–360.

Strober, M., Lampert, C., Morrell, W., Burroughs, J., & Jacobs, C. (1990). A controlled family study of anorexia nervosa: Evidence of family aggregation and lack of shared transmission with affective disorders. *International Journal of Eating Disorders, 9,* 239–253.

Strong, G. K., Torgerson, C. J., Torgerson, D., & Hulme, C. (2011). A systematic meta-analytic review of evidence for the effectiveness of the "Fast ForWord" language intervention program. *Journal of Child Psychology and Psychiatry, 52*(3), 224–235.

Strub, R. L., & Black, F. W. (1981). *Organic brain syndromes: An introduction to neurobehavioral disorders.* Philadelphia: F.A. Davis.

Struckman-Johnson, C. (1988). Forced sex on dates: It happens to men, too. *Journal of Sex Research, 24,* 234–241.

Stuart, G. A., & Llienfeld, S. O. (2007). The evidence missing from evidence-based practice. *American Psychologist, 62,* 615–616.

Sturm, R. A., Duffy, D. L., Zhao, Z. Z., & al., e. (2008). A single SNP in an evolutionary conserved region within intron 86 of the HERC2 gene determines human blue-brown eye color. *American Journal of Human Genetics, 82,* 424–431.

Styron, W. (1992). *Darkness visible: A memoir of madness.* New York: Vintage.

Substance Abuse and Mental Health Services Administration. (2013a). Drug Abuse Warning Network, 2011: National Estimates of Drug-Related Emergency Department Visits. HHS Publication No. (SMA) 13-4760, DAWN Series D-39. Rockville, MD: Substance Abuse and Mental Health Services Administration.

Substance Abuse and Mental Health Services Administration. (2013b). Results from the 2012 National Survey on Drug Use and Health: Summary of National Findings. , NSDUH Series H-46, HHS Publication No. (SMA) 13-4795. Rockville, MD: Substance Abuse and Mental Health Services Administration.

Suchy, Y., Eastvold, A. D., Strassberg, D. S., & Franchow, E. I. (2014). Understanding processing speed weaknesses among pedophilic child molesters: Response style vs. neuropathology. *Journal of Abnormal Psychology, 123,* 273–285.

Suddath, R. L., Christison, G. W., Torrey, E. F., Cassonova, M. F., Weinberger, D. R., et al. (1990). Anatomical abnormalities in the brains of monozygotic twins discordant for schizophrenia. *New England Journal of Medicine, 322,* 789–793.

Sue, D. W., & Sue, D. (2008). *Counseling the culturally different: Theory and practice* (5th ed.). Oxford, UK: John Wiley & Sons.

Sue, S., Yan Cheng, J. K., Saad, C. S., & Chu, J. P. (2012). Asian American mental health: A call to action. *American Psychologist, 67*(7), 532–544.

Sullivan, G. M., Coplan, J. D., Kent, J. M., & Gorman, J. M. (1999). The noradrenergic system in pathological anxiety: A focus on panic with relevance to generalized anxiety and phobias. *Biological Psychiatry, 46,* 1205–1218.

Sullivan, J. M. (2000). Cellular and molecular mechanisms underlying learning and memory impairments produced by cannabinoids. *Learning and Memory, 7,* 132–139.

Sullivan, P. F. (1995). Mortality in anorexia nervosa. *American Journal of Psychiatry, 152,* 1073–1075.

Sullivan, P. F., Daly, M. J., & O'Donovan, M. (2012). Genetic architectures of psychiatric disorders: The emerging picture and its implications. *Nature Reviews Genetics, 13*(8), 537–551.

Sullivan, P. F., Neale, M. C., & Kendler, K. S. (2000). Genetic epidemiology of major depression: Review and metaanalysis. *American Journal of Psychiatry, 157,* 1552–1562.

Suls, J., & Bunde, J. (2005). Anger, anxiety, and depression as risk factors for cardiovascular disease: The problems and implications of overlapping affective dispositions. *Psychological Bulletin, 131,* 260–300.

Sun, D., Phillips, L., Velakoulis, D., Yung, A., McGorry, P. D., Wood, S. J., et al. (2009). Progressive brain structural changes mapped as psychosis develops in "at risk" individuals. *Schizophrenia Research, 108*(1–3), 85–92.

Surles, R. C., Blanch, A. K., Shern, D. L., & Donahue, S. A. (1992). Case management as a strategy for systems change. *Health Affairs, 11,* 151–163.

Sussman, S. (1996). Development of a school-based drug abuse prevention curriculum for high-risk youth. *Journal of Psychoactive Drugs, 28,* 169–182.

Sussman, S., Dent, C. W., McAdams, L., Stacy, A. W., Burton, D., & Flay, B. R. (1994). Group self-identification and adolescent cigarette smoking: A 1-year prospective study. *Journal of Abnormal Psychology, 103,* 576–580.

Sussman, S., Dent, C. W., Simon, T. R., Stacy, A. W., Galaif, E. R., Moss, M. A., Craig, S., & Johnson, C. A. (1995). Immediate impact of social influence-oriented substance abuse prevention curricula in traditional and continuation high schools. *Drugs and Society, 8,* 65–81.

Sussman, S., Stacy, A. W., Dent, C. W., Simon, T. R., & Johnson, C. A. (1996). Marijuana use: Current issues and new research directions. *Journal of Drug Issues, 26*, 695–733.

Sussman, T., Dent, C. W., & Lichtman, K. L. (2001). Project EX: Outcomes of a teen smoking cessation program. *Addictive Behaviors, 26*, 425–438.

Sutcliffe, J. P., & Jones, J. (1962). Personal identity, multiple personality, and hypnosis. *International Journal of Clinical and Experimental Hypnosis, 10*, 231–269.

Sutker, P. B., & Adams, H. E. (2001). *Comprehensive handbook of psychopathology* (3rd ed.). New York: Kluwer Academic/Plenum.

Sutker, P. B., Uddo, M., Brailey, K., Vasterling, J. J., & Errera, P. (1994). Psychopathology in war-zone deployed and nondeployed Operation Desert Storm troops assigned grave registration duties. *Journal of Abnormal Psychology, 103*, 383–390.

Sutphen, C. L., Fagan, A. M., & Holtzman, D. M. (2014). Progress update: Fluid and imaging biomarkers in Alzheimer's disease. *Biological Psychiatry, 75*, 520–526.

Suzuki, K., Takei, N., Kawai, M., Minabe, Y., & Mori, N. (2003). Is taijin kyofusho a culture-bound syndrome? *American Journal of Psychiatry, 160*(7), 1358.

Swain, J., Koszycki, D., Shlik, J., & Bradwein, J. (2003). Pharmacological challenge agents in anxiety. In D. Nutt & J. C. Ballenger (Eds.), *Anxiety Disorders* (pp. 269–295). Malden, MA: Blackwell.

Swanson, J. W., Holzer, C. E., Ganju, V. K., & Jono, R. T. (1990). Violence and psychiatric disorder in the community: Evidence from the Epidemiological Catchment Area surveys. *Hospital and Community Psychiatry, 41*, 761–770.

Swanson, J., Hinshaw, S. P., Arnold, L. E., Gibbons, R., Marcus, S., Hur, K., et al. (2007). Secondary evaluations of MTA 36-month outcomes: Propensity score and growth mixture model analyses. *Journal of the American Academy of Child and Adolescent Psychiatry, 46*, 1002–1013.

Swanson, J., Kinsbourne, M., Nigg, J., et al. (2007). Etiologic subtypes of attention-deficit/hyperactivity disorder: Brain imaging, molecular genetic and environmental factors and the dopamine hypothesis. *Neuropsychology Review, 17*, 39–59.

Swanson, J., McBurnett, K., Christian, D. L., & Wigal, T. (1995). Stimulant medications and the treatment of children with ADHD. In T. H. Ollendick & R. J. Prinz (Eds.), *Advances in Clinical Child Psychology* (Vol. 17, pp. 265–322). New York: Plenum.

Sweet, J. J., Carr, M. A., Rossini, E., & Kasper, C. (1986). Relationship between the Luria-Nebraska Neuropsychological Battery and the WISC-R: Further examination using Kaufman's factors. *International Journal of Clinical Neuropsychology, 8*, 177–180.

Sweet, R. A., Mulsant, B. H., Gupta, B., Rifai, A. H., Pasternak, R. E., et al. (1995). Duration of neuroleptic treatment and prevalence of tardive dyskinesia in late life. *Archives of General Psychiatry, 52*, 478–486.

Szasz, T. S. (1999). *Fatal freedom: The ethics and politics of suicide*. Westport, CT: Praeger.

Szczypka, M. S., Kwok, K., Brot, M. D., Marck, B. T., Matsumoto, A. M., Donahue, B. A., & Palmiter, R. D. (2001). Dopamine production in the caudate putamen restores feeding in dopamine-deficient mice. *Neuron, 30*, 819–828.

Szechtman, H., & Woody, E. Z. (2004). Obsessive-compulsive disorder as a disturbance of security motivation. *Psychological Review, 111*, 111–127.

TADS team. (2007). The treatment for adolescents with depression study (TADS): Long term effectiveness and safety outcomes. *Archives of General Psychiatry, 64*, 1132–1144.

Tallal, P., Miller, S. L., Bedi, G., Byma, G., Wang, X., Nagarajan, S. S., Schreiner, C., Jenkins, W. M., & Merzenich, M. M. (1996). Language comprehension in languagelearning impaired children improved with acoustically modified speech. *Science, 271*, 81–84.

Tallmadge, J., & Barkley, R. A. (1983). The interactions of hyperactive and normal boys with their mothers and fathers. *Journal of Abnormal Child Psychology, 11*, 565–579.

Talmi, D. (2013). Enhanced emotional memory: Cognitive and neural mechanisms. *Current Directions in Psychological Science, 22*, 430–436.

Tambs, K., Czajkowsky, N., Roysamb, E., Neale, M. C., Reichborn-Kjennerud, T., Aggen, S. H., et al. (2009). Structure of genetic and environmental risk factors for dimensional representations of DSM-IV anxiety disorders. *British Journal of Psychiatry, 195*, 301–307.

Tarbox, S. I., Addington, J., Cadenhead, K., Cannon, T., Cornblatt, B., Perkins, D., et al. (2013). Premorbid functional development and conversion to psychosis in clinical high-risk youths. *Development and Psychopathology, 25* (1171–1186).

Tarrier, N., Taylor, K., & Gooding, P. (2008). Cognitive-behavioral interventions to reduce suicide behavior. *Behavior Modification, 32*, 77–108.

Task Force on Promotion and Dissemination of Psychological Procedures. (1995). Training in and dissemination of empirically-validated psychological treatments: Report and recommendations. *The Clinical Psychologist, 48*, 3–23.

Taylor, A., & Kim-Cohen, J. (2007). Meta-analysis of gene–environment interactions in developmental psychopathology. *Development and Psychopathology, 19*, 1029–1037.

Taylor, C. B., Hayward, C., King, R., Ehlers, A., Margraf, J., Maddock, R., et al. (1990). Cardiovascular and symptomatic reduction effects of alprazolam and imipramine in patients with panic disorder: Results of a double-blind, placebo-controlled trial. *Journal of Clinical Psychopharmacology, 10*, 112–118.

Taylor, C. T., & Alden, L. E. (2011). To see ourselves as others see us: An experimental integration of the intra and interpersonal consequences of self-protection in social anxiety disorder. *Journal of Abnormal Psychology, 120*, 129–141.

Taylor, J., Iacono, W. G., & McGue, M. (2000). Evidence for a genetic etiology of early-onset delinquency. *Journal of Abnormal Psychology, 109*, 634–643.

Taylor, S., Asmundson, G. J., & Jang, K. L. (2011). Etiology of obsessive-compulsive symptoms and obsessive-compulsive personality traits: Common genes, mostly different environments. *Depression and Anxiety, 28*, 863–869.

Taylor, S., Jang, K. L., & Asmundson, G. J. (2010). Etiology of obsessions and compulsions: A behavioral-genetic analysis. *Journal of Abnormal Psychology, 119*, 672–682.

Teachman, B. A., & Allen, J. P. (2007). Development of social anxiety: Social interaction predictors of implicit and explicit fear of negative evaluation. *Journal of Abnormal Child Psychology, 35*, 63–78.

Teasdale, J. D. (1988). Cognitive vulnerability to persistent depression. *Cognition and Emotion, 2*, 247–274.

Teasdale, J. D., Segal, Z. V., Williams, J. M. G., Ridgeway, V. A., Soulsby, J. M., & Lau, M. A. (2000). Prevention of relapse/recurrence in major depression by mindfulness-based cognitive therapy. *Journal of Consulting and Clinical Psychology, 68*, 615–623.

Tedeschi, R. G., Park, C. L., & Calhoun, L. G. (1998). Posttraumatic growth: Conceptual issues. In R. G. Tedeschi, C. L. Park & L. G. Calhoun (Eds.), *Posttraumatic growth: Positive changes in the aftermath of trauma* (pp. 1–22). Thousand Oaks, CA: Sage Press.

Telch, M. J., & Harrington, P. J. (unpublished manuscript). Anxiety sensitivity and unexpectedness of arousal in mediating affective response to 35% carbon dioxide inhalation.

Telch, M. J., Shermis, M. D., & Lucas, J. A. (1989). Anxiety sensitivity: Unitary personality trait or domain-specific appraisals? *Journal of Anxiety Disorders, 3*, 25–32.

Teper, E., & O'Brien, J. T. (2008). Vascular factors and depression. *International Journal of Geriatric Psychiatry, 23*, 993–1000.

ter Kuile, M. M., Both, S., & van Lankveld, J. J. (2012). Sexual dysfunctions in women. In P. Sturmey & M. Hersen (Eds.), *Handbook of rvidence-based practice in clinical psychology, adult disorders* (Vol. 2, pp. 413–436). Hoboken, NJ: John Wiley & Sons.

ter Kuile, M. M., & Reissing, E. D. (2014). Lifelong vaginismus. In Y. M. Binik & K. S. K. Hall (Eds.), *Principles and practice of sex therapy* (5th ed., pp. 177–194). New York: Guilford Press.

Teri, L., Gibbons, L. E., McCurry, S. M., Logsdon, R. G., Buchner, D. M., Barlow, W. E., et al. (2003). Exercise plus behavioral management in patients with Alzheimer disease: A randomized controlled trial. *Journal of the American Medical Association, 290*, 2015–2022.

Terry, R. D. (2006). Alzheimer's disease and the aging brain. *Journal of Geriatric Psychiatry and Neurology, 19*, 125–128.

Thapar, A., Langley, K., Owen, M. J., & O'Donovan, M. C. (2007). Advances in genetic findings on attention deficit hyperactivity disorder. *Psychological Medicine, 37*, 1681–1692.

Thapar, A., Rice, F., Hay, D., Boivin, J., Langley, K., van den Bree, M., et al. (2009). Prenatal smoking might not cause attention-deficit/hyperactivity disorder: evidence from a novel design. *Biological Psychiatry, 66*(8), 722–727.

Thase, M. E., & Rush, A. J. (1997). When at first you don't succeed: Sequential strategies for antidepressant nonresponders. *Journal of Clinical Psychiatry, 58*, 23–29.

The ESEMeD/MHEDEA 2000 investigators. (2004). Disability and quality of life impact of mental disorders in europe: Results from the European study of the epidemiology of mental disorders (ESEMeD) project. *Acta Psychiatrica Scandinavica, 109*, 38–46.

The WHO World Mental Health Survey Consortium. (2004). Prevalence, severity, and unmet need for treatment of mental disorders in the World Health Organization world mental health surveys. *Journal of the American Medical Association, 291*, 2581–2590.

Theobald, H., Bygren, L. O., Carstensen, J., & Engfeldt, P. A. (2000). Moderate intake of wine is associated with reduced total mortality and reduced mortality from cardiovascular disease. *Journal of Studies on Alcohol, 61*, 652–656.

Thibaut, F., De La Barra, F., Gordon, H., Cosyns, P., & Bradford, J. M. (2010). The World Federation of Societies of Biological Psychiatry (WFSBP) guidelines for the biological treatment of paraphilias. *World Journal of Biological Psychiatry, 11*, 604–655.

Thoits, P. A. (1985). Self-labeling processes in mental illness: The role of emotional deviance. *American Journal of Sociology, 92*, 221–249.

Thomas, C. A., Turkheimer, E., & Oltmanns, T. F. (2003). Factorial structure of pathological personality as evaluated by peers. *Journal of Abnormal Psychology, 112,* 81–91.

Thomas, G., Reifman, A., Barnes, G. M., & Farrell, M. P. (2000). Delayed onset of drunkenness as a protective factor for adolescent alcohol misuse and sexual risk taking; A longitudinal study. *Deviant Behavior, 21,* 181–200.

Thompson, P. M., Hayashi, H. M., Simon, S. L., et al. (2004). Structural abnormalities in the brains of human subjects who use methamphetamine. *Journal of Neuroscience, 24,* 6028–6036.

Thomson, A. B., & Page, L. A. (2007). Psychotherapies for hypochondriasis. *Cochrane Database of Systematic Reviews, Issue 4,* CD006520.

Tiefer, L. (2001). A new view of women's sexual problems: Why new? Why now? *Journal of Sex Research, 38,* 89–96.

Tiefer, L. (2003). Female sexual dysfunction (FSD): Witnessing social construction in action. *Sexualities, Evolution and Gender, 5,* 33–36.

Tiefer, L., Hall, M., & Tavris, C. (2002). Beyond dysfunction: A new view of women's sexual problems. *Journal of Sex and Marital Therapy, 28,* 225–232.

Tienari, P., Wynne, L. C., Laksy, K., Moring, J., Nieminen, P., Sorri, A., et al. (2003). Genetic boundaries of the schizophrenia spectrum: Evidence from the Finnish adoptive family study of schizophrenia. *American Journal of Psychiatry, 160,* 1587–1594.

Tienari, P., Wynne, L. C., Moring, J., et al. (2000). Finnish adoptive family study: Sample selection and adoptee DSM-III diagnoses. *Acta Psychiatrica Scandinavica, 101,* 433–443.

Timko, C., Moos, R. H., Finney, J. W., & Lesar, M. D. (2001). Long-term outcomes of alcohol use disorders: Comparing untreated individuals with those in Alcoholics Anonymous and formal treatment. *Journal of Studies on Alcohol, 61,* 529–540.

Timpano, K. R., Broman-Fulks, J. J., Glaesmer, H., Exner, C., Rief, W., Olatunji, B. O., et al. (2013). A taxometric exploration of the latent structure of hoarding. *Psychological Assessment, 25,* 194–203.

Tjaden, P., & Thoennes, N. (2006). Extent, nature, and consequences of rape victimization: Findings from the National Violence Against Women Survey. Washington, DC: National Institute of Justice.

Tobler, N. S., Roona, M. A., Ochshorn, P., Marshall, D. G., Streke, A. V., & Stackpole, K. M. (2000). School-based adolescent drug prevention programs: 1998 metaanalysis. *Journal of Primary Prevention, 20,* 275–336.

Tolin, D. F., & Foa, E. B. (2006). Sex differences in trauma and posttraumatic stress disorder: A quantitative review of 25 years of research. *Psychological Bulletin, 132,* 959–992.

Tolin, D. F., & Villavicencio, A. (2011). Inattention, but not OCD, predicts the core features of hoarding disorder. *Behaviour Research and Therapy, 49,* 120–125.

Tolin, D. F., Frost, R. O., Steketee, G., Gray, K., & Fitch, K. (2008). The economic and social burden of compulsive hoarding. *Psychiatry Research, 160,* 200–211.

Tolin, D. F., Kiehl, K. A., Worhunsky, P., Book, G. A., & Maltby, N. (2009). An exploratory study of the neural mechanisms of decision making in compulsive hoarding. *Psychological Medicine, 39,* 325–336.

Tolin, D. F., Stevens, M. C., Villavicencio, A. L., Norberg, M. M., Calhoun, V. D., Frost, R. O., et al. (2012). Neural mechanisms of decision making in hoarding disorder. *Archives of General Psychiatry, 69,* 832–841.

Tolin, D. F., Worhunsky, P., & Maltby, N. (2004). Sympathetic magic in contamination-related OCD. *Journal of Behavior Therapy and Experimental Psychiatry, 35,* 193–205.

Tompkins, M. A., & Hartl, T. L. (2009). *Digging out: Helping your loved one manage clutter, hoarding, and compulsive acquiring.* Oakland, CA: New Harbinger.

Tondo, L., Isacsson, G., & Baldessarini, R. (2003). Suicidal behaviour in bipolar disorder: risk and prevention. *CNS Drugs, 17,* 491–511.

Tonigan, J. S., Miller, W. R., & Connors, G. J. (2000). Project MATCH client impressions about Alcoholics Anonymous: Measurement issues and relationship to treatment outcome. *Alcoholism Treatment Quarterly, 18,* 25–41.

Tonstad, S., Tonnesen, P., Hajek, P., Williams, K. E., Billing, C. B., & Reeves, K. R. (2006). Varenicline Phase 3 Study Group. Effect of maintenance therapy with varenicline on smoking cessation: a randomized controlled trial. *JAMA, 296,* 64–71.

Torgersen, S. (1986). Genetics of somatoform disorder. *Archives of General Psychiatry, 43,* 502–505.

Torgersen, S., Lygren, S., Øien, P. A., Skre, I., Onstad, S., Edvardsen, J., et al. (2000). A twin study of personality disorders. *Comprehensive Psychiatry, 41,* 416–425.

Torgersen, S., Myers, J., Reichborn-Kjennerud, T., Roysamb, E., Kubarych, T. S., & Kendler, K. S. (2012). The heritability of Cluster B personality disorders assessed both by personal interview and questionnaire. *Journal of Personality Disorders, 26,* 848–866.

Torres, A. R., Prince, M. J., Bebbington, P. E., Bhurga, D., Brugha, T. S., Farrell, M., et al. (2006). Obsessive-compulsive disorder: Prevalence, comorbidity, impact, and help-seeking in the British National Psychiatric Morbidity Survey of 2000. *American Journal of Psychiatry, 163,* 1978–1985.

Torrey, E. F. (2014). *American psychosis: How the federal government destroyed the mental illness treatment system.* Oxford, UK: Oxford University Press.

Torrey, E. F., Kennard, A. D., Eslinger, D., Lamb, R., & Pavle, J. (2010). More mentally ill persons are in jails and prisons than hospitals: A survey of the state. Treatment Advocacy Center and the National Sheriffs' Association., Washington DC.

Torrey, E. F., Zdanowicz, M. T., Kennard, A. D., Lamb, H. R., Eslinger, D., Biasotti, M. C., & Fuller, D. A. (2014). The treatment of persons with mental illness in prisons and jails: A state survey. Washington, DC: Treatment Advocacy Center.

Torti, F. M., Gwyther, L. P., Reed, S. D., Friedman, J. Y., & Schulman, K. A. (2004). A multinational review of recent trends and reports in dementia caregiver burden. *Alzheimers Disease and Associated Disorders, 18,* 99–109.

Totterdell, P., & Kellett, S. (2008). Restructuring mood in cyclothymia using cognitive behavior therapy: An intensive time-sampling study. *Journal of Clinical Psychology, 64,* 501–518.

Toufexis, A., Blackman, A., & Drummond, T. (1996, April 29). Why Jennifer got sick. *Time Magazine.*

Touyz, S., Le Grange, D., Lacey, H., Hay, P., Smith, R., Maguire, S., et al. (2013). Treating severe and enduring anorexia nervosa: A randomized controlled trial. *Psychological Medicine, 43*(12), 2501–2511.

Tran, G. Q., Haaga, D. A. F., & Chambless, D. L. (1997). Expecting that alcohol will reduce social anxiety moderates the relation between social anxiety and alcohol consumption. *Cognitive Therapy and Research, 21,* 535–553.

Treadway, M. T., & Zald, D. H. (2011). Reconsidering anhedonia in depression: Lessons from translation neuroscience. *Neuroscience and Biobehavioral Reviews, 35,* 537–555.

Treat, T. A., & Viken, R. J. (2010). Cognitive processing of weight and emotional information in disordered eating. *Current Directions in Psychological Science, 19,* 81–85.

Treynor, W., Gonzalez, R., & Nolen-Hoeksema, S. (2003). Rumination reconsidered: A psychometric analysis. *Cognitive Therapy and Research, 27,* 247–259.

Trierweiler, S. J., Neighbors, H. W., Munday, C., Thompson, E. E., Binion, V. J., & Gomez, J. P. (2000). Clinician attributions associated with the diagnosis of schizophrenia in African American and non-African American patients. *Journal of Consulting and Clinical Psychology, 68,* 171–175.

Trimpey, J., Velten, E., & Dain, R. (1993). Rational recovery from addictions. In W. Dryden & L. K. Hill (Eds.), *Innovations in rational-emotive therapy* (pp. 253–271). Thousand Oaks, CA: Sage.

Trinder, H., & Salkovaskis, P. M. (1994). Personally relevant instrusions outside the laboratory: Long-term suppression increases intrusion. *Behaviour Research and Therapy, 32,* 833–842.

Trivedi, M. H., Rush, A. J., Wisniewski, S. R., Nierenberg, A. A., Warden, D., Ritz, L., et al. (2006). Evaluation of outcomes with citalopram for depression using measurement-based care in STAR*D: Implications for clinical practice. *American Journal of Psychiatry, 163,* 28–40.

True, W. R., Rice, J., Eisen, S. A., Heath, A. C., Godlberg, J., Lyons, M. J., et al. (1993). A twin study of genetic and environmental contributions to liability for posttraumatic stress symptoms. *Archives of General Psychiatry, 50,* 257–264.

True, W. R., Xiam, H., Scherrer, J. F., Madden, P., Bucholz, K. K., et al. (1999). Common genetic vulnerability for nicotine and alcohol dependence in men. *Archives of General Psychiatry, 56,* 655–662.

Trull, T. J., Jahng, S., Tomko, R. L., Wood, P. K., & Sher, K. J. (2010). Revised NESARC personality disorder diagnoses: gender, prevalence, and comorbidity with substance dependence disorders. *J Pers Disord, 24,* 412–426.

Trull, T. J., Solhan, M. B., Tragesser, S. L., Jahng, S., Wood, P. K., Piasecki, T. M., et al. (2008). Affective instability: Measuring a core feature of borderline personality disorder with ecological momentary assessment. *Journal of Abnormal Psychology, 117,* 647–661.

Tsai, D. C., & Pike, P. L. (2000). Effects of acculturation on the MMPI-2 scores of Asian American students. *Journal of Personality Assessment, 74,* 216–230.

Tsai, G., Parssani, L. A., Slusher, B. S., Carter, R., Baer, L., et al. (1995). Abnormal excitatory neurotransmitter metabolism in schizophrenic brains. *Archives of General Psychiatry, 52,* 829–836.

Tsai, J. L. (2007). Ideal affect: Cultural causes and behavioral consequences. *Perspectives on Psychological Science, 2,* 242–259.

Tsai, J. L. (2014). [personal communication].

Tsai, J. L., Butcher, J. N., Vitousek, K., & Munoz, R. (2001). Culture, ethnicity, and psychopathology. In H.E. Adams & P.B. Sutker (Eds.). *The Comprehensive Handbook of Psychopathology* (pp.105–127). New York, NY: Plenum Press.

Tsai, J. L., et al. (2001). Culture, ethnicity, and psychopathology. In H. E. Adams & P.B. Sutkey (Eds). *Comprehensive handbook of psychopathology* (3rd. ed., pp. 105–127). New York: Kluwer Academic/Plenum.

Tsai, J. L., Knutson, B. K., & Fung, H. H. (2006). Cultural variation in affect valuation. *Journal of Personality and Social Psychology, 90,* 288–307.

Tsai, J. L., Knutson, B. K., & Rothman, A. (2006). *The pursuit of ideal affect: Variation in mood-producing* behavior. *Journal of Personality and Social Psychology, 90,* 288-307.

Tsuang, M. T., Lyons, M. J., Meyer, J. M., Doyle, T., Eisen, S. A., et al. (1998). Co-occurrence of abuse of different drugs in men: The role of drug-specific and shared vulnerabilities. *Archives of General Psychiatry, 55,* 967–972.

Tully, L. A., Arseneault, L., Caspi, A., Moffitt, T. E., & Morgan, J. (2004). Does maternal warmth moderate the effects of birth weight on twins' attention-deficit/hyperactivity disorder (ADHD) symptoms and low IQ? *Journal of Consulting and Clinical Psychology, 72,* 218–226.

Turk, D. C. (2001). Treatment of chronic pain: Clinical outcomes, cost-effectiveness, and cost benefits. *Drug Benefit Trends, 13,* 36–38.

Turkheimer, E. (1998). Heritability and biological explanation. *Psychological Review, 105,* 782–791.

Turkheimer, E. (2000). Three laws of behavior genetics and what they mean. *Current Directionsin Psychological Science, 9,* 160–164.

Turkheimer, E., Haley, A., Waldron, M., D'Onofrio, B., & Gottesman, I. I. (2003). Socioeconomic status modifies the heritability of IQ in young children. *Psychological Science, 6,* 623–628.

Turkington, D., Kingdom, D., & Turner, T. (2002). Effectiveness of a brief cognitive-behavioural intervention in the treatment of schizophrenia. *British Journal of Psychiatry, 180,* 523–527.

Turner, C. F., Ku, S. M., Rogers, L. D., Lindberg, J. H., & Pleck, F. L. (1998). Adolescent sexual behavior, drug use, and violence: Increased reporting with computer survey technology. *Science, 280,* 867–873.

Turner, C. M. (2006). Cognitive-behavioural theory and therapy for obsessive-compulsive disorder in children and adolescents: Current status and future directions. *Clinical Psychology Review, 26,* 912–948.

Turner, E. H., Matthews, A. M., Linardatos, E., Tell, R. A., & Rosenthal, R. (2008). Selective publication of antidepressant trials and its influence on apparent efficacy. *New England Journal of Medicine, 358,* 252–260.

Turner, S. M., Beidel, D. C., & Townsley, R. M. (1990). Social phobia: Relationship to shyness. *Behaviour Research and Therapy, 28,* 297–305.

Twenge, J. M., & Foster, J. D. (2010). Birth cohort increases in narcissistic personality traits among American college students, 1982–2009. *Social Psychological and Personality Science, 1,* 99–106.

Tyrer, H., Tyrer, P., & Barrett, B. (2013). Influence of dependent personality status on the outcome and health service costs of health anxiety. *International Journal of Social Psychiatry, 59,* 274–280.

Tyrer, P. (2013). The classification of personality disorders in ICD-11: Implications for forensic psychiatry. *Criminal Behaviour and Mental Health, 23,* 1–5.

Tyrer, P., & Bateman, A. W. (2004). Drug treatments for personality disorder. *Advances in Psychiatric Treatment, 10.*

Tyrka, A. R., Waldron, I., Graber, J. A., & Brooks-Gunn, J. (2002). Prospective predictors of the onset of anorexic and bulimic syndromes. *International Journal of Eating Disorders, 32,* 282–290.

U.S. Bureau of the Census. (2010). Population estimates: U. S. Census Bureau, Population Division.

U.S. Department of Education. (2013). Digest of education statistics, 2012 (Vol. NCES Number: 2014015).

U.S. Department of Health and Human Services Administration for Children and Families. (2010, January). Head Start Impact Study. Final Report. Washington, DC.

U.S. Department of Health and Human Services. (1999). Mental Health: A report of the Surgeon General—Executive summary, Rockville, MD: U.S. Department of Health and Human Services, Substance Abuse and Mental Health Services Administration, Center for Mental Health Services, National Institutes of Health, National Institute of Mental Health.

U.S. Department of Health and Human Services. (2001). Mental Health: Culture, Race, and Ethnicity—A supplement to mental health: A report of the Surgeon General. Rockville, MD: U.S. Department of Health and Human Services, Substance Abuse and Mental Health Services Administration, Center for Mental Health Services.

U.S. Department of Health and Human Services. (2001a). Mental Health: Culture, Race, and Ethnicity—A supplement to mental health: A report of the Surgeon General. Rockville, MD: U.S. Department of Health and Human Services, Substance Abuse and Mental Health Services Administration, Center for Mental Health Services.

U.S. Department of Health and Human Services. (2001b). The Surgeon General's call to action to prevent and decrease overweight and obesity. Rockville, MD: U.S. Department of Health and Human Services, Public Health Service, Office of the Surgeon General. Available from: U.S. Government Printing Office, Washington, DC.

U.S. Department of Health and Human Services. (2002). Supplement to Mental Health: A Report of the Surgeon General (SMA-01-3613). Retrieved July 2, 2002, from http://www.mentalhealth.org/Publications/allpubs/SMA01-3613/sma-01-3613.pdf.

U.S. Department of Health and Human Services. (2006). The health consequences of involuntary exposure to tobacco smoke: A report of the Surgeon General. Atlanta, GA: Department of Health and Human Services, Centers for Disease Control and Prevention, Coordinating Center for Health Promotion.

U.S. Department of Health and Human Services. (2008). 2008 National healthcare disparities report (Table 15-13-11.11b).

U.S. Department of Health and Human Services. (2014). The Health Consequences of Smoking—50 Years of Progress. A Report of the Surgeon General. Atlanta, GA: U.S. Department of Health and Human Services, Centers for Disease Control and Prevention, National Center for Chronic Disease Prevention and Health Promotion, Office on Smoking and Health.

Uchinuma, Y., & Sekine, Y. (2000). Dissociative identity disorder (DID) in Japan: A forensic case report and the recent increase in reports of DID. *International Journal of Psychiatry in Clinical Practice, 4,* 155–160.

Uher, R., & McGuffin, P. (2010). The moderation by the serotonin transporter gene of environmental adversity in the etiology of depression: 2009 update. *Molecular Psychiatry, 15,* 18–22.

UK ECT Review Group. (2003). Efficacy and safety of electro-convulsive therapy in depressive disorders: A systematic review and meta-analysis. *The Lancet, 361,* 799–808.

Unger, J. B., Boley Cruz, T., Schuster, D., Flora, J. A., & Anderson Johnson, C. (2001). Measuring exposure to proand anti-tobacco marketing among adolescents: Intercorrelations among measures and associations with smoking status. *Journal of Health Communication, 6,* 11–29.

Unschuld, P. G., Buchholz, A. S., Varvaris, M., van Zijl, P. C., Ross, C. A., Pekar, J. J., et al. (2014). Prefrontal brain network connectivity indicates degree of both schizophrenia risk and cognitive dysfunction. *Schizophrenia Bulletin, 40*(3), 653–664.

Urada, D., Evans, E., Yang, J., & Conner, B. T., et al. (2009). Evaluation of proposition 36: The substance abuse and crime prevention act of 2000: 2009 report. Retrieved from http://www.uclaisap.org/prop36/html/reports.html.

Ursu, S., Kring, A. M., Germans Gard, M., Minzenberg, M., Yoon, J., Ragland, D., et al. (2011). Prefrontal cortical deficits and impaired cognition-emotion interactions in schizophrenia. *American Journal of Psychiatry, 168,* 276–285.

Valencia, M., Racon, M. L., Juarez, F., & Murow, E. (2007). A psychosocial skills training approach in Mexican outpatients with schizophrenia. *Psychological Medicine, 37,* 1393–1402.

Valenti, A. M., Narendran, R., & Pristach, C. A. (2003). Who are patients on conventional antipsychotics? *Schizophrenia Bulletin, 29,* 195–200.

Valenzuela, M. J., & Sachdev, P. (2006). Brain reserve and dementia: A systematic review. *Psychological Medicine, 36,* 441–454.

Van Ameringen, M. A., Lane, R. M., Walker, J. R., & et al. (2001). Sertreline treatment of generalized social phobia: A 20-week, double-blind, placebo-controlled study. *American Journal of Psychiatry, 158,* 275–281.

van den Biggelaar, A. H., Gussekloo, J., de Craen, A. J., Frolich, M., Stek, M. L., van der Mast, R. C., et al. (2007). Inflammation and interleukin-1 signaling network contribute to depressive symptoms but not cognitive decline in old age. *Experimental Gerontology, 42,* 693–701.

van den Broucke, S., Vandereycken, W., & Vertommen, H. (1995). Marital communication in eating disorders: A controlled observational study. *International Journal of Eating Disorders, 17,* 1–23.

van der Sande, R., Buskens, E., Allart, E., van der Graaf, Y., & van Engeland, H. (1997). Psychosocial intervention following suicide attempt: A systematic review of treatment interventions. *Acta Psychiatrica Scandinavica, 96,* 43–50.

van Elst, L. T. (2003). Frontolimbic brain abnormalities in patients with borderline personality disorder: A volumetric magnetic resonance imaging study. *Biological Psychiatry, 54,* 163–171.

van Erp, T. G. M., Saleh, P. A., Huttunen, M., et al. (2004). Hippocampal volumes in schizophrenic twins. *Archives of General Psychiatry, 61,* 346–353.

van Lankveld, J. J., Granot, M., Weijmar Schultz, W. C., Binik, Y. M., Wesselmann, U., Pukall, C. F., et al. (2010). Women's sexual pain disorders. *Journal of Sexual Medicine, 7,* 615–631.

Van Meter, A. R., Moreira, A. L. R., & Youngstrom, E. A. (2011). Meta-analysis of epidemiologic studies of pediatric bipolar disorder. *Journal of Clinical Psychiatry, 72*(9), 1250–1256.

Van Oppen, P., de Haan, E., Van Balkom, A. J. L. M., Spinhoven, P., Hoogdiun, K., & van Dyck, R. (1995). Cognitive therapy and exposure in vivo in the treatment of obsessive compulsive disorder. *Behaviour Research and Therapy, 33,* 379–390.

van Orden, K. A., Cukrowicz, K. C., Witte, T. K., Braithwaite, S. R., & Joiner, T. E. (2010). The interpersonal theory of suicide. *Psychological Review, 117,* 575–600.

van Orden, K. A., Witte, T. K., Gordon, K. H., Bender, T. W., & Joiner, T. E. (2008). Suicidal desire and the capability for suicide: Tests of the interpersonal-psychological theory of suicidal behavior among adults. *Journal of Consulting and Clinical Psychology, 76,* 72–83.

van Os, J., Kenis, G., & Rutten, B. P. (2010). The environment and schizophrenia. *Nature, 468*, 203–212.

Vance, S., Cohen-Kettenis, P., Drescher, J., Meyer-Bahlburg, H., Pfafflin, F., & Zucker, K. (2010). Opinions about the DSM gender identity disorder diagnosis: Results from an international survey administered to organizations concerned with the welfare of transgender people. *International Journal of Transgenderism, 12*, 1–14.

Vandermosten, M., Boets, B., Poelmans, H., Sunaert, S., Wouters, J., & Ghesquiere, P. (2012). A tractography study in dyslexia: neuroanatomic correlates of orthographic, phonological and speech processing. *Brain, 135*(Pt 3), 935–948.

Vanwesenbeeck, I., Bakker, F., & Gesell, S. (2010). Sexual health in the Netherlands: Main results of a population survey among Dutch adults. *International Journal of Sexual Health, 22*, 55–71.

Vazire, S., Naumann, L. P., Rentfrow, P. J., & Gosling, S. D. (2008). Portrait of a narcissist: Manifestations of narcissism in physical appearance. *Journal of Research in Personality, 42*, 1439–1447.

Veale, D. (2000). Outcome of cosmetic surgery and "DIY" surgery in patients with body dysmorphic disorder. *Psychiatric Bulletin, 24*, 218–221.

Veale, D. (2004). Advances in a cognitive behavioural model of body dysmorphic disorder. *Body Image, 1*, 113–125.

Veehof, M. M., Oskam, M. J., Schreurs, K. M., & Bohlmeijer, E. T. (2011). Acceptance-based interventions for the treatment of chronic pain: a systematic review and meta-analysis. *Pain, 152*, 533–542.

Velakoulis, D., Pantelis, C., McGorry, P. D., Dudgeon, P., Brewer, W., et al. (1999). Hippocampal volume in firstepisode psychoses and chronic schizophrenia: A high resolution magnetic resonance imaging study. *Archives of General Psychiatry, 56*, 133–141.

Vemuri, P., Lesnick, T. G., Przybelski, S. A., Knopman, D. S., Mielke, M. M., Roberts, R. O., et al. (2014). Association of lifetime intellectual enrichment with cognitive decline in the older population. *Journal of the American Medical Association, Neurology, 71*, 1017–1024

Ventura, J., Neuchterlein, K. H., Lukoff, D., & Hardesty, J. D. (1989). A prospective study of stressful life events and schizophrenic relapse. *Journal of Abnormal Psychology, 98*, 407–411.

Videbech, P., & Ravnkilde, B. (2004). Hippocampal volume and depression: A meta-analysis of MRI studies. *American Journal of Psychiatry, 161*, 1957–1966.

Vieta, E., Martinez-De-Osaba, M. J., Colom, F., Martinez-Aran, A., Benabarre, A., & Gasto, C. (1999). Enhanced corticotropin response to corticotropin-releasing hormone as a predictor of mania in euthymic bipolar patients. *Psychological Medicine, 29*, 971–978.

Vila-Rodriguez, F., Panenka, W. J., Lang, D. J., Thornton, A. E., Vertinsky, T., Wong, H., et al. (2013). The hotel study: multimorbidity in a community sample living in marginal housing. *American Journal of Psychiatry, 170*(12), 1413–1422.

Villanti, A. C., McKay, H. S., Abrams, D. B., Holtgrave, D. R., & Bowie, J. V. (2010). Smoking-Cessation Interventions for U.S. Young Adults: A systematic review. *American Journal of Preventive Medicine, 39*(6), 564–574.

Villemure, C., & Bushnell, M. C. (2009). Mood influences supraspinal pain processing separately from attention. *Journal of Neuroscience 29*, 705–715.

Vinkers, D. J., Gussekloo, J., Stek, M. L., Westendorp, R. G. J., & van der Mast, R. C. (2004). Temporal relation between depression and cognitive impairment in old age: Prospective population based study. *British Medical Journal, 329*, 881.

Virtanen, M., Vahtera, J., Batty, G. D., Tuisku, K., Pentti, J., Oksanen, T., et al. (2011). Overcrowding in psychiatric wards and physical assaults on staff: Data-linked longitudinal study. *British Journal of Psychiatry, 198*, 149–155.

Virués-Ortega, J. (2010). Applied behavior analytic intervention for autism in early childhood: Meta-analysis, meta-regression and dose–response meta-analysis of multiple outcomes. *Clinical Psychology Review, 30*, 387–399.

Visser, S. N., Danielson, M. L., Bitsko, R. H., Holbrook, J. R., Kogan, M. D., Ghandour, R. M., et al. (2014). Trends in the parent-report of health care provider-diagnosed and medicated attention-deficit/hyperactivity disorder: United States, 2003–2011. *Journal of the American Academy of Child and Adolescent Psychiatry, 53*(1), 34–46.e32.

Vitaliani, R., Mason, W., Ances, B., Zwerdling, T., Jiang, Z., & Dalmau, J. (2005). Paraneoplastic encephalitis, psychiatric symptoms, and hypoventilation in ovarian teratoma. *Annals of Neurology, 58*(4), 594–604.

Vitaliano, P. P., Zhang, J., & Scanlan, J. M. (2003). Is caregiving hazardous to one's physical health? A meta-analysis. *Psychological Bulletin, 129*, 946–972.

Vitousek, K., & Manke, F. (1994). Personality variables and disorders in anorexia nervosa and bulimia nervosa. *Journal of Abnormal Psychology, 103*, 137–147.

Vittengl, J. R., Clark, L. A., Dunn, T. W., & Jarrett, R. B. (2007). Reducing relapse and recurrence in unipolar depression: A comparative meta-analysis of cognitive-behavior therapy's effects. *Journal of Consulting and Clinical Psychology, 75*, 475–488.

Vogt, D., Smith, B., Elwy, R., Martin, J., Schultz, M., Drainoni, M. L., et al. (2011). Predeployment, deployment, and postdeployment risk factors for posttraumatic stress symptomatology in female and male OEF/OIF veterans. *Journal of Abnormal Psychology, 120*, 819–831.

Vohs, K. D., & Heatherton, T. F. (2000). Self-regulatory failure: A resource-depletion approach. *Psychological Science, 11*(3), 249–254.

Volk, D. W., Austin, M. C., Pierri, J. N., et al. (2000). Decreased glutamic acid decarboxylase67 messenger RNA expression in a subset of prefrontal cortical gamma-aminobutyric acid neurons in subjects with schizophrenia. *Archives of General Psychiatry, 57*, 237–248.

Volkow, N. D., Wang, G. J., Fischman, M. W., & Foltin, R. W. (1997). Relationship between subjective effects of cocaine and dopamine transporter occupancy. *Nature, 386*, 827–830.

Volkow, N. D., Wang, G. J., Fowler, J. S., Logan, J., Jayne, M., Franceschi, D., Wong, C., Gatley, S. J., Gifford, A. N., Ding, Y. S., & Pappas, N. (2002). "Nonhedonic" food motivation in humans involves dopamine in the dorsal striatum and methylphenidate amplifies this effect. *Synapse, 44*, 175–180.

Volkow, N. D., Wang, G. J., Kollins, S. H., Wigal, T. L., Newcorn, J. H., Telang, F., et al. (2009). Evaluating dopamine reward pathway in ADHD: Clinical implications. *Journal of the American Medical Association, 302*(10), 1084–1091.

Volkow, N. D., Wang, G. J., Newcorn, J. H., Kollins, S. H., Wigal, T. L., Telang, F., et al. (2011). Motivation deficit in ADHD is associated with dysfunction of the dopamine reward pathway. *Molecular Psychiatry, 16*(11), 1147–1154.

Vøllestad, J., Nielsen, M. B., & Nielsen, G. H. (2012). Mindfulness- and acceptance-based interventions for anxiety disorders: A systematic review and meta-analysis. *British Journal of Clinical Psychology, 51*, 239–260.

Volpicelli, J. R., Rhines, K. C., Rhines, J. S., Volpicelli, L. A., et al. (1997). Naltrexone and alcohol dependence: Role of subject compliance. *Archives of General Psychiatry, 54*, 737–743.

Volpicelli, J. R., Watson, N. T., King, A. C., Shermen, C. E., & O'Brien, C. P. (1995). Effects of naltrexone on alcohol "high" in alcoholics. *American Journal of Psychiatry, 152*, 613–617.

von Krafft-Ebing, R. (1902). *Psychopathia sexualis*. Brooklyn, NY: Physicians and Surgeons Books.

Voon, V., Derbyshire, K., Ruck, C., Irvine, M. A., Worbe, Y., Enander, J., et al. (2014, in press). Disorders of compulsivity: A common bias towards learning habits. *Molecular Psychiatry*.

Vrshek-Schallhorn, S., Doane, L. D., Mineka, S., Zinbarg, R. E., Craske, M. G., & Adam, E. K. (2013). The cortisol awakening response predicts major depression: Predictive stability over a 4-year follow-up and effect of depression history. *Psychological Medicine, 43*(3), 483–493.

Vrshek-Schallhorn, S., Mineka, S., Zinbarg, R. E., Craske, M. G., Griffith, J. W., Sutton, J., et al. (2013). Refining the candidate environment: Interpersonal stress, the serotonin transporter polymorphism, and gene–environment interactions in major depression. *Clinical Psychological Science, 2*(3), 235–248.

Wade, T. D., Bulik, C. M., Neale, M., & Kendler, K. S. (2000). Anorexia nervosa and major depression: Shared genetic and environmental risk factors. *American Journal of Psychiatry, 157*, 469–471.

Wade, W. A., Treat, T. A., & Stuart, G. A. (1998). Transporting an empirically supported treatment for panic disorder to a service clinic setting: A benchmarking strategy. *Journal of Consulting and Clinical Psychology, 66*, 231–239.

Wahl, O. F. (1999). Mental health consumers' experience of stigma. *Schizophrenia Bulletin, 25*, 467–478.

Wahlbeck, K., Cheine, M., Essali, A., & Adams, C. (1999). Evidence of clozapine's effectiveness in schizophrenia: A systemic review and meta-analysis of randomized trials. *American Journal of Psychiatry, 156*, 990–999.

Wakefield, J. C. (1992). Disorder as dysfunction: A conceptual critique of DSM-III-R's definition of mental disorder. *Psychological Review, 99*, 232–247.

Wakefield, J. C. (1999). Philosophy of science and the progressiveness of DSM's theory—neutral nosology: Response to Follette and Houts, Part 1. *Behaviour Research and Therapy, 37*, 963–969.

Wakefield, J. C. (2011). Should uncomplicated bereavement-related depression be reclassified as a disorder in the DSM-5? Response to Kenneth S. Kendler's statement defending the proposal to eliminate the bereavement exclusion. *Journal of Nervous and Mental Disease, 199*, 203–208.

Wakefield, M., & Chaloupka, R. (2000). Effectiveness of comprehensive tobacco control programmes in reducing teenage smoking in the USA. *Tobacco Control, 9*, 177–186.

Waldinger, M. D., Quinn, P., Dilleen, M., Mundayat, R., Schweitzer, D. H., & Boolell, M. (2005). A multinational population survey of intravaginal ejaculation latency time. *Journal of Sexual Medicine, 2*, 492–497.

Walitzer, K. S., & Dearing, R. L. (2006). Gender differences in alcohol and substance use relapse. *Clinical Psychology Review, 26*, 128–148.

Walker, E. F., Davis, D. M., & Savoie, T. D. (1994). Neuromotor precursors of schizophrenia. *Schizophrenia Bulletin, 20*, 441–451.

Walker, E. F., Grimes, K. E., Davis, D. M., & Adina, J. (1993). Childhood precursors of schizophrenia: Facial expressions of emotion. *American Journal of Psychiatry, 150,* 1654–1660.

Walker, E. F., Kestler, L., Bollini, A., & Hochman, K. (2004). Schizophrenia: Etiology and course. *Annual Review of Psychology, 55,* 401–430.

Walker, E. F., Mittal, V., & Tessner, K. (2008). Stress and the hypothalamic pituitary adrenal axis in the developmental course of schizophrenia. *Annual Review of Clinical Psychology, 4,* 189–216.

Walker, E. F., Trotman, H. D., Pearce, B. D., Addington, J., Cadenhead, K. S., Cornblatt, B. A., et al. (2013). Cortisol levels and risk for psychosis: initial findings from the North American prodrome longitudinal study. *Biological Psychiatry, 74*(6), 410–417.

Walkup, J. T., Albano, A. M., Piacentini, J., Birmaher, B., Comptom, S. N., Sherrill, J. T., et al. (2008). Cognitive behavioral therapy, sertaline, or a combination in childhood anxiety. *New England Journal of Medicine, 359,* 2753–2766.

Waller, D. A., Kiser, S., Hardy, B. W., Fuchs, I., & Feigenbaum, L. P. (1986). Eating behavior and plasma betaendorphin in bulimia. *American Journal of Clinical Nutrition, 4,* 20–23.

Wallis, J. D. (2007). Orbitofrontal cortex and its contribution to decision-making. *Annual Review of Neuroscience, 30,* 31–56.

Walsh, B. T., Agras, S. W., Devlin, M. J., et al. (2000). Fluoxetine for bulimia nervosa following poor response to psychotherapy. *American Journal of Psychiatry, 157,* 1332–1334.

Walsh, B. T., Seidman, S. N., Sysko, R., & Gould, M. (2002). Placebo response in studies of major depression: Variable, substantial, and growing. *Journal of American Medical Association, 287,* 1840–1847.

Walsh, B. T., Wilson, G. T., Loeb, K. L., Devin, M. J., et al. (1997). Medication and psychotherapy in the treatment of bulimia nervosa. *American Journal of Psychiatry, 154,* 523–531.

Walsh, T., McClellan, J. M., McCarthy, S. E., Addington, A. M., Pierce, S. B., et al. (2008). Rare structural variants disrupt genes in neurodevelopmental pathways in schizophrenia. *Science, 320,* 539–543.

Walters, G. L., & Clopton, J. R. (2000). Effect of symptom information and validity scale information on the malingering of depression on the MMPI-2. *Journal of Personality Assessment, 75,* 183–199.

Wang, C.-Y., Xiang, Y-T., Cai, Z-J., Bo, Q-J., Zhao, J-P., Liu, T-Q., Wang, G-H., Weng, S-M., et al. (2010). Risperidone maintenance treatment in schizphrenia: A randomized, controlled trial. *American Journal of Psychiatry, 167,* 676–685.

Wang, K., Zhang, H., Ma, D., Bucan, M., Glassner, J. T., Abrahams, B. S., Salyakina, D., et al. (2009). Common genetic variants on 5p14.1 associate with autism spectrum disorders. *Nature, 459,* 528–533.

Wang, M. Q., Fitzhugh, E. C., Eddy, J. M., Fu, Q., et al. (1997). Social influences on adolescents' smoking progress: A longitudinal analysis. *American Journal of Health Behavior, 21,* 111–117.

Wang, P. S., Aguilar-Gaxiola, S., Alonso, J., Angermeyer, M. C., Borges, G., Bromet, E. J., et al. (2007). Use of mental health services for anxiety, mood, and substance disorders in 17 countries in the WHO world mental health surveys. *The Lancet, 370,* 841–850.

Wang, P. S., Lane, M. C., Olfson, M., Pincus, H. A., Wells, K. B., & Kessler, R. C. (2005). Twelve-month use of mental health services in the United States: Results from the National Comorbidity Survey Replication. *Archives of General Psychiatry, 62,* 629–640.

Wang, P. S., Simon, G. E., Avorn, J., Azocar, F., Ludman, E. J., McCulloch, J., et al. (2007). Telephone screening, outreach, and care management for depressed workers and impact on clinical and work productivity outcomes: A randomized controlled trial. *Journal of the American Medical Association, 298,* 1401–1411.

Wansink, B., & Payne, C.R. (2009). The *Joy of Cooking* too much: 70 years of calorie increases in classic recipes. *Annals of Internal Medicine, 150,* 291.

Ward, T. B., & Beech, A. (2006). An integrated theory of sexual offending. *Aggression and Violent Behavior, 11,* 44–63.

Warwick, H. M. C., & Salkovskis, P. M. (2001). Cognitive-behavioral treatment of hypochondriasis. In D. R. Lipsitt & V. Starcevic (Eds.), *Hypochondriasis: Modern perspectives on an ancient malady* (pp. 314–328). London: Oxford University Press.

Waszczuk, M. A., Zavos, H. M., Gregory, A. M., & Eley, T. C. (2014). The phenotypic and genetic structure of depression and anxiety disorder symptoms in childhood, adolescence, and young adulthood. *Journal of the American Medical Association, Psychiatry, 71,* 905-916.

Waters, A., Hill, A., & Waller, G. (2001). Internal and external antecedents of binge eating episodes in a group of women with bulimia nervosa. *International Journal of Eating Disorders, 29,* 17–22.

Watkins, E. R. (2008). Constructive and unconstructive repetitive thought. *Psychological Bulletin, 134,* 163–206.

Watkins, P. C. (2002). Implicit memory bias in depression. *Cognition and Emotion, 16,* 381–402.

Watson, D. (2005). Rethinking the mood and anxiety of disorders: A qualitative hierarchical model for DSM-V. *Journal of Abnormal Psychology, 114,* 522–536.

Watson, D. (2009). Differentiating the mood and anxiety disorders: A quadripartite model. *Annual Review of Clinical Psychology, 5,* 221–247.

Watson, D., & Clark, L. A. (1994). Introduction to the special issue on personality and psychopathology. *Journal of Abnormal Psychology, 103,* 3–5.

Watson, D., O'Hara, M. W., & Stuart, S. (2008). Hierarchical structures of affect and psychopathology and their implications for the classification of emotional disorders. *Depression and Anxiety, 25,* 282–288.

Watson, J. B., & Rayner, R. (1920). Conditioned emotional reactions. *Journal of Experimental Psychology, 3,* 1–14.

Watson, S., Thompson, J. M., Ritchie, J. C., Ferrier, I. N., & Young, A. H. (2006). Neuropsychological impairment in bipolar disorder: The relationship with glucocorticoid receptor function. *Bipolar Disorders, 8,* 85–90.

Watt, N. F. (1974). Childhood and adolescent roots of schizophrenia. In D. Ricks, A. Thomas & M. Roll (Eds.), *Life history research in psychopathology* (Vol. 3). Minneapolis: University of Minnesota Press.

Watt, N. F., Stolorow, R. D., Lubensky, A. W., & McClelland, D. C. (1970). School adjustment and behavior of children hospitalized for schizophrenia as adults. *American Journal of Orthopsychiatry, 40,* 637–657.

Watters, E. (2010). *Crazy like us: The globalization of the America psyche.* New York: Free Press.

Watts, A. L., Lilienfeld, S. O., Smith, S. F., Miller, J. D., Campbell, W. K., Waldman, I. D., et al. (2013). The double-edged sword of grandiose narcissism: Implications for successful and unsuccessful leadership among U.S. presidents. *Psychological Science, 24,* 2379–2389.

Weaver, I. C. G., Cervoni, N., Champagne, F. A., D'Allesio, A. C., Shakti, S., Seck, J. R., Dymov, S., Szyf, M., &

Meaney, J. J. (2004). Epigenetic programming by maternal behavior. *Nature Neuroscience, 7,* 847–854.

Webster, C., Douglas, K., Eaves, D., & Hart, S. (1997). *HCR-20: Assessing risk for violence (Version 2).* Vancouver, British Columbia, Canada: Simon Fraser University.

Webster, J. J., & Palmer, R. L. (2000). The childhood and family background of women with clinical eating disorders: A comparison with women with major depression and women without psychiatric disorder. *Psychological Medicine, 30,* 53–60.

Webster, R., & Holroyd, S. (2000). Prevalence of psychotic symptoms in delirium. *Psychosomatics, 41,* 519–522.

Webster-Stratton, C. (1998). Preventing conduct problems in Head Start children: Strengthening parenting competencies. *Journal of Consulting and Clinical Psychology, 66,* 715–730.

Webster-Stratton, C., Reid, M. J., & Hammond, M. (2001). Preventing conduct problems, promoting social competence: A parent and teacher training partnership in Head Start. *Journal of Clinical Child Psychology, 30,* 283–302.

Wechsler, D. (1968). *Escala de Inteligencia Wechsler para Adultos.* New York: Psychological Corporation.

Wegner, D. M., Schneider, D. J., Carter, S. R., & White, T. L. (1987). Paradoxical effects of thought suppression. *Journal of Personality and Social Psychology, 53,* 5–13.

Wehr, T. A., Duncan, W. C., Sher, L., Aeschbach, D., Schwartz, P. J., Turner, E. H., et al. (2001). A circadian signal of change of season in patients with seasonal affective disorder. *Archives of General Psychiatry, 58,* 1108–1114.

Wehr, T. A., Turner, E. H., Shimada, J. M., Lowe, C. H., Baker, C., & Leibenluft, E. (1998). Treatment of a rapidly cycling bipolar patient by using extended bed rest and darkness to stabilize the timing and duration of sleep. *Biological Psychiatry, 43,* 822–828.

Weickert, C. S., Straub, R. E., McClintock, B. W., et al. (2004). Human dysbindin (DTNBP1) gene expression in normal brain and in schizophrenic prefrontal cortex and mid brain. *Archives of General Psychiatry, 61,* 544–555.

Weierich, M. R., & Nock, M. K. (2008). Posttraumatic stress symptoms mediate the relation between childhood sexual abuse and nonsuicidal self-injury. *Journal of Consulting and Clinical Psychology, 76,* 39–44.

Weinberger, D. R. (1987). Implications of normal brain development for the pathogenesis of schizophrenia. *Archives of General Psychiatry, 44,* 660–669.

Weinberger, D. R., Berman, K. F., & Illowsky, B. P. (1988). Physiological dysfunction of dorsolateral prefrontal cortex in schizophrenia: 3. A new cohort and evidence for a monoaminergic mechanism. *Archives of General Psychiatry, 45,* 609–615.

Weinberger, D. R., Cannon-Spoor, H. E., Potkin, S. G., & Wyatt, R. J. (1980). Poor premorbid adjustment and CT scan abnormalities in chronic schizophrenia. *American Journal of Psychiatry, 137,* 1410–1413.

Weiner, B., Frieze, L., Kukla, A., Reed, L., Rest, S., & Rosenbaum, R. M. (1971). *Perceiving the causes of success and failure.* New York: General Learning Press.

Weiner, D. B. (1994). Le geste de Pinel: The history of psychiatric myth. In M. S. Micale & R. Porter (Eds.), *Discovering the history of psychiatry.* New York: Oxford University Press.

Weinstein, H. (2002, February 19). Killer's sentence of death debated. *Los Angeles Times,* pp. A1, A14.

Weisberg, R. B., Brown, T. A., Wincze, J. P., & Barlow, D. H. (2001). Causal attributions and male sexual arousal: The impact of attributions for a bogus erectile difficulty on sexual arousal, cognitions, and affect. *Journal of Abnormal Psychology, 110,* 324–334.

Weisberg, R. W. (1994). Genius and madness? A quasi-experimental test of the hypothesis that manic-depression increases creativity. *Psychological Science, 5,* 361–367.

Weisman, A. G., Nuechterlein, K. H., Goldstein, M. J., & Snyder, K. S. (1998). Expressed emotion, attributions, and schizophrenia symptom dimensions. *Journal of Abnormal Psychology, 107,* 355–359.

Weisman, C. S., & Teitelbaum, M. A. (1985). Physician gender and the physician–patient relationship: Recent evidence and relevant questions. *Social Science and Medicine, 20,* 1119–1127.

Weiss, G., & Hechtman, L. (1993). *Hyperactive children grown up* (2nd ed.). New York: Guilford Press.

Weiss, L. A., Shen, Y., Korn, J. M., et al. (2008). Association between microdeletion and microduplication at 16p11.2 and autism. *New England Journal of Medicine, 358,* 667–675.

Weissman, A., & Beck, A. T. (1978). *Development and validation of the Dysfunctional Attitude Scale: A preliminary investigation.*

Weisz, J. R., McCarty, C. A., & Valeri, S. M. (2006). Effects of psychotherapy for depression in children and adolescents: A meta-analysis. *Psychological Bulletin, 132,* 132–149.

Weisz, J. R., Sigman, M., Weiss, B., & Mosk, J. (1993). Parent reports of behavioral and emotional problems among children in Kenya, Thailand and the United States. *Child Development, 64,* 98–109.

Weisz, J. R., Suwanlert, S. C., Wanchai, W., & Bernadette, R. (1987). Over- and under-controlled referral problems among children and adolescents from Thailand and the United States: The wat and wai of cultural differences. *Journal of Consulting and Clinical Psychology, 55,* 719–726.

Weisz, J. R., Weiss, B., Suwanlert, S., & Wanchai, C. (2003). Syndromal structure of psychopathology in children of Thailand and the United States. *Journal of Consulting and Clinical Psychology, 71,* 375–385.

Wells, A. (1998). Cognitive therapy of social phobia. In N. Tarrier, A. Wells & G. Haddock (Eds.), *Treating complex cases: The cognitive-behavioural approach* (pp. 1–26). Chicester, UK: John Wiley & Sons.

Wells, C. E., & Duncan, G. W. (1980). *Neurology for Psychiatrists.* Philadelphia: F. A. Davis.

Wells, K. C., Epstein, J. N., Hinshaw, S. P., et al. (2000). Parenting and family stress treatment outcomes in attention deficit hyperactivity disorder (ADHD): An empirical analysis in the MTA study. *Journal of Abnormal Child Psychology, 28,* 543–553.

Wender, P. H., Kety, S. S., Rosenthal, D., Schulsinger, F., Ortmann, J., & Lunde, I. (1986). Psychiatric disorders in the biological and adoptive families of adopted individuals with affective disorders. *Archives of General Psychiatry, 43,* 923–929.

Westen, D. (1998). The scientific legacy of Sigmund Freud: Toward a psychodynamically informed psychological science. *Psychological Bulletin, 124,* 333–371.

Westen, D., Novotny, C. M., & Thompson-Brenner, H. (2004). The empirical status of empirically supported psychotherapies: Assumptions, findings, and reporting in controlled clinical trials. *Psychological Bulletin, 130,* 631–663.

Wetherill, R. R., Jagannathan, K., Lohoff, F. W., Ehrman, R., O'Brien, C. P., Childress, A. R., & Franklin, T. R. (2014). Neural correlates of attentional bias for smoking cues: modulation by variance in the

dopamine transporter gene. *Addiction Biology, 19*(2), 294–304.

Whisman, M. A. (2007). Marital distress and DSM-IV psychiatric disorders in a population-based national survey. *Journal of Abnormal Psychology, 116,* 638–643.

Whisman, M. A., & Bruce, M. L. (1999). Marital dissatisfaction and incidence of major depressive episode in a community sample. *Journal of Abnormal Psychology, 108,* 674–678.

Whisman, M. A., & Uebelacker, L. A. (2006). Impairment and distress associated with relationship discord in a national sample of married or cohabiting adults. *Journal of Family Psychology, 20,* 369–377.

Whisman, M. A., Sheldon, C. T., & Goering, P. (2000). Psychiatric disorders and dissatisfaction with social relationships: does type of relationship matter? *Journal of Abnormal Psychology, 109,* 803–808.

Whitaker, A. H., van Rossen, R., Feldman, J. F., Schonfeld, I. S., Pinto-Martin, J. A., Torre, C., Shaffer, D., & Paneth, N. (1997). Psychiatric outcomes in low birth weight children at age 6 years: Relation to neonatal cranial ultrasound abnormalities. *Archives of General Psychiatry, 54,* 847–856.

Whitaker, R. (2002). *Mad in America.* Cambridge, MA: Perseus.

White, K. S., & Barlow, D. H. (2004). Panic disorder and agoraphobia. In D. H. Barlow (Ed.), *Anxiety and its disorders: The nature and treatment of anxiety and panic* (pp. 328-379). New York: Guilford Press.

White, S. W., Oswald, D., Ollendick, T., & Scahill, L. (2009). Anxiety in children and adolescents with autism spectrum disorders. *Clinical Psychology Review, 29,* 216–229.

Whittal, M. L., Agras, S. W., & Gould, R. A. (1999). Bulimia nervosa: A meta-analysis of psychosocial and pharmacological treatments. *Behavior Therapy, 30,* 117–135.

Whittle, S., Lichter, R., Dennison, M., Vijayakumar, N., Schwartz, O., Byrne, M. L., et al. (2014). Structural brain development and depression onset during adolescence: A prospective longitudinal study. *The American Journal of Psychiatry, 171*(5), 564–571.

Wiborg, I. M., & Dahl, A. A. (1996). Does brief dynamic psychotherapy reduce the relapse rate of panic disorder? *Archives of General Psychiatry, 53,* 689–694.

Widiger, T. A., Frances, A., & Trull, T. J. (1987). A psychometric analysis of the social-interpersonal and cognitiveperceptual items for schizotypal personality disorder. *Archives of General Psychiatry, 44,* 741–745.

Wiech, K., & Tracey, I. (2009). The influence of negative emotions on pain: behavioral effects and neural mechanisms. *NeuroImage, 47,* 987–994.

Wildes, J. E., Emery, R. E., & Simons, A. D. (2001). The roles of ethnicity and culture in the development of eating disturbance and body dissatisfaction: A meta-analytic review. *Clinical Psychology Review, 21,* 521–551.

Wilfley, D. E., Welch, R. R., Stein, R. I., Spurrell, E. B., Cohen, L. R., et al. (2002). A randomized comparison of group cognitive-behavioral therapy and group interpersonal psychotherapy for the treatment of overweight individuals with binge eating disorder. *Archives of General Psychiatry, 59,* 713–721.

Wilhelm, S., Buhlmann, U., Hayward, L. C., Greenberg, J. L., & Dimaite, R. (2010). A cognitive-behavioral treatment approach for body dysmorphic disorder. *Cognitive and Behavioral Practice, 17,* 241–247.

Wilhelm, S., Phillips, K. A., Didie, E., Buhlmann, U., Greenberg, J. L., Fama, J. M., et al. (2014). Modular cognitive-behavioral therapy for body dysmorphic dis-

order: A randomized controlled trial. *Behavior Therapy, 45,* 314–327.

Wille, R., & Boulanger, H. (1984). 10 years' castration law in Schleswig-Holstein. *Beitrage zur gerichtlichen Medizin, 42,* 9–16.

Willemsen-Swinkels, S. H. N., Buitelaar, J. K., Weijnen, F. G., & van Engeland, H. (1995). Placebo-controlled acute dosage naltrexone study in young autistic children. *Psychiatry Research, 58,* 203–215.

Williams, J. (2003). Dementia and genetics. In R. Plomin, J. D. DeFries & , et al. (Eds.), *Behavioral genetics in the postgenomic era* (pp. 503–527). Washington, DC: American Psychological Association.

Williams, J., Hadjistavropoulos, T., & Sharpe, D. (2006). A meta-analysis of psychological and pharmacological treatments for body dysmorphic disorder. *Behaviour Research and Therapy, 44,* 99–111.

Williams, J. M. G., Watts, F. N., MacLeod, C., & Mathews, A. (1997). *Cognitive psychology and emotional disorders* (2nd ed.). New York: John Wiley & Sons.

Williams, J. W., Plassman, B. L., Burke, J., Holsinger, T., & Benjamin, S. (2010). Preventing Alzheimer's disease and cognitive decline. *Evidence Report/Technology Assessment No. 193.* Rockville, MD: Duke Evidence-based Practice Center.

Williams, P. A., Allard, A., Spears, L., Dalrymple, N., & Bloom, A. S. (2001). Brief report: Case reports on naltrexone use in children with autism: Controlled observations regarding benefits and practical issues in medication management. *Journal of Autism and Developmental Disorders, 31,* 103–108.

Wills, T. A., & Cleary, S. D. (1999). Peer and adolescent substance use among 6th–9th graders: Latent growth analysis of influence versus selection mechanisms. *Health Psychology, 18,* 453–463.

Wills, T. A., Sandy, J. M., & Yaeger, A. M. (2002). Stress and smoking in adolescence: A test of directional hypotheses. *Health Psychology, 21,* 122–130.

Wilsnack, R. W., Vogeltanz, N. D., & Wilsnack, S. C., et al. (2000). Gender differences in alcohol consumption and adverse drinking consequences: Cross-cultural patterns. *Addiction, 95,* 251–265.

Wilson, A. J., & Dehaene, S. (2007). Number sense and developmental dyscalculia. In D. Coch (Ed.), *Human behavior, learning and the developing brain: Atypical development* (pp. 212–238). New York: Guilford Press.

Wilson, D. (2011, April 13). As generics near, makers tweak erectile drugs. *New York Times,* p. B11.

Wilson, G. T. (1995). Psychological treatment of binge eating and bulimia nervosa. *Journal of Mental Health (UK), 4,* 451–457.

Wilson, G. T., & Fairburn, C. G. (1998). Treatments for eating disorders. In P. Nathan & J. M. Gorman (Eds.), *A guide to treatments that work* (pp. 501–530). London: Oxford University Press.

Wilson, G. T., Loeb, K. L., Walsh, B. T., Labouvie, E., Petkova, E., Liu, X., & Waternaux, C. (1999). Psychological and pharmacological treatment of bulimia nervosa: Predictors and processes of change. *Journal of Consulting and Clinical Psychology, 67,* 451–459.

Wilson, G. T., & Pike, K. M. (2001). Eating disorders. In D. H. Barlow (Ed.), *Clinical handbook of psychological disorders* (3rd ed., pp. 332–375). New York: Guilford Press.

Wilson, G. T., & Sysko, R. (2009). Frequency of binge eating episodes in bulimia nervosa and binge eating disorder: Diagnostic considerations. *International Journal of Eating Disorders, 42,* 603–610.

Wilson, G. T., Wilfley, D. E., Agras, S., & Bryson, S. W. (2010). Psychological treatments of binge eating disorder. *Archives of General Psychiatry, 67*, 94–101.

Wilson, R. S., Scherr, P. A., Schneider, J. A., Tang, Y., & Bennett, D. A. (2007). Relation of cognitive activity to risk of developing Alzheimer's disease. *Neurology, 69*, 1191–1920.

Wimo, A., Winblad, B., Aguero-Torres, A., & von Strauss, E. (2003). The magnitude of dementia occurrence in the world. *Alzheimer Disease and Associated Disorders, 17*, 63–67.

Winchel, R. M., Stanley, B., & Stanley, M. (1990). Biochemical aspects of suicide. In S. J. Blumenthal & D. J. Kupfer (Eds.), *Suicide over the life cycle: Risk factors, assessment and treatment of suicidal patterns* (pp. 97–126). Washington, DC: American Psychiatric Press.

Wincze, J. P., & Barlow, D. H. (1997). *Enhancing sexuality: A problem-solving approach.* Boulder, CO: Graywind Publications.

Wincze, J. P., Steketee, G., & Frost, R. O. (2007). Categorization in compulsive hoarding. *Behaviour Research and Therapy, 45*, 63–72.

Wingfield, N., Kelly, N., Serdar, K., Shivy, V. A., & Mazzeo, S. E. (2011). College students' perceptions of individuals with anorexia and bulimia nervosa. *International Journal of Eating Disorders, 44*, 369–375.

Winkleby, M. A., Cubbin, C., Ahn, D. K., & Kraemer, H. C. (1999). Pathways by which SES and ethnicity influence cardiovascular risk factors. In N. E. Adler & M. Marmot (Eds.), *Socioeconomic status and health in industrial nations: Social, psychological, and biological pathways* (Vol. 896). New York: New York Academy of Sciences.

Winkleby, M. A., Kraemer, H. C., Ahn, D. K., & Varady, A. N. (1998). Ethnic and socioeconomic differences in cardiovascular disease risk factors. *Journal of the American Medical Association, 280*, 356–362.

Wirshing, D. W., Wirshing, W. C., Marder, S. R., Liberman, R. P., & Mintz, J. (1998). Informed consent: Assessment of comprehension. *American Journal of Psychiatry, 155*, 1508–1511.

Wirz-Justice, A., Quinto, C., Cajochen, C., Werth, E., & Hock, C. (1999). A rapid-cycling bipolar patient treated with long nights, bedrest and light. *Biological Psychiatry, 45*, 1075–1077.

Wisner, K. L., Sit, D. K., McShea, M. C., Rizzo, D. M., Zoretich, R. A., Hughes, C. L., et al. (2013). Onset timing, thoughts of self-harm, and diagnoses in postpartum women with screen-positive depression findings. *Journal of the American Medical Association Psychiatry, 70*, 490–498.

Witlox, J., Eurelings, L. S. M., de Jonghe, J. F. M., Kalisvaart, K. J., Eikelenboom, P., & van Gool, W. A. (2010). Delirium in elderly patients and the risk of postdischarge mortality, institutionalization, and dementia. *Journal of the American Medical Association, 304*, 443-451.

Wittchen, H. U., Gloster, A. T., Beesdo-Baum, K., Fava, G. A., & Craske, M. G. (2010). Agoraphobia: A review of the diagnostic classificatory position and criteria. *Depression and Anxiety, 27*, 113–133.

Wittchen, H. U., & Jacobi, F. (2005). Size and burden of mental disorders in Europe—A critical review and appraisal of 27 studies. *European Neuropsychopharmacology, 15*, 357–376.

Wolf, E. J., Miller, M. W., Reardon, A. F., Ryabchenko, K. A., Castillo, D., & Freund, R. (2012). A latent class analysis of dissociation and posttraumatic stress disorder: Evidence for a dissociative subtype. *Archives of General Psychiatry, 69*, 698–705.

Wolf, M., Bally, H., & Morris, R. (1986). Automaticity, retrieval processes, and reading: A longitudinal study in average and impaired readers. *Child Development, 57*, 988–1000.

Wolfe, V. V. (1990). Sexual abuse of children. In A. S. Bellack, M. Hersen & A. E. Kazdin (Eds.), *International handbook of behavior modification and therapy* (2nd ed., pp. 707–729). New York: Plenum.

Wolitzky, D. (1995). Traditional psychoanalytic psychotherapy. In A. S. Gurman & S. B. Messer (Eds.), *Essential psychotherapies: Theory and practice.* New York: Guilford Press.

Wolitzky-Taylor, K. B., Horowitz, J. D., Powers, M. B., & Telch, M. J. (2008). Psychological approaches in the treatment of specific phobias: A meta-analysis. *Clinical Psychology Review, 28*, 1021–1037.

Wolpe, J. (1958). *Psychotherapy by reciprocal inhibition.* Stanford, CA: Stanford University Press.

Wolraich, M. L., Wilson, D. B., & White, J. W. (1995). The effect of sugar on behavior or cognition in children: A meta-analysis. *Journal of the American Medical Association, 274*, 1617–1621.

Women's Health Initiative Screening Committee. (2004). Effects of conjugated equine estrogen in postmenopausal women with hysterectomy: The Women's Health Initiative randomized controlled trial. *Journal of the American Medical Association, 291*, 1701–1712.

Wonderlich, S. A., Crosby, R. D., Mitchell, J. E., Thompson, K. M., Redlin, J., Demuth, G., Smyth, J., & Haseltine, B. (2001). Eating disturbance and sexual trauma in childhood and adulthood. *International Journal of Eating Disorders, 30*, 401–412.

Wonderlich, S. A., Gordon, K. H., Mitchell, J. E., Crosby, R. D., Engel, S. G., & Walsh, B. T. (2009). The validity and clinical utility of binge eating disorder. *International Journal of Eating Disorders, 42*, 687–705.

Wonderlich, S. A., Wilsnack, R. W., Wilsnack, S. C., & Harris, T. R. (1996). Childhood sexual abuse and bulimic behavior in a nationally representative sample. *American Journal of Public Health, 86*, 1082–1086.

Woo, J. S., Brotto, L. A., & Gorzalka, B. B. (2011). The role of sex guilt in the relationship between culture and women's sexual desire. *Archives of Sexual Behavior, 40*, 385–394.

Woodberry, K. A., Giuliano, A. J., & Seidman, L. J. (2008). Premorbid IQ in schizophrenia: A meta-analytic review. *American Journal of Psychiatry, 165*, 579–587.

Woodmansee, M. A. (1996). The guilty but mentally ill verdict: Political expediency at the expense of moral principle. *Notre Dame Journal of Law, Ethics and Public Policy, 10*, 341–387.

Woods, S. W., Addington, J., Cadenhead, K. S., Cannon, T. D., Cornblatt, B. A., Heinssen, R., . . . McGlashan, T. H. (2009). Validity of the prodromal risk syndrome for first psychosis: findings from the North American Prodrome Longitudinal Study. *Schizophrenia Bulletin, 35*, 894-908. doi: 10.1093/schbul/sbp027

Woodside, D. B., Bulik, C. M., Halmi, K. A., et al. (2002). Personality, perfectionism, and attitudes towards eating in parents of individuals with eating disorders. *International Journal of Eating Disorders, 13*, 290–299.

Woody, E. Z., & Szechtman, H. (2011). Adaptation to potential threat: The evolution, neurobiology, and psychopathology of the security motivation system. *Neuroscience and Biobehavioral Reviews, 35*, 1019–1033.

Woody, S. R., & Teachman, B. A. (2000). Intersection of disgust and fear: Normative and pathological views. *Clinical Psychology: Science and Practice, 7*, 291–311.

World Health Organization. (2001). *World health report: New understanding, new hope.* Geneva: Author.

Wouda, J. C., Hartman, P. M., Bakker, R. M., Bakker, J. O., van de Wiel, H. B. M., & Schultz, W. C. (1998). Vaginal plethysmography in women with dyspareunia. *Journal of Sex Research, 35*, 141–147.

Wright, I. A., Rabe-Hesketh, S., Woodruff, P. W., Davis, A. S., Murray, R. M., & Bullmore, E. T. (2000). Meta-analysis of regional brain volumes in schizophrenia. *American Journal of Psychiatry, 157*, 16–25.

Writing Group for the Women's Health Initiative Investigators. (2002). Risks and benefits of estrogen plus progestin in healthy postmenopausal women. Principal results from the Women's Health Initiative randomized controlled trial. *Journal of the American Medical Association, 288*, 321–333.

Wu, L. T., Pilowsky, D. J., & Schlenger, W. E. (2004). Inhalant abuse and dependence among adolescents in the United State. *Journal of the American Academy of Child and Adolescent Psychiatry, 43*, 1206–1214.

Wykes, T., Huddy, V., Cellard, C., McGurk, S., & Czobor, P. (2011). A meta-analysis of cognitive remediation for schizophrenia: Methodology and effect sizes. *American Journal of Psychiatry, 168*, 472–485.

Wykes, T., Steel, C., Everitt, T., & Tarrier, N. (2008). Cognitive behavior therapy for schizophrenia: Effect sizes, clinical models, and methodological rigor. *Schizophrenia Bulletin, 34*, 523–537.

Wylie, K. R. (1997). Treatment outcome of brief couple therapy in psychogenic male erectile disorder. *Archives of Sexual Behavior, 26*, 527–545.

Wylie, K. R., & MacInnes, I. (2005). Erectile dysfunction. In R. Balon & R. T. Segraves (Eds.), *Handbook of sexual dysfunctions and paraphilias.* Boca Raton, Fl: Taylor and Francis Group.

Xia, J., Merinder, L. B., & Belgamwar, M. R. (2011). Psychoeducation for schizophrenia. *Schizophrenia Bulletin, 37*, 21–22.

Yaffe, K., Fiocco, A. J., Lindquist, K., Vittinghoff, E., Simonsick, E. M., Newman, A. B., et al. (2009). Predictors of maintaining cognitive function in older adults. *Neurology, 72*, 2029-2035.

Yang, Y., & Raine, A. (2009). Prefrontal structural and functional brain imaging findings in antisocial, violent, and psychopathic individuals: A meta-analysis. *Psychiatry Research: Neuroimaging, 174*, 81–88.

Yehuda, R., & LeDoux, J. (2007). Response variation following trauma: A translational neuroscience approach to understanding PTSD. *Neuron, 56*, 19–32.

Yerkes, R. M., & Dodson, J. D. (1908). The relation of strength of stimulus to rapidity of habit formation. *Journal of Comparative and Neurological Psychology, 18*, 459–482.

Yirmiya, N., & Sigman, M. (1991). High functioning individuals with autism: Diagnosis, empirical findings, and theoretical issues. *Clinical Psychology Review, 11*, 669–683.

Yoast, R., Williams, M. A., Deitchman, S. D., & Champion, H. C. (2001). Report of the Council on Scientific Affairs: Methadone maintenance and needle-exchange programs to reduce the medical and public health consequences of drug abuse. *Journal of Addictive Diseases, 20*, 15–40.

Yonkers, K. A., Bruce, S. E., Dyck, I. R., & Keller, M. B. (2003). Chronicity, relapse, and illness-course of panic disorder, social phobia, and generalized anxiety disorder: Findings in men and women from 8 years of follow-up. *Depression and Anxiety, 17*, 173–179.

York Cornwell, E., & Waite, L. J. (2009). Social disconnectedness, perceived isolation, and health among older adults. *Journal of Health and Social Behavior, 50*, 31–48.

Young, J., Goey, A., Minassian, A., Perry, W., Paulus, M., & Geyer, M. (2010). GBR 12909 administration as a mouse model of bipolar disorder mania: Mimicking quantitative assessment of manic behavior. *Psychopharmacology, 208*(3), 443–454.

Young, M. A., Watel, L. G., Lahmeyer, H. W., & Eastman, C. I. (1991). The temporal onset of individual symptoms in winter depression: Differentiating underlying mechanisms. *Journal of Affective Disorders, 22*, 191–197.

Younglove, J. A., & Vitello, C. J. (2003). Community notification provisions of "Megan's Law" from a therapeutic jurisprudence perspective: A case study. *American Journal of Forensic Psychology, 21*, 25–38.

Youngstrom, E. A., Freeman, A. J., & Jenkins, M. M. (2009). The assessment of children and adolescents with bipolar disorder. *Child and Adolescent Psychiatric Clinics of North America, 18*, 353-390. doi:310.1016/j.chc.2008.1012.1002.

Yung, A. R., McGorry, P. D., McFarlane, C. A., & Patton, G. (1995). The PACE Clinic: Development of a clinical service for young people at high risk of psychosis. *Australian Psychiatry, 3*, 345–349.

Yung, A. R., Phillips, L. J., Hok, P. Y., & McGorry, P. D. (2004). Risk factors for psychosis in an ultra high-risk group: psychopathology and clinical features. *Schizophrenia Research, 67*, 131–142.

Yung, A. R., Woods, S. W., Ruhrmann, S., Addington, J., Schultze-Lutter, F., Cornblatt, B. A., et al. (2012). Whither the attenuated psychosis syndrome? *Schizophrenia Bulletin, 38*(6), 1130–1134.

Zanarini, M. C., Frankenburg, F. R., Hennen, J., Reich, D. B., & Silk, K. R. (2004). Axis I comorbidity in patients with borderline personality disorder: 6-year follow-up and prediction of time to remission. *American Journal of Psychiatry, 161*, 2108–2114.

Zanarini, M. C., Frankenburg, F. R., Reich, D. B., & Fitzmaurice, G. M. (2011). Attainment and stability of sustained symptomatic remission and recovery among patients with borderline personality disorder and axis II comparison subjects: A 16-year prospective follow-up study. *American Journal of Psychiatry, AiA*, 1–8.

Zanarini, M. C., Skodol, A. E., Bender, D., Dolan, R., Sanislow, C., Schaefer, E., et al. (2000). The Collaborative Longitudinal Personality Disorders Study: Reliability of axis I and II diagnoses. *Journal of Personality Disorders, 14*, 291–299.

Zane, M. D. (1984). Psychoanalysis and contextual analysis of phobias. *Journal of the American Academy of Psychoanalysis, 12*, 553–568.

Zanov, M. V., & Davison, G. C. (2009). A conceptual and empirical review of 25 years of cognitive assessment using the Articulated Thoughts in Simulated Situations (ATSS) think-aloud paradigm. *Cognitive Therapy and Research, 34*, 282-291.

Zanov, M. V., & Davison, G.C. (2010). A conceptual and empirical review of 25 years of cognitive assessment using the Articulated Thoughts in Simulated Situations (ATSS) think-aloud paradigm. Cognitive Therapy and Research, 34, 282–291.

Zapf, P. A., & Roesch, R. (2011). Future directions in the restoration of competency to stand trial. *Current Directions in Psychological Science, 20*(1), 43–47.

Zapolski, T. C., Pedersen, S. L., McCarthy, D. M., & Smith, G. T. (2014). Less drinking, yet more problems: understanding African American drinking and related problems. *Psychological Bulletin, 140*(1), 188–223.

Zarit, S. H. (1980). *Aging and mental disorders: Psychological approaches to assessment and treatment*. New York: Free Press.

Zarit, S. H., & Zarit, J. M. (2011). *Mental disorders in older adults: Fundamentals of assessment and treatment* (2nd ed.). New York: Guilford Press.

Zeier, J. D., & Newman, J. P. (2013). Feature-based attention and conflict monitoring in criminal offenders: Interactive relations of psychopathy with anxiety and externalizing. *Journal of Abnormal Psychology, 122*, 797–806.

Zellner, D. A., Harner, D. E., & Adler, R. L. (1989). Effects of eating abnormalities and gender on perceptions of desirable body shape. *Journal of Abnormal Psychology, 98*, 93–96.

Zhang, T. Y., & Meaney, M. J. (2010). Epigenetics and the environmental regulation of the genome and its function. *Annual Review of Psychology, 61*, 439–466.

Zheng, H., Sussman, S., Chen, X., Wang, Y. Xia, J., Gong, J., Liu, C., Shan, J., Unger, J., & Johnson, C. A. (2004). Project EX—A teen smoking cessation initial study in Wuhan, China. *Addictive Behaviors, 29*, 1725–1733.

Zhou, J., & Seeley, W. W. (2014). Network dysfunction in Alzheimer's disease and frontotemporal dementia: Implications for psychiatry. *Biological Psychiatry, 75*, 565–573.

Ziegler, F. J., Imboden, J. B., & Meyer, E. (1960). Contemporary conversion reactions: A clinical study. *American Journal of Psychiatry, 116*, 901–910.

Zilboorg, G., & Henry, G. W. (1941). *A history of medical psychology*. New York: W. W. Norton.

Zimmer, D. (1987). Does marital therapy enhance the effectiveness of treatment for sexual dysfunction? *Journal of Sex and Marital Therapy, 13*, 193–209.

Zimmer, L., & Morgan, J. P. (1995). *Exposing marijuana myths: A review of the scientific evidence*. New York: The Lindemith Center.

Zimmerman, M., & Mattia, J. I. (1999). Differences between clinical and research practices in diagnosing borderline personality disorder. *American Journal of Psychiatry, 156*, 1570–1574.

Zimmerman, M., Rothschild, L., & Chelminski, I. (2005). The prevalence of DSM-IV personality disorders in psychiatric outpatients. *The American journal of psychiatry, 162*, 1911-1918.

Zipfel, S., Wild, B., Gross, G., Friederich, H. C., Teufel, M., Schellberg, D., et al. (2014). Focal psychodynamic therapy, cognitive behaviour therapy, and optimised treatment as usual in outpatients with anorexia nervosa (ANTOP study): randomised controlled trial. *The Lancet, 383*(9912), 127–137.

Zohar, A. H., & Felz, L. (2001). Ritualistic behavior in young children. *Journal of Abnormal Child Psychology, 29*, 121–128.

Zubin, J., & Spring, B. (1977). Vulnerability: A new view of schizophrenia. *Journal of Abnormal Psychology, 86*, 103–126.

Name Index

Subject Index